PSYCHOLOGY

Lester Sdorow
Allentown College

Wm. C. Brown Publishers

Dubuque, Iowa

Book Team

Editor *Michael Lange*
Developmental Editor *Carla J. Aspelmeier*
Production Editor *Gloria G. Schiesl*
Designer *Heidi J. Baughman*
Art Editor *Janice M. Roerig*
Photo Editor *Michelle Oberhoffer*
Permissions Editor *Karen L. Storlie*
Visuals Processor *Amy Saffran*

 Wm. C. Brown Publishers

President *G. Franklin Lewis*
Vice President, Publisher *George Wm. Bergquist*
Vice President, Publisher *Thomas E. Doran*
Vice President, Operations and Production *Beverly Kolz*
National Sales Manager *Virginia S. Moffat*
Advertising Manager *Ann M. Knepper*
Marketing Manager *Kathy Law Laube*
Production Editorial Manager *Colleen A. Yonda*
Production Editorial Manager *Julie A. Kennedy*
Publishing Services Manager *Karen J. Slaght*
Manager of Visuals and Design *Faye M. Schilling*

Cover and interior design by Stuart D. Paterson

Cover: Scala/Art Resource, N.Y., Monet, Impression, Sunrise, (1872) Paris, Marmottan.

The credits section for this book begins on page C–1, and is considered an extension of the copyright page.

Library of Congress Catalog Card Number: 89–83395

ISBN 0–697–07649–0

Printed in the United States of America by Wm. C. Brown Publishers, 2460 Kerper Boulevard, Dubuque, IA 52001

10 9 8 7 6 5 4 3 2 1

To the memory of my father,
Harvey Sdorow, who was—and remains—
a source of inspiration to me.

BRIEF CONTENTS

EXPANDED CONTENTS

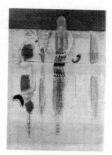

CHAPTER

3

PSYCHOBIOLOGICAL PROCESSES 54

CHAPTER

4

SENSATION AND PERCEPTION 96

CHAPTER

5

CONSCIOUSNESS 144

CHAPTER
6

LEARNING   182

CHAPTER
7

MEMORY   216

CHAPTER
8

THINKING AND LANGUAGE 254

CHAPTER
9

INTELLIGENCE 290

CHAPTER
10

MOTIVATION 322

CHAPTER
11

EMOTION 358

CHAPTER
12

DEVELOPMENT 388

CHAPTER
13

CHAPTER
14

CHAPTER 15

CHAPTER 16

CHAPTER
17

CHAPTER
18

PREFACE

n regard to authors, it has been said that there is the book one intended to write, the book one thought was written, and the book one actually wrote. What *was* the book I intended to write? To accomplish all that I originally intended, the book would easily have been twice as long as it is now. A century ago, William James, disturbed at the length of his now-classic *The Principles of Psychology,* gave his own stinging review of it, calling it, among other things, "a bloated tumescent mass." Though I do not share this view of his book, to which I find myself drawn repeatedly (and from which I quote liberally), I quickly discovered that I would somehow have to pursue my goals without producing a bloated, tumescent mass. This required that I manipulate a kind of intellectual "Rubik's cube" of goals, which could only be achieved by considering each of them in light of the others.

The Goals

To Do Justice to the Breadth of Psychology My students often express amazement at the breadth of psychology. While one psychologist might devote a career to studying how brain cells function in schizophrenia, another might devote a career to studying the social factors that account for human love. And, while one psychologist studies the perceptual abilities of newborn infants, another studies language abilities in chimpanzees. Because of this breadth, I was forced to be selective in what I included in the text. Nonetheless, I believe the text presents a fair, though not encyclopedic, sampling of the discipline.

To Present Material in Sufficient, but not Excessive, Detail Again, compromise was in order. As a teacher and student, I have disliked texts that go to extremes. At one extreme are texts that present a relatively large number of topics in staccato fashion, providing superficial coverage. At the other extreme are texts that present relatively few topics in an elaborate, in-depth fashion. Some texts even jump back and forth between superficial coverage and highly detailed coverage. Though my discussions of topics naturally vary somewhat in degree of coverage, I have made an effort to discuss most of them in moderate detail. This provides enough information to assure student comprehension, while permitting coverage of a sufficient number of topics to assure a good representation of the entire discipline. The main exceptions to this approach are topics covered in-depth in the "Thinking About Psychology" sections (discussed below).

To Encourage Appreciation of the Research Process Several years ago, as a member of my college's academic affairs committee, I joined with faculty from a variety of disciplines in revising our curriculum to include components showing how professionals think in different disciplines. For three years we read literature on the topic, listened to guest speakers with expertise about the issue, and wrestled with differing views on what such a curriculum would require. One consequence of this process was the decision to have each discipline offer an introductory "Modes of Thought" course, emphasizing how professionals go about their business. The emphasis would be on "how we know," as well as "what we know," in each discipline.

I was assigned the task of developing a modes of thought course in introductory psychology. My development of the course and my writing this text have benefited each other. Both aim at encouraging students to appreciate the research process. You will find that in doing so I have once again tried to strike a balance. I have chosen to discuss research studies in moderate detail. For a concrete example, you might turn to the discussion in chapter 8 of a study on how nonartists form concepts of artistic styles from paintings without being able to state the defining features that distinguish one style from another. Or, turn to chapter 16 and read the discussion of a study on how the immune system can be suppressed by classical conditioning. This moderately detailed discussion of research studies contrasts both with texts that present little more than research findings and with texts that describe actual research studies in great detail.

To provide students with enough background to appreciate the research process, chapter 2 is devoted to introducing the student to psychology as a science, the methods of psychology, and the use of statistics. It includes a concrete example of the scientific method by showing how it relates to a classic study of interpersonal attraction. I have chosen to present a discussion of statistics in chapter 2, instead of relegating it to an appendix. Chapter 2 also includes data from a hypothetical study and tells how to calculate descriptive statistics using that data. The chapter also explains the use of inferential statistics, but does not include calculations of them. Few nonpsychology majors would benefit from calculating inferential statistics, and psychology majors will get experience calculating all the inferential statistics they need in upper-level courses.

To Promote Critical Thinking I believe that students should know scientific methodology and scientific findings, and how to evaluate critically what they read by relying on objective, rational evaluation of empirical evidence. Students find that learning to think critically benefits them in their daily lives when confronted by claims made by friends, relatives, politicians, advertisers, or anyone else regarding the nature of various aspects of reality. Almost every page of the text has the student think about popular claims, provide alternative explanations for research findings, or think of possible implications of research findings. For an example of how I have integrated critical thinking within the text, turn to the discussion of hypnosis as an altered state of consciousness in chapter 5, or to a few "Thinking About Psychology" sections. Most of them are extended examples of critical thinking.

To Present Psychology in Context Based on comments from reviewers, "Psychology in Context" would be an appropriate title for this text. In contrast, I have found, with some admirable exceptions, that introductory psychology texts present psychology as though it developed in "ivory towers" divorced from any historical or personal context. Throughout this text you will find numerous ways in which topics are given a historical grounding.

For example, chapter 5 introduces the topic of hypnosis by discussing its origins in the practice of mesmerism in late eighteenth-century France. Chapter 9 traces the nature-nurture debate regarding intelligence back to the flood of immigrants in the early twentieth century. And chapter 10 highlights changing values concerning sexuality by discussing the case of an article submitted to the *Journal of the American Medical Association* in 1899 that was not published until 1983.

I have also taken care to show that psychology is a human endeavour, practiced by people with emotions as well as intellects, and that scientific progress depends on serendipity as well as on cool calculation. For example, chapter 1 discusses William James's effort to have Harvard grant the doctoral degree to Mary Whiton Calkins, who, as a woman, was denied the degree despite fulfilling all the requirements for it. Chapter 3 reveals that the first demonstration of the chemical basis of communication among nerve cells came to Otto Loewi in a dream. Chapter 6 explains why the name Pavlov rings a bell, while the name Twitmyer does not. Chapter 9 counters the myth of the mentally gifted as pitiable in light of the case of William James Sidis. And chapter 13 shows how Alfred Adler's concept of the inferiority complex might be rooted in his own sickly childhood.

To Present a Balanced View of Psychology This is not a psychoanalytic book, a behavioristic book, a humanistic book, a cognitive book, or a psychobiological book. It is a bit of each, which reflects my belief that an introductory psychology textbook should introduce students to a variety of perspectives, rather than reflecting the author's favored one. Having taught for thirteen years at small liberal arts colleges, I have been called upon to teach courses in virtually all areas of psychology, including the history of psychology. This has increased my appreciation of alternative perspectives, and the ways in which they have waxed and waned in their dominance over the decades. The student is introduced to the major perspectives in chapter 1 and continues to encounter them throughout the text, with the most obvious examples in the chapters on personality, psychological disorders, and therapy.

To Present Psychology in a Scholarly Way For students to respect psychology as a science, the textbook they use must be scholarly. Though popular examples are sprinkled throughout the text, they are not used as substitutes for evidence provided by scientific research. A perusal of the reference list at the end of the text reveals that the text is up to date in its coverage of research studies, yet does not slight classic studies. Of course, solving my intellectual Rubik's cube prevented me from including every important classic study or every recent, "cutting edge" study. By referring to the *Reference Diskettes* that are available as supplements to the text, you will appreciate the need for selectivity in choosing references to include in any given chapter.

You might also note that, to make the reader's task more pleasant, I have purposefully steered away from a practice that is annoying to me as a reader: presenting multiple references for the same research finding. While this practice might be appropriate in a journal article, it reduces readability in an introductory psychology text. Some authors include within a single set of parentheses several references, each with several authors. They may even do this more than once in a single paragraph. To avoid chopping up my prose, I have purposely limited myself to a single reference for each set of parentheses. Readers who desire more information about a given topic will enjoy the *Reference Diskettes,* which contain files listing numerous research articles keyed to each major section of each chapter.

To Show the Relevance of Psychology to Everyday Life I enjoy books that give me a sense of the author. I believe that the examples I use in showing the relevance of psychology to everyday life will provide you with this sense. The examples come from sports, politics, student life, arts, literature, history, biography, entertainment, and virtually every area of life. Moreover, instead of showing the relevance of psychology by using the common practice of tacking on "applications boxes," I have interwoven the examples into the body of the text. For example, chapter 5 provides research-based suggestions for overcoming insomnia; chapter 6 discusses how operant conditioning is used to train animals; and chapter 7 discusses ways to improve one's memory.

The Content and Special Features

Organization Though a textbook should stand as a well-written work of literature, it is, foremost, a pragmatic teaching and learning tool. Because of this, I have kept, more or less, to the traditional chapters we have come to expect in an introductory psychology textbook. Perhaps the most distinctive exception is the separation of chapters 1 and 2, which often appear as a single chapter. I believe that this is desirable for providing an adequate background of the history of psychology, the fields of psychology, and the science of psychology.

Because I have never encountered convincing evidence of a single "best" sequencing of chapters (I am continually devising new orders in my own course), the chapters have been written so that they can be covered in any order desired. To facilitate this, I have refrained from grouping chapters together into "Parts," which might otherwise make some instructors and students uncomfortable if an instructor desired to present the chapters in a different order. Within chapters, instructors will also be free to assign or eliminate particular "Thinking About Psychology" sections.

Integration of Concepts Throughout the Text Though each chapter is devoted to a different field of psychology, many concepts covered in one chapter cut across other fields. Thus, many concepts introduced in one chapter are then given expanded coverage in other chapters. For example, the concept of nature versus nurture appears in several chapters in discussions of language, intelligence, and personality. And the role of neurotransmitters is discussed in the chapters on psychobiological processes, memory, psychological disorders, and therapy, among others.

Thinking About Psychology In the senior seminar course I teach, called "Current Issues in Psychology," students read numerous journal articles and some popular articles on a host of controversial topics, which they then discuss or debate. Because of the success of this course—students enjoy sinking their teeth into controversial issues—I have adapted it for this text in many of the topics covered in the "Thinking About Psychology" sections. To provide adequate discussion of each "Thinking About Psychology" topic, I devote several pages to it. The topics covered are not attempts to inflict my beliefs on students, but to present as fairly as possible the status of a particular issue or application.

Most of the topics in these sections illustrate how psychologists think critically about issues such as hemispheric specialization, ESP, unconscious influences, ape language, personality consistency, effectiveness of psychotherapy, and Type A behavior. Other "Thinking About Psychology" sections illustrate the connection of research to practical reality, as in the sections discussing motivation and sport, biofeedback, and prejudice. And some of the sections illustrate how ethics, values, and politics are related to science, as in the sections on the ethical treatment of animals, the nature-nurture controversy concerning intelligence, the study of sex differences, the insanity defense, and the effect of pornography on aggression.

Marginal Glossary Early in my teaching career, I disliked marginal glossaries, in part because the textbook I was using included definitions of many words that were not peculiar to psychology. They were perfectly good, though perhaps unusual, English words that could be looked up in a dictionary. I felt that including such words in a marginal glossary was condescending to students. More recently, I have come to believe that a marginal glossary that limits itself to defining the meaning of psychological terms is a valuable component of a textbook.

Moreover, the marginal glossary eliminates the need to torture one's prose into the formal tones of a dictionary definition when introducing new concepts. In developing the marginal glossary, terms that are defined in the margins are printed in boldface. The marginal definitions are also collected in a glossary at the end of the text, which provides a handy reference for students who reencounter these terms in other chapters.

Illustrations I have made a purposeful effort to select or design illustrations that truly illustrate and reinforce concepts, or show what eminent psychologists look like. The illustrations have not been chosen merely for their artistic merit, though I believe they make the book aesthetically appealing.

Annotated Reading Lists Following each chapter is a list of recommended readings that provide more elaborate coverage of topics discussed in the chapter. Most are scholarly books, many are journal articles, and a few are popular articles. The student or instructor might wish to consult these for additional information.

Careers in Psychology Appendix My only compromise with my dislike for including appendixes (I believe information should be incorporated in the body of the text, if it is included at all) is the inclusion of one on careers in psychology. The material is a bit tangential to include in chapter 1. This should prove useful for psychology majors and may even help other students decide whether or not to consider majoring in psychology.

Other Features Each chapter begins with an *outline* to provide a skeleton around which to place the content of the chapter. And each chapter ends with a *summary* that captures the essential points made in each major section of the chapter. Following the summary are lists of *important concepts* and *important people,* including the pages on which they are discussed. All of the text citations are collected in a *reference section* in the back of the book. Also included are a *name index* and a *subject index.*

Now you know "the book I think I have written." After you have read the book, I would welcome your comments informing me about "the book I have actually written."

A Special Note to the Student

More than twenty years ago I was in the position you may be in right now—enrolled in my first psychology course. Serendipity (fortunate accident) played a part in my enrolling in my first psychology course. I was an English major looking for an elective course to fit in my schedule. I had not even considered taking psychology—that is, until one day, while sitting in my dormitory room listening to the latest Beatles album (yes, I'm from *that* era) and perusing the course listings, I listened to my roommate Wilbur rave about how terrific his introductory psychology course was. Trusting his judgment, I enrolled in that course and, as they say, the rest is history.

I changed my major to psychology and have never regretted it—though I never lost my love for English. Of course, most students who take introductory psychology courses are not psychology majors and most of them will never take another psychology course. In writing this textbook, I have kept the student in mind. Just as my teaching does, this text reflects my attempt to include qualities that I have preferred in the teachers I have had and in the texts I have read. I have preferred teachers who were well-organized, who explained concepts clearly, who provided interesting examples of concepts, and who used visual aids. Thus, I believe you will find the text coherent; written in a clear, conversational tone; packed with interesting, concrete examples of each concept; and easier to comprehend because of its judicial use of illustrations. I also hope that psychology will appeal to you as an intellectual pursuit. I would enjoy reading your comments about aspects of this text that you have enjoyed and any suggestions you have for improving it.

Supplementary Materials

Wm. C. Brown Publishers has gathered a group of talented individuals with many years of experience in teaching introductory psychology to create supplementary materials to assist instructors and students who use this text. The supplements are designed to make it as easy as possible to customize the entire package for the unique needs of individual professors and their students. Wm. C. Brown Publishers has provided a complete package of supplements, and have added some outstanding aids that have never been offered with any other textbook of this kind.

Instructor's Course Planner, the key to this teaching package, was prepared by Steven A. Schneider of Pima Community College and Richmond Johnson of Moravian College. The *ICP* is conveniently packaged in a three-ring binder so that lecture notes or classroom material can be added. This flexible planner provides separate teaching units for every major topic in the textbook. These topic-by-topic teaching units coordinate lecture suggestions, classroom activities, quizzes, handouts, discussion questions, test items, and directions for using the transparencies. Each chapter in the *ICP* also includes numerous activities designed to give students opportunities for further exploration of chapter topics plus film suggestions and aids for encouraging discussion.

Test Item File, by Seth Kalichman of the University of South Carolina and Don Hockenbury of Tulsa Junior College, is very comprehensive. It includes more than 2,000 multiple-choice test questions that are keyed to the text and learning objectives, and designated as factual, conceptual, or applied.

Supplementary Test Item Files, containing over 1,000 items each, will be offered to continued adopters of the text. A second *Test Item File* will be published during the Summer of 1991 for continuing adopters, followed by a third Test Item File that will be published in the Summer of 1992.

Student Study Guide, by Richmond Johnson of Moravian College, includes learning objectives, a guided review, student learning activities, and practice tests. The author has worked to create a *Student Study Guide* that encourages critical thinking while helping students to study more effectively and more efficiently.

Transparency Set of 175 acetate transparencies, most in full color, includes graphics from the text and outside sources. These transparencies have been expressly designed to help in classroom teaching and organizing lectures.

Reference Diskettes are available to all adopters and include over 8,000 journal and book references arranged in files coordinated with each major heading in the textbook. A sample of the *Reference Diskettes* has been included with each sample copy of the text. The complete set of five diskettes is available in either IBM 5.25 or 3.5 inch size.

The Critical Thinker, written by Richard Mayer and Fiona Goodchild of the University of California–Santa Barbara, uses excerpts from introductory psychology textbooks to show students how to think critically about psychology. It is available at no charge to first-year adopters of the textbooks or can be purchased separately.

A Conversation with William James, written by William Calhoun at the University of Tennessee, is a companion volume to the textbook that can be purchased for instructional use. It contains a brief biography of James and eight fictional conversations between James and a small group of students. This very brief book is meant to further encourage critical thinking, introduce the next generation of psychologists to the works of William James through excerpts from his own writing, and celebrate the one hundredth anniversary of James' two-volume *The Principles of Psychology.*

Psycom, *Psychology on Computer: Simulations, Experiments, and Projects,* is an interactive software package for introductory psychology, which is available for the Apple IIe and IIc, and the IBM PC. The various activities teach students to collect data, analyze it, and discuss the results within the context of scientific study. Results of the experiments can be tabulated for individual students or the entire class. A brief student workbook accompanies the software, providing background reading, instructions, worksheets, and other material necessary to complete the projects.

Acknowledgments

The greatest joy in writing this book has been the discovery that everyone at Wm. C. Brown who has been associated with this book has an intrinsic interest in producing texts of high quality. Their sense of pride in their work was everpresent. Moreover, they made a naturally stressful process fun. Michael Lange, psychology editor, has shepherded the project with his remarkable combination of intelligence, insight, and commitment to a book that would fit into a liberal arts curriculum. Sandy Schmidt, former developmental editor, improved the writing and the presentation of material and acted as a valued source of moral support. Gloria Schiesl, production editor, coordinated the work of all the individuals who contributed to the production of the book.

Laura Beaudoin, copy editor, showed her talents for tightening prose and improving diction. Toni Michaels, photo researcher, kept plugging away for just the right photo, and Michelle Oberhoffer, photo editor, was as excited as I was when we found just the right ones. Janice Roerig, art editor, and Stuart Paterson and Heidi Baughman, designers, are responsible for the beautiful appearance of the book. Karen Storlie, permissions editor, made my life infinitely easier by her conscientious performance of a tedious task.

My long-time mentor, Richmond Johnson, who honored me by agreeing to co-sponsor the first Annual Lehigh Valley Undergraduate Psychology Conference, honored me again by infusing his thirty years of teaching experience into writing a truly distinctive study guide.

Any of the good qualities of this text owe themselves in great measure to the many reviewers who read this text in part or in whole. I have valued, seriously considered, and even savored, each of their suggestions. They include:

Thomas R. Alley	Clemson University
J. S. Caldwell	California State University, Chico
J. B. Clement	Daytona Beach Community College
Kenneth Coffield	University of Alabama
Richard T. Comstock	Monroe Community College
Patricia Crane	San Antonio College
Joseph Culkin	Queensborough Community College
Thomas Evans	John Carroll University
William F. Ford	Bucks County Community College
Grace Galliano	Kennesaw College
William Glassman	Ryerson Polytechnical Institute
Richard Haude	University of Akron
Peter Hill	Grove City College
Morton Hoffman	Metropolitan State College
James E. Jans	Concordia University
Richmond Johnson	Moravian College
Seth Kalichman	University of South Carolina
Cindy Kennedy	University of Dayton
Melvyn King	SUNY—Cortland
T. C. Lewandowski	Delaware County Community College
Inez Livingston	Eastern Illinois College
Leonard Mark	Miami University
Kevin Moore	DePauw University
James Mosely	University of Calgary
W. Stephen Royce	University of Portland
Ina Samuels	University of Massachusetts
Steven Schneider	Pima Community College
Thomas J. Schoeneman	Lewis & Clark College
R. Lance Shotland	Pennsylvania State University
Dale Simmons	Oregon State University
Frank Vattano	Colorado State University
Deborah Du Nann Winter	Whitman College

I also owe a special note of thanks to my former students Phyllis Carpenito, Regina Damiano, Ellen Farrell, Laurie Harford, Edward Lucas, and Linda Potosnak for their valuable assistance in performing routine library chores and in scouring the library for hard to find items. Ultimately, this text is the product of my personal, as well as academic, relationships. I would like to thank my colleagues Charles Levinthal, who served as my doctoral dissertation mentor and who began my teaching career by permitting me to serve as his teaching assistant; the late Julia Vane, who developed in me an appreciation for the "soft" side of psychology; James Doyle, who gave me my first full-time faculty position and has given me sound advice on how to survive writing a textbook; and my fellow psychology faculty members at Allentown College: Martha Boston, Joseph Lambert, and Gregg Amore, who have given me their enthusiastic support, lessening the stress of having to fulfill my responsibilities as teacher, department chairperson, and college citizen at the same time that I was writing my text.

Other friends and relatives also deserve thanks. My brother Eric Sdorow has long been my best friend. Constance Sutilla has been a source of constant direction and emotional support. Sal and Marilyn Vicenzino have been more like surrogate parents—excited about my successes and valued guides in my youth. Neil, Shirley, Caryn, and Kenneth Stark developed my early interest in both science and literature. And Sol and Evelyn Barkin and Joe and Pauline Katz have been surrogate aunts and uncles who early in life stimulated my love of reading and humor.

Of course, foremost in my mind are my parents, Mildred and Harvey Sdorow, who made all this possible. My joy at my accomplishment is tempered greatly by the premature death of my father, who at times served as an informal editor, constantly on the phone with me to talk about my latest book-related escapade. I hope that he would be proud of what I have created.

PSYCHOLOGY

CHAPTER
1

THE NATURE OF PSYCHOLOGY

Chapter Opening Art:
Mark Rothko. *Vessels of Magic.* 1946.

D o lie detectors really detect lies? Is there a personality type that is prone to heart attacks? Do eyewitnesses give accurate testimony? Do children of working mothers suffer ill effects? Are chimpanzees capable of using language? Does pornography incite aggression against women? The science that seeks the answers to these—and thousands of other—diverse questions about human and animal behavior and mental processes is psychology.

But what is psychology? The word *psychology* was coined in the sixteenth century from Greek terms meaning "the study of the soul" (La Pointe, 1970), reflecting the religious basis of early interest in psychology. Psychology has continued to be defined by its subject matter, which has changed over time. By the late nineteenth century, when psychology emerged as a science, it had become "the science of mental life" (James, 1890/1950, Vol. I, p. 1). Psychologists studied the mind by having their research subjects describe their mental experiences, including their thoughts, emotions, and sensations. But during the early twentieth century many psychologists—believing that a true science can study only directly observable, measurable events—abandoned the study of mental experiences in favor of the study of overt behavior. Consequently, beginning in the 1920s, psychology was commonly defined as "the scientific study of behavior." This definition lasted until the 1960s, when interest in studying the mind returned and led to the current, broader definition of **psychology** as "the science of behavior and mental processes."

But what makes psychology a "science"? Psychology is a science because it relies on the *scientific method* (which will be discussed in chapter 2). Keep in mind that sciences are "scientific" because they share a common method, *not* because they share a common subject matter. Physics, chemistry, biology, and psychology differ in their subject matter, yet each uses the scientific method.

Psychology The science of behavior and mental processes.

The Scientific Study of Behavior and Mental Processes
Psychologists from a variety of fields of psychology might be interested in studying the skateboarder. For example, a *psychobiology* researcher might be interested in how his brain controls his actions. A *learning* researcher might be interested in how he perfected his skill. A *motivation* researcher might be interested in why he decided to become a skateboarder. A *health psychology* researcher might be interested in the effects of skateboarding on physical and psychological well-being. And a *social psychology* researcher might be interested in the effect of the crowd on his performance.

THE HISTORY OF PSYCHOLOGY

Like any other science, psychology evolved over time, influenced by developments in other disciplines and by its social and historical context.

The Roots of Psychology

The main historical roots of psychology are in philosophy and science, particularly physiology. When physiologists of the late nineteenth century began to use the scientific method to study the mind, psychology became an independent scientific discipline. As a science, psychology relies on objective, systematic observation as its primary source of knowledge. In contrast, philosophy relies on rational argument as its primary source of knowledge. Of course, at times psychologists and other scientists also use rational argument. But they make sure to test the validity of the conclusions they reach by testing them in the physical world.

The philosophical roots of psychology reach back to the philosophers of ancient Greece, most notably Plato (427–347 B.C.) and Aristotle (384–322 B.C.), who were interested in the origin of knowledge. Plato favored a position called **rationalism,** which assumes that true knowledge comes only through correct reasoning and not through the senses. Plato was suspicious of the senses as sources of knowledge, because we can be "fooled" by our senses, as in the case of illusions created by magicians. Though Aristotle, like Plato, accepted the importance of reasoning, he was also willing to accept sensory experience as an important source of knowledge—a position called **empiricism.**

Following the era of ancient Greece, in the early Christian and Medieval eras, answers to psychological questions were more often provided by theologian-philosophers than by secular philosophers. One of the leading authorities was Saint Augustine (354–430), who wrote of his views concerning memory, emotion, and motivation in his classic work *Confessions.* But neither he nor other authorities used the scientific method to study psychological processes such as these (Pratt, 1962).

With the coming of the Renaissance, extending from the fourteenth to the seventeenth centuries, authorities relied less on theology and, once again, more on philosophy to provide answers to psychological questions. The spirit of the Renaissance inspired René Descartes (1596–1650), the great French philosopher-mathematician. Descartes opposed the authority of theologians and insisted, as had Plato, that reasoning was the best means of gaining true knowledge. Other philosophers joined Descartes in rejecting the authority of theologians in dealing with psychological issues but disagreed with the rationalists' sole reliance on reasoning. One of the most renowned of these philosophers was the Englishman John Locke (1632–1704), who favored empiricism. According to Locke, each of us is born a blank slate—or *tabula rasa*—that is written on by life experiences conveyed through the senses.

By the mid-nineteenth century, philosophers—whether rationalists or empiricists—appeared to reach the limits of their ability to answer questions about the nature of psychological processes. In contrast, physiologists were making progress in answering these questions. As a consequence, psychology began to look less to philosophy and more to science for guidance. For example, in the mid-nineteenth century, popular belief, based on rational argument, held that nerve impulses travel the length of a nerve as fast as electricity travels along a wire—that is, almost instantaneously. This belief was contradicted by research by the German physiologist Hermann von Helmholtz (1821–1894).

Rationalism The philosophical position that true knowledge comes through correct reasoning.

Empiricism The philosophical position that true knowledge comes through the senses.

René Descartes (1596–1650) "I . . . have had many experiences that have gradually sapped the faith I had in the senses."

Gustav Fechner (1801–1887)
". . . body and mind parallel each other; changes in one correspond to changes in the other."

Psychophysics The study of the relationship between the physical characteristics of stimuli and the conscious psychological experiences they produce.

Helmholtz found that nerve impulses take a measurable fraction of a second to travel along a nerve. He demonstrated this in an experiment in which he had subjects press a button as soon as they felt a touch on the toe or thigh. A clock recorded their reaction times. Subjects took a fraction of a second longer to react to a touch on the toe than to a touch on the thigh. Helmholtz attributed this difference in reaction time to the longer distance that nerve impulses must travel from the toe to the spinal cord and then on to the brain. This indicated that the nerve impulse is not instantaneous. No amount of philosophical arguing could have made that discovery.

Some of Helmholtz's contemporaries were more interested in the scientific study of mental processes. The most noteworthy of these scientists was the German mystic-philosopher-physicist Gustav Fechner (1801–1887). Fechner invented a technique called **psychophysics** for quantifying the relationship between physical stimulation and mental experience. Psychophysics deals with questions such as, How much change must there be in the intensity of a light for a person to experience a change in its brightness? Psychophysics contributed to the transition of psychology from being a child of philosophy and physiology to becoming an independent science with its own subject matter. Psychophysics has also had important applications during the past century. For example, the scientists who perfected television relied on psychophysics to determine the relationship between characteristics of the television picture and the viewer's mental experience of qualities such as color and brightness (Baldwin, 1954).

The Growth of Psychology

Hermann Ebbinghaus once said, "Psychology has a long past, but only a short history" (Boring, 1957, p. ix). Ebbinghaus (1850–1909) was a pioneer in psychology. He realized that though people have been interested in psychological topics since the era of ancient Greece, psychology did not become a separate science until the late nineteenth century. The early growth of this new discipline was marked by the appearance of competing approaches championed by charismatic leaders. These approaches were known as *schools* of psychology, which included *structuralism, functionalism, psychoanalysis, behaviorism,* and *Gestalt psychology.*

Structuralism The early school of psychology that sought to identify the components of the conscious mind.

Structuralism The first school of psychology—**structuralism**—emerged in the late nineteenth century. Structuralists were inspired by the efforts of biologists, chemists, and physicists to analyze structures into cells, molecules, and atoms. Following the lead of these scientists, structuralists sought to analyze the mind into its component parts by studying conscious mental experience.

Structuralism grew from the work of the German physiologist Wilhelm Wundt (1832–1920). In 1875 Wundt set up a laboratory at the University of Leipzig in a small room that served in part as a dining hall for impoverished students. Wundt's request for a more impressive laboratory had been rejected by the school's administrators, who did not want to promote a science they believed would drive students crazy by encouraging them to examine the contents of their minds (Hilgard, 1987). Beginning in 1879 Wundt's laboratory became the site of formal research conducted by many of the most renowned European and American psychologists. The American Psychological Association recognized Wundt's contributions by celebrating 1979 as psychology's centennial year. Wundt was such a prolific writer that he wrote more than 50,000 pages during his career, despite being virtually blind and relying on his students to do his reading and writing for him.

Wilhelm Wundt (1832–1920)
Wundt, third from left, is shown surrounded by colleagues in his laboratory at the University of Leipzig in Germany in 1912. His establishment of the laboratory in 1879 marked the formal beginning of experimental psychology.

In studying the mind, structuralists analyzed complex mental experiences into what they considered to be the three basic mental elements: images, feelings, and sensations. In a typical research study, a structuralist would present a subject with a stimulus and then ask the subject to report the images, feelings, and sensations evoked by the stimulus. As you are aware from your own experience, stimuli such as paintings, musical passages, and familiar smells do evoke combinations of images, feelings, and sensations.

Wundt's method of having subjects report the mental experiences evoked by specific stimuli was called **analytic introspection.** This was a meticulous—and tedious—procedure. Wundt required his subjects to perform 10,000 introspections before letting them take part in his research. And when a subject was finally permitted to participate, a single introspective report in response to a stimulus that had been presented for little more than a second might take twenty minutes (Lieberman, 1979).

Structuralism was formalized and popularized by Wundt's student Edward Titchener (1867–1927). Titchener, an Englishman, introduced structuralism to the United States after joining the faculty of Cornell University. Among his contributions was research analyzing tastes, which eventually led to the discovery that even a complex taste depends on combinations of the four basic tastes of sweet, sour, salty, and bitter (Webb, 1981). Despite Titchener's contributions, structuralism became not only the first school of psychology to appear, but the first to disappear. This was caused, in part, by its reliance on introspection, which limited structuralism to studying conscious mental experience in relatively intelligent, verbally skillful adult human beings.

Psychologists also found introspection to be unreliable, because introspective reports in response to a particular stimulus by a given subject were inconsistent from one presentation of the stimulus to another. Similarly, introspective reports were inconsistent from one subject to another. And, perhaps most important, the very act of introspecting changed the conscious experience that was being reported. For example, suppose that you were asked to report your mental experience while you were angry. Your anger would weaken simply because you were observing it, making your verbal report of your anger experience inaccurate (Titchener, 1910).

Functionalism The American school of psychology known as **functionalism** arose, in part, as a response to structuralism. Functionalists criticized the structuralists for limiting themselves to analyzing the contents of the

Analytic Introspection A research method in which highly trained subjects report the contents of their conscious mental experiences.

E. B. Titchener (1867–1927)
"Since all the sciences are concerned with the one world of human experience, it is natural that scientific method, to whatever aspect of experience it is applied, should be in principle the same."

How does conscious mind help you survive?

Functionalism The early school of psychology that studied how the conscious mind helps the individual adapt to the environment.

William James (1842–1910)
"Consciousness, then, does not appear to itself chopped up in bits. Such words as *chain* or *train* do not describe it fitly as it presents itself in the first instance. It is nothing jointed; it flows. A *river* or a *stream* are the metaphors by which it is most naturally described. *In talking of it hereafter, let us call it the stream of thought, of consciousness, or of subjective life.*"

Mary Whiton Calkins (1863–1930) "I am more deeply convinced that psychology should be conceived as the science of the self, or person, as related to its environment, physical and social."

mind. The functionalists preferred, instead, to study how the mind affects what people do. While structuralists would study the components of tastes, functionalists would study how the sense of taste affects behavior. This reflected the influence of Charles Darwin's (1809–1882) theory of evolution, which stressed the role of inherited characteristics in helping the individual adapt to the environment. According to Darwin, through *natural selection* characteristics that promote the survival of the individual are more likely to be passed down to offspring, because individuals with such characteristics would be more likely to live long enough to reproduce. The functionalists assumed that the conscious mind evolved because it promoted the survival of individual human beings. Your conscious mind helps you survive because it permits you to evaluate your current circumstances and select the best course of action to adapt to those circumstances (Rambo, 1980). Recall a time when you tasted food that had gone bad. You quickly spit it out, demonstrating the functional value of the sense of taste.

Perhaps the most famous functionalist was William James (1842–1910), the great American psychologist and philosopher. James viewed the mind as a stream, which, as in the case of a real stream, cannot be meaningfully broken down into separate parts. Thus, he believed that the mind—or *stream of consciousness*—was not suited to the kind of analytic study favored by the structuralists. In 1875, the same year that Wundt established his laboratory at Leipzig, James established a psychology laboratory at Harvard University. But unlike Wundt, James used his laboratory for demonstrations rather than for experiments. In fact, James was both uninterested in laboratory research and critical of psychologists who studied narrow behaviors or mental experiences in the laboratory (Jacobson, 1979). James urged them, instead, to study how people function in the world outside of the laboratory.

Though he conducted no experiments, James made several contributions to the progress of psychology. His classic textbook *The Principles of Psychology* (1890/1950) emphasized the interrelationship of philosophy, physiology, and psychology. His theory of emotion, which will be discussed in chapter 11, is still influential today. And his encouragement helped his student Mary Whiton Calkins (1863–1930) to become one of several women, including Margaret Floy Washburn (1871–1939) and Christine Ladd Franklin (1847–1930), to achieve prominence as functionalists even in the face of sex discrimination. Washburn was a pioneer in the study of animal behavior and Franklin was a pioneer in the study of vision and hearing. But it was Calkins who became the most eminent of the early women psychologists.

In 1905 Calkins was elected the first female president of the American Psychological Association—despite her lack of a Ph.D. Though Calkins had completed all the requirements for a Ph.D. at Harvard University, and William James and other members of the faculty had approved her doctoral thesis, she was refused the degree because Harvard did not offer degrees to women. As a matter of principle, she refused a degree from Harvard's sister school, Radcliffe. Calkins's lack of a Ph.D. did not prevent her from making important contributions to psychology. She put forth one of the first theories of personality, developed a still widely used method of testing memory, and promoted the integration of structuralism and functionalism (Russo & Denmark, 1987).

As a group, the functionalists increased the variety of subjects used in psychological research by studying animals, children, and uneducated people. The functionalists also broadened the subject matter of psychology to include topics such as memory, thinking, and personality. And, unlike the structuralists, who limited their research to the laboratory (Leahey, 1981), the functionalists engaged in research applied to everyday situations. For example, John Dewey (1859–1952) applied psychology to improving education, and

Whose theory of emotion encouraged female students?

Hugo Munsterberg (1863–1916) applied psychology to increasing industrial productivity.

Because functionalists dared to move psychology out of the laboratory into the everyday world, they felt the wrath of structuralists, such as Titchener, who insisted that psychology could be a science only if it remained in the laboratory. Titchener even made the exaggerated claim that G. Stanley Hall (1844–1924), the leader of the functionalist school, was held in contempt by his psychology colleagues for using unorthodox research methods, such as questionnaires, and for using unorthodox subjects, such as people with psychological disorders (Goodwin, 1987). Despite Titchener's criticisms, most psychologists today would applaud the functionalists for diversifying the kinds of research methods, research subjects, and research settings used by psychologists.

Where did Psychoanalysis originate?

Psychoanalysis Unlike structuralism and functionalism, which originated in universities, **psychoanalysis** originated in medicine. Sigmund Freud (1856–1939), the founder of psychoanalysis, was an Austrian physician and physiologist. Psychoanalysis grew from Freud's attempts in the late nineteenth century to treat female patients suffering from physical symptoms, such as paralyzed legs, inability to speak, or loss of body sensations, that had no apparent physical causes. Based on his treatment of patients suffering from such symptoms of the disorder known as *conversion hysteria,* Freud concluded that the disorder was the result of unconscious psychological conflicts about sex caused by cultural prohibitions against sexual enjoyment by women. These conflicts were "converted" into the physical symptoms seen in conversion hysteria.

Freud's case studies of patients eventually led him to assume that unconscious conflicts, usually related to sex or aggression, were prime motivators of human behavior. Though Freud's recognition of the importance of unconscious motives was not new, he was the first person to include the unconscious mind in a formal psychological theory. Freud believed that all behavior—whether normal or abnormal—was influenced by unconscious motives. This belief is called **psychic determinism.** In his book *The Psychopathology of Everyday Life,* Freud (1920) explained how even apparently unintentional behaviors could be explained by psychic determinism. Psychic determinism explains misstatements popularly known as "Freudian slips," as in the case of the radio announcer who began a bread commercial by saying, "For the breast in bed . . . I mean, for the best in bread. . . ." As a leading psychologist noted, because of Freud's notion of psychic determinism, "the forgotten lunch engagement, the slip of the tongue, the barked shin could no longer be dismissed as accident" (Bruner, 1956, p. 465).

In addition to shocking the public by claiming that human beings were motivated by chiefly unconscious—often sexual—motives (Rapp, 1988), Freud stirred up controversy by claiming that early childhood experiences were the most important factors in the development of the personality. Freud believed that memories of early childhood experiences stored in the unconscious mind affect behavior later in childhood and adulthood. According to Freud, these unconscious influences explain the irrationality in much of human behavior and the origin of psychological disorders.

Freudian psychoanalysis has been so extraordinarily influential that a 1981 survey of chairpersons of graduate psychology departments found that the respondents considered Freud to be the most important figure in the history of psychology (Davis, Thomas, & Weaver, 1982). Nonetheless, psychoanalysis has been subjected to severe criticism. Critics have pointed out that the unconscious mind can be too easily used to explain any behaviors for which

what are Freudian slips?

Francis Sumner (1895–1954)
G. Stanley Hall, the leader of the functionalist movement, made one of his many contributions to psychology by sponsoring the graduate education of Francis Sumner. When he received his doctorate from Clark University in 1920, Sumner, a functionalist, became the first black to receive a Ph.D. in psychology in the United States. Sumner went on to develop the undergraduate psychology program at Howard University, which has graduated more blacks who have become psychologists than has any other school. Sumner was also one of the most prolific contributors to *Psychological Abstracts,* the basic library research tool for scholars and students of psychology. He wrote almost 2,000 abstracts of articles written in English, French, Spanish, German, and Russian (Bayton, 1975).

Psychoanalysis The early school of psychology that emphasized the importance of unconscious causes of behavior.

Psychic Determinism The Freudian assumption that all behaviors are influenced by unconscious motives.

who found Psychoanalysis?

used case studies

Sigmund Freud (1856–1939)
Freud is shown in 1909 with a group of eminent psychologists during his only visit to the United States to attend the famous Clark University psychology conference. (Seated left to right: Freud, his host G. Stanley Hall, and Carl Jung. Standing left to right: Abraham Brill, Ernest Jones, and Sandor Ferenczi.) Freud's theory of psychoanalysis revolutionized psychological thinking by emphasizing the importance of sexual motivation, unconscious processes, and early childhood experiences.

there are no obvious causes. William James had expressed this very concern even before Freud's views had become widely known. James warned that the unconscious "is the sovereign means for believing whatever one likes in psychology and of turning what might become a science into a tumbling ground for whimsies" (James, 1890/1950, Vol. I, p. 163).

Psychoanalysis has also been criticized for failing to provide adequate research evidence for its claims of the importance of sexual motives, unconscious processes, and early childhood experiences (Hobson, 1985). In fact, Freud never tested his theory scientifically. Instead, he based his theory on notes written hours after seeing patients, which made his conclusions subject to his own memory lapses and personal biases. Furthermore, Freud violated good scientific practice by generalizing to all people the results of his case studies of people with psychological disorders.

Despite these shortcomings, Freud's views have influenced the psychological study of topics as diverse as motivation, dreams, creativity, development, personality, and psychotherapy. Freud's views have also inspired the works of artists, writers, and filmmakers, including Eugene O'Neill's play *Mourning Becomes Electra* (1931) and the classic science fiction film *Forbidden Planet* (1956).

Behaviorism

> Psychology as the behaviorist views it is a purely objective experimental branch of natural science. Its theoretical goal is the prediction and the control of behavior. Introspection forms no essential part of its methods, nor is the scientific value of its data dependent on the readiness with which they lend themselves to interpretation in terms of consciousness. (Watson, 1913, p. 158)

This statement heralded the beginning of the school of psychology called **behaviorism,** founded by John B. Watson (1878–1958). The statement appeared in an article entitled "Psychology as the Behaviorist Views It," which rejected the position shared by structuralists, functionalists, and psychoanalysts that the mind is the proper object of study for psychology. Watson and

Behaviorism The early school of psychology that rejected the study of mental processes in favor of the study of overt behavior.

[handwritten margin notes: "What is the theoretical goal of Psych.?" and "Who founded behaviorism? What is it?"]

Drawing by Donald Reilly;
© 1983 The New Yorker
Magazine, Inc.

"I will, however, say this for Freud—he got a lot of people thinking."

other behaviorists were emphatic in their opposition to the study of mental experience. Ivan Pavlov (1849–1936), a renowned Russian physiologist and behaviorist, even threatened to fire anyone in his laboratory who used terms that referred to the mind (Fancher, 1979). (You will read about Pavlov's contributions to psychology in chapter 6.)

To behaviorists such as Watson and Pavlov the proper subject matter for psychological research is observable behavior, which, unlike mental experiences, can be recorded and subjected to verification by other scientists. While other psychologists might study the mental experience of "anger," behaviorists would prefer to study the observable behavior of "aggression." You should note that though Watson denied that mental processes could affect behavior, he did not deny the existence of the mind (Gray, 1980). Thus, he would not have denied that human beings have the mental experience called "hunger," but he would have denied that the mental experience of hunger *causes* eating. Instead, he would have favored explanations of eating that placed its causes in the body (such as low blood sugar) or the environment (such as a tantalizing meal) instead of in the mind (such as feeling famished).

Watson impressed his colleagues enough to be elected president of the American Psychological Association in 1915, and behaviorism later became so popular that Edwin Boring, an eminent historian of psychology, wrote, "For a while in the 1920s it seemed as if all America had gone behaviorist" (Boring, 1957, p. 645). But, in 1920, just as behaviorism was becoming dominant, Watson dropped out of academic psychology. He had been forced to leave his faculty position at Johns Hopkins University because of a scandalous divorce following his affair with his graduate student, Rosalie Rayner, whom he later married.

After leaving Johns Hopkins, Watson eventually joined the J. Walter Thompson advertising agency and by 1924 had risen to vice-president. Watson developed market research techniques, experiments to determine brand appeal, and sophisticated advertising campaigns. He even introduced the use

John B. Watson (1878–1958)
"Psychology . . . needs introspection as little as do the sciences of chemistry and physics."

of sex to sell products. In one advertising campaign, he associated "Pebeco" toothpaste with sex appeal (Buckley, 1982). Watson was an attractive and charismatic person who popularized his brand of psychology by writing and giving speeches even after leaving academic psychology. His faith in the importance of the environment in controlling behavior is best expressed in his classic proclamation on child development:

> Give me a dozen healthy infants, well-formed, and my own specified world to bring them up in and I'll guarantee to take any one at random and train him to become any type of specialist I might select—doctor, lawyer, artist, merchant-chief and, yes, even beggarman and thief, regardless of his talents, penchants, tendencies, abilities, vocations, and race of his ancestors. (Watson, 1930, p. 104)

Apparently, no parents rushed to offer their infants to Watson to be trained as specialists. Despite some of its excesses, behaviorism injected optimism into psychology by favoring the democratic view that human beings are minimally limited by heredity and easily changed by experience. Behaviorists assumed that all people, regardless of their hereditary background, could improve themselves and their positions in life. And Watson and his fellow behaviorists were more than willing to suggest ways in which to bring about such improvements through their books, articles, and public speeches. Watson even hoped to establish a utopian society based on behavioristic principles (Morawski, 1982).

Behaviorism was also responsible for a decline in the study of the mind. In fact, from 1930 to 1960 it was relatively rare to encounter the term *mind* in psychological research articles (Mueller, 1979). But, as mentioned earlier, during the past two decades the mind has returned as a legitimate object of study. And the weakened influence of behaviorism is also shown by renewed respect for the constraints that heredity places on the behavior of human beings.

Gestalt Psychology The German psychologist Max Wertheimer (1880–1943) founded the school of **Gestalt psychology,** which joined its rival school of functionalism in opposition to structuralism. Wertheimer used the word *gestalt,* meaning "form" or "shape," to underscore his belief that we perceive wholes rather than simply combinations of individual elements. A famous Gestalt psychology saying asserts that "the whole is different from the sum of its parts." And Wertheimer ridiculed structuralism as "brick and mortar psychology" for its attempts at analyzing mental experience into its separate components.

The founding of Gestalt psychology can be traced to a train trip taken by Wertheimer in 1912. While aboard the train he thought of the phenomenon of illusory motion—apparent motion in the absence of actual motion. At a stop Wertheimer left the train and bought a toy stroboscope, which rapidly presents a series of pictures that are slightly different from one another, producing the illusion of motion. On returning to his laboratory, he continued studying illusory motion by using a more sophisticated device called a *tachistoscope,* which can flash visual stimuli for a fraction of a second. Wertheimer had the tachistoscope flash two lines in succession, first a vertical line and then a horizontal line. When the interval between flashes was just right, a single line appeared to move from vertical to horizontal. He called this the *phi phenomenon.*

According to Wertheimer, the phi phenomenon showed that the mind does not passively respond to discrete external stimuli but, instead, organizes stimuli into coherent wholes. Thus, perception is more than a series of individual sensations. If the mind did passively respond to discrete stimuli, in observing

Gestalt Psychology The early school of psychology that claimed that we perceive and think about wholes rather than simply combinations of separate elements.

Wertheimer's demonstration you would first see the vertical line appear and disappear and then the horizontal line appear and disappear. You experience illusory motion whenever you attend a movie, which is simply a series of still pictures presented in rapid succession. (The psychological processes that account for the perception of illusory movement will be discussed in chapter 7.)

As another example of the organizing ability of the mind, consider a melody. A given melody can be perceived regardless of whether it is sung, hummed, or whistled and regardless of whether it is played on a banjo or by a symphony orchestra. Thus, a melody is not merely the product of a series of particular sensations produced by a particular source. Instead, a melody depends on the mind's active processing of different sensations that may be produced by a variety of sources. Gestalt psychology gave a new direction to psychology by emphasizing the active role of the mind in organizing sensations into meaningful perceptions. The Gestalt psychologists also applied their concepts to studies of problem solving, which you will read about in chapter 8.

Though founded by Wertheimer, Gestalt psychology was popularized by his colleague Wolfgang Kohler (1887–1967). Kohler and other Gestalt psychologists introduced Gestalt psychology to the United States after fleeing Nazi Germany. Kohler, a Christian college professor, had provoked the Nazis by writing and speaking out against their oppression of Jewish scientists and professors, including Albert Einstein (Henle, 1978). After emigrating to the United States during the Nazi era, Kohler was later elected president of the American Psychological Association in 1959. In his presidential address, Kohler (1959) urged Gestaltists and behaviorists to create a psychology that included the best aspects of both of their schools. As you will read later in this chapter, the so-called cognitive perspective in psychology reflects Kohler's advice by combining aspects of behaviorism and Gestalt psychology.

Max Wertheimer (1880–1943)
". . . the comprehension of whole-properties and whole-conditions *must* precede consideration of the real significance of parts."

Contemporary Psychological Perspectives

According to Thomas Kuhn (1970), a leading philosopher of science, as a science matures it develops a unifying *scientific paradigm,* or model, that determines its appropriate goals, methods, and subject matter. Though there are

TABLE 1.1	**Early Schools of Psychology**		
School	Subject	Goal	Methods
Structuralism	Conscious experience	Analyzing the structure of the mind	Analytic introspection
Functionalism	Conscious experience	Studying the functions of the mind	Introspection and measures of performance
Psychoanalysis	Unconscious motivation	Understanding personality	Clinical case studies
Behaviorism	Observable behavior	Controlling behavior	Observation and experimentation
Gestalt Psychology	Conscious experience	Demonstrating the holistic nature of the mind	Introspection and demonstrations

Psychoanalytic Perspective
The psychological viewpoint, descended from psychoanalysis, that places less emphasis on biological motives and more emphasis on the importance of interpersonal relationships.

what are the 5 psychological perspectives?

Karen Horney (1885–1952)
"When we realize the great import of cultural conditions on neuroses, the biological and physiological conditions, which are considered by Freud to be their root, recede into background."

B. F. Skinner (1904–   ) "I am a radical behaviorist simply in the sense that I find no place in the formulation for anything which is mental."

no longer separate schools of psychology with charismatic leaders and loyal followers, psychology still lacks a unifying scientific paradigm to which most psychologists subscribe. Instead, there are rival psychological *perspectives* (which in some cases have been influenced by the schools of psychology that were dominant in the early twentieth century): the *psychoanalytic perspective,* the *behavioral perspective,* the *humanistic perspective,* the *cognitive perspective,* and the *psychobiological perspective.*

The Psychoanalytic Perspective The **psychoanalytic perspective** is a descendant of the psychoanalytic school of psychology. The decline of the psychoanalytic school began when two of Sigmund Freud's students, Carl Jung (1875–1961) and Alfred Adler (1870–1937), developed psychoanalytic theories that disagreed with important aspects of his theory. Jung, Adler, and other so-called *neo-Freudians* such as Erich Fromm, Karen Horney, Erik Erikson, and Harry Stack Sullivan placed less emphasis on the biological drives of sex and aggression and more emphasis on the importance of social relationships. The views of the neo-Freudians will be discussed in later chapters.

Though the psychoanalytic perspective downplays the importance of biological drives, it accepts the importance of early childhood experiences and the unconscious mind. During the past two decades researchers have devised techniques—sometimes ingenious ones—that permit the scientific study of unconscious mental processes. (You will read about research on the unconscious mind in chapter 5.) The success of these techniques has led some psychologists to claim that "no psychological model that seeks to explain how human beings know, learn, or behave can ignore the concept of unconscious psychological processes" (Shevrin & Dickman, 1980, p. 432).

The Behavioral Perspective Like the psychoanalytic perspective, the **behavioral perspective** descended from an earlier school of psychology—behaviorism. The leading behaviorist is the American psychologist B. F. Skinner (1904–   ), probably the best-known contemporary psychologist. But it took many years for Skinner to achieve prominence. In fact, by the end of World War II in 1945 he had sold only eighty copies of his landmark book, *The Behavior of Organisms,* which had been published in 1938—an average of only ten copies a year.

Skinner was impressed by the work of John B. Watson. Like Watson, he has urged psychologists to ignore mental processes and to limit psychology to the study of observable behavior. Skinner and other strict behaviorists still refuse to treat introspective reports of mental experiences as appropriate subject matter for psychological research. But in contrast to Watson, who stressed the role of environmental stimuli in controlling behavior, Skinner has stressed the role of the consequences of behavior in controlling behavior. Animals and people tend to repeat behaviors that have been followed by positive consequences. Consider your performance in school. If your studying (a behavior) pays off with an A on an exam (a positive consequence), you will be more likely to study in the future. In Skinner's terms, your behavior has been "positively reinforced."

Skinner, like Watson, is a utopian. In 1948 Skinner published *Walden Two,* a book describing a utopian society based on behavioral principles. In Skinner's utopia, society would be run by benevolent behaviorists who would control behavior primarily by providing positive reinforcement for desirable behaviors. The tiny community of Twin Oaks, Virginia, is based on principles presented in *Walden Two.* Though there is yet no behavioral utopia, the behavioral perspective has contributed to improvements in education, child

Did Skinner believe in mental process (mind) or behavior?

rearing, industrial productivity, and therapy for psychological disorders, which will be discussed in later chapters.

Despite Skinner's continued efforts, the influence of the behavioral perspective has waned in recent years in the face of growing dissatisfaction with the lack of attention that strict behaviorists give to mental processes. This has prompted some behaviorists to begin studying the relationship between mental processes such as images and thoughts, which cannot be directly observed, and overt behavior, which can. These psychologists are called *cognitive behaviorists,* whose most influential leader has been Albert Bandura (1925–). (The strict behaviorist position of Skinner and the cognitive behaviorist position of Bandura will be discussed in later chapters.)

The Humanistic Perspective Because it provided the first important alternative to the psychoanalytic and behavioral perspectives, the **humanistic perspective** has been called the "third force" in psychology. It was founded by the American psychologist Abraham Maslow (1908–1970) in the 1950s to promote the view that human beings have free will and are not merely pawns in the hands of unconscious motives or environmental stimuli. Maslow had begun as a behaviorist, but eventually he rejected its narrow focus on observable behavior and the influence of the environment. Maslow's views were echoed by the American psychologist Carl Rogers (1902–1987). Both assumed that the subject matter of psychology should be the individual's unique subjective experience of the world.

Maslow and Rogers held a positive view of human nature, emphasizing the natural motivation of each person to reach his or her potential—a tendency called *self-actualization.* (Maslow's theory of human motivation will be discussed in chapter 10.) Humanistic psychology has also been a prime mover in the the field of psychotherapy, most notably through the efforts of Carl Rogers. His *person-centered therapy,* one of the chief kinds of psychotherapy, will be discussed in chapter 15. Though person-centered therapy has been the subject of extensive scientific research, other aspects of humanistic psychology, such as techniques that promote so-called personal growth experiences and consciousness raising, have been criticized for having little scientific support (Wertheimer, 1978). This lack of scientific rigor has contributed to the relatively minor impact that humanistic psychology has had on mainstream psychology, a fact lamented by Rogers (1985) near the end of his life. Despite its scientific shortcomings, humanistic psychology has made a valuable contribution in promoting the study of positive aspects of human experience, such as love, altruism, and healthy personality development.

The Cognitive Perspective Recent decades have witnessed a so-called cognitive revolution in psychology, leading to the emergence of a **cognitive perspective.** The cognitive perspective combines aspects of Gestalt psychology and behavioral psychology. Like Gestalt psychologists, cognitive psychologists emphasize the active role of the mind in organizing perceptions, in processing information, and in interpreting experiences. And, like behavioral psychologists, cognitive psychologists emphasize the need for objective, well-controlled laboratory studies. Thus, cognitive psychologists infer mental processes from observable behaviors, without relying on introspective reports alone. But, unlike strict behavioral psychologists, who claim that mental processes, such as thoughts, cannot affect behavior, cognitive psychologists believe that mental processes can, indeed, affect behavior (O'Connor, 1981).

The cognitive perspective owes much to the work of the Swiss psychologist Jean Piaget (1896–1980), who put forth a cognitive-developmental theory of

Behavioral Perspective The psychological viewpoint, descended from behaviorism, that emphasizes the importance of studying environmental influences on overt behavior, yet, in some cases, permits the study of mental processes.

Humanistic Perspective The psychological viewpoint that holds that the proper subject matter of psychology should be the individual's subjective experience of the world.

Abraham Maslow (1908–1970)
"I suppose it is tempting, if the only tool you have is a hammer [that is, the behaviorist's sole reliance on studying overt behavior], to treat everything as if it were a nail."

Cognitive Perspective The psychological viewpoint that favors the study of how the mind organizes perceptions, processes information, and interprets experiences.

which perspective is pervaded in every field of Psych?

Jean Piaget (1896–1980)
"To understand how the budding intelligence constructs the external world, we must first ask whether the child, in its first months of life, conceives and perceives things as we do, as objects that have substance, that are permanent and of constant dimensions."

what are Psychbio. primarily interested in?

Psychobiological Perspective
The psychological viewpoint that supports the study of the relationship between biological and psychological factors.

Roger Sperry (1913–   )
"The new mentalist position of behavioral and cognitive science seems to hold promise, not only as a more valid paradigm for all science but also for all human belief."

the child's mental development. (You will read about Piaget's research in chapter 12.) The cognitive perspective has also been influenced by the computer revolution of the past three decades, which stimulated research viewing the human brain as an information processor. While some cognitive psychologists use computer programs to create models of human thought processes, others use their knowledge of human thought processes to improve computer programs, as in the case of computer chess programs. As you will realize while reading later chapters, the cognitive perspective pervades almost every field of psychology.

The Psychobiological Perspective   Though the schools of psychology in the early twentieth century had their roots in nineteenth-century physiology, there was never a strictly biological school of psychology. But, in recent decades, growing interest in the biological basis of behavior and mental processes, combined with the development of sophisticated research equipment, has led to the emergence of a biological approach to psychology: the **psychobiological perspective.**

Psychobiologists are primarily interested in studying the brain, the hormonal system, and the effects of heredity on psychological functions. Though most psychobiologists rely on animals as subjects, some of the most important psychobiological studies have used human subjects. For example, in the course of surgery on the brains of epilepsy victims to reduce their seizures the Canadian neurosurgeon Wilder Penfield (1891–1976) mapped the areas of the brain that control movement and that process sensory information. And in 1981 the American psychobiologist Roger Sperry (1913–   ) was awarded a Nobel Prize for his studies of epilepsy victims whose left and right brain hemispheres had been surgically separated from each other. Sperry and his colleagues found that each hemisphere was superior to the other in performing particular psychological functions. Chapter 3 will describe the research of Penfield, Sperry, and other psychobiologists.

To appreciate the differences among the psychological perspectives, consider how each might explain your psychology professor's classroom behavior. Suppose you find that your professor is an unusually "happy" person—smiling, cracking jokes, and complimenting students on their brilliant insights. A psychoanalytic psychologist might assume that your professor is happy because he or she has successfully expressed unconscious aggressive urges in socially acceptable ways, perhaps by playing racquetball or creating extremely difficult exams. A behavioral psychologist might assume that your professor is happy because he or she has received positive reinforcement, such as students who remain alert and interested during lectures. A humanistic psychologist might assume that your professor is happy because he or she has a sense of self-actualization, having reached his or her potential as a friend, spouse, parent, artist, athlete, and psychology professor. A cognitive psychologist might assume that your professor is happy because he or she has an optimistic outlook on life, marked by positive thoughts about himself or herself, the world, and the future. And a psychobiologist might assume that your professor is happy because he or she has unusually high levels of brain chemicals associated with positive moods.

You should note (and keep in mind while reading the upcoming chapters) that each psychological perspective is worthwhile and has something to contribute to our fund of knowledge. You are certainly aware that just because an athlete prefers to play basketball it does not mean that he or she necessarily devalues other sports. Likewise, just because a psychologist favors one perspective does not mean that he or she necessarily discounts the value of the others. In fact, many psychologists favor an *eclectic* orientation, in which they combine aspects of several perspectives in forming their own psychological viewpoints. For example, Roger Sperry (1988) incorporates aspects of the behavioral, cognitive, and psychobiological perspectives in his approach to psychology.

FIELDS OF SPECIALIZATION IN PSYCHOLOGY

Since the era of Wilhelm Wundt and William James, as psychology has evolved as a science, its fields of specialization have multiplied. Today there are a wide variety of fields in which psychologists work, both in the laboratory and in everyday settings. Wundt and James would not recognize today's psychology. But, while Wundt, the laboratory-based structuralist, would be outraged that psychology has given birth to many nonlaboratory specialties, James, the pragmatic functionalist, would be elated that psychology has been applied to everyday life. Wundt would be delighted by the academic fields of psychology, tied more closely to the laboratory, and James would be delighted by the applied fields of psychology, tied more closely to the world outside of the laboratory.

Academic Fields of Specialization

Most of the chapters in this text discuss academic fields of specialization in psychology, usually practiced by psychologists working at colleges or universities. In fact, as indicated in figure 1.1, colleges and universities are the main employment settings for psychologists. Because each field of psychology contains subfields, which, in turn, contain sub-subfields, a budding psychologist

Laboratory Research
Experimental and physiological psychology are areas in which precise, careful, experimental strategies are followed. Shown here is a researcher investigating the nervous system. She is using a fluorescence-activated cell sorter to analyze the functions of single cells in the nervous system.

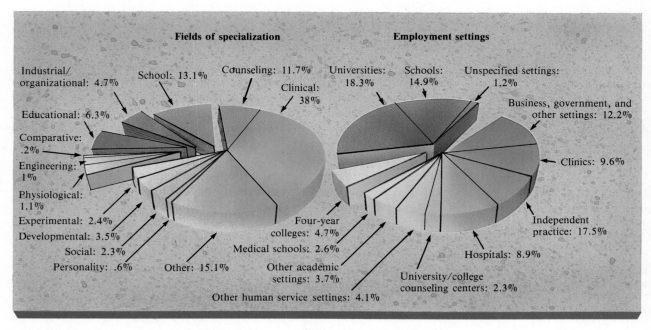

FIGURE 1.1
Fields of Specialization and Employment Settings of Psychologists The pie graph on the left presents the percentage of psychologists working in major fields of specialization. The pie graph on the right presents the percentage of psychologists who work in particular employment settings (Stapp, Tucker, & VandenBos, 1985).

What's largest field of academic specialization in psyd?

Experimental Psychology The field primarily concerned with laboratory research on basic psychological processes, including perception, learning, memory, thinking, language, motivation, and emotion.

Physiological Psychology The field that emphasizes the biological basis of overt behavior and mental processes.

Comparative Psychology The field that studies similarities and differences in the physiology, behaviors, and abilities of animals, including human beings.

Personality Psychology The field that focuses on factors accounting for the differences in behavior and enduring personal characteristics among individuals.

Social Psychology The field that examines the effects that people have on one another.

Developmental Psychology The field that studies physical, cognitive, and psychosocial changes across the life span.

Basic Research Research aimed at finding answers to psychological questions for their own sakes.

Applied Research Research aimed at applying research findings to solve practical problems and to improve the quality of life.

Clinical Psychology The field that applies psychological principles to the prevention, diagnosis, and treatment of psychological disorders.

Counseling Psychology The field that applies psychological principles to help individuals deal with personal problems, generally less severe ones than those seen by clinical psychologists.

Psychiatry The field of medicine that diagnoses and treats psychological disorders by using medical or psychological forms of therapy.

has hundreds of potential specialties from which to choose. For example, a psychologist specializing in the field of social psychology might be interested in the subfield of social attraction, with particular interest in the sub-subfield of dating behavior.

The largest field of academic specialization in psychology is **experimental psychology.** Experimental psychologists restrict themselves primarily to laboratory research on basic psychological processes, including perception, learning, memory, thinking, language, motivation, and emotion. You should note that though this field is called experimental psychology, it is not the only field that uses experiments. Psychologists in almost all fields of psychology use experiments in their research.

Psychologists in the field of **physiological psychology** study the biological basis of behavior and mental processes. A physiological psychologist might study the functions of particular brain structures, the effects of mind-altering drugs, or the ability of the brain to recover from injury. The related field of **comparative psychology** studies similarities and differences in the physiology, behaviors, and abilities of animals, including human beings.

The field of **personality psychology** is concerned with differences in behavior between individuals. It seeks answers to questions such as, Under what circumstances will people behave consistently from one situation to another? Psychologists in the related field of **social psychology** study the effects of people on one another. While one social psychologist might study the reasons why people commit murder, another might study the reasons why people donate to charities.

The field of **developmental psychology** is home to psychologists who study the factors responsible for physical, cognitive, and social changes that take place across the life span. A developmental psychologist interested in the beginning of the life span might study the perceptual abilities of newborn infants. In contrast, a developmental psychologist interested in the end of the life span might study whether intellectual abilities decline in old age.

Applied Fields of Specialization

While many academic psychologists prefer to conduct **basic research,** aimed at finding answers to psychological questions for their own sakes, other psychologists prefer to conduct **applied research,** aimed at applying research findings to improve the quality of life. Keep in mind that basic research and applied research are not mutually exclusive. Many psychologists conduct both kinds of research, and findings from basic research often find applications outside of the laboratory.

As indicated in figure 1.1, two of the largest fields of applied psychology are **clinical psychology** and **counseling psychology,** which deal with the prevention, diagnosis, and treatment of psychological disorders. Clinical psychology and counseling psychology are so similar that even practitioners of one or the other now find it difficult to distinguish between the two. But clinical psychology and counseling psychology are distinctly different from the medical field called **psychiatry.** A psychiatrist is a physician who has served a residency in psychiatry, emphasizing a medical approach to treating psychological disorders. Because psychiatrists are physicians, they may prescribe drugs or other medical treatments for treating psychological disorders.

Psychology also has other well-established applied fields. Psychologists who specialize in **school psychology** evaluate students for proper class place-

(a)

(b)

(c)

FIGURE 1.2
Emerging Fields of Applied Psychology In recent years, several new fields of applied psychology have emerged. Psychologists who practice *program evaluation* assess programs, such as advertising campaigns, sponsored by health, social, industrial, educational, and governmental organization. Psychologists in the field of *sport psychology* (a) help amateur and professional athletes, such as slalom skiers, improve their performance. *Forensic psychology* applies psychological principles to the law, as in improving jury selection procedures or in training police officers in how to respond to incidents of domestic violence. *Environmental psychology* (b) applies research findings to improve the physical environment, as in designing neighborhoods to reduce noise, crowding, and other sources of stress. And *health psychology* (c) contributes to the prevention of physical illness by promoting adherence to healthy behaviors, including regular aerobic exercise, such as rowing.

ment, set up programs to improve student academic performance and school behavior, and provide counseling, often in cooperation with parents and teachers, to students who are having problems in their personal or academic lives. School psychologists are found in elementary schools, junior high schools, and high schools. The allied field of **educational psychology** aims to improve the educational process, including curriculum, teaching, and administration of programs. Educational psychologists are usually faculty members at colleges or universities.

Psychologists who practice **industrial/organizational psychology** work to increase productivity in businesses, industries, and government agencies by improving working conditions, methods for hiring and training employees, and management techniques of administrators. Specialists in **engineering psychology** are experts in *human factors,* the aspects of human behavior and mental processes that must be considered when designing equipment and instruments. An engineering psychologist might assist in the design of the instrument panel of an airplane, the warning system in a nuclear power plant, or the barrier system at a railroad crossing. Figure 1.2 illustrates several emerging areas of applied psychology: **program evaluation, sport psychology, forensic psychology, environmental psychology,** and **health psychology.**

School Psychology The field that applies psychological principles to improving the academic performance and social behavior of students in elementary, junior high, and high schools.

Educational Psychology The field that applies psychological principles to improving curriculums, teaching methods, and administrative procedures.

Industrial/Organizational Psychology The field that applies psychological principles to improve productivity in businesses, industries, and government agencies.

Engineering Psychology The field that applies psychological principles to the design of equipment and instruments.

Program Evaluation The field that applies psychological principles in evaluating programs sponsored by health, social, educational, industrial, and governmental organizations.

Sport Psychology The field that applies psychological principles to help amateur and professional athletes improve their performance.

Forensic Psychology The field that applies psychological principles to improve the legal system, including the work of police and juries.

Environmental Psychology The field that applies psychological principles to improve the physical environment, including the design of buildings and the reduction of noise.

Health Psychology The field that applies psychological principles to the prevention and treatment of physical illness.

THINKING ABOUT PSYCHOLOGY

What Is the Popular Image of Psychology?

You now know that psychology is a century-old science that studies human and animal behavior and mental processes in both academic and applied settings. But, unless you took a psychology course when you were in high school, you probably did not have that image of psychology when you began this course. You might have confused psychologists with psychiatrists, viewing all psychologists as "shrinks" who treat people with interpersonal problems. Your main contact with psychology might have come from "Dr. Ruth" Westheimer's radio and television shows about human sexuality. Or perhaps your image of psychology came from watching television soap operas in which every other character seems to suffer from amnesia, multiple personalities, or some other kind of unusual psychological disorder.

If you did have an inaccurate image of psychology when you began this course, you are not alone. Throughout its century of existence, psychology has suffered from a distorted image of what it is and what psychologists do. The portrayal of psychology by the media and the influence of important public opinion makers has contributed to this problem.

Psychology and the Media

Since its founding in the late nineteenth century, psychology has been popularized through the mass media. In the late nineteenth and early twentieth centuries, psychology was popularized through public speeches, best-selling books, and, especially, magazine articles. In late nineteenth-century Germany, Wilhelm Wundt wrote articles on psychology for family magazines. And, in early twentieth-century America, William James and John B. Watson wrote articles for magazines such as *Cosmopolitan* and *Atlantic Monthly* (Viney, Michaels, & Ganong, 1981). In the early twentieth century, many psychologists were pleased that the media informed the public of the growth of applied psychology, showing its usefulness in business, industry, education, and therapy. But early psychologists were also distressed by the media's tendency to confuse psychology with the study of mind reading, fortune-telling, and the spirit world (Benjamin, 1986).

Contemporary psychologists have also been frustrated by the popular image of psychology presented by the media. Consider the following headline: "Horoscopes Really True, Says Psychologist," which appeared in a reputable newspaper. The article inaccurately reported research findings by the psychologist, who had gone to great pains to explain that her research had shown that astrology is worthless (Fichten, 1984). Because of this tendency of some reporters to distort, oversimplify, or sensationalize psychological findings, some psychologists believe that they should communicate as little as possible with the press. But other psychologists insist that those who want to promote an accurate popular image of psychology should find ways to improve the accuracy of media coverage instead of simply refusing to communicate with reporters (McCall, 1988).

The advent of radio in the 1930s and of television in the 1950s provided means of communicating a more accurate portrayal of psychology to a broader audience than could newpapers and magazines. In the 1950s psychologists realized that the new medium of television could be an especially useful way to inform the public about psychology. Because many of the early television stations were affiliated with universities, academic psychologists were the first to offer programs about psychology. Beginning in the fall of 1950 the University of Michigan offered a televised psychology course portraying human behavior and mental experience as legitimate realms of scientific investigation (McKeachie, 1952). By the mid-1950s similar televised academic psychology courses were offered by at least eight major universities (Harris, 1955). And in 1956 the University of Missouri offered perhaps the first television show on applied psychology. The weekly show discussed, in a nonsensationalistic way, topics such as breaking bad habits, developing self-confidence, and getting along with others (McKinney & Hillix, 1956).

Psychologists in the 1950s considered television to be the best medium for popularizing psychology in an objective, nonsensationalistic manner. Televised psychology was even criticized—not for being too sensationalistic (as it is today) but, instead, for being too dry and fact-oriented (Aronov, 1955). Regardless of the dramatic value of the presentations, television was being used to convey an accurate image of psychology as a science that studied all facets of human and animal behavior and mental experience.

But this changed with the emergence of media psychologists, psychologists who provided psychological advice for personal problems. The appearance of media psychologists on radio and television stations throughout the United States has given the impression that psychologists merely offer homespun, common-sense advice about personal problems. The first national media psychologist of the television era was Joyce Brothers, who has been in the public eye for more than three decades through her books, newspaper columns, and radio and television appearances. In 1956 Brothers was praised by fellow psychologists for enhancing the public image of psychology through her appearance on the popular television quiz show "The $64,000 Question." But Brothers earned this praise not for demonstrating her expertise as a psychologist but, instead, for demonstrating her knowledge of the history of boxing (Aichner, 1956).

In many cases, media psychologists have done more harm than simply reinforcing the inaccurate belief that all psychologists are therapists. Some media psychologists have created a negative portrait of psychologists as being more interested in providing entertainment than in helping people. Consider the following advertisement placed in the *Los Angeles Times* by the producer of a psychology television show: "Personal problems. Do you have problems involving love, sex, marriage, divorce, or drugs and want a consultation with a psychologist on a television show?" A psychologist who auditioned to host the show was told to be entertaining, not therapeutic, in handling the guests—whom the producer called the "problems" (Goleman, 1981).

Despite the tendency to promote psychology as little more than an entertaining way of offering therapy, the media does sometimes present psychology in a more accurate and flattering light. Academic psychology, rarely presented on local or network television, was presented in an accurate, positive way (while still being entertaining) by the Public Broadcasting System's series "The Brain," which first aired in 1984, and "The Mind," which first aired in 1988. These series presented psychology as a science that studies a variety of topics, rather than as merely a form of therapy that treats people with bizarre personal problems.

The media have also at times demonstrated that psychology does more for people than provide entertainment. Consider the case of the Kansas City hotel catastrophe on July 17, 1981. Two aerial walkways in the Hyatt Regency Hotel collapsed on a crowd of more than 2,000 people attending a dance in the lobby, killing 111 and injuring more than 200. Psychologists used radio, television, and newspapers to inform the public of what reactions to expect, ways to cope with emotional distress, and resources available in the community. These actions helped reduce the suffering of victims and their families, with more than 500 people seeking help at community mental-health centers within the first month after the disaster (Gist & Stolz, 1982).

The "Golden Fleece Award"

Media representation of psychology is not the only factor accounting for the inaccurate, sometimes negative popular image of psychology. Another factor is the demeaning of psychology by otherwise responsible leaders. Take the case of former Senator William Proxmire of Wisconsin and his "Golden Fleece Award." Beginning in 1975 and continuing until his retirement in 1988, Proxmire bestowed the award on the researchers whose federally funded research he considered the greatest waste of taxpayers' money. He publicized the award in his own newsletter, in national magazines, and on radio and television talk shows. Those whose research he attacked rarely received even a fraction of Proxmire's print space or airtime to rebut his charges.

Among Proxmire's favorite recipients were psychologists. His very first award went to two psychologists who had received funding for their research on romantic love. In giving the award, Proxmire claimed that love was a mystery that could not be studied scientifically and that even if it could be Americans would not want to hear the answers. He showed his ignorance of psychology as a science and of the possible benefits of such research in improving marital relationships, reducing the incidence of child abuse, and lowering the divorce rate (Shaffer, 1977).

In many instances Proxmire's awards went to research that simply sounded strange to him. One award winner was a study entitled "Sex Life in the Screw Worm." Aside from winning the Golden Fleece Award, the study helped save the cattle industry millions of dollars by eliminating a harmful parasitic worm (Walgren, 1982). In another case, Proxmire was sued for defamation by a researcher whose work on aggression in monkeys was given a Golden Fleece Award because he "made a monkey out of the American taxpayer." The psychologist won an apology and an out-of-court financial settlement from Proxmire. In giving his awards Proxmire discounted the fact that scientists, who have the expertise to make such judgments, evaluate the merits of applications for federal research grants in a highly competitive process. Proxmire would not even let the American Psychological Association provide him with background information explaining the purpose of psychological research studies that he criticized (Kiesler & Lowman, 1980). (This might remind you of those who refused to look through Galileo's telescope because they were not interested in changing their belief that the Earth was the center of the universe.)

As you can see, the popular image of psychology has often failed to reflect accurately its scientific nature and the wide variety of fields in which psychologists conduct research and apply their findings. In chapter 2 you will learn how psychologists go beyond common sense in finding answers to questions about human and animal behavior and mental experience. You will also learn how to evaluate critically claims made by psychologists and other scientists, as well as by politicians and other nonscientists. After reading this text and attending your class lectures you should have a more accurate impression

The Golden Fleece Awards
Before his retirement in 1988, Senator William Proxmire awarded a monthly "Golden Fleece Award" to the federally funded research project that he believed was the biggest waste of taxpayers' money. Proxmire's awards were based more on his own common sense than on the scientific merits of the award recipients. Because Proxmire often unfairly bestowed his award on research projects in psychology, he promoted an inaccurate, negative popular image of psychology.

of psychology as being a science with a diverse subject matter. You should also come to realize that the world of psychology is complex, exciting, and challenging.

SUMMARY

THE HISTORY OF PSYCHOLOGY

Psychology is the scientific study of behavior and mental processes. Psychology is a science because it relies on the scientific method; it differs from other sciences only in its subject matter. The roots of psychology are in philosophy and physiology. When nineteenth-century physiologists began to use the scientific method to study psychological processes, psychology emerged as an independent science. The commonly accepted founding date for psychology is 1879, when Wilhelm Wundt established the first formal psychology laboratory.

The late nineteenth century and early twentieth century were associated with the rise of schools of psychology, which differed in their approaches to the study of psychology. Structuralism, led by Wundt and Edward Titchener, sought to analyze the mind into its component parts by studying conscious mental experience. Functionalism, led by William James and G. Stanley Hall, arose in opposition to stucturalism and favored the study of how the conscious mind helps the individual adapt to the environment. Psychoanalysis, led by Sigmund Freud, was an outgrowth of medicine and studied the influence of unconscious sexual and aggressive motives on behavior. Behaviorism, led by John B. Watson and Ivan Pavlov, rejected the study of the mind in favor of the study of observable behavior, insisting that a science can only study observable, measurable events. And Gestalt psychology, led by Max Wertheimer and Wolfgang Kohler, favored the study of mental processes and emphasized the active role of the mind in perceiving wholes rather than combinations of separate components.

There is yet no unifying scientific paradigm in psychology. Instead there are competing psychological perspectives. The psychoanalytic perspective, favored by neo-Freudians, places less emphasis on the influence of the biological motives of sex and aggression and more emphasis on the influence of interpersonal relationships. The strict behavioral perspective, championed by B. F. Skinner, rejects the study of mental experiences in favor of the study of observable behavior. But cognitive behaviorists accept the study of mental experiences as long as they are carefully tied to observable behavior. The humanistic perspective, founded by Abraham Maslow and Carl Rogers, arose as a "third force" in opposition to both psychoanalysis and behaviorism. It favors the study of subjective mental experience and the belief that human beings are not merely puppets controlled by unconscious drives and environmental stimuli. The cognitive perspective, influenced by the work of Jean Piaget, views the brain as an active processor of information. The psychobiological perspective, exemplifed by the work of Roger Sperry, favors the study of the biological basis of behavior and mental experiences.

FIELDS OF SPECIALIZATION IN PSYCHOLOGY

During its century of existence, psychology has seen the emergence of a wide variety of academic and applied fields of specialization. The academic fields of specialization are primarily concerned with basic research, which aims to add to our fund of knowledge about behavior and mental processes. The major academic fields of specialization are experimental psychology, physiological psychology, comparative psychology, personality psychology, social psychology, and developmental psychology. The applied fields of specialization are primarily concerned with applied research, which aims to improve the quality of life. Among the major fields of applied psychology are clinical psychology, counseling psychology, school psychology, educational psychology, industrial/organizational psychology, and engineering psychology. Emerging fields of applied psychology include program evaluation, sport psychology, forensic psychology, environmental psychology, and health psychology.

THINKING ABOUT PSYCHOLOGY: WHAT IS THE POPULAR IMAGE OF PSYCHOLOGY?

During its century of existence, psychology has often been the victim of a distorted, sometimes negative popular image. Much of this has come from misrepresentations in the media and the assumption that all psychologists treat people with personal problems. The popular image of psychology has been tarnished by influential public figures who are ignorant of the nature of psychology as a science. Most notable among these individuals has been William Proxmire, whose "Golden Fleece Award" has often been unfairly bestowed on psychological research studies.

IMPORTANT CONCEPTS

Analytic introspection 7
Applied research 18
Basic research 18
Behavioral perspective 14
Behaviorism 10
Clinical psychology 18
Cognitive perspective 15
Comparative psychology 18
Counseling psychology 18
Developmental psychology 18
Educational psychology 19
Empiricism 5

Engineering psychology 19
Environmental psychology 19
Experimental psychology 18
Forensic psychology 19
Functionalism 7
Gestalt psychology 12
Health psychology 19
Humanistic perspective 15
Industrial/organizational psychology 19
Personality psychology 18
Physiological psychology 18
Program evaluation 19

Psychiatry 18
Psychic determinism 9
Psychoanalysis 9
Psychoanalytic perspective 14
Psychobiological perspective 16
Psychology 4
Psychophysics 6
Rationalism 5
School psychology 18
Social psychology 18
Sport psychology 19
Structuralism 6

IMPORTANT PEOPLE

Alfred Adler 14
Aristotle 5
Mary Whiton Calkins 8
Charles Darwin 8
René Descartes 5
Gustav Fechner 6
Christine Ladd Franklin 8
Sigmund Freud 9–10
Hermann von Helmholtz 5–6
Karen Horney 14

William James 8
Carl Jung 14
Wolfgang Kohler 13
John Locke 5
Abraham Maslow 15
Ivan Pavlov 11
Wilder Penfield 16
Jean Piaget 15–16
Plato 5

Carl Rogers 15
B. F. Skinner 14
Roger Sperry 16
Francis Sumner 9
Edward Titchener 7
Margaret Floy Washburn 8
John B. Watson 10–11
Max Wertheimer 12–13
Wilhelm Wundt 6–8

RECOMMENDED READINGS

For More on the History of Psychology:

Benjamin, L. T. (Ed.). (1988). *A history of psychology: Original sources and contemporary research.* New York: McGraw-Hill.
A collection of articles on the history of psychology and excerpts from works by eminent psychologists.

Fancher, R. E. (1979). *Pioneers of psychology.* New York: Norton.
A fascinating account of the lives and works of those who contributed to the development of psychology.

Guthrie, R. V. (1976). *Even the rat was white.* New York: Harper & Row.
A discussion of the history of research on differences between blacks and whites and a survey of the contributions of black psychologists.

Hilgard, E. R. (1987). *Psychology in America: A historical survey.* San Diego: Harcourt Brace Jovanovich.
A comprehensive textbook on the history of American psychology.

Kessen, W., & Cahan, E. D. (1986). A century of psychology: From subject to object to agent. *American Scientist, 74,* 640–649.
An article presenting a concise discussion of the history of changes in psychology's main subject matter.

Scarborough, E. S., & Furumoto, L. (1987). *Untold lives: The first generation of American women psychologists.* New York: Columbia University Press.
A discussion of the often-overlooked contributions of early women psychologists, including intriguing accounts of their professional lives.

Wertheimer, M. (1987). *A brief history of psychology.* New York: Holt, Rinehart & Winston.
A brief outline of the history of psychology from ancient Greece through the twentieth century.

For More Information on Careers for Psychology Majors:

American Psychological Association. (1986). *Careers in psychology.* Washington, DC: American Psychological Association.
A booklet describing a variety of careers in psychology. (You can obtain a free copy by writing to Order Department, American Psychological Association, P.O. Box 2710, Hyattsville, MD 20784)

American Psychological Association. (revised annually). *Graduate study in psychology and associated fields.* Washington, D.C.: American Psychological Association.
A manual describing hundreds of graduate programs, as well as helpful hints on selecting and applying to programs that suit your academic background and personal interests.

Fretz, B. R., & Stang, D. J. (1980). *Preparing for graduate study in psychology: Not for seniors only!* Washington, DC: American Psychological Association.
Helpful hints on long-range preparation for graduate study in psychology.

Woods, P. (Ed.). (1986). *The psychology major.* Washington, DC: American Psychological Association.
A collection of articles on the undergraduate psychology curriculum, career preparation, and employment trends in psychology.

Woods, P. J., & Wilkinson, C. S. (Eds.). (1987). *Is psychology the major for you?* Washington, DC: American Psychological Association.
A book advising you on how to plan your undergraduate years.

For More on the Popular Image of Psychology:

Benjamin, L. T. (1986). Why don't they understand us?: A history of psychology's public image. *American Psychologist, 41,* 941–946.
An interesting discussion of the popular image of psychology, mainly during its first half century.

McCall, R. B. (1988). Science and the press: Like oil and water. *American Psychologist, 43,* 87–91.
A discussion of the relationship between scientists and reporters.

For More Further Information about Any Aspect of Psychology, Write:

American Psychological Association
1200 17th Street, N.W.
Washington, DC 20036

CHAPTER
2

PSYCHOLOGY AS A SCIENCE

The Scientific Method
Sources of Knowledge
Steps in Using the Scientific Method

Goals of Psychological Research
Description
Prediction
Explanation
Control

Methods of Psychological Research
Descriptive Research
Case Studies
Naturalistic Observation
Surveys
Correlational Research
Experimental Research
Control
Generalizability

Statistical Analysis of Research Data
Descriptive Statistics
Inferential Statistics

Thinking About Psychology

What Are the Ethics of Psychological Research?
Ethical Treatment of Human Subjects
Ethical Treatment of Animal Subjects

Chapter Opening Art:
Vasily Kandinsky.
Composition 8. July
1923.

As you learned in chapter 1, psychology is the science of behavior and mental processes. But you may be wondering, Why do psychologists prefer the scientific method? and, How do they employ it? After learning the answers to these questions, you will appreciate the scientific basis of the research findings and issues discussed throughout this text. You will also become a more critical and objective judge of claims made by scientists, advertisers, politicians, and other people in your daily life.

THE SCIENTIFIC METHOD

Psychologists and other scientists favor the scientific method as their way of obtaining knowledge. To appreciate why they do, first consider popular alternative sources of knowledge.

Sources of Knowledge

Briefly turn back to chapter 1 and reread the questions on the first page. How would you find the answers to those questions? You might rely on *common sense, authority, reasoning,* or *observation.* When you rely on common sense, you assume that if people agree that something is true then it must be true. Though you may sometimes find common sense to be correct, it too often presents conflicting versions of the "truth." For example, which of these contradictory bits of common-sense wisdom about interpersonal attraction is true: "Opposites attract" or "Birds of a feather flock together"? In using common sense, you might declare, "*Everyone* knows that opposites attract!" To which a friend might counter, "You're wrong. *Everyone* knows that birds of a feather flock together!"

The use of the scientific method to resolve the conflict between these common-sense views about interpersonal attraction will be described later in the chapter. For now, to begin to appreciate how scientific findings may contradict common sense, consider the popular belief that we can identify a drunken person by simply observing his or her behavior. To test this belief, psychologists had bartenders, social drinkers, and police officers observe drinkers and judge whether they were legally drunk or sober. Of the ninety-

Sources of Knowledge What accounts for interpersonal attraction? In seeking the answer to this question and the answers to all sorts of questions about human and animal behavior, each of us relies on common sense, authority, reasoning, and observation. But psychologists, as scientists, rely on the scientific method as the best source of knowledge.

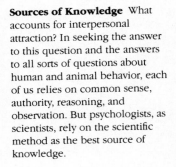

one persons who served as judges, only five were accurate—and all five were police officers with special training in the detection of drunken behavior. Thus, without special training, even people with experience in observing drinkers may be unable to determine whether a person is drunk or sober. This finding is important, because many states hold party hosts and tavern owners legally responsible for the actions of people who become drunk at their parties or taverns (Langenbucher & Nathan, 1983). Figure 2.1 presents another, perhaps surprising, example of the shortcomings of common sense.

In seeking knowledge, you might also appeal to authority. But, as in the case of common sense, authorities may be wrong or contradict one another. Suppose that you wrote to those noted authorities "Dear Abby" and "Ann Landers," asking them to resolve your conflict about the nature of interpersonal attraction. Dear Abby might reply, "My experts tell me that 'opposites attract.' So, you're probably going to marry someone very different from you." But Ann Landers might reply, "My experts tell me that 'birds of a feather flock together.' So, you're probably going to marry someone just like you."

The subjectivity of authorities when answering questions about human behavior was dramatically demonstrated in the case of John Hinckley, who tried to assassinate President Ronald Reagan in 1981. During Hinckley's trial, some psychiatrists testified that he was sane, while others testified that he was insane. Because the jury believed those who claimed that he was insane, and therefore not legally responsible for his actions, Hinckley was committed to a mental hospital—St. Elizabeth's Hospital in Washington, D.C.—instead of being convicted and placed in a prison.

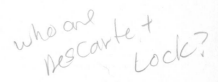

who are Descartes + Lock?

Centuries ago, the inadequacy of the appeal to authority as a source of knowledge led René Descartes (1596–1650) to declare that "the first rule [is] never to accept anything as true unless I recognized it to be certainly and evidently such." As you may recall from chapter 1, Descartes insisted that true knowledge comes through correct reasoning. In arguing the interpersonal attraction issue, you might say, "I believe that 'opposites attract' for the following reasons. . . ." In response, your friend might say, "I believe that 'birds of a feather flock together' for the following reasons. . . ." Of course, the accuracy of either position would depend on the truthfulness of the reasons— or *premises*—given in support of it. If even one of your premises is wrong, you might reason correctly yet reach a false conclusion, as in the following example:

FIGURE 2.1
Common Sense Should you change your answers on multiple-choice tests? Student common sense would say no. You have probably heard the folk wisdom, "Don't change your answers on exams, because you'll be more likely to change a right answer to a wrong answer than a wrong answer to a right answer." You might be surprised that scientific research has consistently found that students are slightly more likely to change a wrong answer to a right answer than a right answer to a wrong answer (Skinner, 1983).

> All mentally retarded people are unable to read.
>
> Helen is mentally retarded.
>
> Therefore, Helen is unable to read.

Though this example uses proper reasoning, its conclusion may be false, because its first premise is not true—many mentally retarded people *can* read.

As you also learned in chapter 1, long before Yogi Berra offered the profound insight, "You can observe a lot just by watchin'," John Locke (1632–1704) countered Descartes by insisting that true knowledge comes through observation—that is, through the senses:

> Let us suppose the mind to be, as we say, white paper, void of all characters, without any ideas; how comes it to be furnished? . . . To this I answer, in one word, from EXPERIENCE. In that all knowledge is founded, and from that it ultimately derives itself. (Locke, 1690/1924, p. 42)

In following Locke's suggestion to use observation as your source of knowledge, you might report that "after observing dozens of campus couples, I have found that 'opposites attract'." Of course, your friend might report that "after observing dozens of campus couples, I have found that 'birds of a feather flock together'." Thus, observation, by itself, may sometimes be an unreliable source of knowledge. Because of the weaknesses of common sense, authority, reasoning, and observation as sources of knowledge, scientists prefer the **scientific method,** which is based on certain assumptions about physical reality and follows a formal series of steps.

Albert Einstein was fond of saying, "God does not play dice with the universe." In using the scientific method, psychologists and other scientists share his assumption that there is *order* in the universe, meaning that there are lawful, rather than haphazard, relationships among events. In looking for these lawful relationships, scientists also share the assumption of *determinism,* which holds that every event has natural, potentially observable causes. This rules out free will and supernatural influences as causes of behavior. B. F. Skinner (1971) championed determinism as the explanation for all behavior in his controversial book, *Beyond Freedom and Dignity.* Yet, as pointed out a century ago by William James (1890/1950), scientists may be committed to determinism in conducting their research, while being tempted to assume the existence of free will in their everyday lives (Immergluck, 1964). They may succumb to this temptation because, if carried to its logical extreme, the assumption of strict determinism would lead them to unpalatable conclusions about human behavior. For example, Mother Theresa would not deserve praise for her work with the poor and Adolf Hitler would not deserve blame for his acts of genocide, because neither was free to choose otherwise. But, of the psychological perspectives, the only one that makes room for the influence of free will is the humanistic perspective.

Aside from (usually) assuming that the universe is an orderly place in which events—including behaviors—are governed by determinism, scientists assume that open-minded *skepticism* is the best attitude when judging the merits of claims of all kinds. Open-minded skepticism requires maintaining a delicate balance between cynicism and gullibility, neither rejecting claims outright nor accepting them uncritically. This skeptical attitude requires research evidence for all claims.

Skepticism is especially important in psychology, because many psychological "truths" are tentative. They are subject to change as the result of subsequent research, in part because psychological research findings depend on the times and places in which the research takes place (Scarr, 1985). What is generally true of human behavior at one time may be false at another time,

Scientific Method A source of knowledge based on the assumption that knowledge comes from the objective, systematic observation and measurement of particular factors and the events they influence.

and what is generally true of human behavior in one culture may be false in another culture. For example, acceptable sex-role behavior for Americans has changed dramatically over the past few decades, and acceptable sex-role behavior in America is not the same as it is in Japan. Thus, psychologists never claim to know the "absolute truth" about human behavior.

Steps in Using the Scientific Method

Given that psychologists are skeptical about claims not supported by solid research, how do they employ the scientific method in obtaining knowledge? The scientific method can be divided into three main steps: *preparing* the study, *conducting* the study, and *analyzing* the resulting data (figure 2.2). These steps were used by psychologist Donn Byrne and his colleagues (Byrne, Ervin, & Lamberth, 1970) in studying the issue of the moment: "Do opposites attract?" or "Do birds of a feather flock together?"

In preparing to conduct his study, Byrne identified his problem of interest, reviewed the relevant research literature, decided on the research procedure to use, and stated his research hypothesis. A **hypothesis** (from the Greek word for *supposition*) is a prediction of the outcome of a study. In Byrne's study the problem concerned the relationship between interpersonal similarity and interpersonal attraction. After reviewing the literature relevant to that problem, Byrne decided to conduct a *field study* in which male and female college students were studied in a real-life setting instead of in a laboratory. Based on his review of the literature, Byrne hypothesized that males and females with similar attitudes would be more likely to be attracted to each other.

Byrne then proceeded to carry out his research procedure and collect data. He had his subjects complete questionnaires assessing a variety of their attitudes as part of an alleged "Computer Dating" program. He told them that

Hypothesis A testable prediction about the relationship between two or more variables, typically concerning the outcome of a research study.

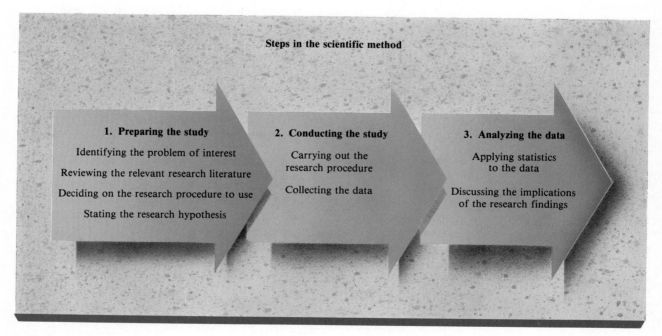

Steps in the scientific method

1. **Preparing the study**

Identifying the problem of interest

Reviewing the relevant research literature

Deciding on the research procedure to use

Stating the research hypothesis

2. **Conducting the study**

Carrying out the research procedure

Collecting the data

3. **Analyzing the data**

Applying statistics to the data

Discussing the implications of the research findings

FIGURE 2.2
The Scientific Method

their responses would be used to pair them with an opposite-sex student who shared their attitudes. But the students were actually paired so that some partners were similar in attitudes while others were dissimilar. The couples were then sent to the student union for a snack. After this brief get-acquainted "date," they were asked to rate their partners, providing Byrne with his research data.

Byrne analyzed the resulting data and discussed its relationship to his research hypothesis. In analyzing the data, Byrne, like almost all researchers, used **statistics,** which are special mathematical techniques used to determine whether the data support the researcher's hypothesis. In this case, Byrne found that his data supported his research hypothesis: partners who had similar attitudes rated each other as more desirable dates than did partners with dissimilar attitudes. Thus, in this study, the scientific method showed that, contrary to some people's common sense, authorities, reasoning, and observation, opposites do not attract.

Byrne, like other scientists, shared his findings by having them published in a professional journal. Scientists also share their findings by presenting papers at research conferences. Even undergraduate psychology majors may present the results of their research projects at undergraduate psychology research conferences.

Statistics Mathematical techniques used to summarize research data or to determine whether the data support the researcher's hypothesis.

[handwritten: What are psych goals in conducting research?]

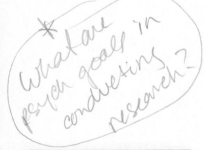

Undergraduate Psychology Research Conferences The scientific commitment of psychology is evident at the undergraduate psychology research conferences held each spring throughout the United States. These conferences provide an opportunity for students to present their research and to attend presentations by other students.

[handwritten: what are V?]

Operational Definition The definition of behaviors or qualities in terms of the procedures used to measure them.

GOALS OF PSYCHOLOGICAL RESEARCH

What goals do psychologists have in conducting their research? As scientists, their goals are *description, prediction, explanation,* and *control.*

Description

Consider Type A behavior, which has been implicated in the development of cardiovascular disease. In *describing* the behavior of people who exhibit this behavior pattern, a psychologist would note that they tend to act in a hostile manner, work under constant time pressure, and do several things at once. Psychologists, like other scientists, are *systematic* in what they describe. They only describe things that are relevant to their study, instead of arbitrarily describing everything that they observe. The need to be systematic in what you describe is expressed well in a statement concerning criminal investigations made by the fictional detective Sherlock Holmes to his friend Dr. Watson:

> A fool takes in all the lumber [facts] that he comes across, so that the knowledge which might be useful to him gets crowded out, or at best is jumbled up with a lot of other things. . . . It is of the highest importance, therefore, not to have useless facts elbowing out the useful ones. (Doyle, 1930)

In science, descriptions must be more than systematic—they must be precise. Precise descriptions require the use of concrete, rather than abstract, language. For example, describing a friend as "generous" would be acceptable in everyday conversation but would be too imprecise for scientific communication. Scientists solve this problem by using **operational definitions,** which define behaviors or qualities in terms of the procedures used to measure them. Thus, you might operationally define "generous" as "donating more than 5 percent of one's salary to charity." And a psychologist might operationally define "Type A behavior" as "a score above five on the Framingham Type A Behavior Scale."

occurrences

Prediction

Psychologists are not content merely to describe phenomena. They also make predictions in the form of hypotheses about changes in behavior, mental experiences, and physiological processes. Hypotheses are usually derived from **theories,** which integrate diverse research findings. Because it is impossible to know all the factors affecting a person or animal at any given time, it is rarely possible for psychologists ever to be certain about their predictions, whether in the laboratory or in everyday life (Manicas & Secord, 1983).

For example, though you might be correct in predicting that people who exhibit the Type A behavior pattern will be more *likely* to suffer heart attacks than will other people, you could not predict with *certainty* whether a given Type A person will suffer a heart attack. But this is no different from the situation in other sciences, which can only make predictions with varying degrees of probability of being correct (Hedges, 1987). Seismologists know that California will experience a major earthquake in the near future, but they cannot predict the exact day—or even the exact decade—when it will occur.

where are hypoth derived from?

Theory An integrated set of statements that summarizes and explains research findings, and from which research hypotheses may be derived.

Explanation

When you are asked to "explain" yourself, you are being asked to state the causes of your behavior. Similarly, in *explaining* changes in overt behaviors, mental experiences, and physiological processes, psychologists are looking for the causes of those events. A psychologist's favored perspective will determine where he or she looks for causes. Psychologists who favor the cognitive, humanistic, or psychoanalytic perspective will usually look for causes in the *mind.* Psychologists who favor the behavioral perspective will usually look for causes in the *environment.* And psychologists who favor the psychobiological perspective will usually look for causes in the *brain.*

Consider possible explanations for a businesswoman's Type A behavior. A cognitive psychologist might assume that her Type A behavior is caused by her belief that she must be perfect and in control of every aspect of her life. A humanistic psychologist might assume that her Type A behavior is caused by feelings of inadequacy and the need to live up to standards that are not her own. A psychoanalytic psychologist might assume that her Type A behavior is caused by her unconscious desire to please her parents. A behavioral psychologist might assume that her Type A behavior is caused by her taking on too many responsibilities and failing to delegate unimportant ones to other people. And a psychobiologist might assume that her Type A behavior is caused by an imbalance in certain brain chemicals that help regulate motivation. Keep in mind that each perspective is worthwhile and can potentially contribute to our uncovering the causes of a given psychological phenomenon.

In looking for the causes of psychological phenomena, be sure not to confuse **causation** with **correlation.** Correlation refers to the degree of association among events, behaviors, and characteristics. When two things are correlated, one can be used to predict the other, though one does not necessarily cause the other. For example, there is a *positive correlation* between educational level and the likelihood of developing a deadly form of skin cancer called malignant melanoma ("Melanoma risk and socio-economic class," 1983). This means that as a person's educational level rises, the probability of getting the disease also rises. You would be correct in predicting that people who attend college will be more likely to develop malignant melanoma than will people who never go beyond high school.

Which types of perspectives will Psych. favor that look for causes in mind? — environment? — brain?

Causation The demonstration of an effect of particular factors on other factors.

Correlation The degree of relationship among events, behaviors, or characteristics.

But does this mean that you should drop out of school today in order to avoid malignant melanoma? The answer is no, because the positive correlation between educational level and malignant melanoma does not necessarily mean that attending college *causes* malignant melanoma. Other factors common to people who attend college, rather than their mere presence in college, may cause them to develop the disease. Perhaps they increase their likelihood of malignant melanoma by lying in the sun more often than people who only have a high school education.

Psychologists, too, are careful about confusing causation and correlation. They are aware that if two events are positively correlated the first might cause the second, the second might cause the first, or other factors might cause both. In regard to Type A behavior, does Type A behavior cause heart attacks, do cardiovascular abnormalities cause Type A behavior, or do other factors cause both Type A behavior and heart attacks?

Control ~behavior

Psychologists go beyond describing, predicting, and explaining psychological phenomena. They also try to *control* them. When psychologists discover the factors that cause a phenomenon, they can then exert control in the laboratory or in everyday life. For example, a program of behavior modification might enable people with Type A behavior to change their maladaptive habits, making them less hostile, less pressured for time, and more able to do one thing at a time.

"What's even more astonishing is it coincides exactly with the World Series."

METHODS OF PSYCHOLOGICAL RESEARCH

Given that psychologists favor the scientific method as their primary source of knowledge, what are the ways in which they use it in their research? And, once they have collected their data, how do they make sense of it? Psychologists use research methods enabling them to describe, predict, explain, or control relationships among overt behaviors, mental experiences, physiological processes, and environmental events (figure 2.3). *Descriptive research* pursues the goal of description, *correlational research* pursues the goal of prediction, and *experimental research* pursues the goals of explanation and control.

[handwritten: what are the goals of the 3 researches?]

Descriptive Research

Descriptive research is "descriptive" because the researcher simply records what he or she has systematically observed. In using descriptive research, psychologists employ *case studies, naturalistic observation,* and *surveys.*

Case Studies A **case study** is an in-depth study of a person in which the researcher obtains as much information as possible about the person's thoughts, feelings, social relationships, and life experiences. The case study is often used in clinical studies of abnormal behavior. In fact, Sigmund Freud pioneered the use of the case study in developing his theory of psychoanalysis. In using the case study method to study obesity, you might obtain information on the life history and current beliefs, feelings, and behaviors of an obese person.

A best-selling book and television movie tells the true story of a woman called Sybil, who suffered from the rare psychological disorder known as *multiple personality,* in which the victim shifts from one distinct personality to another. Sybil had sixteen separate personalities, including males and females

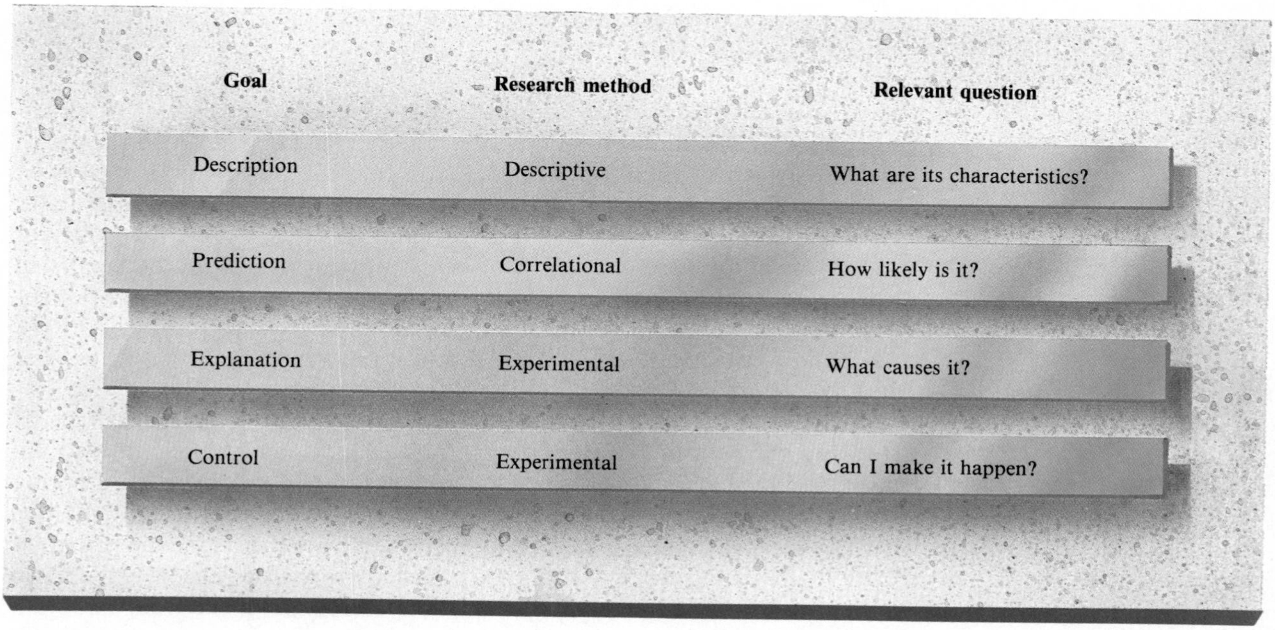

[handwritten: what is ↓]

Descriptive Research Research that involves the recording of behaviors that have been observed systematically.

Case Study An in-depth study of an individual.

Goal	Research method	Relevant question
Description	Descriptive	What are its characteristics?
Prediction	Correlational	How likely is it?
Explanation	Experimental	What causes it?
Control	Experimental	Can I make it happen?

FIGURE 2.3
The Goals and Methods of Psychology

The Case Study In the movie *Sybil,* Sally Field portrayed a young woman with sixteen different personalities. The movie was based on the case study of a woman who developed a multiple personality disorder, apparently as a consequence of extreme childhood abuse. The photograph shows Sybil (*left*) and her psychotherapist (as portrayed by Joanne Woodward).

and adults and children. In seeking help for her disorder, Sybil attended 2,354 psychotherapy sessions, during which she and her psychiatrist discovered that her disorder was apparently the result of a childhood filled with physical and psychological torture inflicted by her mother.

The case study is useful in examining rare phenomena, as in cases of multiple personality. But each of us is affected by so many factors that the case study method cannot determine the particular factors that caused the phenomenon of interest for the researcher. Though it might seem reasonable to assume that Sybil's traumatic childhood experiences caused her to defend herself by developing multiple personalities, it is scientifically incorrect to do so. Other factors, unrelated to how she was treated by her mother, may have caused her disorder. It is even conceivable that her mother began mistreating her only *after* discovering that Sybil had multiple personalities.

This is related to another shortcoming of the case study—the results of a single case study, no matter how compelling, cannot be generalized to all people. Even if Sybil's disorder was caused by traumatic childhood experiences, is it not possible that other people with multiple personalities have not had traumatic childhoods? (By the way, as you will learn in chapter 14, case studies have shown that people with multiple personalities usually do share traumatic childhoods.)

Naturalistic Observation The recording of the behavior of subjects in their natural environments, with little or no intervention by the researcher.

Naturalistic Observation In **naturalistic observation** subjects are observed in their natural environments, whether in a classroom, a shopping mall, or an African jungle. To make sure that the observations represent natural behavior, the observer refrains as much as possible from influencing the subjects he or she is observing. In other words, the observer should be *unobtrusive*. So, if you were studying the eating behaviors of obese and nonobese students in your school cafeteria, you would not announce your intention over the loudspeaker. Otherwise, your subjects might not behave as they normally do. An obese person who normally ate cake and ice cream for dessert might eat jello instead.

In some instances, researchers have devised clever, unobtrusive ways of studying behavior in natural settings. In one study, curators determined the most popular exhibit at Chicago's Museum of Science and Industry by noting which floor tiles wore out the fastest. They found that the tiles at many exhibits did not need to be replaced for many years, while the tiles at the most popular exhibit—hatching chicks—had to be replaced every six weeks (Webb, Campbell, Schwartz, & Sechrest, 1966). Had the researchers walked from exhibit to exhibit carrying clipboards and recording the number of people at each exhibit, they might have affected the number of people at particular exhibits, perhaps increasing the number at some and decreasing it at others.

Naturalistic observation is not limited to the study of human beings. Some of the best-known studies using naturalistic observation have been conducted by Jane Goodall, who has spent years observing chimpanzees in the wilds of Tanzania. To prevent the chimpanzees from acting abnormally because of her presence, Goodall spends her initial observation periods letting them get used to her. Eventually, they barely notice her and continue with their normal everyday routines. Goodall has made observations about chimpanzee behavior that have never been made in zoos or laboratories, such as their use of sticks as tools for a variety of purposes (Goodall, 1986).

As you can see, one of the advantages of naturalistic observation is the potential discovery of phenomena not found in more artificial settings, such as the laboratory. But researchers using naturalistic observation, like those using the case study, must not be hasty in generalizing their findings. For example, naturalistic observation has shown that short-term changes in the habitats of animals brought about by floods, droughts, or food shortages may temporarily alter their normal behavior patterns (Lewin, 1986). And, like the case study, naturalistic observation cannot determine the causes of a phenomenon. There are simply too many factors at work in a naturalistic setting. In using naturalistic observation you might find that obese people eat higher-calorie desserts than do nonobese people, but you would be unable to determine what causes them to do so.

Surveys When psychologists wish to collect a great amount of information about behaviors, opinions, attitudes, life experiences, and personal characteristics from many people, they use surveys. A **survey** asks subjects a series of questions about the topic of interest, such as product preferences or political opinions. Surveys are commonly in the form of written *questionnaires* or personal *interviews*. You have probably been asked to respond to several surveys in the past year, whether enclosed in the "You May Have Already Won!" offers that you receive in the mail or conducted by your student government association to get your views on dormitory visitation policies.

If you employed surveys in studying obesity, you might ask many obese and nonobese people a series of questions about their beliefs, feelings, habits, and family backgrounds in regard to eating, exercise, and other relevant topics. But, as is true of the case study and naturalistic observation, you cannot use the information you obtain to determine what *causes* obesity. You could not possibly decide which, if any, of the factors you surveyed causes obesity.

The prevalence of surveys—and the annoyance they induce—is not new. A century ago, William James (1890/1950) was so irritated by the prevalence of surveys that he called them "one of the pests of life." Today, the most ambitious of these "pests" is still the United States Census, which is conducted every ten years (most recently in 1990). Others you are familiar with are the Gallup public opinion polls and the Nielsen television ratings survey.

Good surveys use clearly worded questions that do not bias the respondent to answer in a particular way. But surveys are limited by the willingness of respondents to answer honestly and by their tendencies to give socially desirable responses. For example, in responding to a questionnaire, obese people might report eating less and exercising more than they actually do.

Because of practical and financial constraints, surveys rarely include everyone of interest. Instead, researchers will administer a survey to a **sample** of people who represent the **population** of interest. In conducting an obesity survey at your school, you might administer it to a sample of one hundred students. But for the results of your survey to be generalizable to the entire student population at your school, your sample must be representative of the student body on factors such as age, sex, and any other characteristics that

Naturalistic Observation
Jane Goodall's naturalistic observations of chimpanzees in the wild have contributed to our understanding of their everyday habits, many of which had never been observed in zoos or laboratories.

Survey A set of questions related to a particular topic of interest administered through an interview or questionnaire.

What are surveys used for?

Sample A group of subjects selected from a population.

Population A group of individuals who share certain characteristics.

The Survey Just as biased sampling affected the results of polls on voter preference during the 1936 presidential campaign, it did the same in 1948. The editor of the *Chicago Daily Tribune* was so confident in a poll placing Thomas Dewey well ahead of Harry Truman that on the night of the election he published an edition proclaiming Dewey the winner. He was more than a little embarrassed when Truman won. The photo shows Truman gleefully displaying the premature headline after learning that he had won.

Random Sampling The selection of a sample from a population so that each member of the population has an equal chance of being included.

Correlational Research Research that studies the degree of relationship among events, behaviors, or characteristics.

Negative Correlation A relationship in which scores on one variable increase as scores on another decrease.

might be relevant. This is best accomplished by **random sampling,** which makes each member of the population equally likely to be included in the sample. You could perform random sampling by using a special computer program to randomly select subjects or by simply mixing slips of paper with the names of all potential subjects in a bowl and, without looking, selecting one hundred.

The need for a sample to be representative of its population was dramatically demonstrated in a poll conducted by the *Literary Digest* during the 1936 presidential election. Based on the poll, the *Literary Digest* predicted that Alf Landon, the Republican candidate, would defeat Franklin Roosevelt, the Democratic candidate. As you know, Roosevelt defeated Landon. But why was the poll wrong? Evidently, the people included in the survey represented a *biased sample* not representative of those who voted. This occurred because the subjects were selected from the telephone book—telephones were a luxury to many people at the time. As a result, those who had telephones tended to be wealthier than those who did not. Because Republican candidates attracted wealthier voters than did Democratic candidates, people who had telephones were more likely to favor the Republican Landon than the Democrat Roosevelt. That was not the only occasion on which a presidential election poll was inaccurate. In 1948 President Harry Truman was elated to learn that another biased election poll had been wrong.

Correlational Research *what is it used for ?*

When psychologists want to predict one event from another, rather than simply describe a phenomenon, they turn to **correlational research.** In regard to obesity, you know that the more people exercise, the thinner they tend to be. This indicates that there is a **negative correlation** between exercise and body weight. As one increases, the other decreases. But, as mentioned earlier, correlation does not imply causation. Though it is possible that exercise causes thinness, it is also possible that thinness causes exercise. Thin people may find it less strenuous, less painful, and less embarrassing to exercise than do obese people.

Because of the difficulty in distinguishing causal relationships from correlational ones, correlational research has stimulated controversies in important areas of research. Consider the issue of intelligence. Is it best explained by nature (heredity) or by nurture (experience)? There is a **positive correlation** between intelligence and genetic closeness. Thus, identical twins tend

Causation versus Correlation People who exercise regularly tend to be thinner than those who do not. But does exercise *cause* thinness? Perhaps not. Thin people may simply be more likely to exercise than are fat people. So, a negative *correlation* between exercise and body weight does not imply that exercise *causes* weight loss. Only experimental research can determine whether there is such a causal relationship.

to be most similar in intelligence, ordinary siblings moderately similar in intelligence, and unrelated people least similar in intelligence. But does this positive correlation mean that heredity *causes* differences in intelligence? Perhaps another factor—different degrees of similarity in life experiences—causes the differences. This issue will be discussed at length in chapter 9.

Experimental Research

So far, you have learned about research methods that do *not* permit you to determine the causes of events. You will now learn about one that does—the **experimental research** method, which permits psychologists to determine the causes of changes in overt behaviors, mental experiences, and physiological processes. The simplest experiment uses two equivalent groups of subjects. One group is exposed to a condition and the second group is not. The group exposed to the condition is called the **experimental group,** and the group not exposed to the condition is called the **control group.**

Consider an experiment on the effect of swimming on weight loss (figure 2.4). The experimental group swims daily for ten weeks, while the control group does not. As the experimenter, you would try to keep constant all other factors that might affect the two groups. By treating both groups the same except on the condition to which the experimental group is exposed, you would be able to conclude that any resulting significant difference in weight loss between the experimental group and the control group was probably caused by the experimental group's participation in swimming.

The components of an experiment are called variables. A **variable** is an event, behavior, condition, or characteristic that has two or more values. Examples of variables would include age, height, temperature, and intelligence. Every experiment includes at least one *independent variable* and at least one

Positive Correlation A relationship in which scores on two variables increase and decrease together.

Experimental Research Research that manipulates one or more variables, while controlling others, to determine the effects on behavior, mental processes, or physiological activity.

Experimental Group The subjects in an experiment who are exposed to the experimental condition of interest.

Control Group The subjects in an experiment who are not exposed to the experimental condition of interest.

Variable An event, behavior, condition, or characteristic that has two or more values.

Group	Independent variable	Dependent variable
(Subjects are randomly assigned to the groups)	(Exercise)	(Weight loss)
Experimental	Swims	Pounds lost
Control	Does not swim	Pounds lost

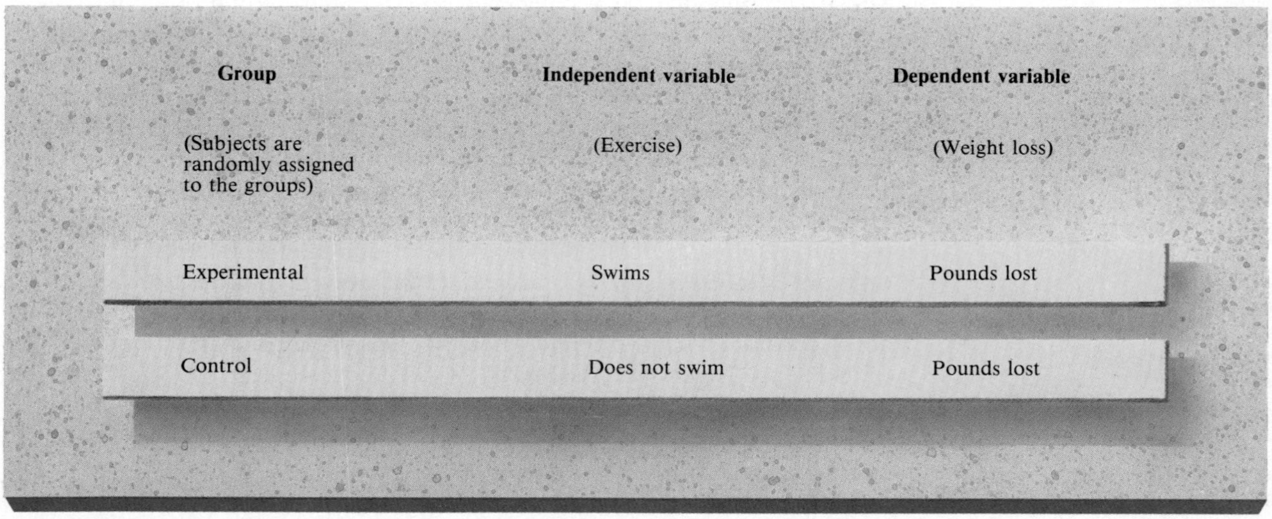

FIGURE 2.4

A Basic Experimental Research Design
Consider a two-group experiment on the effects of exercise on weight loss conducted by a health psychologist. The experimental group is exposed to condition in which subjects swim daily for ten weeks, while the equivalent control group is not. The groups are equivalent because the subjects have been randomly assigned to them. The experimenter would assume that a significant difference in weight loss between the two groups at the end of the ten weeks was caused by the exposure of the experimental group to the swimming condition.

Independent Variable A variable manipulated by the experimenter to determine its effect on another, dependent, variable.

Dependent Variable A variable showing the effect of the independent variable.

dependent variable. The **independent variable** is *manipulated* by the experimenter, who decides on its values before the experiment begins. In the exercise and weight-loss experiment, "exercise" is an independent variable with two values: "swimming" and "no swimming." The experimenter is interested in the independent variable's influence on the **dependent variable.** In determining cause-effect relationships, the independent variable would be the *cause* and changes in the dependent variable would be the *effect.* In the exercise and weight-loss experiment, "weight loss" is a dependent variable with many possible values: "two pounds," "seven pounds," and so on.

As an experimenter, you would try to hold constant all factors other than the independent variable so that the effects of those factors are not confused with the effect of the independent variable. In the exercise and weight-loss experiment, you would not want differences between the experimental group and the control group in diet, drugs, and other forms of exercise to cause changes in the dependent variable that you would mistakenly attribute to the independent variable.

Quasiexperimental Research The use of experimental research methods in situations in which the researcher may not be able to randomly assign subjects to the experimental and control conditions.

In some cases, for practical or ethical reasons, experimenters cannot assign subjects to an experimental group and a control group. For example, if you wanted to determine the effects of parental loss on children's social development it would be unethical to conduct a true experiment, which would require taking some children away from their parents. In such cases, researchers turn to **quasiexperimental research** methods, which do not require that the subjects be assigned to conditions by the experimenter. In conducting a quasiexperimental study, you might compare the social development of children who have already lost a parent and children who have not. Quasiexperimental research methods are especially popular in the emerging field of *program evaluation,* which was described in chapter 1.

Control (1) The ability to manipulate factors to bring about particular events. (2) The procedure by which experimenters keep extraneous variables from affecting dependent variables.

Extraneous Variable A variable that may affect the dependent variable against the wishes of the experimenter.

Control As noted earlier, an experimenter must do more than simply manipulate an independent variable and record changes in a dependent variable. The experimenter must also **control** any **extraneous variables** whose effects would be confused with those of the independent variable. These variables may be associated with the experimental procedure itself, the subjects of the experiment, or the experimenter.

In carrying out the procedure in the exercise and weight-loss experiment, you would not want the effects of any extraneous procedural variables to affect weight loss. You would want the subjects treated the same way, except that those in the experimental group would swim. But suppose that a locker-room attendant gave some of those in the swimming group amphetamines (so-called diet pills) after each exercise session. If the experimental group showed greater weight loss than the control group, the results might be attributable not to differences in exercising but, instead, to differences in drug use.

As an example of the importance of controlling extraneous procedural variables, consider what happened when the Pepsi-Cola company conducted one of its "Pepsi Challenge" taste tests ("Coke-Pepsi slugfest," 1976). Coca-Cola drinkers were asked to taste each of two unidentified cola drinks and state their preference. The cola drinks were Coca-Cola and Pepsi-Cola. The brand of cola drink was the independent variable, and the preference was the dependent variable. To prevent the tasters from knowing which cola they were tasting, Pepsi-Cola was put in a cup labeled *M* and Coca-Cola was put in a cup labeled *Q.* To the delight of Pepsi-Cola stockholders the results showed that most of the subjects preferred Pepsi-Cola.

The Pepsi-Cola company proudly—and loudly—advertised this as evidence that even Coca-Cola drinkers preferred Pepsi-Cola. But, knowing the pitfalls of experimentation, the Coca-Cola company *replicated* (repeated) the experiment, this time filling both cups with Coca-Cola. The results showed that most of the subjects preferred the cola in the cup labeled *M*. Evidently, the Pepsi Challenge had not demonstrated that Coca-Cola drinkers preferred Pepsi-Cola. It had only demonstrated that Coca-Cola drinkers preferred the letter *M* to the letter *Q*. The effect of the letters on the dependent variable had been confused with that of the independent variable—the kind of cola.

If you were asked to design a Coke-Pepsi challenge, how would you control the effect of the letter of the cup? Take a minute to think about this question before reading on. One way to control the effect of the letter would be to use cups without letters on them. Of course, the experimenter would have to keep track of which cup contained Coke and which contained Pepsi. A second way to control the effect of the letter would be to label each of the colas *M* on half of the taste trials and *Q* on the other half of the taste trials. As you can see, two ways to control extraneous procedural factors are to eliminate them or to assure that they affect all conditions equally.

Experimenters must also control extraneous subject variables that might produce effects that would be confused with those of the independent variable. Suppose that in the exercise and weight-loss experiment the subjects in the experimental group initially differed from the subjects in the control group on several factors, including health status, eating habits, and exercise practices. These initial subject differences might affect weight loss during the course of the study, giving the false impression that exercise (the independent variable) caused a significant difference between the two groups in weight loss (the dependent variable).

To avoid the problem of subject differences and maximize the chance that the experimental group and the control group will be initially equivalent on as many subject factors as possible, experimenters rely on **random assignment** of subjects to groups. In random assignment, subjects are as likely to be assigned to one group as to another. In the exercise and weight-loss experiment, you might randomly assign your subjects to the groups by flipping a coin. Given a sufficiently large number of subjects, random assignment will make the two groups initially equivalent on a host of subject factors.

Random Assignment The assignment of subjects to experimental and control conditions so that each subject is as likely to be assigned to one condition as to another.

After randomly assigning subjects to the experimental group and the control group, you would still have to control other subject factors. One of the most important of these is **subject bias,** the tendency of people who know they are participants in a study to behave in a way other than they normally do. As in the case of naturalistic observation, you might choose to be unobtrusive, exposing people to the experimental condition without their awareness. If this were impossible, you might choose to misinform the subjects about the true purpose of the study. In the exercise and weight-loss experiment, you might tell the subjects that the purpose of the study is to determine the effect of swimming on academic performance. This might prevent those in the exercise group from changing their eating habits in an effort to lose as much weight as possible. (The ethical issues involved in using such deception will be discussed later in the chapter.)

Subject Bias The tendency of people who know they are subjects in a study to behave in a way other than they normally would.

Experimenters must not only control extraneous variables associated with the research procedure or the research subjects, they must also control extraneous variables associated with themselves. Of greatest concern is **experimenter bias,** which occurs when the experimenter's expectancies about the outcome of a study affects the results through his or her unintentional actions. These actions might include (among others) facial expressions (perhaps smiling at subjects in one group and frowning at those in another), mannerisms (perhaps shaking hands with subjects in one group but not with those in another), or tone of voice (perhaps speaking in an animated voice to subjects in one group and speaking in a monotone voice to subjects in another).

Experimenter Bias The tendency of experimenters to let their expectancies alter the way they treat their subjects or record the behavior of their subjects.

FIGURE 2.5
Experimenter Bias A graph of
the results of the Rosenthal and
Fode (1963) experiment showing
that allegedly "maze-bright" rats
ran mazes faster than allegedly
"maze-dull" rats.

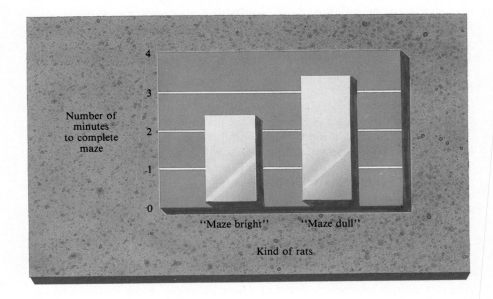

Experimenter bias has been studied most extensively by Robert Rosenthal and
his colleagues, who have demonstrated its effects in many studies since the
early 1960s (Harris & Rosenthal, 1985).

Experimenter bias may even affect the results of experiments using animals
as subjects. In an early experiment (Rosenthal & Fode, 1963), twelve students
acted as experimenters in a study of maze learning in rats. Six of the students
were told that their rats were specially bred to be "maze bright," while the
other six were told that their rats were specially bred to be "maze dull." In
reality, the rats did not differ in their inborn maze-learning potential. Nonetheless, the results showed that the "maze-bright" rats ran the mazes faster
than did the "maze-dull" rats (figure 2.5). Because there was no evidence of
cheating or misrecording of data by the students, the researchers attributed
the results to experimenter bias. The students' expectancies apparently influenced the manner in which they handled the rats, somehow leading the rats
to perform in accordance with the expectancies.

How might experimenter bias affect the results of the exercise and weight-
loss study? The experimenter might act more friendly and encouraging toward
the subjects in the experimental group, perhaps motivating them to swim more
than they would have otherwise, thereby leading to greater weight loss in this
group. One way to control experimenter bias would be to have those who
interact with the subjects be unaware of the research hypothesis, eliminating
the influence of the experimenter's expectancies on the subjects' performance.

Generalizability While experimenters are primarily concerned with controlling procedural, subject, and experimenter factors that might have unwanted effects on the independent variable, they are also concerned with
the issue of **generalizability.** In considering this issue, experimenters ask,
Will the findings of my experiment hold true for other people (or animals)
and in other settings? In other words, an experimenter might ask, Will the
findings of my exercise and weight-loss experiment with students here at
Grimley College hold true for different people swimming in pools other
than the one at the Grimley Physical Fitness Center? You might also ask,
Would people who are more obese than those in my study benefit as much

Generalizability The extent to
which the results of a research
study hold true for other people
or animals and in other settings.

from swimming? and Would other forms of aerobic exercise, such as running, bicycling, or cross-country skiing, have the same effect as swimming did in my study?

Experimenters are rarely sure that their findings can be generalized to other people or animals, because they can rarely take a random sample of the population of interest. Moreover, one of the great limitations on generalizing psychological research findings from studies using human subjects is the reliance on college students, who tend to differ from the general population in age, intelligence, and many other characteristics. But even psychologists who study animals are limited in their ability to generalize their findings to other animals by their reliance on albino rats and other rodents. The artificial conditions of laboratory settings may also limit the generalizability of research findings to other settings. The narrow range of research subjects and settings used in much of psychological research has provoked a call for psychologists to study a wider variety of subjects in a wider variety of settings (Sears, 1986).

Given the impossibility of knowing whether the results of a single experiment will generalize to other people or animals and to other settings or circumstances, psychologists rely on **replication** to determine whether their research is generalizable. In fact, Byrne's computer dating study was conducted to determine whether the results of laboratory studies on the effects of attitude similarity could be generalized to a real-life setting. And recall the study that found that people without special training in detecting drunken behavior are unable to judge accurately whether a person is drunk or sober. How can we know whether those findings generalize to people in the "real world"? We are somewhat more confident in them because they have been replicated in another experiment conducted by a different researcher, using different subjects, in a different research setting (Beatty, 1984).

Similarly, you would be more confident in the generalizability of your exercise and weight-loss experiment if it were replicated. If people of varying degrees of obesity, performing any of a variety of kinds of aerobic exercise, in any of a variety of settings, succeed in losing weight, then your findings have greater generalizability than you might have initially believed. The results of numerous studies show that this is, in fact, the case (Thompson, Jarvie, Lahey, & Cureton, 1982). As you can see, the issue of generalizability is more of an *empirical* question, answered by additional research, than it is a *rational* question, answered by reasoning alone.

Now that you have been introduced to the descriptive, correlational, and experimental methods of research, you should be able to recognize them as you read about the research described in later chapters. As you read, try to determine which method was used, as well as its possible strengths and weaknesses. You are now ready to learn how psychologists analyze the data generated by their research methods.

Replication The repetition of a research study, usually with some alterations in its subjects, methods, or setting, to determine whether the principles derived from earlier findings hold up under similar circumstances.

STATISTICAL ANALYSIS OF RESEARCH DATA

How would you make sense out of the data generated by the exercise and weight-loss experiment? In analyzing the data, you would have to do more than simply state that "Jane Rogers lost two pounds, Steve White gained one pound, Sally Jones lost eight pounds," and so on. You would have to identify overall patterns in the data and whether the data support the research hypothesis that inspired the experiment. As mentioned earlier, to make sense out of their data psychologists rely on mathematical techniques called statistics. Psychologists use *descriptive statistics* to summarize data and *inferential statistics* to test their research hypotheses.

Descriptive Statistics

Descriptive Statistics Statistics that summarize research data.

Measure of Central Tendency A statistic that represents the typical score in a set of scores.

Mode The score that occurs most frequently in a set of scores.

Median The middle score in a set of scores that have been ordered from lowest to highest.

In trying to make sense of your data, you would use **descriptive statistics** such as *measures of central tendency* and *measures of variability* to summarize it. If you were interested in predicting one set of data from another, you would also use *measures of correlation.* A **measure of central tendency** is a single number used to represent a set of scores. The measures of central tendency include the *mode,* the *median,* and the *mean.* Psychological research uses the mode least often, the median somewhat more often, and the mean most often.

The **mode** is the score that occurs most frequently in a set of scores. As shown in table 2.1, in the exercise and weight-loss experiment the mode for the experimental group is 6 pounds and the mode for the control group is 2 pounds. The **median** is the middle score in a set of scores. Thus, in the exercise and weight-loss experiment the median score for each group is the eighth score. The median for the experimental group is 11 pounds and the median for the control group is 3 pounds.

TABLE 2.1   Descriptive Statistics from a Hypothetical Experiment on the Effect of Exercise on Weight Loss

| Experimental group ("swim") | | | | Control group ("no swim") | | | |
Subject	Loss	d (deviation from mean)	d^2	Subject	Loss	d (deviation from mean)	d^2
1	9	−2.07	4.28	1	2	−2.2	4.84
2	21	9.93	98.60	2	11	6.8	46.24
3	6	−5.07	25.70	3	2	−2.2	4.84
4	6	−5.07	25.70	4	5	.8	.64
5	15	3.93	15.44	5	8	3.8	14.44
6	12	.93	.86	6	0	−4.2	17.64
7	2	−9.07	82.26	7	2	−2.2	4.84
8	13	1.93	3.72	8	7	2.8	7.84
9	18	6.93	48.02	9	2	−2.2	4.84
10	17	5.93	35.16	10	4	− .2	.04
11	5	−6.07	36.84	11	3	−1.2	1.44
12	6	−5.07	25.70	12	0	−4.2	17.64
13	11	− .07	.00	13	1	−3.2	10.24
14	15	3.93	15.44	14	12	7.8	60.84
15	10	−1.07	1.14	15	4	− .2	.04
	Sum = 166		Sum = 418.86		Sum = 63		Sum = 196.40

Mode = 6 lbs.

Median = 11 lbs.

Mean = $\dfrac{166}{15}$ = 11.07 lbs.

Range = 21 − 2 = 19 lbs.

Variance = $\dfrac{418.86}{15}$ = 27.92 lbs.

Standard deviation = $\sqrt{27.92}$ = 5.28 lbs.

Mode = 2 lbs.

Median = 3 lbs.

Mean = $\dfrac{63}{15}$ = 4.20 lbs.

Range = 12 − 0 = 12 lbs.

Variance = $\dfrac{196.40}{15}$ = 13.09 lbs.

Standard deviation = $\sqrt{13.09}$ = 3.62 lbs.

You are most familiar with the **mean,** which is the *arithmetic average* of a set of scores. You may have used the mean to calculate gas mileage, exam averages, and baseball batting averages. The mean lets you know whether a given score is at, above, or below the average score. In the exercise and weight-loss experiment the mean for the experimental group is 11.07 pounds and the mean for the control group is 4.20 pounds.

One of the problems in using measures of central tendency is that they can be used selectively to create misleading impressions. Suppose you had the following psychology exam scores: 23, 23, 67, 68, 69, 70, 91. The mode (the most frequent score) would be 23, the median (the middle score) would be 68, and the mean (the average score) would be 58.7. In this case, if you valued a high grade in the course, you would prefer the median as representative of your performance. But what if you had the following scores: 23, 67, 68, 69, 70, 91, 91? The mode would be 91, the median would be 69, and the mean would be 68.4. In that case, if you valued a high grade in the course, you would prefer the mode as representative of your performance.

Product advertisers, government agencies, and political parties are also prone to this selective use of measures of central tendency, as well as other statistics, to support their claims. But the use of statistics to mislead is not new. Its prevalence in the nineteenth century prompted Benjamin Disraeli, the eminent British prime minister, to declare, "There are three kinds of lies: lies, damned lies, and statistics." Even a basic understanding of statistics will make you less likely to be fooled by claims based on the selective use of statistics.

In order to best represent a distribution of scores, psychologists do more than report a measure of central tendency. They also report a **measure of variability,** which describes the degree of dispersion of the scores. Do the scores tend to bunch together? Or are they evenly distributed? Commonly used measures of variability include the *range* and the *standard deviation.*

The **range** is the difference between the highest and lowest scores in a set of scores. In table 2.1 the range of the experimental group is $21 - 2 = 19$ pounds, and the range of the control group is $12 - 0 = 12$ pounds. But the range can be misleading, because one extreme score can create a false impression. Suppose that a friend reports that the range of weight loss in his group is 37 pounds, ranging from 3 pounds to 40 pounds. You might conclude that there was a great deal of variability in the distribution of scores. But what if he then reported that one subject lost 40 pounds and the others lost no more than 5 pounds? Obviously, the variability of scores would be much less than you had concluded.

Because of their need to employ more meaningful measures of variability than the range, psychologists prefer to use the standard deviation. The **standard deviation** represents the degree of dispersion of scores around their mean. The standard deviation is the square root of a measure of variability called the *variance.* Table 2.1 shows that the standard deviation of the experimental group is 5.28 pounds, while the standard deviation of the control group is 3.62 pounds. Thus, the distribution of scores in the experimental group has a larger mean and standard deviation than does the distribution of scores in the control group.

While the mean and standard deviation are useful in describing individual sets of scores, a **measure of correlation** is useful in quantifying the degree of association between two or more sets of scores. As you learned earlier, a correlation may be *positive* or *negative,* and it may range from 0 to 1.00. In a *positive correlation* between two sets of scores, relatively high scores on one

Mean The arithmetic average of a set of scores.

Measure of Variability A statistic describing the degree of dispersion in a set of scores.

Range A statistic representing the difference between the highest and lowest scores in a set of scores.

Standard Deviation A statistic representing the degree of dispersion of a set of scores around their mean.

Measure of Correlation A statistic that assesses the degree of association between two or more sets of scores.

What is the difference between neg + zero correlation? (handwritten margin note)

set are associated with relatively high scores on the other, and relatively low scores on one set are associated with relatively low scores on the other. There is a positive correlation between height and weight and between high school average and college grade point average.

In a *negative correlation* between two sets of data, relatively high scores on one set are associated with relatively low scores on the other. There is a negative correlation between driving speed and gas mileage and between adult age and hours of nightly sleep. A *zero correlation* indicates that there is no relationship between one set of scores and another. As noted earlier, you would find an approximately zero correlation between the intelligence of two groups of strangers. The types of correlations are illustrated in figure 2.6.

FIGURE 2.6
Correlations In a *positive correlation*, scores on the measures increase and decrease together. An example would be the relationship between SAT verbal scores and college grade point average (GPA). In a *negative correlation*, scores on one measure increase as scores on the other measure decrease. An example would be the relationship between age and nightly sleep. In a *zero correlation*, scores on one measure are unrelated to scores on the other. An example would be the relationship between the number of times people brush their teeth during the day and the number of house plants they have.

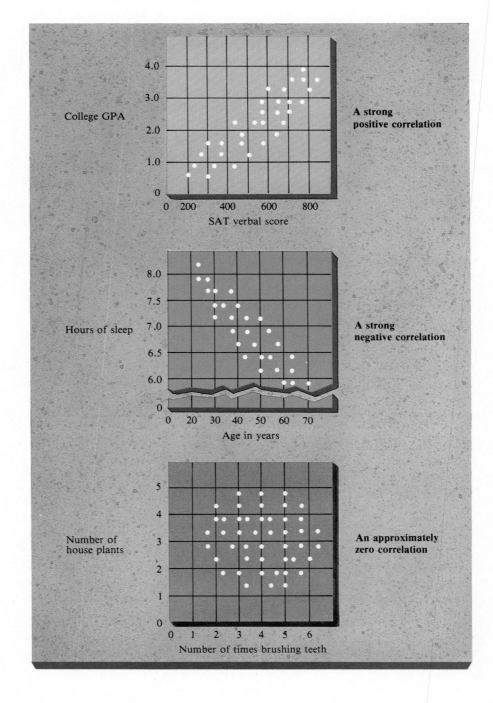

The higher the correlation between two variables, the better will be your ability to use scores on one variable to predict scores on the other. For example, suppose you found a correlation of −.83 between the number of hours people swim a week and their average body weight. This would mean that you would be fairly confident in predicting that as the number of hours of swimming increases the average body weight decreases. But if, instead, you found a correlation of −.21, you would have little confidence in making that prediction.

Inferential Statistics

In the exercise and weight-loss experiment, the experimental group lost more weight than did the control group. But is the difference in weight loss between the two groups large enough for you to conclude with confidence that exercise was responsible for the difference? Perhaps the difference could have happened by chance—that is, because of a host of random factors other than swimming. To determine whether the independent variable, rather than chance factors, caused the changes in the dependent variable, psychologists use **inferential statistics.**

If there is a low probability that the difference between groups on the dependent variable is attributable to chance (that is, to random factors), the difference is **statistically significant** and is attributed to the independent variable. In the exercise and weight-loss experiment, you would expect that chance factors would account for some changes in the weights of subjects in both groups during the course of the study. For the difference in average weight loss between the two groups to be considered statistically significant, it would have to be significantly larger than would be expected by chance alone. Psychologists usually accept a difference as statistically significant when there is no more than a 5 percent (one in twenty) probability that the difference is the product of chance factors.

There are advanced statistical methods that allow psychologists to determine whether a difference between groups on a dependent variable is statistically significant. You would analyze the data in the exercise and weight-loss experiment with an inferential statistic called the **t-test,** which is used to compare two sets of scores. In this case, you would compare the scores of the experimental group and the control group. If the t-test found that the difference in weight loss between the groups was great enough to be statistically significant, you would conclude that the difference is not due to chance and that your research hypothesis is supported: swimming is an effective means of weight loss.

In comparing more than two groups, psychologists often use a statistical procedure called the **analysis of variance.** If you had included a third group in the exercise and weight loss study (perhaps one that dieted), you would use the analysis of variance to analyze the data. Special tables are used to determine whether the result of the t-test or analysis of variance is large enough to be statistically significant. There are a host of other statistical techniques, beyond the scope of this text, that researchers use to analyze their data.

As you read the research studies discussed in later chapters, keep in mind that virtually all were analyzed by descriptive statistics and inferential statistics. You should also note that *statistical* significance does not necessarily imply *practical* significance. For example, a variety of relaxation techniques have been used in treating high blood pressure. While studies have found that some of these techniques can induce statistically significant decreases in blood pressure, those decreases may not be of practical significance. In other words, they may not be large enough to produce clinically important changes in blood pressure.

Inferential Statistics Statistics used to determine whether the results of experiments are due to the effects of their independent variables.

Statistical Significance A low probability (usually less than 5 percent) that the results of a research study are due to chance factors.

t-test An inferential statistic used to determine whether two sets of scores are significantly different from each other.

Analysis of Variance An inferential statistical procedure used to determine whether two or more sets of scores are different from each other.

THINKING ABOUT PSYCHOLOGY

What Are the Ethics
of Psychological
Research?

Psychologists must be as concerned with the ethical treatment of their subjects as they are with the quality of their research methods and statistical analyses. Because of these ethical concerns, the American Psychological Association (1981) has a formal code of ethics covering the treatment of both human and animal subjects.

Ethical Treatment of Human Subjects

The first code of ethics for the treatment of human subjects in psychological research was developed in 1953, partly in response to the Nuremberg war crimes trials following World War II, which disclosed the cruel medical experiments performed by Nazi physicians on prisoners of war and concentration camp inmates (Reese & Fremouw, 1984). Today, the United States government requires institutions that receive federal research grants to establish committees that review research proposals to assure the ethical treatment of human subjects.

According to the American Psychological Association's code of ethics, first, the researcher must inform potential subjects of all aspects of the research procedure that might influence their decision to participate. Second, potential subjects (whether college students, mental patients, or prison inmates) must not be forced to participate in a research study. Third, subjects must be permitted to withdraw from the study at any time. Fourth, the researcher must protect the subjects from physical harm and mental distress. Fifth, if a subject does experience harm or distress, the researcher must try to alleviate it. Sixth, information gained from subjects must be kept confidential.

Despite their code of ethics, psychologists sometimes confront ethical dilemmas in their treatment of human subjects. Of chief concern is the use of deception in research studies, which is commonly used to reduce subject bias. To avoid subject bias, psychologists sometimes do not inform people that they are being studied or misinform them about the true nature of the study. Recall that the "Computer Dating" study used deception by falsely claiming that all participants would be matched with partners who shared their attitudes. Today, for this to be considered ethical, the researcher would have to demonstrate that the research is sufficiently important and that it could not be conducted without the use of deception. Moreover, at the completion of the study, the subjects would have to be debriefed—that is, informed of the deception and reasons for its use. Can you think of a way in which the "Computer Dating" study could have tested its hypothesis without using deception?

One of the most controversial uses of deception in psychological research was in a study conducted by psychologist David Rosenhan (1973) in which eight normal persons, including Rosenhan, gained admission to several mental hospitals by complaining that they were hearing voices. After being admitted, these "pseudopatients" stopped complaining of voices and acted normally during their weeks of confinement. Rosenhan found that only real patients detected the pseudopatients—the hospital staffs never did. He concluded that professional staff members may consider all residents of a mental hospital to be abnormal, regardless of their behavior.

Rosenhan pointed out that the study would have been impossible had it not used deception and that the findings were important enough to justify the deception. According to Rosenhan, it is important to know that normal people might be kept in mental hospitals because of the inability of professionals to identify them. But Diana Baumrind (1985), a long-time critic of deceptive research, claimed that even the positive findings of studies that use deception do not either outweigh the resulting distress of subjects who learn that they have been fooled or the resulting distrust of psychological researchers.

Ethical Treatment of Animal Subjects

At the 1986 Annual Meeting of the American Psychological Association in Washington, D.C., animal rights activists picketed in the streets and disrupted talks, including one by the eminent psychologist Neal Miller, a defender of the use of animals in psychological research. *Animal rights* supporters oppose all laboratory research using animals, regardless of its scientific merit or practical benefits. Animal rights supporters go beyond *animal welfare* supporters, who would permit laboratory research on animals when its potential benefits outweighed any pain and distress caused to animals (Rollin, 1985).

The American Psychological Association's ethical standards for the treatment of animals are closer to those of animal welfare supporters than animal rights supporters. The standards require that animals be treated with respect, housed in clean cages, and given adequate food and water. Researchers must also subject their animal subjects to as little pain and distress as possible and, when necessary, terminate their lives in a humane, painless way. Moreover, all institutions that receive research grants from the federal government must have committees that judge whether research proposals for experiments using animal subjects meet ethical standards (Holden, 1987).

But, you may ask, with so many human beings available, why would psychologists be interested in studying animals? First, some psychologists are simply intrigued by animal behavior and wish to learn more about it. For example, to learn about the process of echolocation, you would have to study bats rather than college students. Second, it is easier to control the extraneous variables that might affect the behavior of an animal. You would not have to worry about subject bias effects when studying pigeons. Third, developmental changes across the life span can be studied more efficiently in animals. If you were interested in the effects of the complexity of the early childhood environment on memory in old age, you might take seventy years to complete a study using human subjects but only three years to complete a study using rats.

Fourth, research on animals can generate hypotheses that are then tested using human subjects. B. F. Skinner's research on learning in rats and pigeons stimulated research on learning in human beings. Fifth, research on animals may benefit both animals and human beings. Psychologists are working on techniques to make coyotes feel nauseated by the taste of sheep, perhaps someday protecting the sheep from coyotes and the coyotes from angry sheep ranchers. Sixth, certain procedures that may be ethically permissible with animal subjects are not ethically permissible with human subjects. If you wanted to conduct an experiment in which you studied the effects of surgically removing a particular brain structure, you would be limited to the use of animals as subjects.

But these reasons have not convinced animal rights activists of the merits of psychological research on animals. During the past decade some animal

The Ethical Treatment of Animal Subjects Animal rights activists have picketed meetings of the American Psychological Association to oppose research using animals as subjects. Psychologists have responded by pointing to the benefits of animal research and the strict ethical standards that they follow in conducting research with animals.

rights activists have vandalized animal research laboratories and even stolen animals from their laboratory cages. Most activists, however, have been content to lobby for stronger laws limiting animal research or to picket meetings of animal researchers. Prior to the meeting at which he was harassed by activists, Neal Miller (1985) had pointed out that for every dog and cat used in laboratory research, ten thousand are abandoned by their owners, and that, in contrast, few psychology experiments inflict pain or distress on animals. He urged animal rights activists to spend more time helping the millions of abandoned pets that are killed in pounds, starve to death, or die after being struck by vehicles.

Miller (1985) has also enumerated the ways in which animal research contributes to human welfare. Findings from animal research have contributed to progress in the treatment of pain; the development of behavior therapy for phobias; the rehabilitation of victims of neuromuscular disorders, such as Parkinson's disease; the understanding of neurological disorders associated with aging, such as Alzheimer's disease; and the development of drugs for treating anxiety, depression, and schizophrenia.

While reasonable people may disagree about the ethical limits of psychological research on animals, the attention given to such research may be out of proportion to its extent and to the pain and distress it causes. Only 5 percent of psychologists conduct research with animals. Of their animal subjects, 95 percent are mice, rats, and birds, while about 1 percent are dogs, cats, monkeys, and chimpanzees—the kinds of animals to which people feel the greatest emotional attachment (Gallup & Suarez, 1985). Moreover, few psychological studies inflict pain or distress on their subjects. In fact, a survey by Neal Miller of all articles describing research with animals published over a five-year period in journals of the American Psychological Association found no evidence of cruel treatment (Miller & Coile, 1984). And, despite the special attention that psychological research receives from animal rights activists, a government report praised the American Psychological Association's ethical standards for the care and use of animals in research as superior to that of any other science (Fisher, 1986). No responsible psychologist would condone a cavalier disregard for the pain and suffering of laboratory animals.

SUMMARY

THE SCIENTIFIC METHOD

Psychologists prefer the scientific method to other sources of knowledge, which include common sense, authority, reasoning, and observation. The scientific method is based on the assumptions of order, determinism, and skepticism. In using the scientific method to perform a research study, a psychologist would first prepare the study, then conduct the study, and finally analyze the resulting data. Researchers test predictions known as hypotheses.

GOALS OF PSYCHOLOGICAL RESEARCH

In conducting research, psychologists pursue the goals of description, prediction, explanation, and control. Scientific descriptions are systematic and rely on operational definitions. Scientific predictions are probabilistic, not certain. Scientific explanations state the causes of events and avoid confusing causation with correlation. And scientists exert control over events by manipulating the factors that cause them.

METHODS OF PSYCHOLOGICAL RESEARCH

Psychologists use descriptive, correlational, and experimental research methods. Descriptive research methods pursue the goal of description through case studies, naturalistic observation, and surveys. Valid surveys use a random sample of respondents selected from the population of interest. Correlational research pursues the goal of prediction by uncovering relationships between events. And experimental research pursues the goals of explanation and control by manipulating an independent variable and measuring its effect on a dependent variable. In quasiexperimental research, the researcher cannot assign subjects to the experimental group and control group and, therefore, must use groups that have already been formed.

Experimenters try to control all factors whose effects might be confused with those of the independent variable. These factors may be associated with the experimental procedure itself, the subjects of the experiment, or the experimenter. Random assignment of subjects is used to make the experimental group and control group equivalent before exposing them to the independent variable. Experimenters must also control for subject bias and experimenter bias. A final concern of experimenters is whether their results are generalizable from their subjects and settings to other subjects and settings. Experimenters rely on replication to determine whether their research is generalizable.

STATISTICAL ANALYSIS OF RESEARCH DATA

Psychologists make sense of their data by using mathematical techniques called statistics. They use descriptive statistics to summarize data and inferential statistics to test their research hypotheses. Descriptive statistics include measures of central tendency (including the mode, median, and mean), measures of variability (including the range and standard deviation), and measures of correlation. Inferential statistics include the t-test and the analysis of variance. Researchers must determine whether their inferential statistics yield statistically significant results.

THINKING ABOUT PSYCHOLOGY:
WHAT ARE THE ETHICS OF PSYCHOLOGICAL RESEARCH?

The American Psychological Association has a code of ethics for the treatment of human subjects and animal subjects. In research using human subjects, researchers must obtain informed consent, not force anyone to participate, permit subjects to withdraw at any time, protect subjects from physical harm and mental distress, alleviate any inadvertent harm or distress, and keep information obtained from the subjects confidential. The use of deception in research has been controversial.

The use of animals in research has also been controversial. Animal rights supporters oppose all research on animals, while animal welfare supporters permit research on animals as long as the animals are treated humanely and the potential benefits of the research outweigh any pain and distress caused the animals. Though only 5 percent of the members of the American Psychological Association conduct research on animals, most psychologists support the use of animals in research because of the benefits of such research to both human beings and animals. Moreover, there is little evidence that psychologists treat their research animals in less than a humane way.

IMPORTANT CONCEPTS

Analysis of variance 47
Case study 35
Causation 33
Control 40
Control group 39
Correlation 33
Correlational research 38
Dependent variable 40
Descriptive research 35
Descriptive statistics 44
Experimental group 39
Experimental research 39
Experimenter bias 41
Extraneous variable 40
Generalizability 42

Hypothesis 31
Independent variable 40
Inferential statistics 47
Mean 44
Measure of central tendency 44
Measure of correlation 45
Measure of variability 45
Median 44
Mode 44
Naturalistic observation 36
Negative correlation 38
Operational definitions 32
Population 37
Positive correlation 38
Quasiexperimental research 40

Random assignment 41
Random sampling 38
Range 45
Replication 43
Sample 37
Scientific method 30
Standard deviation 45
Statistical significance 47
Statistics 32
Subject bias 41
Survey 37
Theory 33
t-test 47
Variable 39

IMPORTANT PEOPLE

Diana Baumrind 49
René Descartes 29

Jane Goodall 37
John Locke 30

Neal Miller 49, 50
David Rosenhan 48

RECOMMENDED READINGS

For More on All Aspects of Psychology as a Science:

Wood, G. (1986). *Fundamentals of psychological research.* Glenview, IL: Scott, Foresman.
A standard textbook discussing methods of psychological research and data analysis.

For More on Methods of Psychological Research and Data Analysis:

Agnew, N. M., & Pyke, S. W. (1987). *The science game* (4th ed). Englewood Cliffs, NJ: Prentice-Hall.
A light-hearted presentation of the research methods used by scientists.

Huck, S. W., & Sandler, H. M. (1979). *Rival hypotheses: Alternative interpretations of data-based conclusions.* New York: Harper & Row.
A fun little book presenting one hundred brief summaries of research studies, advertising claims, and a variety of other findings. The reader is asked to use his or her critical thinking ability to provide alternative explanations for the findings.

Kimble, C. A. (1978). *How to use (and misuse) statistics.* Englewood Cliffs, NJ: Prentice-Hall.
An interesting discussion of some basic statistics, providing examples of how they can be misused to support misleading claims.

Siegel, M. H., & Ziegler, H. P. (Eds.). (1982). *Psychological research: The inside story.* Englewood Cliffs, NJ: Prentice-Hall.
Autobiographical vignettes by eminent psychologists describing what inspired them to conduct research in their chosen areas of interest and the social and practical factors that helped and hindered them along the way.

Stanovich, K. E. (1986). *How to think straight about psychology.* Glenview, IL: Scott, Foresman.
A book discussing how to become a more critical consumer of psychological research findings.

For More on Ethics in Psychological Research:

American Psychological Association (1981). Ethical principles of psychologists. *American Psychologist, 36,* 633–638.
An article presenting the ethical principles governing the professional practice of psychology and the treatment of human and animal research subjects.

Rollin, B. E. (1989). *The unheeded cry: Animal consciousness, animal pain, and scientific change.* New York: Oxford University Press.
A balanced presentation of issues regarding the use of animals in scientific research by a leading authority on research ethics.

CHAPTER
3

PSYCHOBIOLOGICAL PROCESSES

Chapter Opening Art: Joseph Stella. *Brooklyn Bridge.*

What is ↓

Psychobiology The field that studies the relationship between psychological and physiological processes.

Neuron A cell specialized for the transmission of information in the nervous system.

Central Nervous System The division of the nervous system consisting of the brain and the spinal cord.

Peripheral Nervous System The division of the nervous system composed of the nerves, which conveys sensory information to the central nervous system and motor commands from the central nervous system to the glands and muscles.

Brain The portion of the central nervous system located in the skull, and which plays important roles in sensation, movement, and information processing.

Spinal Cord The portion of the central nervous system located in the spine, and which plays a role in body reflexes and in communicating information between the brain and the peripheral nervous system.

Nerve A bundle of axons that conveys information to and from the central nervous system.

Somatic Nervous System The division of the peripheral nervous system that sends messages from the sensory organs to the central nervous system and messages from the central nervous system to the skeletal muscles.

Autonomic Nervous System The division of the peripheral nervous system that controls automatic, involuntary physiological processes.

Sympathetic Nervous System The division of the autonomic nervous system that arouses the body to prepare it for action.

Parasympathetic Nervous System The division of the autonomic nervous system that calms the body and serves maintenance functions.

As you read this page, your eyes are informing your brain about what you are reading. At the same time, your brain is interpreting the meaning of that information and storing some of it in your memory. And, when you reach the end of the page, your brain will direct your hand to turn to the next page. But how do your eyes inform your brain about what you are reading? How does your brain interpret and store the information it receives? and, How does your brain direct the movements of your hand? The answers to these questions are provided by the field of **psychobiology,** which studies the relationship between psychological processes (such as memory) and physiological processes (such as brain activity).

Interest in psychobiology is not new. A century ago, Sigmund Freud predicted that researchers would eventually discover the physiological processes underlying his theory of psychoanalysis. At about the same time, William James (1890/1950), in one of the first popular textbooks on psychology, stressed the close association between psychology and biology. As mentioned in chapter 1, James was influenced by Charles Darwin's (1859/1959) theory of evolution, which holds that individuals who are biologically well-adapted to their environments will be more likely to survive, to reproduce, and, as a result, to pass on their physical characteristics to succeeding generations.

Thus, the human brain has evolved into its present form because it helped people in thousands of earlier generations to adapt successfully to their environments. Because of the remarkable flexibility of the human brain in helping us adapt to different environments, the brain that helped ancient people survive without automobiles, grocery stores, or electric lights is the same brain that today helps people survive in the arctic, outer space, and New York City.

THE NERVOUS SYSTEM

what is chief means of communication in body?

The brain is part of the _nervous system,_ the chief means of communication within the body. The nervous system is composed of **neurons,** cells that are specialized for the transmission of information. The two divisions of the nervous system are the **central nervous system** and the **peripheral nervous system** (figure 3.1). The central nervous system contains the **brain** and the **spinal cord.** The peripheral nervous system comprises the **nerves,** which provide a means of communication between the central nervous system and the glands, sensory organs, skeletal muscles, and internal body organs.

The peripheral nervous system contains the somatic nervous system and the autonomic nervous system. The **somatic nervous system** includes _sensory nerves,_ which send messages from the sensory organs to the central nervous system, and _motor nerves,_ which send messages from the central nervous system to the skeletal muscles. The **autonomic nervous system** controls automatic, involuntary processes such as sweating, heart contractions, and intestinal activity by the effects of its two divisions: the sympathetic nervous system and the parasympathetic nervous system. While the **sympathetic nervous system** arouses the body to prepare it for action, the **parasympathetic nervous system** calms the body to conserve its energy.

Imagine that you are playing a tennis match. Your sympathetic nervous system would speed up your heart rate to pump more blood to your muscles, stimulate the release of sugar from your liver into your bloodsteam to raise your level of energy, and induce sweating to keep you from overheating. As you cooled down after the match, your parasympathetic nervous system would slow your heart rate and constrict the blood vessels in your muscles to divert blood for use by your internal organs. Chapter 11 describes the role of the autonomic nervous system in emotional responses, and chapter 16 explains how chronic activation of the sympathetic nervous system may contribute to the development of stress-related diseases. To understand how the autonomic nervous system and all other parts of the nervous system carry out their functions, you must first understand the workings of the *neuron*.

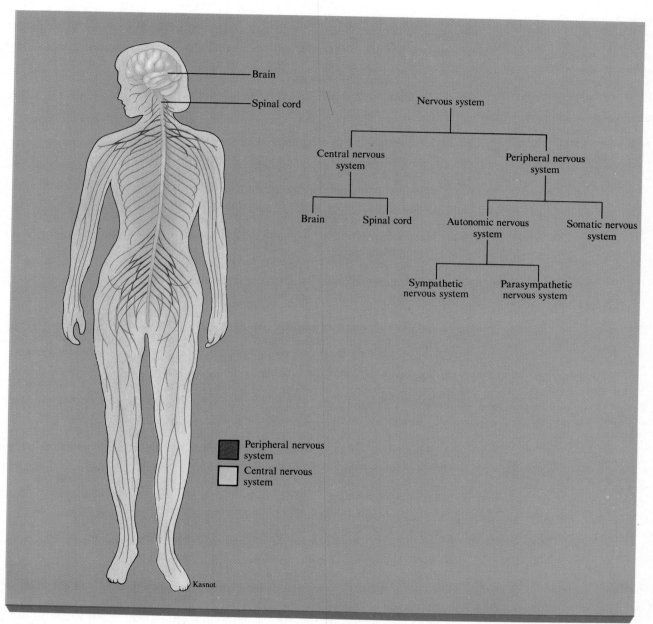

FIGURE 3.1
The Organization of the Nervous System The nervous system comprises the brain, spinal cord, and nerves.

THE NEURON

You are able to read this page because *sensory neurons* are relaying input from your eyes to your brain. You will be able to turn the page because *motor neurons* from your spinal cord are sending directions from your brain to the muscles of your hand. And you will be able to recall information from the page because *interneurons* in your brain are converting the information into memories. **Sensory neurons** send messages along *sensory nerves* to the brain or spinal cord. **Motor neurons** send messages along *motor nerves* to the glands, the cardiac muscle, and the skeletal muscles, as well as to the smooth muscles of the arteries, small intestine, and other internal organs. And **interneurons** are the means of communication between neurons in the brain and spinal cord. Though psychologists are more interested in the functions of the neuron, the nervous system contains many more *glial cells,* which serve several functions. Glial cells (Greek for "glue") act as a physical support structure for the neurons, provide them with nutrition, remove waste materials, help regenerate damaged neurons in the peripheral nervous system, and facilitate the carrying of messages by neurons.

To appreciate the role of neurons in communication, consider the functions of the spinal cord, a long, tubelike structure enclosed in the protective spinal column and extending from the brain to the tip of the spine. Neurons in the spinal cord convey sensory messages from the body to the brain and motor messages from the brain to the body. The sensory and motor functions of the spinal cord were suspected as long ago as the second century, when the Greek physician Galen noted that victims of spinal cord injuries suffered limb paralysis or loss of body sensations. You may know people who have injured their spinal cords in diving accidents or automobile accidents, causing them to lose the ability to move their limbs or feel body sensations below the point of the injury.

In 1730 the English scientist Stephen Hales demonstrated that the spinal cord also plays a role in limb reflexes. Hales decapitated a frog (to eliminate any input from the brain) and then pinched one of its legs. The leg reflexively pulled away. He concluded that the pinch had sent a signal to the spinal cord, which, in turn, sent a signal to the leg, eliciting its withdrawal. We now know that this limb-withdrawal **reflex** involves sensory neurons that convey signals from the site of stimulation to the spinal cord, where they transmit their signals to interneurons in the spinal cord (figure 3.2). The interneurons then send signals to motor neurons, which stimulate certain muscles to contract and pull the limb away from the source of stimulation.

The fact that the limb-withdrawal reflex does not require input from the brain is advantageous. If it did require that signals be sent to the brain and that the brain then send signals down the spinal cord directing the limb to withdraw, you would take a fraction of a second longer to pull your hand away from a hot pot or your foot away from a misplaced thumbtack—making you more susceptible to injury. Of course, a split second after you withdraw your limb from a hot pot or your foot from a thumbtack, your brain receives input from neurons in the spinal cord that causes you to say "Ouch!" (or something even more colorful).

To understand how neurons communicate information, you should first become familiar with the structure of the neuron. Figure 3.3 is a photograph of a neuron taken with an electron microscope and a drawing of a neuron showing its main structures. The **soma** (or *cell body*) contains the nucleus of the neuron, which directs the neuron to act as a nerve cell rather than as a fat cell or muscle cell. The **dendrites** (from the Greek word for "tree") are short, branching fibers that receive messages. And the **axon** is a thin fiber that sends messages. Axons range in length from a tiny fraction of an inch (as in the

Sensory Neuron A neuron that sends messages from sensory receptors toward the central nervous system.

Motor Neuron A neuron that sends messages from the central nervous system to glands, cardiac muscle, or skeletal muscles.

Interneuron A neuron that conveys messages between neurons in the brain or spinal cord.

Reflex An automatic, involuntary motor response to sensory stimulation.

Soma The part of the neuron that serves as its control center.

Dendrites The branchlike structures of the neuron that receive neural impulses.

Axon The relatively long fiber of the neuron that conducts neural impulses.

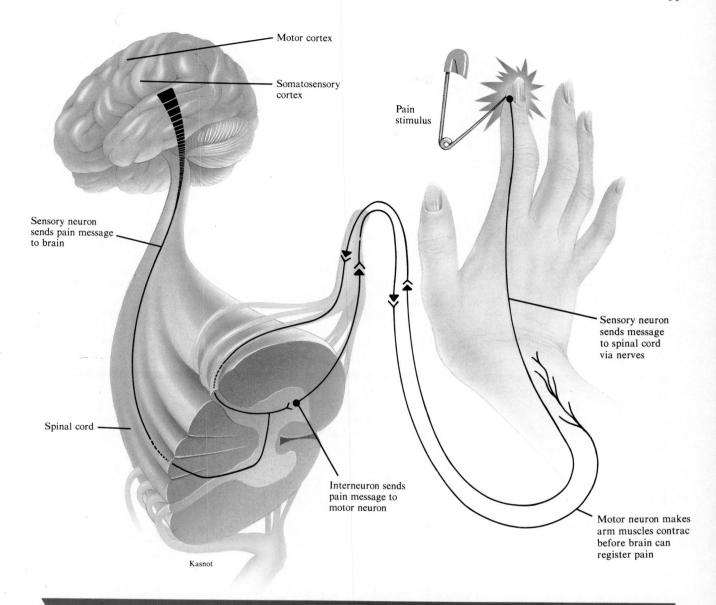

Motor cortex

Somatosensory
cortex

Pain
stimulus

Sensory neuron
sends pain message
to brain

Sensory neuron
sends message
to spinal cord
via nerves

Spinal cord

Interneuron sends
pain message to
motor neuron

Motor neuron makes
arm muscles contrac
before brain can
register pain

Kasnot

FIGURE 3.2
The Limb-Withdrawal Reflex
When your hand touches an object that stimulates pain receptors in the skin, sensory neurons convey this information to interneurons in the spinal cord, which send signals along motor neurons that make certain muscles contract and pull your hand away.

brain) to more than three feet in length (as in the legs of a seven-foot-tall basketball player). Just as bundles of wires form telephone cables, bundles of axons form the nerves of the peripheral nervous system.

The Neural Impulse

How does the neuron convey information? It took centuries of investigation by some of the most brilliant minds in the history of science to find the answer. Until the discovery of the neuron in the nineteenth century, scientists were limited to considering the functions of nerves. In doing so, they were often influenced by their other research interests.

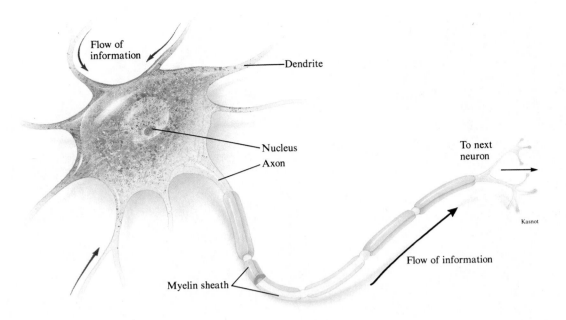

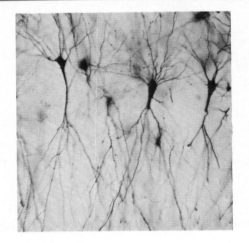

FIGURE 3.3
The Neuron Both the photograph and the drawing show the structure of a neuron. Neurons have dendrites that receive signals from other neurons or sensory receptors, a cell body that controls cellular functions, and an axon that conveys signals to glands, muscles, or other neurons.

In the seventeenth century, René Descartes (1596–1650) was intrigued by moving statues in the royal gardens of King Louis XIII, which were controlled hydraulically by fluid-filled tubes. This led Descartes to speculate that the body is controlled in a similar way by fluids, which he called *vital spirits,* flowing through the nerves. He assumed that our limbs move when vital spirits expand the muscles that control them. Descartes even built his own hydraulic statue to study, which he brought along on an ocean voyage. But the ship's captain, on seeing the statue moving about on deck, accused it of being the work of the devil and threw it overboard—cutting short Descartes's research vacation (Wilson, 1964).

Decades later, another great thinker, the English physicist Isaac Newton (1642–1727), put forth an alternative view based on his research on the nature of vibrating strings. Newton believed that information is conveyed in the nervous system by the vibration of nerves (Gregory, 1987). He concluded that our limbs move because of nerve vibrations that stimulate the muscles that control them. Though later research showed Descartes's and Newton's views to be wrong, you will soon see that there was a grain of truth in both.

There was more than a grain of truth in the view of the Italian physicist Luigi Galvani (1737–1798), who, in 1786, gave one of the first demonstrations of the electrical nature of neuronal activity. Galvani found that by touching the leg of a freshly killed frog with two different metals, such as iron and brass, he could create an electric current that made the leg twitch. He believed he had discovered the basic life force—electricity. Some of Galvani's followers, who hoped to use electricity to raise the dead, obtained the fresh corpses of hanged criminals and stimulated them with electricity. To their disappointment, they failed to induce more than the flailing of limbs (Hassett, 1978). Another of Galvani's contemporaries, Mary Shelley, used lightning as the means of reviving the dead in her classic novel, *Frankenstein.*

Though Galvani and his colleagues failed to demonstrate that electricity was the basic life force, they put scientists on the right track toward understanding how information is communicated in the nervous system. But it took more than two centuries of additional research before researchers identified the exact mechanisms. We now know that neuronal activity, whether involved in hearing a doorbell, throwing a softball, or recalling a childhood memory, depends on the electrical-chemical processes of *axonal conduction* and *synaptic transmission.*

Axonal Conduction In 1952 the English scientists Alan Hodgkin and Andrew Huxley, using techniques that permitted them to study individual neurons, discovered the electrical-chemical nature of the processes underlying **axonal conduction,** the transmission of a *neural impulse* along the length of the axon. Hodgkin and Huxley found that in its inactive state, the neuron maintains an electrical **resting potential,** produced by differences between the *intracellular fluid* inside of the neuron and the *extracellular fluid* outside of the neuron. These fluids contain positively charged particles and negatively charged particles called *ions.* The main positive ions are *sodium* and *potassium,* and the main negative ions are *proteins* and *chloride.*

Axonal Conduction The transmission of a neural impulse along the length of an axon.

Resting Potential The electrical charge of a neuron when it is not firing a neural impulse.

The *neuronal membrane,* which separates the intracellular fluid from the extracellular fluid, is *selectively permeable* to ions. This means that some ions pass back and forth through tiny channels in the membrane more easily than do others. Because ions with like charges repel each other and ions with opposite charges attract each other, you might assume that the extracellular fluid and intracellular fluid would end up with the same relative concentrations of positive ions and negative ions. But, because of several complex processes, the intracellular fluid ends up with an excess of negative ions and the extracellular fluid ends up with an excess of positive ions. Because this makes the inside of the resting neuron negative relative to the outside, the membrane is said to be *polarized*—just like a battery. For example, at rest the inside of a motor neuron has a charge of −70 millivolts relative to its outside. (A millivolt is one-thousandth of a volt.)

When a neuron is stimulated sufficiently by other neurons or by a sensory organ, it stops "resting" (figure 3.4). The neuronal membrane becomes more permeable to positively charged sodium ions, which, attracted by the negative ions inside, rush into the neuron. This makes the inside of the neuron less electrically negative relative to the outside, a process called *depolarization.* As sodium continues to rush into the neuron, and the inside becomes less and less negative, the neuron reaches its *firing threshold* (about −60 millivolts in the case of a motor neuron) and an *action potential* occurs at the point where the axon leaves the cell body.

FIGURE 3.4
The Action Potential During an action potential, the inside of the axon becomes electrically positive relative to its outside, but quickly returns to its normal resting state, with the inside again electrically negative relative to its outside.

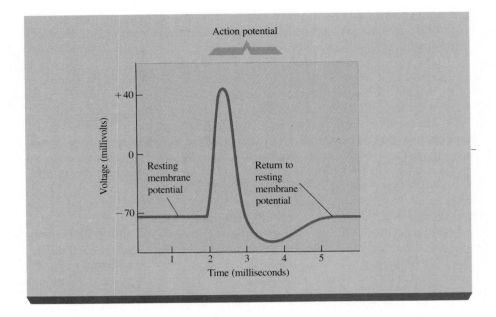

Action Potential A series of changes in the electrical charge across the axonal membrane that occurs after the axon has reached its firing threshold.

An **action potential** is a change in the electrical charge across the axonal membrane, with the inside of the membrane becoming more electrically positive than the outside and reaching a charge of +40 millivolts. Once an action potential has occurred, that point on the axonal membrane immediately restores its resting potential through a process called *repolarization*. During repolarization, the inside of the neuron again becomes electrically negative relative to the outside, beginning with positive potassium ions leaving the neuron.

If an axon fails to depolarize enough to reach its firing threshold and produce an action potential, no neural impulse occurs—not even a weak one. If you have ever been under general anesthesia, you became unconscious because you were given a drug that prevented the axons in your brain that are responsible for the maintenance of consciousness from depolarizing enough to fire off action potentials (Nicoll & Madison, 1982). When an axon does reach its firing threshold and an action potential has occurred, a neural impulse travels the entire length of the axon, as sodium ions rush in at each successive point along the axon (figure 3.5). This is known as the **all-or-none law.** It is

All-or-None Law The principle that once a neuron reaches its firing threshold a neural impulse travels at full strength along the entire length of its axon.

analogous to firing a gun: if you do not pull the trigger hard enough, nothing happens; but if you do pull the trigger hard enough, the gun fires and a bullet travels down the entire length of its barrel.

As you can see, when a neuron reaches its firing threshold a neural impulse travels along its axon, as each point on the axonal membrane depolarizes (producing an action potential) and then repolarizes (restoring its resting potential). Note that this process of depolarization-repolarization is so rapid that an axon may conduct up to one thousand neural impulses a second. The loudness of sounds you hear, the strength of your muscle contractions, and the level of arousal of your brain all depend on the number of neurons involved in those processes and the rate at which they conduct neural impulses.

The speed at which the action potential travels along the axon varies from less than one meter a second to more than one hundred meters a second. The speed depends on several factors, most notably whether the axon is surrounded by sheaths of a white fatty substance called **myelin,** which is produced by glial cells. At frequent intervals along myelinated axons, there are tiny areas not surrounded by myelin. These are called *nodes of Ranvier,* after the French anatomist Louis Antoine Ranvier, who first identified them in 1871.

Myelin A fatty substance that forms a sheath around many axons.

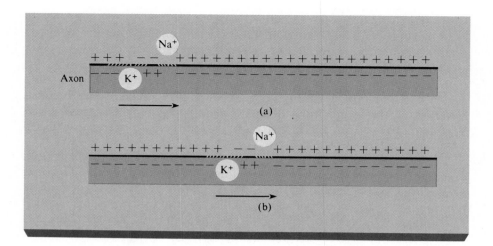

FIGURE 3.5
The Neural Impulse This drawing shows changes in the electrical charge across the axonal membrane as each point successively depolarizes and fires an action potential and then repolarizes and restores its resting potential.

In myelinated axons, such as those forming much of the brain and spinal cord, as well as the motor nerves that control our muscles, the action potential jumps from node to node, instead of traveling from point to point along the entire axon. This explains why myelinated axons conduct neural impulses faster than nonmyelinated axons.

If you were to look at a freshly dissected brain, you would find that the inside appeared mostly white and the outside appeared mostly gray, because the inside contains many more neurons with myelinated axons. You would be safe in concluding that the brain's *white matter* conveyed information faster than its *gray matter.* In the disease called *multiple sclerosis,* portions of the myelin sheaths in neurons of the brain and spinal cord are destroyed, often causing muscle weakness, sensory disturbances, and cognitive deterioration as a result of the disruption of normal axonal conduction (Devins & Seland, 1987).

To summarize, a neuron maintains a *resting potential* during which its inside is electrically negative relative to its outside. Stimulation of the neuron makes positive sodium ions rush in and *depolarize* the neuron (that is, make the inside less negative relative to the outside). If the neuron depolarizes enough, it reaches its *firing threshold* and an *action potential* occurs. During the action potential, the inside of the neuron becomes electrically positive relative to the outside. Because of the *all-or-none law,* a *neural impulse* is *conducted* along the entire length of the axon. After an action potential has occurred at a point on the axonal membrane, potassium leaves the axon and its resting potential is eventually restored.

Synaptic Transmission If all the neuron did was to conduct a series of neural impulses along its axon, we would have an interesting, but useless, phenomenon. The reason that we are able to see a movie, feel a mosquito bite, think about the past, or ride a bicycle is because neurons can also communicate with one another by the process of **synaptic transmission.** The question of *how* neurons communicate with one another provoked a heated debate in the late nineteenth century. The Italian anatomist Camillo Golgi (1843–1926) led those who argued that neurons were physically connected to one another, while his rival, the Spanish anatomist Santiago Ramón y Cajal (1852–1934), led those who argued that neurons were physically separate from one another. Ramón y Cajal won the debate by using a microscopic technique (ironically, developed by Golgi) to show that neurons communicate with each other across tiny gaps. In 1897 the English physiologist Charles Sherrington (1857–1952) coined the term **synapse**

Santiago Ramón y Cajal (1852–1934) "The stature of a scholar is the sum of the original facts which he has discovered."

Synaptic Transmission The conveying of a neural impulse from one neuron to another.

Synapse The junction between a neuron and another neuron, a gland, a muscle, or a sensory organ.

(from the Greek word for "junction") to refer to these gaps. You should note that there are also synapses between neurons and glands, between neurons and muscles, and between neurons and sensory organs.

As is usually the case with scientific discoveries, the demonstration that neurons were separated by synapses led to still another question. How could unconnected neurons communicate with one another? At first, some scientists assumed that the neural impulse somehow jumped across the synapse, just as sparks jump across the gap in a spark plug. But the correct answer came in 1921—in a dream.

The dreamer was Otto Loewi, an Austrian physiologist who had been searching without success for the mechanism of synaptic transmission. Loewi awoke from his dream and carried out the experiment that it suggested. He removed the beating heart of a freshly killed frog and placed it in a solution of salt water. By electrically stimulating the *vagus nerve* to the heart, he made the heart beat slower. He then put another beating heart in the same solution. The second heart also began to beat slower, though he had not stimulated its vagus nerve. If you had made this discovery, what would you have concluded?

Neurotransmitters Chemicals secreted by neurons, which provide the means of synaptic transmission.

Loewi concluded, correctly, that the nerve he had stimulated had released a chemical into the solution. It was this chemical, which he later identified as *acetylcholine,* that slowed the beating of both hearts. Acetylcholine is one of a group of chemicals called **neurotransmitters** that transmit neural impulses across the synapse. Neurotransmitters are stored in round packets called *synaptic vesicles* in the intracellular fluid of tiny branches projecting from the end of axons.

Once again, the discovery of the chemical nature of synaptic transmission led to the question, How? Subsequent research revealed the processes involved in synaptic transmission (figure 3.6). First, when a neural impulse reaches the end of an axon, it causes a chemical reaction that makes some synaptic vesicles release neurotransmitter molecules into the synapse. Second, the molecules diffuse across the synapse and reach the dendrites (or, sometimes, the cell body or axon) of another neuron. Third, the molecules attach to tiny areas on the neuronal membrane called *receptor sites.* Fourth, the molecules interact with the receptor sites to excite the neuron, slightly depolarizing the neuron by permitting sodium ions to enter it. But, for a neuron to depolarize enough to reach its firing threshold, it must be excited by neurotransmitters released by many other neurons. To further complicate the process, a neuron may also be affected by neurotransmitters that *inhibit* it from depolarizing. Thus, a neuron will fire an action potential only when the effects of *excitatory* neurotransmitters sufficiently exceed the effects of *inhibitory* neurotransmitters.

Neurotransmitters do not remain attached to the receptor sites, continuing to affect them forever. Instead, after the neurotransmitters have done their job, they disengage from the receptor sites and are then either broken down by substances called *enzymes* or taken back into the neurons that had released them—a process called *reuptake.*

Of the neurotransmitters, acetylcholine, the one released in Loewi's experiment, is the best understood. It is the neurotransmitter at synapses between the neurons of the parasympathetic nervous system and the organs they control, such as the heart. In the brain, acetylcholine is the neurotransmitter at many of the synapses involved in the processing of memories. The functions of a neurotransmitter can be disrupted, however. For example, chemicals in marijuana disrupt synapses involved in memory processes, so people who smoke it may have difficulty forming memories (Miller & Branconnier, 1983).

Acetylcholine also acts as the neurotransmitter at synapses between motor neurons and muscle fibers, where it stimulates muscle contractions. *Curare,* a poison used on the darts that Amazon Indians shoot from their blowguns,

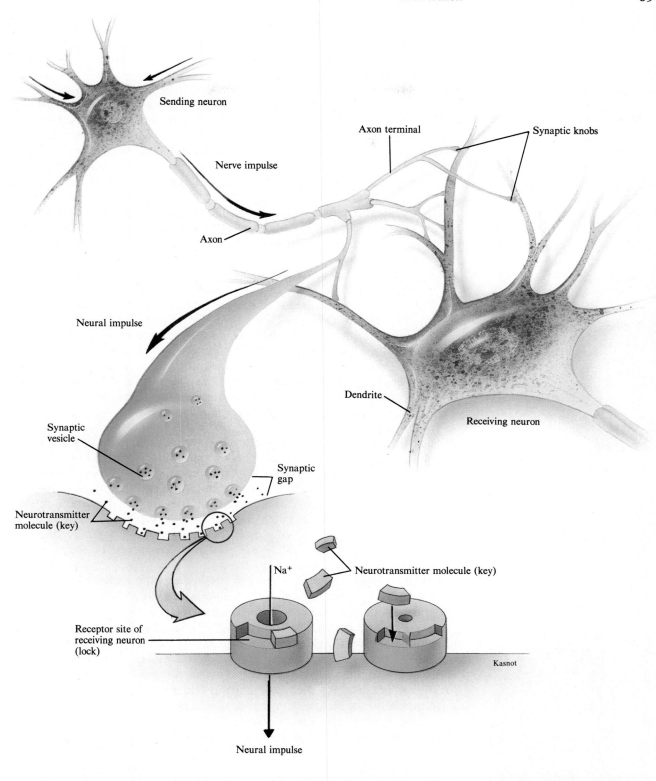

Sending neuron

Nerve impulse

Axon

Axon terminal

Synaptic knobs

Neural impulse

Dendrite

Receiving neuron

Synaptic
vesicle

Synaptic
gap

Neurotransmitter
molecule (key)

Neurotransmitter molecule (key)

Na^+

Receptor site of
receiving neuron
(lock)

Kasnot

Neural impulse

FIGURE 3.6
**Synaptic Transmission between
Neurons** When a neural impulse reaches
the end of an axon, it stimulates synaptic
vesicles to release neurotransmitter
molecules into the synapse. The molecules
diffuse across the synapse and interact with
receptor sites on another neuron, causing
sodium ions to leak into that neuron. The
molecules then disengage from the receptor
sites and are broken down by enzymes or
taken back into the axon.

Endorphins Neurotransmitters that play a role in pleasure, pain relief, and other functions.

paralyzes muscles by preventing acetylcholine from attaching to receptor sites on muscle fibers. The resulting muscle paralysis, which stops the breathing muscles from working, causes death by suffocation.

During the past few years, neurotransmitters called **endorphins** have generated much research and publicity because of their possible roles in relieving pain and inducing feelings of euphoria. The endorphin story began in 1973, when Candace Pert and Solomon Snyder of Johns Hopkins University discovered opiate receptors in the brains of animals. Opiates are pain-relieving drugs (or *narcotics*), including morphine, codeine, and heroin, derived from the opium poppy. Pert and Snyder discovered the opiate receptors by injecting animals with a morphinelike drug and then using special microscopic techniques to examine tissue from their brains. They found that the drug had attached itself to receptors in certain areas of the brain that are associated with pain perception and emotionality. If you had been a member of Pert and Snyder's research team, what would you have inferred from this observation?

Pert and Snyder inferred that the brain must manufacture its own opiatelike chemicals. If it did not, then why had it evolved its own opiate receptors?—certainly not in anticipation of the availability of morphine, codeine, and heroin. This inspired the search for opiatelike chemicals in the brain. The search bore fruit in Scotland when Hans Kosterlitz and colleagues (Hughes et al., 1975) found an opiatelike chemical in brain tissue taken from animals. They called this chemical *enkephalin* (meaning "in the head"). Enkephalin and similar chemicals discovered in the brain were later dubbed "endogenous morphine" (meaning "morphine from within"). This was then abbreviated into the now-popular term *endorphin*.

Once researchers had located the receptor sites for the endorphins and had isolated endorphins themselves, they then wondered, Why has the brain evolved its own source of opiatelike neurotransmitters? With many scientists hot on its trail, the answer was not long in coming. Researchers found that endorphins act at synapses in the brain that inhibit pain impulses. Evidently, endorphins evolved, at least in part, because they provided pain relief. Perhaps the first animals blessed with endorphins were better able to function in the face of pain caused by diseases or injuries, making them more likely to survive long enough to reproduce and pass this physical trait on to successive generations (Levinthal, 1988).

Evidence supporting this speculation has come from experiments such as the intriguingly titled "Opioid-like Analgesia in Defeated Mice." (What do you think William Proxmire, whose Golden Fleece Award you read about in chapter 1, would say after hearing that title?) The researchers first recorded how long mice would allow radiant heat from a light bulb to be focused on their tails before flicking their tails away from it. The mice were then paired with aggressive mice, who attacked and defeated them. The losers' tolerance for the radiant heat was then tested again. The results showed that defeated mice increased the length of time they would permit their tails to be heated. But if the defeated mice were given a drug called *naloxone,* which blocks the pain-relieving effects of morphine, they flicked their tails as quickly as they had done before being defeated. The researchers concluded that the naloxone had blocked the pain-relieving effects of the endorphins (Miczek, Thompson, & Shuster, 1982).

Perhaps athletes who continue playing despite painful injuries do so because their injuries stimulate increased endorphin activity, thereby relieving their pain. Endorphins may also reduce the pain of giving birth, because endorphins have been found in the placenta, which connects the fetus to the mother. The level of endorphins increases as labor approaches (Arehart-Treichel, 1981). There is also evidence that endorphins may be responsible

Candace Pert "Our brains probably have natural counterparts for just about any drug you could name."

The Runner's High The euphoric "exercise high" experienced by long-distance runners may be caused by the release of endorphins in the brain.

for the feelings of euphoria in the "exercise high" experienced by many people who run, swim, or bicycle (Carr et al., 1981). The mechanisms by which endorphins relieve pain and create euphoria are discussed in chapter 4.

Acetylcholine and the endorphins are not the only neurotransmitters that have been identified. Your ability to perform smooth voluntary movements depends on the neurotransmitter *dopamine.* The physiological arousal you experience when under stress is associated with activity in neurons that release the neurotransmitter *norepinephrine.* And when you fall asleep, you owe it to activity in neurons that release the neurotransmitter *serotonin.* These and other neurotransmitters are discussed in upcoming chapters.

Hormonal Influences

Neurotransmitters are not the only chemical messengers. There are also **hormones,** which are chemicals secreted by glands in the **endocrine system** (figure 3.7). The endocrine glands secrete hormones into the bloodstream, which transports them to their sites of action. The hormones play a role in many physiological functions (table 3.1). The **pituitary gland,** an endocrine gland protruding from the underside of the brain, regulates many of the other endocrine glands by secreting hormones that affect those glands. For example, the pituitary gland secretes hormones that regulate the secretion of sex hormones by the *gonads.* Chapter 10 describes the role of the sex hormones in sexual development and sexual behavior.

Certain hormones have direct effects on neural transmission. For example, secretion of the *antidiuretic hormone* by the pituitary gland stimulates neurons in brain structures involved in the formation of memories (Port, Mikhail, Kline, & Patterson, 1985). And the *adrenal glands,* which lie on top of your kidneys, secrete the hormones *epinephrine* and *norepinephrine* (which also act as neurotransmitters), which stimulate activity at synapses in the sympathetic nervous system, thereby arousing the body to take action. Because hormones are slower acting than neurotransmitters, you may have noticed that your feelings of emotional arousal, whether caused by an attractive person or a harrowing drive in a winter storm, last for a while after the source of the arousal is no longer present.

Hormones Chemicals, secreted by endocrine glands, that play a role in a variety of functions, including synaptic transmission.

Endocrine System Glands that secrete hormones into the bloodstream.

Pituitary Gland An endocrine gland that regulates many of the other endocrine glands by secreting hormones that affect those glands.

FIGURE 3.7
The Endocrine System
Hormones secreted by the
endocrine glands affect
metabolism, behavior, and mental
processes.

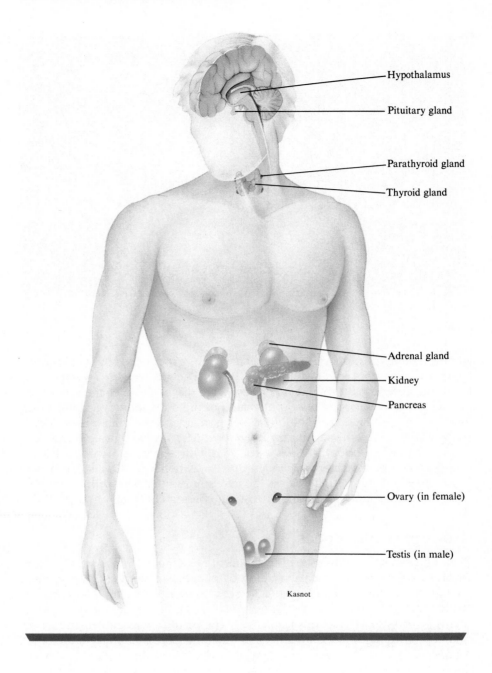

Hypothalamus

Pituitary gland

Parathyroid gland

Thyroid gland

Adrenal gland

Kidney

Pancreas

Ovary (in female)

Testis (in male)

Kasnot

TABLE 3.1   Functions of the Major Hormones

Gland	Hormone	Function
Hypothalamus	Releasing hormones	The hypothalamus is a brain structure that regulates the release of pituitary hormones
Pituitary		
Anterior (front lobe)	Adrenocorticotropic hormone (ACTH)	Stimulates hormone secretion by the adrenal cortex
	Gonadotropic hormones	Regulate the gonads (testes and ovaries)
	Growth hormone	Stimulates growth
	Prolactin	Stimulates milk production in nursing women
	Thyroid-stimulating hormone	Stimulates hormone secretion by the thyroid gland
Posterior (rear lobe)	Antidiuretic hormone	Promotes water retention by the kidneys, as well as playing a role in the formation of memories
	Oxytocin	Stimulates contractions of the uterus during labor and secretion of milk during nursing
Adrenal		
Cortex (outer layer)	Aldosterone	Regulates excretion of sodium and potassium
	Cortisol	Regulates metabolism and response to stress
Medulla (inner layer)	Epinephrine and norepinephrine	Contribute to physiological arousal associated with activation of the sympathetic nervous system
Gonads		
Testes	Testosterone	Regulates development of the male reproductive system, secondary sex characteristics, and sex drive
Ovaries	Estrogens	Regulate development of the female reproductive system and secondary sex characteristics
	Progesterone	Regulates changes in the uterus to maintain pregnancy
Kidneys	Renin	Regulates aldosterone secretion and blood pressure
Pancreas	Insulin	Decreases blood sugar
	Glucagon	Increases blood sugar
Thyroid	Thyroxine	Regulates metabolism and growth

THE BRAIN

"Tell me, where is fancy bred, in the heart or in the head?" (*The Merchant of Venice,* act III, scene 2). The answer to this question from Shakespeare's play may be obvious to you. You know that your brain, and not your heart, is your feeling organ—the site of your mind. But you have the advantage of centuries of research, which have made the role of the brain in all psychological processes obvious to even those who have not studied it. Of course, the cultural influence of erroneous beliefs may dominate—just imagine the response of a person who received a gift of Valentine's Day candy in a brain-shaped box.

The ancient Egyptians associated the mind with the heart, discounting the importance of the apparently inactive brain. In fact, when the pharoah Tutankhamen ("King Tut") was mummified to prepare him for the afterlife, his heart and other body organs were carefully preserved, but his brain was discarded. The Greek philosopher Aristotle (384–322 B.C.) also believed that the heart was the site of the mind, because when the heart stops, mental activity stops (Laver, 1972). But the Greek physician-philosopher Hippocrates (460–377 B.C.), based on his observations of the effects of brain damage, did locate the mind in the brain:

> Some people say that the heart is the organ with which we think and that it feels pain and anxiety. But it is not so. Men ought to know that from the brain and from the brain alone arise our pleasures, joys, laughter, and tears. (Penfield, 1975, p. 7)

Does this mean that Hippocrates was brilliant and Aristotle foolish? On the contrary, each man used the tools available to him—observation and reason—to come to logical, intelligent conclusions. Had subsequent research supported Aristotle's position, we would credit him with the foresight that we now credit to Hippocrates. As you read this chapter and later chapters, you will encounter seemingly foolish beliefs about psychological and physiological processes that have been held by some of the greatest thinkers in history. Try to place those thinkers in the context of their times, rather than in the context of the present. Though we may now know that certain past beliefs are

The Human Brain
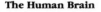

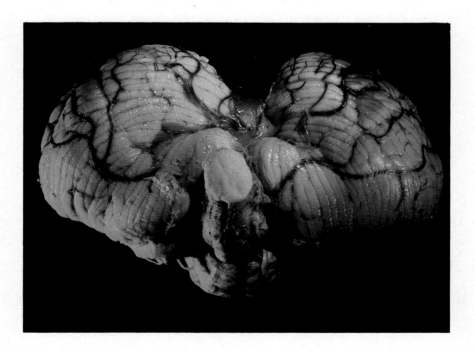

wrong, we should not conclude that those who believed them were foolish. Keep in mind that psychology students in the next century may consider some of our beliefs about the functions of the brain "foolish" as well.

Functions of the Brain

The human brain's appearance does not hint at its complexity. Holding it in your hands, you might not be impressed by either its three-pound weight or its walnutlike appearance. You might be more impressed to learn that it contains billions of neurons, perhaps hundreds of billions (Goodman & Bastiani, 1984). And you might be astounded to learn that a given brain neuron may communicate with thousands of others, leading to a virtually infinite number of pathways for messages to take in the brain.

As you read, you will find that much of what we know about this incredibly complex organ comes from studies of the effects of brain damage, electrical stimulation of the brain, recording of the electricity produced by brain activity, and computer scanning of the brain. As an example, consider the **electroencephalograph (EEG),** which records the pattern of electrical activity produced by neuronal activity in the brain. The EEG has a peculiar history, going back to the turn of the century on a day when an Austrian scientist named Hans Berger fell off a horse and narrowly escaped serious injury. That evening he received a telegram telling him that his sister felt he was in danger.

The telegram inspired Berger to investigate the possible association between *mental telepathy* (the alleged, though scientifically unsupported, ability of one mind to communicate directly with another) and electrical activity in the brain. In 1924, after years of experimenting on animals and on his son Klaus, Berger succeeded in perfecting a procedure for recording electrical activity from the brain. He attached small metal disks called *electrodes* to Klaus's scalp and connected them with wires to a device that recorded changes in the patterns of electrical activity in his brain.

Though Berger failed to find physiological evidence supporting the existence of mental telepathy, he identified two distinct rhythms of electrical activity. He called the relatively slow rhythm associated with a relaxed, unfocused mental state the *alpha rhythm* and the relatively fast rhythm associated with an active, alert mental state the *beta rhythm* (figure 3.8). You will now learn about the brain functions that have been revealed by EEG recordings and other research techniques.

Electroencephalograph (EEG) A device used to record patterns of electrical activity produced by neuronal activity in the brain.

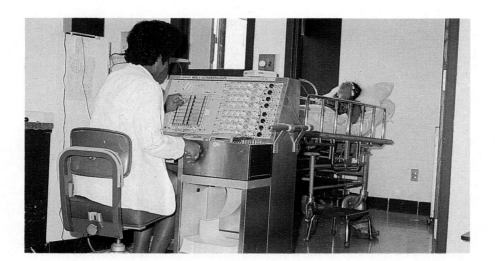

FIGURE 3.8
The Electroencephalograph (EEG) The EEG records patterns of electrical activity from the brain. The fast beta brain-wave pattern is associated with the alert, active mental state you might be in while taking an exam. The slower alpha brain-wave pattern is associated with the relaxed, unfocused mental state you might be in just after lying down to go to sleep.

Functions of the Hindbrain Your ability to survive from moment to moment depends on your *hindbrain,* which is located at the base of the brain (figure 3.9). Of all the hindbrain structures, the most crucial to your survival is the **medulla,** which connects the brain and spinal cord. At this moment your medulla is regulating your breathing, heart rate, and blood pressure. And, when called upon, your medulla will induce coughing, vomiting, or swallowing. By inducing vomiting, for example, the medulla prevents people who drink too much alcohol too fast from poisoning themselves. Because the medulla controls so many vital functions, damage to it can be fatal, as in the 1968 assassination of presidential candidate Robert Kennedy, who was shot through the medulla.

Just above the medulla lies the bulbous structure called the **pons.** As will be explained in chapter 5, the pons regulates the sleep-wake cycle by its effect on consciousness. If you have ever been the unfortunate recipient of a blow to the head that knocked you out, your loss of consciousness may have been caused by the blow's effect on your pons (Hayes et al., 1984).

The pons (which means "bridge" in Latin) connects the **cerebellum** (meaning "little brain") to the hindbrain. The cerebellum controls the timing

Medulla A hindbrain structure that regulates breathing, heart rate, blood pressure, and other life functions.

Pons A hindbrain structure that regulates the sleep-wake cycle.

Cerebellum A hindbrain structure that controls the timing of well-learned movements.

FIGURE 3.9
The Structure of the Human Brain The structures of the hindbrain, midbrain, and forebrain serve a variety of life-support, sensorimotor, and cognitive functions.

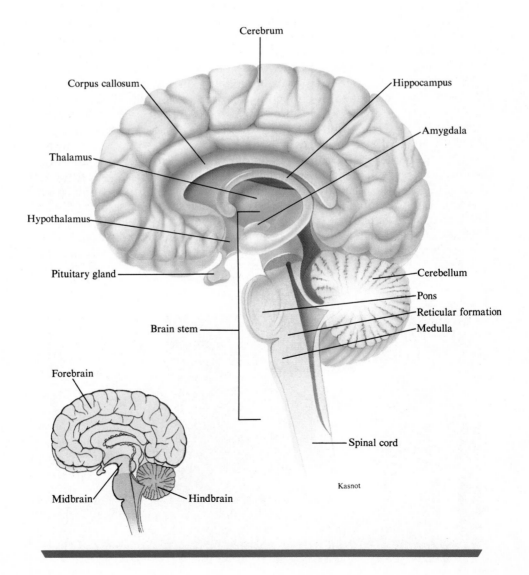

of well-learned sequences of movements that are too rapid to be controlled consciously, as in running a sprint, singing a song, or playing the piano. As you are aware from your own experience, conscious efforts to control normally automatic sequences of movements such as these may disrupt them. A pianist who thinks of each key he or she is striking while playing a well-practiced piece would be unable to maintain proper timing.

Passing through the hindbrain into higher regions of the brain is the **reticular formation,** a diffuse network of neurons that helps maintain vigilance and an optimal level of brain arousal. The role of the reticular formation in maintaining vigilance is shown by the "cocktail party phenomenon," in which you may be engrossed in a conversation but still notice when your name is mentioned by someone elsewhere in the room. Experimental evidence supporting the role of the reticular formation in brain arousal came in 1949 from a study by Giuseppe Moruzzi and Horace W. Magoun in which they awakened sleeping cats by stimulating the reticular formation electrically (Moruzzi & Magoun, 1949).

> **Reticular Formation** A diffuse network of neurons extending from the hindbrain through the midbrain and into the forebrain that helps maintain vigilance and an optimal level of brain arousal.

You become aware of the reticular formation's importance in helping you maintain an optimal level of brain arousal whenever you perform poorly on a task (Gardner, 1986). You have probably noticed that when your level of arousal is too high, you do not perform well on exams, in sports, or in public speaking. If you are extremely anxious during an exam, you may go blank on some questions—only to have the answers pop into your mind after you have left the classroom, become more relaxed, and, as a result, returned to your optimal level of brain arousal. At other times, you may experience too low a level of brain arousal, as when bored by studying. In that case, you might find that playing music in the background helps you raise your level of brain arousal enough for you to maintain your concentration (Patton, Routh, & Stinard, 1986).

As you can see, the structures of the hindbrain let you carry out some of the most basic life functions. Your hindbrain is responsible for your ability to maintain your vital processes, to follow a sleep-wake cycle, to move effectively, to maintain your vigilance, and to adjust your level of brain arousal to an optimal level.

Functions of the Midbrain The *midbrain,* a relatively small region lying between the hindbrain and the forebrain, mediates certain reflexes and promotes smooth movements. Forming the roof of the midbrain is a structure called the **tectum,** which mediates reflexive responses to visual and auditory stimuli (Meredith & Stein, 1985). Suppose that a hidden prankster has thrown a snowball at your head. By responding to input from your eyes, your tectum would detect the snowball and enable you to duck your head before you even realized that the object was a snowball.

> **Tectum** A midbrain structure that mediates reflexive responses to visual and auditory stimuli.

The graceful movements of gymnasts, ballet dancers, and trapeze artists depend on the midbrain structure called the **substantia nigra,** which acts in conjunction with other brain structures to promote smooth voluntary body movements. Less dramatic abilities, such as writing and walking, also rely on the substantia nigra. Many older adults who suffer from *Parkinson's disease,* a degenerative disease of the substantia nigra (Lewin, 1984), have difficulty performing even these simple acts. Victims of Parkinson's disease may walk with a shuffling gait, have difficulty starting and stopping movements, and exhibit hand tremors when simply holding a cup of coffee.

> **Substantia Nigra** A midbrain structure that promotes smooth voluntary body movements.

Functions of the Forebrain As you progress up from the midbrain, you reach the *forebrain,* which plays a role in thinking, learning, memory, emotion, and personality. It helps you adapt to changes in the environment by integrating information from your senses and your memory. Evidence supporting the importance of the forebrain in emotion and personality has come from case studies of people with damage to it, as in the celebrated case of Phineus Gage. On a fall day in 1848, Gage, a twenty-five-year-old Vermont railroad foreman, was clearing away rocks. While he was using an iron tamping rod to pack a gunpowder charge into a rock, a spark ignited the gunpowder. The resulting explosion hurled the rod through Gage's left cheek, into his forebrain, and out the top of his skull. Miraculously, Gage survived, recuperated, and lived twelve more years, with little apparent change in his intellectual abilities. But his personality and emotionality changed drastically. Instead of the friendly, popular, hardworking man he had been before the accident, he became an ornery, disliked, irresponsible bully. Gage's friends believed he had changed so radically that "he was no longer Gage" (Blakemore, 1977).

This case study led to the conclusion that the forebrain structures damaged by the tamping rod are important in emotion and personality. But, as explained in chapter 2, it is difficult to determine causality from a case study. Perhaps Gage's emotional and personality changes were not caused by the brain damage itself, but, instead, by Gage's psychological response to his traumatic accident or by changes in how other people responded to him. Nonetheless, this provided at least circumstantial evidence of the forebrain's importance in emotion and personality, which has been supported by experimental research.

Hypothalamus A forebrain structure that helps to regulate aspects of motivation and emotion, including eating, drinking, sexual behavior, body temperature, and stress responses through its effects on the pituitary gland and the autonomic nervous system.

On the underside of the forebrain is a structure that is important in emotion and a host of other functions—the **hypothalamus.** The hypothalamus helps regulate eating, drinking, emotion, sexual behavior, and body temperature. It exerts its influence by regulating the secretion of hormones by the pituitary gland and by signals sent along neurons to body organs controlled by the autonomic nervous system.

The importance of the hypothalamus in emotionality was discovered by accident. Psychologists James Olds and Peter Milner (1954) of McGill University in Montreal inserted fine wire electrodes into the brains of rats to study the effects of electrical stimulation of the reticular formation. They had trained the rats to press a lever to obtain food rewards. During the experiment, when the rats pressed the lever they obtained mild electrical stimulation of their brains. To the experimenters' surprise, the rats, even when hungry or thirsty, would ignore food and water in favor of pressing the lever—sometimes thousands of times an hour, until they dropped from exhaustion up to twenty-four hours later (Olds, 1956).

Phineas Gage's Skull and the Tamping Rod that Pierced His Forebrain

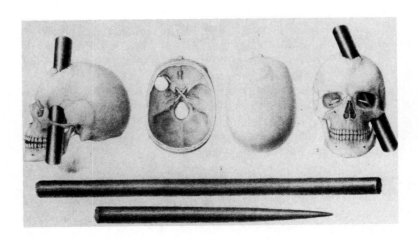

Olds and Milner examined brain tissue from the rats and discovered that they had mistakenly inserted the electrodes near the hypothalamus, not the reticular formation. Though there is no way for a rat to describe how it feels, Olds and Milner concluded that they had discovered a "pleasure center" in that region. Later research studies have shown that the hypothalamus is but one structure in an interconnected group of brain structures that induces feelings of pleasure when stimulated.

Located above the hypothalamus is the **thalamus** ("hypo" means "below" in Greek), an egg-shaped structure at the border between the left and right halves of the brain. The portion of the brain extending from the medulla through the thalamus is called the *brainstem.* The thalamus serves as a kind of sensory relay station, sending taste, body, visual, and auditory sensations on to other areas of the brain for further processing. The visual sensations from this page are being relayed by your thalamus to areas of your brain that specialize in the processing of visual information. The one sense that does not relay information through the thalamus is the sense of smell. Sensory information from smell receptors in the nose goes directly to areas of the brain that process smells.

Thalamus A forebrain structure that acts as a sensory relay station for taste, body, visual, and auditory sensations.

Surrounding the thalamus and lining the border between the left and right halves of your brain is the **limbic system,** a group of structures that interact with other brain structures in promoting the survival of the individual and, therefore, the continuation of the species. The limbic system structure called the **amygdala** continuously evaluates information from the immediate environment, thereby inducing appropriate emotional responses (Henke, 1988). If you saw a pit bull dog running toward you, your amygdala would help you quickly decide whether the dog was friendly, vicious, or simply roaming around. Depending on your evaluation of the situation, you might feel happy and pet the dog, feel afraid and jump on top of your desk, or feel relief and go back to studying.

Limbic System A group of forebrain structures that promote the survival of the individual and, as a result, the continuation of the species by its influence on emotion, motivation, and memory.

Amygdala A limbic system structure that evaluates information from the immediate environment, contributing to feelings of fear, anger, or relief.

In 1966 the amygdala was implicated in the notorious Texas tower massacre (Holmes, 1986), in which a young man named Charles Whitman shot forty-seven people, killing sixteen and wounding thirty-one. He shot most of his victims from the roof of the main administration building of the University of Texas, before dying in a shoot-out with police. In a diary found after his death, Whitman complained about uncontrollable homicidal impulses. An autopsy of his brain found that he had a tumor pressing on his amygdala. Were police, physicians, and reporters right in attributing his murderous rampage to this tumor? Possibly, though, as pointed out in chapter 2, you must be careful not to confuse correlation with causation. Perhaps the presence of the tumor and Whitman's rampage were purely coincidental.

While your amygdala helps you evaluate information from your environment, the brain structure that plays the greatest role in letting you form memories of that information (such as what you are now reading) is the **hippocampus** (Barnes, 1987). Much of what we know about the hippocampus comes from case studies of people who have suffered damage to it. The most famous of these is a man known as H. M. (Scoville & Milner, 1957), whose hippocampus was surgically removed in 1953 to relieve his uncontrollable epileptic seizures. Since the surgery H. M. has formed few new memories, though he can recall events that occurred before his surgery. You will read more about H. M. in chapter 7.

Hippocampus A limbic system structure that contributes to the formation of memories.

Damage to the hippocampus has also been implicated in the memory loss exhibited by victims of *Alzheimer's disease.* Victims of this disease, which often strikes in late middle age, suffer from degeneration of the neurons forming pathways between the hippocampus and other brain areas (Coyle, Price, & DeLong, 1983). Because Alzheimer's disease is marked by the inability to form

"It's times like this that our larger brains seem curiously unimportant."

new memories, a victim might be able to recall his third birthday party but not what he ate for breakfast this morning.

Almost completely covering the brain is the crowning achievement of brain evolution—the **cerebral cortex** of the forebrain. Cortex means "bark" in Latin, and, just as the bark is the outer layer of the tree, the cerebral cortex is the thin outer layer of the uppermost portion of the forebrain called the *cerebrum.* The cerebral cortex of human beings and other mammals has evolved folds called *convolutions,* which give it the appearance of kneaded dough (figure 3.10). The convolutions permit more cerebral cortex to fit inside the

Cerebral Cortex The outer covering of the forebrain.

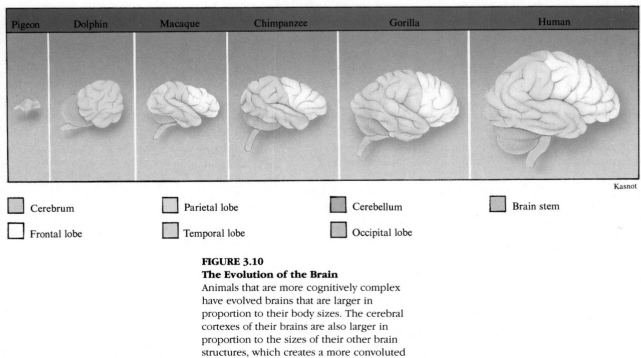

Brain evolution

| Pigeon | Dolphin | Macaque | Chimpanzee | Gorilla | Human |

Kasnot

▢ Cerebrum   ▢ Parietal lobe   ▢ Cerebellum   ▢ Brain stem

▢ Frontal lobe   ▢ Temporal lobe   ▢ Occipital lobe

FIGURE 3.10
The Evolution of the Brain
Animals that are more cognitively complex have evolved brains that are larger in proportion to their body sizes. The cerebral cortexes of their brains are also larger in proportion to the sizes of their other brain structures, which creates a more convoluted brain surface.

skull. This is necessary because evolution has assigned so many complex brain functions to the mammalian cerebral cortex that the brain has, in a sense, outgrown the skull in which it is housed. If the cerebral cortex were smooth instead of convoluted, the human brain would have to be enormous to permit the same amount of surface area and would have to be encased in a skull so large that it would give us the ludicrous appearance of creatures from science fiction movies. The unusually large cerebral cortex of the human brain provides more area for the processing of information, which contributes to the greater flexibility of human beings in adapting to their environments.

The cerebrum is divided into a left half and a right half called the **cerebral hemispheres.** The cerebral cortex covering each hemisphere is divided into four regions, which are called *lobes:* the *frontal lobe,* the *temporal lobe,* the *parietal lobe,* and the *occipital lobe* (figure 3.11). The lobes have **primary cortical areas** that serve motor or sensory functions. The lobes also have **association areas** that integrate information from the primary cortical areas and

Cerebral Hemispheres The left and right halves of the cerebrum.

Primary Cortical Areas Areas of the cerebral cortex that serve motor or sensory functions.

Association Areas Areas of the cerebral cortex that integrate information from the primary cortical areas and other brain areas.

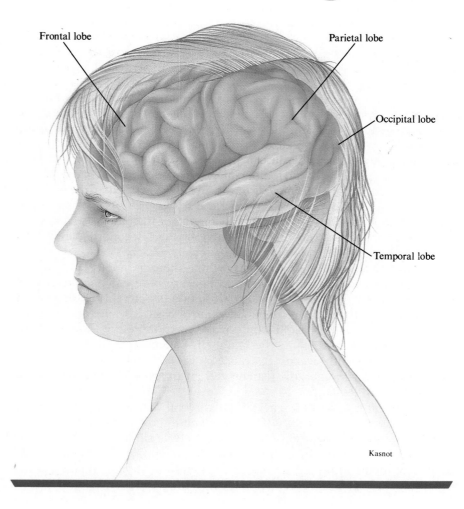

Frontal lobe

Parietal lobe

Occipital lobe

Temporal lobe

Kasnot

FIGURE 3.11
The Lobes of the Brain The cerebral cortex covering each cerebral hemisphere is divided into four lobes: the frontal lobe, the temporal lobe, the parietal lobe, and the occipital lobe.

Frontal Lobe A lobe of the cerebral cortex responsible for motor control and higher mental processes.

Motor Cortex The area of the frontal lobes that controls specific voluntary body movements.

Parietal Lobe A lobe of the cerebral cortex responsible for processing body sensations and perceiving spatial relations.

Somatosensory Cortex The area of the parietal lobes that processes body sensations.

Temporal Lobe A lobe of the cerebral cortex responsible for processing hearing.

Auditory Cortex The area of the temporal lobes that processes hearing.

Wilder Penfield (1891–1976)
"The mind remains, still, a mystery that science has not solved."

other brain areas in processes such as speaking, solving problems, and recognizing objects.

With the layout of the cerebral cortex in mind, you are ready to begin a tour of its lobes. Your tour begins in 1870, when the German physicians Gustav Fritsch and Eduard Hitzig demonstrated that electrical stimulation of a strip of cerebral cortex along the rear of the right or left **frontal lobe** of a dog would induce limb movements on the opposite side of the body. The area they stimulated is now called the **motor cortex.** In more grisly demonstrations, carried out on European battlefields, Fritsch and Hitzig stimulated the motor cortex of soldiers dying from gaping head wounds. This again induced movements of limbs on the opposite side of the body, demonstrating that the motor cortex controls movements on the opposite side of the body in both animals and human beings. This is known as *contralateral control.*

Figure 3.12 presents a "map" of the motor cortex of the frontal lobe, showing that each part of the motor cortex controls the movement of a particular contralateral body part. Note that the map is upside down, with the head represented at the bottom and the feet represented at the top. You might also be struck by the disproportionate sizes of the body parts as represented on the map. The map is distorted because each body part is represented in proportion to the precision of its movements, not in proportion to its actual size. Because your fingers move with great precision in manipulating objects, the region of the motor cortex devoted to your fingers is disproportionately large relative to the regions devoted to body parts that move with less precision, such as your arms.

While the primary cortical areas of the frontal lobes control movements, the primary cortical areas of the other lobes process sensory information. You will notice in figure 3.12 that the primary cortical area of the **parietal lobes** runs parallel to the motor cortex of the frontal lobes. This area is called the **somatosensory cortex,** because it processes information related to body senses such as pain, touch, and temperature. As in the case of the motor cortex, the somatosensory cortex forms a distorted, upside-down map of the body and receives input from the opposite side of the body. Each body part is represented in proportion to its sensory precision, rather than its size. This is why the region devoted to your highly sensitive lips is disproportionately large relative to the region devoted to your less sensitive back.

You may be wondering how we know that there are motor and sensory "maps" on the cerebral cortex. We know because of research conducted by neurosurgeon Wilder Penfield (1891–1976) of the Montreal Neurological Institute in the course of brain surgery to remove tissue causing epileptic seizures. During surgery, Penfield would make incisions around the skull and remove the top of it, exposing the brain. His patients required only a local anesthetic at the skull incisions, because incisions in the brain itself do not cause pain. This permitted the patients to remain awake during surgery and to converse with Penfield.

To avoid cutting through parts of the cerebral cortex that play a role in important functions, Penfield (1975) identified them by administering weak electrical stimulation to points on the cortex. While stimulation of one point might make the left forefinger rise, stimulation of another point might make the patient report a tingling feeling in the right foot. After stimulating points across the entire cerebral cortex of many patients, Penfield made the remarkable discovery that the regions governing movement and body sensations formed distorted upside-down maps of the body.

The **temporal lobes** also have their own primary cortical area, the **auditory cortex,** important in the process of hearing. The auditory cortex of each lobe receives input from both ears but more so from the contralateral ear. Particular regions of the auditory cortex are responsible for processing sounds

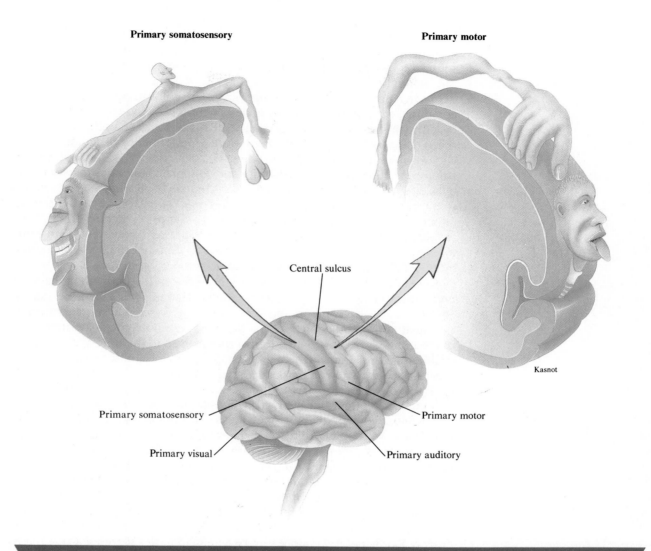

Primary somatosensory

Primary motor

Central sulcus

Kasnot

Primary somatosensory

Primary motor

Primary visual

Primary auditory

FIGURE 3.12
The Motor Cortex and the
Somatosensory Cortex Both the motor
cortex and the somatosensory cortex form
distorted, upside-down maps of the
contralateral side of the body.

From T. L. Peele, *Neuroanatomical Basis for*
Clinical Neurology, 2d ed. Copyright © 1961
McGraw-Hill Book Company.

of particular frequencies. As you listen to a symphony, certain areas of the
auditory cortex would respond more to the low-pitched sound of a tuba, while
other areas would respond more to the high-pitched sound of a flute.

Moving to the back of the brain, you would reach the **occipital lobes,** which
contain the **visual cortex.** The visual cortex makes sense out of the input to
your eyes. Visual sensations from objects in your *right visual field* are processed in your left occipital lobe and visual sensations from objects in your
left visual field are processed in your right occipital lobe.

As stated earlier, our knowledge of the functions of the cerebral cortex and
other brain areas comes primarily from studies of brain damage, electrical
stimulation of the brain, and EEG recordings of brain activity. In recent years,
researchers have added a new tool, **positron emission tomography (PET**
scan), which allows them to determine the amount of activity in particular

Occipital Lobe A lobe of the
cerebral cortex responsible for
processing vision.

Visual Cortex The area of the
occipital lobes that processes
visual input.

Positron-Emission
Tomography (PET Scan) A
brain-scanning technique that
produces color-coded pictures
showing the relative activity of
different brain areas.

regions of the brain. In using the PET scan, researchers inject radioactive glucose (a type of sugar) into a subject. Because neurons rely on glucose as a source of energy, the most active areas of the brain take up the most glucose. The amount of radiation emitted by each area of the brain is measured by a donut-shaped device encircling the head. This information is analyzed by a computer, which generates color-coded pictures showing the relative amount of activity in different brain regions. The PET scan has been useful in revealing the precise patterns of brain activity during performance of motor, sensory, and cognitive tasks (figure 3.13) (Phelps & Mazziotta, 1985). Two other brain-scanning techniques, more useful for showing brain structures than brain activity, are *computerized tomography* (or *CT scan*) and *magnetic resonance imaging* (or *MRI scan*). The CT scan takes many X-rays of the brain from different orientations and uses a computer to compose a picture of particular brain structures. The MRI scan records the responses of different brain structures to a powerful magnetic field and uses a computer to compose an even more detailed picture of the brain than does the CT scan.

In reading about the brain, you may have gotten the impression that each area functions independently of the others. That is not so. Consider the association areas that compose most of the cerebral cortex. These areas integrate information from other areas of the brain. For example, the association areas of the frontal lobes integrate information involved in thinking, planning, and problem solving. Damage here may interfere with the ability to use alternative means of solving a problem (Freedman & Oscar-Berman, 1986). This indicates that the association areas of the frontal lobes are especially important in helping us adapt our behavior to changes in the environment.

The integration of different brain areas underlies many psychological functions. Even your ability to recognize faces depends on the interaction of association areas running along the underside of the occipital, parietal, and temporal lobes. We know this because electrical recordings from this region of the brains of sheep and monkeys show that it becomes more active when they are shown the faces of people or animals. For example, certain cells in the visual cortex of sheep respond to the faces of sheep, other cells to the faces of sheep dogs, and still other cells to the faces of human beings (Kendrick & Baldwin, 1987). Moreover, people who have suffered damage to this region in both cerebral hemispheres exhibit *prosopagnosia,* the inability to

FIGURE 3.13
The PET Scan The red areas of these PET scans reveal the regions of the brain that have absorbed the most glucose, indicating that they are the most active regions during the performance of particular tasks (Phelps & Mazziotta, 1985).

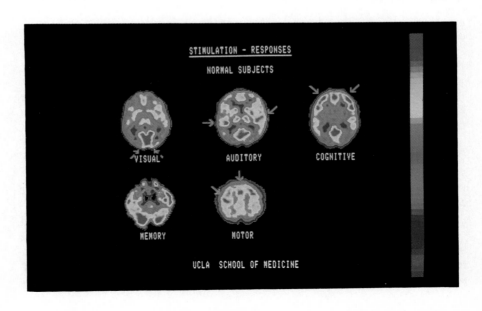

recognize familiar faces (Tranel & Damasio, 1985). Imagine a woman with prosopagnosia. She might recognize her husband's voice, while failing to recognize his face. Every time they met, he would have to announce who he was. Why do you suppose we have evolved cortical association areas devoted to such a narrow function? Perhaps we have done so because the ability to distinguish friend from foe has survival value for us.

To gain more of an appreciation of the way in which cortical association areas interact, consider the process of speech, one of the most distinctly human abilities. Speech depends on the interaction of the association cortex of the frontal and temporal lobes. In most left-handed people and almost all right-handed people, the left cerebral hemisphere is superior to the right in processing speech. The speech area of the frontal lobe, **Broca's area,** is named for its discoverer, the French physician Paul Broca. In 1861 Broca treated a man named "Tan," who was given that nickname because he had a severe speech disorder that made "tan" one of the few syllables he could pronounce clearly. After Tan died of an infection, Broca performed an autopsy that found damage to a small area of the left frontal lobe of his brain. Broca concluded that this area of the brain controls speech, a conclusion that was born out in later studies of the brains of people with similar speech disorders.

Broca's Area The area of the frontal lobe responsible for the production of speech.

Tan's speech disorder is now called *Broca's aphasia.* Though victims of Broca's aphasia retain the ability to comprehend speech, they speak in a telegraphic style that can only be comprehended by listeners who pay careful attention to what is being said. To illustrate this, when one victim of Broca's aphasia was asked about a family dental appointment, he said, "Monday . . . Dad and Dick . . . Wednesday nine o'clock . . . doctors and teeth" (Geschwind, 1979, p. 186). The speaker expressed the important thoughts but failed to express the connections between them. Nonetheless, you probably got the gist of the statement.

Speech also depends on an area of the temporal lobe cortex called **Wernicke's area,** named for the German physician Karl Wernicke. In contrast to Broca's area, which controls the production of speech, Wernicke's area controls the meaningfulness of speech. In 1874, Wernicke reported that patients with injuries at the rear of the left temporal lobe spoke fluently but had difficulty comprehending speech and made little or no sense to even the most attentive listener. This became known as *Wernicke's aphasia.*

Wernicke's Area The area of the temporal lobe responsible for the comprehension of speech.

Consider the following statement by a victim of Wernicke's aphasia describing a picture of two boys stealing cookies behind a woman's back: "Mother is away here working her work to get her better, but when she's looking the two boys looking in the other part. She's working another time" (Geschwind, 1979, p. 186). The statement sounds more grammatical than the telegraphic speech of the victim of Broca's aphasia, but it is impossible to comprehend— it is virtually meaningless.

The consensus among researchers is that speech production requires the interaction of Wernicke's area, Broca's area, and the motor cortex (figure 3.14). Wernicke's area selects the words that will convey your meaning and then communicates them to Broca's area. Broca's area then selects the muscle movements to express those words and communicates them to the region of the motor cortex that controls the speech muscles. Finally, the motor cortex communicates these directions through motor nerves to the appropriate muscles, and you speak the intended words. As you can see, speaking phrases as simple as "let's go out for pizza" involves the interaction of several areas of your brain.

Though we now take it for granted that different areas of the brain interact with one another, the extent to which psychological functions can be localized in particular areas of the brain has been a controversial issue for the past two centuries. The controversy began when the Viennese physician-anatomist

FIGURE 3.14
Speech and the Brain
Wernicke's area, Broca's area, and the motor cortex interact in producing speech.

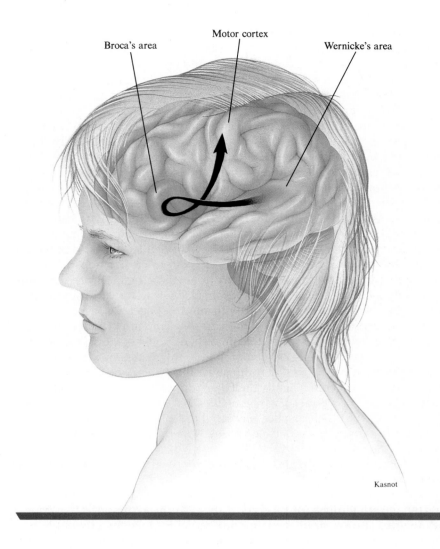

Broca's area   Motor cortex   Wernicke's area

Kasnot

Franz Joseph Gall (1758–1828) expressed the belief that particular regions of the cerebral cortex control particular psychological functions. Gall's interest in the localization of psychological functions began in childhood, when he observed that a classmate with a superior memory had protruding eyes. From that limited sample, Gall erroneously inferred that memory relies on the cerebral cortex located just behind the eyes. Gall assumed that the more cerebral cortex in that region, the better the memory—and the more the eyeballs would be pushed out of their sockets.

Gall went on to devise a system for associating the bumps and depressions of the skull with intellectual abilities and personality traits (figure 3.15). Gall assumed, incorrectly, that the bumps and depressions of the skull reflected the amount of brain tissue lying under them. And, as he did in the case of memory, Gall often jumped to conclusions based on isolated cases. For example, he identified the "combativeness" area of the brain from bumps on the head of a drunken, quarrelsome companion. Gall's student Johann Spurzheim popularized the system as **phrenology** (Greek for "science of the mind")

Though Gall and Spurzheim gave demonstrations of phrenology throughout Europe (McCoy, 1985), they and their followers failed to provide scientific support for their claims. On one occasion, before a demonstration of phrenology on the preserved brain of a genius, a practical joker replaced it with the brain of a mentally retarded person. Despite this exchange, the phre-

Phrenology A discredited technique for determining intellectual abilities and personality traits by examining the bumps and depressions of the skull.

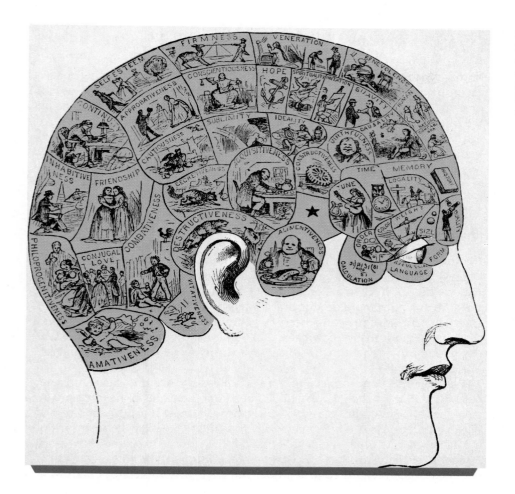

FIGURE 3.15
Phrenology Phrenologists such as Gall and Spurzheim developed maps of the head indicating the supposed functions of areas of the brain underlying particular places on the skull.

nologist proceeded to praise the intellectual qualities of the brain (Fancher, 1979). You might recognize this as an instance of experimenter bias, which was discussed in chapter 2. Despite its scientific shortcomings, phrenology stimulated interest in studying the functions of specific areas of the brain.

The decline of phrenology in the early nineteenth century was accompanied by research suggesting that psychological functions require the interaction of different areas of the brain. This position was championed first by the French physiologist Pierre Flourens and in the twentieth century by the psychologist Karl Lashley (1890–1958). Lashley based his belief on experiments in which he trained rats to run mazes to find food and then destroyed specific areas of their cerebral cortex. He found that the destruction of any given area had only a slight effect on their performance. Lashley (1950) concluded that psychological processes, particularly memory, are not localized in specific areas of the brain but require the interaction of diverse areas. More recent experiments on rats support Lashley's position that memory requires the interaction of diverse areas of the brain (Meyer, Gurklis, & Cloud, 1985).

Today, most psychobiologists would favor a position between Gall's and Lashley's, viewing the brain as a collection of structures that interact flexibly with one another, according to the demands of the situation. Thus, each psychological function requires the interaction of several brain areas but will be disrupted by damage to one or more of those areas. The interaction of Wernicke's area, Broca's area, and the motor cortex in the production of speech is in the spirit of this position. Speech requires the combined action of those areas and will be disrupted by damage to any one of them.

Recovery of Functions after Brain Damage

Based on what you have read so far, and perhaps on what you have observed during your life, you know that brain damage can produce devastating effects, including paralysis, sensory loss, memory disruption, and personality deterioration. But what is the chance of recovery from such damage? It depends on the kind of animal whose brain has been damaged. Though certain kinds of fish and amphibians recover from brain damage by regenerating damaged neurons, mammals, including human beings, do not. Human beings can only regenerate damaged neurons in the peripheral nervous system. Human beings and other mammals depend on factors other than the regeneration of neurons for the recovery of lost brain functions. This also holds true for the spinal cord, which, as part of the central nervous system, is composed of the same tissue as the brain. Thus, damaged spinal cord neurons also do not regenerate.

Plasticity The ability of intact brain areas to take over the functions of damaged ones.

Brain Plasticity In human beings, the most important factor in the recovery of functions that have been lost because of brain damage is **plasticity**—the ability of intact brain areas to take over the functions of damaged ones. In an experiment demonstrating plasticity, researchers surgically destroyed portions of the somatosensory cortex of monkeys. They later found that the somatosensory cortical "map" shifted to intact adjacent areas of the parietal lobes, thereby restoring the ability to experience body sensations (Fox, 1984).

But what mechanisms account for such plasticity? One mechanism is *collateral sprouting*—the growth of branches from the axons of nearby undamaged neurons into the pathways normally occupied by the axons of the damaged neurons. The undamaged neurons then take over the functions of the damaged ones. The younger the individual, the more likely this is to occur. A second mechanism of plasticity is *equipotentiality*—the ability of more than one area of the brain to control a given function. When the area controlling a function is damaged, another area may simply take over for it (Nonneman & Corwin, 1981).

This is shown by the amazing recovery of some children who have had an entire cerebral hemisphere removed, usually because of uncontrollable, life-threatening epilepsy (Shulins, 1987). In some cases, the remaining hemisphere takes over the functions of the missing hemisphere. Though such children may experience some sensory and motor deficits, they may function well intellectually and even go on to success in college. Because of the greater plasticity of young brains, this degree of recovery does not occur in adults who have had a cerebral hemisphere removed.

Brain Graft The transplantation of brain tissue or, in some cases, adrenal gland tissue into a brain to restore functions lost because of brain damage.

Brain Grafts Though plasticity may restore some lost functions, many people who have suffered brain damage do not recover their lost functions. This has led to research on possible ways to repair damaged brains. While some of these ways have included attempts to induce the same processes that permit neurons of the peripheral nerves to regenerate (Liuzzi & Lasek, 1987) or to administer certain chemicals that promote the growth of axons (Kromer, 1987), the most widely publicized, and controversial, way has been to use **brain grafts**—the transplanting of healthy tissue into damaged brains.

Though Mary Shelley's vision of transplanting entire brains is still a topic better suited for science fiction, researchers have been studying the use of brain tissue transplants to treat Parkinson's disease. In one of the earliest studies, researchers destroyed neurons in the substantia nigra of rats, inducing movement disturbances like those seen in victims of Parkinson's disease. The researchers then transplanted tissue from the substantia nigra of healthy fetal rats into the brains of the brain-damaged rats. After several weeks, the recipients showed a reduction in their symptoms, indicating that the transplanted tissue may have taken over the lost functions of the damaged tissue (Perlow et al., 1979).

Studies in which fetal brain tissue has been transplanted to human victims of brain damage have failed to produce any significant restoration of lost functions. In the future, if brain grafts are perfected, brain damage caused by strokes, tumors, diseases, or accidents may be treated by brain tissue transplants. But, as you might imagine, this possibility has already sparked controversy about where we would get such tissue. From animals? From aborted fetuses? From terminally ill patients? As discussed in chapter 2, scientists must confront ethical, as well as technical, issues in conducting their research.

Because initial efforts to transplant human fetal brain tissue into the brains of victims of Parkinson's disease have met with both technical and ethical problems, researchers have turned to transplanting cells from the brain-damaged person's adrenal glands into his or her own brain. Cells from the *adrenal medulla,* the inside portion of the adrenal gland, produce *dopamine,* the neurotransmitter lacking in the brains of victims of Parkinson's disease. In 1982 researchers in Sweden reported disappointing results following the first such adrenal transplants.

It was not until five years later that researchers in Mexico City announced the first successful use of adrenal transplants. They reported that two victims of Parkinson's disease who had received transplants of their own adrenal gland tissue showed marked reductions in their symptoms (Madrazo et al., 1987). But subsequent replications of this study with patients elsewhere, including in the United States, have failed to produce such dramatic improvements (Lewin, 1988). Though brain grafts have yet to demonstrate their worth, researchers may be on the verge of breakthroughs that hold promise for restoring functions that have been lost as the result of brain damage.

THINKING ABOUT PSYCHOLOGY

Do the Cerebral Hemispheres Serve Different Functions?

You may have seen popular reports in the media during the past few years alleging that the cerebral hemispheres control different psychological functions, leading to the notion of "left-brained" and "right-brained" people. Though most researchers would not assign complete responsibility for a particular psychological function to just one hemisphere, they have reached agreement on some of the psychological functions for which each hemisphere is primarily responsible (figure 3.16). The left hemisphere is superior in performing verbal, analytical, rational, and mathematical functions, while the right hemisphere is superior at performing spatial, holistic, emotional, and artistic functions (Springer & Deutsch, 1985).

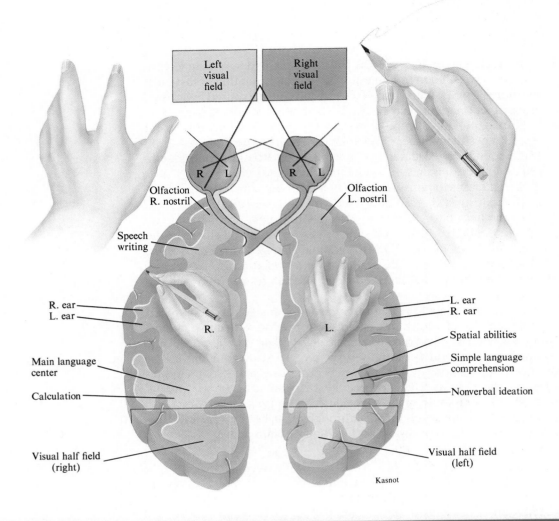

FIGURE 3.16
Hemispheric Specialization Each cerebral hemisphere has psychological functions at which it excels. But keep in mind that the performance of virtually all functions requires the interaction of both hemispheres.

Thus, in a sense, the left hemisphere would be better at giving directions to a driver by speaking, while the right hemisphere would be better at giving directions by drawing a map. But how have psychologists identified the functions of the cerebral hemispheres? They have done so by studying the damaged brain, the intact brain, and the split brain.

Evidence from the Damaged Brain

Case studies of people who have suffered damage to one cerebral hemisphere, often as the result of a stroke, are the oldest source of evidence on hemispheric specialization. As you read earlier, in the 1860s Paul Broca found that damage to the left hemisphere was associated with the disruption of speech, providing evidence of the importance of the left hemisphere in verbal

abilities. In the 1880s, the English neurologist John Hughlings Jackson found that damage to the right hemisphere was associated with the disruption of spatial perception, which underlies the ability to read books, draw pictures, or put together puzzles (Levy, 1985).

A profound example of the role of the right hemisphere in spatial perception is the *neglect syndrome,* a disorder caused by damage to the right parietal cortex. The victim of this disorder acts as though the left side of his or her world does not exist (Posner, Inhoff, Friedrich, & Cohen, 1987). A man with this syndrome might shave the right side of his face, but not the left, and might eat the pork chop on the right side of his plate but not the potatoes on the left. Figure 3.17 shows self-portraits painted by an artist who exhibited the neglect syndrome.

Evidence from the Intact Brain

Because it may be unwise to generalize findings from studies of the damaged brain to the intact brain, psychologists interested in hemispheric specialization have devised several ways to conduct experiments on the intact brain. One of the chief methods has been to have subjects perform tasks while an EEG records the electrical activity of their cerebral hemispheres. Studies have found that people produce greater electrical activity in the left hemisphere while performing verbal tasks, such as solving verbal analogy problems, and greater electrical activity in the right hemisphere while performing spatial tasks, such as mentally rotating geometric forms (Loring & Sheer, 1984). A more recent approach to studying hemispheric specialization in the intact brain uses the PET scan to create color-coded pictures of the relative activity in regions of the left hemisphere and right hemisphere. Figure 3.18 shows the results of one such study.

Evidence from the Split Brain

While studies of damaged brains and intact brains have provided most of the evidence on cerebral hemispheric specialization, the most fascinating approach has been the study of people with so-called *split brains*—brains whose

FIGURE 3.17
The Neglect Syndrome These self-portraits painted by the German artist Anton Raderscheidt were painted over a period of time following a stroke that damaged the cortex of his right parietal lobe. As his brain recovered, his attention to the left side of his world returned (Wurtz, 1982).

Two months after the stroke

Three and one-half months after the stroke

Six months after the stroke

Nine months after the stroke

hemispheres have been surgically separated from each other. Though split-brain research is only a few decades old, the idea was entertained in 1860 by Gustav Fechner, who was introduced to you in chapter 1 as an early contributor to the founding of psychology. Fechner claimed that if a person could survive the surgical separation of the cerebral hemispheres, he or she would have two separate minds in one head (Springer & Deutsch, 1985). But Fechner's contemporary, William McDougall, argued that such an operation would not divide the mind, which he considered indivisible. McDougall even volunteered to test Fechner's claim by having his cerebral hemispheres surgically separated if he ever became incurably ill.

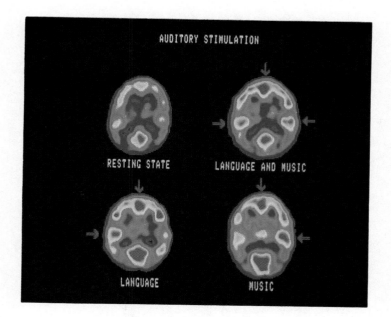

FIGURE 3.18
The PET Scan and Hemispheric Specialization The red areas of these PET scans show that the left hemisphere is more active when we listen to speech, and the right hemisphere is more active when we listen to music (Phelps & Mazziotta, 1985).

Though McDougall never underwent split-brain surgery, it was performed in the early 1960s, when neurosurgeons Joseph Bogen and Phillip Vogel severed the **corpus callosum** of epileptics to reduce seizure activity that had not responded to drug treatments. As illustrated in figure 3.19, the corpus callosum is a thick bundle of axons that provides a means of communication between the cerebral hemispheres. The surgery worked by preventing seizure activity in one hemisphere from spreading to the other. The patients recovered and behaved normally, though one jokingly complained of a splitting headache. Split-brain patients behave normally in their everyday lives, but special testing procedures have revealed an astonishing state of affairs: their left and right hemispheres can no longer communicate with each other. Each acts independently of the other.

During the past three decades, psychobiologist Roger Sperry (1982), of the California Institute of Technology, and his colleagues, most notably Michael Gazzaniga and Jerre Levy, have been at the forefront of split-brain research. You may recall from chapter 1 that Sperry won a Nobel Prize in 1981 for this research. In a typical study of a split-brain patient, information is presented to one hemisphere and the subject is asked to give a response that depends on either the left hemisphere or the right hemisphere. In one study, a split-brain patient performed a block-design task in which he had to arrange multicolored blocks so that their upper sides formed a pattern that matched the pattern printed on a card in front of him (figure 3.20). When the subject performed with his left hand, he did well, but, when he performed with his right hand, he did poorly. Can you figure out why that happened?

Because the left hand is controlled by the right hemisphere, which is superior in perceiving spatial relationships, such as those in designs, he performed well with his left hand. And, because the right hand is controlled by the left hemisphere, which is inferior in perceiving spatial relationships, he performed poorly with his right hand—even though he was right-handed. At times, when his right hand was having a hard time completing the design, his left hand would sneak up on it and try to help. This led to a bizarre battle for control of the blocks—as if each hand belonged to a different person (Gazzaniga, 1967).

Corpus Callosum A thick bundle of axons that provides a means of communication between the cerebral hemispheres, which is severed in so-called split-brain surgery.

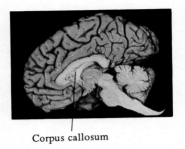

Corpus callosum

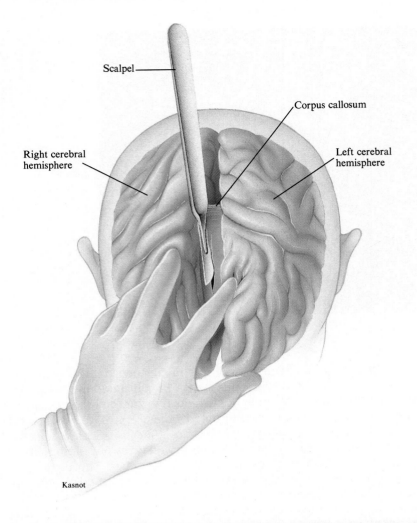

Scalpel

Corpus callosum

Right cerebral hemisphere

Left cerebral hemisphere

Kasnot

FIGURE 3.19
Split-Brain Surgery Severing the corpus callosum disconnects the cerebral hemispheres from each other. Note that in "split-brain" surgery, the entire brain is not split. That would cut through the hindbrain structures that control vital functions, causing immediate death.

Despite such dramatic findings, Jerre Levy believes that researchers, including Gazzaniga, have exaggerated the extent to which each hemisphere regulates particular psychological processes. Gazzaniga (1983) claims that complex cognitive ability is almost entirely a function of the left hemisphere, while Levy (1983) insists that the right hemisphere also contributes to such ability. Levy believes that both hemispheres are involved in verbal and spatial functions and in the analytic and holistic processing of information. Levy views the left hemisphere as analytic for spatial tasks and the right hemisphere as holistic for spatial tasks. Thus, as you look at an object, your left hemisphere may process details of the object, while your right hemisphere may process the object as a whole.

And Levy views the right hemisphere as analytic for verbal tasks and the left hemisphere as holistic for verbal tasks. Thus, as you read, your right hemisphere may process individual letters, while your left hemisphere may process whole syllables (Levy, 1985). Levy's position has been supported by an ex-

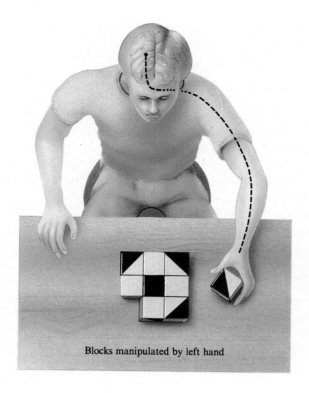

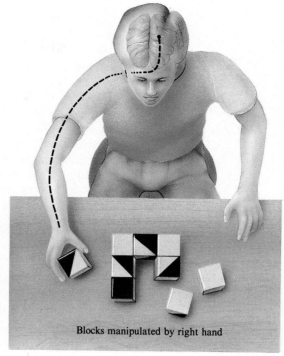

Blocks manipulated by left hand

Blocks manipulated by right hand

Kasnot

Pattern to copy

Pattern to copy

FIGURE 3.20

A Split-Brain Study Gazzaniga (1967) had a split-brain patient arrange multicolored blocks to match a design printed on a card in front of him. The patient's left hand performed better than his right, because the left hand is controlled by the right hemisphere, which is superior at perceiving spatial relationships. You would be able to perform a block-design task equally well with either your right or left hand because your intact corpus callosum would let information from your spatially superior right hemisphere help your left hemisphere control your right hand.

periment that found that the left hemisphere is more active during analytic spatial perception and the right hemisphere is more active during holistic spatial perception (Barchas & Perlaki, 1986). As always, only additional scientific research will resolve the Levy-Gazzaniga debate, which, you might note, is an example of the continual controversy over the degree to which psychological functions are localized in particular areas of the brain.

Aside from questions concerning the degree to which each cerebral hemisphere is involved in specific psychological functions, how should we interpret the findings of split-brain research? Roger Sperry supports Fechner's prediction, made more than a century ago, by claiming, "Everything we have seen so far indicates that the surgery has left these people with two separate minds, that is, two separate spheres of consciousness" (Springer & Deutsch, 1985, p. 256). But other psychologists side with William McDougall in denying that severing the corpus callosum literally divides one mind into two (Robinson, 1982).

And beyond the question of whether split-brain patients have one mind or two is the question, What *is* the mind? Descartes favored a position called *dualism,* which views the mind as an immaterial substance, separate from the material brain. He believed that the *pineal gland,* located at the center of the brain, was the point at which the mind and brain interact. Other philosophers have favored a position called *monism,* viewing the mind and brain as a single substance. Most monists believe that the mind and brain are both matter, with the mind dependent for its existence on brain activity.

Roger Sperry favors that view, and claims that the mind emerges from brain activity:

> I don't see any way for consciousness to emerge or be generated apart from a functioning brain. Everything indicates that the human mind and consciousness are inseparable attributes. (Baskin, 1983, p. 98)

In contrast, Wilder Penfield, the eminent brain mapper, favored a position closer to that of Descartes, though he did not implicate the pineal gland. Penfield claimed that the mind is not dependent on the brain for its existence (a view that he used to support his belief that the mind survives death):

> For my own part, after years of striving to explain the mind on the basis of brain action alone, I have come to the conclusion that it is simpler (and far easier to be logical) if one adopts the hypothesis that our being does consist of two fundamental elements. (Penfield, 1975, p. 80)

Of course, though psychologists can use the scientific method to determine the mental functions of the brain, they cannot use it to determine whether the mind exists apart from the brain—one of the ultimate religious and philosophical questions.

SUMMARY

THE NERVOUS SYSTEM

The field of psychobiology studies the relationship between psychological processes and physiological processes. The nervous system is composed of cells called neurons and serves as the main means of communication within the body. The nervous system is divided into the central nervous system, which comprises the brain and the spinal cord, and the peripheral nervous system, which comprises the nerves of the somatic nervous system and the autonomic nervous system. The autonomic nervous system is subdivided into the sympathetic nervous system, which arouses the body, and the parasympathetic nervous system, which conserves energy.

THE NEURON

The nervous system carries information along sensory neurons, motor neurons, and interneurons, as in the limb-withdrawal reflex mediated by the spinal cord. The neuron generally receives signals through its dendrites and sends signals along its axon.

The neuron maintains a resting potential during which its inside is electrically negative relative to its outside, as a result of a relatively higher concentration of negative ions inside. Sufficient stimulation of the neuron causes it to depolarize (become less electrically negative) and reach its firing threshold. This produces an action potential, which causes a neural impulse to travel along the entire length of the axon.

The neural impulses stimulate the release of neurotransmitter molecules into the synapse. The molecules cross the synapse and attach to receptor sites on glands, muscles, or other neurons. These molecules exert either an excitatory or an inhibitory influence. In recent years, the neurotransmitters known as endorphins have inspired research because of their role in pain relief.

Hormones, secreted into the bloodsteam by endocrine glands, also serve as a means of communication within the body. Hormones participate in functions as diverse as sexual development and responses to stress. Most endocrine glands are regulated by hormones secreted by the pituitary gland.

THE BRAIN

The functions of the brain have been revealed by studies of the effects of brain damage, electrical stimulation of the brain, recording of the electricity produced by brain activity, and computer scanning of the brain. The brain is commonly divided into the hindbrain (including the medulla, pons, and cerebellum), the midbrain (including the tectum and the substantia nigra), and the forebrain (including the hypothalamus, the thalamus, the limbic system, and the cerebral cortex). The medulla regulates vital functions, such as breathing, the pons regulates the sleep-wake cycle, and the cerebellum controls the timing of well-learned sequences of movements. Extending up from the hindbrain through the midbrain is the reticular formation, which regulates brain arousal and helps maintain vigilance. The tectum mediates visual and auditory reflexes, and the substantia nigra promotes smooth movements.

The hypothalamus regulates the pituitary gland, emotion, and motives such as eating, drinking, and sex. The thalamus relays sensory information (except smell) to various regions of the brain for further processing. The limbic system structure called the amygdala continuously evaluates the immediate environment for potential threats, and the limbic system structure called the hippocampus processes information into memories.

The cerebral cortex covers the brain and is divided into the frontal, temporal, parietal, and occipital lobes. Well-defined areas of the lobes regulate movements and process sensory information. But most areas of the cerebral cortex, the association areas, are devoted to integrating information from different brain areas, such as those devoted to speech. In the past decade, positron emission tomography (PET scan) has contributed to our understanding of the functions of different areas of the brain. Researchers have historically disagreed about the extent to which particular psychological functions are localized in particular areas of the brain.

Neurons in the central nervous system do not regenerate. Recovery of functions after brain damage shows the brain's plasticity—the ability of undamaged areas to take over the functions of damaged ones. An exciting, and controversial, topic of research is the possibility of using brain grafts to restore brain functions in people who have suffered brain damage.

THINKING ABOUT PSYCHOLOGY: DO THE CEREBRAL HEMISPHERES SERVE DIFFERENT FUNCTIONS?

Each cerebral hemisphere has psychological functions at which it excels, though both play a role in virtually all functions. Studies of the effects of damage to one hemisphere, of the degree of activity in each hemisphere, and of people whose hemispheres have been surgically disconnected show that the left hemisphere is usually superior at verbal tasks and the right hemisphere is usually superior at spatial tasks. Researchers argue whether people with "split brains" have two separate minds.

IMPORTANT CONCEPTS

Action potential 62
All-or-none law 62
Amygdala 75
Association areas 77
Auditory cortex 78
Autonomic nervous system 56
Axon 58
Axonal conduction 61
Brain 56
Brain graft 84
Broca's area 81
Central nervous system 56
Cerebellum 72
Cerebral cortex 76
Cerebral hemispheres 77
Corpus callosum 89
Dendrites 58
Electroencephalograph (EEG) 71
Endocrine system 67
Endorphins 66
Frontal lobe 78

Hippocampus 75
Hormones 67
Hypothalamus 74
Interneuron 58
Limbic system 75
Medulla 72
Motor cortex 78
Motor neuron 58
Myelin 62
Nerve 56
Neuron 56
Neurotransmitters 64
Occipital lobe 79
Parasympathetic nervous system 56
Parietal lobe 78
Peripheral nervous system 56
Phrenology 82
Pituitary gland 67
Plasticity 84
Pons 72
Positron emission tomography (PET scan) 79

Primary cortical areas 77
Psychobiology 56
Reflex 58
Resting potential 61
Reticular formation 73
Sensory neuron 58
Soma 58
Somatic nervous system 56
Somatosensory cortex 78
Spinal cord 56
Substantia nigra 73
Sympathetic nervous system 56
Synapse 63
Synaptic transmission 63
Tectum 73
Temporal lobe 78
Thalamus 75
Visual cortex 79
Wernicke's area 81

IMPORTANT PEOPLE

Hans Berger 71
Paul Broca 81
Charles Darwin 56
René Descartes 60
Gustav Fritsch and Eduard Hitzig 78
Franz Joseph Gall and Johann Spurzheim 82

Michael Gazzaniga 89
Alan Hodgkin and Andrew Huxley 61
Karl Lashley 83
Jerre Levy 89
Otto Loewi 64
James Olds and Peter Milner 74

Wilder Penfield 78
Candace Pert and Solomon Snyder 66
Santiago Ramon y Cajal 63
Roger Sperry 89
Karl Wernicke 81

RECOMMENDED READINGS

For More on All Aspects of Psychobiological Processes:

Levinthal, C. F. (1990). *Introduction to physiological psychology* (3rd ed.). Englewood Cliffs, NJ: Prentice-Hall. A comprehensive psychobiology textbook expanding on many of the topics covered in this chapter.

For More on the Neuron, Endorphins, and Other Neurotransmitters:

Levinthal, C. F. (1988). *Messengers of paradise.* New York: Doubleday. A thought-provoking book describing recent research on the endorphins and the author's speculation on their evolutionary origins.

Panksepp, J. (1986). The neurochemistry of behavior. *Annual Review of Psychology, 37,* 77–107.

A thorough discussion of the neurotransmitters and their functions.

For More on the Brain:

Bloom, F. E., Lazerson, A., & Hofstadter, L. (1988). *Brain, mind, and behavior* (2nd ed.). New York: Freeman. A readable, beautifully illustrated book based on the PBS television series "The Brain."

Fine, A. (1986, August). Transplantation in the central nervous system. *Scientific American,* pp. 52–58B. A concise, well-written discussion of the use of transplants in treating damage to the brain and spinal cord.

Penfield, W. (1975). *The mystery of the mind.* Princeton, NJ: Princeton University Press. Penfield's own account of his many decades of research on the localization of brain functions.

Sacks, O. (1985). *The man who mistook his wife for a hat and other clinical tales.* New York: Summit. A fascinating collection of case studies of people who have suffered neurological damage, as related by their neurologist.

For More on Hemispheric Specialization:

Springer, S. P., & Deutsch, G. (1985). *Left brain, right brain* (2nd ed.). San Francisco: Freeman. An interesting, widely praised book discussing hemispheric specialization, including studies of the damaged brain, the intact brain, and the split brain, as well as the origins and cultural context of handedness.

CHAPTER
4

SENSATION AND PERCEPTION

Chapter Opening Art:
Carol Colburn. *After the Rain*.

Helen Keller Because she was deaf and blind, Helen Keller relied on her senses of touch and smell to perceive the world. She used her fingers to read Braille well enough to earn a college degree, and she used her nose to recognize people by their scents.

what is sensory

Sensation The process that detects stimuli from the body or surroundings.

Perception The process that organizes sensations into meaningful patterns.

Sensory Receptors Specialized cells that detect stimuli and convert their energy into neural impulses.

Sensory Transduction The process by which sensory receptors convert stimuli into neural impulses.

Psychophysics The study of the relationship between the physical characteristics of stimuli and the conscious psychological experiences they produce.

Absolute Threshold The minimum amount of stimulation that an individual can detect through a given sense.

elen Keller, though deaf and blind, still lived a rich, fulfilling life by using her other senses. But imagine losing *all* of your senses. Your mind would be aware of nothing except itself, and your life would be filled with danger, boredom, and loneliness. You would be unable to smell a gas leak, watch television, or communicate with other people. And you would be without the body and skin sensations that would normally protect you from injury or death, such as feeling the loss of balance caused by tripping over a rock or the burning of your hand caused by leaning on a hot stove.

What is sensation?

SENSORY PROCESSES

Sensory processes are so important that, as you learned in chapter 1, the first scientific studies by psychologists in the nineteenth century were concerned with sensation. Today many psychologists distinguish between *sensation* and *perception*. Sensation begins with a *stimulus* (plural, *stimuli*), a form of energy (such as light waves or sound waves) that can affect sensory organs (such as the eyes or the ears). **Sensation** is the process that detects stimuli from our bodies or surroundings. **Perception** is the process that organizes sensations into meaningful patterns. While visual sensation enables you to detect the black marks on this page, visual perception enables you to organize the black marks into letters and words. Though psychologists distinguish between sensation and perception, the two processes overlap and there is no distinct point at which sensation ends and perception begins.

Sensation depends on specialized cells called **sensory receptors,** which detect stimuli and convert them into neural impulses. This process is called **sensory transduction.** There are receptors that serve each of our senses, including the visual, auditory, smell, taste, skin, and body senses. Some animals have receptors that serve unusual senses. Sharks have receptors that detect weak electrical fields emanating from fish, on which they then prey (Kalmun, 1982). And whales and dolphins navigate by using receptors that sense variations in the Earth's magnetic field. In fact, disruptions of their magnetic sense may account for the periodic strandings of whales and dolphins on beaches (Weisburd, 1984).

What is psychophysics

Sensory Thresholds

How intense must a sound be for a person to detect it? How much change in light intensity must occur for a person to notice it? These questions are the subject matter of **psychophysics,** the study of the relationship between the physical characteristics of stimuli and the conscious psychological experiences they produce. Psychophysics was developed more than a century ago by the German scientist Gustav Fechner (1801–1887) and his brother-in-law Ernst Weber (1795–1878).

The minimum amount of stimulation that can be detected is called the **absolute threshold.** For example, a cup of coffee would require a certain amount of sugar before you could detect a sweet taste. Because the absolute threshold for a particular sensory experience will vary from trial to trial, psychologists formally define the absolute threshold as the minimum level of stimulation that can be detected 50 percent of the time. Thus, if you were presented with a low-intensity sound thirty times and you detected it fifteen times, that level of intensity would be your absolute threshold for sound. Figure 4.1 presents absolute thresholds for several common sensory experiences.

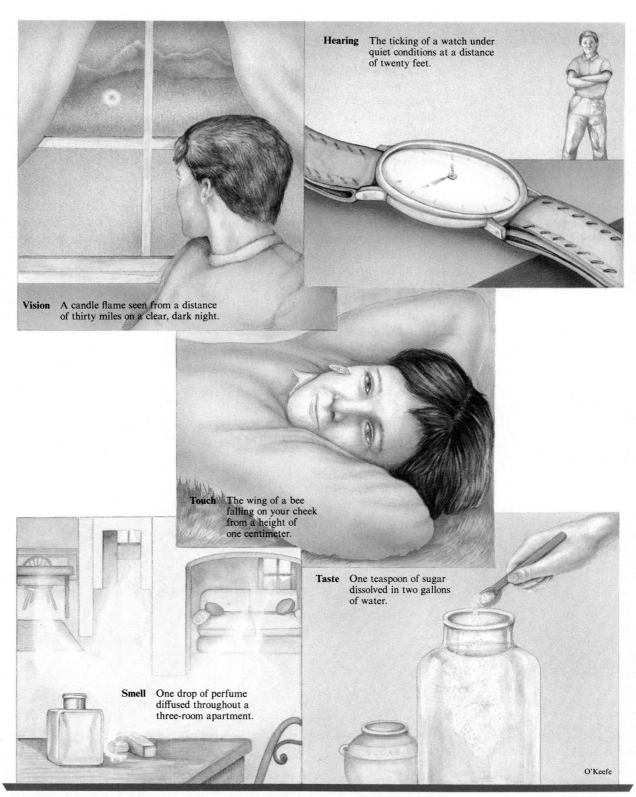

Hearing   The ticking of a watch under quiet conditions at a distance of twenty feet.

Vision   A candle flame seen from a distance of thirty miles on a clear, dark night.

Touch   The wing of a bee falling on your cheek from a height of one centimeter.

Taste   One teaspoon of sugar dissolved in two gallons of water.

Smell   One drop of perfume diffused throughout a three-room apartment.

O'Keefe

FIGURE 4.1
Absolute Thresholds These absolute thresholds illustrate the remarkable sensitivity of our senses (Galanter, 1962, p. 97).

Signal Detection Theory The theory holding that the detection of a stimulus depends on both the intensity of the stimulus and the physical and psychological state of the individual.

Difference Threshold The minimum amount of change in stimulation that can be detected.

Just Noticeable Difference (jnd) Weber and Fechner's term for the difference threshold.

Weber-Fechner Law The principle that the amount of change in stimulation needed to produce a just noticeable difference is a constant proportion of the original stimulus.

what is Weber-Fechner law

The absolute threshold is also influenced by factors other than the intensity of the stimulus. Because of this, researchers have devised **signal detection theory,** which assumes that the detection of a stimulus depends on both the intensity of the stimulus and the physical and psychological state of the observer. One of the most important characteristics of an observer is his or her *response bias*—how predisposed the person is to report the presence of a particular stimulus. Consider walking down a street at night. Your predisposition to detect a sound would depend, in part, on your estimate of the probability of being mugged. So, you would be more likely to detect a sound of a given intensity in a dangerous neighborhood than in a safe neighborhood.

In addition to detecting stimuli, we must be able to detect *changes* in the amount of stimulation we receive. The minimum amount of change in stimulation that can be detected is called the **difference threshold.** For example, a cup of coffee would require a certain amount of additional sugar before you could detect an increase in its sweetness. And, you would have to increase or decrease the intensity of the sound from your compact disk player a certain amount before you could detect a change in the loudness of the music. Like the absolute threshold, the difference threshold for a particular sensory experience will vary from trial to trial. Therefore, psychologists formally define the difference threshold as the minimum change in stimulation that can be detected 50 percent of the time.

Weber and Fechner referred to the difference threshold as the **just noticeable difference** (or **jnd**). They found that the amount of change in stimulation needed to produce a jnd is a constant proportion of the original stimulus. This became known as the **Weber-Fechner law.** For example, because the jnd for weight is about 2 percent, a person holding a fifty-pound weight will notice a change if at least one pound is added or subtracted from that weight. But a person holding a one hundred-pound weight would require the addition or subtraction of at least two pounds to notice a change. The Weber-Fechner law holds better for stimuli of moderate intensity than for stimuli of extremely low or high intensity.

Sensory Adaptation

Given that each of your senses is constantly bombarded by stimulation, why do you notice only certain stimuli? One reason is that if a stimulus remains constant in intensity, you will gradually stop noticing it. For example, after diving into a swimming pool you might shiver with cold. Yet, a few minutes

Sensory Adaptation Because of sensory adaptation, our sensory receptors respond less and less to a constant stimulus. Sensory adaptation permits the members of the Polar Bear Club to celebrate the New Year at the beach without feeling intolerably cold.

later you might invite those at poolside to join you because "the water's fine." On entering a friend's dormitory room you might be struck by the repugnant stench of month-old garbage. Yet, a few minutes later you might not notice the odor at all. This tendency of our sensory receptors to respond less and less to a constant stimulus is called **sensory adaptation.**

Sensory adaptation enables us to detect potentially important changes in our surroundings while ignoring unchanging aspects of it. Once you have determined that pool water is cold or that your friend's room smells, it would serve little purpose to continue noticing those stimuli—especially when more important changes might be occurring elsewhere in your surroundings. Of course, you will not completely adapt to extremely intense sensations, such as severe pain or freezing cold. This is adaptive, because to ignore such stimuli might be harmful or even fatal.

Sensory Adaptation The tendency of the sensory receptors to respond less and less to a constant stimulus.

VISION

Because of our dependence on vision, psychologists have conducted more research on it than on all the other senses combined. **Vision** lets us sense objects by the light reflected from them into our eyes. *Light* is the common name for the **visible spectrum,** a narrow band of energy within the *electromagnetic spectrum* (figure 4.2). The *wavelength* of a light determines its hue, the primary determinant of its color. The wavelength is the distance between two wave peaks, measured in *nanometers* (billionths of a meter). Light varies in wavelength from 380 nanometers to 760 nanometers. The shortest wavelengths of light will appear violet, while the longest wavelengths will appear red.

While human beings have receptors that can sense only the visible spectrum, some animals have receptors that can detect other forms of electromagnetic energy. Many birds and insects have visual receptors that are sensitive to the relatively short wavelengths of *ultraviolet* light (Chen, Collins, & Goldsmith, 1984), which affects human beings primarily by causing sunburn. And rattlesnakes have receptors located in pits below their eyes that are sensitive to the relatively long wavelengths of *infrared* light, which conveys heat. This enables rattlesnakes to hunt at night by detecting the heat emitted by nearby prey (Newman & Hartline, 1982).

Returning to the visible spectrum, the *amplitude*—the height—of light waves determines the brightness of a light. When you use a dimmer switch

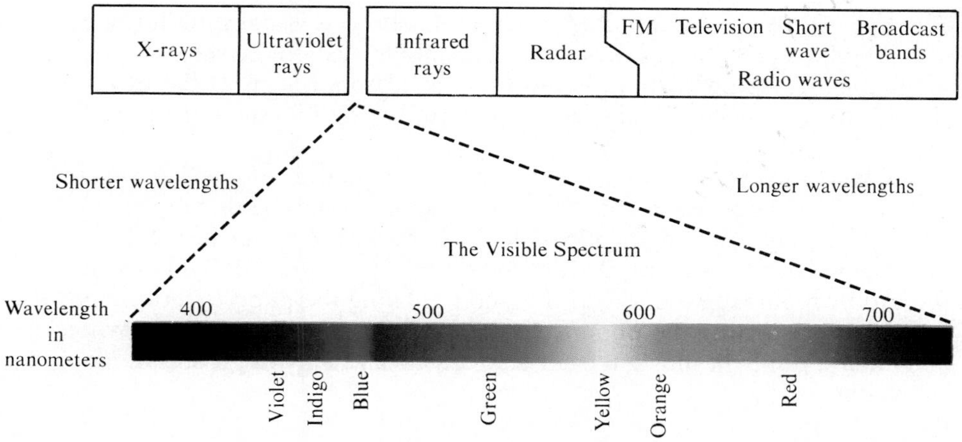

Vision The sense that detects objects by the light reflected from them into the eyes.

Visible Spectrum The portion of the electromagnetic spectrum that we commonly call light.

FIGURE 4.2
The Visible Spectrum The human eye is sensitive to only a narrow slice of the electromagnetic spectrum. This visible spectrum appears in rainbows, when sunlight is broken into its component colors as it passes through raindrops in the atmosphere.

FIGURE 4.3
A Color Solid The qualities of hue, brightness, and saturation can be represented three-dimensionally. Hue is represented by points along the circumference of the color solid; brightness is represented by points on the vertical axis; and saturation is represented by points along the horizontal axis.

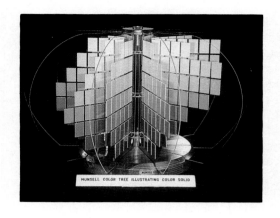

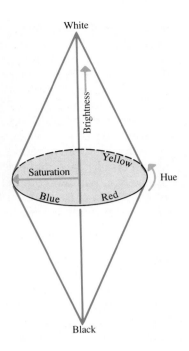

to control a light bulb, you change the amplitude of the light waves emitted by the bulb, thereby changing the brightness of the light you see. The *purity* of a light's wavelength determines its saturation, or vividness. A completely saturated red light would have no other wavelengths except those producing red. Figure 4.3 illustrates the effect of hue, brightness, and saturation on visual experience.

The Visual System

Vision depends on the interaction of the eyes and the brain. The eyes sense objects and then convey this information to the brain, where visual perception takes place. But what accounts for this? Some ancient Greek authorities believed that vision depended on the illumination of objects by light rays emitted by the eyes. But Aristotle presented a telling argument against this belief. If vision depends on light rays emitted by the eyes, why do we not see well in the dark (Mueller & Rudolph, 1966)? Now consider what modern research has discovered about visual processes.

The Eye The eye is a fluid-filled structure that detects visual stimuli (figure 4.4). The "white" of your eye is a tough membrane called the **sclera,** which maintains the shape of the eye and protects it from injury. At the front of the sclera is the round, transparent **cornea,** which focuses light into the eye.

Are you blue-eyed? brown-eyed? green-eyed? Your eye color is determined by the color of your **iris,** a donut-shaped band of muscles behind the cornea. (Iris was the ancient Greek goddess of the rainbow.) At the center of the iris is an opening called the **pupil.** The iris controls the amount of light entering the eye by regulating the size of the pupil, dilating the pupil to let in more light and constricting the pupil to let in less light. Your pupils dilate when you enter a dimly lit movie theater and constrict when you go outside on a sunny day.

Sclera The tough, white outer membrane of the eye.

Cornea The round, transparent area at the front of the sclera that allows light to enter the eye.

Iris The donut-shaped band of muscles behind the cornea that gives the eye its color and controls the size of the pupil.

Pupil The opening at the center of the iris that controls how much light will enter the eye.

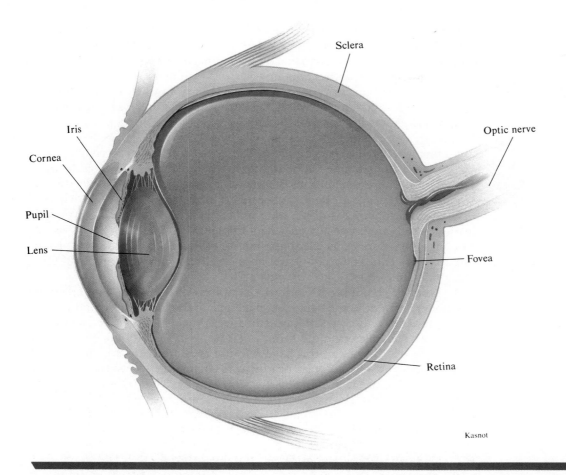

FIGURE 4.4
The Human Eye

You can demonstrate the pupillary response to light by first noting the size of your pupils in your bathroom mirror. Next turn out the light for thirty seconds. Then turn on the light and look in the mirror. Note how much larger your pupils have become and how quickly they begin to constrict in response to the light.

Because our pupils also dilate when we see something we find attractive, merchants in some cultures have traditionally applied this knowledge in bargaining with customers. For example, Chinese jade dealers ask higher prices on items that evoke the greatest pupil dilation in their customers. And we also find people with dilated pupils more attractive (Hess, 1975). This may explain, in part, why we find Disney cartoon characters so endearing—they have large pupils. The attractiveness of large pupils was known to many Renaissance women of the fourteenth to seventeenth centuries, who enhanced their appearance by bathing their eyes with a pupil-dilating drug called *belladonna* (which means "beautiful woman" in Italian).

After passing through the pupil, light is focused by the **lens** onto the **retina,** the light-sensitive inner membrane of the eye. Tiny muscles connected to the lens control **accommodation,** which makes the lens thicken to focus light from close objects or flatten to focus light from distant objects. One of the reasons that it is dangerous to drink and drive is that alcohol disrupts accommodation, causing blurred vision (Miller, Pigion, & Martin, 1985).

Lens The transparent structure behind the pupil that focuses light onto the retina.

Retina The light-sensitive inner membrane of the eye that contains the receptor cells for vision.

Accommodation The process by which the thickness of the lens in the eye changes to focus images of objects located at different distances from the retina.

Why don't we see upside down?

What are

Rods Receptor cells of the retina that play an important role in night vision and peripheral vision.

Cones Receptor cells of the retina that play an important role in daylight vision and color vision.

Fovea A small area at the center of the retina that contains only cones and provides the most acute vision.

What do

Smooth Pursuit Movements
Eye movements that track objects.

allow us to do?

Saccadic Movements
Continuous small darting movements of the eyes that bring new portions of scenes into focus on the foveae.

In the early seventeenth century, René Descartes studied the nature of the image focused on the retina. He wondered whether the lens of the eye, as did similar lenses, would focus an upside-down image. He scraped the back of a cow eyeball until it was thin enough to be transparent and found that images of scenes focused on the retina were upside down. But why then do we not see the world upside down? We do not because the brain flips retinal images over to make them appear right-side up.

It took centuries before scientists discovered how the image focused on the retina is transmitted to the brain. The retina contains cells called *photoreceptors,* which generate neural impulses when they are stimulated by light (figure 4.5). These neural impulses are sent on to the brain. There are two kinds of photoreceptors: **rods** and **cones,** whose names reflect their shapes. Each eye has about 120 million rods and about 6 million cones. As you will learn, the rods are especially important in night vision and peripheral vision, while the cones are especially important in daylight vision and color vision. The rods and cones transmit neural impulses to *bipolar cells,* which, in turn, transmit neural impulses to *ganglion cells.*

The rods are more prevalent in the periphery of the retina and the cones are more prevalent in the center. A small area in the center of the retina, the **fovea,** contains only cones. Because the fovea provides our most acute vision, we try to focus images on the fovea when we wish to note tiny details. You are able to read words on this page because they are being focused on the foveae of your eyes. In contrast, nearby words being focused on the periphery of your retina appear blurred. Foveal vision is more acute (that is, more able to make out fine details) because each cone transmits neural impulses to one bipolar cell. In contrast, a bipolar cell may receive neural impulses from many rods, making peripheral vision less acute. One reason that people vary in the acuity of their vision is that the density of the cones in their foveae varies (Curcio, Sloan, Packer, Hendrickson, & Kalina, 1987).

We use eye movements to keep objects of interest focused on the fovea. **Smooth pursuit movements** permit us to track moving objects—sometimes with amazing precision. A professional baseball player may have to track a baseball thrown by a pitcher at more than ninety miles an hour from a distance of about sixty feet. Though professional baseball players have superior visual tracking ability, research using sophisticated equipment has shown that even a professional batter cannot track a fastball all the way from the pitcher's hand until it strikes his bat. The ball travels the last five feet so fast that smooth pursuit movements cannot track it. Thus, it is impossible to "keep your eye on the ball" all the way from the pitcher's hand to home plate. If this is so, why are some hitters, such as Ted Williams, perhaps the greatest hitter ever, able to see the ball strike the bat? They are able to do so because their brains automatically calculate both the speed and the trajectory of the ball based on their extensive experience in batting, allowing them to anticipate the point in space where the bat will meet the ball (Bahill & LaRitz, 1984).

The smooth pursuit movements used in tracking objects are not the only kind of eye movements. As you scan a scene, such as this page, your eyes make continuous darting movements. These **saccadic movements** bring new portions of scenes into focus on your foveae. After each saccadic movement, the eyes fixate on an object for about a quarter of a second (Rayner, Slowiaczek, Clifton, & Bertera, 1983). We pick up visual information only during these fixations. The time needed to make saccadic movements and to extract information during fixations limits the fastest readers to a maximum of 1,000 words a minute—a phenomenal rate. Yet, speed-reading programs claim that they can increase your reading speed to 10,000 words a minute. How do they do so? By teaching you to skim what you read. Though skimming will increase

rods + cods are photoreceptors

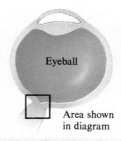

Eyeball

Area shown
in diagram

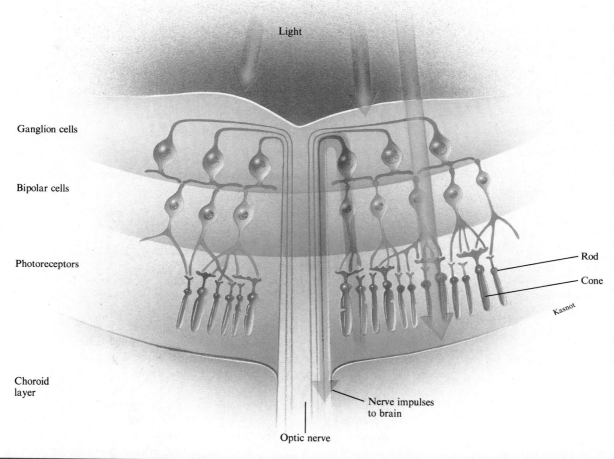

Light

Ganglion cells

Bipolar cells

Photoreceptors

Rod

Cone

Kasnot

Choroid
layer

Nerve impulses
to brain

Optic nerve

FIGURE 4.5

The Cells of the Retina Light must first pass through layers of ganglion cells and bipolar cells before striking the rods and cones. Neural impulses from the rods and cones are transmitted to the bipolar cells, which, in turn, transmit neural impulses to the ganglion cells. The axons of the ganglion cells form the optic nerves, which transmit neural impulses to the brain.

the speed at which you turn pages, it will hurt your comprehension (Homa, 1983).

The retinal images of the words you read, or of any object on which your eyes are focused, are transmitted to the brain along axons of the ganglion cells, which form the **optic nerve.** In the seventeenth century, the French scientist Edmé Mariotte placed a small disk on a screen, closed one eye, stared at the disk, and moved back and forth until the image of the disk disappeared

How is what you read transmitted to your brain?

Optic Nerve The nerve formed from the axons of ganglion cells that carries visual impulses from the retina to the brain.

FIGURE 4.6
Finding Your Blind Spot
Because your retina has no rods or cones at the point where the optic nerve leaves the eye, your retina is "blind" at that spot. To find your blind spot, hold this book at arm's length, close your right eye, and focus your left eye on the black dot. Move the book slowly toward you. When the book is about a foot away, the image of the ladybug should disappear. It disappears when it becomes focused on your blind spot. You do not normally notice your blind spot because your eyes see different views of the same scene, your eyes are constantly focusing on different parts of the scene, and your brain fills in missing details of the scene.

O'Keefe

Blind Spot The point, lacking any rods or cones, at which the optic nerve leaves the eye.

Optic Chiasm The point under the frontal lobes at which some axons from each of the optic nerves cross over to the opposite side of the brain.

Visual Cortex The area of the occipital lobes that processes visual input.

(Mueller & Rudolph, 1966). By doing so, he demonstrated the existence of the **blind spot,** the point at which the optic nerve leaves the eye. It is "blind" because it contains no rods or cones. To repeat Mariotte's demonstration, follow the procedure suggested in figure 4.6.

The Brain   Figure 4.7 traces the path of neural impulses from the eyeballs into the brain. The optic nerves travel under the frontal lobes of the brain and meet at a point called the **optic chiasm.** (*Chiasm* comes from the Greek word for "X.") At the optic chiasm, axons from the half of each optic nerve nearest the nose cross to the opposite side of the brain. The remaining axons continue on the same side of the brain. Most axons of the optic nerves reach the *thalamus,* the sensory relay station of the brain, which transmits visual information to the **visual cortex** of the *occipital lobes.* As you may recall from chapter 3, images of objects in the right visual field project to the left occipital lobe, and images of objects in the left visual field project to the right occipital lobe. The visual cortex integrates visual information about objects, including their shape, color, distance, and movement (Livingstone & Hubel, 1988).

Unfortunately, many people suffer from blindness. Because most cases of blindness result from damage to the eyes or the optic nerves, blind people usually have an intact visual cortex. This has led to research aimed at developing devices that would restore vision by directly stimulating the visual cortex. Researchers have developed a crude electronic system consisting of a television camera connected to an eight-by-eight matrix of sixty-four electrodes placed on the visual cortex. Stimulation of these electrodes produces a pattern of spots of light representing the outlines of objects seen by the camera. In initial demonstrations, blind people using this device were able to recognize common objects, including letters (Dobelle, Madejovsky, Evans, Roberts, & Girvin, 1976). Perhaps more sophisticated devices will one day permit blind people to read textbooks, paint pictures, and drive automobiles.

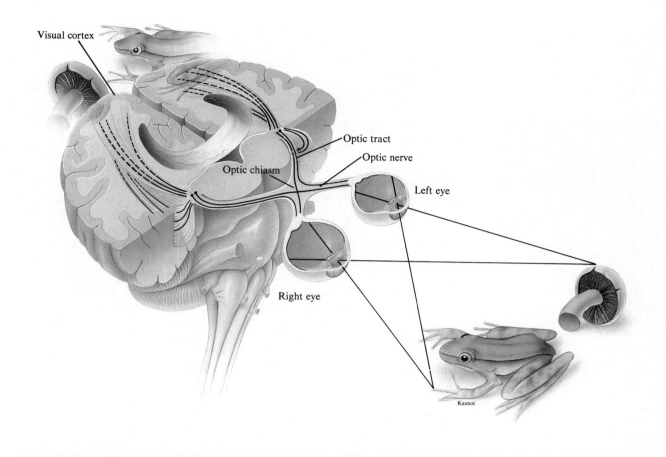

FIGURE 4.7

The Visual Pathway Images of objects in the right visual field are focused on the left side of each retina, and images of objects in the left visual field are focused on the right side of each retina. This information is conveyed along the optic nerves to the optic chiasm and then on to the thalamus. The thalamus then relays the information to the visual cortex of the occipital lobes. Note that images of objects in the right visual field are processed by the left occipital lobe and images of objects in the left visual field are processed by the right occipital lobe.

Visual Sensation

People with normal vision are able to see because of processes taking place in their retinas. Visual sensations depend on chemicals called *photopigments.* Rod vision depends on the photopigment **rhodopsin,** and cone vision depends on the photopigment **iodopsin.** Light striking the rods or cones breaks down their photopigments, which generates neural impulses that are transmitted to the bipolar cells and on to the ganglion cells that form the optic nerves. After being broken down by light, the photopigments are resynthesized—more rapidly in dim light than in bright light.

While the cones function better in normal light than in dim light, the rods function better in dim light than in normal light. Because of this, in normal light we try to focus fine details on the fovea. In contrast, in dim light we try to focus fine details just off the fovea. If you look directly at a star in the night sky, you will be unable to see it because it will be focused on the foveae of

Rhodopsin The photopigment that accounts for rod vision. *dim light*

Iodopsin The photopigment that accounts for cone vision. *normal light*

Dark Adaptation The process by which the eyes become more sensitive to light when under low illumination.

A *Green* Fire Truck? Because the rods are more sensitive to the green end of the visual spectrum than to the red end, green objects look brighter in dim light than do red objects. So, while red fire trucks look bright in the daylight, they look grayish in dim light. This has led some fire departments to increase the evening visibility of their trucks by painting them a yellowish green color.

your eyes. To see the star, you would have to tilt your head, focusing the star on the rod-rich periphery of your retinas. The photoreceptors are also important in the processes of *dark adaptation* and *color vision*.

Dark Adaptation When you enter a darkened movie theater, you have difficulty finding a seat because your photoreceptors have been bleached of their photopigments by the light in the lobby. But your eyes adapt by increasing their rate of synthesizing rhodopsin and iodopsin, gradually increasing your ability to see the seats and people in the theater. The cones reach their maximum sensitivity after about ten minutes of dim light. But your rods continue to adapt to the dim light, reaching their maximum sensitivity in about thirty minutes. So, you owe your ability to see in dim light to your rods. Figure 4.8 illustrates this process of **dark adaptation,** the process by which your eyes become more sensitive to light.

The preceding discussion should make you realize why motorists should dim their high beams when approaching oncoming traffic and why passengers should not turn on the dome light to read road maps. High beams shining into your eyes and dome lights illuminating the inside of your vehicle will bleach your rods, impairing your ability to see objects that might be ahead of you. You should also note that the cones are most sensitive to the red portion of the visible spectrum, while the rods are most sensitive to the green portion. This explains why shortly after dusk (when we shift from cone vision to rod vision) a red jacket will look dull while a patch of green grass will look vibrant.

Color Vision Color enhances the quality of our lives, as shown by our concern with the colors of our clothes, furnishings, and automobiles. While primates such as apes, monkeys, and human beings have good color vision,

FIGURE 4.8
Dark Adaptation When you enter a dark room your photoreceptors adapt by becoming more sensitive to light. The cones reach their maximum sensitivity in about ten minutes, and the rods reach their maximum sensitivity in about thirty minutes. Though the cones adapt to the dark faster than do the rods, the rods become more sensitive than do the cones. This means that the absolute threshold of rods becomes much lower than that of cones.

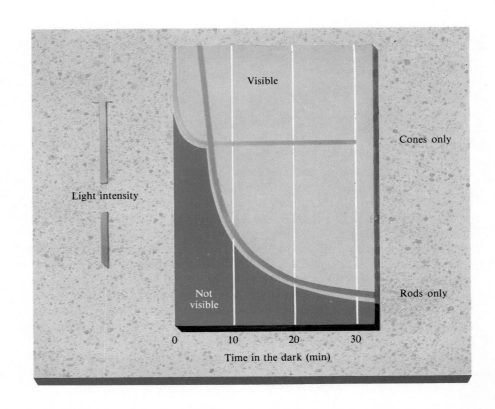

most other mammals, such as dogs, cats, and cows, have little or no color vision. Most birds and fish also have good color vision. In contrast, fish that live in the depths of the ocean have no color vision. Color vision would be useless in dim light, because, as mentioned earlier, cones only function well in bright light (Levine & MacNichol, 1982).

But what processes account for color vision? The first answer came in 1802 when the English physicist Thomas Young presented the **trichromatic theory** of color vision, a theory elaborated in the 1850s by the German physiologist Hermann von Helmholtz. Today the trichromatic theory is also called the *Young-Helmholtz theory*. The theory assumes that the retina has three kinds of receptors—which we now know are cones—maximally sensitive to *red, green,* or *blue* light.

A century after Helmholtz put forth his theory, George Wald (1964) provided evidence for it in research that earned him a Nobel Prize. Wald found that some cones would send neural impulses when stimulated by red light, other cones when stimulated by blue light, and still other cones when stimulated by green light (figure 4.9). The colors we experience depend on the relative degree of stimulation of the cones. For example, stimulation of red and green cones produces the sensation of yellow. Figure 4.10 illustrates the principles of mixing colored lights and mixing colored pigments, which differ from each other.

In the 1870s, the German physiologist Ewald Hering proposed an alternative theory of color vision, the **opponent-process theory,** in part to explain the phenomenon of **afterimages,** images that persist after the removal of a stimulus (figure 4.11). If you stare at a red or blue surface for a minute and then stare at a white surface, you will see an afterimage that is the complementary color. Staring at red will lead to a green afterimage, and staring at blue will lead to a yellow afterimage.

The opponent-process theory assumes that there are *red-green, blue-yellow,* and *black-white* opponent processes (with the black-white opponent process determining the brightness of what we see). Stimulation of one process inhibits the other. When stimulation stops, this inhibition is removed and the complementary color is seen as a brief afterimage. This explains why staring at red leads to a green afterimage and staring at blue leads to a yellow afterimage. This also explains why we cannot perceive reddish greens or bluish yellows—complementary colors cannot be experienced simultaneously because each inhibits the other.

Do Bulls See Red? Because bulls are color blind, the red cape used by matadors is used for dramatic effect—a bull will charge a cape of any color.

Trichromatic Theory The theory that color vision depends on the relative degree of stimulation of red, green, and blue receptors.

Opponent-Process Theory The theory that color vision depends on red-green, blue-yellow, and black-white opponent processes in the brain.

Afterimage A visual image that persists after the removal of a stimulus.

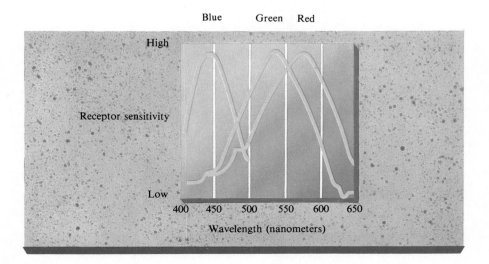

FIGURE 4.9
Relative Sensitivity of the Cones The three kinds of cones (red, green, and blue) each respond to a wide range of wavelengths of light. But each is maximally sensitive to particular wavelengths. The red cones are maximally sensitive to long wavelengths, the green cones to medium wavelengths, and the blue cones to short wavelengths. According to the trichromatic theory, the perceived color of a light depends on the relative amount of activity in each of the three kinds of cones.

FIGURE 4.10
Color Mixing In additive mixing, lights of different colors are combined. As you can see, (a) mixing red, green, and blue lights of equal intensity yields white. In subtractive mixing, pigments of different colors are combined. Because each color absorbs certain wavelengths of light, (b) combining red, yellow, and blue pigments of equal intensity yields black.

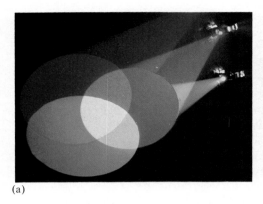
(a)

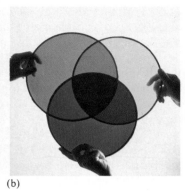
(b)

FIGURE 4.11
Color Afterimages Stare at the dot in the center of the flag for at least thirty seconds. Then stare at a sheet of white paper. You should then see an afterimage of "old glory" with its normal red, white, and blue colors. These colors are complementary to those of the green, black, and yellow flag. Such complementary afterimages support the opponent-process theory of color vision.

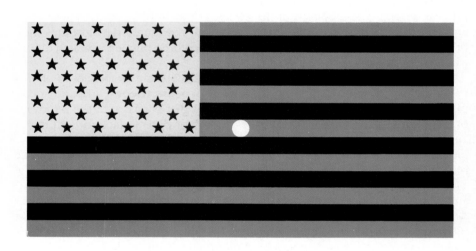

FIGURE 4.12
Testing for Color Blindness A person with red-green color blindness is unable to see the number in this pattern. A complete test of color blindness would present a series of patterns such as this.

The above has been reproduced from Ishihara's Tests for Colour Blindness published by Kanehara & Co., Ltd., Tokyo, Japan, but tests for color blindness cannot be conducted with this material. For accurate testing, the original plates should be used. Graham-Field is the exclusive distributor in the United States and Canada.

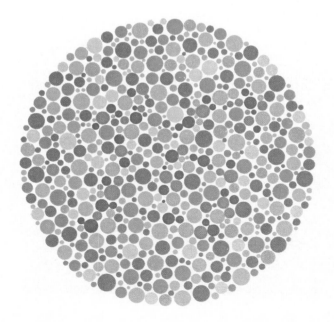

Psychologist Russell DeValois and his colleagues (1966) have provided evidence supporting the opponent-process theory. For example, certain cells in the thalamus send impulses when the cones that send them input are stimulated by red and stop sending impulses when the cones that send them input are stimulated by the complementary color of green. Other cells in the thalamus send impulses when the cones that send them input are stimulated by green and stop sending impulses when the cones that send them input are stimulated by red.

The opponent-process theory also explains another phenomenon that the trichromatic theory cannot: **color blindness.** People with normal color vision are *trichromats*—they have three kinds of photopigments (red, blue, and green). Most people who are color blind are *dichromats*—they lack one kind of photopigment. The most common kind of color blindness is the inability to distinguish between red and green. People with red-green color blindness have cones with blue pigment, but their red and green cones both have either red or green pigment.

Color Blindness The inability to distinguish between certain colors, most often red and green.

About 2 percent of males and less than 1 percent of females are red-green color blind. Males are more likely to be color blind because color blindness is a recessive trait carried on the X chromosome. This means that any male who inherits the trait on his single X chromosome will be color blind. In contrast, a female must inherit the trait on *both* of her X chromosomes to be color blind (Mollon, 1982). Few dichromats suffer from blue-yellow color blindness and even fewer suffer from total color blindness. People with total color blindness are called *monochromats.* Because many people have red-green color blindness, traffic lights always have the red light on top so that color-blind people will know when to stop and when to go. See if you can pass the color-blindness test in figure 4.12.

But how does color blindness support the opponent-process theory? It does so because, while dichromats will fail to distinguish between the complementary colors of red and green or blue and yellow, they will never fail to distinguish between red and blue, red and yellow, green and blue, or green and yellow. Today the trichromatic theory and the opponent-process theory are both used to explain color vision (Boynton, 1988). Information from the red, green, and blue cones of the retinas is relayed to the opponent-process ganglion cells and then further integrated in the thalamus and visual cortex.

FIGURE 4.13
Figure-Ground Perception As you view this picture you will note that it seems to reverse. At one moment you see a vase, and at the next moment you see the profiles of two faces. What you see depends on what you see as figure and what you see as ground.

Figure-Ground Perception The distinguishing of an object (the figure) from its surroundings (the ground).

FIGURE 4.14
Gestalt Principles of Form Perception These patterns illustrate the role of (a) closure, (b) proximity, and (c) similarity in form perception.

Visual Perception

Visual sensations provide the raw materials that are organized into meaningful patterns by *visual perception*. But is visual perception based on inborn mechanisms that automatically convert sensations into perceptions of external stimuli? Or, instead, do we have to learn through experience to convert sensations into accurate perceptions? The *ecological theory* of James J. Gibson (1979) supports the former, while the *constructivist theory* traditionally held by perception researchers favors the latter. As you will learn in chapter 12, recent research on newborn infants' perceptual abilities has lent support to Gibson's theory. Despite this, most perception researchers believe that we "construct" our perceptions based on inferences that we make from our sensations (Cutting, 1987). These inferences are based on our experience with objects in the physical environment.

Form Perception   To perceive *forms* (meaningful shapes or patterns) we must distinguish a *figure* (that is, an object) from its *ground* (that is, its surroundings). This is known as **figure-ground perception.** The words on this page are figures against the ground of the white paper. The vase in figure 4.13 shows how figure and ground may sometimes be ambiguous. This shows that perception is an active process that tries to interpret sensory input. Gestalt psychologists were the first to study the principles governing form perception, several of which are illustrated in figure 4.14.

The principle of *proximity* states that stimuli that are close together will tend to be perceived as parts of the same form. The principle of *similarity* states that stimuli that are similar to one another will tend to be perceived as parts of the same form. The principle of *closure* states that we tend to fill in

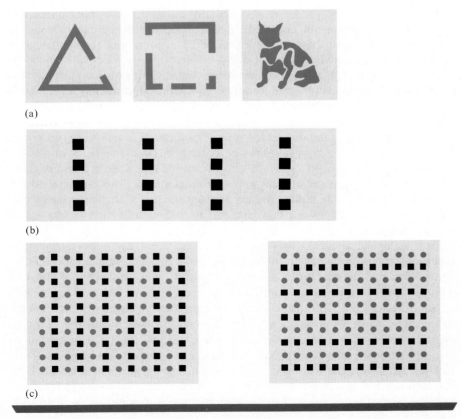

(a)

(b)

(c)

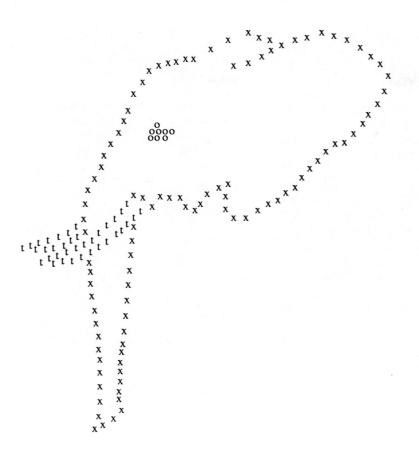

FIGURE 4.15
The Whole Is Different from the Sum of Its Parts According to Gestalt psychologists, you see a picture of an elephant instead of a random grouping of dots because your brain imposes organization on what it perceives. Your perception of the elephant depends on each of the Gestalt principles of similarity, proximity, closure, and continuity. As you will learn later in the chapter, your perception of the elephant also depends on your previous experience. A person from a culture unfamiliar with elephants might be unable to perceive the dots as a meaningful form.

minor gaps in forms that we perceive. And the principle of *continuity* states that we tend to group stimuli into forms that follow continuous lines or patterns.

According to Gestalt psychologists, forms are perceived as wholes, rather than merely constructed from their parts. Recall the famous Gestalt saying, mentioned in chapter 1, that "the whole is different from the sum of its parts." Thus, in figure 4.15 you see an image of an elephant rather than only a pattern of marks. Though there is evidence supporting the Gestalt position that forms are perceived holistically (Navon, 1974), there is also evidence that forms can be perceived through the analysis of their features (Oden, 1984).

Consider the letter *A.* Do we perceive it holistically as a single shape, or analytically as a combination of lines of various lengths and angles? According to Gestaltists we perceive it holistically, but according to the **feature-detector theory** of David Hubel and Torsten Wiesel we may construct our perception of the letter *A* from its component lines and angles. Hubel and Wiesel (1979) base their theory on studies (for which they won a 1981 Nobel Prize) in which they implanted microelectrodes into the visual cortex of cats and presented them with lines of various sizes, orientations, and locations (figure 4.16). They found that certain cells responded to specific features of images on the retina, such as lines of particular lengths, lines at particular angles, and lines in particular locations. Hubel and Wiesel concluded that we construct our visual perceptions from activity in such *feature-detector cells.*

Research has shown that some feature-detector cells in the visual cortex respond to amazingly specific combinations of features. You may recall from

Feature-Detector Theory The view that we construct our perceptions from neurons of the brain that are sensitive to specific features of stimuli.

David Hubel and Torsten Wiesel Hubel and Wiesel are shown celebrating the Nobel Prize they were awarded for their research on visual feature detectors in the brain.

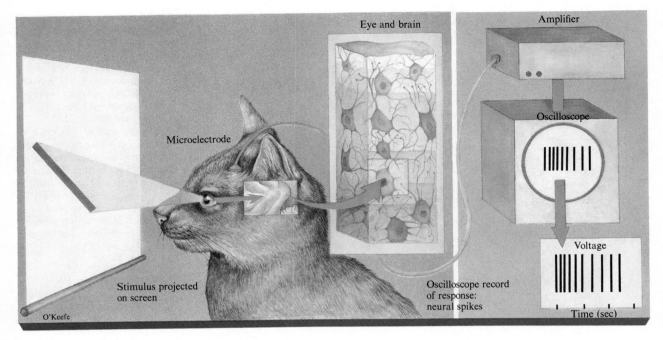

FIGURE 4.16
Feature-Detector Cells David Hubel and Torsten Wiesel showed cats various stimuli and used microelectrodes to record the electrical responses of particular neurons in the visual cortex. A given neuron might respond only to a line of a given length, orientation, and location.

Illusory Contours The perception of edges that do not actually exist, as though they were the outlines of real objects.

Depth Perception The perception of the relative distance of objects.

Binocular Cues Depth perception cues that require input from the two eyes.

chapter 3 that different cells in the visual cortex of sheep respond to the faces of sheep, sheep dogs, and human beings (Kendrick & Baldwin, 1987). Feature-detector cells in the visual cortex even provide an anatomical basis for the **illusory contours** shown in figure 4.17, responding to the contours as if they were the edges of real objects (von der Heydt, Peterhans, & Baumgartner, 1984).

Depth Perception If we lived in a two-dimensional world, form perception would be sufficient. But because we live in a three-dimensional world, we must have some way to judge the distance of objects. This is provided by **depth perception.** But, given that the images on our retinas are two-dimensional, how is it that we perceive depth? We do so by using a variety of visual cues: *binocular cues* and *monocular cues.* **Binocular cues** require the interaction of both eyes—people who are blind in one eye have slightly impaired depth perception. The two main binocular cues are *convergence* and *retinal disparity.*

Convergence is the degree to which the eyes turn inward to focus on an object. As you can demonstrate for yourself, the closer the object, the greater the convergence of the eyes. Hold your forefinger vertically as you move it toward, and then away from, your nose. You may notice changes in the tension of your eye muscles. Your brain translates the degree of muscle tension into an estimate of the distance of the object on which you are focusing.

Retinal disparity is the degree of difference between the images of an object that are focused on the two retinas. The closer the object, the greater the retinal disparity. You can demonstrate retinal disparity for yourself by, again, pointing a forefinger vertically between your eyes and then alternately opening and closing each eye. Note that if you move your finger away from your nose

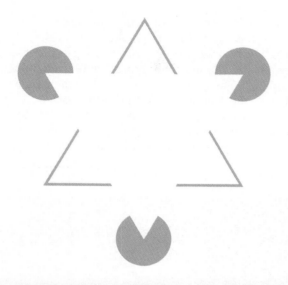

FIGURE 4.17
Illusory Contours Seeing a complete triangle when only its corners exist is an example of the Gestalt principle of closure. Feature-detector cells in the visual cortex respond to such illusory contours as if they were real, supporting the Gestalt position that the brain imposes organization on stimuli.

the degree of retinal disparity decreases. Certain cells in the visual cortex detect the degree of retinal disparity, which the brain uses to estimate the distance of an object focused on your retinas (Mustillo, 1985).

If you have ever seen a "3–D" movie, you have experienced the practical application of retinal disparity. A 3–D movie is shot by two projectors, each filming slightly different views of scenes. The two movies are then shown simultaneously. Viewers who wear special 3–D eyeglasses will see one movie with the left eye and the other movie with the right eye. This creates an impression of depth by mimicking the phenomenon of retinal disparity. If you watch the movie without wearing the special 3–D eyeglasses, you will see a blurred image caused by both versions of the film simultaneously striking both of your retinas.

While binocular cues to depth require two eyes, **monocular cues** require only one. Thus, a person who is blind in one eye still has many cues to use in determining the distance of an object. One monocular cue to depth is accommodation, which you learned earlier is the change in the thickness of the lens that enables you to focus images of objects on the retina. Because closer objects cause increased thickness of the lens, the brain assumes that the greater the thickness of the lens the closer the object being focused on the retina. A second monocular cue is *motion parallax,* the tendency to perceive ourselves passing objects closer to us faster than objects farther from us. You may have noticed this when you drive on rural highways. You perceive yourself passing nearby telephone polls faster than distant farmhouses.

The remaining monocular cues are called *pictorial cues* because they are used by artists to give the impression of depth in their drawings and paintings (figure 4.18). Leonardo da Vinci formalized pictorial cues 500 years ago by teaching his art students how to use them to make their paintings look more realistic (Haber, 1980). He noted that objects that overlap other objects appear closer, a cue known as *interposition.* Because your psychology professor "overlaps" the blackboard you know that he or she is closer to you than is the blackboard. Comparing the *relative size* of objects also provides cues to their distance. If two of your friends are the same height and one appears smaller on your retinas, that friend will be perceived as farther away.

Monocular Cues Depth perception cues that require input from only one eye.

You have probably noticed that parallel objects, such as railroad tracks, seem to get closer together as they get farther away. This cue is called *linear perspective.* During World War II, naval aviation cadets flying at night sometimes crashed into airplanes ahead of them, apparently because of a failure to judge the distance of those planes. This problem was solved by taking advantage of linear perspective. The traditional single taillight was replaced by two taillights set a standard distance apart. As a consequence, when pilots noticed the taillights of an airplane appear to move farther apart they realized that they were getting closer to that airplane (Fiske, Conley, & Goldberg, 1987).

(a)

(b)

(c)

(d)

FIGURE 4.18
Pictorial Cues to Depth Artists make use of pictorial cues to portray depth in their drawings and paintings. These cues include (a) overlap, (b) aerial perspective, (c) texture gradient, and (d) linear perspective.

An object's *distance from the horizon* provides another cue to its distance. Objects that appear closer to the horizon seem to be farther away. If you paint a picture, you can create depth by placing more distant objects higher on your canvas. *Shading patterns* provide cues to distance because areas that are in shadow tend to recede, while areas that are in light tend to stand out. Painters use this to make balls, balloons, and oranges appear round.

The *texture gradient* cue influences depth perception because an object's texture is coarser when you are near it and finer when you are far from it. When looking across a field, you can see every blade of grass near you, but only an expanse of green far away from you. And the cue of *aerial perspective*—the clarity of objects—influences depth perception because distant objects appear hazier. A mountain will appear farther away on a hazy day than on a clear day.

Motion Perception   Given that we live in a three-dimensional world in which objects move through space, we must not only perceive forms and depth, but we must also perceive motion. The traditional view of motion perception attributes it to the progressive movement of images across the retina, which stimulates a series of different photoreceptors. The brain interprets this as motion. An alternative to this view, put forth by James Gibson (1968), claims that motion is produced by changes in the flow of patterns of light on the retinas, not by the successive stimulation of different photoreceptors in so-called retinal painting. Neither view has yet achieved a consensus among researchers.

Gestalt psychologists were especially interested in *apparent motion*—the appearance of motion when none is actually occurring (Petersik, 1989). As described in chapter 1, in 1912 Max Wertheimer, the founder of Gestalt psychology, had a brainstorm that led him to discover that when two light bulbs were turned on and off in succession, at just the right interval, a single light appeared to move from one bulb to the other. He called this apparent motion the **phi phenomenon.** You have experienced the phi phenomenon if you have ever seen the message board in New York's Times Square or a warning sign composed of light bulbs at a highway construction site. Both produce messages by turning light bulbs on and off in desired sequences at just the right intervals.

The phi phenomenon is related to the kind of apparent motion called *stroboscopic motion,* which is produced by successively flashing slightly different views of a scene at rapid speed. This is the basis of movies. A movie projector's shutter rapidly exposes successive frames of a film, with each frame slightly different from the one before it. The brain blends these images into a continuous flow of motion—the "motion" in motion pictures.

Just as there are feature-detector cells for form perception and depth perception, there are others for motion perception (Regan, 1982). Some motion-detector cells are highly specific. In fact, frogs have retinal ganglion cells that respond only to small, dark, moving objects. These so-called bug detectors are useful evolutionary adaptations, because a frog's diet consists mainly of insects (Lettvin, Maturana, McCulloch, & Pitts, 1959).

Perceptual Constancies   Because you can move and objects in your environment can move, the image of a given object focused on your retinas will vary in size, shape, and brightness. Yet, because of *perceptual constancy,* you will continue to perceive the object as stable in size, shape, and brightness. As an object gets farther away from you, it produces a smaller image on your retinas. If you know the actual size of an object, **size constancy** makes you interpret a change in its retinal size as a change in its distance rather than as a change in its size. When you see an automobile a block away, it does not seem smaller than one that is half a block away,

apparent emotion in absence of actual emotion ex: cartoons

Phi Phenomenon   Apparent motion caused by the presentation of different stimuli in rapid succession.

Size Constancy   The perceptual process that makes an object appear to remain the same size despite changes in the size of the image it casts on the retina.

FIGURE 4.19
Shape Constancy As a door opens, its image on your retinas changes in shape. Yet, because of shape constancy, you continue to perceive the door as a rectangle.

Shape Constancy The perceptual process that makes an object appear to maintain its normal shape regardless of the angle from which it is viewed.

Brightness Constancy The perceptual process that makes an object maintain a particular level of brightness despite changes in the amount of light reflected from it.

Visual Illusion A misperception of physical reality usually caused by the misapplication of visual cues.

Moon Illusion The misperception that the moon is larger when it is at the horizon than when it is overhead.

even though the more distant automobile will produce a smaller image on your retinas.

Shape constancy assures that an object of known shape will appear to maintain its normal shape regardless of the angle from which you view it (figure 4.19). Close this book and hold it at varying orientations. Unless you look directly at the cover or back of the book, it will never cast a rectangular image on your retinas, yet you will continue to perceive it as rectangular. Shape constancy occurs because your brain compensates for the slant of an object relative to your line of sight (Wallach & Marshall, 1985).

Though the amount of light reflected from given objects varies over time, we perceive the objects as having a constant brightness. This is known as **brightness constancy.** A white shirt will appear equally bright in dim light or bright light, while a black shirt will appear equally dull in dim light or bright light. But brightness constancy is relative to other objects. If you look at a white shirt in dim light in the presence of other objects in the same light, it will maintain its brightness. In contrast, if you look at the white shirt by itself, perhaps by viewing a large area of it through a tube, it will appear duller in dim light and brighter in sunlight.

Visual Illusions In Edgar Allen Poe's short story "The Sphinx" a man is horrified by an insect on his window that he mistakes for a monstrous animal on a distant mountain. Because the man perceived the creature as far away, he assumed that it was relatively large. And, because he had never seen such a creature, he assumed that it was a monster. This shows how the misapplication of a visual cue, in this case size constancy, can produce a **visual illusion.** Researchers study visual illusions because they provide dramatic examples of the normal processes involved in visual perception.

From ancient times to modern times, people have been mystified by the the **moon illusion,** in which the moon appears larger when it is at the horizon than when it is overhead (figure 4.20). This is an illusion because the size of the image of the moon on the retinas is the same whether the moon is at the horizon or overhead. The most widely accepted explanation of the moon illusion was first put forth by the Greek astronomer Ptolemy in the second century A.D. His explanation, based on the principle of size constancy, is called the *apparent-distance hypothesis* (Kaufman & Rock, 1962). This hypothesis assumes that we perceive the sky as a flattened dome, with the sky

FIGURE 4.20
The Moon Illusion Psychologists have failed to agree on an explanation of why the moon looks larger when it is at the horizon than when it is overhead in the sky.

at the horizon appearing farther away than it does overhead. Because the image of the moon on the retina is the same size, whether the moon is overhead or at the horizon, the brain assumes that the moon must be larger at the apparently more distant location—the horizon. But more recent research has found that, contrary to the apparent-distance hypothesis, the sky looks *farther away* overhead than it does at the horizon. So, if the apparent-distance hypothesis were correct, the moon should appear larger *overhead* than it does at the horizon (Baird & Wagner, 1982).

An alternative explanation for the moon illusion, the *relative-size hypothesis,* attributes it to the different amounts of space surrounding the moon overhead and at the horizon. Because the moon is surrounded by more empty space when overhead than when at the horizon, it appears smaller when it is overhead (Restle, 1970). Despite many studies of the moon illusion, researchers have yet to agree on the best explanation for it. Figures 4.21 and 4.22 present other visual illusions that have stimulated numerous research studies.

(a)

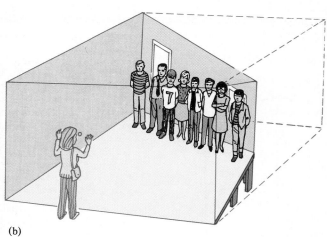

(b)

FIGURE 4.21
The Ames Room (a) The giant children on the right are actually shorter than the tiny adult on the left. (b) The floor plan of the Ames room shows that the individuals on the left are much farther away than the individuals on the right, and the floor to ceiling height is greater on the left than on the right. When viewed with one eye through a peephole, the effect is to make each of the persons seem like they are standing the same distance away in a normal rectangular room. The illusion occurs because the individuals on the right fill more of the space between the floor and the ceiling and because we assume that when two objects are the same distance away the object that produces a smaller image on our retinas is, in fact, smaller.

(b)

O'Keefe

FIGURE 4.22
The Müller-Lyer Illusion
Perhaps the most widely studied illusion was developed a century ago by Franz Müller-Lyer. (a) Note that the vertical line on the right appears longer than the vertical line on the left. Take a ruler and measure both lines. You will find that the lines are equal in length. (b) Though no explanation has achieved universal acceptance (Mack et al., 1985), the most widely accepted explanation depends on size constancy and the resemblance of the figure on the right to the inside corner of a room and the resemblance of the figure on the left to the outside corner of a building. Given that the lines project images of equal length on the retina, the line that appears farther will be perceived as longer. Because the corner of a room appears farther than the corner of a building, the line on the right appears farther and, therefore, longer than the line on the left (Gillam, 1980).

(a)

Experience and Perception As you have just read, visual perception depends on the interaction of the eyes and the brain. But it also depends on life experiences, as demonstrated by studies of *sensory restriction*. In one study, kittens were raised in darkness except for five hours a day spent in a large tube whose walls were covered with either horizontal or vertical lines. Because the kittens also wore a large saucer-shaped collar, they could not even see their own bodies.

After five months their vision was tested under normal lighting by waving a rod in front of them either vertically or horizontally. Kittens that had been exposed to vertical lines swatted at the vertical rod but not at the horizontal rod. And kittens that had been exposed to horizontal lines swatted at the horizontal rod but not at the vertical rod. Recordings of the activity in single neurons in the visual cortex showed that particular neurons responded to either vertical or horizontal lines, depending on the lines to which the kittens had been exposed during the previous five months (Blakemore & Cooper, 1970).

While studies such as this one show that the development of visual perception can be influenced by the effect of experience on visual pathways, other studies show that visual perception can be influenced by life experiences that do not physically alter visual pathways. This was demonstrated by an anthropologist named Colin Turnbull (1961) who visited the Bambuti pygmies of central Africa. Turnbull drove one of the pygmies, who lived in a dense forest, to an open plain. Looking across the plain at a herd of grazing buffalo, the pygmy asked Turnbull to tell him what kind of insects they were. Turnbull responded by driving the pygmy to the herd. As the "insects" got bigger and bigger, the pygmy accused Turnbull of witchcraft for turning the insects into buffalos. Because he had never experienced large objects at a distance, the pygmy had a limited appreciation of size constancy. To him the tiny images on his retinas could only be insects. Because of the understandable failure to apply size constancy appropriately, the pygmy mistook the distant buffalo for a nearby insect, while the man in Poe's short story mistook the nearby insect for a distant monster.

To gain an even greater appreciation for the influence of cultural experience on visual perception, consider the *Ponzo illusion* (figure 4.23). As in the case of most illusions, the Ponzo illusion is caused by the misapplication of perceptual cues. As you read earlier, linear perspective is a cue to depth. Because the train tracks appear to come together in the distance, the horizontal bar higher in the figure appears farther away than the one lower in the figure.

"Its a hell of a lot more impressive from a distance!"

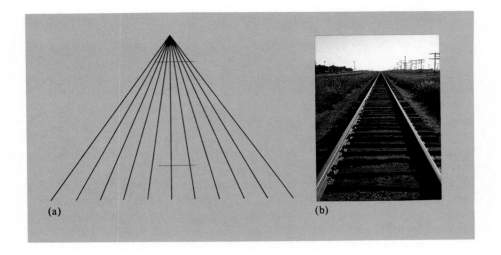

(a)   (b)

If you measure the bars, you will find that they are actually equal in length. Yet, because both bars produce images of equal length on your retinas, the bar that appears farther away seems to be longer. Experiences with monocular cues to depth, such as linear perspective, influence responses to the Ponzo illusion. Rural Ugandan villagers, who have little experience with such cues, are less susceptible to the Ponzo illusion than are Ugandan college students, who have more experience with such cues in art, photographs, and motion pictures (Leibowitz & Pick, 1972).

HEARING

Audition The sense of hearing.

Like the sense of vision, the sense of hearing or **audition** provides us with information about objects at a distance from us. Sound is produced by vibrations carried by air, water, or other mediums. Because sound requires a medium through which to travel, it cannot travel in a vacuum. (Of course, this has not prevented the *Star Trek* and *Star Wars* movies from increasing their dramatic effect by including the sounds of massive explosions and roaring rocket engines in the vacuum of outer space.) Sound vibrations create a successive bunching and spreading of molecules in the sound medium (figure 4.24). A *sound wave* is composed of a series of these bunching-spreading cycles. The height of a sound wave is its *amplitude,* and the number of sound wave cycles that pass a given point in a second is its *frequency.* Sound frequency is measured in *hertz (Hz),* named for the nineteenth-century German physicist Heinrich Hertz. A 60-Hz sound wave would have a frequency of sixty cycles a second.

FIGURE 4.24
Sound Waves Vibrations from objects that produce sounds cause successive compression and expansion of the air around them. Sound waves vary in their amplitude and frequency. Most sounds are not pure but instead are composed of sound waves with different amplitudes and frequencies.

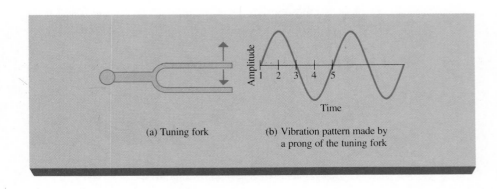

(a) Tuning fork   (b) Vibration pattern made by a prong of the tuning fork

FIGURE 4.25
The Human Ear

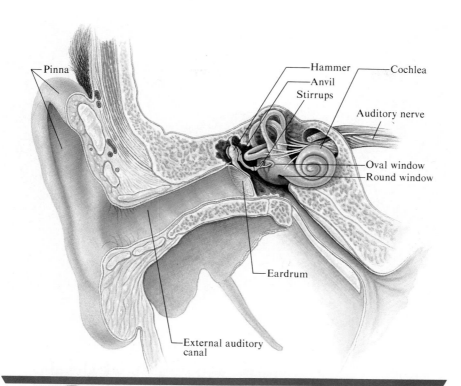

The Auditory System

Sound waves are sensed and perceived by the *auditory system,* which begins with the *ear.* The ear is divided into an outer ear, a middle ear, and an inner ear (figure 4.25). The *outer ear* includes the *pinna,* the oddly shaped flap that we commonly call the "ear." Though the pinna plays a small role in human hearing, some animals, such as deer, have large, movable pinnas that help them detect and locate faint sounds. Sound waves gathered by the pinna pass through the *external auditory canal* and reach the **tympanic membrane,** commonly called the *eardrum.* Sound waves make the eardrum vibrate. Our hearing is responsive to even the slightest movement of the eardrum. If our hearing were any more acute, we would hear the air molecules that are constantly bouncing against the eardrum (von Békésy, 1957).

The eardrum separates the outer ear from the *middle ear.* Vibrations of the eardrum are conveyed to the bones, or *ossicles,* of the middle ear. The ossicles are three tiny bones connected to one another by ligaments. The Latin names of the ossicles reflect their shapes: the *malleus (hammer),* the *incus (anvil),* and the *stapes (stirrup).* Vibrations of the stapes are conveyed to the *oval window* of the *inner ear.* The oval window is a membrane that is part of a spiral structure called the **cochlea** (from a Greek word meaning "snail").

Vibrations of the oval window send waves through a fluid-filled chamber that runs the length of the cochlea (figure 4.26). These waves set in motion the **basilar membrane,** which also runs the length of the cochlea. The movement of the basilar membrane causes bending of *hair cells* protruding from it. The bending triggers impulses that travel along the axons of the neurons that form the **auditory nerve.** Auditory impulses eventually reach the thalamus, which relays them to the **auditory cortex** of the temporal lobes of the brain. Sounds of particular frequencies stimulate particular cells of the auditory cortex, which the brain interprets as pitch (Romani, Williamson, & Kaufman, 1982).

Tympanic Membrane The eardrum; a membrane separating the outer and inner ears that vibrates in response to sound waves that strike it.

Cochlea The spiral, fluid-filled structure of the middle ear that contains the receptor cells for hearing.

Basilar Membrane A membrane running the length of the cochlea that contains the auditory receptor (hair) cells.

Auditory Nerve The nerve that conducts impulses from the cochlea to the brain.

Auditory Cortex The area of the temporal lobes that processes sounds.

The Pinna This girl is experiencing the amplification of sounds that large pinnas provide to animals such as deer.

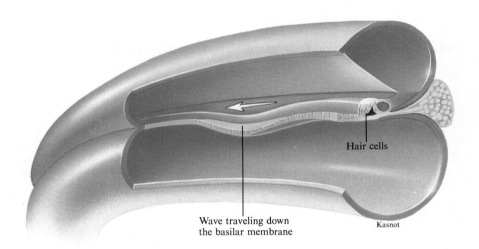

Hair cells

Wave traveling down
the basilar membrane

Kasnot

FIGURE 4.26
The Human Cochlea Waves traveling
through a fluid-filled chamber that run the
length of the cochlea set in motion the
basilar membrane. This causes bending of
hair cells that cover the basilar membrane.

Auditory Perception

How do vibrations conveyed to the basilar membrane create complex auditory experiences? Your ability to perceive voices, music, and sounds of all kinds depends on *pitch perception, loudness perception, timbre perception,* and *sound localization.*

Pitch Perception The frequency of a sound is the main determinant of its perceived *pitch,* which varies from the low pitch of a tuba to the high pitch of a flute. When you use the tone control on a radio, stereo, or television, you alter the frequency of the sound waves emanating from the speakers. This, in turn, alters the pitch of the sound. People with so-called perfect pitch can identify more than fifty musical notes, each representing a different sound frequency (Klein, Coles, & Donchin, 1984).

Animals vary in the range of frequencies they can hear. Human beings hear sounds ranging from 20 Hz to 20,000 Hz. Because elephants can hear sounds only up to 10,000 Hz, they cannot hear higher-pitched sounds that human beings can hear. Dogs, in turn, who can hear sounds up to about 45,000 Hz, can hear higher-pitched sounds than human beings can hear (Heffner, 1983). Dog whistles take advantage of this by producing sounds with frequencies above 20,000 Hz but below 45,000 Hz.

What accounts for **pitch perception?** In 1863 Hermann von Helmholtz put forth the **place theory,** which assumes that particular points on the basilar membrane vibrate maximally in response to sound waves of particular frequencies. Georg von Békésy, a Hungarian scientist, won the Nobel Prize in 1961 for his research supporting the place theory. Békésy took the cochlea from an ear of a human cadaver, stimulated its oval window, and noted the response of the basilar membrane through a hole cut in the cochlea. He found that as the frequency of the stimulus increased, the point of maximal vibration on the basilar membrane moved closer to the oval window. And as the frequency of the stimulus decreased, the point of maximal vibration moved farther from the oval window (von Békésy, 1957). The place theory is also supported by research findings on the high-frequency hearing loss that tends to accompany aging, which is associated with the destruction of hair cells near the oval window (McFadden & Wightman, 1983).

But the place theory cannot explain pitch perception much below about 1,000 Hz, because such low-frequency sound waves do not make the basilar membrane vibrate maximally at any particular point. Instead, the entire basilar membrane vibrates equally. Because of this limitation, perception of sounds below 1,000 Hz is explained best by a theory first put forth by the English physicist Ernest Rutherford in 1886. His **frequency theory** assumes that the basilar membrane vibrates as a whole in direct proportion to the frequency of the sound waves striking the eardrum. The neurons of the auditory nerve will, in turn, fire at the same frequency as the vibrations of the basilar membrane. But, because neurons can fire up to 1,000 times a second, the frequency theory holds only for sounds up to 1,000 Hz.

Still another theory, the **volley theory** (Wever & Bray, 1937), explains pitch perception between 1,000 Hz and 5,000 Hz. The volley theory assumes that sound waves in this range induce certain auditory neurons to fire in volleys, one after another. Though no single neuron can fire at more than 1,000 Hz, the brain may interpret the firing of volleys of particular auditory neurons as

Pitch Perception The subjective experience of the highness or lowness of a sound, which corresponds most closely to the frequency of the sound waves that compose it.

Place Theory The theory of pitch perception assuming that hair cells at particular points on the basilar membrane are maximally responsive to sound waves of particular frequencies.

Frequency Theory The theory of pitch perception assuming that the basilar membrane vibrates as a whole in direct proportion to the frequency of the sound waves striking the eardrum.

Volley Theory The theory of pitch perception assuming that sound waves of particular frequencies induce auditory neurons to fire in volleys, with one volley following another.

Georg von Békésy (1899–1972) "[The ear] is so sensitive that it can almost hear the random rain of air molecules bouncing against the eardrum. Yet in spite of its extraordinary sensitivity, the ear can withstand the pounding of sound waves strong enough to set the body vibrating."

representing sound waves of particular frequencies up to 5,000 Hz (Zwislocki, 1981). For example, the pitch of a sound wave with a frequency of 4,000 Hz might be coded by a particular group of five neurons each firing at 800 Hz. While there is some overlap among the theories, frequency theory best explains the perception of low-pitched sounds, place theory best explains the perception of high-pitched sounds, and volley theory best explains the perception of medium-pitched sounds.

Loudness Perception Sounds vary in *loudness,* as well as in pitch. The loudness of a sound depends mainly on the amplitude of its sound waves. When you use the volume control on a radio, stereo, or television you are regulating the amplitude of the sound waves emanating from the speakers. **Loudness perception** depends on both the number of hair cells on the basilar membrane that are stimulated and the firing thresholds of the hair cells that are stimulated. Hair cells with higher firing thresholds require more intense stimulation. As a consequence, the firing of hair cells with higher firing thresholds increases the perceived loudness of a sound.

The unit of sound intensity is the *decibel* (or *dB*). The faintest detectable sound has an absolute threshold of 0 dB. Table 4.1 presents the decibel levels of some everyday sounds. Exposure to high-decibel sounds promotes hearing loss. Chronic exposure to loud sounds first destroys hair cells nearest the oval window, which respond to high-frequency sounds.

Loud sounds are so prevalent in most American communities that even infants show some destruction of their hair cells (Schneider, Trehub, & Bull, 1980). The loss of hair cells continues through childhood and into adulthood as we continue to be exposed to loud music, vehicles, and machinery. For example, after years as lead singer for the rock group The Who, known for its loud music, Roger Daltrey suffered hearing loss for high-frequency sounds (Cohen, 1981). And, as mentioned earlier, elderly Americans, after a lifetime of exposure to loud sounds, tend to have poor high-frequency hearing. In contrast, the typical eighty-year-old in certain African tribes, whose surroundings rarely produce loud sounds, has better hearing than the typical thirty-year-old American (Raloff, 1982).

In extreme cases, exposure to loud sounds, as well as exposure to infections or injuries, may lead to deafness. In **conduction deafness** the ossicles lose their flexibility and no longer adequately convey sound waves to the tympanic membrane. Conduction deafness can be treated by surgery or by wearing a hearing aid that amplifies sounds. In **nerve deafness,** the hair cells of the basilar membrane are damaged. Nerve deafness does not respond well to surgery or hearing aids. But research on *cochlear implants,* which provide electronic stimulation of the basilar membrane, promises to restore at least rudimentary hearing in people with nerve deafness (figure 4.27).

Timbre Perception Sounds vary in timbre, as well as in pitch and loudness. **Timbre** is the quality of a sound, reflecting its particular mixture of sound waves, that permits us to identify the source of the sound, whether a voice, a musical instrument, or even—to the chagrin of students—a fingernail scratching across a blackboard. The timbre of that spine-chilling sound is similar to the warning cry of macaque monkeys. Perhaps our squeamish response to that sound when we hear it in class reflects an inborn vestigial response inherited from our distant animal ancestors who used it to signal the presence of predators (Halpern, Blake, & Hillerbrand, 1986).

Timbre also permits us to identify musical instruments and to evaluate their relative quality. Because musical notes of the same frequency will differ in timbre when played on different instruments, no two instruments produce exactly the same sounds. This lets you distinguish a violin from a guitar and

Loudness Perception The subjective experience of the intensity of a sound, which corresponds most closely to the amplitude of the sound waves composing it.

Conduction Deafness Hearing loss usually caused by deterioration of the ossicles of the middle ear.

Nerve Deafness Hearing loss caused by damage to the hair cells of the basilar membrane or the axons of the auditory nerve.

Timbre The subjective experience that identifies a particular sound and corresponds most closely to the mixture of sound waves composing it.

TABLE 4.1   Sound Levels (Decibels)

Harmful to hearing	140	Jet engine (25 m distance)
	130	Jet takeoff (100 m away) Threshold of pain
	120	Propeller aircraft
Risk hearing loss	110	Live rock band
	100	Jackhammer/pneumatic chipper
	90	Heavy-duty truck Los Angeles, third-floor apartment next to freeway Average street traffic
Very noisy	80	Harlem, second-floor apartment
Urban	70	Private car Boston row house on major avenue Business office Watts—8 mi. from touch down at major airport
	60	Conversational speech or old residential area in L.A.
Suburban and small town	50	San Diego—wooded residential area
	40	California tomato field Soft music from radio
	30	Quiet whisper
	20	Quiet urban dwelling
	10	Rustle of leaf
	0	Threshold of hearing

Because the decibel scale is a logarithmic measure of sound intensity, values don't add in the usual way: a 60 dB sound played atop another 60 dB sound corresponds to 63 dB noise. And a 10 dB difference means one sound is 10 times louder than the other, so that the ratio between 140 dB and 0 dB is roughly 100 trillion to 1. Readings for cities represent levels actually measured by EPA and expressed as a day-night average.

Reprinted with permission from SCIENCE NEWS, the weekly newsmagazine of science, copyright 1982 by Science Service, Inc.

a cheap violin from an expensive violin (Hutchins, 1981). Though both instruments might be playing the same note, they would also produce different mixtures of sound waves accompanying the note that has been played.

Sound Localization   Merely identifying sounds is not sufficient. We must also locate them. Human beings have an impressive ability to localize sounds, with the ability to locate a voice at a crowded party or an instru-

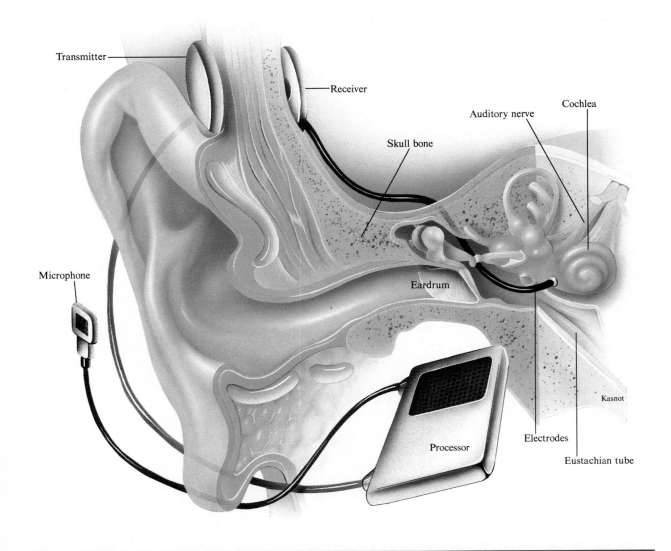

Transmitter

Receiver

Auditory nerve

Cochlea

Skull bone

Microphone

Eardrum

Kasnot

Processor

Electrodes

Eustachian tube

FIGURE 4.27

The Bionic Ear Cochlear implants are based on the place theory of hearing. Electrodes are attached to different points along the basilar membrane. A microphone worn behind the ear picks up sounds and transmits them to a microprocessor. The microprocessor then analyzes the sounds into their component frequencies and sends impulses through the electrodes to stimulate the places on the basilar membrane that respond to those frequencies (Loeb, 1985).

Sound Localization The process by which the individual determines the location of a sound.

ment in a large orchestra. But some animals have even more impressive **sound localization** abilities. A barn owl can capture a mouse in the dark merely by following the faint sounds produced by its movements (Knudsen, 1981).

We are aided in localizing sounds by having two ears. Even though sounds travel at 750 miles an hour, sounds that come from points other than those equidistant between our two ears reach one ear slightly before the other. Such sounds are also slightly more intense at the nearer ear, because the head blocks some of the sound waves as they move from one side of the head to the other. The auditory cortex has cells that respond to these differences in intensity and arrival time, permitting the brain to determine the location of a sound (Phillips & Brugge, 1985).

Stereophonic sound takes advantage of our ability to localize sounds. Consider a stereo with its two speakers. Different voices or musical instruments are played through each speaker. If the speakers are separated from each other, the sound gives the impression that musicians are singing or playing at separate locations in front of you—as they would on stage at a concert.

CHEMICAL SENSES

In front of the Monell Chemical Senses Center in Philadelphia stands a six-foot-tall gold-plated statue of a face with a nose and a mouth but with no eyes or ears. This statue symbolizes the senses that are studied by Monell scientists—the *chemical senses* of smell and taste.

Olfaction The sense of smell, which detects molecules carried in the air.

Smell

Helen Keller identified her friends by their smell and could even tell whether a person had recently been in a kitchen, garden, or hospital room by his or her smell (Ecenbarger, 1987). Though most of us do not rely on the sense of smell to that extent, the sense of smell (or **olfaction**) is important to all of us. It warns us of dangers, such as fire, deadly gases, or spoiled food, and enables us to enjoy the pleasant odors of food, nature, and other people.

Odors are so important to Americans that they spend millions of dollars on perfumes, colognes, and deodorants to make themselves more socially attractive. There may even be a "sweet smell of success," at least as perceived by women. This was demonstrated in a study in which female job interviewers gave higher ratings to male and female job applicants who wore fragrances. In contrast, male interviewers gave *lower* ratings to applicants who wore fragrances (Baron, 1983).

Smell and Marketing
Manufacturers of household products realize that our purchasing decisions are often influenced by our sense of smell.

What accounts for our ability to smell fragrances? Molecules carried in inhaled air stimulate smell receptor cells on the nasal membrane high up in the nasal passages (figure 4.28). Neural impulses from the receptor cells travel along the short *olfactory nerves* to the brain. Smell is the only sense that is not first processed in the thalamus before being processed in other brain centers. The *limbic system,* an important emotional center of the brain that was discussed in chapter 3, receives many neural connections from the olfactory nerves. This may account for the powerful emotional effects of certain odors. As Rudyard Kipling noted, "Smells are surer than sounds or sights to make your heart-strings crack" (Gibbons, 1986, p. 324).

Though researchers have not yet reached agreement on a set of basic odors, the most common system of categorizing odors recognizes seven: *ethereal* (dry-cleaning fluid), *camphoraceous* (mothballs), *musky* (musk cologne), *floral* (roses), *pepperminty* (peppermint candy), *pungent* (vinegar), and *putrid* (rotten eggs). According to this system, all other odors are mixtures of these basic odors. Smell receptors responsive to particular odors are sensitive to molecules of specific sizes, shapes, or electrical charges (Amoore, 1963). But this system has failed to receive consistent research support (Schiffman, 1974).

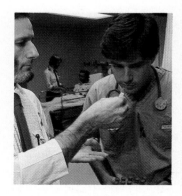

Smell and Medical Diagnosis
Dr. Lewis Goldfrank, chief of emergency medicine at New York City's Bellevue Hospital, trains his staff to recognize quickly the odors of poisons and diseases—odors that may be given off by incoming patients.

Our sense of smell has a remarkably low absolute threshold—we can detect tiny amounts of chemicals diffused in the air. For example, a recent smell survey by *National Geographic* magazine used less than an ounce of a particular chemical to include a sample of its odor with 11 million copies of the survey (Gibbons, 1986). Our exquisite ability to identify familiar odors was demonstrated in a study of male and female college students who washed them-

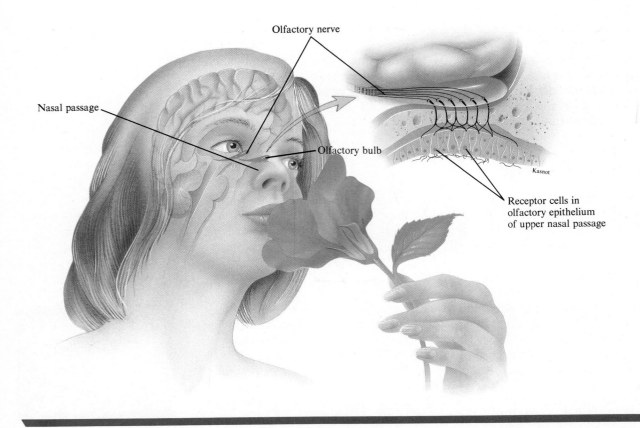

FIGURE 4.28
The Olfactory Pathways Molecules from the flower are inhaled and reach receptor cells high up in the nasal passages. This stimulates the olfactory nerves, which send impulses to brain regions that process the sense of smell.

selves with only water and used no soap, deodorant, or perfume for twenty-four hours. They were then given a T-shirt to wear as an undergarment for twenty-four hours. Afterwards thirteen out of sixteen males and nine out of thirteen females were able to identify their own shirts by sniffing the shirts through an opening in a box (Russell, 1976).

Though smell is important to human beings, it is of greater importance to lower animals. For example, the amazing ability of salmon to return to their home streams to spawn depends on their following the familiar odors of the soil and plants on the banks of the rivers that mark the correct route home (Gibbons, 1986). Researchers have been especially interested in the effects of secretions called **pheromones** on the sexual behavior of animals. This has led some fragrance manufacturers to add animal sex pheromones to perfumes and colognes. But before you run out to purchase a pheromone fragrance, you should note that research findings on the effects of sex pheromones on human beings have been inconsistent. In one study males and females exposed to pig sex pheromones rated photographs of females as more beautiful (Maugh, 1982). But a similar study using photographs of males failed to find such an effect (Filsinger, Braun, Monte, & Linder, 1984).

Pheromones Odorous chemicals secreted by animals that affect the behavior of other animals.

Taste

Gustation The sense of taste, which detects molecules dissolved in the saliva.

Our other chemical sense, the sense of taste (or **gustation**), protects us from harm and enhances our enjoyment of life by preventing us from ingesting poisons and by enabling us to savor food and beverages. Taste depends on thousands of **taste buds,** which line the grooves between bumps on the surface of the tongue called *papillae.* The taste buds contain receptor cells that send neural impulses when stimulated by molecules dissolved in saliva. Taste buds die and are replaced every few days, so the taste buds that are destroyed when you burn your tongue with hot food or drink are quickly replaced. But because replacement of taste buds slows with age, elderly people may find food less flavorful than they did earlier in life (Cowart, 1981).

There is more agreement among researchers about the basic tastes than about the basic odors. The basic tastes are *sweet, salty, sour,* and *bitter.* Figure 4.29 shows that different areas of the tongue are maximally sensitive to each of the basic tastes. The front of the tongue is most sensitive to sweet and salty, the sides most sensitive to salty and sour, and the back most sensitive to bitter. All other tastes are combinations of these basic tastes and appear to depend on the pattern of stimulation of the taste receptors (Rogers, 1985).

As in the case of smell, gustation appears to depend on the shape of molecules stimulating taste receptors. Taste researchers use this knowledge when they develop artificial sweeteners. Taste receptors in different areas of the

Taste Buds Structures lining the grooves of the tongue that contain the taste receptor cells.

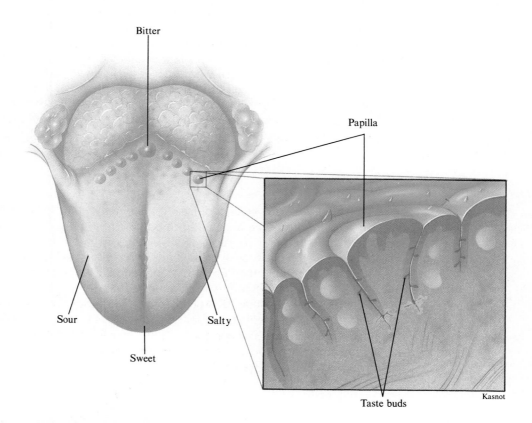

FIGURE 4.29
The Basic Tastes All areas of the tongue are sensitive to each of the four basic tastes, but certain areas are more sensitive to particular tastes. The tip of the tongue is most sensitive to sweet tastes and salty tastes, the sides of the tongue are most sensitive to salty and sour tastes, and the back of the tongue is most sensitive to bitter tastes.

Stereochemical Theory The theory of taste assuming that taste receptors in different areas of the tongue are maximally responsive to molecules of different shapes.

[handwritten margin notes: diff? flavor — smell + taste, taste — 4 tastes]

tongue are maximally sensitive to molecules of particular shapes. This **stereochemical theory** of taste was anticipated by the Epicurean poet Lucretius in the first century B.C.

> Simple tis to see that whatsoever
> Can touch the senses pleasingly are made
> Of smooth and rounded elements, whilst those
> Which seem the bitter and the sharp, are held
> Entwined by elements more crook'd, and so
> Are wont to tear their way into our senses
> And rend our body as they enter in.
> (Ziporyn, 1982, p. 277)

Do not confuse taste with *flavor,* which is more complex. While taste depends on sensations from the mouth, flavor relies on taste *and* smell. If you closed your eyes and held your nose, you would be unable to detect a difference between a piece of apple and a piece of potato. Because smell is especially important in flavor, you may find that your food lacks flavor when you have a head cold interfering with your ability to smell.

Even a food's texture and temperature affect its flavor. Consider the flavor of pizza. People prefer the taste and smell of particular combinations of sauce, cheese, and spices on their pizza. But people also vary in their texture preferences, with some preferring a soft crust and others a crisp crust. Moreover, some people insist on eating their pizza as soon as it comes hot out of the oven, while others enjoy leftover pizza eaten cold right out of the refrigerator.

Animals, as well as people, have flavor preferences. Scientists have taken advantage of this by developing an artificial grape flavor that is appealing to pigs and cattle but revolting to birds. By spreading the flavor on feed grain, farmers are able to save their grain for livestock instead of seeing it stolen by birds (Detjen, 1986).

SKIN SENSES

Skin Senses The senses of touch, temperature, and pain.

We rely on our **skin senses** of touch, temperature, and pain to identify objects, communicate feelings, and protect us from injury. Though there are a variety of receptors that produce skin sensations, there is no simple one-to-one relationship between specific kinds of receptors and specific skin senses. For example, though the cornea has only one kind of receptor, it is sensitive to touch, temperature, and pain. It appears that the pattern of stimulation of receptors, not the specific kind of receptor, determines skin sensations. Neural impulses from the skin receptors reach the thalamus, which relays them to the **somatosensory cortex** of the brain. As you may recall from chapter 3, the somatosensory cortex is a strip of cortex on the parietal lobe that processes sensory information from the body.

Somatosensory Cortex The area of the parietal lobes that processes information from sensory receptors in the skin.

Touch

Your sense of *touch* enables you to identify objects rapidly and accurately even when you cannot see them, such as removing a dime from among the pennies, nickels, and quarters in your pocket. Touch sensitivity depends on the concentration of receptors, with the most sensitive areas of the skin including the lips, face, tongue, hands, and genitals. The sense of touch is so precise that it can be used as a substitute for vision. In 1824 a blind Frenchman named Louis Braille developed the *Braille* system of reading and writing, which uses patterns of raised dots to represent letters. More recently, the Braille concept has been extended to provide a substitute for vision. One approach to this is called *tactile sensory replacement* (figure 4.30). The blind person wears a camera on his or her eye glasses and a special electronic vest covered with a grid of tiny Teflon cones. Outlines of images provided by the camera are impressed onto the skin by vibrations of the cones. People who have used the device have been able to identify familiar objects (Hechinger, 1981).

Temperature

In 1927 psychologist Karl Dallenbach "mapped" the temperature receptors of the skin. He drew a grid on the skin and successively touched each square in the grid with a warm probe and then a cold probe. He found that each spot was sensitive to warm or cold, but not both, leading him to conclude that the skin has separate receptors for warm and for cold. But what of receptors for sensing *hot* objects? Subsequent research has failed to find any. Instead, hot objects stimulate both the cold receptors and the warm receptors. Figure 4.31 shows how cold and warm sensations can combine to induce hot sensations.

Since Dallenbach's early study, research has shown that temperature receptors detect *changes* in temperature. While cold receptors detect decreases in skin temperature, warm receptors detect increases (Darian-Smith, 1982). Unless the skin is extremely hot or cold, which would induce pain sensations, the temperature receptors adapt, as when you enter a bathtub filled with hot water. At first you would feel uncomfortably hot, but your skin would quickly adapt to it and you would eventually stop noticing it.

In the late seventeenth century, John Locke gave a clever demonstration of how temperature sensations depend on detecting changes in skin temperature. To repeat Locke's demonstration, take three bowls and fill one with cold water, one with hot water, and one with lukewarm water. Place one hand in the cold water and the other in the hot water. Keep them submerged for a few minutes to allow temperature adaptation to occur. Then place both hands in the lukewarm water. The water will feel hot to the hand that had been in cold water and cold to the hand that had been in hot water. Thus, the temperature receptors would be responding to the change in temperature, not to the actual temperature of the bowl of lukewarm water.

Pain

The sense of *pain* protects us from injury or even death. People born without a sense of pain, or who lose the sense of pain through nerve injuries, may cut or burn themselves without realizing it. Because intense pain or even mild chronic pain can be one of the most distressing of all experiences, many researchers are studying the factors that cause pain and possible ways of relieving pain.

Pain Factors An injury or intense stimulation of sensory receptors induces pain. So, bright lights, loud noises, hot spices, and excessive pressure, as well as cuts, burns, and bruises, are painful. Many pain receptor neurons transmit pain impulses by releasing the neurotransmitter *substance P* from their axons. In fact, the pain of arthritis varies with the amount of substance P released by neurons from the joints (Levine et al., 1984).

The most influential theory of pain is the **gate-control theory** formulated by the psychologist Ronald Melzack and the biologist Patrick Wall (1965). The theory assumes that pain impulses pass through a part of the spinal cord called the *substantia gelatinosa,* which provides a "gate" for pain impulses (figure 4.32). Stimulation of neurons that convey touch sensations closes the gate to input from neurons that convey pain sensations. This may explain why

FIGURE 4.30
Tactile Sensory Replacement
This man is "seeing" with his skin. Images provided by the camera he is wearing on his glasses are impressed onto his skin by tiny vibrating Teflon cones. People who have used this device have been able to identify objects with distinctive shapes (Hechinger, 1981).

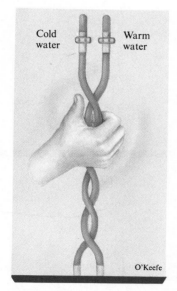

FIGURE 4.31
Paradoxical Hot If cold water circulates through one coil and warm water through the other, a person grasping the coils will feel a hot sensation and quickly let go. This demonstrates that hot sensations are produced by the combined stimulation of receptors responsive to cold and receptors responsive to warmth.

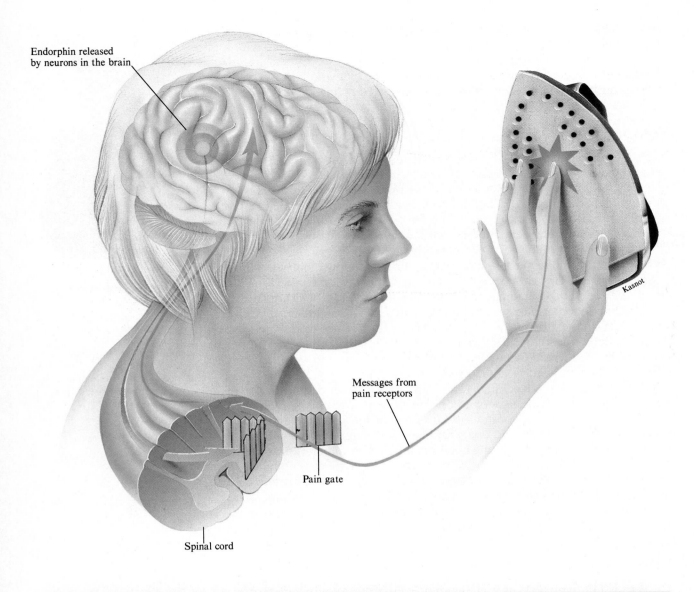

Endorphin released
by neurons in the brain

Kasnot

Messages from
pain receptors

Pain gate

Spinal cord

FIGURE 4.32
The Gate-Control Theory of Pain
Endorphins released by neurons in the
brain may stimulate other neurons to send
send signals that close the "pain gate" in
the spinal cord.

Gate-Control Theory The
theory that pain impulses can be
blocked by the closing of a
neuronal gate in the spinal cord.

rubbing a shin that you have banged against a table will relieve the pain. The
closing of the pain gate is stimulated by the secretion of *endorphins,* which,
as described in chapter 3, are the body's own natural opiates. Endorphins may
reduce the transmission of pain impulses by inhibiting activity in the paingate
of the spinal cord (Ruda, 1982).

Neural impulses descending from the brain can also open or close the gate,
explaining why anxiety, relaxation, and other psychological factors can influence pain perception. This may explain the so-called Anzio effect, in which
wounded soldiers returning from the fierce World War II battle of Anzio in
Italy needed less morphine than did civilians with similar wounds. Because
the soldiers interpreted their wounds as tickets away from the battlefield, they
experienced their pain as less intense (Wallis, 1984). Perhaps this occurred

because their brains sent neural impulses to the substantia gelatinosa, closing the pain gate.

Pain Relief Chronic pain affects millions of Americans. Back pain alone afflicts about 80 percent of Americans at some time in their lives (Dolce & Raczynski, 1985). The pain of injuries, cancer, headaches, and backaches makes pain control an important topic of research in both medicine and psychology. The most popular approach to relieving severe pain relies on drugs such as morphine, which affects sites in the brain. Even **placebo** "sugar pills," supposedly inactive substances that are substituted for pain-relieving drugs, can relieve pain. Placebos work by stimulating the release of endorphins.

Other techniques that do not rely on drugs or placebos also relieve pain by stimulating the release of endorphins. For example, the technique of **acupuncture,** popular in China for more than two thousand years, relies on the insertion of fine needles into various sites on the body, often distant from the site of the pain. A similar, modern approach to pain relief relies on **transcutaneous nerve stimulation** (**TENS**), involving electrical stimulation of sites on the body. As in the case of placebos, acupuncture and TENS relieve pain by stimulating the release of endorphins. Still another approach, *hypnosis,* relieves pain but not by stimulating the release of endorphins. We know this because the pain-relieving effects of hypnosis are not inhibited by injections of the drug *naloxone,* which blocks the effects of endorphins (Watkins & Mayer, 1982).

Even distracting thoughts or distracting stimuli provide pain relief. You may find it helpful to distract yourself from pain by imagining pleasant scenes, listening to music, or watching television. But distraction works best for mild, rather than intense, pain. A combination of techniques is often most effective. For example, in prepared-childbirth classes pregnant women learn to control their pain by relaxing their muscles, breathing deeply, and distracting themselves by imagining pleasant scenes (McCaul & Malott, 1984).

Placebo An inactive substance that may induce some of the effects of the drug for which it has been substituted.

Acupuncture The technique that involves the insertion of fine needles into various sites on the body to provide pain relief, apparently by stimulating the release of endorphins.

Transcutaneous Nerve Stimulation (TENS) The use of electrical stimulation of sites on the body to provide pain relief, apparently by stimulating the release of endorphins.

BODY SENSES

While your skin senses help you judge the state of your skin, your *body senses* make you aware of the position of your limbs and enable you to maintain your equilibrium. The body senses, the *kinesthetic sense* and the *vestibular sense,* are often taken for granted and have inspired less research than the other senses. But they are crucial for functioning in everyday life.

The Kinesthetic Sense

Your **kinesthetic sense** informs you of the position of your joints, the tension in your muscles, and the movement of your arms and legs. This information is provided by special receptors in your joints, muscles, and tendons. To demonstrate the role of kinesthetic receptors in informing you of the position of your body parts, close your eyes and move your arms about freely. Even with your eyes closed you will be able to sense the location of your arms.

If your leg has ever "fallen asleep" (depriving you of kinesthetic sensations) and collapsed on you when you stood up, you know that the kinesthetic sense helps you maintain enough tension in your legs to stand erect. Your kinesthetic sense also protects you from injury. If you are holding an object that is too heavy, kinesthetic receptors signal you to put down the object to prevent injury to your muscles and tendons.

Kinesthetic Sense The sense that provides information about the position of the joints, the degree of tension in the muscles, and the movement of the arms and legs.

The Vestibular Sense

Vestibular Sense The sense that
provides information about one's
position in space and helps in the
maintenance of balance.

Semicircular Canals The curved
vestibular organs of the inner ear
that detect movements of the
head in any direction.

While the kinesthetic sense informs you of the state of your body parts, your **vestibular sense** informs you of your position in space, helping you maintain your balance and orientation. The chief vestibular organs are the **semicircular canals** of the inner ear, which are three fluid-filled tubes oriented in different planes (figure 4.33). This permits the semicircular canals to detect the movement of your head in any direction.

When your head moves in a given direction, the fluid in the tube oriented in that direction lags behind movement of the walls of the canal. This makes hair cells protruding into the fluid bend in the direction opposite to the direction of head movement (Hudspeth, 1983). The bending of hair cells triggers neural impulses that are relayed to your *cerebellum,* which helps you maintain your equilibrium. The neural pathways to your cerebellum allow you to maintain your balance as you move through space.

Your vestibular sense not only helps you maintain your equilibrium, it may also induce motion sickness, including carsickness, airsickness, and seasickness. In fact, the word *nauseous* comes from the Greek word for "seasick." The sixth-century B.C. philosopher Anacharsis suffered from such severe seasickness that he divided human beings into three categories—the living, the dead, and the seasick. Seasickness has plagued such eminent persons as Julius Caesar, Charles Darwin, and Admiral Horatio Nelson. Lawrence of Arabia even

FIGURE 4.33
The Semicircular Canals When your head moves, fluid movement in the semicircular canals stimulates hair cells that send neural impulses to the brain.

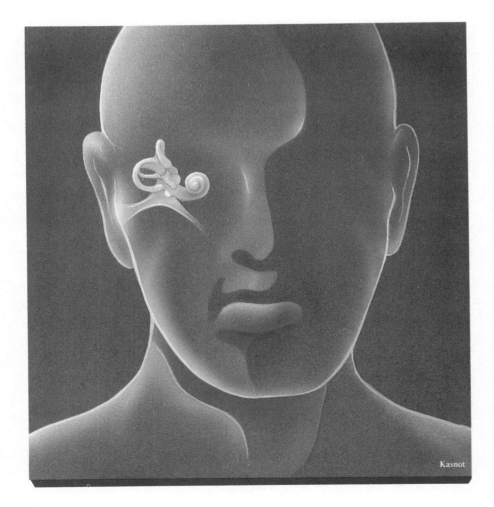

Kasnot

experienced bouts of motion sickness in the middle of the desert—when riding a camel (Swain, 1984).

Though the mechanisms underlying motion sickness are still debated, an influential view holds that motion sickness is induced by conflict between visual and vestibular sensations. Suppose you are in a cabin aboard a ship in a rough sea. Your eyes tell you that you are not moving in relationship to one aspect of your environment—your cabin. But your vestibular sense tells you that you *are* moving in relationship to another aspect of your environment—the ocean (Parker, 1980). But why would conflict between visual and vestibular sensations induce nausea? One hypothesis is that the motion-induced disruption of the normal association between visual and vestibular sensations is similar to that produced by toxins, such as those in spoiled food, that induce nausea (Treisman, 1977).

The Body Senses The kinesthetic sense and the vestibular sense provide gymnasts, as well as dancers, athletes, and other performers, with exquisite control over their body movements.

THINKING ABOUT PSYCHOLOGY

Why Do Psychologists Discount ESP?

As you have just read, perception depends on the stimulation of sensory receptors by various kinds of energy. But you have certainly heard claims supporting the possibility of perception independent of sensory receptors, so-called **extrasensory perception** (or **ESP**). The field that studies ESP is called **parapsychology** (with *para* meaning "besides"), indicating its failure to achieve widespread acceptance among psychologists.

Despite this, a Gallup poll found that most teenagers, ranging from junior high school students to college freshmen, believe in the existence of ESP (Frazier, 1984). Even older adults believe in its existence, as shown in a 1986 lawsuit in which a woman who made a living as a psychic contended that a CAT scan at Temple University Hospital made her lose her ESP abilities. A jury, impressed by the testimony of police officials who claimed that she had helped them solve crimes by using ESP, awarded her $988,000 for the loss of her livelihood (Tulsky, 1986). Given such public support for ESP, why do most psychologists discount it? Before answering this question, first consider several of the *paranormal* abilities studied by parapsychologists.

Alleged Paranormal Abilities

Almost two decades ago, members of the rock group The Grateful Dead had their audiences at a series of six concerts in Port Chester, New York, try to transmit mental images of slides to a person sleeping in a dream laboratory miles away at Maimonides Hospital in Brooklyn. When the sleeper awoke he described the content of his dreams. Independent judges rated his dream reports as being more similar to the content of the slides shown at the concerts than were the dream reports of another person who had not been designated as a receiver of the images (Ullman, Krippner, & Vaughan, 1973). This was reported as a successful demonstration of **mental telepathy,** the ability to perceive the thoughts of others without any sensory contact with them.

Extrasensory Perception (ESP) *The ability to perceive events without the use of sensory receptors.*

Parapsychology *The study of extrasensory perception, psychokinesis, and related phenomena.*

Mental Telepathy *The ability to perceive the thoughts of others without any sensory contact with them.*

Reprinted by permission of NEA, Inc.

FRANK AND ERNEST ©by Bob Thaves

Clairvoyance The ability to perceive objects or events without any sensory contact with them.

Closely related to mental telepathy is **clairvoyance,** the ability to perceive objects or events without any sensory contact with them. You might be considered clairvoyant if you could identify all of the objects in your psychology professor's drawer without looking in it. In a typical demonstration of clairvoyance, a clairvoyant might "read" the serial number of a dollar bill in a subject's wallet. While mental telepathy and clairvoyance deal with the present, **precognition** is the ability to perceive events in the future. Psychics, such as Jean Dixon, make careers of writing tabloid newspaper columns in which they predict events of national interest.

Precognition The ability to perceive events in the future.

Psychokinesis (PK) The ability to control objects with the mind alone.

Closely allied with these ESP abilities is **psychokinesis** (or **PK**), the ability to control objects with the mind alone. Our use of "body English" to influence the movements of dice, roulette wheels, baseballs, golf balls, or bowling balls reflects a superstitious belief in PK. Perhaps you have seen a television performance by Uri Geller, who gives demonstrations in which he bends spoons, fixes watches, or takes photographs by apparently using mental power alone.

REPRINTED COURTESY OMNI MAGAZINE © 1989.

"Never mind that—can you bend the spoon?"

Problems with Paranormal Research

Parapsychology has had many prominent supporters. Mark Twain and William James were early members of the Society for Psychical Research, with James even serving as its president. But credit for making parapsychology a legitimate area of scientific research to some scientists goes to J. B. Rhine (1895–1980) of Duke University, who started a program of experimental research on paranormal phenomena in the 1930s (Mauskopf & McVaugh, 1981). Several leading British universities have also lent credibility to parapsychology by sponsoring paranormal research. Edinburgh University in Scotland even set up the first chair in parapsychology with a $750,000 grant from the estate of the author Arthur Koestler (Dickson, 1984).

Despite the popular acceptance of parapsychology, most psychologists remain skeptical. One reason is that many supposed instances of paranormal phenomena turn out to be the result of poorly controlled demonstrations. In a case reported by the magician James "The Amazing" Randi, a Quebec woman claimed that she could influence fish by PK. Every time she put her fingers on one side of an aquarium, the fish would swim to the opposite side. Randi responded, "She calls it psychic, I call it frightened fish." He suggested that she put paper over a side of the aquarium and then test her ability again. After trying Randi's suggestions and noting that the fish no longer swam to the opposite side, she exclaimed, "It's marvelous! The power doesn't penetrate brown paper!" (Morris, 1980, p. 106).

Supporters of parapsychology may also too readily accept chance events as evidence of paranormal phenomena (Diaconis, 1978). For example, at some time you have probably decided to call a friend, picked up the phone, and found your friend already on the other end of the line. Does this mean that mental telepathy made you call each other at the same time? Not necessarily. Perhaps you and your friend call each other often and at the same time of day, so from time to time you might call each other at exactly the same moment by mere coincidence.

Another blow against the credibility of parapsychology is that some impressive demonstrations have later been found to involve fraud. In a widely publicized case of fraud, the noted psychic Tamara Rand claimed to have predicted the 1981 assassination attempt on President Reagan in a videotape made before the attempt and shown on the *Today* show after it. This was considered evidence of precognition—until James Randi discovered that she had made the videotape *after* the assassination attempt ("A psychic Watergate," 1981).

Of great concern is the passing off of magic tricks as instances of paranormal phenomena. Randi sponsored an elaborate hoax that demonstrated the inability of parapsychology researchers to detect such tricks. In 1979 James McDonnell, the chairman of the board of the McDonnell-Douglas corporation, gave $500,000 to Washington University in St. Louis to establish a parapsychology research laboratory. A respected physics professor was put in charge of the project. Randi sent two magicians, aged seventeen and eighteen, to the university. After demonstrating their PK "abilities" during 120 hours of testing over a three-year period, the two were proclaimed the only subjects to have true PK ability.

Despite this proclamation, both had relied soley on magic—in some cases, beginner's level magic. For example, they demonstrated PK by moving a clock across a table by using an ultrathin thread held between their thumbs. Because of demonstrations such as these, Randi has urged parapsychologists to permit magicians to observe their research so that magic tricks are not mistaken for paranormal phenomena ("Psychic Abscam," 1983). Since 1965 Randi has had an ongoing offer of $10,000 to anyone who can demonstrate a true paranormal ability under controlled conditions. Though many persons have tried, none has yet earned the money.

James "The Amazing" Randi and His Two Protégés

Parapsychologists defend their research by insisting that critics often discount positive findings by *assuming* that they are impossible and, therefore, must be due to some other factor, such as poor controls, magic tricks, or outright fraud (Child, 1985). But even parapsychologists agree that, from the standpoint of science, the greatest weakness of parapsychology research findings is that they are rarely replicable. As you may recall from chapter 2, scientists discount events that cannot be replicated under similar conditions.

A final criticism of paranormal phenomena is that there is no satisfactory explanation for them. For example, efforts to detect any unusual form of energy radiating from people who claim to have paranormal abilities have failed (Balanovski & Taylor, 1978). But supporters of parapsychology believe that scientists should not reject it just because paranormal phenomena violate accepted scientific paradigms (Rockwell, 1979). They remind scientists to be skeptical rather than cynical, because many phenomena that are now scientifically acceptable were once considered impossible and unworthy of study.

For example, prior to the nineteenth century, reports of rocks falling from the sky were discounted by scientists, who did not even bother to investigate them. In 1807, after hearing of a report by two Yale University professors of a rock shower in Connecticut, President Thomas Jefferson, a scientist himself, said, "Gentlemen, I would rather believe that those two Yankee professors would lie than to believe that stones fell from heaven" (Diaconis, 1978). Today, even young children know that such stones are meteorites that have, indeed, fallen from the sky. Nonetheless, because alleged paranormal abilities are so unusual and inexplicable, even noncynical psychologists will continue to discount them unless they are provided with much more compelling evidence than has been provided so far (Hoppe, 1988).

SUMMARY

SENSORY PROCESSES

Sensation is the process that detects stimuli from our bodies or surroundings. Perception is the process that organizes sensations into meaningful patterns. Psychophysics is the study of the relationship between the physical characteristics of stimuli and the conscious psychological experiences they produce. The minimum amount of stimulation that can be detected is called the absolute threshold. According to signal detection theory, the detection of a stimulus depends on both the intensity of the stimulus and the psychological state of the observer. The minimum amount of change in stimulation that can be detected is called the difference threshold. The Weber-Fechner law states that the amount of change in stimulation needed to produce a just noticeable difference is a constant proportion of the original stimulus. The tendency of our sensory receptors to respond less and less to a constant stimulus is called sensory adaptation.

VISION

Vision lets us sense objects by the light reflected from them into our eyes. Light is focused by the lens onto the rods and cones of the retina. Visual input is transmitted by the optic nerves to the brain, ultimately reaching the visual cortex. During dark adaptation the rods and cones become more sensitive to light, with the rods becoming significantly more sensitive than the cones. The trichromatic theory of color vision considers the interaction of red, green, and blue cones. In contrast, the opponent-process theory assumes that color vision depends on activity in red-green, blue-yellow, and black-white cells in the thalamus. Color blindness is usually caused by an inherited lack of a cone pigment. The most common kind of color blindness is red-green.

Form perception depends on distinguishing figure from ground. In studying form perception Gestalt psychologists identified the principles of proximity, similarity, closure, and continuity. While Gestalt psychologists claim that we perceive objects as wholes, other theorists claim that we construct objects from their component parts. This is supported by research showing that the visual cortex has feature-detector cells that respond to specific features of objects.

Depth perception permits us to determine the distance of objects from us. Binocular cues to depth require the interaction of both eyes. The two main binocular cues are convergence of the eyes and retinal disparity. Monocular cues to depth require only one eye. The monocular cues include accommodation, motion parallax, and various pictorial cues (overlap, relative size, linear perspective, distance from the horizon, shading patterns, texture gradient, and aerial perspective).

The traditional view of motion perception attributes it to the progressive movement of images across the retina. James Gibson's alternative view claims that motion perception is produced by changes in the flow of patterns of light on the retinas. Max Wertheimer demonstrated the phi phenomenon, which is apparent motion caused by the rapid presentation of one stimulus after another.

Experience in viewing objects contributes to size constancy, shape constancy, and brightness constancy. The misapplication of depth perception cues and perceptual constancies may contribute to visual illusions. Sensory experience and cultural background both affect visual perception.

HEARING

The sense of hearing, audition, detects sound waves produced by the vibration of objects. Sound waves cause the tympanic membrane to vibrate. The ossicles of the middle ear convey the vibrations to the oval window of the cochlea, which causes waves to travel through fluid within the cochlea. The waves make hair cells on the basilar membrane bend, sending neural impulses along the auditory nerve. Sounds are ultimately processed by the auditory cortex of the temporal lobes.

The frequency of a sound determines its pitch. Pitch perception is explained by the place theory, frequency theory, and volley theory. The intensity of a sound determines its loudness. People may suffer from conduction deafness or nerve deafness. The mixture of sound waves determines a sound's quality, or timbre. Sound localization depends on differences in a sound's arrival time and intensity at the two ears.

CHEMICAL SENSES

The chemical senses of smell and taste detect chemicals in the air we breathe or the substances we ingest. The sense of smell, olfaction, depends on receptor cells on the nasal membrane that respond to particular chemicals. Odorous secretions called pheromones affect the sexual behavior of animals. The sense of taste, gustation, depends on receptor cells on the taste buds of the tongue that respond to particular chemicals. The basic tastes are sweet, salty, sour, and bitter. The stereochemical theory of taste assumes that molecules of particular shapes affect particular taste receptors.

SKIN SENSES

Skin senses depend on receptors that send neural impulses to the somatosensory cortex. Touch sensitivity depends on the concentration of receptors in the skin. While we have separate receptors for cold and warm temperatures, we depend on the simultaneous stimulation of cold and warm receptors to produce hot sensations. Pain depends on both physical and psychological factors. According to the gate-control theory of pain, stimulation of touch neurons closes a spinal "gate," which inhibits neural impulses underlying pain from traveling up the spinal cord. Pain-relieving techniques such as placebos, acupuncture, and transcutaneous nerve stimulation, but not hypnosis, relieve pain by stimulating the release of endorphins.

BODY SENSES

Your body senses make you aware of the position of your limbs and enable you to maintain your equilibrium. The kinesthetic sense informs you of the position of your joints, the tension in your muscles, and the movement of your arms and legs. The vestibular sense informs you of your position in space, helping you maintain your balance and orientation. The chief vestibular organs are the semicircular canals.

THINKING ABOUT PSYCHOLOGY: WHY DO PSYCHOLOGISTS DISCOUNT ESP?

While most of the lay public accepts the existence of paranormal phenomena such as extrasensory perception and psychokinesis, most psychologists do not. Psychologists are skeptical because research in parapsychology has been marked by sloppy procedures, acceptance of coincidences as positive evidence, fraudulent reports, use of magic tricks, failure to replicate studies, and inability to explain paranormal phenomena.

IMPORTANT CONCEPTS

IMPORTANT PEOPLE

Russell DeValois 111
Gustav Fechner 98
James J. Gibson 112
Ewald Hering 109
David Hubel and Torsten Wiesel 113

Ronald Melzack and Patrick Wall 133
James Randi 139
J. B. Rhine 139
Georg von Békésy 125
Hermann von Helmholtz 109, 126

George Wald 109
Ernst Weber 98
Max Wertheimer 117
Thomas Young 109

RECOMMENDED READINGS

For More on All Aspects of Sensation and Perception:

Keller, H. (1970). *Story of my life.* New York: Airmont.
Helen Keller's autobiography, describing how she achieved success and lived a rewarding life despite being blind and deaf.

Matlin, M. W. (1988). *Sensation and perception.* Boston: Allyn & Bacon.
A readable introduction to sensation and perception, expanding on topics covered in this chapter.

For More on Vision:

Coren, S., & Girgus, J. S. (1978). *Seeing is deceiving: The psychology of visual illusions.* Hillsdale, NJ: Erlbaum.
An intriguing presentation of visual illusions and possible explanations for them.

Fineman, M. (1981). *The inquisitive eye.* New York: Oxford University Press.
An interesting discussion of all aspects of vision.

Gibson, J. J. (1979). *The ecological approach to visual perception.* Boston: Houghton Mifflin.
A presentation of Gibson's direct perception theory.

Wolfe, J. M. (Ed.) (1986). *The mind's eye: Readings from Scientific American.* New York: W.H. Freeman.
A collection of articles on vision from *Scientific American.*

For More on Hearing:

Warren, R. M. (1982). *Auditory perception: A new synthesis.* Elmsford, NJ: Pergamon.
A comprehensive textbook on auditory processes.

For More on Chemical Senses:

Dethier, V. G. (1978). Other tastes, other worlds. *Science, 201,* 224–228.
A brief account of historical views of the sense of taste.

Gibbons, B. (1986). The intimate sense of smell. *National Geographic, 170,* 324–361.
A fascinating article about research on the sense of smell and the importance of smell in everyday life.

For More on Skin Senses:

Elton, D., Stanley, G., & Burrows, G. (1983). *Psychological control of pain.* Orlando, FL: Grune & Stratton.
A discussion of the nature of pain and ways of relieving it.

Darian-Smith, I. (1982). Touch in primates. *Annual Review of Psychology, 33,* 155–194.
A review of research on the sense of touch.

For More on Body Senses:

Parker, D. E. (1980, November). The vestibular apparatus. *Scientific American,* pp. 118–135.
A thorough discussion of our vestibular sense, including the nature of motion sickness.

For More on Parapsychology:

Randi, J. (1980). *Flim-flam: The truth about unicorns, parapsychology, and other delusions.* New York: Lippincott & Crowell.
A skeptical evaluation of alleged paranormal phenomena by James "The Amazing" Randi.

Wolman, B. B., Dale, L. A., Schmeidler, G. R., & Ullman, M. (Eds.). (1985). *Handbook of parapsychology.* New York: Van Nostrand Reinhold.
A collection of articles supporting or criticizing research in parapsychology.

CONSCIOUSNESS

Chapter Opening Art:
Marc Chagall. *I and the Village.* 1911.

n January 21, 1959, a New York disc jockey named Peter Tripp began a radiothon to raise money for the March of Dimes fight against polio. He stayed awake for 200 hours—more than eight days—each night broadcasting his three-hour show from an army recruiting booth in Times Square. But, as the days passed, Tripp developed symptoms of psychological disturbance. After four days he experienced hallucinations, seeing a rabbit run across the booth and flames shooting out of a drawer in his hotel room. On the sixth day he began taking stimulant drugs to stay awake. And on the final day he displayed delusional thinking, even insisting that his physician was an undertaker coming to prepare him for burial. After his ordeal, Tripp slept thirteen hours and returned to a state of psychological well-being (Segal & Luce, 1966).

Did Tripp's experience demonstrate that we need to sleep in order to maintain normal psychological functioning? Possibly—but possibly not. First, his experiences were those of a single subject. Perhaps his reactions to sleep deprivation were unique. Second, the delusions he displayed near the end of his ordeal might have been caused by the stimulant drug he used to stay awake rather than by his lack of sleep. As you will read, our knowledge of the effects of sleep deprivation and the effects of stimulant drugs comes from research by psychologists and other scientists interested in the study of *consciousness.*

Two Hundred Hours without Sleep Peter Tripp experienced emotional, perceptual, and cognitive disturbances during his 200-hour radiothon.

Consciousness The awareness of one's own mental activity, including thoughts, feelings, and sensations.

THE NATURE OF CONSCIOUSNESS

But what is consciousness? In 1690 John Locke wrote that "consciousness is the perception of what passes through a man's own mind" (p. 50). Today psychologists share a similar view of **consciousness,** defining it as awareness of one's own mental activity, including thoughts, feelings, and sensations. Two hundred years after Locke, the great psychologist William James (1890/1950) pointed out that consciousness is personal, selective, continuous, and changing. Consider your own consciousness. It is *personal* because you feel that it belongs to you. You do not share it with anyone else. Consciousness is *selective* because you can attend to certain things while ignoring other things. Right now you can shift your attention to a nearby voice, the pressure of this book against your fingers, or the title of this chapter. Consciousness is *continuous* because its contents blend into one another. The mind cannot be broken down into meaningful segments. And consciousness is *changing* because its contents are in a constant state of flux. As much as you might try, you cannot focus on one thing for more than a few seconds without other things drifting through your mind.

Because consciousness is both continuous and changing, James likened it to a stream. Your favorite fishing stream remains the same stream even though the water where you are fishing is constantly being replaced by new water. You may recognize this in the works of James Joyce and other "stream of consciousness" writers, who portray the seemingly random thoughts, feelings, and images that pass through the consciousness of their characters from moment to moment. Even as you read this paragraph, you may notice irrelevant thoughts, feelings, and images passing through your mind. Some may grab your attention, while others may quickly fade away. If you were to write them down as they occur, a person reading them might think you were mad—or at least confused. This also makes stream of consciousness writing difficult to follow without knowing the context of the story.

As a functionalist, James believed that consciousness was an evolutionary development that enhances our ability to adapt to the environment. Today many psychologists agree with James's view and claim that consciousness provides us with a mental representation of the world that permits us to try courses of action in our minds before acting on one (Yates, 1985). This makes us both rational and flexible in adapting to the world, reducing our tendency to engage in aimless, reckless, or impulsive behavior.

One of the ways in which we manipulate mental representations of the world is through **daydreaming,** a state of consciousness in which we voluntarily shift our attention from external stimuli to internal ones generated by the mind. A clever study by psychologist Eric Klinger of the University of Minnesota at Morris found that college students devote several hours a day to daydreaming. Students were given pocket alarms to carry with them all day for several days. The alarms beeped at unpredictable times during the day, but, on the average, beeped every forty minutes. Whenever the students heard the alarm, they noted their mental activity. The results showed that the students spent one-third of their waking hours daydreaming (Bartusiak, 1980).

Given that daydreaming occupies much of our time, what function might it serve? Surveys by Jerome Singer (1975), a leading researcher on daydreaming, have found that, as James would predict, daydreaming permits us to rehearse mentally alternative courses of action. A second reason that people daydream is to keep mentally aroused while in situations in which there is inadequate external stimulation—as any student who has sat through a dull lecture knows too well. A third reason that people daydream is to solve problems. Mark Twain, Edgar Allen Poe, and Robert Louis Stevenson wrote stories inspired by daydreams. And the chemist Friedrich Kekulé, during the drowsy state just before falling asleep, discovered the ringlike structure of the benzene molecule in a daydream of a snake biting its own tail (Schachter, 1976). Of course, there is even a fourth reason to daydream—the pleasure it brings us. This was expressed by the seventeenth-century English writer John Dryden in his poem *Rival Ladies*:

> I strongly wish for what I faintly hope:
> Like the daydreams of melancholy men,
> I think and think on things impossible,
> Yet love to wander in the golden maze.

Today researchers are especially interested in another of the aspects of consciousness identified by James: its selectivity. We refer to the selectivity of consciousness as **attention,** which functions like a television tuner to determine

Daydreaming A state of consciousness that involves shifting attention from external stimuli to self-generated thoughts and images.

Attention The process by which the individual focuses awareness on certain contents of consciousness while ignoring others.

Daydreaming Students may spend one-third of the time daydreaming. One of the reasons for daydreaming is to escape from boring situations.

which stimuli we will notice. Research on attention was inspired in the 1950s by concerns about the ability of air traffic controllers to attend to relevant information and to ignore irrelevant information while directing takeoffs and landings. Research on attention was also inspired by the so-called cocktail party phenomenon, in which you may be engrossed in a conversation at a party, yet be able to shift your attention to another conversation elsewhere in the room (Moray, 1959).

The selectivity of attention was demonstrated in a study in which subjects watched a television screen on which two videotapes were played simultaneously (Neisser & Becklen, 1975). One videotape portrayed two people playing a hand-slapping game and the other portrayed three people bouncing and throwing a basketball. The subjects were told to watch one of the games and to press a response key whenever a particular action occurred. Those watching the hand game had to respond whenever the participants slapped hands with each other. Those watching the ball game had to respond whenever the ball was thrown. The results showed that the subjects made few errors. But when they were asked to watch both games simultaneously, using the right hand to respond to one game and the left hand to respond to the other their performances deteriorated. They made significantly more errors than when attending to just one of the games.

This study showed that the chief advantage of attention—its ability to enable us to focus voluntarily on the most important aspect of our environment—is also a weakness. You realize this when you try to read and watch television at the same time. You must continually shift your attention between the two, interfering with your ability to do either well.

Ironically, after pointing out the importance of attention and other aspects of consciousness, William James became frustrated at his inability to study such a private phenomenon, leading him to write an article entitled "Does Consciousness Exist?" (James, 1904). James's frustration was shared by other psychologists. This eventually led to John B. Watson's classic 1913 article announcing the behaviorist position, which argued that consciousness, being unobservable, cannot be studied scientifically. Watson insisted that "the time seems to have come when psychology must discard all references to consciousness" (Watson, 1913, p. 163).

As discussed in chapter 1, the behaviorist position dominated psychology for about half a century. During that time, relatively few psychologists studied consciousness. But the 1960s brought renewed interest in the study of consciousness as a result of growing interest in Eastern mysticism, widespread use of psychoactive drugs, and the availability of devices that could record physiological changes accompanying altered states of consciousness associated with sleep, hypnosis, meditation, and psychoactive drugs. The current interest in studying altered states of consciousness reflects James's observation that "our normal waking consciousness, rational consciousness as we call it, is but one special type of consciousness, whilst all about it, parted from it by the filmiest of screens, there lie potential forms of consciousness entirely different" (James, 1902/1958, p. 298).

SLEEP AND DREAMS

We spend about one-third of each day in the altered state of consciousness called *sleep*. The daily sleep-wake cycle is the most obvious of our **circadian rhythms,** our twenty-four-hour cycles of psychological and physiological changes. The word *circadian* is derived from the Latin *circa,* meaning "about," and *dies,* meaning "a day." Our circadian rhythm of body temperature parallels our circadian rhythm of brain arousal, with most people beginning the

Circadian Rhythms Twenty-four-hour cycles of psychological and physiological changes, most notably the sleep-wake cycle.

Drawing by Frascino; © 1983 The New Yorker Magazine, Inc.

"If you ask me, all three of us are in different states of awareness."

day at low points on both rhythms and rising on both throughout the day. College roommates who are out of phase with each other in these rhythms are more likely to express dissatisfaction with their relationship than are roommates who are in phase with each other (Watts, 1982). A student who is a "morning person"—already warmed up and chipper at 7:00 A.M.—may find it difficult to socialize with a roommate who can barely crawl out of bed at that time.

What governs our circadian rhythms? One factor is the **pineal gland,** an endocrine gland in the center of the brain that secretes the hormone *melatonin*. Melatonin secretion varies with light levels, decreasing in daylight and increasing in darkness. Sleepiness varies with the level of melatonin in the blood (Fellman, 1985), but the exact mechanism by which melatonin affects the sleep-wake cycle is unclear. And human circadian rhythms, though affected by light, will continue even in total darkness.

When subjects are cut off from cues related to the day-night cycle, perhaps by having them live in a cave or in a windowless room for several weeks, a curious thing happens. For unknown reasons, their sleep-wake cycle changes from twenty-four hours to twenty-five hours in length (figure 5.1). This may explain why "jet lag" is more severe when we fly west to east than when we fly east to west. The symptoms of jet lag, caused by a disruption of the normal sleep-wake cycle, include daytime sleepiness, nighttime insomnia, depressed mood, and lack of motivation (Davis, 1988). Consider a professional baseball player. Eastbound travel would shorten his sleep-wake cycle (so-called **phase advance**), countering the cycle's natural tendency to lengthen. In contrast, westbound travel would lengthen his sleep-wake cycle (so-called **phase delay**), in that case agreeing with the cycle's natural tendency to lengthen. So, phase advance requires more adjustment by the athlete.

The one-quarter of American workers on rotating shifts, including nurses, police officers, and factory workers, also find their sleep-wake cycle disrupted. Because of the natural tendency of the sleep-wake cycle to increase in length, workers on rotating shifts respond better to phase delay than to phase advance. This was demonstrated in a study of industrial workers. Those on a phase-delay schedule moved from the night shift (12 midnight to 8 A.M.) to

Pineal Gland An endocrine gland that affects circadian rhythms through its secretion of the hormone melatonin.

Phase Advance Shortening the sleep-wake cycle, as occurs when traveling from west to east.

Phase Delay Lengthening the sleep-wake cycle, as occurs when traveling from east to west.

FIGURE 5.1
The Extended Sleep-Wake
Cycle When subjects are kept
isolated from cues related to the
normal day-night cycle, they
gradually adopt a twenty-five hour
cycle. They then go to sleep one
hour later each day.

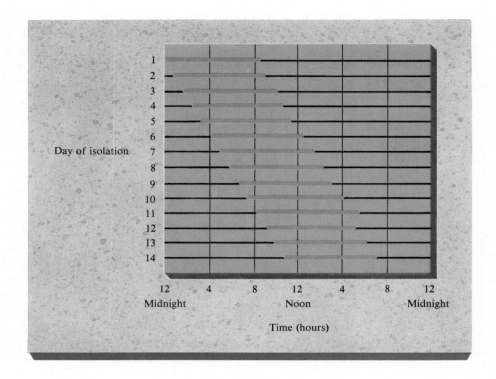

FIGURE 5.1
The Extended Sleep-Wake
Cycle When subjects are kept
isolated from cues related to the
normal day-night cycle, they
gradually adopt a twenty-five hour
cycle. They then go to sleep one
hour later each day.

the day shift (8 A.M. to 4 P.M.) to the swing shift (4 P.M. to 12 midnight). Those on a phase-advance schedule moved in the opposite direction, from the night shift to the swing shift to the day shift. The results showed that workers on a phase-delay schedule had better health, greater satisfaction, higher productivity, and lower turnover (Czeisler, Moore-Ede, & Coleman, 1982).

Patterns of Sleep

Though psychologists are interested in studying the effects of changes in the sleep-wake cycle, they are especially interested in studying sleep itself. Imagine that you are a subject in a sleep study. You would first sleep a night or two in a sleep laboratory to get accustomed to the strange surroundings. You would then sleep several nights in the laboratory while special devices recorded changes in your brain waves, eye movements, heart rate, blood pressure, body temperature, breathing rate, muscle tension, and respiration rate.

The physiological recordings would reveal that when you go to sleep, you do not merely drift into deep sleep, stay there all night, and awaken in the morning. Instead, during a night's sleep, you pass through repeated sleep cycles, with your depth of sleep defined by your characteristic brain-wave patterns (figure 5.2). As you lie in bed with your eyes closed, an EEG recording would show that your brain-wave pattern changes from primarily high-frequency *beta waves,* which mark an alert mental state, to a higher proportion of lower-frequency *alpha waves,* which mark a relaxed, introspective mental state. As you drift off to sleep, you would exhibit slow, rolling eye movements and your brain-wave pattern would show a higher proportion of *theta waves,* which have a lower frequency than alpha waves. You would also exhibit a decrease in other signs of arousal, including heart rate, breathing rate, muscle tension, respiration rate, and body temperature.

The cessation of the rolling eye movements would signify the onset of sleep (Ogilvie, McDonagh, Stone, & Wilkinson, 1988). This initial light stage of sleep is called *stage 1.* After five to ten minutes in stage 1, you would enter the

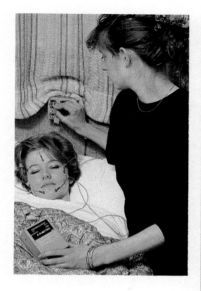

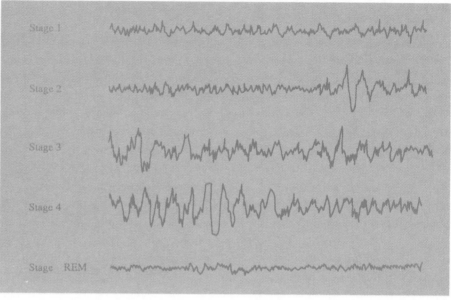

FIGURE 5.2

The Stages of Sleep Studies of subjects in sleep laboratories have found that the stages of sleep are associated with distinctive patterns of brain-wave activity. As we drift into deeper stages of sleep, our brain waves decrease in frequency and increase in amplitude. Note that when we are in REM sleep, our brain-wave patterns are similar to those in the waking state.

slightly deeper *stage 2,* associated with periodic bursts of higher-frequency brain waves known as *sleep spindles.* After ten to twenty minutes in stage 2, you would enter *stage 3,* marked by the appearance of extremely low frequency *delta waves.* When at least 50 percent of your brain waves are delta waves, you would be in *stage 4,* the deepest stage of sleep. After remaining in stages 3 and 4 for perhaps thirty to forty minutes, you would drift up through stages 3, 2, and 1 until, about ninety minutes after falling asleep, you would reach the *rapid eye movement* stage, better known as **REM sleep.**

REM sleep gets its name from the darting eye movements that characterize it. You have probably seen these movements under the eyelids of sleeping people—or even a sleeping pet dog. Because stages 1, 2, 3, and 4 are not characterized by darting eye movements, they are collectively called *non-REM,* or **NREM sleep.** After an initial ten-minute period of REM sleep, you would again drift down into NREM sleep, eventually reaching stage 4. Each complete cycle of NREM-REM sleep takes an average of ninety minutes, meaning that you pass through four or five cycles in a typical night's sleep. Adults generally spend about 25 percent of the night in REM sleep, 5 percent in stage 1, 50 percent in stage 2, and 20 percent in stages 3 and 4. The first half of your night's sleep has relatively more NREM sleep than does the second half, while the second half has relatively more REM sleep than does the first half (figure 5.3). Also, you might not even reach stages 3 and 4 during the second half of the night.

While you are in REM sleep, your heart rate, respiration rate, and brain-wave frequency increase, making you appear to be awake. But you also experience paralysis of your limbs, making it impossible for you to shift your position in bed. Because you would be physiologically aroused, yet immobile, REM sleep is also called *paradoxical sleep.* And because we are paralyzed during REM sleep, sleepwalking (or *somnambulism*) occurs only during

REM Sleep The stage of sleep associated with rapid eye movements, an active brain-wave pattern, and vivid dreams.

NREM Sleep The stages of sleep not associated with rapid eye movements and marked by relatively little dreaming.

[handwritten margin notes:] How long does a complete cycle take? How many do you usually go through

[handwritten note at bottom:] body asleep—brain awake

FIGURE 5.3
A Typical Night's Sleep During a typical night's sleep we pass through cycles involving each of the four stages of NREM sleep and the stage of REM sleep. Note that we obtain our deepest sleep during the first half of the night and that the periods of REM sleep become longer with each successive cycle (Cartwright, 1978).

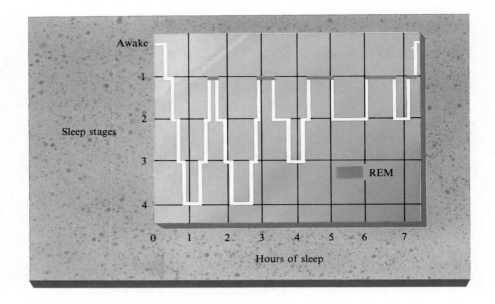

NREM sleep. Despite warnings to the contrary, there is no danger in waking sleepwalkers. The only precaution that should be taken is to protect the habitual sleepwalker by keeping doors and windows locked.

Still another characteristic of REM sleep is erection of the penis or clitoris. Sleep clinics use REM erections to determine whether men who are unable to obtain erections while awake are suffering from a physical or a psychological disorder. If a man has erections while in REM sleep, his problem would be psychological, not physical. Arousal of the sex organs during REM sleep occurs spontaneously and is not necessarily indicative of a sexual dream.

Nonetheless, REM sleep *is* associated with dreaming. We know of this association because of research conducted in the early 1950s by Eugene Aserinsky and Nathaniel Kleitman (1953) of the University of Chicago. When they awakened sleepers exhibiting rapid eye movements, the sleepers usually reported that they had been dreaming. In contrast, when people are awakened during NREM sleep, they rarely report that they had been dreaming. Because the longest REM period occurs during the last sleep cycle of the night, you may often find yourself in the middle of a dream when your alarm clock wakes you in the morning. Though it might be tempting to infer that rapid eye movements reflect the scanning of dream scenes, Aserinsky and his colleagues (1985) have found that they do not. So, if you were dreaming about a tennis match, your eye movements would not necessarily be following the flight of the ball.

Duration of Sleep

As animals go, human beings are moderately long sleepers, with adults averaging seven and one-half hours of sleep a night. In contrast, some animals, such as elephants, sleep as little as two hours a day, and other animals, such as bats, sleep as much as twenty hours a day. Our need for sleep varies across the life span (figure 5.4). While infants may sleep sixteen hours a day, elderly people may sleep less than six hours a day. But adult Americans typically get less than their normal quota of sleep, staying awake to watch television, do schoolwork, or perform other activities. You might go to bed when you want to (perhaps after the late movie) and awaken when you have to (perhaps for an 8 A.M. class), making you chronically sleep deprived. This was supported

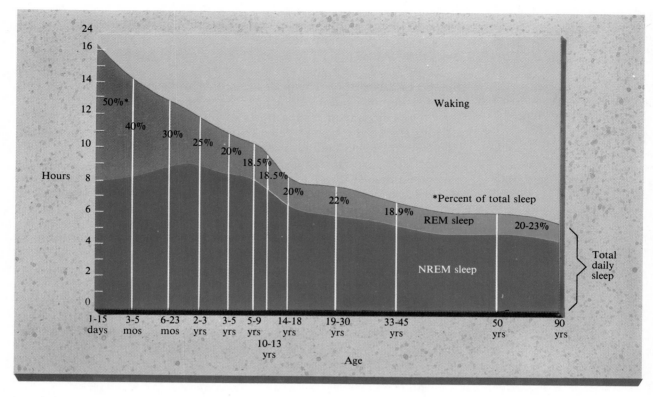

FIGURE 5.4

Sleep Across the Life Span Our amount
of daily sleep decreases across the life span,
decreasing rapidly in infancy and childhood
and more gradually in adulthood. The
proportion of time spent in REM sleep also
decreases across the life span.

Data from H. P. Roffwarg, et al., "Ontogenic
Development of the Human Sleep-Dream Cycle" in
Science, Vol. 152: 608, 29 April 1966. Copyright
1966 by the AAAS. Revised since publication.
Reprinted by permission of the author and the
publisher.

by a study showing that, when given the chance, young adults would sleep
longer than their circumstances normally permitted (Webb & Agnew, 1975).

Of course, many people resort to naps to overcome the effects of abbreviated nighttime sleep. No claim for the benefits of napping has been more
extreme than that made by the eccentric surrealist painter Salvador Dali. Dali
would put a tin plate on the floor, sit on a chair, loosely hold a spoon over the
plate, and fall asleep. As you would expect, as soon as he fell asleep, the spoon
would slip from his grasp and hit the plate, immediately waking him. Dali
claimed that he was refreshed by these extraordinarily brief periods of sleep
(Dement, 1976). Though Dali's claim is probably an exaggeration, napping
can be beneficial. In one study, subjects performed a battery of tests for three
days and nights. Some subjects took periodic naps and others did not. Those
who took naps performed better and felt less sleepy than those who did not
(Webb, 1987).

Sleep Functions

Assuming that you live to be seventy-five, you will have spent up to twenty-
five years asleep. Are you wasting one-third of your life, or does sleep serve
important functions for you? If sleep serves no function, why do we benefit
from naps and why do we eventually succumb to sleep no matter how hard

Function of sleep
& Dreams
Restorative
Problem solving
adaptive inactivity
Wish fulfillment
Freud
MAPP

we try to stay awake? Among the many hypothesized functions of sleep, two are especially prominent: sleep as restorative and sleep as a state of adaptive inactivity.

Sleep as Restorative The most common-sense view of sleep holds that it restores the body and the mind after the wear and tear imposed by waking activities. One way of testing this view is to observe the effects of sleep deprivation. In the case of Peter Tripp, which opened the chapter, sleep deprivation caused hallucinations and delusional thinking, which disappeared after a single night's sleep. In a similar case, Randy Gardner, a seventeen-year-old San Diego high school student, stayed awake 264 hours to get his name in the *Guinness Book of World Records* (a record since broken). He experienced less severe disturbances than Tripp, including some fatigue, irritability, and perceptual distortions. Yet, on his eleventh day without sleep, Gardner beat William Dement, a noted sleep researcher, 100 consecutive times at a pinball game. After fifteen hours of sleep, Gardner awoke restored both physically and mentally (Gulevich, Dement, & Johnson, 1966).

More formal research has also provided evidence of the negative effects of sleep loss and the restorative effects of sleep. In one study, subjects who stayed awake for sixty hours experienced mood disturbances and difficulty performing cognitive tasks, including mental arithmetic (Angus, Heslegrave, & Myles, 1985). Sleep deprivation is especially detrimental to performance on boring tasks or on tasks that require sustained alertness. Fortunately, even if we fail to get our normal nightly quota of sleep during the week (a common problem for college students) we will regain our normal level of alertness after a single night's normal sleep on the weekend (Carskadon & Dement, 1981).

Another source of evidence for the restorative function of sleep is research on the effects of vigorous physical activity on sleep. Sleep, especially deep sleep, increases in duration on the nights after vigorous exercise. A study of runners who participated in a fifty-seven-mile ultramarathon race found that they had a significant increase in sleep, with a significant increase in stage 3 and stage 4 sleep, on the two nights following the race (Shapiro, Bortz, Mitchell, Bartel, & Jooste, 1981). Despite the evidence that sleep has a restorative function, we still do not know exactly *what* sleep restores.

Sleep as Adaptive Inactivity An alternative view, put forth by sleep researcher Wilse Webb (1975), is that sleep evolved because it protected the sleeper from harm. Our prehistoric ancestors who slept at night would be less likely to gain the attention of hungry nocturnal predators. And the limb paralysis accompanying REM sleep may have evolved because it prevented cave dwellers from acting out their dreams, when they might have bumped into trees, fallen off cliffs, or provided dinner for saber-toothed tigers (Chase & Morales, 1983). Evidence for this function of REM sleep comes from studies showing that destruction of a portion of the pons that normally induces REM paralysis in cats produces stalking and attacking movements during sleep, as though they are acting out their dreams (Morrison, 1983).

Another reason to believe that sleep may be a period of adaptive inactivity is because it conserves energy. Evidence supporting this view comes from studies of the food-finding habits of different species. Because the normal duration of sleep for a given species varies with how long it takes members of that species to find their daily food, perhaps animals stay awake only long enough to eat sufficient food to meet their energy needs. Animals may have evolved sleep to conserve energy the remainder of the time. Thus, our need

Wilse Webb "Natural sleep is when you go to bed when you're sleepy and wake up when you're rested. But the modern system of sleeping is to go to bed when you want to and get up when you have to."

for about seven and one-half hours of sleep might mean that our prehistoric ancestors needed about sixteen and one-half hours to find their daily food (Cohen, 1979).

Sleep Disorders

You may take sleep for granted, but millions of people do not. They suffer from sleep disorders such as *insomnia, sleep apnea,* or *narcolepsy.*

Insomnia Millions of Americans suffer from **insomnia,** which is chronic difficulty in either falling asleep (sleep-onset insomnia) or staying asleep all night (sleep-maintenance insomnia). Many insomniacs resort to sedatives, so-called sleeping pills, to fall asleep. But because sleeping pills interfere with the sleep cycle (decreasing REM sleep), eventually lose their effectiveness, and cause harmful side effects (including drug dependence), alternative ways of treating insomnia are preferable.

The shortcomings of drug-induced sleep have led scientists to search for a natural chemical treatment for insomnia. In 1913 a French scientist named Henri Pieron found that transfusions of cerebrospinal fluid from sleepy dogs induced sleep in alert dogs. More recently, scientists isolated a sleep-inducing chemical from human urine. When infused into the brains of rabbits, the chemical, called factor S, causes them to fall sleep. But substance S, composed of several amino acids, is difficult to study—it takes 4.5 tons of urine to isolate one dose (Maugh, 1982).

Instead of turning to sedatives, individuals sometimes devise unusual ways to obtain a good night's sleep. For example, when attending international meetings, Winston Churchill would insist on a room with two beds. During the night, whenever the sheets on the bed he was in got too wrinkled, he would move to the other bed (Segal & Luce, 1966). Psychologists have developed effective treatments for insomnia that rely on neither drugs nor peculiar sleeping habits. You may wish to apply them yourself.

If you suffer from insomnia, you should reduce your presleep arousal by avoiding exercise and caffeine products too close to bedtime. You might also use *paradoxical intention,* in which you try to stay awake while lying in bed.

Insomnia Chronic difficulty in either falling asleep or staying asleep.

Insomnia If you suffer from sleep-onset insomnia, you might benefit from refraining from activities such as eating, reading, or watching television while you are in bed. This will help you associate lying in bed with sleep, rather than with being awake and active.

This might, paradoxically, induce sleep by preventing fruitless, anxiety-inducing efforts to fall asleep. Another technique, *stimulus control,* requires arranging your bedtime situation to promote sleep. First, go to bed only when you feel sleepy. Second, to assure that you will associate lying in bed with sleep, and not with being awake, do not eat, read, watch television, or listen to music while lying in bed. Third, if you toss and turn, get out of bed and return only when you are sleepy. Finally, avoid napping. If you nap during the day you may not feel sleepy enough to fall asleep at your desired bedtime (Ladouceur & Gros-Louis, 1986).

Sleep Apnea A condition in which a person awakens repeatedly in order to breathe.

Sleep Apnea Some people, usually men, experience a form of sleep-maintenance insomnia called **sleep apnea.** When the sleep apnea victim falls asleep, he or she stops breathing. After a minute or so, the individual awakens enough to breathe for several minutes—and then falls asleep again. This sleep-breathe-sleep cycle may occur hundreds of times a night, leading the person to complain of chronic daytime sleepiness. Sleep apnea is caused either by the failure of the respiratory centers of the brain to maintain normal breathing or by constriction of the throat muscles.

In the latter case, a surgeon may provide the sleep apnea victim with a breathing tube inserted through a hole cut into the windpipe. This form of sleep apnea is more common in obese people, as in the so-called Pickwickian syndrome found in obese men whose necks constrict their throats when they are asleep. The syndrome is named for the *Pickwick Papers,* a novel by Charles Dickens in which the obese servant-boy Joe has trouble staying awake during the day (Hall, 1986).

Narcolepsy A condition in which an awake person suffers from repeated, sudden, and irresistible REM sleep attacks.

Narcolepsy If you suffered from **narcolepsy,** you would experience repeated, sudden, and irresistible daytime sleep attacks and immediately fall into REM sleep. Because of its association with REM sleep, narcolepsy is usually accompanied by *cataplexy,* a loss of muscle tension that causes the victim to collapse to the ground. Moreover, strong emotional experiences, whether positive or negative, trigger narcoleptic attacks. This forces victims to maintain a bland emotional life, avoiding both laughing and crying. Though the cause of narcolepsy is unclear, its victims may benefit from stimulant drugs, which prevent drowsiness (Levander & Sachs, 1985).

Dreams

Dream A storylike sequence of visual images, usually occurring during REM sleep.

The most dramatic aspect of sleep is the **dream,** a storylike sequence of visual images commonly evoking strong emotions. Actions that would be impossible in real life may seem perfectly normal in dreams. In a dream, you might find it reasonable to hold a conversation with a dinosaur or to leap across the Grand Canyon. Moreover, everyone dreams—even people who claim they do not. When awakened from REM sleep, people who claim they do not dream will usually report that they were dreaming (Calkins, 1893). Evidently, people confuse their inability to recall dreams with an absence of dreaming. Given that everyone dreams, what do we dream about?

The Content of Dreams Human beings have long been intrigued by dreams, with references to the content of dreams found on Babylonian clay tablets dating from 5000 B.C. The first formal study of the content of dreams was conducted a century ago by Mary Whiton Calkins (1893), who found that she and other subjects tended to dream about mundane personal matters, usually involving familiar people and places. Her findings were supported by the research of Calvin Hall (1966), who analyzed the content of thousands of dreams. Hall, in addition, found that the characters in our dreams are affected by the sex of the dreamer. While females dream about males and females equally, males dream about males about 65 percent of the time. He found this to be true in all cultures, for all ages, and in both laboratory and nonlaboratory settings (Hall, 1984).

When our dreams contain frightening content, they are called **nightmares.** But do not confuse nightmares, which occur during REM sleep, with **night terrors,** which occur during NREM sleep stages 3 and 4. Night terrors are especially common in childhood. The child experiencing a night terror might suddenly sit up in bed, let out a bloodcurdling scream, speak incoherently, and quickly fall back to sleep. Because the child does not recall the night terror, it is more disturbing to the family members who are rudely awakened by it.

The content of dreams may be affected by immediate environmental stimuli, as portrayed by Herman Melville in his novel *Moby Dick.* In describing the effect of Captain Ahab's pegleg on the dreams of his ship's sailors, Melville wrote, "To his weary mates, seeking repose within six inches of his ivory heel, such would have been the reverberating crack and din of that bony step that their dreams would have been of the crunching teeth of sharks." Perhaps you have found yourself dreaming of an ice cream truck ringing its bell, only to awaken suddenly and discover that your dream had been stimulated by the ringing of your telephone. Anecdotal reports of the incorporation of stimuli into dreams have stimulated laboratory research. In one study, researchers sprayed sleepers with a water mist when they were in REM sleep. When the sleepers were awakened, they sometimes reported dreams about a leaky roof, being caught in the rain, or similar such themes. Nonetheless, external stimuli only occasionally have such effects (Dement & Wolpert, 1958).

The Functions of Dreaming REM sleep—dream sleep—is important. If deprived of sleep, subjects increase their proportion of REM sleep when they are again allowed to sleep as long as they like. This is known as the *REM rebound* effect and indicates that dream sleep serves certain, still unclear, functions. People have pondered the function of dreams for thousands of years. The ancient Greeks believed that dreams brought prophecies from the gods, as in Homer's *Iliad* and *Odyssey.* But Aristotle, who at first accepted the divine origin of dreams, later rejected this belief, claiming

Nightmare A frightening REM dream.

Night Terror A frightening NREM experience, common in childhood, in which the individual may suddenly sit up, let out a bloodcurdling scream, speak incoherently, and quickly fall back to sleep, yet usually fail to recall it on awakening.

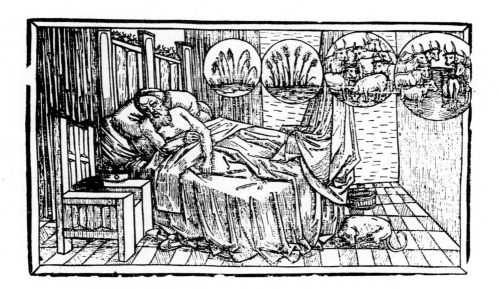

The Dream as Prophecy Belief in the predictive nature of dreams has been common throughout history. This woodcut from the Lubeck Bible of 1494 illustrates Pharaoh's famous dream, which Joseph interpreted as portending seven years of abundance, then famine.

that the gods would not lower themselves to communicate with human beings (Parker, 1987).

Perhaps the most common view of the function of dreaming holds that dreams serve as wish fulfillments. The great fourteenth-century poet Chaucer expressed this view in his poem *The Parliament of Fowls,* in which knights dream of fighting and lovers dream of their romantic partners. Centuries later Sigmund Freud (1900/1955) provided the first formal view of dreaming as wish fulfillment in his classic book *The Interpretation of Dreams.* Freud claimed that dreams serve as safe outlets for unconscious sexual or aggressive impulses that cannot be acted on while awake because of cultural prohibitions. Freud distinguished between a dream's **manifest content,** which is the verbally reported dream, and its **latent content,** which is the dream's true meaning.

But how can we discover a dream's true meaning? According to Freud, a dream's manifest content consists of symbols that disguise its latent sexual or aggressive content. This prevents us from being awakened by dreaming directly about emotionally charged sexual or aggressive material. Thus, trees, rifles, or skyscrapers might serve as phallic symbols representing unconscious sexual impulses. A dream about planting a tree might provide a means of releasing sexual energy. The manifest content of a dream reported by a subject is translated into its latent content during the process of psychoanalysis, which is discussed in chapter 15.

But the failure of psychoanalysts to provide convincing research support for dreaming as a form of disguised wish fulfillment (Fisher & Greenberg, 1985) led researchers to study other possible functions of dreaming. One of those possible functions is problem solving. You may recall reading in chapter 3 how Otto Loewi discovered the chemical nature of neuronal transmission after carrying out an experiment that came to him in a dream. In an earlier case, the nineteenth-century inventor Elias Howe felt frustrated by his inability to determine where to put the hole in the needle of the sewing machine he was perfecting. The answer came to him in a dream in which savages were chasing him with spears. He noticed that each spear had a hole in its tip. This gave Howe the idea of putting a hole in the tip of the sewing machine needle.

Even athletes have solved problems in their dreams. Jack Nicklaus, perhaps the greatest golfer ever, reported that he took ten strokes off his golf game by gripping his clubs in a manner suggested in a dream (Shepard, 1984). Anecdotal reports such as these led Rosalind Cartwright (1978), a leading dream researcher, to conduct research studies of the possible problem-solving function of dreaming. By studying dreams that occur in each of the REM periods across a night's sleep, she has found that they are concerned with developing possible solutions to problems from the preceding day.

The possible problem-solving function of dreaming has also been supported by studies of the ability of dreams to help us deal with emotional, as well as practical, problems. In one such study (Lauer, Riemann, Lund, & Berger, 1987), subjects were shown either a neutral film about the behavior of dolphins and chimpanzees or a disturbing film depicting distressing situations, including a depiction of the massacre of a group of Native Americans and a documentary about the deplorable living conditions in a juvenile prison. On the night following their viewing of the films, subjects who had viewed the disturbing film were more likely to incorporate content from the films into their early dreams and to experience a high degree of personal participation and intense anxiety or aggression. But their later dreams were more likely to be emotionally neutral or positive. This provided evidence that dreaming may help us deal with the impact of disturbing events from the preceding day.

Manifest Content Sigmund Freud's term for the verbally reported dream.

Latent Content Sigmund Freud's term for the true, though disguised, meaning of a dream.

While most dream theorists believe that dreaming serves psychological functions, such as wish fulfillment or problem solving, others view it as merely a by-product of neurological activity. According to the **activation-synthesis theory** of J. Allan Hobson and Robert McCarley (1977), dreams are the by-products of the brain's attempt to make sense of the spontaneous changes in physiological activity generated by the pons during REM sleep. For example, a dream in which you are being chased but cannot run away might reflect the brain's attempt to explain the inability of signals from the motor areas of the brain to stimulate limb movements during the limb paralysis that accompanies REM sleep. Moreover, the strong emotion that we experience in such dreams might be a product of the activation of the limbic system that occurs during REM sleep.

The activation-synthesis theory has been criticized by those who claim that it cannot explain how we can have personally meaningful dreams that are obviously more than the by-products of spontaneous brain activity (Vogel, 1978). Despite almost a century of research, no dream theory has clearly demonstrated its superiority in explaining the functions of dreams. One of the difficulties in dream research is that the same dream can be explained as wish fulfillment, as problem solving, or as the by-product of spontaneous brain activity (figure 5.5).

HYPNOSIS

While sleep is a naturally occurring state of consciousness, **hypnosis** is an induced state of consciousness in which one person responds to suggestions by another person for alterations in perception, thinking, and behavior. Hypnosis originated in the work of the Viennese physician Anton Mesmer (1734–1815), who claimed that he could cure illnesses by transmitting a form of energy he called *animal magnetism* to his patients, a process that became known as *mesmerism.*

In the late eighteenth century, Mesmer became the rage of Paris, impressing Parisians with his demonstrations of mesmerism. His colorful showmanship made him the equivalent of a rock star today. In a typical demonstration, wealthy patients would gather in a luxurious room with thick carpeting, mirrored walls, subdued lighting, and soft music. Mesmer, wearing a flowing purple robe, would direct them to sit around a large oak tub called a baquet, which he had filled with "mesmerized" water, ground glass, and metal filings. The patients were "mesmerized" by holding onto rods protruding from the water and then responding to Mesmer's suggestions to enter a trance state in which they would feel their physical symptoms disappear (Ellenberger, 1970). Today we use the word *mesmerized* to describe a person in a trancelike state and *animal magnetism* to describe a person who has a charismatic personality.

Mesmer's flamboyance and extravagant claims provoked King Louis XVI to appoint a commission to investigate mesmerism. In 1784 the commission, headed by Benjamin Franklin, completed its investigation and concluded that there was no evidence of animal magnetism. They concluded that the effects of mesmerism were attributable to the power of suggestion and the subjects' active imaginations. Mesmer, discredited, moved to Switzerland, where he lived out his life in obscurity.

In 1842 the English surgeon James Braid, who used mesmerism in his practice, concluded that it induced a sleeplike state. He renamed mesmerism *hypnosis,* from Hypnos, the Greek god of sleep. In the late nineteenth century, Sigmund Freud used hypnosis to help his patients gain insight into psychological problems that contributed to their physical symptoms. But Freud aban-

Activation-Synthesis Theory The theory that dreams are the by-products of the brain's attempt to make sense of the spontaneous changes in physiological activity generated by the pons during REM sleep.

Hypnosis An induced state of consciousness in which one person responds to suggestions by another person for alterations in perception, thinking, and behavior.

hyp + med.
what
sim,
diff,

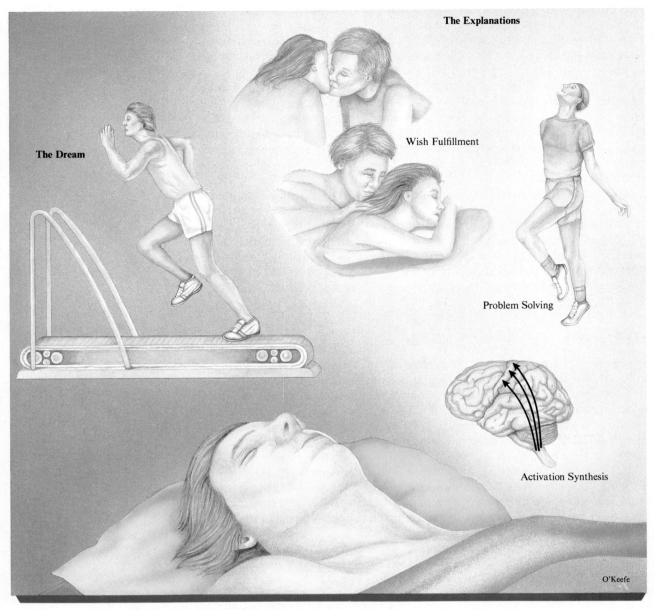

The Explanations

The Dream

Wish Fulfillment

Problem Solving

Activation Synthesis

O'Keefe

FIGURE 5.5
One Dream, Three Explanations *The Dream:* The dreamer dreams that he is running in place and can neither move from that spot nor stop running. *The Explanations:* Wish Fulfillment—The manifest content (the dream as reported) would be translated into its latent content (its true meaning). The dream might reflect the conflict between the dreamer's wish for sex (the desire to move from the spot) and guilt feelings about that wish (the desire to stop running). Problem Solving—The dreamer has been concerned with recent excessive weight gain, but has been unable to decide on the best course of action to lose weight. Perhaps the dream is directing him to take up aerobic exercise. Activation Synthesis—During REM sleep, the pons generates neural impulses that activate random regions of the cerebral cortex. Perhaps it has activated the region of the motor cortex that controls leg and arm movements. Because the dreamer's limbs are paralyzed during REM sleep, he may synthesize the cortical arousal and limb paralysis into a dream about running in place without being able to move or stop.

doned the use of hypnosis after devising what he found to be a more effective technique, psychoanalysis. Despite Freud's rejection of hypnosis, it has achieved widespread acceptance during the past century.

Hypnotic Induction

How do hypnotists induce a hypnotic state? The process depends less on the skills of the hypnotist than on the susceptibility of the subject. People vary in their degree of susceptibility, with highly hypnotizable people having more active fantasy lives and a capacity for absorption in what they are doing (Lynn & Rhue, 1988), whether reading a book, playing a sport, or holding a conversation. Psychologists have developed tests of hypnotizability, which determine the extent to which subjects will comply with hypnotic suggestions after a brief hypnotic induction. A simple suggestion, to indicate some hypnotizability, might direct you to hold your hands in front of you and move them apart, while a more difficult suggestion, to indicate high hypnotizability, might direct you to produce handwriting similar to that of a child.

The aim of hypnotic induction is to create a relaxed, passive, highly focused state of mind. During hypnotic induction the hypnotist might have you focus your eyes on a spot on the ceiling. The hypnotist might then suggest that you notice your eyelids closing, feet warming, muscles relaxing, and respiration slowing. You would gradually relinquish more and more control to the hypnotist over your perceptions, thoughts, and behaviors. But exactly what kinds of effects can hypnosis produce?

Effects of Hypnosis

Many anecdotal reports of the remarkable physical effects of hypnosis have been discredited by experimental research. Perhaps you have heard the claim that a hypnotized person who is given the suggestion that his or her hand has touched a red-hot poker will develop a blister. Experiments have shown that such hypnotic suggestions can, at best, merely promote warming of the skin

Hypnosis Hypnosis is promoted by the willingness of the subject to follow suggestions given by the hypnotist. Here a subject obeys a hypnotic suggestion that her arm is as solid as a board and cannot be bent.

by increasing the flow of blood to it (Spanos, McNeil, & Stam, 1982). None-theless, research has demonstrated a variety of impressive perceptual, cog-nitive, and behavioral effects of hypnosis.

Perceptual Effects Stage hypnotists commonly use hypnosis to induce al-terations in perception, such as convincing subjects that a vial of water is actually ammonia and then observing the subjects jerk their heads away after smelling the vial. But the most important perceptual effect of hypnosis is in pain relief. In the mid-nineteenth century, the Scottish surgeon James Esdaile used hypnosis to induce anesthesia in patients undergoing surgery for the removal of limbs, tumors, or cataracts (Ellenberger, 1970). Research has supported the effectiveness of hypnotically induced pain relief. As you learned in chapter 4, many techniques for pain relief, such as acupuncture, relieve pain by stimulating the release of endorphins. In contrast, hypnosis appears to work by distracting people from their pain (Farthing, Venturino, & Brown, 1984).

Cognitive Effects In 1976, twenty-six elementary school children and their bus driver were kidnapped in Chowchilla, California. After being impris-oned in a buried tractor trailer, the bus driver and two of the children dug their way out and got help. The bus driver, Frank Ray, had seen the license plate number of the kidnappers' van but was unable to recall it. But, after being hypnotized and told to imagine himself watching the kidnapping unfold on television, he was able to recall all but one of the digits of the number. This enabled the police to track down the kidnappers (Smith, 1983).

The Chowchilla case was a widely publicized example of one of the chief cognitive effects of hypnosis, **hypermnesia**—the enhancement of recall. While many studies have demonstrated that hypnosis can enhance recall (Re-linger, 1984), other studies have found that hypnosis may merely increase a person's confidence in the accuracy of his or her recall. In one such study, twenty-seven subjects were hypnotized and then given the suggestion that they had been awakened by a loud noise one night during the preceding week. Later, after leaving the hypnotized state, thirteen of the subjects claimed that the suggested event had actually occurred. Even after being informed of the hypnotic suggestion, six subjects still insisted that they had been awakened by the noise (Laurence & Perry, 1983). This indicates the potential danger of hypnotically enhanced eyewitness testimony. Moreover, hypnotized witnesses feel more confident than nonhypnotized witnesses about the memories they recall—whether their memories are accurate or not—and juries are more im-pressed by confident witnesses (Sheehan & Tilden, 1983).

Behavioral Effects Hypnotists make use of **posthypnotic suggestions,** suggestions for subjects to carry out particular behaviors after leaving hyp-nosis. While this may help some people quit smoking or change other bad habits, what of its possible harmful effects? A century ago debate raged about whether hypnosis could be used to induce criminal or antisocial behavior (Liegois, 1899). Decades later Martin Orne and Frederick Evans (1965) demonstrated that hypnotized subjects could be induced to commit dan-gerous acts. Their study included a group of hypnotized subjects and a group of subjects who simulated being hypnotized. When instructed to do so, subjects in *both* groups plunged their hands into nitric acid, threw the acid in another person's face, and handled a venomous snake. (Note that in both studies a window prevented the subjects from actually touching the snake and that the ''acid'' was actually water.) But, because both groups engaged

Hypermnesia The hypnotic enhancement of recall.

Posthypnotic Suggestions Suggestions directing subjects to carry out particular behaviors or to have particular experiences after leaving hypnosis.

Stage Hypnosis The "human plank" feat has long been a staple of stage hypnosis. But it can be performed by a nonhypnotized person who makes sure to place his or her calves on one chair and head and shoulders on the other.

in dangerous acts, the influence of the research setting, rather than the influence of hypnosis, may have accounted for the results.

Some of the effects of stage hypnosis may also have less to do with hypnosis than with the setting in which they occur. For example, you may have seen a stage hypnotist direct a hypnotized audience volunteer to remain as rigid as a plank while lying extended between two chairs. But highly motivated, nonhypnotized persons can also perform this "human plank" trick. Even the willingness of hypnotized subjects to obey suggestions to engage in bizarre behaviors such as acting like a chicken may be more attributable to the theatrical "anything goes" atmosphere of stage hypnosis than to the effect of hypnosis itself (Meeker & Barber, 1971). You will appreciate this if you have ever watched contestants on the television show "Let's Make a Deal" engage in wacky antics—without even being hypnotized.

The Nature of Hypnosis

In the late 1800s practitioners of hypnosis, most notably in France, disagreed about whether hypnosis induced an altered state of consciousness. One group, led by the French country doctor Ambroise Auguste Liebeault, argued that hypnosis merely induces a normal state of heightened suggestibility (Ellenberger, 1970). Another group, led by the eminent Paris neurologist Jean Martin Charcot, argued that hypnosis induces a state of **dissociation,** in which parts of the mind became separated from one another and form independent streams of consciousness. One stream remains under voluntary control and the other becomes controlled by the hypnotist. This debate lingers on today, with some researchers viewing hypnosis as an altered state of consciousness and others viewing it as a normal state of waking consciousness.

Dissociation A state in which the mind is split into two or more independent streams of consciousness.

Hypnosis as an Altered State Today, the main theory of hypnosis as an altered state is the **neodissociation theory,** a descendant of Charcot's concept of dissociation. This theory originated in a classroom demonstration of hypnotically induced deafness by Ernest Hilgard, who directed a hypnotized blind student to raise an index finger if he heard a sound. When

Neodissociation Theory The theory that hypnosis induces a dissociated state of consciousness.

Hidden Observer Ernest Hilgard's term for the part of the hypnotized person's consciousness that is not under the control of the hypnotist.

blocks were banged near his head, the student did not even flinch. But when asked if some part of his mind had actually heard the noise, his finger rose. Hilgard calls this part of the mind the **hidden observer** (Hilgard, 1978).

Hilgard has used the concept of the hidden observer to explain hypnotically induced pain relief. Hilgard relies on the *cold pressor test,* in which a subject submerges an arm in ice water and is asked every few seconds to estimate his or her degree of pain. Though hypnotized subjects who are told that they will feel no pain report that they feel little or no pain, the hidden observer, when asked, reports that it has experienced intense pain. Hilgard noted that this phenomenon had been reported a century earlier by William James, who observed a hypnotized man who reported no pain when stuck in the hand by a pin. To James's surprise, the man's other hand wrote that a separate part of his mind had experienced the pain. James attributed this "automatic writing" to the dissociation of the man's subconscious mind from his conscious mind (Hilgard, 1973).

Hypnosis as a Normal State The state of dissociation has not gone unchallenged as an explanation for hypnotic effects. The most prominent critics of hypnosis as an altered state are Theodore Barber, Nicholas Spanos, and Martin Orne, who insist that hypnotically induced effects are merely responses to personal factors, such as the subject's motivation, and situational factors, such as the hypnotist's wording of suggestions. By arranging the right combination of factors, the hypnotist increases the likelihood that the subject will comply with hypnotic suggestions.

Consider an experiment that used the cold pressor test, in which the hidden observer was made to give contradictory reports, depending on the hypnotist's suggestions (Spanos & Hewitt, 1980). Some hypnotized subjects were told that the hypnotized part of their mind would feel pain, while the hidden observer would not. Other hypnotized subjects were told that the hypnotized part would not feel pain, while the hidden observer would. When asked to rate the intensity of pain, the hidden observer reported what the subjects had been led to expect. Thus, the hidden observer may merely be a product of the subject's willingness to act as though he or she has experienced suggested hypnotic effects.

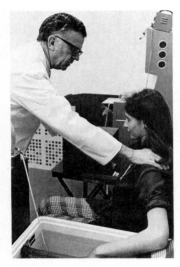

The Hidden Observer Ernest Hilgard uses the cold pressor test to evaluate the ability of hypnosis to prevent the pain that normally accompanies having an arm immersed in ice water. Though the subject may report little or no pain, the "hidden observer" may report severe pain.

Evidence for hypnosis as a form of role playing have also come from studies of hypnotic **age regression,** in which hypnotized subjects are told to return to childhood. A hypnotized adult might talk baby talk or play with an imaginary teddy bear. But a review of research on hypnotic age regression found that subjects do not adopt the true mental, behavioral, and physiological characteristics of children—they merely act as though they are children (Nash, 1987).

Age Regression A hypnotic state in which the individual apparently behaves as he or she did as a child.

In a classic study, Martin Orne (1951) hypnotized college students and suggested that they regress back to their sixth birthday party. He then asked them to describe the people and activities at the party, which they did in great detail. But Orne then asked the subjects' parents to describe the same birthday party. He found that many of the subjects' "memories" had been fabrications. They reported people and events they *assumed* would have been at their sixth birthday party. There was no evidence that they actually reexperienced their sixth birthday party.

Such challenges to hypnosis as an altered state of consciousness have not gone unmet by Hilgard and other of its supporters. Especially strong evidence comes from experiments in which hypnotized subjects experience physiological changes in response to hypnotic suggestions. In one study, hypnotized subjects were given the suggestion that their view of an image on a television screen was blocked by a box. The pattern of electrical activity recorded from their occipital lobes, the site of visual processing in the brain, was similar to what one would expect from people whose view of a television had been blocked by a real box. This indicated that the hypnotic suggestion affected highly specific visual processing in the brain (Spiegel, Cutcomb, Ren, & Pribram, 1985), an effect difficult to attribute to mere suggestibility. Neither side in the debate about the nature of hypnosis has provided sufficient evidence to discount the other side completely.

MEDITATION

Meditation is a procedure that uses mental exercises to achieve a highly focused state of consciousness. Traditionally, meditation has been a religious practice aimed at achieving a mystical union with God or the universe. All major religions, including Buddhism, Christianity, Hinduism, Islam, Judaism, and Taoism, have centuries-old traditions of formal meditative practices. In the past two decades meditation has also gained popularity as a means of promoting physical and psychological well-being.

Meditation A procedure that uses mental exercises to achieve a highly focused state of consciousness.

Common Meditative Practices

The popular forms of meditation share techniques aimed at producing physical relaxation and mental concentration. Suppose that you decided to practice meditation. You would seek a peaceful setting, whether a room, a church, or a forest. While maintaining a comfortable seated position, you would focus on a sound, image, or object. You would also adopt a passive attitude, calmly withdrawing your attention from any intruding images, feelings, or sensations.

Meditation was popularized in the late 1960s by Maharishi Mahesh Yogi, an Indian guru, through the influence of his most famous disciples, the Beatles. They promoted a Westernized form of meditation called **transcendental meditation** (or **TM**). In practicing TM, you concentrate on repeating a sound called a *mantra,* such as "Om," for two twenty-minute periods a day. In the early 1970s, cardiologist Herbert Benson introduced the **relaxation response,** a form of meditation that is identical to TM except that the meditator may mentally repeat a sound other than a mantra, such as the number one or a favorite brief prayer.

Transcendental Meditation (TM) A form of meditation in which the individual relaxes and repeats a sound called a mantra for two 20-minute periods a day.

Relaxation Response A variation of transcendental meditation in which the individual may repeat a sound other than a mantra.

Effects of Meditation

Benson (Wallace & Benson, 1972) has promoted meditation as a technique that induces a unique state of physical and mental relaxation by increasing alpha brain waves and decreasing heart rate, respiration rate, oxygen consumption, and carbon dioxide expiration (figure 5.6). This claim was challenged by David Holmes (1984), whose review of research on meditation found no difference in the physiological arousal of subjects who meditated and subjects who merely rested. For example, an early study found that meditators and people who merely rested did not differ in the level of stress hormones in their blood—a good indicator of arousal level (Michaels, Huber, & McCann, 1976).

Benson responded to Holmes by pointing to studies that showed meditation does have unique effects on arousal (Benson & Friedman, 1985). One study contradicted Holmes by showing that meditators achieved a lower state of physiological arousal than did people who merely relaxed with their eyes

Meditation Athletes may use meditation to alleviate their precompetition anxiety by reducing their levels of mental and physical arousal.

FIGURE 5.6
The Relaxation Response
Oxygen consumption (blue line)
and carbon dioxide elimination
(black line) decrease during
transcendental meditation. Both
of these physiological changes are
signs of relaxation.

From "The Physiology of Meditation"
by R. K. Wallace and H. Benson.
Copyright © 1972 by SCIENTIFIC
AMERICAN, Inc. All rights reserved.

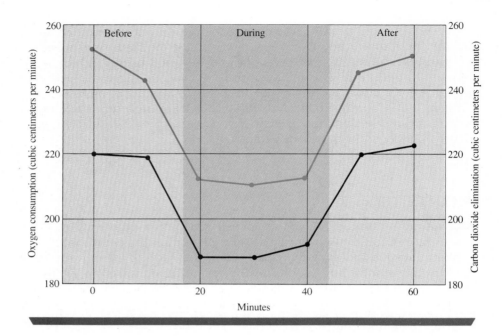

closed (Delmonte, 1984). Whether or not meditation eventually proves to
induce a unique physiological or psychological state, it has demonstrated its
effectiveness in inducing a state of relaxation. This makes it a useful stress-
management technique.

PSYCHOACTIVE DRUGS

Psychoactive Drugs Chemicals
that induce changes in mood,
thinking, perception, and
behavior by affecting neuronal
activity in the brain.

Normal waking consciousness can also be altered by **psychoactive drugs,**
chemicals that induce changes in mood, thinking, perception, and behavior
by affecting neuronal activity. Human beings seem drawn to psychoactive drugs.
Many individuals drink beer to reduce social anxiety, take barbiturates to fall
asleep, use narcotics to feel euphoric, drink coffee to get going in the morning,
or smoke marijuana to enrich the perception of music. The psychoactive drugs
are divided into three categories: *depressants, stimulants,* and *hallucinogens*
(figure 5.7).

Depressants

Depressants Psychoactive drugs
that inhibit activity in the central
nervous system.

The **depressants** reduce arousal by inhibiting activity in the central nervous
system. Chapter 15 discusses two kinds of depressant drugs that are used in
treating psychological disorders: *antianxiety drugs* (or *tranquilizers*), which
are used to relieve anxiety, and *antipsychotic drugs,* which are used to alleviate the symptoms of schizophrenia. This section will discuss several other
kinds of depressants.

Alcohol A depressant, ethyl
alcohol, found in beverages and
commonly used to reduce social
inhibitions.

Alcohol Ethyl **alcohol** has been used—and abused—for thousands of
years. Even the ancient Romans had to pass laws against drunk driving—
of chariots (Whitlock, 1987). Today, a person with a blood alcohol level of
.10 percent is considered legally drunk in most American states. Drunk
drivers (whether they drive chariots or automobiles) are dangerous because they suffer from perceptual distortions, motor incoordination, and
impaired judgment.

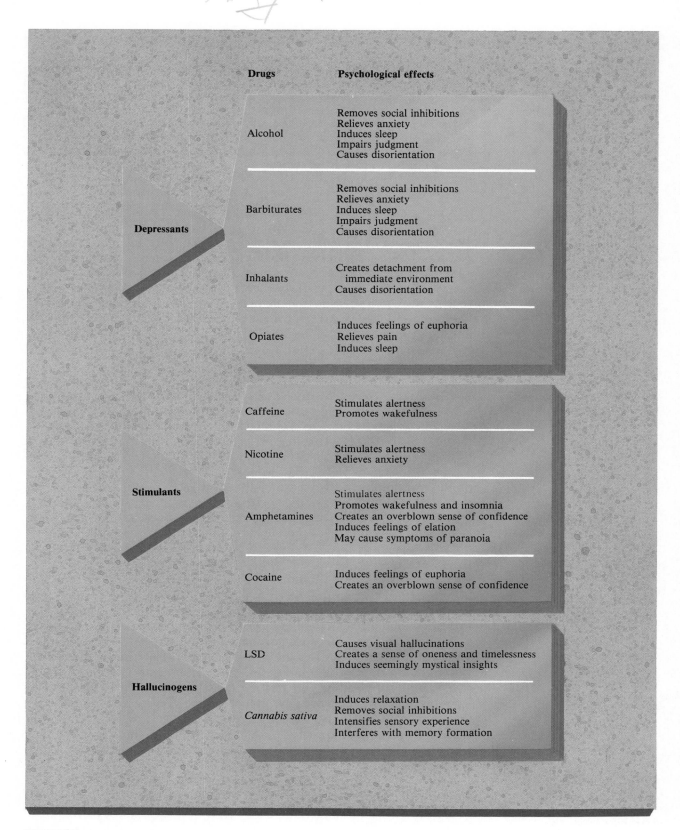

FIGURE 5.7
Psychoactive Drugs

Alcohol Both young and old use alcohol to remove their social inhibitions.

Alcohol exerts its effects by promoting the effectiveness of the neurotransmitter *GABA,* which inhibits neuronal transmission in the brain (Nestoros, 1980). This decreases activity in brain centers that normally inhibit social behaviors such as sex, aggression, or even helpfulness (Steele, Critchlow, & Liu, 1985). You have probably seen sexually proper people become overly affectionate, mild-mannered people become verbally or physically aggressive, and socially shy people become the life of the party after a few drinks. Moreover, because people are aware of alcohol's reputation for removing social inhibitions, they may use it as an excuse for engaging in socially disapproved behaviors, such as casual sex (Hull & Bond, 1986). The person can then blame his or her behavior on the alcohol.

Barbiturates Depressants used to induce sleep or anesthesia.

pen tothal (truth serume)

Barbiturates The **barbiturates** are derived from barbituric acid. Because barbiturates produce effects similar to those of alcohol, they are known as "solid alcohol." Barbiturates work by stimulating GABA receptors (Nicoll & Madison, 1982). The barbiturate Seconal, which acts quickly to induce drowsiness, is used as a sleeping pill. The barbiturate Pentothal is used as a general anesthetic in surgery. Because mild doses of Pentothal induce a drunken, uninhibited state in which the intoxicated person is more willing to reveal private thoughts and feelings, it is popularly known as "truth serum"—though it does not guarantee that the information revealed will be true.

Inhalants Depressants that are inhaled to induce altered states of consciousness.

Inhalants One of the oldest means of inducing an altered state of consciousness is the use of **inhalants,** drugs (including ether, chloroform, and nitrous oxide) that are ingested by inhaling them in vapor form. Greek legend holds that the Oracle at Delphi offered prophecies under the intoxicating influence of natural drug vapors emitted from the ground. In the nineteenth century, the consciousness-altering effects of inhalants appealed to many artists, writers, and intellectuals. William James (1882) used *nitrous oxide* to induce altered states of consciousness in which he hoped to gain philosophical insights into the meaning of life. Peter Mark Roget, whose famous thesaurus you have probably used to find synonyms, was also fond of nitrous oxide. We can merely speculate on how many synonyms came to Roget in an intoxicated state (Brecher, 1972). You may be familiar with nitrous oxide as "laughing gas," which dentists use to induce a dreamy state of anesthesia.

Opiates Depressant drugs, derived from opium, used to relieve pain or to induce a euphoric state of consciousness.

Opiates The opium poppy is the source of **opiates,** which include opium, morphine, heroin, and codeine. The opiates have been prized since ancient times for their ability to relieve pain and to induce euphoria. Sumerian clay tablets from about 4000 B.C. even refer to the opium poppy as "the plant of joy" (Whitlock, 1987). The nineteenth century earned the title of "dope fiend's paradise," because opiates were cheap, legal, and widely available (Brecher, 1972). Nineteenth-century artists and writers used opiates to induce altered states of consciousness. Samuel Taylor Coleridge even wrote his famous poem *Kubla Khan* under the influence of opium.

Many nineteenth-century individuals also relied on the opiates for pain relief. Physicians and druggists prescribed a beverage called *laudanum,* a mixture of opium and alcohol, as a "magic elixir" for many physical and psychological problems. Of course, laudanum merely relieved pain and made the person oblivious to his or her problems. During the Civil War, physicians used *morphine,* the main active ingredient in opium, to ease the pain of wounded soldiers. Morphine was named after Morpheus, the Greek god of dreams, because it induces a dreamy state of consciousness (Julien, 1981).

In 1898 scientists derived a more potent drug from opium—*heroin.* Heroin was named after the Greek god Hero, because it was welcomed as a cure for morphine addiction. But physicians soon found that heroin did not cure morphine addiction, it merely replaced it—with heroin addiction. By the early twentieth century, so many Americans had become addicted to opiates that in 1914 Congress passed the Harrison Narcotic Act banning their nonmedical use. Today, morphine, codeine, and the synthetic opiate Demerol are routinely prescribed to relieve severe pain. The euphoric and pain-relieving effects of the opiates are caused by their binding to endorphin receptors, which act to block pain impulses and stimulate the brain's pleasure centers (Levinthal, 1988).

Stimulants

While the depressant drugs reduce arousal, the stimulant drugs increase it. The **stimulants** include *caffeine, nicotine, amphetamines, cocaine,* and *antidepressants.* The antidepressants, which are used to treat severe depression, are discussed in chapter 15.

Caffeine Many Americans do not go a single day without ingesting **caffeine,** which is found in a variety of products, including coffee, tea, soft

Stimulants Psychoactive drugs that increase central nervous system activity.

Caffeine A stimulant used to increase mental alertness.

Opiates The nineteenth century has been called a "dope fiend's paradise," with even opiate drugs freely available as ingredients in "magic elixirs" and "patent medicines." This advertisement shows that at the turn of the century, both Bayer aspirin and Bayer heroin were legal and readily available. Note that heroin was advertised as a cough suppressant (one of the effects of opiates), though many people used it to induce feelings of euphoria.

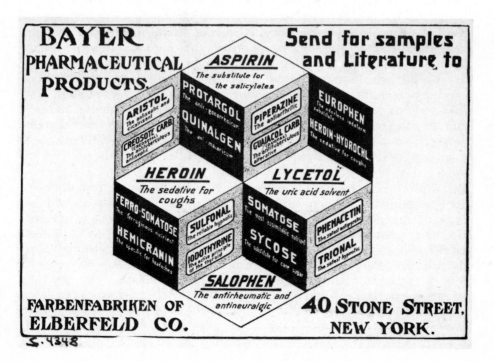

Caffeine and Nicotine Students may drink coffee to obtain caffeine, or smoke cigarettes to stay alert while studying. But excessive caffeine ingestion may cause caffeinism, a condition associated with poor academic performance. And smoking may cause serious illnesses, including cancer and cardiovascular disease.

Nicotine A stimulant used to regulate physical and mental arousal.

Amphetamines Stimulants used to maintain alertness and wakefulness.

Cocaine A stimulant used to induce mental alertness and euphoria.

drinks, chocolate, cold pills, diet pills, and stimulant tablets. The mind-altering effects of caffeine have made it a popular drug for centuries. Chocolate, for example, was considered a gift from the gods by the Aztecs of Mexico, who drank cocoa during their religious rituals. In eighteenth-century Europe, artists, writers, and philosophers gathered at coffee houses to share their ideas under the stimulating influence of caffeine. And in the late nineteenth century coffee use by Americans accelerated after the introduction of the first commercial mix of coffee beans at a Nashville hotel called Maxwell House (Ray, 1983).

Today caffeine is a popular means of maintaining mental alertness. But excessive use of caffeine may induce *caffeinism,* marked by insomnia and high levels of anxiety. Caffeinism is associated with poor academic performance by college students. But it is unclear whether caffeinism causes poor academic performance or academically deficient students tend to ingest large amounts of caffeine (Gilliland & Andress, 1981).

Nicotine "If you can't send money, send tobacco," read a 1776 appeal from General George Washington (Ray, 1983). Washington's troops actually craved **nicotine,** a powerful drug contained in tobacco. Because nicotine's initial effects are those of a stimulant and its later effects are those of a depressant, smokers adjust their intake of nicotine to achieve a desired level of arousal. In one study, ten male smokers performed mental arithmetic under competitive pressure during one session and under noncompetitive pressure during another session. In each session, half of the subjects smoked real cigarettes and half smoked placebo cigarettes (which contain no nicotine). The smokers ingested more nicotine when under competitive pressure than when under noncompetitive pressure. Smoking produced greater reductions in reported anxiety levels in the competitive pressure condition than in the noncompetitive pressure condition. This reduction in anxiety was not a placebo effect, because it held only when the subjects smoked nicotine cigarettes (Pomerleau & Pomerleau, 1987).

Amphetamines The **amphetamines,** synthetic stimulant drugs commonly known as "speed," are more powerful than caffeine and nicotine. The amphetamines, which include Benzedrine, Dexedrine, and Methedrine, exert their effects by stimulating norepinephrine and dopamine receptors. In the 1930s truck drivers discovered that amphetamines would keep them alert during long hauls, thereby letting them drive for many hours without sleeping. During World War II, soldiers used amphetamines to relieve fatigue, and during the past two decades college students have used amphetamines to stay awake while cramming for final exams. Because the amphetamines also suppress appetite and increase the basal metabolic rate, they are commonly used as diet pills. But chronic users may also experience so-called amphetamine psychosis, marked by extreme suspiciousness and, sometimes, violent responses to imagined threats.

Cocaine During the 1980s **cocaine,** a chemical extracted from the coca leaf, became the stimulant drug of choice among those who desired the brief, but intense, feeling of self-confidence and euphoria that it induces. Users snort cocaine in powdered form, smoke it in crystal form (so-called crack), or inject it in solution form. But cocaine was popular long before the 1980s. People of the Andes have used it for more than 5,000 years to induce euphoric feelings and to combat fatigue. Cocaine acts by preventing the reuptake of norepinephrine by neurons that secrete it (Van Dyke & Byck, 1982).

Cocaine may have reached the height of its popularity in the late nineteenth century, when German troops used it to relieve fatigue. Sir Arthur Conan Doyle made his fictional character Sherlock Holmes a cocaine user, and Robert Louis Stevenson relied on cocaine to stay alert while writing two drafts of *The Strange Case of Dr. Jekyll and Mr. Hyde* in six days. Cocaine also joined opium as a popular ingredient in the patent medicines that were sold as cure-alls. And in 1886 an Atlanta druggist named John Pemberton contributed to cocaine's popularity by introducing a stimulant soft drink that contained both caffeine and cocaine, which he named Coca-Cola. Even John B. Watson, the founder of behaviorism, drank Coca-Cola syrup to keep himself alert:

> In my senior year [at Furman University], I was the only man who passed the final Greek exam. I did it only because I went to my room at two o'clock the afternoon before the exam, took with me one quart of Coca-Cola syrup, and sat in my chair and crammed until time for the exam the next day. (Watson, 1961, p. 272)

Unfortunately, cocaine causes harmful side effects, as discovered by Sigmund Freud, who used it himself. In the 1880s, Freud praised cocaine as a wonder drug for inducing local anesthesia, relieving asthma, and curing opiate addiction. But Freud stopped using and prescribing cocaine after discovering its ability to cause paranoia and hallucinations (Byck, 1974). (The dangers of cocaine use also led to its removal as an ingredient in Coca-Cola.)

Hallucinogens

The **hallucinogens** induce extreme alterations in consciousness. Users may experience visual hallucinations, a sense of timelessness, and feelings of depersonalization. Some cultures have relied on hallucinogens to induce mystical states of consiousness. The Aztecs used a "magic mushroom," containing the hallucinogen *psilocybin,* in their religious rituals. And for centuries Native Americans in the Southwest have used the peyote cactus, which contains the hallucinogen *mescaline,* in their religious rituals. Today members of the Native American Church still do so (Ray, 1983). The past two decades have seen the advent of the notorious hallucinogen *phencyclidine,* also known as "PCP" or "angel dust." The drug may induce feelings of depersonalization and paranoia, sometimes leading to violent acts (Julien, 1981). Perhaps the two best-known and most widely used hallucinogens are *LSD* and *cannabis sativa.*

LSD In 1943 Albert Hofmann, a Swiss chemist, accidentally ingested a microscopic amount of the chemical lysergic acid diethylamide (**LSD**), which he had isolated from a fungus called ergot that grows on rye grain. He reported that he felt as though he was losing his mind as "in a twilight state with my eyes closed . . . I found a continuous stream of fantastic images of extraordinary vividness and intensive kaleidoscopic colours" (Julien, 1981, p. 151). LSD exerts its effects by blocking brain receptors for the neurotransmitter serotonin (Jacobs, 1987).

A dose of LSD induces a "trip" lasting up to eight hours that involves visual hallucinations, including shifting patterns of colors, changes in the shapes of objects, and distortions in the sizes of body parts. Users also report a sense of timelessness, a feeling of oneness with the universe, and, at times, mystical insights into the meaning of life. The effects of LSD are so powerful that users may experience a "bad trip," in which the alteration in their consciousness is so disturbing that it induces feelings of panic.

Hallucinogens Psychoactive drugs that induce extreme alterations in consciousness, including visual hallucinations, a sense of timelessness, and feelings of depersonalization.

LSD A hallucinogen derived from a fungus that grows on rye grain.

Cannabis Sativa A hallucinogen derived from the hemp plant and ingested in the form of marijuana or hashish.

Cannabis Sativa The most widely used hallucinogenic drug is tetrahydrocannabinol (or *THC*), which is a constituent of the hemp plant, **cannabis sativa.** While the fibers of the hemp plant have traditionally been used in rope making, hemp has also been popular for two of its other products: *marijuana* and *hashish,* which many people smoke to induce an altered state of consciousness. Marijuana is a combination of the crushed stems, leaves, and flowers of the plant, and hashish is its dried resin.

Marijuana has been used for thousands of years as a painkiller, with the earliest reference to that use in a Chinese herbal medicine book from 2737 B.C. (Julien, 1981). In the nineteenth century, marijuana was a popular way to relieve the pain of headaches, toothaches, and stomachaches (Whitlock, 1987). Today, most marijuana smokers use it for its mind-altering effects, which are related to its concentration of THC. Moderately potent marijuana makes time seem to pass more slowly and induces rich sensory experiences, in which music seems fuller and colors seem more vivid. Highly potent marijuana induces visual hallucinations, in which objects may appear to change their shape.

In 1937, after centuries of unregulated use, marijuana was outlawed in the United States because of claims that it induced bouts of wild sexual and aggressive behavior. Allegations linking the hemp plant to aggressive behavior date back to at least the thirteenth century, when the explorer Marco Polo reported that hashish-smoking members of a Muslim sect murdered their leader's political enemies (Iyer, 1986). Though the word *assassin* may have been derived from the word *hashish,* it is unlikely that hashish provoked these murders, because research has shown that THC does not promote aggression.

This was demonstrated in a study (Myerscough & Taylor, 1985) in which subjects were given low, moderate, or high doses of THC. Those given moderate or high doses became less aggressive on a competitive reaction-time task than those given low doses, indicating that THC does not promote aggression and, instead, may actually inhibit it. But this is not to say that marijuana use is desirable. It would be unwise to drive or to operate machinery while under the influence of marijuana—or any other psychoactive drug. And it has been well documented that marijuana impairs memory as the result of THC's effect on acetylcholine neurons that process memories (Miller & Branconnier, 1983).

Hallucinogens The geometric designs in these weavings by the Huichol Indians of Mexico were inspired by visual hallucinations induced by the ingestion of peyote, a cactus that contains the hallucinogen mescaline. LSD and other powerful hallucinogens can induce similar effects.

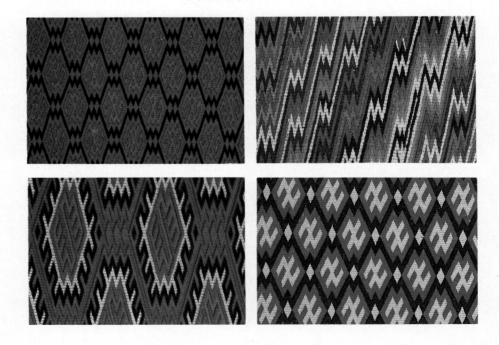

THINKING ABOUT PSYCHOLOGY

Are We Affected by Unconscious Influences?

In his classic psychology textbook, William James (1890/1950) included a section entitled "Can States of Mind Be Unconscious?" that presented ten arguments answering yes and ten arguments answering no. Today, a century later, the extent to which we are affected by unconscious influences still provokes animated debate. But the concept of the unconscious involves any of three different concepts. The first is the Freudian unconscious, a portion of the mind containing thoughts and feelings that influence us without our awareness. The second is subliminal perception, the unconscious perception of stimuli that are too weak to exceed the absolute threshold for detection. And the third is perception without awareness, the unconscious perception of stimuli that do exceed the absolute threshold but that fall outside our focus of attention.

The Freudian Unconscious

During the 1988 National League playoffs between the New York Mets and the Los Angeles Dodgers, relief pitcher Brian Holton of the Dodgers became so nervous that he could not grip the baseball. Suddenly, he found himself singing the lyrics to a folk song, "You take the high road and I'll take the low road." This surprised him because he had never heard the song. But he did find that singing the song relaxed him enough to grip the baseball. When he told his mother about this mysterious behavior, she informed him that his father had sung the song to him when he was a young child.

Anecdotal reports such as this are used by psychoanalytic theorists to support the influence of the Freudian unconscious, which was anticipated by the seventeenth-century philosopher René Descartes and the eighteenth-century philosopher Gottfried von Leibniz, who both claimed that childhood experiences stored in the brain can continue to affect us without our awareness of them. The idea of such unconscious influences became the core of Sigmund Freud's psychoanalytic theory in the late nineteenth and early twentieth centuries.

Freud divided consciousness into three levels: the conscious, the preconscious, and the unconscious (figure 5.8). Freud, as had James, viewed the **conscious** mind as the awareness of fleeting images, feelings, and sensations. The **preconscious** mind contains memories of which we are unaware at the moment, but of which we can become aware at will. And the **unconscious** mind contains repressed feelings and memories of which we are unaware. But, through what Freud called *psychic determinism,* the unconscious mind affects our behavior (see chapter 1). Freud's notion of unconscious motivation is exemplified by slips of the tongue, so-called Freudian slips, in which we replace intended words with sexual or aggressive ones.

Until recently, the Freudian unconscious was considered impossible to study scientifically because evidence of its existence came solely from anecdotal reports and because it seemed impossible to ever study something that could not be directly observed. But later chapters will discuss the use of research methods that, while not necessarily convincing all psychologists of the exis-

Conscious The level of consciousness that includes the mental experiences which we are aware of at a given moment.

Preconscious The level of consciousness that contains feelings and memories which we are unaware of at the moment but which we can become aware of at will.

Unconscious The level of consciousness that contains thoughts, feelings, and memories that influence us without our awareness.

FIGURE 5.8
Levels of Consciousness
According to Sigmund Freud,
there are three levels of
consciousness. The conscious
level contains thoughts, images,
and feelings of which we are
aware. The preconscious level
contains memories that we can
retrieve at will. And the
unconscious level contains
repressed motives and memories
that would evoke intense feelings
of anxiety if we became aware of
them.

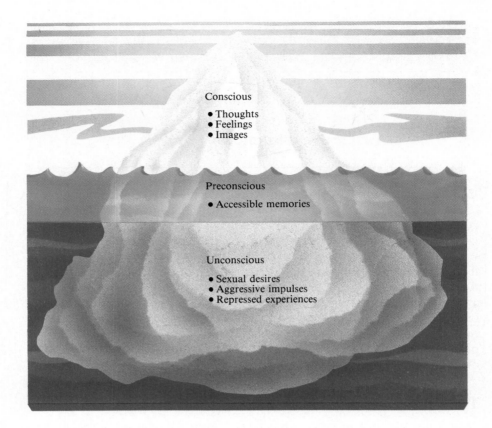

tence of the Freudian unconscious, at least make it subject to scientific research.

Subliminal Perception

Subliminal Perception The
unconscious perception of stimuli
that are too weak to exceed the
absolute threshold for detection.

Research on **subliminal perception** has been considered more scientifically credible because it uses stimuli that can be controlled by the experimenter. In one study, slides of strangers were flashed to subjects by a tachistoscope (see chapter 1) too briefly to exceed the absolute threshold. Because previous research had shown that we prefer stimuli with which we are familiar, the experimenters predicted that if subliminal perception exists, the subjects would later express more positive feelings toward people whose photographs had been presented subliminally. This was, in fact, what occurred (Bornstein, Leone, & Galley, 1987).

Given that we prefer stimuli with which we are familiar, could manufacturers make us like their products more by repeatedly presenting us with subliminal images of them? This is the heart of a controversy that has lasted since the late 1950s. Can subliminal advertising make people buy particular products? The controversy began after a marketing firm inserted the words "Eat Popcorn" and "Drink Coca-Cola" every few frames in movies shown at a theater in Fort Lee, New Jersey. Though those watching the movies could not detect the advertisements, after several weeks, popcorn sales increased 50 percent and Coke sales increased 18 percent (McConnell, Cutter, & McNeil, 1958).

While marketing executives expressed glee at this potential boon to advertising, the public feared that subliminal perception could be used as a means of totalitarian mind control. But psychologists pointed out that the uncontrolled conditions of the study made it impossible to determine the actual reason for the increase in sales. Perhaps sales increased because better movies,

"Good morning, beheaded—uh, I mean beloved."

hotter weather, or more appealing counter displays attracted more customers.

More recently, citizens have expressed concerns about the alleged subliminal messages in rock music recordings, such as Led Zeppelin's "Stairway to Heaven," that supposedly can be heard when the recording is played backwards. Despite the absence of evidence that such messages exist, fear that they might cause crime, satanism, and sexual promiscuity led California and other states to pass laws requiring warnings on recordings that contained subliminal messages. Yet, even if recordings (or movies) contain subliminal messages, there is no evidence that listeners will *obey* them like zombies any more than they will obey messages of which they are aware (Vokey & Read, 1985).

Perception without Awareness

Though there is little evidence that we can be influenced by subliminal perception, there is substantial evidence that we can be influenced by stimuli that are above the absolute threshold but to which we are not attending. The existence of such **perception without awareness** led some psychologists at the turn of the century to assume that suggestions given to people while they sleep might help children study harder or adults quit smoking (Jones, 1900). But subsequent research failed to support such sleep learning (or *hypnopedia*). Any learning that does take place occurs during brief awakenings (Aarons, 1976). So, if you studied for your next psychology exam by playing a tape of class lectures while you were asleep, you would be more likely to disrupt your sleep than to learn significant amounts of material.

But research on attention, the aspect of consciousness that William James called selectivity, has demonstrated the existence of perception without awareness. Consider research on dichotic listening in which the subject, wearing headphones, repeats—or "shadows"—a message being presented to one ear, while another message is being presented to the other ear (figure 5.9). By shadowing one message, the subject is prevented from attending to the other message. Yet, though the subject cannot recall the unattended message, he or she may recall certain qualities of it, such as whether it was spoken

Perception without Awareness The unconscious perception of stimuli that normally exceed the absolute threshold but fall outside our focus of attention.

FIGURE 5.9
Dichotic Listening In studies of dichotic listening, the subject repeats a message presented to one ear while a different message is presented to the other ear.

by a male voice or by a female voice. This demonstrates that our brains process incoming stimuli of which we are unaware (Cherry, 1953).

Evidence of this also comes from studies of people with brain damage, as in cases of prosopagnosia. As you may recall from chapter 3, *prosopagnosia* is characterized by the inability to recognize familiar faces. In one study, two women with prosopagnosia were shown photographs of strangers, friends, and relatives while their galvanic skin response (a measure of arousal) was being recorded. Though the women were unable to name their friends and relatives from the photographs, they gave larger galvanic skin responses to those photographs than to the photographs of strangers. This indicates that intact pathways in the women's brains had distinguished between the faces without the women's conscious awareness (Tranel & Damasio, 1985).

Of course "awareness" is often not an all-or-none phenomenon. There is a continuum between controlled processing and automatic processing of information (Schneider & Shiffrin, 1977). At one extreme, when we focus our attention on one thing, we use **controlled processing,** which involves conscious awareness and mental effort and interferes with the performance of other activities. At the other extreme, when we do one thing while focusing our attention on another, we use **automatic processing,** which does not require conscious awareness and mental effort and does not interfere with the performance of other activities. As we practice a task we need to devote less and less attention to it because we move from controlled processing to automatic processing (Kihlstrom, 1987).

Think back to when you learned to write in cursive. You depended on controlled processing, which required you to focus your complete attention on forming each letter. Today, after years of practice in writing, you make use of automatic processing. This enables you to write notes in class while focusing your attention on the teacher's words rather than on the movements of your pen. The transition from conscious, controlled processing to unconscious, automatic processing holds for numerous behaviors (figure 5.10). Even Michael Jordan had to use controlled processing when he learned to play basketball, focusing his attention on the basketball and little else. Today, he relies on automatic processing, because dribbling no longer requires his attention. Thus, controlled processing limits our attention to one thing. In contrast, automatic processing enables us to perform separate actions simultaneously without our awareness of certain ones.

Controlled Processing
Information processing that involves conscious awareness and mental effort, and that interferes with the performance of other ongoing activities.

Automatic Processing
Information processing that does not require conscious awareness and mental effort, and that does not interfere with the performance of other ongoing activities.

FIGURE 5.10
Controlled Processing and Automatic Processing When we learn a new task, we depend on controlled processing, which makes us focus our attention on that task. With experience we depend less on controlled processing and more on automatic processing. Eventually, we may be able to perform the task while focusing our attention on other tasks.

SUMMARY

THE NATURE OF CONSCIOUSNESS

Consciousness is the awareness of one's own mental activity. William James noted that consciousness is personal, selective, continuous, and changing. Consciousness permits us to manipulate mental representations of the world, as in daydreaming. We daydream to rehearse courses of action, to maintain mental arousal, to solve problems, and to experience pleasure.

SLEEP AND DREAMS

The sleep-wake cycle follows a circadian rhythm. The pineal gland, which responds to changes in light, plays a role in the regulation of circadian rhythms. The depth of sleep is defined by characteristic brain-wave patterns. REM sleep is associated with dreaming. Our nightly sleep duration and the percentage of time we spend in REM sleep decrease across the life span. The functions of sleep are still unclear. One major theory views sleep as restorative. A second major theory views it as adaptive inactivity, either because it protects us from danger when we are most vulnerable or because it conserves energy. The major sleep disorders include insomnia, sleep apnea, and narcolepsy.

The most dramatic aspect of sleep is the dream. Though we may fail to recall our dreams, everyone dreams. Most dreams deal with familiar people and situations. While REM sleep may be disturbed by nightmares, NREM sleep may be disturbed by night terrors. In some cases we may incorporate stimuli in the immediate environment into our dreams. The major theories of dreaming view it as wish fulfillment, as problem solving, or as a by-product of spontaneous brain activity.

HYPNOSIS

Hypnosis is a state in which one person responds to suggestions by another person for alterations in perception, thinking, and behavior. Hypnosis had its origin in mesmerism, a technique promoted by Anton Mesmer to restore the balance of what he called animal magnetism. Hypnotic induction aims at creating a relaxed, passive, highly focused state of mind. Hypnosis is useful in treating pain. While hypnosis may enhance memory, it may also make subjects more confident in inaccurate memories. Under certain conditions, hypnotized people—like nonhypnotized people—may obey suggestions to perform dangerous acts. The effects of stage hypnosis may have as much to do with the theatrical atmosphere as with being hypnotized. Researchers argue whether hypnosis is an altered state of consciousness or merely role playing. Ernest Hilgard has put forth the concept of the "hidden observer" to support his neodissociation theory of hypnosis as an altered state.

MEDITATION

Meditation is a procedure that uses mental exercises to achieve a highly focused state of consciousness. Transcendental meditation and the relaxation response are popular forms of meditation aimed at inducing mental and physical relaxation. As in the case of hypnosis, researchers argue whether meditation produces a unique physiological state.

PSYCHOACTIVE DRUGS

Psychoactive drugs induce changes in mood, thinking, perception, and behavior by affecting neuronal activity. The depressant drugs reduce arousal by inhibiting activity in the central nervous system. The main depressants include alcohol, barbiturates, inhalants, and opiates. The stimulant drugs, which increase arousal, include caffeine, nicotine, amphetamines, and cocaine. The hallucinogens induce extreme alterations in consciousness, including hallucinations, a sense of timelessness, and feelings of depersonalization. The main hallucinogens include psilocybin, mescaline, LSD, and *cannabis sativa* (marijuana and hashish).

THINKING ABOUT PSYCHOLOGY: ARE WE AFFECTED BY UNCONSCIOUS INFLUENCES?

The answer to this question depends on the concept of "unconscious" that is being used. The Freudian unconscious refers to a portion of the mind containing thoughts and feelings that influence us without our awareness. Because the Freudian unconscious deals with unobservable phenomena it has proven difficult to study scientifically. Subliminal perception is the unconscious perception of stimuli that are too weak to exceed the absolute threshold for detection. Research has shown that we can be influenced by subliminal stimuli but has not supported fears that people might obey subliminal messages like zombies. And perception without awareness is the unconscious perception of stimuli that do exceed the absolute threshold but that fall outside our focus of attention. We experience perception without awareness whenever we use automatic, rather than controlled, processing of information.

IMPORTANT CONCEPTS

Activation-synthesis theory 159
Age regression 164
Alcohol 166
Amphetamines 170
Attention 147
Automatic processing 177
Barbiturates 168
Caffeine 169
Cannabis sativa 172
Circadian rhythms 148
Cocaine 170
Conscious 173
Consciousness 146
Controlled processing 177
Daydreaming 147
Depressants 166
Dissociation 163

Dream 156
Hallucinogens 171
Hidden observer 164
Hypermnesia 162
Hypnosis 159
Inhalants 168
Insomnia 155
Latent content 158
LSD 171
Manifest content 158
Meditation 165
Narcolepsy 156
Neodissociation theory 163
Nicotine 170
Nightmare 157
Night terror 157

NREM sleep 151
Opiates 168
Perception without awareness 175
Phase advance 149
Phase delay 149
Pineal gland 149
Posthypnotic suggestions 162
Preconscious 173
Psychoactive drugs 166
Relaxation response 165
REM sleep 151
Sleep apnea 156
Stimulants 169
Subliminal perception 174
Transcendental meditation (TM) 165
Unconscious 173

IMPORTANT PEOPLE

Theodore Barber 164
Herbert Benson 165
Mary Whiton Calkins 156
Rosalind Cartwright 158
Sigmund Freud 158, 171, 173
Calvin Hall 156

Ernest Hilgard 163
J. Allan Hobson and
    Robert McCarley 159
David Holmes 165
William James 146, 164, 168

Anton Mesmer 159
Martin Orne 162, 164
Jerome Singer 147
Nicholas Spanos 164
Wilse Webb 154

RECOMMENDED READINGS

For More on All Aspects of Consciousness:

Wallace, B., & Fisher, L. E. (1983). *Consciousness and behavior.* Newton, MA: Allyn & Bacon.
A readable discussion of each of the main topics of interest to consciousness researchers.

For More on the Nature of Consciousness:

Hilgard, E. (1980). Consciousness in contemporary psychology. *Annual Review of Psychology, 31,* 1–26.
A leading researcher traces changing attitudes toward the study of consciousness during the past century.

Jaynes, J. (1976). *The origin of consciousness in the breakdown of the bicameral mind.* Boston: Houghton Mifflin.
A controversial book that presents evidence to support the author's belief that the conscious mind did not appear until about 3,000 years ago, implying, among other things, that Homer wrote the *Iliad* and the *Odyssey* while unconscious.

For More on Sleep and Dreams:

Cartwright, R. D. (1978). *A primer on sleep and dreaming.* Reading, MA: Addison-Wesley.
Still one of the best available introductions to sleep and dreams.

Coleman, R. M. (1986). *Wide awake at 3:00 A.M.: By choice or by chance?* New York: W.H. Freeman.
An interesting overview of sleep and biological rhythms, emphasizing the application of research findings to daily life.

For More on Hypnosis:

Bowers, K. S. (1983). *Hypnosis for the seriously curious.* New York: Norton.
An introduction to hypnosis, including hypnotic induction, hypnotic effects, and the nature of hypnosis.

Ellenberger, H. F. (1970). *The discovery of the unconscious.* New York: Basic Books.
A fascinating presentation of the history of hypnosis and its implications for the nature of consciousness.

For More on Meditation:

Benson, H., & Proctor, W. (1984). *Beyond the relaxation response.* New York: Times Books.
A discussion of meditation and the physical and psychological benefits of the "relaxation response."

For More on Psychoactive Drugs:

Ray, O. S., & Ksir, C. (1987). *Drugs, society, and human behavior* (4th ed.). St. Louis: Mosby.
A highly readable book describing the physiological and psychological effects of psychoactive drugs, as well as the historical and cultural context of drug use and abuse.

For More on Unconscious Influences:

Bowers, K. S., & Meichenbaum, D. (Eds.). (1984). *The unconscious reconsidered.* New York: Wiley.
A collection of authoritative articles on a variety of topics related to the unconscious mind.

Whyte, L. L. (1978). *The unconsciousness before Freud.* New York: St. Martins Press.
A look at historical views of the unconscious before Freud.

CHAPTER
6

LEARNING

Chapter Opening Art: Henry O. Tanner. *The Banjo Lesson.* 1993.

[handwritten: Def of]

Learning A relatively permanent change in knowledge or behavior as a result of experience.

[handwritten margin notes: reflex, instinct, maturation]

[handwritten margin note: Know 3 kinds of learning]

Tying your shoes. Writing in script. Riding a bicycle. Performing mental arithmetic. Going out on a date. At one time each of these activities seemed difficult—or even impossible—to you. Yet, today you probably take each of them for granted. This indicates the importance of **learning,** which is a relatively permanent change in knowledge or behavior as a result of experience. What you learn is *relatively* permanent because it can be changed by future learning. Because learning influences every aspect of our lives, almost all of the chapters in this text deal with learning in one way or another. You will find that aspects of your life as varied as your motivation to achieve academic success (chapter 10), your adoption of a particular gender role (chapter 12), and your political attitudes (chapter 17) depend on learning.

Do not confuse learning with reflexes, instincts, or maturation. A *reflex* is an inborn response to a specific stimulus, such as withdrawing your hand after touching a hot pot (see chapter 3). An *instinct* is an inborn complex behavior found in members of a species, such as nest building in birds (see chapter 10). And *maturation* is a process by which a behavior appears in the natural course of individual development, such as walking in human infants (see chapter 12).

Psychologists began the scientific study of learning in the late nineteenth century. In keeping with Charles Darwin's theory of evolution, they viewed learning as a means of adapting to the environment. Because Darwin emphasized the continuity between animals and human beings, psychologists began studying learning in animals, hoping to identify principles they might also apply to human learning. As you will read, many of the principles of learning do, indeed, apply to both animals and people.

Psychologists have identified three kinds of learning. The first, *classical conditioning,* considers the learning of associations between stimuli. The second, *operant conditioning,* considers the learning of associations between behaviors and their consequences. And the third, *cognitive learning,* considers learning through the mental manipulation of information.

CLASSICAL CONDITIONING *[handwritten: involves making associations between stimuli]*

Classical conditioning grew out of a tradition that can be traced back to Aristotle, who believed that learning depended on *contiguity*—the occurrence of events close together in time and space (such as lightning and thunder). British philosophers of the seventeenth and eighteenth centuries, most notably John Locke and David Hume, became known as *associationists* because they agreed with Aristotle's view that learning depends on associating contiguous events with one another.

In the early twentieth century, the research of Ivan Pavlov (1849–1936) stimulated worldwide scientific interest in the study of associative learning. Pavlov, a Russian physiologist, won a Nobel Prize in 1904 for his research on digestion in dogs. Because Pavlov was a giant among Russian scientists, he was offered extra food rations during the Russian Revolution. But, being feisty and dedicated to maintaining his research program, he refused to accept any unless he also received food for his dogs (Bolles, 1979).

In his research on digestion, Pavlov would place meat powder on a dog's tongue, stimulating reflexive salivation. He collected the saliva from a tube inserted into one of the dog's salivary glands (figure 6.1). To his surprise, he found that after repeated presentations of the meat powder, the dog would salivate in response to stimuli associated with the meat powder. A dog would salivate to the sight of its food dish, the sight of the laboratory assistant who brought the food, or the sound of the assistant's footsteps. At first Pavlov was

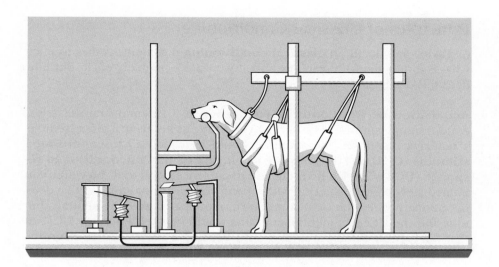

FIGURE 6.1
Pavlov's Research Apparatus
In studying the digestive process, Ivan Pavlov would present a dog with meat powder and collect saliva through a tube inserted into one of the dog's salivary glands. The amount of salivation was recorded by having a stylus write on a rotating drum. Pavlov found that dogs would salivate to stimuli associated with the presentation of food, such as the mere sight of the laboratory assistant who brought the food.

distressed by this phenomenon, which he called "conditional responses," because he could no longer control the onset of salivation by his dogs. But he eventually became so intrigued by the phenomenon that he devoted the rest of his career to studying it.

At the annual meeting of the American Psychological Association in 1904, the same year that Pavlov received his Nobel Prize, E. B. Twitmyer, an American graduate student at the University of Pennsylvania, reported the results of a study on the "knee jerk" reflex. As you may know from your last physical examination, when a physician strikes you with a rubber hammer just below your bent knee, your lower leg will reflexively extend. In his study, Twitmyer rang a bell as a warning that the hammer was about to strike. After repeated trials in which the sound of the bell preceded the hammer strike, the sound of the bell itself caused extension of the lower leg. But, to his disappointment, Twitmyer's presentation was met with indifference. In fact, William James, who chaired Twitmyer's session, was so bored (or so hungry) that he adjourned the session for lunch—without providing the customary opportunity for discussion of Twitmyer's findings (Coon, 1982).

American psychologists did not begin to take note of this kind of learning until John B. Watson described Pavlov's research in his presidential address at the annual meeting of the American Psychological Association in 1914. Because of Pavlov's extensive early research on "conditional responses," the phenomenon earned the name of *classical conditioning*.

Ivan Pavlov (1849–1936)
Pavlov is shown in his laboratory flanked by his assistants and one of his dogs.

Principles of Classical Conditioning

Classical Conditioning A form of learning in which a neutral stimulus comes to elicit a response after being associated with a stimulus that already elicits that response.

Unconditioned Stimulus (UCS) In classical conditioning, a stimulus that automatically elicits a particular "unconditioned" response.

Unconditioned Response (UCR) In classical conditioning, an unlearned, automatic response to a particular "unconditioned" stimulus.

Conditioned Stimulus (CS) In classical conditioning, a neutral stimulus that comes to elicit a particular "conditioned" response after being paired with a particular "unconditioned" stimulus that already elicits that response.

Conditioned Response (CR) In classical conditioning, the learned response given to a particular "conditioned" stimulus.

As Pavlov first noted, in **classical conditioning** a stimulus comes to elicit (that is, bring about) a response that it would not normally elicit. But how does this occur?

Acquisition of the Conditioned Response To demonstrate classical conditioning, you would first have to identify a stimulus that already elicits a reflexive response. The stimulus would be called an **unconditioned stimulus** (**UCS**) and the response would be called an **unconditioned response** (**UCR**). You would then have to present several trials on which you immediately precede the UCS with a *neutral stimulus*—a stimulus that does not normally elicit the UCR. After one or more pairings of the neutral stimulus and the UCS, the neutral stimulus would by itself elicit the UCR. At that point the neutral stimulus would become a **conditioned stimulus** (**CS**) and the response to it would be called a **conditioned response** (**CR**). Pavlov used the UCS of meat powder to elicit the UCR of salivation (figure 6.2). He then used a tone as the neutral stimulus. After several trials on which the tone preceded the meat powder, the tone itself became a CS that elicited the CR of salivation.

Of course, a tone is but one of many potential conditioned stimuli. Among the most important conditioned stimuli are words. In a clever classroom demonstration, a college professor used the word "Pavlov" as a neutral stimulus (Cogan & Cogan, 1984). Student subjects said "Pavlov" just before lemonade powder was placed on their tongues. The UCS of lemonade powder naturally elicited the UCR of salivation. After repeated pairings of "Pavlov" and the lemonade powder, "Pavlov" became a CS that elicited the CR of salivation. Classical conditioning may account, in part, for the power of words to elicit emotional responses. Perhaps the mere mention of the name of someone with whom you have a romantic relationship makes your heart "flutter."

What factors influence classical conditioning? In general, the greater the intensity of the UCS and the greater the number of pairings of the CS and the UCS, the greater will be the strength of conditioning. The time interval between the CS and the UCS also affects acquisition of the CR. In *delayed conditioning,* the CS is presented first and remains at least until the onset of the

FIGURE 6.2
Classical Conditioning Before conditioning, the unconditioned stimulus of meat elicits the unconditioned response of salivation and the neutral stimulus of a tone does not elicit salivation. During conditioning, the tone is repeatedly presented before the meat (UCS), which continues to elicit salivation (UCR). After conditioning, the tone becomes a conditioned stimulus (CS) that elicits salivation as a conditioned response (CR).

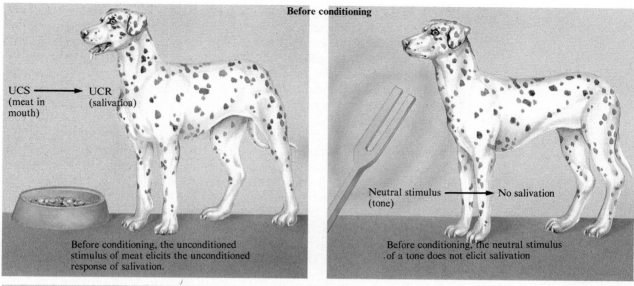

Before conditioning

UCS ⟶ UCR
(meat in   (salivation)
mouth)

Before conditioning, the unconditioned
stimulus of meat elicits the unconditioned
response of salivation.

Neutral stimulus ⟶ No salivation
(tone)

Before conditioning, the neutral stimulus
of a tone does not elicit salivation

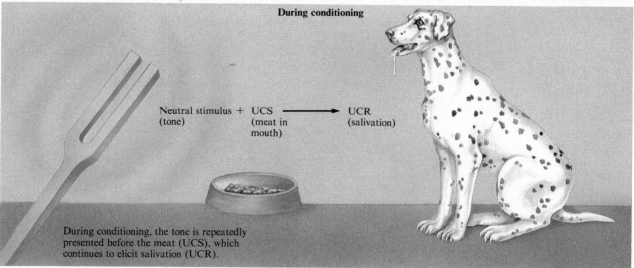

During conditioning

Neutral stimulus + UCS ⟶ UCR
(tone)   (meat in   (salivation)
                mouth)

During conditioning, the tone is repeatedly
presented before the meat (UCS), which
continues to elicit salivation (UCR).

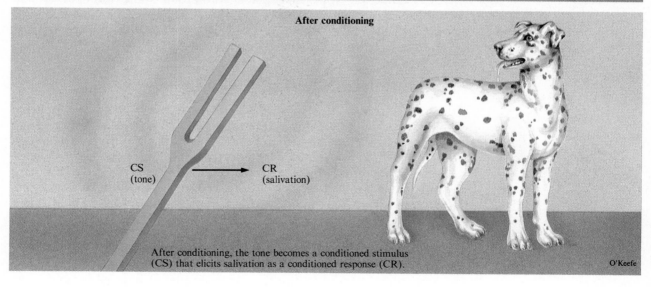

After conditioning

CS ⟶ CR
(tone)   (salivation)

After conditioning, the tone becomes a conditioned stimulus
(CS) that elicits salivation as a conditioned response (CR).

O'Keefe

UCS. In *trace conditioning*, the CS is presented first and ends before the onset of the UCS. In *simultaneous conditioning*, the CS and UCS begin and end together. And in *backward conditioning*, the onset of the UCS *precedes* the onset of the CS. In general, delayed conditioning produces strong conditioning, trace conditioning produces moderately strong conditioning, and simultaneous conditioning produces weak conditioning. Backward conditioning rarely produces any conditioning at all, though there have been some reports of its success (Spetch, Wilkie, & Pinel, 1981).

Stimulus Generalization and Stimulus Discrimination In classical conditioning, the CR may occur in response to stimuli that are similar to the CS. This is called **stimulus generalization.** So, a dog conditioned to salivate to a dinner bell (a CS) might also salivate to a doorbell, a telephone bell, or an ice-cream truck bell. But the dog might eventually salivate only in response to the dinner bell. This would be an instance of **stimulus discrimination,** in which the dog responds to the CS but not to stimuli that are similar to the CS. This would occur if the dog learns that the other bells are not followed by food.

Extinction and Spontaneous Recovery Will the dog forever salivate in response to the dinner bell? Not necessarily. If a CS is repeatedly presented without presenting the UCS, the CR will diminish and eventually stop occurring. This process is called **extinction.** A dog that has learned to salivate to a dinner bell (the CS) would eventually stop doing so unless presentations of the dinner bell were periodically followed by presentations of food (the UCS).

But extinction only inhibits the CR, it does not eliminate it. In fact, after a CR has been subjected to extinction it may reappear later if the CS is reintroduced. For example, suppose that you produced extinction of the CR of salivation by no longer presenting the dog with food after ringing the dinner bell. If you rang the dinner bell a few days later, the dog would again respond by salivating.

This process, by which a CR that has been subjected to extinction will again be elicited by a CS, is called **spontaneous recovery.** In spontaneous recovery, however, the CR is weaker and subject to faster extinction than it was prior to extinction. Thus, after spontaneous recovery, the dog's salivation to the dinner bell would be weaker and subject to faster extinction than it was originally. Figure 6.3 illustrates the acquisition, extinction, and spontaneous recovery of a classically conditioned response.

Applications of Classical Conditioning

In his 1932 novel *Brave New World,* Aldous Huxley warned of a future in which classical conditioning would be used to mold people into narrow social roles. In the novel, classical conditioning is used to make children who have been assigned to become workers repulsed by any interests other than work. This is accomplished by giving them electric shocks whenever they reach for forbidden objects such as books or flowers. Despite such fears of the diabolical use of classical conditioning, it has, in reality, been applied in less ominous ways.

Advertising Products Advertisers know that classical conditioning has the power to make us associate their products with appealing stimuli, such as good times, playful puppies, or sexually attractive people. As you may recall from chapter 1, John B. Watson, after leaving psychology for the field of advertising, became one of the first marketing experts to make sex appeal

---

Stimulus Generalization In classical conditioning, a conditioned response to stimuli that are similar to the conditioned stimulus.

Stimulus Discrimination In classical conditioning, a conditioned response to the conditioned stimulus but not to stimuli similar to it.

Extinction In classical conditioning, the gradual disappearance of the conditioned response when the conditioned stimulus is repeatedly presented without being paired with the unconditioned stimulus.

Spontaneous Recovery In classical conditioning, the reappearance after a period of time of a conditioned response that has been subjected to extinction.

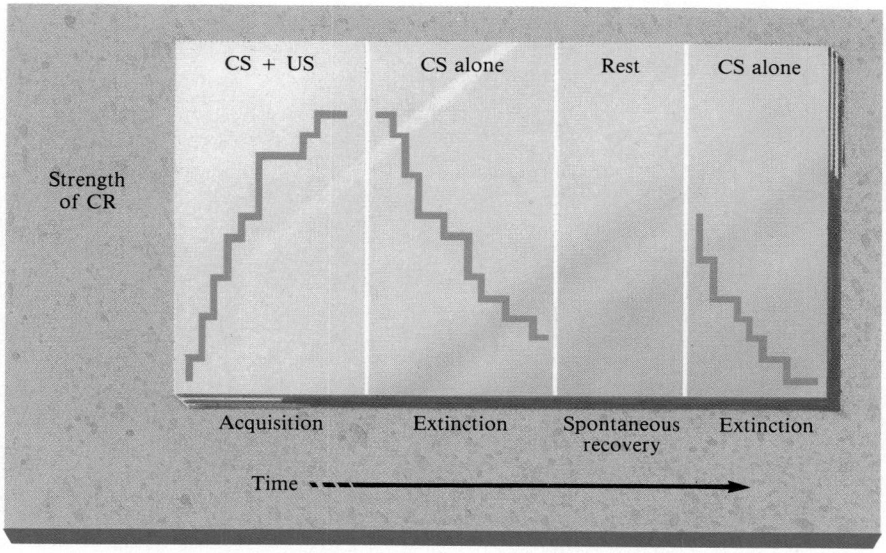
CS + US
CS alone
Rest
CS alone
Strength of CR
Acquisition
Extinction
Spontaneous recovery
Extinction
Time

FIGURE 6.3
Processes in Classical Conditioning In classical conditioning, the pairing of the CS and the UCS leads to acquisition of the CR. When the CS is then presented without the UCS, the CR gradually disappears. After extinction, following a rest period, spontaneous recovery of the CR occurs. But extinction occurs again, even more rapidly than the first time.

a formal aspect of advertising. Today, automobile manufacturers encourage men to buy their automobiles by showing beautiful women in, on, or around the automobiles. Given that automobiles normally do not arouse men sexually, manufacturers hope that the women will elicit mild sexual arousal, which the men will associate with the automobiles, thereby making the automobiles more appealing.

But what evidence is there that sex appeal can be transferred to neutral objects, such as automobiles? Some evidence comes from experiments on animals. In one experiment, male rats were placed in small plastic tubs and were separated by a wire fence from sexually receptive female rats. The female rats (the UCS) induced sexual excitement (the UCR) in the male rats. Eventually, being in the tubs (the CS) came to induce sexual excitement (the CR) in the male rats. As a result, the rats engaged in sex more quickly when placed in the tubs and given access to females (Zamble, Mitchell, & Findlay, 1986). This study also provides support for classical conditioning as a possible cause of *fetishism*, in which people are sexually aroused by unusual objects, such as shoes, nylons, or leather goods. The fetishist may have experienced sexual arousal in the presence of the objects, which eventually come to elicit sexual arousal by themselves. So, in a sense, advertisers who pair their products with sexual stimuli are inducing mild fetishes in responsive people.

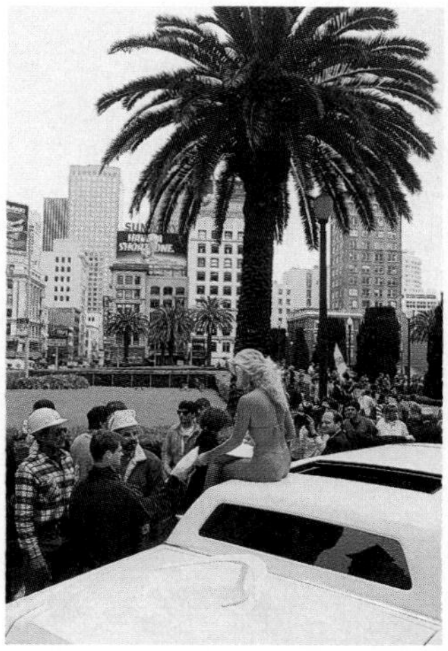

Classical Conditioning and Advertising Advertisers know that they can make products more appealing to consumers by pairing them with sexual stimuli.

Explaining Phobias The role of classical conditioning in fetishism shows its importance in the development of psychological disorders. Almost three hundred years ago, John Locke (1690/1924) observed that children who had been punished in school for misbehaving became fearful of their books and other stimuli associated with school. Today we would say that these children had been classically conditioned to develop school phobias. A *phobia* is an unrealistic or exaggerated fear.

The most famous study of a classically conditioned phobia was conducted by John B. Watson and his graduate student Rosalie Rayner (Watson & Rayner, 1920). Their subject was an eleven-month-old boy they called "Little Albert," who enjoyed playing with animals, including tame white rats. Just as Little Albert would touch a white rat, Watson would make a loud noise behind his head by banging a steel bar with a hammer. Little Albert responded to the noise (the UCS) with fear (the UCR), jumping violently, falling forward, and

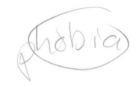

Little Albert John B. Watson and Rosalie Rayner trained Little Albert to fear white rats. Through stimulus generalization, he also came to fear similar-looking objects.

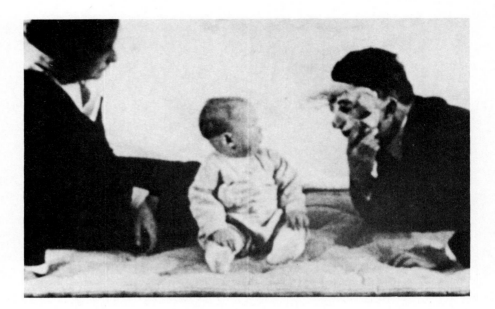

burying his face in the mattress on which he sat. After seven pairings of the rat and the noise, Little Albert responded to the rat (the CS) with fear (the CR) by crying and showing distress in response to it.

When tested several days later, Little Albert also showed stimulus generalization. He responded fearfully to other furlike objects, including a dog, a rabbit, cotton wool, Watson's hair, a sealskin coat, and even a Santa Claus mask. Little Albert moved away before Watson had a chance to try to remove his phobia. As you might suspect from your reading in chapter 2, current ethical standards of psychological research would prevent the experimental induction of phobias in children. Though this study was so haphazardly done that it is not a convincing demonstration of a classically conditioned phobia (Harris, 1979), it led to sounder research studies demonstrating that phobias are, indeed, sometimes learned through classical conditioning (see chapter 14). Chapter 15 describes how classical conditioning can also be used to *rid* people of their phobias.

Explaining Drug Dependence Classical conditioning may even explain dependence on psychoactive drugs. When a psychoactive drug (the UCS), such as heroin, is administered it produces characteristic physiological effects (the UCR). With continued use, higher and higher doses of the drug are required to produce the same physiological effects. This is known as *tolerance.* Tolerance may be, in part, the product of classical conditioning (Baker & Tiffany, 1985). Stimuli associated with the administration of certain drugs act as conditioned stimuli that elicit conditioned physiological responses *opposite* to those produced by the drug. For example, though heroin induces respiratory depression, stimuli associated with its administration induce respiratory excitation. Why would stimuli associated with drug taking elicit effects opposite to those of the drug itself? Perhaps it is an adaptive, compensatory process that prevents the physiological response to the drug from becoming too extreme.

Consider heroin addiction. Tolerance to heroin may occur because stimuli associated with its administration, such as hypodermic needles and particular settings, may act as conditioned stimuli to counter the physiological effects produced by heroin. This may explain why heroin addicts sometimes die of respiratory failure after injecting themselves with their normal dose of heroin

in a setting different from that in which they normally administer the drug. By doing so they remove the conditioned stimuli that elicit conditioned physiological responses and normally counter the unconditioned physiological responses elicited by the drug. As a consequence, the unconditioned physiological responses, particularly respiratory depression, may be stronger than usual—in some cases strong enough to cause a fatal reaction (Siegel, Hinson, Krank, & McCully, 1982).

Explaining Taste Aversions Have you ever eaten a meal, developed a stomach virus several hours later, vomited, and later found yourself repulsed by something you had eaten at the meal? If so, you have experienced the phenomenon of a classically conditioned *taste aversion*. In a clever application of this phenomenon, coyotes have been discouraged from eating sheep (Gustavson, Garcia, Hawkins, & Rusiniak, 1974). Lithium chloride, a drug that causes gastrointestinal distress, is first inserted into sheep carcasses. If a coyote eats this tainted meat, it becomes dizzy and nauseated, associates these feelings with eating sheep, and, consequently, may refrain from killing them. This technique may eventually provide a happy compromise between ranchers who want to kill coyotes and conservationists who want to save them. Unfortunately, in some cases, it may merely inhibit predators from eating, rather than from killing, their prey (Timberlake & Melcer, 1988).

John Garcia "Immediate reinforcement is simply not necessary for learning when illness is the reinforcer."

The classical conditioning of taste aversions is known as the **Garcia effect,** after John Garcia, the researcher who first demonstrated it. At first, psychologists were shocked by this apparent violation of contiguity in classical conditioning. How could the taste of food be associated with nausea occurring hours later? Because Garcia's findings violated the principle of contiguity, editors of research journals refused to publish his studies, claiming that his findings were impossible (Garcia, 1981). Through the persistence of Garcia and his colleagues, who replicated his findings, the Garcia effect is now an accepted psychological phenomenon. This should remind you that scientists should maintain an attitude of skepticism, not cynicism. Of course, being human beings, psychologists, like all scientists, may succumb to their own biases in evaluating findings that contradict their cherished beliefs.

Garcia Effect A conditioned taste aversion produced by pairing a taste with gastrointestinal distress.

Had Garcia been less persistent, we may have been denied a potentially useful tool for combating the nausea-induced loss of appetite experienced by people undergoing cancer chemotherapy. Their loss of appetite makes them eat less and lose weight, weakening them and impairing their ability to fight the disease. Ilene Bernstein (1978) has conducted a program of research on

FIGURE 6.4
Chemotherapy and Conditioned Taste Aversion
Ilene Bernstein (1978) found that children undergoing cancer chemotherapy will develop conditioned taste aversions to a novel flavor of ice cream eaten on the same days that they undergo treatment. Because the nausea induced by the therapy becomes associated with the novel flavor, the children may develop an aversion to the flavor. As the graph shows, when later given the choice of eating Mapletoff or playing a game, children who had eaten Mapletoff on the days when they received therapy were less likely to choose Mapletoff than were children who never ate it or who ate it on days when they did not receive therapy.

From Ilene L. Bernstein, "Learned Taste Aversions in Children Receiving Chemotherapy" in *Science*, Vol. 200:1302–03, 16 June 1978. Copyright 1978 by the AAAS. Reprinted by permission of the author and the publisher.

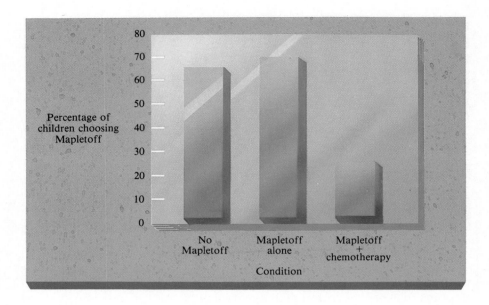

Ilene Bernstein "The demonstration of taste aversions in children receiving chemotherapy treatments may prove to be of importance to physicians who administer treatments which induce nausea and vomiting."

taste aversion in chemotherapy patients. In one study, she assigned children receiving chemotherapy into three groups. One group ate "Mapletoff" ice cream, which has a novel maple-walnut flavor, before each chemotherapy session. The second group ate Mapletoff on days when they did not receive chemotherapy. And the third group never ate Mapletoff. Two to four weeks later the children were given the choice of eating Mapletoff or playing a game.

The results showed that 67 percent of the children who never ate Mapletoff and 73 percent of the children who ate it only on days they did not receive chemotherapy chose Mapletoff (figure 6.4). In contrast, only 21 percent of the children who ate Mapletoff on days they received chemotherapy chose Mapletoff. Based on these findings (and on findings that taste aversion is stronger in response to novel-tasting foods than to familiar-tasting foods), Bernstein has suggested that cancer patients be given a novel-tasting food before receiving chemotherapy. This might lead them to experience taste aversion only in response to the novel food instead of to familiar foods, thereby helping them maintain their appetite for familiar foods.

Biological Constraints on Classical Conditioning

According to Ivan Pavlov (1928, p. 88), "Every imaginable phenomena of the outer world affecting a specific receptive surface of the body may be converted into a conditioned stimulus." Until the past two decades learning theorists agreed with Pavlov's proclamation. They assumed that any stimulus paired with an unconditioned stimulus could become a conditioned stimulus. But we now know that there are inherited biological constraints on the ease with which particular stimuli can be associated with particular responses. This was demonstrated in an early study of classically conditioned taste aversion in which two groups of rats were presented with a CS consisting of three components: saccharin-flavored water, a light, and a clicking sound (Garcia & Koelling, 1966). For one group the CS was followed by a strong electric shock (the US) that induced pain (the UR). For another group the CS was followed by X rays (the US) that induced nausea and dizziness (the UR).

The results showed that the rats that had been hurt by the electric shock developed an aversion to the light and the clicking sound but not to the saccharin-flavored water. In contrast, the rats that had been made to feel ill developed an aversion to the saccharin-flavored water but not to the light and the clicking sound. This indicates that rats have an inborn tendency to associate nausea and dizziness with tastes, but not with sights and sounds, and to associate pain with sights and sounds, but not with tastes. Thus, all stimuli and responses are not equally associable.

OPERANT CONDITIONING

In the late 1890s, while Russian physiologists were studying the relationship between stimuli and responses, an American named Edward Thorndike (1874–1949) was studying the relationship between actions and their consequences. While pursuing a doctoral degree at Harvard University, Thorndike studied learning in chicks by rewarding them with food for successfully negotiating a maze constructed of books. After his landlady objected to Thorndike's raising the chicks in his bedroom, William James, one of his professors, agreed to raise the chicks in his basement—much to the delight of the James children (Thorndike, 1961).

Later, distraught after being rejected by a woman (whom he eventually married), Thorndike left Harvard and completed his studies at Columbia University. While at Columbia he conducted research using cats in so-called puzzle boxes, which were constructed from wooden shipping crates. In a typical puzzle box study, Thorndike (1898) would put a hungry cat in the box and a piece of fish just outside of the box. A sliding latch kept the door to the box closed. The cat could escape by stepping on a pedal that released the latch. At first the cat would perform ineffective actions, such as biting the wooden slats or trying to squeeze between them. Eventually the cat would accidentally perform the correct action, thereby releasing the latch, opening the door, and gaining access to the fish. Thorndike repeated this for several trials and found that as the trials progressed the cat took less and less time to escape, eventually escaping as soon as it was placed in the box.

The results of his puzzle box studies led Thorndike to develop the **law of effect,** which states that a behavior followed by a "satisfying" state of affairs is strengthened and a behavior followed by an "annoying" state of affairs is weakened. In the puzzle box experiments, behaviors that let the cat reach the fish were strengthened and behaviors that kept the cat in the box were weakened. Because Thorndike studied the process by which behaviors are instrumental in bringing about certain consequences, the process became known as **instrumental conditioning.**

Principles of Operant Conditioning

Thorndike's work inspired B. F. Skinner (1904–), perhaps the best-known contemporary psychologist. Skinner calls instrumental conditioning **operant conditioning,** because animals and people learn to "operate" on the environment to produce desired consequences, instead of merely responding reflexively to stimuli. Following in Thorndike's footsteps, Skinner uses boxes, now known as **Skinner boxes,** to study learning in animals. Skinner has devoted his career to studying the different kinds of relationships between behaviors and their consequences, which he calls **behavioral contingencies.** Figure 6.5 summarizes the differences between the behavioral contingencies of *positive reinforcement, negative reinforcement, extinction,* and *punishment.*

Edward Thorndike (1874–1949) "When a certain connection [between a behavior and a consequence] has been followed by a satisfier the connection lasts longer than it does when it has been followed by an annoyer."

Law of Effect Edward Thorndike's principle that a behavior followed by a satisfying state of affairs is strengthened and a behavior followed by an annoying state of affairs is weakened.

Instrumental Conditioning A form of learning in which a behavior becomes more or less probable, depending on its consequences.

Operant Conditioning B. F. Skinner's term for instrumental conditioning.

Skinner Box An enclosure containing a bar or key that can be pressed to obtain food or water, which is used to study operant conditioning in rats, pigeons, or other small animals.

Behavioral Contingencies Relationships between behaviors and their consequences, such as positive reinforcement, negative reinforcement, extinction, and punishment.

Contingency	Behavioral consequence	Probability of behavior	Example
Positive reinforcement	Brings about something desirable	Increases	You study for an exam and receive an A, which makes you more likely to study in the future.
Negative reinforcement	Removes something undesirable	Increases	You go to the dentist to have a cavity filled. This eliminates your toothache, which makes you more likely to visit the dentist in the future when you have a toothache.
Extinction	Fails to bring about something desirable	Decreases	You say hello to a person who repeatedly fails to greet you in return. This leads you to stop saying hello.
Punishment	Brings about something undesirable	Decreases	You overeat at a party and suffer from a severe upset stomach. In the future you become less likely to overeat.

FIGURE 6.5
Behavioral Contingencies

Positive Reinforcement Two centuries ago, while on a fort-building expedition, Benjamin Franklin increased the likelihood of attendance at daily prayer meetings by withholding his men's rations of rum until they had prayed (Knapp & Shodahl, 1974). This showed his appreciation of the power of *reinforcement*. A *reinforcer* is a consequence of a behavior that *increases* the likelihood that the behavior will occur again. In **positive reinforcement** a behavior (for example, praying) that is followed by the *presentation* of a desirable stimulus (for example, rum) becomes more likely to occur in the future. Skinner calls the desirable stimulus a *positive reinforcer.* You are certainly aware of the effect of positive reinforcement in your own life. For example, if you find that studying for exams earns you high grades, you will be more likely to study for exams in the future.

Positive reinforcement is strengthened by increasing the magnitude of the reinforcer, decreasing the interval between the behavior and the reinforcer,

Positive Reinforcement In operant conditioning, an increase in the probability of a behavior that is followed by a desirable stimulus.

Primary Reinforcer In operant conditioning, an unlearned reinforcer, which satisfies a biological need such as air, food, or water.

and increasing the number of pairings of the behavior and the reinforcer. Keep in mind that something that is reinforcing to one person may not be to another. Jello might be a positive reinforcer to one person, yet repugnant to another.

There are two classes of positive reinforcers. A **primary reinforcer** is biological and unlearned, such as air, food, water, and sleep. In contrast, a **secondary reinforcer** (also known as a *conditioned reinforcer*) is learned and becomes reinforcing by being associated with a primary reinforcer through the process of classical conditioning. This was demonstrated in a classic study in which chimpanzees could obtain grapes by inserting tokens into a vending machine (Wolfe, 1936). After using tokens to obtain treats from the "chimp-o-mat," the chimps would steal tokens and hoard them. The tokens had become secondary reinforcers. Among the most powerful secondary reinforcers to human beings are praise, money, and success.

Why do behaviors that have been positively reinforced not occur continually? One reason is that behavior is controlled by discriminative stimuli, a process that Skinner calls *stimulus control*. A **discriminative stimulus** informs an individual when a behavior will be likely to be reinforced. You would be silly to dial a telephone number unless you first heard a dial tone, which acts as a discriminative stimulus to signal you that dialing might result in positive reinforcement—reaching the person whom you are calling.

A second reason that behaviors that have been reinforced do not occur continually is the individual's relative degree of *satiation* in regard to the reinforcer. Reinforcement will be more effective when the individual has been deprived of the reinforcer. In contrast, reinforcement will be ineffective when the individual has been satiated by having free access to the reinforcer. So, water will be more reinforcing to a thirsty person and praise will be more reinforcing to a person who is rarely praised.

Shaping and Chaining Positive reinforcement is useful in increasing the likelihood of behaviors that are already in an individual's repertoire. But how can we use positive reinforcement to promote behaviors that rarely or

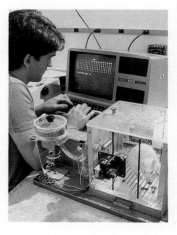

The Skinner Box The computer-controlled stainless steel and plexiglass Skinner box is a far cry from Thorndike's puzzle box. Rats learn to obtain food by pressing a bar and pigeons learn to obtain food by pecking a lighted disc.

Secondary Reinforcer In operant conditioning, a neutral stimulus that becomes reinforcing after being associated with a primary reinforcer.

Discriminative Stimulus In operant conditioning, a stimulus that indicates the likelihood that a particular response will be reinforced.

Source: From B. F. Skinner, "A Case History in Scientific Method" in *American Psychologist*, 11:221–233, 1956.

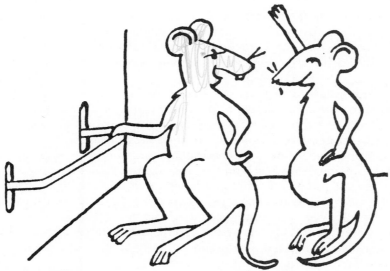

"Boy have I got this guy conditioned! Every time I press the bar down he drops in a piece of food."

never occur? Consider the trained dolphins you have seen jump through hoops held high above the water. How do they learn to perform such a behavior, which is not a part of their natural repertoire? You cannot reinforce a behavior until it occurs. If the trainer waited until the dolphin jumped through a hoop held above the water, he or she might wait forever—dolphins do not naturally jump through hoops held above the water.

Animal trainers rely on a technique called **shaping** to train rats, dolphins, and other animals to perform actions that they would rarely or never perform naturally. In shaping, the individual is reinforced for *successive approximations* of the target behavior and eventually reinforced for the target behavior itself. A dolphin trainer might begin by giving a dolphin a fish for turning toward a hoop held underwater and then, successively, for moving toward the hoop, for coming near the hoop, and for swimming through the hoop. The trainer would then gradually raise the hoop and continue to reward the dolphin for swimming through it. Eventually the trainer would reward the dolphin for swimming through the hoop when it was held partly out of the water, then for jumping through the hoop when it was held slightly above the water, and, finally, for jumping through the hoop when it was held several feet above the water. Figure 6.6 shows that the behavior of animals, such as diving for food, may be shaped by nature, not just by human beings (Galef, 1980).

Shaping is not limited to animals. It is also useful in training people to perform behaviors that are not parts of their behavioral repertoires. Students can even use shaping to influence the behavior of their teachers. In one demonstration a college professor asked her psychology students to shape her behavior during the semester (Chrisler, 1988). They were not to tell her what behavior was being shaped or what positive reinforcers were being used. The students successfully conditioned her to write more often on the blackboard, to increase eye contact with all members of the class, to move about the classroom more frequently, and to give more examples from her own personal life experiences to illustrate concepts. As positive reinforcers, the students used nodding, smiling, eye contact, note taking, and class participation.

What if you wish to teach an individual to perform a complex *series* of behaviors, rather than single behaviors? You might use **chaining,** which involves the reinforcement of each behavior in a series of behaviors. Chaining is accomplished by first reinforcing the final action in the chain and then working backwards, each time adding a behavioral segment to the chain, until the individual performs all of the behavioral segments in sequence. For example, a father could use chaining to teach his child to put on a shirt. The father would begin by putting the shirt on the child and leaving the top button open. He would then work backwards, first reinforcing the child for buttoning the top button, then for buttoning the top two buttons, and so on, until the child could perform the sequence of actions involved in putting on a shirt.

Schedules of Reinforcement

Once an individual has been operantly conditioned to perform a behavior, the performance of the behavior is influenced by its *schedule of reinforcement.* In a **continuous schedule of reinforcement** every instance of a desired behavior is reinforced. A rat in a Skinner box would be on a continuous schedule of reinforcement if it received a pellet of food each time it pressed a bar. Similarly, candy vending machines put you on a continuous schedule of reinforcement. Each time that you insert the correct change, you receive a package of candy. If you do not receive one, you might pound on the machine, but you would not insert more coins. This illustrates another characteristic of continuous schedules of reinforcement—they are subject to rapid extinction when reinforcement stops.

Shaping An operant conditioning procedure involving the positive reinforcement of successive approximations of an initially improbable behavior to eventually bring about that behavior.

Chaining An operant conditioning procedure used to establish a desired sequence of behaviors by positively reinforcing each behavior in the sequence, beginning with the last behavior.

Continuous Schedule of Reinforcement A schedule of reinforcement that provides reinforcement for each instance of a desired response.

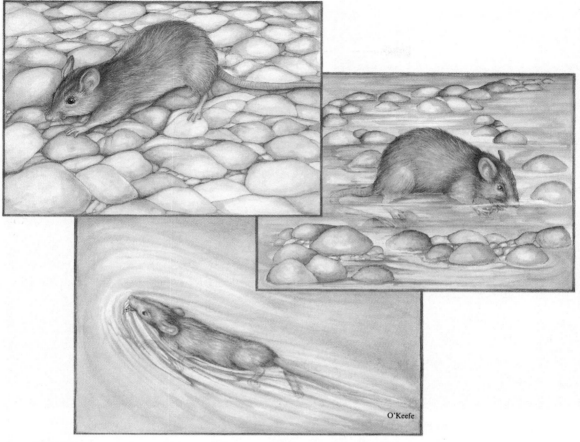

O'Keefe

FIGURE 6.6

Natural Shaping Shaping occurs naturally in the wild. This may explain why wild rats living next to the Po River in Italy will dive to the river bottom to get shellfish to eat, while similar wild rats living next to other rivers will not. The Po River experiences radical changes in depth. At times the rats living next to the Po can scamper across exposed areas of its bed to get shellfish. As the water rises, the rats wade across the river and submerge their heads to get shellfish. Eventually, when the water becomes deeper, they swim across the river and dive to get shellfish. Thus, the natural changes in the depth of the water shape the rats' behavior by reinforcing them with shellfish for successive approximations of diving (Galef, 1980).

In **partial schedules of reinforcement,** reinforcement is not given for every instance of a desired behavior, but only for some instances. Because reinforcement is less predictable in partial schedules, they are more resistant to extinction than are continuous schedules. Partial schedules are further divided into ratio schedules and interval schedules. In a *ratio schedule of reinforcement,* reinforcement is provided after the individual makes a certain number of desired responses. There are two kinds of ratio schedules: fixed and variable. A **fixed-ratio schedule** provides reinforcement after a specific number of desired responses. A rat in a Skinner box might be reinforced with a pellet of food after every five bar presses. And suppose that contestants on a television quiz show receive a prize each time they answer three questions in a row. They, too, would be on a fixed-ratio schedule. Fixed-ratio schedules produce high, steady response rates, with a slight pause in responding after each reinforcement.

Partial Schedule of Reinforcement A schedule of reinforcement that reinforces some, but not all, instances of a desired response.

Fixed-Ratio Schedule of Reinforcement A partial schedule of reinforcement that provides reinforcement after a set number of desired responses.

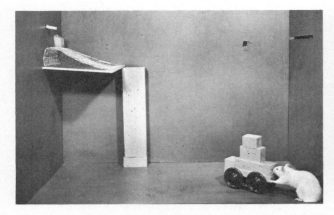
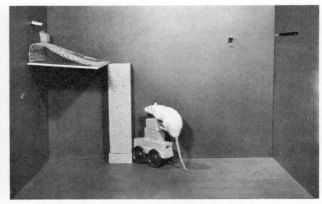

The Rat Olympics Chaining has been used to train animals to perform amazing sequences of actions. Some psychology professors have even instituted so-called "Rat Olympics," in which students compete to train rats to perform the longest sequence of actions (Solomon & Morse, 1981). Here, a rat has learned to obtain food by pushing a cart to reach a stand, climbing onto the cart, jumping up to the top of the stand, and running up a ramp. Note, however, that the rat learned this chain of behaviors backwards, first learning to run up the ramp and finally learning to push the cart.

Variable-Ratio Schedule of Reinforcement A partial schedule of reinforcement that provides reinforcement after varying, unpredictable numbers of desired responses.

Fixed-Interval Schedule of Reinforcement A partial schedule of reinforcement that provides reinforcement for the first desired response made after a set length of time.

Variable-Interval Schedule of Reinforcement A partial schedule of reinforcement that provides reinforcement for the first desired response made after varying, unpredictable lengths of time.

Unlike a fixed-ratio schedule, a **variable-ratio schedule** provides reinforcement after a *varying* number of desired responses. The number of responses required will vary around an average. For example, a rat in a Skinner box might be reinforced with a food pellet after an average of seven bar presses, with the number required varying each time, perhaps five presses one time, ten presses a second time, and six presses a third time. People playing the slot machines in Atlantic City are on a variable-ratio schedule, because they cannot predict how many times they will have to play before they win. Variable-ratio schedules produce high, steady rates of responding, which are more resistant to extinction than are those produced by any other schedule of reinforcement. In fact, by using a variable-ratio schedule of reinforcement, Skinner has conditioned pigeons to peck a lighted disk up to ten thousand times to obtain a single pellet of food. This also explains why compulsive gamblers find it so difficult to quit—they know they will eventually receive positive reinforcement, though they do not know when.

While ratio schedules of reinforcement provide reinforcement after a certain number of desired responses, *interval schedules of reinforcement* provide reinforcement for the first desired response after a period of time. There are two kinds of interval schedules: fixed and variable. A **fixed-interval schedule** reinforces the first desired response after a set period of time. For

example, a rat in a Skinner box might be reinforced with a food pellet for its first bar press after an interval of 30 seconds. Bar presses given during the intervals would not be reinforced.

A fixed-interval schedule produces a drop in responding immediately after a reinforcement and a gradual increase in responding as the time for the next reinforcement approaches. Suppose that you have a biology exam every three weeks. You would study before each exam to obtain a good grade—a positive reinforcer. But you probably would stop studying biology immediately after each exam and not begin studying it again until a few days before the next exam.

A **variable-interval schedule** of reinforcement provides reinforcement for the first desired response made after varying periods of time, which vary around an average. For example, a rat might be reinforced for its first bar press after 19 seconds, then after 37 seconds, then after 4 seconds, and so on, with the interval averaging 20 seconds. If you go out for a day of fishing you are on a variable-interval schedule of reinforcement, because you cannot predict how long you will have to wait until a fish bites. Variable-interval schedules produce slow, steady rates of responding, highly resistant to extinction. An individual may continue to fish even if the fish are few and far between. And teachers who give periodic surprise quizzes make use of variable-interval schedules to promote more consistent studying by their students.

Ratio schedules produce faster responses than do interval schedules, because the number of responses, not the length of time, determines the onset of reinforcement. And variable schedules produce steadier rates of responses than do fixed schedules, because the individual does not know when reinforcement will occur.

Negative Reinforcement In contrast to positive reinforcement, in **negative reinforcement** a behavior that brings about the *removal* of an *aversive* stimulus becomes more likely to occur in the future. Note that both positive and negative reinforcement increase the likelihood of a behavior. Consider the *negative reinforcer* of daydreaming. Because daydreaming lets you escape from boring lectures, you are likely to daydream whenever you find yourself listening to a boring lecture. This form of negative reinforcement is called **escape learning**—learning to *end* something aversive.

Fixed-Interval Schedules of Reinforcement If you receive your mail at the same time every day, say at 11:00 A.M., you would be on a fixed-interval schedule of reinforcement. You would be reinforced the first time you check your mailbox after 11:00 A.M., but you would not be reinforced if you check it before 11:00 A.M.

Negative Reinforcement In operant conditioning, an increase in the probability of a behavior that is followed by the removal of an aversive stimulus.

Escape Learning Learning to perform a behavior that terminates an aversive stimulus, as in negative reinforcement.

Avoidance Learning Learning to prevent the occurrence of an aversive stimulus by giving an appropriate response to a warning stimulus.

Of course your class might be so boring that you stop attending it. This is a form of negative reinforcement called **avoidance learning**—learning to *prevent* something aversive. But, you might be thinking, if negative reinforcement involves engaging in a behavior that removes an aversive stimulus, how could avoidance learning be a form of negative reinforcement? What is the stimulus that is being removed? Evidently, what is being removed is an *internal* aversive stimulus—the emotional distress caused by your anticipation of being in a boring class. Thus, in escape learning the aversive stimulus itself is removed, while in avoidance learning the emotional distress caused by anticipation of that stimulus is removed (Mowrer, 1947).

Extinction In operant conditioning, the gradual disappearance of a response that is no longer followed by a reinforcer.

Extinction and Spontaneous Recovery As in classical conditioning, behaviors learned through operant conditioning are subject to **extinction.** Skinner discovered extinction by accident. In one of his early studies, he conditioned a rat in a Skinner box to press a bar to obtain pellets of food from a dispenser. On one occasion he found that the pellet dispenser had become jammed, preventing the release of pellets. Skinner noted that the rat continued to press the bar, though at a diminishing rate, until it finally stopped pressing at all. Extinction might occur when a student who raises her hand is no longer called on to answer questions. Because she is no longer being positively reinforced for raising her hand, she would eventually stop doing so.

Spontaneous Recovery In operant conditioning, the reappearance after a period of time of a behavior that has been subjected to extinction.

Also as in the case of classical conditioning, a behavior that has been subject to extinction may show **spontaneous recovery**—it may reappear after a period of time. This may have an evolutionary advantage. Suppose that wild animals who visit a certain water hole normally obtain positive reinforcement by finding water there. If they visit the water hole on several successive occasions and find that it has dried up, their behavior will undergo extinction—they will stop visiting the water hole. But after a period of time, the animals might exhibit spontaneous recovery, again visiting the water hole—in case it had become refilled with water.

Punishment In operant conditioning, the process by which an aversive stimulus decreases the probability of a response that precedes it.

Punishment Still another way of reducing the probability of behaviors is **punishment,** in which the consequence of a behavior decreases the likelihood of the behavior. Do not confuse punishment with negative reinforcement. Negative reinforcement is "negative" because it refers to the removal of a stimulus, not because it involves punishment. And negative reinforcement *increases* the probability of a behavior by *removing* something undesirable as a consequence of that behavior, while punishment *decreases* the probability of a behavior by *presenting* something undesirable as a consequence of that behavior. For example, a child who touches a hot stove will be less likely to touch the stove in the future—an example of punishment.

Though punishment can be an effective means of reducing undesirable behaviors, it is rarely used effectively as a form of discipline. Consider some effective and ineffective ways to use punishment in disciplining children. First, punishment for misbehavior should be immediate so that the child will associate the punishment with the misbehavior. A mother (father) should not resort to threats of "wait until your father (mother) gets home," which might separate the misbehavior and punishment by hours. Second, punishment should be strong enough to stop the undesirable behavior but not excessive. You might punish a child for throwing clothes about his room by having him clean his entire room, but you would be using excessive punishment if you had him clean every room in the house. Punishment that is excessive will merely induce resentment aimed at the person who administers the punishment.

Third, punishment should be consistent. If parents truly wish to reduce a child's misbehavior, they must punish it each time that it occurs. Otherwise the child will learn only that his or her parents are unpredictable and that the misbehavior will sometimes lead solely to positive reinforcement. Fourth, punishment should be aimed at the misbehavior, not at the child. Children who are told that they, rather than their behavior, are "bad" may lose self-esteem. A child who is repeatedly called "stupid" for making mistakes while playing softball might feel incompetent and lose interest in softball and other sports. Fifth, punishing undesirable behavior merely suppresses the behavior and tells the child what *not to do*. To make sure that the child learns what *to do*, you must provide positive reinforcement of desirable behavior.

One of the main controversies concerning punishment is the use of physical punishment. As you will read later in the chapter, children imitate parental models. If they observe their parents relying on physical punishment, they may rely on it in dealing with their friends, siblings, and, eventually, their own children. Moreover, child abuse is a major problem in the United States, in part because parents may rely on physical punishment rather than positive reinforcement and nonphysical forms of punishment.

Applications of Operant Conditioning

B. F. Skinner claims that many of our everyday problems could be solved by more widespread use of operant conditioning (Skinner, 1986). As one example, consider the problem of injuries and deaths caused by automobile accidents. As shown in figure 6.7 operant conditioning has proved useful in teaching children to use seat belts, thereby reducing their risk of injury (Roberts & Fanurik, 1986). Now consider several other ways in which operant conditioning has been applied to everyday life.

Animal Training Skinner and his colleagues have been pioneers in using shaping and chaining to train animals to perform behaviors that are not part of their normal repertoires. Perhaps Skinner's most noteworthy accomplishment in animal training occurred during World War II in "Project

Animal Training Animal trainers have used shaping and chaining to train animals to perform an amazing array of behaviors.

FIGURE 6.7
**Positive Reinforcement and
Seatbelt Use** Positive
reinforcement is commonly used
to promote adaptive behaviors.
These graphs show the successful
use of pizza, bumper stickers, and
coloring books as positive
reinforcers for seatbelt use by
elementary schoolchildren.

From M. C. Roberts and D. Fanurik,
"Rewarding Elementary Schoolchildren
for Their Use of Safety Belts" in *Health
Psychology,* 5:185–196, 1986.
Copyright © 1986 by Lawrence
Erlbaum Assoc., Inc., Hillsdale, NJ.
Reprinted by permission.

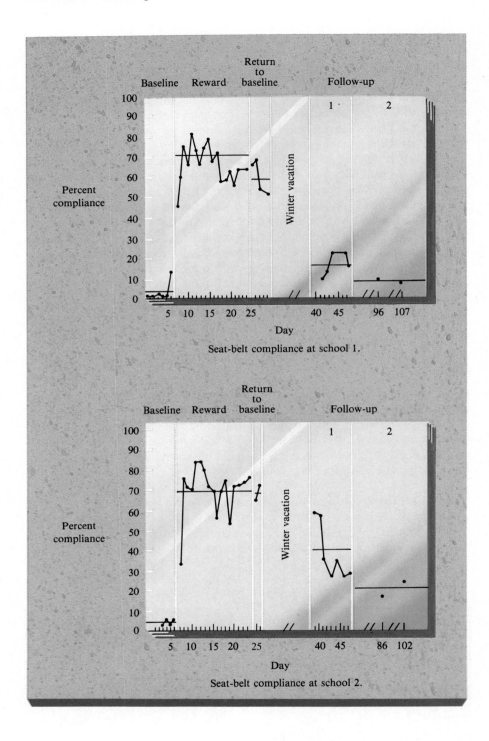

Seat-belt compliance at school 1.

Seat-belt compliance at school 2.

Pigeon." This was a secret project in which Skinner (1960) trained pigeons to guide missiles toward enemy ships by pecking at an image of the target ship shown on a display to obtain food pellets. Though this guidance system proved feasible, the advent of electronic guidance systems made it unnecessary.

More recently, pigeons have been trained to serve as air-sea rescue spotters in the Coast Guard's "Project Sea Hunt" (Stark, 1981). The pigeons are reinforced with food pellets for responding to red, orange, or yellow objects—the common colors of floatation devices. Three pigeons are placed in a compartment under a helicopter so that they look out of windows oriented in different directions. When a pigeon spots an object floating in the sea, it pecks a key, which sounds a buzzer and flashes a light in the cockpit. Pigeons have proved to be superior to human spotters, because they have the ability to focus over a wider area of the sea and to scan the sea for longer periods of time without becoming fatigued.

In another beneficial application of operant conditioning, psychologists have trained capuchin monkeys to serve as aides to physically handicapped people (Mack, 1981). These monkeys act as extensions of the handicapped person. They bring drinks, turn pages in books, turn on television sets, and perform a host of other behaviors for the person. The person directs the monkey by using an optical pointer that focuses a beam of light on a desired object.

Child Rearing In 1945 Skinner shocked the public when he published an article entitled "Baby in a Box" in *Ladies Home Journal,* describing how he and his wife had reared their infant daughter in an enclosure called an *air crib.* The air crib filtered and controlled the temperature of the infant's air supply. It also replaced diapers with a roll of paper that permitted sections to be placed under the baby and discarded when dirty. The parents could even pull down a shade over the front window of the air crib when the baby was ready to go to sleep. Skinner claimed this was a more convenient way to rear infants and allowed more time for social interaction with them. Critics disagreed with Skinner, claiming that Skinner's treatment of his daughter was dehumanizing. Over the past few decades, rumors have claimed that Skinner's daughter's experiences in the air crib eventually led her to sue her father, to become insane, or to commit suicide. In reality, his daughter had a happy childhood and has pursued a successful career as an artist (Langone, 1983).

Though the air crib provoked fears of impersonal child rearing, it was never widely used. Skinner had tried, unsuccessfully, to market the air crib under the brand name "Heir Conditioner." But operant conditioning has proved useful in child rearing. For example, parents have used extinction to eliminate their child's tantrums (Williams, 1959). When parents ignore their child's tantrums, rather than giving in to the child's demand for toys, candy, or attention, the tantrums no longer occur. And teachers have promoted toothbrushing by positively reinforcing children for having clean teeth by posting their names on the classroom wall (Swain, Allard, & Holborn, 1982).

Educational Improvement Teachers have also used positive reinforcement to improve the classroom performance of their students. For example, verbal praise has been used to increase participation in classroom discussions (Smith, Schumaker, Schaeffer, & Sherman, 1982), and since the 1960s positive reinforcement in the form of token economies has been used to promote desirable classroom behaviors (Kazdin, 1982). In a **token economy** teachers use tokens to reward students for appropriate conduct and academic behaviors. The students then use the tokens to purchase items such as toys or privileges such as extra recess time.

Perhaps the most distinctive contribution that operant conditioning has made to education has been **programmed instruction,** which had its origin in the invention of the *teaching machine* by Sidney Pressey of Ohio State University in the 1920s. His machines provided immediate knowledge of results and a piece of candy for correct answers (Benjamin, 1988). But credit for developing programmed instruction is generally given to B. F. Skinner for his invention of a teaching machine that takes the student through a series of questions related to a particular subject, gradually moving the student from simple to more complex questions. After the student answers a question, the

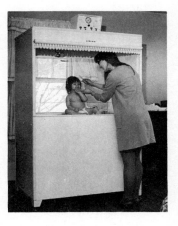

The Air Crib B. F. Skinner's daughter Julie Vargas is shown caring for her daughter Lisa in a sophisticated version of the air crib.

Token Economy An operant conditioning procedure that uses tokens as positive reinforcers in programs designed to promote positive behaviors, with the tokens later used to purchase desired items or privileges.

Programmed Instruction A step-by-step approach, based on operant conditioning, in which the learner proceeds at his or her own pace through more and more difficult material and receives immediate knowledge of the results of each response.

correct answer is revealed. The teaching machine failed to catch on in the 1950s and 1960s because of fears of dehumanization, that it could only teach certain subjects, and that teachers would lose their jobs.

Nonetheless, Skinner (1984) still believes that programmed instruction has several advantages over traditional approaches to education. Programmed instruction provides immediate knowledge of results (positive reinforcement for correct answers and only mild punishment for incorrect answers), eliminates the need for anxiety-inducing exams, and permits the student to go at his or her own pace. Skinner estimates that if schools adopted programmed instruction, students would learn twice as much in the same amount of time. Today's use of **computer-assisted instruction** in our schools is a descendant of Skinner's programmed instruction. Computer programs take the student through a graded series of items at the student's own rate. The programs can even branch off to provide extra help on items that the student finds difficult to master. Though teaching machines and computers have not replaced teachers, they have added another teaching tool to the classroom.

Computer-Assisted Instruction The use of computers to provide programmed instruction.

Understanding and Treating Psychological Disorders Operant conditioning has enhanced our understanding of psychological disorders, particularly depression. As you will read in chapter 14, the concept of **learned helplessness** has gained influence as an explanation for depression through the work of Martin Seligman. Depressed people feel that they have less control over obtaining positive reinforcers and avoiding punishments. As a consequence, they are less likely to try to change their life situations—which further contributes to their feelings of depression. You may have seen this in students who study many hours but still do poorly in school—they may become depressed, stop studying, and even drop out of school.

Learned Helplessness A feeling of futility caused by the belief that one has little or no control over events in one's life, which may make one stop trying and develop feelings of depression.

Operant conditioning has also been used to change abnormal behaviors. This is known as *behavior modification*. For example, token economies have been used to train residents of mental hospitals to dress themselves, to use toilets, to brush their teeth, and to eat with utensils. They use the tokens to purchase merchandise or special privileges. Chapter 15 describes other applications of behavior modification in the treatment of psychological disorders.

Biological Constraints on Operant Conditioning

Around the turn of the century, Edward Thorndike put forth the concept of *belongingness* to explain why he found it easier to train cats to escape from his puzzle boxes by stepping on a pedal than by scratching themselves. Thorndike observed that animals appeared to inherit tendencies to associate the performance of certain behaviors with certain consequences. Cats are more predisposed to escape by performing actions that affect the environment, such as stepping on a pedal, than by performing actions that affect their bodies, such as scratching themselves.

Thorndike's observation had little influence on his contemporaries, and it was not until the 1950s that psychologists rediscovered what he had observed. The psychologists who first made this rediscovery were Keller and Marian Breland, former students of B. F. Skinner who became renowned animal trainers. Since its founding in 1947, their Animal Behavior Enterprises in Hot Springs, Arkansas, has trained animals to perform in zoos, fairs, movies, circuses, museums, amusement parks, department stores, and television commercials.

Instinctive Drift The reversion of animals to behaviors characteristic of their species even when being reinforced for performing other behaviors.

Despite their success in training animals, the Brelands were distressed by the tendency of some animals to "misbehave" (Breland & Breland, 1961). Their misbehavior was actually a reversion to behaviors characteristic of their species, which the Brelands called **instinctive drift.** For example, a chicken trained to hit a baseball by pulling a string to swing a miniature bat and then run to first base for food would, instead, chase after the ball and peck at it. This "misbehavior" of animals has distressed animal trainers, but it demonstrates that animals tend to revert back to *species-specific behaviors* even when being reinforced for other behaviors.

After considering instinctive drift and related problems in operant conditioning, psychologist Martin Seligman (1970) concluded that there is a continuum of **preparedness** for certain behaviors. Behavioral preparedness has been demonstrated in many studies. For example, hamsters more easily learn to dig than to wash their faces to obtain positive reinforcement (Shettleworth & Juergensen, 1980). The continuum of behavioral preparedness ranges from *prepared* to *unprepared* to *contraprepared*. Behaviors for which members of a species are *prepared* have survival value for them and are easily learned by members of that species. Behaviors for which members of a species are *unprepared* have no survival value for them and are difficult to learn by members of that species. And behaviors for which members of a species are *contraprepared* have no survival value for them and are impossible to learn by members of that species. For example, human beings are prepared, chimpanzees are unprepared, and dogs are contraprepared to use language. Human beings can learn to speak, read, write, and use sign language. Chimpanzees can learn to use sign language. And dogs cannot learn any of these language skills.

Preparedness The degree to which members of a species are innately prepared to learn particular behaviors.

COGNITIVE LEARNING

Both classical conditioning and operant conditioning have traditionally been explained by the principle of contiguity—the mere association of events in time and space. Contiguity has been used to explain the association of a CS and a UCS in classical conditioning and the association of a behavior and its consequence in operant conditioning. In the past few decades, the associationistic explanation of learning has been criticized for viewing human and animal learners as passive reactors to "external carrots, whips, and the stimuli associated with them" (Boneau, 1974, p. 308). These critics, influenced by the "cognitive revolution" in psychology, favor the study of cognitive factors in classical conditioning and operant conditioning, as well as the study of learning by observation, which has traditionally been ignored by learning researchers.

Cognitive Factors in Associative Learning

As discussed earlier, the traditional view of classical conditioning and operant conditioning is that they are explained by contiguity alone. But evidence has accumulated that mere contiguity of a neutral stimulus and an unconditioned stimulus is insufficient to produce classical conditioning, and mere contiguity of a behavior and a consequence is insufficient to produce operant conditioning. This evidence has led to cognitive interpretations of associative learning, as in the age of operant conditioning. For example, secondary reinforcers have traditionally been thought to gain their reinforcing ability through mere *contiguity* with primary reinforcers. Cognitive theorists believe, instead, that secondary reinforcers gain their ability to reinforce behaviors because they have reliably *predicted* the occurrence of primary reinforcers (Rose & Fantino, 1978).

Suppose that you are training your dog to "shake hands" by using dog biscuits as positive reinforcers. Just before giving your dog a biscuit, you might offer praise by saying "good dog!" If you did so every time that your dog shook hands, the words "good dog!" might become a secondary reinforcer. The traditional view of operant conditioning would claim that the praise became a secondary reinforcer by its mere contiguity with food. In contrast, the cognitive view would claim that the praise became a secondary reinforcer because it had become a good predictor of the food reward.

Psychologists have also provided cognitive explanations of classical conditioning that rule out mere contiguity as being a sufficient explanation. The most influential of these explanations states that classical conditioning will occur only when the conditioned stimulus permits the individual to reliably predict the occurrence of the unconditioned stimulus. The better the conditioned stimulus is as a predictor, the stronger will be the conditioning. This means that conditioning involves learning relations among events in the environment (Rescorla, 1988). Consider this explanation in relationship to Pavlov's studies of salivation in dogs. The dog learns that a tone is followed by meat powder. The more consistently the tone precedes the meat powder, the more predictable will be the relationship and, as a consequence, the stronger will be the conditioning.

Another source of evidence supporting the cognitive explanation of classical conditioning is the phenomenon of **blocking,** in which a neutral stimulus paired with a CS that already elicits a CR will be less likely to become a CS itself (Kamin, 1969). Suppose that you have conditioned a dog to salivate to the sound of a bell by repeatedly presenting the bell before presenting meat powder. If you then repeatedly paired a light with the bell before presenting the meat powder, the principle of contiguity would make you expect that the light, too, would gain the ability to elicit salivation. But it will not. Instead, the CS (the bell) "blocks" the neutral stimulus (the light) from becoming a conditioned stimulus.

What accounts for blocking? According to one cognitive interpretation, blocking occurs because the neutral stimulus (the light) adds nothing to the prediction of the occurrence of the UCS (the meat powder). The CS (the bell) already predicts the occurrence of the UCS.

Still another source of evidence against a strictly contiguity-based view of classical conditioning comes from research on the Garcia effect. As you learned earlier, individuals who suffer gastrointestinal illness hours after eating novel food may avoid that food in the future. This contradicts the notion that events must be contiguous for us to learn to associate those events with each other.

But how can gastrointestinal distress become associated with the taste of what was eaten hours before? Regurgitation and the taste of stomach contents hours after eating cannot explain this, because some animals that experience the Garcia effect, such as rats, cannot regurgitate. A cognitive explanation of learned taste aversion holds that animals may have evolved a tendency to *expect* to become ill after eating novel foods. Hours later, if they have not become ill, they realize that the food is safe to eat. This may explain why animals in the wild taste small bits of a novel food rather than ingesting it completely—they are testing the food to see if they become ill later. If they do not become ill, they will devour the remaining food.

Observational Learning

Also influenced by the "cognitive revolution" in psychology is a trend in recent decades to view learning less in terms of changes in overt behavior, as in classical or operant conditioning, and more in terms of the acquisition of knowledge (Greeno, 1980). This means that learning can occur without revealing itself in observable behavior. For example, suppose that after studying many hours and mastering the material for a psychology exam, you fail the exam. Should your professor conclude that you had not learned the material? Not necessarily. Perhaps you failed the exam because the questions were ambig-

Blocking The process by which a neutral stimulus paired with a conditioned stimulus that already elicits a conditioned response fails to become a conditioned stimulus itself.

uous or because you were so anxious that your mind "went blank." Your performance on the exam did not reflect how well you had learned the material.

The first psychologist to emphasize the distinction between learning and performance was Edward Tolman (1932), who pointed out that learning can occur without reinforcement of overt actions, a process that he called **latent learning.** In latent learning, learning is not immediately revealed in performance but is revealed later when reinforcement is provided for performance. In a classic study (Tolman & Honzik, 1930), Tolman had three groups of rats run individually through a maze once a day for ten days. One group received food as a reward for reaching the end of the maze and the other two groups did not. The rewarded rats quickly learned to run through the maze with few wrong turns, while the unrewarded rats did not. Beginning on the eleventh day one of the groups of unrewarded rats was also rewarded with food for reaching the end of the maze. The next day that group ran the maze as efficiently as the previously rewarded group, while the remaining, still-unrewarded group continued to perform poorly (figure 6.8). This demonstrated latent learning. The rats in the group that was not rewarded until the eleventh day had learned the route to the end of the maze but only revealed this learning when rewarded for doing so.

More recent research has provided additional support for latent learning. In one study, rats given an opportunity to observe a water maze before swimming through it for a food reward performed better than rats not given such an opportunity (Keith & McVety, 1988). This provided evidence that rats can form what Tolman called "cognitive maps," which are mental representations of physical reality. But they use their cognitive maps only when reinforced for doing so.

In the 1960s research on latent learning stimulated interest in **observational learning,** in which an individual learns a behavior by observing others perform it. Observational learning is important to both animals and human beings in a variety of situations. For example, a rat that observes other rats

Edward Tolman (1886–1959)
"Our system . . . concerns mental processes as functional variables intervening between stimuli, initiating physiological states, and the general heredity and past training of the organism, on the one hand, and final resulting responses on the other."

Latent Learning Learning that occurs without the reinforcement of overt behavior.

Observational Learning
Learning a behavior by observing the consequences that others receive for performing it.

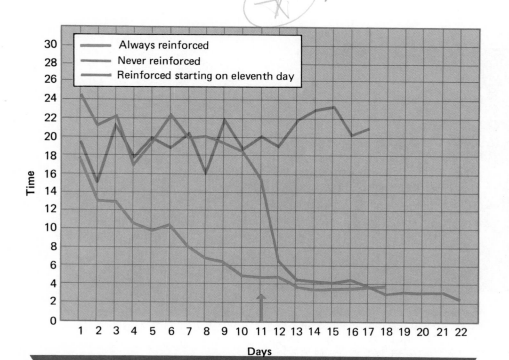

FIGURE 6.8
Latent Learning Rats are capable of latent learning, in which they learn through experience, but do not reveal this learning in overt behavior until they are reinforced for doing so. As the graph illustrates, in the Tolman and Honzik (1930) study, rats that merely explored a maze once a day for ten days were given a food reward for reaching the end of the maze on the eleventh day. On succeeding days they performed as well as rats that had been rewarded on the first ten days, while other rats that had never been rewarded continued to perform poorly.

eating foods will be more likely to eat those foods (Galef, 1986), and a retarded person who observes people eating properly in restaurants will be
morely likely to show proper eating etiquette (Vanden Pol et al., 1981).

Observational learning is central to Albert Bandura's **social learning
theory,** which assumes that social behavior is learned mainly through observation and the mental processing of information. What accounts for observational learning? Bandura (1986) has identified four factors: first, you must
pay *attention* to the model's actions; second, you must *remember* the model's
actions; third, you must have the *ability* to produce the actions; and fourth,
you must be *motivated* to perform the action. Consider a gymnast learning to
perform a flying dismount from the uneven bars. She might learn to perform
this feat by first paying attention to a gymnast who can already perform it. To
be able to try the feat later, the learner would have to remember what the
model did. But to perform the feat the learner must have the strength to swing
from the bars. Assuming that she paid attention to the model, remembered
what the model did, and had the strength to perform the movement, she still
might only be motivated to perform the feat in important competitions.

Observational learning can promote undesirable behavior, as well as desirable behavior. In an early study of observational learning, Bandura (1965)
demonstrated its influence on the aggressiveness of children. Three groups
of preschool children watched a film of an adult punching and verbally abusing
a Bobo doll (figure 6.9). Each group saw a different version of the film. In the
first version the model was rewarded with candy, soda, and praise by another
adult. In the second version the other adult scolded and spanked the model.
And in the third version there were no consequences to the model. The children then played individually in a room with a Bobo doll and other toys. Those
who had seen the model rewarded for being aggressive were more aggressive
in their play than those who had seen the other two versions of the film. This
demonstrated that operant conditioning can occur vicariously, simply through
the observation of others receiving positive reinforcement for engaging in the
target behavior.

Social Learning Theory A
theory that assumes that people
learn social behaviors mainly
through observation and mental
processing of information.

Albert Bandura "Most human
behavior is learned
observationally through
modeling."

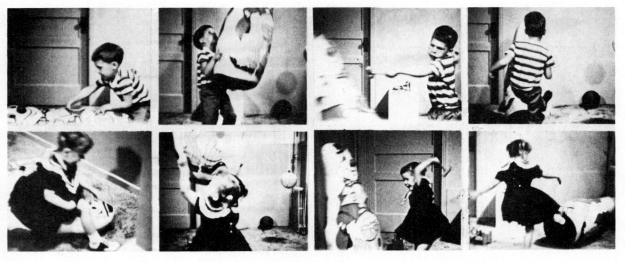

FIGURE 6.9
Observational Learning Children who
observe aggressive behavior being positively
reinforced are more likely to engage in it
themselves (Bandura, 1965).

Studies such as this have contributed to concerns about the effects of movies and television on viewers, particularly on children. This concern may be well founded because children who watch violent programs tend to be more aggressive, while children who watch altruistic programs such as "Mister Rogers' Neighborhood" tend to engage in more positive social behaviors (Huston, Watkins, & Kunke, 1989). Chapter 18 describes research findings on the effects of media violence on children and the effects of pornography on violence against women.

THINKING ABOUT PSYCHOLOGY

Is Biofeedback an Effective Means for Learning Self-Regulation of Physiological Processes?

One day more than two decades ago, the eminent learning researcher Neal Miller stood in front of a mirror trying to teach himself to wiggle one ear. By watching his ear in the mirror, he was eventually able to make it wiggle (Jonas, 1972). The mirror provided Miller with visual *feedback* of his ear's movement. This convinced him that people might learn to control physiological processes that are not normally subject to voluntary control if they were provided with feedback of those processes. Since the 1960s Miller and other psychologists have developed a technique called *biofeedback* to help people learn to control normally involuntary processes such as brain waves, blood pressure, and intestinal contractions.

Biofeedback A form of operant conditioning that enables an individual either to learn to control a normally involuntary physiological process or to gain better control of a normally voluntary one when provided with visual or auditory feedback of the state of that process.

The Nature of Biofeedback

Biofeedback is a form of operant conditioning that enables an individual to learn to control a normally involuntary physiological process or to gain better control of a normally voluntary physiological process when provided with visual or auditory feedback of the state of that process. The feedback acts as a positive reinforcer for changes in the desired direction. How is this accomplished? The first step is to detect changes in electrical activity reflecting changes in the physiological process of interest. This is done by sensors, usually *electrodes,* attached to the body. The second step is to amplify the changes in electrical activity so that they can be recorded and used to generate a feedback signal. The third step is to present the subject feedback indicating the state of the physiological process. The feedback might be in the form of a light that changes in brightness as heart rate changes or a tone that changes in pitch as muscle tension changes.

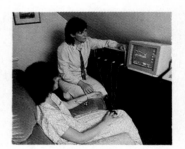

Biofeedback People provided with feedback of physiological processes may gain some control over normally involuntary processes, such as heart rate, or improved control over normally voluntary processes, such as muscle tension.

Historical Background

Though the term *biofeedback* was not coined until 1969, the ability to gain extraordinary self-control of physiological processes was known long before then. For centuries Indian yogis have demonstrated the ability to gain control

Neal Miller "The biofeedback and behavioral medicine techniques already available are preventing unnecessary suffering, correcting disabling conditions, and helping people regain control of their lives."

over involuntary processes, such as heart rate, that are normally regulated by the autonomic nervous system. Perhaps the first study of what we now call biofeedback occurred in 1885 when a Russian researcher reported the case of a patient who could control his heart rate when permitted to observe an ongoing recording of it (Tarchanoff, 1885). But until the 1960s few researchers conducted studies of learned control of normally involuntary physiological processes, in part because influential psychologists such as B. F. Skinner considered it impossible.

Nonetheless, some researchers were undaunted by this pessimistic outlook and continued research on voluntary self-control of physiological processes. Their research bore fruit in the early 1960s with reports of the successful use of physiological feedback in training subjects to control their heart rate (Shearn, 1962) and imperceptible muscle twitches in their hands (Basmajian, 1963). Biofeedback was popularized in the late 1960s by reports of subjects who learned to control their alpha brain-wave patterns (Kamiya, 1969) which, as you read in chapter 5, are associated with a relaxed state of mind. But biofeedback did not become scientifically credible to many psychologists until Neal Miller reported success in training rats to gain voluntary control over physiological responses normally controlled solely by the autonomic nervous system. In his studies, Miller used electrical stimulation of the brain's reward centers (positive reinforcement) or, in some cases, escape or avoidance of shock (negative reinforcement) to train rats to increase or decrease their heart rate, intestinal contractions, urine formation, or blood pressure. Because Miller was an eminent, hard-nosed researcher, serious scientists became more willing to accept the legitimacy of biofeedback. But, for unknown reasons, attempts at replicating these studies have failed (Dworkin & Miller, 1986).

Applications of Biofeedback

Disappointment at the failure to replicate Miller's findings and at the failure of biofeedback to fulfill early promises to induce mystical states of consciousness led to skepticism about its merits. But, though biofeedback has not proven to be an unqualified success, it has not proven to be a total failure. Hundreds of studies have demonstrated the effectiveness of biofeedback in helping people learn to control a variety of physiological processes, including heart rate, brain waves, and gastrointestinal activity. One of its main uses has been in training people to gain better control of their skeletal muscles. Though we normally exert excellent control over our muscles, at times we may want to exert greater control over them. For example, auditory biofeedback has been used to train blind people to adopt more normal looking facial expressions (Webb, 1977).

In some cases, we might want to reduce our level of muscle tension. Biofeedback has helped pregnant women to remain relaxed during labor (Gregg, 1983), gymnasts to relax their hip muscles (Wilson & Bird, 1981), violin players to relieve excess tension in their hands (LeVine & Irvine, 1984), and victims of muscle tension headaches to gain relief by relaxing their neck and forehead muscles (Hart & Cichanski, 1981). In other cases, we might want to increase our level of muscle tension. This is particularly true in physical rehabilitation. Muscle tension biofeedback has been used to restore control of foot movements in stroke victims (Santee, Keister, & Kleinman, 1980) and use of facial muscles after surgery to reconnect the nerves serving those muscles (Nahai & Brown, 1983).

Biofeedback has even been used to help increase muscle strength. In one study bodybuilders were randomly divided into two groups. Both groups worked out on a Cybex leg extension machine three times a week for five weeks. One group received visual and auditory biofeedback while using the machine, while the other group did not. At the end of the training period, the legs of those in the group that received biofeedback were stronger than those in the group that exercised without it. Those who received biofeedback apparently benefited from continuous monitoring of their degree of exertion, which served to increase their motivation to exert greater effort (Croce, 1986).

Evaluating Biofeedback Research

Though biofeedback is widely used by psychologists and health professionals, it is not a panacea. In fact, there is controversy concerning its effectiveness and practicality. To demonstrate the effectiveness of biofeedback one must show that learned self-regulation of physiological processes is caused by the feedback and not by other factors. For example, early biofeedback studies showed that feedback of alpha brain waves could increase these brain waves and induce a state of relaxation. But replications of those early studies showed that the effects were caused by the subjects sitting quietly with their eyes closed. The brain-wave feedback added nothing (Plotkin, 1979).

Moreover, because biofeedback involves the use of sophisticated, scientifically impressive devices, it has the potential to create powerful placebo effects (Furedy, 1987). To control for placebo effects, researchers will provide some subjects with *noncontingent feedback,* which is recorded feedback of the physiological activity of another subject. If the subjects who receive true feedback and the subjects who receive noncontingent feedback show equal improvement in self-regulation of a physiological process, then the improvement would be considered a placebo effect. But noncontingent feedback may be an inadequate control, because some subjects may realize that the feedback is not accurately reflecting changes in the physiological process, especially in studies providing feedback of muscle tension (Burnette & Adams, 1987).

Even when the results of a biofeedback study can be attributed to the feedback, the technique might still not be of practical use. Why is this so? First, the typical biofeedback device costs hundreds or even thousands of dollars. So, clinicians must decide whether the benefits of biofeedback justify its cost, especially when other equally effective, less expensive treatments are available. For example, simple training in relaxation, requiring no costly apparatus, may be as useful as biofeedback-assisted relaxation (Kluger, Jamner, & Tursky, 1985).

Second, laboratory experiments on biofeedback may produce statistically significant results (see chapter 2) that merit being reported but that are too small to be of practical use in clinical settings (Steiner & Dince, 1981). For example, biofeedback may produce a *statistically* significant reduction in blood pressure in a hypertensive person that may too small to be *clinically* meaningful. Third, biofeedback training in a clinician's office may not produce results that last much beyond the training sessions. But, fortunately, subjects who continue to practice what they have learned in therapy sessions will be more likely to maintain the beneficial effects they have obtained (Libo & Arnold, 1983).

Finally, the results of laboratory studies may not be applicable to the clinical setting. For example, an important factor in any treatment program is an empathetic relationship between the therapist and the client, which would usually not exist between a laboratory researcher and a subject. In addition, therapists, unlike experimenters, would rarely if ever rely solely on a biofeedback device in treating disorders. The therapist who uses biofeedback typically achieves success by combining biofeedback with other approaches

Transfer of Biofeedback Training Portable, battery-operated biofeedback devices may help people transfer the physiological self-control they learn in the clinical setting to everyday life.

to therapy. The clinical effectiveness of biofeedback, therefore, will remain controversial until its effectiveness has been demonstrated in well-controlled clinical, as well as laboratory, studies.

SUMMARY

CLASSICAL CONDITIONING

Learning is a relatively permanent change in knowledge or behavior as a result of experience. As demonstrated by Ivan Pavlov, in the kind of learning called classical conditioning, a stimulus (the conditioned stimulus) comes to elicit a response (the conditioned response) that it would not normally elicit by being paired with a stimulus (the unconditioned stimulus) that already elicits that response (the unconditioned response).

In stimulus generalization, the conditioned response occurs in response to stimuli that are similar to the conditioned stimulus. And in stimulus discrimination, the conditioned response occurs only in response to the conditioned stimulus. If the conditioned stimulus is repeatedly presented without presenting the unconditioned stimulus, the conditioned response will diminish and eventually stop. This is called extinction. But, after a period of time, the conditioned stimulus will again elicit the conditioned response. This is called spontaneous recovery.

Classical conditioning has been applied in many ways, including advertising and in explaining phobias, drug dependence, and taste aversions. In the past two decades, research has shown that there are biological constraints on the ease with which stimuli can be associated with one another in classical conditioning.

OPERANT CONDITIONING

While classical conditioning concerns the relationship between stimuli and responses, operant conditioning concerns the relationship between behaviors and consequences. B. F. Skinner has identified four behavioral contingencies to describe the relationship between behaviors and consequences: positive reinforcement, negative reinforcement, extinction, and punishment. In shaping, positive reinforcement is used to increase the likelihood of a behavior that is not in an individual's repertoire. In chaining, positive reinforcement is used to teach an individual to perform a complex series of behaviors.

In operant conditioning, behavior is influenced by schedules of reinforcement. In a continuous schedule, every instance of a desired behavior is reinforced. In partial schedules, reinforcement is not given for every instance. Partial schedules include ratio schedules, which provide reinforcement after a certain number of responses, and interval schedules, which provide reinforcement for the first desired response after a certain interval of time.

In negative reinforcement, a behavior that brings about the removal of an aversive stimulus becomes more likely to occur in the future. Negative reinforcement is implicated in avoidance learning and escape learning. When a behavior is no longer followed by reinforcement it will be subject to extinction. But after a period of time the behavior will reappear—only to be subject to even faster extinction if it is still not reinforced. In punishment, the consequence of a behavior decreases the likelihood of the behavior. To be effective, punishment should be immediate, firm, consistent, aimed at the misbehavior rather than the individual, and coupled with reinforcement of desirable behavior.

Operant conditioning has even more diverse applications than does classical conditioning, which includes animal training, child rearing, educational improvement, understanding psychological disorders, and treating psychological disorders. Like classical conditioning, operant conditioning is subject to biological constraints, because members of particular species are more evolutionarily prepared to engage in certain behaviors than in others.

COGNITIVE LEARNING

Cognitive psychologists have shown that contiguity is not sufficient to explain learning. Mere contiguity of a neutral stimulus and an unconditioned stimulus is insufficient to produce classical conditioning, and mere contiguity of a behavior and a consequence is insufficient to produce operant conditioning. Instead, active cognitive assessment of the relationship between stimuli or the relationship between behaviors and consequences is essential for learning to occur. In latent learning, learning occurs through observation, but it is revealed in overt behavior only when reinforcement is provided for that behavior. Albert Bandura's social learning theory considers how individuals learn through observing the behavior of others.

THINKING ABOUT PSYCHOLOGY: IS BIOFEEDBACK AN EFFECTIVE MEANS FOR LEARNING SELF-REGULATION OF PHYSIOLOGICAL PROCESSES?

Biofeedback is a form of operant conditioning that enables an individual to learn to control a normally involuntary physiological process or to gain better control of a normally voluntary physiological process when provided with visual or auditory feedback of the state of that process. Biofeedback gained scientific credibility through the research of Neal Miller. One of the most successful applications of biofeedback has been in the self-control of skeletal muscle activity, particularly in physical rehabilitation. To demonstrate the effectiveness of biofeedback, researchers must show that learned self-regulation of physiological processes is caused by the feedback and not by other factors, such as placebo effects. For biofeedback to be of practical value, its benefits must justify its cost. Its effects must be of practical, as well as statistical, significance. Moreover, the effects of biofeedback must transfer from the clinical setting to the everyday world for it to be useful in treating disorders.

IMPORTANT CONCEPTS

Avoidance learning 200
Behavioral contingencies 193
Biofeedback 209
Blocking 206
Chaining 196
Classical conditioning 186
Computer-assisted instruction 204
Conditioned response (CR) 186
Conditioned stimulus (CS) 186
Continuous schedule of
    reinforcement 196
Discriminative stimulus 195
Escape learning 199
Extinction 188, 200
Fixed-interval schedule 198

Fixed-ratio schedule 197
Garcia effect 191
Instinctive drift 204
Instrumental conditioning 193
Latent learning 207
Law of effect 193
Learned helplessness 204
Learning 184
Negative reinforcement 199
Observational learning 207
Operant conditioning 193
Partial schedule of reinforcement 197
Positive reinforcement 194
Preparedness 205
Primary reinforcer 195

Programmed instruction 203
Punishment 200
Secondary reinforcer 195
Shaping 196
Skinner box 193
Social learning theory 208
Spontaneous recovery 188, 200
Stimulus discrimination 188
Stimulus generalization 188
Token economy 203
Unconditioned response (UCR) 186
Unconditioned stimulus (UCS) 186
Variable-interval schedule 199
Variable-ratio schedule 198

IMPORTANT PEOPLE

RECOMMENDED READINGS

For More on All Aspects of Learning:

Domjan, M., & Burkhard, B. (1986). *The principles of learning and behavior* (2nd Ed.). Monterey, CA: Brooks/Cole.

A readable, more extensive introduction to most of the topics discussed in this chapter.

For More on Classical Conditioning:

Pavlov, I. P. (1927). *Conditioned reflexes.* New York: Oxford University Press.

A translation of Pavlov's classic work on classical conditioning.

Watson, J. B., & Rayner, R. (1920). Conditioned emotional reactions. *Journal of Experimental Psychology, 3,* 1–14.

The classic, clearly written, account of the classical conditioning of Little Albert.

For More on Operant Conditioning:

Rescorla, R. A. (1988). Pavlovian conditioning: It's not what you think it is. *American Psychologist, 43,* 151–160.

A sophisticated article presenting a cognitive interpretation of classical conditioning.

Skinner, B. F. (1948). *Walden two.* New York: Macmillan.

A controversial novel describing Skinner's vision of a utopian community based on the application of the principles of operant conditioning.

Skinner, B. F. (1938). *The behavior of organisms.* New York: Appleton-Century-Crofts.

The classic book that introduced Skinner's views on the nature of learning.

For More on Cognitive Learning:

Bandura, A. (1986). *Social foundations of thought and action: A social cognitive theory.* Englewood Cliffs, NJ: Prentice-Hall.

A presentation of Bandura's social learning theory, emphasizing the importance of cognitive processes and observational learning.

For More on Biofeedback:

Basmajian, J. V. (1988). Research foundations of EMG biofeedback in rehabilitation. *Biofeedback and Self-Regulation, 13,* 275–298.

A review of the application of muscle biofeedback in rehabilitation, written by the leading researcher in the field.

Hatch, J. P., Fisher, J. G., & Rugh, J. D. (Eds.). (1987). *Biofeedback: Studies in clinical efficacy.* New York: Plenum.

A collection of scholarly articles on a variety of applications of biofeedback.

CHAPTER
7

MEMORY

Chapter Opening Art:
Salvador Dali. *The Persistence of Memory.* 1931.

Flashbulb Memory A vivid, long-lasting memory of a surprising, important, emotionally arousing event.

Memory The process by which information is stored in the brain and later retrieved.

I n 1898 a survey of middle-aged adults asked, "Do you recall where you were when you heard that Lincoln was shot?" Of those surveyed, 71 percent recalled where they were on April 14, 1865, when they first heard that President Lincoln had been shot (Colegrove, 1899). Such vivid, long-lasting memories of surprising, important, emotionally arousing events are commonly called **flashbulb memories** (Brown & Kulik, 1977). You may have some of your own. Perhaps you can recall where you were on January 28, 1986, when the space shuttle *Challenger* exploded after takeoff. You might even recall how you heard the news and your exact feelings at that moment. Older students may recall where they were on November 22, 1963, when they heard of the assassination of President John F. Kennedy. You may even have flashbulb memories of personally momentous events, such as your first kiss or your first day in kindergarten.

What accounts for flashbulb memories? The answer is unclear. Some psychologists believe they are the product of a special brain mechanism that we have evolved that assures that we remember important experiences. But other psychologists disagree, claiming instead that normal memory processes can explain them (McCloskey, Wible, & Cohen, 1988). If an answer to the question is found it will come from research on **memory,** the process by which we store and later retrieve information.

INFORMATION PROCESSING AND MEMORY

During the past three decades memory research has been driven by the so-called cognitive revolution in psychology, which views the brain as an information processor. This is reflected in the most influential model of memory, first put forth by Richard Shiffrin and Richard Atkinson (1969). Their model

Flashbulb Memories Memory researchers are searching for explanations of flashbulb memories of momentous events.

assumes that memory involves the processing of information in three successive stages. **Sensory memory** stores exact replicas of stimuli impinging on each of the senses. Sensory memories last for a brief period—from less than one second (in the case of visual sensory memory) to as long as four seconds (in the case of auditory sensory memory). When we attend to information in sensory memory it is transferred to **short-term memory,** which stores it for about 20 seconds, unless you maintain it through mental rehearsal—as when you repeat a phone number to yourself long enough to dial it. Information transferred from short-term memory into **long-term memory** is stored relatively permanently, in some instances for a lifetime. You can appreciate this by stopping for a moment to recall some early childhood memories. This also indicates that information can move from long-term memory into short-term memory.

The handling of information at each memory stage has been compared to information processing by a computer, which involves encoding, storage, and retrieval. **Encoding** is the placing of information into a form that can be stored in memory. When you strike the keys on a computer keyboard, your actions are translated into a code that the computer understands. **Storage** is the retention of information in memory. Personal computers typically store information on diskettes. **Retrieval** is the recovery of information from memory. When you strike certain keys, you provide the computer with cues that make it recall the information you desire. We are also subject to **forgetting**—the failure to retrieve information from memory. This is analogous to the erasing of information on a diskette. Figure 7.1 summarizes the **information-processing model** of memory.

SENSORY MEMORY

Think back to the last movie you saw. The movie was actually a series of frames, each containing a picture slightly different from the one before it. Given this, why did you see smooth motion instead of a rapidly presented series of individual pictures? You did because of your sensory memory, in this case your

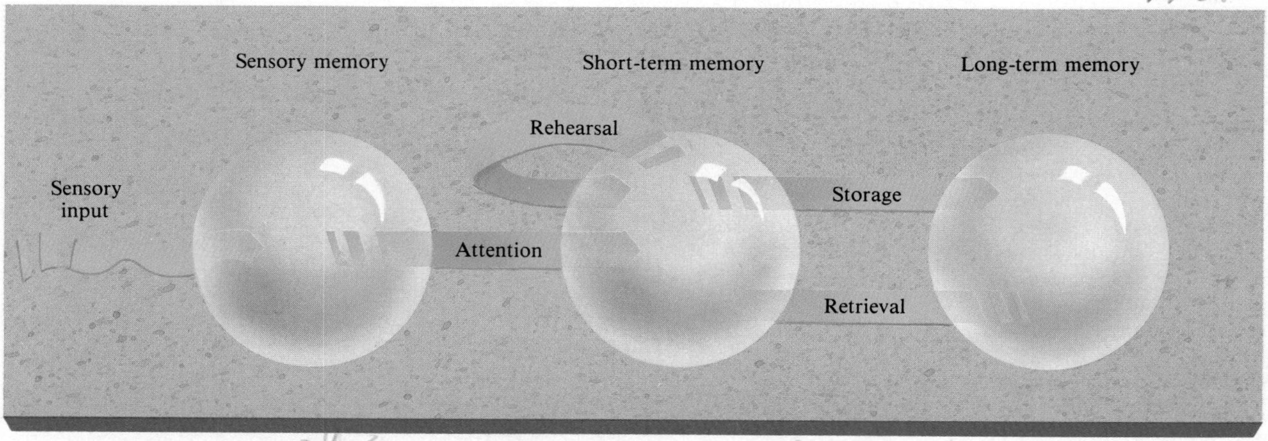

Sensory Memory The stage of memory that briefly, for at most a few seconds, stores exact replicas of sensations.

Short-Term Memory The stage of memory that can store a few items of unrehearsed information for up to about twenty seconds.

Long-Term Memory The stage of memory that can store a virtually unlimited amount of information relatively permanently.

Encoding The placing of information into a form that can be stored in memory.

Storage The retaining of information in memory.

Retrieval The recovering of information from memory.

Forgetting The failure to retrieve information from memory.

Information-Processing Model The view that the processing of memories involves encoding, storage, and retrieval.

FIGURE 7.1

Memory Processes The information-processing model of memory assumes that information passes from sensory memory to short-term memory to long-term memory. Information may also pass from long-term memory to short-term memory. Each of the stages involves information encoding, storage, and retrieval.

visual sensory memory, which stores images for a fraction of a second. Visual sensory memory is called **iconic memory,** because an image stored in it is called an *icon* (from the Greek word for "image"). Because the movie projector presented the frames at a rate that made each successive frame appear just before the previous one left your iconic memory, the successive images blended together and created the impression of smooth motion. You have certainly been at a movie when the projector suddenly presented the frames too rapidly, leading to a mere blur on the screen (as well as hooting and hollering from the audience). You perceived a blur because the successive images overlapped too much in your iconic memory.

Auditory sensory memory serves a similar purpose, blending together successive pieces of auditory information. Auditory sensory memory is called **echoic memory,** because each sound in it is called an *echo.* Echoic memory stores information for longer periods than does iconic memory, storing sounds for as long as four seconds. The greater persistence of information in echoic memory enables you to perceive speech by blending together successive spoken sounds that you hear. If echoic memory storage were as brief as iconic memory storage, speech might sound like a staccato series of separate sounds rather than words and phrases (Cowan, 1984).

Though sensory memory serves each of the senses, almost all studies of it have concerned either iconic memory or echoic memory. Perhaps the most famous experiment on sensory memory was carried out by a Harvard University doctoral student named George Sperling (1960). Until Sperling's experiment, psychologists assumed that sensory memory could store a relatively small amount of information. He tested this assumption by using an ingenious procedure involving iconic memory (figure 7.2).

Each of Sperling's subjects stared at a screen as he projected sets of 12 letters, arranged in three rows of four, onto it. Each presentation lasted for only one-twentieth of a second—a mere flash. Sperling then asked the subject to report as many of the letters as possible. He found that the subjects could accurately report an average of only four or five. The subjects claimed, however, that they had briefly retained an image of the 12 letters, but by the time they had reported a few of them the remaining ones had faded from memory.

Rather than dismiss these claims, Sperling decided to test them experimentally by using a variation of his task. Instead of using *whole report* (asking the subjects to report as many of the 12 letters as possible), he used *partial*

Iconic Memory Visual sensory memory, which lasts up to about a second.

Echoic Memory Auditory sensory memory, which lasts up to about three or four seconds.

FIGURE 7.2
Testing Sensory Memory In Sperling's (1960) study of sensory memory, the subject fixated on a cross. A display of letters was flashed briefly on the screen. At varying times after the display had been flashed (.15, .30, .50, or 1 second), a tone signaled the subject to report the letters in a particular row. This enabled Sperling to determine how many of the letters were stored in sensory memory. By delaying the tone for longer and longer periods, Sperling was also able to determine how quickly images in sensory memory fade.

Source: Data from G. Sperling, *Psychological Monographs,* 74 (whole No. 498), 1960.

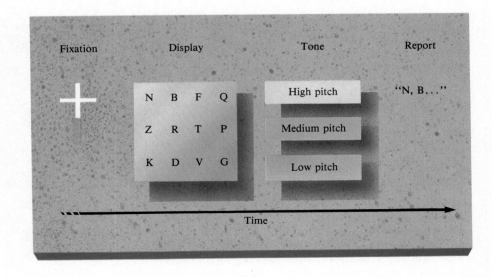

report (asking the subjects to report as many of the four letters as possible in a designated row). The task again included sets of 12 letters arranged in three rows of four. But this time, at the instant that the visual display was terminated, a tone was sounded. The pitch of the tone signaled the subject to report the letters in a particular row: a high tone for the top row, a medium tone for the middle row, and a low tone for the bottom row.

Subjects giving partial reports accurately reported an average of 3.3 of the 4 letters in a designated row. Because the subjects did not know which row would be designated until *after* the display was terminated, the results indicated that an average of 9.9 of the 12 letters were stored in iconic memory. Sperling concluded that virtually all of the information from visual receptors is stored as an image in iconic memory, but, as his subjects had claimed, the image fades rapidly.

This inspired Sperling to seek the answer to another question: How fast does the information in iconic memory fade? He found the answer by repeating his partial report procedure but this time delaying the tone signaling the subject to give a partial report. He varied the delay from one-tenth of a second to one second. As the delay lengthened, the subject's ability to recall letters in a designated row declined more and more. Sperling found that by the time the delay reached one second almost all of the information in iconic memory had faded. Based on Sperling's study, and subsequent research, we know that sensory memory can store virtually all the information provided by our sensory receptors and that this information fades rapidly (though the rate varies among the senses). But we can retain information that is in sensory memory by attending to it and transferring it into short-term memory.

SHORT-TERM MEMORY

When you pay attention to information in your sensory memory or to information retrieved from your long-term memory, the information enters your short-term memory. Because you are paying attention to this sentence, it has entered your short-term memory. In contrast, other information in your sensory memory, such as the feeling of this book against your hands, did not enter your short-term memory until your attention was directed to it. And note that you are able to comprehend the words in this sentence because you have

Sensory Memory If you joined these people at Times Square in New York City, your senses would be bombarded by sights, sounds, and smells. An enormous amount of this stimulation would be stored in your sensory memory. But, at any given moment, you would be consciously aware of only a small portion of the stored information. This selectivity of attention prevents your consciousness from being overwhelmed by external stimuli.

what is another name for short term memory?

retrieved their meanings from your long-term memory. Because we use short-term memory to manipulate information provided by either sensory memory or long-term memory, it is also called *working memory.*

To appreciate the nature of working memory, you might compare it to a baker's table. Just as you would use the table to mix ingredients, you would use working memory to process information to which you are attending. And just as you can get ingredients for the table from a cupboard or from a grocery store, you can transfer information into your working memory from either your long-term memory or your sensory memory. Moreover, just as you can move ingredients from the table to a cupboard, you can transfer information from your working memory into your long-term memory.

Encoding

Information transferred into short-term memory is encoded as sounds or images. But we usually encode information as sounds—even when that information is visual. This was demonstrated in a study in which subjects were shown a short series of letters and were then immediately asked to recall them. The subjects' errors showed that they more often confused letters that sounded alike (for example, *T* and *C*) than letters that looked alike (for example, *Q* and *O*). This indicated that the letters, though presented visually, had been encoded according to their sounds (Conrad, 1962).

Storage

In comparison to sensory memory or long-term memory, short-term memory has a relatively small storage capacity (just as a baker's table has a relatively small storage capacity compared to a grocery store or cupboard). You can demonstrate this for yourself by performing this exercise: read the following numbers once and then (without looking at them) write them in order on a sheet of paper: 6 3 9 1 4 6 5. Next, read the following numbers once and again write them down from memory: 5 8 1 3 9 2 8 6 3 1 7. If you have average short-term memory storage capacity, you probably were able to recall the seven numbers in the first set but not the eleven numbers in the second set.

The normal limit of seven items in short-term memory was the theme of a famous article by psychologist George Miller (1956) entitled "The Magical Number Seven, Plus or Minus Two." Miller pointed out many studies indicating that short-term memory has, on average, a capacity of seven "chunks" of information, with a normal range of five to nine chunks. A *chunk* is a unit of meaningful information, such as a number, a letter, or a word.

what is a chunk?

The ability to chunk individual items of information can increase the amount of information stored in short-term memory. For example, after a five-second look at the positions of pieces on a chessboard, expert chess players are significantly better than novice chess players at reproducing the positions of the pieces. This reflects the greater ability of experts to chunk chess pieces into familiar configurations (Chase & Simon, 1973). Thus, though chess experts do not store more memory chunks in their short-term memory than do novices, their memory chunks contain more information.

In some cases, chunking can dramatically increase the amount of information stored in short-term memory. Consider the case of college student Steve Faloon, who had a normal short-term memory storage capacity. Yet, after 230 hours of practice over a twenty-month period, Faloon increased his short-term memory span from seven to seventy-nine digits. How did he achieve such an amazing accomplishment? He did so by converting series of digits into larger and larger meaningful chunks. Because Faloon was an avid long-distance runner, one of his techniques was to convert sequences of digits into racing times. For example, the sequence 3 4 9 2 became "3 minutes and 49.2 seconds, near world-record mile time." He used other techniques to increase the size of his memory chunks even more, until he could store and recall seventy-nine digits (Ericsson, Chase, & Faloon, 1980).

Given that the typical person can store about seven chunks of information in short-term memory, how long will this information remain stored? Without rehearsal (that is, without repeating the information to ourselves), we can store information in short-term memory for no more than 20 seconds. But if we use *maintenance rehearsal* by repeating the information to ourselves, we can store it in short-term memory for as long as we want. Suppose you are waiting to play basketball and a friend who is playing gives you the combination to his or her locker so that you can get a ball with which to practice shooting. To retain the combination in your short-term memory long enough to use it you would have to repeat it to yourself.

But how do we know that unrehearsed information in short-term memory lasts no longer than 20 seconds? We know because of a study conducted by Lloyd and Margaret Peterson (1959) in which they orally presented *trigrams* consisting of three consonants (for example, "VRG") to their subjects (figure 7.3). To distract the subjects and prevent them from engaging in maintenance rehearsal of a trigram, immediately after a trigram was presented a light indicated that the subject was to count backward from a three-digit number by threes (for example, "657, 654, 651, . . ."). Following an interval varying from

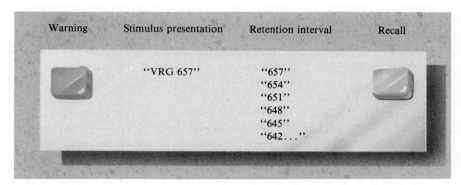

(a)

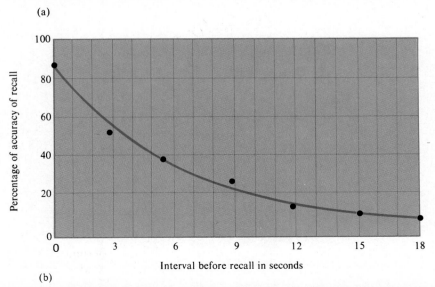

(b)

FIGURE 7.3
The Duration of Short-Term Memory Peterson and Peterson (1959) demonstrated that the information in short-term memory lasts no more than twenty seconds. (a) A warning light signaled that a trial was to begin. The subject then heard a three-letter trigram and a three-digit number. To prevent rehearsal of the trigram, the subject counted backward by threes from the number. After a period of from three to eighteen seconds, a light signaled the subject to recall the trigram. (b) The longer the delay between presentation and recall of the trigram, the less likely the subject was to recall it accurately.

Source (b): Data from *Journal of Experimental Psychology,* 58:193–198, 1959.

3 seconds to 18 seconds, a light indicated that the subject was to recall the trigram. The longer the interval, the less likely the subject was to recall the trigram. And when the interval was 18 seconds, the subject could rarely recall the trigram. Thus, the results indicated that unrehearsed information normally remains in short-term memory for no longer than 20 seconds.

Retrieval

In 1966 psychologist Saul Sternberg published the results of an ingenious experiment that showed how information is retrieved from short-term memory (figure 7.4). Sternberg had subjects memorize sets of digits ranging in length from one to six digits. He called these *memory sets.* On a given trial a subject might see a memory set such as 3 8 1 7. This was immediately followed by presentation of a single *probe digit.* On half of the trials the probe digit (in this example, perhaps an 8) had appeared in the memory set, and on half of the trials the probe digit (in this example, perhaps a 5) had not appeared in the memory set. The subject responded as quickly as possible to the probe digit by pressing either a *yes* button if the probe digit had appeared in the memory set or a *no* button if the probe digit had not appeared in it.

Because the task was relatively easy, subjects made few errors. But Sternberg was not interested in the subjects' errors. Instead, he was interested in the speed of their responses to the probe digits. Sternberg found that the time it took subjects to respond to the probe digit increased proportionally with the number of digits in the memory set. Each digit in the memory set added about 40 milliseconds to the response times.

Based on this finding, Sternberg concluded that the retrieval of information from short-term memory is a *serial,* rather than a *parallel,* search process. This means that the subjects scanned the digits in their short-term memory one at a time in sequence, rather than simultaneously, to decide whether any of them matched the probe digit. If retrieval from short-term memory were a parallel process, the response times would be the same regardless of the number of digits in the memory set.

Sternberg also determined whether the retrieval of information from short-term memory is an *exhaustive* or a *self-terminating* search process. If retrieval

FIGURE 7.4
Retrieval from Short-Term Memory This graph shows the results of the experiment by Sternberg (1966) on the retrieval of items from short-term memory. Because the time that it takes to retrieve items from short-term memory increases by about 40 milliseconds per item, the retrieval of items involves a serial, rather than a parallel, search process.

Data from S. Sternberg, "High-Speed Scanning in Human Memory" in *Science,* Vol. 153:652–54, 5 August 1966. Copyright 1966 by the AAAS. Reprinted by permission of the author and the publisher.

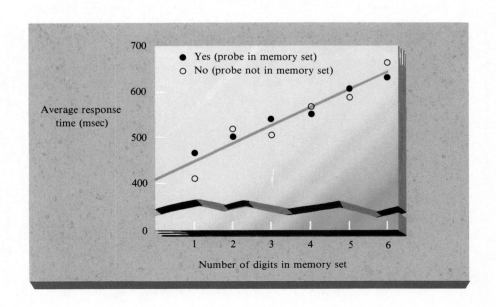

were an exhaustive search process, in searching for an item in short-term memory we would sequentially scan all of the items in short-term memory, even if we encounter the item we are seeking before reaching the last one. If retrieval were a self-terminating process, a *no* response trial would require the subject to compare the probe digit sequentially with each of the digits in the memory set. But a *yes* response trial would require the subject to compare the probe digit sequentially with the digits in the memory set only until the subject found one that matched the probe digit. Sternberg concluded that retrieval from short-term memory is an exhaustive process, because subjects, on average, took as long to respond on *yes* trials as on *no* trials. If retrieval were a self-terminating process, *yes* responses, on average, would have been faster than *no* responses.

Forgetting

We know that we can encode an average of seven chunks of information in short-term memory, that without maintenance rehearsal we can store information for about 20 seconds, and that we retrieve information by a serial, exhaustive search process. But information in short-term memory does not last forever. It is lost through the process of forgetting. Information stored in short-term memory is lost by decay (the mere fading of information over time) and by displacement by new information (Reitman, 1974).

The displacement of information from short-term memory was demonstrated in a study in which subjects called a telephone operator for a long-distance number. They showed poorer recall of the number if the operator said, "Have a nice day" after giving them the number than if the operator did not. The cheery message displaced the phone number from short-term memory (Schilling & Weaver, 1983).

LONG-TERM MEMORY

As mentioned earlier, information moves back and forth between short-term memory and long-term memory. When functioning at its best, long-term memory can store an enormous amount of information with great accuracy. This was demonstrated in the early twentieth century by Hebrew scholars from Poland, who were able to recall the entire contents of the thousands of pages in the twelve-volume *Babylonian Talmud,* a Hebrew holy book. In fact, if a pin was pushed through the pages of a volume, a scholar could recall each of the words pierced by the pin (Stratton, 1917).

In contrast, when functioning at its worst, long-term memory may fail to store information and what the person recalls may be woefully inaccurate. This occurs in **Korsakoff's syndrome,** a brain disorder caused by alcoholism. Victims of Korsakoff's syndrome have difficulty forming new long-term memories and resort to *confabulation*—using plausible guesses to fill in their missing memories. For example, if you asked a Korsakoff's patient about a recent vacation, he or she might tell you about wonderful experiences that, in reality, never took place.

Korsakoff's Syndrome A brain disorder caused by alcoholism and marked by difficulty in forming new long-term memories.

Normal information processing in long-term memory has been compared to a library. Information in a library is *encoded* in materials such as books or magazines, *stored* on shelves in a systematic way, *retrieved* by using cues given by card catalogs, and *forgotten* when it is misplaced or its catalog card lost. Similarly, information in long-term memory is encoded in several ways, stored in an organized manner, retrieved by using cues, and forgotten by the failure to store it adequately or to use appropriate retrieval cues.

Encoding

As William James (1890/1950, p. 686) noted, "A curious peculiarity of our memory is that things are impressed better by active than by passive repetition." To appreciate William James's claim, take a moment to draw the face side of a penny from memory. Next, look at the drawings of pennies in figure 7.5. Which one is accurate? Though you have seen thousands of pennies in your life and may realize that the front of a penny has a date and a profile of Abraham Lincoln, you almost certainly were unable to match every detail. And even when presented with several drawings to choose from, you may have still chosen the wrong one. If you had difficulty, you are not alone. A study of adult Americans found that few could draw a penny from memory, and less than half could recognize the correct drawing of one (Nickerson & Adams, 1979).

What accounts for our failure to remember an image that is a common part of everyday life? The answer depends on the distinction between maintenance rehearsal and elaborative rehearsal. In using **maintenance rehearsal,** we merely hold information in short-term memory without trying to transfer it into long-term memory. In **elaborative rehearsal,** we actively organize information and integrate it with information already stored in long-term memory. Though maintenance rehearsal may encode some information (such as the main features of a penny) into long-term memory, elaborative rehearsal will encode more information (such as the exact arrangement of the features of a penny) into long-term memory (Greene, 1987).

You can experience the benefits of elaborative rehearsal when, while studying your textbook, you are confronted by a new concept that you do not understand. If you make an effort to understand the concept by integrating it with material you have already learned in this course or in previous life experiences, you will be more likely to encode the concept into your long-term memory. For example, when you came across the concept of flashbulb memory, you would have been more likely to encode it into long-term memory if it provoked you to think about your own flashbulb memories.

The superior encoding of information that has been subjected to elaborative rehearsal supports the **levels of processing theory** of Fergus Craik and Robert Lockhart (1972). They believe that the "depth" at which we process

Maintenance Rehearsal Repeating information to oneself to keep it in short-term memory.

Elaborative Rehearsal Actively organizing new information to make it more meaningful, and integrating it with information already stored in long-term memory.

Levels of Processing Theory The theory that the "depth" at which we process information determines how well it is encoded, stored, and retrieved.

FIGURE 7.5
Can You Identify the Real Penny?

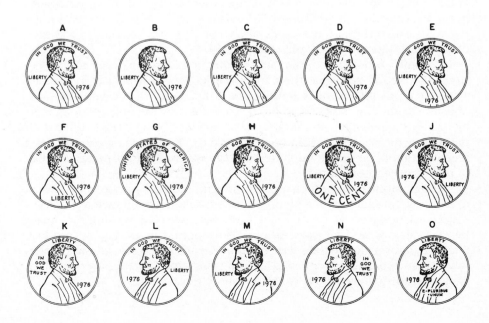

information will determine how well it is encoded and, as a result, how well it is stored in long-term memory. When you process information at a shallow level, you attend to its superficial, sensory qualities—as when you use maintenance rehearsal of a telephone number. In contrast, when you process information at a deep level, you attend to its meaning—as when you use elaborative rehearsal of textbook material. Similarly, if you merely listen to the sound of a popular song over and over on the radio—a shallow level of processing—you may recall the melody but not the lyrics. But if you listen to the lyrics and think about their meaning—a deeper level of processing—you may recall both the words and the melody.

In a study that supported the levels of processing theory, subjects were induced to process words at different levels by asking them different kinds of questions about each word just before it was flashed for a fifth of a second (Craik & Tulving, 1975). Imagine that you are replicating the study, and one of the words is "BREAD." You could induce a shallow level of encoding by asking about how the word *looks,* such as, "Is the word written in capital letters?" You could induce a somewhat deeper level of encoding by asking a question about how the word *sounds,* such as, "Does the word rhyme with head?" And you could induce a much deeper level of encoding by asking a question about what the word *means,* such as, "Does the word fit in the following sentence?": The boy used the ———— to make a sandwich.

After repeating this with several words, the subject would be presented with a list of words and would be asked to identify which of the words had been presented before. Craik and Tulving (1975) found that the deeper the level at which a word had been encoded, the more likely it was to be correctly identified (figure 7.6). Thus, the storage of information in long-term memory may be improved by increasing its depth of processing.

Storage

When information is stored in long-term memory it is encoded as words or images (Paivio & te Linde, 1982). Apparently, because our memory for pictures is better than for words, a picture *is,* in a sense, worth a thousand words. This has been attributed to the storage of pictures as both words and images, while words are stored only as words (Horton & Mills, 1984).

According to influential memory researcher Endel Tulving (1985), we store information in two kinds of long-term memory. The first, **procedural memory,** includes memories of how to perform behaviors, such as making an omelet or using a word processor. The second, **declarative memory,** includes memories of facts. Tulving subdivides declarative memory into semantic memory and episodic memory. **Semantic memory** includes memories of general knowledge, such as the definition of an omelet or the components of a word processor. **Episodic memory** includes memories of personal experiences tied to particular times and places, such as the last time you made an omelet or used a word processor.

Apparently, the brain has evolved different memory systems for storing these different kinds of memory (Sherry & Schachter, 1987). Evidence of this comes from studies of people who have suffered brain damage. They may exhibit deficits in one kind of memory, while the others remain intact. In one case study (Schachter, 1983), a victim of the degenerative brain disorder called Alzheimer's disease was able to play golf (procedural memory) and had good knowledge of the game (semantic memory), but he could not find his tee shots (episodic memory).

But how are memories organized within these systems? Unlike short-term memory, in which a few unorganized items of information can be stored and retrieved efficiently, long-term memory requires that millions of pieces of

Procedural Memory The part of long-term memory that contains memories of how to perform particular actions or skills.

Declarative Memory The part of long-term memory that contains memories of facts.

Semantic Memory The part of declarative memory that contains general information about the world.

Episodic Memory The part of declarative memory that contains memories of personal experiences tied to particular times and places.

FIGURE 7.6
Depth of Processing Craik and
Tulving (1975) found that the
greater the depth of processing of
words the better will be memory
for them. Encoding words
according to their meanings
produced better recognition of
them than encoding them
according to their sounds or
appearances.

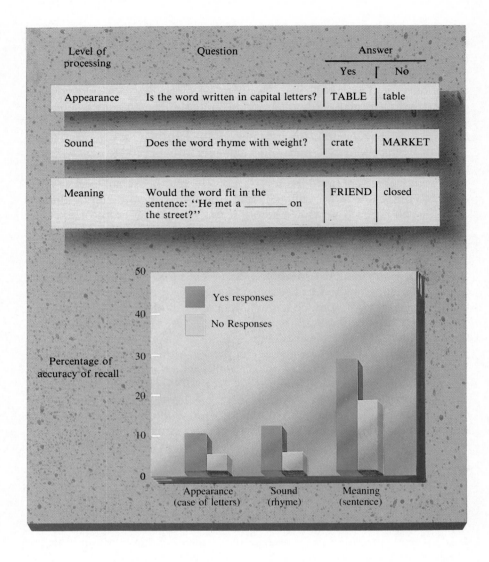

formation be stored in an organized, rather than arbitrary, manner. Otherwise, you might spend years searching your memory until you retrieved the one you wanted, just as you might spend years searching the Library of Congress for Williams James's *The Principles of Psychology* if its books were shelved randomly.

Semantic Network Theory A theory that explains how semantic information is meaningfully organized in long-term memory is **semantic network theory** (figure 7.7), which assumes that memories are stored as nodes interconnected by links. A *node* is a concept such as "pencil," "green," "uncle," or "cold," and a *link* is a connection between two concepts. Related nodes have stronger links between them. The retrieval of a node from memory stimulates activation of related nodes, so-called spreading activation (Collins & Loftus, 1975).

Even young children organize memories into semantic networks. For example, preschool children who enjoy playing with toy dinosaurs and listening to their parents reading to them about dinosaurs may organize their knowledge of dinosaurs into semantic networks (Chi & Koeske, 1983). The dinosaurs would be represented as nodes (for example, "Tyrannosaurus Rex" or "Brontosaurus") and their relationships would be represented by links. The

Semantic Network Theory The theory that memories are stored as nodes interconnected by links representing their relationships.

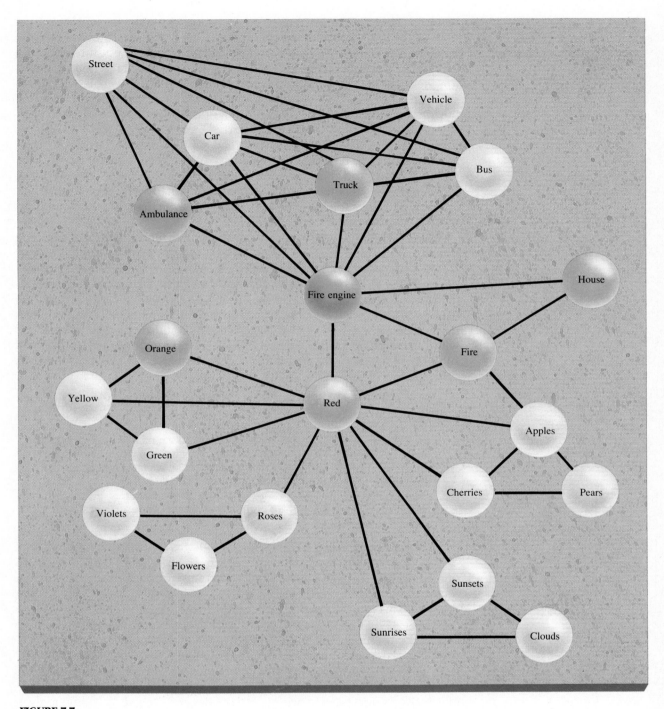

FIGURE 7.7
A Semantic Network According to Collins and Loftus (1975), our long-term memories are organized into semantic networks in which concepts are interconnected by links. The shorter the link between two concepts the stronger the association between them. After a retrieval cue has activated a concept, related concepts will also be activated and retrieved from long-term memory.

retrieval of a dinosaur's name from memory would activate nodes with which it is linked. So, retrieval of "Tyrannosaurus Rex" would be more likely to activate nodes containing the names of other meat-eating dinosaurs than those containing the names of plant-eating dinosaurs.

Schema Theory The theory that long-term memories are stored as parts of schemas, which are cognitive structures that organize knowledge about events or objects.

Schema Theory An alternative to the network theory of memory organization is the **schema theory,** which is used to explain both episodic memory and semantic memory. The schema theory was put forth decades ago by the English psychologist Frederic Bartlett (1932), who found that long-term memories are stored as parts of schemas. A *schema* is a cognitive structure that organizes knowledge about an event or object and that affects the encoding and retrieval of information about that event or object. Schemas would include "birthday party," "class clown," and "Caribbean vacation." In a classic study, Bartlett had subjects read a Native American folktale called "The War of the Ghosts" and then write the story from memory. He found that the subjects recalled the theme of the story but forgot many of its details. Because the folktale had some seemingly illogical content, the subjects added, eliminated, or changed details to fit their own story schemas.

Bartlett's findings were replicated in a study in which college students read a brief biographical passage about either a famous person (Adolf Hitler or Helen Keller) or a fictitious person (Gerald Martin or Carol Harris). Each student's ability to recognize individual sentences that had or had not been included in the original passages was tested one week later. Passages with a famous character yielded more false positive errors—recognition of sentences that were not in the original passage but that could be plausibly associated with the famous person. Thus, knowledge of the topic of a passage affected subsequent memory for it through a reconstructive process based on the schema for Hitler or Keller (Sulin & Dooling, 1974).

Retrieval

> In short, we may search in our memory for forgotten ideas, just as we rummage our house for a lost object. In both cases we visit what seems to us the probable neighborhood of that which we miss. We turn over the things under which, or within which, or alongside which, it may possibly be; and if it lies near them, it soon comes to view. But these matters, in the case of a mental object sought, are nothing but its associatives. (James, 1890/ 1950, Vol. I, p. 654)

The network theory of memory agrees with this statement that the retrieval of memories from long-term memory begins by searching a particular region of memory and then tracing the associations among nodes (memories) in that region, rather than by a haphazard search of information stored in long-term memory. This is analogous to looking for a book in a library. You would use the card catalog to provide you with a retrieval cue (a book number) to help you locate the book you want. Similarly, when you are given a memory retrieval cue, the relevant stored memories are activated, which, in turn, activates other related memories with which they are linked (Anderson, 1983). If, as in short-term memory, retrieval from long-term memory were a serial, exhaustive search process, we might take days or even years to find a given memory.

To illustrate retrieval from a semantic network, suppose that you were given the cue "sensory memory." If your semantic network were well organized, the cue might activate nodes for "Sperling," "iconic," and "partial report." But if your semantic network were less well organized, the cue might also activate nodes for "amnesia," "chunks," or "Korsakoff's." And if your semantic network were poorly organized, the cue might activate nodes completely unrelated to sensory memory, such as "hallucination," "sensory deprivation," or "extrasensory perception."

In contrast to network theory, schema theory assumes that we alter our memories to make them consistent with our schemas. This was supported by

FIGURE 7.8
A Memory Schema Schemas such as stereotypes can affect the recall of information from long-term memory. About half of the subjects who viewed a picture similar to this one later reported that the black man held the razor.

a study in which subjects, who were white, viewed a picture of the inside of a subway car in which a white man holding a straight razor stood facing a black man (figure 7.8). When asked to recall the picture, half of the subjects placed the razor in the hand of the black man. This indicated that their stereotypical schema for blacks as more violent than whites had influenced their memory of the picture (Allport & Postman, 1947).

A more recent example of the schematic nature of memory retrieval, taken from testimony about the 1972 Watergate burglary that led to the resignation of President Nixon, was given by the eminent memory researcher Ulric Neisser (1981). Neisser described how schemas influenced the testimony of John Dean, former legal counsel to President Nixon, before the Senate Watergate Investigating Committee in 1973. Dean began his opening testimony with a 245-page statement in which he recalled the details of dozens of meetings that he had attended over a period of several years. Dean's apparently phenomenal recall of minute details prompted Senator Daniel Inouye of Hawaii to ask skeptically, "Have you always had a facility for recalling the details of conversations which took place many months ago?" (Neisser, 1981, p. 1).

Neisser found that Inouye's skepticism was well founded. In comparing Dean's testimony with tape recordings of those conversations (secretly made by Nixon), Neisser found that Dean's recall of their themes was accurate, but his recall of many of the details was inaccurate. Neisser took this as evidence for Dean's relying on a schema to retrieve memories. The schema reflected

The Schematic Nature of Schemes Comparisons between John Dean's testimony before the Senate Watergate Investigating Committee about meetings with President Nixon in the White House and secret tape recordings of those meetings made by Nixon showed that many of the details of Dean's testimony were inaccurate. Nonetheless, the gist of his testimony was correct. The inaccurate details may have been products of a schema: his knowledge that a burglary had occurred and that Nixon and other officials had tried to cover it up.

Dean's knowledge that there had been a cover-up of the Watergate break-in. Neisser used this to support his conclusion that in recalling real-life events, "Constructive recall is the rule, literal recall is the exception" (Neisser, 1984, p. 33). What Neisser called **constructive recall** is the distortion of memories by adding or changing details to fit a schema. But neither the schema theory nor the network theory has yet emerged as the best explanation of the storage and retrieval of long-term memories. Perhaps a complete explanation will require both.

Forgetting

According to William James (1890/1950, Vol. I p. 680), "If we remembered everything, we should on most occasions be as ill off as if we remembered nothing." James believed that forgetting is adaptive because it rids us of useless information that might interfere with our memory for useful information. But as you are sometimes painfully aware when taking exams, even useful information that has been stored in memory is not always retrievable. We refer to this inability to retrieve previously stored information as forgetting. The first formal research on forgetting was conducted by the German psychologist Hermann Ebbinghaus (1850–1909). Ebbinghaus (1885/1913) studied memory by repeating lists of items over and over until he could recall them in order perfectly. The items he used were called *nonsense syllables* (consisting of a vowel between two consonants, such as "VEM") because they were not real words. He used nonsense syllables instead of words because he wanted a "pure" measure of memory, unaffected by prior associations with real words.

Ebbinghaus found that immediate recall is worse for items in the middle of a list than at the beginning and end of a list (figure 7.9). This differential forgetting is called the **serial-position effect.** The better memory for items at the beginning of a list is called the *primacy effect,* and the better memory for items at the end of a list is called the *recency effect.* Thus, in memorizing a list of terms from this chapter, you would have greater difficulty memorizing terms from the middle of the list than from the beginning or end of the list.

Constructive Recall　The distortion of memories by adding, dropping, or changing details to fit a schema.

Hermann Ebbinghaus (1850–1909)　"Physical states of every kind, sensations, feelings, ideas, which at one time were present and then disappeared from consciousness, have not absolutely ceased to exist. Although an inward glance may not find them, they are not absolutely denied and annulled, but continue to live in a certain way, retained, as one says, in memory."

Serial-Position Effect　The superiority of immediate recall for items at the beginning and end of a list.

FIGURE 7.9
The Serial-Position Effect　A typical serial-position curve, showing that items in the middle of a list are the most difficult to recall.

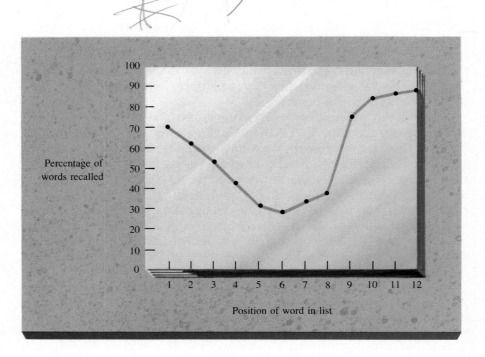

Percentage of words recalled

Position of word in list

What accounts for the serial-position effect? The primacy effect appears to occur because the items at the beginning of a list are subjected to more rehearsal as a learner memorizes the list, firmly placing those items in long-term memory. And the recency effect appears to occur because items at the end of the list remain readily accessible in short-term memory. In contrast, items in the middle of the list are neither firmly placed in long-term memory nor readily accessible in short-term memory (Greene, 1986). Note that this explanation supports Shiffrin and Atkinson's distinction between short-term memory and long-term memory.

Ebbinghaus also introduced the **method of savings,** which is now called *relearning,* as a way to assess memory. In using the method of savings, Ebbinghaus would memorize a list of items until he could recall them perfectly, noting how many trials he needed to achieve perfect recall. After varying intervals, during which he would naturally forget some of the items, Ebbinghaus would again memorize the list until he could again recall it perfectly. He found that it took him fewer trials to relearn a list than to learn it originally. He called the difference between the number of original trials and the number of relearning trials *savings,* because he relearned the material more quickly the second time. The phenomenon of savings demonstrates that even when we cannot recall information, much of it still remains stored in memory. Otherwise, we would take just as long to relearn material as we took to learn it originally.

When you study for a cumulative final exam, you experience savings. Suppose that your psychology course lasts fifteen weeks and you study your notes and readings for six hours a week in order to perform at an A level on exams given during the semester. You would have studied for a total of ninety hours. If you then studied for a cumulative final exam, you would not have to study for ninety hours to rememorize the material to your original level of mastery. In fact, you would have to study for only a fraction of the original number of hours—perhaps as little as a few hours—to master the material again. A possible cause of savings is that relearning improves the *retrieval* of information stored in memory, rather than improving the *storage* of information in memory (MacLeod, 1988).

Ebbinghaus also found that, once we have mastered a list of items, forgetting is initially rapid and then slows. So, if you memorized a list of terms from this chapter for an exam, you would do most of your forgetting in the first few days after the exam. Ebbinghaus's **forgetting curve** even holds for material learned decades earlier, as demonstrated in a study of the retention of Spanish words learned in high school by groups of subjects ranging from recent graduates to individuals who had graduated fifty years earlier. Though some of the subjects had not spoken Spanish in fifty years, they showed surprisingly good retention of some words. Figure 7.10 indicates that forgetting is rapid during the first three years after high school, then remains relatively unchanged. This indicates that after a certain amount of time memories that have not been forgotten may become permanent (Bahrick, 1984).

Decay Theory Plato, who likened memory to an imprint made on a block of wax, believed that memories fade over time just as wax imprints wear away over time. Plato's view anticipated the **decay theory,** which assumes that memories naturally fade over time. But decay theory has received little research support, and a classic study provided evidence against it. John Jenkins and Karl Dallenbach (1924) had two subjects memorize a list of ten nonsense syllables and then either stay awake or immediately go to sleep for varying periods of one, two, four, or eight hours. At the end of each period, the subjects tried to recall the nonsense syllables. The

Method of Savings The assessment of memory by comparing the number of trials needed to memorize a given amount of information and the number of trials needed to memorize it again at a later time.

Forgetting Curve A graph showing that forgetting is initially rapid and then slows.

Decay Theory The theory that forgetting occurs because memories naturally fade over time.

FIGURE 7.10
The Forgetting Curve (*top*)
The results of a study by
Ebbinghaus on memory for
nonsense syllables, (*bottom*) the
results of a study on memory for
Spanish words. Both graphs show
that forgetting is initially rapid
and then levels off. But note that
the forgetting of nonsense
syllables is more rapid than the
forgetting of meaningful items,
such as words.

Source (*top*): Data from Hermann
Ebbinghaus, *Uber das Gedachnis (On
Memory)*, 1885.

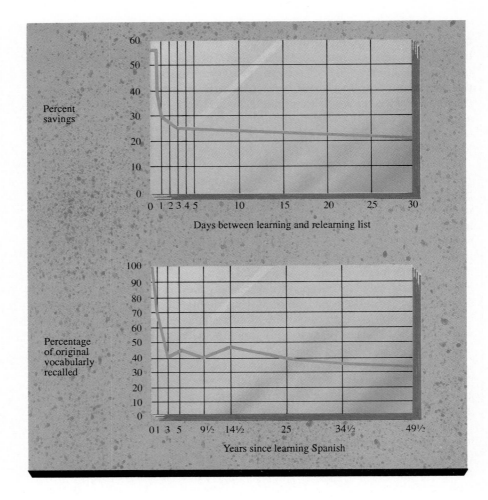

Days between learning and relearning list

Years since learning Spanish

researchers believed that sleep would prevent waking activities from interfering with the memories.

The subjects showed better recall if they slept than if they remained awake
(figure 7.11). Though there was some memory loss during sleep, providing
some support for decay theory, if decay theory were an adequate explanation
of forgetting, the subjects should have shown the same level of recall whether
they remained awake or slept. Jenkins and Dallenbach concluded that the
subjects forgot more if they remained awake because experiences that they
had while they were awake interfered with their memories of the nonsense
syllables. In contrast, the subjects forgot less after sleeping because they had
few experiences while asleep that could interfere with their memories for the
nonsense syllables.

Interference Theory Since Jenkins and Dallenbach's classic study contradicting decay theory, psychologists have come to favor *interference* as
a better explanation of forgetting. **Interference theory** assumes that forgetting results from particular memories interfering with the retrieval of
other memories. In **proactive interference,** old memories interfere with
new memories. You have probably experienced this after moving to a new
home, when your memory of your old phone number interfered with your
ability to recall your new one. In **retroactive interference,** new memories interfere with old ones. Your memory of your new phone number may
interfere with your memory of your old one.

Interference Theory The
theory that forgetting results from
some memories interfering with
the ability to remember other
memories.

Proactive Interference The
process by which old memories
interfere with the ability to
remember new memories.

Retroactive Interference The
process by which new memories
interfere with the ability to
remember old memories.

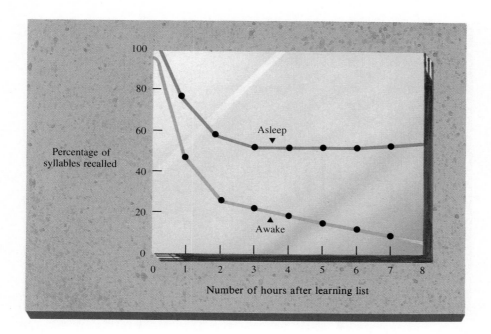

FIGURE 7.11
Interference and Recall Jenkins and Dallenbach (1924) found that when subjects learned a list of nonsense syllables and then slept they forgot less than when they stayed awake.

Source: Data from J. G. Jenkins and K. M. Dallenbach, "Obliviscence During Sleeping and Waking" in *American Journal of Psychology*, 35:605–612, 1924.

You have certainly experienced both kinds of interference when taking an exam. Material you have studied for other courses will interfere with your memories of the material on the exam. Interference is stronger when the materials are similar to each other. So, biology material will interfere more than computer science material with your recall of psychology material. Because of the great amount of material you learn during a semester, proactive interference may be a particularly strong influence on your exam performance (Dempster, 1985).

Motivation Theory Sigmund Freud (1901/1965) claimed that we may forget material through the process of repression. **Repression** is the process by which emotionally threatening experiences, such as viewing a horrible accident or having a painful emotional experience, are banished from the conscious mind to the unconscious mind. Though research findings have tended to discount Freudian repression as an explanation of forgetting (Holmes, 1974), there is some evidence that we *are* more motivated to forget emotionally upsetting experiences.

In an experiment demonstrating motivated forgetting, subjects were shown one of two versions of a training film for bank tellers depicting a simulated bank robbery. In one version, a shot fired by the robbers at pursuers instead hit a boy in the face. The boy fell to the ground, bleeding profusely. In the other version, instead of showing the boy being shot, the bank manager was shown talking about the robbery. When asked to recall details of the robbery, subjects who had seen the violent version had poorer recall of the details of the crime than did subjects who had seen the nonviolent version. Evidently, the content of the violent version motivated subjects to forget what they had seen (Loftus & Burns, 1982).

We may even be motivated to recall past events in ways that make them more consistent with our current circumstances, much as schemas influence our recall of past events. This possibility was investigated in an experiment in which college students were randomly assigned to a study skills group or to a control group that was put on a waiting list (Conway & Ross, 1984). All subjects began by doing a self-evaluation of their study skills. Three weeks later

Repression The process by which emotionally threatening experiences are banished from the conscious mind to the unconscious mind.

Motivated Forgetting
According to Sigmund Freud a person may forget a traumatic event by repressing its memory into the unconscious mind.

all subjects were asked to recall their initial self-evaluations. Members of the study skills group recalled their evaluations as worse than they had reported, but members of the control group recalled theirs accurately. Members of the study skills group also reported greater improvement in their study skills and expected better final grades than did those in the control group. But the actual grades of the two groups did not differ. And six months later members of the study skills group overestimated their academic performance during the period when the program was conducted. The distorted memories of the study skills group may have reflected their motivation to have their participation pay off.

Cue-Dependence Theory Because the retrieval of long-term memories depends on adequate retrieval cues, forgetting can sometimes be explained by the failure to have or to use adequate retrieval cues. This is known as *cue-dependence theory.* At times we may fail to find an adequate cue to activate the relevant portion of a semantic memory network. Consider the **tip-of-the-tongue phenomenon,** in which you cannot quite recall a familiar word but can recall parts of the word, or words similar to it, but are unable to retrieve it from your memory.

Tip-of-the-Tongue Phenomenon The inability to recall information that one knows has been stored in long-term memory.

In a study of this phenomenon, subjects were read only the definitions of rarely used words such as *cloaca* and *nepotism* (Brown & McNeill, 1966). See if you can recall the word referred to by the following definition: "A small boat found in the Far East, propelled by a single oar at the rear, and often covered by a roof of straw mats." Even if you are unable to recall it, you may feel that you know it. The word you are trying to retrieve is *sampan.* The study found that subjects who reported tip-of-the-tongue phenomena often felt as though they knew the words but could not recall them. And the subjects often recalled the first letters of the word, the number of syllables, a word that sounded similar, or a word of similar meaning. Thus, if you failed to recall the word *sampan,* you may have recalled that it began with an *s,* had two syllables, sounded like "sandman," or was something like a small ark.

Encoding Specificity The principle that recall will be best when cues that were associated with the encoding of a memory are also present during attempts at retrieving it.

This supports the concept of **encoding specificity,** which states that recall will be best when cues that were associated with the encoding of a memory are also present during attempts at retrieving the memory (Tulving & Thomson, 1973). In an unusual experiment that demonstrated the effect of the environmental context as a cue for recall, scuba divers memorized lists of words while underwater or on a beach, and then they tried to recall the words while either in the same location or in the other location (Godden & Baddeley, 1975). The subjects communicated with the experimenter through a special intercom system. The results showed that when the subjects memorized and recalled the words in different locations they recalled about 30 percent fewer than when they memorized and recalled the words in the same location (figure 7.12). This is known as **context-dependent memory.** This study even has practical implications. Instructions given to scuba divers should not be limited to dry land, and if divers are making observations about what they observe underwater they should record them there and not wait until they get on dry land (Baddeley, 1982).

The effect of environmental context on recall is not lost on theater directors, who hold dress rehearsals in full costume amid the scenery that will be used during actual performances. And even your academic performance may be affected by environmental cues. Half a century ago a study found that college students performed worse when their exams were given in classrooms other than their normal ones (Abernethy, 1940). Perhaps you have noticed this when you have taken a final exam in a strange room. If you find yourself in that situation, you may improve your performance by mentally reinstating the environmental context in which you learned the material (Smith, 1984).

Note that the environmental context is important only when *recall* is required, not when *recognition* is required. This means that your performance on an essay exam might be impaired if you took an exam in a strange room, but your performance on a multiple-choice test would not. Apparently, tasks requiring recognition include enough retrieval cues of their own, making environmental retrieval cues relatively less important (Eich, 1980).

Our recall of memories depends not only on cues from the external environment but also on cues from our internal states. The effect on recall of the similarity between a person's internal state during encoding and during retrieval is called **state-dependent memory.** For example, when memories are encoded while the person is in a psychoactive drug-induced state, they will

Context-Dependent Memory The tendency for recall to be best when the environmental context present during the encoding of a memory is also present during attempts at retrieving it.

State-Dependent Memory The tendency for recall to be best when one's emotional or physiological state is the same during the recall of a memory as it was during the encoding of that memory.

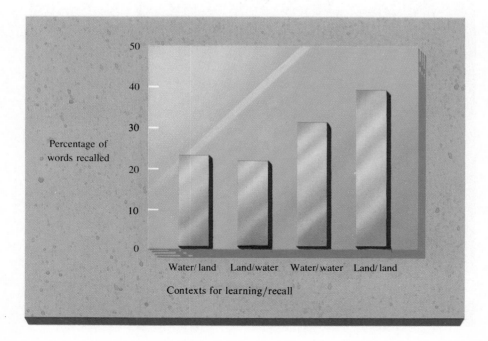

FIGURE 7.12
Context-Dependent Memory
Godden and Baddeley (1975) found that words learned underwater were best recalled underwater and that words learned on land were best recalled on land.

Percentage of words recalled

Water/land   Land/water   Water/water   Land/land

Contexts for learning/recall

be recalled better when in that state. In a government-sponsored study on the effects of marijuana (Eich, Weingartner, Stillman, & Gillin, 1975), one group of subjects memorized a list of words after smoking marijuana, and a second group memorized the same list after smoking a placebo that tasted like marijuana. The groups were "blind"—that is, they did not know whether they were smoking marijuana or a placebo. Four hours later half of each group smoked either marijuana or a placebo and then tried to recall the words they had memorized. Recall was better either when subjects smoked the placebo on both occasions or when they smoked marijuana on both occasions than when they smoked marijuana on one occasion and the placebo on the other. You should *not* conclude that marijuana smoking improves memory. You may recall from chapter 5 that marijuana actually *impairs* memory. And, indeed, in this study the group that smoked the placebo on both occasions performed *better* than the groups that smoked marijuana on either occasion or on both occasions.

Our internal states also reflect our moods, which may play a role in a form of state-dependent memory called *mood-dependent memory,* in which our recall of information that has been encoded in a particular mood will be best when we are in that mood again (Bower, 1981). The mood appears to act as a cue for the retrieval of memories from semantic networks. Thus, if you have an experience while you are in an angry mood, you may be more likely to recall details of that experience when you are again in an angry mood. This effect was observed in a study in which moods were induced by having subjects smell either a pleasant odor (almond extract) or an unpleasant odor (a chemical called pyridine). The subjects were then asked to recall past experiences. Those in the pleasant odor condition recalled a higher percentage of happy memories than did those in the unpleasant odor condition (Ehrlichman & Halpern, 1988). Despite a number of studies that have demonstrated mood-dependent memory, even Gordon Bower, the psychologist who first reported it, has had difficulty in replicating his early research (Bower &

State-Dependent Memory In the movie *City Lights,* a tramp played by Charlie Chaplin is befriended by a drunken millionaire. But when the millionaire sobers up he considers Chaplin an unwanted intruder and has him thrown out. When the millionaire gets drunk again, he once again treats Chaplin as his good friend. This illustrates so-called alcoholic blackout, a form of state-dependent memory.

Mood-Dependent Memory The current moods of these family members may influence the kinds of memories that the photographs evoke. We tend to recall memories that are congruent with our current mood.

Mayer, 1985). So, mood-dependent memory seems to be, at best, an inconsistent phenomenon.

As you may have concluded from what you have read so far, the field of memory research is diverse, fascinating, and filled with promising applications to everyday life. One important application is the improvement of memory.

IMPROVING YOUR MEMORY

A century ago William James (1890/1950) criticized those who claimed that memory ability could be improved by mere practice. To James memory was a fixed, inherited ability and not subject to improvement. He concluded this after finding that practice in memorizing did not decrease the time it took him and other subjects to memorize poetry or other kinds of literature. Though it is unclear whether we can improve our inherited memory ability, we can certainly make better use of the ability we have by improving our study habits and by using memory aids called mnemonic devices.

Improving Study Habits

Given two students with equal memory ability, the one with better study habits will probably perform better in school. To practice good study habits, you would begin by setting up a strict schedule in which you would do the bulk of your studying when you are at your most alert and most motivated—whether in the early morning, late afternoon, or some other time. You should also study in a quiet, comfortable place, free of distractions. If you study in a dormitory lounge with students milling around and holding conversations, you might find yourself distracted from the information being processed in your short-term memory, making it more difficult for you to transfer the information efficiently into your long-term memory.

As for particular study techniques, you might consider using the **SQ3R method** (Robinson, 1970). SQ3R stands for Survey, Question, Read, Recite, and Review. By using the SQ3R method to study chapters in this text, you would organize the material, make it meaningful, and, as a result, improve your recall of it. Note that this method involves elaborative rehearsal, in which you process information at a relatively deep level. This is distinct from rote memorization, in which you process information at a relatively shallow level.

SQ3R Method A study technique that requires the student to survey, question, read, recite, and review course material.

Overlearning In learning a script, actors would not merely memorize it until they recall it perfectly once. Instead, they would overlearn it by making sure that they could recall it perfectly several times. This would aid their recall of the lines and improve their confidence, thereby improving their performance.

Overlearning Studying material beyond the point of initial mastery.

Distributed Practice Spreading out the memorization of information or the learning of a motor skill over several sessions.

Massed Practice Cramming the memorization of information or the learning of a motor skill into one session.

If you have ever found yourself studying for hours, yet doing poorly on exams, it may be the consequence of failing to use elaborative rehearsal.

Suppose that you decide to use the SQ3R method to study the final two sections of this chapter. You should follow several steps. First, *survey* the main headings and subheadings to create an organized framework in which to fit the information you are studying. Second, as you survey the sections ask yourself *questions* to be answered when you read them. For example, you might ask yourself, What is the physiological basis of memory? and Is eyewitness testimony accurate? Third, *read* the material carefully, trying to answer your questions as you move through each section. In memorizing new terms, you might find it especially helpful to say them out loud. A study found that subjects who read terms out loud later remembered more of them than did subjects who read them silently, wrote them down, or heard them spoken by someone else (Gathercole & Conway, 1988). Fourth, after reading a section, *recite* information from it to see whether you understand it. Do not proceed to the next section until you understand the one you are studying. Fifth, periodically (perhaps every few days) *review* the information in the entire chapter by quizzing yourself on it and then rereading anything you fail to recall. You will find yourself experiencing savings—each time you review the material it will take you less time to reach the same level of mastery. This would indicate that you are gaining greater command of the material.

You may also wish to apply other principles to improve your studying. First, *overlearn* the material you are studying. You can accomplish this by studying the material until you feel you know all of it—and then going over it several more times. This will make you less likely to forget it and more confident that you know it (Nelson, Leonesio, Shimamura, Landwehr, & Narens, 1982), perhaps improving your exam performance by making you less anxious. The power of **overlearning** is revealed by the amazing ability that people show for recognizing the names and faces of their high school classmates decades after graduation. This is attributable to their having overlearned the names and faces during their years together in school (Bahrick, Bahrick, & Wittlinger, 1975).

Second, use **distributed practice** instead of **massed practice** (Wickelgren, 1981). If you devote five hours to studying this chapter, you would be better off studying for one hour on five different occasions than studying for five hours on one occasion. You may recognize this as a suggestion to avoid "cramming" for exams. Note how the following explanation by William James for the negative effects of cramming anticipated recent research into the effects of elaborative rehearsal, overlearning, environmental cues, and semantic networks on memory.

> Things learned thus in a few hours, on one occasion, for one purpose, cannot possibly have formed many associations with other things in the mind. . . . Speedy oblivion is the almost inevitable fate of all that is committed to memory in this simple way. . . . Whereas on the contrary, the same information taken in gradually, day after day, recurring in different contexts, considered in various relations, associated with other external incidents, and repeatedly reflected on, grow into a fabric, lie open to so many paths of approach, that they remain permanent possessions. (James, 1890/1950, Vol. I, p. 663)

Mnemonic Devices

As the story goes, about 2,500 years ago the Greek poet Simonides stepped outside of the banquet hall where he was to recite a poem in honor of a Roman nobleman. While Simonides was outside, the hall collapsed, killing all the guests and mangling their bodies beyond recognition. But, by recalling where each guest had been sitting, Simonides was able to identify all of them. He

√ location

called this the **method of loci** (*loci* means "place" in Latin), which he recommended to orators, because paper and pens were too expensive to waste on writing routine speeches (Bower, 1970). The method of loci is useful for memorizing sets of items. You might memorize concrete terms from this chapter by associating them with places and landmarks on your campus, and then retrieving them while taking a mental walk across it (figure 7.13).

The method of loci is one of several **mnemonic devices,** which are techniques for organizing information to make it easier to recall. The word *mnemonic* is derived from Mnemosyne, the Greek goddess of memory. You are familiar with certain mnemonic devices, such as acronyms. An **acronym** is a term formed from the first letters of a series of words. Examples of acronyms include USA, NFL, and even SQ3R. And you are also familiar with the use of rhymes as mnemonic devices, as in "i before e except after c" and "Thirty days hath November. . . ."

Though rhymes are useful mnemonic devices for adults, they may actually impair the memory of young children. In one study, children who listened to stories presented in prose had better recall of them than did children who listened to stories presented in verse. Apparently, the children who listened to verse processed the stories at a shallow level, as sounds, while the children

Method of Loci A mnemonic device in which items to be recalled are associated with landmarks in a familiar place and then recalled during a mental walk from one landmark to another.

Mnemonic Device A technique for organizing information to be memorized to make it easier to remember.

Acronym A mnemonic device that involves forming a term from the first letters of a series of words that are to be recalled.

O'Keefe

FIGURE 7.13
The Method of Loci In using the method of loci to recall a shopping list, you would pair each item on the list with a familiar place. You would then take a mental tour, retrieving items as you go.

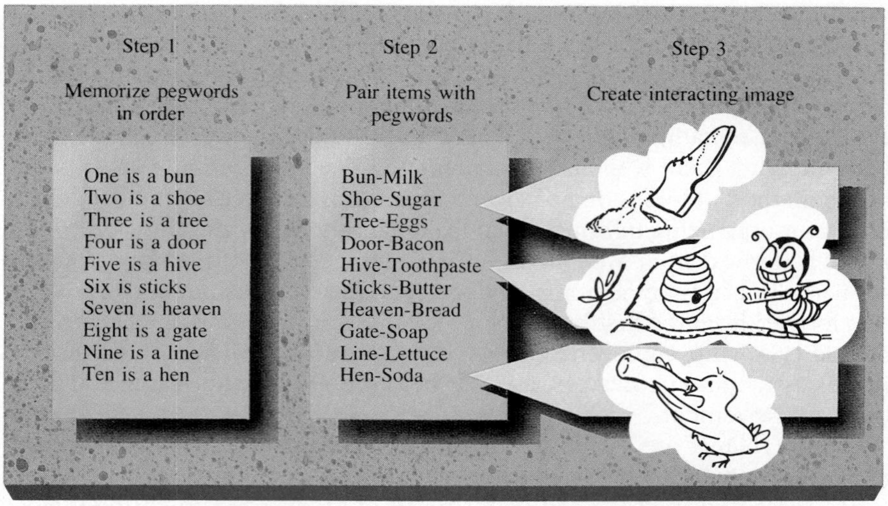

FIGURE 7.14
The Pegword Method The pegword method can be used to recall a grocery list. Each grocery item is paired with a pegword. Thus, the retrieval of a pegword will cue the retrieval of the associated grocery item.

Step 1
Memorize pegwords in order

One is a bun
Two is a shoe
Three is a tree
Four is a door
Five is a hive
Six is sticks
Seven is heaven
Eight is a gate
Nine is a line
Ten is a hen

Step 2
Pair items with pegwords

Bun-Milk
Shoe-Sugar
Tree-Eggs
Door-Bacon
Hive-Toothpaste
Sticks-Butter
Heaven-Bread
Gate-Soap
Line-Lettuce
Hen-Soda

Step 3
Create interacting image

Pegword Method A mnemonic device that involves associating items to be recalled with objects that rhyme with the numbers 1, 2, 3, and so on, to make the items easier to recall.

Link Method A mnemonic device that involves connecting images of items to be memorized in sequence to make them easier to recall.

who listened to prose processed the stories at a deeper level, in terms of their meaning (Hayes, Chemelski, & Palmer, 1982).

A mnemonic device that relies on both imagery and rhyming is the **pegword method,** which begins with memorizing a list of concrete nouns that rhyme with the numbers *1, 2, 3, 4, 5, 6,* and so on. For the pegword method to work well, the image of the pegword object and the image of the object to be recalled should interact, rather than merely being paired side by side (Wollen, Weber, & Lowry, 1972). Suppose that you wanted to remember the grocery list presented in figure 7.14. You might imagine, among other things, sugar being poured from a shoe, bees in a hive brushing their teeth, and a hen drinking from a soda bottle. To recall an item you would merely imagine the pegword that is paired with a particular number, which would act as a cue for retrieving the image of the object that interacted with that pegword. Thus, if you imagined a shoe you would automatically retrieve an image of sugar being poured from the shoe.

Still another mnemonic device that makes use of imagery is the **link method,** which involves taking images of the items to be memorized and connecting them in sequence. One form of the link method is the *narrative method,* in which unrelated items are connected to one another in a story. Figure 7.15 presents an example of the narrative method. In a study showing its effectiveness, two groups of subjects memorized twelve lists of ten nouns. While one group used the narrative method to memorize the nouns, the other group used ordinary mental rehearsal. Both groups showed nearly perfect immediate recall. But when later asked to recall all of the lists, the narrative group recalled an average of 93 percent of the words, while the mental rehearsal group recalled an average of only 13 percent (Bower & Clark, 1969).

THE PHYSIOLOGY OF MEMORY

Though study habits and mnemonic devices depend on overt behavior or mental imagery, they ultimately work by affecting the encoding, storage, and retrieval of memories in the brain. Today, research on the anatomy and chemistry of memory is revealing more and more about its physiological basis.

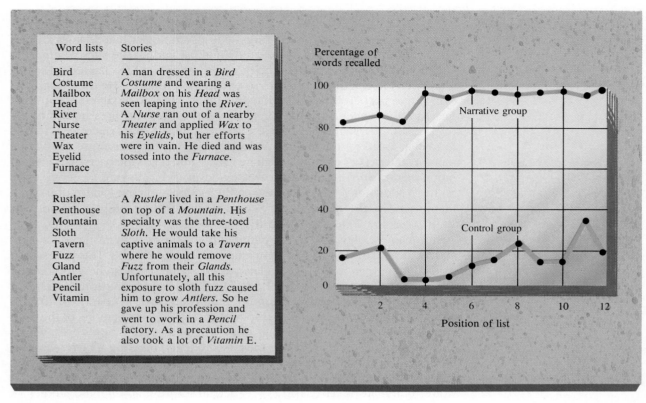

Word lists	Stories
Bird	A man dressed in a *Bird*
Costume	*Costume* and wearing a
Mailbox	*Mailbox* on his *Head* was
Head	seen leaping into the *River*.
River	A *Nurse* ran out of a nearby
Nurse	*Theater* and applied *Wax* to
Theater	his *Eyelids*, but her efforts
Wax	were in vain. He died and was
Eyelid	tossed into the *Furnace*.
Furnace	
Rustler	A *Rustler* lived in a *Penthouse*
Penthouse	on top of a *Mountain*. His
Mountain	specialty was the three-toed
Sloth	*Sloth*. He would take his
Tavern	captive animals to a *Tavern*
Fuzz	where he would remove
Gland	*Fuzz* from their *Glands*.
Antler	Unfortunately, all this
Pencil	exposure to sloth fuzz caused
Vitamin	him to grow *Antlers*. So he
	gave up his profession and
	went to work in a *Pencil*
	factory. As a precaution he
	also took a lot of *Vitamin* E.

FIGURE 7.15
The Narrative Method In using the narrative method to recall a list of words, you would create a story using each of the words. The graph shows the superior recall of subjects who used the narrative method in a study by Bower and Clark (1969).

"When you're young, it comes naturally, but when you get a little older, you have to rely on mnemonics."

The Anatomy of Memory

During the first half of this century, neuropsychologist Karl Lashley carried out an ambitious program of research aimed at finding the sites where individual memories are stored in the brain. As mentioned in chapter 3, Lashley trained rats to run through mazes to obtain food rewards. He then destroyed small areas of their brains and noted whether this made a difference in their maze performance. To Lashley's dismay, no matter what area he destroyed, the rats still negotiated the mazes, showing at most a slight decrement in performance. Lashley concluded that he had failed in his lifelong search for the memory trace—or **engram,** which he had assumed was the basis of individual memories. Lashley revealed his frustration in the following facetious statement: "I sometimes feel, in reviewing the evidence on the localization of the memory trace, that the necessary conclusion is that learning just is not possible" (Lashley, 1950, pp. 477–478).

But many scientists were not daunted by Lashley's pessimistic conclusion and continued to search for the engram—with some success. This persistence paid off more than three decades later when a team of researchers located the site of a specific memory in the brain (McCormick & Thompson, 1984). The researchers first used classical conditioning (described in chapter 6) to train rabbits to blink their eyelids in response to a tone. Presentations of the tone were repeatedly followed by puffs of air directed at the rabbit's eyes, which elicited blinking. Eventually, the tone itself elicited blinking. The researchers then found that electrical stimulation of a tiny site in the cerebellum of the rabbit would produce the conditioned eye blink, while destruction of the site would eliminate it. They had succeeded in locating an engram. Studies of memory formation in *Aplysia,* the sea slug, have also identified a kind of engram involving changes in the transmission of neural impulses at specific synapses as a consequence of learning (Kandel & Schwartz, 1982).

Attempts at identifying the brain structures responsible for memory formation have also born fruit. As discussed in chapter 3, the brain structure called the *hippocampus* plays an important role in memory. One source of evidence of this has come from the case study of a man called H. M. (Scoville & Milner, 1957). H. M. has formed few new memories since undergoing brain surgery in 1953, when he was 27 years old. The surgery, performed to relieve uncontrollable epileptic seizures, removed most of both of his temporal lobes, including almost all of his hippocampus.

As a consequence, H. M. developed **anterograde amnesia,** the inability to form new long-term declarative memories (that is, memories of facts and events). But H. M. retained his ability to recall old memories or to store information in short-term memory. His condition is so severe that he cannot recall events after 1953, leading him to complain that each moment of his life is like waking from a dream. H. M. will meet the same person on repeated occasions, yet have to be reintroduced each time. And he may read the same magazine over and over, without realizing that he read it before. While H. M. cannot form new declarative memories, he can form new procedural memories (that is, memories of how to perform tasks). For example, though H. M. has learned to play tennis since his surgery and has retained that procedural memory, he does not recall ever having taken lessons (Herbert, 1983).

The case of H. M. supports research findings by neuropsychologist Larry Squire and his colleagues that the hippocampus may play a role in the formation of declarative memories but not procedural memories. In one study, subjects suffering from the same form of anterograde amnesia as H. M. were trained to read words in a mirror. Though this is a difficult task, they were able to do so and improved in their abilities over a three-day period (figure 7.16). Despite having the ability to form new procedural memories, the subjects also

Engram A memory trace in the brain.

Anterograde Amnesia A memory disorder in which the individual is unable to form new long-term memories.

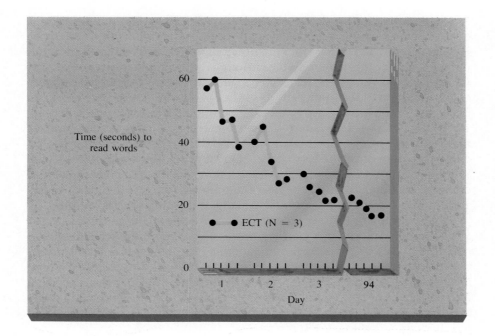

FIGURE 7.16
The Brain and Memory People suffering from anterograde amnesia caused by brain damage may retain their abilities to form new procedural memories, while being unable to form new declarative memories. The graph shows the results of the Cohen and Squire (1980) study, in which amnesia victims successfully learned to perform mirror reading, yet failed to recall having learned how to do it. This indicates that different brain structures are involved in the processing of procedural and declarative memories.

revealed an ability to form new declarative memories—they failed to recall having ever learned the task (Cohen & Squire, 1980). This indicates that procedural memories depend on still unidentified brain structures other than the hippocampus.

The Chemistry of Memory

In 1959 James McConnell and his colleagues shocked the scientific world by reporting the results of an unusual study (McConnell, Jacobson, & Kimble, 1959). They had classically conditioned flatworms to contract their bodies in response to a light by repeatedly pairing presentations of the light with mild electric shocks. They then cut the flatworms in half. Because flatworms can regenerate themselves, both halves grew into whole flatworms. They were then retrained to contract in response to light. As expected, the flatworms that had regenerated from the head (brain) ends showed savings—they took fewer trials to learn to respond to the light than the original flatworms had taken, which provided evidence that prior learning had been retained by the brain end. But, to the researchers' surprise, the flatworms that had regenerated from the tail ends learned to respond to the light as fast as those that had regenerated from the brain ends. This seemed to indicate that the memory of the classically conditioned response had been encoded chemically and distributed throughout the flatworm's body.

These findings led to a series of even more unusual experiments by a variety of researchers, which apparently demonstrated that memories could be transferred from one animal to another. In one study, rats were trained to run to a light compartment instead of to a dark compartment, which they would normally favor, by shocking them whenever they entered the dark compartment. When extracts from the brains of these rats were injected into mice, the mice spent less time in the dark compartment than they normally would. The researchers eventually isolated the proteinlike substance apparently responsible for this effect, which they called *scotophobin*, meaning "fear of the dark" (Unger, Desiderio, & Parr, 1972).

As you might guess, the results of such memory transfer studies created controversy, eventually leading twenty-three researchers to write a letter to the influential journal *Science,* in which they reported their failure to produce memory transfer in eighteen studies in seven different laboratories ("Memory transfer," 1966). But a few years later a published review of the research literature concluded that hundreds of studies of flatworms, goldfish, chickens, mice, rats, and hamsters had demonstrated the transfer of memories (Smith, 1974). Yet, because of the failure of some researchers to replicate those studies, interest in the study of memory transfer has waned. Perhaps interest has declined in part because the very notion of memory transfer seems better suited to science fiction than science. As discussed in chapter 2, scientists in all disciplines, including biology, chemistry, and physics, tend to avoid topics that appear to violate accepted scientific paradigms defining what is conceivable.

In contrast, there is no controversy about whether neurotransmitters play a role in memory, because memory processing requires the transmission of neural impulses from one neuron to another. But the exact relationship between neurotransmitter activity and memory has only recently begun to reveal itself. As you learned in chapter 3, neurotransmitters are chemicals secreted into the synapses between neurons. Of the major neurotransmitters the one that is most strongly implicated in memory processes is *acetylcholine* (Harrell, Barlow, & Parsons, 1987).

Alzheimer's Disease A brain disorder characterized by anterograde amnesia and general mental deterioration.

The most striking evidence of the role of acetylcholine in memory comes from studies of victims of **Alzheimer's disease,** which is characterized by, among other symptoms, severe anterograde amnesia. Autopsies of victims of Alzheimer's disease show degeneration of acetylcholine neurons connecting the hippocampus to other brain areas. In fact, when normal subjects are given drugs that inhibit the activity of acetylcholine neurons, they show memory losses similar to those seen in victims of Alzheimer's disease.

It would seem logical that treatments aimed at increasing acetylcholine levels in the brains of Alzheimer's victims would improve the ability to form new memories. One approach has been to administer *choline*—the dietary substance from which acetylcholine is synthesized and that is found in milk and eggs. Unfortunately, administration of high doses of choline has not been effective in improving the memory of Alzheimer's victims (Bartus, Dean, Beer, & Lippa, 1982). Perhaps the degeneration of acetylcholine neurons prevents the additional choline from having a beneficial effect, just as adding gasoline to the empty tank of a car with no spark plugs would not make it more likely to start.

Other research is providing evidence of the chemical basis of memory. One promising line of research is the investigation of the role of protein synthesis in the brain, which may alter the level of activity along certain neural pathways as a consequence of learning (Davis & Squire, 1984). Another promising line of research has found that memory storage is promoted by administering the stimulant drug amphetamine, which increases the release of epinephrine from the adrenal medulla (which, as mentioned in chapter 3, is the inner portion of the adrenal glands). Because epinephrine does not affect the brain directly, it does not exert its effects directly. There is evidence that it exerts its effects, instead, by stimulating the release of glucose from the liver. Glucose, needed for cell metabolism, has ready access to the brain and may enhance activity in neurons that are involved in ongoing memory processing (Lee, Graham, & Gold, 1988). As you can see, research on the physiology of memory cannot be divorced from the psychology of memory. And physiological research promises to discover ways of improving memory, which would be a boon both to people with intact brains and to people with damaged brains.

THINKING ABOUT PSYCHOLOGY

Should We Trust Eyewitness Testimony?

In August 1979, Father Bernard Pagano went on trial for a series of armed robberies. Seven eyewitnesses had identified him as the so-called gentleman bandit, a polite man who had robbed several convenience stores in Wilmington, Delaware. Father Pagano was arrested after several people who knew him informed the police that he resembled published drawings of the bandit. Seven eyewitnesses shown photographs in which Father Pagano wore his clerical collar identified him as the robber. They may have been influenced by previous police reports expressing the possibility that the perpetrator was a clergyman. Fortunately for Father Pagano, while he was on trial another man, Ronald Clouser, confessed to the crimes (Rodgers, 1982).

As you can see from figure 7.17, there was only a slight resemblance between Father Pagano and Ronald Clouser. The possibility of convicting innocent people or of exonerating guilty people based on inaccurate *eyewitness testimony* has led psychologists to study the factors that affect eyewitness testimony. This concern is not new. Hugo Munsterberg (1908), the first psychologist to study the psychology of law, warned us to consider the imperfections of human memory when evaluating the accuracy of eyewitness testimony.

During the past two decades, many psychologists, most notably Elizabeth Loftus, have conducted numerous studies of the factors affecting the accuracy of eyewitness testimony. Research on eyewitness memories shows that they

FIGURE 7.17
Eyewitness Testimony
Eyewitnesses mistakenly identified Father Bernard Pagano, *left,* as the perpetrator of a series of convenience store robberies actually committed by Ronald Clouser, *right.*

are not like mental tape recordings, which record and play back exactly. Instead, as discussed earlier, eyewitness recollections are reconstructive, altering somewhat the events that they represent.

Characteristics of the Eyewitness

Many studies have investigated the relationship between eyewitness testimony and the characteristics of the eyewitness. For example, studies of the influence of age have found that children are less accurate than adults in their eyewitness accounts of crimes. This is in keeping with the American judicial system's historical distrust of eyewitness accounts by children, originating in the Salem witch trials three centuries ago, when children testified against women accused of being witches. All states now have laws mandating that the testimony of a child be confirmed by another person before it can be accepted as evidence in court.

The assumption that the eyewitness testimony of children is especially subject to the biasing effects of leading questions has been supported by research indicating that misleading information about events can distort children's memories of those events (Ceci, Ross, & Toglia, 1987). Of course, with the present scourge of child abuse, courts must achieve a delicate balance between believing children's testimony and being skeptical of it.

Another important factor in eyewitness testimony is race, because eyewitnesses tend to be more accurate in identifying members of their own race. Consider a study that was carried out at sixty-three convenience stores in a small city. Clerks working in these stores were asked by persons claiming to be law interns to identify two men who had been in the store two hours earlier from photo lineups prepared by local police. One of the men was black and one was white. Almost all of the clerks were white. The ability of the clerks to make accurate identifications of the black man was related to the amount of previous social interaction they had with blacks. Those who had more social interaction with blacks made more accurate identifications (Brigham, Maas, Snyder, & Spaulding, 1982).

Because jurors attribute greater accuracy to the testimony of confident eyewitnesses, another important factor in eyewitness testimony is how confident eyewitnesses are about their memories. In the 1972 case of *Neil v. Biggers* the United States Supreme Court even ruled that one of the criteria that juries should use in judging the accuracy of eyewitness testimony is the degree of confidence expressed by the witness. But this ruling may be misguided, because the level of confidence of the eyewitness is generally unrelated to the accuracy of the eyewitness's testimony (Wells & Lindsay, 1985). As a consequence, it may be unwise for jurists to assume that a confident eyewitness is necessarily an accurate eyewitness.

Still another popular assumption about eyewitness testimony is that victims are more accurate eyewitnesses than are bystanders. Real-life incidents have provided evidence that this assumption is false, and research has shown that there is no consistent tendency for victims to be more, or less, accurate than bystanders in identifying the perpetrators of crimes (Hosch & Cooper, 1982).

Questioning the Eyewitness

One of the main factors influencing the testimony of eyewitnesses is the wording of questions, as demonstrated in a classic series of experiments by Elizabeth Loftus and her colleagues. In one experiment, subjects viewed a film of a two-car automobile accident (Loftus & Palmer, 1974). Some subjects were asked, "About how fast were the cars going when they hit each other?"

Other subjects were asked a similar question, with the word "hit" being replaced by the word "contacted," "bumped," "collided," or "smashed." The subjects' estimates of the speed of the cars were influenced by the severity of the word used in the question (figure 7.18).

A week later, the subjects were asked, "Did you see any broken glass?" Though there had been no broken glass, some subjects in both groups recalled seeing broken glass. But subjects who had been given the question containing the word "smashed" were more likely to report having seen broken glass than were subjects who had been given the question containing the word "hit."

Studies such as this demonstrate that the memories of eyewitnesses may be reconstructions, instead of exact replicas, of the events witnessed and that the retrieval of these memories can be altered by inaccurate information introduced during questioning. This indicates that memory schemas affect eyewitness accounts and supports the practice of barring leading questions in courtroom proceedings.

But there is also evidence that we can prevent misleading information from influencing the memories of eyewitnesses by warning them about the possibility that information will be misleading. This was demonstrated in a study in which subjects were given warnings just prior to the presentation of misleading information about a simulated crime. The subjects viewed slides of a wallet being snatched from a woman's purse and then read descriptions of

Elizabeth Loftus "One reason most of us, as jurors, place so much faith in eyewitness testimony is that we are unaware of how many factors influence its accuracy."

Question	Possible scene recalled	Average estimate of speed
"About how fast were the cars going when they *hit* each other?"		34.0 MPH
"About how fast were the cars going when they *smashed* into each other?"		40.8 MPH

O'Keefe

FIGURE 7.18

Leading Questions The wording of questions can influence the recall of eyewitnesses. As demonstrated in an experiment by Loftus and Palmer (1974), subjects who witnessed a collision between two cars gave different estimates of their speed, depending on the wording of the questions they were asked.

Data from E. F. Loftus and J. C. Palmer, "Reconstruction of Automobile Destruction: An Example of the Interaction Between Language and Memory" in *Journal of Verbal Learning and Verbal Behavior*, 13:585–589, 1974. Copyright © 1974 Academic Press, Orlando, FL. Reprinted by permission of the author and the publisher.

the crime. Subjects who had been given warnings showed greater resistance to the misleading information in the descriptions (Greene, Flynn, & Loftus, 1982). Nonetheless, some psychologists argue that informing jurors of the unreliability of eyewitness testimony may make already skeptical jurors too skeptical, perhaps leading to the exoneration of guilty persons (McCloskey & Egeth, 1983).

Other critics claim that Loftus's studies do not show that memories have been changed, only that retrieval cues present at the time of the incidents are not present at the time of retrieval. This supports the assumption that leading questions may influence the retrieval of memories, not the stored memories themselves. In one study, store clerks were asked to identify a previously encountered customer from an array of photographs. The original context was reinstated by providing physical cues from the encounter and by instructing the clerk to mentally recall events leading up to the customer's purchase. As discussed earlier, mentally reinstating the context in which you learned something may improve your recall of it. In this study, the reinstatement of the original context led to a significant increase in the accuracy of identifications (Krafka & Penrod, 1985). Fortunately, though leading questions may affect the recall of eyewitnesses, recent research indicates that eyewitnesses may be less susceptible to leading questions than has been suggested by previous research (Kohnken & Maass, 1988).

Regardless of the exact extent to which eyewitness testimony can be influenced by misleading information and the reasons for that influence, Elizabeth Loftus believes that eyewitness testimony is, in fact, too easily affected by such information. She expressed this in a statement similar to John B. Watson's claim concerning his ability to condition infants to become any kind of person desired (see chapter 1, p. 12). Loftus remarked: "Give us a dozen healthy memories, well-informed, and our own specified world to handle them in. And we'll guarantee to take any at random and train it to become any type of memory that we might select—hammer, screwdriver, wrench, stop sign, yield sign, Indian chief—regardless of its origin or the brain that holds it" (Loftus & Hoffman, 1989, p. 103).

SUMMARY

INFORMATION PROCESSING AND MEMORY

Memory research has been influenced by the cognitive revolution in psychology. The most widely accepted model of memory assumes that memory processing involves the stages of sensory memory, short-term memory, and long-term memory. At each stage the processing of memories involves encoding, storage, retrieval, and forgetting.

SENSORY MEMORY

Stimulation of sensory receptors produces sensory memories. Visual sensory memory is called iconic memory and auditory sensory memory is called echoic memory. George Sperling found that iconic memory contains more information than had been commonly believed and that almost all of it fades within a second.

SHORT-TERM MEMORY

Short-term memory is called working memory, because we use it to manipulate information provided by either sensory memory or long-term memory. We tend to encode information in short-term memory as sounds. We can store an average of seven chunks of information in short-term memory without rehearsal. Memories in short-term memory last about 20 seconds without rehearsal. Saul Sternberg found that retrieval of information in short-term memory is a serial, exhaustive search process. Forgetting in short-term memory is caused by decay and displacement of information.

LONG-TERM MEMORY

Memories stored in long-term memory are relatively permanent. Elaborative rehearsal of information in short-term memory produces superior long-term memories than does maintenance rehearsal. Craik and Lockhart's levels of processing theory assumes that information processed at deeper levels will be more likely to be stored in long-term memory. Researchers distinguish between procedural, semantic, and episodic memories. Semantic network theory assumes that memories are stored as nodes interconnected by links. Schema theory assumes that memories are stored as cognitive structures that affect the storage and retrieval of information related to them.

Hermann Ebbinghaus began the formal study of memory by employing the method of savings and identified the serial-position effect and the forgetting curve. The main theories of forgetting include decay theory, interference theory, motivation theory, and cue-dependence theory. The main versions of cue-dependence theory are context-dependent memory and state-dependent memory.

IMPROVING YOUR MEMORY

You can improve your memory by improving your study habits and by using mnemonic devices. A useful study technique is the SQ3R method, in which you survey, question, read, recite, and review. Overlearning and distributed practice are also useful techniques. Mnemonic devices are memory aids that organize material to make it easier to recall. The main mnemonic devices include acronyms, the method of loci, the pegword method, and the link method.

THE PHYSIOLOGY OF MEMORY

Although Karl Lashley failed in his search for the engram, researchers have discovered some of the anatomical and chemical bases of memory. The brain structure called the hippocampus and the neurotransmitter called acetylcholine are especially important in memory formation.

THINKING ABOUT PSYCHOLOGY:
SHOULD WE TRUST EYEWITNESS TESTIMONY?

Research on eyewitness testimony by Elizabeth Loftus and her colleagues has shown that it may be inaccurate. One important finding is that the confidence an eyewitness places in his or her memories is not a good indicator of their accuracy. Another important finding is that leading questions can alter the recall of memories by eyewitnesses.

IMPORTANT CONCEPTS

Acronym 241
Alzheimer's disease 246
Anterograde amnesia 244
Constructive recall 232
Context-dependent memory 237
Decay theory 233
Declarative memory 227
Distributed practice 240
Echoic memory 220
Elaborative rehearsal 226
Encoding 219
Encoding specificity 236
Engram 244
Episodic memory 227
Flashbulb memory 218

Forgetting 219
Forgetting curve 233
Iconic memory 220
Information-processing model 219
Interference theory 234
Korsakoff's syndrome 225
Levels of processing theory 226
Link method 242
Long-term memory 219
Maintenance rehearsal 226
Massed practice 240
Memory 218
Method of loci 241
Method of savings 233
Mnemonic device 241
Overlearning 240

Pegword method 242
Proactive interference 234
Procedural memory 227
Repression 235
Retrieval 219
Retroactive interference 234
Schema theory 230
Semantic memory 227
Semantic network theory 228
Sensory memory 219
Serial-position effect 232
Short-term memory 219
SQ3R method 239
State-dependent memory 237
Storage 219
Tip-of-the-tongue phenomenon 236

IMPORTANT PEOPLE

Frederic Bartlett 230
Fergus Craik and Robert Lockhart 226
Hermann Ebbinghaus 232
H. M. 244
Karl Lashley 244

Elizabeth Loftus 247, 249
Ulric Neisser 231
Lloyd and Margaret Peterson 223
Richard Shiffrin and
    Richard Atkinson 218

George Sperling 220
Larry Squire 244
Saul Sternberg 224
Endel Tulving 227

RECOMMENDED READINGS

For More on All Aspects of Memory:

Loftus, E. (1980). *Memory.* Reading, MA: Addison-Wesley.
A readable, comprehensive book covering all aspects of memory, written by a leading memory researcher.

Luria, A. R. (1968). *The mind of a mnemonist.* New York: Basic Books.
A classic book about a Russian man with a phenomenal memory, discussing both the positive and negative consequences of remembering almost everything one sees.

Neisser, U. (1982). *Memory observed: Remembering in natural contexts.* San Francisco: Freeman.
A discussion of memory in everyday life, including an extended discussion of memory's weaknesses as revealed in the Watergate testimony of John Dean.

For More on Improving Your Memory:

Baddeley, A. D. (1982). *Your memory: A user's guide.* New York: Macmillan.
An interesting, well-illustrated discussion of memory, including ways of improving your use of it.

For More on the Physiology of Memory:

Allport, S. (1986). *Explorers of the black box: The search for the cellular basis of memory.* New York: Norton.
A fascinating account of research on the neuronal basis of memory, as well as profiles of the researchers leading the search for it.

Mishkin, M., & Appenzeller, T. (1987, June). The anatomy of memory. *Scientific American,* pp. 80–99.
A popular account of the physiological basis of memory.

For More on Eyewitness Testimony:

Wells, G. L., & Loftus, E. F. (Eds.). (1984). *Eyewitness testimony: Psychological perspectives.* Cambridge, MA: Cambridge University Press.
A collection of articles by authorities on eyewitness testimony, including discussions of factors affecting its accuracy.

THINKING AND LANGUAGE

Chapter Opening Art:
Vasily Kandinsky. *Levels.*
March 1929.

hinking and language are two different, yet interrelated, cognitive activities. In chapter 7 you were introduced to the cognitive activity of memory, which permits you to store and retrieve information. Like memory, thinking and language help you profit from experience and adapt to your environment. Your abilities to think and to use language will permit you to comprehend the information conveyed in this chapter and, perhaps, to apply some of it in your everyday life. After using your thinking and language abilities in reading this chapter, you will have stored in your memory information bearing on questions such as, What is the nature of creativity? What is artificial intelligence? How do children develop language? and Can apes use language?

THINKING

Forming concepts. Solving problems. Being creative. Making decisions. Each of these processes depends on **thinking,** which is the purposeful mental manipulation of words and images. Yet, in 1925, John B. Watson, the "father of behaviorism," claimed that thinking is not a mental activity. Instead, he insisted that it was no more than subvocal speech—activity of the speech muscles that is too subtle to produce audible sounds. There is an intuitive appeal to this claim, because you may sometimes find yourself engaging in subvocal speech—perhaps even while reading this chapter. Moreover, physiological recordings of activity in the speech muscles have shown that some people do subvocalize while thinking (McGuigan, 1970).

But this does not necessarily support Watson's claim that subvocal speech *is* thinking. Convincing evidence against Watson's claim came from a study in which a physician named Scott Smith had himself paralyzed for half an hour by the drug curare (Smith, Brown, Toman, & Goodman, 1947). He did so to assess the possible anesthetic effect of curare. Because curare causes paralysis of all skeletal muscles (see chapter 3), including the breathing muscles, Smith was kept alive by a respirator. After the curare had worn off, he was able to report conversations that had taken place while he had been totally paralyzed. Because Smith was able to think and form memories while his speech muscles were paralyzed, this showed that thinking cannot be dependent on subvocal speech.

Though most behaviorists did not equate thinking with subvocal speech, they agreed with Watson's position that mental processes were not the proper object of study for psychologists. But, by the 1960s, dissatisfaction with the inability of strict behaviorism to explain memory, thinking, and certain other psychological processes contributed to the cognitive revolution, which reintroduced the study of mental processes, or "cognition," to psychology (Pribram, 1985). One of the most basic cognitive processes is *concept formation.*

Concept Formation

If a biology teacher asked you to hold a snake, you would be more willing to hold a "nonpoisonous" snake than a "poisonous" snake. Similarly, you might eat a "nonpoisonous" mushroom but not a "poisonous" mushroom. Your actions would show that you understood the concepts of "poisonous" and "nonpoisonous." A **concept** represents a category of objects, events, qualities, or relations whose members share certain features. "Poisonous" objects share the ability to make you ill or kill you if ingested. During your life you have formed many thousands of concepts, which provide the raw materials for your cognitive processes.

Thinking The mental manipulation of words and images, as in concept formation, problem solving, and decision making.

What does a concept rep.

Concept A category of objects, events, qualities, or relations that share certain features.

Concepts Concepts refer to objects (such as "furniture"), events (such as "holiday"), qualities (such as "tall"), and relationships (such as "opposite").

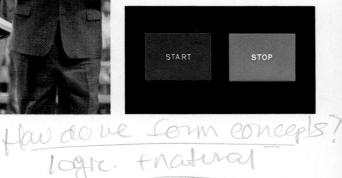

Logical Concepts How do we form concepts? Consider the case of a **logical concept,** which is formed by identifying the specific features possessed by all members of the concept. For example, "Great Lakes state" is a logical concept. Each of its members would have the features of being a state and bordering one or more of the Great Lakes. The book of Leviticus in the Old Testament provides two of the oldest examples of logical concepts. Leviticus distinguishes between "clean" animals, which may be eaten, and "unclean" animals, which may not be eaten. As one example, "clean" sea animals have fins and scales, while "unclean" sea animals do not. This means that bass and trout are "clean" animals, while clams and lobsters are "unclean" animals (Murphy & Medin, 1985).

Logical concepts like those found in Leviticus have typically not been the kinds studied in the laboratory. Instead, laboratory studies have typically used

Logical Concept A concept formed by identifying the specific features possessed by all of its members.

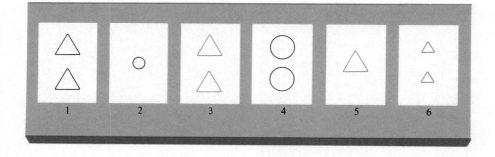

FIGURE 8.1

Concept Formation Laboratory studies of the formation of logical concepts present subjects with a series of examples varying on specific features. The subject's task is to identify the features that compose the concept. The figures in this example can vary in size (small or large), shape (circle or triangle), color (black or magenta), or number (one or two). Given that the odd-numbered cards are members of the concept and the even-numbered cards are not, see how quickly you can identify the concept (The answer appears at the bottom of this page).

Natural Concept A concept, typically formed through everyday experience, whose members may not all possess a common set of features.

Prototype The best representative of a concept.

logical concepts created by the researcher. These studies might present subjects with a series of symbols varying in size, shape, and color. The subject's task is to discover the features that define the concept. For example, a symbol might have to be large, square, and blue to be considered an example of the particular concept. Subjects determine the features of the concept by testing hypotheses about its possible defining features on successive examples that are labeled as either positive or negative examples of it. A positive example would include the defining features of the concept (in this case, large, square, and blue), while a negative example would lack at least one of the defining features (for example, large, square, and red). Try to identify the concept presented in figure 8.1.

Natural Concepts Is baseball a sport? How about table tennis? fishing? shuffleboard? golf? backgammon? bridge? roller derby? You have an intuitive sense of how "sportlike" each of these activities is. "Sport" is an example of a **natural concept,** a concept formed through everyday experience rather than by testing hypotheses. We may be unable to identify the defining features of natural concepts such as "sport." In other words, natural concepts often have "fuzzy boundaries." This led psychologist Eleanor Rosch (1975) to propose that natural concepts are based on prototypes. A **prototype** is considered to be the best representative of a concept.

According to Rosch, the more similarity between an example and a prototype, the more likely we are to consider the example to be a member of the concept represented by the prototype. A robin is a better prototype of a bird than is a penguin. Both have wings, feathers, and hatch from eggs, but only the robin can fly. In regard to the concept "sport," baseball is more prototypical than is golf, which, in turn, is more prototypical than is backgammon. The "fuzziness" of natural concepts may lead to arguments about whether a particular example is a member of a given concept. This was illustrated in 1988 by a series of letters to the editor of *The Sporting News* either supporting or opposing its coverage of Wrestlemania, the Indianapolis 500, and the World Chess Championship. While supporters considered these to be examples of the concept "sport," opponents did not.

Influenced by the work of Rosch, psychologists have become more interested in conducting laboratory studies of natural concept formation, that is, the formation of concepts without logically testing hypotheses about their defining features. Consider the following study of the identification of artistic styles (Hartley & Homa, 1981). Subjects who were naive about artistic styles were shown works by the impressionist painters Manet, Renoir, and Matisse. Later, the subjects were shown more paintings by these artists and by other artists—without being told the identity of the artists.

After viewing the second set of paintings, the subjects were accurate in matching particular paintings with the styles of the artists whose works they

FIGURE 8.2
Prototypes A prototype is the best representative of a concept. Which do you believe is the most prototypical dog? tree? airplane?

had seen in the first set of paintings. The subjects used the first set to form concepts representing the styles of the three artists: a "Manet," a "Renoir," and a "Matisse." This could not be explained as an example of logical concept formation, because the subjects could not identify a set of features that distinguished a Manet from a Renoir from a Matisse. By reflecting for a moment, you may be able to conjure up natural concepts for which you, too, cannot identify a set of defining features.

Problem Solving

One of the most important uses of concepts is in **problem solving,** the thought process that enables us to overcome obstacles in order to reach goals. Suppose that your car fails to start. In looking for a solution to your problem, you might follow a series of steps commonly used in solving problems (Kramer & Bayern, 1984). First, you would identify the problem: "My car won't start." Second, you would gather information relevant to the problem: "Am I out of gas?" "Is my battery dead?" or "Are my ignition wires wet?" Third, you would try out a solution: "I'm not out of gas, so I'll dry off the wires." Finally, you

Problem Solving The thought process by which an individual overcomes obstacles to reach a goal.

would evaluate the result: "The car started, so the wires were, indeed, wet." If the solution failed to work, you might try a different one: "Drying off the wires didn't work, so I'll try a jump start." In addition to following this series of steps, you might sometimes rely on one of several common problem-solving strategies.

Trial and Error The simplest strategy for solving problems is **trial and error,** which involves trying one possible solution after another until one works. As an example, imagine that your psychology professor asks you to get a stopwatch from a laboratory and gives you a ring with ten keys on it. Suppose that on reaching the laboratory you realize that your professor forgot to tell you which key opened the door to the laboratory. You would immediately identify the problem: finding the correct key. After assessing your situation you would probably decide to use trial and error to solve the problem. You would try one key after another until you found one that opened the door.

But, while trial and error is often effective, it is not always efficient. For example, if your professor gave you a ring with fifty keys on it, you might find it more efficient to return and ask your professor to identify the correct key rather than wasting time trying one key after another. Imagine trying to learn to use a word processor by trying various combinations of key strokes until you hit upon the correct ones to perform desired functions. You would probably spend the rest of your life without achieving success.

Insight More than two thousand years ago, the Greek physicist Archimedes was asked to solve a problem: Was King Hiero's new crown made of pure gold? Or had the goldsmith cheated him by mixing cheap metals with the gold? Archimedes discovered a method of solving this problem when he noticed that when he sat in his bathtub the water level rose. He decided to submerge the crown in water, measure the volume of water it displaced, and compare that volume to the volume displaced by an equal weight of pure gold. Though we do not know what Archimedes found, we do know that he relied on **insight,** an approach to problem solving that depends on mental manipulation of information rather than on overt trial and error. Insight is often characterized by an "Aha!" experience—the sudden realization of the solution to a problem (Metcalfe & Wiebe, 1987).

Animals, too, may use insight to solve problems. The classic study of insight in animals was conducted by the Gestalt psychologist Wolfgang Kohler (1887–1968) on the island of Tenerife in the Canary Islands during World War I. Kohler (1925) presented a chimpanzee named Sultan with bananas hanging from the top of his cage, well out of his reach (figure 8.3). But his cage also contained several crates. After trying fruitlessly to reach the bananas by jumping, Sultan suddenly hit upon the solution. He piled the crates on top of one another, quickly climbed to the top, and grabbed a banana—just as the shaky structure came tumbling down.

The assumption that Sultan displayed insight was challenged more than a half century later by several behaviorists (Epstein, Kirshnit, Lanza, & Rubin, 1984). In a tongue-in-cheek study analogous to the one involving Sultan, these behaviorists used food rewards to train a pigeon to first perform the separate acts of moving a tiny box to a specific location, standing on the box, and pecking a plastic, miniature banana. When later confronted with the banana hanging out of reach from the top of its cage, the pigeon at first seemed confused but then suddenly moved the box under the banana, climbed the box, and pecked at the banana to get a food reward (figure 8.4). If the lowly pigeon could

Trial and Error An approach to problem solving in which the individual tries one possible solution after another until one works.

Insight An approach to problem solving that depends on mental manipulation of information rather than overt trial and error, and produces sudden solutions to problems.

FIGURE 8.3
Insight in Apes Kohler (1925) demonstrated that chimpanzees can use insight to solve problems. The chimpanzee Sultan found a way to reach bananas hanging out of reach without engaging in mere trial-and-error behavior.

FIGURE 8.4
Insight in a Pigeon? This pigeon was trained to perform the separate actions of pushing a box to a designated location and climbing on the box to peck a plastic banana. When presented with the box and the banana in separate locations, the pigeon pushed the box under the banana, climbed on the box, and pecked the banana. This showed that an apparent instance of insight may be no more than performing a chain of previously learned behaviors.

engage in supposedly insightful behavior, then perhaps insight in animals—and perhaps in people—is no more than chaining together previously rewarded behaviors.

Algorithms If you use the formula "length times width," you will obtain the area of a rectangle. When you follow a cake recipe, you will produce a cake. Both formulas and recipes are examples of problem-solving strategies called algorithms. An **algorithm** is a rule that, when followed step by step, assures that the solution to a problem will be found. The notion of the algorithm is an offshoot of research in computer science by cognitive psychologists Allen Newell and Herbert Simon (1972). Many computer programs rely on algorithms to process information.

But, like trial and error, an algorithm may be an inefficient means of finding the solution to a problem. To appreciate this, imagine that you are in the middle of a chess game. An algorithm for finding your best move would require tracing all possible sequences of moves from the current position. Because there are an average of 35 different moves that can be made in any single position in the middle of a chess game, you would need literally millions of years to find the best move by tracing all possible sequences of moves. Even using an algorithm to follow all possible sequences of just the next three moves in the middle of a chess game would require the analysis of an average of 1.8 billion moves (Waltz, 1982). Because a formal chess match gives each player only 150 minutes to make 40 moves, even world champions do not rely on algorithms. Instead, they rely on problem-solving strategies called heuristics.

Algorithm A problem-solving rule or procedure that, when followed step by step, assures that a correct solution will be found.

Heuristics A **heuristic** is a general principle, or "rule of thumb," that guides problem solving. Unlike an algorithm, a heuristic does not guarantee the discovery of a solution. But a heuristic may be more efficient than an algorithm, because it rules out many useless alternatives before they are even attempted. Suppose that you are shopping for new shoes. Instead of

Heuristic A general principle, or "rule of thumb," that guides problem solving, though it does not guarantee a correct solution.

Heuristics If you had unlimited time, you could put together a 1,500-piece jigsaw puzzle by taking a piece and trying one piece after another until you found one that fit that piece. You would continue in a similar manner until you completed the puzzle. But you would perform more efficiently if you relied on heuristics. One heuristic might be, "Separate the pieces into piles of similar colors." A second might be, "Find the corner pieces first." And a third might be, "Complete the edges of the puzzle before proceeding to the center."

Mental Set A tendency to use a particular problem-solving strategy that has succeeded in the past but that may interfere with solving a problem requiring a new strategy.

trying on every pair in every store, you would use heuristics. You would only try on shoes in your size and perhaps even try on only brown leather loafers. Similarly, a chess player would rely on heuristics, such as trying to control the center of the board.

Impediments to Problem Solving Before reading on, try to solve the six problems presented in figure 8.5, in which you must use three jars to measure out exact amounts of water. If you are like most subjects, you had no difficulty with the first five problems but ran into difficulty on the sixth problem. In the original water-jar study, the subjects quickly realized that the solution to the first problem was to fill jar B, pour enough water from it to fill jar A, and then pour enough water from jar B to fill jar C twice. This left the desired amount in jar B. The subjects then found that the same strategy worked for each of the next four problems. But when they reached the sixth problem two-thirds were unable to solve it. Those who failed to solve the sixth problem had developed an effective strategy that made the simple solution to it difficult to discover. In contrast, of subjects who were asked to solve only the sixth problem, few had difficulty discovering the simple solution: fill jar A and pour enough water from it to fill jar C, leaving the desired amount in jar A (Luchins, 1942).

This study demonstrated that we are sometimes hindered by a **mental set,** a particular problem-solving strategy that has succeeded in the past but that may interfere with solving a problem that requires a new strategy. In one study (Adelson, 1984), expert computer programmers and novice computer programmers were presented with a programming problem that could be solved by using a simple programming strategy that is more often used by novices. The results showed that the novices were more likely to solve the problem, because the experts tried to use a more sophisticated, but ineffective strategy that they had adopted during their careers as computer programmers. In other words, the experts had developed a mental set that blinded them to the simpler solution.

How can we overcome mental sets? Strategies for overcoming them require that we purposely change habitual approaches to problem solving. One way you might accomplish this is by thinking visually instead of verbally. In developing a computer program, you might draw a diagram of it instead of writing it in words. A second way you might overcome a mental set is by placing the

FIGURE 8.5
Mental Sets Luchins (1942) asked subjects to use jars with the capacities shown in columns A, B, and C to obtain the amounts required in the right-hand column. The first five problems led subjects to overlook a simpler solution in the sixth problem.

Source: Adapted from Abraham S. Luchins, "Mechanization in Problem-Solving: The Effect of Einstellung" in *Psychological Monographs* (6, Whole No. 248), 1942.

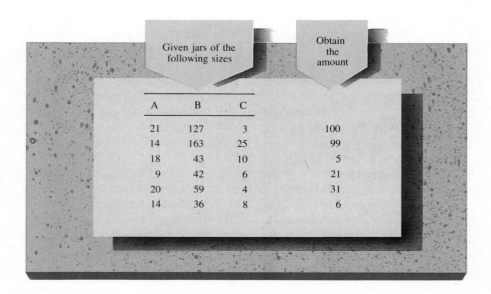

Given jars of the following sizes			Obtain the amount
A	B	C	
21	127	3	100
14	163	25	99
18	43	10	5
9	42	6	21
20	59	4	31
14	36	8	6

problem in a different context. A social psychologist might choose to examine factors that affect social attraction by studying couples in real-life settings instead of in a laboratory setting. And a third way you might overcome a mental set is by making assumptions opposite to those you normally make. This might have helped the expert computer programmers who were unable to solve the problem that the novices were able to solve. See if you can overcome mental sets by solving the problems in figure 8.6 (the solutions to the problems appear in figure 8.7).

Besides mental sets, a second way in which past experience can impede our ability to solve problems is through **functional fixedness,** the inability to realize that a problem can be solved by using a familiar object in an unusual way. The role of functional fixedness in problem solving was demonstrated in a classic study in which each subject was asked to perform the simple task of tying together two long strings hanging from a ceiling. The problem was that the two strings were too far apart for the subject to grasp both at the same time. The room contained a variety of objects, including a table, a chair, an extension cord, and a pair of pliers (figure 8.8).

Subjects were given ten minutes to solve the problem. One obvious solution was to tie the extension cord to one string, grasp the other string, pull the strings toward one another, and then tie them together. Each time the subject identified a solution, the experimenter said, "Now do it a different way." The solution that the experimenter was interested in is illustrated in figure 8.9. Subjects who discovered that solution tied the pliers to one of the strings and started it swinging like a pendulum. They then grabbed the other string, walked toward the swinging pliers, and tied the two strings together (Maier, 1931). To discover that solution, the subjects had to realize that the pliers could be used as a weight and not solely as a tool. Only 39.3 percent of the subjects discovered this solution on their own. Additional subjects discovered it when the experimenter provided a hint by subtly setting one of the strings in motion.

As in the case of mental sets, functional fixedness can be overcome. One of the best ways is to change or ignore the name of familiar objects. In a study demonstrating this, subjects were given a bulb, a switch, a wrench, and batteries. The subjects were told to create a circuit that would light the bulb, even though they had too little wire to complete the circuit. The solution was to use the wrench to complete it. Subjects who were told to use nonsense names

Functional Fixedness The inability to realize that a problem can be solved by using a familiar object in an unusual way.

[handwritten margin note: can't use an article any other way then what it was planed for]

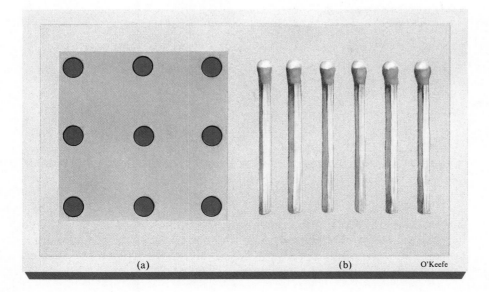

(a)   (b)   O'Keefe

FIGURE 8.6
Problem Solving Test your problem-solving ability on these two brain teasers. Connect the nine dots by drawing four straight lines without lifting your pencil. Use the six matches to form four equilateral triangles. The solutions are given in figure 8.7. Did a mental set affect your performance on either problem?

FIGURE 8.7
Solutions to the Nine-Dot and Six-Matchsticks Problems

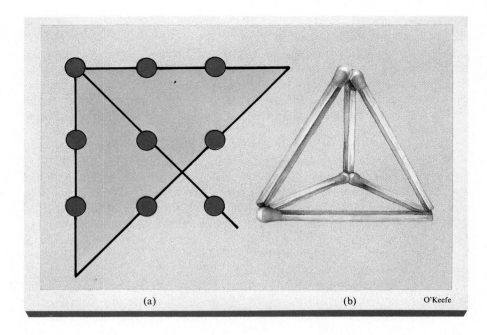

(a)   (b)   O'Keefe

FIGURE 8.8
Functional Fixedness Maier (1931) asked subjects to tie two strings together even though they were too far apart to grasp at the same time. Functional fixedness interfered with finding some of the possible solutions, one of which is illustrated in figure 8.9.

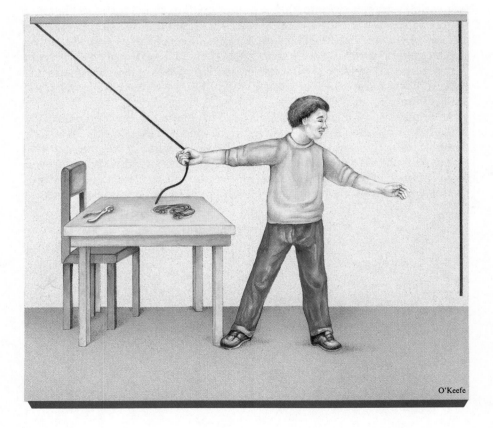

O'Keefe

such as "jod" to refer to the wrench were more likely to solve the problem than were subjects who referred to the wrench as a "wrench" (Glucksberg & Danks, 1968). By using nonsense words to refer to the wrench, the subjects were less likely to think of it as only a mechanical tool.

Creativity

In 1950, in his final address as president of the American Psychological Association, the noted creativity researcher J. P. Guilford expressed disappointment that of the more than 100,000 psychological studies published up until then fewer than 200 dealt with creativity. Since Guilford's address, influenced by the cognitive revolution, there has been a marked increase in the number of scientific studies of creativity (Barron & Harrington, 1981).

But what is creativity? Like other natural concepts, creativity cannot be defined by a specific set of features—that is, it has "fuzzy boundaries." We may be able to distinguish between creative and noncreative accomplishments without being able to indicate exactly what makes one example creative and another noncreative. Psychologists generally define **creativity** as a form of problem solving characterized by novel, useful solutions to problems (Mumford & Gustafson, 1988), whether artistic, scientific, or practical.

Novelty is not sufficient to demonstrate creativity, as expressed in the following statement by the great French mathematician Henri Poincaré (1948, p. 16): "To create consists precisely in not making useless combinations and in making those which are useful and which are only a small minority. Invention is discernment, choice." Thus, if you gave a monkey a paintbrush and a pallet of paint, it might produce novel paintings, but they would not be considered examples of creativity.

Characteristics of Creative People Do creative people share certain characteristics? Creative people tend to have above-average intelligence, but one does not have to be a genius to be highly creative (Nicholls, 1972). Creative people also tend to prefer novelty, favor complexity, and make independent judgments (Barron & Harrington, 1981). Moreover, they show the ability to integrate different kinds of thinking. They are superior at integrating verbal thinking with visual thinking (Kershner & Ledger, 1985) and rational, reality-oriented thinking with irrational, imaginative thinking (Suler, 1980).

Creative people are more motivated by their intrinsic interest in creative tasks than by extrinsic factors, such as fame, money, or approval. In fact, when people are presented with extrinsic reasons for performing intrinsically interesting creative tasks, they may lose their motivation to perform them. This was demonstrated in a study in which young adults involved in creative writing

Creativity A form of problem solving that generates novel, useful solutions to problems.

REPRINTED COURTESY OMNI MAGAZINE © 1986.

"I paint what I see."

FIGURE 8.9
One Solution to the Maier String Problem

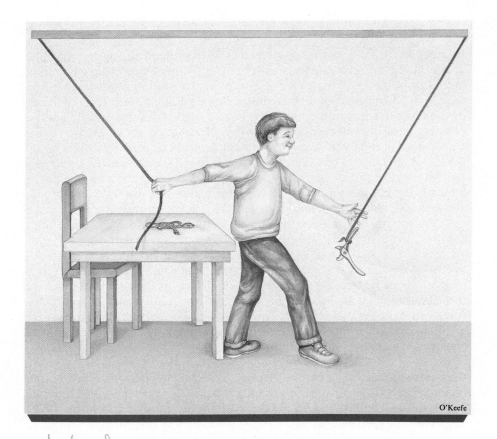

O'Keefe

what kind of thinking is great. thin

concervative

were asked to write two poems. After writing the first poem, one group completed a questionnaire focusing on intrinsic reasons for writing, such as the opportunity for self-expression, while a second group completed a questionnaire focusing on extrinsic reasons for writing, such as gaining public recognition.

When the first poems were judged for their creativity, the two groups did not differ. But when the second poems were judged for their creativity, the poems written by the group exposed to the questionnaire focusing on extrinsic reasons for writing were judged less creative than those written by the group exposed to the questionnaire focusing on intrinsic reasons for writing. These results agree with the experience of the noted American poet Sylvia Plath, who believed that her persistent writer's block was caused by her excessive concern about an extrinsic reason for writing—the recognition of her work by publishers, critics, and the public (Amabile, 1985).

Creativity and Divergent Thinking   How many ways can you use a brick? If the only things you think of are "to build a house," "to build a fireplace," or similar uses, you would exhibit convergent thinking. **Convergent thinking** is the cognitive process that focuses on finding conventional "correct" solutions to problems. If you also thought of less conventional "correct" uses for a brick, such as "to prop open a door," "to save water by putting it in a toilet tank," or "to break a window to enter your home after losing your house key," you would exhibit divergent thinking. **Divergent thinking,** a hallmark of creativity (Guilford, 1984), is the cognitive process in which a person freely considers a variety of potential solutions to artistic, literary, scientific, or practical problems.

Convergent Thinking The cognitive process that focuses on finding conventional solutions to problems.

Divergent Thinking The cognitive process by which an individual freely considers a variety of potential solutions to artistic, scientific, or practical problems.

Consider the *Remote Associates Test* developed by Sarnoff Mednick (1962), which presents subjects with sets of three apparently unrelated words. For each set, subjects are asked to find a fourth word that is related to the other three. To do so, subjects must use divergent thinking. For example, what word would you choose to associate with the words piano, record, and baseball? The word "player" would be one possibility. Mednick believes that the ability to form unusual associations is indicative of creative thinking (Busse & Mansfield, 1980). Try testing your ability to find remote associates using the items in figure 8.10.

Divergent thinking can be cultivated. This type of thinking is promoted by parents who raise their children to be open to a wide variety of experiences (Harrington, Block, & Block, 1987). Even adults can learn to use more divergent thinking. This idea is not lost on industrial leaders, who have their employees attend seminars in which they learn to think more creatively by engaging in divergent thinking (Basadur, Graen, & Scandura, 1986). Divergent thinking is also promoted by positive emotional states (Isen, Daubman, & Nowicki, 1987). When you are angry, anxious, or depressed, you would be more likely to engage in convergent thinking. Thus, teachers who evoke positive emotional states in their students and managers who evoke positive emotional states in their employees may be encouraging creative academic or vocational problem solving.

Decision Making

Each of our days is filled with decisions. They may be minor, such as deciding whether or not to take along a raincoat when leaving home, or major, such as deciding which college to attend. **Decision making** is a form of problem solving in which we try to make the best choice from among alternative judgments or courses of action. In making decisions, we weigh two factors: utility and probability. *Utility* is the value we assign to a given alternative, and *probability* is our estimate of the likelihood that a given alternative will lead to a valued consequence. Though we normally prefer alternatives of both high utility and high probability, we may make exceptions. Consider the decision to purchase state lottery tickets. Though the decision may have low probability, it has high utility (the potential to win millions of dollars), which makes it an attractive decision to many people.

Though decision making seems like a simple matter of rationally calculating the utility and probability of alternative decisions, studies in the 1970s

Decision Making A form of problem solving in which one tries to make the best choice from among alternative judgments or courses of actions.

FIGURE 8.10
The Remote Associates Test
Items like these are included in the Remote Associates Test (Mednick, 1962). For each of the items, find a word that is associated with all three of the given words.

	Given words			Your word?
1.	Worker	Boiled	Core	_____
2.	York	World	Born	_____
3.	Base	Foot	Basket	_____
4.	Range	Climber	Grown	_____

Possible responses: (1) hard; (2) new; (3) ball; (4) mountain.

Amos Tversky and Daniel Kahneman "Most people are . . . very sensitive to the difference between certainty and high probability and relatively insensitive to intermediate gradations of probability."

Representativeness Heuristic In decision making, the assumption that characteristics of a small sample are representative of its population.

Availability Heuristic In decision making, the tendency to estimate the probability of an event by how easily relevant instances of it come to mind.

found that decision making is also subject to certain biases that may keep us from making objective decisions (Karen & Wagenaar, 1985). Biases in decision making have been studied most extensively by cognitive psychologists Amos Tversky and Daniel Kahneman, who have found that our decision making is often biased by our reliance on heuristics.

Heuristics and Decision Making Weather forecasters measure the current humidity, temperature, air pressure, wind velocity, and other factors to predict the weather. Based on the kind of weather that occurred under similar conditions in the past, they predict the probability of particular kinds of weather, such as rain or snow. In doing so, they are making use of what Kahneman and Tversky (1973) call the representativeness heuristic. In using the **representativeness heuristic,** we assume that characteristics of a small sample are representative of its population. Because a sample may not accurately represent its population, the use of the representativeness heuristic does not guarantee that weather forecasts or other decisions will be good ones.

Consider a study of the effect of the representativeness heuristic in regard to the "hot hand" in basketball, in which a player makes several baskets in a row (Gilovich, Vallone, & Tversky, 1985). The study was prompted by a survey that found that both fans and players tended to believe that during a basketball game the chance of making a basket is greater following a made basket than following a miss. The researchers analyzed shooting records of the Boston Celtics and Philadelphia 76ers basketball teams. The results showed that the chance of making a basket after a made basket was no greater than the chance following a miss. Apparently, fans and players alike incorrectly assume that brief runs of successful shooting are representative of a more general tendency to shoot well.

Answer the following question: In English, is the letter *k* more likely to be the first letter or the third letter of a word? Though the letter *k* is more likely to be the third letter, most people decide that it is more likely to be the first letter. This is explained by what Tversky and Kahneman (1973) call the **availability heuristic,** which is the tendency to estimate the probability of an event by how easily relevant instances of the event come to mind. The more easily an instance comes to mind, the more probable we assume the event will be.

But the ease with which instances come to mind may not reflect their actual probability. Instead, instances may come to mind because they are vivid, recent, significant, or easily recalled, rather than because they are highly probable. Thus, because it is easier to recall words, such as "kick" or "kiss," that begin with *k* than words, such as "make" or "hike," that have *k* as their third letter, we conclude that more words begin with *k* than have *k* as their third letter.

The effect of the availability heuristic was shown in a study in which subjects were asked to estimate the prevalence of cheating by welfare recipients. Those who first read a vivid case of welfare cheating overestimated its prevalence (Hamill, Wilson, & Nisbett, 1980). This reflects our tendency to respond to rare, but vivid, news reports of instances of welfare recipients living in luxurious comfort by overestimating the likelihood of welfare cheating. In fact, when we lack the information required for making an objective judgment, the availability of even a single instance of an event may make us overestimate the probability of other occurrences of that event (Lewicki, 1985).

Framing Effects Judges and opposing lawyers must be constantly alert to the use of "leading questions," which may unfairly influence jury decisions. Note the difference in the following comments: "Dr. Jones fails 10 percent of his students" and "Dr. Jones passes 90 percent of his students." Though both statements report the same reality, you might be more in-

clined to enroll in Dr. Jones's course after hearing the second comment. Leading questions are examples of what Kahneman and Tversky call **framing effects,** which are biases introduced in the decision-making process by presenting a situation in a certain manner.

Consider the following study by Kahneman and Tversky (1982) in which people were asked one of the following two questions: "If you lost a pair of tickets to a Broadway play for which you paid forty dollars, would you purchase two more?" or "If you lost forty dollars on your way to purchase tickets at the box office, would you still purchase tickets?" Though in each case the subject would be forty dollars poorer, more subjects answered yes to the second question. Thus, the way in which the questions were framed, not the amount of money they would lose, influenced their decisions. Their subjective evaluation, not the objective situation, influenced their decisions.

Framing Effect In decision making, biases introduced into the decision-making process by presenting an issue or situation in a certain manner.

Artificial Intelligence

Almost two hundred years ago a Hungarian inventor named Wolfgang von Kempelen toured Europe with a chess-playing machine called the Maezel Chess Automaton. The machine defeated almost all the people who dared play against it. Among the Automaton's admirers was the noted American author Edgar Allen Poe, who wrote an essay speculating—incorrectly—on how it worked. After years of defeating one challenger after another, the Automaton's mechanism was finally revealed. Inside it was a legless Polish army officer named Worouski, who was a master chess player ("Program Power," 1981).

During the past three decades, computer scientists have developed machines that can play chess—but without resorting to hiding master chess players inside. These modern chess-playing machines are actually computers that are programmed to play chess. Computer chess programs are the offshoot of studies in **artificial intelligence (AI)**, a field founded by Nobel Prize-winning psychologist Herbert Simon that integrates computer science and cognitive psychology. Those who study AI try to simulate, or even improve on, human thinking by using computer programs. For example, computer scientists have developed a program that answers political questions as though it were either a politically liberal or a politically conservative person (Abelson, 1981).

Artifical Intelligence (AI) A field that integrates computer science and cognitive psychology in studying information processing through the design of computer programs that appear to exhibit intelligence.

Expert System A computer program that displays expertise in a specific domain of knowledge.

AI program is a expert system

Many AI researchers are interested in developing computer programs, so-called **expert systems,** that display expertise in specific domains of knowledge. Computer chess programs have led the way in these efforts. The first computer chess programs were developed in the 1950s at Los Alamos Laboratory in New Mexico and improved steadily during the next two decades until they finally began defeating expert chess players. But, to date, they have yet to defeat a world-class player in a multiple-game match. In 1978 David Levy, the chess champion of Scotland, got a scare when a computer chess program defeated him in the fourth game of a six-game chess match. Levy had made a $2,500 bet that no chess program could defeat him. But Levy won or drew the other five games, and renewed his bet (Ehara, 1980). Despite his victory, Levy and world chess champions appear doomed to eventual defeat by computer chess programs. One ominous sign occurred in 1979 at a backgammon match in Monte Carlo, when a computer program defeated the world back-gammon champion, Luigi Villa of Italy. This was the first time that a computer program defeated a human world champion in an intellectual game ("Teaching a Machine the Shades of Gray," 1981).

When a computer chess program finally defeats a world chess champion, it may be a descendant of a program called Belle. In 1981, at the Virginia Open Chess Tournament, Belle took fourth place in competition against master chess players ("Program Power," 1981). The only rating above master is grand-master, the level achieved by the best chess players in the world. While most computer chess programs have relied on algorithms—searching for all possible sequences of moves several moves deep—to find the best move in a given postion, Belle takes a more sophisticated, human approach by using heuristics. Though Belle can follow potential sequences of moves four moves deep, it does not follow each sequence to its conclusion. Instead, Belle stops following a sequence as soon as it proves inferior to another that has already been identified. This makes Belle perform faster and examine more potentially effective moves in a given time span than do other computer chess programs (Peterson, 1983).

Though computer chess programs are the most well known of expert systems, computer scientists have developed a variety of other systems. Among these expert systems, *Mycin* has helped physicians diagnose infectious diseases, *Prospector* has helped mining companies decide where to dig for minerals, and *Dipmeter* has helped analyze geological data from oil-well drillings (Davis, 1986). Expert systems are helpful because, in narrow domains of knowledge, they can analyze data more quickly and more objectively than can human experts.

Despite the speed and objectivity with which computers process certain kinds of information, they will not process information in many everyday situations as efficiently as human beings until there are computer programs that function more like the human brain. Computer programs perform decision-making processes in *serial,* meaning that they perform one step at a time. In contrast, the human brain performs decision-making processes both in serial and in parallel.

When information is processed in *parallel,* several decision-making steps occur simultaneously and are then integrated. As a consequence, the human brain can perform many kinds of thinking better than the fastest computers. For example, AI scientists have developed a cart that uses a computerized artificial vision system to find its way around obstacles. Human beings, who use both **serial processing** and **parallel processing** of the size, shape, location, and movement of objects can quickly find their way around obstacles. In contrast, the cart must stop after moving three feet so that its computer program can spend fifteen minutes using serial processing to determine its next movement (Waldrop, 1984). Because of the slowness of serial computer

Serial Processing The processing of information one step at a time.

Parallel Processing The processing of different information simultaneously.

programs, it is unlikely that any chess programs will defeat human world chess champions until AI researchers develop advanced chess programs that use both serial and parallel processing (Kurzweil, 1985).

LANGUAGE

Arguing about politics. Reading a newspaper. Using sign language. Each of these is made possible by **language,** a formal system of communication involving symbols—whether spoken, written, or gestured—and rules for combining them. In using language, we rely on spoken symbols to communicate through speech, written symbols to communicate through writing, and gestured symbols to communicate nonverbally through sign language. We use language to communicate with other people, to store and retrieve memories, and to think about the past, present, and future.

But what makes something "language"? The world's several thousand languages share three characteristics: semanticity, generativity, and displacement (Brown, 1973). **Semanticity** indicates that a true language conveys the thoughts of the communicator in a meaningful way to those who understand the language. For example, you know that *anti* at the beginning of a word refers to being against something and *ed* at the end of a word refers to past action. As you will read in chapter 14, the use of language by people with schizophrenia often lacks semanticity—it may be meaningless to other people.

Generativity indicates that those who use a language can combine its symbols in novel ways, rather than being limited to a fixed number of combinations. In fact, each day you say or write sentences that may have never appeared before. This generativity of language accounts for "baby talk," "Brooklynese," and the works of Shakespeare.

Language A formal system of communication involving symbols—whether spoken, written, or gestured—and rules for combining them.

Semanticity The characteristic of language marked by the use of symbols to convey thoughts in a meaningful way.

Generativity The characteristic of language marked by the ability to combine words in novel, meaningful ways.

Language The ability of human beings to use language makes us much more flexible than any animal in communicating with one another. We can communicate complex thoughts through spoken language, written language, or sign language.

Generativity The generativity of language is exemplified in the unique ability of certain orators to use words in ways that can move thousands of people.

Displacement The characteristic of language marked by the ability to refer to objects and events that are not present.

Displacement indicates that a language permits us to refer to objects and events that are not present. The objects and events may be in another place or in the past or future. Thus, you can talk about someone in China, about your fifth birthday party, or about who will win the World Series next year.

Note that *language* is a form of *communication,* but that communication can occur without the use of language. This is true of many animals, which can communicate but cannot use language. Consider a pet dog. The dog may indicate when it is hungry by pacing around its food dish or indicate when it wants to go out by scratching at the door. But does this mean that the dog is using language? No, because the only characteristic of language that the dog would be displaying is semanticity. Dogs do not exhibit generativity or displacement in their communications.

Other animals also communicate without using true language. A bee can communicate the location of nectar-containing flowers to residents of its hive (figure 8.11). When a bee returns to its hive after finding nectar less than fifty yards away, it performs a "circle dance" on the wall of the hive. If the nectar is farther away, the bee does a "waggle dance," moving in a figure-eight pattern. The angle of the straight line in the figure-eight pattern relative to the sun indicates the direction of the nectar, and the duration of the dance indicates the distance of the nectar—the longer the duration, the farther away it is (von Frisch, 1974). But these dances are merely a form of communication, not language. They have semanticity and displacement, but they lack generativity—they cannot be used to indicate anything other than the location of nectar.

As another example of communication without language, consider how monkeys use different alarm calls to signal the presence of particular kinds of predators. In a study of the responses of monkeys to alarm calls, researchers presented monkeys with tape recordings of alarm calls signifying the presence of an eagle, a boa constrictor, or a leopard. The monkeys responded to eagle alarms by looking up, to boa constrictor alarms by looking down, and to leopard alarms by climbing up into trees (Seyfarth, Cheney, & Marler, 1980). Though monkeys use alarm calls to communicate, they are not using true language. The calls have semanticity because they communicate the presence of a particular kind of predator, but they lack generativity and displacement. Monkeys can neither combine their calls in novel ways nor use them to refer to animals that are not present.

In contrast to dogs, bees, and monkeys, human beings do use true language. Without language, we would be severely limited in our ability to communicate with one another. You would not even be reading this book—books

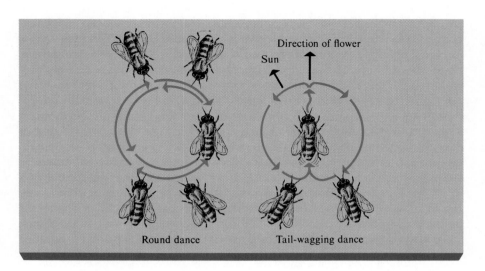

Round dance   Tail-wagging dance

FIGURE 8.11
Communication among Bees A bee that has found flowers containing nectar will return to its hive and do a circle dance if the nectar is within 50 yards of the hive. If the nectar is more than 50 yards away, the bee will do a waggle dance. The bee moves in a figure eight, with the angle of the straight line in the figure eight relative to the sun indicating the location of the nectar.

would not exist. Even the Old Testament book of Genesis recognizes the importance of language. In the story of the Tower of Babel, God punishes human beings for their pride by having them speak different languages—restricting their ability to communicate and engage in cooperative projects, such as building a tower to heaven.

The Structure of Language

English, Japanese, and all other languages have structures governed by rules known as **grammar.** The components of grammar include phonology, syntax, and semantics.

Grammar The set of rules that governs the proper use and combination of language symbols.

Phonology All spoken languages are composed of **phonemes**—the basic sounds of a language. Languages use as few as 20 and as many as 80 phonemes. English contains between 40 and 45 phonemes, with the number varying with the dialect of English that is spoken. Each phoneme is represented by either a letter (such as the *o* sound in the word "g*o*") or a combination of letters (such as the *sh* sound in "*sh*ould"). Words are combinations of phonemes, with each language permitting only certain combinations. As a speaker of English, you intuitively realize that the combination of phonemes in "cogerite" would form an acceptable word in English even though there is no such word. You also intuitively realize that the combination of phonemes in "klputng" would not form an acceptable word in English.

Phoneme The smallest unit of sound in a language.

Because a language may exclude certain phonemes found in other languages, people learning to speak a foreign language have difficulty pronouncing phonemes that are present in the foreign language but not in their native language. For example, even after extensive conversational practice, adults who are native speakers of Japanese and who learn English have great difficulty in distinguishing between *r* sounds, as in "*r*ock," and *l* sounds, as in "*l*ock." Their pronunciation makes both words sound like "lock" (Strange & Dittmann, 1984).

Because children who learn a foreign language have less difficulty pronouncing phonemes not found in their native language, there may be a critical period in childhood after which unused phonemes can no longer be pronounced correctly. Nonetheless, with special training even adults learning a new language may improve their ability to pronounce unfamiliar phonemes. For example, if you say "the" and "theta," you will notice that the *th* sounds

Morpheme The smallest meaningful unit of language.

are slightly different. This distinction is not made by those whose native language is French. Difficulty in perceiving differences between phonemes in a foreign language is accompanied by difficulty in correctly pronouncing those phonemes. But French-speaking Canadians enrolled in a special training program quickly learned to distinguish between the *th* sound in words such as "*the*" and the *th* sound in words such as "*th*eta" (Jamieson & Morasan, 1986).

Individual phonemes and combinations of phonemes form **morphemes,** the smallest meaningful units of language. Words are composed of one or more morphemes. For example, the word "book" is composed of a single morpheme. In contrast, the word "books" is composed of two morphemes: "book," which refers to an object, and "s," which indicates the plural of a word. Among the common morphemes that affect the meaning of words is the *ing* suffix, which indicates ongoing action. Note that the 40 to 45 phonemes in English build more than 100,000 morphemes, which, in turn, build almost 500,000 words. And, using these words, we can create a virtually infinite number of sentences. This shows that one of the outstanding characteristics of language is its generativity.

Syntax The rules that govern the acceptable arrangement of words in phrases and sentences.

Syntax In addition to rules that govern the acceptable combinations of sounds in words, languages have **syntax**—rules that govern the acceptable arrangement of words in phrases and sentences. Because you know English syntax, you would say, "She ate the ice cream," but not, "She the ice cream ate" (though poets do have a "license" to violate normal syntax). And syntax varies from one language to another. In English, adjectives usually precede the nouns they modify, while in Spanish, adjectives usually follow the nouns they modify. The English phrase "the red book" would be "el libro rojo" in Spanish. Therefore, a Spanish-speaking person learning English might say "the book red," while an English-speaking person learning Spanish might say "el rojo libro." As another example of variations in syntax between languages, the English sentence "John hit Bill" would be translated into Japanese as "John Bill hit." This is because the normal order of the verb and the object in Japanese is opposite to their normal order in English (Gliedman, 1983).

Semantics The study of how language conveys meaning.

Deep Structure The underlying meaning of a statement.

Surface Structure The word arrangements used to express thoughts.

Transformational Grammar The rules by which languages generate surface structures from deep structures, and deep structures from surface structures.

Semantics Words must not only be arranged appropriately in phrases and sentences, they must also convey meaning. The study of how language conveys meaning is called **semantics.** The eminent linguist Noam Chomsky has been intrigued by our ability to convey the same meanings through different phrases and sentences. Consider the statements, "The boy fed the horse" and "The horse was fed by the boy." Both express the same meaning but use different syntax. Moreover, if either sentence were spoken in English, Chinese, or Swahili, its meaning would be the same.

Chomsky explains this ability to express the same meaning using different phrases or different languages by distinguishing between a language's deep structure and its surface structure. The **deep structure** is the underlying meaning of a statement, while the **surface structure** is the word arrangements that express the underlying meaning. Chomsky calls the rules by which languages generate surface structures from deep structures and deep structures from surface structures **transformational grammar.** In terms of transformational grammar, language comprehension involves transforming the surface structure, which is the verbal message, into its deep structure, which is its meaning. Thus, the sentences "The boy fed the horse" and "The horse was fed by the boy" are transformed into the same meaning.

Transformational Grammar
Though the messages on this sign differ in their surface structure, with one in English and one in French, they communicate the same message—that is, they have the same deep structure.

The meaning of a statement depends on not only its words and their arrangement but also on factors such as the social context in which the statement is made. The branch of semantics that is concerned with the relationship between language and its social context is called **pragmatics.** To appreciate the relationship between language and social context, consider the following statement made by a student about an upcoming meal in the cafeteria: "I can't wait to have dinner tonight." If spoken in an enthusiastic voice during Thanksgiving week, the statement might mean that the student expects to enjoy a delicious turkey dinner. Yet, if spoken in a sarcastic voice during a normal school week, the same statement might mean that the student expects to be confronted by the cafeteria's notorious "mystery meat."

The importance of the social context in speech comprehension is shown by the difficulty scientists have had in developing computer programs that comprehend speech (Levinson & Liberman, 1981). A program that could comprehend speech would have to consider characteristics of the message, the speaker, and the situation. The importance of employing pragmatics in developing computer programs that can comprehend speech is illustrated in the following conversation between a reporter (R) and a computer "therapist" called Eliza (E) (Gorman, 1985, p. 65):

R: Row, row, row your boat

E: What about your own boat?

R: Gently down the stream

E: Why do you say that?

R: Merrily, merrily, merrily, merrily

E: I am not sure I understand you fully

R: Life is but a dream

E: What does the dream suggest to you?

The Acquisition of Language

What accounts for a child's ability to progress from a crying, gurgling infant to a talkative three-year-old? The process of language acquisition appears to be universal, with infants in all cultures acquiring language in similar ways as they pass through distinct stages (Rice, 1989). Though the timing of the stages may vary among infants, the order does not.

Stages in Language Acquisition For the first months after birth, infants are limited to communicating through crying, which they use to indicate that they are hungry or in pain. Between four and six months of age infants enter the babbling stage. When infants babble they repeat sequences of phonemes, such as "ba-ba-ba." Infants in all cultures begin babbling at about the same age and produce the same range of phonemes, including some that are not part of their parents' language. Even deaf infants begin babbling at the same age as infants who can hear (Lenneborg, Rebelsky, & Nichols, 1965), though their babbling is not normal (Gilbert, 1982). The universality of the onset and initial content of babbling indicates that it is a product of the maturation of an inborn predisposition, rather than a product of experience. Nonetheless, by the age of nine months, infants begin to show the influence of experience, as they begin to limit their babbling to the phonemes of their family's language.

When infants are about one year old, they begin to say their first words. Their earliest words typically refer to objects that interest them. Thus, common early words include "dada," "milk," and "doggie." In using words, older infants exhibit **overextension,** applying words too broadly. Consider an infant who refers to her cat as "kitty." If she also refers to dogs, cows, horses, and other four-legged animals as "kitty," she would be exhibiting overextension. In contrast, if she refers to her cat, but to no other cats, as "kitty," she would

The Growth of Vocabulary
After a child reaches the age of two, vocabulary grows rapidly as the child learns to label more and more objects in the immediate environment.

Underextension The tendency to apply a word to fewer objects or actions than it actually represents.

Holophrastic Speech The use of single words to represent whole phrases or sentences.

Telegraphic Speech Speech marked by reliance on nouns and verbs, while omitting other parts of speech, including articles and prepositions.

Mean Length of Utterance (MLU) The average length of spoken statements, which is used as a measure of language development in children.

be exhibiting **underextension.** As infants gain experience with objects and language, they rapidly learn to apply their words to the appropriate objects.

After learning to say single words, infants begin using them in **holophrastic speech,** which is the use of single words to represent whole phrases or sentences. For example, on one occasion an infant might say "car" to indicate that the family car has pulled into the driveway, while on another occasion the infant might say "car" to indicate that he would like to go for a ride. Between the ages of eighteen and twenty-four months, infants go beyond holophrastic speech by speaking two-word phrases, typically including a noun and a verb in a consistent order. The infant is now showing a rudimentary appreciation of proper syntax, as in "Baby drink" or "Mommy go."

Because, in the two-word stage, infants rely on nouns and verbs and leave out other parts of speech (such as articles and prepositions), their utterances are called **telegraphic speech.** As you know, to save time and money, telegrams leave out connecting parts of speech yet still communicate meaningful messages. Reruns of the television series "The Lone Ranger" provide good examples of telegraphic speech, as spoken by Tonto. Tonto tends to say things such as "Sheriff hurt" or "Him bad." Of course, this reflected the unfortunate Hollywood practice of portraying adult Native Americans as more childlike, more naive, and less intelligent than their white counterparts.

Until they are about two years old, infants use words only to refer to objects that are located in their immediate environments. When children are about two years old, they begin speaking sentences that include parts of speech in addition to nouns and verbs. They also begin to exhibit displacement, as when a two-year-old asks, "Grandma come tomorrow?" After the age of two, children show a rapid increase in their vocabulary and in the length and complexity of their sentences. Psychologist Roger Brown (1973) invented a unit of measurement called the **mean length of utterance (MLU)** to assess a child's level of language maturation. The MLU is calculated by taking samples of a child's statements and finding their average length in words and morphemes. The MLU increases rapidly in early childhood, though there is some variability from one child to another (figure 8.12).

FIGURE 8.12
Mean Length of Utterance
Roger Brown (1973) used the mean length of utterance to assess the language maturity of children. The graph shows changes in the mean length of utterances for three children.

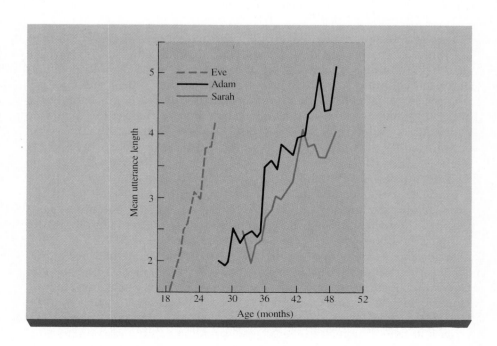

The increased sophistication that young children show in their use of language is partly attributable to their application of language rules, which they learn from listening to the speech of those around them. From the day of their birth, infants are exposed to sophisticated language. In fact, studies have found that, contrary to popular impressions, staff members in hospital nurseries do not rely solely on baby talk and soothing sounds when speaking to newborn infants. Instead, staff members spend much of the time speaking to the infants with normal, though perhaps simple, phrases and sentences (Rheingold & Adams, 1980).

The language rules that children learn are strongly influenced by their mothers' speech (Hoff-Ginsberg, 1986). But English has many exceptions to grammatical rules, which may explain the phenomenon of **overregularization**—the application of grammatical rules without making necessary exceptions. At first children using the past tense will, correctly, say words such as "did," "went," and "brought," which violate the *ed* rule for forming the past tense. They learn these specific words by listening to older children and adults. But as children learn the *ed* rule they say words such as "doed," "goed," or "bringed." Later, when they learn that grammatical rules have exceptions, they learn not to apply the *ed* rule to irregular verbs and again say "did," "went," and "brought" (Kolata, 1987).

How do we know that infants learn rules, rather than a series of specific instances of correct grammar? One source of evidence is a classic study by Jean Berko (1958), who reasoned that if children used correct grammar when confronted with words they have never heard then they must be relying on rules, not rote memory. To test her assumption, Berko developed the "Wugs Test," which included drawings of imaginary creatures called "Wugs" (figure 8.13). Berko found that children would, indeed, apply grammatical rules to novel words.

Is There a Critical Period for Language Acquisition? In 1800 a boy who appeared to be about twelve years old emerged from a forest near Aveyron, France, having somehow survived for many years without human contact (Shattuck, 1980). A physician named Jean Itard named the boy Victor. Victor also became known as the "Wild Boy of Aveyron." Despite extensive training in language, Victor could only say "lait" ("milk"). Similar reports have provided additional evidence of a **critical period** for language acquisition extending from infancy to adolescence, during which language learning is optimal (Colombo, 1982). If people are not exposed to a language until after childhood, they will fail to become proficient in speaking that language.

A more recent and well-documented case described a girl named Genie, who had been raised in isolation. In 1970, thirteen-year-old Genie was discovered by welfare workers in a room in which her father had kept her restrained in a harness and isolated from social contact—and language—since infancy. He communicated with her by growling and barking and beat her whenever she made a sound. By 1981, more than a decade after being returned to society and undergoing intensive language training, Genie had acquired only a rudimentary ability to speak telegraphically while ignoring proper syntax. Like Victor, Genie may have been past her critical period for language acquisition when she returned to society (Pines, 1981). Though the cases of Victor and Genie support the existence of a critical period for language acquisition, you may recall from chapter 2 that it is unwise to generalize from case studies. Perhaps other factors could account for the findings. For example, suppose that Victor and Genie were born with brain disorders that interfered with their ability to acquire language. Even if they had been reared

This is a wug.

Now there is another one.
There are two of them.
There are two _____.

FIGURE 8.13
The Wugs Test Berko (1958) used the "Wugs test" to demonstrate that young children can form the plural of a word they have never seen. This indicates that language acquisition involves learning rules, rather than merely rote memorization of many individual examples.

Overregularization The application of a grammatical rule without making necessary exceptions to it.

Critical Period A period in childhood when experience with language produces optimal language acquisition.

The Wild Boy of Aveyron
Francois Truffaut's movie *The Wild Child* portrayed the case of Victor, the so-called Wild Boy of Aveyron. After living for years in the woods without human contact, Victor failed to develop normal language despite intensive efforts to teach him. This provided evidence that there may be a critical period for language development that ends before adolescence.

from birth in normal family settings, they might still have failed to acquire mature language.

Theories of Language Acquisition   In the thirteenth century Frederick II, emperor of the Holy Roman Empire, tested the popular belief that even if infants were not exposed to language they would eventually begin speaking a recognizable classic language, such as Greek, Latin, or Hebrew. Frederick ordered that several newborn infants be raised without any exposure to speech. But the infants died of illnesses before reaching childhood, bringing the study to a premature halt (Pines, 1981).

Though current ethical standards would prevent such a study today, language researchers still debate the question, Is language acquired solely through learning or is it acquired by the maturation of an inherited predisposition? Those who favor the learning position assume that if it were possible to raise two infants together with no exposure to language, they would not develop true language. In contrast, those who favor language as emerging from an inherited predisposition assume that the same infants might develop a rudimentary form of language with semanticity, generativity, and displacement. According to this position, learning only determines which language an infant will speak, whether English, Dutch, or Navaho.

Language as the Product of Learning   B. F. Skinner (1957) claims that language is acquired through learning, mainly through the positive reinforcement of appropriate speech. For example, a one-year-old child might learn to say "milk" because her parents give her milk and praise her when she says "milk." Similarly, a two-year-old child named Jane might be given a cookie and praise for saying, "Give Jane cookie," but not for saying, "Jane cookie give." As you can see, Skinner assumes that vocabulary and grammar are learned through positive reinforcement.

What support is there for Skinner's position? In one study, two groups of infants between two and seven months old were positively reinforced for producing different phonemes. The infants were reinforced by smiles, "tsk" sounds, and light stroking of the abdomen. One group was reinforced for making vowel sounds, while the other group was reinforced for making consonant sounds. The infants responded by increasing their production of the phonemes for which they were reinforced. This study showed that positive reinforcement may influence language acquisition (Routh, 1969).

Albert Bandura (1977), the influential cognitive-behavioral psychologist, supports the role of observational learning in language acquisition. He assumes that children develop language primarily through imitating the vocabulary and grammatical constructions used by their parents and others in their everyday lives. In one study, adults replied to statements of two-year-old children by purposely using slightly more complex syntax than they normally would. After two months, the children had developed more complex syntax than had children who had not been exposed to the adult models (Nelson, 1977). Additional support for the effect of modeling comes from findings that two-year-olds whose parents read to them acquire language more rapidly than do two-year-olds whose parents do not (Whitehurst et al., 1988).

Language as an Inborn Predisposition   The assumption that language is acquired by learning has been challenged by the linguist Noam Chomsky (1986) and his followers. Chomsky insists that infants are born with the predisposition to develop language. He believes they inherit a language acquisition device, a brain mechanism that makes them sensitive to phonemes, syntax, and semantics. In analyzing the interactions of parents and

Modeling Language   The modeling of language by parents is an important factor in the acquisition of a particular language by the child.

children, Chomsky has found that children progress through similar stages and learn their native languages without formal parental instruction. Children say things that adults never say and their parents do not positively reinforce appropriate grammar in any consistent manner. Moreover, parents will respond to grammatically incorrect statements, too. And even modeling cannot explain all language learning, because observations of children at home show that they vary greatly in the degree to which they imitate what their parents say (Snow, 1981).

But what evidence is there to support Chomsky's position? One source of evidence is the previously mentioned universality in the stages of language acquisition, which indicates that the tendency to develop language is inborn. Studies of deaf children also offer support for Chomsky's position. One study observed deaf children who were neither rewarded for using sign language nor able to learn it from a model. Nonetheless, the children spontaneously developed their own gestural system, in which they communicated by using signs with the characteristics of true language (Goldin-Meadow & Mylander, 1983).

Despite the evidence favoring language as innate and contradicting learning as an explanation for language acquisition, more recent research has provided some support for the learning position. One study tested the assumption made by those who favor Chomsky's position that adults typically ignore children's speech errors and fail to inform them of the distinction between grammatical and ungrammatical sentences. The study found that language acquisition does depend on feedback provided by adults who correct specific instances of improper grammar. Adults do so by repeating a child's grammatically incorrect statements in grammatically correct form or by asking the child to clarify his or her statements (Bohannon & Stanowicz, 1988).

It seems that the positions of Chomsky, Skinner, and Bandura must be integrated in order to explain how language is acquired. We appear to be born with a predisposition to develop language, which provides us with an innate sensitivity to grammar. But we may learn our specific language, including some aspects of its grammar, through positive reinforcement and observational learning.

The Relationship between Language and Thinking

In his novel *1984* George Orwell (1949) envisioned a totalitarian government that controlled its citizens' thoughts by controlling their language. By adding, removing, or redefining words, the government used *Newspeak* to ensure that citizens would not think rebellious thoughts against their leader, "Big Brother." For example, in Newspeak the word "joycamp" was added to refer to a forced labor camp. And the word "free" was redefined to refer only to statements about physical reality, such as "The dog is free from lice," rather than to statements relating to political freedom. Even our own government officials will, at times, resort to euphemisms reminiscent of *Newspeak*. For example, to reduce public outrage about deceptive practices, they have coined the word "misinformation" to replace the word "lying."

The Linguistic Relativity Hypothesis Orwell's view of the influence of language on thought was shared by the linguist-anthropologist Benjamin Lee Whorf (1897–1941), who expressed it in his **linguistic relativity hypothesis,** which assumes that our view of the world is determined by the particular language we speak. Whorf (1956) pointed out that the Eskimo language has many words for snow (such as words distinguishing between falling snow and fallen snow), while the English language has only one.

Noam Chomsky "We should expect heredity to play a major role in language because there is really no other way to account for the fact that children learn to speak in the first place."

Linguistic Relativity Hypothesis The assumption that one's perception of the world is molded by one's language.

The Lingustic Relativity Hypothesis According to Whorf's linguistic relativity hypothesis, a forest ranger who has learned the names of many kinds of trees would, as a consequence, perceive more differences between trees than would people who know the names of few trees.

According to the linguistic relativity hypothesis, the variety of words in the Eskimo language causes people who speak it to perceive differences in snow that people who speak English do not.

Critics argue that, on the contrary, thinking determines language. Perhaps the greater importance of snow in Eskimo culture led them to coin several words for snow, each referring to a different kind. Moreover, English-speaking people to whom snow is important, such as avid skiers, use different adjectives to describe different kinds of snow. Their ability to distinguish between "powdery," "granular," and "crusty" snow indicates that even English-speaking people can perceive wide variations in the quality of snow.

What does formal research have to say about the linguistic relativity hypothesis? In an early study bearing on Whorfs hypothesis (Carmichael, Hogan, & Walter, 1932), subjects were presented with ambiguous drawings of objects that were given either of two labels. When later asked to draw the objects, the subjects drew pictures that looked more like the object that had been named than like the object they had seen (figure 8.14). This supported Whorf's hypothesis.

The most influential studies of the linguistic relativity hypothesis have investigated whether people from cultures with fewer color names can distinguish fewer colors. In one study, researchers compared the color recall ability of English-speaking college students to that of the Dani people of New Guinea. English contains eleven basic, or "focal," color names: red, yellow, green, blue, purple, orange, pink, brown, grey, black, and white. In contrast, the Dani have only two color names: one representing light colors and one representing dark colors.

The subjects were given a series of trials on which they were first shown a colored plastic chip for five seconds. After thirty seconds they were asked to select the chip from among a group of forty chips. The results showed that both the Dani and the college students were superior at recognizing the eleven focal colors than at recognizing nonfocal colors (Heider & Olivier, 1972). This contradicts Whorf's hypothesis, because it indicates that though the Dani only use two color names they are as capable as English-speaking people of perceiving all the focal colors.

Language and Sexism Though language does not *determine* how we think about the world, it may *influence* how we think about the world (Hoffman, Lau, & Johnson, 1986). This is the basis of the current concern about the traditional use of masculine pronouns, such as "his" and "him,"

FIGURE 8.14
The Effect of Labels on Recall
Subjects were shown the pictures in the middle column with one of two different labels. When later asked to draw what they had seen, the subjects drew pictures that were consistent with the labels, not with the pictures (Carmichael, Hogan & Walter, 1932). This indicates that language can affect how we *think* about the world, even though it may not affect how we *perceive* the world.

Source: Data from L. Carmichael, et al., "An Experimental Study of the Effect of Language on the Reproduction of Visually Perceived Form" in *Journal of Experimental Psychology*, Vol. 15:73–86, 1932.

to refer to persons when no sexual identification is intended. Critics of this practice point out that it creates the impression that such statements refer primarily to males (Hyde, 1984).

Consider the statement, "A student may spend four years in graduate school in order to earn his doctoral degree in psychology." This statement refers to both males and females, even though it uses a masculine pronoun. But the statement implies that it is more appropriate for males to earn doctorates in psychology. Years of exposure to such use of the male pronoun to refer to both males and females may promote the belief that certain sex-neutral activities are more suitable for males than for females. Because our use of language can influence the way we think about sex roles, as well as other aspects of everyday life, the linguistic relativity hypothesis may have some merit, as long as it is used to recognize that language influences thinking, though it does not determine it.

THINKING ABOUT PSYCHOLOGY

Can Apes Use Language?

In the early seventeenth century, the philosopher René Descartes argued that language was *the* critical feature that distinguished human beings from other animals. Modern interest in teaching animals cognitive skills normally associated with human beings was stimulated by the case of "Clever Hans," a horse who impressed onlookers by performing arithmetic in Germany in the early twentieth century. Hans was trained to count out the answers to arithmetic problems by tapping one of his hooves until he reached the correct answer. He would count anything present, including persons, hats, or umbrellas. But a psychologist named Oskar Pfungst demonstrated that Hans stopped counting when he noticed tiny movements of his questioner's head, which cued the initiation and termination of counting. When the questioner knew the answer, Hans was correct almost all of the time. But when the questioner did not know the answer, Hans was wrong almost all of the time. So, Hans may have been clever, but he had no idea of how to perform arithmetic (Davis & Memmott, 1982).

As interest in teaching animals to perform arithmetic waned, interest in teaching them language grew. As you read at the beginning of the chapter, animals as diverse as bees, dogs, and monkeys can communicate in limited, stereotyped ways, though they do not use true language, which is characterized by semanticity, generativity, and displacement. But there is one animal that may be capable of acquiring true language—the ape.

Studies of Language in Apes

More than fifty years ago Winthrop and Luella Kellogg (1933) published a book about their experiences raising a chimpanzee named Gua with their infant son, Donald. Even after being exposed to speech as a member of the

Clever Hans An audience watches Clever Hans perform arithmetic calculations in Berlin in 1904.

family, Gua could not speak a single word. Another couple, Cathy and Keith Hayes (1951), had only slightly better results with Viki, a chimpanzee they, too, raised as a member of their family. Despite intensive efforts over a period of several years, they succeeded in teaching Viki to say only four words: "mama," "papa," "cup," and "up." They concluded that the vocal anatomy of apes is not designed for producing speech.

In 1925 the eminent primatologist Robert Yerkes, wondering whether apes have lots to say but no way of saying it, suggested teaching them to use sign language instead of speech. His suggestion was not carried out until 1966, when Allen and Beatrice Gardner (1969) of the University of Nevada began teaching *American Sign Language (ASL)* to a one-year-old chimpanzee named Washoe. They raised Washoe in a trailer next to their house. The Gardners "molded" Washoe's hands into signs to refer to particular actions or objects. They then rewarded her with food and praise for forming signs in the presence of the actions or objects for which the signs stood. To encourage Washoe to use ASL, they never spoke in her presence. After four years of training, Washoe had a repertoire of 132 signs, which she used to name objects and to describe qualities of objects.

Washoe also displayed the ability to generalize her signs to refer to similar things. For example, she used the sign for "open" to refer to doors on a car, a house, and a refrigerator. Washoe even showed an important characteristic of true language—generativity. On seeing a swan for the first time, Washoe made the sign for "water bird." And, after retiring to a chimpanzee colony in Washington State, Washoe was observed teaching ASL to a young chimpanzee she had "adopted" (Cunningham, 1985).

During the past two decades several other apes have been taught to use sign language or other forms of language. Ann and David Premack taught a laboratory chimpanzee named Sarah to use plastic chips of different shapes and colors to represent words (Premack, 1971). Sarah learned to answer questions by arranging the chips in different orders on a board to form sentences. Duane Rumbaugh and Sue Savage-Rumbaugh of the Yerkes Regional Primate Center at Emory University taught a chimpanzee named Lana to use a computer to create sentences by pressing large keys marked by *lexigrams*— geometric forms representing particular words (Rumbaugh, Gill, & von Glasersfeld, 1973). Lana formed sentences by pressing particular keys in a particular order. Lana's language was called "Yerkish" in honor of Robert Yerkes. When Lana made grammatically correct requests, she was rewarded with food, toys, music, or other things she desired.

Criticisms of Ape-Language Studies

Have Washoe, Sarah, and Lana learned to use true language? Do they exhibit semanticity, generativity, and displacement? That is, can they communicate meaningfully, create novel combinations of signs, and refer to objects that are not present? Columbia University psychologist Herbert Terrace, an early supporter of ape language, says no (Terrace, Petitto, Sanders, & Bever, 1979). Terrace taught a chimpanzee named Nim Chimpsky to use sign language. (Nim was named after Noam Chomsky, who does not believe that apes can learn true language.) After five years of training, Nim had mastered 125 signs. At first, Terrace assumed that Nim had learned true language. But after analyzing videotapes of conversations with Nim and videotapes of other apes that had been taught sign language, he concluded that Nim and the other apes had not learned true language.

On what did Terrace base his conclusion? He found that apes merely learned to make signs, arrange forms, or press computer keys in a certain order to

Washoe Allen and Beatrice Gardner taught Washoe to use American sign language. Here Washoe is signing "sweet" in response to a lollipop.

Nim Chimpsky According to Herbert Terrace, even his own chimpanzee, Nim Chimpsky, uses sign language only in response to cues from his trainers. The photo shows Nim learning the sign for "drink."

Criticism of apes Terrace's object

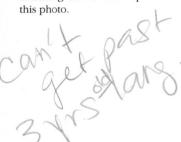

Language or Conditioning? Some researchers argue that apes who have been taught to use language are using true language. But other researchers respond that the apes are merely engaging in behaviors that have been operantly conditioned through positive reinforcement, as in the case of the chimpanzees obtaining cans of Diet Pepsi in this photo.

Can't get past 3 yrs. lang.

obtain rewards. In other words, their use of language was no different from a pigeon who learns to peck a sequence of keys to get food rewards. No researcher would argue that the pigeon is using language. So, the ability of an ape to produce a string of words does not indicate that the ape has learned to produce a sentence. Terrace also claims that the apparent generativity of ape language may be a misinterpretation of ape sign language. For example, Washoe's apparent reference to a swan as a "water bird" may have been a reference to two separate things—a bird and water.

As additional evidence against ape language, Terrace claims that many instances of allegedly spontaneous signing by chimpanzees are merely responses to subtle cues from trainers. Terrace found that Nim communicated primarily in response to prompting by his trainer or by imitating signs recently made by his trainer. Thus, he did not use language in an original or spontaneous way, and his signs may merely be gestures prompted by cues from his trainer that produce consequences he desired—a kind of operant conditioning (Terrace, 1985).

Terrace's attack has not gone unchallenged. Francine Patterson has taught a gorilla named Koko to use more than three hundred signs. Koko has even displayed generativity by referring to a zebra as a "white tiger." She criticizes Terrace for basing his conclusions on his work with Nim and on isolated frames he has examined from films of other apes using ASL. She claims that Nim's inadequate use of language may stem from his having had sixty different trainers, many of whom did not know ASL. This may account for Nim's failure to use sign language in a spontaneous way. In contrast, Patterson reported that Koko had only one primary trainer and used signs more spontaneously than did Nim ("Ape Language," 1981).

In recent years, the strongest evidence supporting ape language comes from studies by Duane Rumbaugh and Sue Savage-Rumbaugh of the Yerkes Primate Research Center in Atlanta. They trained two chimpanzees, Austin and Sherman, to communicate through Yerkish, the language first used by Lana. Austin and Sherman use language in a more meaningful way than previous chimpanzees. In one study, Austin, Sherman, and Lana were taught to categorize three objects (an orange, a beancake, and a slice of bread) as "edible" and three objects (a key, a stick, and a pile of coins) as "inedible." When given other objects, Austin and Sherman, but not Lana, were able to categorize them as edible or inedible. Perhaps Lana could not learn this task because she had been trained to use language to associate labels with specific objects rather than to understand the concepts to which the labels referred (Savage-Rumbaugh, Rumbaugh, Smith, & Lawson, 1980).

Koko While most ape-language researchers have used chimpanzees as subjects, Francine Patterson has taught sign language to the gorilla Koko. Here Koko is signing "love" in response to her pet kitten, All Ball.

Austin and Sherman Duane Rumbaugh and Sue Savage-Rumbaugh have trained two chimpanzees, Austin and Sherman, to use computer keyboards to communicate with each other. Here Sherman responds to Austin's request for bread by obtaining a piece of bread from a tray and handing it to Austin.

Even when housed in different rooms, Austin and Sherman can request objects from each other. This was demonstrated by giving one of the chimpanzees a container from which he could obtain food only by using a tool located in the other chimpanzee's room. The tools included a key for unlocking a box in which there was food or a stick for pushing food out a long, narrow tube. The chimpanzee in the room with the food indicated the tool he needed by striking a particular series of keys on a computer keyboard. The chimpanzee in the room with the tools responded by passing that tool to the other chimpanzee (Marx, 1980).

More recently, Sue Savage-Rumbaugh and her colleagues (1986) have described their work with two pygmy chimpanzees, Kanzi and Mulika, who have achieved language ability superior to that of previous apes. They learned Yerkish by observing other apes pressing appropriate symbols on a keyboard. They can also identify symbols referred to in human speech. Previous apes depended on their particular language system to comprehend human commu-

Kanzi To date, Kanzi is the ape who has shown the most sophisticated use of language. Here he is using Yerkish, a language consisting of geometric symbols.

"Remember, don't talk sex, politics, or religion."

nications. Kanzi and Mulika can even form requests in which other individuals are either the agent or the recipient of action. Previously apes were only able to make spontaneous requests in which *they* were the recipient of action. Moreover, Kanzi and Mulika show displacement, using lexigrams to refer to things that are not present (Savage-Rumbaugh, 1987).

Perhaps future studies using pygmy chimpanzees will succeed where others have failed in demonstrating convincingly that apes are capable of using true language. But even if apes can use true language, no ape has gone beyond the language level of a three-year-old child. Is that the upper limit of ape language ability or is it merely the upper limit using current training methods? Research during the next decade may provide the answer.

SUMMARY

THINKING

Thinking is the purposeful mental manipulation of words and images. Thinking depends on concepts, which are categories of objects, events, qualities, or relations whose members share certain features. A logical concept is formed by identifying specific features possessed by all members of the concept. A natural concept is formed through everyday experiences and has "fuzzy boundaries." The best representative of a concept is called a prototype.

One of the most important uses of concepts is in problem solving, the thought process that enables us to overcome obstacles in order to reach goals. The simplest method of solving problems is trial and error, which involves trying one possible solution after another until finding one that works. The problem-solving strategy called insight depends on the mental manipulation of information. An algorithm is a rule that, when followed step by step, assures that the solution to a problem will be found. A heuristic is a general principle that guides problem solving but does not guarantee the discovery of a solution. A mental set is a problem-solving strategy that has succeeded in the past but that may interfere with solving a problem that requires a new strategy. Our past experience can also impede problem solving through functional fixedness, the inability to realize that a problem can be solved by using a familiar object in an unusual way.

Creativity is a form of problem solving characterized by novel, useful solutions to problems. Creative people tend to have above-average intelligence and are able to integrate different kinds of thinking. Creative people are more motivated by intrinsic interest in creative tasks than by extrinsic factors. Creativity also depends on divergent thinking, in which a person freely considers a variety of potential solutions to creative problems.

Decision making is a form of problem solving in which we try to make the best choice from among alternative judgments or courses of action. Our decisions are influenced by the factors of utility and probability. In using the representativeness heuristic, we assume that characteristics of a small sample are representative of its population. In using the availability heuristic, we estimate the probability of an event by how easily relevant instances of the event come to mind. We are also subject to framing effects, which are biases introduced in the decision-making process by presenting a situation in a certain manner.

Artificial intelligence is a field that integrates computer science and cognitive psychology to try to simulate or improve on human thinking by using computer programs. Computer programs called expert systems display expertise in specific domains of knowledge. Computer scientists are now trying to develop programs that use parallel information processing, as well as serial information processing.

LANGUAGE

True language is characterized by semanticity, generativity, and displacement. The rules of a language are its grammar. Phonemes are the basic sounds of a language, and morphemes are the smallest meaningful units of a language. A language's syntax includes rules governing the acceptable arrangement of words and phrases. Semantics is the study of how language conveys meaning. Noam Chomsky calls the underlying meaning of a statement its deep structure and the words themselves its surface structure. We translate between the two structures by using transformational grammar. The branch of semantics concerned with the relationship between language and its social context is called pragmatics.

Infants in all cultures progress through similar stages of language development. They begin babbling between four and six months of age and say their first words when they are about one year old. At first they use holophrastic speech, in which single words represent whole phrases or sentences. Between the ages of eighteen and twenty-four months, infants begin speaking two-word sentences and use telegraphic speech. As infants learn their language's grammar, they may engage in overregularization, in which they apply grammatical rules without making necessary exceptions. There may be a critical period for language acquisition extending from infancy to adolescence. B. F. Skinner and Albert Bandura believe that language is a learned behavior, while Chomsky believes we have an innate predisposition to develop language.

Benjamin Lee Whorf's linguistic relativity hypothesis assumes that our view of the world is determined by the particular language we speak. But research has shown that though language may influence thinking, it does not determine thinking.

THINKING ABOUT PSYCHOLOGY: CAN APES USE LANGUAGE?

Researchers have taught apes to communicate by using sign language, form boards, and computers. The most well known of these apes have been the gorilla Koko and the chimpanzees Washoe, Sarah, and Lana. Herbert Terrace, the trainer of Nim Chimpsky, claims that apes have not learned true language. Instead, they have learned to give responses that lead to rewards, just as pigeons learn to peck at lights to obtain rewards. Francine Patterson and Duane Rumbaugh and Sue Savage-Rumbaugh have countered by providing evidence that the apes have, indeed, learned true language characterized by semanticity, generativity, and displacement.

IMPORTANT CONCEPTS

IMPORTANT PEOPLE

RECOMMENDED READINGS

For More on All Aspects of Cognition:

Ellis, H. C., & Hunt, R. R. (1989). *Fundamentals of human memory and cognition* (4th ed.). Dubuque, IA: Wm. C. Brown.
A readable, up-to-date textbook on cognition.

Gardner, H. (1985). *The mind's new science: A history of the cognitive revolution.* New York: Basic Books.
An engaging presentation of the origins and status of the cognitive revolution.

For More on Concept Formation:

Smith, E. E., & Medin, D. L. (1981). *Categories and concepts.* Cambridge, MA: Harvard University Press.
A summary of research on concepts and concept formation.

For More on Problem Solving:

Baron, J. B., & Sternberg, R. J. (1987). *Teaching thinking skills.* New York: Freeman.
A series of discussions by experts concerning ways of improving thinking skills.

Mayer, R. E. (1983). *Thinking, problem solving, and cognition.* New York: Freeman.
A scholarly discussion of thinking and the improvement of problem solving.

For More on Creativity:

Amabile, T. M. (1983). *The social psychology of creativity.* New York: Springer-Verlag.
A discussion of creativity, ways of enhancing it, and factors that may reduce intrinsic interest in creative activities.

Weisberg, R. (1986). *Creativity: Genius and other myths.* New York: Freeman.
A thought-provoking account of creativity and major issues concerning its nature.

For More on Decision Making:

Kahneman, D., & Tversky, A. (1982, January). The psychology of preferences. *Scientific American,* pp. 160–173.
An interesting discussion of common biases in decision making, both in the laboratory and in everyday life.

For More on Artificial Intelligence:

McCorduck, P. (1979). *Machines who think: A personal inquiry into the history and prospects of artificial intelligence.* San Francisco: Freeman.
An intriguing discussion of the development of artificial intelligence and the scientists who founded the field.

For More on Language:

Chomsky, N. (1985). *Knowledge of language: Its nature, origin, and use.* New York: Praeger.
A discussion of language by Noam Chomsky, who emphasizes our inborn predisposition to develop it.

Curtiss, S. (1977). *Genie: A psycholinguistic study of a modern-day "wild child."* New York: Academic Press.
A fascinating account of a child who was reared in social isolation and her difficulty in acquiring language in adolescence.

For More on Ape Language:

Premack, D. (1986). *Gavagai! The future history of the ape language controversy.* Cambridge, MA: MIT Press.
A leading researcher presents a sober account of the current status of the ape-language controversy.

CHAPTER
9

INTELLIGENCE

Chapter Opening Art: Paul Klee. *Twittering Machine*. 1922.

Rainman In *Rainman,* Tom Cruise played the younger brother of Dustin Hoffman, who portrayed a man with *autism,* a brain disorder marked by social aloofness, language disturbances, and often, mental retardation.

Intelligence The global capacity to act purposefully, to think rationally, and to deal effectively with the environment.

What school

n the 1988 movie *Rainman,* which won the Academy Award for best picture, Dustin Hoffman played an autistic, mentally retarded man who could perform amazing feats, such as recalling the telephone number of anyone in the telephone book. Hoffman portrayed a so-called idiot savant (French for "learned fool"), a person who is mentally retarded but who has an outstanding ability typically in art, music, memory, or calculating. In one case, a mentally retarded man was able to give the day of the week for any date between 1943 and 1969 (Hill, 1975). He apparently had spent many hours memorizing the day of the week on which each date fell, just as Dustin Hoffman's character spent many hours memorizing the telephone book. Their feats are similar to the ability of children to memorize statistics from the backs of hundreds of baseball cards and then recall any statistic for any player.

You certainly recognize intelligent behavior when you see it: an "idiot savant" who memorizes enormous amounts of material; a student who gets an *A* on a calculus exam; a composer who writes a great symphony; a scientist who discovers a cure for a disease. But recognizing intelligent behavior is easier than defining "intelligence" itself. Though the word *intelligence* comes from the Latin word meaning "to understand," intelligence is a broader concept than that. Yet, finding a universally acceptable definition of intelligence is difficult because intelligence is a natural concept. As you learned in chapter 8, natural concepts are not easily defined by a distinct set of features.

Three decades ago David Wechsler (1958), a leading intelligence researcher, put forth what has become the most widely accepted definition of intelligence. He called **intelligence** the global capacity to act purposefully, to think rationally, and to deal effectively with the environment. In other words, intelligence reflects how well we function. This definition is in the spirit of the first American school of psychology, functionalism, which emphasized the importance of adaptive functioning in everyday life (see chapter 1).

And, indeed, intelligent people tend to function better in society. For example, a recent study of the children of criminals found that the more intelligent the children the less likely they are to become criminals themselves. Apparently, those with a higher level of intelligence perform better in school, become less alienated, and use their educational success as a means to a socially acceptable career (Kandel et al., 1988).

INTELLIGENCE TESTING

Modern interest in the study of intelligence began with the development of tests of mental abilities, which include achievement tests, aptitude tests, and intelligence tests. An **achievement test** assesses knowledge of a particular subject. A cumulative final examination in your psychology course would be an achievement test to assess your knowledge of psychology. An **aptitude test** predicts your potential to benefit from instruction in a particular academic or vocational setting. Aptitude tests are commonly used to screen job applicants and college applicants. In applying to colleges, you probably submitted the results of your performance on either the Scholastic Aptitude Test (SAT) or the American College Test (ACT). Scores on those tests help admissions committees determine whether applicants have the potential to succeed in college. An **intelligence test,** the main topic of this section, is a kind of aptitude test that assesses overall mental ability.

Achievement Test A test that measures knowledge of a particular subject. *Sat*

Aptitude Test A test designed to predict a person's potential to benefit from instruction in a particular academic or vocational setting.

Intelligence Test A test that assesses overall mental ability.

The Early History of Intelligence Testing

The use of tests of mental abilities can be traced as far back as 2200 B.C., when the Chinese used them to identify talented individuals to serve as civil servants (Fox, 1981). But ability testing did not become the subject of scientific study until a century ago, when the scientist Sir Francis Galton (1822–1911) set up his Anthropometric Laboratory at the 1884 International Health Exhibition in London. (The word "anthropometric" means "human measurement.") More than nine thousand visitors paid to be measured on a variety of physical characteristics, including head size, grip strength, visual acuity, and reaction time to sounds (Johnson et al., 1985).

Galton was influenced by his cousin Charles Darwin's theory of evolution. According to Darwin, individuals who are the most physically well adapted to their environments are the most likely to survive and produce offspring with those physical characteristics. Galton similarly assumed that people with superior physical abilities, especially sensory and motor abilities, are better adapted for survival. He viewed them as more intelligent than those with average or inferior physical abilities.

Galton's interest in studying physical differences reflected his interest in studying all sorts of individual differences, including the relative beauty of women from different countries. (In a possible instance of experimenter bias, Galton found that the women of England, his home country, were the most beautiful.) His research on individual differences established the field of **differential psychology,** which is concerned with studying cognitive and behavioral differences among individuals. Galton's anthropometric method was introduced to the United States in 1890 by James McKeen Cattell (1860–1944), who administered Galton's tests to students at the University of Pennsylvania. But anthropometry eventually proved fruitless as a way of measuring general intelligence, because anthropometric measurements, such as grip strength, had little or no relationship to mental measures of intelligence, such as reasoning ability.

The first true test of general intelligence—the *Binet-Simon Scale*—appeared in 1905. It grew out of an 1881 French law requiring all children to attend school even if they could not profit from a standard curriculum (Levine, 1976). But educators found that many children could not perform adequately in normal classes. In 1904 this led the French Minister of Education to ask psychologist Alfred Binet (1857–1911) to develop a test to identify children who required special classes for slow learners.

Binet collaborated with psychiatrist Theodore Simon (1873–1961) to develop a test that could assess the ability of children to perform in school. Binet and Simon began by administering many questions related to language, reasoning, and arithmetic to elementary schoolchildren of all ages. Questions that tended to be answered correctly or incorrectly by children of all ages were eliminated. Questions that were answered correctly by more and more children at each successive age were retained and became the Binet-Simon Scale.

The test was then administered to children who needed to be placed in school. Each student received a *mental age,* based on the number of test items he or she passed—the greater the number of items passed, the higher the mental age. A student with a mental age significantly below his or her chronological age was considered a candidate for placement in a class for slow learners. Binet urged that his test be used solely for class placement. He disagreed with those who claimed that the test measured a child's inherited level of intelligence or that a child's level of intelligence could not be improved by education.

Sir Francis Galton (1822–1911) "Social hindrances cannot impede men of high ability from being eminent . . . [and] social advantages are incompetent to give that status to a man of moderate ability."

Differential Psychology The field concerned with studying cognitive and behavioral variations among individuals.

Alfred Binet (1857–1911) "It will be seen that a profound knowledge of the normal intellectual development of the child would not only be of great interest but useful in formulating a course of instruction really adapted to their aptitudes."

Intelligence Quotient (IQ)
(1) Originally, the ratio of mental age to chronological age; that is, MA/CA × 100. (2) Today, the score on an intelligence test, calculated by comparing a person's performance to norms for his or her age group.

The Binet-Simon Scale proved useful, but the mental age, at times, proved misleading. Suppose that a ten-year-old child had a mental age of eight and a six-year-old child had a mental age of four. Both would be two years below their chronological age, but the six-year-old would be proportionately further behind his or her age peers than would the ten-year-old. This problem was solved by the German psychologist William Stern (1871–1938), who recommended using the ratio of mental age to chronological age to determine a child's level of intelligence. A ten-year-old with a mental age of eight would have a ratio of $8/10 = .80$, and a six-year-old with a mental age of four would have a ratio of $4/6 = .67$, indicating that the six-year-old was relatively further behind his or her age peers. Stern eliminated the decimal point by multiplying the ratio by 100. Thus, .80 becomes 80 and .67 becomes 67. The formula, (mental age/chronological age) x 100, became known as the **intelligence quotient**—or **IQ.** As you can calculate for yourself, a child whose mental age is exactly the same as his or her chronological age would have an IQ of 100, and a child whose mental age is higher than his or her chronological age would have an IQ above 100.

The Binet-Simon Scale was translated into English and first used in the United States by the American psychologist Henry Goddard (1866–1957) at a New Jersey school with the odd name of the Vineland Training School for Feebleminded Boys and Girls. A revised version of the Binet-Simon Scale, more suitable for children reared in American culture, was published in 1916 by Stanford University psychologist Lewis Terman (1877–1956). The American version became known as the *Stanford-Binet Intelligence Scale,* which is still used today. Ironically, the Binet-Simon Scale was neither widely used nor widely known in France until after the Stanford-Binet had become popular in America (Wolf, 1961). Terman also redesigned the Stanford-Binet to make it suitable for testing both children and adults. (The test was revised in 1937, 1960, 1972, and 1986.)

Because the Stanford-Binet is given individually and may take an hour or more to administer, it is not suitable for testing large groups of people in a brief period of time. This became a problem during World War I, when the United States Army sought a way to assess the intelligence of large groups of recruits. The army wanted to reject recruits who did not have the intelligence to perform well and to identify recruits who would be good officer candidates. The solution to this problem was provided by Terman and his student A. A. Otis. They developed two group tests of intelligence—the *Army Alpha Test* and the *Army Beta Test.* The Army Alpha Test was given in writing to recruits who could read English, and the Army Beta Test was given orally to those who could not read English and in pantomine to those who were non-English-speaking immigrants. Descendants of these group intelligence tests, such as the current *Otis-Lennon Mental Abilities Tests,* are still used today for testing many persons at once.

After World War I the Stanford-Binet became the most widely used intelligence test. But the ratio IQ devised by Stern, which was adequate for representing the intelligence of children, proved inadequate for representing the intelligence of adults. Because growth in mental age slows markedly after childhood, the use of the ratio IQ led to the absurdity of people with average or above-average intelligence becoming below average as their chronological age increased. For example, consider the case of a fifteen-year-old girl with a mental age of twenty. She would have an IQ of $(20/15)$ x $100 = 133$. This would put her in the mentally gifted range (that is, above 130). Suppose that at age forty she had retained the mental age of twenty. She would then have an IQ of $(20/40)$ x $100 = 50$. This would put her well within the mentally retarded range (that is, below 70). Yet, she might be a successful lawyer, physician, or professor.

(a)   (b)

The Army Tests More than 1.7 million recruits took either (a) the nonverbal Army Beta Test or (b) the verbal Army Alpha Test during World War I.

This inadequacy of the ratio IQ was overcome by David Wechsler (1896–1981), who replaced Stern's ratio IQ with a *deviation IQ.* The deviation IQ compares a person's intelligence test score with the average score of his or her age peers. Those who perform at exactly the average level of their age peers receive an IQ of 100; those who perform above the average level of their age peers receive an IQ above 100; and those who perform below the average level of their age peers receive an IQ below 100.

In 1939 Wechsler developed his own intelligence test. While working as chief psychologist at Bellevue Hospital in New York City, Wechsler sought a way to assess the intelligence of those with low verbal ability among the derelicts, alcoholics, and emotionally disturbed people he encountered there. Because the Stanford-Binet emphasized verbal ability, it was not suitable for that purpose. This led Wechsler to develop an intelligence test that placed less emphasis on verbal ability, which he called the *Wechsler-Bellevue Intelligence Scale.*

Wechsler later developed versions of his test for use with different age groups, including the *Wechsler Intelligence Scale for Children* (*WISC*) in 1949, for ages six to seventeen, and the *Wechsler Adult Intelligence Scale* (*WAIS*) in 1955, for adults. The Wechsler Scales have been revised periodically, with the most recent revisions being the WISC (called the WISC-R) in 1974 and the WAIS (called the WAIS-R) in 1981. Each of the Wechsler Intelligence Scales contains subtests measuring different aspects of verbal and nonverbal intelligence (figure 9.1). The test taker receives a verbal IQ, a performance (that is, nonverbal) IQ, and an overall IQ.

David Wechsler (1896–1981) "Intelligence, operationally defined, is the aggregate or global capacity of the individual to act purposefully, to think rationally, and to deal effectively with his environment."

Test Construction

principles

But how do psychologists construct intelligence tests? They do so by following several principles of test construction: standardization, reliability, and validity.

Standardization There are two kinds of **standardization.** The first kind assures that the test will be administered and scored in a consistent manner. In giving a test, all test administrators must use the same instructions, the same time limits, and the same scoring system. If they do not, a test taker's score might not accurately reflect his or her ability.

The second kind of standardization establishes **norms**—the standards with which the scores of test takers are compared. Without norms a score on an intelligence test would be a meaningless number. Norms are established by giving the test to samples of hundreds or thousands of people who are representative of the people for whom the test is designed. If a test is to be used in the United States, samples might include representative proportions of males and females; blacks and whites; lower-, middle-, and upper-class members; urban and rural dwellers; and easterners, westerners, northerners, and southerners.

Standardization (1) A procedure assuring that a test is administered and scored in a consistent manner. (2) A procedure for establishing test norms by giving a test to large samples of people who are representative of those for whom the test is designed.

Norms Scores based on the test performances of large numbers of subjects that are used as standards for assessing the performances of individual test takers.

FIGURE 9.1
The Wechsler Adult
Intelligence Scale-Revised The
WAIS-R (1981) includes items
that test both verbal and
nonverbal intelligence.

Verbal subtests

General information
The individual is asked a number of general information questions about
experiences that are considered normal for individuals in our society.
For example, "How many hours apart are eastern standard time and pacific
standard time?"

Similarities
The individual must think logically and abstractly to answer a number of
questions about how things are similar.
For example, "In what way are boats and trains the same?"

Arithmetic reasoning
Problems measure the individual's ability to do arithmetic mentally and include
addition, subtraction, multiplication, and division.
For example, "If oranges are $1.20 per dozen, how much does one orange
cost?"

Vocabulary
To evaluate word knowledge, the individual is asked to define a number of
words. This subtest measures a number of cognitive functions, including
concept formation, memory, and language.
For example, "What does the word *disparate* mean?"

Comprehension
This subtest is designed to measure the individual's judgment and common
sense.
For example, "Why do individuals buy automobile insurance?"

Digit span
This subtest primarily measures attention and short-term memory. The individual is required to repeat numbers forward and backward.
For example, "I am going to say some numbers and I want you to repeat them
backward: 4   7   5   2   8."

Nonverbal subtests

Picture completion
A number of drawings are shown, each with a significant part missing. Within a
period of several seconds, the individual must differentiate essential from
nonessential parts of the picture and identify which part is missing. This subtest
evaluates visual alertness and the ability to organize information visually.
For example, "I am going to show you a picture with an important part
missing. Tell me what is missing."

Picture arrangement
A series of pictures out of sequence are shown to the individual, who is asked to
place them in their proper order to tell an appropriate story. This subtest
evaluates how individuals integrate information to make it logical and meaningful.
For example, "The pictures below need to be placed in an appropriate order
to tell a meaningful story."

Object assembly

The individual is asked to assemble pieces into something. This subtest measures visual-motor coordination and perceptual organization.

For example, "When these pieces are put together correctly, they make something. Put them together as quickly as you can."

Block design

The individual must assemble a set of multi-colored blocks to match designs that the examiner shows. Visual-motor coordination, perceptual organization, and the ability to visualize spatially are measured.

For example, "Use the four blocks on the left to make the pattern on the right."

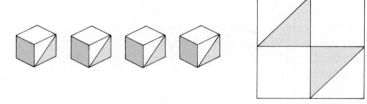

Coding

This subtest evaluates how quickly and accurately an individual can link code symbols and digits. The subtest assesses visual-motor coordination and speed of thought.

For example, "As quickly as you can, transfer the appropriate code symbols to the blank spaces."

Code

●	□	★	△	∕∕
1	2	3	4	5

Test

3	5	2	4	1	2	4	3	5	2	1	4	3	5

When an intelligence test is standardized, the average performance of the standardization group for each age range is given a score of 100, with a standard deviation of about 15. As you learned in chapter 2, the mean is the average for a group of scores, and the standard deviation is a measure of how variable a group of scores are around their mean. Figure 9.2 shows that IQ scores fall along what is called a *normal curve.* For the Wechsler Scales, this means that 68 percent of test takers will score between 85 and 115 and 95 percent will score between 70 and 130. Average intelligence falls between 85 and 115. IQs below 70 fall in the mentally retarded range, and IQs above 130 fall in the mentally gifted range.

Reliability Imagine using a bathroom scale that gave markedly different readings from day to day, perhaps indicating 195 pounds one day, 114 pounds the next day, and 146 pounds the third day. Because your actual weight would not fluctuate that much in three days, the scale would be unreliable and you would no longer use it to measure your weight. Similarly, you would use an intelligence test only if it were reliable. The **reliability** of a test is the degree to which it gives consistent results. Suppose you took an IQ test and scored 105 (average) one month, 62 (mentally retarded) the next month, and 138 (mentally gifted) the third month. Because your level of intelligence normally would not fluctuate that much in three months, you would argue that the test is unreliable.

One way of determining whether a test is reliable is to use the **test-retest method,** in which the same test is given to a group of people on two occasions. The scores on the two occasions are then correlated. A high positive correlation would indicate that the test is reliable. A second way of determining reliability is to use the **split-half method,** in which the test is divided into two halves, usually with the odd items on one half and the even items on the other half. Scores on the two halves are then correlated. Again, a high positive correlation would indicate that the test is reliable. The advantage of the split-half method is that the test is given only once, which rules out any practice effects that might improve scores when subjects are retested using the test-retest method. Because the reliability correlations for the Stanford-Binet and Wechsler Scales are at least .90, the tests are reliable measures of intelligence.

Reliability The degree to which a test gives consistent results.

Test-Retest Reliability Assessing a test's consistency by giving it to a group of people on two occasions and then correlating scores on the first occasion with scores on the second.

Split-Half Reliability Assessing a test's consistency by dividing it into two halves, usually with odd-numbered items in one half and even-numbered items in the other, and then correlating scores on the two halves.

odd # even # score seperately

FIGURE 9.2
The Normal Distribution of IQ Test Scores

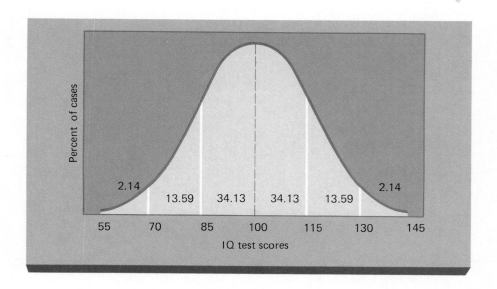

Though standardized IQ tests are reliable, an individual's IQ score may vary over a period of years. The Berkeley Growth Study, conducted at the University of California at Berkeley, contradicted the once-popular belief that intelligence does not change during childhood. The study found that mental ability increases steadily until adolescence, slows down, and then levels off at about the age of twenty (Bayley, 1955).

But what about changes in intelligence in adulthood? One of the major controversies about adult intelligence is whether it declines in old age. While some researchers have presented evidence that intelligence does decline (Horn & Donaldson, 1976), others have presented evidence that it does not (Baltes & Schaie, 1976). One reason for this disagreement is the use of two different research designs: cross-sectional designs and longitudinal designs. In a **cross-sectional design,** groups of people representing different life stages are compared to one another. A cross-sectional study might compare young adults, middle-aged adults, and old adults. In a **longitudinal design,** a single group of people is studied as they pass through different life stages. A longitudinal study might follow the same group of subjects as they pass through young adulthood, middle adulthood, and late adulthood.

While cross-sectional studies tend to find a marked decline in intelligence in old age, longitudinal studies tend to find little or no decline. What might account for these contradictory findings? Cross-sectional studies may be comparing samples of younger people to samples of older people that include more individuals who perform worse on intelligence tests because they are less healthy, less educated, or less motivated to perform well on such tests. This would give the mistaken impression that intelligence declines markedly in old age.

Validity A reliable test would be useless if it were not also valid. **Validity** is the extent to which a test measures what it is supposed to measure. A test with **face validity** appears, on superficial observation, to be valid. A

Cross-Sectional Design A research design in which groups of people representing different life stages are compared to one another.

Longitudinal Design A research design in which the same group of subjects is tested or observed repeatedly over a period of time.

Validity The extent to which a test measures what it is supposed to measure.

Face Validity The extent to which a test appears, on superficial observation, to be valid.

test of cooking aptitude that asked questions such as, What is the effect of baking soda? would have face validity. A test of baking aptitude that asked, How much larger is the area of a square with five-inch sides than a square with three-inch sides? would not. But the apparent face validity of a test does not indicate whether it is, in fact, valid. We might find that many people who know what baking soda does may not know how to bake. And we might find that people who can calculate the area of a square make better bakers, perhaps because they know how to change the amount of ingredients to produce cakes of different sizes. Nonetheless, face validity is important because it will motivate test takers to try their best.

Content Validity The extent to which the items in a test are a representative sample of the knowledge or behavior that is being tested.

Tests should also have **content validity,** meaning that the items they contain are a representative sample of what is being tested. A baking test in which all the questions referred to baking pies would not have content validity, because it would not include questions about other kinds of baking. Similarly, a psychology test on this chapter that only asked questions about this section would not have content validity. As in the case of face validity, content validity improves the motivation of the test taker.

Construct Validity The extent to which a test measures the supposed concept, or construct, it presumably measures.

Another kind of validity, **construct validity,** refers to the extent to which the test measures the supposed concept, or *construct,* it presumes to measure. Thus, people who score high on a test of verbal ability should perform better in reading, writing, and vocabulary than do people who score low on the test. This would provide evidence that the test is a valid measure of the construct of "verbal ability."

Predictive Validity The extent to which a test accurately predicts behavior it is supposed to predict.

Psychologists are especially concerned with a fourth kind of validity, **predictive validity,** meaning that the test accurately predicts behavior related to what the test is supposed to measure. A test of mechanical ability with predictive validity would accurately predict the ability to become an automobile mechanic. The behavior that is being predicted by a test, whether baking, automobile mechanics, or academic performance, is called a *criterion.*

Consider the SAT's ability to predict school performance. The SAT correlates .41 with the criterion of college grade point average. This means that the SAT is a moderately good predictor. But high school grade point average, which correlates .52 with college grade point average, is an even better predictor. Moreover, the combination of the SAT and high school grade point average is a still better predictor, correlating .58 with college grade point average (Linn, 1982). As for intelligence tests, the Stanford-Binet and Wechsler Scales correlate between .40 and .75 with school performance, depending on the aspect of school performance being measured (Aiken, 1982).

These moderately high correlations indicate that the tests are good, but far from perfect, predictors of school performance. Because the correlations are less than a perfect 1.00, factors other than those measured by the SAT or by IQ tests also contribute to school performance. This has made the fairness of tests of mental ability one of the most controversial issues in contemporary psychology.

The Fairness of Intelligence Testing

Before reading on, try to answer the questions in figure 9.3. The less familiar you are with black culture, the less likely you were to answer the questions correctly. There is concern today that IQ tests and other tests of mental ability might be unfair to minority groups, especially blacks, because they are less familiar with their content than are whites. There is general agreement that blacks score, on average, fifteen points lower than whites on IQ tests. There is also general agreement that this difference reflects the consequences of past and present discrimination against blacks. Because blacks are less likely to

1. A "gas head" is a person who has a:
   (a) fast-moving car
   (b) stable of "lace"
   (c) "process"
   (d) habit of stealing cars
   (e) long jail record for arson
2. "Bo Diddley" is a:
   (a) game for children
   (b) down-home cheap wine
   (c) down-home singer
   (d) new dance
   (e) Moejoe call
3. If a pimp is uptight with a woman who gets state aid, what does he mean when he talks about "Mother's day"?
   (a) second Sunday in May
   (b) third Sunday in June
   (c) first of every month
   (d) none of these
   (e) first and fifteenth of every month
4. A "handkerchief head" is:
   (a) a cool cat
   (b) a porter
   (c) an Uncle Tom
   (d) a hoddi
   (e) a preacher
5. If a man is called a "blood," then he is a:
   (a) fighter
   (b) Mexican-American
   (c) Negro
   (d) hungry hemophile
   (e) red man, or Indian
6. Cheap chitlings (not the kind you purchase at a frozen-food counter) will taste rubbery unless they are cooked long enough. How soon can you quit cooking them to eat and enjoy them?
   (a) forty-five minutes
   (b) two hours
   (c) twenty-four hours
   (d) one week (on a low flame)
   (e) one hour

Answers: 1. c 2. c 3. e 4. c 5. c 6. c

FIGURE 9.3
Items from the Chitling Test

Source: Adrian Dove, 1968.

have the same cultural and educational experiences as whites, they tend, on average, to perform more poorly on tests that assume cultural and educational experiences common to whites (Miller-Jones, 1989).

But does this mean that IQ tests are biased against blacks? After decades of controversy, the issue of the validity of IQ tests for blacks reached the courts in the 1970s. In 1979 Judge Robert Peckham of the Federal District Court in San Francisco ruled that without court approval California schools could no longer use IQ tests to place black schoolchildren in classes. His ruling came in the case of *Larry P. v. Wilson Riles* (the California superintendent of education), which was brought in 1971 on behalf of six black children who had been placed in classes for the educable mentally retarded (that is, those with mild mental retardation).

After hearing ten thousand pages of testimony from experts and advocates on both sides of the issue, Peckham ruled that the use of IQ tests violated the civil rights of black children, because a greater proportion of black children than white children was being placed in classes for the mentally retarded. His decision influenced school districts in several other states to abandon the use of IQ tests for deciding the school placement of black children.

But Peckham's decision was also met by arguments that IQ tests are not biased against blacks, because the tests have predictive validity—they accurately predict the performances of both black children and white children in elementary school classes. The differences in IQ scores between black children and white children may reflect the greater likelihood of black children being reared in socially disadvantaged families that do not provide them with the opportunity to gain experiences that are important in doing well on IQ tests and in school (Lambert, 1981). And, a committee of scholars from several academic fields reported to the National Academy of Science that standardized tests are accurate predictors of school and job performance for all groups and, therefore, are not biased against any particular group ("NAS Calls Tests Fair But Limited," 1982).

Nonetheless, the issue has become as much a political issue as a scientific one. On one side are those, such as Judge Peckham, who believe that tests of mental abilities are being used to perpetuate discrimination against blacks by placing black children in slower classes and by preventing black adults from obtaining desirable jobs. They would favor outlawing the use of tests. On the

FIGURE 9.4
**Raven Progressive Matrices
Test** In this "culture-fair" test,
the person is presented with a
series of matrices and must
complete it by selecting the
appropriate symbol from an
accompanying group of symbols.

A5 taken from the Raven *Standard
Progressive Matrices.* Reprinted by
permission of J. C. Raven Limited.

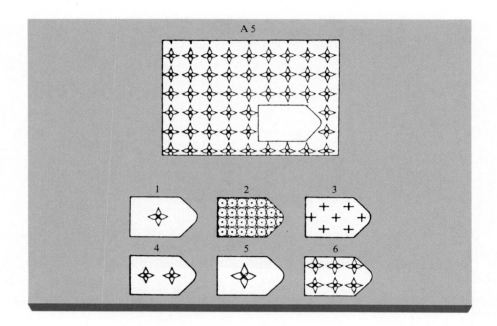

other side are those who believe that blaming IQ tests for revealing the unfortunate consequences of discrimination is like killing the messenger who
brings bad news. They would favor changing the conditions that contribute
to the poorer performances of blacks and other minority groups.

One possible solution presents a compromise: use tests that are not affected by the test taker's cultural background. But efforts to develop "culture-
free" tests in the 1940s (Cattell, 1940) and "culture-fair" tests in the 1950s
(Davis & Eels, 1953) produced disappointing results. These tests presented
test takers with items that emphasized perceptual and spatial abilities, rather
than verbal abilities, and avoided the use of items that would presume an extensive background in a particular culture (figure 9.4). But, just as on traditional intelligence tests, people of higher socioeconomic status perform better
on these nonverbal tests than do people of lower socioeconomic status (Jensen,
1980).

Imagine Alfred Binet's reaction to the controversy that has arisen over the
use of standardized tests, considering that he saw testing as an objective means
of assessing the abilities of students. As Richard Weinberg (1989, p. 100), a
leading intelligence researcher, has noted:

> In the light of the effectiveness of current IQ tests to predict school per-
> formance, it is ironic that tests have been outlawed for the very purpose
> for which they were designed—to prevent subjective judgment and prej-
> udice from being the basis for assigning students to special classes or de-
> nying them certain privileges.

EXTREMES OF INTELLIGENCE

Another controversial issue regarding intelligence is the classification and education of people who fall at either extreme of the range of intelligence. As
you learned earlier, 95 percent of the population will score between 70 and
130 on IQ tests. Of the remaining 5 percent, half will score below 70 and half
will score above 130. Those who score below 70 are usually considered mentally retarded and those who score above 130 are usually considered mentally
gifted—though the classification of a person as mentally retarded or mentally
gifted is not based on IQ scores alone.

A Group Home Mentally retarded people may live in supervised group homes, instead of in large institutions. They learn to become self-reliant, including preparing their own meals.

Mental Retardation

Depending on the criteria used to define **mental retardation,** from slightly more than 3 million to almost 7 million Americans are mentally retarded. The estimate varies because the person's level of adaptive behavior, and not just his or her level of intelligence, needs to be assessed before the person is classified as mentally retarded. In fact, the current trend in classification is to rely more on the person's everyday functioning and less on his or her IQ score (Haywood, Meyers, & Switzky, 1982).

Classification of Mental Retardation We have come a long way in our classification of the mentally retarded. In the early 1900s, the mentally retarded were placed in one of three categories, each referring to an increasing degree of mental retardation: moron (from a Greek word meaning "foolish"), imbecile (from a Latin word meaning "weak-minded"), and idiot (from a Greek word meaning "ignorant"). Fortunately, these terms are no longer used by professionals, but, as you are certainly aware, they have become common terms of disparagement in everyday language.

To be classified as mentally retarded, a person must have an IQ below 70 and difficulties performing in everyday life (Landesman & Ramey, 1989). These include difficulties in self-care (such as eating and dressing), schoolwork (such as reading and arithmetic), and social relationships (such as conversing and developing friendships). Moreover, before a person can be classified as mentally retarded, alternative causes of the person's low IQ score and difficulties performing in everyday life must be ruled out. These alternative causes include physical illnesses, impairment of vision or hearing, and a non-English-speaking family background.

Today, a person who is classified as mentally retarded will fall in one of four categories of mental retardation (American Psychiatric Association, 1987). Those with IQs of 50 to 70 have *mild retardation* and comprise 85 percent of the mentally retarded. They are able to care for themselves, reach a sixth-grade level of education, hold responsible jobs, be married, and serve as adequate parents. Those with IQs of 35 to 49 have *moderate retardation* and comprise 10 percent of the mentally retarded. They may be trained to care for themselves, reach a second-grade level of education, and hold menial jobs, often in sheltered workshops. But they have difficulty maintaining social relationships and they rarely marry.

Mental Retardation Intellectual deficiency marked by an IQ below 70 and difficulties performing in everyday life.

what % in each cat IQ is characterise esp. moderate

The Special Olympics Mentally retarded people have the opportunity to demonstrate their athletic abilities at the Special Olympics.

Cultural-Familial Retardation Mental retardation apparently caused by social or cultural deprivation.

Fetal Alcohol Syndrome A disorder, marked by physical defects and mental retardation, that may affect the offspring of women who drink alcohol during pregnancy.

Cerebral Palsy A movement disorder caused by brain damage, which is often accompanied by mental retardation.

Phenylketonuria (PKU) A hereditary enzyme deficiency that, if left untreated in the infant, causes mental retardation.

Those with IQs between 20 and 34 have _severe retardation_ and comprise 3 to 4 percent of the mentally retarded. They may learn rudimentary language and work skills but may be unable to care for themselves, to benefit from schooling, to hold jobs, or to maintain normal social relationships. And those with IQs below 20 have _profound retardation_ and comprise 1 to 2 percent of those with mental retardation. They may spend their lives in institutions that provide them with no more than custodial care.

Causes of Mental Retardation In 1912 Henry Goddard traced the descendants of a Revolutionary War soldier whom he gave the name Martin Kallikak. The soldier produced two lines of descendants. One line arose from his affair with a mentally retarded tavern maid. The other line arose through his marriage to a respectable woman of normal intelligence. Goddard found that the descendants of the tavern maid included many derelicts, prostitutes, and mentally retarded people. In contrast, the descendants of his wife included few such people.

The differences between the two lines of descendants account for Goddard's use of the name "Kallikak." The name is a combination of the Greek words "kalos" (meaning "good") and "kakos" (meaning "bad"). Goddard concluded that the descendants of the soldier's wife inherited the tendency to be moral and intelligent, while the descendants of the tavern maid inherited the tendency to be immoral and mentally retarded. He ignored the influence of the markedly different sociocultural environments into which the children in each branch of the family were born as the probable causes of the differences.

Today we know that about 75 percent of cases of mental retardation are caused, not by heredity, but by sociocultural deprivation, so-called **cultural-familial retardation** (Scott & Carran, 1987). In fact, almost all mildly retarded persons come from such backgrounds. Their families may fail to provide them with adequate intellectual stimulation, such as discussing current events with them, encouraging them to read, helping them with homework, and taking them on trips to zoos, museums, and other educational settings. They are also more likely to attend inferior schools, to suffer from malnutrition, and to lack adequate medical care—each of which may impair intellectual growth.

Though most cases of mental retardation are caused by sociocultural deprivation, about 25 percent are caused by brain damage. Pregnant women who ingest drugs may cause brain damage in their offspring. For example, women who drink alcohol while pregnant may give birth to children suffering from **fetal alcohol syndrome,** marked by physical deformities and mental retardation. Pregnant women who suffer from certain diseases, particularly _rubella_ (German measles), also have a greater risk of giving birth to mentally retarded offspring. And a newborn infant who fails to breathe for several minutes after birth will experience _anoxia, a_ lack of oxygen to the brain. This may cause **cerebral palsy,** a form of brain damage characterized by movement disorders and often accompanied by mental retardation.

Mental retardation may also be caused by genetic defects. This may occur when a child inherits an organic defect that causes brain damage, as in the case of **phenylketonuria (PKU).** PKU is caused by an inherited lack of the enzyme required to metabolize the amino acid _phenylalanine,_ which is found in milk and other common foods. This eventually causes brain damage, which leads to mental retardation by the age of three. Fortunately, routine screening of newborns in the United States and other countries can detect PKU early enough to protect infants from brain damage by putting them on a diet that eliminates almost all of their intake of phenylalanine.

Some cases of mental retardation are caused by genetic defects that occur during gestation, as in the case of **Down syndrome** (Patterson, 1987). This disorder is named for the English physician Langdon Down, who identified it in 1866. As you probably know, human beings normally have twenty-three pairs of chromosomes, with one member of each pair coming from each parent. A person with Down syndrome has an extra, third chromosome on the twenty-first pair. The extra chromosome can come from either the mother's egg or the father's sperm. The chances of having a child with Down syndrome increase markedly during middle age.

Children with Down syndrome are usually moderately retarded and exhibit distinctive physical characteristics. These include small ears and hands; short necks, feet, and fingers; protruding tongues; and a fold over the eyes, giving them an almond-shaped, oriental appearance. Because of this, Down syndrome was originally called "Mongolism" and victims were called "Mongoloid idiots." This reflected the nineteenth-century belief that victims of the disorder failed to develop beyond what was then assumed to be the more primitive physical and intellectual level of Orientals, such as Mongolians (Gould, 1981).

Education of the Mentally Retarded   Over the centuries the mentally retarded have been treated as everything from children of God, who brought good luck, to subhumans, who were locked up as dangerous (Wolfensberger, 1972). Today psychologists interested in the mentally retarded emphasize their potential to benefit from education and training. One reason that mentally retarded people do not perform as well as non-mentally retarded people is that they fail to use effective methods of information processing. For example, when mentally retarded people are given a series of words or pictures to remember, they tend not to rehearse the items or group them into chunks—techniques that are used by non-mentally retarded people (Campione & Brown, 1979). As you learned in chapter 7, memory is enhanced by the rehearsal and chunking of information.

Today mildly retarded persons are called "educable," and moderately retarded persons are called "trainable." From the 1950s to the 1970s, the educable mentally retarded were placed in special classes in which they received teaching tailored to their levels of ability. But in the 1970s dissatisfaction with the results of this approach led to so-called mainstreaming, which places mentally retarded children in as many normal classes as possible and encourages them to participate in as many activities as possible with nonretarded children. To promote mainstreaming, the Education for All Handicapped Children Act of 1975 mandated that retarded children be given individual instruction in the most normal academic setting that is feasible for them. Today almost one million mentally retarded children are educated in public schools (Schroeder, Schroeder, & Landesman, 1987).

The educational needs of mentally retarded persons are not limited to academic subjects. They may also need training in self-care, including dressing, grooming, feeding, and using the toilet. Behavior modification has been especially useful in training the mentally retarded in self-care. For example, the behavior modification techniques of modeling and positive reinforcement have been used successfully in training mentally retarded people to shower themselves (table 9.1) (Matson, DiLorenzo, & Esveldt-Dawson, 1981). A movement that has paralleled mainstreaming is *normalization,* the transfer of mentally retarded individuals from large institutional settings into community settings so that they may live more normal lives. Given adequate support services, even severely and profoundly retarded people can progress in settings other than large, custodial institutions (Landesman & Butterfield, 1987).

Down Syndrome Many children with Down syndrome can benefit from special education and personalized instruction. Here a mother reads with her Down syndrome child.

Down Syndrome A form of mental retardation associated with certain physical deformities, which is caused by an extra, third chromosome on the twenty-first pair.

TABLE 9.1	A Step-by-Step Approach for Training Mentally Retarded People to Shower Themselves

Task Analyzed Steps of Showering

1. Acquire washcloth
2. Turn on the water
3. Adjust temperature
4. Get wet, then turn water off
5. Wash hair
6. Lather cloth
7. Wash face, ears, and neck
8. Wash shoulders
9. Wash left arm
10. Wash under left arm
11. Wash right arm
12. Wash under right arm
13. Wash chest and stomach
14. Wash genitals
15. Wash left leg and foot
16. Wash right leg and foot
17. Wash back
18. Wash buttocks
19. Rinse off soap
20. Wring out cloth
21. Properly dispose of cloth
22. Get a towel
23. Dry hair
24. Dry face, ears, and neck
25. Dry remainder of body
26. Put towel in hamper
27. Apply deodorant

Reprinted with permission from *Behaviour Research and Therapy,* 19:399–405, J. L. Matson, et al., "Independence Training as a Method of Enhancing Self-Help Skills Acquisition of the Mentally Retarded," copyright © 1981, Pergamon Press plc.

Mental Giftedness

Mental Giftedness Intellectual superiority marked by an IQ above 130 and exceptionally high scores on achievement tests in specific subjects, such as mathematics.

Interest in the study of the mentally retarded has been accompanied by interest, though less extensive, in the study of **mental giftedness.** Sir Francis Galton began the study of the mentally gifted—or "geniuses"—in the late nineteenth century. Lewis Terman, who was introduced earlier, considered Galton himself to be mentally gifted. Terman based his assessment on Galton's early demonstration of outstanding ability, including the ability to recite the alphabet when he was eighteen months old and read classic literature when he was five years old (Terman, 1917). Today the mentally gifted are considered those with IQs above 130 and with exceptionally high scores on achievement tests in specific subjects, such as mathematics (Fox, 1981).

The special needs of the mentally gifted have traditionally received less attention than those of the mentally retarded (Reis, 1989). Perhaps the most well-known organization dedicated to meeting the needs of the mentally gifted is "Mensa," which limits its membership to those who score in the top 2 percent on any standardized intelligence test. One of the reasons for the traditional lack of interest in the mentally gifted was the belief in "early ripe, early rot." This belief assumed that children who are intellectually precocious are doomed to become academic, vocational, and social failures.

The classic case study in support of that viewpoint was that of William James Sidis. Sidis was a mathematically gifted boy who enrolled at Harvard in 1909 at the age of eleven and received national publicity a year later when he gave a talk on higher mathematics to the Harvard Mathematical Club (Montour, 1977). But constant pressure from his father to excel and the glare of publicity eventually led Sidis to retreat from the world. In his early twenties, Sidis left the faculty position he had taken at Rice Institute in Houston and spent the rest of his life working at menial jobs.

Years later, in 1937, James Thurber, writing under a pen name in *The New Yorker,* published a sarcastic article about Sidis entitled "April Fool" (Sidis was born on April 1). Thurber wrote that Sidis was a failure, living in a single room in a rundown section of Boston, which Thurber used as evidence of the dire consequences of being too intelligent at too young an age. Sidis sued Thurber for invasion of privacy and won a modest settlement shortly before dying—in obscurity—in 1944 (Wallace, 1986).

The Study of Genius Contrary to the case of William James Sidis, mentally gifted children do not tend to become failures. In fact, they tend to become more successful in every area of life. The strongest evidence for this comes from a study of mentally gifted children that began in 1921 and that has continued ever since—the *Study of Genius.* The study was begun by Lewis Terman, who used the Stanford-Binet Intelligence Scale to identify California children with IQs above 135. He found more than 1,500 such children between the ages of eight and twelve. Their average IQ was about 150. Reports on Terman's gifted children have appeared every decade or two since 1921. After Terman's death in 1956, the study was continued by Robert and Pauline Sears of Stanford University.

The Study of Genius has shown that mentally gifted children tend to become socially, physically, vocationally, and academically superior adults. They are healthier, more likely to have attended college, more likely to have professional careers, and more likely to have happy marriages. The 1972 report on Terman's subjects, then at an average age of sixty-two, found that they were generally satisfied with life, combining successful careers with rewarding family lives (Sears, 1977).

The Study of Mathematically Precocious Youth Perhaps the best-known recent study of mentally gifted children is the *Study of Mathematically Precocious Youth* being conducted by Camilla Benbow and Julian Stanley (1983) of Johns Hopkins University. Their study provides special programs for adolescents who score above 700 (out of a maximum of 800) on the mathematics subtest of the SAT. The programs offer intensive summer courses in science and mathematics, accelerated courses at universities, and counseling for parents to help them meet the academic and emotional needs of their gifted children. There is no evidence that these gifted children are prone to the personal and social problems that plagued William James Sidis. In fact, a program such as this might have helped him pursue a rewarding career as a mathematician instead of fading into obscurity.

THEORIES OF INTELLIGENCE

Is intelligence a general characteristic that affects all aspects of behavior or are there different kinds of intelligence, with each affecting specific aspects of behavior? Theories of intelligence differ in their answers to this question. Alfred Binet and most of his successors believed that intelligence was a general characteristic. But, today intelligence researchers tend to assume that there are many kinds of intelligence. For example, consider a study of men who spend much of their recreational time at race tracks betting on horse races. The results of the study found that the men's abilities to handicap races accurately was unrelated to their scores on a test of general intelligence, indicating that handicapping horse races taps a separate kind of mental ability (Ceci & Liker, 1986).

William James Sidis "He died alone, obscure, and destitute, and he left a troublesome legacy best termed the 'Sidis Fallacy'—that talent like his rarely matures or becomes productive" (Montour, 1977, p. 265).

Lewis Terman (1877–1956) "Children of IQ 140 or higher are, in general, appreciably superior to unselected children in physique, health, and social adjustment; markedly superior in moral attitudes as measured either by character tests or trait ratings; and vastly superior in their mastery of school subjects."

The Mentally Gifted Children who are mentally gifted, like those who are mentally retarded, benefit from special educational programs to help them develop their abilities.

Factor-Analytic Theories of Intelligence

Alfred Binet viewed intelligence as the general ability to reason and to solve problems in a variety of situations. Binet based this view on his observation that good students tended to do well on all of the tasks included in the Binet-Simon Scale, while poor students tended to do poorly on all of the tasks. At about the time that Binet was developing his intelligence test, the British psychologist Charles Spearman (1863–1945) was developing a theory of intelligence that agreed with Binet's view of intelligence as a general characteristic underlying a variety of behaviors.

Spearman's Theory of General Intelligence   In 1927, after more than two decades of research, Spearman published his conclusions about the nature of intelligence. He used a statistical technique called **factor analysis,** which determines the degree of correlation between performances on various tasks. If performances on certain tasks correlate highly, then they are presumed to reflect the influence of a particular underlying factor. For example, if performances on a vocabulary test, a reading test, and a writing test correlate highly they might reflect the influence of a "verbal ability" factor.

Factor Analysis A statistical technique that determines the degree of correlation between performances on various tasks to determine the extent to which they reflect particular underlying characteristics, which are known as factors.

In using factor analysis, Spearman first gave a large group of people a variety of cognitive tasks. He found that scores on the tasks tended to show high positive correlations with one another. This meant that subjects tended to score high or moderate or low on all the tests. This led Spearman to conclude that performance on all of the tasks depended on the operation of a single underlying factor. He called this factor "g"—a general intelligence factor.

But because the correlations between the tasks correlated less than a perfect 1.00, Spearman concluded that performance on each task also depended, to a lesser extent, on its own specific factor, which he called "s." For example, Spearman explained that scores on vocabulary tests and arithmetic tests tended to be highly positively correlated with each other because vocabulary ability and arithmetic ability are influenced by a general intelligence factor. But because scores on vocabulary tests and arithmetic tests are not perfectly corre-

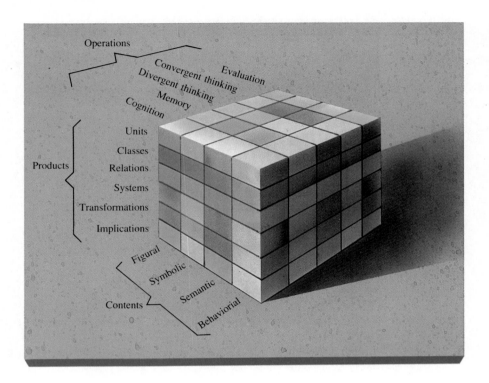

FIGURE 9.5
The Structure of the Intellect
Guilford identified 120 factors
underlying intelligence, based on
the interaction of five kinds of
operations, four kinds of contents,
and six kinds of products.

Source: From J. P. Guilford, "Three
Faces of Intellect" in *American
Psychologist*, 14:469–479, 1959.

lated, each ability must also depend on its own intelligence factor. Nonetheless, Spearman believed that the general intelligence factor was more important than any specific intelligence factor in governing any particular ability.

Thurstone's Theory of Primary Mental Abilities Like Spearman, Louis Thurstone (1887–1955) used factor analysis to determine the nature of intelligence. But, unlike Spearman, Thurstone (1938) concluded that there was no general intelligence factor. Instead, based on a battery of tests that he gave to college students, he identified seven factors, which he called *primary mental abilities*: reasoning, word fluency, perceptual speed, verbal comprehension, spatial visualization, numerical calculation, and associative memory.

Though scores on tests measuring these abilities had moderately high correlations with one another, they did not correlate highly enough for Thurstone to assume the existence of a general underlying intelligence factor. Suppose that you took tests to assess your abilities in reasoning, verbal comprehension, and numerical calculation. Thurstone would insist that your performance on any single test would not reflect the influence of a general intelligence factor but, instead, would reflect the influence of a specific intelligence factor related to the particular ability assessed by that test.

Guilford's Theory of the Structure of the Intellect J. P. Guilford (1897–1987), as had Thurstone, rejected the notion of a general intelligence factor. He did so because of the unevenness he observed in children's abilities. But instead of the mere seven factors identified by Thurstone, Guilford (1959) used factor analysis to identify 120 factors (figure 9.5). Each of these factors represents the interaction among dimensions that Guilford called *cognitive operations* (thought processes), *contents* (information that a person is thinking about), and *products* (results of thinking about the information). Of course, given so many factors, it will take many years of re-

FIGURE 9.6
Life Span Changes in Intelligence While fluid intelligence tends to decline in old age, crystallized intelligence tends to increase (Horn & Donaldson, 1976).

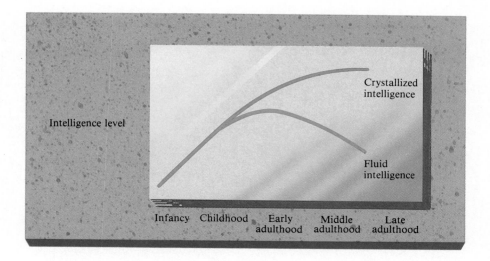

search to determine the merits of Guilford's theory. Up until the time of his death, Guilford hoped to develop ways of improving intelligence, reflecting his belief that intelligence can be improved through education (Comrey, Michael, & Fruchter, 1988).

Horn and Cattell's Two-Factor Theory of Intelligence The most recent theory of intelligence based on factor analysis was developed by John Horn and Raymond Cattell (1966), who identified two intelligence factors. **Fluid intelligence** reflects thinking ability, memory capacity, and speed of information processing. Horn and Cattell believe that fluid intelligence is largely inherited, affected little by training, and declines in late adulthood. In contrast, **crystallized intelligence** reflects the acquisition of knowledge through schooling and everyday experience. Horn and Cattell believe that crystallized intelligence increases or remains the same in late adulthood. Changes in fluid intelligence and crystallized intelligence across the life span are illustrated in figure 9.6.

But Guilford (1980) argued that Horn and Cattell had failed to demonstrate the existence of these two factors. It remains for psychologists to determine which, if any, of the factor-analytic theories of intelligence is the best. But a more telling criticism of factor-analytic theories of intelligence is that they assume that intelligence reflects only those cognitive abilities needed to perform in school. Perhaps a more useful theory of intelligence would consider a broader range of abilities (Frederiksen, 1986). Theories proposed by Robert Sternberg and Howard Gardner have done so.

The Triarchic Theory of Intelligence

As a child, Robert Sternberg performed poorly on IQ tests and suffered from severe test anxiety, yet later he earned a Ph.D. and became one of the leading researchers in cognitive psychology. This contributed to his belief that intelligence is more than the abilities measured by intelligence tests (Trotter, 1986). To determine the views of nonpsychologists about the nature of intelligence, Sternberg and his colleagues (1981) surveyed people reading in a college library, entering a supermarket, or waiting for a train. They were asked to list what they believed were the main characteristics of intelligent people. The

Fluid Intelligence The form of intelligence that reflects reasoning ability, memory capacity, and speed of information processing.

Crystallized Intelligence The form of intelligence that reflects knowledge acquired through schooling and in everyday life.

results showed that the respondents assumed that intelligent people had good verbal skills, good problem-solving abilities, and good social judgment.

During the past decade, Sternberg (1984) has developed a **triarchic theory of intelligence,** which claims that intelligence is composed of three kinds of abilities similar to those reported by the people in his earlier survey. He bases his theory on his observations of how people process information. *Componential intelligence* is similar to the kind of intelligence considered by traditional theories of intelligence. It primarily reflects our verbal reasoning ability. *Experiential intelligence* is the ability to combine different experiences in insightful ways to solve problems. It reflects creativity. An artist, composer, or scientist would exhibit this. According to Sternberg, creative geniuses, such as Leonardo da Vinci and Albert Einstein, have especially high levels of experiential intelligence. *Contextual intelligence* is the ability to function in practical everyday social situations. It reflects "street smarts," as in negotiating the price of a new car.

The triarchic theory recognizes that we must be able to function in settings other than school. Moreover, we may excel in one kind of intelligence without excelling in the other two. Sternberg believes that each of the three kinds of intelligence can be improved by special training, and he is developing ways of testing and improving each (Sternberg, 1986). Though Sternberg's theory goes beyond traditional theories by considering creativity and practical intelligence, as well as academic intelligence, more research is needed to determine its merits.

The Theory of Multiple Intelligences

While Sternberg's theory is based on his study of information processing, Gardner's (1983) **theory of multiple intelligences** is based on his belief that the brain has evolved separate systems for different adaptive abilities that he calls "intelligences." According to Gardner, there are seven types of intelligence, each of which is developed to different degrees in every person: linguistic, logical-mathematical, spatial, musical, bodily-kinesthetic, intrapersonal, and interpersonal. Gardner assumes that the brain pathways underlying these intelligences are developed to different extents and that damage to specific brain pathways interferes with one or more of the intelligences. For example, damage to speech centers interferes with linguistic intelligence and damage to the cerebellum interferes with bodily-kinesthetic intelligence.

Several of Gardner's kinds of intelligence are assessed by traditional intelligence tests. *Linguistic intelligence* is the ability to communicate through language. If you are good at reading textbooks, writing term papers, and presenting oral reports, you would be high in linguistic intelligence. A person with high *logical-mathematical intelligence* would be good at analyzing arguments and solving mathematical problems. And a person with high *spatial intelligence,* such as an architect or carpenter, would be good at perceiving and arranging objects in the environment.

The remaining kinds of intelligence are not assessed by traditional intelligence tests. *Musical intelligence* is the ability to analyze, to compose, or to play music. A person with good *bodily-kinesthetic intelligence* would be able to move effectively, as in dancing or playing sports, or to manipulate objects effectively, as in using tools or driving a car. If you have high *intrapersonal intelligence,* you know yourself well and understand what motivates your behavior. And if you have high *interpersonal intelligence,* you function well in

Triarchic Theory of Intelligence Robert Sternberg's theory of intelligence, which assumes that there are three main kinds of intelligence: componential, experiential, and contextual.

Robert Sternberg "The triarchic theory is an attempt to account for, in a single theory, what in the past has been accounted for by multiple theories often perceived to be in conflict with each other."

Theory of Multiple Intelligences Howard Gardner's theory of intelligence, which assumes that the brain has evolved separate systems for seven kinds of intelligence.

The Theory of Multiple Intelligences Howard Gardner believes that we have evolved seven kinds of intelligence, which are developed to different extents in each of us. Former Congresswoman Barbara Jordan's excellent speaking ability exemplifies linguistic intelligence. Rock musician Sting's proficiency in singing, playing, and composing music exemplifies musical intelligence. And basketball star Michael Jordan's superb athletic ability exemplifies bodily kinesthetic intelligence.

social situations because you are able to understand the needs of other people and to predict their behavior.

As you have certainly observed in your own life, a person may excel in one or more of Gardner's intelligences while being average or below average in others. In extreme cases, we have the idiot savant who excels in painting but cannot read, the child prodigy who excels in mathematics but cannot dance, the student who excels in science but has no friends, and the athlete who excels in sports but cannot write a coherent sentence. Of course, you may have also encountered the so-called Renaissance person, who excels in several, or all, of Gardner's intelligences.

According to Gardner, the extent to which we will succeed in life depends on the extent to which we develop the kinds of intelligence that are needed in our culture. For example, for most people in the United States success depends more on linguistic intelligence than on musical intelligence. In contrast, success in a culture that relies on hunting skills would put a greater premium on spatial intelligence and bodily-kinesthetic intelligence. Gardner's theory is so new that it has yet to generate sufficient research to determine its merits. But it is superior to traditional theories of intelligence in its attention to the kinds of abilities needed to function in everyday, nonacademic settings.

THINKING ABOUT PSYCHOLOGY

Does Intelligence Depend More on Nature or Nurture?

In the 1950s the movie *Bedtime for Bonzo,* starring Ronald Reagan and a chimpanzee named Bonzo, comically questioned whether a chimpanzee raised in a human household would become more intelligent than the typical chimpanzee. And in the 1980s movie *Trading Places,* two upper-class men argued about whether our social positions are determined more by heredity or by environment. They agreed to settle their argument by manipulating a rich white man and a poor black man into trading homes (a mansion versus the street), vocations (big business versus begging), and financial status (wealth versus poverty). Both movies demonstrate the popular concern with the issue of *nature* versus *nurture.*

The phrase "nature versus nurture" was popularized in the 1870s by Sir Francis Galton (Fancher, 1984). As a follower of his cousin Charles Darwin, he assumed that intelligence was inherited. Galton (1869) concluded this after finding that eminent men had a higher proportion of eminent descendants than did noneminent men. This led Galton to champion **eugenics,** the practice of encouraging supposedly superior people to reproduce, while preventing supposedly inferior people from reproducing. Galton's views also influenced the attitudes of psychologists toward immigrants in the early twentieth century.

Eugenics The practice of encouraging supposedly superior people to reproduce, while preventing supposedly inferior people from reproducing.

Early Studies of Immigrants

In 1912 Henry Goddard (1866–1957) was put in charge of testing the intelligence of immigrants arriving at Ellis Island in New York Harbor. Goddard made the astonishing claim that 79 percent of Italians, 80 percent of Hungarians, 83 percent of Jews, and 87 percent of Russians scored in the "feeble-minded" range, which we would today call mildly retarded. Even after later

Nature versus Nurture Even Hollywood movies, such as *Bedtime for Bonzo,* have been concerned with the issue of nature versus nurture.

Immigrant Testing Results of the intelligence-testing program at Ellis Island, New York, in the early twentieth century contributed to the deportation of allegedly "feebleminded" immigrants. But, many of these immigrants did not have the language or cultural background assumed by the tests, making their test scores invalid estimates of their intelligence.

reevaluating his data, he claimed that an average of "only" 40 percent of these groups were feebleminded (Gelb, 1986). Goddard, following in the footsteps of Galton, concluded that these ethnic groups were, by nature, intellectually inferior.

You probably realize that Goddard neglected to consider possible environmental causes for the poor test performance of immigrants. He failed to consider a lack of education, a long ocean voyage below deck, and anxiety created by the testing situation as causes of their poor performance. Moreover, even though the tests were translated into the immigrants' native languages, the translations were often inadequate. Despite the shortcomings of the tests, low test scores were used as the basis for having many supposedly "feebleminded" immigrants deported. This was ironic, because at the 1915 meeting of the American Psychological Association in Chicago a critic of Goddard's program of intelligence testing reported that the mayor of Chicago had taken an IQ test and had scored in the feebleminded range (Gould, 1981). There is no evidence that the mayor was deported.

Further support for Goddard's position was provided by the army's intelligence testing program during World War I, which was headed by Robert Yerkes (1876–1956). One of Yerkes's colleagues, Carl Brigham (1923), published the results of the testing program. He found that immigrants scored lower on the IQ tests than did American-born whites. Brigham assumed that these differences in IQ scores were attributable to differences in heredity. Partly in response to Brigham's findings, Congress passed the Immigration Act of 1924, which restricted immigration from eastern and southern Europe.

But in 1930 Brigham admitted that he had been wrong in assuming that the poorer performance of immigrants was attributable to heredity. He realized that in their everyday lives immigrants may not have had the opportunity to encounter much of the material in the army IQ tests. To appreciate this, consider the following multiple-choice items from the Army Alpha Test: "Crisco is a: patent medicine; disinfectant; toothpaste; food product;" and "Christy Mathewson is famous as a(n): writer; artist; baseball player [the correct answer]; comedian" (Gould, 1981).

Research on the Relative Influence of Heredity and Environment

After three decades of relative indifference to it, the issue of nature versus nurture reemerged in the 1960s when President Lyndon Johnson began *Project Head Start,* which provides preschool children from deprived socioeconomic backgrounds with enrichment programs to promote their intellectual development. Head Start was stimulated, in part, by the finding that blacks scored an average of fifteen points lower than whites on IQ tests. Those who supported Head Start attributed this difference to the poor socioeconomic conditions in which black children were more likely to be reared.

But in 1969 an article by psychologist Arthur Jensen questioned whether programs such as Head Start could significantly boost the intellectual level of deprived children. Jensen's doubts were based on the notion of **heritability,** the extent to which the variability in intelligence within a group can be attributed to heredity. Jensen claimed that intelligence has a heritability of .80, which would mean that 80 percent of the variability in intelligence can be explained by heredity. This led him to conclude that the IQ gap between white and black children was mainly attributable to heredity. But he was accused of making an unwarranted inference. Just because intelligence may have high heritability does not mean that IQ differences *between* blacks and whites are caused by heredity. Moreover, research has found that the heritability of

Heritability The extent to which variability in a characteristic within a group can be attributed to heredity.

intelligence is about .50, not .80 (Weinberg, 1989). Jensen's article led to accusations that he was a racist and to demonstrations against him when he spoke on college campuses.

In the tradition of eugenics, one of Jensen's chief supporters, William Shockley (1972), urged that the federal government pay people with below-average IQ scores (who would be disproportionately black) to undergo sterilization. He recommended paying them one thousand dollars for each IQ point that they scored under 100. Though Shockley was not a psychologist or a social scientist, he gained media attention because he had won a 1956 Nobel Prize for inventing the transistor. Shockley and several other Nobel Prize winners have even deposited their sperm in a "sperm bank" in California for use by women of superior intelligence who wish to produce highly intelligent offspring ("Superkids?," 1980). As you might imagine, Shockley and his followers were accused of following in the steps of Hitler in their desire to create a "super race."

The most vigorous response to Jensen, Shockley, and others who claimed that intelligence is primarily the product of heredity came from Leon Kamin (1974). The biggest blow landed by Kamin was his discovery that important data supporting the hereditary basis of intelligence had been falsified. Sir Cyril Burt (1883–1971), an eminent British psychologist, had reported findings from three studies showing that the correlation in IQ scores between identical twins reared apart was higher than the correlation in IQ of fraternal twins reared together. Because identical twins reared apart have the same genes but different environments, yet had a higher correlation in intelligence than fraternal twins reared together, the data supported the greater influence of heredity on intelligence.

In each of his studies, published in 1943, 1955, and 1966, Burt reported that the correlation in intelligence between identical twins reared apart was .771. But, as Kamin observed, the odds against finding the same correlation to three decimal places in three different studies are so high as to defy belief. Burt's findings were literally too good to be true. Even Burt's official biographer, who began as an admirer and who believed that Burt had not falsified his data, eventually concluded that the data were, indeed, fraudulent (Hearnshaw, 1979).

Family Studies of Intelligence Though the publicity generated by the discovery of Burt's deception struck a blow against the hereditary view of intelligence, other researchers have conducted legitimate family studies of intelligence. As shown in figure 9.7, the closer the relationship between relatives, the more similar they are in intelligence (Bouchard & McGue, 1981). But the closer the genetic relationship between relatives, the more likely they also are to share similar environments. Consequently, the size of the correlation in intelligence between relatives of varying degrees of genetic similarity is, by itself, inadequate for determining whether this similarity is caused primarily by hereditary factors or by environmental factors. Even the higher correlation in intelligence between identical twins than between fraternal twins when the twins are reared together may be attributable to the more similar treatment received by identical twins.

To separate the effects of heredity and environment, researchers have turned to adoption studies. Some of these studies compare the correlation in intelligence between adopted children and their adoptive parents with the correlation in intelligence between adopted children and their biological parents. A review of adoption studies found that the correlation in intelligence between adoptees and their adoptive parents is .19, while the correlation between adoptees and their biological parents is .22. This provides evidence for the genetic basis of intelligence; the genes inherited from the natural parents

The Nurturing of Intelligence
Children from higher socioeconomic classes will be more likely than children from lower socioeconomic classes to receive the intellectual enrichment they need to reach their intellectual potential.

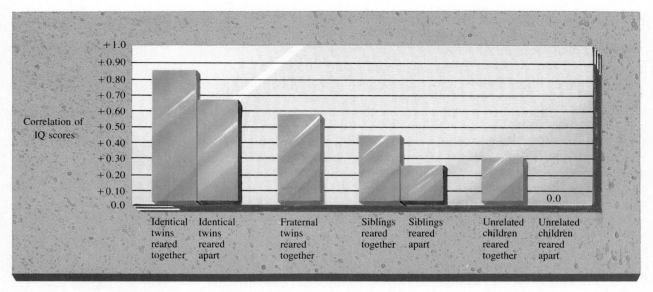

FIGURE 9.7
Heredity versus Environment The correlation in IQ between relatives increases as their hereditary or environmental similarity increases.

Data from T. Bouchard, "Familial Studies of Intelligence: A Review" in *Science*, Vol. 212:1055–59, 29 May 1981. Copyright 1981 by the AAAS. Reprinted by permission of the publisher and the author.

appear to exert at least as strong an influence on adoptees as does the environment provided by their adoptive parents (Bouchard & McGue, 1981).

But some adoption studies have provided support for the effect of environment on intelligence. Sandra Scarr and Richard Weinberg (1976) reported the results of the Minnesota Adoption Study, which included black children adopted by white Minnesota couples of higher socioeconomic status than their biological parents. The study found that the children who had been adopted had an average IQ of 110. This indicated that the environment had a strong effect on their intelligence, because the adoptees scored about twenty points higher than the average IQ of comparable black children reared by their biological parents.

A study of adopted children in France found that these findings also held for white children. The subjects of the study were thirty-two children who had been abandoned at birth by their lower-class parents and adopted at an average age of four months by white professionals. When compared with their siblings who were reared by their biological parents, the adoptees scored an average of fourteen points higher in intelligence and were less likely to be held back in school (Schiff, Duyme, Dumaret, & Tomkiewicz, 1982).

A more recent study in France included eighty-seven adolescents given up at birth and adopted before three years of age into different social classes. The results showed a significant correlation of −.37 between the social class of the adoptive fathers and the repetition of a grade in school. This means that as the social class of the adoptive fathers increased, the likelihood of an adoptee having to repeat a grade decreased. This supported the importance of the environment in determining intellectual performance (Duyme, 1988). Based on their review of adoption studies, Scarr and Weinberg (1983) have concluded that intelligence is influenced by both heredity and environment, with neither dominating the other.

Additional support for the influence of the environment comes from family configuration studies. A survey of all of the 400,000 nineteen-year-old men in

Sandra Scarr "Behavioral differences among individuals . . . can arise in any population from genetic differences, from variations among their environments, or both."

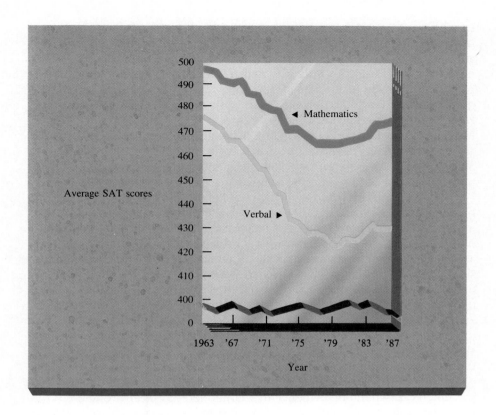

FIGURE 9.8
Trends in SAT Scores As predicted by Zajonc, the downward trend in SAT scores that began in 1963 has reversed itself since 1980.

the Netherlands found that the larger their families and the later their birth order the less intelligent they tended to be (Belmont & Marolla, 1973). This finding has been explained by Robert Zajonc's (1986) **confluence model,** which assumes that each child is born into an intellectual environment that is dependent on the intelligence levels of his or her parents and siblings. The greater the number of children and the smaller the average interval between births, the lower will be what Zajonc calls the *average intellectual environment* into which a child is born. One of the reasons for this drop may be the inevitable reduction in the attention parents give to each of their children following the birth of a child. Zajonc claims that this is not due to the tendency of people from lower socioeconomic classes to have larger families, because the relationship holds even when socioeconomic status is held constant (Zajonc, 1983).

In 1976, in a bold gesture, Zajonc used the confluence model to predict that the decline in SAT scores that had begun in 1963 would stop in 1980 and then begin to rise. Zajonc based his prediction on the fact that high school students who took the SAT between 1963 and 1980 had been born into increasingly larger families during the post-World War II "Baby Boom." But after 1980, high school students who would take the SAT would come from smaller and smaller families. Zajonc's prediction was supported: SAT scores continued to decline until 1980 and then began to rise (figure 9.8).

But at least one aspect of Zajonc's confluence model may not be as powerful as he originally believed. Data from a study by the National Institutes of Health, which included 47,000 women and their 53,000 children, failed to find a relationship between the intelligence of the children and the average interval between the births of children in their families (Brackbill & Nichols, 1982).

Confluence Model The view that each child is born into an intellectual environment that is dependent on the intelligence levels of his or her parents and siblings, with the number of children and the interval between births affecting the intelligence of each successive child.

Project Head Start Intellectual enrichment programs, such as Project Head Start, provide a stimulating preschool environment that better prepares children for success in elementary school.

© 1981 by Sidney Harris—*Discover* magazine.

Intellectual Enrichment Programs Further support for the influence of the environment on intelligence comes from the finding that between 1976 and 1983 the difference between white and black performance on the SAT narrowed (Jones, 1984). This may reflect better educational opportunities provided blacks in recent decades, including intellectual enrichment programs such as Head Start. Socioeconomically deprived children who attend Head Start show an average gain of ten points in their IQ scores (Zigler, Abelson, Trickett, & Seitz, 1982) and make greater gains in their cognitive abilities compared to those not in such programs (Lee, Brooks-Gunn, & Schnur, 1988). Thus, Jensen's (1969) prediction that Head Start would have no effect has been shown to be wrong.

Other countries have also found that intellectual enrichment programs may be beneficial. The most ambitious of all enrichment programs began in 1979 in Venezuela, which even has its own Minister of State for the Development of Intelligence. The program provides good prenatal care and infant nutrition, as well as sensory stimulation of preschoolers and special training in cognitive skills. New mothers watch videocassettes on proper child rearing while in their hospital rooms, schoolchildren attend "Learning to Think" classes, and television commercials promote the need to develop the minds of Venezuelan children (Walsh, 1981). Early results show that the more than four hundred children who participated in a Venezuelan program to teach thinking skills have shown better academic performance than comparable students who did not participate (Herrnstein, Nickerson, de Sánchez, & Swets, 1986).

Despite decades of arguing, neither side of the nature-nurture debate has presented overwhelming evidence that either heredity or environment is the main determinant of intelligence. This has led supporters of each side to assume, illogically, that because the other side has failed to provide overwhelming evidence for its position, their own side must be correct. Nonetheless, a review of research found that the bulk of the evidence leans somewhat in favor of the greater role of environment in accounting for racial differences (Mackenzie, 1984).

Even more evidence of the influence of the environment on intelligence comes from the finding that IQ scores have increased from five to twenty-five points in fourteen nations during the past thirty years, apparently because of better nutrition, education, and health care (Flynn, 1987). And both Galton and Goddard would be surprised to find that today the Japanese, whom they considered intellectually inferior, score significantly higher than Americans on IQ tests, with Japanese children scoring eleven points higher than American children (Lynn, 1982). Their increase in IQ scores parallels their country's increased emphasis on education, with children going to school more hours, attending school more days, and studying more hours than American children.

One leading psychologist has suggested that it may not be in our best interest to study the relative importance of nature and nurture (Sarason, 1984). To do so might discover little of scientific import, while perhaps providing apparent scientific support for discrimination against racial or ethnic minorities. The current trend to view intelligence as comprising a variety of abilities and as being improvable by proper education may change the focus of research from trying to determine whether particular groups are naturally more intelligent than other groups to trying to discover ways of helping all people approach their intellectual potential.

SUMMARY

INTELLIGENCE TESTING

Intelligence is the global capacity to act purposefully, to think rationally, and to deal effectively with the environment. An achievement test assesses knowledge of a particular subject, an aptitude test predicts your potential to benefit from instruction in a particular academic or vocational setting, and an intelligence test is a kind of aptitude test that assesses overall mental ability.

Sir Francis Galton began the study of mental abilities in the late nineteenth century and founded the field of differential psychology. The first true test of general intelligence was the Binet-Simon Scale, which was developed to determine the proper placement of children in school. The American version of the test became known as the Stanford-Binet Intelligence Scale. Today that test and the Wechsler Intelligence Scales are the most popular intelligence tests.

Tests must be standardized so that they are administered in a uniform manner and so that test scores can be compared with norms. A test must also be reliable, giving consistent results over time. And a test must be valid, meaning that it measures what it is supposed to measure.

Controversy has arisen over whether intelligence testing is fair to minority groups, particularly blacks. Those who oppose intelligence testing claim that the tests are biased against blacks because blacks score lower on them than do whites. Those who support their use claim that the tests accurately predict the academic performance of both blacks and whites, attributing the differences in performance to the deprived backgrounds that are more common among black children. Attempts to develop tests that are not affected by the test taker's cultural background have failed.

EXTREMES OF INTELLIGENCE

To be classified as mentally retarded, a person must have an IQ below 70 and difficulties performing in everyday life. The four categories of mental retardation are mild retardation, moderate retardation, severe retardation, and profound retardation. Most cases of mental retardation are caused by cultural-familial factors, while some are caused by brain damage. Most mentally retarded people can benefit from education and training programs.

To be classified as mentally gifted, a person must have an IQ above 130 and demonstrate unusual ability in at least one area, such as art, music, or arithmetic. Lewis Terman's Study of Genius has demonstrated that mentally gifted children tend to become successful in their academic, social, physical, and vocational lives. Benbow and Stanley's Study of Mathematically Precocious Youth identifies children with outstanding mathematical ability, provides them with special programs, and counsels their parents about how to help them reach their potential.

THEORIES OF INTELLIGENCE

Theories of intelligence have traditionally depended on factor analysis, a statistical technique for determining the abilities that underlie intelligence. The theories have differed on the extent to which intelligence is a general factor or a combination of different factors. The most recent factor-analytic theory distinguishes between fluid intelligence and crystallized intelligence.

Robert Sternberg's triarchic theory of intelligence is based on his research on information processing. The theory distinguishes between componential (academic) intelligence, experiential (creative) intelligence, and contextual (practical) intelligence. He also believes that people can be taught to process information more effectively, thereby increasing their levels of intelligence.

Howard Gardner's theory of multiple intelligences is a psychobiological theory, which assumes that the brain has evolved separate systems for different adaptive abilities that he calls "intelligences." They include linguistic, logical-mathematical, spatial, musical, bodily-kinesthetic, intrapersonal, and interpersonal intelligences. All of us vary in the degree to which we have developed each of these kinds of intelligence.

THINKING ABOUT PSYCHOLOGY: DOES INTELLIGENCE DEPEND MORE ON NATURE OR NURTURE?

One of the most controversial issues in psychology has been the extent to which intelligence is a product of heredity or environment. Early studies of immigrants found that many were mentally retarded. The examiners attributed this to hereditary factors rather than a host of cultural and environmental factors that actually accounted for such an astounding finding.

Arthur Jensen created a stir by claiming that heredity is a much more powerful determinant of intelligence than is environment. Studies of twins, adopted children, family configuration effects, and enrichment programs indicate that neither heredity nor environment is a dominant determinant of intelligence. More importantly, there is no widely accepted evidence that differences in intelligence between particular groups are caused by heredity.

IMPORTANT CONCEPTS

Achievement test 292
Aptitude test 292
Cerebral palsy 304
Confluence model 317
Construct validity 300
Content validity 300
Cross-sectional design 299
Crystallized intelligence 310
Cultural-familial retardation 304
Differential psychology 293
Down syndrome 305

Eugenics 313
Face validity 299
Factor analysis 308
Fetal alcohol syndrome 304
Fluid intelligence 310
Heritability 314
Intelligence 292
Intelligence quotient (IQ) 294
Intelligence test 292
Longitudinal design 299
Mental giftedness 306

Mental retardation 303
Norms 295
Phenylketonuria (PKU) 304
Predictive validity 300
Reliability 298
Split-half reliability 298
Standardization 295
Test-retest reliability 298
Theory of multiple intelligences 311
Triarchic theory of intelligence 311
Validity 299

IMPORTANT PEOPLE

Alfred Binet 293
James McKeen Cattell 293
Sir Francis Galton 293, 306, 313
Howard Gardner 311
Henry Goddard 294, 304, 313
J. P. Guilford 309

John Horn and Raymond Cattell 310
Arthur Jensen 314
Sandra Scarr and Richard Weinberg 316
Theodore Simon 293
Charles Spearman 308
William Stern 294

Robert Sternberg 310–311
Lewis Terman 294, 306, 307
Louis Thurstone 309
David Wechsler 292, 295
Robert Zajonc 317

RECOMMENDED READINGS

For More on All Aspects of Intelligence

Sternberg, R. J. (Ed.). (1982). *Handbook of human intelligence.* New York: Cambridge University Press. A compilation of articles by leading researchers in the field of intelligence.

For More on Intelligence Testing:

Anastasi, A. (1988). *Psychological testing* (6th ed.). New York: Macmillan. A standard textbook on all aspects of testing, include intelligence testing.

For More on Extremes of Intelligence:

Haywood, H. C., Meyers, C. E., & Switzky, H. N. (1982). Mental retardation. *Annual Review of Psychology, 33,* 309–342. A review of research on the nature of mental retardation.

Horowitz, F. D., & O'Brien, M. (Eds.). (1985). *The gifted and talented.* Washington, DC: American Psychological Association. A collection of articles by experts on the mentally gifted and talented.

For More on Theories of Intelligence:

Gardner, H. (1983). *Frames of mind: The theory of multiple intelligences.* New York: Basic Books. An interesting presentation of the author's theory that we have seven kinds of intelligence, each developed to different extents in all of us.

Sternberg, R. (1986). *Intelligence applied: Understanding and increasing your intellectual skills.* San Diego: Harcourt Brace Jovanovich. A readable discussion of the triarchic theory of intelligence and ways of improving intelligence.

For More on Nature Versus Nurture:

Eysenck, H. J., & Kamin, L. (1981). *The intelligence controversy.* New York: Wiley. A lively debate on the nature-nurture controversy by two leading authorities.

Fancher, R. E. (1985). *The intelligence men: Makers of the IQ controversy.* New York: Norton. A book tracing the history of intelligence testing, the lives of important figures in the development of intelligence testing, and controversies concerning the nature of intelligence.

Gould, S. J. (1981). *The mismeasure of man.* New York: Norton. A fascinating account of the history of intelligence testing and its misuse in designating particular ethnic groups as intellectually inferior.

MOTIVATION

Chapter Opening Art: Arthur Bowen Davies. *Dances.* 1914.

I n 1972 survivors of an airplane crash in a frigid, isolated region of the Andes mountains of Chile turned to cannibalism, eating the flesh of dead passengers to stay alive (Read, 1974). At the 1988 Olympic Games in Korea, left-handed pitcher Jim Abbott led the United States to a gold medal in baseball, fielding well despite being born without a right hand. Why would civilized people eat human flesh? Why would a one-handed person pursue a baseball career when even excellent two-handed athletes often fail?

In explaining extraordinary behaviors such as these, as well as everyday behaviors, psychologists employ the concept of **motivation,** the psychological process that arouses, directs, and maintains behavior. The Andes survivors were motivated by hunger, which aroused them to find food, directed them to eat the human flesh, and maintained their cannibalism until they were rescued. Jim Abbott was motivated by his need for achievement, which aroused him to excel as a pitcher, directed him to learn how to play baseball with one hand, and maintained his participation despite periodic failures.

Because we cannot directly observe an individual's motivation, we must infer it from behaviors that we observe. We might infer that a person who drinks a quart of water is motivated by a strong thirst and that a person who becomes dictator of a country is motivated by a strong need for power. The concept of motivation is also useful in explaining fluctuations in behavior over time (Atkinson, 1981). If yesterday morning you ate three stacks of pancakes but this morning ate only a piece of toast, your friends would not attribute your change in behavior to a change in your personality. Instead, they would attribute it to a change in your degree of hunger—your motivation.

SOURCES OF MOTIVATION

What are the main sources of motivation? In providing answers to this question, psychologists have implicated *genes, drives,* and *incentives.*

Genes

In the early twentieth century, most psychologists, influenced by Charles Darwin's theory of evolution and led by William McDougall (1871–1938), attributed motivation to instincts. An **instinct** is a complex, inherited (that is, unlearned) behavior pattern characteristic of a species. Instincts, controlled by inherited *genes,* have evolved because they promote the continuation of the genes. Instincts make birds build nests, spiders weave webs, and salmon swim upstream to their spawning grounds. But what of human instincts?

Motivation The psychological process that arouses, directs, and maintains behavior.

Instinct A relatively complex, inherited behavior pattern characteristic of a species.

Motivation After their airplane crashed in the Andes mountains of Chile, why did members of some of the most prominent families in Uruguay turn to cannibalism? Why did Jim Abbott, born without a right hand, strive to become a professional baseball pitcher? Psychologists rely on the concept of *motivation* to explain these, and other, behaviors.

McDougall (1908) claimed that human beings are guided by a variety of instincts, including instincts for "pugnacity," "curiosity," and "gregariousness." As you will read in chapter 13, McDougall's contemporary, Sigmund Freud, based his theory of psychoanalysis on instincts motivating sex and aggression.

In the 1920s, psychologists, influenced by the behaviorist John B. Watson, rejected instincts as factors in human motivation. One reason that instinct theorists lost scientific credibility was their attempt to explain almost all human behavior as instinctive, in some cases compiling lists of thousands of alleged human instincts. Taking this to its extreme, you might say that people paint because of an "aesthetic instinct," play sports because of a "competitive instinct," and pray because of a "religious instinct." Perhaps you enrolled in this course because of your "psychocuriosity instinct."

A second reason that instinct theorists fell out of favor was their failure to *explain* the behaviors they labeled as instinctive. Consider the following hypothetical dialogue concerning an alleged "parenting instinct":

"Why do parents take care of their children?"

"Because they have a parenting instinct."

"But how do you know parents have a parenting instinct?"

"Because they take care of their children."

Such circular reasoning neither explains why parents take care of their children nor provides evidence of a parenting instinct. Each of the assertions is simply used to support the other.

Though instinct theory, as applied to human beings, has fallen into disfavor, some scientists still believe that there is a genetic basis for human social behavior. The chief proponents of this belief work in the field of **sociobiology,** which studies the hereditary basis of human and animal social behavior (Wilson, 1975). For example, sociobiologists claim that the motive of *altruism* (discussed in chapter 18), which is marked by the willingness to sacrifice for others, has evolved because it promotes the survival of the genes. In an extreme case of altruism, a person might sacrifice his or her life, as when a soldier purposely falls on a hand grenade, to save the lives of other people, who may then pass on their genes to many offspring.

Sociobiology The study of the hereditary basis of human and animal social behavior.

But, sociobiology has been criticized for overestimating the role of heredity in human social behavior. Critics fear that acceptance of sociobiology would lend support to the status quo, making us less inclined to change what has been "ordained by nature," such as differences in the social status of men and women, blacks and whites, and rich and poor.

Instincts While gathering acorns is an *instinctive* adaptive behavior in squirrels, shopping for food in a grocery store is a *learned* adaptive behavior in human beings.

Drives

Drive-Reduction Theory The theory that behavior is motivated by the need to reduce drives such as sex or hunger.

Need A motivated state caused by physiological deprivation, such as a lack of food or water.

Drive A state of psychological tension induced by a need.

Homeostasis A steady state of physiological equilibrium.

Following the decline of the instinct theory of human motivation, the **drive-reduction theory** of Clark Hull (1884–1952) dominated psychology during the 1930s and 1940s. According to Hull (1943) a **need** caused by physiological deprivation, such as a lack of food or water, induces a state of tension called a **drive,** which motivates the individual to reduce it. The thirst drive would motivate drinking, the hunger drive would motivate eating, and the sex drive would motivate sexual relations.

Drive reduction aims at restoring **homeostasis,** a steady state of physiological equilibrium. Consider your thirst drive. When your body loses water, perhaps through perspiring, receptor cells in your *hypothalamus* (see chapter 3) respond and make you feel thirsty. Thirst arouses you, signaling you that your body lacks water, and directs you to drink. By drinking you reduce your thirst and restore homeostasis—your body's normal amount of water. Though we are undoubtedly motivated to reduce drives such as thirst, hunger, and sex, drive reduction cannot explain all human motivation. In some cases we perform behaviors that do not reduce physiological drives, as in Jim Abbott's participation in baseball. His behavior shows that we sometimes are motivated by *incentives.*

Incentives

Incentive An external stimulus that pulls an individual toward a goal.

While a drive is an internal state of tension that "pushes" you toward a goal, an **incentive** is an external stimulus that "pulls" you toward a goal. Through experience, we learn that certain stimuli (such as a puppy) are desirable and should be approached, making them *positive* incentives. We also learn that other stimuli (such as elevator music) are undesirable and should be avoided, making them *negative* incentives. Thus, we are pulled toward positive incentives and away from negative incentives.

Incentives are often associated with drives. For example, your thirst drive would motivate you to replenish your body's water, but incentives would determine what you would choose to drink. You could satisfy your need for water by drinking water, lemonade, apple juice, or cherry soda. Your thirst would "push" you to drink, but your favorite flavor would "pull" you toward a particular beverage. As with all incentives, your favorite flavor would depend on learning, which, in this case, would depend on your past experience with a variety of flavors. In the case of the Andes survivors a strong hunger drive made them respond to a weak incentive, human flesh. The opposite may occur in your everyday life. Despite feeling little hunger, you might be motivated to eat in response to a strong incentive, such as an ice cream sundae.

Maslow's Hierarchy of Needs

Hierarchy of Needs Abraham Maslow's arrangement of needs in order of their motivational priority, ranging from physiological needs to the need for self-actualization.

If forced to make a choice, would you prefer enough food to eat or straight As in school? Would you prefer to have a home or close friends? In each case, though both options are appealing, you probably chose the first. This shows that some motives have priority over others and led the humanistic psychologist Abraham Maslow (1970) to develop a **hierarchy of needs** (figure 10.1), which presents the relative priorities of important needs. Maslow uses the term *need* to refer to both physiological and psychological motives. According to Maslow you must first satisfy your basic *physiological* needs such as food and water before becoming motivated to meet your higher needs for *safety and security,* and so on up the hierarchy.

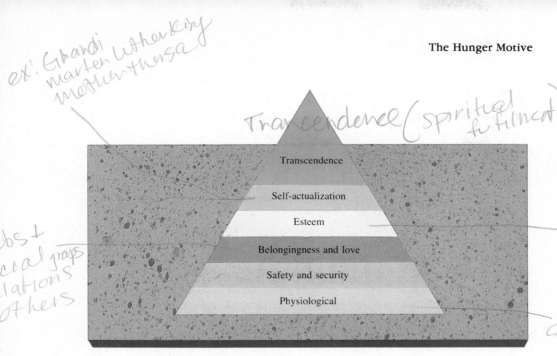

(handwritten annotations:) ex: Ghandi, Marten Luther King, Mother Thersa

Transcendence (spiritual fulfilment)

abst social group relations /others

we spend most of are time in esteem

activity + sleep

PSSBLE SAT

↑ Maslow's Hierarchy

FIGURE 10.1
Maslow's Hierarchy of Needs
Abraham Maslow assumed that our needs are arranged in a hierarchy, with our most powerful needs at the bottom. We will not be motivated by higher needs until our lower needs are met.

As you progress up the hierarchy, you would eventually reach the highest two levels, representing the need for *self-actualization* (achievement of all your potentials) and *transcendence* (spiritual fulfillment). According to Maslow, because few people satisfy all their lower needs, few reach these two levels. Though Maslow died before conducting much research on people who had reached transcendence, he did conduct extensive research on people he considered self-actualized, including Abraham Lincoln and Eleanor Roosevelt (see chapter 13 for a list of the characteristics of self-actualized people).

To appreciate the hierarchy of needs, consider a study conducted during World War II on conscientious objectors (people who refused to perform military service out of a sense of moral conviction). The purpose of the study was to understand the effects of starvation in the hope of finding ways to help the many refugees, prisoners of war, and concentration camp inmates who suffered from it. The subjects volunteered to eat half their normal amount of food for six months. During that period they lost weight, lacked energy, and became apathetic. They also became obsessed by food—daydreaming about it, collecting cookbooks, and talking for hours about recipes. Moreover, as Maslow would have predicted, they lost interest in their higher social need for love and affiliation in favor of their lower physiological need for food, even preferring pictures of food to pictures of their girlfriends (Keys, Brozek, Henschel, Mickelson, & Taylor, 1950).

Though research has supported the existence of the needs included in Maslow's hierarchy, it has shown that we do not pass through the levels of the hierarchy in a fixed sequence (Goebel & Brown, 1981). This may explain why parents will ignore their own safety and run into a burning building to save their children and why martyrs such as Mahatma Gandhi will starve themselves for the sake of others. You will now learn about several of the most extensively studied motives: *hunger, sex, arousal,* and *achievement.*

THE HUNGER MOTIVE

The World War II study on the effects of semistarvation showed the power of the *hunger* motive, which impels you to eat to satisfy your body's need for nutrients. If you have just eaten, food may be the last thing on your mind. But, if you have not eaten for days—or even for a few hours, food may be the *only* thing on your mind.

Factors Regulating Hunger

What accounts for the waxing and waning of hunger? Hunger is regulated by factors in the body and the brain. Taste receptors in the mouth play a role in hunger by sending taste sensations to the brain, informing it of the nutrient content of the food being tasted (Miller, 1984). Your brain will favor the tastes of foods containing nutrients you may lack. If you lack protein you may find yourself hungry for a steak. If you lack sugar you may find yourself hungry for starchy foods such as bread.

Though sensations from your mouth affect hunger, they are not the sole source of it. This was demonstrated in the early nineteenth century when physician William Beaumont reported the case study of Alexis St. Martin, a man who survived a gunshot wound that tore a hole through his abdomen into his stomach. St. Martin was able to regulate his intake of food even when he was fed through the hole, bypassing his mouth (Gibbs, Maddison, & Rolls, 1981).

But how does the stomach affect hunger? In 1912 the physiologist Walter Cannon and his assistant A. L. Washburn set out to answer that question. Washburn swallowed a balloon, which inflated in his stomach (figure 10.2). The balloon was connected by a tube to a device that recorded stomach contractions by measuring changes they caused in the air pressure inside the balloon. Whenever Washburn felt a hunger pang, he pressed a key, producing a mark next to the recording of his stomach contractions.

The recordings revealed that Washburn's hunger pangs were associated with stomach contractions, leading Cannon and Washburn (1912) to conclude that stomach contractions cause hunger. Might they have interpreted their findings another way? Perhaps the opposite was true—Washburn's hunger may have caused stomach contractions. Moreover, given that we now know that stomach contractions occur when the stomach contains food, perhaps the balloon itself caused Washburn's stomach contractions, which he misinterpreted as a sign of hunger. Later research has also revealed that the stomach, like the mouth, is not the sole means of regulating hunger. People who have had their stomachs removed because of cancer or severe ulcers can still experience hunger (Ingelfinger, 1944).

Though the stomach is not necessary for the regulation of hunger, it normally plays an important role. Receptor cells in the stomach detect both the amount and the kind of food it contains. After gorging yourself on a Thanks-

FIGURE 10.2
Cannon's Study of Hunger Pangs Walter Cannon studied the relationship between stomach contractions and hunger pangs by using the device shown in this drawing. The subject pressed a key whenever he felt a hunger pang. A rotating drum recorded both the hunger pangs and stomach contractions (Cannon & Washburn, 1912).

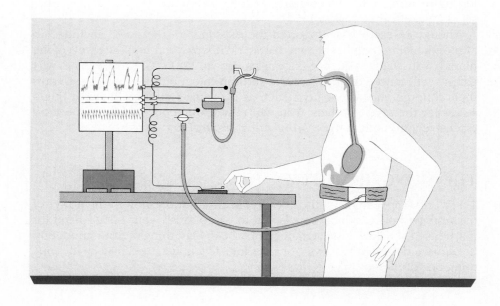

giving dinner, you may become painfully aware of the stretch receptors in your stomach that respond to the presence of large amounts of food. These receptors inform the brain of the amount of food in the stomach by sending neural impulses along the *vagus nerve* to the brain, reducing your level of hunger.

Receptors in the stomach also affect your hunger by detecting the presence of nutrients and communicating that information to the brain. This explains, in part, why filling your stomach with a lettuce salad is not as satisfying as filling it with several slices of pizza. Pizza is richer in nutrients. But information about the nutrient content of the food in the stomach is not sent along the vagus nerve. We know this because of studies of animals in which the vagus nerve is disconnected from the stomach. The animals no longer regulate their eating according to the amount of food in their stomachs but continue to regulate it according to the nutrient content of the food (Gonzalez & Deutsch, 1981). The mechanism underlying this is unclear.

Food stored in the stomach eventually reaches the small intestine, the main site of digestion. The presence of food in the small intestine stimulates it to secrete the hormone *cholecystokinin,* which, in turn, stimulates the vagus nerve to send neural impulses to the brain, reducing your level of hunger (Gosnell & Hsiao, 1984). And still another organ that regulates hunger is the liver. *Glucose receptors* in the liver send neural impulses along the vagus nerve to the brain, informing it of changes in the level of blood sugar. A low level of blood sugar makes you feel hungry, while a high level makes you feel full (Tordoff, Novin, & Russek, 1982).

Of special importance in the regulation of hunger is the hormone **insulin,** which is secreted by the pancreas. Insulin helps blood sugar enter body cells for use in metabolism, makes sweets taste better, and induces feelings of hunger. In fact, hunger depends more on increased levels of insulin than on decreased levels of blood sugar. We know this from studies in which the level of blood sugar has been held constant by a continuous infusion of glucose, while insulin levels are permitted to rise. Subjects in those studies reported increased levels of hunger (Rodin, 1985).

Insulin A hormone secreted by the pancreas that helps blood sugar enter body cells.

Though signals from the body regulate hunger, they do so through their effects on the brain. In 1902 the Viennese physician Alfred Frohlich reported that patients with tumors of the pituitary gland often became obese. (You may recall from chapter 3 that the pituitary gland is the "master gland" of the endocrine system.) Frohlich concluded that the pituitary gland regulates hunger. But later research found that, in reality, the tumors influenced hunger by affecting the **hypothalamus,** which lies just above the pituitary gland (figure 10.3).

Two areas of the hypothalamus are especially important in the regulation of hunger. Electrical stimulation of the *ventromedial hypothalamus* (*VMH*), an area at the bottom-middle of the hypothalamus, inhibits eating, while its destruction induces eating. In the 1940s researchers demonstrated that rats whose VMH had been destroyed would eat until they became grossly obese and would then eat enough to maintain their new, higher level of weight (Hetherington & Ranson, 1942).

While the VMH has been implicated in reducing hunger, the *lateral hypothalamus* (*LH*), comprising areas on both sides of the hypothalamus, has been implicated in increasing it. Electrical stimulation of the LH promotes eating, while its destruction inhibits eating. Rats whose LH has been destroyed will stop eating and starve to death even in the presence of food. Only forced feeding will keep them alive long enough for them to recover their appetite (Anand & Brobeck, 1951). Though early experiments such as these led to the conclusion that the LH acts as our "hunger center" while the VMH acts as our "satiety center," later experiments have shown that these sites are

FIGURE 10.3
The Hypothalamus and
Hunger The lateral hypothalamus
and the ventromedial
hypothalamus play important
roles in regulating hunger.

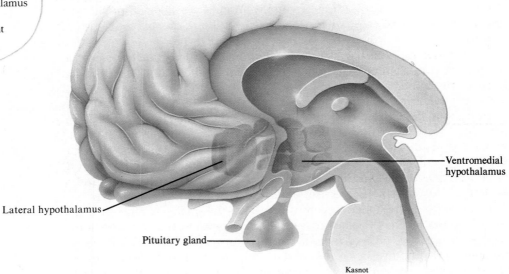

Kasnot

The VMH Rat Destruction of the
ventromedial hypothalamus
induces overeating and gross
obesity. A rat whose ventromedial
hypothalamus has been destroyed
may eat until it becomes three
times its normal weight.

From Teitelbaum, P. "Appetite,"
*Proceedings of the American
Philosophical Society,* 1964, 108,
464–472.

Set Point A specific body weight
that the brain tries to maintain
through the regulation of diet,
activity, and metabolism.

merely important components in the brain's complex system for regulating
hunger and eating (Stricker & Verbalis, 1987). There is no simple "on-off"
switch for eating.

But how does damage to the hypothalamus affect hunger? It does so by
altering the body's **set point,** that is, its normal weight. Damage to the LH
lowers the set point, reducing hunger and making the animal eat less to maintain a lower body weight. In contrast, damage to the VMH raises the set point,
increasing hunger and making the animal eat more to maintain a higher body
weight (Keesey & Powley, 1986). While signals from the body regulate changes
in hunger from meal to meal, the set point regulates changes in hunger over
months or years.

Hunger, especially in human beings, is regulated by external, as well as
internal, factors. Food can act as an incentive to make you feel hungry. The
taste, smell, sight, sound, and texture of food can "pull" you toward it. Have
you ever been watching television, with no appreciable feeling of hunger,

only to become hungry after viewing a commercial showing an enticing array of fast-food donuts? Or perhaps you have felt full after a multicourse dinner and insisted that you could not eat another bite, only to have someone coax you into eating a luscious chocolate dessert. But how can the mere sight of food induce feelings of hunger? One way is by increasing the level of insulin in your blood. In fact, even daydreaming about food can stimulate your pancreas to release insulin, making you hungry and possibly sending you on a hunt for cake, candy, or ice cream (Rodin, 1985).

Obesity

Given the many factors that regulate hunger and eating, why do some people become obese? **Obesity** is defined as a body weight more than 20 percent above normal for one's height and build. An important factor in obesity is the body's set point, which reflects the amount of fat stored in the body. Though fat cells can increase in number and can increase or decrease in size, they cannot decrease in number. Once you have fat cells, they are yours forever. This means that obese people can lose weight only by shrinking the size of their fat cells. Because this induces constant hunger, it is difficult to maintain weight loss for an extended period of time (Kolata, 1985).

Another important factor in obesity is the **basal metabolic rate,** the rate at which the body burns calories just to keep itself alive. The basal metabolic rate accounts for most of the calories that your body uses. This might explain why one of your friends can habitually ingest a milkshake, three hamburgers, and a large order of french fries, yet remain thin, while another will gain weight by periodically ingesting a diet cola, a hamburger without a bun, and a single french fry. While your first friend may have a basal metabolic rate high enough to burn huge amounts of calories, your second friend may have a basal met-

Insulin and Hunger The mere sight of rich, delicious food may stimulate your pancreas to secrete insulin, making you more hungry and, as a consequence, more likely to eat the food.

Obesity A body weight more than 20 percent above normal for one's height and build.

Basal Metabolic Rate The rate at which the body burns calories merely to keep itself alive.

Drawing by Booth; © 1986 The New Yorker Magazine, Inc.

"Let's just go in and see what happens."

abolic rate too low to burn even a modest amount of calories, which forces the body to store much of the ingested food as fat.

Your body alters its metabolic rate to defend its set point, increasing the rate if you eat too much and decreasing the rate if you eat too little. But what determines the set point? Because obesity runs in families, some researchers have looked for a possible genetic basis for the set point. Evidence that heredity helps determine the set point was provided by an analysis of Danish adoption records. The results revealed a strong relationship between the weight of adoptees and their biological parents, but no relationship between the weight of adoptees and their adoptive parents (figure 10.4). This indicates that heredity plays a more important role in obesity than do habits learned from the family in which one is reared (Stunkard et al., 1986).

The set point also seems to be affected by early diet, as shown by the results of a study of 300,000 men who, early in life, had been exposed to a famine in Holland during World War II. The famine followed a German embargo on food entering Holland as punishment for Dutch resistance to Nazi occupation. Men who had been exposed to the famine during a critical period of development, including the third trimester of gestation and the first month after birth, were less likely to become obese than men who had been exposed to the famine at other times during their early development (Ravelli, Stein, & Susser, 1976). The men exposed to the famine during the critical period may have developed lower set points than did the other men.

Researchers have also linked obesity to differences in responsiveness to external food cues. Because a series of studies in the 1960s indicated that obese people feel hungrier and eat more in the presence of external food cues, Stanley Schachter (1971) concluded that obese people are more responsive to those cues. In one study using naturalistic observation, researchers observed people eating in a diner. When a waitress provided an appetizing description of a dessert, obese people were more likely to order it than when she did not. Nonobese people were much less affected by her description of a dessert (Herman, Olmsted, & Polivy, 1983).

Though this supported the belief that obese people are more responsive to food cues, the "externality" of obese people does not seem to cause their obesity. Instead, their obesity seems to cause their externality. Why? Because

FIGURE 10.4

Heredity and Obesity Data from Danish adoption records indicated that there was a positive relationship between the weight of adopted children and their biological parents, but no relationship between the weight of adopted children and their adoptive parents. The graph illustrates the relationship between adoptees and their biological and adoptive mothers. The relationship also holds true for adoptees and their biological and adoptive fathers (Stunkard et al., 1986).

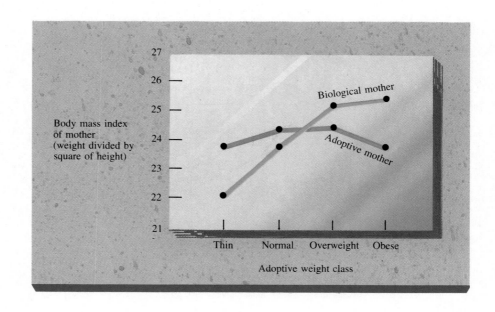

many obese people are constantly dieting, they may be in a chronic state of hunger, making them more responsive to food cues. Moreover, obesity researcher Judith Rodin (1981) has found that obese people may have chronically high levels of insulin, making them hungrier and, as a result, more responsive to food cues. This gives the false impression that obese people are more "external" than nonobese people.

Still another external factor, stressful situations, can induce hunger and, in some cases, overeating. You may have suspected this when observing the voracious appetites that some students exhibit during final exam week. Under such stressful conditions, obese people will be more likely than nonobese people to overeat (Pine, 1985). But how does stress induce overeating? One possibility is by stimulating the brain to secrete *endorphins.* As you learned in chapters 3 and 4, endorphins are neurotransmitters that relieve pain. They also increase when we are under stress and stimulate hunger (Morley & Levine, 1980). Perhaps obese people eat more under stress than do nonobese people because stress induces greater increases in their endorphin levels. As you can see, hunger is associated with many factors (figure 10.5), some of which contribute to obesity. Chapter 16 describes the effects of obesity on health and the approaches used to help obese people lose weight.

Judith Rodin "Almost any overweight person can lose weight; few can keep it off."

Eating Disorders

What do you consider the ideal body? Your answer may depend, in part, on whether you are a male or a female. This was demonstrated in a study in which college students were presented with a set of nine figure drawings ranging from very thin to very heavy. They were asked to indicate which was closest to their current figure, their ideal figure, and the figure they felt was most attractive to the opposite sex. For men, the current, the ideal, and the most attractive figures were almost identical. For women, the current figure was heavier than the most attractive, and the most attractive was heavier than the ideal. The women also thought men liked women thinner than the men actually reported. Moreover, women tended to be less satisfied with their own figures than were men with their own. This may put more pressure on women to lose weight (Fallon & Rozin, 1985).

This pressure may also account, in part, for the greater incidence of dieting among women than among men. And, dieting may contribute to the greater tendency of women to develop eating disorders marked by excessive concern with weight control, most notably *anorexia nervosa* and *bulimia nervosa* (Fallon & Rozin, 1985). In fact, a study that followed 193 adolescent girls for two years found that those who viewed their bodies most negatively were more likely to develop eating disorders. The onset of the disorders might be triggered by the tendency to accumulate body fat during puberty (Attie & Brooks-Gunn, 1989).

In 1983 the popular singer Karen Carpenter died of starvation—despite having access to all the food she could want. She suffered from **anorexia nervosa,** a sometimes fatal disorder in which the victim becomes emaciated after going on a starvation diet. Anorexia nervosa is more common in young women, with no more than 15 percent of cases occurring in males (Bemis, 1978). Victims view themselves as fat even when they are objectively thin. Yet, they are preoccupied with food—talking about it, cooking it, and urging others to eat.

Anorexia Nervosa An eating disorder marked by self-starvation.

The causes of anorexia nervosa are unclear. Possible causes vary from a malfunctioning hypothalamus (Gold, Pottash, Sweeney, Martin, & Davies, 1980) to conflicts concerning social maturation (Strober & Humphrey, 1987). The victims' upbringing may make them have high achievement standards,

FIGURE 10.5
Factors that Affect Hunger and Eating Hunger and eating depend on the interaction of biological factors and external (psychological-environmental) factors.

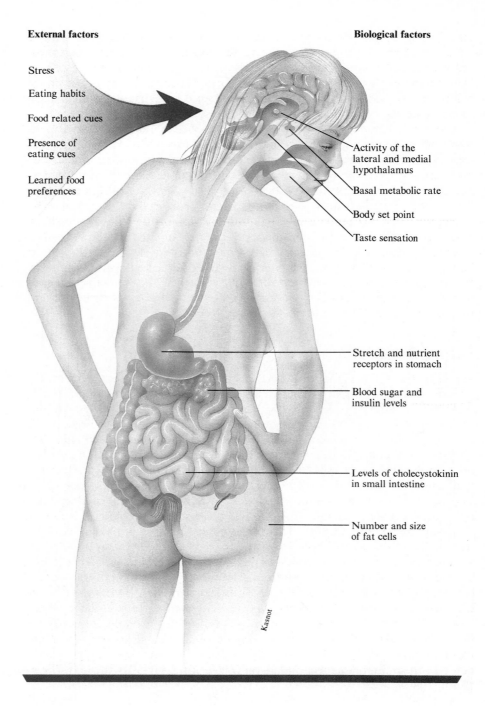

External factors

Stress

Eating habits

Food related cues

Presence of eating cues

Learned food preferences

Biological factors

Activity of the lateral and medial hypothalamus

Basal metabolic rate

Body set point

Taste sensation

Stretch and nutrient receptors in stomach

Blood sugar and insulin levels

Levels of cholecystokinin in small intestine

Number and size of fat cells

Kasnot

while feeling inadequate to meet the demands of puberty, college, or marriage. Women victims even become physically childlike, experiencing cessation of menstruation and loss of their mature figures. Treatment of severe anorexia nervosa may begin with the provision of nourishment through intravenous feeding or feeding through a nasogastric tube. Therapists then try to promote more adaptive ways of thinking about food (Mitchell & Eckert, 1987).

In a related disorder, people go on repeated eating binges in which they ingest up to 30,000 calories at a time—more than a week's worth of calories, perhaps by eating a half gallon of ice cream, a two-pound box of chocolates, a loaf of French bread, and other high carbohydrate foods. Nonetheless, they maintain normal weight by ridding themselves of the food by self-induced vomiting or by using enemas or laxatives (Cunningham, 1984). This binge-purge syndrome is called **bulimia nervosa.** People with bulimia nervosa think obsessively about food and fear becoming obese. As in the case of anorexia nervosa, most victims of bulimia nervosa are young women, with only about 10 percent of victims being men (Striegel-Moore, Silberstein, & Rodin, 1986). The repeated bouts of vomiting lead to medical problems, such as dehydration, tooth decay, or ulcers of the esophagus.

As in the case of anorexia nervosa, the causes of bulimia nervosa are unclear. One possible cause is a low level of the neurotransmitter serotonin, which is associated with depression. Binge eating of carbohydrates may elevate mood by increasing serotonin levels in the brain. This is supported by research showing that antidepressant drugs that increase serotonin levels are useful in treating bulimia nervosa (Agras & McCann, 1987).

People exposed to situations that emphasize weight control are more likely to develop bulimia nervosa. For example, males with bulimia nervosa are likely to be dancers, jockeys, or collegiate wrestlers (Striegel-Moore, Silberstein, & Rodin, 1986). Victims of bulimia nervosa tend to come from families that fail to support social independence and emotional expression (Johnson & Flach, 1985). And, victims of bulimia nervosa may be *restrained eaters,* people who are continually concerned with controlling their desire for food. Our culture has made restrained eating common among women, because constant dieting has become a normal eating pattern for many of them.

How does this explain binging? When restrained eaters eat a "taboo" food, such as ice cream, they may say to themselves, "I've blown my diet, so I might as well keep eating." In contrast, nonrestrained eaters do not share this all-or-nothing belief. They can ingest a rich food, such as a milkshake, without going on eating binges (Weber, Klesges, & Klesges, 1988). An effective approach to treating bulimia nervosa is having the person attend therapy sessions in which he or she receives psychotherapy and learns to eat without vomiting (Leitenberg, Rosen, Gross, Nudelman, & Vara, 1988).

THE SEX MOTIVE

Every February, newsstands sell about 2 million copies of a special issue of *Sports Illustrated,* instead of the 100,000 copies they normally sell. The reason newsstands sell twenty times the normal number of copies is not because the special issue contains fascinating articles about celebrated athletes. As you probably know, the issue is popular because it contains photographs of beautiful women in skimpy bathing suits. This demonstrates both the power of the sex drive and the incentive value of sexual stimuli. Though individuals, such as religious celibates, can live long lives without engaging in sexual intercourse, the survival of the species requires that many individuals engage in it. Had sexual intercourse not evolved into an extremely pleasurable behavior, we would have little inclination to seek it. But what accounts for the power of the sex motive?

Physiological Factors

The most important physiological factors in sexual motivation are sex hormones secreted by the **gonads,** the sex glands. The secretion of sex hormones is controlled by hormones secreted by the pituitary gland, which, in turn, is controlled by hormones secreted by the hypothalamus. Sex hormones direct sexual development as well as sexual behavior. Their influence on sexual development is discussed in chapter 12.

While hormones exert a direct effect on human sexual development, their influence in motivating human sexual behavior is less clear. Research indicates that testosterone motivates both male and female sexual behavior, while

Bulimia Nervosa An eating disorder marked by binging and purging.

Sex as a Drive and an Incentive Would Sports Illustrated have as much success with a "baseball uniform" issue as it has with its "swimsuit" issue?

Gonads The male and female sex glands, the testes and the ovaries.

The World's Longest Kiss While kissing is unknown in some cultures, it is common in others. This photograph shows Eddie Levin and Delphine Crha in Chicago entering the Guinness Book of World Records by kissing for seventeen days and nine hours. (Of course, in this case, the couple was more motivated by their need for achievement than by their desire for romance.)

Paraphilia A way of obtaining sexual gratification that violates legal or cultural norms concerning proper sex objects and sexual practices.

Alfred Kinsey (1894–1956) "The present study was undertaken because the senior author's students were bringing him, as a college teacher of biology, questions on matters of sex. . . . They had found it more difficult to obtain strictly factual information which was not biased by moral, philosophic, or social interpretations."

estrogen contributes little to the sexual motivation of either males or females. Human males or females who, for medical reasons, have been castrated before puberty typically show a weak sex drive as adults. In contrast, castration after puberty typically produces only a slight reduction in the human sex drive (Feder, 1984). And, unlike lower mammals, women do not show a significant increase in sexual motivation at the midpoint of their menstrual cycle, when estrogen levels peak and ovulation occurs (Hoon, Bruce, & Kinchloe, 1982).

Sociocultural Factors

While sex hormones are the main motivators of animal sexual behavior, sociocultural factors are the main motivators of human sexual behavior. Because sexual motivation in animals is rigidly controlled by hormones, members of a given species will vary little in their sexual behaviors. In contrast, because human sexual motivation is influenced more by environmental stimuli and sociocultural factors, we vary markedly in our sexual behavior. For example, breast caressing is a prelude to sexual intercourse among the Marquesan islanders of the Pacific but not among the Sirionian Indians of Bolivia. And, while the Pukapukan children of Polynesia are allowed to masturbate in public, the Cuna children of Panama are whipped if caught masturbating even in private (Klein, 1982). In extreme cases, human beings may engage in **paraphilias,** which are ways of obtaining sexual gratification that violate cultural norms concerning proper sex objects and sexual practices (table 10.1).

In Western cultures, acceptable sexual behavior has varied over time. The ancient Greeks viewed bisexuality as normal and masturbation as a desirable way for youths to relieve their sexual tensions. In contrast, most Americans and Europeans of the Victorian era of the nineteenth century believed that all sexual activity should be avoided except when aimed at procreation. The Victorian emphasis on sexual denial even led John Harvey Kellogg to invent what he claimed was a nutritional "cure" for masturbation—cornflakes (Money, 1986).

The liberalization of attitudes toward sexual behavior that has taken place during the twentieth century was shown in 1983 when the *Journal of the American Medical Association* published an article on human sexuality. This would not be noteworthy except that the article had been submitted for publication in 1899—at the end of the Victorian era. The article was based on a paper concerning female sexuality presented by gynecologist Denslow Lewis (1899/1983) at the annual meeting of the American Medical Association. Lewis described the female sexual response, the need for sex education, the importance of sex for marital compatibility, and techniques for overcoming sexual problems. Lewis even made the radical suggestion (for his time) that wives be encouraged to enjoy sex as much as their husbands did. At the time, the editor of the journal refused to publish the paper, which a prominent physician called "filth" and another editor feared would bring charges of sending obscene material through the mail (Hollender, 1983).

Denslow Lewis's critics would be even more distressed by research in human sexuality that has taken place in the past few decades, beginning with the post–World War II research of Alfred Kinsey. Kinsey, a biologist at Indiana University, found that he was unable to answer his students' questions about human sexual behavior because of a lack of relevant information. This inspired him to conduct surveys of the sexual behavior of men (Kinsey, Pomeroy, & Martin, 1948) and women (Kinsey, Pomeroy, Martin, & Gebhard, 1953).

Kinsey and his colleagues obtained their data from interviews with thousands of men and women and published their findings in two best-selling books. The books (which contained statistics but no pictures) shocked the public, because Kinsey reported that masturbation, homosexuality, premarital

TABLE 10.1	Paraphilias
Fetishism	A person with a *fetish* gains sexual gratification from inanimate objects such as shoes or panties. In an especially bizarre case, a man obtained brassieres by claiming to be an agent of the Environmental Protection Agency and convincing women to remove their brassieres so that he could administer a "breathing test" to determine whether a local atomic power plant had affected breathing capacities (Duke & Nowicki, 1986).
Transvestitism	A *transvestite* gains sexual gratification from dressing in opposite-sex clothing. Because women in American culture have greater freedom to wear male clothing, almost all transvestites are males. Some transvestites work as female impersonators.
Voyeurism	A *voyeur* gains sexual gratification primarily from watching people who are naked or engaged in sex. According to a popular legend, in A.D. 1057 Lady Godiva rode naked through Coventry, England. Her husband, the Lord of Coventry, had decreed that everyone stay indoors and keep their shutters closed. But Tom, the town tailor, peeked at her and was punished for his voyeuristic act contributing the name "Peeping Tom" to our language.
Sadomasochism	In the eighteenth century, the Marquis de Sade, a French nobleman, described the sexual pleasure he obtained from brutalizing women. Thus, a *sadist* gains sexual gratification from inflicting humiliation and pain. In the nineteenth century, Leopold Sacher-Masoch, an Austrian author, wrote novels about men who experienced sexual pleasure from submitting to physical abuse by women. Thus, a *masochist* gains sexual gratification from being forced to submit to bondage, beatings, and humiliation.

sex, extramarital sex, and other sexual behaviors were more common than most people had believed. But scientists warned, correctly, that Kinsey's findings should not be generalized to all people, because his sample was not representative of the American population. His sample included primarily white, well-educated eastern and midwestern people, willing to be interviewed about their sexual behavior. Moreover, what is true of people in one decade may not be true in another. Sexual activity in the decades after Kinsey's survey surged, only to taper off in the 1980s with increased fears concerning AIDS, genital herpes, and other sexually transmitted diseases (Gerrard, 1987).

The shocked response to Kinsey's surveys was mild compared to that generated in the 1950s and 1960s by the research of William Masters and Virginia Johnson. Unlike Kinsey, Masters and Johnson were not content with merely asking people about their sexual motivation and behavior. Instead, they observed ongoing sexual behavior and recorded physiological changes that accompanied it. To study the female sexual response, they even invented a transparent plastic "penis" through which they could photograph genital changes during sexual arousal.

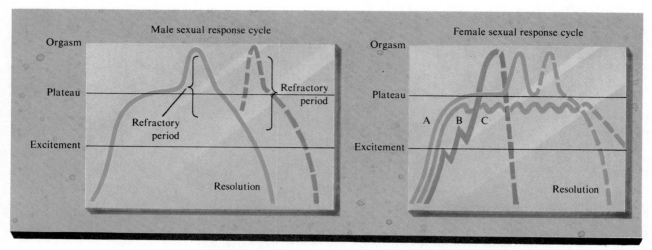

FIGURE 10.6
The Human Sexual Response Cycle Masters and Johnson found that males and females have sexual response cycles comprising four phases: excitement, plateau, orgasm, and resolution. After reaching orgasm, males cannot achieve another orgasm until they have passed through a refractory period. In contrast, pattern A shows that females may experience more than one orgasm during a single cycle. Pattern B shows a cycle during which a woman has reached the plateau stage without proceding to orgasm. Pattern C shows a cycle during which a woman has reached orgasm quickly. Males, too, may experience pattern B and pattern C.

Sexual Response Cycle During sexual activity, the phases of excitement, plateau, orgasm, and resolution.

Based on their study of more than ten thousand orgasms experienced by more than three hundred men and three hundred women, Masters and Johnson (1966) identified four phases in the **sexual response cycle** of both men and women (figure 10.6). During the *excitement phase* mental or physical stimulation causes sexual arousal. In males the penis becomes erect as it becomes engorged with blood. In females the nipples become erect, the vagina becomes lubricated, and the clitoris protrudes as it, too, becomes engorged with blood. During the *plateau phase* heart rate, blood pressure, muscle tension, and respiration rate increase. In males the erection becomes firmer and the testes are drawn closer to the body to prepare for ejaculation. Drops of fluid, possibly containing sperm (and capable of causing pregnancy), may appear at the tip of the penis. In females the body flushes, lubrication increases, the clitoris retracts, the vagina clamps around the penis, and the breasts swell (making the nipples seem to shrink).

During the *orgasm phase* heart rate and breathing rate reach their peaks, males ejaculate *semen* (a fluid containing sperm), and both males and females experience intensely pleasurable sensations induced by rhythmic muscle contractions. Finally, during the *resolution phase,* blood leaves the genitals and sexual arousal lessens. Males then enter a *refractory period,* lasting from minutes to hours, during which they cannot achieve an erection. In contrast, some women who receive continued sexual stimulation may experience multiple orgasms.

Sexual Dysfunctions

Sexual Dysfunction A chronic problem at one or more phases of the sexual response cycle.

Once they had identified the normal phases of the human sexual response, Masters and Johnson became interested in studying **sexual dysfunctions,** which are chronic problems at phases in the sexual response cycle. A man with an *erectile dysfunction* will fail either to attain an erection or to maintain it through the arousal phase. A man exhibiting *premature ejaculation* will reach the orgasm phase too fast for his partner to be sexually satisfied. And a woman experiencing *orgasmic dysfunction* will be unable to reach the orgasm phase.

Based on their research findings, Masters and Johnson (1970) concluded that the psychological causes of sexual dysfunctions are usually sexual guilt, sexual ignorance, or anxiety about sexual performance. In treating sexual dysfunctions, Masters and Johnson first have their clients examined by a physician to rule out any physical causes, such as drugs, diabetes, or hormonal imbalances. They then counsel their clients to help them overcome their sexual guilt, educate them about sexual anatomy, sexual motivation, and sexual behavior, and teach them specific techniques for reducing performance anxiety. Of course, none of these procedures will be of much use unless the clients are sexually attracted to each other.

The main technique in Masters and Johnson's sex therapy is **sensate focusing,** in which the partners at first participate in nongenital caressing, later proceed to genital caressing, and finally proceed to sexual intercourse. The partners are urged to concentrate on pleasurable feelings instead of striving for erections and orgasms. They are also instructed to tell each other what kinds of stimulation they enjoy and what kinds they do not. Masters and Johnson teach their clients other techniques when necessary. They may have a woman with an orgasmic dysfunction practice masturbating to orgasm as a step toward reaching orgasm during sexual intercourse. In treating premature ejaculation, they may have the man's partner repeatedly stimulate his penis just to the point before orgasm to teach him to gain control over the timing of his orgasm.

Masters and Johnson (1970) reported that more than two-thirds of their clients showed improvement. But they were criticized for not operationally defining what they meant by "improvement" and for failing to conduct follow-up studies of their clients to determine whether the positive effects of therapy were long-lasting. Nonetheless, studies of sex therapy by many other therapists have provided convincing evidence of its effectiveness (LoPiccolo & Stock, 1986). More recently, Masters and Johnson have joined other sex researchers in studying the factors that account for **gender identity** and **sexual orientation.**

Gender Identity and Sexual Orientation

In 1953 Christine Jorgensen shocked the world by announcing that "she" was a man who had undergone surgery and hormone treatments to look more like a woman. Though this procedure had been performed since the 1930s, Jorgensen's case was the first widely publicized instance of **transsexualism,** a disorder of gender identity in which a person who is physically a male or female feels psychologically like a member of the opposite sex. The extent to which heredity, hormonal imbalances, or childhood experiences contribute to transsexualism is unknown. Though many transsexuals express satisfaction with the results of sex-change surgery, some suffer serious emotional distress, develop psychological disorders, or even attempt suicide (Abramowitz, 1986).

Transsexualism is much less common than **homosexuality,** a sexual orientation that is marked by a preference for sexual relations with members of one's own sex. Unlike the transsexual, the homosexual does not feel trapped in the body of the wrong sex. Female homosexuals are called *lesbians,* after the island of Lesbos, on which the Greek poet Sappho (c.620–c.565 B.C.) ran a school for women. Sappho killed herself after a student failed to return her love. Today, attitudes toward homosexuality vary among cultures and within a given culture. In 1973, in keeping with increasingly liberal attitudes toward homosexuality in the United States, the American Psychiatric Association voted to eliminate homosexuality from its list of mental disorders.

Masters and Johnson "Aside from obvious anatomic variants, men and women are homogenous in their physiological responses to sexual stimuli."

Sensate Focusing A sex therapy technique that, at first, involves nongenital caressing and gradually progresses to sexual intercourse.

Gender Identity A person's self-perceived sex.

Sexual Orientation One's sexual attraction toward members of either one's own sex or opposite sex.

Transsexualism A condition in which a genetic male or female has the gender identity of the opposite sex.

Homosexuality A consistent preference for sexual relations with members of one's own sex.

Transsexualism Physician and tennis player Richard Raskin felt like a female trapped in a male body. This led him to undergo surgery and hormone treatments to make him look more like a woman. He then created controversy by pursuing a brief career on the women's tennis tour under the new name of Renee Richards.

Given that our reproductive anatomy and cultural norms favor heterosexuality, why are 1 percent of women and 4 percent of men homosexuals (Ellis & Ames, 1987)? Theories of homosexuality abound, with none gaining universal acceptance. Physiological theories of homosexuality implicate hereditary and hormonal factors. Support for the hereditary basis of homosexuality comes from research showing that identical twins (who have the same genes) adopted as infants by different families have a higher likelihood of both becoming homosexuals than do ordinary siblings reared together in the same family (Eckert, Bouchard, Bohlen, & Heston, 1986). Support for the hormonal basis of homosexuality comes from research showing that the administration of estrogen produces a physiological response in homosexual men that is intermediate between that produced in women and in heterosexual men (Gladue, Green, & Hellman, 1984).

But what of possible social factors that might account for sexual orientation? Traditional views have favored the Freudian notion that homosexuality is caused by a dominant, overly affectionate mother and an aloof, unemotional father. Though some homosexuals have such backgrounds, others do not. In fact, there is no evidence that particular childhood experiences alone will cause a person to become a homosexual (Bell, Weinberg, & Hammersmith, 1981).

A controversial theory holds that our sexual orientation, whether heterosexual or homosexual, depends on the sex of the children with whom we are socializing when our sex drive first emerges (Storms, 1981). Reports by homosexuals indicate that their sex drive emerges two to three years before that of heterosexuals, at a time when they are more likely to be socializing exclusively with same-sex peers. Because of this, they may attach their sexual feelings to those children. In contrast, the sex drive of most children emerges later, at a time when they would typically be socializing with members of both sexes. This makes them more likely to attach their sex drive to the culturally approved opposite sex.

Despite numerous studies on the origins of sexual orientation, none has identified any physiological or social factor that, by itself, can explain why one person develops a heterosexual orientation and another a homosexual orientation. Researchers continue to argue about the relative strengths of physiological and sociocultural factors. A review of the research literature concluded that abnormal hormonal activity during a critical period between the middle of the second month and the middle of the fifth month after conception may alter the development of the hypothalamus and predispose some people toward a homosexual orientation (Ellis & Ames, 1987).

But, according to John Money (1987), a leading sex researcher, sexual orientation is more malleable than that finding would indicate. Money points to the Sambia tribe of New Guinea, in which males between the ages of nine and nineteen are encouraged to follow a homosexual orientation to become more manly. Yet, at the age of nineteen the males marry and switch to a heterosexual orientation, indicating that sexual orientation is not regulated strictly by physiological factors.

THE AROUSAL MOTIVE

Though the hunger motive and sex motive seem to dominate American culture, we are also influenced by another biological motive, the **arousal motive.** *Arousal* is the general level of physiological activation of the brain and body. As you learned in earlier chapters, the reticular formation regulates brain arousal and the sympathetic nervous system and endocrine system regulate body arousal. In 1908 researchers reported that animals performed tasks best at a moderate, or *optimal,* level of arousal, and that the more complex the task, the lower the level of optimal arousal (Yerkes & Dodson, 1908). Later researchers, led by Donald Hebb (1955) of McGill University in Montreal, showed that human beings, too, perform best at a moderate level of arousal, with performance deteriorating under excessively high or low arousal levels. This relationship between arousal and performance, represented by an inverted **U**-shaped curve (figure 10.7), became known as the **Yerkes-Dodson law,** after the researchers who first identified it.

Hebb found that optimal arousal is higher for simple tasks than for complex tasks. The optimal level of arousal for doing a simple addition problem would be higher than for a complex geometry problem. Hebb also found that optimal arousal is higher for well-learned tasks than for novel tasks. Your optimal level of arousal for reading is higher now than it was when you were first learning to read. But how does arousal level influence performance?

Arousal Motive The motive to maintain an optimal level of physiological activation.

Yerkes-Dodson Law The principle that the relationship between arousal and performance is best represented by an inverted **U**-shaped curve.

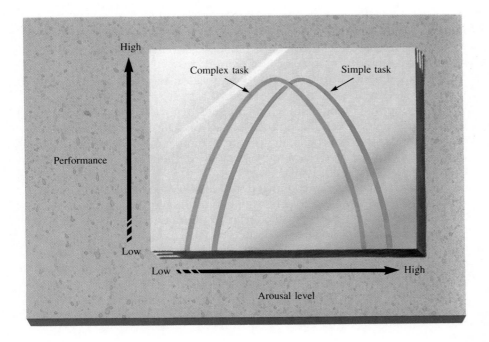

FIGURE 10.7
The Yerkes-Dodson Law The graph depicts the relationship between arousal level and task performance. Note that the best performance occurs at a moderate level of arousal. Performance declines when arousal is below or above that level. Note that the optimal level of arousal becomes lower as the task becomes more complex.

According to Hebb, an optimal level of arousal permits us to concentrate and attend to tasks, such as exams. If you are underaroused your mind may wander to irrelevant details, as when you make careless errors on exams, such as darkening the letter *C* when you meant to darken the letter *B*. But if you are overaroused your focus of attention may become too narrow, reducing your ability to shift to other details that may help you solve a problem, as when you find yourself so anxious that you stare at a particular exam question for several minutes.

Research has tended to support the notion of an optimal level of arousal. In a study of arithmetic performance in third- and fourth-graders under time pressure, low-anxious children performed better than did moderately anxious or high-anxious children (Plass & Hill, 1986). How could the concept of optimal arousal explain these findings? Assume that before performing arithmetic the low-anxious children began *below* their optimal levels of arousal for performing arithmetic, the moderately anxious children began *at* their optimal levels of arousal, and the high-anxious children began *above* their optimal levels of arousal. The additional arousal caused by the arithmetic task may have boosted the arousal of the low-anxious children *to* their optimal levels and the arousal of the moderately anxious children *above* their optimal levels, while the high-anxious children may have been boosted even further above their optimal levels of arousal.

Moreover, for any given task there is no single optimal level of arousal. The optimal level will vary from person to person (Ebbeck & Weiss, 1988). So, an outstanding math student would have a higher optimal level of arousal for performing arithmetic than would a poor math student. As a consequence, the outstanding math student might have to "psych up" before an exam, while the poor math student might have to relax—both in an effort to reach an optimal level of arousal.

Sensory Deprivation

Sensory Deprivation The prolonged withdrawal of normal levels of external stimulation.

Though the amount of arousal each of us prefers varies, we require at least a minimal amount for our brains to function properly. Anecdotal reports from Arctic explorers, shipwrecked sailors, and prisoners in solitary confinement made early psychologists aware that human beings require sensory stimulation for proper perceptual, cognitive, and emotional functioning. **Sensory deprivation** is the prolonged withdrawal of normal levels of external stimulation. When people are subjected to sensory deprivation, they may experience delusions, hallucinations, and emotional arousal caused by the brain's attempt to restore its optimal level of arousal.

The experimental study of sensory deprivation began in the early 1950s when the Defense Research Board of Canada asked Donald Hebb to find ways of countering the "brainwashing" techniques that the Chinese communists used on prisoners of war during the Korean War. During brainwashing, prisoners were deprived of social and physical stimulation. This became so unpleasant that it motivated them to cooperate with their captors just to receive more stimulation (Hebb, 1958).

Hebb and his colleagues conducted studies of sensory deprivation in which each subject was confined to a bed in a soundproofed room with only the monotonous humming of a fan and an air conditioner (figure 10.8). The subjects wore translucent goggles to reduce visual sensations and cotton gloves and cardboard tubes over their arms to reduce touch sensations. They were permitted to leave the bed only to eat or to use the toilet. After many hours of sensory deprivation, some subjects experienced hallucinations, emotional instability, and intellectual deterioration. Though the students who served as volunteers for the study were paid twenty dollars a day for participating (a

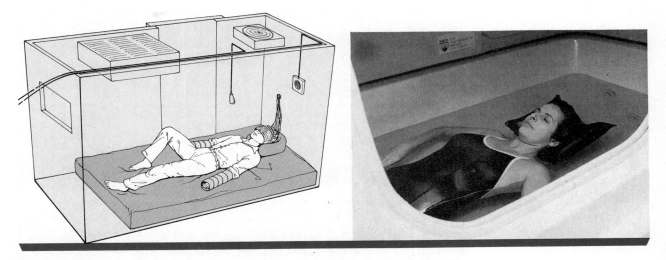

FIGURE 10.8
Sensory Deprivation The sensory deprivation room used in the Canadian studies in the 1950s and the flotation tank that became popular in the 1970s.

large amount at the time), most quit within forty-eight hours. They found the lack of sensory stimulation so aversive that they preferred to forego the monetary incentive in favor of sensory stimulation (Bexton, Heron, & Scott, 1954).

In the 1970s the American psychologist John Lilly popularized another method of sensory deprivation, in which the subject floats in warm saltwater in an enclosed, soundproofed, casketlike tank. While some people became distressed by their experiences in flotation tanks, others reported profound religious experiences. The flotation tank was promoted as a means of achieving relaxation or altered states of consciousness (Hood & Morris, 1981).

Research on sensory deprivation demonstrates that inadequate external stimulation motivates us to seek external stimulation or to generate our own stimulation through alterations in brain activity. This is especially true of people who perform monotonous tasks in relative isolation, such as conducting research in the Arctic, driving long-distance trucking hauls, or living for extended periods in outer space stations. And, as you are certainly aware, even college students will seek external stimulation to combat boring classes and monotonous campus life (Weinstein & Almaguer, 1987).

Sensation Seeking

Would you prefer to ride a roller coaster or lie on a beach? Attend a lively party or have a quiet conversation? Your preferences would depend in part on your degree of **sensation seeking,** your motivation to seek high or low levels of sensory stimulation. While people high in sensation seeking prefer activities that increase their arousal levels, those low in sensation seeking prefer activities that decrease their arousal levels (Zuckerman, Buchsbaum, & Murphy, 1980).

To appreciate the extremes of sensation seeking, consider the childhood disorders of **hyperactivity** and **autism.** Hyperactive children are motivated to seek stimulation. They constantly move about, have difficulty concentrating on tasks, and are easily distracted by irrelevant stimuli. In contrast, autistic children are motivated to avoid stimulation. They dislike changes in their routines, perform repetitive actions such as rocking back and forth, and ignore

Sensation Seeking The extent to which an individual seeks sensory stimulation.

Hyperactivity A condition, arising in childhood, in which the individual is motivated to seek constant stimulation and has difficulty focusing his or her attention.

Autism A condition, arising in infancy, in which the individual is motivated to avoid stimulation, including social interaction.

Sensation Seeking These two groups of people may differ markedly in their degree of sensation seeking.

stimuli other than that to which they are attending. One theory, based on numerous research studies, holds that hyperactive children are physiologically *underaroused* and autistic children are physiologically *overaroused* (Zentall & Zentall, 1983).

How would this explain the behavior of hyperactive and autistic children? Perhaps the behavior of both kinds of children is aimed at helping them maintain an optimal level of arousal, the hyperactive child by seeking stimulation and the autistic child by avoiding stimulation. This may also explain the paradoxical effects of drugs that are prescribed to treat children with these disorders. Stimulant drugs, which make normal children more active, may calm hyperactive children, apparently by raising their levels of arousal enough so that they become less motivated to engage in sensation seeking. And tranquilizing drugs, which make normal children less active, may stimulate autistic children, apparently by lowering their levels of arousal enough so that they become more motivated to engage in sensation seeking (Zentall & Zentall, 1983).

THE ACHIEVEMENT MOTIVE

Achievement Motive The desire for mastery, excellence, and accomplishment.

Human beings are motivated by social, as well as physiological, needs. Interest in studying social motivation was stimulated in the 1930s and 1940s by the work of Henry Murray (1938), who identified a variety of important social motives, including dominance, achievement, and affiliation. Since Murray's pioneering research, psychologists, led by David McClelland and John Atkinson, have been especially interested in studying the **achievement motive,** which is the desire for mastery, excellence, and accomplishment.

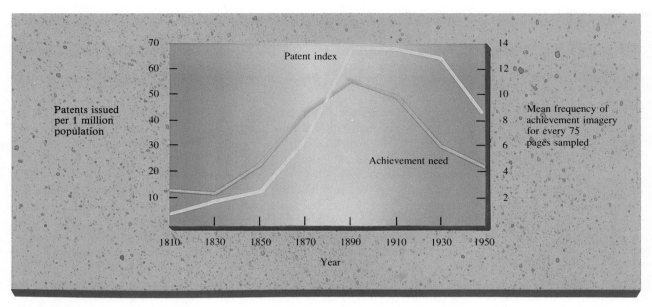

FIGURE 10.9
Achievement Themes and the Patent Index Between 1800 and 1950, there was a strong positive association between the number of achievement themes in children's readers and the number of patents issued by the U.S. Patent Office (DeCharms & Moeller, 1962).

In the context of Maslow's hierarchy of needs, the need for achievement would be associated with one of the higher levels, the need for esteem. This means that the need for achievement would be stronger in cultures, such as the United States, where most people have satisfied their lower needs. But even in the United States the relative importance of the need for achievement has changed over time. Figure 10.9 shows the results of a survey of children's readers published between 1800 and 1950, which found that the number of achievement themes in the readers increased until about 1890 and then decreased through 1950. This was accompanied by a parallel change in the number of patents issued, indicating that changes in a country's achievement motivation may affect its practical achievements (DeCharms & Moeller, 1962). Of course, it is not certain from this data that changes in achievement motivation *caused* changes in practical achievements. You will once again recall that a positive correlation between two variables does not necessarily mean that changes in one *cause* changes in the other.

Changes in the achievement motive over time also differ for males and females. From the late 1950s to the late 1970s American men showed no change in their achievement motivation, while American women showed a marked increase. This has been attributed to the women's movement of the past few decades, which made personal achievement outside of traditional women's fields, such as homemaking, more acceptable for women (Veroff, Depner, Kulka, & Douvan, 1980).

David McClelland ". . . achievement motivation training is very cost effective for improving small business performance. . . ."

Need for Achievement

Henry Murray (1938) referred to the achievement motive as the *need for achievement,* which reveals itself in efforts to meet high standards of performance or to compete successfully against other people. How do psychologists measure the need for achievement? The most common means has been the

Thematic Apperception Test (also known as the *TAT*), developed by Murray and his colleague Christiana Morgan in the 1930s to assess social motivation (Morgan & Murray, 1935). The TAT assumes that our fantasies reveal our motives. The test consists of a series of drawings of people in ambiguous situations (figure 10.10). The subject is asked to tell what is happening in the picture, what led up to it, how the people feel, and how the situation turns out. The responses are scored for any themes that run through them. Individuals with a high need for achievement will tell stories in which people overcome obstacles, work hard to reach goals, and accomplish great things.

What do we know about people who score high on the need for achievement? Research shows that they persist at tasks in the face of difficulties, delay gratification in the pursuit of long-term goals, and achieve greater success than people with a low need for achievement. They also select moderately difficult challenges, neither so easy that they guarantee success nor so difficult that they guarantee failure (McClelland, 1985). Even psychologists with a high need for achievement become more successful, at least as measured by the recognition accorded their research by fellow psychologists. Psychologists with a high need for achievement have their published research cited more often in articles written by other psychologists (Helmreich, Spence, Beane, Lucker, & Matthews, 1980).

The need for achievement varies with the achievement situation. Even people with a high need for achievement rarely seek success in more than a few areas of life. So, your achievement behavior depends on more than just the strength of your need for achievement. Your achievement behavior would also depend on **incentive value,** the perceived rewards that would accompany success in a particular area, and **expectancy,** the perceived probability

Incentive Value In achievement situations, the perceived rewards that would accompany success in a particular area.

Expectancy In achievement situations, the perceived probability of success in a particular area.

FIGURE 10.10
The Thematic Apperception Test What is happening in this picture? What led up to it? How does the person feel? How will it turn out? Your responses to several ambiguous pictures like this might contain themes revealing the strength of your need for achievement.

of success in a particular area (McClelland, 1985). Still another factor that would affect your achievement behavior would be what John Atkinson labeled the **fear of failure,** the motivation to avoid situations that might bring failure (Atkinson & Litwin, 1960).

Consider these factors in regard to your achievement behavior in this course. If you are high in achievement motivation, if you find that a good grade in the course has high incentive value for you, and if you expect that studying hard would be likely to result in a good grade, you would be more likely to work hard in the course. But, if you are high in achievement motivation yet do not value a high grade in psychology (perhaps because it is only an elective course) or believe that you have little chance of success in the course (perhaps because the professor is a notoriously hard grader), you might not work as hard. But what of your fear of failure? If you had a strong fear of failure, you might work harder to avoid doing poorly and being subjected to criticism from your parents. Or, if your fear of failure overcame you, you might choose to take the course "pass-fail."

Research has also shown that the need for achievement may interact with arousal to determine a person's performance. As you read earlier, each of us performs best at his or her optimal level of arousal for a given task. In an arousing situation, such as giving a speech to a class, a student with a low need for achievement might perform well because the situation raises the student to his or her optimal level of arousal. In the same situation a student with a high need for achievement, already at an optimal level of arousal, might perform poorly because the situation raises the student beyond his or her optimal level (Humphreys & Revelle, 1984).

Considering the importance of the need for achievement, why does one person have a high need for achievement and another a low need for achievement? Early upbringing is an important factor. Children whose parents encourage them to be independent in carrying out everyday responsibilities and who reward them for performing well tend to develop a strong need for achievement. In contrast, children whose parents habitually criticize them or punish them for mistakes will tend to develop a strong fear of failure (Teevan & McGhee, 1972).

Given that achievement motivation is learned, can adults raised in a culture that does not foster achievement motivation learn to develop it? In seeking an answer, David McClelland (1978) found that businessmen in a village in India who had participated a decade earlier in a special training program aimed at increasing achievement motivation were more successful than businessmen in a comparable village who had not received the training. The training had consisted of teaching the men to think, talk, and act like achievement-oriented people. They were instructed to plan for the future, to set moderately difficult goals, and to imagine themselves overcoming obstacles and succeeding. Those who had participated in the training started more businesses and became more successful than did those who had not participated.

Goal Setting

Suppose that you are high in the need for achievement in academics, sports, or some other area. How should you go about seeking to fulfill that need? Hundreds of studies, including McClelland's study of Indian businessmen, have demonstrated the importance of **goal setting.** Goals increase motivation and improve performance by providing incentives. Your goals focus your attention, increase your effort, maintain your persistence, and encourage you to develop strategies for reaching them.

But how should you set your goals? Research findings provide several suggestions (Locke & Latham, 1985). Specific, challenging goals (such as, "I will

Fear of Failure The motivation to avoid achievement situations that might bring failure.

Goal Setting The establishment of a particular level of performance to achieve in the future.

increase my studying by one hour a night") produce better performance than do no goals, vague goals (such as, "I will increase the time I spend studying"), easy goals (such as, "I will increase my studying by ten minutes a week"), or mere encouragement to do your best. Feedback of your progress toward a goal (such as keeping a record of how much time you spend studying) will help you reach that goal. And a goal that you set yourself will motivate you more than will a goal imposed on you (as when a parent forces a child to stay home and study everyday after school).

Another effective technique is to use short-term goals to help you reach long-term goals, as was demonstrated in a program aimed at improving children's arithmetic performance. Children who were given short-term goals did better in arithmetic than did those given long-term goals (Bandura & Schunk, 1981). Suppose you have the long-term goal of owning your own business. You would be wise to have short-term goals also. These might include finding a summer job in your field of interest, earning a bachelor's degree, and gaining an entry-level position after graduation.

Intrinsic Motivation

If you have ever written a term paper merely to obtain a grade, you can appreciate William James's distress at having to complete his now-classic 1890 textbook merely to fulfill a contract. According to Edward Thorndike (1961, p. 267), "James wrote the *Principles* with wailing and gnashing of teeth to fulfill a contract with a publishing firm." Though James enjoyed writing, he did not enjoy writing for money. He was not unusual, because research has shown that receiving extrinsic rewards for performing intrinsically rewarding activities, whether writing a textbook or writing a term paper, can make those activities less rewarding and reduce the motivation to perform them. **Intrinsic motivation** is the desire to perform a task for its own sake. In contrast, **extrinsic motivation** is the desire to perform a task to gain external rewards, such as praise, grades, or money. For example, you may be taking this course because you find it interesting (an intrinsic reason) or because it is a graduation requirement (an extrinsic reason).

Intrinsic Motivation The desire to perform a behavior for its own sake.

Extrinsic Motivation The desire to perform a behavior to obtain an external reward, such as praise, grades, or money.

Until the 1970s, most psychologists agreed with B. F. Skinner that rewards (positive reinforcers) increase behavior or, at worst, have no effect on it. But then research began to show otherwise. In one of the first experiments on intrinsic motivation, children were given a period of time during which they could draw. Some of them were then given a certificate as a reward for having drawn. When given a subsequent chance to draw, students who had been rewarded for drawing spent less time at it than did students who had not been rewarded (Lepper, Greene, & Nisbett, 1973).

Later studies have also supported the benefits of intrinsic motivation and the detrimental effects of extrinsic motivation. High school students who are intrinsically interested in intellectual pursuits perform better in their courses (Lloyd & Barenblatt, 1984). And employees governed by extrinsic rewards such as fringe benefits are less motivated than are employees governed by intrinsic rewards such as control over their own work schedules (Notz, 1975).

Given the everyday observation that extrinsic rewards may increase achievement motivation, especially in people who initially have little or no motivation in a particular area, why do extrinsic rewards sometimes decrease achievement motivation? Two theories provide possible answers. **Justification theory** assumes that extrinsic rewards will decrease intrinsic motivation when a person attributes his or her performance to the extrinsic rewards. The children who were rewarded for drawing may have attributed their behavior to the rewards rather than to their interest in drawing.

Justification Theory The theory that an extrinsic reward will decrease intrinsic motivation when a person attributes his or her performance to that reward.

"It was obviously built when the Mayans were feeling good about themselves."

An alternative theory, **cognitive evaluation theory** (Deci, Nezlek, & Sheinman, 1981), holds that a reward perceived as providing *information* about a person's performance in an activity will increase his or her intrinsic motivation to perform that activity. But a reward perceived as an attempt to *control* a person's behavior will decrease his or her intrinsic motivation to perform that activity. Consider a student whose teacher rewards her for doing well in drawing. If the student believes that the reward is being used to provide information about her performance, her intrinsic motivation to perform that activity may increase. But if she believes that the reward is being used to control her behavior (perhaps to make her spend more time drawing), her intrinsic motivation to perform that activity may decrease. So, when you reward people for performing activities that they find intrinsically rewarding you must be careful to use rewards as information rather than as controls.

You should now have a better appreciation of the influence of motivation, particularly the hunger, sex, arousal, and achievement motives, in your everyday

Cognitive Evaluation Theory
The theory that a person's intrinsic motivation will increase when a reward is perceived as a source of information but will decrease when a reward is perceived as an attempt to exert control.

life. To appreciate how motivation affects behavior in an area of life that is important to many people, consider the relationship between motivation and sport.

THINKING ABOUT PSYCHOLOGY

What Is the Relationship between Motivation and Sport?

Sport Psychology The field that applies psychological principles to help amateur and professional athletes improve their performance.

In 1898 psychologist Norman Triplett observed that bicyclists rode faster when competing against another bicyclist than when competing against time. Given the popularity of instinct theories near the turn of the century, you would probably not be surprised that he attributed this performance to stimulation of the "competitive instinct," which released stored energy and increased the bicyclist's level of arousal. This was perhaps the first study in **sport psychology,** the field that studies the relationship between psychological factors and sport performance. If you watched the past summer or winter Olympics, you saw reports about elite athletes who used the services of sport psychologists to help motivate them to perform up to their capabilities. In studying motivation in sport, researchers are especially interested in the arousal motive and the achievement motive.

The Arousal Motive and Sport

The arousal motive, particularly your degree of sensation seeking, will influence your choice of sports. People high in sensation seeking will prefer more exciting, dangerous sports than will people low in sensation seeking. In one study, people who participated in the highly stimulating sports of hang gliding or auto racing scored higher on the Sensation Seeking Scale (Zuckerman, 1979) than did those who participated in the less stimulating sport of intercollegiate bowling (Straub, 1982).

If you have ever played a competitive sport you know what it is to "choke"— to be so anxious that you perform below your normal level of ability. "Choking" occurs when your anxiety makes you attend to normally automatic movements. Recall that the cerebellum coordinates well-learned, automatic sequences of movements, such as those involved in playing a sport. If you consciously attend to those movements, they will be disrupted (Baumeister, 1984). Consider foul shooting in basketball. If you attend to each movement of your arm and hand as you shoot foul shots, you will disrupt the smooth sequence of movements that foul shooting requires. Athletes at an optimal level of arousal are less likely to "choke," as shown in a study of women collegiate basketball players. Those with moderate levels of pregame anxiety performed better than those with low or high levels (Sonstroem & Bernardo, 1982).

Reprinted with special permission of
King Features Syndicate, Inc.

The Yerkes-Dodson law may explain why some athletes perform better during practice than during competition. For example, if you play intramural softball, you may be at your optimal level of arousal during practice, a relatively unstressful situation. But you may rise above your optimal level during a game, a relatively stressful situation. Similarly, the Yerkes-Dodson law may also explain why some athletes perform better during competition than during practice. In that case, you might be below your optimal level of arousal during practice but rise up to your optimal level during a game.

A good coach will realize which of his or her athletes must be "psyched up" and which must be calmed down to achieve an optimal level of arousal during competition. There is no single optimal level of arousal. Each athlete has his or her own optimal level for a given sport (Ebbeck & Weiss, 1988). Thus, Knute Rockne's "win one for the Gipper" pep talks may hurt the performance of moderately or highly aroused athletes. Yet, such pep talks may be good for athletes who are too relaxed before competitions, especially in aggressive sports such as football or weight lifting.

As mentioned earlier, the optimal level of arousal will be lower for complex tasks than for simple tasks. This is also true in sports (Gardner, 1986). Your optimal level of arousal while hitting a golf ball (a relatively complex task) would be lower than your optimal level while playing shuffleboard (a relatively simple task). Moreover, the more skillful the athlete, the higher will be his or her optimal level of arousal. The golfer who makes a putt on the eighteenth green to win the United States Open may be so skillful that he has a higher optimal level of arousal than the golfer who "chokes" in the same situation. This also means that when teaching a beginner to play golf, to ride a bicycle, or to serve a volleyball you should try to keep his or her arousal level from becoming too high. Chapter 16 describes relaxation techniques that athletes can use to attain an optimal level of arousal.

Researchers have become more refined in studying the relationship between arousal and performance by now distinguishing between mental and physical arousal. A study of competitive swimmers found an inverted-U relationship between physical arousal and swimming speed, as predicted by the Yerkes-Dodson law. That is, subjects who had moderate physical arousal swam faster than those who had either low or high physical arousal. But the study failed to find such a relationship between mental arousal and swimming speed. Instead, the lower the swimmers' self-reported mental arousal, the faster they swam (Burton, 1988).

Kathy Ormsby

The Achievement Motive and Sport

On June 4, 1986, six weeks after setting the collegiate record for the ten-thousand-meter run, Kathy Ormsby, though among the leaders, veered off the track midway through the final race at the NCAA championships in Indianapolis. She left the stadium, ran to the nearby White River Bridge, and leaped fifty feet to the river bank. The fall broke her back, damaged her spinal cord, and paralyzed her from the waist down. Besides excelling at running, Ormsby had been her high school's valedictorian (with an average of ninety-nine out of one-hundred), was a premedicine student at North Carolina State University, and was dedicated to living up to the strict standards of behavior required by her religious beliefs. As one of her teachers said, "If a human being can be perfect, I would say that Kathy was perfect" (Dwyer, 1986, p. 8–A). Ormsby was certainly high in her need for achievement.

Ormsby had been overcome periodically by anxiety strong enough to force her to drop out of races. Her friends and coaches believed she succumbed to what they called "her will to succeed." Though her high need for achievement certainly motivated her to compete, she apparently succumbed to her fear of failure, finding it more and more difficult to motivate herself to compete against other elite athletes. Kathy Ormsby's tragic story shows that the achievement motive can be a powerful force in athletic competition, as it is in other areas of life.

Athletes with a high need for achievement are motivated to seek competition that provides a fair test of their abilities. Early evidence for this came from a study in which college students played a game of ringtoss. Those with a high need for achievement were more likely to stand at an intermediate distance from the peg, while those with a low need for achievement were more likely to stand either close to the peg or far from it (Atkinson & Litwin, 1960). Similarly, if you were high in your need for achievement in tennis, you would probably choose to play someone of your own ability. Neither playing a five-year-old child nor playing Martina Navratilova would be a fair test of your ability. In contrast, a person low in need for achievement or high in the fear of failure might prefer to play either someone who barely knows how to grip a racket, which would assure success, or a professional tennis player, which would assure that losing would be attributable to the professional's excellence rather than to personal incompetence.

One way in which superior athletes make competition against lesser athletes more motivating is by giving themselves some sort of handicap, making the competition a moderate challenge, rather than a guaranteed success (Nicholls, 1984). If you are an excellent table tennis player, you might provide a more moderate challenge for yourself by giving a lesser opponent ten points in a twenty-one-point game. Similarly, in the 1960s Wilt Chamberlain, perhaps the most physically imposing athlete in history (he once *averaged* fifty points a game in the National Basketball Association), developed a fade-away jump shot to show that he could succeed even when giving up his greatest asset, his ability to score from near the basket because of his great strength and height (seven feet, one inch). By doing so, he made scoring a moderate, rather than easy, challenge for himself—often to the distress of his coach.

As in other areas of life, goal setting is important in sport motivation. In a study of sit-up performance by children, those who used specific short-term goals improved more than did those who were only told to "do your best" (Hall & Byrne, 1988). And, members of the University of Notre Dame hockey team successfully used goal setting as part of a motivational program to in-

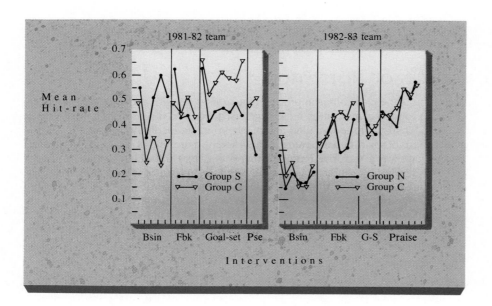

FIGURE 10.11
Goal Setting and Hockey Performance This graph shows the superiority of goal setting in improving the performance of the Notre Dame University hockey team by increasing body checking. Feedback of the number of body checks made and praise for body checking during the 1981–82 and 1982–83 seasons. The mean hit rate refers to the average number of body checks per minute on ice. In regard to interventions, Bsin refers to a baseline period, Fbk refers to a performance feedback period, Goal-set (G-S) refers to a goal-setting period, and Praise (Pse) refers to a praise period. In regard to groups, Group S involved talented seniors, Group N involved new players, and Group C involved subjects who played both seasons. (Anderson et al., 1988).

crease their aggressiveness (figure 10.11). They increased their rate of legal body checking and, perhaps as a consequence, improved their won-loss record (Anderson, Crowell, Doman, & Howard, 1988).

Athletes are also more motivated by intrinsic rewards than by extrinsic rewards. A study of youth basketball players found that boys and girls who were high in their intrinsic motivation to play and low on perceived parental pressure to play enjoyed playing more than did other children (Brustad, 1988). In a study of college athletes, football players on athletic scholarships reported less intrinsic motivation than did those who were not. But among male wrestlers and female athletes, those on athletic scholarships reported *more* intrinsic motivation than those who were not. What could account for these findings? Perhaps football coaches use scholarships more as a means of *control,* while wrestling coaches and coaches of female athletes use scholarships more as a means of *informing* athletes about their competence. Recalling the cognitive evaluation theory, rewards that are perceived as a means of control may decrease instrinsic motivation, while rewards that are perceived as a means of providing information about competence may increase intrinsic motivation (Ryan, 1980).

The importance of intrinsic motivation in sport was expressed in the response of star shortstop Ozzie Guillen of the Chicago White Sox to the idea of including incentive clauses in his playing contract: "I don't want incentives to play, because I like to play. I don't want to go to the All-Star Game because of money" (Isle, 1988, p. 6). As you can see, motivational factors important in other areas of life are also important in sport. Athletes perform best at an optimal level of arousal, which varies with the individual, the sport, and the position. And athletes are influenced by their achievement motive, with their level of motivation enhanced by their need for achievement, proper use of goal setting, and reliance on intrinsic, instead of extrinsic, rewards.

SUMMARY

SOURCES OF MOTIVATION

Motivation is the psychological process that arouses, directs, and maintains behavior. The main sources of motivation include genes, drives, and incentives. Though William McDougall's instinct theory failed to achieve scientific credibility, interest in the hereditary basis of social behavior remains alive today in the field of sociobiology. Instinct theories gave way to the drive-reduction theory of Clark Hull, which assumes that physiological deprivation causes a need, which induces a state of tension called a drive. Drive reduction aims at restoring a steady state of physiological equilibrium called homeostasis. While a drive "pushes" you toward a goal, an incentive is an external stimulus that "pulls" you toward a goal. Abraham Maslow arranged human needs into a hierarchy, with the pursuit of higher needs contingent on the satisfaction of lower ones.

THE HUNGER MOTIVE

Hunger impels you to eat to satisfy your body's need for nutrients. Factors that regulate hunger include taste sensations, stretch and nutrient receptors in the stomach, cholecystokinin secreted by the small intestine, glucose receptors in the liver, and insulin secreted by the pancreas. Areas of the hypothalamus regulate hunger by responding to signals from the body and blood. External food-related cues also influence hunger and eating. The most common eating problem is obesity, which is defined as a body weight more than 20 percent above normal for one's height and body build. Obesity depends on the body's set point, basal metabolic rate, responsiveness to external cues, chronic level of blood insulin, and reaction to stress. Two of the most prevalent eating disorders are anorexia nervosa and bulimia nervosa.

THE SEX MOTIVE

Sex serves as both a drive and an incentive. Sex hormones direct sexual development and sexual behavior. Unlike animals, human adult sexual behavior is controlled more by sociocultural factors than by sex hormones. Formal research on human sexuality began with surveys on male and female sexual behavior conducted by Alfred Kinsey and his colleagues. Later research by William Masters and Virginia Johnson showed that males and females share a similar sexual response cycle. Masters and Johnson also developed sex therapy techniques that have been successful in helping men and women overcome sexual dysfunctions, which are chronic problems at phases in the sexual response cycle. Human beings vary in their gender identity and sexual orientation. Transsexuals feel trapped in the body of the wrong sex and may even seek surgery and hormonal treatments to change their appearance. Homosexuals are sexually attracted to members of their own sex.

THE AROUSAL MOTIVE

Arousal is the general level of physiological activation of the brain and body. The Yerkes-Dodson law holds that there is an optimal level of arousal for the performance of a given task, with the optimal level becoming lower as the task becomes more complex. Studies of sensory deprivation by Donald Hebb and his colleagues show that we are motivated to maintain at least a minimal level of sensory stimulation. People also differ in their degree of sensation seeking, which is the motivation to seek high or low levels of sensory stimulation. One theory holds that hyperactive children are high in sensation seeking because they are chronically below their optimal levels of arousal. The theory also holds that autistic children are low in sensation seeking because they are chronically above their optimal levels of arousal.

THE ACHIEVEMENT MOTIVE

The achievement motive is the desire for mastery, excellence, and accomplishment. Henry Murray and Christiana Morgan introduced the Thematic Apperception Test as a means of assessing the need for achievement. People with a high need for achievement persist at tasks in the face of difficulties, delay gratification in the pursuit of long-term goals, and achieve greater success than people with a low need for achievement. They also prefer moderately difficult challenges. Your actual achievement behavior in a given situation depends on the strength of your need for achievement, as well as the incentive value of success, your expectancy of success, and the strength of your fear of failure in that situation. Goal setting increases motivation and improves performance by providing incentives. The best goals are specific and challenging, with short-term goals useful in the pursuit of long-term goals. The intrinsic motivation to engage in an activity can be reduced by extrinsic rewards. Justification theory and cognitive evaluation theory provide different explanations for the detrimental effects of extrinsic rewards.

THINKING ABOUT PSYCHOLOGY: WHAT IS THE RELATIONSHIP BETWEEN MOTIVATION AND SPORT?

Sport psychology is the field that studies the relationship between psychological factors and sport performance, particularly the influence of motivation. In studying motivation and sport, sport psychologists are especially interested in the relationship between arousal and performance. To keep from "choking" during competition, athletes must learn to keep from rising above their optimal levels of arousal. Athletic performance is also affected by other motivational factors, including the need for achievement, goal setting, and intrinsic motivation.

IMPORTANT CONCEPTS

Achievement motive 344
Anorexia nervosa 333
Arousal motive 341
Autism 343
Basal metabolic rate 331
Bulimia nervosa 334
Cognitive evaluation theory 349
Drive 326
Drive-reduction theory 326
Expectancy 346
Extrinsic motivation 348
Fear of failure 347
Gender identity 339
Goal setting 347

Gonads 335
Hierarchy of needs 326
Homeostasis 326
Homosexuality 339
Hyperactivity 343
Incentive 326
Incentive value 346
Instinct 324
Insulin 329
Intrinsic motivation 348
Justification theory 348
Motivation 324
Need 326

Obesity 331
Paraphilia 336
Sensate focusing 339
Sensation seeking 343
Sensory deprivation 342
Set point 330
Sexual dysfunctions 338
Sexual orientation 339
Sexual response cycle 338
Sociobiology 325
Sport psychology 350
Transsexualism 339
Yerkes-Dodson law 341

IMPORTANT PEOPLE

Walter Cannon and A. L. Washburn 328
Donald Hebb 341
Clark Hull 326
Alfred Kinsey 336
John Lilly 343

Abraham Maslow 326
William Masters and Virginia Johnson 337, 338, 339
David McClelland and John Atkinson 344–345
William McDougall 324

Henry Murray and Christiana Morgan 346
John Money 341
Judith Rodin 333
Stanley Schachter 332

RECOMMENDED READINGS

For More on All Aspects of Motivation:

Mook, D. G. (1987). *Motivation: The organization of action.* New York: Norton.
An introduction to important topics in motivation, including several not covered in this chapter.

For More on the Hunger Motive:

Logue, A. W. (1986). *The psychology of eating and drinking.* New York: Freeman.
A readable book about factors involved in normal and abnormal patterns of eating and drinking.

For More on the Sex Motive:

Hyde, J. S. (1986). *Understanding human sexuality* (3rd ed.). New York: McGraw-Hill.
A comprehensive textbook covering all aspects of human sexual development and sexual behavior.

Masters, W. H., Johnson, V. E., & Kolodny, R. C. (1986). *Sex and human loving.* Boston: Little, Brown.
A presentation of Masters and Johnson's research findings and theoretical positions concerning human sexuality.

For More on the Arousal Motive:

Zuckerman, M. (1979). *Sensation seeking: Beyond the optimal level of arousal.* Hillside, NJ: Erlbaum.
A discussion of sensation seeking by an eminent researcher in the field.

For More on the Achievement Motive:

Deci, E. L., & Ryan, R. M. (1985). *Intrinsic motivation and self-determination in human behavior.* New York: Plenum.
A scholarly book discussing research on factors affecting intrinsic and extrinsic motivation.

Spence, J. T. (Ed.). (1983). *Achievement and achievement motives.* New York: W. H. Freeman.
A collection of articles by leading researchers on the topic of achievement motivation.

For More on Sport Psychology:

Cox, R. H. (1990). *Sport psychology: Concepts and applications* (2nd ed.). Dubuque, IA.: Wm. C. Brown.
An up-to-date textbook covering all aspects of sport psychology.

Cratty, B. J. (1989). *Psychology in contemporary sport* (3rd ed.). Englewood Cliffs, NJ: Prentice-Hall.
A textbook of sport psychology dealing with a variety of topics, including motivation and sport.

EMOTION

Chapter Opening Art:
Marc Chagall. *Green Violinist*. 1923–24.

How do you feel? Anxious about an upcoming exam? Depressed by a recent loss? In love with a wonderful person? Angry at a personal affront? Happy at your favorite team's performance? Your feeling would be an *emotion,* from a Latin word meaning "to set in motion." And, like motives such as sex and hunger, emotions such as anger and love motivate behavior. Though it is easy to recognize an emotion, it is difficult to define the concept itself. This led two emotion researchers to observe, "Everyone knows what an emotion is, until asked to give a definition" (Fehr & Russell, 1984, p. 464).

Despite the difficulty of defining the concept of an emotion, most psychologists agree that **emotion** is a motivated state marked by physiological arousal, expressive behavior, and mental experience (Buck, 1985). Consider an angry man. His heart might pound (a sign of physiological arousal), he might grit his teeth (an expressive behavior), and he might feel enraged (a mental experience). As you learned in chapter 2, in trying to explain psychological phenomena some psychologists prefer to study the biological level, others the behavioral level, and still others the mental level.

THE PHYSIOLOGY OF EMOTION

What is the physiological basis of emotion? To answer this question psychologists look to the autonomic nervous system and the brain.

The Autonomic Nervous System

Both your emotional expression and your emotional experience depend on physiological arousal, which reflects activity in your **autonomic nervous system.** Figure 11.1 illustrates the functions of the two branches of the autonomic nervous system: the **sympathetic nervous system** and the **parasympathetic nervous system.** As mentioned in chapter 3, the interplay of these two systems contributes to the ebb and flow of emotions. Activation of the sympathetic nervous system may stimulate the **fight-or-flight response,** which evolved to enable our prehistoric ancestors to meet sudden physical threats (whether from nature, animals, or people) by either confronting them or running away from them. After a threat has been met or avoided, the sympathetic nervous system becomes less active and the parasympathetic nervous system becomes more active, calming the body.

The fight-or-flight response is triggered by psychological, as well as physical, threats—such as academic demands that we feel inadequate to meet. To appreciate the role of the autonomic nervous system in the emotional response to a psychological threat, imagine that you are about to give a classroom speech that you did not adequately prepare. As you walk to your class, you experience anxiety associated with physiological arousal induced by your sympathetic nervous system.

As you enter the classroom, you become more alert and energetic as your circulatory system diverts blood rich in oxygen and other nutrients from your

Emotion A motivated state marked by physiological arousal, expressive behavior, and mental experience.

Autonomic Nervous System The division of the peripheral nervous system that controls automatic, involuntary physiological processes.

Sympathetic Nervous System The division of the autonomic nervous system that arouses the body to prepare it for action. *activates*

Parasympathetic Nervous System The division of the autonomic nervous system that calms the body and serves maintenance functions.

Fight-or-Flight Response A state of physiological arousal that enables us to meet sudden threats by either confronting them or running away from them.

FIGURE 11.1
The Autonomic Nervous System
Emotional responses involve the interplay of the two branches of the autonomic nervous system: the sympathetic nervous system, which tends to arouse us, and the parasympathetic nervous system, which tends to return us to a calmer state.

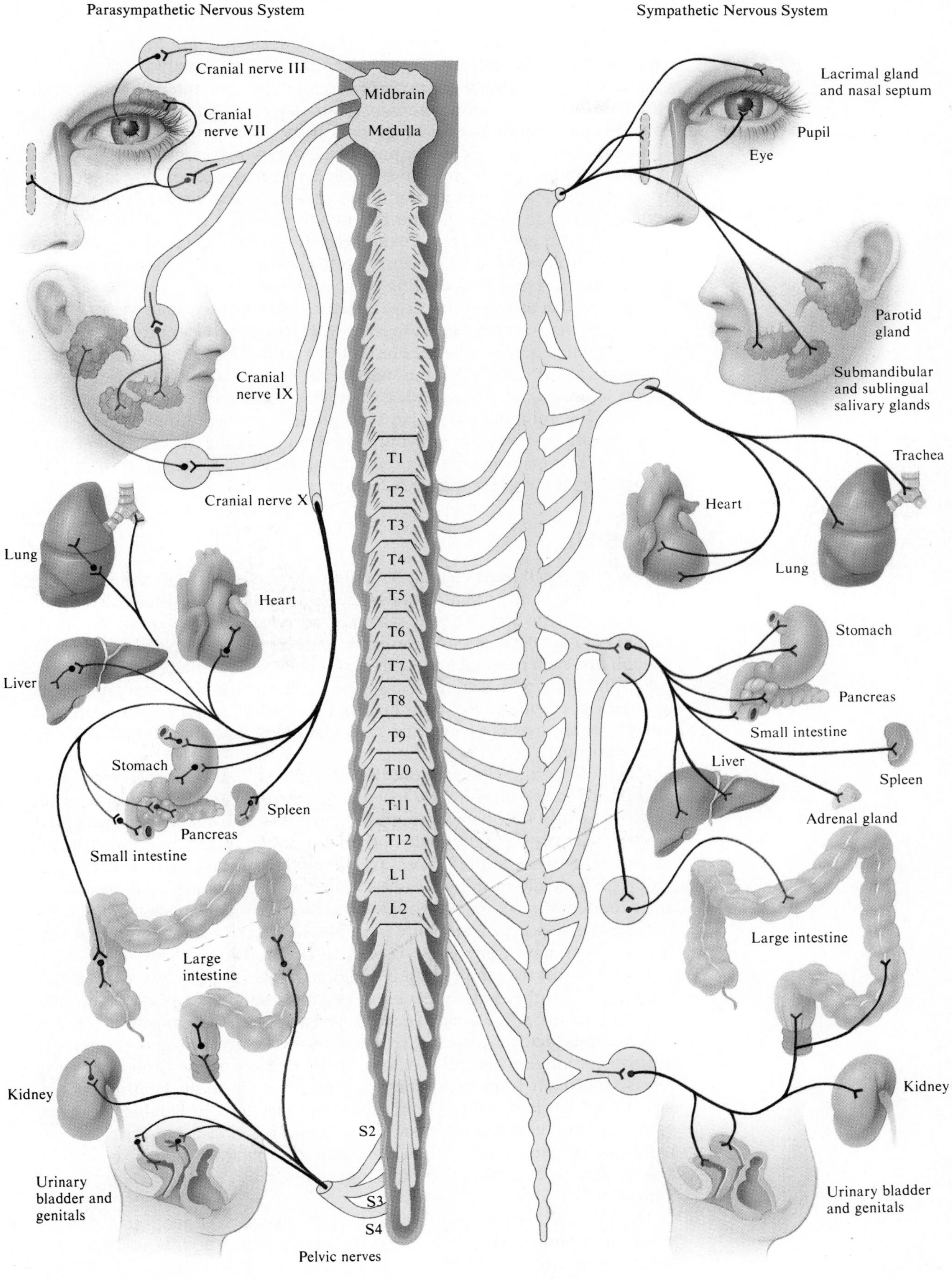

Parasympathetic Nervous System

Sympathetic Nervous System

Cranial nerve III

Cranial nerve VII

Cranial nerve IX

Cranial nerve X

Midbrain

Medulla

T1
T2
T3
T4
T5
T6
T7
T8
T9
T10
T11
T12
L1
L2

S2
S3
S4

Pelvic nerves

Lung

Liver

Heart

Stomach

Spleen

Pancreas

Small intestine

Large intestine

Kidney

Urinary bladder and genitals

Lacrimal gland and nasal septum

Pupil

Eye

Parotid gland

Submandibular and sublingual salivary glands

Trachea

Heart

Lung

Stomach

Pancreas

Small intestine

Liver

Spleen

Adrenal gland

Large intestine

Kidney

Urinary bladder and genitals

Kasnot

stomach and intestines to your brain and skeletal muscles. Your energy increases as your liver releases sugar. Your heart pounds rapidly and strongly in response to the hormone *epinephrine* secreted by your adrenal glands. Your bronchioles dilate to permit more oxygen-rich air to enter your lungs, and you breathe more rapidly as your lungs work harder to expel carbon dioxide.

A classmate may notice your pupils dilating, which improves your vision by letting more light into your eyes. And you may notice your mouth becoming dry, goose bumps appearing on your arms, and beads of perspiration forming on your forehead. Your dry mouth reflects a marked reduction in salivation. Your goose bumps are caused by hairs standing on end—a remnant of threat displays made by our furry prehistoric ancestors. And your perspiration provides a means of cooling off your aroused body.

Suppose that as you sit in class in this anxious, aroused state, your teacher announces that a surprise guest speaker will lecture for the entire class period. You immediately feel relieved and notice your arousal subsides—in part, a consequence of activity in your autonomic nervous system. Your mind becomes less alert, your muscles less energetic, your heartbeat less noticeable, and your breathing more regular. Your pupils constrict to their normal size, your mouth becomes moist, your goose bumps disappear, and you stop sweating. You may become so profoundly relaxed and relieved that you fall asleep during the guest speaker's lecture.

The Brain

As you may recall from chapter 3, autonomic nervous system arousal is regulated by the brain structure called the *hypothalamus*. You may also recall that activity in the brain's *limbic system* and *cerebral cortex* plays an important role in emotional experience. Research findings have converged on the conclusion that each cerebral hemisphere is specialized for the processing of different emotions, with the left hemisphere more involved in positive emotions and the right hemisphere more involved in negative emotions. But keep in mind that this does not mean that particular emotions are processed *solely* in one hemisphere or the other.

Much of our knowledge about the role of each hemisphere in emotional experience comes from studies that have measured the relative degree of activity in each hemisphere during emotional arousal. A study that recorded electrical activity from the brains of ten-month-old infants found that hemispheric differences in the processing of emotions appear early. Greater activation of the left hemisphere was associated with a pleasant facial expression and a tendency to approach people. In contrast, greater activation of the right hemisphere was associated with an unpleasant facial expression and a tendency to withdraw from people (Fox & Davidson, 1988).

Evidence that the left hemisphere is more related to positive emotions and the right hemisphere more related to negative emotions has also been provided by studies of brain damage. Because each cerebral hemisphere inhibits the emotional activity of the other, we normally experience neither intensely positive nor intensely negative emotions. But damage to one hemisphere may release the other from its inhibition. Damage to the right hemisphere, releasing the left hemisphere from inhibition, may lead to laughing, elation, optimism, and other signs of positive emotion. In contrast, damage to the left hemisphere, releasing the right hemisphere from inhibition, may lead to crying, worry, pessimism, and other signs of negative emotion (Leventhal & Tomarken, 1986).

The brain also modulates emotions by its secretion of neurotransmitters, which alter our moods by affecting neuronal activity. The role of these neurotransmitters in moods and mood disorders will be discussed in chapter 14.

For now, consider the role of *endorphins,* the brain's own "opiates" (see chapters 3 and 4), which contribute to pain relief and feelings of euphoria. The emotional thrill we experience from a dance performance, a scene in a movie, or a musical passage may rely on endorphin activity. This was demonstrated in a study of college students who listened to a musical passage and then received an injection of either naloxone (a drug that will block the effects of endorphins) or a placebo (in this case, a saline solution that will not block the effect of endorphins).

Neither the subject nor the experimenter knew whether the subject had received naloxone or a placebo (an application of the **double-blind technique**). This prevented subject bias or experimenter bias from affecting the results. After receiving the injection, the subject again listened to the musical passage. When asked to estimate the intensity of their emotional thrill in response to the music, the subjects who had received naloxone reported a significant decrease in intensity. The subjects who had received a placebo reported no such decrease. Because naloxone blocks the effects of endorphins, but a placebo does not, the findings support the role of endorphins in positive emotional experiences (Goldstein, 1980).

Double-Blind Technique A research technique in which neither the experimenter nor the subjects know which subjects have received an active treatment and which subjects have received a placebo treatment.

THE EXPRESSION OF EMOTION

How do you know how your fellow students feel? And how do they know how *you* feel? Because our emotional experiences are private, they cannot be directly observed by other people. Instead, emotions must be inferred from descriptions of them or from expressive behaviors. Behaviors that express emotions include vocal qualities, body movements, and facial expressions.

Vocal Qualities

When you speak, your voice, as well as your words, conveys emotion. In fact, you can use the same spoken words to express different emotions by simply altering the vocal qualities of your speech. Thus, the same statement can sound sincere or sarcastic, depending on its vocal qualities. We communicate our emotional state in part through changes in the rate, pitch, and loudness of our

Endorphins and Emotions The emotional thrills experienced by these concertgoers may be caused by the release of endorphins in their brains.

Conveying Emotions through Gestures Every culture conveys emotions through gestures, but a gesture that has a positive meaning in one culture may have a negative meaning in another (Ekman et al., 1984).

speech. For example, when you are happy your voice will show an increase in pitch (just recall the last time you heard the voices of two people greeting each other after being apart for a long time). Changes in vocal qualities indicative of changes in emotion tend to be consistent from one person to another and from one culture to another (Frick, 1985). Perhaps these common vocal patterns evolved in our prehistoric, prelanguage ancestors as a universal means of communicating emotional states in everyday social interactions.

Body Movements

If you have observed the gestures of impatient drivers in heavy traffic on a hot summer day, you know that body movements may convey emotions. Even movements of the whole body may do so. The performances of ballet dancer Mikhail Baryshnikov or basketball player Magic Johnson are especially appealing because their movements convey emotions.

But how do we know that we are responding to their movements rather than simply to their facial expressions or physical appearances? The importance of body movements in expressing emotion has been demonstrated in studies that have eliminated other emotional cues. In one study (Walk & Homan, 1984), college students watched a videotape of people performing dances portraying different emotions. To eliminate the influence of facial expressions and physical appearance, the dancers wore lights on their joints and danced in total darkness. Thus, the subjects saw only the movement of lights. Nonetheless, the subjects accurately identified the emotions represented by the dances. This indicates that the emotional cues provided by body movements are distinct from those provided by facial expressions or physical appearance.

Facial Expressions

Philip D. Chesterfield, an eighteenth-century British statesman, noted that our faces give away our emotions: "Look in the face of the person to whom you are speaking if you wish to know his real sentiments, for he can command his words more easily than his countenance." Research has supported his belief by showing that facial expressions convey both the intensity and the pleasantness of our emotional states. Many card players realize this, leading them to maintain an expressionless "poker face" to avoid revealing the strength of their hands. But card players should note that any judgment of emotions from a person's facial expression depends, in part, on the facial expressions of other people who may be present. For example, an expressionless face will seem sad when presented next to a happy face, but it will seem happy when presented next to a sad face (Russell & Fehr, 1987). So, if everyone else maintains a sad face, the person with a poker face will seem happy—as though he or she has a good hand. And if everyone else maintains a happy face, the person with a poker face will seem sad—as though he or she has a poor hand.

Charles Darwin (1872/1965) believed that facial expressions evolved to communicate emotions and help individuals distinguish friend from foe. His belief was supported in an experiment that measured how quickly subjects could detect an angry or happy face in a crowd (Hansen & Hansen, 1988). The subjects reported that a single angry face seemed to emerge from the crowd faster than a single happy face. The results supported the subjects' impressions. They were able to detect an angry face faster than a happy face. Why might we have evolved the ability to detect angry faces more quickly than other faces? Perhaps because it promotes our survival by motivating us to take more immediate action to confront or to escape from a person displaying an angry face.

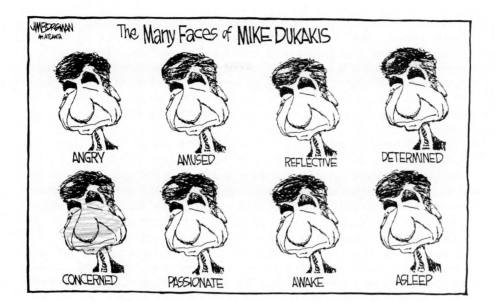

The Poker Face and Politics
During the 1988 presidential campaign, Michael Dukakis was criticized for not being emotionally expressive. Evidently, a poker face may be advantageous to a gambler but not to a presidential candidate.
Reprinted with special permission of King Features Syndicate, Inc.

FIGURE 11.2
The Universality of Facial Expressions Support for the inborn, universal nature of facial expressions representing the basic emotions comes from studies showing similar facial expressions in people from different cultures, such as these people from Kenya, the United States, and Peru.

Additional evidence for Darwin's belief that facial expressions are inborn evolutionary adaptations comes from studies showing that young infants produce facial expressions for the basic emotions of joy, fear, anger, disgust, sadness, and surprise, as shown in figure 11.2 (Izard, Huebner, Risser, McGinnes, & Dougherty, 1980). The hereditary basis of facial expressions was supported decades ago in a case study of a ten-year-old girl who had been born deaf and blind. Despite her inability to see normal facial expressions or to receive oral instructions on how to form them, she displayed appropriate facial expressions for the basic emotions (Goodenough, 1932).

Further support for Darwin's evolutionary view of facial expressions comes from studies showing that facial expressions for the basic emotions are common across cultures. The subjects in one study were members of the Fore tribe of New Guinea, who had almost no contact with Westerners prior to the study

FIGURE 11.3
Can a Smile Influence Voters?
During the 1984 presidential campaign, Peter Jennings showed more positive facial expressions when speaking about Ronald Reagan than when speaking about Walter Mondale. Tom Brokaw and Dan Rather showed no such bias. People who watched Jennings were more likely to vote for Reagan than were people who watched Brokaw or Rather (Mullen et al., 1986). Could those voters have been influenced by Jennings's smiles?

(Ekman & Friesen, 1971). The tribesmen listened to descriptions of a series of emotion-arousing situations representing joy, fear, anger, disgust, sadness, or surprise. The descriptions included situations such as, "He is looking at something that smells bad" and "Her friends have come and she is happy." After each description, the tribesmen viewed a set of three photographs of Western faces expressing different emotions, from which they selected the face portraying the emotion of the person in the description they had just heard.

The tribesmen correctly identified expressions portraying joy, anger, sadness, and disgust but failed to distinguish between expressions portraying fear and surprise. Perhaps the tribesmen's expressions for fear and surprise did not differ because similar situations evoke both fear and surprise in their culture (such as an enemy or a wild animal suddenly appearing from out of the jungle). This study was replicated, with similar results, in a more recent study of people in ten different cultures from around the world (Ekman et al., 1987).

Regardless of the extent to which evolution has determined our facial expressions, they play an important role in our everyday lives—and may even influence our political views. In fact, the facial expressions of our favorite television anchors may affect our preferences for political candidates (figure 11.3). A study conducted during the 1984 presidential campaign found that NBC's Tom Brokaw, CBS's Dan Rather, and ABC's Peter Jennings did not show biases in what they said about Ronald Reagan and Walter Mondale. But Jennings showed a facial bias. Unlike Brokaw and Rather, Jennings exhibited significantly more positive facial expressions when speaking about Reagan than when speaking about Mondale.

A telephone survey found that voters who regularly watched Jennings were significantly more likely to vote for Reagan than were those who watched Brokaw or Rather. The researchers concluded that Jennings's biased facial expressions may have made some viewers more favorable toward Reagan. Of course, as emphasized in chapter 2, we must be careful to avoid making hasty inferences about causation. Perhaps Jennings's facial expressions did not affect viewers' preferences. Instead, those who already favored Reagan may have preferred to watch Jennings because he smiled more when talking about him (Mullen et al., 1986).

THE EXPERIENCE OF EMOTION

Though we have hundreds of words for emotions, there seem to be only a few basic emotions, from which all others are derived. One of the most influential models of emotion, devised by Robert Plutchik (1980), considers joy, fear, anger, disgust, sadness, surprise, acceptance, and anticipation to be the basic emotions. More complex emotions arise from mixtures of these basic ones (figure 11.4).

Charles Darwin assumed that the basic emotions evolved because they promoted our survival. For example, disgust (which means "bad taste") may have evolved to prevent us from ingesting poisonous substances. This may explain why human beings in all cultures exhibit an early feeling of disgust at the sight and smell of feces—the "universal disgust object" (Rozin & Fallon, 1987). Note that disgust involves each of the major aspects of emotion: physiological change (intestinal contractions causing nausea), expressive behavior (a contorted face), and mental experience (a feeling of revulsion). And the facial expression of disgust now has a social meaning as well, expressing revulsion at something that someone has said or done.

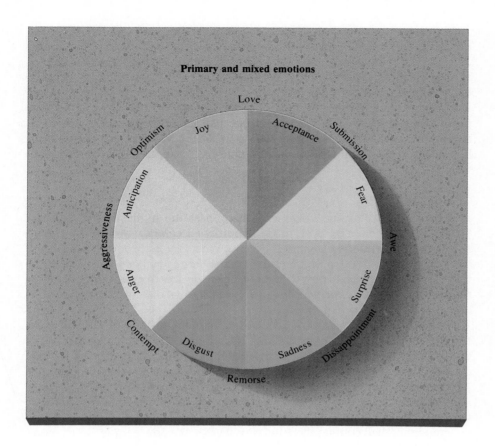

Primary and mixed emotions

FIGURE 11.4
Plutchik's Emotion Wheel
According to Robert Plutchik (1980), there are eight primary emotions, composed of four pairs of opposites: joy and sadness, acceptance and disgust, fear and anger, and surprise and anticipation. We cannot experience opposites simultaneously. Thus, you could not feel joyful and sad at the same time. The closer together that emotions are on the wheel, the more similar they are to each other. Mixtures of adjacent emotions produce other emotions. For example, the mixture of joy and acceptance produces love, and the mixture of anger and disgust produces contempt.

REPRINTED WITH PERMISSION FROM PSYCHOLOGY TODAY MAGAZINE. Copyright © 1980 (PT Partners, L.P.).

The experience of emotion varies in both its intensity and its pleasantness. There is also a positive correlation between the intensity levels of positive and negative emotions (Diener, Larsen, Levine, & Emmons, 1985). While people who tend to experience intensely pleasant emotions (such as elation) also tend to experience intensely unpleasant emotions (such as despair), people who tend to experience mildly pleasant emotions (such as gladness) also tend to experience mildly unpleasant emotions (such as disappointment). Some people, particularly introspective people, are prone to experience unpleasant emotions, apparently because they brood about the negative side of events, others, and themselves. Perhaps people who are prone to experience pleasant emotions do so because they dwell less on the negative side of life (Watson & Clark, 1984).

Folk wisdom holds that just as certain people are prone to experience unpleasant emotions, certain days—particularly so-called blue Monday—are more likely to induce unpleasant emotions. A study of the "blue Monday effect" had people who insisted that their moods were lowest on Mondays keep daily diaries of their emotional states (Stone, Hedges, Neale, & Satin, 1985). The results showed that a given person's emotional state tended to be similar on Monday, Tuesday, Wednesday, and Thursday. But, as you might expect, the person's emotional state on weekends—Friday, Saturday, and Sunday—tended to be more positive than on weekdays. Evidently our "blue Mondays" owe their "blueness" to a return to our normal weekday emotional state, rather than to something unique about Mondays. In essence, we may have "blue Mondays," but we also have equally blue Tuesdays, Wednesdays, and Thursdays. We simply notice the contrast between "bright Sunday" and "blue Monday" more.

FIGURE 11.5
Happiness and the Declaration of Independence Thomas Jefferson believed that happiness was so important that he viewed its pursuit as one of the three unalienable rights of human beings.

Social Comparison Theory
The theory that happiness is the result of estimating that one's life circumstances are more favorable than those of others.

Adaptation Level Theory The theory that happiness depends on comparing one's present circumstances with one's past circumstances.

Though people tend to view pleasant emotions, such as happiness, as normal and unpleasant emotions, such as depression, as abnormal (Sommers, 1984), until the past two decades psychologists had conducted many more studies of unpleasant emotions. In fact, *Psychological Abstracts,* the main library research tool of psychologists, did not include the term "happiness" in its index until 1973 (Diener, 1984). To counter the traditional overemphasis placed on unpleasant emotions, and because unpleasant emotions such as anxiety and depression are discussed elsewhere in this text, this chapter will be limited to discussing the pleasant emotions of happiness and amusement.

Happiness

Philosophers have always considered happiness the highest good (Diener, 1984). Thomas Jefferson even made happiness a central issue in the Declaration of Independence (figure 11.5). But what factors promote happiness? Charles Montesquieu, an eighteenth-century French philosopher, noted: "If one only wished to be happy, this could be easily accomplished; but we wish to be happier than other people, and this is always difficult, for we believe others to be happier than they are."

One of the most influential theories of happiness—**social comparison theory**—shares Montesquieu's assumption about the nature of happiness. The theory considers happiness to be the result of estimating that one's life circumstances are more favorable than those of others, as when you discover that your grade is one of the highest in the class. You can even make yourself happier with your own life by purposely comparing it with the lives of those who are less fortunate (Wills, 1981). One factor in social comparison that is less important than commonly believed is wealth. Wealthy people are no more happy than nonwealthy people, provided that the nonwealthy people have at least the basic necessities of life, such as a job, home, and family (Diener, 1984).

According to **adaptation level theory,** your happiness depends not only on comparing yourself with other people but also on comparing yourself with yourself. Your current happiness depends in part on comparing your present circumstances and your past circumstances. But, as your circumstances improve, your standard of happiness becomes higher. This can have surprising emotional consequences for a person who gains sudden financial success. Life's small pleasures may no longer make that person happy. His or her standard of happiness may become too high, as demonstrated by a study of Illinois state lottery winners (Brickman, Coates, & Janoff-Bulman, 1978). Despite winning from fifty thousand dollars to one million dollars, these winners were no happier than they were in the past. In fact, they found less enjoyment in formerly satisfying everyday activities, such as watching television, shopping for clothes, or talking with a friend. So, although comparing our circumstances with those of less fortunate people may make us happier, improvements in our own circumstances may make us adopt higher and higher standards of happiness—making happiness more and more elusive. In recognizing this problem, the nineteenth-century clergyman Henry Van Dyke remarked, "It is better to desire the things we have than to have the things we desire."

Amusement

Happiness is enhanced by amusement. And amusement is usually evoked by humor, whether from friends, funny movies, situation comedies on television, or stand-up comedians in nightclubs. Though philosophers have long argued about the nature of humor, psychologists have only recently begun to study it scientifically (Martin & Lefcourt, 1984). One surprising finding has been that

humorous people may not feel as extraverted as they act. Consider the class clown, who sees humor in everything. Though that person might be popular, he or she may not be as sociable as you might expect. Instead, the class clown may use humor as a way to avoid close personal relationships. For example, humorous adolescents may use humor to maintain their social distance from other people (Prasinos & Tittler, 1981). You may have been frustrated at one time or another by such people, who joke about everything, rarely converse in a serious manner, and never disclose their personal feelings. Evidence that some people use humor to maintain their social distance may explain anecdotal reports that many comedians, who may appear socially outgoing in public performances, are socially reclusive in their private lives.

Aside from the possibility that humorous people may not be as gregarious as they seem, what makes their humor amusing? One factor is the social context in which humor is expressed. Consider comedians who perform in nightclubs before audiences who have been drinking alcoholic beverages. Comedians who use blunt, simple humor will seem funnier to those who are inebriated, because alcohol tends to make that kind of humor seem more amusing. But comedians who use subtle, complex humor will seem less funny to inebriated people, because alcohol makes that kind of humor seem less amusing (Weaver, Masland, Kharazmi, & Zillmann, 1985). This also means that if you drank a few beers you would probably find a Three Stooges movie more amusing and a Woody Allen movie less amusing.

But what accounts for our responses to humor while in a sober state? According to C. L. Edson, a twentieth-century American newspaper editor, "We love a joke that hands us a pat on the back while it kicks the other fellow down the stairs." Edson's comment indicates that he favored the **disparagement theory** of humor, first put forth by the seventeenth-century English philosopher Thomas Hobbes. Hobbes claimed that we feel amused when humor makes us feel superior to other people (Nevo, 1985). Research supporting Hobbes's position has also found that we are especially amused when we dislike those to whom we are made to feel superior (Wicker, Barron, & Willis, 1980). Satirists, newspaper columnists, and television commentators take this approach by disparaging certain commonly disliked groups, such as greedy lawyers, crooked politicians, and phony evangelists.

Disparagement Theory The theory that humor is amusing when it makes one feel superior to other people.

"It's nice to see he hasn't lost his sense of humor."

Incongruity Theory The theory that humor is amusing when it brings together incompatible ideas in a surprising outcome that violates one's expectations.

In the eighteenth century, the German philosopher Immanuel Kant put forth an alternative theory of humor, the **incongruity theory.** Incongruous humor brings together incompatible ideas in a surprising outcome that violates our expectations (Wicker et al., 1980). As an example of incongruous humor, consider the following statement by Woody Allen: "I don't know if I believe in an afterlife, but I'm taking a change of underwear" (Raskin, 1985). The incongruity theory explains why many jokes require timing and may lose something on the second hearing—bad timing or repetition may destroy the incongruity (Kuhlman, 1985).

Release Theory The theory that humor is amusing when it raises one's level of anxiety and then suddenly lowers it.

Another theory of humor, **release theory,** is based on Sigmund Freud's claim that humor is an outlet for anxiety caused by repressed sexual or aggressive energy, as explained in his book *Jokes and Their Relationship to the Unconscious* (Freud, 1905). Humor may raise your level of anxiety and then suddenly lower it, providing you with relief so pleasurable that it may make you laugh (McCauley, Woods, Coolidge, & Kulick, 1983). This explains the popularity of humor that plays on our sexual anxieties by weaving a story that ends with a sudden punch line, as in the following joke: "A genie grants one wish to an aging spinster. The woman requests that her male cat be transformed into a prince. Once the miracle is performed, the prince says to her with a quavering voice, 'Now aren't you sorry you had me altered?'" (Raskin, 1985).

The field of humor research is relatively young, and more research is required to uncover the factors that make people find amusement in one kind of humor but not in another. Such research might explain why some people (most notably, the French) find Jerry Lewis amusing, while others do not.

THEORIES OF EMOTION

How do we explain emotional experience? Theories of emotion vary in the emphasis they place on physiology, behavior, and cognition.

Theories of Humor Humor researchers have found that humor is based on disparagement, incongruity, or release. If you have seen Don Rickles hurl insults at his audience or Joan Rivers make critical remarks about prominent people, you have observed performances that support the disparagement theory of humor. The incongruity theory of humor gains support from comedians such as Jay Leno, Carol Leifer, and David Letterman, who play on our sense of the absurd to make us laugh. And comedians such as Eddie Murphy and Buddy Hackett, who rely on sexual humor, exemplify the release theory of humor, which assumes that the sudden release of sexual feelings induces a feeling of amusement.

Physiological Theories of Emotion

Though all theories of emotion recognize the importance of physiological factors, certain theories emphasize them. In the late nineteenth century the American psychologist William James (1884) claimed that physiological changes precede emotional experiences. Because a Danish physiologist named Carl Lange made the same claim at about the same time, it became known as the **James-Lange theory** (figure 11.6).

The main implication of the James-Lange theory is that particular emotional events stimulate specific patterns of physiological changes, each evoking a specific emotional experience. According to James (1890/1950, pp. 449–450):

> Common-sense says, we lose our fortune, are sorry and weep; we meet a bear, are frightened and run; we are insulted by a rival, are angry and strike . . . the more rational statement is that we feel sorry because we cry, angry because we strike, afraid because we tremble.

Your own experience may provide circumstantial evidence supporting this theory. If you have ever barely avoided an automobile accident, you may have noticed your pulse racing and your palms sweating and moments later found yourself overcome by fear.

The James-Lange theory provoked criticism from the American physiologist Walter Cannon (1927). First, Cannon noted that individuals had poor ability to perceive many of the physiological changes induced by the sympathetic nervous system. How could the perception of physiological changes be the basis of emotional experiences when we are unable to perceive many of those changes? Second, Cannon noted that different emotions were associated with the same pattern of physiological arousal. How could different emotions be

James-Lange Theory The theory that specific patterns of physiological changes evoke specific emotional experiences.

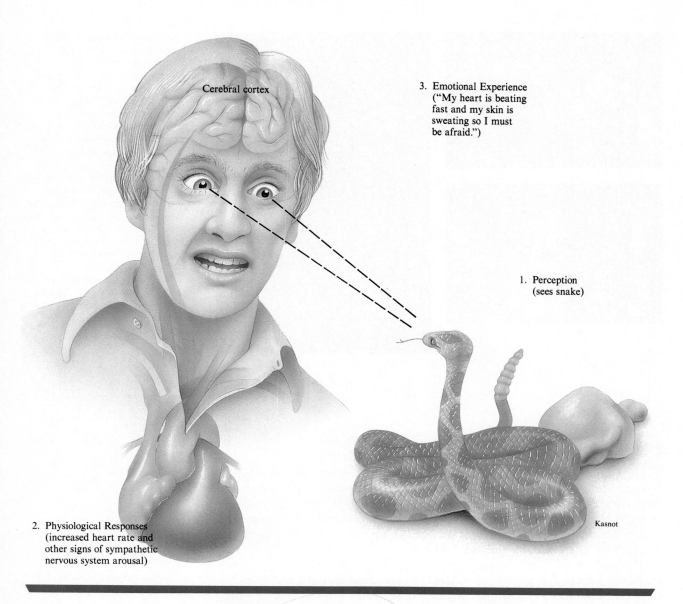

Cerebral cortex

3. Emotional Experience ("My heart is beating fast and my skin is sweating so I must be afraid.")

1. Perception (sees snake)

Kasnot

2. Physiological Responses (increased heart rate and other signs of sympathetic nervous system arousal)

FIGURE 11.6
James-Lange Theory According to the James-Lange theory of emotion, the perception of an event or object induces physiological changes that evoke an emotional experience.

evoked by the same pattern of arousal? And third, Cannon found that physiological changes dependent on the secretion of hormones by the adrenal glands were too slow to be the basis of all emotions. How could a process that takes several seconds account for apparently instantaneous emotional experiences?

Because of Cannon's criticisms, the James-Lange theory fell into disfavor for several decades. But recent research findings have lent some support to it. In one study professional actors were directed to adopt facial expressions representing fear, anger, disgust, sadness, surprise, and happiness (Ekman, Levenson, & Friesen, 1983). The subjects were told which muscles to contract or relax but were not told which emotions they were expressing. Physiological

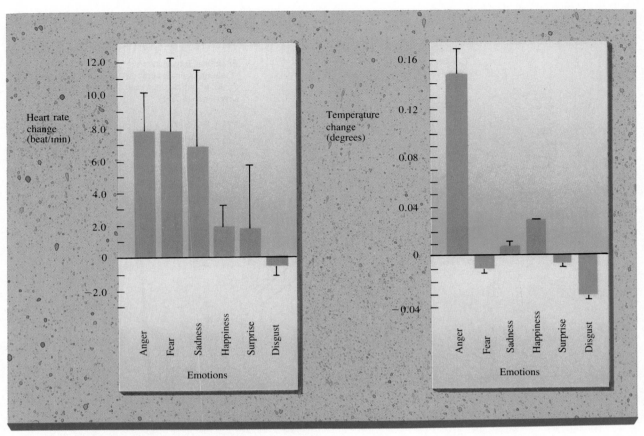

FIGURE 11.7
Specificity of Autonomic Response Patterns As illustrated in this graph, heart rate and finger temperature vary between emotions. For example, anger is associated with marked increases in both heart rate and finger temperature, while fear is associated with a marked increase in heart rate and a slight decrease in finger temperature.

From P. Ekman, et al., "Autonomic Nervous System Activity Distinguishers Among Emotions" in *Science*, Vol. 221:1208–10, 16 September 1983. Copyright 1983 by the AAAS. Reprinted by permission of the publisher and the author.

recordings of heart rate and skin temperature were taken as they maintained the facial expressions. The results showed that the facial expression of fear induced a large increase in heart rate and a slight decrease in finger temperature, while the facial expression of anger induced a large increase in both heart rate and finger temperature (figure 11.7). (Finger temperature varies with the amount of blood flow through the fingers, with a decrease in blood flow causing a decrease in temperature and an increase in blood flow causing an increase in temperature.)

Note that, in everyday language, when we are afraid we have "cold feet" and when we are angry our "blood is boiling." The difference in the patterns of physiological arousal between fear and anger support the James-Lange theory's assumption that emotional changes follow physiological changes and that particular emotions are associated with particular patterns of physiological arousal.

After rejecting the James-Lange theory of emotion, Walter Cannon (1927) and his colleague Philip Bard (1934) put forth their own theory, giving equal

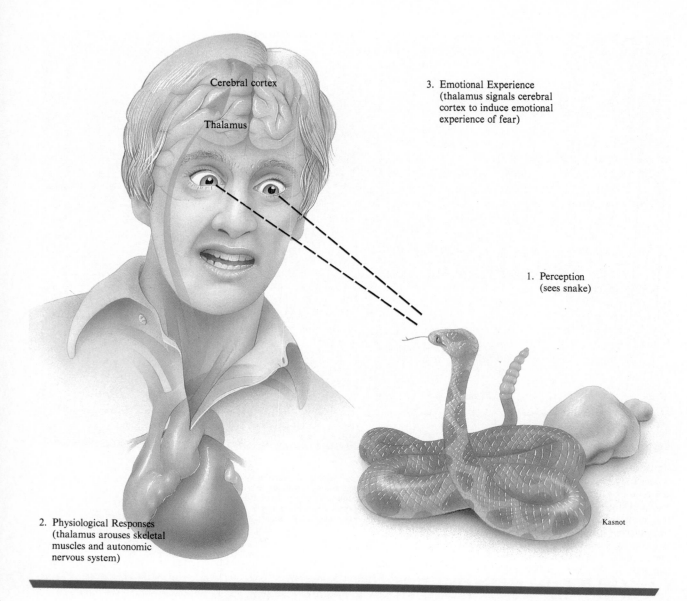

3. Emotional Experience
(thalamus signals cerebral
cortex to induce emotional
experience of fear)

Cerebral cortex

Thalamus

1. Perception
(sees snake)

2. Physiological Responses
(thalamus arouses skeletal
muscles and autonomic
nervous system)

Kasnot

FIGURE 11.8
The Cannon-Bard Theory According to
the Cannon-Bard theory of emotion, when
we perceive an event or object the thalamus
relays that information to the cerebral
cortex, the skeletal muscles, and the organs
of the autonomic nervous system. The
cerebral cortex is responsible for the
particular emotion we experience, while
muscle tension and autonomic nervous
system arousal account for the intensity of
our emotional experience.

Cannon-Bard Theory The
theory that an emotion is
produced when an event or object
is perceived by the thalamus,
which conveys this information
simultaneously to the cerebral
cortex and the skeletal muscles
and autonomic nervous system.

weight to physiological changes and cognitive processes. The **Cannon-Bard theory** claims that an emotion is produced when an event or object is perceived by the brain structure called the thalamus (see chapter 3) which conveys this information simultaneously to the cerebral cortex and to the skeletal muscles and autonomic nervous system (figure 11.8).

The cerebral cortex then uses memories of past experiences to determine the nature of the perceived event or object, providing the subjective experience of emotion. Meanwhile, the muscles and sympathetic nervous system provide the physiological arousal that determines emotional intensity. Unlike the James-Lange theory, the Cannon-Bard theory assumes that different emotions are associated with the same state of physiological arousal. The Cannon-Bard theory has failed to gain research support, because the thalamus does not appear to play the role the researchers envisioned. But if you simply replace the thalamus with the brain's hypothalamus and limbic system, the theory *is* supported by research findings.

Research on victims of spinal cord damage has provided support for the Cannon-Bard theory, while contradicting the James-Lange theory. A study found that even people with spinal cord injuries that prevent them from perceiving their body arousal experience distinct, often intense emotions (Chwalisz, Diener, & Gallagher, 1988). This violates the James-Lange theory's assumption that emotional experience depends on the perception of bodily arousal, while supporting the Cannon-Bard theory's assumption that emotional experience depends mainly on the brain's perception of ongoing events.

In anticipating another theory of emotion, Plato, in his *Phaedo,* states:

> How strange would appear to be this thing that me call pleasure! And how curiously it is related to what is thought to be its opposite, pain! The two will never be found *together* in a man, and yet if you seek the one and obtain it, you are almost bound always to get the other as well, just as though they were both attached to one and the same head. . . . Wherever the one is found, the other follows up behind. So, in my case, since I had pain in my leg as a result of the fetters, pleasure seems to have come to follow it up.

If Plato were alive today, he might favor the **opponent-process theory** of emotion, which holds that the mammalian brain has evolved mechanisms that counteract strong positive or negative emotions by evoking an opposite emotional response (figure 11.9). According to Richard Solomon (1980), who first put forth the theory, the opposing emotion begins sometime after the onset of the first emotion, weakens the first emotion, and lasts longer than the first emotion. If we experience the first emotion on repeated occasions, it grows weaker while the opposing emotion grows stronger.

Opponent-Process Theory The theory that the brain counteracts a strong positive or negative emotion by evoking an opposite emotional response.

Suppose that you took up skydiving. The first time you parachuted from an airplane you would probably feel terror. After surviving the jump, your feeling of terror would be replaced by a feeling of relief. As you jumped again and again, your original feeling of terror would weaken into a milder feeling of anticipation as you prepared to jump. And your initial postjump feeling of relief would eventually intensify into a feeling of exhiliration that would appear more and more quickly after jumping.

The opponent-process theory may also explain the depression that often follows the joy of childbirth and the giddiness that often follows the anxiety

Post-Exam Euphoria The opponent-process theory may explain why college students who, as freshmen, were terrified before their first final exam and relieved after it, will, as seniors, be anxious before a final exam and euphoric after it.

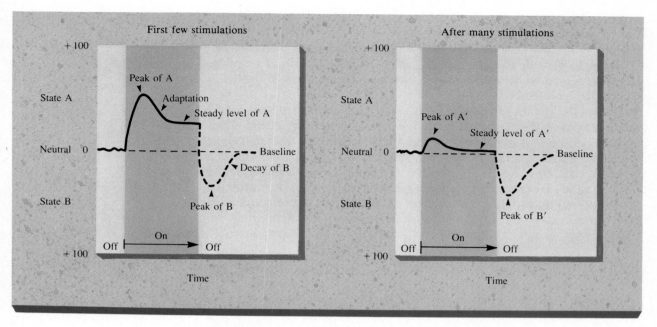

FIGURE 11.9

Opponent-Process Theory According to the opponent-process theory of emotion, when we experience an emotion (A) an opposing emotion (B) will counter the first emotion, dampening the experience of that emotion (as indicated by the steady level of A being lower than the peak of A). As we experience the first emotion (A') on repeated occasions, the opposing emotion (B') becomes stronger and the first emotion weaker, which leads to an even weaker experience of the first emotion (as indicated by the steady level of A' being lower than the peak of A'). For example, the first time you drove on a highway you may have experienced fear, followed by a feeling of relief. As you drove on highways on repeated occasions, your feeling of fear eventually gave way to a feeling of mild arousal (Solomon, 1980).

of final exam week. The theory may even explain why some blood donors become seemingly "addicted" to donating blood. When a person first donates blood he or she may experience fear. After donating blood the person may experience a pleasant feeling known as the "warm glow" effect. If the person repeatedly donates blood, the anticipatory fear weakens and the "warm glow" strengthens, leading the person to donate blood in order to induce the "warm glow" (Piliavin, Callero, & Evans, 1982).

The opponent-process theory implies that our brains are programmed against hedonism, because people who experience intense pleasure are doomed to experience intense displeasure. This provides support for those who favor the "happy medium"—moderation in everything, including emotional experiences.

Behavioral Theories of Emotion

Benjamin Franklin said, "A cheerful face is nearly as good for an invalid as healthy weather." Have you ever received the advice, "Put on a happy face" or "Keep a stiff upper lip" from people trying to help you overcome adversity? Both of these bits of advice are common-sense versions of the **facial-feedback theory** of emotion, which holds that our facial expressions affect our emotional experiences. As you learned in the discussion of the James-Lange theory of emotion, adopting a facial expression characteristic of a particular emotion may induce that emotion (Ekman, Levenson, & Friesen, 1983). But

Facial-Feedback Theory The theory that particular facial expressions induce particular emotional experiences.

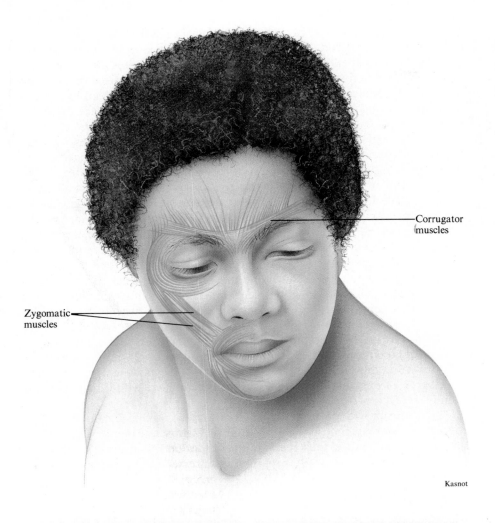

Zygomatic muscles

Corrugator muscles

Kasnot

FIGURE 11.10
The Facial-Feedback Theory
According to the facial-feedback theory of emotion, particular patterns of sensory feedback from facial expressions evoke particular emotions. Thus, sensory feedback from the corrugator muscles, which are active when we frown, may contribute to unpleasant emotional experiences. Similarly, sensory feedback from the zygomatic muscles, which are active when we smile, may contribute to pleasant emotional experiences.

unlike the James-Lange theory, which is primarily concerned with the effect of sympathetic nervous system arousal on emotion, the facial-feedback theory is limited to the effect of facial expressions.

The facial-feedback theory was put forth in 1907 by the French physician Israel Waynbaum and recently has been restated in various versions. Waynbaum assumed that particular facial expressions alter the flow of blood to particular regions of the brain, thereby evoking particular emotional experiences. For example, smiling might increase the flow of blood to regions of the brain that elevate mood. It remains for research to test Waynbaum's theory (Zajonc, 1985).

Contemporary facial-feedback theorists, led by Paul Ekman, assume that evolution has endowed us with facial expressions that provide different patterns of sensory feedback of muscle tension levels to the brain, thereby evoking different emotions (figure 11.10). Support for the theory has come from studies that have found that emotional experiences follow facial expressions rather than precede them, and that sensory neurons convey information from facial muscles directly to the hypothalamus, which plays an important role in emotional arousal (Zajonc, 1985).

Despite support from many studies, the facial-feedback theory has not received universal support. The effect of facial feedback on emotional experience tends to be small (Matsumoto, 1987), and some studies have found that emotional experience depends more on feedback from internal organs than on feedback from facial muscles (Buck, 1980). Apparently, feedback from facial expressions is just one of several factors governing our emotional experiences.

Though facial expressions may not be the sole cause of emotions, they can contribute to emotional experience. (Try smiling and then frowning and note the subtle difference they induce in your mood.) In one study, female subjects were asked to imagine three pleasant scenes and three unpleasant scenes (McCanne & Anderson, 1987). The three pleasant scenes were, "You get a 4.0 grade point average," "You inherit a million dollars," and "You meet the man of your dreams." The three unpleasant scenes were, "Your mother dies," "You lose a really close friendship," and "You lose a limb in an accident."

The subjects imagined each scene three times. The first time they simply imagined the scene. The second time they imagined the scene while maintaining increased muscle tension in one of two different muscle groups, either muscles that control smiling or muscles that control frowning. The subjects learned to tense only the target muscles through the use of biofeedback (discussed in chapter 6). The third time they imagined the scene, the subjects were instructed to suppress muscle tension in either their smiling muscles or their frowning muscles. On each occasion, the subjects were asked to report the degree of enjoyment or distress they experienced while imagining the scene.

The results provided partial support for the facial-feedback theory. Subjects reported less enjoyment when imagining pleasant scenes while suppressing activity in their smiling muscles. And they reported less distress when imagining unpleasant scenes while suppressing activity in their frowning muscles.

Cognitive Theories of Emotion

The most recent theories of emotion emphasize the importance of cognition—thinking. They assume that our emotional experiences depend on our subjective interpretation of situations in which we find ourselves. Stanley Schachter's **two-factor theory** views emotional experience as the outcome of two factors: physiological arousal and the attribution of a cause for that arousal (figure 11.11). According to Schachter, when you experience physiological arousal, you search for its source. Your attribution of a cause for your arousal determines the emotion that you experience. For example, if you experience intense physiological arousal in the presence of an appealing person, you might attribute your arousal to that person, and, as a result, feel that you are in love with him or her.

The two-factor theory resembles the James-Lange theory in assuming that emotional experience follows physiological arousal. But it is different from the James-Lange theory in assuming that all emotions involve similar patterns of physiological arousal, which makes it similar to the Cannon-Bard theory. But while the Cannon-Bard theory assumes that emotional experience and physiological arousal occur simultaneously, the two-factor theory assumes that emotion follows the attribution of a cause for physiological arousal.

The original experiment supporting the two-factor theory provided evidence that when we experience physiological arousal we seek to identify its source, which, in turn, determines our emotional experience (Schachter & Singer, 1962). Male college students who served as subjects were told that they were getting an injection of a new vitamin called "Suproxin" to assess its effect on visual perception. In reality, they received an injection of the hor-

Two-Factor Theory The theory that emotional experience is the outcome of physiological arousal and the attribution of a cause for that arousal.

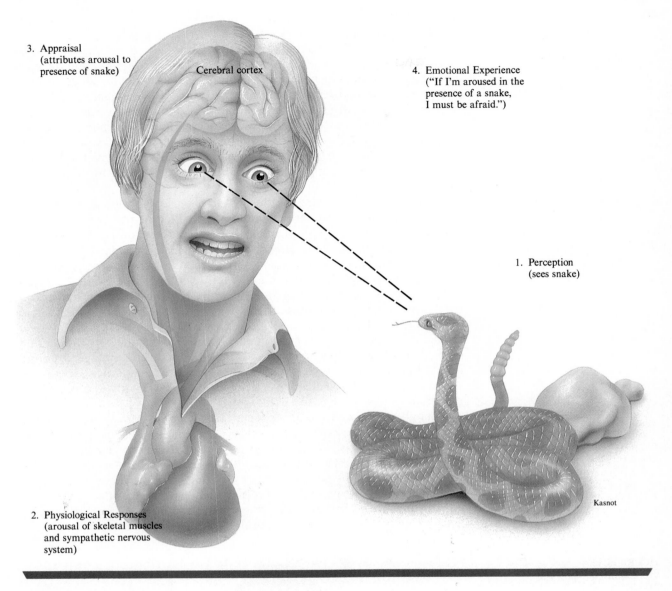

3. Appraisal
(attributes arousal to
presence of snake)

Cerebral cortex

4. Emotional Experience
("If I'm aroused in the
presence of a snake,
I must be afraid.")

1. Perception
(sees snake)

2. Physiological Responses
(arousal of skeletal muscles
and sympathetic nervous
system)

Kasnot

FIGURE 11.11
The Two-Factor Theory According to the two-factor theory of emotion, when we experience physiological arousal we seek its cause in our immediate situation. The nature of the situation determines the emotional label that we attach to our arousal.

mone epinephrine, which activates the sympathetic nervous system. The epinephrine caused hand tremors, flushed faces, pounding hearts, and rapid breathing. Some subjects were told to expect these changes (the *informed group*). Some subjects were told to expect itching, numb feet, and headache (the *misinformed group*), and some were told nothing about the effects (the *uninformed group*).

Each subject then waited in a room with the experimenter's accomplice, a male who acted either happy or angry. When acting happy, the accomplice was cheerful and threw paper airplanes, played with a hula hoop, and shot paper wads into a wastebasket. When acting angry, the accomplice was upset, stomped around, and complained about a questionnaire given by the experimenter, which included questions about the bathing habits of the respondent's family and the sex life of his mother.

The subject's emotional response was assessed by observing him through a one-way mirror and by having him complete a questionnaire about his feelings. The results showed that the informed subjects were unaffected by the accomplice, while the misinformed subjects and uninformed subjects experienced emotions similar to those of the accomplice. Schachter concluded that the misinformed subjects and the uninformed subjects attributed their physiological arousal to the situation they were in, responding positively when the accomplice acted happy and responding negatively when the accomplice acted angry.

Since the original studies of the two-factor theory in the early 1960s, research has produced inconsistent findings. Consider the theory's assumption that unexplained physiological arousal can just as well provoke feelings of joy as feelings of sadness, depending on the person's interpretation of the source of the arousal. This was contradicted by a study in which subjects received injections of epinephrine without being informed of its true effects. The subjects tended to experience negative emotions, regardless of their immediate social environment. Even those in the presence of a happy person tended to experience unpleasant emotions (Marshall & Zimbardo, 1979). A review of research on Schachter's two-factor theory concluded that the only assumption of the theory that has been consistently supported is that physiological arousal misattributed to an outside source will *intensify* an emotional experience. There is little evidence that such a misattribution will *cause* an emotional experience (Reisenzein, 1983).

Though Schachter's two-factor theory has failed to gain strong support, it has stimulated interest in the cognitive basis of emotion. The purest cognitive theory of emotion is the **cognitive appraisal theory** of Richard Lazarus (1984), which downplays the role of physiological arousal. The cognitive appraisal theory, like the two-factor theory, assumes that our emotion at a given time depends on our interpretation of the situation we are in at that time (figure 11.12). But, unlike the two-factor theory, the cognitive appraisal theory ignores the role of physiological arousal.

Cognitive Appraisal Theory
The theory that one's emotion at a given time depends on one's interpretation of the situation one is in at that time.

FIGURE 11.12
The Cognitive Appraisal Theory According to the cognitive appraisal theory of emotion, our interpretation of events, rather the events themselves, determines our emotional experiences. Thus, the same event may evoke different emotions in different people, as in this exhilarated boy and his terrified mother riding on a ferris wheel.

This view of emotion is not new. In *Hamlet,* Shakespeare wrote, "There is nothing either good or bad, but thinking makes it so." So, you might appraise an impending exam as threatening, while your friend might appraise it as challenging. Consequently, the exam might make you feel anxious while making your friend feel eager.

An early study by Lazarus and his colleagues supported the cognitive appraisal theory of emotion (Speisman, Lazarus, Mordkoff, & Davison, 1964). The subjects watched a film about a tribal ritual in which adolescents had incisions made in their penises. The subjects' level of emotional arousal was measured by recording their heart rate and skin conductance (an increase in the electrical conductivity of the skin caused by sweating). Subjects watched the same film but heard different soundtracks. Those in the *silent group* saw the film without a soundtrack. Those in the *traumatic group* were told that the procedure was extremely painful and emotionally distressing. Those in the *intellectualization group* were told about the procedure in a detached, matter-of-fact way, with no mention of feelings. And those in the *denial group* were told that the procedure was not painful and that the boys were overjoyed by the ritual because it signified their entrance into manhood.

Recordings of the subjects' physiological arousal showed that the traumatic group experienced greater arousal than the silent group, which, in turn, experienced greater arousal than the denial and intellectualization groups (figure 11.13). These findings indicate that subjective appraisal of the situation, rather than the objective situation itself, accounted for the subjects' emotional arousal.

Though more recent studies have provided additional support for the assumption that your interpretation of a situation will affect your emotional state

FIGURE 11.13
Cognitive Appraisal and Emotion The graph shows that the emotional responses of subjects who viewed a film of a ritual in which adolescents had incisions made in their penises depended on the nature of the sound track. Those who heard a sound track that described the procedure as traumatic experienced the greatest emotional arousal (Speisman et al., 1964).

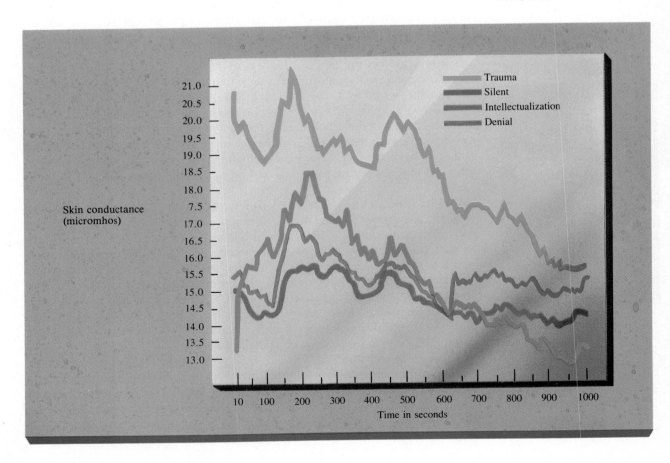

(Smith & Ellsworth, 1985), the cognitive appraisal theory has been challenged by Robert Zajonc (1984) and others, who insist that cognitive appraisal is not essential to the experience of emotion. For example, you have probably taken an instant liking or disliking to a person without knowing why. And, as you may recall from the discussion of subliminal perception in chapter 5, research findings show that we can respond emotionally to stimuli of which we are unaware, indicating that emotional experience can take place without cognitive appraisal.

What can we conclude from the variety of contradictory theories of emotion? The best that we can conclude is that none of them is adequate to explain emotion, though each describes a process that contributes to it. Moreover, when considered together, the theories illustrate the importance of the physiological, expressive, and experiential components of emotion.

THINKING ABOUT PSYCHOLOGY

Do Lie Detectors Tell the Truth?

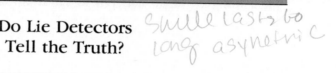 *smile lasts 60 long asymetric*

As discussed earlier, in everyday life we may infer a person's emotional state from his or her expressive behavior. We may even infer whether the person is lying. If you have ever detected a seemingly phony smile from a salesperson or politician, you probably noted certain cues indicating that the smile was insincere. Perhaps the smile lasted too long—a sign of insincerity. Or perhaps you noticed that the smile was asymmetrical. Posed expressions, including smiles, will usually be more pronounced on the left side of the face than on the right side (Rinn, 1984).

The detection of lies from expressive behavior has a long history. The Old Testament describes a case in which King Solomon resolved a dispute between two women claiming to be the mother of the same infant. Solomon proposed cutting the infant in half, then giving one half to each woman. One woman calmly agreed to this, but the other pleaded with Solomon to give the infant to her adversary. Solomon reasoned that the pleading woman had to be the real mother, because she was willing to lose the infant rather than see it killed.

While King Solomon inferred lying from expressive behavior, lie detection has historically been based on the assumption that liars will display increased physiological arousal. In the fifteenth century, interrogators for the Inquisition required suspected heretics to swallow pieces of bread and cheese. If the food stuck to the person's palate, he or she was considered guilty. As you will recall, the arousal of the sympathetic nervous system that accompanies emotionality reduces salivation, leading to a dry mouth. A dry mouth would make it more difficult to swallow food. As you can imagine, a person brought before the Inquisition would experience increased arousal—whether or not he or she was a heretic—and would be convicted of heresy.

Modern lie detection began in 1895 with the work of Cesare Lombroso, an Italian criminologist who questioned suspects while recording their heart rate and blood pressure. He assumed that if they showed marked fluctuations in heart rate and blood pressure while responding to questions they were lying (Kleinmuntz & Szucko, 1984b).

The Polygraph Test The polygraph test assumes that patterns of changes in physiological responses, such as heart rate, blood pressure, breathing patterns, and electrodermal activity, will reveal whether a person is lying.

Procedures in Lie Detection

Today the lie detector, or **polygraph test,** typically measures breathing patterns, heart rate, blood pressure, and electrodermal activity. Electrodermal activity reflects the amount of sweating, with greater emotionality associated with more sweating. Though the polygraph test is used to detect lying, no pattern of physiological responses, by itself, indicates lying. Instead, the test detects physiological arousal produced by activation of the sympathetic nervous system. As David Lykken, an expert on lie detection, has said, "The polygraph pens do no special dance when we are lying" (Lykken, 1981, p. 10).

Given that there is no pattern of physiological responses that indicates lying, how is the recording of physiological arousal used to detect lies? The typical polygraph test given to a criminal suspect begins with an explanation of the test and the kinds of questions to be asked. The subject is then asked *control questions,* which are designed to provoke lying about minor transgressions common to almost everyone. For example, the suspect might be asked, "Have you ever stolen anything from an employer?" It is a rare person who has not "stolen" at least an inexpensive item, yet many people would answer no, creating an increase in physiological arousal. And even if the suspect answers yes to a control question, he or she would probably experience some increase in physiological arousal in response to that question.

The subject's physiological response to control questions is compared to his or her physiological response to *relevant questions,* which are concerned with facts about the crime, such as, "Did you steal money from the bank safe?" Polygraphers assume that a guilty person will show greater physiological arousal in response to relevant questions, while an innocent person will show greater physiological arousal in response to control questions (figure 11.14). The typical polygraph test asks about twelve relevant questions, which are repeated three or four times.

Polygraph Test The "lie detector" test, which assesses lying by measuring changing patterns of physiological arousal in response to particular questions.

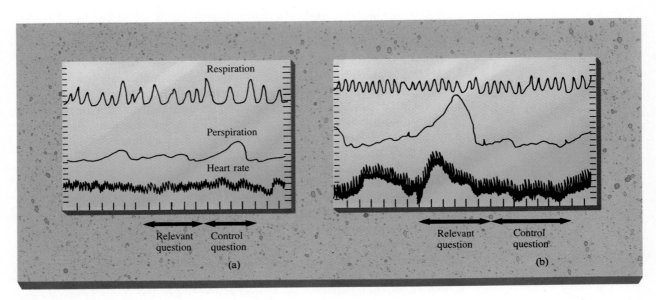

(a)   (b)

FIGURE 11.14
Relevant Questions versus Control Questions The polygraph test compares physiological responses to relevant and control questions. The record on the left (a) is that of a person who responded less strongly to a question relevant to a crime than to an emotionally arousing control question not relevant to the crime. Such responses indicate to the examiner that the person is telling the truth. The record on the right (b) is that of a person who responded more strongly to a question relevant to a crime than to an emotionally arousing control question not relevant to the crime. Responses such as this indicate to the examiner that the person is lying.

Issues in Lie Detection

The use of the polygraph test has provoked controversy because it is far from a perfect measure of lying. One difficulty is that the accuracy of the polygraph depends, in part, on the subject's physiological reactivity. People with low reactivity will exhibit a smaller difference in their responses to control and relevant questions than will people with high reactivity. This might cause an unemotional criminal to be declared innocent and an emotional innocent person to be declared guilty (Waid, Wilson, & Orne, 1981).

Criminals are also aware of countermeasures that can make them appear innocent on a polygraph test. Consider the case of Floyd Fay, an innocent man convicted in 1978 of murdering his best friend and sentenced to life in prison after failing a polygraph test that he had taken voluntarily. Two years later a county defender tracked down the real murderer. While in prison, Fay became an expert on lie detection and taught prisoners how to beat the polygraph test. Of twenty-seven inmates who had admitted their guilt to him, twenty-three passed their polygraph tests (Kleinmuntz & Szucko, 1984b).

What techniques do criminals use to fool the polygraph machine? One technique uses the properly timed induction of pain. For example, suppose that during control questions you bite your tongue or step on a tack hidden in your shoe. This would increase your level of physiological arousal in response to control questions, thereby reducing the difference in your physiological responses to control questions and relevant questions (Honts, Hodes, & Raskin, 1985).

Though aware that criminals can fool the polygraph machine, critics of the test are more concerned with the possibility that the polygraph will find innocent people guilty. In the 1980s millions of Americans were subjected to polygraph tests in criminal cases, employment screening, employee honesty checks, and security clearances (Kleinmuntz & Szucko, 1984b). In 1983 President Reagan gave an executive order to use the polygraph test to identify federal employees who reveal classified information. But a report commissioned by Congress found that the polygraph test was invalid in the situations favored by Reagan. The report concluded that the only justifiable use of the polygraph test is in criminal cases (Saxe, Dougherty, & Cross, 1985).

In June of 1988 President Reagan, confronted with overwhelming opposition to the unrestricted use of polygraph tests, signed a law banning their use for preemployment screening by private employers. But the law still permits the use of polygraph tests in ongoing investigations of specific incidents. And drug companies, security services, government agencies, and private companies that have contracts with government intelligence agencies are exempt from the ban on the use of polygraph tests in preemployment screening (Bales, 1988).

What evidence led to the widespread opposition to the unrestricted use of the polygraph? Though supporters of the polygraph test claim accuracy rates of 90 percent or better (Raskin & Podlesny, 1979), research findings indicate that it is much less accurate than that. In one study the polygraph printouts of fifty thieves and fifty innocent people were presented to six professional polygraphers from leading lie detector companies. The results showed that the polygraphers correctly identified 76 percent of the guilty persons and 61 percent of the innocent persons (figure 11.15). Though their performance was better than chance, this also meant that they incorrectly identified 24 percent of the guilty persons as innocent and 39 percent of the innocent persons as guilty (Kleinmuntz & Szucko, 1984a). The polygraph test's high rate of false

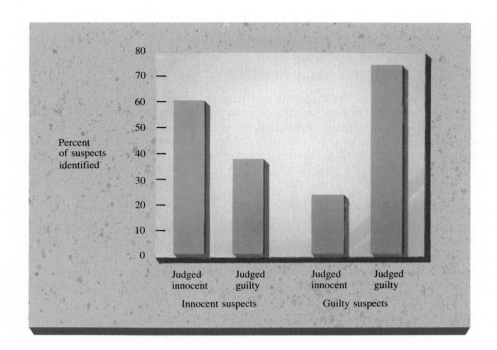

FIGURE 11.15
**The Validity of Polygraph
Testing** The study by Kleinmuntz
and Szucko (1984) found that the
polygraph test is far from
foolproof in determining guilt or
innocence. About one-third of
innocent suspects were judged
guilty and about one-quarter of
guilty suspects were judged
innocent.

positives (that is, identifying innocent persons as guilty) can have tragic consequences for those who are unjustly denied jobs, fired from jobs, or prosecuted for crimes.

A promising alternative to the polygraph test is the **Guilty Knowledge Test,** developed by David Lykken (1974). If you have ever played the board game *Clue,* you have some understanding of the test. In contrast to the polygraph test, Lykken's test assesses knowledge about a transgression, rather than alleged anxiety about it. The Guilty Knowledge Test is useful only when details of the transgression are known to the transgressor but not to innocent people. Consider its use in a bank robbery. A suspect would be asked questions concerning the victim, the site of the crime, and the commission of the crime. Instead of being asked, "Did you steal money from the bank safe?" the suspect would be asked, "Was the money stolen from the _____?" This question would be asked several times, each time with different words completing the statement. In this case, the words might be *bank safe, teller's drawer,* and *armored car.*

The Guilty Knowledge Test assumes that a guilty person (knowing details of the crime), but not an innocent person, will show greater physiological arousal in response to the relevant words than in response to the irrelevant words. If a person shows greater physiological reactivity to the relevant words in a *series* of statements (a single positive instance would be insufficient), that person would be considered guilty. Of course, examiners should not know any details of the crime. Otherwise, they might affect the suspect's physiological response to relevant words, perhaps by saying those words louder. Despite the Guilty Knowledge Test's potential superiority, it has yet to stimulate sufficient research to convince polygraph users to switch to it.

Guilty Knowledge Test A method that assesses lying by measuring physiological arousal in response to words that are relevant to a transgression and physiological arousal in response to words that are irrelevant to that transgression.

SUMMARY

THE PHYSIOLOGY OF EMOTION

Emotion is a motivated state marked by physiological arousal, expressive behavior, and mental experience. Emotional arousal depends on activity in the autonomic nervous system and the limbic system of the brain. While the left cerebral hemisphere plays a greater role in positive emotions, the right cerebral hemisphere plays a greater role in negative emotions. Neurotransmitters, including endorphins, alter our moods by affecting neuronal activity.

THE EXPRESSION OF EMOTION

We express our emotions behaviorally through changes in vocal qualities, body movements, and facial expressions. Charles Darwin believed that facial expressions evolved to communicate emotions and help individuals distinguish friend from foe. The hereditary basis of facial expressions is supported by research showing cross-cultural consistency in the relationship between particular facial expressions and particular emotions.

THE EXPERIENCE OF EMOTION

Robert Plutchik considers the basic emotions to be joy, fear, anger, disgust, sadness, surprise, acceptance, and anticipation. Emotions vary in their intensity and pleasantness, with people who tend to experience intensely pleasant emotions also likely to experience intensely unpleasant emotions. Psychologists have only recently begun to study pleasant emotions, such as happiness and amusement, to the same extent as unpleasant emotions. According to social comparison theory, happiness is the result of estimating that one's life circumstances are more favorable than those of others. And according to adaptation level theory, happiness depends on estimating that one's current life circumstances are more favorable than one's past life circumstances. Amusement is evoked by humor. Humor is explained by disparagement theory, incongruity theory, and release theory.

THEORIES OF EMOTION

Psychologists have devised a variety of theories to explain emotional experience. The James-Lange theory assumes that physiological changes precede emotional experiences, with different patterns of physiological arousal associated with different emotions. The Cannon-Bard theory claims that the thalamus perceives an event and communicates this information to the cerebral cortex (which provides the subjective experience of emotion) and stimulates the physiological arousal characteristic of emotion. According to the opponent-process theory, the brain has evolved mechanisms that counteract strong positive or negative emotions by evoking an opposite emotional response. If the first emotion is repeated, the opposing emotion gradually strengthens and the first emotion gradually weakens.

According to the facial-feedback theory, different emotions are caused by sensory feedback from different facial expressions. The two-factor theory views emotional experience as the consequence of attributing physiological arousal to a particular aspect of one's immediate environment. Cognitive appraisal theory ignores the role of physiological arousal and considers emotional experience to be solely the result of a person's interpretation of his or her current circumstances.

THINKING ABOUT PSYCHOLOGY: DO LIE DETECTORS TELL THE TRUTH?

The lie detector, or polygraph, assumes that differences in physiological arousal in response to control questions and relevant questions can be used to determine whether a person is lying. Critics point out that the polygraph can be fooled and that it is unreliable, because it finds a large proportion of guilty people innocent and an even larger proportion of innocent people guilty. A promising alternative to the traditional polygraph test is the Guilty Knowledge Test, which depends on the guilty person's physiological arousal to important facts about his or her transgression.

IMPORTANT CONCEPTS

Adaptation level theory 368
Autonomic nervous system 360
Cannon-Bard theory 374
Cognitive appraisal theory 380
Disparagement theory 369
Double-blind technique 363
Emotion 360

Facial-feedback theory 376
Fight-or-flight response 360
Guilty Knowledge Test 385
Incongruity theory 370
James-Lange theory 371
Opponent-process theory 375

Parasympathetic nervous system 360
Polygraph test 383
Release theory 370
Social comparison theory 368
Sympathetic nervous system 360
Two-factor theory 378

IMPORTANT PEOPLE

Walter Cannon 371
Charles Darwin 364
Paul Ekman 377

William James 371
Richard Lazarus 380
David Lykken 383

Robert Plutchik 366
Stanley Schachter 378
Richard Solomon 375

RECOMMENDED READINGS

For More on All Aspects of Emotion:
Carlson, J. G., & Hatfield, E. (1989). *Psychology of emotion.* Belmont, CA: Wadsworth.
A textbook discussing the physiology, expression, and experience of emotion.

For More on the Physiology of Emotion:
Miller, L. (1988, February). The emotional brain. *Psychology Today,* pp. 34–42.
A popular account of the role of the cerebral hemispheres in the processing of emotions.

For More on the Expression of Emotion:
Darwin, C. (1872/1965). *The expression of the emotions in man and animals.* Chicago: University of Chicago Press.
A classic, readable book describing the adaptive functions of human and animal emotional expressions.

Ekman, P. (1985). *Telling lies: Clues to deceit in the marketplace, politics, and marriage.* New York: Norton.
An interesting discussion of the role of gestures and facial expressions in everyday deception written by a noted researcher in the field of nonverbal communication.

For More on the Experience of Emotion: '
Plutchik, R. (1980). *Emotion: A psychoevolutionary synthesis.* New York: Harper & Row.
A presentation of the author's views on emotion, emphasizing emotion as the product of evolution.

For More on Theories of Emotion:
Leventhal, H., & Tomarken, A. J. (1986). Emotion: Todays problems. *Annual Review of Psychology, 37,* 565–610.
A review of issues in the study of emotion, with emphasis on the major theories of emotion.

For More on Lie Detectors:
Kleinmuntz, B., & Szucko, J. J. (1984). Lie detection in ancient and modern times: A call for contemporary scientific study. *American Psychologist, 39,* 766–776.
A fascinating survey of the history of lie detection.

Lykken, D.T. (1981). *A tremor in the blood: Uses and abuses of the lie detector.* New York: McGraw-Hill.
A discussion of scientific, ethical, and legal issues in the use of the polygraph test written by a leading authority in the field.

CHAPTER
12

Development

The Nature of Developmental Psychology
Basic Issues in Developmental Psychology
Research Designs in Developmental Psychology

Prenatal Period
The Germinal Stage
The Embryonic Stage
The Fetal Stage

Childhood
Physical Development
Cognitive Development
  Sensorimotor Stage
  Preoperational Stage
  Concrete Operational Stage
Psychosocial Development
  Child-Rearing Practices
  Social Relationships
  Gender-Role Development

Adolescence
Physical Development
Cognitive Development
Psychosocial Development

Adulthood
Physical Development
Cognitive Development
Psychosocial Development
  Early Adulthood
  Middle Adulthood
  Late Adulthood

Thinking About Psychology

Are There Significant Sex Differences?
  Motor Differences
  Cognitive Differences
  Psychosocial Differences

Chapter Opening Art: Edward Potthast. *Children at Shore.*

ach of us changes markedly across the life span. You are not the same today as you were in infancy. And you are not the same today as you will be in old age. What changes occur from the moment of our conception until the moment of our death? What factors account for these changes? The answers to these questions are provided by the field of **developmental psychology,** which studies the physical, cognitive, and psychosocial changes that take place across the life span.

THE NATURE OF DEVELOPMENTAL PSYCHOLOGY

Before reading about research on human development, you will first learn about two of the main issues in developmental psychology. You will then read about the difference between two research designs that are commonly used by developmental psychologists.

Basic Issues in Developmental Psychology

Is development a gradual process or are there abrupt changes at certain points in the life span? Is development determined more by *nature* or by *nurture?* These are two of the basic issues in developmental psychology. While many researchers believe that development is a gradual, cumulative process, some prominent theorists claim that development occurs in stages, with qualitative, rather than quantitative, differences between the stages. As you will soon read, the influential Swiss psychologist Jean Piaget believed that children go through distinct stages of cognitive development, with the child's thinking being qualitatively different at each stage.

As for the second issue, psychologists differ in the importance they assign to nature and nurture. Almost a century ago, early developmental psychologists were influenced by Charles Darwin's theory of evolution. This led them to stress the importance of heredity in the maturation—that is, the natural unfolding—of inborn traits and abilities that would help the individual adapt to life situations (Vidal, Buscaglia, & Voneche, 1983). The advent of behaviorism in the 1920s led psychologists to play down the role of heredity and to stress the role of life experiences. In the past two decades, however, there has been renewed interest in studying the role of heredity in human development.

As discussed in chapter 9, studies of adopted children reared apart have been important sources of evidence concerning the relative contributions of heredity and environment to human development. Research has consistently found that adoptees are more psychologically similar to their biological parents than to their adoptive parents, providing evidence that supports psychologists who stress the importance of heredity. One such study provided support for the hereditary basis of criminality. The study found no relationship between the criminal behavior of 14,427 adoptees convicted of crimes and the criminal behavior of their adoptive parents, but it did find a significant positive correlation between the criminal behavior of the adoptees and the criminal behavior of their biological parents (Mednick, Gabrielli, & Hutchings, 1984).

Nonetheless, regardless of the influence of heredity on development, experience is also important. Heredity and experience interact—they do not act independently. For example, heredity may have provided you with the potential to be a Nobel Prize winner, but without adequate academic experiences you might, instead, not even perform well enough to graduate from college. As you proceed through this chapter, you will find that heredity and environment interact to affect individual development. In fact, research findings in-

"Not guilty by reason of genetic determinism, Your Honor."

dicate that heredity and experience each accounts for about 50 percent of the differences in psychological development among individuals (Plomin, Loehlin, & DeFries, 1985).

Research Designs in Developmental Psychology

Though developmental psychologists use the same research designs as other psychologists, they also rely on two research designs that are unique to developmental psychology. These are longitudinal research and cross-sectional research, which you encountered in the discussion of changes in intelligence presented in chapter 9. **Longitudinal research** follows the same group of subjects over a period of time, typically ranging from months to years. In contrast, **cross-sectional research** considers groups of subjects of different ages at the same point in time.

Suppose that you wanted to study changes in the social maturity of college students (see figure 12.1). If you chose to use a longitudinal design, you might assess the social maturity of an incoming class of freshmen and then note changes in their social maturity during their four years in college. If, instead, you chose to use a cross-sectional design, you might compare the current social maturity of freshmen, sophomores, juniors, and seniors.

Cross-sectional designs are used more often, because longitudinal designs are time consuming, are affected by subjects dropping out as the study progresses, and are dependent on the willingness of researchers and sources of financial support to continue them. Though cross-sectional designs do not have these limitations, they may produce misleading findings if certain age groups in the study are affected by unique life circumstances. Suppose that you conduct a cross-sectional study and find that older adults are more prejudiced against minorities than are younger adults. Does this mean that we

Longitudinal Research A research design in which the same group of subjects is tested or observed repeatedly over a period of time.

Cross-Sectional Research A research design in which groups of subjects of different ages are compared at the same point in time.

"In extenuation, Your Honor, I would like to suggest to the court that my client
was inadequately parented."

become more prejudiced with age? Not necessarily. Perhaps, instead, older
adults were raised at a time when prejudice was more acceptable than it is
today. They simply may have retained attitudes they developed in their youth.
Similarly, children who experienced the Great Depression, World War II, the
"Woodstock era" of the 1960s, or the "Reagan revolution" of the 1980s may
have developed somewhat differently than will children reared in the 1990s.

PRENATAL PERIOD

It is amazing to think that you, Julius Caesar, Oprah Winfrey, and anyone who
has ever lived began as a single cell. The formation of that cell begins the
prenatal period, which lasts about nine months and is divided into the *germinal stage,* the *embryonic stage,* and the *fetal stage.* Figure 12.2 presents
several scenes from prenatal development.

The Germinal Stage

Germinal Stage The prenatal
period that lasts from conception
through the second week.

The **germinal stage** begins with conception, which occurs when a *sperm*
from the male fertilizes an egg (or *ovum*) from the female in one of her two
fallopian tubes, forming a one-cell *zygote.* The zygote contains twenty-three
pairs of chromosomes, one member of each pair coming from the sperm and
the other from the ovum. The chromosomes, in turn, contain genes that govern
the development of the individual. The zygote immediately begins a trip down
the fallopian tube during which, through repeated cell divisions, it is transformed into a larger, multicelled structure. By the end of the first week, the
structure consists of more than one hundred cells. The structure eventually
reaches the uterus and attaches to its wall, a process that is usually completed
by the end of the second week. This marks the beginning of the embryonic
stage.

10 yrs.   20 yrs.   30 yrs.   40 yrs.   50 yrs.

Cross-sectional

10 yrs.   30 yrs.   50 yrs.

20 yrs.   40 yrs.   60 yrs.

FIGURE 12.1
Longitudinal and Cross-Sectional Research In longitudinal research, the same subjects are studied over time, usually for a period of years. In cross-sectional research, subjects representing different age groups are studied at the same time. The example illustrates a hypothetical longitudinal study in which racial prejudice was measured in the same subjects every ten years for a period of forty years and a hypothetical cross-sectional study in which racial prejudice was measured in different subjects who were ten, twenty, thirty, forty, fifty, and sixty years old.

Lasts

The Embryonic Stage

The **embryonic stage** lasts from the second week through the eighth week of prenatal development. The embryo increases in size and begins to develop specialized organs, such as the eyes, heart, and brain. What accounts for this

Embryonic Stage The prenatal period that lasts from the end of the second week through the eighth week.

FIGURE 12.2

Prenatal Development Prenatal development is marked by rapid growth and differentiation of structures. (a) At four weeks, the embryo is about 0.2 inches long, has a recognizable head, arm buds, leg buds, and a heart that has begun beating. (b) At eight weeks—the end of the embryonic stage, the embryo has features that make it recognizable as distinctly human, including a nose, a mouth, eyes, ears, hands, fingers, feet, and toes. This marks the beginning of the fetal stage. (c) At sixteen weeks, the fetus is about seven inches long and makes movements that can be detected by the mother. The remainder of the fetal stage involves extremely rapid growth.

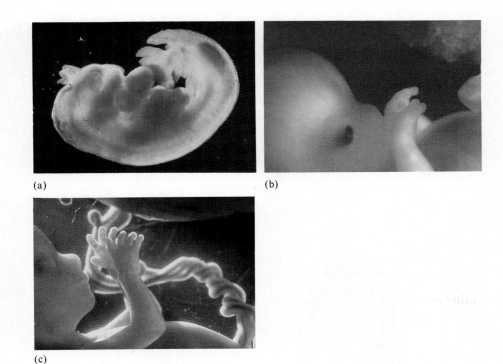

(a)

(b)

(c)

rapid, complex process? The development and location of body organs is regulated by genes that have been inherited from the mother and father. The genes determine the kinds of cells that will develop and direct the actions of *cell-adhesion molecules.* These molecules direct the movement of cells and determine which cells will adhere to one another, thereby determining the size, shape, and location of organs in the embryo (Edelman, 1984). By the end of the embryonic stage, development has progressed to the point that the heart is beating and the approximately one-inch-long embryo has facial features, limbs, fingers, and toes.

But what determines whether an embryo becomes a male or a female? Embryos that have inherited two X chromosomes are genetic females, and embryos that have inherited one X and one Y chromosome are genetic males. Near the end of the embryonic period, male embryos secrete the hormone *testosterone,* which stimulates the development of male sexual organs. If testosterone is not secreted, the newborn male's external genitals will look like those of a female. In contrast, the secretion of excessive amounts of testosterone in female embryos leads to the development of masculine-looking external genitals. This phenomenon was discovered in 1865 by an Italian anatomist who autopsied a man who lacked testes, only to find that in addition to a penis the man had ovaries, a uterus, and a vagina. The "man" was actually a genetic female whose adrenal glands had secreted an excessive amount of testosterone during prenatal development, causing her clitoris to enlarge into a penislike organ (Miller, 1984).

The Fetal Stage

The presence of a distinctly human appearance marks the beginning of the **fetal stage,** which lasts until birth. By the fourth month after conception, pregnant women report movement by the fetus. And by the seventh month all of the major organs are functional, which means that an infant born even two or three months prematurely will have a good chance of surviving. The final three months of prenatal development are associated with a great increase in the size of the fetus.

Fetal Stage The prenatal period that lasts from the end of the eighth week through birth.

Though prenatal development usually proceeds in an orderly fashion and produces a normal infant, in some cases genetic defects produce distinctive physical and psychological syndromes. As explained in chapter 9, the genetic disorder called *Down syndrome* is associated with mental retardation and abnormal physical development. Prenatal development, particularly during the embryonic stage and early fetal stage, can also be disrupted by noxious substances passed from the pregnant woman to the embryo or fetus. During prenatal development, nutrients are provided and wastes are removed by the *placenta,* which is attached to the wall of the uterus. Unfortunately, noxious substances, including many viruses and drugs, can also pass from the placenta into the bloodstream of the embryo or fetus. For example, exposure to the German measles (*rubella*) virus, particularly in the first three months of prenatal development, can cause defects of the eyes, ears, and heart.

Drugs such as nicotine, alcohol, and heroin can also cause abnormal physical and psychological development. **Fetal alcohol syndrome** may afflict the offspring of women who drink alcohol during pregnancy. Women who drink alcohol while pregnant may also produce offspring who appear normal in infancy but show ill effects years later. This was demonstrated in a study that followed the offspring of mothers who drank the equivalent of three alcoholic drinks a day while pregnant. At the age of four, these children scored almost five IQ points lower than their peers whose mothers had not ingested alcohol during pregnancy. This difference in IQ existed even after equating the children on other factors, including their racial backgrounds, their parents' ed-

Fetal Alcohol Syndrome A disorder, marked by physical defects and mental retardation, that may afflict the offspring of women who drink alcohol during pregnancy.

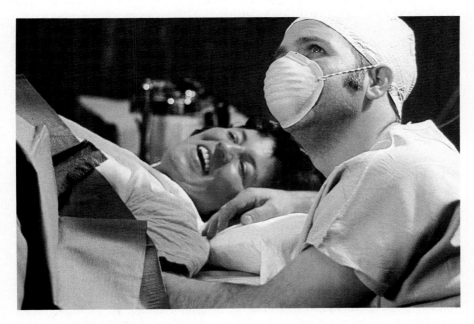

Natural Childbirth The recognition that in modern society the once natural act of childbirth had become a technological, medical procedure has led to interest in returning to more personal, natural methods of childbirth. One of the most popular methods was introduced in 1951 by a French obstetrician named Lamaze. The *Lamaze method* includes attendance at childbirth classes during the last three months of pregnancy, at which the parents are informed of the physical changes that occur during gestation and of what to expect during labor and delivery. The parents are instructed in how to control pain through special breathing techniques, muscular relaxation, and mental distraction. The father also serves as a labor coach to the mother during delivery. The effectiveness of natural childbirth methods such as the Lamaze method in reducing pain and improving maternal attitudes toward childbirth has not been adequately assessed. Evidence of its positive effects has generally come from anecdotal reports, rather than from controlled experiments (Wideman & Singer, 1984).

ucational levels, and their attendance in preschool classes. Other studies have found that women who drink even small amounts of alcohol during pregnancy may produce offspring who fail to reach their intellectual potentials (Streissguth, Barr, Sampson, Darby, & Martin, 1989). Perhaps the wisest course of action is for expectant mothers to refrain from all alcohol (and other drug) consumption.

Though researchers have traditionally shown little interest in the possible perceptual and cognitive abilities of the fetus, clever research studies have revealed that near the end of prenatal development the fetus can hear sounds and form memories of them. In one study, sixteen pregnant women read out loud, twice a day, the Dr. Seuss poem *The Cat in the Hat* during the last forty-five days of their pregnancies. Later, a newborn infant could, by sucking on a nipple in different patterns, turn on a recording of its mother reading either *The Cat in the Hat* or *The King, the Mice, and the Cheese.* Infants whose mothers had read *The Cat in the Hat* out loud during pregnancy sucked more to hear the recording of that poem than to hear the recording of the other poem (Kolata, 1984b). This indicates that, while in the womb, the infants had heard their mothers reading *The Cat in the Hat* and had formed memories that enabled them to recognize the sound qualities of the story. Of course, it would be a bit much to infer that the infants recognized the story itself.

CHILDHOOD

Childhood The period that extends from birth until the onset of puberty.

Infancy The period that extends from birth through two years of age.

In 1877 Charles Darwin published a diary describing the physical and psychological development of his infant son. This was one of the first formal studies of child development. More than a century later, hundreds of studies of child development are published each year. **Childhood** extends from birth until puberty and begins with **infancy,** a period of rapid physical, cognitive, and psychosocial development, extending from birth to age two. During the past century childhood has been recognized as a distinct period of the life span that is qualitatively different from adulthood. Many developmental psychologists devote their careers to studying the changes in physical, cognitive, and psychosocial development that occur during childhood.

Physical Development

Though newborn infants are dependent on caregivers for their survival, they exhibit reflexes that promote their survival, such as blinking, coughing, or searching for a nipple with their lips when their cheeks are touched. But through *maturation,* which is the gradual unfolding of inherited behavior patterns, the infant quickly develops motor skills that go beyond mere reflexes. The typical infant is crawling by the sixth month and walking by the thirteenth month. Though infant motor development follows a consistent sequence, dependent on maturation rather than on learning, the timing of motor milestones will vary somewhat among infants (figure 12.3).

Infancy is also a period of rapid brain development, during which many synaptic connections are formed and many others are eliminated. Though these changes are influenced by heredity, animal studies indicate that they may also be influenced by experience. In one study (Camel, Withers, & Greenough, 1986), a group of infant rats spent thirty days in an enriched environment and another group spent thirty days in an impoverished environment. In the enriched environment, the rats were housed together in two large toy-filled cages, one containing water and one containing food, which were attached to the opposite ends of a maze. The pattern of pathways and dead ends through the maze was changed daily. In the impoverished environment, the rats were housed individually in small, empty cages.

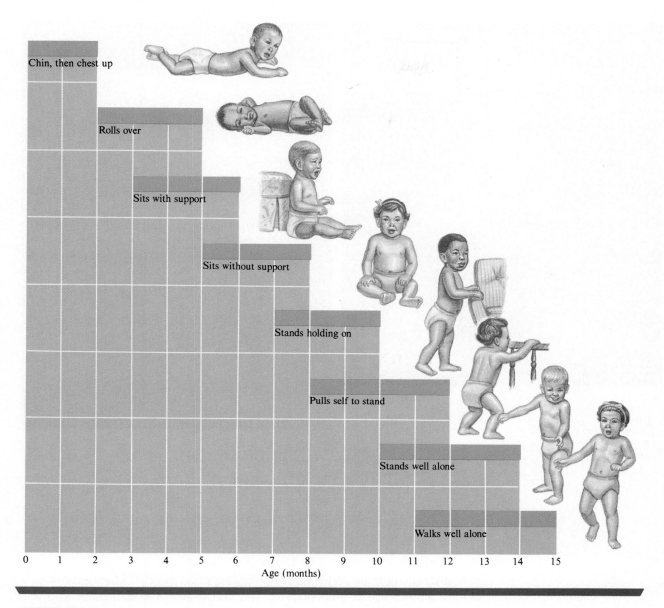

Chin, then chest up

Rolls over

Sits with support

Sits without support

Stands holding on

Pulls self to stand

Stands well alone

Walks well alone

0   1   2   3   4   5   6   7   8   9   10   11   12   13   14   15
Age (months)

FIGURE 12.3

Motor Milestones Infancy is a period of rapid motor development, during which the infant begins with a set of motor reflexes and, over the course of little more than a year, develops the ability to manipulate objects and move independently through the environment. You should note that the ages at which normal children reach motor milestones vary somewhat from child to child, but the sequence of motor milestones does not. Motor development depends not on training, but on the maturation of inherited abilities.

Later, microscopic examination of the brains of the rats found that those exposed to the enriched environment had longer and more numerous dendrites on their neurons than did those exposed to the impoverished environment. Studies such as these, which demonstrate the importance of experience in the development of the brain, have inspired attempts to improve the cognitive abilities of mentally retarded children through programs that provide them with enriched environments involving high levels of sensory, motor, and cognitive stimulation (Rosenzweig, 1984). The effectiveness of these programs remains to be determined.

Childhood as a Modern Invention
Childhood has been a privileged period of
life in our culture only since the late
nineteenth century. Until then children
were treated as smaller, less-experienced
adults with no special needs or rights.

After infancy, the child's growth rate slows and most children grow two or three inches a year until puberty. The child's motor coordination also improves. Children learn to perform more sophisticated motor tasks, such as using scissors, tying their shoes, riding bicycles, and playing sports. The development of motor skills also affects the development of cognitive skills. For example, the ability of children to express themselves through language depends on the development of motor abilities that permit them to speak and to write.

Cognitive Development

A century ago, in describing what he believed was the chaotic mental world of the newborn infant, William James (1890/1950, Vol. I, p. 488) claimed, "The baby, assailed by eyes, ears, nose, skin, and entrails at once, feels it all as one great blooming, buzzing confusion." But other authorities believed that newborn infants could not be assailed in that way, because they were assumed to be born blind and deaf (Gibson, 1987). During the past three decades, research studies have shown that neither view was correct. Newborn infants have more highly developed sensory, perceptual, and cognitive abilities than had traditionally been believed. Their mental world is not a blooming, buzzing confusion and they are neither blind nor deaf (unless they have a physical defect).

Researchers have discovered that infants have relatively well-developed sensory abilities. Ingenious studies have permitted researchers to infer what infants perceive, even though the infants cannot say what they perceive. For example, as shown in figure 12.4, thirty-six-hour-old infants can imitate sad, happy, and surprised facial expressions (Field, Woodson, Greenberg, & Cohen, 1982). And by six months of age most infants can perceive depth. Figure 12.5 describes the use of the *visual cliff* in testing infant depth perception.

Infancy is also a time of rapid cognitive development. Jean Piaget (1896–1980), a Swiss psychologist, put forth the first formal theory of cognitive development. Piaget (1952) noted that, beginning in infancy, children pass

what believe

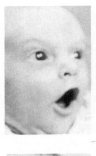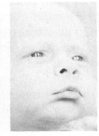
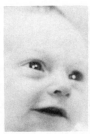

FIGURE 12.4
Abilities of Newborn Infants
Newborn infants not only see better than has been traditionally assumed, they can also imitate facial expressions. A study of two-day-old infants found that they could imitate facial expressions of sadness, happiness, and surprise (Field et al., 1982).

FIGURE 12.5
The Visual Cliff Eleanor Gibson and Richard Walk (1960) developed the *visual cliff* to test infant depth perception. The visual cliff consists of a thick sheet of glass placed on a table. The "shallow" end of the visual cliff has a checkerboard surface an inch or so below the glass. The "deep" end of the visual cliff has a checkerboard surface several feet below the glass. An infant who has reached the crawling stage will crawl from the center of the table across the shallow end, but not across the deep end, to reach his or her mother. This indicates that by the age of six months infants can perceive depth. Of course, this does not preclude the possibility that infants have depth perception even before they can crawl.

through four distinct, increasingly sophisticated cognitive stages. He found that, while going through these stages, children are active manipulators, rather than passive receivers, of information. In doing so, they make more and more sense of the world around them.

Sensorimotor Stage Piaget called infancy the **sensorimotor stage,** during which the child learns to coordinate sensory experiences and motor behavior. Parents are often all too aware of the exploits of the infant in developing sensorimotor coordination, as when the infant scoops up food and only sometimes manages to deposit it in his or her mouth instead of on the floor. By the age of nine months, sensorimotor coordination becomes sophisticated enough for the infant to grab a moving object by aiming his or her reach somewhat ahead of the object instead of where the object appears to be at that moment (von Hofsten, 1983). The successful manipulation of objects during this stage not only aids in the development of sensorimotor coordination, it also contributes to the infant's sense of mastery and competence (MacTurk, McCarthy, Vietze, & Yarrow, 1987).

Piaget claimed that experiences with the environment help the infant form **schemas,** which are mental models incorporating the characteristics of persons, objects, events, or situations. This means that infants do more than merely gather information about the world. Their experiences actively change the way in which they think about the world. Schemas permit infants to adapt their behaviors to changes in the environment. But what makes schemas themselves change? They change as the result of **assimilation** and **accommodation.**

Infants *assimilate* when they fit information into their existing schemas and *accommodate* when they revise their schemas to fit new information. Consider the schema "food." You have probably observed the indiscriminate way in which young infants place objects of all kinds in their mouths. By tasting and chewing on the different objects, infants learn which are food and which are not. For example, an infant learns early in life to assimilate milk into the schema "food." But if the infant later drinks milk that has gone sour, he or she will accommodate by revising the schema to exclude sour milk.

Young infants share an important schema in which they assume that the removal of an object means that the object no longer exists. If an object is hidden by a piece of cloth, for example, the young infant will not look for it—even after watching the object being hidden. To the young infant, out of sight means out of mind (figure 12.6). As infants gain experience with the coming and going of objects in the environment, they accommodate and develop the schema of **object permanence**—the realization that objects that are not in view may still exist.

After the age of eight months, most infants will demonstrate their appreciation of object permanence by searching for an object that they have seen being hidden from view. This indicates that they have reached the point at which they can retain mental images of physical objects even after the objects are no longer in sight. But other researchers have questioned Piaget's belief that young infants fail to search for hidden objects because they lack a schema for object permanence. Perhaps, instead, they lack the memory ability needed to recall the location of an object that has been hidden from view (Bjork & Cummings, 1984).

Preoperational Stage According to Piaget, when the child reaches the age of two and leaves infancy, the sensorimotor stage gives way to the **preoperational stage,** which lasts until about the age of seven. The stage is called preoperational because the child cannot perform *operations*—mental

Jean Piaget (1896–1980) "As the child's thought evolves, assimilation and accommodation are differentiated and become increasingly complementary."

Sensorimotor Stage The Piagetian stage, from birth through the second year, during which the infant learns to coordinate sensory experiences and motor behavior.

Schema A mental model incorporating the characteristics of particular persons, objects, events, or situations.

Assimilation The cognitive process that interprets new information in light of existing schemas.

Accommodation The cognitive process that revises existing schemas to incorporate new information.

Object Permanence The realization that objects exist even when they are no longer visible.

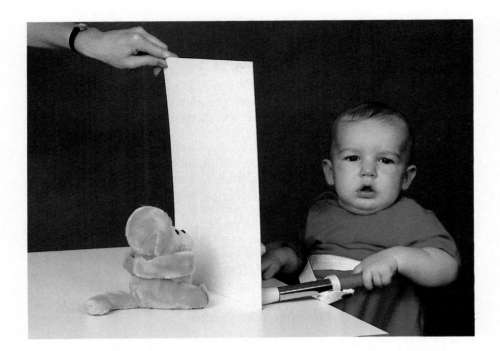

FIGURE 12.6
Object Permanence After young infants see an object being hidden from view, they act as though it no longer exists. This indicates that they lack the concept of *object permanence*—the realization that an object that is no longer in view may still exist.

manipulations of reality that are reversible. For example, the young school-age child does not realize that addition is the reverse of subtraction. But the preoperational stage does see improvements in the child's use of language, including a rapid growth in vocabulary and a more sophisticated use of grammar.

The preoperational child develops the ability to reason but may reason in ways unlike those of older children. For example, the young preschool child engages in **transductive reasoning.** The child reasons that if two objects have a characteristic in common, then the objects are identical. So, all vehicles with wheels are "cars" and all four-legged animals are "doggies." During the preoperational stage the child also learns to overcome what Piaget called **egocentrism,** which is the inability to perceive physical reality from the perspective of another person. Children exhibit egocentrism when they draw a picture of their family but fail to include themselves in the drawing. You exhibited egocentrism as a child if your parents ever asked you to get out of the way when you stood between them and the television. You did not realize that you were blocking their view.

You should note that, contrary to popular belief, children who play hide-and-seek by covering their eyes with their hands are not so egocentric that they assume that other people cannot see them. Though children who cover their eyes may say that other people cannot see them, they actually mean that other people cannot see their faces. They are aware that other people can still see their bodies (Flavell, Shipstead, & Croft, 1980).

Concrete Operational Stage At the age of seven the child enters what Piaget calls the **concrete operational stage,** which lasts until about the age of twelve. The child learns to reason logically but is limited to reasoning about objects that are physically present. For example, when you first learned to do arithmetic problems you were unable to perform mental calculations. Instead, you counted by using your fingers or other objects.

Preoperational Stage The Piagetian stage, extending from age two until age seven, during which the child's use of language becomes more sophisticated but the child has difficulty in the logical mental manipulation of information.

Transductive Reasoning The assumption that if two objects have a characteristic in common, then the objects are identical.

Egocentrism The inability to perceive physical reality from the perspective of another person.

Concrete Operational Stage The Piagetian stage, extending from age seven until age twelve, during which the child learns to reason logically about objects that are physically present.

FIGURE 12.7
Conservation During the concrete operational stage, the child exhibits conservation. The child comes to realize that changing the form of something does not change its amount. In a classic demonstration used by Piaget, a child is shown two containers holding equal amounts of liquid. When the fluid in one container is poured into a tall, narrow container, the preoperational child will believe that container contains more fluid than the short, wide container. In contrast, the concrete operational child realizes that both containers hold the same amount of fluid.

Transitive Inferences The application of previously learned relationships to infer new relationships.

Conservation The realization that changing the appearance of something does not change its amount or number.

Social Attachment A strong, enduring emotional tie between an infant and a caregiver.

An important kind of reasoning ability that develops during this stage is the ability to make **transitive inferences**—the application of previously learned relationships to infer new relationships. For example, suppose that a child is told that John is taller than Paul, and that Paul is taller than James. A child who can make transitive inferences will correctly conclude that John is taller than James. Though Piaget claimed that the ability to make transitive inferences develops by age eight, research has shown that children as young as four can do so (Breslow, 1981).

During the concrete operational stage, the child also develops a schema that Piaget called **conservation**—the realization that changing the form or arrangement of something does not change its amount. Suppose that a child is shown two balls of clay of equal size. One ball is then rolled out into a snake, and the child is asked whether one or the other has more clay. The child who has not learned conservation will reply either that the snake has more clay because it is longer or that the ball has more clay because it is fatter. Figure 12.7 presents a classic means of testing whether a child has developed the schema of conservation. The importance of experience in the development of conservation was demonstrated in a study of children in a Mexican village whose parents were pottery makers. The children, who normally helped their parents in making clay pottery, learned conservation earlier than other children (Price-Williams, Gordon, & Ramirez, 1969).

During the concrete operational stage, some children are found to have *learning disabilities.* This means that they have at least average intelligence but have difficulty performing cognitive tasks such as reading, writing, spelling, or arithmetic. Their cognitive abilities seem to mature more slowly than normal. But special education and the realization by parents and teachers that the learning disabled child is not mentally retarded may enable the child to become a successful—or even eminent—adult. For example, in school Albert Einstein did poorly in arithmetic, Thomas Edison had difficulty writing, and General George Patton had so much difficulty reading that he had to memorize whole lectures in order to pass exams. Even the actor Tom Cruise has become a movie star despite suffering from a reading disability that interferes with his ability to learn scripts (Schulman, 1986). Piaget's fourth stage of cognitive development—that is, the formal operational stage—will be discussed in the section of the chapter dealing with adolescence.

Psychosocial Development

Just as Piaget believed that the child passes through stages of cognitive development, Sigmund Freud believed that the child passes through stages of personality development. His theory is discussed in chapter 13. Erik Erikson, another psychoanalyst, put forth a theory of personality, or "psychosocial," development encompassing the entire life span in which each stage of development involves a crisis that must be overcome. Each stage and its associated crisis is described in table 12.1.

Erikson believed that the major crisis of the first year of infancy is *trust versus mistrust.* One of the most important factors in helping the infant develop trust is **social attachment,** a strong emotional tie to a caregiver. Freud had assumed that an infant will become attached to his or her mother because she provides nourishment through nursing. Freud's assumption was brought into question by research conducted by Harry Harlow and his colleagues on social attachment in rhesus monkeys. In one study, Harlow separated infant monkeys from their parents and peers and raised them for six months with two "surrogate mothers." The surrogates were wire monkeys with wooden heads. One surrogate was covered with terry cloth and the other was left bare.

what did Freud say?

TABLE 12.1   Erikson's Stages of Psychosocial Development

Age	Conflict	Successful resolution
First Year	Trust vs. mistrust	The infant develops a sense of security
Second Year	Autonomy vs. shame and doubt	The infant achieves a sense of independence
3–5 Years	Initiative vs. guilt	The child finds a balance between spontaneity and restraint
6 Years–Puberty	Competence vs. inferiority	The child attains a sense of self-confidence
Adolescence	Identity vs. role confusion	The adolescent experiences a unified sense of self
Young Adulthood	Intimacy vs. isolation	The adult forms close personal relationships
Middle Adulthood	Generativity vs. stagnation	The adult promotes the well-being of others
Late Adulthood	Integrity vs. despair	The adult enjoys a sense of satisfaction by reflecting on a life well lived

Adapted from *Childhood and Society,* Second Edition, by Erik H. Erikson, by permission of W. W. Norton & Company, Inc. Copyright 1950, 1963 by W. W. Norton & Company, Inc. Copyright renewed 1978 by Erik H. Erikson.

Harlow found that the monkeys preferred to cling to the cloth-covered surrogate, even when milk was provided by a nipple available only from the wire surrogate (figure 12.8). Harlow concluded that physical contact is a more important factor than nourishment in promoting infant attachment to the mother (Harlow & Zimmerman, 1959).

Of course, ethical standards would prevent the replication of Harlow's research with human infants (and, perhaps, even with infant monkeys). Much of what we know about attachment in human infants comes from research by Mary Ainsworth (1979) and her colleagues on the relationship between infants and their mothers. In Western cultures, mothers are more nurturant in providing for their children's physical needs, while fathers are more likely to play with their children (Bronstein, 1984). Thus, the mother is more likely to be the primary caregiver. In assessing the mother's influence on the child, Ainsworth makes a distinction between *securely attached* and *insecurely attached* infants.

The securely attached infant seeks physical contact with the mother yet will freely leave her to play and to explore, using the mother as a secure base. In contrast, insecurely attached infants cling to their mothers, act highly anxious when separated from them, and may be unresponsive when reunited with them. Mothers who are more sensitive, accepting, and affectionate toward their infants than are other mothers have infants who are more securely attached (Goldsmith & Alansky, 1987). And infants who are securely attached are, in turn, more likely to become sociable children (LaFreniere & Sroufe, 1985).

According to Erikson, during the second year the child experiences a crisis pitting *autonomy versus shame and doubt.* The child explores the physical environment, begins to learn self-care skills such as feeding, and tries out budding motor and language skills. In doing so, the child develops a greater sense of independence from his or her parents. But parents who do not permit the child to have enough independence or criticize the child's awkward efforts will promote feelings of shame and doubt.

Erik Erikson (1902–) "I shall present human growth from the point of view of the conflicts, inner and outer, which the vital personality weathers, re-emerging from each crisis with an increased sense of inner unity."

FIGURE 12.8
Social Attachment Harry Harlow found that infant monkeys became more attached to a terrycloth-covered wire surrogate mother than to a bare-wire surrogate mother. Even when fed only from a bottle protruding from the bare-wire surrogate mother, the infant monkeys preferred to cling to the terrycloth-covered surrogate mother. Apparently, social attachment depends more on physical contact than on the provision of nourishment (Harlow & Zimmerman, 1959).

At the age of three, the child enters the stage that involves what Erikson calls *initiative versus guilt.* The child shows initiative in play, social relationships, and in exploration of the environment. But the child also learns to control his or her impulses, feeling guilt for actions that go beyond limits set by parents. So, at this stage, parents may permit their child to rummage through drawers but not to throw clothing around the bedroom.

At the age of six, and continuing until about the age of twelve, Erikson observed that the child faces a crisis that involves *industry versus inferiority.* The industrious child who achieves successes during this stage is more likely to feel competent. This is important, because children who feel academically and socially competent are happier than other children (Blechman, Tinsley, Carella, & McEnroe, 1985). A sense of industry is also promoted by confidence in one's physical abilities. A study of fourth and fifth graders found that those who believed they were more physically able were more likely to participate in sports (Roberts, Kleiber, & Duda, 1981). A child who develops a sense of inferiority may lose interest in academics, avoid social interactions, or fail to participate in sports.

Child-Rearing Practices One of the most important factors in psychosocial development is the child-rearing practices of the parents, particularly their approach to discipline. *Permissive* parents set few rules and rarely punish misbehavior. Permissiveness is undesirable, because children will be less likely to adopt positive standards of behavior. At the other extreme, *authoritarian* parents set strict rules and rely on punishment. They respond to questioning of their rules by saying, "Because I say so!" Studies have found that physical punishment is not an effective means of disciplining children. There is no evidence that "sparing the rod" will spoil the

Drawing by Weber; © 1984 The New
Yorker Magazine, Inc.

"I find there's a lot of pressure to be good."

child (Cordes, 1984). One of the dangers of a reliance on physical discipline is that it will mushroom into child abuse. Abused children have poorer self-esteem and are more socially withdrawn (Kaufman & Cicchetti, 1989). They also tend to be more aggressive and less empathetic toward children in distress (Main & George, 1985). This may partly explain the cycle in which abused children become child abusers themselves as adults.

The most effective approach to discipline is the *authoritative* approach (Baumrind, 1983). Authoritative parents tend to be warm and loving, yet they still insist that their children behave appropriately. They encourage independence within well-defined limits, show a willingness to explain the reasons for their rules, and permit their children to express verbal disagreement with them. By maintaining a delicate balance between freedom and control, authoritative parents help their children internalize standards of behavior. Children who have authoritative parents are more likely to become socially competent, independent, and responsible.

Another important, and controversial, factor in child rearing is *day care.* Until recently, widely available day care was found only in countries in which mothers traditionally work outside the home, such as China, Israel, and the Soviet Union. The recent increase in the United States in the number of women who work outside the home has led to an increase in the number of preschool children who spend their weekdays in day-care centers. During the past twenty years, popular books and magazine articles have often presented a negative view of day care. But studies have shown that day care, so long as it is of high quality, does not have adverse effects on the preschool child's physical health, maternal attachment, social relationships, intellectual development, and emotional well-being (Etaugh, 1980).

Moreover, children's emotional well-being and cognitive development are affected less by the absence of their mothers during the day than by the overall amount of time their mothers spend with them when they are home. Though mothers who are employed full time spend less time with their infants and preschoolers during the week, they usually compensate for this by interacting with them more on weekends (Hoffman, 1989).

But what of school-age children whose parents both work? While many preschool children may spend their days in day-care centers, many school-age children become so-called latchkey children. When these children return home from school, they care for themselves until one of their parents returns home from work. Extreme concern about the possible negative effects of being a latchkey child may be unwarranted. For example, there appear to be no differences in the self-esteem and social adjustment of latchkey children and children who have a parent at home (Rodman, Pratto, & Nelson, 1985).

Social Relationships   Children are also affected by social factors other than their parents' child-rearing practices. An important factor is the quality of their parents' marital relationship. A study of four- and five-year-old children with parents experiencing marital discord found that the children tended to be socially withdrawn and to play less with other children. They also had unusually high levels of stress hormones in their urine, indicating that they were under chronically high levels of stress. This may explain why such children interact less with other children. They may do so to counter their chronically high levels of arousal (Gottman & Katz, 1989). As explained in chapter 10, we may either seek or avoid external stimulation in order to maintain an optimal level of arousal.

In some cases marital discord leads to divorce. Because about half of all marriages end in divorce, many children will spend at least part of childhood in single-parent households. This often has negative effects on children. A study of a national sample of 1,197 children found, based on reports by parents, teachers, and children, that children of divorce tend to suffer more emotional distress, to perform worse in school, and to have poorer peer relations. This applies especially to girls and to young children (Allison & Furstenberg, 1989).

Many children must also adjust to adoptive parents. Though it is popularly believed that adopted children are at a greater risk of social maladjustment than other children, research has failed to confirm this. In fact, adopted children tend to be more confident and view others more positively than do children who live with their biological parents. Adopted children also tend to view their adoptive parents as more caring, helpful, and protective than do children who live with their biological parents (Marquis & Detweiler, 1985).

Of course, children are affected by their relationships with friends and siblings as well as their relationships with parents. Few children develop friendships before the age of three and 95 percent of childhood friendships are with members of the same sex (Hartup, 1989). Boys and girls differ in the kinds of relationships they have with their peers, with girls tending to have fewer and more intimate friendships than do boys (Berndt & Hoyle, 1985). Adequate peer relationships are important, because children with poor peer relationships are at risk for later difficulties. This is especially true of children who behave aggressively and who are less accepted by their peers. They become more likely to drop out of school and to engage in criminal behavior (Parker & Asher, 1987).

Among our most important peers are our siblings. Sibling birth order is a factor in social development, with firstborn children usually being less socially popular than last-born children. This may occur because the firstborn interacts more with adults than with siblings, compared to the last-born interacting extensively with both parents and siblings. As a consequence, the last-born may be more likely to develop social skills that are well-suited for interacting with peers (Baskett, 1984). Despite the advantages of having siblings, the popular belief that an only child suffers because of the absence of siblings is unfounded. An only child is usually superior to all except firstborn children and children from two-child families in intelligence and academic achievement (Falbo & Polit, 1986).

Of course, children with siblings experience relationships that the only child does not. For example, sibling rivalry cannot occur without a sibling. In sibling rivalry, the children compete for parental attention and approval, as well as competing to outdo each other in social, academic, athletic, or vocational endeavors. Provided that parents keep it from becoming excessive, sibling rivalry is normal and provides a means of learning positive competition and resolution of conflicts (Bank & Kahn, 1982). Vestiges of sibling rivalry may even last into adulthood. Consider the brothers William James, the great psychologist, and Henry James, the great novelist. Despite their great mutual admiration and affection, they were lifelong rivals. This was highlighted in 1905, when William was elected to the prestigious Academy of Arts and Letters—three months after Henry's election. William declined membership because his "younger and shallower and vainer brother" had already been elected (Adams, 1981).

Gender-Role Development One of the most important aspects of psychosocial development in childhood is the development of **gender roles,** which are behavior patterns that are considered to be appropriate for males or females in a given culture. Gender roles vary across cultures and over

Gender Roles The behaviors that are considered to be appropriate for males or females in a given culture.

Sibling Rivalry Henry James, the novelist, and William James, the psychologist, had an intense sibling rivalry.

time. This once again demonstrates the tentativeness of research findings, which was discussed in chapter 2. During the nineteenth century, as the United States moved from an agricultural country to an industrial country, men began to play the "good provider" role and women began to play the "homemaker" role. No longer did the typical husband and wife work together on the family farm or in the family business. Instead, the husband went off to work, while the wife took care of the home and children. Because the family's income depended on the husband's job, his role increased in stature, while the wife's role decreased in stature (Bernard, 1981). American women began entering the job market in large numbers during World War II, when many men were serving in the armed forces. Today, most married women work outside the home at least part-time. Nonetheless, this has yet to lead to a drastic revision of traditional gender roles. For example, even when the wife and husband both work, most housework is still performed by the wife (Atkinson & Huston, 1984).

What factors account for the development and maintenance of gender roles? The first formal theory of gender-role development was put forth by Sigmund Freud. He assumed that the resolution of what he called the Oedipus conflict (see chapter 13) at age five or six led the child to adopt the gender of the same-sex parent. The Oedipus conflict begins with the child's sexual attraction to the opposite-sex parent. According to Freud, because the child fears punishment for desiring the opposite-sex parent, the child instead identifies with the same-sex parent. But studies of children show that gender identity develops by the age of three, long before the resolution of the Oedipus conflict, and that gender identity develops even in children who live in one-parent households. Because of the lack of research support for Freud's theory most researchers favor more recent theories of gender-role development.

Social learning theory stresses the importance of observational learning and positive reinforcement. Thus, social learning theorists assume that the child learns gender-relevant behaviors by observing gender-role models and by being rewarded for appropriate gender-role behavior. This process of gender typing begins on the very day of birth. In one study new parents were interviewed within twenty-four hours of the birth of their first child. Though there are no observable differences in the physical appearance of male and female newborns whose genitals are covered, parents were more likely to describe newborn daughters as cuter, weaker, and less coordinated than newborn sons (Rubin, Provenzano, & Luria, 1974). An influential review of research on sex differences found, however, that parents reported that they did not treat their sons and daughters differently (Maccoby & Jacklin, 1974). Of course, parents may believe they treat their sons and daughters the same, while actually treating them differently.

Traditional gender roles may also be perpetuated by the presence of men and women in positions in which they model stereotypic gender roles. For example, as long as women are more likely to be homemakers and men are more likely to be workers outside the home, children will be more likely to view these as appropriate gender-related behaviors. Moreover, educational approaches to changing gender roles will be less effective than will be the increased presence of males and females in nontraditional gender roles (Eagly, 1984). When it comes to gender roles, "do as I do" may be more powerful than "do as I say."

Cognitive Developmental Theory A theory of gender-role development that assumes the child must first understand the concept of gender before adopting behaviors that are gender related.

Lawrence Kohlberg (1966) put forth a **cognitive-developmental theory** of gender roles based on Piaget's theory of cognitive development. According to Kohlberg, the child must first understand the concept of male and female genders before adopting behaviors that are gender related. This occurs at about

Gender Roles According to social learning theory, children learn gender-role behaviors by being rewarded for performing those behaviors and by observing adults, particularly parents, engaging in them.

the age of three. Those with the best-developed sense of gender will be the most likely to act in accordance with gender roles. In essence, the child assimilates and accommodates information into the schemas of male and female.

This was supported in a study of forty-three twenty-one- to forty-month-old children who were asked to discriminate between pictures of males and females. Those who could discriminate between males and females were more likely to prefer same-sex peers and to show gender-related differences in their aggressiveness, with the boys acting more aggressively than the girls (Fagot, Leinbach, & Hagan, 1986). But there is also evidence contradicting Kohlberg's theory of gender-role development. For example, even children with low levels of gender awareness emulate same-sex models in preference to opposite-sex models. This provides stronger support for the social learning theory of gender-role development (Bussey & Bandura, 1984).

As a compromise between social learning theory and cognitive-developmental theory, Sandra Bem (1981) put forth a **gender schema theory,** which combines aspects of both. She believes that the process by which gender identity develops is best explained by cognitive-developmental theory, but the adoption of specific behaviors that are appropriate to the male and female genders is best explained by social learning theory. The theory holds that social learning leads the child to adopt specific gender-related behaviors that are integrated into a gender schema, which then leads the child to perform behaviors that are consistent with that schema.

Gender Schema Theory A theory of gender role development that combines aspects of social learning theory and cognitive-developmental theory.

ADOLESCENCE

Childhood blends into **adolescence.** The concept of adolescence is a modern invention, which appeared in industrialized countries to ease the transition between carefree childhood and responsible adulthood. Adolescence is unknown in many nonindustrialized countries, in which adulthood begins with the onset of puberty and is commonly celebrated with initiation rites.

Adolescence The transition period lasting from the onset of puberty to the beginning of adulthood.

PuBerty The period of rapid physical change that occurs during adolescence, including the development of the ability to reproduce sexually.

Physical Development

Recall your own adolescence. What you might recall most vividly are the rapid physical changes associated with **puberty.** Puberty is marked by a rapid increase in height (figure 12.9), with girls showing a growth spurt between the ages of ten and twelve and boys between the ages of twelve and fourteen. The physical changes of puberty also include the maturation of *primary sex characteristics* and *secondary sex characteristics* as a consequence of the increased secretion of the male sex hormone testosterone at twelve or thirteen and the female sex hormone estrogen at ten or eleven.

Boys have their first semen ejaculation between the ages of thirteen and fifteen, and girls have their first menstrual period between the ages of eleven and thirteen. In 1900, the average age of *menarche,* the onset of menstruation, was fourteen, but improved health and nutrition has reduced it to the age of twelve and a half. These physical changes can be distressing if the adolescent is unprepared for them or made to feel self-conscious by parents or peers. Early maturation has different effects on boys and girls. Girls who mature early may feel self-conscious and tend to develop more chunky figures. Boys who mature early may be more self-confident and sociable (Petersen, 1988).

What triggers the onset of puberty? Researchers are not sure, but one factor may be the *pineal gland,* which was first suspected almost a century ago. In 1898 the German physician Otto Heubner reported the case of a four-year-old boy who died after experiencing unusually early puberty. An autopsy revealed that a brain tumor had destroyed the boy's pineal gland, which is located in the center of the brain. Heubner reasoned that the pineal gland normally releases a substance that suppresses the onset of puberty. Researchers have since identified that substance as the hormone *melatonin.* A sudden decrease in the secretion of melatonin may initiate the physiological changes of puberty (Kolata, 1984a). Additional research is needed to determine whether this is, in fact, the trigger for puberty.

FIGURE 12.9
The Adolescent Growth Spurt
Puberty brings with it a rapid increase in height. Note that females experience an earlier growth spurt than males.

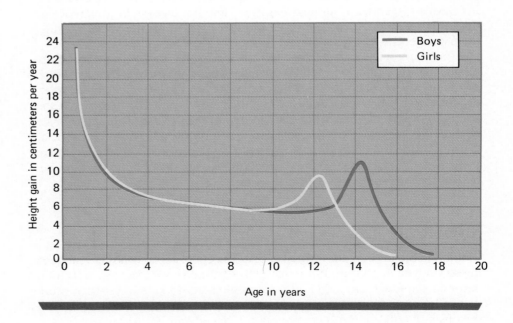

Puberty Because adolescents enter puberty at different times, junior high school classes will include students varying greatly in height and physical maturity. As a consequence, a typical junior high school class may appear to include a wider age range than it actually does.

Cognitive Development

According to Piaget, the adolescent is not only physically but also cognitively different from the child. At about the age of twelve, many, but not all, adolescents reach the **formal operational stage.** The stage is characterized by the ability to use abstract reasoning in the absence of concrete objects and to solve problems by testing hypotheses instead of by trial and error. For example, suppose that you had a row of three chairs and three persons to fill those chairs and were asked to determine how many different ways you could sit the three persons in the three chairs. A child in the concrete operational stage would need to have the three persons and the three chairs physically present to solve the problem. In contrast, an adolescent in the formal operational stage would be able to solve the problem mentally.

In the past two decades, Piaget's theory of cognitive development has come to influence research on moral development. This arose following dissatisfaction with Sigmund Freud's theory of moral development. According to Freud, moral values arise from the resolution of the Oedipus conflict at the age of five or six. By identifying with the same-sex parent, the child internalizes that parent's moral values. There is little research support for Freud's view of moral development (Hunt, 1979).

An alternative to the psychosexual theory of moral development has been provided by social learning theory. According to social learning theory, moral values arise primarily through the rewarding of good behavior and the punishing of bad behavior—most notably by the child's parents. The psychosexual theory and social learning theory of moral development are called *socialization theories,* because they both assume that morality is a set of values transmitted from generation to generation.

In contrast, the *cognitive-developmental theory* of Lawrence Kohlberg (1981) assumes that moral reasoning parallels the child's cognitive development and will be similar from one culture to another among individuals who have reached the same level of cognitive development. Moreover, moral

Formal Operational Stage The Piagetian stage, beginning at about age twelve, marked by the ability to use abstract reasoning and to solve problems by testing hypotheses.

development does not end in childhood. Instead, it continues through adolescence. Kohlberg's theory is based on Piaget's (1932) proposal that a person's level of moral development depends on his or her level of cognitive development. Kohlberg assumes that as a person becomes cognitively more complex, he or she also reaches more complex, higher levels of moral reasoning.

Kohlberg, agreeing with Piaget, developed a stage theory of moral development. Kohlberg determines the individual's level of moral reasoning by presenting a series of stories, each of which includes a moral dilemma. The person must suggest a resolution of the dilemma and give reasons for choosing that resolution. The person's stage of moral development depends not on the resolution but, rather, on the reasons given for that resolution. Your moral reasoning in resolving the following dilemma proposed by Kohlberg would determine your level of moral development:

> In Europe, a woman was near death from a very bad disease, a special kind of cancer. There was one drug that the doctors thought might save her. It was a form of radium that a druggist in the same town had recently discovered. The drug was expensive to make, but the druggist was charging ten times what the drug cost him to make. He paid two hundred dollars for the radium and charged two thousand dollars for a small dose of the drug. The sick woman's husband, Heinz, went to everyone he knew to borrow the money, but he could get together only about one thousand dollars, which was half of what it cost. He told the druggist that his wife was dying and asked him to sell it cheaper or let him pay later. But the druggist said, "No, I discovered the drug, and I am going to make money from it." So Heinz got desperate and broke into the man's store to steal the drug for his wife. (Kohlberg, 1981, p. 12)

The levels of moral development represented by particular responses to this dilemma are presented in table 12.2. Kohlberg has identified three levels of moral development: the *preconventional, conventional,* and *postconventional* levels. Each level contains two stages, making a total of six stages of moral development. As we progress to higher levels of moral reasoning, we become more concerned with the actor's motives than with the consequences of the actor's actions. This was supported by a study of moral judgments about aggressive behavior, which found that high school and college students at higher stages of moral reasoning were more concerned with the aggressor's motivation than were students at lower stages (Berkowitz, Mueller, Schnell, & Padberg, 1986).

People at the **preconventional level** of moral reasoning, usually children, are mainly concerned with the consequences of moral behavior to themselves. In stage 1, the person has a *punishment and obedience orientation,* in which moral behavior serves to avoid punishment. In stage 2, the child has an *instrumental relativist orientation,* in which moral behavior serves to get rewards or favors in return, as in "you scratch my back and I'll scratch yours."

People at the **conventional level** of moral reasoning, usually reached in late childhood or early adolescence, uphold conventional laws and values by favoring obedience to parents and authority figures. Kohlberg calls stage 3 the *good boy–nice girl orientation,* because the child assumes that moral behavior is desirable because it gains social approval, especially from parents. Kohlberg calls stage 4 the *society-maintaining orientation,* in which the adolescent views moral behavior as a way to do one's duty, show respect for authority, and maintain the social order.

At the end of adolescence, some of those who have reached the formal operational stage also reach the **postconventional level** of morality. At this level of moral reasoning, people make moral judgments based on ethical prin-

Preconventional Level In Kohlberg's theory, the level of moral reasoning characterized by concern with the consequences that behavior has to oneself.

Conventional Level In Kohlberg's theory, the level of moral reasoning characterized by concern with upholding laws and values and by favoring obedience to authority.

Postconventional Level In Kohlberg's theory, the level of moral reasoning characterized by concern with obeying mutually agreed upon laws and by the need to uphold human dignity.

TABLE 12.2   Kohlberg's Theory of Moral Development

Levels	Stages	Moral Reasoning in Response to the Heinz Dilemma	
		In Favor of Heinz's Stealing the Drug	Against Heinz's Stealing the Drug
I. Preconventional level: Motivated by self-interest	Stage 1 *Punishment and obedience orientation:* Motivation to avoid punishment	"If you let your wife die, you will get in trouble."	"You shouldn't steal the drug because you'll be caught and sent to jail if you do."
	Stage 2 *Instrumental relativist orientation:* Motivation to obtain rewards	"It wouldn't bother you much to serve a little jail term, if you have your wife when you get out."	"He may not get much of a jail term if he steals the drug, but his wife will probably die before he gets out, so it won't do him much good."
II. Conventional level: Motivated by conventional laws and values	Stage 3 *Good boy–nice girl orientation:* Motivation to gain approval and to avoid disapproval	"No one will think you're bad if you steal the drug, but your family will think you're an inhuman husband if you don't."	"It isn't just the druggist who will think you're a criminal, everyone else will too."
	Stage 4 *Society-maintaining orientation:* Motivation to fulfill one's duty and to avoid feelings of guilt	"If you have any sense of honor, you won't let your wife die because you're afraid to do the only thing that will save her."	"You'll always feel guilty for your dishonesty and lawbreaking."
III. Postconventional level: Motivated by abstract moral principles	Stage 5 *Social-contract orientation:* Motivation to follow rational, mutually agreed-upon principles and maintain the respect of others	"If you let your wife die, it would be out of fear, not out of reasoning it out."	"You would lose your standing and respect in the community and break the law."
	Stage 6 *Universal ethical principle orientation:* Motivation to uphold one's own ethical principles and avoid self-condemnation	"If you don't steal the drug, . . . you would have lived up to the outside rule of the law but you wouldn't have lived up to your own standards of conscience."	"If you stole the drug, . . . you'd condemn yourself because you wouldn't have lived up to your own conscience and standards of honesty."

ciples that may conflict with self-interest or with the maintenance of social order. In stage 5, the *social-contract orientation,* the person assumes that adherence to laws is in the long-term best interest of society but that unjust laws may sometimes have to be overturned. The U.S. Constitution is based on this view. Stage 6, the highest stage of moral reasoning, is called the *universal ethical principle orientation.* People at this stage assume that moral reasoning must uphold human dignity and their consciences—even if that brings them into conflict with their society's laws or values. Thus, an abolitionist who helped escaped slaves flee from plantations in the nineteenth century would be acting at this highest level of moral reasoning.

Kohlberg's theory has received some support from research studies. For example, a study of adolescents on an Israeli kibbutz found that, as predicted by Kohlberg's theory, their stages of moral development were related to their stages of cognitive development (Snarey, Reimer, & Kohlberg, 1985). But Kohlberg's theory has been criticized on several grounds. First, the theory explains moral reasoning, not moral action. A person's moral actions may not reflect his or her moral reasoning. Yet, there has been some research support for a positive relationship between moral reasoning and moral actions. One study found that people at higher stages of moral reasoning do tend to behave more honestly and more altruistically (Blasi, 1980).

A second criticism is that the situation, not just the person's level of moral reasoning, plays a role in moral decision making and moral actions. This was demonstrated in a study of male college students who performed a task in which their goal was to hold a stylus above a light moving in a triangular pattern—a tedious, difficult task. When provided with a strong enough temptation, even those at higher stages of moral reasoning succumbed to cheating (Malinowski & Smith, 1985).

Another criticism of Kohlberg's theory argues that the postconventional level of morality condemns those with conservative views of morality to no higher than the conventional level of morality. As one critic argues, Kohlberg's theory might as well be the view of "an articulate liberal secular humanist" (Shweder, 1982, p. 423). As evidence of this, college students at the postconventional level of morality are more likely to hold liberal moral positions, such as opposing capital punishment (de Vries & Walker, 1986). This apparent bias against conservative morality was also supported by a study of college students who defined themselves as either politically left wing or right wing. The students completed a measure of moral reasoning twice—once from their own political perspective and once from the other political perspective. As expected, the left-wingers scored higher on moral development than did the right-wingers when they responded from their own perspective. But when the right-wingers responded from what they believed was the left-wing perspective, they scored higher than when they responded from their own perspective (Emler, Renwick, & Malone, 1983). This indicates that either conservatives tend to function at a lower level of moral reasoning than do liberals or Kohlberg's theory of moral development is biased against conservative views of morality.

Besides the accusation of being biased toward a liberal view of morality, Kohlberg's theory has been accused of being biased toward a male view of morality. The main proponent of this criticism has been Carol Gilligan (1982). She claims that Kohlberg's theory favors the view that morality is concerned with legal *justice*—a male orientation—rather than with social *care*—a female orientation. She believes that women's moral reasoning is colored by their desire to relieve distress, while men's moral reasoning is colored by their desire to uphold laws. The results of a recent study supported Gilligan's claim that males and females differ in their notions of morality. As she would have predicted, males tended to have a justice orientation and females tended to have a care orientation. In addition, the more feminine the male, the more likely he was to favor a care orientation (Ford & Lowery, 1986).

Other critics insist that Kohlberg's theory may not have generality beyond Western industrialized cultures. This criticism has been countered by Kohlberg and his colleagues (Snarey, Reimer, & Kohlberg, 1985). They found that when people in other cultures are interviewed in their own languages, using moral dilemmas based on situations that are familiar to them, Kohlberg's theory holds up well. In other cultures, the stages of moral reasoning unfold in the order claimed by Kohlberg, though postconventional moral reasoning is not found in all cultures. Kohlberg's theory has become the most influential theory of moral development, but an adequate theory of moral development will probably have to include elements from socialization theories as well (Gibbs & Schnell, 1985).

Psychosocial Development

Adolescence is especially important in Erikson's psychosocial theory of development. Erikson (1963) believed that the most important task of adolescence was to resolve the crisis of *identity versus role confusion*. The adolescent develops a sense of identity by adopting personal values and social behaviors, but generally this does not occur before he or she experiments with a variety of values and social behaviors—often to the displeasure of parents. If you observe groups of adolescents, you will see styles, beliefs, and actions that may contrast markedly with adult norms. Erikson believes this is a normal part of answering questions related to one's identity. Who am I? What do I believe? What are my goals? Of course, in extreme cases, adolescents may adopt identities that encourage them to engage in delinquent behaviors. This is more common in adolescents with parents who set few rules, fail to discipline them, and fail to supervise their behavior (Loeber & Dishion, 1983). Erikson's theory of adolescence has received support from studies showing that adolescents do tend to move from a state of role confusion to a state of identity achievement (Constantinople, 1969).

Because the adolescent is dependent on parents, while at the same time seeking to be an independent person, adolescence has traditionally been con-

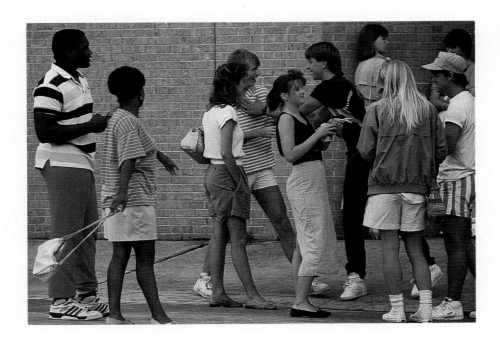

Identity Formation During adolescence, our peers play a large role in the development of our sense of identity.

sidered a time of conflict between parents and children. In fact, G. Stanley Hall (1904), the first great developmental psychologist, called adolescence a period of "storm and stress." But most adolescents have positive relations with their parents, and positive relations with parents promote more satisfactory relations with peers (Gold & Yanof, 1985).

But the onset of puberty is associated with an important conflict: that between the biological urge to engage in sexual relations and societal values against premarital sex. The proportion of adolescents engaging in sex increased from the 1930s to the 1980s, with most males and females now engaging in premarital sex before leaving their teens. Careless adolescent sexual activity makes teenage pregnancy a great problem, due to ignorance of birth control and failure to practice it. This leads to abortions, fatherless offspring, and inadequate care of offspring. Though American and European adolescents have similar sex rates, Americans have many more unwanted pregnancies, due to their failure to use contraceptives. This begins from the very first sexual experience, when most American adolescents do not use contraceptives (Brooks-Gunn & Furstenberg, 1989).

Adolescence is also a period when many individuals begin using drugs, including alcohol, nicotine, cocaine, and marijuana. More than two-thirds of high school seniors use alcohol regularly (Newcomb & Bentler, 1989). Drug use by adolescents is related to the use of drugs by their peers and parents. For example, adolescents are more likely to begin smoking if their peers and parents smoke (Chassin, Presson, Sherman, Montello, & McGrew, 1986). Drug use by adolescents is also related to emotional distress. A study of college students found that those experiencing uncontrollable and stressful negative life events were more likely than other students to resort to alcohol and other drugs to reduce their emotional distress (Newcomb & Harlow, 1986).

ADULTHOOD

Adulthood The period beginning when the individual assumes responsibility for his or her own life.

Until the past two decades, developmental psychologists have been more interested in studying development in childhood and adolescence than in studying development in adulthood. In Western cultures, **adulthood** begins when adolescents become independent from their parents and assume responsibility for their own lives. Of course, there is no single age that automatically signifies the onset of adulthood. Even the legal ages for voting, drinking, marrying, or assuming a variety of other adult responsibilities vary. Interest in adulthood development has brought an increased realization that development continues across the entire life span and is associated with physical, cognitive, and psychosocial changes.

Physical Development

Adults reach their physical peak in their late twenties, when they begin a slow physical decline that does not accelerate appreciably until old age. Beginning in the twenties, the basal metabolic rate also decreases, accounting in part for the tendency to gain weight in adulthood. This makes attention to a diet and exercise especially important for adults. Though heart, lung, and muscle capacities decline gradually through early and middle adulthood, diet and exercise can counter these changes somewhat. A prime example of this is Kareem Abdul Jabbar, who, by meticulous attention to maintaining a healthy diet and a state of physical fitness, played twenty years of professional basketball. He retired in 1989 at the age of forty-two. But peak performances in most sports occur in the early to late twenties. For example, on the average, baseball players

(a)

(b)

(c)

Aging and Physical Well-Being These people show that proper diet and exercise can help us maintain our physical well-being as we age. (a) By following a strict dietary and exercise routine, forty-one-year-old Dr. Gregg Amore won the 1988 "Mr. North America" body-building championship in the over-thirty-five-age class. He did so while fulfilling his roles as husband and father, running the family farm, and serving as director of counseling at Allentown College. (b) Even individuals in their eighties, such as marathon runner Ruth Rothfarb, can compete in athletics. (c) And downhill skiing, too, can be enjoyed by the elderly, including these two men in their seventies.

peak at twenty-eight years of age, distance runners peak at twenty-seven, and high jumpers peak at twenty-four (Horn, 1988).

As men age, they produce fewer and fewer sperm, yet they can still father children into old age. But they may have increasing difficulty in achieving penile erections (Doyle, 1989). When women reach their late forties or early fifties, they experience *menopause*—the cessation of the menstrual cycle. They experience a reduction in estrogen secretion, they stop ovulating, and, consequently, they can no longer become pregnant. The reduction in estrogen may cause sweating, hot flashes, and brittle bones, as well as atrophy of the vagina, uterus, and mammary glands. Women may view menopause negatively or positively. On the negative side, a woman may be distressed that she can no longer bear children. On the positive side, she may be pleased that she no longer menstruates monthly and no longer needs to use birth control.

Marked changes in physical abilities usually do not occur until late adulthood. The older adult will exhibit deterioration in heart output, lung capacity, reaction time, muscular strength, and motor coordination (Maranto, 1984).

Older adults tend to become farsighted and to lose their high-pitched hearing. Eventually, no matter how well we take care of our bodies, all of us die. Though the upper limit of the human life span seems to be about 120 years, few people live to even 100. This is so rare that weatherman Willard Scott has made a practice of wishing happy birthday on the "Today" show to people celebrating their 100th birthday. But why is death inevitable? Death seems to be genetically programmed into our cells. In old age, the ability of cells to repair and reproduce themselves simply gives out. This may occur because our cells can divide, and thereby restore the body, no more than fifty times, a limit that is approached in old age (Hayflick, 1980).

Cognitive Development

Developmental psychologists are especially concerned with cognitive changes in late adulthood. As discussed in chapter 9, the apparent decline in intelligence in the elderly is found more often in cross-sectional studies than in longitudinal studies. This indicates that the decline in intelligence found in cross-sectional studies may not be attributable solely to aging. And, as also discussed in chapter 9, any decline is more pronounced for fluid intelligence than for crystallized intelligence. The decline in fluid intelligence is associated with a slowing in the speed of information processing (Hertzog, 1989).

But do any other factors account for the poorer performance of older people on cognitive tasks? One factor that explains why older adults do more poorly than adolescents and young adults on cognitive tasks is that they have not attended school for many years. Consider the results of a study that compared the recall ability of college students of traditional age, their peers not attending college, and older people not attending college. The average age of the younger groups was twenty-two years and the average age of the older group was sixty-nine. The three groups were equal in verbal intelligence.

The results showed that the recall ability of the college group was better than that of the other two groups. But the older people who were not attending college did not differ from the younger people who were not attending college. This indicates that it may be the failure to use one's memory, rather than simply brain deterioration accompanying aging, that accounts for the inferior performance of the elderly on tests of recall. So, the adage "use it or lose it" may have some validity when it comes to the maintenance of cognitive abilities (Ratner, Schell, Crimmins, Mittelman, & Baldinelli, 1987).

Though aging does bring some slowing of cognitive processes, the greater experience that older adults may have in performing a particular task can prevent a decline in performance on that task. For example, older chess players, who have presumably experienced a decline in fluid intelligence, perform as well as younger players of equal ability. Evidently, the older players use their chess-playing experience to search more efficiently for the best moves (Charness, 1981).

B. F. Skinner (1983) has suggested ways to help older adults compensate for any decline in their perceptual and cognitive abilities. He has created what he calls a "prosthetic environment." For example, he suggests that elderly persons who cannot see well enough to read books should listen to recordings of books, and elderly persons who notice their memories failing should begin writing reminders to themselves.

Cognitive deterioration in old age is attributable in part to the loss of brain neurons. But the growth of dendrites from surviving neurons in the aging brain can compensate somewhat for this loss (Turkington, 1986). Perhaps the most devastating cause of cognitive deterioration associated with neuronal loss is Alzheimer's disease (see chapter 7), which affects up to two million Americans, the great majority over the age of sixty. About 100,000 victims die each year. The disease was first identified in 1907 by the German neurologist Alois Alzheimer in patients who had gradually lost their cognitive abilities over a period of years.

Alzheimer's disease begins with memory loss for recent events and progresses to the point that the victim cannot recognize family members or remember his or her own name, has difficulty performing cognitive tasks such as arithmetic, and exhibits personality deterioration. The disease is associated with the destruction of acetylcholine neurons. As discussed in chapter 3, acetylcholine neurons play a role in memory. The causes of Alzheimer's disease are unknown. Possible causes include heredity, toxins, and infections. As mentioned in chapter 7, preliminary, and so far unsuccessful, efforts are being made to treat the disease by providing victims with the dietary substance choline, which is a precursor of acetylcholine, in an effort to increase acetylcholine levels in the brain (Wurtman, 1985).

Back to School The myth that rapid intellectual decline is a normal aspect of aging is countered by the increasing numbers of older adults beginning college careers. The older adults who may now be in your classes were rare only a decade ago.

Psychosocial Development

Social development continues through early, middle, and late adulthood. Early adulthood extends from about age twenty to about age forty, middle adulthood extends from about age forty to about age sixty, and late adulthood extends from about age sixty on. The similarities exhibited by people within these periods are related to common social experiences associated with particular periods, such as employment, marriage, parenthood, widowhood, and retirement. Of course, events that are unique in each person's life may also play a role in psychosocial development. For example, chance encounters in each of our lives contribute to our unique development (Bandura, 1982). You might reflect on chance encounters that influenced your choice of a college or your meeting your current boyfriend or girlfriend.

Early Adulthood Though Sigmund Freud paid little attention to adult development, he did note that normal adulthood is defined by the ability to love and to work. Erik Erikson agreed that the capacity for love is an important aspect of early adulthood and claimed that the first major task of adulthood is the development of *intimacy versus isolation*. Intimate relationships involve a strong sense of emotional attachment and personal commitment. A study of college women supported Erikson's belief that the development of the capacity for intimacy depends on the successful formation of a personal identity in adolescence. Women who were capable of high intimacy felt more secure and confident as separate individuals and responded with less distress to separations from persons to whom they were attached (Levitz-Jones & Orlofsky, 1985).

About 95 percent of young adults experience the intimate relationship of marriage. But what characteristics do they look for in potential spouses? Both men and women tend to seek spouses who are kind, loyal, honest, considerate, intelligent, affectionate, and interesting. In addition, men tend to be more concerned than women with the potential spouse's physical attractiveness, and women tend to be more concerned than men with the potential spouse's earning capacity (Buss & Barnes, 1986).

Freud predicted that men will prefer wives like their mothers and women will prefer husbands like their fathers. This was supported by a study of 577 brides and 403 grooms of mixed ethnic parentage in Hawaii. The ethnic groups included white, black, Hawaiian, Portugese, Chinese, Korean, Filipino, and Japanese. As predicted by Freud, males were more likely to marry into their mothers' ethnic groups and females were more likely to marry into fathers' ethnic groups (Jedlicka, 1980). This provides some support for the lyrics "I want a girl [boy] just like the girl [boy] who married dear old dad [mom]."

What determines whether a marriage will succeed? Marital happiness depends, in part, on the relative dominance of the spouses. The happiest marriages are those in which neither spouse is dominant over the other. But marriages in which the wife is dominant are more unhappy than marriages in which the husband is dominant, perhaps reflecting traditional gender-role norms (Gray-Little & Burks, 1983). Another important factor in marital happiness is the willingness to discuss marital issues. Active discussions of marital issues by couples result in more effective problem solving than does avoidance of such issues (Miller, Lefcourt, Holmes, Ware, & Saleh, 1986). Marital happiness is also related to work. Wives who work outside the home are more satisfied than those who do not. But, possibly because of the continued strength of the traditional male gender role, husbands of working women feel less adequate as family breadwinners (Staines, Pottick, & Fudge, 1986).

Unfortunately, for many couples marital happiness is an elusive state. About half of first marriages end in divorce. In extreme cases, divorce is the consequence of wife abuse. Yet, many abused wives remain married. What determines whether an abused wife will leave her husband? Abused wives are more likely to leave if they have outside employment, if they have shorter, less committed relationships, if their children are also being abused, and if they have a history of previous separations (Strube, 1988).

For most married couples, parenthood is a major part of early adulthood. Some women experience *postpartum depression,* severe depression following the birth of a child. Though this may be, in part, a consequence of hormonal changes, it may also be the result of a decrease in participation in rewarding social activities brought about by new parental responsibilities (Atkinson & Rickel, 1984). Raising children can be one of the greatest joys in life, but it can also be one of life's greatest stresses. Because women still tend to be the primary caregiver, their parental responsibilites tend to be especially stressful. But mothers who receive emotional support from their husbands show less distress in response to their children (Levitt, Weber, & Clark, 1986).

Middle Adulthood   In 1850 few Americans lived beyond what we now call early adulthood. The average life span was only forty years (Shneidman, 1989). But improved sanitation, nutrition, and health care have almost doubled that life span. What was the end of life more than a century ago is today simply the beginning of middle adulthood. According to Erik Erikson, the main task of middle adulthood is resolving the crisis of *generativity versus stagnation.* Those who achieve generativity become less self-absorbed, more productive, and more concerned about the well-being of the world and future generations. In fact, as illustrated in figure 12.10, the transition between early and middle adulthood, from the late thirties to the early forties, is a time when leaders and creative people tend to make their most outstanding contributions (Simonton, 1988).

Experiences as parents during early adulthood lay the groundwork for the achievement of generativity in middle adulthood (Snarey, Son, Kuehne, Hauser, & Vaillant, 1987). But middle adulthood also brings transitions associated with one's children. You may be surprised to learn that parents become more distressed and experience more marital unhappiness after their first child leaves home than after their last child leaves home. In fact, after the last child has left home, parents tend to be more relaxed and experience improved marital relations (Harris, Ellicott, & Holmes, 1986). Perhaps the notion of an "empty nest syndrome" (after the last child has left home) should be replaced by the notion of a "partly-empty nest syndrome" (after the first child has left home).

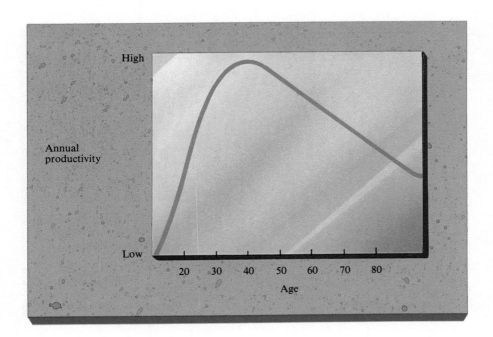

FIGURE 12.10
Age and Achievement
Outstanding creative and leadership achievement peaks in the late thirties and early forties (Simonton, 1988).

Late Adulthood As more people live into their seventies and beyond, developmental psychologists have become more interested in studying late adulthood. In 1900 only one person in thirty was over sixty-five. By 1970 one person in nine was over sixty-five, and by 2020 one person in five will be over sixty-five (Eisdorfer, 1983). While this increase in the elderly population will bring new concerns about physical needs, it will also bring new concerns about psychosocial needs.

Erikson claimed that the main psychosocial task of late adulthood is to resolve the crisis of *integrity versus despair.* A sense of integrity results from reflecting back on a meaningful life. But old age can be more than a time of reflection. Changes in work laws enable people to work beyond the traditional retirement age of sixty-five, providing the opportunity to continue meaningful work. For those who prefer not to work, retirement usually brings physically healthy couples greater marital happiness than at any other time during their marriages.

For those who remain healthy and mentally active, late adulthood has been called the "Indian summer" of life. Consider a follow-up study of men from Lewis Terman's study of the mentally gifted, which began in 1921 and is discussed in chapter 9. At the time of the follow-up study, the men averaged seventy years of age (Shneidman, 1989). This and other studies have shown that personal growth and accomplishment can continue well into late adulthood. You have probably encountered lively, active older people in your own life. For example, in December 1988, the number-one nationwide best-seller was *Gracie,* written by the then ninety-two-year-old comedian George Burns. And Burns had been booked years earlier to perform at the Palladium Theatre in London on his one-hundreth birthday in 1996.

Eventually we all must confront two of the greatest social challenges of old age—the death of our loved ones and our own death. The loss of a spouse is especially stressful. Both widows and widowers are more likely to suffer depression, illness, and death than are their peers with living spouses, perhaps because of the loss of the emotional and practical support previously provided by their spouses. But widowers are more devastated than widows, apparently because widows receive greater social support from others—particularly from their friends (Stroebe & Stroebe, 1983).

Accomplishment in Old Age
Old age is not necessarily a
barrier to performing well in
demanding fields. Until his death
in 1989, Representative Claude
Pepper of Florida lived a vigorous
life, championing the cause of
"senior citizens" well into his
eighties.

Hospice Movement The
movement to provide care for the
terminally ill in settings that are
as close to everyday life as
possible, and that emphasizes the
need to reduce pain and
suffering.

Near-Death Experiences The
experiences reported by persons
as they die or by persons who
have apparently died and then
been revived.

Though, as Benjamin Franklin observed in 1789, "in this world nothing's
certain but death and taxes," we can at least improve the way in which we
confront death. Prior to the twentieth century, death was accepted as a public
part of life. People died at home surrounded by loved ones. In contrast, the
twentieth century has been characterized by denial of death and isolation of
the dying person (Robinson, 1981). Today, people commonly die alone, in
pain, in hospital rooms, and attached to life-support systems.

One of the most promising developments in our approach to death and
dying is the **hospice movement,** founded in the 1950s by the British physician Cicely Saunders, who was disturbed by her colleagues' inability to respond sensitively to dying patients. The hospice movement was introduced
to the United States in 1962 in Connecticut. As indicated in figure 12.11, the
hospice provides comprehensive care for the dying patient in a hospital, residential, or home setting and differs in several ways from the traditional
twentieth-century approach to dying (Butterfield-Picard & Magno, 1982).

But what of the psychological experiences of the dying? The person who
has done the most to promote interest in studying the experiences of dying
persons is Elizabeth Kübler-Ross (1969). Based on her observations of thousands of dying patients, she identified five stages experienced by terminally
ill patients: *denial, anger, bargaining, depression,* and *acceptance.* At first,
terminally ill patients deny their medical diagnoses, then become angry at
their plight, bargain with God to let them live, suffer depression at the thought
of dying, and finally come to accept their impending deaths. Kübler-Ross,
however, has found that not all terminally ill patients go through all the stages
or go through them in the same order (Kübler-Ross, 1974). Her research has
inspired others to study the process of dying.

Some researchers, including Kübler-Ross, have also studied so-called **near-
death experiences,** which are the experiences of persons as they die or of
persons who have apparently died and then been revived. These persons may

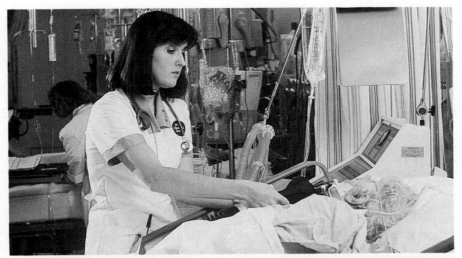

FIGURE 12.11
The Hospice During the last three decades, the hospice movement has provided many dying patients with a more dignified and humane death and their families with practical and emotional support. The patient and his or her family are given primary responsibility for decisions concerning the patient, including when to discontinue artificial life support. Emphasis is placed on relieving the patient's physical pain and psychological distress, preferably in as homelike an environment as possible.

report any of a remarkable set of experiences. Some report that their minds left their bodies, permitting them to view themselves. They may report traveling through a tunnel with a light at the end and meeting deceased friends and relatives. Others report seeing beings of light, such as a Christ figure, who present them with a review of their lives and then send them back to live a better life. Many report that the experience is pleasant and that they would have preferred to stay.

Of course, this evidence is based on anecdotal reports. Scientific study of these experiences is difficult for both ethical and practical reasons—though Thomas Edison believed it would be possible to measure the energy of the mind as it left the dying body to enter the hereafter. Critics of supposed near-death experiences claim that they may simply be hallucinations induced by drugs, fever, anoxia, anesthesia, or the emotional and physiological changes accompanying dying (Siegel, 1980). For each of us, the ultimate mystery will be answered by our own experience, not by scientific research.

THINKING ABOUT PSYCHOLOGY

Are There Significant Sex Differences?

In the nineteenth century, scientific interest in the question of whether or not significant sex differences exist was stimulated by Darwin's theory of evolution. His theory promoted the belief that males and females evolved physical and psychological differences that help them function in particular roles (Shields, 1975). Beginning in the 1960s, assumptions about sex differences began to be evaluated through scientific research.

There is controversy concerning the extent and importance of psychological sex differences. In addition, there is controversy concerning the relative importance of heredity and environment in accounting for any such differences. Researchers concerned with this controversy are often advocates of one side or the other, which brings into question their objectivity even more than the objectivity of researchers in less emotionally charged areas (Wittig, 1985). Keep in mind that, as discussed in chapter 2, the biases of researchers can influence their research findings.

Motor Differences

In early childhood boys are slightly better than girls at motor tasks, and both boys and girls improve their motor abilities through childhood. This means that during childhood females have the potential to compete equally with males in sports. But, after puberty, females level off in their motor abilities, while males continue to improve. Thus, the disparity between males and females on many motor tasks, including athletics, will be significantly greater after puberty. But what accounts for sex differences in motor abilities? Some differences are attributable to males' greater experience in competitive games requiring agility, balance, and jumping. But other differences appear to be more related to biological differences, particularly differences in tasks requiring strength or throwing ability (Thomas & French, 1985).

Cognitive Differences

In studying cognitive differences between males and females, researchers have concentrated on differences in verbal, spatial, and mathematical abilities. Females tend to be superior to males in verbal abilities, as measured by their speaking, spelling, vocabulary, and reading comprehension. Yet, contrary to the popular stereotype, men are more talkative than women (Hyde & Linn, 1988). Though research has tended to find that men are superior on spatial tasks, such as manipulating mental images of objects, the adequacy of this research and the notion of a general spatial ability has been questioned by researchers who are not convinced by such findings (Caplan, MacPherson, & Tobin, 1985).

Perhaps the most widely accepted sex difference is that males are, on the average, better than females in mathematics. A national talent search by Camilla Benbow and Julian Stanley (1983) found that among seventh and eighth graders who took the mathematics subtest of the Scholastic Aptitude Test (SAT) males performed better. Among those scoring higher than seven hundred (out of eight hundred) males outnumbered females thirteen to one. Could this be attributed to males having more experience in mathematics? Benbow and Stanley say no, because they found no difference in the number of mathematics courses taken by males and females. Because they found no life experiences that could explain their findings, Benbow and Stanley concluded that there might be a biological basis for this difference.

Their conclusion has provoked controversy. Critics argue that the sex differences in mathematical abilities reported by Benbow and Stanley may be attributable to mathematically gifted girls having been less willing to take part in the study, to girls having less experience in activities associated with mathematics other than classes in mathematics, and to cultural norms that teach girls that mathematics is a pursuit more appropriate for boys (Tomizuka & Tobias, 1981). Also, boys do not perform better than girls on all measures of mathematical ability. Though boys receive higher scores on mathematics achievement tests, girls receive higher grades in mathematics courses. What could account for this? One possible explanation is the finding that girls tend to perform better than boys in familiar situations, such as in the classroom, while boys tend to perform better than girls in novel situations, such as on standardized tests (Kimball, 1989).

If cognitive sex differences do exist, what factors might account for them? One factor might be hormonal differences. In one study, females exposed to abnormally high levels of prenatal testosterone did better than other females on tests of spatial ability, participated more on tasks involving spatial manipulation, and participated less on tasks involving verbal activity (Resnick, Berenbaum, Gottesman, & Bouchard, 1986).

Cognitive sex differences have also been attributed to differences in brain structures. But efforts to associate cognitive differences with differences in brain structures have produced mixed results. A decade ago researchers who examined the brains of deceased men and women found that a portion of the corpus callosum called the splenium was larger in women than in men (as explained in chapter 3, the corpus callosum is a bundle of axons that provides a means of communication between the cerebral hemispheres). In discussing the results of their study, the researchers concluded that the larger female splenium might explain why females seem to make more equal use of the cognitive abilities associated with the two cerebral hemispheres (DeLacoste-Utamsing & Holloway, 1982). But a replication of this study, which used magnetic resonance imaging to examine the brains of living people, found no sex differences in the size of the splenium. Moreover, the relationship, if any, between the size of the splenium and its role in hemispheric communication is unknown (Byrne, Bleier, & Houston, 1988).

Perhaps cognitive sex differences are caused more by social, rather than biological, factors. This may explain why studies conducted during the past twenty years show a narrowing of cognitive sex differences between males and females (Jacklin, 1989). It is inconceivable that males and females have become physiologically more alike in that short period of time. A much more likely explanation for this decrease in sex differences is the recent cultural movement to provide more similar treatment of male and female children.

Psychosocial Differences

The nineteenth-century psychologist Sir Francis Galton once remarked, "One notable peculiarity in the character of woman is that she is capricious and coy, and has less straightforwardness than the man" (Buss, 1976, p. 284). Today, psychologists would discount as sexist and unscientific statements such as this, which was based on Galton's assumption that heredity accounted for differences in social behavior between males and females. Though research has found several differences in the social behavior of males and females, the extent to which these are attributable to biological differences is unclear.

Females exposed prenatally to high levels of testosterone, either because of an endocrine disorder or because their mothers received testosterone injections while pregnant, tend to develop a tomboyish appearance and to become more aggressive in play. But these girls are usually born with masculine-looking genitals, which are surgically corrected. Perhaps the more masculine behavior of these girls is caused not by their prenatal exposure to testosterone but, instead, by their parents' responses to their having masculine genitals initially and to the girls' own responses to being informed of their early condition. But this explanation is also questionable, because parents report that they do not treat these girls any differently than they treat their other daughters (Hines, 1982).

Females have a reputation for being more emotionally sensitive than males. For example, women are considered more empathetic than men. But this apparent difference depends on how empathy is measured. When asked to report on their level of empathy, females score higher than males. But when empathy is measured by physiological arousal or overt behavior, sex differences disappear. Evidently, social expectations that females will be more emotionally sensitive than males create differences in their self-reports but not in their actual behavior (Eisenberg & Lennon, 1983).

Just as females are reputed to be more empathetic than males, males are reputed to be more aggressive than females. But, again, this difference depends on how aggressiveness is measured. Males are somewhat more physically aggressive than females, as in fighting, sports, or crime. But males and females do not differ in their verbal aggressiveness (Eagly & Steffen, 1986). Males are also reputed to be more dominant in social situations. But sex differences in social dominance may reflect differences in social status, rather than sex differences. For example, men may be more influential and women more influenceable because men are more likely than women to hold high-status positions (Eagly, 1983).

As in the case of cognitive differences, evidence supporting the biological basis of sex differences in social behavior implicates hormonal differences. For example, highly masculine females may have higher levels of testosterone and perceive themselves as more self-directed, action oriented, and less socially caring than other females (Baucom, Besch, & Callahan, 1985). Again, despite studies providing evidence supporting a biological basis for sex differences in social behavior, life experiences appear to be more important in accounting for those differences (Deaux, 1985).

After two decades of extensive research, no sex differences have emerged that are large enough to predict with confidence how particular males and females will behave. This means that decisions concerning the suitability of particular males or females for specific academic or vocational positions should not be influenced by assumptions concerning sex differences in cognitive or social behavior. The relatively few demonstrated sex differences and the decrease in the size of sex differences over the past few decades have led psychologist Roy Baumeister (1988) to argue that we should no longer study them. Why study differences that are too few or too small to have practical significance? And why study sex differences when reports of even small differences may support discrimination against one sex or the other? This view was countered by psychologist Sandra Scarr (1988), who believes objective scientific research on sex differences should continue, even if it may potentially discover differences that we would prefer do not exist. As you can see, research on sex differences is as much a social and political issue as it is a scientific one.

SUMMARY

THE NATURE OF DEVELOPMENTAL PSYCHOLOGY

The field that studies the physical, cognitive, and psychosocial changes that take place across the life span is called developmental psychology. One of the important issues in developmental psychology is whether development is a gradual process or a process marked by abrupt changes. A second important issue is whether development is determined more by nature or nurture. Developmental psychologists rely on longitudinal studies and cross-sectional studies.

PRENATAL PERIOD

The prenatal period is divided into the germinal, embryonic, and fetal stages. The development of body organs is governed by cell-adhesion molecules. Women who drink alcohol during pregnancy may have offspring who suffer from fetal alcohol syndrome. During the third trimester, the fetus can form memories of sounds that it has heard.

CHILDHOOD

Infancy extends from birth to two years old, and childhood extends from infancy until puberty. Motor development follows a consistent sequence, though the timing of motor milestones will vary somewhat among infants. Jean Piaget found that children pass through distinct cognitive stages of development. During the sensorimotor stage, the infant learns to coordinate sensory experiences and motor behavior and forms schemas that represent aspects of the world. The preoperational stage is marked by transductive reasoning and egocentrism. In the concrete operational stage, the child learns to make transitive inferences and to appreciate conservation.

Erik Erikson put forth an influential theory of psychosocial development. He believed that the life span consists of eight distinct stages, each associated with a crisis that must be overcome. An important factor in infant development is social attachment, a strong emotional tie to a caregiver. Permissive or authoritarian child-rearing practices are less effective than authoritative ones. Children who receive high-quality day care do not appear to suffer ill effects from being separated from their parents. And adopted children are at least as well adjusted as children raised by their biological parents. Gender-role development is explained by social learning theory, cognitive-developmental theory, and gender schema theory.

ADOLESCENCE

Adolescence is a transition period between childhood and adulthood that begins with puberty. Some adolescents enter Piaget's formal operational stage. The most influential theory of moral development has been Lawrence Kohlberg's cognitive-developmental theory. His theory is based on Piaget's proposal that a person's level of moral development depends on his or her level of cognitive development. Kohlberg proposes that we pass through preconventional, conventional, and postconventional levels of moral development. Carol Gilligan argues that Kohlberg's theory is biased toward a masculine view of morality. Adolescence is also a time of identity formation, in which the individual becomes more and more influenced by peers.

ADULTHOOD

Adulthood begins when adolescents become independent from their parents. Adults reach their physical peak in their late twenties, at which point they begin a gradual decline that does not accelerate appreciably until old age. Middle-aged women experience menopause. Though aging brings some slowing of cognitive processes, people who continue to be mentally active show less cognitive decline than do other people. Some adults succumb to the degenerative brain disorder called Alzheimer's disease.

About 95 percent of adults marry, but half of today's marriages will end in divorce. The most successful marriages are those in which neither spouse is dominant and in which the spouses discuss, rather than avoid, marital issues. Contrary to popular belief, after the last child has left home, parents tend to improve their emotional and marital well-being. Elizabeth Kübler-Ross stimulated interest in the study of death and dying. She found that dying people go through the stages of denial, anger, bargaining, depression, and acceptance. The hospice movement has promoted more humane, personal, and homelike care for the dying patient.

THINKING ABOUT PSYCHOLOGY: ARE THERE SIGNIFICANT SEX DIFFERENCES?

Research on sex differences has found no consistent differences in male and female brains. Boys and girls differ little in their physical abilities until puberty, when boys begin to improve more than girls. Females tend to have better verbal abilities, while males tend to have better spatial and mathematical abilities. Males also tend to be more physically aggressive than females. Research on sex differences is controversial, because of fears that its findings might be used to promote discrimination. Sex differences are based on group averages and are so small that they should not be used to make decisions about individuals.

IMPORTANT CONCEPTS

IMPORTANT PEOPLE

RECOMMENDED READINGS

For More on All Aspects of Development:

Santrock, J. W. (1989). Life-span development (3rd ed.). Dubuque, IA: Wm. C. Brown.
A textbook focusing on the physical, cognitive, and social development at each stage of the life span.

For More on Infancy:

Klaus, M. H., & Klaus, P. (1985). *The amazing newborn.* Reading, MA: Addison-Wesley.
A survey of the many, often surprising, perceptual and cognitive abilities of the newborn infant.

Lamb, M. E., & Bornstein, M. H. (1987). *Development in infancy: An introduction* (2nd ed.). New York: Random House.
A textbook covering all aspects of infant development.

For More on Childhood:

Sroufe, A. L., & Cooper, R. G. (1987). *Child development: Its nature and course.* New York: Random House.
A comprehensive textbook of development in childhood.

For More on Adolescence:

Erikson, E. H. (1968). *Identity: Youth and crisis.* New York: Norton.
Erik Erikson's classic book on adolescent development.

Santrock, J. W. (1987). *Adolescence* (3rd ed.). Dubuque, IA: Wm. C. Brown.
A textbook providing thorough coverage of physical, cognitive, and psychosocial development in adolescence.

For More on Adulthood:

Woodruff-Pak, D. S. (1988). *Psychology and aging.* Englewood Cliffs, NJ: Prentice-Hall.
A textbook describing physical, cognitive, and psychosocial factors in aging.

For More on Sex Differences:

Doyle, J. A. (1989). *The male experience* (2nd. ed.). Dubuque, IA: William C. Brown.
A fascinating discussion of the male gender role, including its historical development in Western culture.

Eagly, A. H. (1987). *Sex differences in social behavior: A social-role explanation.* Hillsdale, NJ: Erlbaum.
A thorough review of research on psychological similarities and differences between males and females.

Hyde, J. S. (1985). *Half the human experience* (3rd ed.). Lexington, MA: Heath.
A scholarly presentation of research on the female gender role.

CHAPTER
13

PERSONALITY

Chapter Opening Art:
Jackson Pollock. *Male
and Female*.

Personality An individual's unique, relatively consistent pattern of thoughts, feelings, and behaviors.

The word *personality* comes from the Latin word *persona,* meaning mask. Just as masks distinguished one character from another in ancient Greek and Roman plays, your personality distinguishes you from other people. Your **personality** is your unique, relatively consistent pattern of thoughts, feelings, and behaviors. To appreciate the uniqueness of each personality, first consider the following personality description (Ulrich, Stachnik, & Stainton, 1963):

> You have a strong need for other people to like and admire you. You have a tendency to be critical of yourself. You have a great deal of unused capacity, which you have not turned to your advantage. . . . Disciplined and controlled on the outside, you tend to be worrisome and insecure inside. . . . At times you are extraverted, affable, and sociable; at other times, you are introverted, wary, and reserved.

Do you recognize yourself in this description? Study after study has shown that when people are given personality tests and then presented with mock personality descriptions like this one, which include statements that are true of almost everyone, they tend to view the descriptions as accurate. This is especially true when the descriptions are flattering (Johnson, Cain, Falke, Hayman, & Perillo, 1985). The tendency to accept personality descriptions based on statements that are true of almost everyone is known as the "Barnum effect" (Meehl, 1956). This reflects P. T. Barnum's saying, "There's a sucker born every minute, and his observation, "A good circus has a little something for everybody."

Several years ago, in a study that made the same point about astrological personality descriptions, a researcher placed a newspaper advertisement offering a free personalized horoscope. Of the 150 who responded, 141 (or 94 percent) said they recognized themselves in the "personalized" description. Actually, each of the respondents received the same personality description—the personality profile of a mass murderer in France (Waldrop, 1984). Thus, useful personality descriptions must distinguish one person from another, instead of simply stating characteristics that most people have in common. You should no more accept a personality description that fails to recognize your distinctive combination of personal characteristics than you would accept a physical description that merely states that you have a head, a torso, two eyes,

The Actual Self and the Ideal Self Picasso's 1932 painting of a *Girl Before A Mirror* depicts the actual self and the ideal self.

Pablo Picasso, *Girl Before a Mirror,* 1932, oil on canvas, 64 × 51¼". Collection, The Museum of Modern Art, N.Y. Gift of Mrs. Simon Guggenheim.

ten toes, and other physical characteristics shared by almost everyone. Given that each of us has a unique personality, how do we explain our distinctive patterns of thoughts, feelings, and behaviors? Several psychological approaches have attempted to answer this question.

THE PSYCHOBIOLOGICAL APPROACH

Some personality researchers have warned that "any theory that ignores the evidence for the biological underpinnings of human behavior is bound to be an incomplete one" (Kenrick & Dantchik, 1983, p. 302). They recognize the importance of the *psychobiological approach* to personality. The biological underpinnings of personality have been recognized by ancient and modern thinkers alike. The Greek physician and philosopher Hippocrates (460–377 B.C.) presented an early biological view of personality. He claimed that **temperament,** a person's predominant emotional state, reflects the relative levels of body fluids he called *humors.* Hippocrates associated blood with a cheerful, or *sanguine,* temperament; phlegm with a calm, or *phlegmatic,* temperament; black bile with a depressed, or *melancholic,* temperament; and yellow bile with an irritable, or *choleric,* temperament.

More recently, the eighteenth and nineteenth centuries saw the advent of phrenology and physiognomy. As described in chapter 3, *phrenology* is the study of the bumps of the skull. Phrenologists assumed that specific areas of the brain control specific personality characteristics and that the bumps and depressions of the skull indicate the size of those brain areas (figure 13.1).

Temperament A person's characteristic emotional state, first apparent in early infancy and possibly inborn.

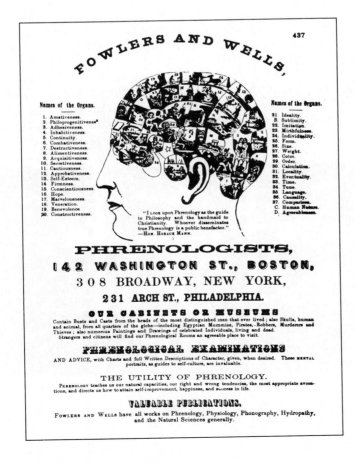

FIGURE 13.1
Phrenology This nineteenth-century advertisement shows the brain sites that phrenologists believed were associated with particular personality and intellectual characteristics.

Physiognomy, the study of the face, held that personality was revealed by the features of the face. Physiognomy became so popular that it almost prevented Charles Darwin from embarking on the historic voyage that inspired his theory of evolution. In 1836 the captain of the H.M.S. *Beagle* threatened to reject Darwin as the ship's naturalist because he thought Darwin's nose was the wrong shape for a sailor (Fancher, 1979). Because research findings failed to support either phrenology or physiognomy, psychologists lost interest in them. The early twentieth century saw increasing interest in the study of the relationship between physique and personality.

Physique and Personality

The following passage from Shakespeare's *Julius Caesar* (act I, scene 2) expresses Caesar's belief that one's physique reveals one's personality:

> Let me have men about me that are fat;
> Sleek-headed men and such as sleep o'nights:
> Yond Cassius has a lean and hungry look;
> He thinks too much: Such men are dangerous.

The study of the relationship between physique and personality began with the work of the German psychiatrist Ernst Kretschmer (1925). But the researcher who did the most to advance the scientific study of this relationship was the American physician William Sheldon (1899–1977).

In formulating his *constitutional theory* of personality, Sheldon (Sheldon & Stevens, 1942) examined photographs of thousands of male college students. He identified three kinds of physiques, which he called **somatotypes.** The *ectomorph* has a thin, frail body; the *mesomorph* has a muscular, strong body; and the *endomorph* has a fat, soft body. Based on personality assessments, Sheldon associated each somatotype with a particular temperament. He called the shy, restrained, and introspective temperament of the ectomorph *cerebrotonia*; the bold, assertive, and energetic temperament of the mesomorph *somatotonia;* and the relaxed, sociable, and easygoing temperament of the endomorph *viscerotonia.* Because other researchers failed to support Sheldon's findings, psychologists interested in the biological basis of personality turned away from somatotyping. More recently, they have become interested in studying the relationship between heredity and personality.

Somatotype A person's body type, whether an ectomorph (thin), a mesomorph (muscular), or an endomorph (fat).

Somatotypes William Sheldon would view Woody Allen as an ectomorph, Arnold Schwarzenneger as a mesomorph, and John Candy as an endomorph. Does each exhibit the temperament associated with his somatotype? If so, does that necessarily verify the theory of somatotypes?

Heredity and Personality

A century ago Francis Galton insisted that "nature prevails enormously over nurture" (Holden, 1987, p. 598). Today those, like Galton, who believe that heredity molds personality assume that evolution has provided us with inborn behavioral tendencies that differ somewhat from person to person (Buss, 1984). The study of the relationship between heredity and behavior is called **behavioral genetics.** Research in this field has shown that even newborn infants exhibit differences in temperament—some are placid, while others are irritable (Matheny, Riese, & Wilson, 1985). But how might these initial differences in temperament contribute to the development of differences in personality? They do so by affecting how infants respond to other people and, in turn, how other people respond to them. For example, a placid infant would be less responsive to other people. As a consequence, others would be less responsive to the infant. This might predispose the infant to become less sociable later in childhood.

Behavioral Genetics The study of the relationship between heredity and behavior.

Psychobiological Assessment of Personality

With the decline of interest in the study of somatotypes, those who favor the psychobiological approach are more interested in assessing the relationship between heredity and personality. In general, the closer the genetic relationship between two persons the more alike they will be in personality characteristics. Because this relationship may reflect common life experiences, rather than common genetic inheritance, researchers have resorted to adoption studies to determine the relative contributions of heredity and life experiences. Children who were adopted as infants tend to be more similar in temperament to their biological mothers than to their adoptive mothers. One study found that adopted infants and their biological mothers were more similar in their degrees of shyness than were adopted infants and their adoptive mothers (Daniels & Plomin, 1985). This indicates that parent-child personality similarity is influenced more by common heredity than by common life experiences.

Studies of identical twins reared apart provide additional evidence of the hereditary basis of personality. Identical twins have 100 percent of their genes in common, while fraternal twins have 50 percent in common. This may explain why identical twins who are adopted and reared by different families are more similar in personality than are fraternal twins who are reared by their biological parents—even three decades after adoption (Tellegen et al., 1988). Since 1979, psychologist Thomas Bouchard of the University of Minnesota has conducted the most comprehensive study of identical twins reared apart. He has found amazing behavioral similarities between some of the twins.

Consider the case of Oskar Stohr and Jack Yufe, who were born in Trinidad to a Jewish father and a Catholic mother. The twins were separated shortly after birth and reared in vastly different life circumstances. Oskar was raised in Germany as a Nazi and a Catholic by his maternal grandmother, while Jack was raised in Trinidad as a Jew by his father. Decades later, when they arrived at the airport in Minneapolis to take part in Bouchard's study, both Jack and Oskar sported mustaches, wire-rimmed glasses, and two-pocket shirts with epaulets. Bouchard found that they both preferred sweet liqueurs, stored rubber bands on their wrists, flushed the toilet before using it, read magazines from back to front, and dipped buttered toast in their coffee (Holden, 1980).

Though there are no "flush toilet before using" genes, the men's identical genetic inheritance may have provided them with similar temperaments that predisposed them to develop certain behavioral similarities.

Status of the Psychobiological Approach

Research has failed to find the strong relationship between somatotype and personality reported by Sheldon. One of the main problems with Sheldon's research was that *he* rated both the somatotypes and the temperaments of his subjects. This provided room for experimenter bias, perhaps influencing his ratings to support his theory. Nonetheless, there is a modest relationship between physique and personality. For example, mesomorphic males tend to be extraverted, self-confident, and emotionally stable (Tucker, 1983). Of course, these relationships do not indicate that physique differences *cause* personality differences. Perhaps, instead, personality differences affect dietary and exercise habits, thereby causing differences in physique.

But what of the *heritability* of personality, which is the extent to which the variation in personality within a group is caused by heredity? Estimates of the heritability of personality vary from about 25 percent (Scarr, Webber, Weinberg, & Wittig, 1981), indicating that environment is more important than he-

Identical Twins Reunited When reunited at the age of thirty-nine as part of Thomas Bouchard's study, identical twins Jim Lewis and Jim Springer revealed remarkable similarities even though they had been adopted into different homes at four weeks of age. Both liked arithmetic but not spelling, drove Chevrolets, had dogs named Toy, chewed their fingernails to the nub, served as deputy sheriffs, enjoyed vacationing in Florida, married women named Linda, and got divorced and then married women named Betty. Both also enjoyed mechanical drawing and carpentry. The photo shows them in their basement workshops, where both had built white benches that encircle trees in their backyards.

Separated at birth, the Mallifert twins meet accidentally.

redity, to about 60 percent (Tellegen et al., 1988), indicating that heredity is more important than environment. And what of Bouchard's research on identical twins reared apart? Care must be taken in drawing conclusions from the amazing behavioral similarities in some of the twins he has studied. Imagine that you and a fellow student were both asked fifteen thousand questions (as Bouchard does over a six-day period). You would undoubtedly find some surprising similarities between the two of you, even though you were not genetically related. This was demonstrated in a study that found many similarities between pairs of strangers. For example, one pair of women found that they were both Baptists, nursing students, active in tennis and volleyball, fond of English and mathematics, not fond of shorthand, and partial to vacations at historic places (Wyatt, Posey, Welker, & Seamonds, 1984). Given the evidence for both genetic and environmental influences, the best bet is probably to assume that they both strongly influence the development of personality.

THE PSYCHOANALYTIC APPROACH

The *psychoanalytic approach* to personality has its roots in the psychobiological approach. Early psychoanalytic theorists were biologists and physicians who assumed that unknown brain mechanisms accounted for personality. Even Sigmund Freud, the founder of psychoanalysis, hoped to one day find the biological basis of the psychological processes contained in his theory (Knight, 1984).

Sigmund Freud (1856–1939) and Anna Freud (1895–1982) Even after his death, Freud's theory was championed by his daughter Anna, who pursued a career as a psychoanalyst.

Conscious The level of consciousness that includes the mental experiences which we are aware of at a given moment.

Preconscious The level of consciousness that contains feelings and memories which we are unaware of at the moment, but which we can become aware of at will.

Unconscious The level of consciousness that contains thoughts, feelings, and memories that influence us without our awareness and that we cannot become aware of at will.

Repression A defense mechanism that banishes threatening conscious experiences into the unconscious mind.

Psychosexual Theory

Sigmund Freud (1856–1939) was born in Moravia (now part of Czechoslovakia) to Jewish parents and moved to Vienna when he was four years old. Though Freud desired a career as a biology professor, antisemitism limited his choice of professions to law or medicine. He chose medicine, eventually becoming a neurologist. Freud became one of the most influential figures of the twentieth century, yet he refused to capitalize on his fame by taking advantage of commercial opportunities. These included financial enticements to write articles for *Cosmopolitan* magazine and to serve as a Hollywood consultant on movies about famous love affairs (Pervin, 1984). Instead, Freud remained in Vienna until the Nazis began burning his books and threatening his safety. In 1938 he emigrated to England, where he died the following year after suffering for many years from mouth cancer.

Early in his career, Freud became interested in psychiatry after studying with the French neurologist Jean Charcot, who demonstrated the power of hypnosis in treating *conversion hysteria.* This disorder was characterized by physical symptoms such as deafness, blindness, or paralysis without any physical cause. Charcot used hypnotic suggestion to help his patients, almost always women, regain the use of their lost senses or paralyzed limbs. Freud was also intrigued by reports that psychiatrist Josef Breuer had successfully used a so-called talking cure to treat conversion hysteria. Breuer found that by encouraging his patients to talk freely about whatever came into their minds they became aware of the psychological causes of their physical symptoms, leading to the disappearance of the symptoms.

Freud's personality theory reflected his time—the Victorian era of the late nineteenth century. The Victorians valued rationality and self-control as characteristics that separated human beings from animals. Freud attributed the symptoms of conversion hysteria in his female patients to unconscious sexual conflicts, which were symbolized in their symptoms. For example, paralyzed legs might symbolize a sexual conflict. Freud's claim that sexuality, an animal drive, was an important determinant of human behavior shocked and disgusted many of his contemporaries. Yet, though Freud argued against the extreme sexual inhibition of his time, he recognized the undesirability of sexual promiscuity (McCarthy, 1981).

Later in his career Freud expanded his theory to include inhibited aggression, as well as inhibited sexuality, as an important determinant of human behavior. This led him to claim that we are motivated by a life instinct, *Eros,* and a death instinct, *Thanatos.* Eros and Thanatos, as well as many other terms used by Freud, are Greek words, reflecting his fascination with the culture of ancient Greece. Appropriately, Freud's ashes reside in one of his favorite Greek urns at a crematorium in London (Tourney, 1965).

Levels of Consciousness As described in chapter 5, Freud divided the mind into three levels. The **conscious** is merely the "tip of the iceberg," representing a tiny part of the mind. The contents of the conscious mind are in a constant state of flux as feelings, memories, and perceptions enter and leave. Just below the conscious mind lies the **preconscious,** which includes accessible memories—memories that we can recall at will. The **unconscious,** the bulk of the mind, lies below both the conscious mind and the preconscious mind. It contains material we cannot recall at will.

Freud claimed that threatening thoughts or feelings are subject to **repression,** the banishment of conscious material into the unconscious. Because Freud assumed that unconscious thoughts and feelings are the most important influences on our behavior, he proclaimed: "The theory of repression is the cornerstone on which the whole structure of psychoanalysis rests" (Freud, 1914/1957, p. 16). The notion of repressed thoughts and feelings led to the concept of **psychic determinism,** which holds that all behavior is influenced by unconscious motives. Psychic determinism is exhibited in *Freudian slips,* unintentional statements that may reflect our repressed feelings. This would be the case if one person said to another, "I loathe you . . . I mean I love you."

The Structure of Personality Freud distinguished three structures of personality (figure 13.2). The **id** is unconscious and consists of our inborn biological drives. In demanding immediate gratification of drives, most notably sex and aggression, the id obeys the **pleasure principle.** In regard to sex, the id says, "Now!" The word "id" is Latin for "it," reflecting the impersonal nature of the id. The classic science fiction movie *Forbidden Planet* portrays the impersonal, amoral nature of the id by having the unconscious anger of a mad scientist transformed into a being of pure energy, which runs amok on an alien planet, blindly killing anyone in its path.

Through life experiences we learn that acting on every sexual or aggressive impulse is socially maladaptive. As a consequence, each of us develops an **ego,** Latin for "I." The ego obeys the **reality principle,** directing us to express sexual and aggressive impulses in socially acceptable ways. In regard to sex, the ego says, "Not now, later!" As for aggression, suppose that a teacher refuses to change your grade on an exam that was graded with an incorrect answer key. Your ego would encourage you to argue with the teacher, rather than punching the teacher in the nose.

Psychic Determinism The Freudian assumption that all behaviors are influenced by unconscious motives.

Id In Freud's theory, the part of the personality that contains inborn biological drives and that seeks immediate gratification.

Pleasure Principle The process by which the id seeks immediate gratification of its impulses.

Ego In Freud's theory, the part of the personality that helps the individual adapt to external reality by making compromises between the id, the superego, and the environment.

Reality Principle The process by which the ego directs the individual to express sexual and aggressive impulses in socially acceptable ways.

Drawing by Modell; © 1981 The New Yorker Magazine, Inc.

"And then I say to myself, 'If I really wanted to talk to her, why do I keep forgetting to dial 1 first?' "

FIGURE 13.2
The Structure of Personality
Freud divided the personality into the id, ego, and superego. The id is entirely unconscious and demands immediate gratification of its desires. The ego is partly conscious and partly unconscious. This permits it to balance the id's demands with the external demands of social reality and the moralistic demands of the superego, which is also partly conscious and partly unconscious.

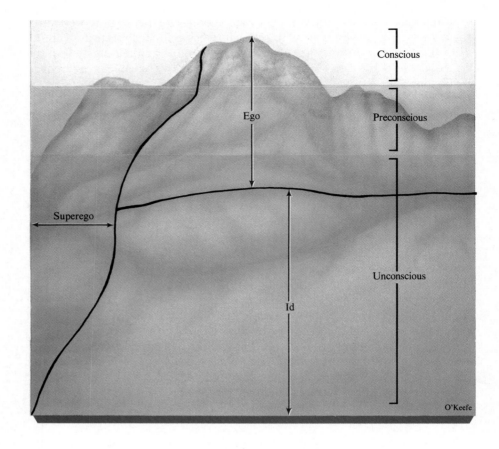

Superego In Freud's theory, the part of the personality that acts as a moral guide telling us what we should and should not do.

The **superego,** Latin for "over the I," counteracts the id, which is concerned only with immediate gratification, and the ego, which is concerned only with adapting to reality. The superego acts as our moral guide. It contains the *conscience,* which makes us feel guilty for doing or thinking wrong, and the *ego ideal,* which makes us feel good for doing or thinking good. In regard to sex, the superego says, "Not now, wait until you are married!" Children whose parents do not teach them right from wrong may develop a superego too weak to inhibit aggressive behavior. As discussed in chapter 14, children, such as Charles Manson, who fail to develop a strong superego may develop an antisocial personality. To Freud, your personality is the outcome of the continual battle for dominance among the id, ego, and superego.

Defense Mechanism In Freud's theory, a process that distorts reality to prevent the individual from being overwhelmed by anxiety.

Defense Mechanisms The ego may resort to **defense mechanisms,** which distort reality, to protect itself from the anxiety caused by id impulses, particularly those of sex and aggression. The ego may also use defense mechanisms to relieve the anxiety caused by unpleasant personal experiences and unacceptable personal characteristics. Each of us uses defense mechanisms to varying extents, which contributes to the distinctiveness of each of our personalities. But, defense mechanisms may also prevent the individual from recognizing and dealing with the true source of his or her anxiety. As noted in chapter 14, excessive reliance on defense mechanisms characterizes certain psychological disorders.

Freud viewed *repression* as the main defense mechanism, common to all the others. As mentioned earlier, repression is the banishment of threatening thoughts, feelings, and memories into the unconscious mind. The memory of a traumatic event, such as an auto accident, may be repressed to relieve the anxiety that the memory produces. Because all defense mechanisms involve repression, we are not aware when we are using them.

We sometimes rely on especially immature kinds of defense mechanisms. In using *denial,* we simply refuse to admit a particular aspect of reality. A smoker may deny that smoking causes cancer. And, as discussed in chapter 12, terminally ill patients may initially reduce their anxiety by denying they are dying. In resorting to the defense mechanism of *regression,* the individual displays immature behaviors that have relieved anxiety in the past. A ten-year-old may respond to school pressures by engaging in baby talk or thumb sucking. An adult may respond to job frustrations by crying or throwing temper tantrums.

Some defense mechanisms rely on changing our perception of reality. When we resort to *rationalization,* we provide socially acceptable reasons for our inappropriate behavior. For example, a student whose semester grades include one D and four Fs may blame the four Fs on studying too much for the course in which he received a D. People who use *intellectualization* reduce anxiety by reacting to emotional situations in a detached, unemotional way. Instead of reacting to the death of a loved one by crying, they may react by saying, "Everyone must die sometime." Intellectualization is a useful defense mechanism for medical personnel, who must continually deal with death and illness.

In some cases, defense mechanisms direct sexual or aggressive drives in safer directions. If we cannot accept our own undesirable feelings, we may resort to *projection,* attributing our undesirable feelings to others. Rapists may use projection to excuse their behavior by claiming that their victims were sexually provocative. Because a person who uses *displacement* fears the consequences of expressing his or her feelings toward a particular person, he or she will express them toward someone less threatening. A worker who hates his boss, but fears criticizing him, may, instead, constantly criticize his wife.

Shakespeare wrote in *Hamlet,* "The lady doth protest too much, methinks." He was referring to what we now call *reaction formation*—acting in a manner opposite to our true feelings. A mother who engages in "smother love" may hide her animosity toward her child by constantly doting on him and hugging him in public. Samuel Johnson, the famous eighteenth century writer and dictionary editor, reported a classic example of reaction formation. A pair of proper ladies who met him at a literary tea commented, "We see, Dr. Johnson, that you do not have those naughty words in your dictionary." Johnson replied, "And I see, dear ladies, that you have been looking for them" (Morris & Morris, 1985, p. 101).

Defense mechanisms may also promote marked changes in one's life-style. In using *compensation,* a person may react to a personal deficiency by developing another talent. Perhaps Napoleon compensated for his shortness by becoming a conqueror. Even Stevie Wonder may have compensated for his blindness by working to become a great singer and composer. According to Freud, the most successful defense mechanism is *sublimation,* the expression of sexual or aggressive impulses through indirect, socially acceptable outlets. The sex drive may be sublimated through creative activities, such as painting, ballet dancing, or composing music. And the aggressive drive may be sublimated through sports such as football, lacrosse, or field hockey.

Psychosexual Development Freud assumed that personality development depended on changes in the distribution of sexual energy, which he called **libido,** in regions of the body he called *erogenous zones.* Stimulation of these regions produces pleasure. Thus, he was concerned with stages of *psychosexual development.* Failure to progress smoothly through a par-

Libido Freud's term for the sexual energy of the id.

Fixation In Freud's theory, the failure to mature beyond a particular stage of psychosexual development.

Oral Stage In Freud's theory, the stage of personality development, between birth and age one, during which the infant gains pleasure from oral activities and faces a conflict over weaning.

Anal Stage In Freud's theory, the stage of personality development, between ages one and three, during which the child gains pleasure from defecation and faces a conflict over toilet training.

Phallic Stage In Freud's theory, the stage of personality development, between ages three and five, during which the child gains pleasure from the genitals and must resolve the Oedipus complex.

Oedipus Complex In Freud's theory, a conflict, during the phallic stage, between the child's desire for the parent of the opposite sex and fear of punishment from the same-sex parent.

Electra Complex A term used by some psychoanalysts, but not by Freud, to refer to the Oedipus complex in females.

Latency Stage In Freud's theory, the stage, between age five and puberty, during which there is little psychosexual development.

Genital Stage In Freud's theory, the last stage, associated with puberty, during which the individual develops erotic attachments to others.

ticular stage causes **fixation,** a tendency to continue to engage in behaviors associated with that stage. Freud called the first year of infancy the **oral stage** of development, because the infant gains pleasure from oral activities such as biting, sucking, and chewing. The most important social conflict of this stage is *weaning.* An infant inadequately weaned might become fixated at the oral stage. An infant who receives too much oral gratification may develop an *oral dependent* personality, marked by passivity, dependency, and gullibility. Later in life, the infant will "swallow anything," sometimes even becoming a "sucker." An infant who, instead, receives too little oral gratification, may develop an *oral aggressive* personality, marked by cruelty and sarcastic, "biting" remarks.

The one-year-old child enters the **anal stage.** The child obtains pleasure from defecation and experiences an important conflict regarding toilet training. Freud claimed that inadequate toilet training may lead to fixation at the anal stage. The characters in the movie and television series "The Odd Couple" exhibit two kinds of anal fixation. Felix represents the *anal retentive* personality, associated with severe, premature toilet training and marked by compulsive cleanliness and orderliness. Oscar represents the *anal expulsive* personality, associated with lenient, delayed toilet training and marked by sloppiness and carelessness.

Freud claimed that between the ages of three and five the child passes through the **phallic stage,** in which pleasure is gained from the genitals. This stage is associated with the **Oedipus complex,** which is the child's desire for the parent of the opposite sex while fearing punishment from the parent of the same sex. Freud noted this conflict in Sophocles's play *Oedipus Rex,* in which Oedipus, abandoned as an infant, later kills his father and marries his mother—without knowing who they are. Freud believed that the Oedipus story reflected a universal truth—the sexual attraction of each child for the opposite-sex parent. Resolution of the conflict leads to identification with the same-sex parent. The boy gives up his desire for the mother because of his *castration anxiety*—his fear that his father will punish him by removing his genitals. The girl, because of *penis envy,* becomes angry at her mother, whom she believes caused the removal of her penis, and becomes attracted to her father. This is known as the **Electra complex,** after a Greek character who helped kill her mother. But, fearing the loss of maternal love, the girl identifies with her mother, hoping to still attract her father. Through the process of *identification,* boys and girls adopt parental values and develop a superego.

Freud called the period between age five and puberty the **latency stage.** He was relatively uninterested in this stage because he believed the child experiences little psychosexual development during it. Instead, the child develops social skills and friendships. Finally, during adolescence, the child reaches the **genital stage** and becomes sexually attracted to other people. To Freud, the first three stages are the most important determinants of personality development. He assumed that personality is essentially fixed by the age of five. Figure 13.3 summarizes the psychosexual stages of development.

Individual Psychology

Because Freud's intellectual descendants made alterations in his theory, they became known as *neo-Freudians.* Figure 13.4 presents the views of several of the most renowned of them. One of the most influential of Freud's followers was Alfred Adler (1870–1937). In 1902 Adler, a Viennese physician, joined the regular Wednesday evening group discussions of psychoanalysis at Freud's home and became a devoted disciple. But in 1911 Adler broke with Freud over revisions he made in Freud's theory that deemphasized the importance

FIGURE 13.3
The Psychosexual Stages of Development

Stage	Age	Characteristics
Oral	Birth to 1	Gratification from oral behaviors, such as sucking, biting, and chewing. Conflict over weaning.
Anal	1 to 3	Gratification from defecation. Conflict over toilet training.
Phallic	3 to 5	Gratification from genital stimulation. Resolution of the Oedipus complex
Latency	5 to puberty	Sexual impulses repressed. Development of friendships.
Genital	Puberty on	Gratification from genital stimulation. Development of intimate relationships.

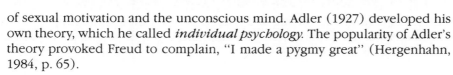

of sexual motivation and the unconscious mind. Adler (1927) developed his own theory, which he called *individual psychology.* The popularity of Adler's theory provoked Freud to complain, "I made a pygmy great" (Hergenhahn, 1984, p. 65).

FIGURE 13.4
The Neo-Freudians The neo-Freudians accepted the importance of unconscious motives, but placed greater emphasis on the ego's relationship to society than on the id's demand for gratification.

Karen Horney (1885–1952) A German immigrant to the United States, she was the first eminent female psychoanalyst. Horney claimed that the personality develops from the child's attempt to seek security by overcoming the *basic anxiety* caused by feeling isolated and helpless in a potentially hostile world. According to Horney (1937), we try to relieve basic anxiety by socially moving toward, against, or away from people. Normally, this means that we become sociable, competitive, or shy. But in extreme cases we exhibit *neurotic trends,* in which we might relieve basic anxiety by being submissive, aggressive, or reclusive. Horney also criticized Freud's view that women feel inferior to men because of penis envy. Instead, she insisted that women envy men's traditionally superior rights and social status.

Harry Stack Sullivan (1892–1949) One of the pioneers of modern American psychiatry, he lived a lonely and unhappy life, which may partly account for his theory's emphasis on the importance of healthy social relationships. Sullivan (1953) claimed that human beings have a tendency to either accept or reject their experiences as part of themselves. If we reject our unpleasant experiences and, as a consequence, fail to work at improving the inadequate relations that cause them, we may become divorced from ourselves and develop maladaptive ways of handling anxiety. Sullivan applied his theory to the process of psychiatry and to possible ways of easing international tensions.

Alfred Adler (1870–1937) "I began to see clearly in every psychological phenomenon the striving for superiority."

Adler's childhood experiences influenced his theory of personality. He was a sickly child, crippled by rickets and suffering repeated bouts of pneumonia. He also saw himself as inferior to his stronger and healthier older brother. Adler assumed that because children feel small, weak, and dependent on others, they develop an *inferiority complex.* This motivates them to compensate by *striving for superiority* in some way—that is, developing certain abilities to their maximum extent. For example, Theodore Roosevelt may have compensated for his childhood frailty by becoming a rugged outdoorsman—as Alfred Adler did by becoming an eminent psychoanalyst.

Adler believed that striving for superiority is healthiest when it promotes active concern for the welfare of others, which he called *social interest.* Both a physician and a criminal strive for superiority, but the physician expresses this motive in a socially beneficial way. Striving for superiority may lead to

Erich Fromm (1900–1980) A German immigrant, he is best known for his popular book *The Art of Loving* (1956), which applies psychoanalytic concepts to the understanding of love. Fromm based his theory on the individual's conflict between the need for freedom and the anxiety that freedom brings. In capitalistic societies, people may reduce their anxiety by giving up some of their freedom by developing a *marketing orientation,* in which they alter themselves to please other individuals. We may adopt hairstyles, musical interests, and political beliefs merely to advance our standing with other people. In totalitarian countries, people may reduce the anxiety that freedom brings by letting the government control their social, vocational, and political lives. Fromm (1941) discussed this tendency in his book *Escape from Freedom.*

Erik Erikson (1902–) The child of Danish parents, he was reared in Germany and moved to the United States later in his childhood. His father had abandoned his mother before his birth. She remarried soon after Erik's birth, but Erik was not told of his biological father until years later. This may have influenced Erikson's (1968) emphasis on the importance of developing a sense of identity in adolescence and his interest in writing psychobiographies. Psychobiographies apply psychoanalytic principles to understanding the personality development of famous people, including Martin Luther and Mahatma Gandhi. The preceding chapter discussed Erikson's contributions to the study of human development across the life span.

overcompensation, as in what Adler called *masculine protest.* This means that men (and women) may try to prove themselves by dominating others rather than by developing their own abilities. Napoleon may have overcompensated for his shortness by dominating most of the known world—the ultimate in masculine protest.

According to Adler, in striving for superiority we develop a *style of life* based on *fictional finalism.* This means that we are motivated by beliefs that may not be objectively true. A person guided by the belief that "nice guys finish last" might exhibit a style of life in which he or she acts in a ruthless, competitive way. In contrast, a person guided by the belief that "it is more blessed to give than to receive" might exhibit a style of life in which he or she acts in a helpful, altruistic way.

Analytic Psychology

Freud's favorite disciple was Carl Jung (1875–1961). Though Jung, a native of Switzerland, came from a family in which the men traditionally pursued careers as religious pastors, he obeyed a dream that directed him to pursue a career in medicine (Byrne & Kelley, 1981). He later decided to become a psychoanalyst after reading Freud's *The Interpretation of Dreams* (1900/1955). Freud and Jung carried on a lively correspondence, and Freud hoped that Jung would become his successor as head of the psychoanalytic movement. But in 1914 they parted over revisions Jung made in Freud's theory, especially Jung's deemphasis of the sex motive. Jung called his version of psychoanalysis *analytic psychology.*

Though Jung agreed with Freud that each of us has his or her own unconscious mind—the **personal unconscious**—he claimed that we also share a common unconscious mind—the **collective unconscious.** Jung held that the collective unconscious contains inherited memories passed down from generation to generation. He called these memories **archetypes,** which are images representing important aspects of the accumulated experience of humankind. Jung claimed that archetypes influence our dreams, religious symbols, and artistic creations. For example, the characters in the *Star Wars* movies represent archetypes (figure 13.5).

Jung (1959/1969) even connected the archetype of God to reports of flying saucers. Widespread reports of flying saucer sightings began in the late 1940s, following the horrors of World War II and the advent of the atomic bomb. According to Jung, these sightings stemmed from the desire of people, in-

Carl Jung (1875–1961) "While the personal unconscious is made up essentially of contents which have at one time been conscious but which have disappeared from consciousness through having been forgotten or repressed, the contents of the collective unconscious have never been in consciousness, and therefore have never been individually acquired, but owe their existence exclusively to heredity."

FIGURE 13.5
Archetypes The Star Wars movies have characters that may represent Jungian archetypes. The evil Darth Vader may represent the archetype of the shadow, our animal nature. The elderly Obi-Wan Kenobi may represent the archetype of the wise old man. The adventurer Luke Skywalker may represent the archetype of the hero. And the mysterious Force may represent the archetype of God.

spired by the archetype of God, to have a more powerful force than themselves save humankind from self-destruction. Even the round shape of the flying saucer represented the archetypal image of God-like unity and perfection of the self. Beginning in the 1950s with the movie *The Day the Earth Stood Still* and continuing on with movies such as *Close Encounters of the Third Kind,* science fiction movies have reflected the Jungian theme of powerful aliens arriving in flying saucers to save us from ourselves.

The archetype of the *mother* is a theme in the novel *Narcissus and Goldmund,* written by Jung's friend Hermann Hesse (1930/1968), whom he also psychoanalyzed. The novel describes how the archetype of the mother guides Goldmund in his constant search for the perfect woman and his fondness for images of the Madonna. Two other archetypes, the self and the persona, are interrelated. While the *self* is the true, private personality, the *persona* is the somewhat false social "mask" that we wear in public. According to Jung, a psychologically healthy individual has a persona that is not too incongruent with his or her self. The incongruence between the self and the persona is the theme of the movie *Zelig,* in which Woody Allen plays a human chameleon who alters his persona—and even his physical appearance—to suit the people he is with.

Personal Unconscious In Jung's theory, the individual's own unconscious mind, which contains repressed memories.

Collective Unconscious In Jung's theory, the unconscious mind that is shared by all human beings and that contains archetypal images passed down from our prehistoric ancestors.

Archetypes In Jung's theory, inherited images that are passed down from our prehistoric ancestors and that reveal themselves as universal symbols in art, dreams, and religion.

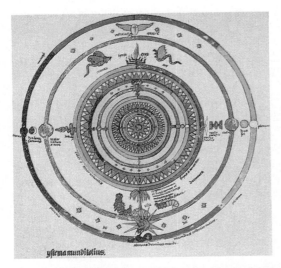

The Mandala Balanced, circular paintings such as these have been found in cultures throughout history and throughout the world. Jung claimed that this showed the influence of the archetype of the self, which symbolizes unity and wholeness.

Jung also distinguished between the *anima,* the female archetype, and the *animus,* the male archetype. According to Jung, each of us is influenced by both the anima and the animus. A psychologically healthy person, whether male or female, must maintain a balance between the two. A "macho" male who acts tough and rarely expresses tender emotions would be unhealthy, as would a "prissy" female who acts passive and has little control over her emotions. Jung even contributed to our everyday language by distinguishing between two personality types. While **extraverts** are socially outgoing and pay more attention to the surrounding environment, **introverts** are socially reserved and pay more attention to their private mental experiences. Jung applied this concept in his own life, viewing Freud as an extravert and Adler as an introvert (Monte, 1980).

Psychoanalytic Assessment of Personality

A century ago, Sir Arthur Conan Doyle popularized the use of handwriting analysis, or *graphology,* by writing stories in which the detective Sherlock Holmes used it to solve crimes. Graphologists claim that features of one's handwriting, such as the size, shape, and slant of letters, reveal aspects of one's personality. Today, because of the lack of experimental evidence supporting the claims of graphologists, few psychologists use graphology to assess personality. In one study, graphologists did no better than chance in predicting the success of bank employees based on samples of their handwriting (Ben-Shakhar, Bar-Hillel, Bilu, Ben-Abba, & Flug, 1986). Graphology is an ancestor of modern psychoanalytic assessment techniques, which are called **projective tests,** because they are based on the assumption that we will "project" our repressed feelings onto ambiguous stimuli. Today the most popular projective tests are the *Rorschach Test* and the *Thematic Apperception Test.*

The Rorschach Test Have you ever seen animal shapes in cloud formations? Have you ever argued about images in abstract paintings? If so, you will have some appreciation for the *Rorschach Test,* which asks subjects to report what they see in inkblots. This technique was used centuries ago by Leonardo da Vinci, who evaluated the creativity of young artists by having them create meaningful forms from ambiguous figures (Kaplan & Saccuzzo, 1982). The Rorschach Test was developed in 1921 by the Swiss psychiatrist Hermann Rorschach (1884–1922), who died before he was able to conduct much research with it. The test consists of ten bilaterally symmetrical inkblots. Some of the inkblots are in black and white, while others include colors.

In responding to the inkblots, the person tells what he or she sees in each one and then reports the features of the inkblot that prompted the response. The scoring of the responses is based on four criteria. The first criterion is the location to which the person responds. Does the person respond to the whole inkblot or to parts of the inkblot? The second criterion is the characteristics of the response. Does the person respond to form, to colors, or to shading? The third criterion is the content of the response. Does the person see plants, animals, human beings, or inanimate objects? And the fourth criterion is the commonality of the response. Is it common or is it unusual?

After scoring each response, the examiner uses clinical judgment and one of several available scoring systems to write a profile of the person's motives and conflicts. Such profiles have been used for purposes as diverse as diagnosing psychological disorders (Parker, Hanson, & Hunsley, 1988) and understanding the motivation of clowns, actors, and comedians (Fisher & Fisher, 1981).

Extravert A person who is socially outgoing and prefers to pay attention to the external environment.

Introvert A person who is socially reserved and prefers to pay attention to his or her private mental experiences.

Projective Test A Freudian personality test based on the assumption that individuals will project their unconscious feelings when responding to ambiguous stimuli.

The Rorschach Test The basic assumption of the Rorschach Test is that what we report seeing in a series of inkblots will reveal our unconscious motives and conflicts.

The Thematic Apperception Test Look at the card. What do you think is happening? What led up to it? How does the person feel? How will it turn out? If you took the Thematic Apperception Test (TAT) you would be shown a series of ambiguous pictures and asked to answer these questions. Themes in your stories would be assumed to reveal your unconscious motives and conflicts.

The Thematic Apperception Test The *Thematic Apperception Test (TAT)* was created by the American psychiatrist Henry Murray and his associate Christiana Morgan (Morgan & Murray, 1935). The TAT consists of cards containing black-and-white pictures of people in ambiguous situations. The examiner asks several questions about each one. What is happening in the card? What events led up to that situation? Who are the people in the card? How do they feel? How does the situation turn out? Murray assumed that the person's responses would reveal his or her most important needs, such as the need for sex, power, achievement, or affiliation.

Over the past fifty years, psychologists have used the TAT for a variety of purposes. During World War II psychologists even used it to select spies for the Allies (Hjelle & Ziegler, 1981). Psychologists typically use the TAT to determine important motives. For example, in one study the TAT revealed that men tended to be motivated by the fear of social intimacy, while women tended to be motivated by the fear of social isolation (Pollak & Gilligan, 1982).

Status of the Psychoanalytic Approach

Though the psychoanalytic approach has been the most influential approach to the study of personality, it has received only mixed support from research findings. Adler's theory of personality has influenced cognitive psychology and humanistic psychology by its emphasis on the importance of our subjective experience of reality. His concept of a style of life that reflects our striving for superiority has an important descendant in the current interest in *Type A behavior,* discussed at length in chapter 16 as a possible factor in coronary heart disease. Type A behavior is marked by hostility, competitiveness, and compulsive activity. A person who exhibits Type A behavior may be combating feelings of inferiority (Cooney & Zeichner, 1985). In fact, Meyer Friedman, the cardiologist who first identified the Type A behavior pattern in his patients, reported: "About 70 percent of our sample said they received inadequate parental love and then tried to compensate by being aggressive and overcompetitive" ("Type A," 1984, p. 109).

And what of Jung's theory? His theory has been attacked because his concept of archetypes violates known mechanisms of inheritance by assuming that memories can be inherited. Yet, as explained in chapter 14, we have an inborn predisposition to develop phobias of snakes, heights, and other situations that were dangerous to our prehistoric ancestors. Jung's concept of personality types has received more research support than has his concept of archetypes. One study compared the styles of extraverted painters and introverted painters. Extraverted painters tended to use realistic styles, reflecting their greater attention to the external environment. In contrast, introverted painters tended to use abstract styles, reflecting their greater attention to private mental experience (Loomis & Saltz, 1984).

Of all the psychoanalytic theories of personality, Freud's has been the most influential, but it has received limited support for its concepts (Fisher & Greenberg, 1985). For example, the assumption that repression keeps painful, unpleasant experiences out of conscious awareness was supported by a study showing that people who use repression as a defense mechanism are less likely to recall emotionally unpleasant personal experiences (Hansen & Hansen, 1988). In contrast, there has been little support for Freud's concept of Thanatos, which assumes that we have an unconscious desire to harm ourselves. Though there is evidence that we may harm ourselves by engaging in self-defeating behaviors, there is no evidence that we engage in deliberate self-destructiveness (Baumeister & Scher, 1988). Research has also failed to support the existence of the Oedipus complex and has shown that the anal retentive personality is more related to impatient and punitive parents than to harsh toilet training (Hunt, 1979). Perhaps the greatest weakness of the theory is that many of its terms refer to processes that are neither observable nor measurable. Who has ever seen an id? How can we measure libido? As noted in chapter 2, we cannot conduct experiments on concepts that are not operationally defined.

Despite the mixed support for psychoanalytic concepts, the psychoanalytic approach has contributed to our understanding of personality. First, it has revealed that much of our behavior is governed by irrational motives of which we are unaware. Second, it has stimulated interest in studying sexual behavior and sexual development. Third, it has demonstrated the importance of early childhood experiences. Fourth, it has been responsible for the emergence of psychological therapies. And fifth, it has influenced the works of artists, writers, and filmmakers. These contributions are discussed in several of the chapters in this text.

THE DISPOSITIONAL APPROACH

Personality theorists have traditionally assumed that personality is stable over time and consistent across situations. The *dispositional approach* to personality attributes this apparent stability and consistency to relatively enduring personal characteristics called *types* and *traits*.

Type Theories

In his book *Characters,* the Greek philosopher Theophrastus (*c.*372–287 B.C.) wondered why Greeks differed in personality despite sharing the same culture and geography. He concluded that personality differences arise from inborn predispositions to develop particular personality *types* dominated by a single characteristic. His list of personality types included the Flatterer, the Faultfinder, and the Tasteless Man. Like Theophrastus, some people rely on personality typing when they call certain individuals "nerds" or "jocks." Such people would expect different behavior from a "nerd" than from a "jock."

Today the most influential theory of personality types is Hans Eysenck's *three-factor theory* (Eysenck & Eysenck, 1985). Eysenck (1916–   ), a German psychologist, fled to England after refusing to become a member of Hitler's secret police. Eysenck used the statistical technique of factor analysis (see

Personality Types Hollywood filmmakers have made millions of dollars from movies portraying the stereotypical personality type known as the "nerd."

FIGURE 13.6
Eysenck's Primary Personality Dimensions This drawing shows the interaction of Eysenck's personality dimensions of extraversion/introversion and stability/instability. Note that the four combinations of the dimensions produce the four temperaments identified by Hippocrates more than two thousand years ago.

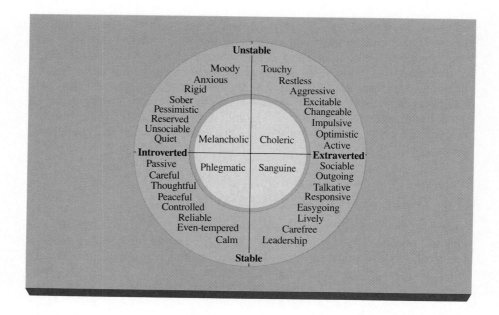

chapter 9) in identifying three dimensions of personality. By measuring where a person falls on these dimensions, we can determine his or her personality type.

The dimension of *stability/instability* measures *neuroticism,* which reflects a person's level of anxiety. While stable people are calm, even-tempered, and reliable, unstable people are moody, anxious, and unreliable. The dimension of *tough minded/tender minded* measures *psychoticism,* which reflects a person's sociability. While tough-minded people are hostile, impersonal, and insensitive, tender-minded people are friendly, empathetic, and cooperative.

The dimension of *introversion/extraversion,* first identified by Jung, has stimulated the most research interest. For example, research has shown that there are significantly more introverts among expert chess players than in the general population. Because introverted chess champions may be uncomfortable in social situations, they prefer to avoid victory parties, press conferences, and autograph hounds. They may even feel compelled to leave the chess scene itself. In 1972 the American Bobby Fischer generated unprecedented interest in chess with his brilliant play in winning the World Chess Championship, only to retire into seclusion soon after (Olmo & Stevens, 1984). In general, extraverts tend to be happier and more satisfied with life than introverts (Costa & McCrae, 1980). Figure 13.6 illustrates the interaction of the dimensions of extraversion/introversion and stability/ instability. Note that the interaction of these two dimensions yields four personality types—the very ones identified by Hippocrates more than two thousand years ago.

Trait Theories

Instead of describing personality in terms of distinctive types, trait theorists describe personality in terms of distinctive combinations of personal characteristics. A **trait** is a relatively enduring, cross-situationally consistent personality characteristic that is inferred from a person's behavior. Eysenck's theory can be viewed as either a type theory or a trait theory, because the personality types in his theory are products of the interaction of certain trait dimensions. The two most influential trait theories are those of Gordon Allport (1897–1967) and Raymond Cattell (1905–   ). Early in his career, Allport had a brief meeting in Vienna with Sigmund Freud that convinced him that psychoanal-

Trait A relatively enduring, cross-situationally consistent personality characteristic that is inferred from a person's behavior.

ysis was not the best approach to the study of personality. Confronted with a silent Freud, Allport broke the silence by describing a boy he had met on a train who had complained of dirty people and whose mother had acted annoyed at his behavior. Freud responded, "And was that little boy you?" Allport concluded that psychoanalysis was too concerned with psychic determinism—finding hidden motives for even the most mundane behaviors (Allport, 1967).

Allport began his research by identifying all the English words that refer to personal characteristics. In 1936 Allport and his colleague Henry Odbert counted almost 18,000 such words in an unabridged dictionary. By eliminating synonyms and words referring to relatively temporary states (such as "hungry"), they reduced the list to about 4,500 words. Allport then grouped the words into almost 200 clusters of related words, which became the original personality traits in his theory.

Allport distinguished three kinds of traits. *Cardinal traits* are similar to personality types, in that they affect every aspect of the person's life. For example, altruism is a cardinal trait in the personality of Mother Theresa. Because cardinal traits are rare, you probably know few people whose lives are governed by them. The most important traits are *central traits,* which affect many aspects of our lives, but which do not have the pervasive influence of cardinal traits. When you refer to someone as kind, humorous, or conceited, you are usually referring to a central trait. The least important traits are *secondary traits,* because they affect relatively narrow aspects of our lives. Preferences for wearing cuffed pants, reading western novels, or eating chocolate ice cream would reflect secondary traits.

Raymond Cattell, a native of England who spent most of his career in the United States, further refined the trait theory of personality. By using factor analysis, Cattell identified sixteen basic traits, which he called *source traits.* These traits became the basis of a widely used personality test that will be described later in the chapter. More recently, researchers using factor analysis have reduced the number of basic traits to five (Digman & Inouye, 1986). *Surgency* resembles Eysenck's factor of introversion/extraversion, and *emotional stability* resembles his factor of stability/instability. *Agreeableness* indicates whether a person is good-natured, *conscientiousness* indicates whether a person is responsible, and *openness to experience* indicates whether a person is interested in artistic and intellectual pursuits.

Dispositional Assessment of Personality

The dispositional assessment of personality relies on tests of personality types or traits. These are called *objective tests,* because they present subjects with straightforward statements rather than with ambiguous stimuli, as in projective tests. For example, the objective test called the *Profile of Mood States* has shown that elite athletes tend to share a so-called iceberg profile (figure 13.7).

Tests of Personality Types One of the most popular objective tests is the *Myers-Briggs Type Indicator* (Briggs & Myers, 1943), which is unusual in that it is a dispositional test based on a psychoanalytic theory. The test assesses personality types derived from Jung's analytic theory of personality. The subject is presented with pairs of statements and selects the statement in each pair that is closest to how he or she usually acts or feels. A typical item would be, "At parties, do you (a) sometimes get bored or (b) always have fun?" An introvert would be more likely to select (a) and an extravert, (b). The test has been used for a variety of purposes. One study found that football defensive backs were more introverted than other players (Schurr, Ruble, Nisbet, & Wallace, 1984).

FIGURE 13.7
The "Iceberg Profile" Studies using the objective personality test called the Profile of Mood States have consistently found that elite athletes share an iceberg-shaped personality profile. They score higher than average on personal vigor, while scoring at or below average on negative characteristics: tension (anxiety), depression, anger, fatigue, and confusion. Thus, elite athletes appear to be psychologically healthier than the average person. The graph shows the personality profiles of world-class rowers, wrestlers, and runners (milers and marathoners).

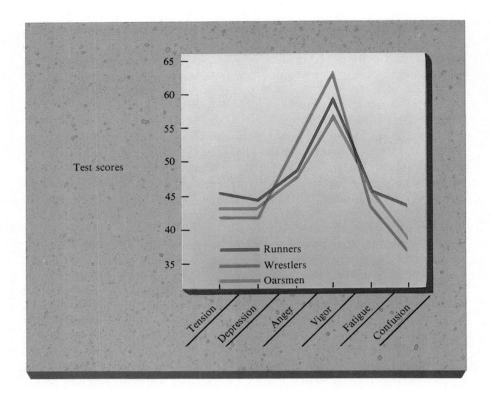

Tests of Personality Traits The most widely used of all personality tests is the *Minnesota Multiphasic Personality Inventory* (*MMPI*), which measures personality traits. The MMPI was developed at the University of Minnesota by psychologist Starke R. Hathaway and psychiatrist John C. McKinley (1943) to diagnose psychological disorders. McKinley had suspected that many medical patients had psychological, rather than physical, problems.

Hathaway and McKinley used the *empirical method* of test construction, which retains only those questions that discriminate between people who differ on the characteristics of interest. Hathaway and McKinley collected one thousand statements, which they administered to seven hundred people, including nonpatients, medical patients, and psychiatric patients. The subject responded "True," "False," or "Cannot Say" to each statement, depending on whether the statement was true of him or her. Hathaway and McKinley kept those statements that tended to be answered the same way by people with particular psychiatric disorders. For example, the MMPI includes the statement "Nothing in the newspaper interests me except the comics" solely because significantly more depressed people than nondepressed people responded "True" to that statement (Holden, 1986).

Because trait tests constructed using the empirical method may include items that seem silly or unrelated to the test's purpose (that is, they may lack *face validity*), they have been easy targets for satirical commentary. Art Buchwald, the political columnist-humorist, even created his own personality test with true-false statements such as "I was an imaginary playmate" and "I believe I smell as good as most people" (Vance, 1965). Yet, if either of those statements discriminated between those with a particular psychiatric disorder and those without it, the statement would be acceptable for inclusion with the 550 statements already in the MMPI.

The MMPI has ten clinical scales measuring important personality traits (table 13.1). For example, *hypochondriasis* measures concern with bodily functions and symptoms, and *paranoia* measures suspiciousness and delu-

TABLE 13.1   Scales of the MMPI

Scales	Content
Clinical Scales	
Hypochondriasis	Items identifying people who are overly concerned with bodily functions and symptoms of physical illness.
Depression	Items identifying people who feel hopeless and who experience slowing of thought and action.
Hysteria	Items identifying people who avoid problems by developing mental or physical symptoms.
Psychopathic deviancy	Items identifying people who disregard accepted standards of behavior and have shallow emotional relationships.
Masculinity-femininity	Items identifying people with stereotypically male or female interests.
Paranoia	Items identifying people with delusions of grandeur or persecution who also exhibit pervasive suspiciousness.
Psychasthenia	Items identifying people who feel guilt, worry, and anxiety and who have obsessions and compulsions.
Schizophrenia	Items identifying people who exhibit social withdrawal, delusional thoughts, and hallucinations.
Hypomania	Items identifying people who are overactive, easily excited, and recklessly impulsive.
Social introversion	Items identifying people who are emotionally inhibited and socially shy.
Validity Scales	
Cannot say	Items that are not answered, which may indicate evasiveness.
Lie	Items indicating an attempt to make a positive impression.
Frequency	Items involving responses that are rarely given by normal people, which may indicate an attempt to seem abnormal.
Correction	Items revealing a tendency to respond defensively in admitting personal problems or shortcomings.

From S. R. Hathaway and J. C. McKinley, *Minnesota Multiphasic Personality Inventory (MMPI)*. Copyright © 1943 University of Minnesota Press, Minneapolis, MN.

sions of persecution. The MMPI also has four *validity scales* that test for eva- siveness, defensiveness, lying to look good, and faking to look bad. For example, the "Lie Scale" contains statements that describe common human failings to which almost all people respond "True." So, a person who responded "False" to statements such as "I sometimes have violent thoughts" might be lying to create a good impression.

Psychologists commonly use the MMPI to screen applicants for positions in which people with serious psychological disorders might be dangerous, such as police officers or nuclear power plant operators. Though the MMPI has proved to be a valid means of diagnosing psychological disorders (Parker, Hanson, & Hunsley, 1988), today it tends to diagnose a higher proportion of people as psychologically disordered than it did in the past. Does this mean that more people have psychological disorders today than in the past? Or does it mean that the MMPI's norms are outdated? The latter seems to be the case. As one critic noted, "Whoever takes the MMPI today is being compared with the way a man or woman from Minnesota endorsed those items in the late 1930s and early 1940s" (Herbert, 1983, p. 228). Because of this, the MMPI has been restandardized to avoid comparing people today with the narrow segment of society that served as the standardization group half a century ago—people from a farm or small town with an eighth-grade education and with an average age of thirty-five years (Adler, 1989).

Another popular test for measuring personality traits is the *16 Personality Factor Questionnaire (16 PF)*, which measures the sixteen source traits identified by Raymond Cattell (1949). Psychologists typically use the 16 PF for general personality testing rather than for diagnosing psychological disorders. The 16 PF contains 187 multiple-choice statements. A typical item would be, "I feel mature in most things:" (a) "True," (b) "Uncertain," (c) "False." The person's scores on each of the source traits are plotted on a graph to provide a personality profile, which may be used by employers or career counselors to determine whether the profile is similar to those of people who have been successful in particular professions (figure 13.8).

Status of the Dispositional Approach

Though the dispositional approach to personality has been useful in *describing* personality differences, it has been less successful in *explaining* those differences. Suppose that the results of testing with the Myers-Briggs Type Indicator reveal that one of your friends is an "extravert." Someone might ask, "Why is she an extravert?" You might respond, "Because she likes to socialize." The person might then ask, "Why does she like to socialize?" To which you might reply, "Because she is an extravert." This circular reasoning would not explain why your friend is an extravert.

One of the few dispositional theories that tries to explain personality is Eysenck's three-factor theory, which holds that the dimension of introversion/extraversion depends on our customary level of physiological arousal. While introverts have high levels of arousal, extraverts have low levels. As you learned in chapter 10, we have a tendency to try to adopt a moderate level of arousal. This might explain why introverts avoid stimulation while extraverts seek it. For example, introverted students prefer to work in quieter conditions than do extraverted students. In one study, students were permitted to choose the level of noise they would hear while performing a memory task. Extraverted students chose more intense levels than did introverted students. Moreover, students who were permitted to choose their own noise levels performed better than students who were assigned noise levels higher or lower than they preferred (Geen, 1984).

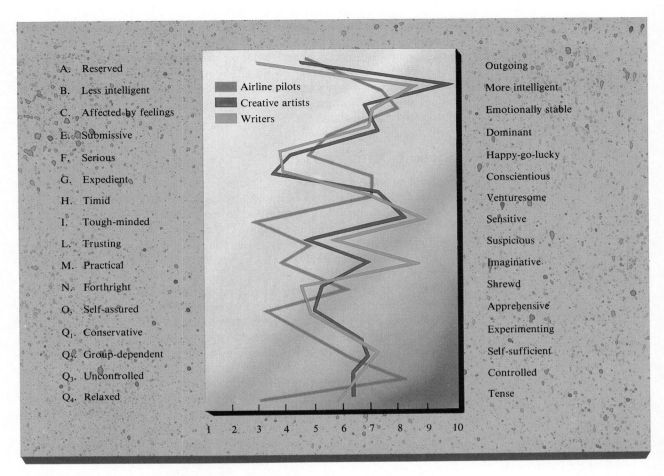

FIGURE 13.8
The 16 PF Test The graph presents
personality profiles of writers, creative artists,
and airline pilots based on the sixteen
personality traits in Cattell's 16 PF Test. The
left-hand and right-hand columns present
the opposite extremes of each trait. Average
scores fall about equidistant between these
extremes. Note the differences between the
profile of airline pilots and the profiles of
the other two groups.

THE BEHAVIORAL APPROACH

Those who favor the *behavioral approach* to personality discount biological
factors, unconscious influences, and dispositional traits. Instead, they stress
the importance of learning and environmental factors.

Operant Conditioning Theory

To B. F. Skinner (1953), whose *operant conditioning theory* is described in
chapter 6, there is nothing exceptional about personality. What we call *personality* is merely a person's unique pattern of behavior. You might say that
a fellow student has a "gregarious" personality because you have observed
the student engage in behaviors such as initiating conversations, going to parties every weekend, and monopolizing the dormitory telephone.

According to Skinner, we are what we do. And what we do in a particular situation depends on our history of reinforcement and punishment in that situation and similar situations. We tend to engage in behaviors for which we have been reinforced and to avoid engaging in behaviors for which we have been punished. How would Skinner explain a gregarious personality? He would assume that a gregarious person has a history of being reinforced for being socially outgoing.

Social Cognitive Theory

Social cognitive theory builds a bridge between Skinner's strict behavioral approach to personality and the cognitive approach to personality, which will be discussed later in the chapter. Social cognitive theory is similar to traditional behavioral theories in stressing the role of reinforcement and punishment in the development of personality. But social cognitive theory is different from traditional behavioral theories in arguing that behavior is affected by cognitive processes.

Social cognitive theory was developed by Albert Bandura (1925–), who served as president of the American Psychological Association in 1974. Other social cognitive theories have been developed by Julian Rotter and Walter Mischel. Their views will be discussed later in the chapter. Bandura's theory of personality grew out of his research on observational learning, which is described in chapter 6. According to Bandura, we learn many of our behavioral tendencies by observing other people obtaining rewards or punishments for particular behaviors. Bandura's (1986) theory of personality also emphasizes the concept of **reciprocal determinism,** which reflects his belief that neither personal dispositions nor environmental factors can by themselves explain behavior. Instead, personality traits, environmental factors, and overt behavior affect one another (figure 13.9).

One of the most important aspects of personality to consider in reciprocal determinism is **self-efficacy,** which is the extent to which a person believes that he or she can perform behaviors that are necessary to bring about a desired outcome. Self-efficacy determines our choice of activities, our intensity of effort, and our persistence in the face of obstacles and unpleasant experiences, in part by reducing the anxiety that might interfere with performance of the activity (Bandura, Reese, & Adams, 1982).

But what determines whether you will have a feeling of self-efficacy in a given situation? The first determinant is *previous success*. You would have a greater feeling of self-efficacy in your psychology course if you have done well

Reciprocal Determinism
Bandura's belief that personality traits, environmental factors, and overt behavior affect each other.

Self-Efficacy In Bandura's theory, a person's belief that he or she can perform behaviors that are necessary to bring about a desired outcome.

FIGURE 13.9
Reciprocal Determinism
Bandura's concept of reciprocal determinism considers the mutual influence of the person's characteristics, behavior, and situation. Each of the three factors can affect the other two.

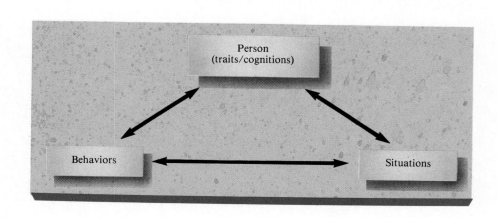

in previous courses. The second determinant is *vicarious experience*. You would have a greater feeling of self-efficacy if you know other students who have succeeded in the course. The third determinant is *verbal persuasion*. You would have a greater feeling of self-efficacy if you gave yourself pep talks or your advisor convinced you that you have the ability to do well in the course. And the fourth determinant is *physiological arousal*. You would have a greater feeling of self-efficacy if you were at an optimal level of arousal (see chapter 10). If you are too aroused while making a classroom speech and notice your tense muscles, increased heart rate, and irregular breathing pattern, you might become so distracted that you mispronounce words or forget your place.

Behavioral Assessment of Personality

There are two main behavioral approaches to the assessment of personality. One approach examines overt behavior, while the other examines cognitions that are closely connected to overt behavior.

Assessment of Overt Behavior Theorists who favor the examination of overt behavior believe that we should note what people actually do or say they would do in specific situations rather than simply record their responses to personality tests. In *behavioral observation* the subject is observed in real or simulated conditions related to work, school, recreation, or other situations of interest. Behavioral observation is more likely to produce valid findings when it involves several observers who know the person and who observe the person in the situation of interest on several occasions (Moskowitz & Schwarz, 1982).

Behavioral Observation
Behavioral observation is useful in determining how individuals will behave in real-life situations. The responses of this astronaut to isolation, weightlessness, and simulated emergencies will help determine whether she will be permitted to take part in space flights.

During a *situational interview,* the interviewer asks the subject how he or she would act in specific situations. As a consequence, for example, instead of reporting that a potential employee is "conscientious," the interviewer might report that the person would probably not let shoddy products pass on the assembly line. Suppose you are given a situational interview after applying for a job as a summer camp counselor. The interviewer might ask how you would handle homesick campers, campers who refuse to participate in activities, or fellow counselors who use drugs. Research findings support the usefulness of the situational interview in predicting how an employee will do on the job (Latham & Saari, 1984).

Another form of behavioral assessment uses the *experience sampling method.* In using this method, a person carries a portable beeper that beeps at random times. On hearing the beep, the person reports his or her experiences and behaviors at that time. This reveals relationships between specific situations and the person's thoughts, feelings, and behaviors (Hormuth, 1986).

Cognitive-Behavioral Assessment As an example of the *cognitive-behavioral assessment* of personality consider the *Internal-External Locus of Control Scale,* which was developed by Julian Rotter (1966) to measure what he calls the locus of control. Your *locus of control* is the extent to which you believe that you are in control of events in your life or that such events are controlled by factors beyond your control. Rotter's concept of the locus of control has been so influential that his original study is one of the most frequently cited studies in the recent history of psychology (Sechrest, 1984). The scale contains twenty-nine pairs of statements, including six that merely disguise the purpose of the test. A typical relevant pair would be similar to the following: "The more effort you expend, the more likely you are to succeed" and "Luck is more important than hard work in job advancement." Your responses would determine whether you have an internal or an external locus of control. Just as your sense of self-efficacy might affect your behavior in real-life situations, your locus of control might determine whether you try to exert control over real-life situations.

The locus of control has been used in a variety of studies. One study found that drivers with an internal locus of control have fewer fatal accidents, perhaps because they are more cautious, attentive, and adept at avoiding aversive situations (Montag & Comrey, 1987). Researchers in another study wondered why tornadoes kill more residents of Alabama than Illinois, given that the incidence of tornadoes in those states is similar. The researchers found that Alabamans tended to have an external locus of control, while Illinoisans tended to have an internal locus of control. As a consequence, Alabamans may take fewer precautions than Illinoisans when given warnings about impending tornadoes (Sims & Baumann, 1972). Evidently, Alabamans were more fatalistic and attributed events to external factors, such as luck, fate, or God's will.

Status of the Behavioral Approach

Skinner's operant conditioning theory of personality has been praised for making psychologists more aware of the influence of learning and environmental factors on personality. But the theory has been criticized for viewing the person as a passive responder to the environment and for failing to consider the importance of cognitive factors. The social cognitive theorists have corrected these shortcomings by recognizing the importance of cognitive processes, as well as environmental factors. Bandura's concept of self-efficacy, in particular, has been supported by research findings in a variety of areas. One study found that a person's feeling of self-efficacy in mathematics influenced his or her arithmetic anxiety and decision whether to major in mathematics (Hackett, 1985). Another study found that people with feelings of self-efficacy for long-distance running are more likely to enter marathon races, train hard for those races, and continue running despite the pain and fatigue they experience (Okwumabua, 1985).

Of practical importance is the finding that self-efficacy can be enhanced by training. In one case, a training program enhanced the self-efficacy of maintenance workers in regard to job attendance relative to a control group of workers who did not attend the program. The results of the study also showed that the higher the worker's feeling of self-efficacy, the better was his or her job attendance. Those with high self-efficacy were better able to overcome social and personal obstacles to job attendance (Frayne & Latham, 1987).

THE COGNITIVE APPROACH

Like the social cognitive theory, the *cognitive approach* to personality recognizes the influence of thoughts on behavior. But this approach pays more attention to subjective experience and less attention to objective situations than does the social cognitive theory.

Personal Construct Theory

The most influential cognitive theory of personality is the *personal construct theory* of George Kelly (1905–1967). Kelly, who spent his childhood on a Kansas farm, was educated in both physics and psychology. His background in physics influenced his view of human beings as lay scientists who continually test hypotheses about social reality. He called each of these hypotheses a *personal construct* (Kelly, 1963). According to Kelly, your characteristic pattern of personal constructs determines your personality.

Kelly believed that personal constructs are bipolar, meaning that they involve opposite extremes. So, people are either shy or outgoing, safe or dangerous. Suppose you held the personal construct that "strangers are dangerous." It might make you behave suspiciously toward strangers. Just as scientists retain hypotheses only if they prove accurate, we retain our personal constructs only as long as we believe they are accurate. If you found that elderly strangers are not dangerous, you might revise your personal construct to hold that "young strangers are dangerous."

Kelly called our ability to apply different personal constructs to a given situation *constructive alternativism,* which he divided into three phases: the *circumspection-preemption-control cycle.* During the *circumspection phase* we evaluate constructs that may be relevant to a particular person or situation. During the *preemption phase* we decide which construct is most relevant to the situation. And during the *control phase* we follow a course of action based on the chosen construct.

As an example, suppose that someone comes to your door to ask for a contribution to a high school marching band. During the circumspection phase, you would evaluate and choose among several bipolar constructs to determine which is relevant to the situation. You would consider whether the person seemed honest or dishonest and whether the charity seemed worthy or unworthy. During the preemption phase, you might determine that the person was honest and that the charity was worthy. During the control phase these constructs would make you more likely to contribute to the charity.

George Kelly (1905–1967)
"[Personal] constructs are used for prediction of things to come, and the world keeps rolling along and revealing these predictions to be either correct or misleading."

Cognitive Assessment of Personality

The most popular form of cognitive assessment of personality is the *Role Construct Repertory Test* (*REP Test*), which Kelly derived from his personal construct theory. The REP Test presents the subject with sets of three persons whom the subject knows. The subject must specify a way in which two of the persons are similar to each other and different from the third. A psychologist might present an individual with sets of three persons who play roles of importance to the individual, such as "father," "best friend," and "disliked teacher." The individual then specifies a way in which two of the persons are similar to each other and different from the third. If you were the individual, you might report that your father and your best friend are both sincere, while your most disliked teacher is insincere.

The psychologist repeats this process with several sets of persons. A therapist would take your responses and determine how many constructs you used to distinguish between people. These constructs would be the ones you use to perceive social reality, such as "sincere-insincere." If you relied on too few constructs, you might be inflexible and view people according to stereotypes. In contrast, if you relied on too many constructs, you might be confused and perform poorly in social situations because you would have difficulty predicting people's behavior.

Status of the Cognitive Approach

Fixed-Role Therapy A kind of therapy, derived from Kelly's personality theory, that encourages clients to adopt roles that promote new, more adaptive personal constructs.

Kelly contributed a method of psychotherapy called **fixed-role therapy,** which encourages clients to adopt roles that promote new, more adaptive constructs. And his REP Test has been adapted for use in market research to determine the subjective criteria that consumers use in evaluating products (Jankowicz, 1987). After his death, Kelly's theory, which has been called "a classic ahead of its time," was carried on chiefly by a small group of his followers (Rorer & Widiger, 1983, p. 456). Yet, his theory stimulated renewed interest in cognitive factors in personality and influenced the development of social cognitive theory.

Nonetheless, the cognitive approach to personality has attracted psychologists who believe that thoughts are more important than unconscious motives or environmental stimuli in determining behavior. But traditional behavioral theorists argue that thoughts do not influence behavior. And psychoanalytic theorists criticize cognitive theories for ignoring the irrational, emotional bases of behavior.

THE HUMANISTIC APPROACH

In the nineteenth century the philosopher Jean-Jacques Rousseau praised the "noble savage"—the natural, unspoiled human being, uncorrupted by civilization. Rousseau believed that human beings have an inborn tendency to be good. The *humanistic approach* to personality, which emerged in the 1950s, is a descendant of Rousseau's belief, because humanistic personality theorists believe that human beings are naturally good. This contrasts with psychoanalytic personality theorists, who believe that human beings are predisposed to be selfish and aggressive, and behavioral personality theorists, who believe that human beings are neither naturally good nor naturally evil.

The humanistic approach also contrasts with the psychoanalytic and behavioral approaches by accepting conscious mental experience as its subject matter. This makes the humanistic approach more similar to the cognitive approach though somewhat more concerned with emotional experience. Moreover, the humanistic approach assumes that we have free will, meaning that our every action is not compelled by id impulses or environmental stimuli.

Self-Actualization Theory

Humanistic theories of personality have some of the flavor of the theories of Jung and Adler in that they view human beings as goal directed and governed by their subjective view of reality. The first humanistic theory of personality was that of Abraham Maslow (1970), whose theory of motivation is discussed in chapter 10. Maslow, who was reared in Brooklyn, was directed by his parents to attend law school. One day, finding himself in a course in which he had no interest, Maslow bolted from the classroom.

Maslow never returned to law school. Instead, against his parents' wishes, he decided to pursue a career in psychology. This willingness to fulfill one's own needs, rather than those of other people, became a hallmark of humanistic theories of personality. As you may recall from chapter 10, Maslow believed that our second highest need is **self-actualization,** the predisposition to try to reach our potentials. The concept of self-actualization is a descendant of Adler's concept of striving for superiority (Crandall, 1980). But who is self-actualized? Maslow presented several candidates, including President Abraham Lincoln, psychologist William James, and humanitarian Eleanor Roosevelt. Table 13.2 presents a list of characteristics shared by self-actualized people.

Self-Actualization In Maslow's theory, the individual's predisposition to try to reach his or her potentials.

TABLE 13.2   Characteristics of Self-Actualized Persons

Realistic orientation

Self-acceptance and acceptance of others and the natural world as they are

Spontaneity

Problem-centered rather than self-centered

Air of detachment and need for privacy

Autonomous and independent

Fresh rather than stereotyped appreciation of people and things

Generally have had profound mystical or spiritual, though not necessarily religious, experiences

Identification with humankind and a strong social interest

Tendency to have strong intimate relationships with a few special, loved people rather than superficial relationships with many people

Democratic values and attitudes

No confusion of means with ends

Philosophical rather than hostile sense of humor

High degree of creativity

Resistance to cultural conformity

Transcendence of environment rather than always coping with it

From A. H. Maslow, *The Farther Reaches of Human Nature.* Copyright © 1971 Viking Press, New York, NY.

Maslow decided on these characteristics after testing, interviewing, or reading the works of individuals he considered self-actualized.

Self Theory

Carl Rogers (1902–1987) "It has been my experience that persons have a basically positive direction."

Carl Rogers (1902–1987) was born in Oak Park, Illinois, to a devoutly religious family. His religious upbringing led him to enter Union Theological Seminary in New York City. But Rogers left the seminary to pursue a career in psychology, eventually serving as president of the American Psychological Association in 1946. His *self theory* of personality has its roots in the works of William James and Mary Whiton Calkins.

Rogers pointed out that self-actualization requires acceptance of one's *self,* which is your answer to the question, "Who are you?" But each of us experiences incongruence between the self and personal experience. This causes anxiety, which, in turn, motivates the person to reduce the incongruence. As explained in chapter 14, people who have a great incongruence between the self and experience may develop psychological disorders.

How does incongruence between the self and experience develop? According to Rogers, a child who does not receive *unconditional positive regard*—that is, complete acceptance—from parents will develop incongruence by denying aspects of his or her experience. To gain acceptance from parents the child may express thoughts, feelings, and behaviors that are acceptable to the parents. For example, a boy whose parents insist that "boys don't cry" may learn to deny his own painful physical and emotional experiences to gain parental approval. Such *conditions of worth* lead the child to become rigid and anxious because of a failure to accept his or her experiences. Instead of self-actualizing, such children may adopt a life-style of conformity and ingratiation (Baumeister, 1982) or blame their failures and shortcomings on external factors to protect their self image (Snyder & Higgins, 1988).

Psychologically healthy people also have congruence between the self (the person they perceive themselves to be) and the *ideal self* (the person they would like to be). People with a great incongruence between the self and the ideal self have more self-doubts and fewer social skills. In contrast, people with a small incongruence between the self and the ideal self are more confident, socially poised, and able to deal with the problems of everyday life (Gough, Fioravanti, & Lazzari, 1983).

Humanistic Assessment of Personality

How do humanistic psychologists assess personality? Two of the main techniques are the *Personal Orientation Inventory* and the *Q-sort.*

The Personal Orientation Inventory Psychologists who wish to assess self-actualization often use the *Personal Orientation Inventory* (*POI*) (Shostrom, 1962). The POI determines the degree to which a person's values and attitudes agree with those of Maslow's description of self-actualized people, such as being governed by one's own motives and principles. The inventory contains items that force the person to choose between options, such as (a) "Impressing others is most important" and (b) "Expressing myself is most important." The POI has been especially popular in sport psychology research, as in a study that found that female athletes were more self-actualized than male athletes (Gundersheim, 1982).

The Q-Sort The *Q-sort,* derived from Rogers's self theory, measures the degree of congruence between a person's self and ideal self. If you took a Q-sort test, you would be given a pile of cards with a self-descriptive statement on each. A typical statement might be, "I feel comfortable with strangers." You would put the statements in several piles, ranging from a pile containing statements that are most characteristic of your self to a pile containing statements that are least characteristic of your self. You would then follow the same procedure for your ideal self, creating a second set of piles. The greater the positive correlation between your self and your ideal self, as indicated by the degree of overlap between the two sets of piles, the greater the congruence between your self and your ideal self. Some psychotherapists use this method to determine whether therapy has increased the congruence between a client's self and ideal self.

Status of the Humanistic Approach

The past decade has seen research on a variety of "selves." A recent view of the self considers the relationship between three selves: the *actual self,* the *ideal self,* and the *ought self.* Incongruence between the actual self (which represents the self in Rogers's theory) and the ideal self will make a person feel depressed. This incongruence is expressed in Woody Allen's remark, "My only regret in life is that I am not someone else." Incongruence between the actual self and the ought self (which is similar to Freud's ego ideal in representing beliefs about one's moral duties) will make a person feel anxious (Higgins, 1987).

Still another self has been proposed—the *undesired self.* The undesired self includes personal experiences and personal qualities that we dislike. One study found that happiness depends more on the degree of incongruence between the actual self and the undesired self than on the degree of congruence between the actual self and the ideal self (Ogilvie, 1987). Only additional research will determine the exact relationship between each of the "selves" that have been proposed.

The humanistic approach has been praised for countering the tendency of psychologists to study the negative aspects of human experience by encouraging psychologists to study love, creativity, and other positive aspects of human experience. The humanistic approach has also renewed interest in studying conscious mental experience, which was the original subject matter of psychology a century ago (Singer & Kolligian, 1987). In fact, the humanistic approach might best reflect popular views of personality. A survey of people in everyday life found that most people believe that others would know them best if others knew their private mental experiences rather than their overt behavior (Andersen & Ross, 1984).

The humanistic approach has also contributed to the recent interest in self-development, including the emphasis on improving one's physical appearance. For example, improving physical appearance through weight training enhances the self-esteem of both men (Tucker, 1982) and women (Trujillo, 1983). But the humanistic approach has not escaped criticism. Critics accuse it of divorcing the person from both the environment and the unconscious mind and for failing to operationally define and experimentally test abstract concepts such as self-actualization. Some critics wonder whether the pursuit of self-actualization, however it is defined, may produce unhappiness in those who lack the skill or resources to achieve it (Geller, 1984). And the assumption of the innate goodness of human beings has been called naive by the influential humanistic psychologist Rollo May (1982), who believes that innately good human beings would not have created the evil that the world has known.

Maslow and Rogers have even been accused of unintentionally promoting self-centeredness by emphasizing the importance of self-actualization, without placing an equal emphasis on social responsibility (Geller, 1982). They have even been accused of encouraging the so-called me generation of Americans that emerged in the 1970s and 1980s, many of whose members were supposedly more interested in self-development than in contributing to the well-being of others. But this accusation is countered by research showing that people who have developed a positive self-regard tend to have a greater regard for others (Epstein & Feist, 1988). Though the humanistic approach to personality has received its share of criticism, Rogers has been widely praised for his contributions to the advancement of psychotherapy, which is discussed in chapter 15. Today, no single approach to personality dominates the others. Each makes a valuable contribution to our understanding of personality.

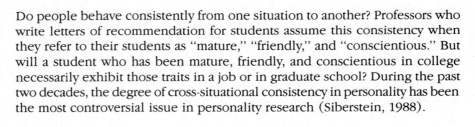

THINKING ABOUT PSYCHOLOGY

Is Personality Consistent?

Do people behave consistently from one situation to another? Professors who write letters of recommendation for students assume this consistency when they refer to their students as "mature," "friendly," and "conscientious." But will a student who has been mature, friendly, and conscientious in college necessarily exhibit those traits in a job or in graduate school? During the past two decades, the degree of cross-situational consistency in personality has been the most controversial issue in personality research (Siberstein, 1988).

Personality as Inconsistent

The current debate over the consistency of personality began in 1968 with the publication of a book in which social cognitive theorist Walter Mischel reported that personality is much less consistent from one situation to another than was commonly believed. Mischel found that the correlation between behaviors presumed to represent the same underlying personality trait rarely exceeded a relatively low .30. This means that you could not predict with confidence whether a person who scored high on the trait of "generosity" would behave in a generous manner in a given situation. For example, a person who scored high on a test measuring "generosity" might donate to the Salvation Army but might not pick up the check in a restaurant—though both behaviors would presumably reflect the trait of generosity. Based on his review of research findings, Mischel concluded that our behavior is influenced more by the situations in which we find ourselves than by the personality characteristics that we possess.

Though Mischel stimulated the current debate over the issue of personality consistency, the issue is not new. Forty years before Mischel published his findings, psychologists reported research findings showing that children's honesty was inconsistent across situations. A child might cheat on a test but

Personality Consistency
Perhaps the most controversial issue in personality research during the past two decades has been the extent to which personality is consistent from one situation to another. If you have watched *Leave It to Beaver,* you know that Eddie Haskell is unbearably polite in the presence of Mr. and Mrs. Cleaver, but a wise guy in the presence of Wally and Beaver. Research findings have convinced some personality researchers that our behavior is influenced more by the situation we are in than by the personality characteristics we possess.

not in an athletic event or lie at school but not at home (Hartshorne & May, 1928). Another early study found that college students were inconsistent in their punctuality across situations. A student might arrive on time for recreation or entertainment but might arrive late for church services or an 8 A.M. class (Dudycha, 1936).

If personality is inconsistent across situations, why do we perceive it to be consistent in our everyday lives? There are several reasons for this perception. First, we may confuse the consistency of behavior in a given situation over time with the consistency of that behavior across different situations (Mischel & Peake, 1982). If a fellow student is consistently humorous in your psychology class, you may mistakenly infer that she is humorous at home, at parties, and in the dormitory. Second, we tend to avoid situations that are inconsistent with our personalities (Snyder, 1983). If you view yourself as "even-tempered," you may avoid situations that might make you lose your temper, such as political discussions.

Third, our first impression of a person may make us discount later behavior that is inconsistent with that impression (Hayden & Mischel, 1976). If someone acts friendly toward you the first time you meet but acts rude to you the next time you meet, you might say that she was "not herself" today. And fourth, our perception of cross-situational consistency in others may reflect a powerful situational factor—our presence in their environment (Lord, 1982). If others adapt their behavior to our presence, we may erroneously infer that they are consistent across situations.

Walter Mischel "If human behavior is determined by many interacting variables—both in the person and in the environment— then a focus on any one of them is likely to lead to limited predictions and generalizations."

Personality as Consistent

These attacks on cross-situational consistency have provoked responses from those who claim there is more cross-situational consistency than Mischel and his allies believe (Kenrick & Funder, 1988). First, individuals do show consistency on certain traits. But how do we know *which* traits? One way to find out is to ask. People who claim to be consistent on a given trait tend to exhibit behaviors reflecting that trait across situations (Zuckerman et al., 1988). In one study, students were asked to judge how consistent they were on the trait of "friendliness." Those who claimed to be friendly across situations were more consistently friendly than were students who did not claim to be, as verified by their peers, parents, and other observers (Bem & Allen, 1974).

Second, cross-situational consistency in behavior depends on whether a person is a *high self-monitor* or a *low self-monitor*. High self-monitors are concerned about how people perceive them and adapt their behaviors to fit specific situations, while low self-monitors are less concerned about how people perceive them and do not adapt their behaviors as much to fit specific situations. This means that low self-monitors will show greater cross-situational consistency in their behaviors than will high self-monitors (Gangestad & Snyder, 1985).

Third, many of the studies that Mischel reviewed were guaranteed to find low cross-situational consistency, because they either correlated trait test scores with single instances of behaviors or correlated single instances of behaviors with each other. This would be like trying to predict your exact score on your next psychology test from your score on the Scholastic Aptitude Test or from your score on a biology test. Most likely the prediction would be wrong, because many factors influence your performance on any given academic test. Similarly, many factors other than a given personality trait influence your behavior in a given situation.

Psychologists have achieved greater success in demonstrating cross-situational consistency by using *behavioral aggregation*. In aggregating behaviors, you would observe a person's behavior across several situations. You would then determine how the person typically, but not necessarily always, behaves—much in the same way that you would find your average on several exams to determine your typical performance in a course. A "humorous" person would be humorous in many, but not all, situations. When we predict how a person will typically behave, instead of how that person will behave in a specific situation, the correlation between traits and behaviors becomes a relatively high .60 or more (Epstein & O'Brien, 1985).

When behavioral aggregation was applied to the Hartshorne and May (1928) study, the correlation between the trait of honesty and behaviors reflecting honesty rose considerably. Similarly, when behavioral aggregation was applied to the Dudycha (1936) study, college students showed much greater cross-situational consistency in their punctuality. More recent studies using behavioral aggregation have demonstrated cross-situational consistency for other traits, such as social dominance (Moskowitz, 1982).

In the past few years, the cross-situational consistency debate has died down. The trend is for researchers to agree that the best approach is to consider the interaction of the person, the situation, and the behavior in assessing cross-situational consistency (Diener & Larsen, 1984). Of course, some situations (such as being in church) are so powerful that almost all people—regardless of their personalities—will behave the same way in them (Monson, Hesley, & Chernick, 1982).

SUMMARY

THE PSYCHOBIOLOGICAL APPROACH

Your personality is your unique, relatively consistent pattern of thoughts, feelings, and behaviors. Closely related to personality is temperament, a person's most characteristic emotional state. Sheldon's constitutional theory holds that different temperaments are associated with different physiques, or somatotypes. Research in behavioral genetics has found evidence of the hereditary basis of temperament and other aspects of personality.

THE PSYCHOANALYTIC APPROACH

Freud's psychosexual theory emphasizes the conflict between biological drives and sociocultural prohibitions in the development of personality. Freud divided the mind into conscious, preconscious, and unconscious levels. He also distinguished between the personality structures called the id, the ego, and the superego. According to Freud, we progress through oral, anal, phallic, latency, and genital stages of development. These stages depend on changes in the distribution of sexual energy.

Freud's intellectual descendants altered his theory, generally downplaying the importance of sexuality and emphasizing the importance of social relationships. Alfred Adler's theory of individual psychology assumes that personality develops from our attempts to overcome early feelings of inferiority. Carl Jung's theory of analytic psychology assumes that we are influenced by both a personal unconscious and the archetypes in a collective unconscious. Neo-Freudians such as Karen Horney, Erich Fromm, Harry Stack Sullivan, and Erik Erikson have made further changes in Freud's theory. In assessing personality, Freudians may use the Rorschach Test and the Thematic Apperception Test to uncover unconscious motives and conflicts.

THE DISPOSITIONAL APPROACH

The dispositional approach to personality attributes the consistency we see in personality to relatively enduring personality attributes. Hans Eysenck's three-factor theory sees personality as dependent on the interaction of three dimensions: stability/instability, tough minded/tender minded, and introversion/extraversion. In his trait theory of personality, Gordon Allport distinguished three kinds of traits: cardinal traits, central traits, and secondary traits. Raymond Cattell, in his trait theory, identified sixteen source traits. Personality types are measured by tests such as the Myers-Briggs Type Indicator, and personality traits are measured by tests such as the MMPI or the 16 PF.

THE BEHAVIORAL APPROACH

B. F. Skinner's operant conditioning theory assumes that what we call personality is merely a person's unique pattern of behavior. Albert Bandura's social cognitive theory argues that cognitive processes influence behavior. His concept of reciprocal determinism points out the mutual influence of personality characteristics, overt behavior, and environmental factors. One of the most important personality characteristics is self-efficacy, the extent to which a person believes that he or she can perform behaviors that are necessary to bring about a desired outcome. Behavioral assessment is accomplished through behavioral observation, the situational interview, and the experience-sampling method. Julian Rotter's Internal-External Locus of Control Scale is one of the main cognitive-behavioral assessment techniques.

THE COGNITIVE APPROACH

The most influential cognitive theory of personality is the personal construct theory of George Kelly. He assumed that we continually test hypotheses about social reality. These hypotheses are called personal constructs. We alter our personal constructs through the process of constructive alternativism. The person's unique pattern of personal constructs is measured by the Role Construct Repertory Test.

THE HUMANISTIC APPROACH

Abraham Maslow's self-actualization theory is based on his hierarchy of needs. He assumes that we have a need to develop all of our potentials. Maslow identified the characteristics of eminent people whom he believed were self-actualized. Carl Rogers's self theory holds that psychological well-being depends on the congruence between one's self and one's experience. Other researchers point to the importance of congruence between the actual self, the ideal self, and the ought self. Self-actualization is measured by the Personal Orientation Inventory. Congruence between the self and the ideal self is measured by using the Q-sort.

THINKING ABOUT PSYCHOLOGY: IS PERSONALITY CONSISTENT?

In 1968 Walter Mischel stimulated controversy by claiming that situations are more important determinants of behavior than are personality traits. He based this conclusion on studies finding that the individual's behavior is not consistent across different situations. Researchers have spent the past two decades debating whether personality is consistent. The conclusion appears to be that personality is not as inconsistent as Mischel originally claimed nor as consistent as personality theorists had previously claimed. Our behavior is the product of the interaction between personal characteristics and environmental situations. In some cases, powerful personality characteristics will dominate environmental situations. In other cases, powerful environmental situations will dominate personality characteristics.

IMPORTANT CONCEPTS

Anal stage 442
Archetypes 446
Behavioral genetics 435
Collective unconscious 446
Conscious 438
Defense mechanism 440
Ego 439
Electra complex 442
Extravert 448
Fixation 442
Fixed-role therapy 462
Genital stage 442

Id 439
Introvert 448
Latency stage 442
Libido 441
Oedipus complex 442
Oral stage 442
Personality 432
Personal unconscious 446
Phallic stage 442
Pleasure principle 439
Preconscious 438
Projective test 448

Psychic determinism 439
Reality principle 439
Reciprocal determinism 458
Repression 438
Self-actualization 463
Self-efficacy 458
Somatotype 434
Superego 440
Temperament 433
Trait 452
Unconscious 438

IMPORTANT PEOPLE

Alfred Adler 442
Gordon Allport 452
Albert Bandura 458
Thomas Bouchard 435
Raymond Cattell 452
Erik Erikson 445
Hans Eysenck 451

Sigmund Freud 438
Erich Fromm 445
Karen Horney 444
Carl Jung 446
George Kelly 461
Abraham Maslow 463

Walter Mischel 466
Carl Rogers 464
Julian Rotter 460
William Sheldon 434
B. F. Skinner 457
Harry Stack Sullivan 444

RECOMMENDED READINGS

For More on All Aspects of Personality:

Ryckman, R. M. (1989). *Theories of personality* (4th ed.). Belmont, CA: Brooks/Cole.
A comprehensive textbook presenting all the major theoretical positions, as well as background information on eminent personality theorists.

For More on the Psychobiological Approach:

Holden, C. (1987). The genetics of personality. *Science, 237,* 598–601.
A popular article discussing research on the inheritance of personality characteristics, including research on similarities between identical twins who have been reunited after having been adopted by separate families.

Sheldon, W. H., & Stevens, S. S. (1942). *The varieties of temperament: A psychology of constitutional differences.* New York: Harper.
A presentation of the somatotype theory, supporting the relationship between physique and temperament.

For More on the Psychoanalytic Approach:

Fisher, S., & Greenberg, R. P. (1985). *The scientific credibility of Freud's theories and therapy.* New York: Columbia University Press.
An objective consideration of the evidence supporting and contradicting Freud's theory of psychoanalysis.

Freud, S. (1940/1969). *An outline of psychoanalysis.* New York: Norton.
A summary of Freud's theory written near the end of his life.

For More on the Dispositional Approach:

Cattell, R. B. (1982). *The inheritance of personality and ability.* New York: Academic Press.
A presentation of Cattell's trait theory of personality, also emphasizing the biological origins of personality.

Eysenck, H. J., & Eysenck, M. W. (1985). *Personality and individual differences.* New York: Plenum.
A presentation of Hans Eysenck's theory of personality types, emphasizing the biological origins of personality.

For More on the Behavioral Approach:

Bandura, A. (1986). *Social foundations of thought and action: A social-cognitive theory.* Englewood Cliffs, NJ: Prentice-Hall.
A discussion of Bandura's social cognitive theory, which emphasizes the person-behavior-environment relationship.

Skinner, B. F. (1953). *Science and human behavior.* New York: Macmillan.
An early, but still relevant, discussion of Skinner's operant learning theory, which assumes that personality is no more than learned behavior patterns.

For More on the Cognitive Approach:

Kelly, G. A. (1955). *The psychology of personal constructs.* New York: Norton.
A summary of Kelly's personal construct theory, which holds that personality develops through the testing and revising of hypotheses about everyday events and behaviors.

For More on the Humanistic Approach:

Maslow, A. H. (1970). *Motivation and personality.* New York: Harper & Row.
A presentation of Maslow's self-actualization theory, which sees each of us as having a natural tendency to develop in a positive way.

Rogers, C. R. (1980). *A way of being.* Boston: Houghton Mifflin.
A presentation of Rogers's self theory, which emphasizes the importance of being true to one's self.

For More on Personality Consistency:

Epstein, S., & O'Brien, E. J. (1985). The person-situation debate in historical and current perspective. *Psychological Bulletin, 98,* 513–537.
An article reviewing the history of the debate over personality consistency.

CHAPTER
14

PSYCHOLOGICAL DISORDERS

Chapter Opening Art:
Willem De Kooning.
Excavation. 1950.

Between 1972 and 1978, a successful, civic-minded Chicago building contractor named John Wayne Gacy murdered thirty-three boys and young men and buried them under his house. After his capture, Gacy expressed no remorse and, instead, reported that his acts of cold-blooded murder had given him pleasure. Gacy's personal history indicated that he had an *antisocial personality disorder* (Darrach & Norris, 1984).

Following a pregame workout in April 1978, players on the Texas Rangers baseball team were shocked to find pitcher Roger Moret standing immobile, grasping a shower slipper in one hand and staring into his locker. Moret held the pose for almost an hour before being taken to a mental hospital, where he was diagnosed as having a psychological disorder called *catatonic schizophrenia* (Rabun, 1978).

On January 22, 1987, at a televised news conference, Pennsylvania treasurer R. Budd Dwyer committed suicide by putting the barrel of a pistol in his mouth and pulling the trigger. Dwyer had suffered from severe *depression* following his conviction on charges of corruption (Cusick, 1987).

THE NATURE OF PSYCHOLOGICAL DISORDERS

Hardly a week goes by without the news media reporting instances of extreme psychological disorders such as these. But how do we determine whether a person has a psychological disorder? What are the causes of psychological disorders? And how are psychological disorders classified? Answers to these questions are provided by psychologists and others in the field of **psychopathology,** which is the study of psychological disorders.

Psychopathology The study of psychological disorders.

Criteria for Psychological Disorders

In the early 1980s, interviewers from the National Institute of Mental Health went door to door in Baltimore, St. Louis, and New Haven and conducted the most ambitious survey ever done on the prevalence of psychological disorders in the United States. Their interviews with more than ten thousand persons found that about 20 percent of adult Americans have one or more psychological disorders (Robins et al., 1984). You probably know people whose patterns of moods, thoughts, and actions make you suspect that they are among that 20 percent. But what are the criteria for determining that a person has a psychological disorder? The main criteria are abnormality, maladaptiveness, and personal distress.

Abnormality Abnormal behavior deviates from the behavior of the "typical" person—the *norm.* A norm may be qualitative or quantitative. *Qualitatively* abnormal behavior deviates from culturally acceptable behavior, perhaps even seeming bizarre. A railroad conductor who announces train stops would be normal, while a passenger who announces train stops would be abnormal. *Quantitatively* abnormal behavior deviates from the statistical average, that is, it is higher or lower than the average. A woman who washes her hands three times a day would be normal, while a woman who washes her hands thirty times a day would be abnormal.

But, by itself, abnormality is not a sufficient criterion for determining the presence of a psychological disorder. If *qualitative* abnormality were sufficient, then a Nobel Prize winner, an Olympic decathlon champion, and even your student government president would be considered psychologically disordered. And if *quantitative* abnormality were sufficient, then even a physician who washes her hands thirty times a day in the course of seeing patients would be considered psychologically disordered. Thus, the context in which deviant behavior occurs must be considered before deciding that it is symptomatic of a psychological disorder.

Maladaptiveness According to the criterion of *maladaptiveness,* you would have a psychological disorder if your behavior seriously disrupted your social, academic, or vocational life. As an example, consider a person with the psychological disorder called *agoraphobia,* characterized by the fear of being in public places. Such a person might be afraid to leave home, perhaps leading to alienation of friends, failure in school, or loss of a job. But maladaptive behavior is not always a sign of a psychological disorder. Though cramming for exams, failing to eat fruits and vegetables, or driving ninety miles per hour on a busy highway are maladaptive behaviors, they would not necessarily be symptomatic of a psychological disorder.

Drawing by Handelsman; © 1983 The New Yorker Magazine, Inc.

"I don't know how you and I would be rated by the psychiatrists in the Soviet Union, but I'd say we're fairly sane by New York standards."

Does this Man Have a Psychological Disorder? For three decades, the blind musician and poet "Moondog," whose real name was Louis Thomas Hardin, was a fixture on the streets of midtown Manhattan in New York City. Though Moondog certainly deviated from cultural norms, there was no evidence that his behavior was maladaptive. On the contrary, he made enough money to live on by playing homemade instruments and offering copies of his poetry to passersby. And there was no evidence that his behavior caused him personal distress. In fact, he claimed that truly distressed people were those who tried to adapt themselves to the demands of modern society.

Personal Distress The criterion of *personal distress* assumes that our subjective feelings of anxiety, depression, or other emotions determine whether we have a psychological disorder. For example, in 1973, as the result of lobbying by homosexual rights groups and reconsideration by mental-health professionals, the American Psychiatric Association declared that a homosexual should be considered psychologically disordered only if he or she felt distressed at being a homosexual, so-called ego-dystonic homosexuality. Until then, homosexuality *was* considered a psychological disorder, primarily because it was considered both abnormal and maladaptive. But even personal distress is not in itself always a sufficient criterion. Individuals, such as John Wayne Gacy, may have psychological disorders without being distressed by their own behavior.

Given that a single criterion may not be sufficient, the presence of behavior that is abnormal, maladaptive, and personally distressing is the strongest indication that a person has a psychological disorder. But note that there is no single point at which a person moves from being psychologically healthy to being psychologically disordered. Instead, there is a continuum ranging from psychologically healthy to psychologically disordered. So, there is a degree of subjectivity in even the best answers to the question, How abnormal, maladaptive, or personally distressing must a person's behavior be before we determine that he or she has a psychological disorder? And even when psychologists agree on the presence of a particular psychological disorder, they may disagree on its causes; that is, they favor different *viewpoints* in determining the causes of psychological disorders.

Viewpoints on Psychological Disorders

Since ancient times human beings have tried to explain what we now call psychological disorders. The ancient Greeks attributed them to the actions of gods and evil spirits. But the physician Hippocrates (460–377 B.C.) argued that psychological disorders had natural causes. As mentioned in chapter 13, Hippocrates believed that temperament was regulated by the relative amounts of fluids he called humors, which included blood, phlegm, black bile, and yellow bile. According to Hippocrates, imbalances in these humors caused psychological disorders by their effects on the brain.

Despite the efforts of Hippocrates and his followers, supernatural explanations remained dominant through the Middle Ages and the Renaissance. Some authorities believe that many of the thousands of women who were executed as witches, both in Europe and in the infamous Salem, Massachusetts, witch trials of 1692, actually had psychological disorders. They behaved in such bizarre ways that others became convinced they were in league with the devil. Of course, this conjecture is based on written records of the trial interpreted three centuries later. Other authorities evaluating the same records find the evidence inadequate to conclude that the accused witches suffered from psychological disorders (Spanos, 1985).

The late sixteenth century saw the beginning of opposition to the supernatural view of psychological disorders from religious leaders, most notably the Spanish nun Teresa of Avila. She saved a group of nuns from being punished as witches after they had inexplicably begun yelling and jumping about with wild abandon, a phenomenon known as *tarantism* or *St. Vitus's dance*. She convinced the religious authorities that the nuns were not possessed but, rather, were "as if sick." That is, they were suffering from "mental illness."

The sixteenth-century Swiss physician Phillipus Paracelsus also rejected the supernatural perspective. Instead of attributing unusual behavior to demons, he attributed it to the moon. Paracelsus called people who exhibited unusual behavior *lunatics* (from the Latin word for "moon"). Though even today almost

The Supernatural Perspective This painting depicts a scene from the Salem witchcraft trials of 1692. The unusual behavior of accused witches was attributed to their being in league with the devil. Some authorities believe that many persons executed as witches were actually suffering from psychological disorders.

Lunacy Paracelsus claimed that the moon could affect behavior, as shown in this engraving depicting "moonstruck" women.

half of all college students believe that the full moon can make people behave strangely, there is no scientific evidence that the moon affects our behavior (Rotton & Kelly, 1985).

During the past two centuries, the growing influence of science as a source of knowledge led to a decline in supernatural explanations of psychological disorders. Current viewpoints on psychological disorders attribute them to natural causes. The viewpoints differ in the extent to which they attribute psychological disorders to biological, mental, or environmental factors (table 14.1).

TABLE 14.1	The Major Viewpoints on Psychological Disorders
Viewpoint	**Causes of Psychological Disorders**
Biomedical	Inherited or acquired brain disorders involving imbalances in neurotransmitters or damage to brain structures.
Psychoanalytic	Unconscious conflicts over impulses such as sex and aggression, originating in childhood.
Behavioral	Positive reinforcement of inappropriate behaviors and punishment of appropriate behaviors.
Cognitive	Irrational or maladaptive thinking about one's self, life events, and the world in general.
Humanistic	Incongruence between one's actual self and public self as a consequence of trying to live up to the demands of others.
Diathesis-Stress	A biological predisposition interacting with stressful life experiences.

The Biomedical Viewpoint A century ago, Sigmund Freud remarked, "In view of the intimate connection between things physical and mental, we may look forward to a day when paths of knowledge will be opened up leading from organic biology and chemistry to the field of neurotic phenomena" (Taulbee, 1983, p. 45). As a biologist and physician, Freud would approve of the *biomedical viewpoint,* which favors the study of the biological causes of psychological disorders (which include so-called neurotic phenomena) and can be traced back to the humoral theory of Hippocrates.

Modern interest in the biological causes of psychological disorders was stimulated in the late nineteenth century when researchers discovered that a disorder called *general paresis,* marked by severe mental deterioration, was caused by infection with syphilis. Researchers in the nineteenth century also found that toxic chemicals, such as mercury, could induce psychological disorders. In fact, the Mad Hatter in *Alice in Wonderland* exhibits psychological symptoms caused by exposure to the mercury that was used in making felt hats. This was the origin of the phrase "mad as a hatter" (Broad, 1981).

Today biomedical researchers are especially interested in the role of brain chemistry and brain damage in the development of psychological disorders. Just as some researchers search for the underlying biological causes of physical illness, others look for underlying biological causes of psychological symptoms. The biomedical perspective (also called the *medical model*) has contributed a vocabulary used by both physicians and many mental-health professionals, including terms such as "cure," "patient," "treatment," "diagnosis," "mental illness," and "mental hospital."

The Psychoanalytic Viewpoint The *psychoanalytic viewpoint* grew out of the biomedical perspective. Instead of looking for underlying biological causes, the psychoanalytic viewpoint looks for unconscious causes of psychological disorders. As discussed in chapter 13, Sigmund Freud emphasized the continual conflict between inborn sexual and aggressive drives that demand expression and the rules of society that inhibit their expression. These conflicts may be repressed into the unconscious mind, leading to feelings of anxiety caused by the unreleased sexual or aggressive energy. Freud claimed that we use defense mechanisms to relieve this anxiety. If our defense mechanisms are either inadequate or too rigid, we may develop psychological disorders.

The Behavioral Viewpoint As discussed in previous chapters, the *behavioral viewpoint* arose in opposition to psychological perspectives that looked for mental causes of behavior. Those who favor the behavioral perspective, most notably B. F. Skinner, look to the environment and to faulty learning for the causes of psychological disorders. A psychological disorder may arise when a person is rewarded for inappropriate behavior. Social cognitive theorists, such as Albert Bandura, would add that we may develop a psychological disorder by observing other people's behavior. For example, a person may develop a phobia (an unrealistic fear) of dogs either after being bitten by a dog or after observing someone else being bitten by a dog.

The Cognitive Viewpoint The Greek Stoic philosopher Epictetus (A.D. ca. 60–ca. 120) taught that "men are disturbed not by things, but by the views which they take of things." This is the central assumption of the *cognitive viewpoint,* which holds that psychological disorders arise from irrational beliefs about oneself and the world, leading to emotional disturbances and maladaptive behaviors. Yet, recent studies indicate that people with psychological disorders may think *more* rationally and objectively than other people about themselves and the world (Taylor & Brown, 1988). That is, people not suffering from psychological disorders may view the world through "rose-colored glasses."

The Humanistic Viewpoint As noted in chapter 13, psychologists such as Abraham Maslow and Carl Rogers, who favor the *humanistic viewpoint,* emphasize the importance of self-actualization, which is the fulfillment of one's potentials. Psychological disorders are the result of blocked self-actualization. This means that people may fail to reach their potential because others, especially their parents, discourage them from expressing their true desires, thoughts, and interests. This *conditional positive regard* may lead the person to develop a public self-image that is favorable to others but markedly different from his or her private self-image. The distress caused by the failure to behave in accordance with one's own desires, thoughts, and interests may lead to the development of psychological disorders. Thus, the humanistic viewpoint sees psychological disorders as reasonable responses to unreasonable demands placed on the individual.

The Diathesis-Stress Viewpoint No single viewpoint provides an adequate explanation of psychological disorders. This has led to the emergence of the **diathesis-stress viewpoint,** which holds that each of us varies in his or her biological predisposition to develop psychological disorders.

Diathesis-Stress Viewpoint The assumption that psychological disorders are consequences of the interaction of a biological, inherited predisposition (diathesis) and exposure to stressful life experiences.

This predisposition is called a *diathesis,* which is determined mainly by heredity. A person with a strong predisposition to develop psychological disorders may succumb to even relatively low levels of psychological stress. In contrast, a person with a weak predisposition to develop psychological disorders may resist even extremely high levels of psychological stress.

Classification of Psychological Disorders

Since ancient times, authorities have distinguished a variety of psychological disorders, each characterized by its own set of symptoms. Hippocrates devised the first system for classifying psychological disorders, which included *mania* (overexcitement), *melancholia* (severe depression), and *phrenitis* (disorganized thinking). In 1883 the German psychiatrist Emil Kraepelin devised the first modern classification system, combining Hippocrates's categories of mania and melancholia into a disorder called *manic depression* and renaming phrenitis *dementia praecox.* Today manic depression is called *bipolar disorder* and dementia praecox is called *schizophrenia.*

The DSM-III-R   These and other psychological disorders are included in the most widely used system of classification of psychological disorders: the revised third edition of the *Diagnostic and Statistical Manual of Mental Disorders,* better known as the *DSM-III-R,* which is published by the American Psychiatric Association. The DSM-III-R, which was published in 1987, is a revised version of the DSM-III, which was published in 1980 and preceded by the DSM-II in 1968 and the DSM-I in 1952. The DSM-III-R provides a means of communication among mental-health practitioners, helps practitioners choose the best treatment for particular disorders, and offers a framework for research on the causes of disorders.

The DSM-I and the DSM-II, which were based on psychoanalytic theory, divided disorders into neuroses and psychoses. **Neuroses** were disorders involving anxiety, moderate disruption of social relations, and relatively good contact with reality. **Psychoses,** in contrast, were disorders involving thought disturbances, bizarre behavior, severe disruption of social relations, and relatively poor contact with reality. The DSM-III-R has dropped this psychoanalytic orientation and, instead, considers the interaction of biological, psychological, and social factors in diagnosing psychological disorders (Linn & Spitzer, 1982).

The DSM-III-R provides five axes for diagnosing psychological disorders. Axis I contains sixteen major categories of psychological disorders (table 14.2). Axis II contains developmental disorders and personality disorders. Axis III contains medical conditions that might affect the person's psychological disorder. Axis IV contains a rating (from one to six) of the degree of social stress the person has been under during the past year. And Axis V contains a rating (from ninety to one) of both the person's current level of functioning and highest level of functioning during the past year.

Neuroses A general category, no longer widely used, that comprises psychological disorders associated with maladaptive attempts to deal with anxiety but with relatively good contact with reality.

Psychoses A general category, no longer widely used, that comprises severe psychological disorders associated with thought disturbances, bizarre behavior, severe disruption of social relations, and relatively poor contact with reality.

TABLE 14.2 The DSM-III-R: Axis I Disorders and Multiaxial Evaluation

Axis I: Clinical Syndromes

1. **Disorders usually first evident in infancy, childhood, or adolescence**
   Disorders that appear before adulthood. Examples include stuttering, enuresis (bedwetting), and anorexia nervosa (self-starvation).

2. **Organic mental syndromes and disorders**
   Disorders that are caused by aging, drugs, toxins, or diseases. Examples include delirium (extreme mental confusion) and dementia (a marked deterioration of the intellect).

3. **Psychoactive substance use disorders**
   Disorders that involve dependence on psychoactive drugs to the detriment of everyday functioning. Examples include dependency on alcohol, heroin, cocaine, or marijuana.

4. **Schizophrenia**
   Disorders associated with marked disorganization of perception, cognition, emotionality, and behavior. Examples include catatonic schizophrenia and paranoid schizophrenia.

5. **Delusional disorder**
   Disorders involving paranoid delusional thinking, without the extreme deterioration of schizophrenia. Examples include delusions of grandeur or persecution.

6. **Psychotic disorders not elsewhere classified**
   Disorders that are less severe than schizophrenia or mood disorders, but which involve similar symptoms. Examples include schizophreniform disorder and schizoaffective disorder.

7. **Mood disorders**
   Disorders marked by severe emotional disturbances. Examples include major depression and bipolar disorder.

8. **Anxiety disorders**
   Disorders associated with extreme anxiety. Examples include generalized anxiety disorder, panic disorder, phobic disorders, and obsessive-compulsive disorder.

9. **Somatoform disorders**
   Disorders involving physical symptoms, such as paralysis or sensory loss, without a physical cause. Examples include hypochondriasis and conversion disorder.

10. **Dissociative disorders**
    Disorders in which conscious awareness is separated from personally relevant thoughts, feelings, and memories. Examples include psychogenic amnesia, psychogenic fugue, and multiple personality.

11. **Sexual disorders**
    Disorders characterized by unusual sexual practices or by sexual dysfunctions. Examples of unusual sexual practices include exhibitionism and fetishism. Examples of sexual dysfunctions include male erectile disorder and inhibited female orgasm.

12. **Sleep disorders**
    Disorders marked by disruption of the sleep-wake cycle. Examples include insomnia and hypersomnia.

13. **Factitious disorders**
    Disorders in which the person fakes symptoms of physical or psychological disorders. Examples include factitious pain and Munchausen syndrome (self-induced illnesses and repeated attempts to gain admission to hospitals).

14. **Impulse control disorders not elsewhere classified**
    Disorders associated with an inability to resist the impulse to commit certain acts. Examples include compulsive gambling and kleptomania (compulsive stealing).

15. **Adjustment disorder**
    Disorders in which the person fails to adapt adequately to important stressors. Examples include the failure to adapt well to a divorce or to a financial setback.

16. **Psychological factors affecting physical condition**
    Stress-related psychological factors that may cause or worsen physical conditions. Examples of physical conditions affected by psychological factors include asthma, headaches, and gastric ulcers.

An example of multiaxial evaluation on the DSM-III-R

Axis I	Alcohol dependence
Axis II	Antisocial personality disorder
Axis III	Alcoholic cirrhosis of the liver
Axis IV	Psychosocial stressors: divorce Severity: 4—severe(acute event)
Axis V	Current level of functioning: 35 Highest level of functioning in the past year: 50

Though the DSM-III-R is an improvement over previous diagnostic systems, it has met with some criticism (McReynolds, 1989). Preliminary research indicates that the DSM-III-R categories have only modest reliability and validity (concepts discussed in chapter 9), so they have yet to demonstrate their usefulness as a means of diagnosing psychological disorders (Eysenck, Wakefield, & Friedman, 1983). And a survey of psychologists found that most rejected the DSM-III-R for being too dependent on the medical model and insufficiently sensitive to interpersonal factors (Smith & Kraft, 1983).

There is also concern that the DSM-III-R may be biased against women. For example, the *dependent personality disorder* has been accused of being an exaggeration of stereotypical female behavior. One critic (with tongue somewhat in cheek) wonders why there is no similar category for an "independent personality disorder," representing an exaggeration of stereotypical male behavior (Kaplan, 1983). Defenders of the DSM-III-R report that though certain personality disorders, such as the dependent personality disorder, are diagnosed more often in women, others, such as the *antisocial personality disorder,* are diagnosed more often in men, and that there is no overall tendency for females to be diagnosed as having personality disorders more often than are men (Kass, Spitzer, & Williams, 1983).

Criticisms of the Diagnosis of Psychological Disorders Criticisms of psychological diagnosis itself abound, as in a classic study conducted by David Rosenhan (1973). Rosenhan had eight normal persons, including himself, gain admission to mental hospitals by calling the hospitals for appointments and complaining of hearing voices saying "empty, hollow, thud"—a symptom of a serious psychological disorder called schizophrenia. These "pseudopatients" were admitted to twelve hospitals in five states, with their stays ranging from seven to fifty-two days.

During their stays they behaved normally, did not complain of hearing voices, and sometimes wrote hundreds of pages of notes about their experiences in the hospitals. Though no staff members discovered they were faking, several real patients expressed the belief that they were journalists or professors investigating mental hospitals. Rosenhan concluded that the diagnosis of psychological disorders is influenced more by preconceptions and by the context in which we find a person than by any objective characteristics of the person, as in the following conversation from *Alice in Wonderland*:

> "I don't want to go among mad people," Alice remarked.
> "Oh, you can't help that," said the Cat: "we're all mad here. I'm mad. You're mad."
> "How do you know I'm mad?" said Alice.
> "You must be," said the Cat, "or you wouldn't have come here."

But Rosenhan's study provoked criticisms that he had misinterpreted the results of his study. First, the admission of the pseudopatients to the mental hospitals was justified, because people who report hearing voices that do not actually exist are exhibiting symptoms of schizophrenia. Second, schizophrenics may go long periods of time without displaying obvious symptoms of schizophrenia. Thus, the staff members who observed the pseudopatients during their stays had no reason to conclude that they were faking. Nonetheless, the power of the label "mentally ill" to influence judgment of a person was supported by another study. When subjects observed people labeled as mental patients (who actually were not) or similar people not given that label, they were more likely to rate the alleged mental patients as being "unusual" (Piner & Kahle, 1984).

Other critics of the classification of psychological disorders point to the use of diagnostic labels to discredit or persecute people with unpopular ideas.

During the 1964 presidential campaign between Lyndon Johnson and Barry Goldwater, a poll of psychiatrists from across the United States found that most of those who opposed Goldwater diagnosed him as suffering from paranoid schizophrenia—a serious psychological disorder marked by irrational suspiciousness and a high potential for violence. Goldwater apparently earned this label merely because his political beliefs were unpopular with many of those who responded to the poll (Eron, 1966).

The best-known critic of diagnostic labels is psychiatrist Thomas Szasz (1960), who has gone so far as to call mental illness, including schizophrenia, a "myth." He believes that the behaviors that earn the label of mental illness are "problems in living." According to Szasz, labeling people as mentally ill wrongly places the blame for their "problems in living" on the victims, rather than on the intolerable social conditions that cause their problems. As indicated in the following comment, Szasz's claim that mental illness is a myth has provoked hostile responses from other mental-health practitioners:

> This myth has a seductive appeal for many persons, especially if they do not have to deal clinically with individuals and their families experiencing the anguish, confusion, and terror of schizophrenia. Unfortunately, informing schizophrenics and their relatives that they are having a mythological experience does not seem to be appreciated by them and is not particularly helpful. (Kessler, 1984, p. 380)

Most mental-health professionals do not view psychological disorders as myths. In fact, the DSM-III-R describes more than two hundred disorders. Among the most important categories of disorders are anxiety disorders, somatoform disorders, dissociative disorders, mood disorders, schizophrenic disorders, and personality disorders. Figure 14.1 indicates the prevalences of several important psychological disorders.

Thomas Szasz "Mental illness is a myth, whose function it is to disguise and thus render more palatable the bitter pill of moral conflicts in human relations."

ANXIETY DISORDERS

You have certainly experienced anxiety when learning to drive, taking an important exam, or going on a first date with someone. *Anxiety* is a feeling of apprehension accompanied by increased sympathetic nervous system activity, producing increases in sweating, heart rate, and breathing rate. Though anxiety is a normal part of our everyday lives, in **anxiety disorders** it becomes intense, chronic, and disruptive of everyday functioning. About 10 to 15 percent of adult Americans suffer from anxiety disorders (Robins et al., 1984).

Anxiety Disorders Psychological disorders marked by persistent anxiety that disrupts everyday functioning.

Generalized Anxiety Disorder

While we normally experience anxiety in response to stressful situations, the person with a **generalized anxiety disorder** is in a constant state of anxiety that exists independently of any particular stressful situation. Because the person is constantly anxious, with no apparent source of the anxiety, the anxiety is said to be "free floating." The person worries constantly about almost everything, including work, school, finances, and social relationships.

What accounts for the development of a generalized anxiety disorder? One possibility is heredity, because anxiety disorders run in families, with the children of individuals with anxiety disorders, such as generalized anxiety disorder, seven times more likely to suffer from them than is the general population. It remains to be determined whether this is more attributable to common heredity or to common life experiences (Turner, Beidel, & Costello, 1987).

Generalized Anxiety Disorder An anxiety disorder marked by a persistent state of anxiety that exists independently of any particular stressful situation.

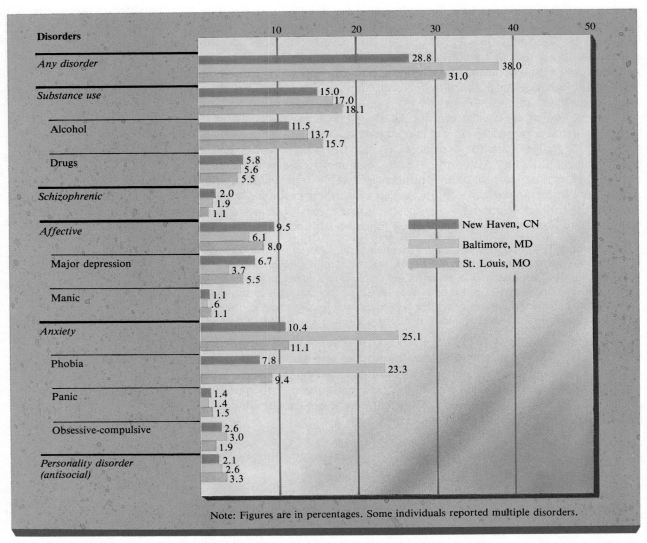

Disorders	New Haven, CN	Baltimore, MD	St. Louis, MO
Any disorder	28.8	38.0	31.0
Substance use	15.0	17.0	18.1
Alcohol	11.5	13.7	15.7
Drugs	5.8	5.6	5.5
Schizophrenic	2.0	1.9	1.1
Affective	9.5	6.1	8.0
Major depression	6.7	3.7	5.5
Manic	1.1	.6	1.1
Anxiety	10.4	25.1	11.1
Phobia	7.8	23.3	9.4
Panic	1.4	1.4	1.5
Obsessive-compulsive	2.6	3.0	1.9
Personality disorder (antisocial)	2.1	2.6	3.3

Note: Figures are in percentages. Some individuals reported multiple disorders.

FIGURE 14.1
Lifetime Prevalence of Some Major Psychological Disorders A survey of people in three American cities found that about one-third had experienced one or more DSM-III-R categories. Note that the prevalence of certain disorders varied markedly from city to city (Robins et al., 1984).

The humanistic viewpoint provides a different point of view. One humanistic explanation holds that anxiety arises from a discrepancy between the actual self and the ought self, which are described in chapter 13 (Higgins, 1987). This means that a generalized anxiety disorder may be caused by failing to live up to desirable standards of behavior.

Panic Disorder

Panic Disorder An anxiety disorder marked by sudden, unexpected attacks of overwhelming anxiety, often associated with the fear of dying or "losing one's mind."

In describing the motivation for his painting *The Scream,* Norwegian artist Edvard Munch (1863–1944) remarked, "I was walking . . . and I felt a loud, unending scream piercing nature" (Blakemore, 1977, p. 155). Both the painting and the statement indicate that Munch had experienced a **panic disorder,** which is marked by sudden, unexpected attacks of overwhelming anx-

Panic Edvard Munch's painting *The Scream* (1893) conveys the intense anxiety and terror characteristic of a panic attack.

iety, accompanied by dizziness, trembling, cold sweats, heart palpitations, shortness of breath, fear of dying, and fear of going crazy. A person suffering a panic attack may also feel detached from his or her own body or feel that other people are not real. Though panic attacks usually last only a few minutes, they are so distressing that more people seek therapy for panic disorder than for any other psychological disorder (Boyd, 1986).

One biomedical explanation of panic disorder attributes it to the effect of *hypoglycemia* (low blood sugar) on the brain. But this explanation has failed to gain research support. In one study, people prone to panic disorders were given insulin intravenously to create hypoglycemia. Though all of them developed hypoglycemia, none developed the intense anxiety associated with panic disorder (Schweizer, Winokur, & Rickels, 1986).

According to cognitive theorists, anxiety disorders result from faulty thinking. For example, people prone to panic disorders engage in catastrophic thinking, misattributing physical symptoms of mild arousal to serious physical or psychological problems. This leads them to experience overwhelming anxiety (Rapee, Mattick, & Murrell, 1986). Note how much this explanation has in common with Schachter's two-factor theory of emotion (chapter 11).

Phobias

Phobia An anxiety disorder marked by excessive or inappropriate fear.

Simple Phobia A phobia of a specific object or situation.

Social Phobia A phobia of situations that involve public scrutiny.

Agoraphobia A phobia associated with fear of being in public, usually because the person fears the embarrassment of a panic attack.

The word **phobia** comes from Phobos, the Greek god of fear, and refers to the experience of excessive or inappropriate fear. The person realizes that the fear is irrational but cannot control it. A **simple phobia** is an intense, irrational fear of a specific object or situation. People with simple phobias may go to great lengths to avoid the object or situation that they fear. Table 14.3 lists common simple phobias.

People with **social phobias** fear public scrutiny, perhaps leading them to avoid playing sports, making telephone calls, or performing in plays (so-called stage fright). You have gotten a hint of this experience if you have noticed your mouth becoming dry, your palms sweating, and your heart beating strongly just before making an oral presentation in class.

Agoraphobia is a fear of being in public, usually because the person fears the embarrassment of having a panic attack witnessed by other people. A person with agoraphobia might avoid parties, sporting events, and shopping malls. In fact, the word "agoraphobia" comes from the Greek term for "fear of the marketplace." In extreme cases the person might become a prisoner in his or her own home—terrified to leave for any reason. Because agoraphobia disrupts every aspect of the victim's life, it is the most common phobia seen by psychotherapists.

According to Martin Seligman (1971), evolution has biologically prepared us to develop phobias of potentially dangerous natural objects, such as fire, snakes, and heights. Early human beings who feared these things were more likely to avoid them and, as a result, were more likely to live long enough to reproduce. This may explain why phobias involving potentially dangerous natural objects, such as snakes, are more persistent than are phobias involving usually safe natural objects, such as flowers (McNally, 1987).

TABLE 14.3   Simple Phobias

Phobia	Source of Phobia
Acrophobia	High places
Ailurophobia	Cats
Algophobia	Pain
Aquaphobia	Water
Arachnophobia	Spiders
Astraphobia	Lightning storms
Claustrophobia	Enclosed places
Cynophobia	Dogs
Hematophobia	Blood
Hydrophobia	Fear of water
Monophobia	Being alone
Mysophobia	Dirt
Nyctophobia	Darkness
Ocholophobia	Crowds
Thanatophobia	Death
Triskaidekaphobia	Number thirteen
Xenophobia	Strangers
Zoophobia	Animals

Psychoanalysts believe that phobias are caused by anxiety displaced from a feared object or situation onto another object or situation. By displacing the anxiety, the person keeps the true source unconscious. The classic psychoanalytic case is that of Little Hans, a five-year-old boy who was afraid to go outside because of his fear of horses. After listening to the background of the case, Sigmund Freud attributed the phobia to inadequate resolution of the Oedipus complex. Freud claimed that Hans had an incestuous desire for his mother and a fear of being punished for it by being castrated by his father. Hans displaced his fear of his father to horses, permitting him to keep his incestuous feelings unconscious.

In contrast, behavioral theorists claim that phobias are learned responses to frightening situations, either through personal experience or through observation. For example, Little Hans's phobia could have been attributed to a horrifying incident that he witnessed in which horses harnassed to a wagon fell and then struggled to get to their feet (Stafford-Clark, 1965).

Obsessive-Compulsive Disorder

Have you ever been unable to keep a commercial's jingle from continually running through your mind? If so, you have experienced a mild *obsession,* which is a persistent, recurring thought. Have you ever repeatedly checked your alarm clock to make sure it was set the night before an early-morning exam? If so, you have experienced a mild *compulsion,* which is a repetitive action that you feel compelled to perform. People whose obsessions and compulsions interfere with their daily functioning suffer from an **obsessive-compulsive disorder.**

Biomedical researchers have found that people with obsessive-compulsive disorders have chronically high levels of physiological arousal. This may make them overreact to mildly stressful situations and engage in obsessive-compulsive behavior to reduce their arousal (Turner, Beidel, & Nathan, 1985). You may have experienced this in a mild form when you felt anxious about school work, spent an hour rearranging your room, and felt less anxious as a consequence.

"But that's what you said yesterday—'Just one more cord'!"

Drawing by Woodman; © 1986 The New Yorker Magazine, Inc.

Obsessive-Compulsive Disorder An anxiety disorder in which the person has recurrent, intrusive thoughts (obsessions) and recurrent urges to perform ritualistic actions (compulsions).

According to psychoanalysts, obsessive-compulsive disorders are caused by fixation at the anal stage, resulting from harsh toilet training. This causes repressed anger directed at the parents. The child defends against the guilt generated by these feelings of anger and later transgressions by repeating certain thoughts and actions over and over. The obsessions and compulsions often have symbolic meaning, as portrayed in Shakespeare's *Macbeth* when Lady Macbeth engages in compulsive handwashing after murdering King Duncan.

Behavioral theorists view obsessions and compulsions as ways of avoiding anxiety-inducing situations. So, you might compulsively clean and organize your room to avoid the anxiety of studying for exams and writing term papers. In providing a cognitive explanation of obsessive-compulsive disorders, some theorists point to the so-called God or scum phenomenon, which afflicts people who believe they are failures unless they are perfect. In that case, obsessive-compulsive behaviors might be attempts at gaining complete control over oneself and one's immediate environment (Pacht, 1984).

SOMATOFORM DISORDERS

Somatoform Disorders
Psychological disorders characterized by physical symptoms in the absence of disease or injury.

The **somatoform disorders** (somatoform means "bodylike") are characterized by physical symptoms in the absence of disease or injury. The symptoms are caused, instead, by psychological factors. Do not confuse somatoform disorders with *malingering,* in which the person purposely invents symptoms in order to be relieved of certain responsibilities. The person with a somatoform disorder truly believes he or she has symptoms of a real physical disorder.

Hypochondriasis

Hypochondriasis A somatoform disorder in which the person interprets the slightest physical changes as evidence of a serious illness.

A person with the somatoform disorder called **hypochondriasis** interprets the slightest physical changes in his or her body as evidence of a serious illness. Hypochondriacs may go from physician to physician, searching for the one physician who will finally diagnose the serious disease that they are sure is causing their symptoms. Medical students may experience a mild form of hypochondriasis in the so-called medical student syndrome, in which a mere sore throat might convince them they have cancer. As you read about the various psychological disorders, you should beware of developing a similar "psy-

From R. Chast, *The Sciences,* 10 September 1985. Copyright © R. Chast.

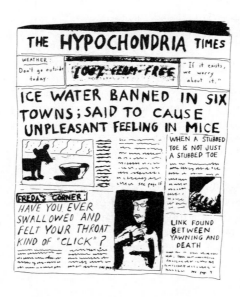

chology student syndrome," in which you interpret your normal variations in mood, thinking, and behavior as symptoms of a psychological disorder. Of course, if your symptoms become distressing, prolonged, or disruptive of your life, you should consider seeking professional counseling.

What accounts for hypochondriasis? Behavioral theorists point to both positive reinforcement, such as being lavished with attention, and negative reinforcement, such as relief from work responsibilities. Cognitivists note that people who develop hypochondriasis fear disease so much that they become overly vigilant about bodily changes, leading them to notice and exaggerate even the slightest changes (Barsky & Klerman, 1983).

Conversion Disorder

A person with the somatoform disorder called **conversion disorder** exhibits loss or alteration of a physical function without any apparent physical cause. In typical cases, the person exhibits muscle paralysis, such as difficulty in speaking, or sensory loss, such as an inability to feel an object on the skin. But the apparently lost function is actually intact. In one study, a girl who suffered for a year with "paralyzed" legs began using them after merely being provided with biofeedback providing her with evidence of activity in her leg muscles (Klonoff & Moore, 1986). Physicians suspect the presence of a conversion disorder when a patient displays *la belle indifference*—a lack of concern that people with conversion disorders commonly display toward their symptoms. A conversion disorder may also be diagnosed by a physician who notices that a patient's symptoms are anatomically impossible (figure 14.2).

Theories explaining conversion disorder have a long and sometimes bizarre history. An Egyptian papyrus dating from 1900 B.C. attributed the disorder, which was believed to be limited to women, to a wandering uterus (Jones, 1980). Hippocrates accepted this explanation and called the disorder *hysteria,* from the Greek word for uterus. Because Hippocrates believed that the uterus wandered when a woman was sexually frustrated, he prescribed marriage as a cure.

Conversion Disorder A somatoform disorder in which the person exhibits motor or sensory loss or the alteration of a physiological function without any apparent physical cause.

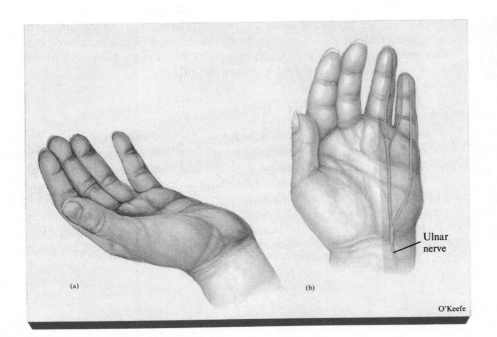

(a)   (b)   Ulnar nerve

O'Keefe

FIGURE 14.2
Conversion Disorder (*a*) A person with "glove anesthesia" will complain of numbness in the hand from the wrist to the tips of the fingers. This is easily diagnosed as a conversion disorder because damage to the sensory nerves of the hand will not produce this pattern of sensory loss. Different areas of the hand are served by the ulnar, radial, and median nerves. If a given nerve is injured, there will be numbness in only a portion of the hand. For example, damage to the ulnar nerve will produce numbness along the outer edge of the hand (*b*).

The "wandering womb" view was challenged in the late nineteenth century when Sigmund Freud claimed that hysteria resulted from anxiety generated by repressed sexual impulses. The anxiety was converted into symbolic physical symptoms, such as paralyzed legs, that enabled a woman to avoid acting on her sexual impulses. Freud called such disorders *conversion hysteria.* Today, to avoid the implication that the disorder is strictly a female problem, it is simply called *conversion disorder.* Though conversion disorders occur more often in women, they also occur in men. For example, unemployed Appalachian coal miners show an increased incidence of conversion disorders, perhaps because it helps them save face for being out of work (Jones, 1980).

Biomedical researchers have found that somatoform disorders run in families. This may have a hereditary basis, because the concordance rate for identical twins is three times greater than for fraternal twins (29 percent versus 10 percent). The *concordance rate* is the likelihood that a person will develop a psychological disorder given that a particular relative has that disorder. But it is unclear whether the higher concordance rate for identical twins simply reflects greater similarity in their life experiences (Torgersen, 1986).

DISSOCIATIVE DISORDERS

In **dissociative disorders,** the person's conscious awareness becomes separated from certain of his or her thoughts, feelings, and memories. The dissociative disorders include psychogenic amnesia, psychogenic fugue, and multiple personality.

Psychogenic Amnesia

While being interrogated about his assassination of Robert F. Kennedy in 1968, Sirhan Sirhan was unable to recall the incident (Bower, 1981). He apparently suffered from **psychogenic amnesia,** the inability to recall personally significant memories. The lost memories are usually related to a traumatic event, such as witnessing a catastrophe. Victims of psychogenic amnesia typically regain the lost memories after a period of hours or days.

The psychoanalytic viewpoint assumes that the repression of painful memories causes psychogenic amnesia. This was supported by a study showing that people who viewed slides of normal and disfigured faces accompanied by verbal descriptions had poorer recall of the verbal descriptions associated with the disfigured faces (Christianson & Nilsson, 1984).

Psychogenic Fugue

In September 1980, a young woman was found wandering in Birch State Park in Florida. She did not know who she was or where she was from. After a nationally televised appearance on a morning television show, she was reunited with her family in Illinois. She suffered from **psychogenic fugue,** marked by the memory loss characteristic of psychogenic amnesia and by fleeing from one's home. (The word "fugue" comes from the Latin word meaning "to flee.") The person may adopt a new identity, only to emerge from the fugue state months or years later, recalling nothing that has happened during the intervening time period.

Dissociative Disorders Psychological disorders in which thoughts, feelings, and memories become separated from conscious awareness.

Psychogenic Amnesia A dissociative disorder marked by the inability to recall personally significant memories.

Psychogenic Fugue A dissociative disorder marked by the memory loss characteristic of psychogenic amnesia, the loss of one's identity, and fleeing from one's home.

Psychogenic Fugue In September 1980, this young woman was found naked and starving in Birch State Park in Florida. She could not recall who she was or where she was from— a case of psychogenic fugue. Those who took care of her called her "Jane Doe." Even after being reunited with an Illinois couple who claimed to be her parents, she was unable to recall her identity or her past.

Multiple Personality

In 1812 Benjamin Rush, the father of American Psychiatry, reported the following summary of his case study of a minister's wife:

> In her paroxysms of madness she resumed her gay habits, spoke French, and ridiculed the tenets and practices of the sect to which she belonged. In the intervals of her fits she renounced her gay habits, became zealously devoted to the religious principles and ceremonies of the Methodists, and forgot everything she did and said during the fits of her insanity. (Carlson, 1981, p. 668)

This was one of the first well-documented cases of **multiple personality,** in which a person has two or more distinct personalities that alternate with one another, as in the story of Dr. Jekyll and Mr. Hyde. The multiple personalities may include males and females, children and adults, and moral and immoral characters. A quiet, retiring middle-aged woman may alternate with a flamboyant, promiscuous young woman. Each personality may have its own way of walking, writing, and speaking. You are probably familiar with two cases of multiple personality that were made into movies based on best-selling books: the story of Chris Sizemore, portrayed by Joanne Woodward in *The Three Faces of Eve* and the story of Sybil Dorsett, portrayed by Sally Field in *Sybil.*

Multiple Personality A dissociative disorder in which the person has two or more distinct personalities that alternate with one another.

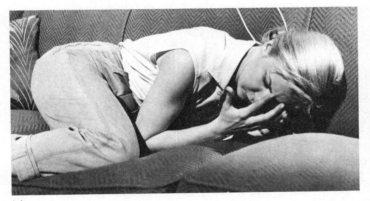

(a)

(c)

(b)

(d)

Multiple Personality In the 1957 film *The Three Faces of Eve,* Joanne Woodward portrayed a woman with three different personalities. The personality named Eve White (*a*) was prim and proper; the personality named Eve Black (*b*) was sexually promiscuous; and the personality named Jane (*c*) was a balanced compromise between the other two. More than two decades later, a woman named Chris Sizemore (*d*) revealed that she was the woman portrayed by Joanne Woodward. After years of therapy she was finally able to maintain a single, integrated personality—instead of the twenty-two she displayed at one point in her life.

In some cases, the original personality may not be aware of the others—as in the notorious case of Billy Milligan. In 1977 Milligan raped four women on the campus of Ohio State University. His defense was that he was unaware that one of his alleged twenty-four personalities, a lesbian, had committed the rapes—for which another of his personalities, a child, had confessed. Milligan became the first person to use a multiple personality disorder as the basis for a successful insanity defense, though some experts suspected that he was faking (Langone, 1981).

People who develop multiple personalities almost always had traumatic childhood experiences. As a child, Chris Sizemore saw a man drown, saw a man cut to pieces in a sawmill, and was forced to kiss her grandfather's corpse. Sybil Dorsett's mother locked her in closets and sexually tortured her. And Billy Milligan's stepfather physically abused him and threatened to bury him alive if he told anyone.

Because of a marked increase in reported cases of multiple personality in the 1980s, some cognitive researchers believe multiple personalities are being overdiagnosed and are merely the product of role playing, just as the "hidden observer" in hypnosis (which is discussed in chapter 5) may be a case of role playing. This possibility was demonstrated in a study in which students were hypnotized and asked to reveal the hidden personality of an accused multiple murderer called Harry or Betty Hodgins. Eighty percent did so. This indicates that at least some reputed cases of multiple personality disorder may be no more than role playing, whether intentional or not (Spanos, Weekes, & Bertrand, 1985).

MOOD DISORDERS

Mood Disorders Psychological disorders marked by prolonged periods of extreme depression or elation, often unrelated to the person's current situation.

We all experience repeated, mild fluctuations in our emotions, such as becoming briefly depressed after failing an exam or briefly elated after getting an A. But people with **mood disorders** experience prolonged periods of extreme depression or elation, often unrelated to their current circumstances, that disrupt their everyday functioning.

Major Depression

Major Depression A mood disorder marked by depression so intense and prolonged that the person may be completely unable to function in everyday life.

We normally feel depressed after personal losses or failures, with the frequency and intensity of depressive episodes varying from person to person. Winston Churchill was so hounded by depression that he called it the "black dog" that followed him around. And depression is so common and distressing that 250,000 persons wrote to Ann Landers requesting a pamphlet on depression that she had offered in one of her columns (Holden, 1986).

People with **major depression** experience depression that is so intense and so prolonged that it causes extreme distress and disrupts their lives. They may express despondency, helplessness, and loss of self-esteem. They may also suffer from insomnia, lose interest in food, feel constantly fatigued, abandon good grooming habits, withdraw from social relations, find it difficult to concentrate, and fail to perform up to their normal academic and vocational standards. About 2 to 3 percent of men and about 4 to 9 percent of women suffer from major depression (APA, 1987).

You should be aware that people suffering from major depression are more susceptible to suicide. Though some suicides are done for honor, as in the Japanese ritual of hara-kiri, or to escape intolerable pain, as in cases of terminal cancer, most are associated with major depression. There are more than 200,000 suicide attempts each year in the United States, with more than 25,000 fatalities. Three times more females than males attempt suicide, but three times more males than females succeed. This occurs because males tend to use more lethal means, such as gunshots to the head, while females tend to use less lethal means, such as overdoses of depressant drugs.

During your lifetime, you will probably know people who you suspect are contemplating suicide. Studies have shown that one of the main factors that keeps suicidal people from attempting suicide is social support, which may reduce the effect of negative events on the suicidal person (Slater & Depue, 1987). According to Edwin Shneidman (1987), one of the leading experts on suicide, about 80 percent of people who attempt suicide give signs before their attempts. This makes it important to take threats seriously and take appropriate actions to prevent suicide attempts. Though there is no guaranteed way to prevent suicide, table 14.4 presents several steps you can take to dissuade a suicidal person from attempting it.

Bipolar Disorder

A biblical story describes how King Saul stripped off his clothes in public, exhibited alternating bouts of elation and severe depression, and eventually committed suicide. Though the story attributes his behavior to evil spirits, psychologists might attribute it to a bipolar disorder. A **bipolar disorder,** formerly called *manic depression,* is characterized by periods of mania alternating with longer periods of major depression, typically separated by days or weeks of normal moods.

Mania (from the Greek term for "madness") is characterized by euphoria, hyperactivity, grandiose ideas, annoying talkativeness, unrealistic optimism, and inflated self-esteem. Manic people may also overestimate their own abilities, perhaps leading them to make rash business deals or to leave a sedentary job to train for the Olympics. At some time in their lives, .4 to 1.2 percent of adults have a bipolar disorder, which is equally common in males and females (APA, 1987).

Bipolar Disorder A mood disorder marked by periods of mania alternating with longer periods of major depression.

Mania A mood disorder marked by euphoria, hyperactivity, grandiose ideas, annoying talkativeness, unrealistic optimism, and inflated self-esteem.

TABLE 14.4   Suicide Prevention

1. Because suicide attempts are, indeed, usually cries for help, the mere act of providing an empathetic response may reduce the immediate likelihood of an actual attempt. Just talking about a problem may reduce its apparent dreadfulness and help the person realize possible solutions other than suicide.

2. Broaden the suicidal person's options to more than a choice between death and a hopeless, helpless life. You might have the person make a list of options and then rank them in order of preference. Suicide may no longer rank first.

3. An immediate goal should be to relieve the psychological pain of the person by intervening, if possible, with those who might be contributing to the pain, whether friends, lovers, teachers, or family members.

4. Encourage the person to seek professional help, even if you have to make the appointment for the person and accompany him or her to it. Many cities have twenty-four-hour suicide hotlines or walk-in centers to provide emergency counseling.

Causes of Mood Disorders

What accounts for mood disorders? Each of the major viewpoints offers its own explanations.

The Biomedical Viewpoint   The mood disorders have a biological basis, apparently influenced by heredity. Consider the concordance rate in twins. If an identical twin suffers from major depression, the other twin will have a 40 percent chance of suffering from it. If a fraternal twin suffers from major depression, the other twin will have only a 10 percent chance of suffering from it (Allen, 1976). Because identical twins have the same genetic inheritance, while fraternal twins are no more genetically alike than ordinary siblings, this provides evidence of a hereditary predisposition to develop major depression. But heredity alone cannot explain depression. If it could, when one identical twin suffers from major depression, the other would have a 100–percent chance of suffering from it. Thus, differences in life experiences also play an important role in determining whether a person with a hereditary predisposition actually develops major depression.

There is also evidence of a hereditary basis for bipolar disorder, as provided by a study of the Amish community in Lancaster County, Pennsylvania. Because the Amish have a culturally isolated community, only marrying among themselves, they provide an excellent opportunity to study the influence of heredity on psychological disorders. Janice Egeland and her colleagues (1987) found that Amish people suffering from bipolar disorder share a defective gene on the eleventh chromosome. But, because only 63 percent of those with this defect develop the disorder, differences in life experience must also play a role. Moreover, there must be other mechanisms for the inheritance of bipolar disorder because a study of three other North American family groups in which bipolar disorder follows a hereditary pattern failed to find a defective gene on the eleventh chromosome (Detera-Wadleigh et al., 1987).

The hereditary predisposition to develop mood disorders may manifest itself by its effect on neurotransmitters. Major depression is related to abnormally low levels of *serotonin* or *norepinephrine* in the brain (McNeal & Cimbolic, 1986). One study measured levels of a chemical by-product of serotonin in the cerebrospinal fluid of depressed people who had tried suicide. Of those with above-average levels, none subsequently committed suicide. Of those with below-average levels, 20 percent subsequently did (Traskman, Asberg, Bertilsson, & Sjostrand, 1981). Antidepressant drugs, often prescribed for suicidal people, act by increasing levels of serotonin and norepinephrine.

Serotonin appears to moderate norepinephrine's relationship to both mania and major depression. Depression is associated with a combination of low levels of serotonin and low levels of norepinephrine, while mania is associated with a combination of low levels of serotonin and high levels of norepinephrine. Mania is also associated with unusually high levels of brain arousal, perhaps related to these neurotransmitter levels (figure 14.3).

The Psychoanalytic Viewpoint   The traditional psychoanalytic view holds that the loss of a parent or rejection by a parent early in childhood predisposes the person to experience depression whenever he or she suffers a personal loss, such as a job or a lover, later in life. Because the child feels it is unacceptable to express anger at the lost or rejecting parent, the child turns the anger on himself or herself, creating feelings of guilt and self-loathing (Freud, 1917/1963). Research studies have provided little support for this explanation. For example, both depressed and nondepressed adults are equally likely to have suffered the loss of a parent in childhood (Crook & Eliot, 1980).

Heredity and Bipolar Disorder
The Amish community of Lancaster County, Pennsylvania, has provided the opportunity for determining the hereditary basis of bipolar disorder. The Amish keep good genealogical records and rarely marry anyone from outside their community. Janice Egeland and her colleagues (1987) found that bipolar disorder was linked to a specific genetic defect in an extended family in the Amish community.

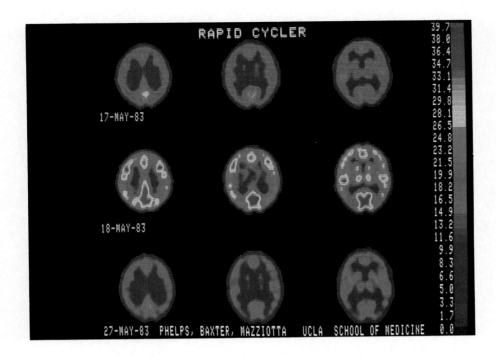

FIGURE 14.3
Brain Activity in Bipolar Disorder These PET scans show the brain activity of a rapid-cycling bipolar patient. The patient cycled between mania and depression every twenty-four to forty-eight hours. The top and bottom sets of scans were obtained during periods when the patient was depressed. The middle set of scans was obtained during a manic period. Note that the red areas indicate significantly higher brain activity during the manic period (Phelps & Mazziotta, 1985).

The Behavioral Viewpoint Behavioral explanations of depression emphasize the role of learning and environmental factors. One of the most influential behavioral theories of depression is Peter Lewinsohn's *reinforcement theory,* which assumes that depressed people lack the social skills to gain normal social reinforcement from others and, instead, provoke negative reactions from them. For example, depressed people stimulate less smiling, fewer statements of support, more unpleasant facial expressions, and more negative remarks from others than do nondepressed people (Gotlib & Robinson, 1982). Lewinsohn points out that the depressed person is caught in a vicious cycle in which reduced social reinforcement leads to depression and depressed behavior further reduces social reinforcement (Youngren & Lewinsohn, 1980).

Another influential behavioral theory of depression is based on Martin Seligman's notion of *learned helplessness,* which results from experiences that indicate one has little control over the events in one's life. This may explain why women are more likely to become depressed than men. Sociocultural factors may provide women with less control over events in their lives. Perhaps because of this, men are more likely to engage in behaviors that reduce their depression, while women are more likely to ruminate about their depression, which may serve only to intensify it (Nolen-Hoeksema, 1987).

Today, Seligman and his followers explain depression in terms of the attributions we make for events in our lives. Depressed people attribute negative events in their lives to stable, global, and internal factors (Abramson, Seligman, & Teasdale, 1978). A *stable factor* is unlikely to change. A *global factor* affects almost all areas of one's life. And an *internal factor* is a characteristic of one's self rather than of the environment. So, you would be more likely to become depressed if you attributed your failure on an exam to your lack of intelligence (a stable, global, internal factor) rather than to an unfair exam (an unstable, specific, external factor).

Research on learned helplessness and depression has tended to find that, as predicted, depressed people make internal, stable, and global attributions for negative events in their lives (Sweeney, Anderson, & Bailey, 1986). For example, college freshmen who attribute their poor academic performance to internal, stable, and global factors become more depressed than students who attribute their own poor academic performance to external, unstable, and specific factors (Peterson & Barrett, 1987).

The Cognitive Viewpoint The most influential cognitive view of depression is Aaron Beck's (1967) *cognitive theory*. Beck has found that depressed people exhibit what he calls a *negative triad*: they have a negative view of themselves, their current circumstances, and their future possibilities. This negative outlook is maintained because depressed people overgeneralize from negative events. For example, depressed people tend to assume that a single failure means that they are incompetent (Carver & Ganellen, 1983).

One problem with cognitive theories of depression is the difficulty in determining whether the patterns of thought that characterize depressed people are the cause of their depression or the result of their depression. To determine this would require prospective studies, which follow groups of people over a period of time to determine whether depressed thinking styles precede, accompany, or follow the onset of depression. Because there is more evidence that depressed thinking styles accompany or follow the onset of depression, they may not be the cause of depression (Brewin, 1985).

This conclusion was supported by an experiment in which groups of depressed people received either daily doses of antidepressant drugs or twice-weekly psychotherapy sessions. Both groups showed decreases in depression and more positive views of themselves and the world. Because even those who received only drugs showed cognitive improvement, perhaps nondepressed styles of thinking are simply a consequence of feeling good and depressed styles of thinking are simply a consequence of feeling bad (Simons, Garfield, & Murphy, 1984).

As mentioned earlier in the chapter, people with psychological disorders may have more objective beliefs about themselves and the world. This seems to be true of depressed people. Nondepressed people, but not depressed people, overestimate the likelihood that positive events, and underestimate the likelihood that negative events, will happen to them than to other people (Crocker, Alloy, & Kayne, 1988). This leads to the surprising conclusion that if you are not depressed, it may mean that you have an unrealistically positive view of yourself and the world.

The Humanistic Viewpoint Those who favor the humanistic viewpoint attribute depression to the frustration of self-actualization. More specifically, depressed people suffer from incongruence between the actual self and the ideal self (Higgins, 1987). The actual self is the person's subjective appraisal of his or her own qualities. The ideal self is the person's subjective judgment of the person he or she would like to become. If the actual self has qualities that are too distinct from those of the ideal self, the person becomes depressed.

SCHIZOPHRENIA

In his middle age, Edvard Munch, the founder of modern expressionist painting (and whose painting *The Scream* you saw earlier in the chapter), began acting in odd ways. He became a social recluse, believed his paintings were his children, and claimed they were too jealous to be exhibited with other paintings (Wilson, 1967). Munch's actions were symptoms of **schizophrenia,** a severe psychological disorder characterized by markedly impaired social, emotional, cognitive, and perceptual functioning.

Schizophrenia A class of psychological disorders characterized by grossly impaired social, emotional, cognitive, and perceptual functioning.

The modern classification of schizophrenia began in 1860 when the Belgian psychiatrist Benedict Morel used the Latin term *demence precoce* (meaning "mental deterioration of early onset") to describe the behavior of a brilliant, outgoing thirteen-year-old boy who gradually withdrew socially and deteriorated intellectually. In 1911 the Swiss psychiatrist Eugen Bleuler coined the term "schizophrenia" (from the Greek terms for "split mind") to refer to this disorder, reflecting his belief that it involved a splitting apart of the normally integrated functions of perceiving, feeling, and thinking. Note that the popular notion of a "split personality" refers to people suffering from schizophrenia, not those suffering from a multiple personality disorder.

About 1 percent of Americans (that is, more than two million) have schizophrenia, which is equally prevalent in males and females. Schizophrenic patients occupy half of the beds in mental hospitals and cost the American economy billions of dollars each year. Despite the prevalence, severity, and cost of schizophrenia, making it the "cancer" of psychological disorders, relatively little money is spent on research into its causes, prevention, and treatment. While the government spends three hundred dollars a day for each cancer victim, it spends less than twenty dollars a day for each victim of schizophrenia (Holden, 1987).

Characteristics of Schizophrenia

To be diagnosed as schizophrenic, a person must display several symptoms of it for at least six months (APA, 1987). People with schizophrenia often experience *hallucinations,* which are perceptual experiences in the absence of relevant stimulation. The great Spanish painter Francisco Goya (1746–1848) had visual hallucinations that drove him to paint pictures of ghosts, witches, and vampires on the walls of his home (Wilson, 1967). But schizophrenic hallucinations are usually auditory, typically voices that may ridicule the person or order the person to commit antisocial acts.

Schizophrenia is also characterized by cognitive disturbances. Schizophrenic people have difficulty focusing their attention and are easily distracted by irrelevant stimuli. This inability to focus attention may account for the cognitive fragmentation that is a hallmark of schizophrenia. Because this cognitive fragmentation is also evident in their language, you might find it frustrating to converse with a schizophrenic person. A schizophrenic person's speech might include invented words called *neologisms,* such as, "The children have to have this 'accentuative' law so they don't go into the 'mortite' law of the church" (Vetter, 1969, p. 189). The schizophrenic person's speech might also include a meaningless jumble of words called a *word salad,* such as, "The house burnt the cow horrendously always" (Vetter, 1969, p. 147).

Among the most distinctive cognitive disturbances in schizophrenia are delusions. A *delusion* is a belief that is held despite compelling evidence to the contrary, such as Edvard Munch's belief that his paintings were his children and were jealous of other paintings. The most common delusions are delusions of influence, such as the belief that one's thoughts are being beamed to all parts of the universe (*thought broadcasting*). Less common are *delusions of grandeur,* in which the person believes that he or she is a famous or powerful person. The fascinating book *The Three Christs of Ypsilanti* (Rokeach, 1964) describes the cases of three men in a single mental hospital who had the same delusion of grandeur—each claimed to be Jesus Christ.

Schizophrenic people typically have flat or inappropriate emotionality. Emotional flatness is shown by an unchanging facial expression, a lack of expressive gestures, and an absence of vocal inflections. Emotional inappropriateness is shown by bizarre actions, such as laughing when someone is

The Paintings of Louis Wain
Wain (1860–1939) was a British artist who gained acclaim for his paintings of cats in human situations. But, after developing schizophrenia, he no longer painted with a sense of humor. Instead, his paintings revealed his mental deterioration, becoming progressively more fragmented and bizarre.

seriously injured. Schizophrenia is often associated with unusual motor behavior, such as tracing patterns in the air or holding poses for hours.

As in the case of Edvard Munch, schizophrenic people are usually socially withdrawn, with few, if any, friends. This may first appear in childhood. Mark David Chapman, who murdered John Lennon, was a reclusive child who lived in a world of imaginary little people who he claimed lived in the walls of his living room and who looked up to him as their king (Huyghe, 1982).

Kinds of Schizophrenic Disorders

Disorganized Schizophrenia A type of schizophrenia marked by severe personality deterioration and extremely bizarre behavior.

Diagnosticians distinguish several kinds of schizophrenic disorders. The most severe kind is **disorganized schizophrenia.** People with disorganized schizophrenia show marked personality deterioration, speak gibberish, dress outlandishly, laugh inappropriately, perform ritualized movements, and engage in obscene behavior. The bizarreness of their behavior and the incoherence of their speech may make it impossible for them to maintain normal social relationships.

Catatonic schizophrenia is characterized by unusual motor behavior, often alternating between catatonic excitement and catatonic stupor. In *catatonic excitement* the person paces frantically, speaks incoherently, and engages in stereotyped movements. In *catatonic stupor* the person may become mute and barely move, possibly freezing in positions for hours or days. The person may even exhibit "waxy flexibility," in which he or she can be moved from one frozen pose to another.

Paranoid schizophrenia is characterized by hallucinations, delusions, suspiciousness, and argumentativeness. This disorder was portrayed in the World War II novel and movie *The Caine Mutiny,* in which Captain Queeg (played by Humphrey Bogart) developed paranoid delusions in the face of wartime stress. He accused his crew of conspiring against him, going so far as to conduct a full-scale investigation to determine who stole strawberries from the ship's kitchen. Because a paranoid schizophrenic may feel threatened by other people, he or she may become violent. Cases that do not fall neatly into any of the three categories of schizophrenia just described are commonly lumped into a category called **undifferentiated schizophrenia.**

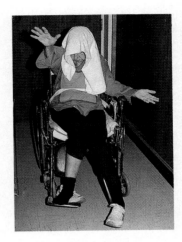

Catatonic Schizophrenia A person with catatonic schizophrenia may maintain bizarre postures.

Causes of Schizophrenia

No single viewpoint can explain all cases of schizophrenia or why some people with certain risk factors develop schizophrenia and others do not. Note that even when a risk factor is identified it is unclear whether the factor causes schizophrenia, whether schizophrenia causes the factor, or whether other factors cause both the apparent risk factor and schizophrenia. Moreover, schizophrenia is best explained by the diathesis-stress viewpoint, which sees it as the outcome of the interaction between a biological predisposition and stressful life experiences. For example, children who have both a hereditary predisposition to become schizophrenic and the stress of losing their fathers are more likely to develop schizophrenia (Walker, Hoppes, Emory, Mednick, & Schulsinger, 1981).

The Biomedical Viewpoint Biomedical theories of schizophrenia emphasize genetic, biochemical, and neurological causes. Schizophrenia runs in families—the closer the genetic relationship to a schizophrenic, the more likely a person is to become schizophrenic. The concordance rates for schizophrenia appear to have a strong hereditary basis (figure 14.4) (Faraone & Tsuang, 1985). Yet, for example, the higher concordance rate for identical twins than for fraternal twins might be caused by the more similar treatment that identical twins receive, rather than by their identical genetic endowment.

To assess the relative contributions of heredity and experience, researchers have turned to adoption studies. Many of these studies have been conducted in Denmark, where the government maintains excellent birth and adoption records. The studies have tended to support the genetic basis of schizophrenia. For example, schizophrenia is more common in the biological relatives of adoptees, children adopted from schizophrenic parents have a greater risk of schizophrenia than do children adopted from normal parents, and children of normal parents adopted by schizophrenic parents do not show an increased risk of schizophrenia (Buchsbaum & Haier, 1983).

Given the hereditary basis of schizophrenia, what biological differences might exist among people who develop schizophrenia and those who do not? In the 1950s researchers isolated a chemical they called *taraxein* from the blood of schizophrenics, which produced symptoms of schizophrenia when transfused into normal volunteers (Heath, Martens, Leach, Cohen, & Feigley,

Catatonic Schizophrenia A type of schizophrenia marked by unusual motor behavior, such as bizarre actions, extreme agitation, or immobile stupor.

Paranoid Schizophrenia A type of schizophrenia marked by hallucinations, delusions, suspiciousness, and argumentativeness.

Undifferentiated Schizophrenia A catchall category for cases that do not fall neatly into any single type of schizophrenia.

FIGURE 14.4
Heredity and the Lifetime Risk of Schizophrenia The
concordance rates for
schizophrenia between people
become higher as their genetic
similarity becomes greater. This
provides evidence supportive of
the hereditary basis of
schizophrenia, but cannot by
itself rule out the influence of the
degree of similarity in life
experiences (Gottesman &
Shields, 1982).

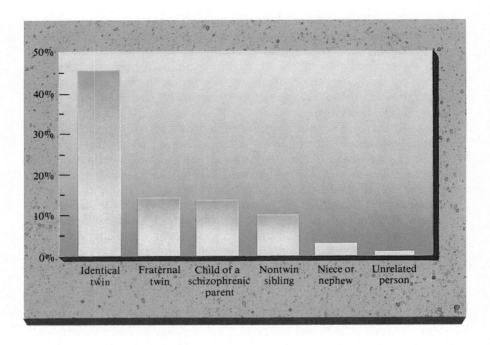

1958). The assumption that chemicals in the blood caused schizophrenia led researchers to use kidney dialysis to rid the blood of them. Though initial studies produced promising findings, researchers have failed to replicate them. In one study, schizophrenics were randomly assigned to receive either active dialysis or placebo (that is, fake) dialysis. Because the study used a double-blind procedure, neither the subjects nor those asked to evaluate their behavior knew whether they had received active or placebo dialysis. The researchers found no difference in symptoms between those who received active dialysis and those who received placebo dialysis (Vanherweghen, Linkowski, & Mendlewicz, 1983).

Though research on blood chemistry has not been fruitful, studies have found a relationship between schizophrenia and brain chemistry, particularly high levels of the neurotransmitter *dopamine*. What evidence is there to support this view? First, drugs that are used to treat schizophrenia work by blocking dopamine receptors. Second, drugs such as amphetamines, which increase dopamine levels in the brain, can induce schizophrenic symptoms in normal people. Third, *L-dopa,* a drug used to treat Parkinson's disease because it increases dopamine levels in the brain, can induce schizophrenic symptoms in Parkinson's victims (Nicol & Gottesman, 1983). Because dopamine neurons play a role in attention and in information processing, perhaps abnormally high levels of dopamine disrupt these psychological functions in schizophrenia.

Another promising area of research on the causes of schizophrenia involves the study of neurological dysfunctions. Schizophrenics tend to have atrophy of brain tissue, creating enlarged cerebral ventricles, the fluid-filled chambers inside the brain (figure 14.5) (Mirsky & Duncan, 1986). Particular kinds of neurological disorders may be associated with particular sets of schizophrenic symptoms. According to Nancy Andreasen, there are two kinds of schizophrenic syndromes, characterized by either positive symptoms or negative symptoms, which are associated with different neurological dysfunctions (Andreasen, Olsen, Dennert, & Smith, 1982). *Positive symptoms* are active symptoms that include hallucinations, delusions, thought disorders, and bizarre

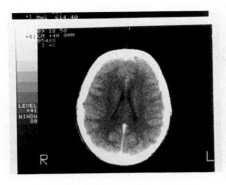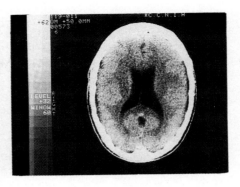

FIGURE 14.5
Schizophrenia and Neurological Dysfunctions CAT scans of the brains of people with schizophrenia often show atrophy and enlarged ventricles. Notice that the ventricles (the dark areas) in the schizophrenic brain on the right are much larger than those in the normal brain on the left.

behaviors. People with positive symptoms experience acute episodes, show progressively worsening symptoms, respond well to drug treatment, show increased numbers of dopamine receptors, and reveal no brain structure pathology. In contrast, *negative symptoms* are passive symptoms that include mutism, apathy, flat affect, social withdrawal, intellectual impairment, poverty of speech, and inability to experience pleasure. People with negative symptoms experience chronic disorders, respond poorly to drug treatment, do not show dopamine hyperactivity, and have enlarged brain ventricles and atrophy of the cerebral cortex (Seidman, 1983).

The Psychoanalytic Viewpoint According to the psychoanalytic viewpoint, people who become schizophrenic fail to overcome their dependence on their mothers and, as a result, become fixated at the oral stage. This gives them a weak ego that may fail to defend them against the anxiety caused by unconscious id impulses and external stressors. Instead they cope with anxiety by resorting to behaviors characteristic of the oral stage, such as fantasy, silly actions, incoherent speech, and irrational thinking.

Recent research, in the spirit of the psychoanalytic viewpoint, has found that parents high in what is known as *expressed emotion* may contribute to the maintenance or relapse of schizophrenia in their child. Parents who are high in expressed emotion criticize their child, are hostile toward the child, and become emotionally overinvolved with the child's well-being. Parents who criticize their child are especially harmful (Hahlweg et al., 1989). Because of this, schizophrenic children who avoid contact with their parents tend to exhibit better psychological adjustment than do schizophrenic children who maintain contact with their parents (Koenigsberg & Handley, 1986).

The Behavioral Viewpoint Behavioral theories of schizophrenia, which emphasize the role of learning, assume that schizophrenics are rewarded for behaving in bizarre ways (Ullmann & Krasner, 1975). This was portrayed in the 1974 movie *A Woman Under the Influence,* in which a woman (played by Gena Rowlands) makes bizarre sounds in order to be rewarded with attention from her boorish husband (played by Peter Falk). Even upon her return from a mental hospital her husband urges her to make the same sounds—in front of a houseful of people at a welcome-home party. Behavioral theorists also assume that a person who engages in bizarre behavior provokes social rejection from others, which, in turn, contributes to the suspiciousness and social withdrawal characteristic of schizophrenia.

The Cognitive Viewpoint Proponents of the cognitive viewpoint emphasize disturbances of attention and thinking as the main factors in schizophrenia. As the noted schizophrenia researcher Eugen Bleuler observed earlier this century, people with schizophrenia seem "incapable of

Nancy Andreasen "Patients with ventricular enlargement tend to have a preponderance of negative symptoms, while patients without ventricular enlargement tend to have a preponderance of positive symptoms."

holding the train of thought in the proper channel'' (Baribeau-Braun, Picton, & Gosselin, 1983). Children exposed to parents who communicate in confusing, irrational ways are predisposed to develop the irrational thought patterns of schizophrenia (Doane, West, Goldstein, Rodnick, & Jones, 1981).

The Humanistic Viewpoint According to the humanistic viewpoint, schizophrenia reflects the most extreme incongruence between the public self and the actual self. This has been supported most strongly by psychiatrist R. D. Laing (1967), who claims that schizophrenia results when a person develops a false public self to confront an intolerable life situation. This retreat from reality permits the person to experience his or her actual self. The schizophrenic person's bizarre thinking, language, and behavior are indicative of this retreat from reality. Laing recommends that family, friends, and professionals permit the schizophrenic person to go on what he calls a ''voyage of self-discovery'' into his or her actual self, rather than interfering with that process through the administration of drugs or commitment to a mental hospital.

Laing's critics claim that he romanticizes schizophrenia, in the same way that nineteenth-century poets romanticized tuberculosis, by implying that it is somehow noble to be crazy. One of Laing's chief critics is Mark Vonnegut, son of the noted writer Kurt Vonnegut. Mark had been a follower of Laing's until he suffered several episodes of schizophrenia, as described in his autobiography *The Eden Express* (1975). When Mark recovered, he did not describe a voyage of self-discovery. Instead, he described a horrifying experience that he would have been better off without. Mark's disillusionment with Laing's view of schizophrenia led him to write an article for *Harper's* magazine entitled, ''Why I Want to Bite R. D. Laing'' (Vonnegut, 1974).

PERSONALITY DISORDERS

Personality Disorders
Psychological disorders characterized by enduring, inflexible, maladaptive patterns of behavior.

Axis II of the DSM-III-R includes the **personality disorders,** which are long-standing inflexible, maladaptive patterns of behavior (table 14.5). People with personality disorders provoke negative reactions from others. For example, people with a *narcissistic personality* offend other people by displaying a grandiose sense of self-importance and by being completely preoccupied with themselves. The disorder is named for Narcissus, the mythological youth who fell in love with his own reflection in a pool of water. The most central characteristic of the narcissistic personality is the tendency to exploit other people (Emmons, 1987).

The Antisocial Personality Disorder

Antisocial Personality Disorder A personality disorder marked by impulsive, manipulative, often criminal behavior, without any feelings of guilt in the perpetrator.

Because of its harmful effect on society, the personality disorder that has inspired the most interest is the antisocial personality disorder, which is found in about 3 percent of American males and almost 1 percent of American females. In the nineteenth century the antisocial personality disorder was called *moral insanity,* and for most of this century it was called *psychopathy* or *sociopathy.* The **antisocial personality disorder** is characterized by maladaptive behavior beginning in childhood, including lying, stealing, truancy, vandalism, fighting, drug abuse, physical cruelty, academic failure, and early sexual activity. Adults with an antisocial personality may not conform to social expectations. They may fail to hold a job, to honor financial obligations, or to fulfill parental responsibilities.

TABLE 14.5   Personality Disorders

Disorders Characterized By:	Symptoms
Odd or Eccentric Behavior	
Paranoid personality disorder	Unrealistic mistrust and suspiciousness of people.
Schizoid personality disorder	Problems in forming emotional relationships with others.
Schizotypal personality disorder	Oddities of thinking, perception, communication, and behavior not severe enough to be diagnosed as schizophrenia.
Dramatic, Emotional, or Erratic Behavior	
Antisocial personality disorder	Continually violating the rights of others, being prone to impulsive behavior, and feeling no guilt for the harm done to others.
Borderline personality disorder	Instable in mood, behavior, self-image, and social relationships.
Histrionic personality disorder	Overly dramatic behavior, self-centered, and craving attention.
Narcissistic personality disorder	Grandiose sense of self-importance, insists on being the center of attention, and lacks empathy for others.
Anxious or Fearful Behavior	
Avoidant personality disorder	Hypersensitive to potential rejection by others, causing social withdrawal despite a desire for social relationships.
Dependent personality disorder	Fails to take responsibility for own life, instead relying on others to make decisions.
Obsessive-compulsive personality disorder	Preoccupied with rules, schedules, organization, and trivial details, and unable to express emotional warmth.
Passive-aggressive personality disorder	Unassertive, indirect resistance to demands, as in forgetting, procrastinating, being late, and being inefficient.

Because people with antisocial personalities can be charming, lie with a straight face, and talk their way out of trouble, they may pursue careers as shyster lawyers, crooked politicians, and phoney evangelists. Two hallmarks of the antisocial personality are impulsive behavior, such as reckless driving or promiscuous sexual relations, and a remarkable lack of guilt for the pain and suffering they inflict on others.

In extreme cases, people with antisocial personalities engage in criminal activities yet fail to change their behavior even after being punished for it.

The Antisocial Personality
Charles Manson was born to a teenage prostitute, raised first by her, then by an aunt and uncle, and again by her. He left home at fourteen, repeatedly ran afoul of the law, and escaped from numerous juvenile detention centers. In the late 1960s he used his charismatic personality to develop a cult following in California. In August 1969, he convinced his followers to invade an exclusive area of Los Angeles and murder and mutilate pregnant actress Sharon Tate and five other persons. Since his imprisonment, Manson has expressed no sense of remorse for his crime. He is an extreme example of a person with an antisocial personality disorder. He behaved impulsively, failed to learn from punishment, enjoyed harming other people, and expressed no guilt concerning his actions.

Criminals with antisocial personalities violate the conditions of their release more than do comparable prisoners without antisocial personalities (Hart, Kropp, & Hare, 1988). Fortunately for society, criminals with antisocial personalities tend to "burn out" after age forty and commit fewer crimes than do other criminals (Hare, McPherson, & Forth, 1988).

Causes of the Antisocial Personality Disorder

The antisocial personality disorder is the only personality disorder that has been subjected to a substantial amount of research as to its causes. In recent years, studies have provided evidence of a physiological basis for it. People with antisocial personalities have unusually low levels of physiological arousal. As discussed in chapter 10, we seem to have a predisposition to try and maintain an optimal level of physiological arousal. Perhaps the unusually low levels of arousal of people with antisocial personalities motivate them to engage in behaviors that increase their levels of arousal. While some learn to increase their arousal by engaging in auto racing and other socially acceptable activities, others learn to do so by committing bank robberies and other antisocial activities.

But what makes one person with a low level of physiological arousal seek thrills through auto racing and another seek thrills through robbing banks? In explaining the antisocial personality disorder, psychoanalysts stress the influence of abusive parents or physically absent parents, who make the child feel rejected. Because such children have no emotional ties to their parents, they fail to develop an adequate superego, including a conscience. Behaviorists believe that the antisocial personality disorder is caused by parents who reward, or fail to punish, their children for engaging in antisocial behaviors such as lying, stealing, or aggression. Such parents may also, through their own actions, teach their children to use charm and social manipulation to get their way. Adults with antisocial personalities may even try to manipulate juries into accepting their plea of *insanity* as an excuse for their commission of crimes.

THINKING ABOUT PSYCHOLOGY

Should We Retain the Insanity Defense?

More than two thousand years ago, Plato noted that "someone may commit an act when mad or afflicted with disease. . . . let him pay simply for the damage; and let him be exempt from other punishment" (Carson, Butcher, & Coleman, 1988, p. 33). Today, Plato would face opposition from those who argue against the insanity defense. In recent years, spurred by the successful insanity plea of John Hinckley following his attempted assassination of President Reagan, many people have criticized the insanity defense as a miscarriage of justice.

Hinckley claimed that he had been motivated by his desire to impress actress Jodie Foster. After being declared insane and committed to St. Elizabeth's Hospital in Washington, D. C., Hinckley wrote a letter that was published in *Newsweek* in which he claimed, "Sending a John Hinckley to a mental hospital instead of prison is the American way" (Hinckley, 1982, p. 30). In criticizing Hinckley's successful use of the insanity defense, columnist William F. Buckley wrote, "And realism [concerning the decision] begins by sticking out our tongues at the judge and jurors who went along with the expensive charade" (Buckley, 1982, p. 917). Many Americans shared his opinion.

The Nature of the Insanity Defense

Both supporters and opponents of the insanity defense may misunderstand it. **Insanity** is a legal, not a psychological or psychiatric, term attesting that a person is not responsible for his or her own actions. In criminal cases this is usually determined by a jury. The insanity defense was first used in 1843 in the case of Daniel M'Naghten, a paranoid schizophrenic man who tried to murder the English Prime Minister Robert Peel, who he believed was persecuting him. But M'Naghten killed Peel's secretary Edward Drummond by mistake. After a controversial trial, M'Naghten was ruled not guilty by reason of insanity and was committed to a mental hospital.

Queen Victoria was so upset by this verdict that she asked the House of Lords to review the case. It upheld the decision and the M'Naghten rule became a guiding principle in English law. The rule holds that a person is not guilty if, at the time of a crime, the suspect did not know what he or she was doing or that what he or she was doing was wrong. The M'Naghten verdict led an

Insanity A legal term attesting that a person is not responsible for his or her own actions, including criminal behavior.

The Insanity Defense John Hinckley, Jr.'s successful use of the insanity defense following his assassination attempt on President Reagan stimulated debate on the use of this defense in criminal cases.

Englishman named Thomas Campbell to write the following widely published poem (Perr, 1983, p. 873):

> Ye people of England: exult and be glad
> For ye're now at the will of the merciless mad.
> [The insane are]
> A privileg'd class, whom no statute controls
> And their murderous charter exists in their souls.
> Do they wish to spill blood—they have only to play
> A few pranks—get asylum'd a month and a day
> Then heigh! to escape from the mad-doctor's keys,
> And to pistol or stab whomsoever they please.

Today in the United States the most widely used standard for determining insanity is that of the American Law Institute. The standard comprises two rules. The *cognitive rule,* similar to the M'Naghten rule, says that a person was insane at the time of a crime if the person did not know what he or she did or did not know that it was wrong. The *volitional rule,* which assumes the reality of free will, says that a person was insane at the time of a crime if the person was not in voluntary control of his or her behavior. As described in chapter 3, an autopsy performed on Charles Whitman, the so-called Texas Tower killer, revealed that he had a brain tumor of the limbic system, a region of the brain that helps control aggression. Had Whitman gone to trial, he might have used the volitional rule as his defense, claiming that the tumor made him unable to control his behavior.

An 1881 cartoon bitterly portrays the insanity defense of Charles Guiteau, assassin of President James Garfield. Guiteau, in jester's outfit, chuckles beneath Garfields's coffin. Gentlemen in the background howl over law books. A jury found Guiteau guilty.

Source: From *Harper's Weekly,* December 10, 1881.

Controversy Concerning the Insanity Defense

Controversy concerning the use of the insanity defense in American courts did not begin with the case of John Hinckley. An earlier case that created a controversy was that of Ezra Pound, a renowned American poet who broadcast propaganda for Italy against the Allies during World War II. After the War he was accused of treason, but he escaped punishment by successfully pleading insanity. Pound was committed to St. Elizabeth's Hospital, where he was treated like a celebrity and given special privileges. Critics of the insanity verdict in Pound's case claimed that the hospital supervisor led a conspiracy that encouraged Pound to fake symptoms of paranoid schizophrenia so he would be declared insane (Torrey, 1981).

In recent decades, several cases involving the insanity defense, including that of John Hinckley, have provoked controversy. In 1979, in a widely publicized case, former San Francisco city supervisor Dan White murdered mayor George Moscone and city supervisor Harvey Milk. White's lawyer claimed that White had been insane at the time of the killings because eating junk food so altered his blood sugar level that it made him lose voluntary control over his behavior. This became known as the "Twinkie defense." A compromise verdict was reached, and White was sentenced to seven years for manslaughter. After his release, White committed suicide.

Despite outrage over alleged abuses of the insanity defense, it is used in less than 1 percent of felony crimes and is rarely successful (Holden, 1983). For example, Sirhan Sirhan was convicted of first-degree murder and sentenced to life in prison, despite expert testimony that he was schizophrenic. In another noteworthy case in which the insanity defense failed, Kenneth Bianchi, the so-called Hillside Strangler, who raped and murdered at least ten women on the West Coast in 1977, pleaded insanity because of an alleged multiple personality. In a 1984 Public Broadcasting System documentary, psychiatrists debated whether Bianchi truly had multiple personalities. Those who believed that Bianchi was faking his disorder noted that he had a collection of introductory psychology textbooks that contained descriptions of cases of multiple personality. When it appeared that his plea would fail, Bianchi agreed to a plea bargain and was sentenced to life in prison (Fisher, 1984).

The notoriety of cases such as those of John Hinckley, Dan White, and Kenneth Bianchi prompted a reevaluation of the insanity defense by state legislatures and professional organizations. Some states have abandoned the insanity defense entirely, while others have adopted a rule of *guilty but mentally ill,* requiring that an insane person who committed a crime be placed in a mental hospital until he or she is no longer mentally ill, at which time the person would serve the remaining time in prison. There is also a trend toward placing the burden on the defendant to prove that he or she was insane at the time of the crime, rather than placing it on the prosecution to prove that the defendant was sane.

The American Psychiatric Association, the American Psychological Association, and the American Bar Association have their own positions regarding the insanity defense. The American Psychiatric Association was so embarrassed by the contradictory testimony of psychiatrists in the Hinckley trial that it published its first statement ever on the insanity defense. The statement says that the insanity defense is a legal and moral question, not a psychiatric one, and that psychiatrists should testify only about a defendant's mental status and motivation—not about a defendant's responsibility for a crime (Herbert, 1983). The American Psychological Association has taken a more cautious approach, calling for more research before any changes are made in the current use of the insanity defense. It opposes efforts to eliminate the insanity defense or to replace it with a plea of guilty but mentally ill (Mervis, 1984).

The American Bar Association would eliminate the volitional (that is, free will) rule in the insanity defense. Thus, the American Bar Association would still retain the cognitive rule. A person who did not know what he or she was doing could still use the insanity defense. As the American Bar Association explains:

> Someone who knowingly stole a radio, for example, would be legally responsible even if he believed it was issuing instructions to him from Mars. Mental illness would only be a defense if a person were so psychotic that he thought he was squeezing an orange when he was strangling a child. (Holden, 1983, p. 994)

The volitional rule has come under especially strong attack because it may be impossible to determine whether a person has acted from free will or from an irresistible impulse. For example, imagine that a woman on trial for murder attributes her criminal action to irresistible violent impulses caused by the premenstrual syndrome. The jury would be left with the task of determining whether her symptoms had been so severe at the time of the crime that they made her lose voluntary control over her behavior—not to mention the possible support that such a defense would give to bias against women (Turkington, 1984). Will legislatures completely overturn our long tradition of not holding people with severe psychological disorders responsible for criminal actions? Only future legal decisions will decide.

SUMMARY

THE NATURE OF PSYCHOLOGICAL DISORDERS

Researchers in the field of psychopathology study psychological disorders. The criteria for determining the presence of a psychological disorder include abnormality, maladaptiveness, and personal distress. The major viewpoints on the causes of psychological disorders include the biomedical, psychoanalytic, behavioral, cognitive, and humanistic perspectives. The more recent diathesis-stress viewpoint sees psychological disorders as products of the interaction between biological predisposition and stressful life experiences.

The *Diagnostic and Statistical Manual of Mental Disorders* (DSM-III-R), published by the American Psychiatric Association, is the accepted standard for classifying psychological disorders. But the DSM-III-R's reliability and validity have yet to be demonstrated. Some authorities, such as psychiatrist Thomas Szasz and psychologist David Rosenhan, have criticized the wisdom of using any kind of classification system at all.

ANXIETY DISORDERS

Anxiety disorders are associated with anxiety that is intense, chronic, and disruptive of everyday functioning. Generalized anxiety disorder is a constant state of anxiety that exists independently of any particular stressful situation. A panic disorder is marked by sudden, unexpected attacks of overwhelming anxiety, accompanied by dizziness, trembling, cold sweats, heart palpitations, shortness of breath, fear of dying, and fear of going crazy.

Phobias are excessive or inappropriate fears. A simple phobia involves a specific object or situation. A social phobia involves fear of public scrutiny. And agoraphobia involves fear of being in public, usually because the person fears being embarrassed by having a panic attack. People whose obsessions and compulsions interfere with their daily functioning suffer from an obsessive-compulsive disorder. An obsession is a persistent, recurring thought, and a compulsion is a repetitive action that one feels compelled to perform.

SOMATOFORM DISORDERS

The somatoform disorders are characterized by physical symptoms in the absence of disease or injury. The symptoms are caused, instead, by psychological factors. A person with hypochondriasis interprets the slightest physical changes in his or her body as evidence of a serious illness. A person with a conversion disorder exhibits loss or alteration of a physical function without any apparent physical cause.

DISSOCIATIVE DISORDERS

In dissociative disorders, the person's conscious awareness becomes separated from certain of his or her thoughts, feelings, and memories. A person with psychogenic amnesia is unable to recall personally significant memories. A person with psychogenic fugue suffers from psychogenic amnesia and flees from home. And a person with multiple personality has two or more distinct personalities that alternate with one another.

MOOD DISORDERS

Mood disorders involve prolonged periods of extreme depression or elation, often unrelated to objective circumstances. People with major depression experience depression that is so intense and prolonged that it causes extreme distress and disrupts their lives. In such cases, suicide is always a concern. People who attempt suicide usually give warnings, so their threats should be taken seriously. In bipolar disorder, the person alternates between periods of mania and major depression. Mania is characterized by euphoria, hyperactivity, grandiose ideas, annoying talkativeness, unrealistic optimism, and inflated self-esteem.

SCHIZOPHRENIA

Schizophrenia is characterized by a severe disruption of perception, cognition, emotionality, behavior, and social relationships. The most serious kind of schizophrenia is disorganized schizophrenia, marked by a complete collapse of the personality and the intellect. Catatonic schizophrenia is marked by unusual motor behavior. Paranoid schizophrenia is marked by hallucinations, delusions, suspiciousness, and argumentativeness.

PERSONALITY DISORDERS

Personality disorders are long-standing, inflexible, maladaptive patterns of behavior. Of greatest concern is the antisocial personality disorder, associated with lying, stealing, fighting, drug abuse, physical cruelty, and lack of responsibility. Persons suffering from this disorder also behave impulsively, fail to learn from punishment, and express no remorse for the pain and suffering they inflict on others.

THINKING ABOUT PSYCHOLOGY: SHOULD WE RETAIN THE INSANITY DEFENSE?

Insanity is a legal term attesting that a person is not responsible for his or her own actions. The insanity defense was first used in 1843 in the case of Daniel M'Naghten. Today the insanity defense is based on two rules. The cognitive rule says that a person was insane at the time of a crime if the person did not know what he or she did or did not know that it was wrong. The volitional rule says that a person was insane at the time of a crime if the person was not in voluntary control of his or her behavior. The successful use of the insanity defense by John Hinckley, Jr., the would-be assassin of President Reagan, has sparked debate over the merits of the insanity defense. Despite this controversy, the insanity defense is rarely used and is even more rarely successful.

IMPORTANT CONCEPTS

Agoraphobia 486
Antisocial personality disorder 502
Anxiety disorders 483
Bipolar disorder 493
Catatonic schizophrenia 499
Conversion disorder 489
Diathesis-stress viewpoint 479
Disorganized schizophrenia 498
Dissociative disorders 490
Generalized anxiety disorder 483
Hypochondriasis 488

Insanity 505
Major depression 492
Mania 493
Mood disorders 492
Multiple personality 491
Neuroses 480
Obsessive-compulsive disorder 487
Panic disorder 484
Paranoid schizophrenia 499
Personality disorders 502

Phobia 486
Psychogenic amnesia 490
Psychogenic fugue 490
Psychopathology 474
Psychoses 480
Schizophrenia 496
Simple phobia 486
Social phobia 486
Somatoform disorders 488
Undifferentiated schizophrenia 499

IMPORTANT PEOPLE

Nancy Andreasen 500
Aaron Beck 496
Sigmund Freud 478, 487, 490

R. D. Laing 502
Peter Lewinsohn 495
David Rosenhan 482

Martin Seligman 486, 495
Thomas Szasz 483

RECOMMENDED READINGS

For More on All Aspects of Psychological Disorders:

Coleman, J. C., Butcher, J. N., & Carson, R. C. (1988). *Abnormal psychology and modern life* (8th ed.). Glenview, IL: Scott Foresman.
A classic and comprehensive textbook on psychological disorders.

For More on the Nature of Psychological Disorders:

Andreasen, N. C. (1984). *The broken brain: The biological revolution in psychiatry.* New York: Harper & Row.
An interesting discussion of the biomedical viewpoint on psychological disorders.

Bromberg, W. (1953). *Man above humanity.* Philadelphia: Lippincott.
An intriguing presentation of the history of popular and professional views on psychological disorders.

For More on Anxiety Disorders:

Agras, W. S. (1985). *Panic: Facing fears, phobias, and anxiety.* New York: Freeman.
An interesting account of the causes and treatment of panic, phobia, and debilitating anxiety.

Rachman, S. J., & Hodgson, R. J. (1980). *Obsessions and compulsions.* Englewood Cliffs, NJ: Prentice-Hall.
A discussion of obsessive-compulsive disorders.

For More on Somatoform Disorders:

Barsky, A. J., & Klerman, G. L. (1983). Overview: Hypochondriasis, bodily complaints, and somatic styles. *American Journal of Psychiatry, 140,* 273–283.
A comparison of alternative explanations of hypochondriasis.

Jones, M. M. (1980). Conversion disorder: Anachronism or evolutionary form? A review of the neurologic, behavioral, and psychoanalytic literature. *Psychological Bulletin, 87,* 427–441.
A discussion of the possible causes of conversion disorder.

For More on Dissociative Disorders:

Schreiber, F. R. (1974). *Sybil.* New York: Warner Books.
An account of a woman who developed sixteen personalities.

Sizemore, C. C., & Pittillo, E. S. (1977). *I'm Eve.* New York: Jove/HBJ.
A personal account of Sizemore's battle with multiple personalities, which was the basis for *The Three Faces of Eve.*

For More on Mood Disorders:

Beck, A. T. (1976). *Cognitive therapy and emotional disorders.* New York: International Universities Press.
A discussion of psychological disorders, with emphasis on the cognitive theory of depression.

Endler, N. S. (1982). *Holiday of darkness.* New York: Wiley.
A psychologist provides a personal account of his battle against severe depression.

For More on Schizophrenia:

Mirsky, A. F., & Duncan, C. C. (1986). Etiology and expression of schizophrenia: Neurobiological and psychosocial factors. *Annual Review of Psychology, 37,* 291–319.
A scholarly review of the possible causes of schizophrenia.

Torrey, E. F. (1988). *Surviving schizophrenia: A family manual.* New York: Harper & Row.
A readable discussion of the nature of schizophrenia, its treatment, and its effect on relatives of victims.

For More on Personality Disorders:

Cleckley, H. (1976). *The mask of sanity* (5th ed.). St. Louis: Mosby.
A classic book on the antisocial personality disorder.

For More on the Insanity Defense:

Caplan, L. (1984, July 2). The insanity defense. *The New Yorker,* pp. 45–78.
A popular account of the heated debate concerning the insanity defense.

CHAPTER
15

THERAPY

Chapter Opening Art:
Richard Diebenkorn.
Ocean Park No. 66.
1973.

n everyday life, when we feel anxious or depressed, or behave in a maladaptive way, we can generally rely on our own resources to carry us through. We may analyze the causes of our distress or our ineffective behavior, try to change the way we think about our current circumstances, or change the way we behave. By doing so, we usually relieve our distress and function better. On occasion, we may seek the advice of friends, relatives, or acquaintances to help overcome our problems.

You may have also received help from members of important informal helping groups, such as bartenders, hairdressers, and taxi drivers. Hairdressers may even attend special training programs to make them better informal counselors (Cowen, 1982). Despite the help you may receive from others in your everyday life, at some time in your life you may become so distressed or behave so maladaptively that you develop a psychological disorder requiring professional therapy. Modern therapy for psychological disorders has come a long way since its ancient origins.

THE HISTORY OF THERAPY

If you visit the Smithsonian Institute in Washington, you will encounter a display of ancient skulls with holes cut in them. The holes were produced by **trephining,** which is the use of sharp stones to chip holes in the skull, presumably to let out evil spirits that accounted for abnormal behavior. Though you might be struck by the apparent cruelty of this treatment, it followed logically from the presumed cause of the behavior. From ancient times until today, the kinds of therapy used in treating psychological disorders have been logically derived from the presumed causes of those disorders.

The Greek philosopher Hippocrates (460–377 B.C.) turned away from the supernatural explanation of psychological disorders in favor of a naturalistic explanation. As discussed in chapter 13, Hippocrates believed that many psychological disorders were caused by imbalances in fluids that he called humors, which included blood, phlegm, black bile, and yellow bile. This led him to recommend treatments aimed at restoring their balance. For example, be-

Trephining An ancient technique that involved the use of sharp stones to chip holes in the skull, presumably to let out evil spirits that caused abnormal behavior.

Trephining This skull shows the effect of trephining, in which sharp rocks were used to chip holes in the skull to let out evil spirits that allegedly accounted for bizarre thinking and behavior. The growth of new bone around the holes in some trephined skulls indicates that many people survived the surgery.

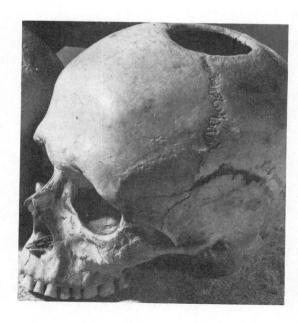

cause Hippocrates believed an excess of blood caused the agitated state of mania, he treated mania with bloodletting. As you would expect, people who lost blood became less agitated.

Naturalistic treatments remained popular but were challenged during the early Christian era by treatments based on supernatural explanations of psychological disorders. The New Testament even describes an incident in which Jesus cured a madman by banishing demons from him and casting them into a herd of pigs. Until the Middle Ages, treatments for psychological disorders were generally humane, at worst involving mild forms of exorcism that might hurl insults at the devil. But by the late Middle Ages treatments more often involved physical punishment—literally trying to "beat the devil out of him."

This inhumane treatment continued into the Renaissance, which also saw the advent of the *insane asylum*. Though some of these institutions were pleasant communities in which residents received humane treatment, most were no better than prisons in which inmates lived under deplorable conditions. The most humane asylum was the town of Geel in Belgium, where people with mental disorders lived in the homes of normal townspeople, moved about freely, and worked to support themselves. Today the town of Geel continues to provide humane care for people with psychological disorders.

But few asylums were as pleasant as Geel. The most notorious asylum was St. Mary's of Bethlehem in London. This was a nightmarish place where inmates were treated like animals in a zoo. On weekends, families would go on outings to the asylum, pay a small admission fee, and be entertained by the antics of the inmates. Visitors called the male inmates of St. Mary's "Tom Fools," contributing the word *tomfoolery* to our language (Morris & Morris, 1985). And the asylum became known as "Bedlam," reflecting the cockney pronunciation of Bethlehem. The word *bedlam* eventually came to mean any confused, uproarious scene.

In 1792 inhumane conditions in French insane asylums and the positive model of Geel spurred the physician Phillippe Pinel to institute what he called **moral therapy** at the Bicetre asylum in Paris. Pinel, who was superintendent

Moral Therapy An approach to therapy, developed by Phillippe Pinel, that provided mental patients with humane treatment.

Bedlam William Hogarth's (1697–1764) engraving depicts the asylum of St. Mary's of Bethlehem (better known as "Bedlam") in London, notorious for the inhumane treatment of its residents. Even Shakespeare referred to the bedlam of Bedlam in *King Lear* (Act II, Scene 3):
The country gives me proof and precedent
Of Bedlam beggars, who, with roaring voices,
Strike in their numb'd and mortified bare arms
Pins, wooden pricks, nails, sprigs of rosemary;
And . . .
Sometimes with lunatic bans, sometimes with prayers,
Enforce their charity.

of the asylum, unchained the inmates, provided them with nourishment, and treated them with kindness. He even instituted the revolutionary technique of speaking with them about their problems. When the first inmate was released, a powerful man who had been chained in a dark cell for forty years after killing an attendant with a blow from his manacles, onlookers were surprised (and relieved) when he simply strolled outside, gazed up at the sky, and exclaimed, "Ah, how beautiful" (Bromberg, 1954, p. 83).

Pinel's moral therapy spread throughout Europe and was introduced to the United States by Benjamin Rush (1745–1813), a signer of the Declaration of Independence and the founder of American psychiatry. As part of moral therapy, Rush prescribed work, travel, and reading. But he also prescribed physical treatments. For example, because Rush believed that depressed people had too little blood in their brains, he whirled them around in special chairs to force blood from their bodies into their heads. Figure 15.1 shows treatment devices that were popular in the nineteenth century.

In the 1840s Dorothea Dix (1802–1887), a Massachusetts school teacher, shocked Congress with reports of the brutal treatment of the inmates of insane asylums. Her efforts led to the building of many state mental hospitals throughout the United States, often in rural settings, that provided good food, social activities, and employment on farms. Unfortunately, over time many of these mental hospitals became human warehouses, providing custodial care and little else.

In the early twentieth century, public concern about the deplorable conditions in state mental hospitals grew after the publication of the book *A Mind that Found Itself* by a Yale graduate named Clifford Beers (1908/1970). The book described the unnecessary physical abuse he suffered during his three years in the Connecticut State Hospital while suffering from a psychological disorder. Beers founded the mental-health movement, which promotes the humane treatment of people with mental disorders. The mental-health movement has seen mental hospitals joined by group homes, private practices, and counseling centers as alternative treatments for psychological disorders.

Pinel Unchaining the Inmates of an Asylum Phillippe Pinel shocked and frightened many of his fellow French citizens by freeing the inmates of insane asylums and providing them with humane treatment. When opponents asked, "Citizen, are not you yourself crazy, that you would free these beasts?" Pinel replied, "I am convinced that these *people* are not incurable if they can have air and liberty" (Bromberg, 1954, p. 83).

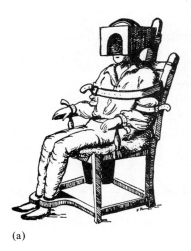

(a)

(b)

(c)

FIGURE 15.1
Nineteenth-Century Treatment Devices Benjamin Rush invented (*a*) the "tranquilizing chair" to calm manic patients. Other devices that were popular in the nineteenth century included (*b*) the "crib," which was used to restrain violent patients, and (*c*) the "circulating swing," which was used to restore balance to allegedly out-of-balance body fluids.

Dorothea Dix (1802–1887)
"Were I to recount the one hundreth part of the shocking scenes of sorrow, suffering, abuse, and degradation to which I have been witness—searched out in jails, in poorhouses, in pens and block-houses, in caves, in cages and cells, in dungeons and cellars; men and women in chains, frantic, bruised, lacerated, and debased, your souls would grow sick at the horrid recital."

The Mental Hospital Many of the mental hospitals built through the efforts of Dorothea Dix are still used today.

Psychotherapy The treatment of psychological disorders through psychological, as opposed to biomedical, means, generally involving verbal interaction with a professional therapist.

Today, specially trained professionals offer therapy for psychological disorders. Psychological therapy, or **psychotherapy,** involves the verbal interaction of a professional counselor with one or more persons suffering from a psychological disorder. Though there are many orientations to psychotherapy, most psychotherapists favor an *eclectic orientation,* which combines the best features of different orientations (Smith, 1982). The first of the orientations to psychotherapy was the psychoanalytic orientation.

THE PSYCHOANALYTIC ORIENTATION

From 1880 to 1882 the Austrian physician Josef Breuer (1842–1925) treated a young woman known as Anna O., who suffered from symptoms of conversion hysteria (described in chapter 14). She displayed impaired vision, paralyzed legs, and difficulty swallowing, without any physical causes. Breuer found that when Anna O. spoke freely about her condition she obtained relief from her symptoms. She called this her "talking cure" or "chimney sweeping." As she spoke freely she often recalled emotionally distressing childhood experiences. By talking about them, she obtained emotional release, followed by a reduction in her physical symptoms.

Catharsis In psychoanalysis, the release of repressed emotional energy as a consequence of insight into the unconscious causes of one's psychological problems.

Breuer called this process of emotional release **catharsis.** In 1882 Breuer abruptly broke off therapy with Anna O. after finding that she had become sexually and emotionally attached to him—even claiming to be pregnant with his child. Later, after recovering, Anna O., whose real name was Bertha Pappenheim (1859–1936), became a philanthropist, a founder of the social work profession, and a leader in the women's rights movement.

The Nature of Psychoanalysis

After Breuer related the case of Anna O. to him, Sigmund Freud turned from medicine to the study of psychological disorders. According to Freud, childhood emotional conflicts repressed into the unconscious mind cause overt symptoms, including those of conversion hysteria. Freud's aim was to make the person gain insight into these repressed conflicts, thereby inducing ca-

Sigmund Freud's Study During psychoanalytic therapy sessions, Freud had his patient recline on a couch while he sat out of sight. Freud believed that this helped the patient be more relaxed and less inhibited while talking freely about emotionally threatening topics.

tharsis and relieving the underlying conflict. This led Freud to develop a more elaborate system of therapy—**psychoanalysis.**

Traditional Freudian psychoanalysis takes place with the client reclining on a couch and the therapist sitting nearby, just out of sight. Freud claimed that this arrangement relaxes the client, thereby reducing inhibitions about discussing emotional topics. He also believed that the arrangement allows the therapist to better attend to what that client is saying. But some authorities argue that Freud preferred this arrangement because he was shy and disliked making eye contact with his clients (Corsini, 1984).

Freud usually saw clients for less than a year, and he even cured the composer Gustav Mahler of impotence in one four-hour session that provided Mahler with insight into the cause of his problem (Goleman, 1981). Today, traditional Freudian psychoanalysts may see clients three to five times a week for years. In the movie *Sleeper,* the noted psychoanalysis client Woody Allen pokes fun at the lengthiness of traditional psychoanalysis. After being kept frozen for two hundred years, Allen awakens and remarks, "If I had kept seeing my analyst, I'd almost be cured by now." Though Freudian psychoanalysis does not always take years, at one hundred dollars or more a session it is beyond the reach of most people.

Techniques in Psychoanalysis

An important goal of psychoanalytic techniques is to make the client's unconscious conflicts conscious. The process by which the client uses the therapist's interpretations of what he or she says to gain insight into the unconscious conflicts that are causing his or her problem is called *working through.* The main technique of psychoanalysis is the **analysis of free associations.** In free association, the client is urged to report anything that comes to mind—no matter how trivial, bizarre, or embarrassing it seems. By engaging in free association, clients overcome defenses that prevent them from becoming aware of their unconscious conflicts. The process of free association was used as long ago as ancient Greece. In the play *The Clouds,* written by Aristophanes, Socrates uses free association to help a man gain self-knowledge.

Psychoanalysis A type of psychotherapy, developed by Sigmund Freud, aimed at uncovering the unconscious causes of psychological disorders.

Analysis of Free Associations In psychoanalysis, the process by which the therapist interprets the underlying meaning of the client's uncensored reports of anything that comes to mind.

Psychoanalysis Today Though most psychotherapists now favor seated, face-to-interaction with their clients, some psychoanalytic psychotherapists still sit out of sight of the client, who reclines on a couch.

Analysis of Resistances In psychoanalysis, the process by which the therapist interprets client behaviors that interfere with therapeutic progress toward uncovering unconscious conflicts.

Analysis of Dreams In psychoanalysis, the process by which the therapist interprets the symbolic, manifest content of dreams to reveal their true, latent content to the client.

Analysis of Transference In psychoanalysis, the process by which the therapist interprets the feelings expressed by the client toward the therapist as being indicative of the feelings typically expressed by the client toward important people in his or her personal life.

Behavior Therapy The therapeutic application of the principles of learning in order to change maladaptive behaviors.

In the **analysis of resistances,** the psychoanalyst notes behaviors that interfere with therapeutic progress. Signs of resistance include arriving late, missing sessions, talking about insignificant topics, or bringing up important matters just before the end of a session. By interpreting the meaning of the client's resistances, the therapist helps the client uncover the unconscious conflicts that provoke them. Suppose a client changes the topic whenever the therapist asks him about his father. The therapist might interpret this as a sign that the client has unconscious emotional conflicts concerning his father.

As explained in chapter 5, Freud believed that the **analysis of dreams** was the "royal road to the unconscious." He claimed that dreams symbolized unconscious sexual and aggressive conflicts. Having the client free associate about the content of a series of dreams allows the psychoanalyst to interpret the symbolic, or *manifest,* content of the client's dreams to reveal the true, or *latent,* content—the real meaning.

The key to a psychoanalytic cure is the **analysis of transference** (Miller, 1983). *Transference* is the tendency of the client to act toward the therapist as he or she acts toward important people, such as parents, in everyday life. Transference may be positive or negative. In *positive transference* the client expresses feelings of approval and affection toward the therapist—as Anna O. did toward Breuer. In *negative transference* the client expresses feelings of disapproval and rejection toward the therapist—such as criticizing the therapist's skill. By interpreting transference, the therapist helps the client gain insight into the social origins of current emotional problems.

Traditional Freudian psychoanalysis inspired many offshoots. Freud's students Carl Jung and Alfred Adler broke with him and developed their own versions of psychoanalysis. During succeeding decades, neo-Freudians such as Karen Horney, Erich Fromm, and Harry Stack Sullivan developed their own forms of psychoanalytic therapy. Today few therapists are strict Freudians. Instead, many practice what is called *psychoanalytic psychotherapy,* employing aspects of psychoanalysis in face-to-face, once-a-week therapy lasting months instead of years. These therapists also rely more on rational discussions of past and present social relationships than on trying to uncover hidden conflicts through techniques such as free association and dream analysis.

Psychoanalysis, in its various forms, has gone from being the choice of most therapists in the 1950s to being the choice of about 15 percent in the 1980s (Smith, 1982). One of the main reasons for this trend is that other less costly and less time-consuming therapies are at least as effective as psychoanalysis (Fisher & Greenberg, 1985).

THE BEHAVIORAL ORIENTATION

In 1952 British psychologist Hans Eysenck coined the term **behavior therapy** to refer to treatments that emphasize changing maladaptive behaviors rather than providing insight into unconscious conflicts. According to Eysenck, knowing why you are depressed will not necessarily make you less depressed. Unlike traditional psychoanalysts, behavior therapists ignore unconscious conflicts, emphasize the present rather than the past, and assume that therapy can be accomplished in weeks rather than in years.

Psychoanalytic therapists responded to the challenge of this new form of therapy by insisting that merely eliminating maladaptive behaviors without dealing with the supposed underlying, unconscious causes would produce *symptom substitution*—the replacement of one maladaptive behavior by another. But studies have shown that directly changing maladaptive behaviors does not induce substitute maladaptive behaviors (Kazdin, 1982). Behavior therapists change maladaptive behaviors by applying the principles of classical conditioning, operant conditioning, and social learning theory.

Classical Conditioning Therapies

As explained in chapter 6, in classical conditioning a stimulus paired with another stimulus that elicits a response may itself come to elicit that response. Therapies based on classical conditioning emphasize the importance of stimuli in controlling behavior. The goal of these therapies is the removal of the stimuli that control maladaptive behaviors or the promotion of more adaptive responses to those stimuli.

Counterconditioning The technique of **counterconditioning** attempts to replace unpleasant emotional responses to stimuli with pleasant ones. The procedure is based on the assumption that we cannot simultaneously experience an unpleasant feeling, such as anxiety, and a pleasant feeling, such as relaxation. Counterconditioning was introduced by John B. Watson's student Mary Cover Jones (1896–1987). As described in chapter 6, Watson conditioned a boy called Little Albert to fear a white rat by pairing it with a loud sound. Watson also proposed that the fear could be eliminated by pairing the rat with a pleasant stimulus, such as pleasurable stroking (Watson & Rayner, 1920).

Pioneers of Behavior Therapy
Joseph Wolpe (1988), who developed systematic desensitization, called Mary Cover Jones "the founding mother of behavior therapy" for introducing the use of counterconditioning in treating phobias.

It was Jones who took Watson's suggestion and tried to rid a three-year-old boy named Peter of a rabbit phobia he had developed naturally. Jones presented Peter with milk and crackers and then brought a caged rabbit closer and closer to him. The pleasant feelings that Peter experienced in response to his favorite snack gradually became associated with the rabbit. After several sessions, Peter lost his fear of the rabbit and even enjoyed holding it in his lap (Jones, 1924).

Today the most widely used form of counterconditioning is **systematic desensitization,** developed by Joseph Wolpe (1958) for treating phobias. Systematic desensitization comprises three steps. The first step is for the client to practice *progressive relaxation,* a technique developed in the 1930s by Edmund Jacobson to relieve anxiety. To learn progressive relaxation, you would sit in a comfortable chair and practice successively tensing and relaxing each of your major muscle groups, including those of your head, arms, body, and legs, until you gained the ability to relax your entire body.

The second step is the construction of an *anxiety hierarchy,* consisting of a series of anxiety-inducing scenes related to the person's phobia. The client lists ten to twenty scenes, rating them on a one-hundred-point scale from least to most anxiety inducing. A rating of zero would mean that the scene induces no anxiety, while a rating of one hundred would mean that the scene induces intolerable anxiety. Suppose that you have a spider phobia. You might rate a photo of a spider a five, a spider on your arm a sixty, and a spider on your face an eighty-five. Table 15.1 presents an example of an anxiety hierarchy.

The third step is to pair the scenes in the anxiety hierarchy with muscle relaxation. You would begin by closing your eyes, relaxing your muscles, and imagining the least anxiety-inducing scene on your anxiety hierarchy. After doing this for fifteen to twenty seconds, you would stop and rate the level of anxiety now produced by the scene. You would repeat this process until the scene evoked little or no anxiety. And you would do this for each of the scenes in your hierarchy in succession.

Of course, the ultimate test of systematic desensitization would be your ability to face the actual source of your phobia (Foa & Kozak, 1986). This might be accomplished by proceeding to *in vivo desensitization,* in which the client is exposed to actual situations involving successively higher items

Counterconditioning A behavior therapy technique that applies the principles of classical conditioning to replace undesirable responses to stimuli with desirable ones.

Systematic Desensitization A form of counterconditioning that trains the client to maintain a state of relaxation in the presence of anxiety-inducing stimuli.

TABLE 15.1   A Test-Anxiety Hierarchy

Initial Rating of Distress	Fear-Inducing Scene
0	Registering for next semester's courses
5	Going over the course outline in class
20	Hearing the instructor announce that the midterm exam will take place in three weeks
30	Discussing the difficulty of the exam with fellow students
45	Reviewing your notes one week before the exam
50	Attending a review session three days before the exam
60	Listening to the professor explain what to expect on the exam the day before the exam
65	Studying alone the day before the exam
70	Studying with a group of students the night before the exam
75	Overhearing superior students expressing their self-doubts concerning the exam
80	Realizing that you are running out of study time at 1:00 A.M. the night before the exam
90	Entering the class before the exam and having the professor remind you that one-third of your final grade depends on the exam
95	Reading the exam questions and discovering that you do not recognize several of them
100	Answering the exam questions while hearing other students hyperventilating and muttering about them

on his or her anxiety hierarchy. Systematic desensitization has been successful in treating a wide variety of phobias, including the fear of blood (Elmore, Wildman, & Westefeld, 1980), the fear of dentists (Klepac, 1986), and even the fear of magnetic resonance imaging in patients undergoing that radiological procedure (Klonoff, Janata, & Kaufman 1986).

Given the success of systematic desensitization in treating phobias, what accounts for its effectiveness? One study implicated the endorphins (Egan, Carr, Hunt, & Adamson, 1988). As discussed in chapter 3, the endorphins are the brain's own opiates, capable of inducing feelings of euphoria. The subjects in the study were people with simple phobias (see chapter 14). Prior to sessions of systematic desensitization, half of the subjects received intravenous infusions of naloxone, a drug that blocks the effect of endorphins, and half received intravenous infusions of a placebo, a salt solution with no specific effect.

Because the study used the double-blind method, neither the subjects nor the experimenter knew which subjects received naloxone and which received the placebo. This controlled for any subject or experimenter biases. The results showed that the subjects who received the placebo displayed a decrease

In Vivo Desensitization A phobia sufferer may gain relief through in vivo desensitization, involving gradual exposure to more and more anxiety-inducing situations related to the phobia. This man, suffering from a fear of heights (acrophobia), may have begun therapy by simply looking out of a first floor window. He has progressed to the point that he is able to walk onto the roof of a tall building. But note that he still holds tightly to the ledge. He should eventually be able to peer over the ledge without having to grasp it.

in their phobias, while those who received naloxone did not. Because naloxone blocks the effects of the endorphins, the results support the possible role of endorphins in systematic desensitization. The pleasant feelings produced by the endorphins may become conditioned to the formerly fear-inducing stimuli.

Aversion Therapy The goal of aversion therapy is to make a formerly pleasurable, but maladaptive, behavior unpleasant. In this sense, aversion therapy is the reverse of systematic desensitization. In **aversion therapy** a stimulus that normally elicits a maladaptive response is paired with an unpleasant stimulus, leading to a reduction in the maladaptive response. Aversion therapy was introduced in the 1930s to treat alcoholism by administering painful electrical shocks to alcoholic patients in the presence of the sight, smell, and taste of alcohol. Today aversion therapy for alcoholism uses drugs that make the individual feel deathly ill after drinking alcohol. The drugs interfere with the metabolism of alcohol, leading to the buildup of a toxic chemical that induces nausea and dizziness.

Aversion Therapy A form of behavior therapy that inhibits maladaptive behavior by pairing it with an unpleasant stimulus.

A study of 685 alcoholics treated with aversion therapy using illness-inducing drugs found that two-thirds were abstinent one year later and one-third were abstinent three years later (Wiens & Menustik, 1983). In treating alcoholism, aversion therapy using drugs is superior to aversion therapy using electric shocks. This supports the concept of *behavioral preparedness* discussed in chapter 6. We seem to have an inborn tendency to associate intestinal distress with tastes such as alcohol rather than with external sources of pain such as electric shocks (Cannon & Baker, 1981). Aversion therapy has also been used to treat a variety of other behavioral problems, including smoking, bedwetting, overeating, and sexual abuse of children.

Operant Conditioning Therapies

Treatments based on operant conditioning change maladaptive behaviors by controlling the consequences of those behaviors. This is known as **behavior modification** and is based on the work of learning theorist B. F. Skinner. Popular forms of behavior modification rely on the behavioral contingencies of positive reinforcement and punishment.

Behavior Modification The application of the principles of operant conditioning to change maladaptive behaviors.

Positive Reinforcement One of the most important uses of positive reinforcement has been in treating patients in mental hospitals. Residents of mental hospitals have traditionally relied on the staff to take care of all their needs. This often leads to passivity, a decrease in self-care, and a general decline in what would normally be considered dignified behavior. But "talking therapies" such as psychoanalytic therapy have proved ineffective in improving the behavior of hospitalized patients suffering from schizophrenia or mood disorders.

Token Economy An operant conditioning procedure that uses tokens as positive reinforcers in programs designed to promote positive behaviors, with the tokens later used to purchase desired items or privileges.

The development of the so-called token economy provided a way to overcome this problem (Ayllon & Azrin, 1968). The **token economy** provides tokens (often plastic poker chips) as positive reinforcement for desirable behaviors, such as taking showers, making beds, or wearing appropriate clothing. The patients use the tokens to purchase items such as books or candy and privileges such as television or passes to leave the hospital grounds. The use of the token economy has proved successful in mental hospitals and other settings, including classrooms and community residences for the mentally retarded (Kazdin, 1982). Of course, participants in token economies must be weaned from them. This may occur naturally, as improved self-image and social relations alone become sources of positive reinforcement for appropriate behavior.

Punishment Though less desirable than positive reinforcement, punishment can also be effective in changing maladaptive behaviors. In fact, it may sometimes be the only way to prevent inappropriate, or even dangerous, behavior. In using punishment, the therapist would provide negative consequences for maladaptive behavior. A controversial application of punishment has been the use of mild electric shocks to reduce head banging, self-biting, and other self-destructive behaviors in autistic children, who do not respond to talking therapies (figure 15.2). Before using punishments such as mild electric shocks therapists must first present their rationale and gain approval from parents and fellow professionals. Once the self-injurious behavior has stopped, the therapist uses positive reinforcement to promote more appropriate behaviors. The combination of punishment and positive reinforcement has proved highly effective in treating autistic children, though it does not make them behave as normal children do (Lovass, 1987).

FIGURE 15.2
Punishment and Autism This autistic child wears a device developed at Johns Hopkins University called the Self-Injurious Behavior Inhibiting System, which delivers a mild electric shock to his leg whenever he bangs his head. This and similar devices have been used with success to reduce self-injurious behavior by autistic children. As you can imagine, the use of such devices has sparked controversy (Landers, 1987).

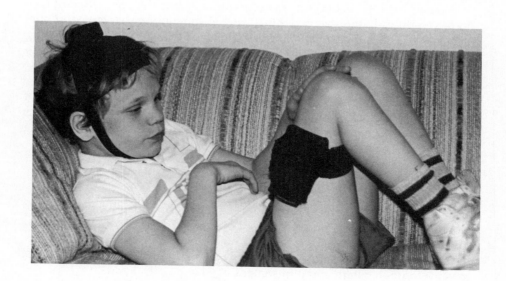

Social Learning Therapies

In treating Peter's rabbit phobia, Mary Cover Jones (1924) sometimes let Peter observe children playing with a rabbit. In doing so, Jones made use of social learning, which was discussed in chapter 6. Therapists who use social learning have their clients watch other people model adaptive behaviors either in person or on videotape. Clients learn to acquire social skills or to overcome phobias by performing the behavior that is being modeled (figure 15.3). Therapists may also use **participatory modeling,** in which the therapist models the

Participatory Modeling A form of social learning therapy in which the client learns to perform more adaptive behaviors by first observing the therapist model the desired behaviors.

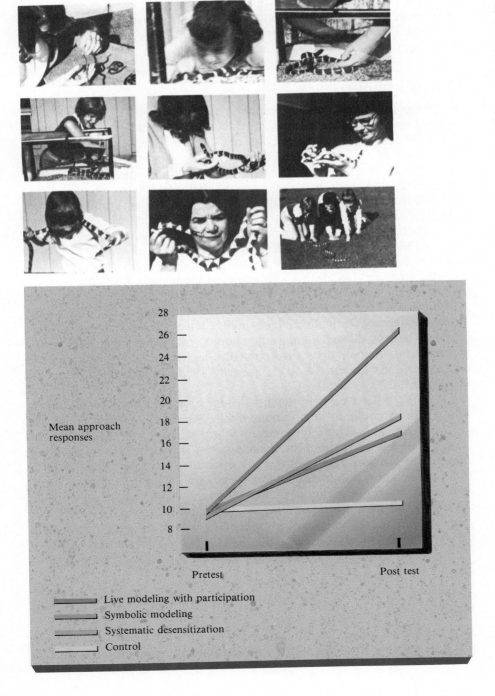

FIGURE 15.3
Modeling and Phobias People may learn to overcome their phobias by observing other people either handle objects they are afraid to handle or perform in situations in which they are afraid to perform. The graph shows the results of a study comparing the effectiveness of three kinds of therapy for snake phobia. The control group received no therapy. As you can see, all three therapies produced more approaches to the snakes than did the control condition. But participant modeling produced more improvement than did symbolic modeling (in which subjects watched models on film) or systematic desensitization (Bandura, Blanchard, & Ritter, 1969).

Albert Ellis "It is my contention . . . that all effective psychotherapists, whether or not they realize what they are doing, teach or induce their patients to reperceive or rethink their life events and philosophies and thereby to change their unrealistic and illogical thought, emotion, and behavior."

Rational-Emotive Therapy (R-E-T) A type of cognitive therapy, developed by Albert Ellis, that treats psychological disorders by forcing the client to give up irrational ways of thinking.

Paradoxical Intention A therapy technique that requires clients to perform the very acts that would normally cause them emotional distress.

desired behavior while the client watches. The client then tries to perform the behavior. Participatory modeling has been successful in treating phobias, including fears of dogs and cats (Ladouceur, 1983).

THE COGNITIVE ORIENTATION

"There is nothing either good or bad, but thinking makes it so," wrote Shakespeare in *Hamlet*. Shakespeare's belief is reflected in the fastest growing orientation to therapy—the cognitive orientation (Smith, 1982). Cognitive therapists believe that events, in themselves, do not cause maladaptive emotions and behaviors. Instead, it is our interpretation of events that does so. Given this assumption, cognitive therapists assume that changes in thinking can produce changes in maladaptive emotions or behaviors. Because cognitive therapies may include aspects of behavior therapy, they are commonly called *cognitive behavior therapies.*

Rational-Emotive Therapy

The former psychoanalytic psychotherapist Albert Ellis (1913–   ) developed the first form of cognitive therapy, which he calls **rational-emotive therapy (R-E-T).** A survey of therapists found that in recent decades Ellis has been second only to Carl Rogers in his influence on the field of psychotherapy (Smith, 1982). Ellis's therapy is based on his *A-B-C theory* of emotion, in which A is an activating event, B is an irrational belief, and C is an emotional consequence. Ellis (1962) points out that most of us believe that A causes C, when, in fact, B causes C. Imagine that you fail an exam (A) and experience depression (C). Ellis would attribute your depression not to your failure but to an irrational belief, such as the belief (B) that you must be perfect. Thus, your irrational belief, not your failure, causes your depression. Table 15.2 lists common irrational beliefs that Ellis claims guide many of our lives.

Though many therapists who use R-E-T develop warm, empathetic relationships with their clients, Ellis himself is more interested in demolishing, sometimes harshly, the irrational ideas of his clients. After identifying a client's irrational beliefs, Ellis challenges the client to provide evidence supporting them. Ellis then contradicts any irrational evidence, almost demanding that the client agree with him. Table 15.3 presents a verbatim transcript illustrating the use of R-E-T.

Ellis, like other cognitive therapists, may give behavioral homework to clients. For example, to demonstrate vividly that their irrational beliefs are unfounded, Ellis may have his clients perform acts that would normally embarrass them and cause them emotional distress. This technique is called **paradoxical intention.** Its use in treating insomnia is described in chapter 5. Ellis might employ paradoxical intention by encouraging a client who is afraid of stuttering to try stuttering in public. When the client discovers that his or her world has not come to an end because of the stuttering, he or she may give up this irrational belief and, consequently, experience less emotional distress (Shohan-Salomon & Rosenthal, 1987). The changes in beliefs produced by R-E-T are, indeed, associated with relief from emotional distress (Smith, 1983).

Cognitive Therapy

As discussed in the preceding chapter, the psychiatrist Aaron Beck assumes that depression is caused by negative beliefs about oneself, the world, and the

---

TABLE 15.2   Common Irrational Beliefs

1. It is a dire necessity for an adult human being to be loved or approved by virtually every significant other person in his or her community.

2. One should be thoroughly competent, adequate, and achieving in all possible respects if one is to consider oneself worthwhile.

3. Certain people are bad, wicked, or villainous and should be severely blamed and punished for their villainy.

4. It is awful and catastrophic when things are not the way one would very much like them to be.

5. Human unhappiness is externally caused and people have little or no ability to control their sorrows and disturbances.

6. If something is or may be dangerous or fearsome one should be terribly concerned about it and should keep dwelling on the possibility of its occurring.

7. It is easier to avoid than to face certain life difficulties and self-responsibilities.

8. One should be dependent on others and need someone stronger than oneself on whom to rely.

9. One's past history is an all-important determiner of one's present behavior and because something once strongly affected one's life, it should indefinitely have a similar effect.

10. One should become quite upset over other people's problems and disturbances.

11. There is invariably a right, precise, and perfect solution to human problems and it is catastrophic if this perfect solution is not found.

From A. Ellis, *Reason and Emotion in Psychotherapy.* Copyright © 1962 Lyle Stuart Inc., Secaucus, NJ. Reprinted with permission.

Cognitive Therapy A type of therapy, developed by Aaron Beck, that aims at eliminating exaggerated negative beliefs.

future (Beck, Rush, Shaw, & Emery, 1979). Depressed people blame themselves rather than their circumstances for misfortunes, attend more to negative events than to positive events, and have a pessimistic view of the future. Depressed people also overgeneralize from minor negative events. The goal of Beck's **cognitive therapy** is to change such exaggerated beliefs in treating psychological disorders, most notably depression.

Beck is less directive in his approach than is Ellis. Beck employs a Socratic approach, in which he asks clients questions that lead them to recognize their irrational beliefs. Beck asks clients to keep a daily record of their thoughts and urges them to note irrational beliefs and replace them with rational ones. A client who claims, "I am an awful student and will never amount to anything," might be encouraged to think, instead, "I am doing poorly in school because I do not study enough. If I change my study habits, I will graduate and pursue a desirable career." To promote positive experiences, Beck may give the client homework assignments that guarantee success, such as beginning by having someone who feels socially incompetent speak to a close friend on the telephone. Cognitive therapy has been especially successful in treating depression, which was its original purpose (Rush, Beck, Kovacs, Weissenburger, & Hollon, 1982).

Aaron Beck "The depressed person has a global negative view of himself [herself], the outside world, and the future."

TABLE 15.3   Rational-Emotive Therapy

This transcript illustrates how the rational-emotive therapist (T) challenges the client (C) to change irrational beliefs. The client is a twenty-three-year-old young woman experiencing intense feelings of guilt for not living up to her parents' strict standards.

C: Well, this is the way it was in school, if I didn't do well in one particular thing, or even on a particular test—and little crises that came up—if I didn't do as well as I had wanted to do.

T: Right. You beat yourself over the head.

C: Yes.

T: But why? What's the point? Are you supposed to be perfect? Why the hell shouldn't human beings make mistakes, be imperfect?

C: Maybe you always expect yourself to be perfect.

T: Yes. But is that *sane*?

C: No.

T: Why do it? Why not give up that unrealistic expectation?

C: But then I can't accept myself.

T: But you're saying, "It's shameful to make mistakes." *Why* is it shameful? Why can't you go to somebody else when you make a mistake and say, "Yes, I made a mistake"? Why is that so awful?. . .

C: It might all go back to, as you said, the need for approval. If I don't make mistakes, then people will look up to me. If I do it all perfectly—

T: Yes, that's part of it. That, is the erroneous belief; that if you never make mistakes everybody will love you and that it is necessary they do. That's right. That's a big part of it. But is it true, incidentally? Suppose you never did make mistakes—*would* people love you? They'd sometimes hate your guts, wouldn't they?

Reprinted by permission, Science and Behavior Books, Inc. Palo Alto, California, 1971.

Cognitive Behavior Modification

Cognitive Behavior Modification A type of therapy, developed by Donald Meichenbaum, that promotes more positive thinking.

Donald Meichenbaum goes beyond Ellis and Beck in his emphasis on promoting positive thinking in his clients through the use of **cognitive behavior modification.** Meichenbaum has received support from recent studies, discussed in chapter 14, that show that people with psychological disorders tend to be objective and rational in their beliefs. People without such disorders tend to hold irrational beliefs, viewing themselves and the world more positively than is merited by objective reality.

In applying what he calls *stress inoculation training*, Meichenbaum (1985) helps clients change their pessimistic thinking into optimistic thinking when in stressful situations. The therapist first explores the client's characteristic ways of thinking and responding in particular situations that create distress. The therapist may model more appropriate thought patterns and behaviors for the client to consider. The client then rehearses the thought patterns by saying them out loud and, if feasible, rehearses the behaviors. The client next

Drawing by Ziegler; © 1984 The New Yorker Magazine, Inc.

proceeds to test the new thought patterns and behaviors in real-life situations and reports back to the therapist on their effect. Cognitive behavior modification has achieved success, such as helping patients face the prospect of cardiac catheterization (Kendall et al., 1979) and pianists overcome performance anxiety (Kendrick, Craig, Lawson, & Davidson, 1982).

THE HUMANISTIC ORIENTATION

About 10 percent of psychotherapists practice some form of *humanistic therapy,* making it one of the most popular approaches to therapy (Smith, 1982). Unlike the psychoanalytic orientation, the humanistic orientation emphasizes the present rather than the past and conscious experience rather than unconscious experience. Unlike the behavioral orientation, the humanistic orientation emphasizes the importance of subjective mental experience rather than objective environmental circumstances. And unlike the cognitive orientation, the humanistic orientation encourages the expression of emotion rather than its control. Moreover, the humanistic orientation emphasizes the responsibility of the person for change—we are free to overcome our past experiences and present circumstances.

Person-Centered Therapy

The most popular kind of humanistic therapy is **person-centered therapy,** formerly called *client-centered therapy.* It was developed in the 1950s by Carl Rogers (1902–1987), who had practiced psychoanalytic psychotherapy, as one of the first alternatives to psychoanalysis. As mentioned earlier, a survey of therapists found that Rogers has been the most influential of all contemporary psychotherapists (Smith, 1982). While the rational-emotive therapist is *directive* in challenging the irrational beliefs of clients, the person-centered therapist is *nondirective* in permitting clients to find their own answers to their problems. This is in keeping with the humanistic concept of self-actualization (Rogers, 1951).

Since person-centered therapists give no advice, how do they help their clients? They do so by promoting self-acceptance. As discussed in chapter 14, humanistic psychologists assume that psychological disorders arise from an incongruence between a person's public self and private self. This makes

Person-Centered Therapy A type of humanistic therapy, developed by Carl Rogers, that helps clients find their own answers to their problems.

TABLE 15.4   Person-Centered Therapy

This transcript illustrates how the person-centered therapist (T) acts as a psychological mirror, reflecting back the feelings expressed in statements by the client (C). The client feels anxious about taking responsibility for her life. Notice how the therapist is less directive than the one in the transcript of rational-emotive therapy in table 15.3.

C: Um-hum. That's why I say . . . (*slowly and very thoughtfully*) well, with that sort of foundation, well, it's really up to me. I mean, it seems to be really apparent to me that I can't depend on someone else giving me an education. (very softly) I'll really have to get it myself.

T: It really begins to come home—there's only one person that can educate you—a realization that perhaps nobody else can give you an education.

C: Um-hum. (long pause—while she sits thinking) I have all the symptoms of fright (*laughs softly*).

T: Fright: That this is a scary thing, is that what you mean?

C: Um-Hum (*very long pause—obviously struggling with feelings in herself*)

T: Do you want to say any more about what you mean by that? That it really does give you the symptoms of fright?

C: (*laughs*) I, uh . . . I don't know whether I quite know. I mean . . . well, it really seems like I'm cut loose (*pause*), and it seems that I'm very—I don't know—in a vulnerable position, but I, uh, I brought this up and it, uh, somehow it almost came out without saying it. It seems to be . . . it's something I let out.

T: Hardly a part of you.

C: Well, I felt surprised.

T: As though, "Well for goodness sake, did I say that?" (*both chuckle*).

the person distort reality or deny feelings, trying to avoid the anxiety caused by failing to act in accordance with those feelings. The goal of person-centered therapy is to help the client reduce this incongruence by accepting and expressing true feelings.

The therapist accomplishes this through reflection of feelings, genuineness, accurate empathy, and unconditional positive regard. Note that a close friend or relative whom you consider a "good listener" and valued counselor probably exhibits these characteristics, too. *Reflection of feelings* is the main technique of person-centered therapy. The therapist is an active listener who serves as a therapeutic mirror, attending to the emotional content of what the client says and rephrasing it for the client. This helps the client recognize true feelings. By being *genuine* the therapist acts in a warm, honest, and sincere manner rather than in a detached, closed, and superior manner. This makes the client more willing to express true feelings. The client also becomes more willing to share feelings when the therapist shows *accurate empathy,* which means that the therapist's words and actions indicate true understanding of how the client feels.

Perhaps the most difficult task for the person-centered therapist is maintaining *unconditional positive regard.* In doing so, the therapist accepts the person as he or she is and remains nonjudgmental—no matter how personally distasteful may be the client's thoughts, feelings, and actions. This enables the client to freely express and deal with even the most distressing aspects of his or her private self. Note that this does not mean that the therapist must approve of the client's behavior, only that the therapist must accept the client's personal experience. Table 15.4 presents a verbatim transcript illustrating the use of person-centered therapy.

Though Rogers urged therapists to be nondirective, even he was unable to fulfill that ideal perfectly. A study of films and recordings of therapy sessions involving Rogers showed that he was warm, empathic, accepting, and nondirective as long as the client was expressing insight into his or her problems. He became less so when the client failed to express insight. At times, Rogers even became directive (Truax, 1966).

Gestalt Therapy

Imagine a therapy that combines aspects of psychoanalysis, R-E-T, and client-centered therapy and you might conceive of **Gestalt therapy.** Fritz Perls (1893–1970), a former psychoanalytic psychotherapist and the founder of Gestalt therapy, claimed, "The idea of Gestalt therapy is to change paper people to real people" (Perls, 1973, p. 120). To Perls paper people were those out of touch with their true feelings, making them live "inauthentic lives." Like psychoanalysis, Gestalt therapy seeks to bring unconscious feelings into conscious awareness. Like person-centered therapy, Gestalt therapy attempts to increase the client's emotional expressiveness. And like rational-emotive therapy, Gestalt therapy may be confrontational in forcing clients to change maladaptive ways of thinking and behaving.

Despite its name, Gestalt therapy is not related to Gestalt psychology (Henle, 1978), which is discussed in chapter 1, except in emphasizing the need to achieve wholeness of the personality. Gestalt therapists insist that clients take responsibility for their own behavior, rather than blaming other people or events for their problems, and that clients live in the here and now, rather than being concerned about events occurring at other places and times. Gestalt therapists also assume that people who are aware of their feelings can exert greater control over their reactions to events. The Gestalt therapist notes any signs that the client is not being brutally honest about his or her feelings, at times by observing the client's nonverbal communication—posture, gestures, facial expressions, and tone of voice. For example, a client who denies feeling anxious while tightly clenching his fists would be accused of lying about his emotions.

One way that Gestalt therapists help clients develop emotional awareness is through a variety of psychological exercises. In the *two-chair exercise,* the client alternately sits in one chair and then another, with each chair representing an aspect of himself or herself, such as the extravert and the introvert, and proceeds to carry on a dialogue between the two aspects. The two-chair exercise has proved effective in relieving emotional distress (Greenberg & Dompierre, 1981). But Perls has been criticized for promoting self-centeredness and emotional callousness, as in his "Gestalt prayer" (Perls, 1972, p. 70): "I do my thing and you do your thing. I am not in this world to live up to your expectations. And you are not in this world to live up to mine. You are you and I am I. And if by chance we find each other, it's beautiful. If not, then it can't be helped."

Gestalt Therapy A type of humanistic therapy, developed by Fritz Perls, that encourages the client to become aware of his or her true feelings and to take responsibility for his or her own actions.

Fritz Perls (1893–1970) Fritz Perls, the founder of Gestalt therapy, was a refugee from Nazi Germany who attracted loyal followers to his center at Esalen Institute in Big Sur, California in the 1960s in the hope of becoming "authentic people." Perls was a charismatic person who thought as highly of himself as did his followers, claiming that "I believe I am the best therapist for any type of neurosis in the States, maybe in the world" (Prochaska, 1984, p. 128).

THE SOCIAL RELATIONS ORIENTATION

The therapeutic orientations that have been discussed so far involve a therapist and a client. In contrast, the *social relations orientation* assumes that, because many psychological problems involve interpersonal relationships, other people must be brought into the therapy process.

Group Therapy

In 1905 Joseph Pratt, a Boston physician, found that his tuberculosis patients gained relief from emotional distress by meeting in groups to discuss their feelings. This marked the beginning of *group therapy*. But group therapy did not become an important form of therapy until World War II, when a limited number of therapists found themselves faced with more people in need of therapy than they could see individually (Hersen, Kazdin, & Bellack, 1983). Because group therapy allows a therapist to see more people (usually six to twelve in a group) in less time, more people can receive help at less cost per person. Group therapy provides participants with a range of role models, encouragement from others with similar problems, feedback about their own behavior, assurance that their problems are not unique, and the opportunity to try out new behaviors.

Psychoanalytic Group Therapies Group therapies derived from psychoanalysis stress insight and emotional catharsis. In 1910 Jacob Moreno (1892–1974), a Romanian psychiatrist, introduced the psychoanalytic group therapy called *psychodrama,* and in 1931 he coined the term *group therapy*. **Psychodrama** aims at achieving insight and catharsis through acting out real-life situations. The therapist functions as a director, making observations and offering suggestions. One technique of psychodrama is *role reversal,* in which a participant plays the role of a family member or other important person. This provides insight into the other person's motives and empathy for that person's feelings. Psychodrama appears to be about as effective as other kinds of group therapy (Garfield, 1983).

Psychodrama A form of psychoanalytic group therapy, developed by Jacob Moreno, that aims at achieving insight and catharsis through acting out real-life situations.

Psychodrama Psychodrama emphasizes the importance of emotional expression and emotional insight.

A more recent form of group therapy inspired by psychoanalysis is **transactional analysis (TA),** popularized in the 1960s by psychiatrist Eric Berne (1910–1970) in his best-selling book *Games People Play* (1964). Berne claimed that we act according to one of three roles: child, parent, or adult. These resemble the Freudian personality structures of id, superego, and ego. The *child,* like the id, acts impulsively and demands immediate gratification. The *parent,* like the superego, is authoritarian and guides moral behavior. And the *adult,* like the ego, promotes rational and responsible behavior.

Each role is adaptive in certain situations and maladaptive in others. For example, being childish is appropriate at parties but not at job interviews. According to Berne, our relationships involve *transactions*—social interactions between these roles. *Complementary transactions,* in which both individuals act according to the same role, are usually best. *Crossed transactions,* as when one person acts as a child and the other acts as an adult, are usually worst. Figure 15.4 presents examples of complementary and crossed transactions.

The goal of TA is to analyze transactions between group members. These are the "games" that people play, which reflect our *life scripts*—the pervasive

Transactional Analysis (TA) A form of psychoanalytic group therapy, developed by Eric Berne, that helps clients change their immature or inappropriate ways of relating to other people.

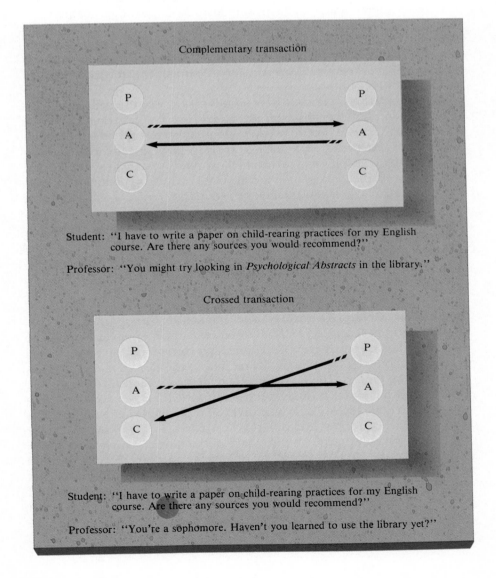

Student: "I have to write a paper on child-rearing practices for my English course. Are there any sources you would recommend?"

Professor: "You might try looking in *Psychological Abstracts* in the library."

Student: "I have to write a paper on child-rearing practices for my English course. Are there any sources you would recommend?"

Professor: "You're a sophomore. Haven't you learned to use the library yet?"

FIGURE 15.4
Transactional Analysis
According to Eric Berne (1964), our social relationships involve transactions in which we act as a parent, adult, or child. In a complementary transaction, two persons act according to the same role. In a crossed transaction, two persons act according to different roles.

themes that we follow in our social relations. For example, a woman might have a life script that supports her feelings of worthlessness and continually play games that provoke responses from others that support that script. It is difficult to determine the effectiveness of TA because it has stimulated relatively little research. One study found that it was inferior to behavior therapy in treating alcoholism (Olson, Ganley, Devine, & Dorsey, 1981).

Social Skills Training A form of behavioral group therapy that improves the client's social relationships by improving his or her interpersonal skills.

Behavioral Group Therapies Psychologists who favor behavioral group therapies assume that changes in overt behavior will bring relief of emotional distress. A popular form of behavioral group therapy, also used in individual therapy, is **social skills training.** Its goal is to improve social relationships by improving social skills, such as cultivating friendships or carrying on conversations. Participants are encouraged to rehearse new behaviors in the group setting. Members of the group may model more effective behaviors. And shaping may be used to develop more effective behaviors gradually. Social skills training has been successful in helping children overcome shyness (Van Hasselt, Griest, Kazdin, Esveldt-Dawson, & Unis, 1984), adolescents overcome social anxiety (Blair & Fretz, 1980), and adults overcome depression (Thase et al., 1984).

Assertiveness Training A form of social skills training that teaches clients to express their feelings directly, instead of passively or aggressively.

A form of social skills training called **assertiveness training,** introduced in 1949 by Andrew Salter, helps people learn to express their feelings constructively in social situations. Many people experience poor social relations because they are unassertive. They are unable to ask for favors, to say no to requests, or to complain about poor service. By learning to express their feelings, formerly unassertive people relieve their anxiety and have more rewarding social relationships.

Members of assertiveness training groups try out assertive behaviors in the group situation. The therapist typically models assertive behaviors, aggressive behaviors, and passive behaviors to permit group members to distinguish between them. *Assertive* people express their feelings directly and constructively. *Aggressive* people express their feelings directly but with a hostile edge. And *passive* people express their feelings indirectly, as in pouting.

One assertiveness training technique is the *broken record,* in which those who have trouble saying no practice repeating brief statements rejecting requests. The therapist and group members critique each participant's attempts at assertive behaviors. Assertiveness training has been successful in improving the communication skills of people as diverse as athletes (Connelly, 1988), working women (Stake & Pearlman, 1980), and college students (Wolff & Desiderato, 1980).

Humanistic Group Therapies The humanistic group therapies encourage awareness and acceptance of emotional experiences. In the late 1940s, studies of small-group relationships carried out at the National Training Laboratories in Bethel, Maine, led to the development of sensitivity training groups. The early sensitivity groups, called *training groups* (or *T-groups*), helped businesspeople improve their relationships with workers and colleagues. Today sensitivity groups are also popular with the clergy, police, educators, and other professionals.

Sensitivity groups include twelve to twenty members. Participants explore their own feelings and become aware of how their actions affect the feelings of others. They learn to rely on reason and cooperation instead of coercion and manipulation. A study of the effectiveness of sensitivity groups found that social skills training was superior to sensitivity training in improving social skills and reducing social anxiety (Monti, Curran, Corriveau, DeLancey, & Hagerman, 1980).

A relative of sensitivity training is the **encounter group,** an offshoot of the *human potential movement* that arose in the 1950s and declined in the early 1970s (Finkelstein, Wenegrat, & Yalom, 1982). Encounter groups typically involve people who have had little or no prior contact with one another. The groups may meet for hours or days. Compared with sensitivity training groups, encounter groups are more concerned with the open expression of emotions than with improving social relationships. Encounter groups promote crying, cursing, and verbal abuse. They may also encourage physical touching as a means of overcoming social isolation.

Studies of encounter groups indicate that their slight beneficial effects may be temporary (Kilmann & Sotile, 1976) and that they may attract people ill-suited for intense emotional confrontations. Some participants are even emotionally harmed by their experiences (Hartley, Roback, & Abramowitz, 1976). But the encounter group movement did lead to the emergence of *self-help groups* for drug abusers, widowed people, and others with specific shared problems. The groups are conducted by people who have experienced those problems; for example, some self-help groups for phobia sufferers are run by former phobics (Ross, 1980).

Encounter Group A derivative
of humanistic therapy in which
group members learn to be
themselves by openly expressing
their true feelings to one another.

Family Therapy

While group therapy usually brings together unrelated people, **family therapy** brings together members of the same family. The basic assumption of family therapy is that a family member with problems related to his or her family life cannot be treated apart from the family. The main goals of family therapy are the constructive expression of feelings and the establishment of rules that family members agree to follow. In family therapy, one of the family members—known as the *identified patient*—is assumed to bear the brunt of the family's problems. Typically, the family is brought together for family therapy after that person has entered individual psychotherapy.

Family therapy attempts to improve communications and relationships between family members, who learn to provide and accept feedback from each other. The therapist helps family members establish an atmosphere in which

Family Therapy A form of
group therapy that encourages the
constructive expression of
feelings and the establishment of
rules that family members agree
to follow.

Family Therapy In family therapy, family members gain insight into their maladaptive patterns of interaction and learn to change them into healthier ones.

no one is blamed for family problems. A popular form of family therapy is *structural family therapy,* developed by Salvadore Minuchin (1974). Minuchin emphasizes the emotional "boundaries" between family members. Boundaries that are too rigid create inadequate contact between family members. And boundaries that are too diffuse create oppressive familiarity between family members.

The structural family therapist assesses the structure of the family members' interactions, perhaps even observing the family at home. The therapist then draws diagrams of these relationships and discusses how certain of the relationships are maladaptive. Perhaps the family is too child oriented or perhaps a parent and child are allied against the other parent. The goal of the therapist is to have the family replace these maladaptive relationships with more effective ones. Family therapy improves both the relationships between family members and the behavior of individual family members (Hazelrigg, Cooper, & Borduin, 1987).

THE BIOMEDICAL ORIENTATION

Though Sigmund Freud practiced psychoanalysis, he predicted that, as science progressed, therapies for psychological disorders would become more and more biological (Trotter, 1981). During the past few decades, the *biomedical orientation* has, indeed, become an important approach to therapy. It is based on the assumption that psychological disorders are associated with brain disturbances and, consequently, will respond to treatments that alter brain activity. Biomedical treatments can only be offered by psychiatrists and other physicians.

Psychosurgery

While attending a professional meeting in 1935, Portugese psychiatrist Egas Moniz was impressed by a report indicating that agitated chimpanzees became calmer after undergoing brain surgery that separated their frontal lobes from the rest of the brain. Moniz wondered whether such **psychosurgery,** might also benefit agitated mental patients. He convinced neurosurgeon Almeida Lima to perform *prefrontal lobotomies* on such patients. Lima drilled holes in the patient's temples, inserted scalpels through the holes, and cut away portions of the frontal lobes. Moniz reported many successes in calming agitated patients. But in 1944 a former psychosurgery patient shot Moniz through the spinal cord, paralyzing him for life. In 1949 Moniz won the Nobel Prize for inventing psychosurgery, then considered a humane alternative to locking agitated patients in rooms or restraining them in straitjackets (Valenstein, 1980).

Psychosurgery was introduced to the United States and popularized in the 1940s by neurosurgeon Walter Freeman and psychiatrist James Watts. They favored a technique called *transorbital leucotomy* (figure 15.5), in which the patient's eyesocket was anesthetized and a mallet was used to drive a surgical pick into the frontal lobe. The pick was then levered back and forth to separate portions of the lobe from the rest of the brain. By 1979, psychosurgery had been performed on about thirty-five thousand mental patients in the United States.

But the use of psychosurgery has declined markedly. One reason is its unpredictability. Aside from the normal risks of brain surgery, psychosurgery produced unpredictable effects. While some patients became apathetic, others became violent, as in the case of the patient who shot Moniz. A second reason for its decline was the advent of drug therapies in the 1950s and 1960s, which provided safer, more effective, and more humane treatment. And a third reason for its decline was public opposition to what seemed to be a barbaric means of behavior control. Today, psychosurgery is rarely used in the United States and, when it is used, more often involves the use of electrodes inserted deep into the brain of an uncontrollably violent person. A current sent through the electrodes destroys small amounts of tissue in areas of the limbic system that promote aggression (Gonzalez, 1980).

Psychosurgery The treatment of psychological disorders by the destruction of specific areas of the brain.

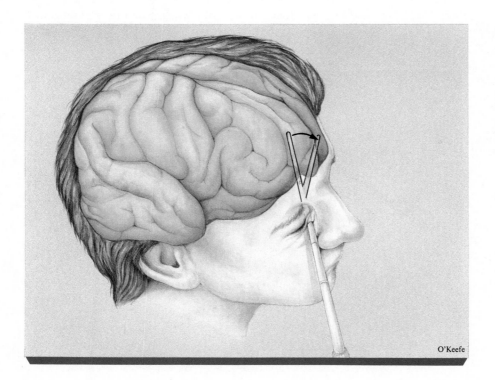

O'Keefe

FIGURE 15.5
Transorbital Leucotomy In the form of psychosurgery called transorbital leucotomy, a surgeon would use a mallet to drive a surgical pick through the thin bone of the eye socket into the brain. The surgeon would then lever the pick back and forth, severing portions of the frontal lobes from the rest of the brain.

Electroconvulsive Therapy

In the early nineteenth century, Benjamin Rush employed "shock therapy" in treating patients. He would first use a dirty surgical instrument to make an incision in the patient's neck. The resulting infection produced a large boil. Rush would then shock the patient by unexpectedly popping open the boil with a needle. He reported that many patients showed a decrease in their symptoms after such treatments.

Modern shock therapy began in 1933, when the Austrian physician Manfred Sakel found that schizophrenic patients showed improvement following convulsions induced by insulin overdoses. In 1935 Hungarian psychiatrist Ladislas Meduna noted that schizophrenia and epilepsy rarely occurred in the same person. He inferred that the induction of brain seizures might relieve the symptoms of schizophrenia. Meduna used the drug camphor to induce seizures, but he found that though the treatments relieved some patients' symptoms, they injured or even killed other patients.

In 1938, on a visit to a slaughterhouse, Italian psychiatrist Ugo Cerletti watched pigs rendered unconscious by electric shocks. Cerletti reasoned that electric shock might be a safe alternative to drug-induced shock therapy in calming agitated patients. Cerletti and his fellow psychiatrist Lucio Bini introduced **electroconvulsive therapy** (**ECT**), which induces brain seizures through the application of a brief electrical current. While ECT was originally used for treating agitated patients, it proved more successful in elevating the mood of severely depressed patients who fail to respond to drug therapy.

A psychiatrist administers ECT by attaching electrodes to the temples of a patient who is under general anesthesia and who has been given a muscle relaxant (figure 15.6). The muscle relaxant prevents injuries that might be caused by violent contractions of the muscles. A burst of electricity of 70 to 150 volts is passed through the brain for perhaps half a second. This induces a brain seizure, which is followed by a period of unconsciousness lasting up to thirty minutes. The patient typically receives three treatments a week for several weeks (Scovern & Kilmann, 1980).

In treating severe depression, ECT can be more effective than antidepressant drugs. Because ECT produces more rapid improvement than antidepres-

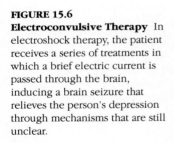

Electroconvulsive Therapy (ECT) A biomedical therapy in which brief electrical currents are used to induce brain seizures in victims of major depression.

FIGURE 15.6
Electroconvulsive Therapy In electroshock therapy, the patient receives a series of treatments in which a brief electric current is passed through the brain, inducing a brain seizure that relieves the person's depression through mechanisms that are still unclear.

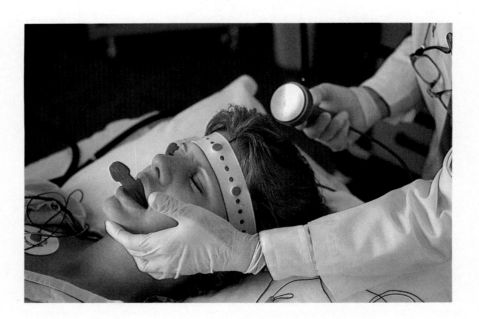

sant drugs, it is the treatment of choice for depressed people in imminent danger of committing suicide (Scovern & Kilmann, 1980). But ECT's mechanism of action is unclear. As explained in chapter 14, depression is associated with low levels of norepinephrine. The most widely accepted explanation is that ECT stimulates an increase in the level of norepinephrine in the brain (Masserano, Takimoto, & Weiner, 1981). Some studies have found that ECT may work by increasing the level of endorphins in the brain (Alexopoulos et al., 1983), perhaps lifting the depressed person's mood.

In recent years ECT has provoked controversy concerning its safety and effectiveness. In the past, the violence of the convulsions induced by ECT would often break bones and tear muscles. Today muscle relaxants prevent such damage. But ECT does cause *retrograde amnesia*—the forgetting of events that occurred from minutes to days prior to the treatment. In 1982 the potential side effects of ECT and fears that ECT could be used to control people against their will led the citizens of Berkeley, California, to ban its use. But citizens who argued that this violated the rights of those who might benefit from ECT convinced a California superior court judge to remove the ban (Cunningham, 1983). Those who favor the availability of ECT were heartened by a report from the National Institute of Health stating that ECT is rarely fatal and rarely produces long-lasting memory losses (Holden, 1985). The debate about the desirability of ECT remains as much an ethical, emotional, and political issue as a scientific one.

Drug Therapy

Since its introduction in the 1950s, drug therapy has become the most widely used form of biomedical therapy. It has been responsible for freeing patients from restraints and padded cells and permitting many more to live in normal communities. As discussed in chapter 14, psychological disorders are associated with abnormal levels of neurotransmitters in the brain. Drug therapies work by restoring neurotransmitters to more normal levels. But a common criticism of drug therapies is that they relieve symptoms without changing the person's ability to adjust to everyday stressors. This means that concurrent psychotherapy may be desirable to help clients learn more adaptive ways of thinking and behaving.

Antianxiety Drugs Because of their calming effect, the **antianxiety drugs** were originally called *tranquilizers.* Today the most widely prescribed are the *benzodiazepines,* such as *diazepam* (Valium). In fact, the prevalence of anxiety disorders makes the antianxiety drugs the most widely prescribed of all psychoactive drugs. The benzodiazepines work by stimulating special receptors in the brain that enhance the effects of the neurotransmitter GABA (Greenblatt, Shader, & Abernethy, 1983). GABA reduces brain activity. The benzodiazepines may also produce side effects, including drowsiness, depression, and dependence.

Antianxiety Drugs Psychoactive drugs, commonly known as minor tranquilizers, that are used to treat anxiety disorders.

Antipsychotic Drugs For centuries, physicians in India prescribed the snakeroot plant for calming agitated patients. Beginning in the 1940s a chemical derivative of the plant, *reserpine,* was used to reduce symptoms of mania and schizophrenia. But reserpine fell into disfavor because of its tendency to cause depression and low blood pressure. The 1950s saw the development of safer **antipsychotic drugs** called *phenothiazines,* such as *chlorpromazine* (Thorazine), for treating people with schizophrenia. French physicians had noted that the drug, used to sedate patients before surgery, calmed psychotic patients.

Antipsychotic Drugs Psychoactive drugs, commonly known as major tranquilizers, that are used to treat schizophrenia.

The phenothiazines relieve the positive symptoms of schizophrenia but not the negative ones (Killian, Holzman, Davis, & Gibbons, 1984). As discussed in chapter 14, positive symptoms include hallucinations, disordered thinking, and bizarre behavior, while negative symptoms include apathy and social withdrawal. The phenothiazines work by blocking brain receptor sites for the neurotransmitter dopamine (Sternberg, Van Kammen, Lerner, & Bunney, 1982). Unfortunately, long-term use of antipsychotic drugs can cause the bizarre motor side effects that characterize *tardive dyskinesia,* which include grimacing, lip smacking, and limb flailing (Gardos, Cole, Salomon, & Schniebolk, 1987).

Antidepressant Drugs   The first **antidepressant drugs** were the *MAO inhibitors.* They were originally used to treat tuberculosis but were prescribed as antidepressants after physicians noted that they induced euphoria in tuberculosis patients. The MAO inhibitors work by blocking enzymes that normally break down the neurotransmitters serotonin and norepinephrine. This increases the levels of those neurotransmitters in the brain, elevating the patient's mood.

But the MAO inhibitors fell into disfavor because they can cause dangerously high blood pressure in patients who eat foods (such as cheeses) or drink beverages (such as beer) containing the amino acid tyramine. The MAO inhibitors have largely been replaced by the *tricyclic antidepressants,* such as *imipramine* (Tofranil). The tricyclics increase the levels of serotonin and norepinephrine in the brain by preventing their reuptake by brain neurons. Though the tricyclics are effective in treating depression ("Task Force on the

Antidepressant Drugs
Psychoactive drugs that are used to treat major depression.

Drawing by Handelsman; © 1981 The New Yorker Magazine, Inc.

"Your tale is very sad, Ben. I'm almost sorry I took an anti-depressant."

Use of Laboratory Tests in Psychiatry," 1985), they take two to four weeks to have an effect. This means that suicidal patients given antidepressants must be watched carefully during that period.

Antimania Drugs In the 1940s, Australian physician John Cade observed that the chemical lithium calmed agitated guinea pigs. He then tried it on patients and found that it calmed those suffering from mania (Tosteson, 1981). Psychiatrists prescribe the antimania drug *lithium carbonate* to prevent the extreme mood swings of bipolar disorder. Lithium works by normalizing the flow of ions across the membranes of brain neurons (Tosteson, 1981). Psychiatrists must be vigilant in monitoring patients taking lithium because of its ability to produce severe side effects, including seizures, brain damage, and irregular heart rhythms (Honchar, Olney, & Sherman, 1983).

COMMUNITY MENTAL HEALTH

As discussed earlier, for most of the nineteenth and twentieth centuries state mental hospitals served as the primary sites of treatment for people with serious psychological disorders. But, since the 1950s, there has been a movement toward **deinstitutionalization,** which involves the treatment of people in community settings instead of in mental hospitals. The number of patients in mental hospitals has declined from a high of 559,000 in 1955 to fewer than 140,000 in the early 1980s (figure 15.7) (Bassuk, 1984).

What accounts for this trend? First, the introduction of drug treatments made it more feasible for mental patients to function in the outside world. Second, mental hospitals had become underfunded, understaffed, and overcrowded. Many were little more than human warehouses, with patients wasting away their lives with no hope of improvement. Community-based treatment seemed to be a cheaper, superior alternative. Third, increasing concern for the legal rights of mental patients made it more difficult to have people committed to mental hospitals and to keep them there after they had been committed. And

Deinstitutionalization The movement toward treating people with psychological disorders in community settings instead of in mental hospitals.

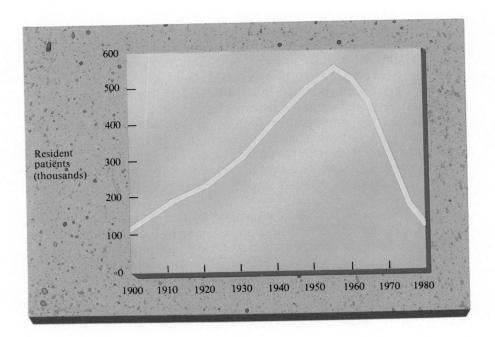

FIGURE 15.7
Deinstitutionalization As a result of deinstitutionalization, the number of patients in state mental hospitals in 1980 was less than one-fourth the number in 1955.

The Crisis Intervention Center The community mental-health system is aided by crisis intervention centers. These centers handle emergencies such as rape cases, wife abuse, suicide threats, or other problems that require immediate help.

fourth, the Community Mental Health Centers Act of 1963, advocated by President Kennedy, mandated the establishment of federally funded centers in every community in the United States. These centers were to provide services to prevent and treat psychological disorders, further reducing the need for mental hospitals.

Community mental-health centers provide a variety of services. One service is outpatient counseling, which permits people to receive therapy while living and working in the community. A second service is short-term inpatient treatment. Instead of being committed to a state hospital possibly hours away from home, a person experiencing major depression might spend a brief period of time in a local center, receiving drug therapy, counseling, and practical assistance. A third service is twenty-four-hour emergency care. This might include a suicide hotline, a shelter for battered wives, and a shelter for runaways. And a fourth service is consultation and education provided to courts, police, and public welfare agencies. For example, a trained counselor might present a program on drug-abuse prevention to schoolchildren.

Community mental-health centers have three main goals regarding the prevention of psychological disorders. *Primary prevention* helps prevent psychological disorders by fostering social support systems, eliminating sources of stress, or strengthening the person's ability to deal with stressors (Gesten & Jason, 1987). This might be promoted by reducing unemployment and making available low-cost housing. *Secondary prevention* provides early treatment for people at immediate risk of developing psychological disorders, sometimes through *crisis intervention*. Community mental-health centers often go into action following disasters in which people are killed or communities are ravaged. When a Philadelphia neighborhood was destroyed by fire after a bomb was dropped on a house occupied by members of a radical organization called MOVE, community mental-health centers provided counseling for children who had been trapped in their schools and terrified by the fire and gunshots. *Tertiary prevention* helps people who have full-blown psychological disorders. Among the main community approaches to tertiary prevention are community residences, or *halfway houses,* that provide homelike, structured environments in which former mental hospital patients readjust to independent living.

Unfortunately, deinstitutionalization has worked better in theory than in practice. Communities too often provide inadequate aftercare for discharged mental patients. Even when funding is available for treatment facilities such as halfway houses, homeowners often oppose the placement of such facilities in their neighborhoods (Turkington, 1984). And the policies of private and government insurance programs concerning reimbursement for the treatment of psychological disorders encourage hospitalization instead of less costly and more effective community-based treatments. For example, insurance programs that fully reimburse patients for hospital stays may require partial payment for outpatient treatments (Kiesler, 1982). As a consequence, former mental hospital patients who lack family support may have little choice but to live on the street. Many of the homeless people on the streets of major cities and, increasingly, on the streets of smaller cities are former residents of mental hospitals.

The potential benefits of adequate support for deinstitutionalization are evident in the results of a study comparing community care for former mental hospital patients in the comparable cities of Portland, Oregon, and Vancouver, British Columbia. Portland provides few community mental-health services, while Vancouver provides many private and public services. One year after their discharge, formerly hospitalized schizophrenics in Vancouver were less likely than those in Portland to have been readmitted and more likely to be employed and to report a greater sense of psychological well-being. Because

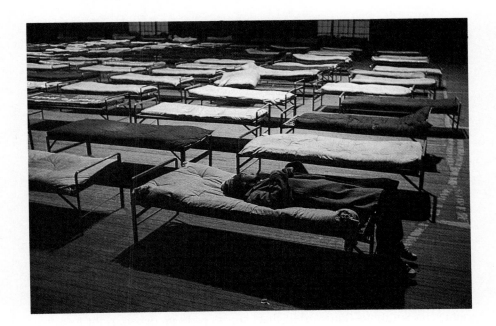

The Homeless Mentally Ill The deinstitutionalization movement, the lack of community mental health services, and the lack of low-cost housing have contributed to the homelessness problem. This photograph shows a homeless person sleeping in an armory shelter in New York City.

the two groups were initially equivalent, the greater progress of the Vancouver group was attributed to community services rather than to initial differences between the groups (Beiser, Shore, Peters, & Tatum, 1985).

The inadequacies of deinstitutionalization have provoked legal actions. Homeless mental patients in Denver, New York, and Los Angeles have sued to receive housing, treatment, and supervision to enable them to remain in the community. In other cases, people who have been judged ready for discharge but who have not been discharged because of inadequate housing and community services have sued to receive community housing, treatment, and supervision (Cunningham, 1984). But some critics, frustrated by the inadequacy of services for former mental hospital patients, urge limited deinstitutionalization, reasoning that people would be better off confined in mental hospitals than living in boxes, subways, or doorways (Thomas, 1981).

THE RIGHTS OF THE THERAPY CLIENT

Does a resident of a mental hospital have the right to refuse treatment? Does a resident of a mental hospital have the right to receive treatment? Is what a client reveals to a therapist privileged information? These questions have generated heated debate during the past three decades.

The Rights of Hospitalized Patients

As mentioned, concern for the rights of patients in mental hospitals has contributed to the deinstitutionalization movement in the United States. People who are committed to mental hospitals lose many of their rights, including their rights to vote, to marry, to divorce, and to sign contracts. Revelations about past psychiatric practices in the Soviet Union show the extent to which the commitment process can be abused. Soviet psychiatrists have used unusual diagnoses, such as "reformist delusions" and "schizophrenia with religious delirium," to commit political dissidents to mental hospitals (Faraone, 1982).

In the United States, ideally only people who are judged to be dangerous to themselves or others can be involuntarily committed to mental hospitals. The need to demonstrate that a person is dangerous before being committed was formalized by the United States Supreme Court in the 1979 case of *Addington v. Texas*. Commitment usually requires two psychiatrists to document that the person is dangerous. During the commitment process, the person has the right to a lawyer, to call witnesses, and to a hearing or a jury trial. The final decision on commitment is made by a judge or jury, not a psychiatrist.

Court decisions have also ruled that people committed to mental hospitals have both a right to receive treatment and a right to refuse treatment. In 1975, in the widely publicized case of *Donaldson v. O'Connor,* the United States Supreme Court ruled that mental patients have a right to more than custodial care. The case was brought by Kenneth Donaldson, who had been confined for fifteen years in a Florida mental hospital without treatment. Legal decisions such as this contributed to the deinstitutionalization movement by making it more difficult to keep mental patients hospitalized against their will. If treatment for a patient is unavailable in the hospital, the patient has the right to be released.

In 1983, in the case of *Rogers v. Commissioner of Mental Health,* the Massachusetts Supreme Court ruled that mental patients have a right to refuse treatment, unless a court judges them to be incompetent to make their own decisions (Gutheil, 1985). When the case was first brought, critics claimed that such a ruling would merely give mental patients the right to "rot with their rights on" (Appelbaum & Gutheil, 1980). This decision has helped fuel the deinstitutionalization movement by contributing to the tendency of mental hospitals to provide little more than custodial care.

Johnny M. After a traumatic childhood, "Johnny M." became emotionally disturbed and was committed to a mental hospital. As part of deinstitutionalization, he was discharged from the hospital and lived for awhile in a single room. After his building was converted into condominiums, he was left destitute to live on the streets.

The Right to Confidentiality

But what of the rights of individuals receiving therapy? One of the most important of their rights is the right to confidentiality. In general, therapists are ethically bound to keep confidential the information revealed by their clients. But the extent to which this information is privileged varies from state to state. In recent decades the most significant legal decision concerning confidentiality was the *Tarasoff decision*—a ruling by the California Supreme Court that a therapist who believes that a client might harm a particular person must personally warn that person. The ruling came in the case of Prosenjit Poddar, who murdered his former girlfriend Tatiana Tarasoff.

In 1969 Poddar had informed his therapist at the counseling center of the University of California at Berkeley that he intended to kill Tarasoff. The therapist reported the threat to the campus police, who ordered Poddar to stay away from Tarasoff. Two months later Poddar murdered her, leading her parents to sue the therapist, the police, and the university. In 1976 the court ruled in favor of the parents—the therapist should have warned Tarasoff about Poddar's threat (Everstine et al., 1980).

This decision upholding the *duty to warn* influenced similar decisions in other states and has provoked concern among therapists for several reasons. First, no therapist can reliably predict whether a threat made by a client is a serious threat (Rubin & Mills, 1983). If a student in a moment of anger says to a therapist, "I could just *kill* my psychology professor," should the therapist immediately warn the professor? Second, it may be impractical to warn potential victims. In one case, a client warned that he was going to kill "rich people"—he then murdered a wealthy couple. Considering the duty to warn, this prompted a therapist to ask whether a sign should have been posted reading, "All rich people watch out!" (Fisher, 1985).

Third, given the duty to warn, a therapist and a client might feel inhibited about discussing the client's hostility toward certain people, making the client even more likely to commit an act of violence. This possibility was the basis of a 1988 ruling by the Court of Appeals in North Carolina in the case of *Currie v. United States.* The court ruled that psychiatrists did not have a duty to commit people to mental hospitals for threatening acts of violence. The case concerned a 1982 murder in which Leonard Avery, who was under the care of Veteran's Administration psychiatrists, shot a fellow IBM employee after making threats against IBM. The victim's relatives sued, claiming that the psychiatrists should have committed Avery after he made threats against IBM. The court ruled that such a duty would prevent psychiatrists and clients from discussing hostile feelings, perhaps *increasing* the probability of violence (Bales, 1988).

THE SELECTION OF A THERAPIST

At times in your life, you or someone you know will face psychological problems that require more than friendly advice. When personal problems disrupt your social, academic, and vocational life, or when you experience severe and prolonged emotional distress, you might be wise to seek the help of a therapist. You could receive therapy from a psychologist, a psychiatrist, or a variety of other kinds of therapists (table 15.5). Just as there is no single way to find a physician, there is no single way to find a therapist.

You may have a friend, relative, or professor who can recommend a therapist or counseling center to you. Your college counseling center might be a good place to start. Other potential sources of help or referral include community mental-health centers, psychological associations, and mental-health

TABLE 15.5   Kinds of Therapists

Clinical Psychologist	A clinical psychologist has earned a doctoral degree in clinical psychology, including training in both research and clinical skills, and has served a one-year clinical internship. Clinical psychologists typically work in private practice, counseling centers, or mental hospitals.
Counseling Psychologist	A counseling psychologist has either a master's degree or a doctoral degree in counseling psychology. Counseling psychologists tend to have less training in research skills and tend to treat less severe or more narrow problems than do clinical psychologists. Thus, counseling psychologists might limit themselves to counseling families, married couples, or college students. Counseling psychologists typically work in private practice, mental-health centers, or college counseling centers. In fact, college counselors are more likely to be counseling psychologists, while hospital psychologists are more likely to be clinical psychologists (Watkins, Lopez, Campbell, & Himmell, 1986).
Pastoral Counselor	A pastoral counselor is a layperson or a member of the clergy who has earned a master's degree in pastoral counseling. Pastoral counselors combine spiritual and psychological counseling in their work in settings such as prisons, churches, hospitals, or counseling centers. Some people prefer seeing a pastoral counselor, because they find it less stigmatizing than seeing a clinical or counseling psychologist (Bales, 1986).
Psychiatrist	A psychiatrist is a physician who has served a three- or four-year residency in a mental hospital or a psychiatric ward of a general hospital. Though psychiatrists often rely on biomedical therapies, particularly drug therapy, some restrict their practices to psychotherapy. Psychiatrists usually work in private practice, psychiatric wards, or mental hospitals. A psychoanalyst is a psychiatrist (or, sometimes, a psychologist) with special training in psychoanalytic psychotherapy. Psychoanalysts receive their training at psychoanalytic institutes and almost always work in private practice.
Psychiatric Nurse	A psychiatric nurse is a registered nurse who has a master's degree (M.S.N.) in nursing and specialized training in psychiatric care. Psychiatric nurses usually work under the supervision of psychiatrists in psychiatric wards or mental hospitals.
Psychiatric Social Worker	A psychiatric social worker has a master's degree (M.S.W.) in social work and training in the counseling of individuals and families. Psychiatric social workers work in hospitals, private practice, human service agencies, and mental-health centers.
Paraprofessional	A paraprofessional may lack an advanced degree—or anything more than a high school diploma—but has special training in counseling people with certain problems, such as obesity, drug abuse, or criminal conduct. Paraprofessionals are often people who have overcome the problem that they treat and who work under professional supervision in mental-health centers or in self-help groups that help people with that problem.

associations. You can find many of these organizations, as well as private practitioners, listed in the Yellow Pages.

After finding a therapist, try to assess the therapist's credentials, reputation, therapeutic approach, and interpersonal manner as best you can. Does the therapist have legitimate academic and clinical training? Do you know anyone who will vouch for the therapist's competence? Does the therapist's approach make sense for your problem? Do you feel comfortable talking with the therapist? The therapist should be warm, open, concerned, and empathetic. If you find that you lack confidence in the therapist, feel free to seek help elsewhere. But, once in therapy, do not expect instant miracles. Nonetheless, if you make little progress after a reasonable length of time, feel free to end the relationship.

THINKING ABOUT PSYCHOLOGY

Is Psychotherapy
Effective?

In 1952 Hans Eysenck published an article that sparked a debate on the effectiveness of psychotherapy that has continued to this day. Based on his review of twenty-four studies of psychotherapy with neurotics (people usually suffering from anxiety or depression), Eysenck concluded that about two-thirds of those receiving psychotherapy improved. This would have provided strong evidence supporting the effectiveness of psychoanalysis (then the dominant form of psychotherapy) had Eysenck not also found that about two thirds of control subjects who had received *no* therapy also improved. He called improvement without therapy **spontaneous remission** and attributed it to beneficial factors occurring in the person's everyday life. Because those who received no therapy improved about as much as those who received therapy, Eysenck concluded that psychotherapy is ineffective.

Spontaneous Remission The improvement of some victims of psychological disorders without their undergoing formal therapy.

Eysenck's article provoked criticisms of its methodological shortcomings. One shortcoming was that many of the untreated people were under the care of physicians who prescribed drugs for them and provided informal counseling. Another shortcoming was that the treated groups and untreated groups were not equivalent, differing in educational level, socioeconomic status, and motivation to improve. This meant that the control group may have had a better initial prognosis than the treatment group. Still another shortcoming was that Eysenck overestimated the rate of spontaneous remission, which other researchers have found is closer to 40 percent than to 70 percent (Bergin & Lambert, 1978).

Evaluation of Psychotherapy

During the decades since Eysenck's article, hundreds of studies have assessed the effectiveness of psychotherapy. But this is a difficult scientific endeavor. For one thing, the definition of "effective" varies with the approach to therapy used. Psychoanalytic therapy would look for insight into unconscious conflicts originating in childhood and a resulting cathartic release of repressed emotions. Behavioral therapy would look for changes in maladaptive behaviors. R-E-T would look for rational changes in thinking. And person-centered therapy would look for greater acceptance of oneself, warts and all.

Moreover, who is to judge whether these changes have occurred? A survey of client satisfaction with psychotherapy found that about three-quarters of those who responded said that they were "satisfied" (Lebow, 1982). But clients, and therapists, may be biased in favor of reporting improvement. In some cases, friends, family members, teachers, or employers will also be asked for their assessment of the client to provide cross-validation of client and therapist assessments of improvement.

What has the admittedly imperfect research on the effectiveness of psychotherapy found? The general conclusion drawn from research conducted since Eysenck issued his challenge is that both psychotherapy and placebo therapy are more effective than no therapy, but, importantly, psychotherapy is more effective than placebo therapy. Placebo effects in psychotherapy are caused by factors such as the client's faith in the therapist's ability and the client's expectancy of success (Critelli & Neumann, 1984).

Mary Lee Smith and her colleagues (1980) published a comprehensive review that summarized the results of 475 studies on the effectiveness of psychotherapy. They found that, on the average, the typical psychotherapy client is better off than 80 percent of untreated persons. And, there is little overall difference in the effectiveness of the various approaches to therapy (figure 15.8). So, psychotherapy does work, but no single kind stands out as the best. If any kind of psychotherapy stands out as *somewhat* more effective than the others, it is behavioral therapy (Giles, 1983).

More recently, preliminary results of an ambitious ten-million-dollar study sponsored by the National Institute of Mental Health have lent further support

FIGURE 15.8
The Effectiveness of Psychotherapy Research has found that psychotherapy is effective, but that no approach is consistently better than any other approach. This graph shows the effectiveness of different kinds of therapy relative to no treatment. For example, people given psychodynamic (that is psychoanalytic) psychotherapy show, on the average, significantly greater improvement than about 80 percent of untreated people (Smith, Glass, & Miller, 1980).

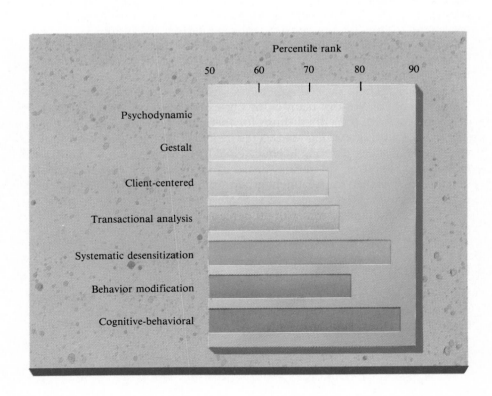

to the effectiveness of psychotherapy. The study randomly assigned 239 severely depressed subjects into four groups. Twenty-eight therapists were trained in each of the psychotherapy treatments, which were offered at three different universities—the University of Pittsburgh, the University of Oklahoma, and the George Washington University. One group received Beck's cognitive therapy. A second group received interpersonal psychotherapy (a derivative of psychoanalytic therapy). A third group received the antidepressant drug imipramine. And a fourth group received a placebo treatment involving a placebo pill and a minimal amount of social support from a therapist.

The participants were assessed after sixteen weeks of therapy and again at a follow-up eighteen months later. As expected, all of the groups improved, with the three forms of active therapy eliminating depression in 50 to 60 percent of the subjects and the placebo therapy eliminating depression in 29 percent of the subjects. There were no differences in effectiveness between the three active forms of therapy. Though drug therapy relieved symptoms more quickly, the two psychotherapies eventually caught up (Mervis, 1986).

Factors in the Effectiveness of Psychotherapy

Given the consensus that psychotherapy is effective and that no approach is significantly more effective than any other approach, researchers are faced with the question, What factors account for the effectiveness of psychotherapy? In trying to answer this question, researchers study therapy characteristics, client characteristics, and therapist characteristics.

Therapy Characteristics A review by Lester Luborsky and his colleagues (1971) of therapy, client, and therapist factors found that the worst predictor of success in therapy was the nature of the therapy itself. The only important therapy characteristic was the number of therapy sessions—the more sessions, the more improvement. A more recent review of fifteen studies of psychotherapy using more than 2,400 clients found that 50 percent of clients improved by eight sessions and 75 percent improved by twenty-six sessions (figure 15.9). Additional sessions added little to the

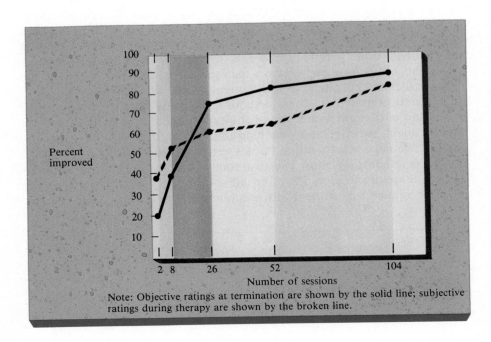

FIGURE 15.9
The Length of Therapy and Therapy Effectiveness As the number of therapy sessions increases, the percentage of clients who improve increases. But after the twenty-sixth session, additional sessions help relatively few clients. Note that there is a slight difference between objective ratings of improvement given by therapists and subjective ratings given by the clients themselves, though the general trend is similar for both (Howard, Kopta, Krausse, & Orlinsky, 1986)

Percent improved

Number of sessions

Note: Objective ratings at termination are shown by the solid line; subjective ratings during therapy are shown by the broken line.

therapeutic outcome, indicating that most clients gain maximum benefit from relatively brief psychotherapy (Howard, Kopta, Krausse, & Orlinsky, 1986).

Client Characteristics The review by Luborsky and his colleagues (1971) found that the best predictor of success was client characteristics. Clients were more likely to improve if they had more education, higher intelligence, and higher socioeconomic status. Improvement was also greatest in those with less severe disorders, more adequate personalities, and greater motivation to change.

Therapist Characteristics The review by Luborsky and his colleagues (1971) found that the second-best predictor of success was therapist characteristics. Clients were more likely to improve if their therapists had more experience and were perceived as empathetic. The client's perception of therapist empathy, in particular, has been consistently identified as an important factor in the effectiveness of psychotherapy (Free, Green, Grace, Chernus, & Whitman, 1985), a factor first noted by Carl Rogers. In fact, Rogers began the formal study of the research process by taping his therapy sessions and analyzing his interactions with clients (Gendlin, 1988). This might surprise those who criticize the humanistic perspective as being unscientific.

The greater importance of therapist empathy than the kind of professional training has been supported by research showing that empathetic people may be as effective as trained psychotherapists in treating psychological problems. In one study, Vanderbilt University students with anxiety-inducing problems were treated by either professional psychotherapists or empathetic professors. The results showed that the psychotherapists and the professors were equally effective in helping the students (Strupp & Hadley, 1979).

Additional support for the importance of personal, as well as professional, skills came from a review of research on the effectiveness of *paraprofessionals,* people who usually have less training and experience than professionals but who help in the treatment of specific problems. The review found that paraprofessionals are at least as effective as professionals (Hattie, Sharpley, & Rogers, 1984). This indicates that certain personal characteristics of therapists, rather than their training and experience, may determine their effectiveness. But, in general, studies indicate that professional training does add something to the therapeutic process, making well-trained therapists more effective than less-trained "caring people" (Bowers & Clum, 1988). For example, professional therapists are more effective than paraprofessionals in reducing the emotional distress of chemotherapy patients (Carey & Burish, 1987).

Researchers are refining their methods to study the more precise question, What kind of therapy, offered by what kind of therapist, is helpful for what kind of client, experiencing what kind of problem, in what kind of circumstances? We must wait for future studies testing interactions among these factors to determine the most effective combinations. For example, perhaps systematic desensitization offered by an empathetic psychologist will prove superior for a college student with a public-speaking phobia.

SUMMARY

THE HISTORY OF THERAPY

People with psychological disorders may seek professional therapy. Modern therapy has come a long way since its ancient origins. In trephining, sharp holes were cut in the skull to release evil spirits that were alleged to cause abnormal behavior. Hippocrates introduced a more naturalistic form of treatment, recommending procedures to restore the balance of body humors. The Renaissance saw the appearance of insane asylums. While some, such as Bedlam, were awful places, others, such as Geel, provided humane treatment. Near the end of the eighteenth century, Phillippe Pinel released asylum inmates and championed moral therapy. Moral therapy was introduced to America by Benjamin Rush, who also used unusual devices for treating certain disorders. Through the efforts of Dorothea Dix, state mental hospitals were built throughout the United States. But they became crowded and deteriorated into mere human warehouses. In the early twentieth century, a book by Clifford Beers, describing his horrible experiences in a mental hospital, led to the founding of the mental-health movement, promoting the prevention and humane treatment of psychological disorders.

THE PSYCHOANALYTIC ORIENTATION

After hearing Joseph Breuer's report of the benefits of catharsis in the case of Anna O., Sigmund Freud developed psychoanalysis. The main procedures in psychoanalysis are the analysis of free associations, dreams, resistances, and transference. The goal of these procedures is to have the client gain insight into unconscious conflicts and experience catharsis.

THE BEHAVIORAL ORIENTATION

The behavioral orientation emphasizes the importance of learning and environmental influences. Two of the main kinds of behavioral therapy based on classical conditioning are systematic desensitization, useful in treating phobias, and aversion therapy, useful in making formerly pleasurable, but maladaptive, behavior unpleasant. One of the main uses of the operant conditioning principle of positive reinforcement is the token economy, especially useful in institutional settings. The operant conditioning principle of punishment is useful in eliminating behaviors, such as self-injurious behavior in autistic children. Albert Bandura's social learning theory has contributed participant modeling as a way to overcome phobias.

THE COGNITIVE ORIENTATION

The cognitive orientation assumes that thoughts, rather than events themselves, cause psychological disorders. In Albert Ellis's rational-emotive therapy, the client learns to change irrational thinking. Aaron Beck developed cognitive therapy to help depressed people think less negatively about themselves, the world, and the future. And Donald Meichenbaum uses stress inoculation training to help people be more optimistic when in stressful situations.

THE HUMANISTIC ORIENTATION

The humanistic orientation emphasizes the importance of being aware of one's emotions and feeling free to express them. Carl Rogers's person-centered therapy, a form of nondirective therapy, helps clients come up with their own solutions to their problems. In contrast, Fritz Perls's Gestalt therapy is more directive in making clients face their true feelings and act on them.

THE SOCIAL RELATIONS ORIENTATION

The social relations orientation assumes that people cannot be treated as isolated individuals. In group therapy, people, usually strangers, are brought together for therapy. Group therapy derived from the psychoanalytic approach includes psychodrama and transactional analysis. Group therapy derived from the behavioral approach includes social skills training and assertiveness training. And group therapy derived from the humanistic approach includes sensitivity groups and encounter groups. In family therapy, family members gain insight into their unhealthy patterns of interaction and learn to change them.

THE BIOMEDICAL ORIENTATION

The biomedical orientation uses medical procedures to treat psychological disorders. The main procedures include psychosurgery (rarely used today), electroconvulsive therapy for depression, and drug therapy. Psychiatrists may prescribe antianxiety drugs, antipsychotic drugs, antidepressant drugs, and antimanic drugs.

COMMUNITY MENTAL HEALTH

The community mental-health movement was stimulated by deinstitutionalization, the treatment of people in community settings instead of in mental hospitals. Commmunity mental-health centers aid in both the prevention and treatment of psychological disorders. But the failure to provide adequate housing and services for former mental hospital patients has contributed to the growing homelessness problem.

THE RIGHTS OF THE THERAPY CLIENT

Laws require that formal procedures be followed before a person is committed to a mental hospital. Once in a mental hospital, patients have the right to refuse treatment and the right to receive treatment. What clients reveal in therapy sessions is normally confidential, but legal cases have led to the concept of the duty to warn.

THE SELECTION OF A THERAPIST

There are many kinds of therapists, including both professionals and paraprofessionals. You should be as careful in selecting a therapist as you are in selecting a physician.

THINKING ABOUT PSYCHOLOGY: IS PSYCHOTHERAPY EFFECTIVE?

In 1952 Hans Eysenck challenged the world of psychotherapy by claiming that people who received psychotherapy improved no more than did people who received no therapy. Subsequent research has shown that psychotherapy is better than no therapy and better than placebo therapy. But no single kind of therapy stands out as clearly superior to the rest. More sophisticated research is required to determine the ideal combinations of therapy, therapist, client, and problem factors.

IMPORTANT CONCEPTS

IMPORTANT PEOPLE

RECOMMENDED READINGS

For More on All Aspects of Therapy:

Corsini, R. J. (Ed.). (1989). *Current psychotherapies* (4th ed.). Itasca, IL: Peacock.

A collection of chapters written by prominent therapists, describing their approaches to psychotherapy.

Zeig, J. K. (Ed.). (1987). *The evolution of psychotherapy.* New York: Brunner/Mazel.

A collection of articles on all forms of psychotherapy written by outstanding proponents of them and based on presentations they made at the largest conference on psychotherapy ever held, which attracted seven thousand psychotherapists and earned the name of "the Woodstock of psychotherapy."

For More on the History of Therapy:

Reisman, J. M. (1976). *A history of clinical psychology.* New York: Irvington.

A fascinating account of the history of psychotherapy from ancient times into the twentieth century.

For More on the Psychoanalytic Approach:

Fisher, S., & Greenberg, R. P. (1985). *The scientific credibility of Freud's theories and therapy.* New York: Columbia University Press.

A review of research on psychoanalytic theory, including the practice of psychoanalysis.

For More on the Behavioral Approach:

O'Leary, K. D., & Wilson, G. T. (1987). *Behavior therapy: Application and outcome* (2nd ed.). Englewood Cliffs, NJ: Prentice-Hall.

A presentation of major behavior therapy techniques and their effectiveness in treating particular disorders.

For More on the Cognitive Approach:

Meichenbaum, D. (1985). *Stress-inoculation training.* New York: Pergamon Press.

A discussion of how to change our patterns of thinking to adapt better to stressful situations.

For More on the Humanistic Approach:

Rogers, C. R. (1961). *On becoming a person: A therapist's view of psychotherapy.* Boston: Houghton Mifflin.

A discussion of client-centered (now known as person-centered) therapy by its inventor.

For More on the Social Relations Approach:

Bentovim, A., Barnes, G. G., & Cooklin, A. (Eds.). (1988). *Family therapy* (2nd ed.). New York: Academic Press.

A textbook discussing the principles and practice of family therapy.

For More on the Biomedical Approach:

Valenstein, E. S. (1986). *Great and desperate cures: The rise and decline of psychosurgery and other radical treatments for mental illness.* New York: Basic Books.

A thought-provoking presentation of the uses and abuses of biomedical treatments of psychological disorders.

For More on Community Mental Health:

Bassuk, E. L. (1984, July). The homelessness problem. *Scientific American,* pp. 40–45.

A readable article discussing the negative effect of deinstitutionalization on the homelessness problem.

For More on the Rights of the Therapy Client:

Simon, C. (1988, June). Boundaries of confidence. *Psychology Today,* pp. 23–26.

A discussion of the dilemma between the rights of the therapy client and the rights of society in regard to confidentiality.

For More on the Effectiveness of Psychotherapy:

Garfield, S. L., & Bergin, A. E. (Eds.). (1986). *Handbook of psychotherapy and behavior change* (3rd ed.). New York: Wiley.

A review of issues and research findings regarding all of the major approaches to psychotherapy.

CHAPTER 16

Psychology and Health

Chapter Opening Art:
Henri Matisse. *La
Negresse.*

D o you overeat? smoke cigarettes? prefer alcoholic beverages? drive recklessly? exercise rarely? fail to follow your physician's medical recommendations? respond inefficiently to stressful situations? These are among the leading causes of death in the United States. In fact, according to the National Academy of Sciences, half of the mortality from the ten leading causes of death is strongly influenced by life-style (Hamburg, 1982).

This conclusion would not have been true at the turn of the century, when most Americans died from infectious diseases such as influenza, pneumonia, or tuberculosis. But the development of vaccines and antibiotics and improved public sanitation practices led to a decline in the importance of infectious diseases and a surge in the importance of unhealthy or dangerous behaviors as factors contributing to illness and death. Today, we are more likely to become ill or die because of our own actions than because of viruses or bacteria invading our bodies. So, you are more likely to hear of a smoker who has died from lung cancer than of a person struck down by polio—an all too common event until the development of the Salk vaccine in the 1950s.

The field of psychology that studies the role of behavioral factors in the promotion of health and the prevention of illness and injury is called **health psychology.** Health psychologists favor a *biopsychosocial model* of health and illness, emphasizing the interaction of biological, psychological, and social factors. In contrast, the traditional biomedical approach neglects psychological and social factors. Health psychologists study the relationship between stress and illness, the effects of health-impairing habits, and reactions to illness.

STRESS AND ILLNESS

In the 1960s, students attending Penn State University, recognizing their isolation in peaceful, rural State College, Pennsylvania, dubbed State College and its surroundings "Happy Valley." The students were vindicated two decades later, in 1988, when a California psychologist named Robert Levine reported the results of his survey of living conditions in the United States. He concluded that State College had the distinction of being the least stressful place to live in the United States (Rossi, 1988).

What is *stress?* According to the Austrian-born Canadian endocrinologist Hans Selye, the father of stress research, **stress** is the physiological response of the body to physical and psychological demands. Such demands are known as **stressors.** Though stress has been implicated as a factor in illness, some degree of stress is normal, necessary, and unavoidable. As Selye has noted, "Complete freedom from stress is death" (Selye, 1980, p. 128). Stress acts as a motivator to make us adjust our behavior to meet changing demands—for example, studying for an upcoming exam, wearing a sweater in cold weather, or seeking companionship when lonely. Stress can even be pleasurable, as when attending a party, shooting rapids on a raft, or playing a game of Scrabble. Selye called unpleasant stress *distress* and pleasant stress *eustress* (from the Greek for "good stress").

Sources of Stress

There are three general categories of stressors. One category includes frustrations. **Frustration** occurs when you are blocked from reaching a goal. Minor frustrations include waiting in line at a movie theater or performing poorly on an exam. Major frustrations include losing one's job or flunking out of school. A second category of stressors includes pressures. **Pressure** occurs when you

Behavioral Causes of Illness and Death Half of the mortality from the leading causes of death in the United States is influenced by unhealthy or dangerous behaviors, such as overeating, failing to exercise, and overexposing oneself to the sun.

Health Psychology The field that applies psychological principles to the prevention and treatment of physical illness.

Stress The body's physiological adjustment to physical and psychological demands.

Stressor A physical or psychological demand to which the body must adjust.

Frustration The emotional state induced when one is blocked from reaching a goal.

Pressure The emotional state induced when one is confronted by personal responsibilities.

must fulfill responsibilities that tax your abilities. You experience pressure when you write a research paper or work to pay for your tuition.

Even great athletes experience pressure during competition. Consider the pressure of playing in a professional sports championship. A review of baseball World Series records from 1924 through 1982 and National Basketball Association championship records from 1967 through 1982 found that, contrary to popular belief, the home team in the deciding game of a championship series is more likely to lose than to win (Baumeister & Steinhilber, 1984). Thus, there seems to be a home-field *disadvantage* in deciding games. In contrast, in earlier, nondeciding games, the home team does maintain a home-field advantage.

What could explain the difference in home-team performance between early games and deciding games? The researchers attributed this to the increased *pressure* of playing important games before home fans. This pressure makes home-team players more self-conscious, which, in turn, makes them pay attention to their performance of skilled movements that they normally perform automatically with little or no conscious awareness. As a result, the home-team players may become less fluid in their movements and more prone to perform below their normal levels of ability. For example, in baseball the home teams made significantly more errors in seventh games than in earlier games. And in basketball the home team's shooting percentage was significantly lower in seventh games than in earlier games. Evidently, the pressure of performing before wildly cheering home fans may cause members of the home team to "choke."

A third category of stressors includes conflicts. **Conflict** occurs when you are torn between two or more potential courses of action. In an *approach-approach conflict,* you are torn between two desirable courses of action. This might occur when one friend invites you to go to a party and another invites you to attend a concert. This is the least stressful kind of conflict, because both options are desirable. In an *avoidance-avoidance conflict,* you are forced to choose between two unpleasant courses of action. You may experience this when deciding whether to go to the dentist or suffer with a toothache. Though you might delay making a choice for as long as possible, the conflict is re-

Conflict The emotional state induced when one is torn between two or more potential courses of action.

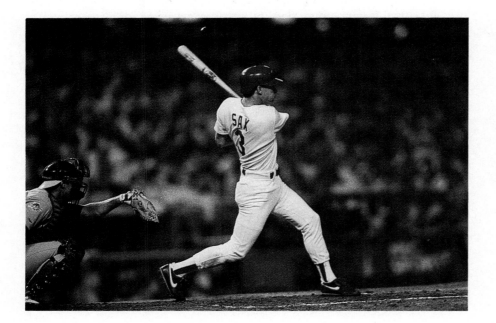

Pressure and the Home Field Disadvantage In deciding games of the World Series, the pressure of playing before home fans may interfere with the home team's performance. The players may become so self-conscious that they attend to normally automatic, unconscious movements. As a result, they may lose their normal timing and coordination, hampering their performance.

Drawing by Lorenz; © 1981 The New Yorker Magazine, Inc.

solved when one option forces you to choose it. An unbearable toothache would eventually make you go to the dentist.

In an *approach-avoidance conflict,* you are simultaneosly drawn to and repelled by the same goal. College seniors may experience this when they consider their upcoming graduation, which has both desirable and undesirable aspects. In an approach-avoidance conflict, you would vacillate, sometimes moving toward the goal, at other times moving away from it. When you are far from the goal, your approach tendency will be relatively stronger than your avoidance tendency (figure 16.1). In contrast, when you near the goal, your avoidance tendency will be relatively stronger than your approach tendency.

Consider engaged couples, who commonly experience an approach-avoidance conflict. At first, when they get engaged, their approach tendency is much stronger than their avoidance tendency. But, as they get closer and closer to the wedding day, they may begin to get "cold feet" as they think more about the negative aspects of marriage. In extreme cases, the avoidance tendency may become so strong that the bride or groom fails to appear at the wedding ceremony.

Frustrations, pressures, and conflicts are often associated with chronically stressful situations, including poverty, unhappy marriages, or diseases such as diabetes. Though health psychologists study the effects of chronic stress, they show a preference for studying the effects of more acute events, including life changes, such as moving, and daily hassles, such as failing an exam. Of course, chronic stressors, life changes, and daily hassles are interrelated and may affect one another (Eckenrode, 1984).

Life Changes Throughout life each of us must adjust to *life changes,* which may be pleasant (such as graduation from college) or unpleasant (such as the death of a loved one). Interest in the relationship between life changes and illness began when Thomas Holmes and Richard Rahe (1967) developed the *Social Readjustment Rating Scale.* Holmes and Rahe asked medical patients to report positive and negative life changes that had occurred during the months before they became ill. This generated a list of forty-three kinds of life changes (table 16.1).

Another sample of people were then asked to rate, on a one-hundred-point scale, the degree of life change, or *adjustment,* required by each of the forty-three. Each kind of life change was rated relative to marriage, which Holmes and Rahe gave the arbitrary value of fifty. Note that the death of a spouse has

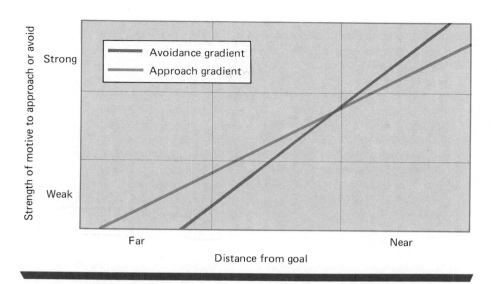

FIGURE 16.1
Approach-Avoidance Conflict
In an approach-avoidance conflict, both the approach and avoidance tendencies increase in strength the closer you get to a goal. But the avoidance tendency increases more rapidly. Vacillation between approach and avoidance will be greatest at the point where the two tendencies are of about equal strength. In the graph, this is the point where the approach and avoidance gradients cross.

the highest rating—one hundred points—while minor violations of the law have the lowest rating—eleven points. Also note that the scale includes both negative events, such as the foreclosure of a mortgage or loan, and positive events, such as Christmas.

A person's *life change score* is the sum of the scores for his or her life changes that occurred in a given period of time, generally the past year. Holmes and Rahe found that people who had a total life change score of more than three hundred points in the preceding year were more than twice as likely to become ill as people who had a total of less than three hundred points. Though Holmes and Rahe assumed that adjustment to changes brought about by life events—whether positive or negative—induced stress, subsequent research has shown that it is the nature of the events, rather than change itself, that induces stress. Negative life changes tend to induce stress, while neutral or positive life changes do not (Monroe, 1982).

Hundreds of studies have also shown that exposure to negative life changes is associated with illness. For example, because unemployment is the most powerful predictor of death from cardiovascular disease, people who have lost their jobs may become truly "heart sick" (Liem & Rayman, 1982). People who experience traumatic events, such as war or natural disasters, may experience **posttraumatic stress disorder,** which may appear from months to years after the event and is marked by anxiety, detachment, nightmares, insomnia, survivor guilt, and flashbacks of the event. Though posttraumatic stress disorder may occur following any of a variety of events, including rape, kidnapping, earthquakes, and airplane crashes, it has been most widely publicized in regard to the minority of Vietnam War veterans who developed symptoms years after returning to the United States (Kaylor, King, & King, 1987).

Posttraumatic stress disorder is associated with an increased risk of physical illness. For example, in 1980 a natural disaster struck the state of Washington—the eruption of the Mount Saint Helen's volcano in the Cascade Mountains. Though more than one hundred miles from the volcano, the town of Othello was covered by volcanic ash. Residents of that farming community suffered the distress of having their fields covered with ash, the fear of the effects of the ash on their health, and the dread that the volcano would erupt again. During the six months following the disaster, a local medical clinic reported an almost 200-percent increase in stress-related illnesses among the residents of Othello. There was also an almost 20-percent increase in the local death rate (Adams & Adams, 1984).

Posttraumatic Stress Disorder
People who experience unusually stressful events may develop a posttraumatic stress disorder marked by emotional and physical symptoms. Interest in this disorder was stimulated by symptoms experienced by veterans of the Vietnam War.

Posttraumatic Stress Disorder
A syndrome of physical and psychological symptoms that appears as a delayed response after exposure to an extremely emotionally distressing event.

TABLE 16.1   Social Readjustment Rating Scale

Life Event	Mean Value
Death of spouse	100
Divorce	73
Marital separation	65
Jail term	63
Death of close family member	63
Personal injury or illness	53
Marriage	50
Fired at work	47
Marital reconciliation	45
Retirement	45
Change in health of family member	44
Pregnancy	40
Sex difficulties	39
Gain of new family member	39
Business readjustment	39
Change in financial state	38
Death of close friend	37
Change to different line of work	36
Change in number of arguments with spouse	35
Mortgage or loan for major purchase (home, etc.)	31
Foreclosure on mortgage or loan	30
Change in responsibilities at work	29
Son or daughter leaving home	29
Trouble with in-laws	29
Outstanding personal achievement	28
Spouse begins or stops work	26
Begin or end school	26
Change in living conditions	25
Revision of personal habits	24
Trouble with boss	23
Change in work hours or conditions	20
Change in residence	20
Change in schools	20
Change in recreation	19
Change in church activities	19
Change in social activities	18
Mortgage or loan for lesser purchase (car, TV, etc.)	17
Change in sleeping habits	16
Change in number of family get-togethers	15
Change in eating habits	15
Vacation	13
Christmas	12
Minor violations of the law	11

Reprinted with permission from *Journal of Psychosomatic Research*, 11, T. H. Holmes and R. H. Rahe, "The Social Readjustment Scale," Copyright 1967, Pergamon Press plc.

Daily Hassles A decade ago Richard Lazarus and his colleagues investigated the possibility that the hassles of everyday life, and not only life changes, are associated with stress (Kanner, Coyne, Schaefer, & Lazarus,

1981). Everyday hassles include forgetting one's keys, being stuck in traffic, or dealing with a rude salesperson. Such hassles are associated with subsequent health problems, including headaches, sore throats, and influenza (DeLongis, Folkman, & Lazarus, 1988).

Life changes may, in fact, promote illness indirectly by increasing everyday hassles (Weinberger, Hiner, & Tierney, 1987). Suppose that a man gets divorced—a major life change. The stress he experiences might be a product of not only the divorce itself but also of the new daily hassles with which he must now cope. Perhaps he must for the first time shop for his own food, cook his own meals, do his own laundry, and iron his own shirts. His adrenal glands may respond by increasing their secretion of the hormones cortisol, epinephrine, and norepinephrine (Brantley, Dietz, McKnight, Jones, & Tulley, 1988). Though these hormones make us better able to adapt to stressors, they also impair our resistance to disease.

Most research on the relationship between daily hassles and illnesses makes it difficult to determine whether they are merely correlated or whether hassles actually promote illness. This is so because there have been few *prospective* studies of the relationship between hassles and health. A prospective study would investigate whether a person's current level of hassles is predictive of his or her future health. One of the few prospective studies of the effect of daily hassles found that they may, in fact, promote illness. On two occasions, adolescent girls who served as subjects in the study were asked to indicate whether each of twenty commonly experienced circumstances had occurred in their lives and whether they rated its occurrence as positive or negative. They also completed an illness symptoms checklist and a personality test measuring depression. The results showed that negative circumstances were associated with depression and poor health. But this was true only when the girls also reported low levels of positive circumstances. Apparently, positive circumstances may buffer the effects of negative ones, making them have less of an effect (Siegel & Brown, 1988).

Effects of Stress

Stress, whether caused by chronic circumstances, life changes, or daily hassles, is marked by physiological arousal and, in some cases, reduced resistance to disease. In the nineteenth century, noted English physician Daniel Hack Tuke wrote one of the first books on the physiological effects of psychological stressors, *Illustrations of the Influence of the Mind on the Body* (Weiss, 1972). More than a century later, Tuke's intellectual descendants study the effects of both physical and psychological stressors on physiological arousal. As explained in chapter 11, physical and psychological stressors evoke the *fight-or-flight response,* involving activation of the sympathetic nervous system and secretion of stress hormones by the adrenal glands.

In the mid-1930s, Hans Selye (1936), hoping to discover a new sex hormone, injected rats with extracts from ovaries. He found that the rats developed enlarged adrenal glands and atrophied spleens, thymus glands, and lymph nodes. Selye later observed that rats displayed this same response to a variety of stressors, including cold, heat, injuries, and infections. This indicated that his initial findings were not necessarily caused by a sex hormone. Selye also found that animals and people, in reacting to stressors, go through three stages, which he called the **general adaptation syndrome.** During the first stage, the *alarm reaction,* the body prepares to cope with the stressor by increasing activity in the sympathetic nervous system and adrenal glands (the fight-or-flight response). Selye noted that during the alarm stage different stressors produced similar symptoms, such as fatigue, fevers, headaches, and loss of appetite.

General Adaptation Syndrome As first identified by Hans Selye, the body's stress response, which includes the stages of alarm, resistance, and exhaustion.

Hans Selye (1907–1982) "Even prehistoric man must have recognized a common element in the sense of exhaustion that overcame him in conjunction with hard labor, agonizing fear, lengthy exposure to cold or heat, starvation, loss of blood, or any kind of disease."

If the body continues to be exposed to the stressor, it enters the *stage of resistance,* during which it becomes more resistant to the stressor. The stage of resistance is like the second wind you may experience while playing a sport or while studying for a final exam. During a second wind, your initial fatigue gives way to a feeling of renewed energy and well-being. Though resistance to a given stressor increases during the resistance stage, resistance to disease may decline. During final exam week you may be able to cope well enough to study for all your exams despite a decrease in sleep, exercise, recreation, and normal meals, but soon after the finals are over you may come down with the flu.

In rare cases, a person under chronic stress succumbs and enters the *stage of exhaustion.* At this point, the person's resistance to disease collapses and death may follow. Though Selye believed that all stressors produce similar patterns of physiological responses, research has shown that different stressors may produce different patterns (Krantz & Manuck, 1984). Your physiological response to rush-hour traffic may be different from your physiological response to a job interview.

Stress and Noninfectious Diseases As noted in chapter 11, the fight-or-flight response evolved to help animals and human beings cope with periodic stressors, such as wild fires or animal attacks. Unfortunately, in twentieth-century America we are subjected to continual, rather than periodic, stressors. The infrequent saber-toothed tiger attack has been replaced by rush-hour traffic jams, three exams on one day, and threats of muggers on city streets. The repeated activation of the fight-or-flight response takes its toll on the body, possibly causing or aggravating noninfectious diseases, such as stomach ulcers (Young, Richter, Bradley, & Anderson, 1987).

Of all the diseases that are influenced by stress, coronary heart disease has received the most attention from health psychologists. As discussed later in the chapter, coronary heart disease is caused by **atherosclerosis,** which is promoted by cholesterol deposits in the coronary arteries. Even the stress of

Atherosclerosis The narrowing of arteries caused by the accumulation of fatty deposits.

everyday college life may affect the level of cholesterol in your blood. In fact, college students merely anticipating an upcoming exam show significant increases in their levels of blood cholesterol (Van Doornen & van Blokland, 1987). Stress may also promote coronary heart disease by stimulating the repeated elevation of heart rate and blood pressure. This may damage the walls of the coronary arteries by increasing blood turbulence and levels of stress hormones in the blood, making the walls of the coronary arteries more susceptible to the buildup of cholesterol plaques (Krantz & Manuck, 1984). The effect of atherosclerosis on the coronary arteries is illustrated in figure 16.2.

Stress and Infectious Diseases In 1884 a physician writing in a British medical journal observed that the depression experienced by mourners at funerals predisposes them to develop illnesses (Baker, 1987). A century later, a research study provided a scientific basis for this observation. As shown in figure 16.3, the study found that men whose wives had died of breast cancer showed impaired functioning of their immune systems during the first two months of their bereavement (Schleifer, Keller, Camerino, Thornton, & Stein, 1983). The realization that stressful events, such as the death of a loved one, can impair the immune system led to the emergence of **psychoneuroimmunology,** the interdisciplinary field that studies the relationship between stress factors and illness. This field recognizes the interaction of psychological, neurological, and immunological factors in causing disease.

Though many of the mechanisms by which stress suppresses the immune system remain to be determined, one mechanism is well established (figure 16.4). Stress prompts the hypothalamus to secrete a hormone that stimulates the pituitary gland to secrete adrenocorticotropic hormone (ACTH), which then stimulates the adrenal cortex to secrete corticosteroids. The hypothalamus also increases activity in the sympathetic nervous system, which stimulates the adrenal medulla to secrete the hormones epinephrine and norepinephrine. As noted earlier, while corticosteroids, epinephrine, and norepinephrine make us more resistant to stressors, they also impair our immune systems.

The cells chiefly responsible for the immunological response to infections are white blood cells called B-lymphocytes and T-lymphocytes. While *B-lymphocytes* attack invading bacteria, *T-lymphocytes* attack viruses, cancer cells, and foreign tissues. The immunosuppressive effects of stress hormones may explain why Apollo astronauts returning to Earth from stressful trips to the moon showed impaired immune responses (Jemmott & Locke, 1984).

But you do not have to go to the moon to experience stress-induced suppression of your immune response, as demonstrated in a study of dental students. The students recorded their daily mood three times a week for eight weeks. On each occasion a sample of their saliva was taken and mixed with an *antigen* (a substance that induces an immune response). The results showed that their B-lymphocyte response to the antigen was stronger on days on which they were in a good mood than on days on which they were in a bad mood (Stone, Cox, Validimarsdottir, Jandorf, & Neale, 1987).

The relationship between stress and the immune system is of special importance to victims of *acquired immune deficiency syndrome (AIDS)*, who suffer stress induced by both their illness and hostile social reactions to them. Such stress might further impair the functioning of their immune systems, making them even more vulnerable to potentially fatal infections (Kiecolt-Glaser & Glaser, 1988).

There is also evidence that the immune response may be subject to classical conditioning, meaning that normally neutral stimuli may come to enhance it or to suppress it. A leading researcher in this area has been Robert

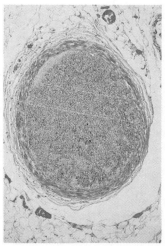

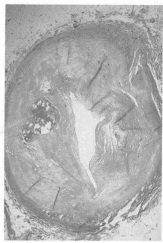

FIGURE 16.2
Atherosclerosis Diets high in cholesterol contribute to atherosclerosis, which narrows coronary arteries and predisposes the person to heart attacks. The top photograph shows a cross-section of a healthy artery, and the bottom photograph shows a cross-section of an atherosclerotic artery.

Psychoneuroimmunology The interdisciplinary field that studies the relationship between psychological factors and physical illness.

FIGURE 16.3
Bereavement and the Immune Response During the first two months after the deaths of their wives, widowers show a decrease in the proliferation of lymphocytes in response to doses of antigens (Schleifer et al., 1983).

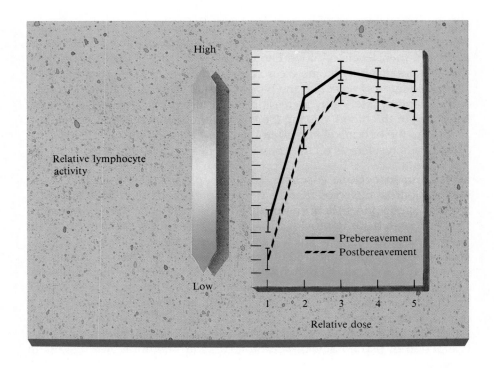

FIGURE 16.4
Stress Pathways When the cerebral cortex processes stressful memories or stressful input from the immediate environment, it stimulates a physiological response by way of the endocrine system and the sympathetic nervous system. Both pathways involve the hypothalamus. The hypothalamus signals the pituitary gland, which secretes adrenocorticotropic hormone (ACTH). ACTH, in turn, stimulates the adrenal cortex to secrete corticosteroid hormones, which mobilize the body's energy stores, reduce tissue inflammation, and inhibit the immune response. The hypothalamus also sends signals through the sympathetic nervous system to the adrenal medulla, which, in turn, stimulates the release of epinephrine and norepinephrine. These hormones contribute to the physiological arousal characteristic of the "fight-or-flight" response.

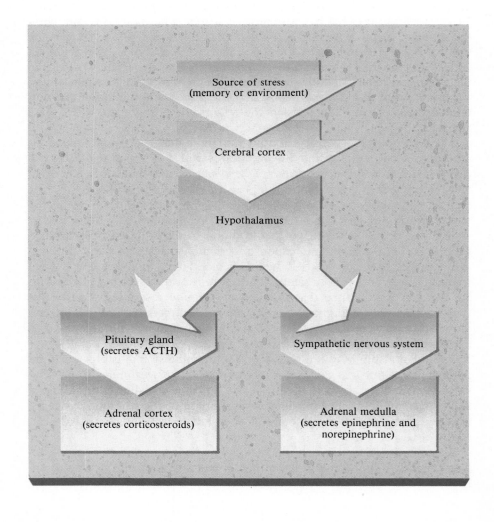

Ader. In a study demonstrating conditioned suppression of the immune response, Ader and his colleague Nicholas Cohen (1982) gave tastes of saccharin-flavored water to mice and then injected them with a drug called cyclophosphamide, which induces nausea. As expected, the mice developed an aversion to sweet-tasting water. But when some of the mice were later forced to drink sweet-tasting water, several of them developed illnesses and died. Ader and Cohen attributed this to another effect of cyclophosphamide—the suppression of the immune response. They apparently had conditioned suppression of the mice's immune response, with the sweet-tasting water serving as the conditioned stimulus (figure 16.5). Perhaps classical conditioning may one day be applied to suppress undesirable immune responses, such as those that occur in allergic reactions, or to enhance the immune responses in people who have low resistances to infections. Though this is not yet possible, it is hypothetically feasible.

Stress and Cancer Stress has also been linked to cancer. While stress may indirectly promote cancer by encouraging cancer-inducing behaviors, such as smoking tobacco, eating high-fat foods, and drinking too much alcohol, stress may also directly interfere with the immune system's ability to defend against cancer. You should note, however, that there is no evidence that stress can make normal cells become cancerous. Though stress does not *cause* cancer, it does interfere with the immune system's ability to destroy cancerous cells (Justice, 1985).

In the second century A.D., the Roman physician Galen noted that depressed women were more likely to develop cancer than were happy women. Modern research has produced inconsistent findings concerning this apparent relationship between emotions and cancer. In one study, medical students who had been given personality tests in medical school were followed retrospectively for thirty years. Of those who were emotionally expressive, less than 1 percent developed cancer. Those who were loners, and presumably more emotionally controlled, were sixteen times more likely to develop cancer

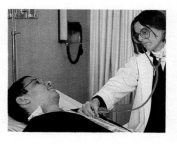

Stress and AIDS The stress of their illness combined with the stress of hostile responses to them may further impair the immune response of AIDS victims, increasing their susceptibility to life-threatening infections.

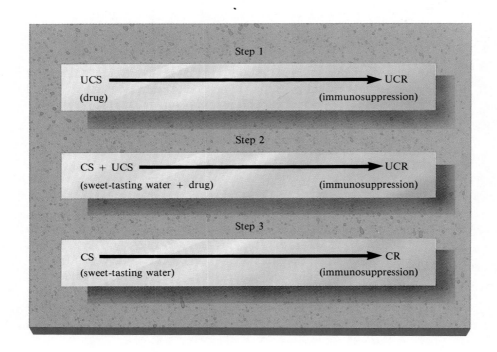

FIGURE 16.5
Conditioned Immuno-suppression When Ader and Cohen (1982) paired saccharin-sweetened water with cyclophosphamide, a drug that suppresses the immune response, they found that the sweet-tasting water itself came to elicit immunosuppression. (See chapter 6 for a discussion of the relationship between the UCS, UCR, CS, and CR.)

than were those who were emotionally expressive (Shaffer, Graves, Swank, & Pearson, 1987).

But research linking emotion and cancer has been countered by research failing to find such an association. A study of 6,848 people followed from 1965 to 1982 in Alameda County, California, found a relationship between depression and death from causes other than cancer but no relationship between depression and cancer incidence or mortality (Kaplan & Reynolds, 1988). It remains for future research to determine the circumstances under which our emotions promote the development of cancer.

Assuming that our emotions can influence the progress of cancer, what mechanisms might account for it? One possibility is that unpleasant emotional arousal impairs the body's defenses against cancer cells. In fact, during periods when they are under intense academic pressure, medical students exhibit a reduction in the activity of *natural killer cells,* the lymphocytes responsible for detecting and destroying cancer cells. This appears to be the result of a decrease in the production of *interferon,* a chemical needed for the proper functioning of natural killer cells (Glaser, Rice, Speicher, Stout, & Kiecolt-Glaser, 1986).

Mediation of Stress

More than two thousand years ago, Hippocrates recognized the relationship between individual factors and physiological responses when he observed that it is more important to know what sort of person has a disease than to know what sort of disease a person has (Rees, 1983). Because of variability among individuals, a given stressor will not evoke the same physiological response in every person. Our reactions to stress are mediated by a variety of factors.

Physiological Reactivity People differ in their physiological reactivity to stressors. In one study, men with mild hypertension played the Pac Man videogame while their heart rate and blood pressure were measured. Those who displayed high heart-rate acceleration while playing the game also displayed greater increases in blood pressure. Blood tests showed that high accelerators had higher levels of blood cholesterol than did low accelerators. This may explain the greater risk of atherosclerosis in people with greater physiological reactivity (Jorgensen, Nash, Lasser, Hymowitz, & Langer, 1988).

Reactivity, in turn, depends on other factors. Differences in cardiovascular reactivity between males and females indicate that sex is a factor. Males react to stressors with greater increases than females in cardiovascular activity and in the secretion of stress hormones. This may explain, in part, the greater vulnerability of males to coronary heart disease (Stoney, Davis, & Matthews, 1987). Physically fit people are less likely to develop essential hypertension, perhaps because they show less physiological reactivity. For example, they respond to stressors with smaller increases in stress-hormone secretion than do physically unfit people (Sothmann, Horn, Hart, & Gustafson, 1987).

Still another factor in physiological reactivity is the use of stimulant drugs, which evoke greater physiological reactivity to stressors. This was demonstrated in a study of medical students. The study took place during an eight-day period of low stress, when the students had no exams, and an eight-day period of high stress, when they had final exams. On each day, half the students received a caffeine tablet and half received a placebo. Their heart rates and blood pressures were then measured over a forty-minute period. Immediately after each period, blood samples were drawn and tested for levels of cortisol and cholesterol.

The results showed that the subjects had higher heart rates during the exam period and that those who received caffeine during either period showed increased blood pressure, cortisol levels, and cholesterol levels. During the exam period, those who received caffeine had blood pressure in the borderline hypertensive range. Apparently, people who ingest caffeine during periods of work stress may experience greater physiological reactivity (Pincomb, Lovallo, Passey, Brackett, & Wilson, 1987). This study might make you wary of drinking cup after cup of coffee during final exams, because of caffeine's tendency to increase your physiological reactivity to stressors.

Cognitive Appraisal Richard Lazarus believes that one of the reasons the same stressor may induce high stress in one person and mild stress in another is that the two appraise the stressor differently. This is known as *cognitive appraisal*. In *primary appraisal* you judge whether a particular situation is stressful. After judging that a situation is stressful, you would engage in *secondary appraisal* by estimating whether you have the ability to cope with the stressor (Lazarus, DeLongis, Folkman, & Gruen, 1985). Consider your upcoming final exams. Students who perceive them as highly demanding and who lack confidence in their abilities to perform well on them will experience greater stress than will students who perceive their upcoming exams as moderately demanding and who are confident of their abilities to perform well on them.

Explanatory Style As discussed in chapter 14, depressed people have a pessimistic explanatory style. They attribute unpleasant events to *stable, global,* and *internal* characteristics of themselves. In other words, depressed people attribute unpleasant events to their own unchanging, pervasive, personal characteristics—such as a lack of intelligence. The possible role of a pessimistic explanatory style in the promotion of illness was supported by a follow-up study of graduates of the Harvard University classes of 1942 to 1944. Graduates who had pessimistic explanatory styles at the age of twenty-five became less healthy between the ages of forty-five and sixty—even though all of the graduates had been healthy at age twenty-five.

What might account for the effect of a pessimistic explanatory style on illness? The researchers hypothesized that this style might make people less likely to curb negative life events, leading to more numerous and more severe negative life events. A pessimistic explanatory style might also lead to poor health habits, suppression of the immune system, and withdrawal from sources of social support. Each of these factors can contribute to the development of illness (Peterson, Seligman, & Vaillant, 1988).

Suzanne Kobasa "Hardiness has an active emphasis in that it predisposes persons to interact more intensely with stressful events in order to transform them into less stressful forms."

Hardiness A personality characteristic, marked by feelings of commitment, challenge, and control, that promotes resistance to stress.

Personal Hardiness In studying executives working under high stress, psychologist Suzanne Kobasa found that some were more likely to succumb to illness than others. After giving a group of executives a battery of personality tests and following them for a period of five years, she found that those who were illness resistant tended to share a constellation of personality characteristics that made them more hardy than those who were not illness resistant (Kobasa, Maddi, & Kahn, 1982). People high in personal **hardiness** are more resistant to stressors and, consequently, are less susceptible to stress-related illness.

What characteristics are shared by people high in hardiness? Hardy people face stressors with a sense of commitment, challenge, and control. People who feel a sense of *commitment* are actively involved in practical activities and social relationships, rather than being alienated from them. Hardy students are committed to their course work and friendships rather than being alienated from them. People who feel a sense of *challenge* view life's stressors as opportunities for personal growth rather than as burdens to be endured. Hardy students would view term papers as chances to improve in their knowledge, thinking, and writing, rather than as unpleasant demands on their time. And people who feel a sense of *control* believe they have the personal resources to cope with stressors, rather than merely being helpless in the face of them. Hardy students would believe that their abilities and efforts will lead to academic success, rather than believing that nothing they do will make a difference. Figure 16.6 presents examples of the three components of hardiness.

But how does hardiness reduce susceptibility to illness? Hardiness appears to do so by affecting health habits. People high in personal hardiness, compared to people low in it, are more likely to maintain good health habits in the face of stress (Wiebe & McCallum, 1986). Perhaps hardy students are more resistant to illness because they are more likely to eat well, take vitamins, exercise more, and seek medical attention for minor ailments even when confronted by social, financial, and academic stressors.

Feeling of Control   As you have learned, a feeling of control mediates our responses to stressors. Even research unrelated to personal hardiness has demonstrated the importance of feelings of control in mediating the stress

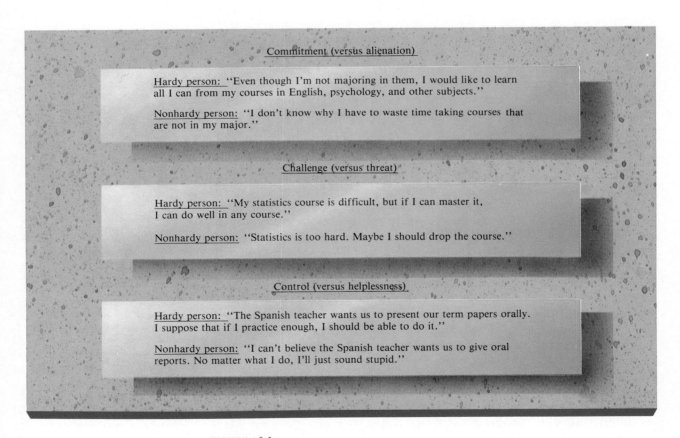

FIGURE 16.6
Personal Hardiness People who score high in personal hardiness have a sense of commitment, challenge, and control instead of a sense of alienation, threat, and helplessness.

response. While the talent for doing nothing under stress is desirable in astronauts, as expressed in the following excerpt from Tom Wolfe's book *The Right Stuff,* (1979, p. 151), it may be unhealthy. The impaired immune response displayed by Apollo astronauts on their return to Earth might reflect their passive voyage through thousands of miles of outer space:

> The pilot's, particularly the hot pilot's, main psychological bulwark under stress was his knowledge that he controlled the ship and could always do something. . . . This obsession with active control, it was argued, would only tend to cause problems on Mercury [space] flights. What was required was a man whose main talent was for doing nothing under stress.

People who work at demanding jobs with little control over job stressors are more likely to develop coronary heart disease (Krantz, Contrada, Hill, & Friedler, 1988). And residents of homes for the elderly who are given greater responsibility for self-care and everyday activities live longer and healthier lives than do residents whose lives are controlled by staff members, apparently because they maintain stronger immune responses (Rodin, 1986). Consider the "good patient" in the hospital, who adopts a passive, compliant role—leaving his or her recovery up to nurses and physicians. The poorer recuperative powers of such patients are associated with their feelings of **learned helplessness**—the feeling that one has little control over events in one's life, based on past experiences with uncontrollable negative events, and that this helplessness is due to one's own shortcomings rather than to external circumstances (Raps, Peterson, Jonas, & Seligman, 1982).

Learned Helplessness A feeling of futility caused by the belief that one has little or no control over events in one's life, which may make one stop trying and develop feelings of depression.

In a best-selling book describing his recovery from a massive heart attack, Norman Cousins, former editor of the *Saturday Review,* claims that his insistence on taking personal responsibility for his recovery—including devising his own rehabilitation program—helped him regain his health. In contrast, as Cousins noted in his book, "good patients" discover that "a weak body becomes weaker in a mood of total surrender" (Cousins, 1983, p. 223).

The ultimate act of surrender in response to a lack of control is the phenomenon of **burnout**—a state of mental, emotional, and physical exhaustion caused by subjection to chronic uncontrollable stressors. Mental exhaustion is associated with difficulty concentrating or paying attention. Emotional exhaustion is associated with depression and apathy. And physical exhaustion is associated with fatigue and a lack of energy. Burnout strikes people who have worked hard but who feel their efforts have had little effect. They may respond by becoming cynical, unmotivated, and socially aloof.

Burnout A state of cognitive, emotional, and physical exhaustion caused by exposure to chronic uncontrollable stressors.

Burnout is especially common among human service providers, including nurses, teachers, and counselors. A study of public school teachers in Iowa found that the greater the number of stressful events they experienced, the more likely they were to suffer burnout. But teachers who felt they were receiving social support and recognition of their contributions from supervisors were less vulnerable to burnout (Russell, Altmaier, & Van Velzen, 1987).

Sense of Humor As Norman Cousins (1983) pointed out, people have long recognized the beneficial effect of a sense of humor on health. The seventeenth-century physician Thomas Sydenham noted that "the arrival of a good clown exercises more beneficial influence upon the health of a town than twenty asses laded with drugs." When Cousins (1979) found himself suffering from a rare, often incurable neuromuscular disease, he sped his recovery by watching Marx Brothers movies and episodes of the television show "Candid Camera." Research has supported Cousins's belief, showing that people with a sense of humor experience less stress. While laughter itself may relieve stress and reduce depression by inducing physical relaxation, a sense of humor may also make stressors seem less negative and may evoke social support from other people (Nezu, Nezu, & Blissett, 1988).

Social Support   Misery may indeed love company. People with social support are less likely to suffer illness. Social support may be tangible, in the form of money or practical help, or intangible, in the form of advice or encouragement. Social support mediates the effects of stressful life events, promotes recovery from illness, and increases adherence to medical regimens (Heitzmann & Kaplan, 1988). Even people with genital herpes, marked by recurrent painful sores on the genitals, who receive social support related to their illness have fewer recurrences. The opportunity to talk about, rather than hide, their illness seems to be especially important in relieving distress and reducing recurrences (Vander Plate, Aral, & Magder, 1988).

There is evidence that social support also has an effect on the immune response. In one study, samples of saliva were taken from healthy college students five days before their first final exam and fourteen days after their last final exam. The samples were analyzed for the level of immunoglobulin A, an antibody that provides immunity against infections of the upper respiratory tract, gastrointestinal tract, and urogenital system. Salivary concentrations of immunoglobulin A during the final exam period were lower than before. Students who reported more adequate social support during the preexam period had consistently higher immunoglobulin A concentrations than did their peers who reported less adequate social support (Jemmott & Magloire, 1988).

Formal Methods of Coping with Stress

While certain routine behaviors and social interactions may reduce stress, formal methods of coping with stress provide additional weapons against it. Among the most important of these methods are relaxation, exercise, and stress-

Stress and Social Support People with adequate social support are less likely to develop stress-related illnesses.

Humor and Health Norman Cousins relied on Marx Brothers' movies to help him recover from a rare neuromuscular disease. Research has shown that a sense of humor reduces our response to stressors and may help us maintain our health or recover from illness.

management programs. Each is effective in decreasing physiological indicators of stress, such as heart rate and blood pressure (Bruning & Frew, 1987).

Relaxation Because stress is associated with physiological arousal, health psychologists emphasize the importance of relaxation training. Several techniques have proved effective in reducing physiological arousal. These include hypnosis (Wadden & Anderton, 1982), meditation (Barr & Benson, 1984), biofeedback (McGrady, Woerner, Bernal, & Higgins, 1987), and paced (slow, rhythmic) breathing (Fried, 1987). But the most popular relaxation technique is **progressive relaxation,** which involves practice in successively tensing and relaxing each of the major muscle groups of the body. By doing so, the person learns to distinguish muscle tension from relaxation and, eventually, to relieve muscle tension by immediately relaxing tense muscles. As illustrated in figure 16.7, progressive relaxation has been remarkably effective in reducing symptoms of physiological arousal, including high blood pressure (Hoelscher, 1987).

Progessive relaxation may even enhance the immunological response. Consider the following experiment involving medical students. Blood samples were taken from students one month before midterm exams and then on the day of the exams. Half of the students were randomly assigned to participate in regular relaxation practice during the month between the two measurement days. The results showed that the students who were not assigned to practice relaxation, compared to the students who were, displayed a significantly greater decrease in natural killer cell activity between the first and second measurements (Kiecolt-Glaser et al., 1986). As you learned earlier, natural killer cells are one of the body's main defenses against cancer cells.

Exercise Almost three decades ago, President Kennedy, a physical fitness proponent, noted, "The Greeks knew that intelligence and skill can only function at the peak of their capacity when the body is healthy and strong—that hearty spirits and tough minds usually inhabit sound bodies" (Silva &

Progressive Relaxation A procedure that involves the successive tensing and relaxing of each of the major muscle groups of the body.

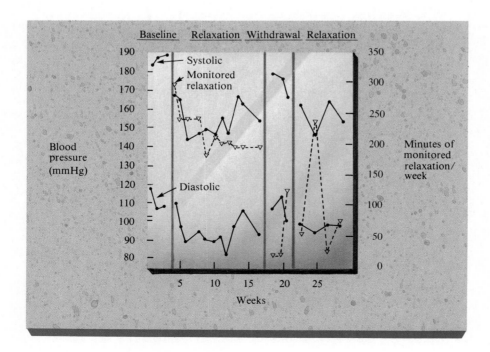

FIGURE 16.7
Relaxation and Blood Pressure The graph shows the results of a study in which a subject practiced relaxation. As you can see, relaxation practice was associated with lower systolic and diastolic blood pressure readings. When relaxation practice was withdrawn, blood pressure rose (Hoelscher, 1987).

Weinberg, 1984, p. 416). Kennedy would certainly approve of the recent trend toward greater personal fitness among adults. As mentioned earlier, physically fit people are less physiologically reactive to stressors and less vulnerable to illnesses.

How does exercise mediate the response to stress? Exercise has a direct effect by reducing physiological reactivity and an indirect effect by increasing one's sense of control over stressors. The beneficial effect of exercise was demonstrated in a longitudinal study that found that adolescents under high life stress who exercised regularly had a significantly lower incidence of illness than did adolescents who exercised little (Brown & Siegel, 1988). The results are presented in figure 16.8.

Stress-Management Programs The past decade has seen an increase in stress-management programs, typically combining relaxation training, regular exercise, and cognitive-behavioral therapy. But, for some people, less ambitious stress-management programs have also proved effective. A simple, but effective, approach to stress management involves merely writing about stressful experiences. In a study of college students, half were assigned to write about traumatic experiences and half were assigned to write about superficial topics for four consecutive days. Those who wrote about their traumatic experiences had lower physiological arousal and better functioning of their immune systems. And, as indicated in figure 16.9, those who wrote about their traumatic experiences also made fewer visits to the college health center (Pennebaker, Kiecolt-Glaser, & Glaser, 1988).

HEALTH-IMPAIRING HABITS

Habits as varied as smoking, overeating, avoiding exercise, and failing to wear seat belts sharply increase the chances of illness, injury, or death. Yet, a study of college students found that they tended to have an "It can't happen to me" attitude. Their estimate of the probability that their own risky behaviors would

FIGURE 16.8
Exercise and Illness A study of the relationship between exercise and illness found that adolescents who exercised little and adolescents who exercised regularly did not differ in their incidence of illness when under low life stress. In contrast, when under high life stress those who exercised regularly had a significantly lower incidence of illness than did those who exercised little (Brown & Siegel, 1988).

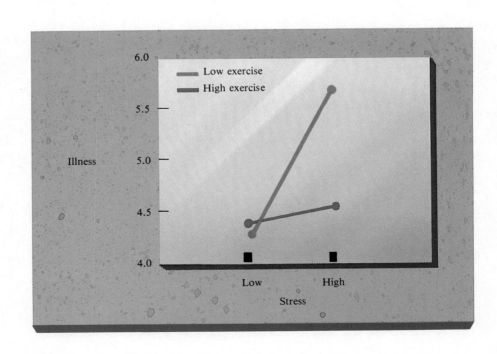

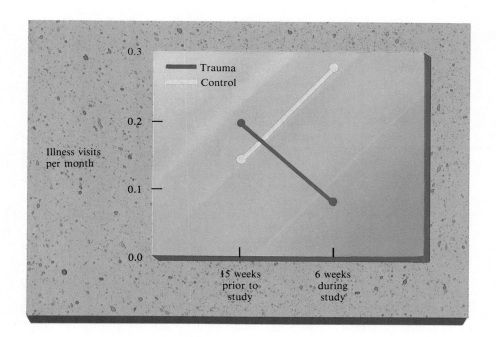

FIGURE 16.9
Writing and Illness College students who wrote about their emotionally distressing (traumatic) experiences made fewer visits to their college health center than did comparable students who did not write about their experiences (Pennebaker et al., 1988).

lead to illness or injury underestimated the actual probability. Because of our inability to estimate the true riskiness of our behaviors, programs aimed at changing health-impairing habits must not only point out risky behaviors but also make participants realize that those habits make them more susceptible to unhealthy consequences than they might believe (Weinstein, 1984).

Unsafe Behavior

Accidents are common causes of injury and death in the United States. Traffic accidents take an especially heavy toll. Police and ambulance attendants know too well that the failure to use seat belts contributes to the physical toll of traffic accidents. This has led health psychologists to develop programs to increase the use of seat belts. A program in Ottawa, Ontario, had the highway patrol periodically enforce mandatory seat-belt use laws for one year. These enforcement periods were publicized by the local media. The program led to a significant increase in seat-belt use and a significant decrease in traffic accident casualties. During the same period, drivers in the comparable city of Kingston, Ontario, which did not take part in the program, showed no change in their seat-belt use and in their traffic accident casualties (Jonah & Grant, 1985).

Lack of Exercise

Exercise has several beneficial effects. People who exercise are healthier and less likely to suffer from infectious diseases than are those who do not. Exercise may reduce the risk of infectious diseases by increasing the level of a chemical factor that increases the effectiveness of immune system cells that fight bacterial infections (Cannon & Kluger, 1983). But exercise is even more important in preventing obesity and cardiovascular disease. Aerobic exercise (such as running, swimming, bicycling, brisk walking, or cross-country skiing) combats obesity by using up calories, raising the basal metabolic rate, and inhibiting the appetite. Aerobic exercise also reduces the cardiovascular risk

Exercise People who exercise are more stress resistant and disease resistant than people who do not. The well-publicized benefits of exercise account for the popularity of exercise "gurus" such as Jack LaLanne, Richard Simmons, and Jane Fonda.

factors of obesity, high blood pressure, and high blood cholesterol (Martin & Dubbert, 1985). Even weight training, a nonaerobic exercise, may reduce the risk of cardiovascular disease by decreasing the level of fats in the blood of previously sedentary men and women (Goldberg, Elliot, Schutz, & Kloster, 1984).

Unfortunately, of those who begin formal progams of aerobic exercise, about 50 percent will drop out within six months. Moreover, people who are obese or who have symptoms of cardiovascular disease—the very people who might benefit most from exercise—are less likely to exercise (Dishman & Gettman, 1980). This failure of both healthy and unhealthy people to maintain programs of exercise has prompted health psychologists to study ways of increasing exercise adherence. In one study, groups of people engaged in jogging, aerobic dancing, or pre-ski training for ten weeks. Some of the participants in each of the three groups also took part in a special program to increase their exercise adherence. The program made participants more aware of obstacles to exercise and taught them how to cope with periodic exercise lapses, rather than having an all-or-none attitude. Instead of giving up after exercise lapses, exercisers were urged to return immediately to their exercise programs. The results showed that those who participated in the adherence program, compared to those who did not, were, indeed, more likely to adhere to their exercise programs (Belisle, Roskies, & Levesque, 1987).

Smoking

Mark Twain once remarked, "To cease smoking is the easiest thing I have ever done; I ought to know because I've done it a thousand times." As Twain did a century ago, today health psychologists recognize the addictive nature of nicotine. Though smokers claim that they smoke to relieve anxiety or to make them more alert, they actually smoke to avoid the unpleasant symptoms of nicotine withdrawal, which include irritability, hand tremors, heart palpitations, and difficulty concentrating. Thus, addicted smokers smoke to regulate the level of nicotine in their bodies (Leventhal & Cleary, 1980). Under stressful circumstances, as when expressing one's opinions in social interactions (Gilbert & Spielberger, 1987), smokers report that smoking reduces their anxiety, perhaps because stress makes their bodies crave higher levels of nicotine.

Smoking causes harmful side efects through the actions of tars and other substances in cigarette smoke. Smoking causes fatigue by reducing the blood's ability to carry oxygen, making smoking an especially bad habit for athletes. But, more importantly, smoking contributes to the deaths of 300,000 Americans each year from stroke, cancer, emphysema, and heart disease. In fact, each cigarette smoked reduces the typical smoker's life span by fifteen minutes. Given that a pack of cigarettes contains twenty cigarettes, "pack-a-day" smokers reduce their life spans about one day for every five days they smoke. And smokers who have high cholesterol levels reduce their life spans even more (Perkins, 1985).

Despite the harmful effects of smoking, governments permit it—and even profit from it. In 1565 King James I of England, who considered smoking a despicable habit, chose to tax cigarettes rather than ban them, a practice governments still follow today (Whitlock, 1987). Smoking is especially difficult to resist because it may become associated with many everyday situations, as in the case of smokers who light a cigarette when answering the telephone, after eating a meal, or upon leaving a class.

The ill effects of smoking make programs to prevent the onset of smoking and to help smokers quit smoking imperative. Many smoking-prevention programs are based in schools and provide information about the immediate and long-term social and physical consequences of smoking. Students learn that smoking, in the short term, causes bad breath, yellow teeth and fingers, and weakened stamina. They also learn that smoking, in the long term, causes cancer, emphysema, and cardiovascular disease. Smoking-prevention programs also teach students how to resist peer pressure and advertisements encouraging them to begin smoking. Overall, smoking-prevention programs have been effective, reducing the number of new smokers among participants by 50 percent (Flay, 1985). But programs to help people stop smoking have been less successful than programs to prevent smoking, mainly because of the addictive power of nicotine.

Health psychologists employ a variety of techniques to help people stop smoking. *Nicotine gum* provides the nicotine that smokers crave without the harmful chemicals contained in tobacco smoke. Of course, nicotine gum does not help smokers overcome their addiction to nicotine. The technique of *nicotine fading* gradually weans the smoker off nicotine by having him or her use cigarettes with lower and lower nicotine content until the content has been reduced by 90 percent. At that point the smoker might find it easier to quit smoking completely.

In the technique of *rapid smoking,* a form of aversion therapy (see chapter 15), the smoker is forced to take a puff every six to eight seconds for several minutes. This induces feelings of nausea and dizziness, and after several sessions, the person may develop an aversion to smoking. But rapid smoking may induce heart-beat irregularities, making it potentially dangerous for smokers with cardiac problems.

Self-management programs use behavior modification to promote smoking cessation. They encourage smokers to avoid stimuli that act as cues for smoking, such as coffee breaks, alcoholic beverages, and other smokers. Smokers may also take part in *contingency contracting,* in which they are rewarded for a reduction in smoking. For example, a smoker who quits might be rewarded by his or her spouse with a vacation trip. Self-management programs show promise, with up to 50 percent of participants still refraining from smoking a year after completing their programs (Kamarck & Lichtenstein, 1985).

Poor Nutrition

The relationship between diet and health has been known since biblical days. In the book of Daniel in the Old Testament, the Babylonian king Nebuchadnezzar orders that captured Judean boys of noble descent be given food and wine from his royal table. Daniel, one of the captured boys, begs the chief eunuch not to make the boys violate religious dietary laws by forcing them to eat "unclean" foods and drink "unclean" beverages from the table:

> But he [the eunuch] warned Daniel, "I am afraid of my lord the king: he has assigned you food and drink, and if he sees you looking thinner in the face than the other boys of your age, my head will be in danger with the king because of you." At this Daniel turned to the guard whom the chief eunuch had assigned to Daniel, Hananiah, Mishael, and Azariah. He said, "Please allow your servants a ten days' trial, during which we are given only vegetables to eat and water to drink. You can then compare our looks with those of the boys who eat the king's food; go by what you see, and treat your servants accordingly." The man agreed to do what they asked and put them on ten days' trial. When the ten days were over they looked and were in better health than any of the boys who had eaten their allowance from the royal table; so the guard withdrew their allowance of food and the wine they were to drink, and gave them vegetables. (Daniel, 1:3–17)

This passage demonstrates both Daniel's surprising scientific sophistication and his realization that diet influences physical health. It demonstrates Daniel's scientific sophistication because he recommended using an "experimental group," which would eat a vegetarian diet, and a "control group," which would eat a normal diet. Today health psychologists, as did Daniel, recognize the importance of diet in health and illness.

Health psychologists are especially concerned with the relationship between diet and cardiovascular disease. A high-fat diet is one of the main risk factors in cardiovascular disease. High-fat diets contribute to high levels of cholesterol in the blood, which promotes atherosclerosis by the build up of plaque deposits that narrow the arteries. The narrowing of cerebral arteries and coronary arteries reduces blood flow, promoting strokes and heart attacks. Health psychologists have developed programs combining nutritional education and behavior modification to help people reduce their risks of cardiovascular disease by adopting healthier eating habits. Though these programs are effective in improving eating habits, their long-term effectiveness has yet to be demonstrated (Jeffery, 1988).

A high-fat diet also contributes to obesity. As explained in chapter 10, obesity is an important risk factor in illness for both men and women. Yet, in Western cultures, a leaner figure has been stylish for women only since the early twentieth century—and a muscularly toned figure only in the past decade. For the preceding six hundred years cultural standards favored a more rounded figure (Bennett & Gurin, 1982). You have probably seen this in Renaissance paintings depicting the ideal woman as having a plump figure. Figure 16.10 depicts changes in cultural views concerning the ideal female figure. Even today certain cultures favor overweight women. Members of the Anay tribe of Nigeria, for example, encourage their women to gain as much weight as possible—with women weighing more than four hundred pounds considered the most beautiful ("Overweight," 1986).

But current Western standards of beauty and concern with the health-impairing effects of obesity make weight loss a major American preoccupation. Weight reduction seems deceptively easy. You simply make sure that you burn more calories than you ingest. Yet, less than 5 percent of obese people maintain their weight losses long enough to be considered "cured" (Brow-

FIGURE 16.10
The Ideal Female Figure
In Western cultures the ideal female figure has changed over the centuries and over recent decades. The ideal has at times been represented by the Rubenesque nude of the early seventeenth century, the voluptuous actress Marilyn Monroe of the 1950s, and the muscular athlete Florence Griffith-Joyner of the 1980s.

nell, 1982). But some obesity researchers criticize this pessimistic view for reflecting the experiences of people who have been in formal weight-loss programs. In contrast, almost two-thirds of people who try to lose weight on their own succeed. Perhaps those who seek treatment for obesity are a select group of people who are the least likely to succeed (Schachter, 1982).

How do people control their weight? A common but relatively ineffective approach is dieting. People who diet may drastically reduce their caloric intake for weeks or months. Unfortunately, as dieters lose weight their basal metabolic rate slows (Foreyt, 1987), forcing them to diet indefinitely to maintain their lower levels of weight—an impossible feat. Because dieting alone cannot last for a lifetime, the dieter eventually returns to the same eating habits that contributed to his or her obesity. Moreover, dieting is unhealthy, with 25 percent of diet-induced weight loss consisting of lean body tissue, including skeletal muscle (Brownell, 1982).

Failing to change their eating habits, obese people may resort to medical treatments to control weight. The most common medical treatments are diet pills, usually amphetamines. Amphetamines promote weight loss by their effects on the hypothalamus, though the exact mechanism is unknown (Paul, Hulihan-Giblin, & Skolnick, 1982). But amphetamines eventually lose their effectiveness and can cause insomnia, high blood pressure, and symptoms of paranoid schizophrenia.

More extreme medical treatments for obesity rely on surgery. In fact, *morbid obesity,* in which the person is more than one hundred pounds above normal weight, is best treated by surgical means, which have a 50 to 60 percent success rate (Kral & Kissileff, 1987). Some obese people undergo stomach stapling to reduce the size of the stomach. Because the smaller stomach fills up faster, feelings of fullness occur before the person can ingest large amounts of food. Another surgical approach bypasses most of the small intestine with a tube so that food has less chance to be digested in the small intestine (Castelnuovo-Tedesco, Weinberg, Buchanan, & Scott, 1982). Though effective in treating morbid obesity, these are risky procedures that can produce potentially fatal side effects.

Formal psychological approaches to weight loss rely on behavior therapy in conjunction with aerobic exercise, which markedly raises the heart rate. Aerobic exercise promotes weight loss not only by burning calories during the exercise but also by raising the metabolic rate for hours afterward. This counters diet-induced decreases in the basal metabolic rate. Weight loss through aerobic exercise is also healthier than through dieting alone, because only 5 percent of weight loss will be lean tissue (Brownell, 1982). Unfortunately, despite the effectiveness of aerobic exercise in weight control, half of those who enroll in formal exercise programs drop out within a few months (McMinn, 1984).

In behavior therapy programs participants monitor their eating behaviors, change maladaptive eating habits, and correct misconceptions about eating. An ambitious experiment randomly assigned 123 mildly to moderately obese adults to one of five conditions: (1) behavior therapy alone; (2) behavior therapy plus a posttreatment maintenance program that included contact with

Morbid Obesity People who are more than 100 pounds above their normal weight are considered morbidly obese. Some cases of morbid obesity are truly astounding. In a widely publicized case, comedian and nutritionist Dick Gregory helped Walter Hudson, a man weighing more than 1000 pounds, lose several hundred pounds. Gregory learned of the man when he heard news reports describing how he had become wedged in a doorway and had escaped only after having the doorway cut from around him. In many cases of extreme obesity, the person spends his or her entire life trapped indoors, barely able to walk and possibly unable to fit through doorways.

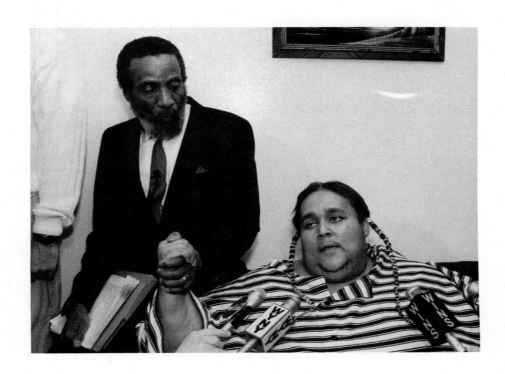

a therapist; (3) behavior therapy plus posttreatment therapist contact plus a social influence maintenance program; (4) behavior therapy plus posttreatment therapist contact plus aerobic exercise; and (5) behavior therapy plus posttreatment therapist contact plus aerobic exercise plus a social influence maintenance program.

The social influence maintenance program provided peer support, offered money for adherence, and required lecturing to other people interested in weight control. The posttreatment programs were twenty-six biweekly sessions during the year following treatment for obesity. At an eighteen-month follow-up, all four conditions that combined behavior therapy with a posttreatment maintenance program yielded significantly greater long-term weight loss than did behavior therapy alone (Perri et al., 1988). This demonstrates the need for continued support after the completion of weight-loss programs.

REACTIONS TO ILLNESS

Despite your best efforts to adapt to stress and to live a healthy life-style, you may periodically suffer from illnesses. Some health psychologists study how people cope with illness and try to develop ways to promote better coping strategies to reduce patient distress and to increase patient adherence to medical regimens.

Patient Distress

Illness, especially chronic illness or illness requiring surgery, induces distress in patients. In some cases, relatively simple procedures can reduce illness-related distress. In one study, children undergoing chemotherapy for cancer were divided into an experimental group that played videogames during their chemotherapy and a control group that did not. Children in the experimental group reported less anxiety and nausea (figure 16.11). The children who played videogames were apparently distracted from the unpleasant sensations caused by the chemotherapy (Redd et al., 1987).

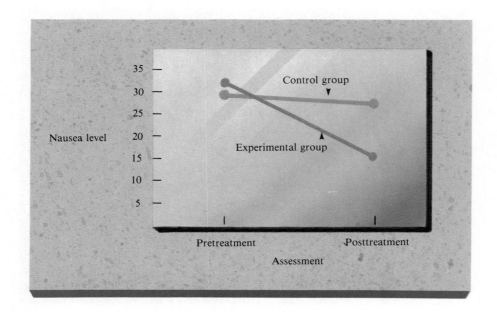

FIGURE 16.11
Controlling Patient Distress
Children who played videogames while undergoing cancer chemotherapy (the experimental group) showed a marked reduction in nausea. In contrast, children who did not play videogames while undergoing cancer chemotherapy (the control group) showed little change in nausea (Redd et al., 1987).

Adult surgery patients may also benefit from relatively simple procedures. Patients about to undergo coronary-bypass surgery who have a hospital roommate who has just undergone successful surgery of any kind will be less anxious before surgery, walk more after surgery, and go home sooner than similar patients who have a roommate who is only scheduled to undergo surgery. Apparently, merely observing a person who has survived surgery has a calming effect on patients about to undergo surgery. Moreover, people who have undergone surgery may reduce the distress of patients about to undergo surgery by letting them know what to expect and suggesting ways to cope with the situation (Kulik & Mahler, 1987).

Adherence to Medical Regimens

Recovery from illness often depends on following a medical regimen laid out by a physician. A medical regimen might include a prescription drug, a restricted diet, or an exercise program. But patients may fail to follow a treatment regimen because they do not understand the physician's instructions, find the regimen too complex to follow, experience unpleasant side effects, or simply dislike the physician. In some cases, patients may stop adhering to the regimen prematurely because they fail to notice any symptoms. Consider a patient with essential hypertension (chronic high blood pressure) who must take medication, watch her diet, and follow an exercise program. Because we have, at best, a modest ability to sense the level of our blood pressure (Pennebaker & Watson, 1988), the patient may fail to follow her prescribed medical regimens. She may assume, incorrectly, that because she does not feel like she has high blood pressure, she actually does not have high blood pressure. The failure of many patients to adhere to medical regimens has led health psychologists to study the effectiveness of various procedures in promoting adherence. In one study, women were given a reward of either a one-dollar lottery ticket or a Susan B. Anthony dollar for performing breast self-examination. Those who received the reward were more likely to engage in self-examination than were those who did not receive a reward (Grady, Goodenow, & Psorkin, 1988).

Patient-Physician Relationship
Physicians who are empathetic have patients who are more satisfied and more cooperative than do physicians who are matter-of-fact in their relationships with patients.

As you have just read, health psychologists have demonstrated that we play an active role in maintaining our health, succumbing to diseases, and recovering from illness. Though some diseases and injuries are unavoidable, we can no longer view ourselves as being the passive victims of viruses, bacteria, carcinogens, or accidents. By learning to adapt effectively to stressors, to eliminate risky behaviors, and to adopt health-promoting behaviors, we can greatly reduce our chances of illness, injury, and death. For example, the manner in which we adapt to everyday stressors may influence our tendency to develop coronary heart disease, as demonstrated by research on Type A behavior.

THINKING ABOUT PSYCHOLOGY

Does Type A Behavior Promote Coronary Heart Disease?

On November 2, 1988, "Iron Mike" Ditka, the tough head coach of the Chicago Bears football team and former star tight end, was hospitalized with a mild heart attack. In a televised interview on ESPN, Ditka's physician reported that Ditka had none of the common physical risk factors for coronary heart disease, such as smoking, obesity, or lack of exercise. His only risk factor was a psychological one: *Type A behavior.*

Mike Ditka When Mike Ditka, the intense, aggressive head coach of the Chicago Bears, suffered a heart attack during the 1988 football season, his only risk factor was a Type A behavior pattern.

Characteristics of Type A Behavior

In the mid-1950s two San Francisco cardiologists, Meyer Friedman and Ray Rosenman (1974), noted that their waiting room chairs were worn along the front edges. They interpreted this as a sign of the impatience of their patients, who spoke rapidly and interrupted frequently during conversations. The patients were also easily angered, highly competitive, and driven to do more and more in less and less time. Friedman and Rosenman called this syndrome of behaviors **Type A behavior.** In contrast, *Type B behavior* is characterized by patience, an even temper, and willingness to do a limited number of things in a reasonable amount of time. The Type A person might also show *time urgency* by changing lanes to advance a single car length, *chronic activation* by staying active most of every day, and *multiphasic activity* by reading, eating, and watching television at the same time (Wright, 1988). Based on their research findings, Friedman and Rosenman boldly concluded:

> In the absence of Type A Behavior Pattern, coronary heart disease almost never occurs before seventy years of age, regardless of the fatty foods eaten, the cigarettes smoked or the lack of exercise. But when this behavior pattern is present, coronary heart disease can easily erupt in one's thirties or forties. (Friedman & Rosenman, 1974, p. ix)

In 1975 Friedman and Rosenman reported the results of a study on coronary heart disease that began in 1960 and ended in 1969—the Western Collaborative Group Study. They studied 3,154 middle-aged men who were free of heart disease at the beginning of the study. Each of the men was categorized as Type A or Type B based on a procedure called the Structured Interview. The subjects answered questions related to Type A behavior and the examiner noted behavioral manifestations of Type A behavior during the interview, such as rapid speech, hostile comments, or interrupting the examiner. The results showed that during the eight and one-half years of the study the men classified as Type A were more than twice as likely to develop coronary heart disease as the men classified as Type B (Rosenman et al., 1975).

Type A Behavior A syndrome, marked by impatience, hostility, and extreme competitiveness, that has been associated with the development of coronary heart disease.

Multiphasic Activity The Type A behavior pattern is associated with multiphasic activity, in which the person engages in several activities at once as part of a continual effort to do more and more in less and less time.

Type A behavior is not merely a style of responding to the environment—
it may induce the very environmental situations that evoke it. This was demonstrated in a study comparing Type A and Type B police radio dispatchers
during work shifts. Type A's generated more job pressures by initiating more
work tasks for themselves and attending to multiple tasks at the same time.
Moreover, perhaps following the adage, "If you want something done give it
to a busy person," their coworkers and supervisors looked to them when there
were additional tasks to be performed. So, Type A people may create work
conditions that promote a driven, time-urgent, impatient behavioral style (Kirmeyer & Biggers, 1988). Similarly, a Type A student might take a course over-
load, work a full-time job, serve on several student committees, and participate
in intramural sports at the same time.

But the strength of the relationship between Type A behavior and coronary
heart disease was brought into question by results of a twenty-two-year follow-
up study from the Western Collaborative Group Study, which found no relationship between Type A behavior and coronary heart disease mortality. In
fact, Type A's who had suffered a heart attack had a somewhat *lower* risk of a
second heart attack. Of course, this may have been a result of other factors,
such as greater medical attention given to Type A than to Type B heart-attack
victims (Ragland & Brand, 1988). And, though these results indicate that the
overall pattern of Type A behavior is unrelated to coronary heart disease, research findings have been converging on a specific component of the Type A
behavior pattern, *antagonistic hostility,* as most related to coronary heart disease. Antagonistic hostility is characterized less by outbursts of anger and more
by acting in a rude, condescending, and uncooperative manner (Dembroski
& Costa, 1988).

Effects of Type A Behavior

Assuming that antagonistic hostility or some other aspect of Type A behavior,
rather than the overall pattern of Type A behavior, promotes coronary heart
disease, how might it do so? One way might be through the effects of stress
hormones. Redford Williams and his colleagues (1982) had Type A and Type

**Hostility and Coronary Heart
Disease** Research studies have
converged on antagonistic
hostility as the component of the
Type A behavior pattern that is
most strongly associated with the
development of coronary heart
disease.

B male college students perform the stressful task of counting aloud backward by 17s from 7,683. The first to finish would win a prize. The results showed that the Type A's displayed a significantly greater increase in levels of the adrenal gland stress hormones cortisol, epinephrine, and norepinephrine. These stress hormones promote the buildup of cholesterol plaques on the walls of arteries, narrowing them, and increasing the risk of heart attacks due to atherosclerosis. Perhaps, in everyday life, Type A's induce similar physiological responses in themselves by their willingness to subject themselves to stressful competitive situations.

Another possible factor mediating the effect of Type A behavior on coronary heart disease is the tendency of Type A people to ignore symptoms of illness. In fact, prior to being hospitalized with his heart attack, Mike Ditka had ignored pain earlier in the week and at a team workout shortly before his assistant coaches forced him to seek medical attention. His job meant more to him than his health. This tendency of Type A's to discount illness first appears in childhood. Type A children are less likely to complain of symptoms of illness, and Type A children who have surgery miss fewer days of school than do Type Bs (Leikin, Firestone, & McGrath, 1988).

But certain Type A's may be more stress resistant than others. For example, a study of human service employees found that Type A's who were high in hardiness, discussed earlier in the chapter, were less susceptible to the negative effects of Type A behavior. In fact, Type A's who scored high in hardiness experienced less psychological distress and burnout than did Type B's who scored low in hardiness (Nowack, 1986).

Development of Type A Behavior

Once researchers identified the characteristics of Type A behavior and its harmful effects, they became interested in studying how Type A behavior develops. Though there is only weak evidence of a hereditary basis for Type A behavior, there is evidence that the pattern runs in families. In a study of male and female adolescents, those who scored high on the hostility component of Type A behavior and also had a parent suffering from essential hypertension showed a greater elevation in blood pressure in response to stressful tasks than did subjects who had a parent suffering from essential hypertension but who did not score high on hostility (McCann & Matthews, 1988).

Karen Matthews, a leading researcher on Type A behavior, points to child-rearing practices as the primary origin of Type A behavior. Parents of Type A children encourage them to try harder even when they do well and offer them few spontaneous positive comments. Type A children may be given no standards except "do better," making it difficult for them to develop internal standards of achievement. They may then seek to compare their academic performances with that of the best child in their class. This may contribute to the development of the hard-driving component of the Type A behavior pattern (Matthews & Woodall, 1988). You probably know fellow students who not only want A's on exams but want the highest grade in the class.

Modification of Type A Behavior

Because of the possible association between Type A behavior and coronary heart disease, its modification would be wise. But a paradox of Type A behavior is that Type A persons are not necessarily disturbed by their behavior. Why change a behavior pattern that is rewarded in our competitive society? Programs to modify Type A behavior in those who are willing to participate try to alter specific components of the Type A behavior pattern, particularly impatience, hostility, and competitiveness. One such program has been suc-

Karen Matthews "Type A children's awareness of high standards . . . may maintain their struggle to strive after everescalating goals."

cessful in reducing Type A behavior in people especially prone to Type A behavior—university teachers. Teachers received cognitive behavior modification and assertiveness training in eight two-hour group sessions. The participants learned to modify their maladaptive beliefs and attitudes related to anger, impatience, hostility, and competitive drive. They also learned to express themselves assertively, rather than passively or aggressively. A follow-up found that the participants displayed less impatience and less hostility a year later (Thurman, 1985).

As you can see, though the worn edges of Friedman's and Rosenman's waiting-room chairs have inspired much research, many questions about Type A behavior as a risk factor in coronary heart disease remain to be answered. Which aspects of the Type A behavior pattern promote coronary heart disease? What physiological mechanisms account for the relationship between Type A behavior and coronary heart disease? Why do some people adapt the Type A behavior pattern while others adapt the Type B pattern? How can we best modify the Type A behavior pattern?

SUMMARY

STRESS AND ILLNESS

Health psychology is the field of psychology that studies the role of behavioral factors in the promotion of health and the prevention of illness and injury. One of the main topics of interest to health psychologists is stress, the physiological response of the body to physical and psychological demands. The main categories of stress are frustration, pressure, and conflict. They are associated with chronic situations, life changes, and daily hassles.

Hans Selye identified a pattern of physiological response to stress called the general adaptation syndrome, which includes the alarm reaction, the stage of resistance, and the stage of exhauston. Stress has been linked to noninfectious diseases, infectious diseases, and cancer. The field that studies the relationship between stress factors and illness is called psychoneuroimmunology.

The relationship between stress and illness is mediated by a variety of factors. These include physiological reactivity, cognitive appraisal, explanatory style, personal hardiness, feeling of control, sense of humor, and social support. Formal methods of coping with stress include relaxation, exercise, and stress-management programs.

HEALTH-IMPAIRING HABITS

Most deaths in the United States are associated with unhealthy habits. These include unsafe behavior, lack of exercise, smoking, and poor nutrition. Programs aimed at changing these habits hold promise as ways of reducing the incidence of illness and death.

REACTIONS TO ILLNESS

Health psychologists study how people cope with illness and try to develop ways to promote better coping strategies to reduce patient distress and to increase patient adherence to medical regimens. The patient-practitioner relationship is an important factor in adherence.

THINKING ABOUT PSYCHOLOGY: DOES TYPE A BEHAVIOR PROMOTE CORONARY HEART DISEASE?

People who display Type A behavior are easily angered, highly competitive, and driven to do more and more in less and less time. They also show time urgency, chronic activation, and multiphasic activity. Research studies indicate that at least some components of the Type A behavior pattern are related to the development of coronary heart disease. Recent research has converged on antagonistic hostility as the most important component.

Type A behavior may increase the risk of coronary heart disease by increasing blood pressure and levels of stress hormones such as cortisol, epinephrine, and norepinephrine. Type A behavior originates in childhood and is associated with parents who encourage their children to do better and better without providing clear standards of achievement. Programs aimed at reducing the risk of coronary heart disease by altering the Type A behavior pattern show promise, but their effect on the incidence of coronary heart disease remains to be determined.

IMPORTANT CONCEPTS

SOCIAL COGNITION

Chapter Opening Art:
Auguste Renoir. *Le Moulin de la Galette.* 1876.

n the 1890s, bicycle racing was a major spectator sport in the United States. As mentioned in chapter 10, Norman Triplett (1898), a bicycling fan, noted that those who raced against other riders seemed to go faster than those who raced against the clock. He decided to study the effect of competitors on the performance of others by having boys spin fishing reels as fast as they could, either competing against time or against another boy. He found that they performed faster when competing against another boy. This is generally recognized as the first experiment in **social psychology**—the field of psychology that studies social relationships.

Though social psychology textbooks appeared in the first decade of this century (Pepitone, 1981), social psychology did not become a distinct field of psychology until after World War II, when researchers became interested in the formal study of social cognition and social influence. Though there is some overlap between social cognition and social influence, *social cognition* is more concerned with how we perceive, interpret, and predict behavior, while *social influence* is more concerned with the effects that we have on one another's behavior. One of the main topics in social cognition is **social attribution,** the process by which we determine the causes of social behavior.

SOCIAL ATTRIBUTION

As first noted in the 1940s by social psychologist Fritz Heider (1944), when we engage in social attribution we weigh the relative influence of a person and the person's circumstances. When you decide that a person is responsible for his or her own behavior, you are making a *dispositional attribution.* And when you decide that a person's circumstances are responsible for his or her behavior, you are making a *situational attribution.*

To appreciate this, imagine that you are a member of a jury at a murder trial. The prosecutor might try to convince you that the defendant is guilty of first-degree murder by providing evidence that the defendant is a vengeful person with a violent temper. In response, the defense attorney might insist that the defendant is innocent and merely acted in self-defense by pointing out that he had been repeatedly threatened by the victim. Thus, while the prosecutor would emphasize characteristics of the defendant, the defense attorney would emphasize the defendant's circumstances.

But when do we engage in social attribution? Researchers disagree on the answer to this question. Some have found that we engage in social attribution continually and unconsciously, regardless of the behavior we are observing (Winter & Uleman, 1984). Others have found that we engage in it only when confronted with personally important or unexpected behaviors (Weiner, 1985b). This might occur when a good student does poorly on an exam or when an underdog team wins a baseball game.

Kelley's Principles of Social Attribution

There were so many studies of social attribution in the 1970s that it became known as "the decade of attribution theory in social psychology" (Weiner, 1985b, p. 74). Perhaps the most influential attribution theorist of the 1970s was Harold Kelley, who identified factors that determine whether we make dispositional attributions or situational attributions for given behaviors. Kelley (1973) found that social attributions depend on three important factors: consistency, distinctiveness, and consensus. **Consistency** is the extent to which a person behaves in the same way in a given situation on different occasions. **Distinctiveness** is the extent to which a person behaves in the same way

Social Psychology The field that studies the effects that people have on one another's thoughts, feelings, and behaviors.

Social Attribution The cognitive process by which we infer the causes of both our own and other people's social behavior.

Consistency The extent to which a person behaves in the same way in a given situation on different occasions.

Distinctiveness The extent to which a person behaves in the same way across different situations.

across different situations. And **consensus** is the extent to which, in a given situation, other people perform the same behavior as the person being observed.

These three factors interact in determining whether we make dispositional or situational attributions (figure 17.1). Consider a fellow student who sits through a history lecture without asking any questions or participating in any discussions. If she rarely speaks in that course (high consistency), if she rarely speaks in other courses (low distinctiveness), and if other students speak during that lecture (low consensus), you would probably make a dispositional attribution, perhaps attributing her behavior to shyness. As in this example, we tend to make dispositional attributions when there is high consistency, low distinctiveness, and low consensus for a given behavior. In contrast, we tend to make situational attributions when there is low consistency, high distinctiveness, and high consensus.

Weiner's Attributional Dimensions

While Kelley's theory of attribution dominated the 1970s, it was joined in the 1980s by Bernard Weiner's (1985a) theory of attribution. Weiner and his colleagues found that estimating the relative importance of dispositional factors and situational factors is important but cannot by itself explain all social attributions. Weiner identified three dimensions that govern social attribution. The *internal-external dimension* refers to the degree to which we make dispositional or situational attributions for behaviors. The *stable-unstable dimension* refers to the degree to which we attribute behaviors to a factor that is stable or unstable. And the *controllable-uncontrollable dimension* refers to the degree to which we attribute behaviors to a factor that is controllable or uncontrollable.

Figure 17.2 illustrates the interaction of the stable-unstable dimension and the internal-external dimension. To appreciate the interaction of Weiner's three dimensions in attributions for success and failure, consider a study that examined the attributions made by competitive gymnasts. Following a gymnastics meet, those who received high scores, but not those who received low scores, from judges tended to attribute their performance to internal, stable, and controllable factors (McAuley, 1985).

Weiner and his colleagues (1987) found that the internal-external and controllable-uncontrollable dimensions influence the effectiveness of the everyday excuses we make. Students were asked for the kind of excuses they used or did not use when they arrived late for an appointment or failed to do something expected of them. They were also asked to describe how other people reacted to their excuses. The students' excuses generally relied on external/uncontrollable factors (for example, "I was stuck behind a school bus that stopped every block") and avoided internal/controllable factors (for example, "I overslept"). The students found that the first kind of excuse evoked less hostility than did the second kind. You might have found this yourself when explaining why you missed an exam or handed a paper in late.

But would the students' excuses really produce the effects they reported? A follow-up experiment by the same researchers found that the answer was yes. They had a student confederate of theirs arrive late and keep subjects waiting for fifteen minutes. In some cases, the student gave an excuse based on an external, uncontrollable factor, such as, "The professor in my class gave an exam that ran way over time." In other cases, the student gave an excuse based on an internal, controllable factor, such as, "I was talking to some friends in the hall." Subjects in the latter condition reported more anger and irritation, viewed the person as less dependable, and reported less desire to see the person again.

Consensus The extent to which, in a given situation, other people perform the same behavior as the person being observed.

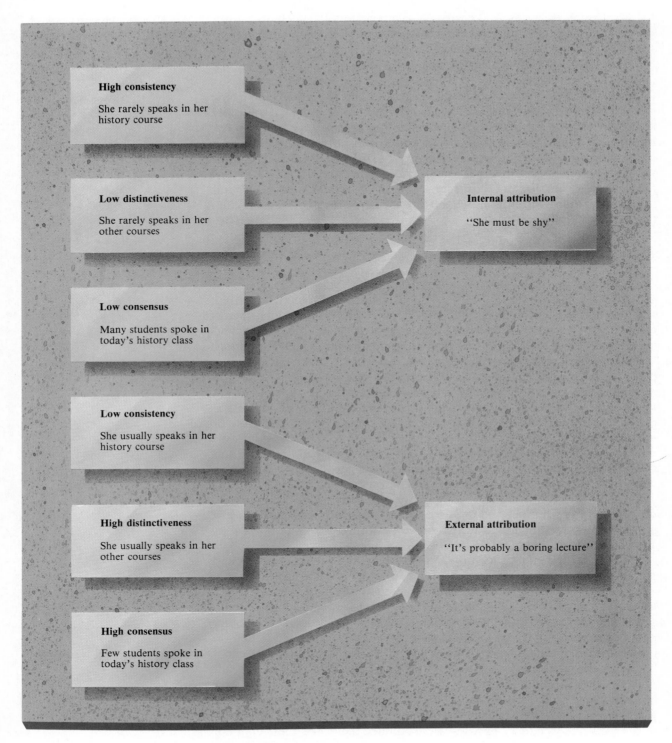

FIGURE 17.1
**Dispositional and Situational
Attribution** In deciding why a student did
not speak in a history class, Kelley (1973)
would have us consider the factors of
consistency, distinctiveness, and consensus.
These are only two of the many possible
combinations of the three factors.

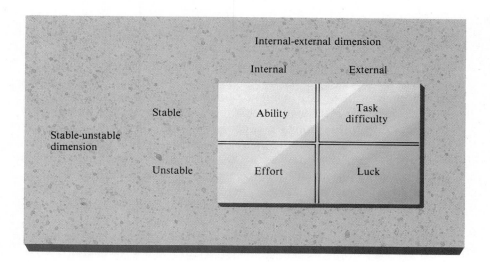

FIGURE 17.2
Dimensions of Social Attribution According to Weiner, we may explain our successes and failures by attributing them to internal or external causes that are either stable or unstable.

In another example of the practical effects of Weiner's dimensions, college counselors made use of the stable-unstable dimension in a program aimed at improving the academic performance of college freshmen who were doing poorly. The program tried to convince freshmen that their low grades were caused by unstable factors instead of stable factors. Freshmen were given data informing them that students tend to improve their grades after the freshman year. They were also shown videotapes of juniors and seniors reporting that their grade point averages had increased since their freshman years. Freshmen who were exposed to this information were significantly less likely to leave college and had significantly greater increases in grade point average during their sophomore years than did those who were not exposed to it (Wilson & Linville, 1982).

Biases in Social Attribution

If human beings were as rational and objective as Mr. Spock in *Star Trek,* the social attribution process would be a straightforward affair. But, being somewhat irrational and nonobjective, we exhibit biases in the social attributions we make.

The Actor-Observer Bias A survey of advice columns, including "Dear Abby" and "Ann Landers," found that people who write for advice tend to attribute their own problems to situational factors, while attributing other people's problems to dispositional factors (Schoeneman & Rubanowitz, 1985). This tendency for observers to make dispositional attributions for the behavior of others but situational attributions for their own behavior is called the **actor-observer bias.**

Even explanations for our choices of majors or romantic partners are subject to the actor-observer bias. When male college students were asked to give reasons for their best friends' choices of a major and a girl friend, they were more likely to give reasons related to their best friends' personal characteristics. For example, they might note that a friend needed a challenging major and someone who was intelligent. In contrast, when male college students were asked to give reasons for their own choices of a major and a girl friend, they were more likely to give reasons related to appealing characteristics of

Actor-Observer Bias The tendency of observers to make dispositional attributions for the behaviors of others but to make situational attributions for their own behaviors.

their majors and girl friends. For example, they might note that their majors provided career opportunities or that their girl friends were intelligent (Nisbett, Caputo, Legant, & Marecek, 1973).

Why are we subject to the actor-observer bias? One explanation is that we usually have greater knowledge of the circumstances that influence our own behaviors than of those that influence other people's behaviors. As an example, suppose that a student is consistently absent from her introductory psychology course. Her professor might attribute the absences to her unreliable nature. In contrast, the student might attribute her absences to dull lectures. Thus, the greater awareness that the student has of the circumstances affecting her behavior may lead her to make a situational attribution for her absences. In contrast, the professor, being aware of only the student's behavior, may be biased toward making a dispositional attribution for her absences (Eisen, 1979).

Nonetheless, there is evidence that the actor-observer bias is more related to differences in salience than to differences in the knowledge of circumstances. *Salience* refers to the extent to which something grabs our attention. When observing another person's behavior, the person is more salient than his or her circumstances. In contrast, when observing our own behavior, our circumstances are more salient than ourselves (Watson, 1982).

The Self-Serving Bias   A study of college students found that those who received high grades (such as A's or B's) tended to make dispositional attributions for them, attributing their success to their own efforts and abilities. In contrast, students who received lower grades (such as C's, D's, or F's) tended to make situational attributions for their grades, attributing their lack of success to bad luck and difficult tests (Bernstein, Stephan, & Davis, 1979). This tendency to make dispositional attributions for our positive behaviors and situational attributions for our negative behaviors is called the **self-serving bias.**

The self-serving bias has been applied successfully in a program aimed at relieving public speaking anxiety. College students were asked to read speeches in front of a camera. Some of the students were told they would be

Self-Serving Bias The tendency to make dispositional attributions for one's successes and situational attributions for one's failures.

The Actor-Observer Bias If you were the driver of the car that struck the one on the right, you would probably blame the accident on situational factors, such as a blowout. Yet, if you saw someone else have the accident, you would probably blame it on dispositional factors, such as carelessness.

exposed to subliminal noise that would make them feel unpleasantly aroused, while other students were told that the experience of reading the speech would make them feel unpleasantly aroused. The results showed that students who believed that their natural nervousness was caused by the subliminal noise spoke more fluently than did those who were only told that they would naturally be nervous. Thus, the attribution of personal distress to a specific situational, instead of a personal dispositional, factor may improve our performance in stressful situations (Olson, 1988).

One of the chief explanations for the self-serving bias is that it helps us maintain our self-esteem (Harvey & Weary, 1984). This may account for the differences in the attributions made by winners and losers in sports. A study using Weiner's internal-external and stable-unstable dimensions found that baseball players and football players were more likely to attribute wins to dispositional factors, such as their own efforts or abilities, but were more likely to attribute losses to situational factors, such as bad luck or poor officiating (Lau & Russell, 1980). Perhaps Casey Stengel, the colorful manager of some of the awful New York Mets teams of the 1960s, was protecting his self-esteem when he claimed that he coached well but his team played lousy.

IMPRESSION FORMATION

In addition to determining the causes of behavior, we spend much of everyday life making judgments about the personal characteristics of people and the social phenomena with which they are associated. This is known as **impression formation.**

Impression Formation The process of making judgments about the personal characteristics of others.

Social Schemas

"College professor." "Rock concert." "Bill Cosby." "Eskimo." Each of these is an example of a **social schema,** which is composed of the presumed characteristics of a role, event, person, or group. Social schemas bring order to

Social Schema A cognitive structure comprising the presumed characteristics of a role, event, person, or group.

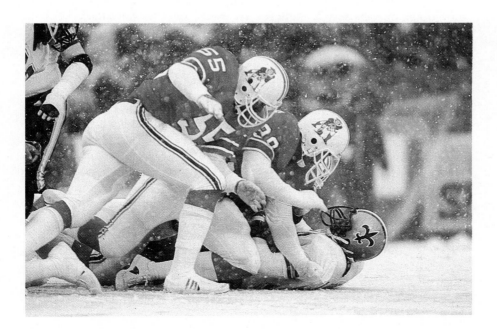

The Self-Serving Bias The winners of this game would probably attribute their success to their effort and ability. In contrast, the losers would probably attribute their failure to poor officiating or the harsh weather conditions.

what might otherwise be a chaotic social world by permitting us to interpret and predict the behavior of others. For example, if you did not have a social schema of "college professor," you would have no reason to expect your professor to behave any differently than the academic dean, the athletic director, or the college president.

When we revise a schema to make it agree with new, incongruent information, we engage in *accommodation*. But our social schemas are resistant to change because of *assimilation,* the process by which we make new information fit an existing schema. Accommodation and assimilation are described in the discussion of Jean Piaget's theory of cognitive development in chapter 12. When a person's behavior is consistent with a social schema, we tend to attribute the behavior to the social schema, but when a person's behavior is inconsistent with a social schema, we tend to attribute the behavior to situational factors—instead of making the social schema accommodate the new information (Kulik, 1983). For example, if your psychology professor began singing in class instead of lecturing, you would not revise your schema of "college professor" to include singing. Instead, you might assume that your professor heard some good news that day.

A social schema may have powerful effects on our social perception. As an example, think of the words "spokesperson" and "mouthpiece." Would you expect different behaviors from individuals described by these terms? The social schema for "mouthpiece" includes negative characteristics that the social schema for "spokesperson" does not. The possible negative impression created by the label "mouthpiece" was the basis of a lawsuit on behalf of Frank Sinatra's attorney against *Barron's Business and Financial Weekly,* which referred to the attorney as "Sinatra's mouthpiece." The results of a survey showing that the term "mouthpiece" created a negative impression in the minds of readers were introduced as evidence in court. Though the judge accepted the validity of this evidence, *Barron's* won the case on the grounds of freedom of the press (Kramer, Buckhout, Eugenio, & Cohen, 1985).

Social schemas may even influence our memories of people. In one study, subjects watched a videotape of a woman engaged in a variety of activities, including drinking beer and listening to classical music. For half the subjects, the woman was identified as a waitress. For the other half of the subjects, she was identified as a librarian. When asked to recall what she had done in the videotape, the subjects were influenced by their social schemas for "waitress" and "librarian." Those who believed she was a waitress were more likely to recall her drinking beer. In contrast, those who believed she was a librarian were more likely to recall her listening to classical music (Cohen, 1981).

First Impressions

When we first meet a person, we may have little information about the individual other than his or her sex, race, apparent age, and physical appearance. Each of these characteristics may activate a particular social schema, which, in turn, will create a first impression of that person. A first impression functions as a social schema to guide our predictions of a person's behavior and our desire to interact with that person. First impressions are important in many situations and have been shown to be important in determining whether college roommates will become friends (Berg, 1984).

First impressions may be based on as little as a person's facial features, as shown by a study in which subjects were asked to match photographs of faces to a list of occupations. Certain faces were consistently matched with "honest occupations" such as engineer, physician, or clergy, while certain other faces

Drawing by Handelsman; © 1984 The
New Yorker Magazine, Inc.

"The basis of our defense will be that a man of your standing in the community,
whatever else he may be, is certainly no thief."

were consistently matched with "dishonest occupations" such as rapist, armed robber, or mass murderer (Goldstein, Chance, & Gilbert, 1984). If this type of bias is shared by people in general, we may unfairly favor or disfavor particular people because of the social schemas evoked by their faces. You can appreciate how undesirable this would be in certain situations, such as jury trials.

A classic experiment by Harold Kelley (1950) demonstrated the importance of a first impression on our evaluation of a person. Undergraduates were given a written description of a guest lecturer as "a rather warm person, industrious, critical, practical, and determined" or the same description with the word "warm" replaced by the word "cold." After the lecture, which provided the opportunity for questions and discussion, the students were asked for their impressions of the lecturer. Students who had been told that the lecturer was warm rated him as more informal, sociable, and humorous than did those who were told he was cold. Those who had been told the lecturer was warm also asked more questions and participated in more discussions with him. This indicated that the students assimilated the lecturer's behavior into the schema they had been given.

First Impressions Do these people bring different thoughts and feelings to mind? Your first impressions of them might determine how you initially act toward them.

Self-Fulfilling Prophecy

Self-Fulfilling Prophecy The tendency for one person's expectations to make another person behave in accordance with those expectations.

One of the important effects of first impressions is the **self-fulfilling prophecy,** which is the tendency for one person's expectations to influence a second person to behave in accordance with those expectations. This occurs because the social schema we have of the other person will make us act a certain way toward that person, which, in turn, will make the person respond in accordance with our expectations (Darley & Fazio, 1980). In everyday life, if we expect someone to be shy, our actions may influence the person to act in a shy manner. And if we expect someone to be outgoing, our actions may influence the person to act in an outgoing manner.

Self-fulfilling prophecy was demonstrated in an experiment in which undergraduates were given the opportunity to get acquainted with a person who they were told was either another student or a psychotherapy client. During their meetings, those who believed that their partners were psychotherapy clients treated the person more negatively than did those who believed that their partners were fellow students. Moreover, the partner behaved in a less socially desirable way when the student believed that the partner was a psychotherapy client (Sibicky & Dovidio, 1986).

SOCIAL ATTRACTION

In forming our impressions of other people, we also develop *social attraction* for some of them. At this point in the semester, there are students in your psychology course whom you like more than others. You have probably become friendly with certain students, while being indifferent to others. And you may have even developed a romantic relationship with someone in particular. Social psychologists interested in social attraction seek answers to questions such as, Why do we like certain people more than others? and What is the nature of romantic love?

What accounts for liking? P F

Liking

Think of the students in your psychology class whom you like. Research studies have discovered several factors that stand out as the most likely reasons for your liking particular ones.

Proximity Almost two decades ago, a psychologist made an initially mystifying observation. Trainees at the Maryland State Police Academy whose last names began with letters near each other in the alphabet were more likely to become friends. Before reading on, you might wish to play intellectual sleuth and think of a hypothetical explanation for that finding. When the researcher investigated further, he found a simple explanation. The trainees were assigned to their rooms and classroom seats in alphabetical order. As a consequence, those close to one another in the alphabet were more likely to become friends because of *proximity,* their distance from one another (Segal, 1974).

Research has consistently supported the importance of proximity in the development of friendships, as in a classic study of the residents of apartments in a housing project for married students at the Massachusetts Institute of Technology. The closer students lived to one another, the more likely they were to become friends. In fact, 41 percent of the students reported that their best friends lived next door. Because the students were randomly assigned to apartments, their initial degree of liking for one another could not explain the findings (Festinger, Schachter, & Back, 1950).

Proximity provided the Maryland police trainees and the MIT students with the opportunity to interact and get to know each other. Perhaps you are more friendly with students who sit near you in class or live near you at home or in a dormitory than with other students. You will also tend to choose to be near people you like: eating together, going to parties together, and walking to class together. This provides even more opportunities for proximity to increase your mutual liking.

Familiarity Proximity makes us more familiar with certain people. But, contrary to the popular saying, familiarity tends to breed liking, not contempt. As explained in chapter 5, the more familiar we are with a stimulus, whether a car, a painting, or a professor, the more we will come to like it. So, in general, the more that we interact with people, the more we tend to like them (Moreland & Zajonc, 1982). Of course, this **mere exposure effect** holds only when the people with whom we interact do not behave in negative ways. The effect of familiarity on liking is not lost on politicians, who enhance their popularity by making repeated television appearances, or manufacturers, who increase sales through repeated advertisements of particular products.

The mere exposure effect was supported by a clever experiment using female college students as subjects. Two photographs of each subject were presented to the subject and to a friend or lover. While one photograph was a true image of the subject, the second was a mirror image—what the subject would see when looking at herself in a mirror. Mirror images and normal photographic images differ because our faces are not perfectly symmetrical—the left and right sides look different. Each subject, friend, and lover was asked to choose which of the two photographs he or she liked better. Friends and lovers were more likely to choose the true image, while subjects were more likely to choose the mirror image. This supported the mere exposure effect,

Proximity The development of interpersonal liking depends on proximity.

Mere Exposure Effect The tendency to like stimuli, including people, more as we are exposed to them repeatedly.

Familiarity We tend to increase our liking of people, such as Johnny Carson, as we become more familiar with them.

because the friends and lovers were more familiar with the true images of the subjects, while the subjects were more familiar with their own mirror images (Mita, Dermer, & Knight, 1977). You could easily replicate this experiment by using your friends as subjects.

Physical Attractiveness Proximity not only permits us to become familiar with people, it also permits us to notice how attractive they are. We tend to like physically attractive people more than physically unattractive people. In an early experiment, college freshmen took part in a computer dating study. They completed personality and aptitude tests and were told that they would be paired on their responses. In reality, they were paired randomly. Independent judges rated the physical attractiveness of each student. The couples then attended a dance that lasted several hours and afterward rated their partners on a questionnaire. The results showed that physical attractiveness was the most important factor in determining whether subjects liked their partners and whether they desired to date them again (Walster, Aronson, Abrahams, & Rottman, 1966).

What makes someone attractive? Facial features are especially important. People with "baby faces," which have small chins, small noses, large eyes, and high eyebrows, are considered especially attractive and, consequently, are especially well liked. Men with baby faces are rated as kinder, warmer, and more honest than are men with more mature faces (Berry & McArthur, 1985). The preference for attractive faces appears in infancy, as in a study in which infants from two to eight months old were shown pairs of slides of the faces of women who were previously rated as attractive or unattractive. The infants spent more time looking at the attractive faces. This shows that attractiveness is not totally dependent on learning, perhaps indicating that we may have an inborn tendency to respond positively to faces with particular features. In this study, the infants preferred smooth, rounded faces (Langlois et al., 1987).

But physical attractiveness is also relative—a person of average attractiveness will appear less attractive when in the presence of highly attractive people. Consider a study conducted in a men's dormitory. Residents of the dormitory were asked to rate a photograph of a woman of average physical attractiveness on her desirability as a date. Some of the residents who were shown the pho-

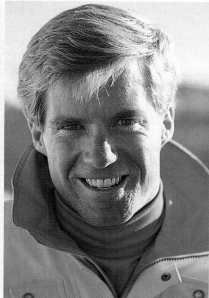

Physical Attractiveness As you can see from these photographs of attractive people, standards of physical attractiveness vary from culture to culture.

tograph were watching the television show "Charlie's Angels," which had three attractive women as its co-stars. Other residents who were shown the photograph were not watching "Charlie's Angels." Those who had been watching the television show rated the woman as less attractive than did those who had not been watching the show (Kenrick & Gutierres, 1980). So, when you are with friends who are more attractive than you, others may view you as less attractive than when they see you alone. Of course, when you are with friends who are less attractive than you, others may view you as more attractive than when they see you alone.

Physical attractiveness also has practical benefits. For example, physically attractive people tend to have more successful careers (Dickey-Bryant, Lautenschlager, Mendoza, & Abrahams, 1986). But attractiveness may backfire on some women, as shown by a study in which subjects judged the levels of ability of male and female managers. While attractive men were judged higher in ability than less attractive men, attractive women were judged lower in ability than less attractive women (Heilman & Stopeck, 1985). This may reflect the unfortunate cultural stereotype of the beautiful woman relying solely on her physical attractiveness to get ahead.

Similarity Do "opposites attract" or do "birds of a feather flock together"? You may recall the experiment discussed in chapter 2 that showed we are more attracted to people whose attitudes are similar to our own (Byrne, Ervin, & Lamberth, 1970). But this interpretation has been challenged by research showing that people are likely to associate with people who hold similar attitudes because they are repulsed by those who have dissimilar ones. Life's circumstances simply place us in religious, political, recreational, and educational settings where we are likely to associate with people who share our attitudes (Rosenbaum, 1986).

Donn Byrne has proposed a compromise, two-stage model of relationship formation. We may initially exclude people from further consideration if they

fix what did they find?

are unattractive, act negatively toward us, or express dissimilar attitudes. We then rely on similarity of attitudes to determine with whom to seek relationships from among those who are most similar to us (Byrne, Clore, & Smeaton, 1986). And, more recently, Byrne and his colleagues found that when dissimilar attitudes were held constant, attraction between undergraduates who had never met before increased as their similarity in attitudes regarding issues such as welfare spending, "soft-core" pornography, and draft registration for women increased (Smeaton, Byrne, & Murnen, 1989).

Self-Disclosure To determine whether we share similar attitudes, we must engage in **self-disclosure,** in which we disclose our beliefs, feelings, and experiences. The importance of self-disclosure in interpersonal attraction is shown by the tendency of people who engage in it to have more satisfactory social relationships (Franzoi, Davis, & Young, 1985). Relationships are promoted by both the reciprocation of self-disclosure and by gradual increases in self-disclosure. But when people disclose highly personal information to us too early in a relationship, we may become uneasy, suspicious, and like them less (Huston & Levinger, 1978). If someone you have just met has ever presented you with his or her whole life story, you may have felt uncomfortable and uninterested in pursuing the relationship.

Our degree of self-disclosure to another person depends on our sex and our expectation of meeting the person again. This was demonstrated in a study in which male and female college students were invited to take part in research on the "acquaintance process." They were placed in same-sex pairs and asked to discuss topics such as "things in my past or present of which I am ashamed," "aspects of my personality that I dislike," and "my disappointments with the opposite sex."

The results showed that when men expected to interact with their partners in the future, they made self-disclosures that were more intimate and emotional. In contrast, when women expected to interact with their partners in the future they made self-disclosures that were less intimate and emotional. The reasons for these differences between men and women are unclear. The researchers pointed to the possibility that women are more likely to believe that revealing intimate information will hurt future working relationships or are more likely to suffer anxiety when they expect to interact with a person in the future, causing them to reveal less about themselves (Shaffer & Ogden, 1986). Whether the researchers' interpretation of the results is correct can only be determined by future research.

Romantic Love

what is main factors of Romantic Relations

Though love may make the world go round, there were few scientific studies of romantic love until the 1970s. Yet, some people believe that the scientific study of romantic love either is doomed to failure or invades an area of life that is better left as an everlasting mystery. In fact, Senator William Proxmire gave his first Golden Fleece Award to a study of romantic love that was supported by an eighty-four thousand dollar grant from the National Science Foundation. As discussed in chapter 2, Proxmire gave the award to studies that *he* believed were the greatest waste of taxpayers' money. In bestowing his first award, Proxmire claimed, "Right at the top of the things we don't want to know is why a man falls in love with a woman" (Adler & Carey, 1980, p. 89).

Despite Proxmire's criticisms, social psychologists have continued to conduct research on romantic love. Unlike Proxmire, they realize that the findings of such research might be used to help prevent and relieve the emotional and physical suffering that is produced by unhappy romantic relationships, in-

---

Self-Disclosure The extent to which we reveal our private beliefs, feelings, and experiences to others.

Passionate Love Love characterized by intense emotional arousal and sexual feelings.

Companionate Love Love characterized by feelings of affection and commitment to a relationship with another person.

cluding spouse abuse, child abuse, and divorce. What have researchers discovered about the nature of romantic love?

Theories of Love Elaine Hatfield (formerly Walster), undaunted by earning the first Golden Fleece Award for research she conducted with her colleague, Ellen Berscheid, makes a distinction between passionate love and companionate love (Hatfield, 1988). **Passionate love,** commonly known as sexual love, involves intense emotional arousal, including sexual feelings. **Companionate love** involves feelings of affection and commitment to the relationship. Romantic relationships tend to decline in passionate love and increase in companionate love.

More research has been conducted on passionate love than on companionate love. According to Berscheid and Hatfield, passionate love depends on three factors. First, the culture must promote the notion of passionate love. Passionate love has been important in Western cultures only since the Middle Ages, and, even today, some cultures have no concept of it. Second, the person must experience a state of intense emotional arousal. Third, the emotional arousal must be associated with a romantic partner (Berscheid & Walster, 1974).

Their theory of romantic love incorporates aspects of Stanley Schachter's two-factor theory of emotion. As explained in chapter 11, Schachter's theory assumes that you will experience a particular emotion when you perceive that you are physiologically aroused and attribute that arousal to an emotionally relevant aspect of the situation in which you find yourself. The two-factor theory of romantic love assumes that it is the result of being physiologically aroused in a situation that promotes the labeling of that arousal as romantic love.

The two-factor theory of romantic love was supported by a clever experiment that took place on two bridges in Vancouver, British Columbia. One bridge, the Capilano River Bridge, was 5 feet wide, 450 feet long, and 230 feet above rocky rapids. It had low handrails and was constructed of wooden boards attached to wire cables, which made it prone to wobble back and forth, inducing fear-related physiological arousal in those who walked across it. The other bridge, over a tiny tributary of the Capilano River, was wide, solid, immobile, and only 10 feet above the stream. These characteristics made that bridge less likely to induce arousal in those who walked across it.

Ellen Berscheid (*top*) and **Elaine Hatfield** (*bottom*) "The evidence suggests that most individuals docilely accept the prescription that beauty and sexual and romantic passion are inexorably linked."

Romantic Love For romantic love to last after passionate love has waned, romantic partners must maintain the deep affection that characterizes companionate love.

FIGURE 17.3
Love and Arousal Physiological arousal in the presence of an appropriate person can intensify feelings of romantic love.

Triangular Theory of Love
Robert Sternberg's theory that love comprises passion, intimacy, and decision/commitment.

Whenever a man walked across one of the bridges, he was met by an attractive woman who was the experimenter's accomplice. The woman would ask each man to participate in a psychology course project concerning the effects of scenic attractions on creative expression. Each man was shown a picture of a man and a woman in an ambiguous situation and was asked to write a brief dramatic story about the picture. The woman then gave the man her phone number in case he later wanted to ask her any questions about the study. The results showed that the men who were on the bridge that induced physiological arousal, compared with the men on the bridge that was less likely to induce arousal, wrote stories with more sexual content and were more likely to call the woman later (Dutton & Aron, 1974).

According to the two-factor theory of romantic love, the men on the bridge that induced arousal had attributed their arousal to the presence of the attractive woman, leading them to experience romantic feelings toward her. But this interpretation of the results has been rejected by some researchers, who offer an alternative interpretation that assumes that the presence of the woman reduced the men's fear of the bridge, which, as a consequence, conditioned them to find her more attractive (Riordan & Tedeschi, 1983).

Nonetheless, results of studies similar to the Capilano River study that have ruled out conditioned fear reduction as a possible cause of their results have supported the two-factor theory of romantic love. In one such study, men who were physiologically aroused by exercise while in the presence of an attractive woman were more attracted to that woman than were men who were not physiologically aroused by exercise (White, Fishbein, & Rutstein, 1981). Based on the two-factor theory of romantic love, why would you expect the exhilaration experienced by the couple in figure 17.3 to increase their romantic feelings for each other?

A somewhat more elaborate theory of love has been proposed by Robert Sternberg (1986), whose triarchic theory of intelligence is discussed in chapter 9. Sternberg also thinks in threes when it comes to love, as evidenced by his **triangular theory of love**, which states that love has three components. *Passion* encompasses drives that lead to romance, physical attraction, and sexual relations. *Intimacy* encompasses feelings of closeness, bondedness, and connectedness. And *decision/commitment* encompasses, in the short term, the decision that one loves another, and, in the long term, the commitment to maintain that love.

According to Sternberg, the intensity of love depends on the individual strengths of these three components, while the kind of love that is experienced depends on the strengths of the three components relative to one another. For example, strong passion combined with little intimacy and weak decision/commitment is associated with infatuation, while strong passion and great intimacy combined with weak decision/commitment is associated with romantic love. Intimacy and decision/commitment without passion is associated with companionate love. Figure 17.4 presents the kinds of love associated with different combinations of the three components of Sternberg's theory. Because the triangular theory of love is relatively new, it has not yet generated enough research to determine its merits.

Promoting Romantic Love What factors promote romantic love? As with liking someone, similarity is an important factor in romance. We tend to date and to marry people who are similar to us in attractiveness (Murstein, 1972), as well as in age, race, religion, ethnic background, and educational level (Buss, 1985). Yet, when asked to rate the factors that make someone attractive as a romantic partner, males and females rate a sense of humor as the most important (Buss, 1988). As in the case of liking, self-disclosure plays an important role in romantic love. A study of eighteen-year-old dating

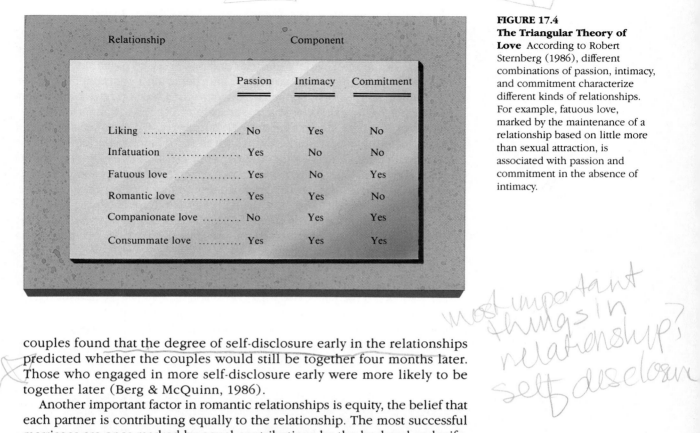

Relationship   Component

	Passion	Intimacy	Commitment
Liking	No	Yes	No
Infatuation	Yes	No	No
Fatuous love	Yes	No	Yes
Romantic love	Yes	Yes	No
Companionate love	No	Yes	Yes
Consummate love	Yes	Yes	Yes

FIGURE 17.4
The Triangular Theory of Love According to Robert Sternberg (1986), different combinations of passion, intimacy, and commitment characterize different kinds of relationships. For example, fatuous love, marked by the maintenance of a relationship based on little more than sexual attraction, is associated with passion and commitment in the absence of intimacy.

couples found that the degree of self-disclosure early in the relationships predicted whether the couples would still be together four months later. Those who engaged in more self-disclosure early were more likely to be together later (Berg & McQuinn, 1986).

Another important factor in romantic relationships is equity, the belief that each partner is contributing equally to the relationship. The most successful marriages are ones marked by equal contributions by the husband and wife, in which neither one dominates the relationship (Gray-Little & Burks, 1983). This also means that romantic relationships that last are marked by mutual consideration, in which each partner displays the ability to look at situations from the point of view of the other (Davis & Oathout, 1987). In inequitable relationships, liking declines because a partner who believes he or she is receiving too few rewards will become resentful, and a partner who believes he or she is receiving too many rewards will become guilty (Walster, Walster, & Traupmann, 1978).

Even the mere promise of equity may be important in promoting romantic relationships. A survey of eight hundred advertisements placed by individuals seeking romantic partners found that the advertisers tended to seek equitable relationships. But men and women differed in complementary ways in the rewards they offered and sought. Men tended to seek attractive women, while offering financial security in return. In contrast, women tended to seek financially secure men, while offering physical attractiveness in return (Harrison, 1977). Of course, this survey was conducted more than a decade ago. Perhaps changes in traditional sex roles during the past decade would make such advertisements less likely today. You may wish to conduct an informal survey of recent advertisements to determine whether males and females seek and offer the same rewards that they did in the 1970s.

SOCIAL ATTITUDES

What are your feelings about the insanity defense? Surprise parties? Abstract art? Fraternity members? Your answers to these questions would reveal your attitudes. **Attitudes** are evaluations of ideas (such as dormitory curfews), events (such as surprise parties), objects (such as abstract art), or people (such

Attitude An evaluation, containing cognitive, emotional, and behavioral components, of an idea, event, object, or person.

as fraternity members). In the 1930s the noted psychologist Gordon Allport claimed that the attitude was the single most important concept in social psychology. Though the attitude may no longer maintain such a lofty position, it is still one of the most widely studied concepts in social psychology.

Attitudes have emotional, cognitive, and behavioral components (figure 17.5) (Breckler, 1984). To appreciate this, imagine that you have been asked to participate in a market research survey of attitudes toward a new low-cholesterol, fast-food hamburger called "Burger-Lo." The market researcher would determine your attitude toward Burger-Lo by measuring one or more of the three components of your attitude. Your *emotional* response might be measured by a questionnaire asking you to rate your feelings about Burger-Lo's taste, aroma, texture, and appearance. Your *cognitive* response might be measured by asking you to describe the thoughts that Burger-Lo brings to mind, such as, "It's better than a Big Mac." And your *behavioral* response might be measured by observing whether you choose Burger-Lo over several other fast-food hamburgers in a blind taste test.

The Formation of Attitudes

How are our attitudes formed? Some are formed through *classical conditioning.* An attitude that is formed through classical conditioning may be acquired by the pairing of something desirable or undesirable with the object

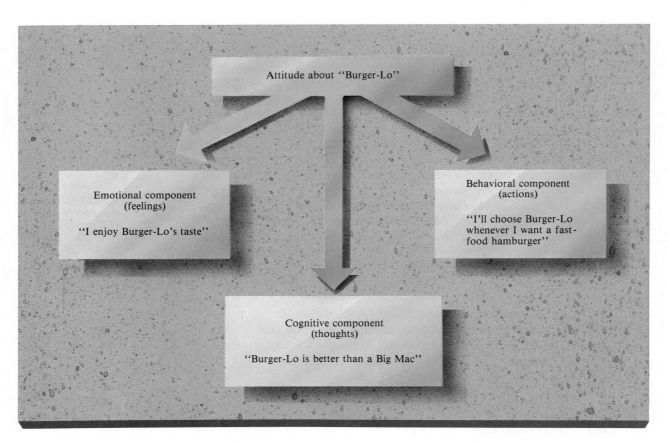

FIGURE 17.5
The Components of Attitudes Attitudes have emotional, cognitive, and behavioral components.

of the attitude. If Burger-Lo tastes good, you will associate that experience with Burger-Lo and develop a positive attitude toward it.

Attitudes may also be formed through *operant conditioning,* by positive reinforcement or punishment, as in an experiment conducted at the University of Hawaii (Insko, 1965). Undergraduates were contacted by telephone and asked whether they agreed or disagreed with each of a series of statements favoring or opposing a proposed "Springtime Aloha Week." The caller positively reinforced certain statements by saying "good." For half of the telephone calls, the caller said "good" whenever the student agreed with a statement favoring the proposal. For the other half, the caller said "good" whenever the student agreed with a statement opposing the proposal.

One week later the students were given a "Local Issues Questionnaire." Among the items in the questionnaire was a question asking whether they favored or opposed the proposed Springtime Aloha Week. The responses to that question showed that students who earlier had been reinforced for making statements favoring the Springtime Aloha Week were more likely to favor it, while students who earlier had been reinforced for making statements opposing the Springtime Aloha Week were more likely to oppose it.

According to *social learning theory,* many of our attitudes are learned through observing others, particularly our parents, our peers, and characters on television shows, being punished or positively reinforced for expressing particular behaviors. Suppose that a child repeatedly observes her parents responding positively to her older sister for expressing certain political or religious attitudes. Because she would want to receive the same positive responses from her parents, she might adopt similar attitudes.

The Art of Persuasion

In 1956 Edward Schein published a book describing the results of his interviews with United Nations soldiers who, as prisoners during the Korean War, had been subjected to so-called brainwashing. One of the main techniques of brainwashing was to use mild persuasion and small rewards to encourage prisoners to express positive attitudes toward communism and negative attitudes toward the United States. At first, prisoners would make mild statements, perhaps to receive cigarettes. They would then be encouraged to express stronger and stronger attitudes. Eventually, they might write letters or make recordings in which they strongly supported the communist "liberators" and harshly attacked the capitalist "warmongers." Some prisoners even freely chose to remain in North Korea after the war's end.

Publicity about brainwashing and fears that it could be used by totalitarian governments to control citizens stimulated interest in studying factors that influence persuasion and resistance to it. **Persuasion** is the intentional attempt to influence the attitudes of other people. Today researchers have little interest in studying brainwashing but much interest in studying the use of persuasion in our everyday lives, whether by friends, relatives, advertisers, or politicians. Note that persuasion is a topic that indicates the overlap between social cognition and social influence.

Persuasive messages may take a *central route* or a *peripheral route.* A message that takes a central route relies on clear, explicit arguments concerning the issue at hand. This encourages active consideration of the merits of the arguments. In contrast, a message that takes a peripheral route relies on factors other than the merits of the arguments, such as characteristics of the source or the situational context. But what determines whether the central route or the peripheral route will be more effective? An important factor is the relevance of the message to the listener. When a message has high relevance to

Persuasion The intentional attempt to influence the attitudes of other people.

The Power of Persuasion We are continually exposed to persuasive messages in our everyday lives.

the listener, the central route will be more effective. When a message has low relevance to the listener, the peripheral route will be more effective.

This was demonstrated in a study of student attitudes toward recommended policy changes at a university that would be instituted either the following year (high relevance) or in ten years (low relevance). Students who were asked to respond to arguments about policy changes that would be instituted the following year were influenced more by the quality of the arguments (central route) than by the expertise of the source (peripheral route). In contrast, students who were asked to respond to arguments about policy changes that would be instituted in ten years were influenced more by the expertise of the source than by the quality of the arguments (Petty, Cacioppo, & Goldman, 1981). The central and peripheral routes are related to the main factors in persuasion: the source, the message, the context, and the receiver.

The Source of the Message One of the important peripheral factors in persuasion is the source of the message. The greater the *credibility* of the source, the greater the persuasiveness of the message. Politicians realize this and gain votes by having credible supporters praise their merits and criticize their opponents' faults (Calantone & Warshaw, 1985). But what determines a source's credibility? Two of the most important factors are the source's expertise and trustworthiness.

We perceive sources as especially trustworthy when their messages are contrary to what we would expect from them (Wood & Eagly, 1981). For example, as noted in chapter 9, Sir Cyril Burt's biographer concluded that Burt had fabricated data supporting a strong genetic basis for intelligence. The author of an article discussing Burt's biography claimed, "The conclusion carries more weight because the author of the biography, Professor Leslie Hearnshaw, began his task as an admirer" (Hawkes, 1979, p. 673). If Hearnshaw had been a critic of Burt's work, his conclusion would have been less credible.

Sources that are *attractive*, because they are likable or physically appealing, are also more persuasive. Advertisers take advantage of this by having attractive actors appear in their commercials. Even the appeal of politicians is influenced by their attractiveness. In fact, Richard Nixon's unattractive appearance during a debate with John Kennedy may have cost him the 1960 presidential election. Nixon's five-o'clock shadow and tendency to perspire made him less attractive, and thus less convincing, to voters who watched the debate on television. In fact, surveys found that those who watched the debate on television rated Kennedy the winner, while those who listened to the debate on the radio rated Nixon the winner (Weisman, 1988). Having learned from Nixon's mistake, today's politicians make sure that they appear as attractive as possible on television.

We are also more likely to be persuaded by sources who are *similar* to us in ways that are relevant to the object of the message. Consider a study that was conducted in the paint department of a large store. When the salesman claimed that he did the same amount of painting as the customer, the customer was more likely to purchase the paint recommended by the salesman— even when it was a higher-priced paint than the customer had intended to buy (Brock, 1965). Likewise, you would be more likely to purchase a record recommended by a friend with your taste in music than one recommended by a friend who does not share your taste.

The Nature of the Message Characteristics of the message itself may take the central or the peripheral route. It may surprise you to learn that it is not always desirable to present only arguments that support your position. This was first discovered by social psychologist Carl Hovland and his colleagues in the waning days of World War II, following the surrender of Germany. The military asked Hovland for advice on how to convince soldiers that the war against Japan would take a long time to win. The researchers presented soldiers with a fifteen-minute talk presenting either one-sided or two-sided arguments to members of the armed forces. In the one-sided message, they presented only arguments about why the war would not be over soon, such as the distance and the fighting spirit of the Japanese. In the two-sided argument, they presented both that argument *and* arguments explaining why the war might end earlier, such as Allied air su-

Physical Attractiveness and Persuasion Richard Nixon's relatively unattractive appearance during a televised debate with John F. Kennedy may have contributed to his defeat in the 1960 presidential election.

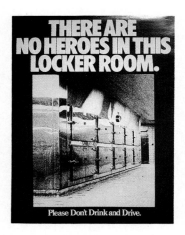

The Appeal to Fear Persuasive appeals that rely on fear can be effective if the supposed threat is severe, its likelihood high, and we can do something to prevent or eliminate it.

periority. Before and after the messages, the subjects were given surveys including questions about how long they believed the war would last.

The results showed that those who originally believed the war would take a long time to win were more influenced by the one-sided argument and became more extreme in their attitudes. But those who originally believed there would be an early end to the war were more influenced by the two-sided argument (Hovland, Lumsdaine, & Sheffield, 1949). As you can see, if the listener already favors your position, arguments favoring your position alone will be more persuasive. But if the listener opposes your position, arguments that seem to present both sides of the issue will be more persuasive. Two-sided arguments such as these are effective because they enhance the credibility of the source and, as a consequence, decrease counterarguing by the listener.

But what of messages that induce fear, as well as provide information? Messages that try to induce intense fear tend to be ineffective, because they make the listener discredit the source and ignore the message. The 1930s movie *Reefer Madness* became little more than a campy classic because it tried to convince viewers that smoking marijuana, which does have some harmful effects, could convert peaceful people into rapists and murderers. For an appeal to fear to be effective, the supposed threat must be severe, the likelihood of the threat must be high, and the listener must be able to engage in an action that will prevent or eliminate the threat (Rogers & Mewborn, 1976). The importance of these factors in making an appeal to fear effective was the basis of a campaign to convince people to get tetanus shots. The targets of the campaign were more likely to get tetanus shots when they were convinced of the danger of tetanus, of the likelihood that they would get tetanus if injured, and of the effectiveness of inoculations in preventing tetanus (Dabbs & Leventhal, 1966).

The Situational Context of the Message Have you ever wondered why business people prefer to discuss deals with clients over lunch or dinner? They do so, in part, because they realize that a pleasant setting combined with food and drink increases their ability to persuade clients to purchase products or services (Janis, Kaye, & Kirschner, 1965). This occurs because

Pleasure and Persuasion We are less resistant to persuasive appeals when we are in a pleasant setting. Business people know this and make a point of taking their clients out to fine restaurants.

the situational context of a message promotes the peripheral route of persuasion. Another important aspect of the situational context is the presence of distractions. Distractions work by reducing the receiver's ability to think of counterarguments.

An early experiment examining the influence of distractions on the effectiveness of persuasive messages presented members of college fraternities with two films, each arguing strongly against fraternities. One film simply showed a speaker giving the speech. The other film presented the voice of the same speaker giving the speech accompanied by an irrelevant unnarrated film about art. The results showed that fraternity members who watched the distracting presentation were more persuaded by the speaker's arguments than were fraternity members who only watched the speaker. Apparently, the irrelevant film distracted listeners enough to interfere with their ability to think of counterarguments against the speaker's position (Festinger & Maccoby, 1964).

The Receiver of the Message During the Watergate hearings, supporters of President Nixon were less likely to watch the televised hearings than were people who had supported his 1972 campaign opponent, George McGovern (Sweeney & Gruber, 1984). This showed how our biases may determine whether we attend to particular persuasive messages. The intelligence level of the receiver is also important, because it helps determine whether a message will be more effective using the central or the peripheral route.

People of relatively high intelligence are more likely to be influenced by messages supported by rational arguments—the central route—while people of relatively low intelligence are more likely to be influenced by messages supported by factors other than rational arguments—the peripheral route. Relatively intelligent people are more likely to attend to rational arguments because they are better able to comprehend them (Eagly & Warren, 1976). A marketing firm for a client, such as a computer company, whose potential customers are relatively high in intelligence might be advised to use rational arguments to persuade people to purchase a product.

Attitudes and Behavior

Common sense tells us that if we know a person's attitudes we can accurately predict his or her behavior. But research studies have shown that the relationship is not that simple. For one thing, our behavior may not always agree with our attitudes. Perhaps more surprisingly, our behavior may sometimes affect our attitudes.

The Influence of Attitudes on Behavior Until the late 1960s, most social psychologists accepted the common-sense notion that our behavior is consistent with our attitudes. But researchers began to find that this is not always so (Cooper & Croyle, 1984). You have seen this exhibited dramatically by television evangelists who preach sexual denial while themselves engaging in a variety of extramarital sexual relations.

Though widespread interest in the inconsistency between attitudes and behaviors is only two decades old, evidence supporting the inconsistency between attitudes and behaviors appeared as early as the 1930s, when psychologist Richard LaPiere (1934) traveled with a young Chinese couple for 10,000 miles throughout the United States. They ate at 184 restaurants and stayed at 66 hotels, motels, and other places. Though anti-Chinese feelings were strong at that time, only 1 of the 250 establishments refused them service.

Six months after the journey, LaPiere wrote to each of the establishments, asking whether they would serve Chinese people. Of the 128 that replied, 118 (92 percent) said they would not. LaPiere concluded that this demonstrated that our behaviors do not necessarily agree with our attitudes. But the study had a major flaw. The people who served them (waiters and desk clerks) may not have been the same people who responded to LaPiere's letter (owners and managers). But what determines whether our attitudes and behaviors will be consistent?

Attitude-behavior consistency is influenced by the extent to which the receiver adapts his or her behavior to different situations. As discussed in chapter 13, the extent to which we adapt our behavior to fit different situations is called *self-monitoring.* High self-monitors adapt their behaviors to fit different situations. In contrast, low self-monitors behave in a relatively consistent manner across situations. And those who are low self-monitors show greater consistency between their attitudes and their behaviors than do those who are high self-monitors (Ajzen, Timko, & White, 1982). For example, low self-monitors show a more consistent relationship between their religious attitudes and their religious behaviors than do high self-monitors. This means that low self-monitors tend to behave in accordance with their religious attitudes regardless of the situation they are in (Zanna, Olson, & Fazio, 1980).

A general attitude is a better predictor of general behavioral tendencies than it is of specific behaviors. For example, your attitude toward safe driving may not predict whether you will obey the speed limit tomorrow morning, but it will predict your general tendency to engage in safe driving behaviors over time, such as checking your tire pressure, using turn signals, and obeying the speed limit. In contrast, a specific attitude is a better predictor of specific behaviors than it is of general behavioral tendencies. For example, your attitude toward the environmentalist Sierra Club (a specific attitude) would be a better predictor of your active participation in Sierra Club activities (a set of specific behaviors related to that attitude) than it would be of your attitude toward the environment (a general attitude). This shows that your attitudes and behaviors are more consistent with one another when they are at similar levels of specificity (Weigel, Vernon, & Tognazzi, 1974).

The Influence of Behavior on Attitudes   In the mid-1950s, Leon Festinger and his colleagues (1956) were intrigued by a sect whose members believed they would be saved by aliens in flying saucers at midnight prior to the day of a prophesized worldwide flood. But neither the aliens nor the flood ever arrived. Did the members lose their faith? On the contrary, their faith was strengthened. They simply concluded that the aliens had rewarded their faith by saving the world from the flood. The sect's members simply changed their belief in order to justify their action.

The ability of the sect's members to relieve the emotional distress that they experienced when the prophecy failed to come true stimulated Festinger's interest in attitude change and his development of the theory of **cognitive dissonance.** Cognitive dissonance is an unpleasant state of tension associated with high physiological arousal (Elkin & Leippe, 1986), which is caused by the realization that one has cognitions that are inconsistent with one another. This would occur in a cigarette smoker who believes that smoking is dangerous. We are motivated to reduce the unpleasant arousal associated with cognitive dissonance by making our cognitions consistent. Thus, a smoker might stop smoking or simply discount reports that link smoking to disease.

The more we feel responsible for the inconsistencies between our cognitions, the stronger will be our feelings of cognitive dissonance and the more motivated we will be to change them. This was the finding of the first experimental study of cognitive dissonance, conducted by Festinger and J. Merrill

Cognitive Dissonance Theory Leon Festinger's theory that attitude change is motivated by the desire to relieve the unpleasant state of tension caused when one holds cognitions that are inconsistent with each other.

Carlsmith (1959). In that experiment students were asked to perform boring tasks, one of which was to arrange small spools on a tray, dump the tray, and arrange the spools again and again for half an hour. Each student was paid either one dollar or twenty dollars to tell the next student that the task was enjoyable. After the experiment was over the students were asked to express their attitudes toward the task. Their responses violated what common sense would have predicted. Those who were paid less (one dollar) tended to rate the task as interesting, while those who were paid more (twenty dollars) tended to rate the task as boring (figure 17.6).

What could account for this finding? According to the theory of cognitive dissonance, the students experienced unpleasant arousal because their claims that the task was interesting did not agree with their beliefs that the task was boring. But those who were paid twenty dollars to lie about the task experienced weaker cognitive dissonance because they could justify their lies by attributing them to the large payment they received. In contrast, those who were paid only one dollar to lie experienced stronger cognitive dissonance because they could not attribute their lies to such a small payment. Consequently, those who were paid only one dollar reduced the dissonance between their cognitions by changing their attitudes toward the task, rating it as more interesting than it actually was.

The cognitive dissonance interpretation of attitude change has been challenged by another theory: Daryl Bem's (1967) self-perception theory. According to **self-perception theory,** attitude change is not motivated by our need to reduce cognitive dissonance. Instead, we infer our attitudes from our behavior in the same way that we infer other people's attitudes from their behaviors. When we observe someone behaving under no apparent external constraints, we use the behavior to make inferences about the person's attitudes. Likewise, when the situation we are in does not place constraints on our behavior, we may infer our own attitudes from our behavior. As an example, self-perception theory may explain why we tend to favor our home

Leon Festinger "The human organism tries to establish internal harmony, consistency, or congruity among his [her] opinions, attitudes, knowledge, and values."

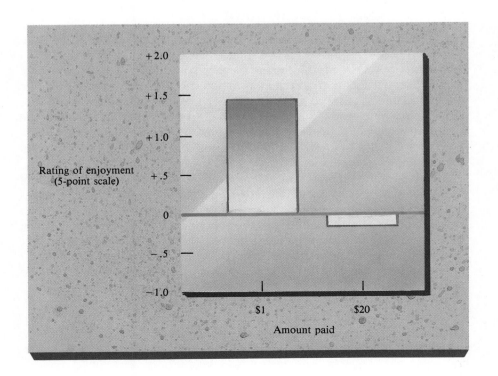

FIGURE 17.6
Cognitive Dissonance Subjects who were paid one dollar for telling other people that a boring task was interesting later rated the task as more enjoyable than did subjects who were paid twenty dollars for telling the same white lie.

Source: Data from L. Festinger and J. M. Carlsmith, "Cognitive Consequences of Forced Compliance" in Journal of Abnormal and Social Psychology, 58, 1959.

sports teams. Because of our proximity to them, we are more likely to attend our home teams' games, watch our home teams on television, and read about them in the newspaper. Because we perceive ourselves engaging in these behaviors, we may infer that we like our home teams.

But how does self-perception theory explain why students who were paid one dollar for lying would show greater attitude change than students who were paid twenty dollars? According to Bem, the students would not experience cognitive dissonance. Instead, they would determine whether their behaviors were attributable to themselves or to the situation. The students who were paid twenty dollars would attribute their behaviors to being paid a relatively large sum of money. They would have no reason to attribute their behaviors to their attitudes. In contrast, the students who were paid one dollar would be unable to attribute their behaviors to such a small sum of money. Consequently, those students would attribute their behaviors to their attitudes, perhaps saying to themselves, "If I told another student that the task was interesting and I was not induced to do so by a large amount of money, then the task must have been interesting to me."

Neither the theory of cognitive dissonance nor self-perception theory has emerged as the clearly superior explanation of the effect of behavior on attitudes. But each seems to be superior in certain circumstances. While cognitive dissonance theory appears to be better at explaining the effect of behavior on well-defined attitudes, self-perception theory appears to be better at explaining the effect of behavior on poorly defined attitudes (Chaiken & Baldwin, 1981).

THINKING ABOUT PSYCHOLOGY

Why Are People Prejudiced?

About twenty years ago, third-grade teacher Jane Elliott of Riceville, Iowa, gained national attention for a demonstration she gave of the devastating psychological effects of social prejudice. She divided her students, who all were white, into a blue-eyed group and a brown-eyed group. On the first day of the demonstration, Elliott declared that blue-eyed people are superior to brown-eyed people. The next day, she declared that brown-eyed people were superior to blue-eyed people.

Members of the superior group were given privileges, such as sitting where they wanted in class, going to lunch early, and staying late at recess. Members of the inferior group were made to wear identification collars and were not permitted to play with members of the superior group. Elliott reported that during the two-day demonstration, students who were made to feel inferior became depressed and performed poorly on classwork (Leonard, 1970). If prejudice could have this effect in an artificial, temporary situation, imagine the effect that prejudice has on children who are its targets in everyday life.

Prejudice is a negative attitude toward a person based on his or her membership in a particular group. The behavioral component of prejudice is **discrimination,** which involves treating persons differently, usually negatively, based only on their group membership. Women may be denied access to cer-

Prejudice An attitude, usually negative, toward a person based on his or her membership in a particular group.

Discrimination The treatment of a person differently, usually negatively, based on his or her group membership.

tain jobs, blacks prevented from living in certain neigborhoods, and handi-capped children prevented from enrolling in regular classes.

Factors Promoting Prejudice

What factors account for the origin and maintenance of prejudice? As with all attitudes, learning plays an important role. Parents, peers, and the media all provide input, informing us of the supposed characteristics of particular groups and which groups deserve to be disparaged. Research has been especially concerned with certain factors.

Stereotypes Men. Women. Blacks. Whites. Jews. Christians. If you believe that virtually all members of any of these groups share a set of character-istics that is unique to that group, you are guilty of stereotyping. A **stereo-type** is a social schema that incorporates characteristics, both positive and negative, that supposedly belong to almost all members of a group. Ste-reotypes are used to make predictions about the behavior of group mem-bers. We are likely to rely on stereotypes in making decisions about the behavior of others when we have little else but their group memberships on which to base our decisions.

Consider a study in which subjects were presented with the identical job applications of male and female applicants for sex-neutral, traditionally male, or traditionally female jobs. There was no difference in recommendations of males and females for the sex-neutral job. But, as would be expected based on male and female stereotypes, male applicants were favored for the tradi-tionally male job and female applicants were favored for the traditionally fe-male job. This discrimination was reduced when additional information was provided showing that the applicant had qualities that violated sex stereotypes (Glick, Zion, & Nelson, 1988).

You may recall from earlier in the chapter that one of the most important factors in interpersonal attraction is attitude similarity. Prejudiced people per-ceive stereotyped groups as having attitudes that are different from those of their own groups. When people believe that a member of another race has attitudes similar to their own, they will be less prejudiced toward that person. In a study of this phenomenon, subjects were asked to choose a work partner. When they were given information about another's race and attitudes, their choices were influenced more by their similarity in attitudes than by their sim-ilarity in race (Rokeach & Mezei, 1966).

As you will also recall from earlier in the chapter, our expectations may induce a *self-fulfilling prophecy.* A classic experiment, showing how social ste-

Stereotype A social schema that incorporates characteristics, both positive and negative, supposedly shared by almost all members of a group.

Prejudice and Social Learning
Adult models play a powerful role in determining whether children will become prejudiced against members of other groups.

reotypes may create self-fulfilling prophecies, investigated the influence of teachers' expectations on the performance of schoolchildren. The teachers were told that a new intelligence test indicated that certain of their students were "late bloomers" and would show a marked increase in intelligence by the end of the school year. The label "late bloomer" was actually assigned randomly to about 20 percent of the students. Yet, at the end of the school year, the "late bloomers" showed a significantly greater increase in intelligence than did the students who were not given that label. Apparently, the teachers' expectations led them to treat the "late bloomers" differently than the other students, thereby creating a self-fulfilling prophecy (Rosenthal & Jacobson, 1968). Likewise, teachers who believe that boys will be better at arithmetic than girls or that white children will be better at reading than black children may create self-fulfilling prophecies.

Authoritarian Personality A personality type marked by the tendency to obey superiors while dominating subordinates, to favor one's own group while being prejudiced against other groups, and to be unwilling to admit one's own faults while placing them on members of other groups.

The Authoritarian Personality The horrors of Nazism in the 1930s and 1940s led to a major research program at the University of California at Berkeley aimed at identifying the personality characteristics associated with fascist tendencies (Adorno, Frenkel-Brunswik, Levinson, & Sanford, 1950). Based on the results of tests and interviews with adult Californians, the researchers discovered what they called the authoritarian personality. People with an **authoritarian personality** tend to be obedient to their superiors and domineering over their subordinates (*authoritarianism*), in favor of their own groups and prejudiced against other groups (*egocentrism*), and unwilling to accept their own faults and willing to place them on members of other groups (*projection*).

The researchers also found factors that predispose people to develop authoritarian personalities. Such people tend to have parents who gave them little affection, relied on physical punishment, and refused to accept any back talk when they were children. This pattern of child rearing induces frustration, which leads to feelings of anger. Unable to direct this anger against their parents, children may displace it onto members of minority groups, who become the targets of prejudice and serve as scapegoats. You may recognize this as a Freudian interpretation of the development of the authoritarian personality.

But a later research study questioned whether the authoritarian personality was the main cause of prejudice. This study, conducted in the late 1950s, found that there was more prejudice against blacks in South Africa and the southern United States than in the northern United States. Yet, there was no difference in the degree of authoritarianism of southerners, northerners, and South Africans. Consequently, authoritarianism could not account for the greater racial prejudice that existed among southerners at that time. The researcher who conducted the study concluded that the greater racial prejudice among southerners was attributable to cultural norms that supported racial prejudice at that time (Pettigrew, 1959). This is a more ominous explanation of prejudice, because it implies that all people, regardless of their parents' style of discipline, are susceptible to becoming prejudiced.

Reducing Prejudice

Social psychologists are not content to study the causes of prejudice. They are also concerned with finding ways to reduce it. But this is a difficult process, because we are hesitant to revise our judgments based on stereotypes. We modify our stereotypes gradually through individual experiences and by creating subtypes to accommodate instances that we cannot easily assimilate. The latter occurs when a person says, "Some of my best friends are . . .," which only means that the speaker believes there are some exceptions to the stereotypes he or she holds. Evidently, we do not necessarily revise our stereotypes after experiencing a few dramatic exceptions to them (Weber & Crocker, 1983).

Equal Status Contact In the 1950s, the influential psychologist Gordon Allport (1954) insisted that prejudice could be reduced by increasing social contact between members of different social groups. At about the same time, in 1954, in the landmark case of *Brown v. The Board of Education of Topeka,* the United States Supreme Court ruled that "separate but equal" schools did not provide black children with the same benefits as white children. The Court's decision was influenced by research showing that segregated schools hurt the self-esteem of black children, increased interracial prejudice, and encouraged whites to view blacks as inferior.

But events during the past three decades have shown that social contact alone may not produce the effects predicted by Allport and the Supreme Court. For contact between groups to reduce prejudice, the contact must be between group members of equal status. If the contact is between group members of unequal status, then prejudice may actually increase. The effectiveness of equal status contact in reducing racial prejudice was supported by a study of black children and white children who spent a week at a summer camp. The children were between eight and twelve years old and were of equally low socioeconomic status. At the end of the week, children of both races had more positive attitudes toward children of the other race (Clore, Bray, Itkin, & Murphy, 1978). Under such equal status conditions, black children are more likely to experience enhanced self-esteem, to improve academic performance, and to experience less prejudice from white children (Cook, 1985).

Intergroup Cooperation One of the best ways to reduce prejudice is to promote intergroup cooperation, as in the so-called jigsaw method. The inventors of this method assigned elementary schoolchildren of different ethnic groups into mixed groups and gave each group different lessons to learn, which they had to use later to solve problems. Those who partici-

Equal Status Contact Contact between members of different groups will be more likely to reduce prejudice if the people have equal educational, organizational, or socioeconomic status.

Intergroup Cooperation
Prejudice may be reduced when
members of different groups
cooperate in working on the same
task.

pated in this study became more friendly with and less prejudiced against
one another (Aronson & Bridgeman, 1979).

But, because of attributional biases, intergroup cooperation does not always
reduce prejudice. If cooperative efforts fail, members of one group may attribute responsibility for this to members of the other group. And if cooperative efforts succeed, members of one group may attribute responsibility for
the success to a favorable situation, rather than giving any credit to members
of the other group (Brewer & Kramer, 1985). Thus, in certain cooperative situations, members of a cooperating group may be caught in a no-win, "Catch-
22" situation. As you can see, though prejudice can be overcome, it is difficult
to do so.

SUMMARY

SOCIAL ATTRIBUTION

Social psychology is the field of psychology that studies social relationships. The process by which we determine the causes of social behavior is called social attribution.
When you decide that a person is responsible for his or her own behavior, you are
making a dispositional attribution. And when you decide that a person's circumstances
are responsible for his or her behavior, you are making a situational attribution.

Harold Kelley identified three factors that interact in determining whether we make
dispositional or situational attributions: consistency, distinctiveness, and consensus.
Weiner's more ambitious theory of attribution looks at the interaction of the internal-
external, stable-unstable, and controllable-uncontrollable dimensions. Major biases in
social attribution include the actor-observer bias and the self-serving bias.

IMPRESSION FORMATION

Impression formation is the process by which me make judgments about the personal characteristics of people. This often depends on social schemas, which are composed of the presumed characteristics of a role, event, person, or group. Changes in our schemas depend on the interaction of accommodation and assimilation. Our first impressions play an important role in impression formation, in some cases creating a self-fulfilling prophecy.

SOCIAL ATTRACTION

Psychologists interested in studying social attraction are concerned with the factors that make us like or love other people. Liking depends on the factors of proximity, familiarity, physical attractiveness, similarity, and self-disclosure. Researchers who study love distinguish between passionate love and companionate love. According to Ellen Bersheid and Elaine Hatfield, romantic love depends on cultural support for the concept of love, a state of physiological arousal, and the presence of an appropriate person to love. Robert Sternberg's triangular theory of love explains how the interaction of passion, intimacy, and decision/commitment create different kinds of love or liking. Among the most important factors in promoting love are similarity, self-disclosure, and equity.

SOCIAL ATTITUDES

Attitudes are evaluations of ideas, events, objects, or people. Attitudes have emotional, cognitive, and behavioral components. Classical conditioning, operant conditioning, and social learning theory explain how attitudes are learned. We are often subject to persuasive messages aimed at getting us to change our attitudes. Persuasive messages may take a central route or a peripheral route, which are related to the message itself, the source of the message, the situational context of the message, and the receiver of the message.

Sources that are more credible and attractive are more persuasive. Under certain circumstances, two-sided messages will be more effective than one-sided messages. Persuasion is more effective in a pleasant setting. The biases and intelligence level of the receiver also determine the effectiveness of persuasive messages. But our attitudes may not always accurately predict our behavior, and our behavior may sometimes affect our attitudes, a phenomenon that is explained by cognitive dissonance theory and self-perception theory.

THINKING ABOUT PSYCHOLOGY:
WHY ARE PEOPLE PREJUDICED?

Prejudice is a negative attitude toward a person based on his or her membership in a particular group. The behavioral component of prejudice is discrimination. Among the important factors promoting prejudice are stereotypes and the authoritarian personality. Prejudice may be reduced when there is equal status contact and intergroup cooperation.

IMPORTANT CONCEPTS

Actor-observer bias 593
Attitude 605
Authoritarian personality 616
Cognitive dissonance theory 612
Companionate love 603
Consensus 591
Consistency 590
Discrimination 614

Distinctiveness 590
Impression formation 595
Mere exposure effect 599
Passionate love 603
Persuasion 607
Prejudice 614
Self-disclosure 602
Self-fulfilling prophecy 598

Self-perception theory 613
Self-serving bias 594
Social attribution 590
Social psychology 590
Social schema 595
Stereotype 615
Triangular theory of love 604

IMPORTANT PEOPLE

Leon Festinger 612
Elaine Hatfield and Ellen Berscheid 603

Harold Kelley 590, 597
Robert Sternberg 604

Bernard Weiner 591

RECOMMENDED READINGS

For More on All Aspects of Social Cognition:

Aronson, E. (1987). *The social animal* (5th ed.). New York: Freeman.
A readable, award-winning book on social psychology.

Baron, R. A., & Byrne, D. (1987). *Social psychology: Understanding human interaction* (5th ed.). Boston: Allyn & Bacon.
A comprehensive textbook covering all topics in social psychology.

For More on Social Attribution:

Harvey, J. H., & Weary, G. (1981). *Perspectives on attributional processes*. Dubuque, IA: Wm. C. Brown.
A discussion of the factors that determine our perception of the causes of behaviors.

For More on Impression Formation:

Fiske, S. T., & Taylor, S. E. (1984). *Social cognition*. Reading, MA: Addison-Wesley.
A scholarly presentation of research on impression formation, social attribution, and other topics in social cognition.

For More on Interpersonal Attraction:

Hatfield, E., & Sprecher, S. (1986). *Mirror, mirror: The importance of looks in everyday life*. Albany, New York: SUNY Press.
An engaging look at the relationship between physical attractiveness and social interactions.

Sternberg, R. J., & Barnes, M. L. (Eds.). (1988). *The psychology of love*. New Haven, CT: Yale University Press.
An interesting collection of articles on the factors that promote and maintain romantic relationships.

For More on Social Attitudes:

Petty, R. E., & Cacioppo, J. T. (1981). *Attitudes and persuasion: Classic and contemporary approaches*. Dubuque, IA: Wm. C. Brown.
A thorough discussion of the processes of attitude formation and attitude change.

For More on Prejudice:

Dovidio, J. F., & Gaertner, S. L. (Eds.). (1986). *Prejudice, discrimination, and racism*. Orlando, FL: Academic Press.
A collection of articles on the causes, effects, and prevention of prejudice and discrimination, with special emphasis on the problem of racism.

CHAPTER
18

SOCIAL INFLUENCE

Chapter Opening Art:
Joan Miro. *The Birth of the World.* Montroig, 1925.

623

o leaders share certain personal characteristics? Are people more violent in warm weather? When will a bystander help someone in an emergency? These are some of the questions that interest psychologists who study **social influence,** the effects of social relationships on thinking, feeling, and behaving. As you read this chapter, you will realize that social influence cannot be divorced from social perception, the topic of chapter 17. You will also note a theme that runs through this chapter: the behaviors of individuals in groups are often different from their behaviors when they are alone.

Social Influence The effects of social relationships on thinking, feeling, and behaving.

RELATIONSHIPS IN GROUPS

In the late 1940s, hoping to understand the social factors that contributed to the Great Depression, the rise of European dictatorships, and World War II, social psychologists became more interested in studying the factors that affect relationships between members of groups (Zander, 1979). This remains an important area of research in social psychology.

Characteristics of Groups

Group A collection of two or more persons who have mutual influence on each other.

Norm A rule of proper social behavior that guides group members.

Role A social position that is associated with norms that determine the proper behavior of individuals who hold that position.

In everyday life we refer to any collection of people as a "group." But social psychologists favor a narrower definition of a **group** as a collection of two or more persons who interact and have mutual influence. Examples of groups would include a sorority, a softball team, and the board of trustees of your school. Groups are governed by **norms,** which are the rules of behavior that guide group members. Social **roles** are the behaviors expected of people who hold certain positions in a group. As an example, social *norms* direct orchestra members to dress in particular ways, play particular kinds of music, and acknowledge the audience at particular times. Similarly, social *roles* require the orchestra conductor to direct musicians and the musicians to follow the conductor's directions.

Our social norms are influenced by the groups with which we identify—commonly called *reference groups.* The influence of reference groups was illustrated in a classic study conducted by Theodore Newcomb (1943) at Bennington College in Vermont in the 1930s. The students at Bennington, a women's college, came from wealthy, conservative families. With their families as their most important reference groups, freshmen tended to be conservative. So, it was not surprising that in the 1936 presidential election between conservative Alf Landon and liberal Franklin Roosevelt 62 percent of the freshmen supported Landon. What was surprising, however, was that only 15 percent of the juniors and seniors supported him.

What accounted for this difference? Because their professors tended to expose them to more liberal ideas, students tended to become more and more liberal. These students then became a liberal reference group for freshmen, reinforcing the influence of their professors. Twenty-five years later, a follow-up study by Newcomb and his colleagues (1967) found that the graduates tended to retain their liberal views. This occurred, in part, because they had continued to associate with more liberal people. They married liberal men, kept in contact with liberal classmates, and participated in activities sponsored by liberal organizations.

While the Bennington study showed the powerful influence of social norms, another classic study showed that social roles, too, have a powerful influence on behavior. In that study, social psychologist Phillip Zimbardo assigned male students to be "guards" and "prisoners" at a mock prison in a basement at Stanford University for a two-week period. The guards wore uniforms and strictly enforced all rules. The prisoners wore prison garb and spent much of their time locked up in cells. Zimbardo had to end the study after only six days, because the guards and prisoners began taking their roles too seriously. The guards became authoritarian, verbally abusive, and physically intimidating, while the prisoners became fearful and passive-aggressive. Zimbardo feared that some of the students might get hurt if he permitted the study to continue (Zimbardo, Haney, & Banks, 1973).

Because the students had been selected for their high emotional stability, Zimbardo concluded that the results were attributable not to the kind of people he used but, rather, to the powerful social roles of "guard" and "prisoner." You can certainly appreciate the implications of this study. If these roles could exert such strong effects in a mock prison, imagine their effects in real prisons. Even good-natured people who become guards may act cruelly when they are on the job, and even pleasant people who become prisoners may act belligerently. Perhaps much of our behavior is controlled by our social roles, rather than our personality characteristics.

Decision Making in Groups

As members of groups, we are often called upon to make group decisions. A family must decide which new house to buy. College administrators must decide which proposed new academic majors to approve. And the Congress must decide on air pollution standards. Decisions made by groups are not simply the outcome of rational give and take, with the wisest decision automatically emerging. They are affected by other factors as well.

Group Polarization In the 1950s, social critic William H. Whyte (1956) claimed that groups, notably those within business and governmental organizations, tended to make safe, compromise decisions instead of risky, extreme decisions. Whyte assumed that this tendency explained why organizations failed to be as creative and innovative as individuals. In the 1960s his view was challenged by studies that found a tendency for group decisions to be *riskier* than decisions made by individuals. The first study asked individuals to make decisions about hypothetical problems. They then took part in group discussions to reach group decisions. The results showed that decisions made by individuals were, on the average, safer than the decisions made by groups composed of those same individuals (Stoner, 1961). The tendency for group decisions to be riskier than would be made by their individual members was found in other studies and became known as the *risky shift* (Wallach, Kogan, & Bem, 1962).

But more recent research has shown that groups tend to make decisions in either a risky *or* a cautious direction, rather than in only a risky direction. The

Social Roles The study by Zimbardo, Haney, and Banks (1973) showed the powerful influence of social roles. The photograph on the left shows student participants being "arrested." The photograph on the right shows a "guard" taking his role a bit too seriously.

Group Polarization The tendency for groups to make more extreme decisions than their members would make as individuals.

tendency for groups to make more extreme decisions than their members would make as individuals is called **group polarization.** In one study, when groups of high school students either high or low in racial prejudice discussed racial issues, those who were low in prejudice became less prejudiced and those who were high in prejudice became more prejudiced (Myers & Bishop, 1970).

What accounts for group polarization? There are two theories that have received support from research findings, indicating that group polarization may depend on both. *Persuasive argumentation theory* assumes that group members who initially hold a moderate position about an issue will move in the direction of the most persuasive arguments, which will eventually move the group toward either a risky or a cautious decision. According to *social comparison theory,* group members want to be viewed as socially desirable, perhaps by agreeing with the average tendency of group members. As a consequence, when a group member determines the position that the group seems to favor, that member will adopt a slightly more extreme position in that direction. If each member of the group does this, the group will eventually reach either a risky decision or a cautious decision (Isenberg, 1986).

Groupthink On January 28, 1986, the space shuttle *Challenger* exploded shortly after taking off from Cape Canaveral, killing all of the crew members and shocking the hundreds of spectators and millions of television viewers excited by the presence of the first teacher-astronaut, Christa McAuliffe. The committee that investigated this tragedy reported that the explosion was caused by a faulty joint in one of the rocket boosters. The decision to launch the shuttle had been made despite warnings from engineers that the joint might fail (Zaldivar, 1986). This ill-fated decision has been attributed to groupthink.

Groupthink The tendency of small, cohesive groups to place unanimity ahead of critical thinking in making decisions.

The term **groupthink,** coined by psychologist Irving Janis, refers to a decision-making process in small, cohesive groups that places unanimity ahead of critical thinking. Groupthink is promoted by several factors: the desire to maintain group harmony, a charismatic leader, feelings of invulnerability, discrediting of contrary evidence, fear of criticism for disagreeing, isolation from outside influences, and disparaging outsiders as incompetent. In criticizing

Group Polarization One of the most important situations in which group polarization is desirable is in jury deliberations. We expect the members of juries to start with neutral positions concerning the defendant and then, after deliberation, to move to a more extreme position—deciding that the defendant is either guilty or innocent.

Groupthink President Kennedy discusses foreign policy with his advisors. Their decision in the ill-fated Bay of Pigs invasion showed characteristics of groupthink.

the decision to launch the *Challenger,* Senator John Glenn of Ohio, the first American to orbit the Earth, referred to feelings of invulnerability among the officials who made the decision: "The mindset of a few people in key positions at NASA had changed from an optimistic and supersafety conscious 'can do' attitude, when I was in the program, to an arrogant 'can't fail' attitude" (Zaldivar, 1986, p. 12-A).

Janis (1983) used two decisions by President Kennedy, both involving Cuba, to illustrate groupthink and how to overcome it. On April 17, 1961, 1,400 Cuban exiles who had been trained by the CIA landed at the Bay of Pigs in an attempt to overthrow Fidel Castro. But within three days about 200 of the invaders were killed and the rest captured. According to Janis, President Kennedy and his advisors had succumbed to groupthink. Kennedy, a strong leader, played an active role in group discussions, the group failed to seek outside opinions, and they ignored contrary information about the expected strength of Cuban resistance to the invasion.

During the Cuban missile crisis of October 1962, President Kennedy showed that he had learned from the Bay of Pigs fiasco. He and his advisors avoided groupthink in reaching a decision on how to convince the Soviet Union to remove its nuclear missile bases from Cuba. This was a monumental decision, because it was the closest the United States has ever come to nuclear war. Kennedy permitted his advisors to hold some meetings without him. His advisors invited contributions from outside experts. And members of the advisory group were encouraged to play "devil's advocate" by countering all proposals. Kennedy and his advisors decided to assure the Soviet Union that the United States would not invade Cuba in return for the removal of the nuclear missiles. This proposal was accepted and a possible nuclear confrontation was avoided.

Minority Influence Does the majority always determine the outcome of group decision making? In general, the answer is yes. The majority has the power to convince group members to go along with its decision, in part because of its ability to criticize and socially ostracize those who dissent. Yet, under certain circumstances, minorities may influence group decisions. If you are part of a minority and wish to influence group decisions, you should follow several well-established principles.

First, you must present rational, rather than emotional, reasons for your position. As discussed in chapter 17, this means that you must take the central, rather than peripheral, route of persuasion to make the majority consider your position. Second, you must appear absolutely confident in your position, with no wavering at all. If you are unsure of your position, majority members will discount it. Third, you must be consistent in your position over time. Again, if you are inconsistent, your opponents will discredit you. Fourth, you must have patience. Though majorities may initially dismiss minority positions, the passage of time may make them ponder the evidence you have provided and gradually change their positions. Fifth, try to bring at least one other person over to your side. A minority of two is much more influential than a minority of one (Nemeth, 1986).

Group Leadership

Leader A group member who exerts more influence on the group than does any other member.

Group decisions are often made by a group **leader,** a person who exerts more influence on the group than does any other group member. The role of a leader is to define the group's goals, plan the group's activities, and direct the group's actions.

Characteristics of Leaders What makes certain people become leaders? In 1904, Lewis Terman put forth what is now known as the "great person" theory of leadership to explain why certain people became leaders. He assumed that such people have characteristics that predispose them to become leaders. If that were true, by now research should have discovered a set of "leadership traits" common to people who become leaders. But research has failed to do so.

Though leaders tend to share few personality traits, they do tend to be taller than average and to be male. Yet, there are many exceptions to both of these tendencies. For example, Napoleon was shorter than average and Margaret Thatcher has served for years as Prime Minister of Great Britain. Though there is still a cultural bias against women leaders, when group members believe that women members of a group are competent, they are more willing to permit women to emerge as leaders. This was demonstrated in a study of four-person groups consisting of men and women who were asked to make decisions about different problems. When the groups were given no information about the backgrounds of group members, men were more likely to dominate the groups, offering more opinions and providing more information. When the groups were told that the women were competent (for example, by portraying them as highly intelligent), there were no sex differences in the emergence of discussion leaders (Wood & Karten, 1986).

Because of the failure to identify personality characteristics shared by leaders, most psychologists now assume that leadership is situation specific, with leaders emerging who meet the requirements of specific situations. For example, the crisis of World War II led to the emergence of Winston Churchill as the leader of Great Britain. Yet, in peacetime, both before and after World War II, the British people rejected Churchill as their leader. The characteristics that made him a great leader during a wartime crisis were apparently not those valued by the British during peacetime.

Leaders People emerge as leaders when their personal characteristics fit the circumstances they are in. This is true of military leaders such as George Patton, political leaders such as Corazon Aquino, and business leaders such as Lee Iacocca.

Effective Leadership What makes a leader effective? Perhaps the most influential explanation is provided by Fred Fiedler's (1971) **contingency theory of leadership,** which states that the effectiveness of a leader is a function of the interaction between his or her style of leadership and the favorableness of the situation. So, neither the person nor the situation alone determines a leader's effectiveness. Fiedler distinguishes two kinds of leaders. A *task-oriented leader* assumes that group members will perform well when they receive constant supervision from their leader. A *relationship-oriented leader* assumes that group members will perform well when they receive emotional support from their leader. The favorableness of the situation depends on the group atmosphere, the clarity of the task, and the leader's degree of authority. The most favorable situation is one in which the relationship between the leader and the group members is good rather than bad; the task is clearly defined rather than ambiguous; and the leader has a strong, rather than a weak, position of authority.

According to the contingency theory of leadership, a task-oriented leader will be more effective in either a highly favorable situation or a highly unfavorable situation, while a relationship-oriented leader will be more effective in a moderately favorable situation. Fiedler assumes that in a highly unfavorable situation the group needs the guidance provided by a task-oriented leader, while in a highly favorable situation the group will appreciate the task-oriented leader's tendency to be concerned only with task performance. In a moderately favorable situation, group members respond better to a leader who provides emotional support with a modest degree of direction. The contingency theory of leadership has received mixed support, with laboratory experiments providing stronger support for it than have field studies (Peters, Hartke, & Pohlmann, 1985). It remains to be seen whether the positive findings of laboratory studies will generalize to real-life leadership situations.

Contingency Theory of Leadership The theory that the effectiveness of a leader is a function of the interaction between the style of leadership and the favorableness of the leadership situation.

Group Effects on Performance

One of the first topics to be studied by social psychologists was the influence of groups on the task performances of their members. Social psychologists have been especially interested in studying the effects of *social facilitation* and *social loafing* on performance.

"I can't solve your problem. I *am* the problem."

Social Facilitation As mentioned at the beginning of chapter 17, almost a century ago Norman Triplett (1898) observed that people performed faster when competing against other people than when performing alone. A quarter-century later, psychologist Frank Allport (1920) found that people performed a variety of tasks better when working in the same room than when working in separate rooms. The presence of other people, not just the presence of a competitor, appeared to improve performance. Allport called the improvement in performance caused by the presence of other people **social facilitation.**

Social Facilitation The improvement in a person's task performance when in the presence of other people.

But later studies found that the presence of others may sometimes *impair* performance, a process called *social inhibition.* A review of 241 studies involving almost 24,000 subjects found that the presence of other people improves performance on simple tasks and impairs performance on complex tasks. Moreover, the presence of other people improves performance on well-learned tasks and impairs performance on poorly learned tasks (Bond & Titus, 1983). For example, in one study, children tried to balance on a teeterboard for as long as possible. In the presence of other people, children who were highly skilled performed better and children who were poorly skilled performed worse than when performing alone (MacCracken & Stadulis, 1985).

What would account for these findings? The most influential explanation for both social facilitation and social inhibition is the *drive theory* of Robert Zajonc (1965). According to Zajonc the presence of other people increases physiological arousal, which energizes the performer's most well-learned responses to a task. For those who are good at a task, the most well-learned responses will be effective ones. Consequently, those people will perform *better* in the presence of others. In contrast, for those who are not good at a task, the most well-learned responses will be ineffective ones. Consequently, those people will perform *worse* in the presence of others. This has practical implications. When you are learning to perform a new task, whether playing golf or playing the piano, you should practice as much as possible alone before seeking to play in the presence of other people.

But how does the presence of other people increase arousal? Two influential theories provide different explanations. The *distraction-conflict theory* assumes that arousal increases because of the greater effort required to attend to a task while being distracted by other people. In contrast, the *evaluation-apprehension theory* assumes that arousal increases because of concern with having one's performance evaluated. Consider a study in which male and female runners were timed (without their knowledge) as they ran along a ninety-yard segment of a footpath. One-third of the subjects ran alone, one-third encountered a female facing them at the halfway point, and one-third encountered a female seated with her back to them at the halfway point. Only the group that encountered a female facing them showed a significant acceleration between the first and second halves of the segment (Worringham & Messick, 1983).

Both theories could provide explanations for this finding. According to the distraction-conflict theory, the woman facing the runners was more distracting to them than was the woman with her back to them. In contrast, according to the evaluation-apprehension theory, the woman facing the runners made them more concerned with being evaluated than did the woman with her back to them. Neither theory has emerged as clearly superior to the other. Perhaps a combination of both would best explain social facilitation and social inhibition.

Social Loafing In the 1880s a French agricultural engineer named Max Ringelmann found that people exerted less effort when working in groups than when working alone. He had men pull on a rope attached to a meter that measured the strength of their pull. As the number of men pulling increased from one to eight, the average strength of each man's pull decreased. Ringelmann attributed this to a loss of coordination when working with other people, a phenomenon that became known as the *Ringelmann effect* (Kravitz & Martin, 1986).

More recently, the Ringelmann effect has been attributed to a decrease in the effort exerted by individuals when working together, a phenomenon known as **social loafing.** This reflects the old saying, "Many hands make light the work." Social loafing has been demonstrated in many studies. In one experiment, high school cheerleaders cheered either alone or in pairs. Sound-level recordings found that individual cheerleaders cheered louder when cheering alone than when cheering together (Hardy & Latané, 1988).

Note that unlike social facilitation, which occurs when people believe their individual performances are being scrutinized, social loafing occurs when people believe their performances are not being scrutinized. According to the concept of the *diffusion of responsibility,* social loafing occurs when group members feel anonymous and believe that their individual performances do not matter. This makes them less motivated to exert their maximum effort. Because of this, committees are often inefficient in accomplishing their goals, with each member able to claim, "I thought _____ was going to do it." This also means that a good way to reduce social loafing is to convince group members that their individual efforts will be evaluated. Years ago legendary Ohio State University football coach Woody Hayes used that technique to motivate his linemen, whose performance normally received little attention. Hayes videotaped every play, rated each lineman's performance, and held weekly press conferences to announce the lineman of the week and to present special helmet decals to linemen for outstanding performances (Williams, Harkins, & Latané, 1981).

An alternative explanation of social loafing is provided by *equity theory,* which assumes that social loafing occurs because group members tend to expect their fellow group members to loaf. This makes members exert less

Social Facilitation and Social Inhibition Because of social facilitation, a professional bicycle racer may perform better in the presence of other people. In contrast, because of social inhibition, a child learning to ride a bicycle may perform better when practicing alone.

Social Loafing A decrease in the individual effort exerted by group members when working together on a task than when working independently.

Social Loafing Because of social loafing, these individuals will probably exert less effort than they would if they pulled by themselves.

Conformity Behaving in accordance with group norms when there is little or no overt pressure to do so.

Conformity Our tendency to conform knows no boundaries of age.

effort in order to establish an equitable division of labor. For example, waiters who believe that their fellow waiters will set up fewer tables, serve fewer customers, and clear fewer tables will establish equity by behaving in that very manner themselves. When members of a work group are convinced that their fellow members will not loaf, social loafing is eliminated (Jackson & Harkins, 1985). Apparently, both the diffusion of responsibility and the desire for equity play a role in social loafing.

INTERPERSONAL INFLUENCE

The groups we belong to influence our behavior in ways that range from subtle prodding to direct demanding. Among the most important kinds of interpersonal influence are *conformity, compliance,* and *obedience.*

Conformity

Do you dress the way you do because your friends dress that way? Do you hold certain religious beliefs because your parents hold them? If you answered yes to these questions, you might be exhibiting **conformity,** which means behaving in accordance with group norms with little or no overt pressure to do so. The power of conformity was demonstrated in a classic series of experiments conducted by psychologist Solomon Asch in the 1950s. In a typical experiment, a male college student who had volunteered to be a research subject was told that he would be taking part in a study of visual perception. He was seated around a table with six other "subjects," who were actually the experimenter's confederates. The experimenter presented a series of trials in which he displayed two large white cards (figure 18.1). One card contained three vertical lines of different lengths. The second card contained a single vertical line clearly equal in length to one of the three lines on the first card.

On each of eighteen trials, the participants were asked, one person at a time, to choose the line on the first card that was the same length as the line on the second card. The lengths of the lines varied from trial to trial. On the first two trials each confederate chose the correct line. But on the third trial, and on eleven of the succeeding trials, the confederates chose a line that was clearly *not* the same length as the single line. On the first few bogus trials, the subject appeared uncomfortable but usually chose the correct line. But over the course of the twelve bogus trials the subject sometimes conformed to the erroneous choices made by the confederates.

The results showed that, overall, the subjects conformed on 37 percent of the bogus trials. Three-quarters of the subjects conformed on at least one bogus trial. In replications of the experiment, Asch varied the number of confederates from one to fifteen persons. As illustrated in figure 18.2, he found that the subject's tendency to conform increased dramatically until there were three confederates, with additional confederates producing little additional increase in conformity (Asch, 1955).

Why did the subjects conform to the obviously erroneous judgments of strangers? Some claimed they really saw the lines as equal and others believed that the confederates knew something they did not. But their main reason for conforming was their need for social approval—they feared social rejection. The subjects, as do many people, found it difficult to be the lone dissenter in a group. In variations of the experiment in which one of the confederates joined the subject in dissenting, the subjects conformed on less than one-tenth, rather than on one-third, of the bogus trials (Asch, 1955). Thus, dissent is more likely when we have fellow dissenters.

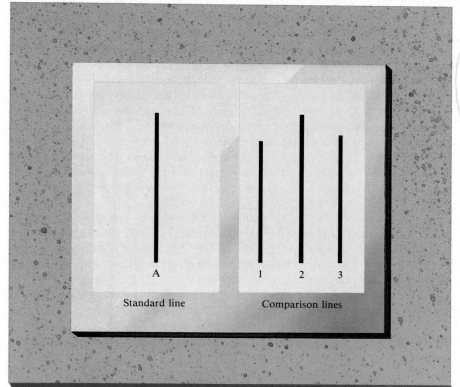

Standard line

Comparison lines

A   1   2   3

FIGURE 18.1
The Asch Study Subjects in Solomon Asch's studies had to decide which of three lines was equal in length to another line. The photograph on the right shows the confusion of subject number 6 when other subjects chose the wrong line.

Source (b): From Solomon E. Asch, "Studies of Independence and Conformity: A Minority of One Against a Unanimous Majority" in *Psychological Monographs* (90, Whole No. 416), 1956.

conforming + the need for social approval

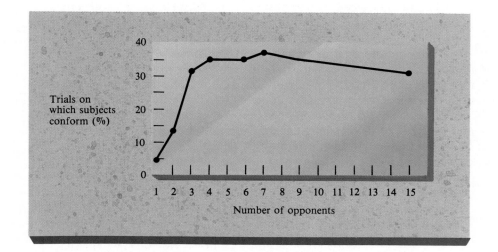

Trials on which subjects conform (%)

Number of opponents

FIGURE 18.2
Conformity and Group Size Asch (1955) found that conformity increased dramatically as the number of opponents increased to three. Adding more opponents did little to increase conformity.

From "Opinions and Social Pressure" by Solomon Asch. Copyright © 1955 by SCIENTIFIC AMERICAN, Inc. All rights reserved.

Compliance

We are continually bombarded with requests. A friend might want to borrow your car. A fellow student might ask you to help move laboratory equipment. An advertiser might urge you to purchase a particular deodorant. The process by which a person agrees to a request that is backed by little or no threat of punishment is called **compliance.**

The Foot-in-the-Door Years ago, it was common for salespersons to go door-to-door trying to sell encyclopedias, vacuum cleaners, or other products. Every salesperson knew that a person who complied with the small request to be permitted inside to discuss or demonstrate a product would then be more likely to comply with the larger request to purchase the product. This became known as the **foot-in-the-door technique.**

The foot-in-the-door technique, which can be used in a variety of social interactions, can produce extraordinary degrees of compliance. In one study, women were surveyed by telephone to ask them questions about the brand of soap they used. Three days later they were called again, as were a group of women who had not received the first call. This time the caller asked each woman for permission to send a team of men who would rummage through her cabinets to record the household items that she used. Of those who had complied with the first (small) request, 53 percent agreed to permit a team to visit their homes. Of those who received only the second (large) request, just 22 percent agreed to permit a team to visit their homes (Freedman & Fraser, 1966).

Why is the foot-in-the-door technique effective? Self-perception theory provides an answer (Eisenberg, Cialdini, McCreath, & Shell, 1987). As explained in chapter 17, self-perception theory assumes that we infer our personal characteristics from observing our own behaviors. If you freely comply with a small, worthwhile request, you will view yourself as the kind of person who does favors for others. Because you wish to be consistent with your self-perception, you will be more likely to comply with other requests.

The Door-in-the-Face Salespeople also know that those who refuse to purchase a particular item will be more likely to comply with a request to purchase a less expensive item. Suppose that a Girl Scout rang your doorbell and asked you to buy a case of girl scout cookies. If you turned down that request and she then asked you to buy one box of cookies, you would be more likely to buy one box (a small request) than you would have been if she had not first asked you to buy a case (a large request). Fostering compliance by presenting a smaller request after a larger request has been denied is called the **door-in-the-face technique.**

We resort to the door-in-the-face technique in our everyday lives in situations such as negotiating salaries, selling our homes, or convincing professors to give us extra time to complete term papers. Even charities use the technique. In one study, potential volunteers were asked to commit themselves to serve as a Big Brother or Big Sister at a juvenile detention center for two hours a week for two years. After they rejected this large request, they were subjected to a much smaller request—to chaperone a group of low-income children on a single two-hour visit to a zoo. The subjects were more likely to comply with this request than were those who had not been asked earlier to serve as a Big Brother or Big Sister (Cialdini et al., 1975).

The door-in-the-face technique depends on social norms that require that concessions offered by one negotiating party must be met by concessions from the other party. The willingness of one person to reduce the size of an initial request would be considered to be a concession, imposing social pressure on

Compliance Behaving in accordance with a direct request that is backed by little or no threat of punishment.

Foot-in-the-Door Technique Increasing the likelihood that someone will comply with a request by first getting them to comply with a smaller request.

Door-in-the-Face Technique Increasing the likelihood that someone will comply with a request by first getting them to reject a larger request.

The Foot-in-the-Door Technique If you have ever been in a major city or large airport, you have probably observed panhandlers use the foot-in-the-door technique. A panhandler might ask a passerby for a quarter to call home. If the passerby complies, the panhandler might then ask for a dollar for busfare home. A passerby who complies with the smaller request will be more likely to comply with the larger request than will one who is subjected only to the larger request.

the person who had refused the first request to comply with the second one (Cann, Sherman, & Elkes, 1975).

Obedience

Would you assist in the cold-blooded murder of innocent people if your superior ordered you to? This question deals with the limits of **obedience**—the following of orders given by an authority. The limits of obedience were at the heart of the Nuremberg war crime trials held after World War II. The defendants were Nazis accused of "crimes against humanity" for their complicity in the executions of millions of innocent people during World War II, most notably the genocide of six million Jews. The defendants claimed that they were only following orders.

Obedience Behaving in accordance with orders given by an authority.

A more recent example of the dangers of blind obedience occurred in 1977. To avoid a government investigation of his practices, the Reverend Jim Jones fled California with members of his "People's Temple" and established "Jonestown" in Guyana. The group's norms included blind obedience to Jones. When reports reached friends and relatives of his followers that Jones was keeping some of them against their wills, Congressman Leo Ryan responded by flying to Guyana. Ryan convinced Jones to release those who wished to return home. But as Ryan and several followers were about to board a plane for the United States, gunmen obeying orders from Jones opened fire, killing Ryan and several other people. Jones then ordered his followers to kill themselves by drinking from a large bowl of Kool-Aid laced with cyanide. Most obeyed willingly. Those who refused were shot by followers who then killed themselves. Jones killed himself with a gunshot to his head. More than nine hundred people, including infants and children, died in the bloodbath (Matthews, Harper, Fuller, Nater, & Lubenow, 1978).

Are people who obey orders to hurt innocent people unusually cruel, or are most human beings susceptible to obeying such orders? This question led psychologist Stanley Milgram (1963) of Yale University to conduct one of the most famous—and controversial—of all psychology experiments. Milgram's subjects were adult men who had responded to an advertisement for volunteers to participate in a study of the effects of punishment on learning. On arriving at the laboratory, each subject was introduced to a pleasant, middle-aged man who would also participate in the experiment. In reality, the man was a confederate of the experimenter. The experimenter asked both men to draw a slip of paper out of a hat to determine who would be the "teacher" and who would be the "learner." The drawing was rigged so that the subject was always the teacher.

The subject communicated with the learner over an intercom as the learner performed a memory task while strapped to an electrified chair in another room (figure 18.3). The subject sat at a control panel with a series of switches with labels ranging from "Slight Shock" (15 volts) to "Danger: Severe Shock" (450 volts) in 15–volt increments. The experimenter instructed the subject to administer an increasingly strong electric shock to the learner whenever he made an error. At higher shock levels, the learner would cry out in pain or beg the teacher to stop. Many subjects responded to the learner's distress with sweating, trembling, and stuttering. If the subject hesitated to administer a shock, the experimenter might say, "You have no other choice, you must go on," and remind the teacher that he, the experimenter, was responsible for any ill effects.

How far do you think you would have gone as the teacher? To Milgram's surprise, two-thirds of the subjects reached the maximum level of shock, and *none* stopped before reaching 300 volts—the point at which the learner frantically banged on the wall and stopped answering questions. Surveys of psy-

The Jonestown Massacre
Obedience to Jim Jones led to the murders or suicides of more than nine hundred members of his "People's Temple."

Public Announcement

WE WILL PAY YOU $4.00 FOR ONE HOUR OF YOUR TIME

Persons Needed for a Study of Memory

•We will pay five hundred New Haven men to help us complete a scientific study of memory and learning. The study is being done at Yale University.

•Each person who participates will be paid $4.00 (plus 50c carfare) for approximately 1 hour's time. We need you for only one hour: there are no further obligations. You may choose the time you would like to come (evenings, weekdays, or weekends).

•No special training, education, or experience is needed. We want:

Factory workers	Businessmen	Construction workers
City employees	Clerks	Salespeople
Laborers	Professional people	White-collar workers
Barbers	Telephone workers	Others

All persons must be between the ages of 20 and 50. High school and college students cannot be used.

•If you meet these qualifications, fill out the coupon below and mail it now to Professor Stanley Milgram, Department of Psychology, Yale University, New Haven. You will be notified later of the specific time and place of the study. We reserve the right to decline any application.

•You will be paid $4.00 (plus 50c carfare) as soon as you arrive at the laboratory.

TO:
PROF. STANLEY MILGRAM, DEPARTMENT OF PSYCHOLOGY, YALE UNIVERSITY, NEW HAVEN, CONN. I want to take part in this study of memory and learning. I am between the ages of 20 and 50. I will be paid $4.00 (plus 50c carfare) if I participate.

NAME (Please Print). . . . .

ADDRESS . . . .

TELEPHONE NO. . . . . Best time to call you . . . .

AGE . . . . OCCUPATION . . . . SEX . . . . . .
CAN YOU COME:

WEEKDAYS . . . . EVENINGS . . . . . . WEEKENDS . . . .

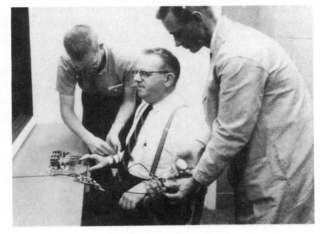

FIGURE 18.3
Milgram's Study of Obedience
Milgram advertised for people who would be willing to take part in a study of memory. The photographs show the "shock generator" that he used and a subject helping the experimenter attach electrodes to the learner's arm.

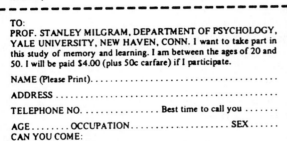

chiatrists and Yale students had predicted that less than 2 percent of the subjects would reach the maximum level. By the way, the learner never received a single shock. In fact, his responses were all played on a tape recorder.

Could the prestige of Yale University and the legitimacy of a laboratory study have affected the subjects? Milgram repeated the study in a run-down office building, he did not wear a laboratory coat, and he made no reference to Yale. He obtained impressive results nonetheless. Of those participating, 48 percent reached the maximum level of shock. Did physically separating the teacher and the learner have an effect? Somewhat. Figure 18.4 shows that when the teacher sat near the learner, 40 percent reached the maximum. Even when the teacher had to force the learner's hand down onto a shock grid, 30 percent still reached the maximum (Milgram, 1974). Milgram's original experiment has also been successfully replicated in several other countries, indicating that extreme obedience to authority is common across cultures (Shanab & Yahya, 1977).

Milgram's research has disturbing implications. The line that separates Nazi war criminals and the followers of Jim Jones from us may be thinner than we would like to believe. Many of us, given orders by someone we consider to be a legitimate authority whom we assume will be responsible for our actions, might be willing to harm an innocent person. Despite the insight it provided into the nature of obedience, Milgram's research provoked criticism, most notably from Diana Baumrind (1964). She claimed that Milgram's use of deception increased distrust of psychological researchers and that his subjects' self-esteem was damaged by the realization that they might harm an innocent person merely because an authority figure ordered them to.

In response to these criticisms, Milgram reported that 84 percent of the subjects in his study were glad they had participated, that there was no evidence that any of them developed long-term emotional distress, and that the importance of the findings made the use of deception worthwhile (Milgram, 1964). Today's increased concern with the rights of research subjects, in part a response to studies like Milgram's, would make it unlikely for any researchers to conduct similar experiments.

ENVIRONMENTAL PSYCHOLOGY

Winston Churchill once said, "We shape our buildings, and afterwards our buildings shape us" (McCurdy, 1981, p. 21). This was born out in 1972 when the forty-three eleven-story apartment buildings of the Pruitt-Igoe Housing Project in St. Louis were demolished. They had become too dangerous and dilapidated for their twelve thousand residents to live in. Yet, when the first residents had moved into the new project in the late 1950s, it had been hailed as a modern, attractive place for low-income people to live.

Why had such a drastic change taken place in little more than a decade? Many of the social problems associated with Pruitt-Igoe were caused by flaws in its design. There were many hiding places, such as elevators and stairways, for muggers and rapists but few public places for residents to interact. Long corridors with many apartments promoted impersonal relationships. And children playing outside were often out of sight of their parents. Consequently, the residents lived in constant fear and social isolation. As crime increased and the buildings deteriorated, the residents gave up hope of ever improving the situation. This led authorities to condemn the project and then obliterate it.

In the late 1960s, at the same time that Pruitt-Igoe was reaching the end of its life span, the field of environmental psychology was emerging—partly in response to the need for sounder urban planning. **Environmental psychology** is the study of the interrelationship between the physical environ-

Environmental Psychology The field that applies psychological principles to improve the physical environment, including the design of buildings and the reduction of noise.

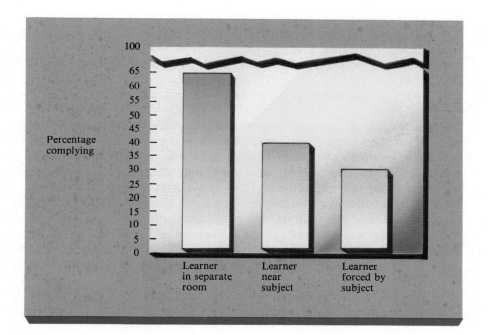

FIGURE 18.4
Proximity and Obedience As you can see, subjects in Milgram's studies were more willing to give maximum shocks when the subject and learner were in separate rooms. They were less willing when they sat near the subject. And they were the least willing when they had to force the subject's hand onto a shock grid.

Percentage complying

100
65
60
55
50
45
40
35
30
25
20
15
10
5
0

Learner in separate room

Learner near subject

Learner forced by subject

Environmental Psychology
The application of principles derived from environmental psychology might have prevented the deplorable conditions that led to the demolition of the Pruitt-Igoe Housing Project in St. Louis.

ment and human behavior and experience (Holahan, 1986). Among the major topics of research in environmental psychology are the effects of social space, noise, and temperature.

Social Space

Our everyday social interactions take place in physical space, generally referred to as *social space*. In 1959, E. T. Hall published a book that initiated the study of the role of social space in interpersonal relationships, known as **proxemics.**

Proxemics The study of the role of social space in interpersonal relationships.

Personal Space The distance at which we prefer to carry out the everyday social relations that are neither formal nor intimate.

Personal Space Most studies of social space have been concerned with what Hall called **personal space,** the distance at which we prefer to carry out the everyday social relations that are neither formal nor intimate. When our personal space is invaded, we experience anxiety (Holahan, 1986). But the preferred size of personal space varies from one culture to another. For example, South Americans prefer closer conversational distances than do North Americans, who, in turn, prefer closer conversational distances than do Japanese (Sussman & Rosenfeld, 1982). People involved in international relations, whether in business, politics, or education, must realize this. Otherwise, they might be offended by someone who violates their personal space or who keeps backing away from them as they try to get closer.

Territories All of our social interactions take place in *territories* to which we feel attached to varying degrees. The more attached we feel to a territory the more protective we are of it. At one extreme we have *primary territories,* such as our homes, which we may defend violently against intruders. At the other extreme we have *public territories,* such as our local supermarket, which we assume are open to all people. In between these extremes we have *secondary territories,* such as our seats in a movie theater, which we will defend against intruders but usually by nonviolent means. We may leave markers, such as our coats, to protect our secondary territories from intruders. You have certainly done this to protect your seat in class, in a movie theater, or at an athletic event.

Violations of secondary territories may disturb us. A study conducted in a library found that males and females responded differently to invasions of their secondary territories, the tables at which they were working. While males responded more negatively when someone sat down across from them, females responded more negatively when someone sat down next to them. To prevent invasions of their secondary territories, students will erect "barricades." Males are more likely to pile up books in front of them and females are more likely to pile up books next to them. This might reflect the tendency for males to prefer face-to-face interactions with people they like, but not strangers, and for females to prefer side-to-side interactions with people they like, but not strangers (Fisher & Byrne, 1975). You might wish to take a stroll through your own library to see whether the results of this study hold true at your school.

Crowding If you took a ten-minute walk in Manhattan, you might pass through an area containing more than 200,000 people (Milgram, 1970). Despite this, you might not feel crowded. Environmental psychologists recognize this and, therefore, distinguish between crowding and social density. **Social density** is the number of persons in a given area, while **crowding** is an unpleasant state of arousal that is a subjective response to social density (Stokols, 1972). Interest in the scientific study of crowding and social density began in the early 1960s, after publication of an experiment showing the harmful effects of high social density on rats. In that experiment, rats living in holding pens containing an overabundance of rats developed abnormal social behaviors, including neglecting their young, becoming socially withdrawn, and practicing cannibalism (Calhoun, 1962).

Human beings, too, respond negatively to social density, which they may experience as crowding. A study of the effects of crowding compared residents of crowded neighborhoods and uncrowded neighborhoods. The residents worked on a challenging cognitive task while their blood pressure and heart rate were recorded. Crowded residents showed greater increases in blood pressure and heart rate and took longer to return to baseline than did uncrowded residents. This indicated that residents of crowded neighborhoods may show chronic changes in their physiological responses, perhaps predisposing them to cardiovascular disease (Fleming, Baum, Davidson, Rectanus, & McArdle, 1987).

Social Density The number of persons in a given area.

Crowding An unpleasant state of arousal that is a subjective response to social density.

Crowding and Social Density
Crowding is a subjective response to social density. Though the people in these scenes are being subjected to high levels of social density, the people on the beach may feel less crowded than the people in the elevator.

Even office workers are affected by crowding. They feel uncomfortable and dissatisfied when there are many workers in the same office, when the workers are seated close to one another, and when their work areas are not surrounded by partitions. In one study, when office workers moved from an open-plan office to either a partitioned office or a lower social density open-plan office, their feelings of being crowded decreased and their satisfaction with their jobs increased (Oldham, 1988).

As you may already know from personal experience, college dormitory residents are especially prone to feelings of crowding. A study of college dormitory residents found that those with rooms on long corridors experienced more feelings of crowding than students with rooms on short corridors, because the long corridors exposed residents to more uncontrolled encounters with visitors and unfamiliar residents. The residents of long corridors reacted to this by becoming socially withdrawn (Baum, Aiello, & Calesnick, 1978). This situation was corrected in a later study by making a simple architectural alteration—dividing a long corridor by a central lounge area with doors on both ends (figure 18.5). As a result, the residents experienced less crowding and, consequently, became less socially withdrawn because they gained a greater sense of control over their social interactions (Baum & Davis, 1980). Thus, the principles of environmental psychology can be applied to solve practical problems in our everyday environments, including where we work and where we live.

FIGURE 18.5
Psychology and Architecture
Baum and Davis (1980) found that simply dividing a long corridor by a central lounge reduced feelings of crowding and improved the quality of life of dormitory residents.

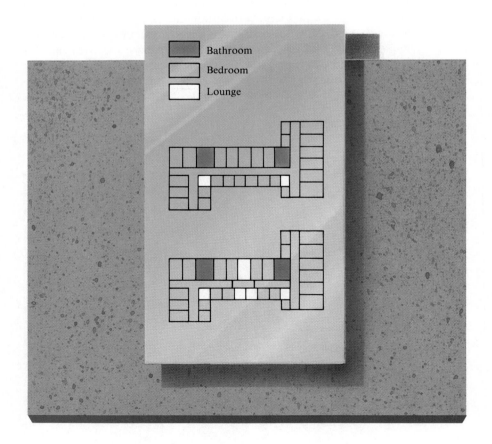

Noise

importance of + what (handwritten)

Urban living brings not only crowding but also noise. Exposure to chronic noise has both physiological and psychological effects, as in a study of Los Angeles's four noisiest schools, located in the air corridor of Los Angeles International Airport. In comparison with students of similar racial and socioeconomic backgrounds from three quiet schools, the students from the noisy schools had higher blood pressure, performed more poorly on cognitive tasks, and were more likely to give up before finishing tasks. Even when tested a year after the implementation of a noise abatement plan, the students still showed only slight improvements in their perseverance, cognitive performance, academic achievement, and ability to hear teachers (Cohen, Evans, Krantz, Stokols, & Kelly, 1981). This indicates that urban planners should attempt to create buffer zones around residential areas to protect residents from the ill effects of noise.

effects of noise (handwritten)

Temperature

Our environments also vary in temperature, which may do more than make us change the clothing we wear. For example, violent crimes increase in hot weather, with hotter cities experiencing more violent crimes than do cooler cities. One explanation of this relationship makes use of Schachter's two-factor theory of emotion (see chapter 11). Uncomfortably hot temperatures produce unpleasant arousal. If people attribute this feeling to other people in their immediate environment, they may increase their feelings of hostility toward them, increasing the likelihood of aggression (Anderson, 1987).

A study of riots found that the relationship between temperature and violence may be *curvilinear* (figure 18.6). There was a positive relationship between temperature and violence until the temperature reached the mid-80s Fahrenheit. But, as temperature increased further, there tended to be a de-

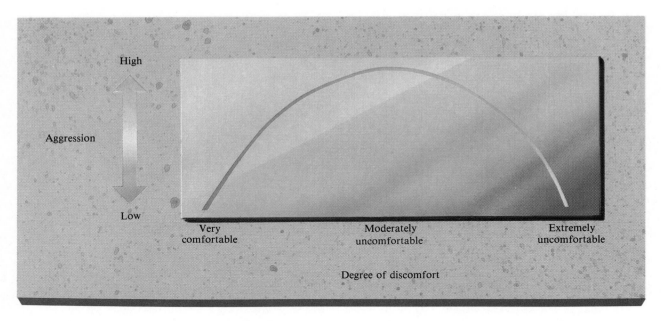

FIGURE 18.6
A Curvilinear Model of Temperature and Violence Baron and Ransberger (1978) found that increases in temperature were associated with increases in violence. But beyond a certain point, further increases in temperature were associated with decreases in violence.

crease in violence. Perhaps when the temperature becomes too hot, people become so uncomfortable that they lose interest in all kinds of physical activity, including aggression (Baron & Ransberger, 1978). But, as shown in figure 18.7, a study of the number of rapes and murders in Houston over a two-year period found a *linear* relationship between temperature and aggression (Anderson & Anderson, 1984). This means that as the temperature increases, the probability of aggression continues to increase. Only additional research will discover the conditions under which the relationship between temperature and violence is linear and the conditions under which the relationship is curvilinear.

PROSOCIAL BEHAVIOR

On a spring day in 1986, one-year-old Jennifer Kroll, of West Chicago, Illinois, fell into her family's swimming pool. Jennifer's mother, after pulling Jennifer out of the pool and discovering that she was not breathing, ran outside and began screaming for help. Her screams were heard by James Patridge, who had been confined to a wheelchair since losing his legs in a land-mine explosion in Vietnam. Patridge responded by rolling his wheelchair toward the pool, until he encountered heavy brush, forcing him to crawl the final twenty yards. Patridge revived Jennifer by using cardiopulmonary resuscitation ("God's Hand," 1986). Patridge's heroic act led to offers of financial rewards, which he declined to accept, saying that saving Jennifer's life was reward enough.

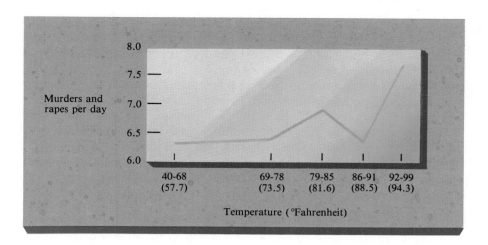

FIGURE 18.7
A Linear Model of
Temperature and Violence
Anderson and Anderson (1984)
found that as temperature
increased violent acts increased,
even at extremely high
temperatures.

Altruism

Patridge's act is an example of **prosocial behavior**—helping others in need. His behavior is also an example of **altruism**—helping others without the expectation of a reward in return. But are altruistic acts truly selfless? Perhaps people who engage in apparently altruistic behaviors do receive some kind of rewards. The most famous person to make this claim was Abraham Lincoln. During a train trip, Lincoln looked out his window and saw several piglets drowning. He ordered the train to stop so that the piglets could be saved. When praised for his action, Lincoln discounted altruism as his motive, claiming, instead, that his act was motivated by the selfish desire to avoid a guilty conscience (Batson, Bolen, Cross, & Neuringer-Benefiel, 1986).

Social psychologists interested in the study of altruism have been especially concerned with the emotion of empathy. **Empathy** is the ability to feel the emotions that someone else feels. Some researchers have found that prosocial behavior associated with feelings of empathy is truly altruistic, while

Prosocial Behavior Behavior that helps others in need.

Altruism The helping of others without the expectation of a reward.

Empathy The ability to experience the emotions that someone else feels.

Prosocial Behavior People will sometimes go to extreme lengths to help animals, as well as people. In the fall of 1988, the efforts of Eskimos and other people to free whales that had been trapped in ice off the coast of Alaska gained worldwide attention and support.

FIGURE 18.8
The Murder of Kitty Genovese
On returning home from work, Kitty Genovese (1) drove into a parking lot, noticed a man, and walked toward a police call box (2) but was attacked by the man. The man left twice but returned to attack her again (3) and again (4). None of the thirty-eight neighbors who heard her screams intervened to save her.

noticing the victim

what contributes to

Bystander Intervention The act of helping someone who is in immediate need of aid.

prosocial behavior associated with feelings of distress, but not empathy, is not (Schroeder, Dovidio, Sibicky, Matthews, & Allen, 1988). But what of people whose prosocial behavior is associated with feelings of both distress and empathy?

This question was the concern of a study in which subjects were given the opportunity to help a person in need. The subjects were given questionnaires that measured their levels of sadness and their levels of empathy for the person. The results showed that the subjects' willingness to help was related more to their sadness scores than to their empathy scores, indicating that they acted more out of a desire to reduce their own distress than out of a desire to reduce the distress of the other person. In fact, when the subjects were given a "mood fixing" placebo that allegedly made it impossible for them to alter their moods, fewer subjects were willing to help, even when they had high empathy scores (Cialdini et al., 1987). This study provided scientific support for President Lincoln's belief that altruistic behavior may not always be truly selfless.

Bystander Intervention

Regardless of his motivation, James Patridge's rescue of Jennifer was an all too infrequent example of **bystander intervention,** the act of helping someone who is in immediate need of help. Interest in the study of bystander intervention was stimulated by a widely publicized tragedy in which bystanders failed to help save a woman's life. At 3:20 A.M. on March 13, 1964, a twenty-eight-year-old woman named Kitty Genovese was returning home from her job as a bar manager. As she walked to her apartment building in the New York City borough of Queens, she was attacked by a mugger who repeatedly stabbed her (figure 18.8). Her screams awakened neighbors, who turned on their lights and rushed to look out their windows. The assailant left twice, returning each time to continue his attack until, finally, Kitty Genovese died. How would you have responded had you been one of her neighbors?

The neighbors' response may shock you. At no time during these three separate attacks, which took thirty minutes to complete, did any of the thirty-eight people who observed them through their windows try to help Kitty Genovese or even call the police. When questioned by police and reporters, none of the witnesses could adequately explain why he or she had not called the police. Their reasons included feeling tired, assuming it was a lover's quarrel, and believing that "it can't happen here" (Gansberg, 1964).

The murder of Kitty Genovese gained national attention, and the apparent apathy of her neighbors was taken as a sign of the indifferent, impersonal nature of residents of big cities. But, appalled by the tragedy, social psychologists John Darley and Bibb Latané rejected this common-sense explanation as too simplistic. Instead, they conducted a series of research studies to determine the factors that affect the willingness of bystanders to intervene in emergencies. Darley and Latané found that bystander intervention involves a series of steps (figure 18.9). The intervention process may continue through each of these steps or be halted at any one.

Noticing the Victim To intervene in an emergency, you must first notice the event or the victim. James Patridge heard the screams of Jennifer Kroll's mother, and neighbors heard the screams of Kitty Genovese.

Interpreting the Situation as an Emergency The same event may be interpreted as an emergency or as a nonemergency. James Patridge was confronted by a fairly unambiguous situation. He interpreted the screams of Jennifer's mother as a sign that there was an emergency. In contrast, there was some ambiguity in Kitty Genovese's situation. In fact, when there is an

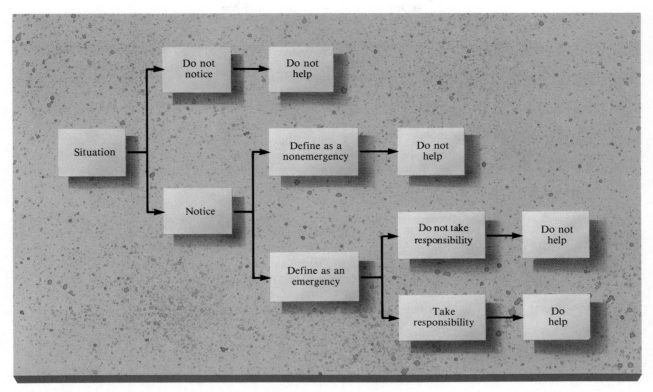

FIGURE 18.9
Steps in Bystander Intervention
According to Bibb Latané and John Darley
(1968), bystanders go through certain steps

before intervening in emergencies. The
possibility of intervening may be inhibited
at any of these steps.

apparent confrontation between a man and a woman, bystanders tend to assume that it is a lover's quarrel rather than a true emergency (Shotland & Straw, 1976). Because almost all of Kitty Genovese's neighbors interpreted the situation as a nonemergency, at that point there was little likelihood that she would be helped.

An experiment conducted by Latané and Darley (1968) found that in ambiguous situations, we may look to others for guidance in determining whether a true emergency exists. Male undergraduates were brought to a waiting room to fill out a questionnaire before participating in a discussion of urban life. Suddenly, the room began to fill with smoke that entered through a vent. Of the subjects who were alone, 75 percent reported the smoke. But of those in a room with two people (confederates of the experimenter) who did not react, only 10 percent reported it. They apparently assumed the other two knew more than they did. In the case of Kitty Genovese, when neighbors noticed that no one else had intervened, they may have assumed that intervention was not necessary.

Taking Personal Responsibility After interpreting the situation as an emergency, Patridge took responsibility for intervening. But not even those who may have interpreted Kitty Genovese's situation as an emergency took responsibility for helping her. Darley and Latané discovered a surprising reason for this. Contrary to what you might expect, as the number of bystanders *increases,* the likelihood of a bystander intervening *decreases.*

The influence of the number of bystanders on bystander intervention was demonstrated in an early study by Darley and Latané (1968). They had college students meet to discuss the problems they faced in attending school in New York City. Each student was led to a room and told to communicate with other students over an intercom. The subject was told that there was a total of two, three, or six students taking part in the discussion. But the other students were always the experimenter's confederates. In fact, the remarks of the other students were, in reality, tape recordings. Early in the session the subject heard another student apparently having an epileptic seizure and crying out for help. Figure 18.10 shows that of those subjects who believed they were a lone bystander, 85 percent sought help for the stricken person. Of those who believed they were one of two bystanders, 62 percent sought help. And of those who believed they were one of five bystanders, only 31 percent sought help.

One reason for this is the *diffusion of responsibility:* as the number of bystanders increases, the responsibility felt by each one decreases. So, the students who were exposed to a mock epileptic seizure felt less responsibility for helping the victim when they believed other bystanders were present. In contrast to Kitty Genovese's neighbors, who assumed that other neighbors had been awakened, Patridge may have assumed that no one else could intervene, leaving him with the responsibility.

Deciding on a Course of Action The decision to intervene depends, in part, on whether the bystander feels competent to meet the demands of the situation (Clark & Word, 1974). Patridge decided to wheel himself toward the pool and then crawl to it. Because Patridge had training in cardiopulmonary resuscitation, while Jennifer Kroll's mother did not, he felt more competent to try to revive Jennifer. Though none did so until after Kitty Genovese was dead, her neighbors might have at least considered calling the police when they heard her screams.

Taking Action Patridge propelled himself to Jennifer's side and revived her. Kitty Genovese's neighbors could have yelled, helped her, or called police. Patridge believed the potential benefits of intervention outweighed the potential costs. As discussed in chapter 10, Abraham Maslow assumed that people are more motivated by the need for safety than by the need for

FIGURE 18.10
Diffusion of Responsibility
Darley and Latané (1968) found that as the number of bystanders increased, the likelihood of any of them going to the aid of a woman apparently experiencing an epileptic seizure decreased.

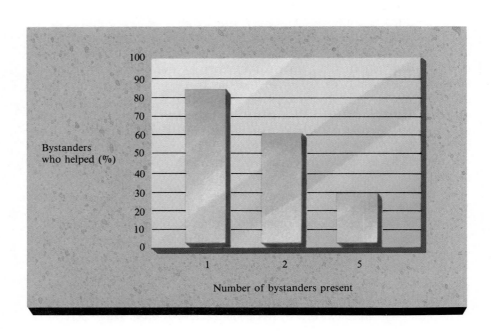

The Batman of Birmingham
For some people, prosocial behavior is a way of life. Willie J. Perry, known as "the Batman of Birmingham," travels the streets of Birmingham, Alabama, in his "rescue ship," seeking to help stranded motorists or anyone in trouble.

self-esteem. This may explain why bystanders who believe that intervening in an emergency would place them in danger (as some may have believed in the case of Kitty Genovese) are less likely to intervene, even if failure to do so would lower their self-esteem.

This was supported by a study of bystander reactions to an apparently dangerous emergency. The bystanders were subjects who had been invited to participate in an experiment. But during the session the experimenter was apparently injured in an explosion. Of course, it was a mock explosion. The results showed that subjects who were more motivated by the need for safety were less likely to intervene than were those who were more motivated by the need for self-esteem (Wilson & Petruska, 1984). The characteristics of the victim also influence bystander intervention. One of the most important characteristics is the degree to which the victim appears responsible for his or her predicament. You may recognize this as an example of social attribution, which is discussed in chapter 17. If we make dispositional attributions for a person's predicament, we will be less likely to help than if we make situational attributions for it (Weiner, 1980). So, we will be more likely to help someone who has collapsed because of an apparent sudden illness (a situational attribution) than someone who has collapsed because of running into a wall while behaving recklessly (a dispositional attribution).

As you can now appreciate, bystander intervention is not simply the product of a particular personality type. Instead, it is a complex process that depends on the interaction between characteristics of the victim, the bystander, and the situation.

Raoul Wallenberg During World War II, Raoul Wallenberg, a Swedish Christian, risked his life to help thousands of Jews escape from Hungary and avoid being murdered by Nazis. He took personal responsibility for rescuing them, had the skill to do so, and dared to take action. After the war, he was captured by the Soviet Union and is presumed to have died in custody.

AGGRESSION

Unfortunately, human beings are capable of antisocial, as well as prosocial, behavior. The most extreme form of antisocial behavior is **aggression,** which is behavior aimed at causing harm to someone else. American society is marked by frequent acts of extreme aggression. In fact, in the United States one woman is raped every six minutes and one person is murdered every twenty-three minutes (Siegel, 1983). What accounts for the prevalence of such violent acts?

Aggression Behavior that is intended to hurt someone either physically or psychologically.

Theories of Aggression

One class of theories views aggression as the product of an inborn tendency. A second class of theories views aggression as the product of experience.

Aggression as Inborn   The earliest theories of aggression claimed that it was instinctive. An *instinct* is an inborn tendency, unaffected by learning, to engage in a relatively complex behavior that characterizes members of a species—such as nest building in birds. After observing the extraordinary violence of World War I, Sigmund Freud concluded that human aggression is caused by an instinct that he called *Thanatos* (Greek for "death"). Thanatos made human beings self-destructive, which, in extreme cases, promotes suicide. But Thanatos may also be turned against others in the form of aggression.

According to Freud, Thanatos causes a buildup of aggressive energy, which must be released periodically through a process called *catharsis* to prevent outbursts of extreme violence. You might experience catharsis by playing football, field hockey, or another aggressive sport. If you have ever watched professional ice hockey, you know that those who regulate the sport assume that allowing players to have fist fights will make them less likely to engage in more serious fighting. But research has failed to support the belief that aggression can be reduced through catharsis. In fact, people who engage in aggression usually become *more* likely to engage in it (Geen, Stonner, & Shope, 1975).

A more recent instinct theory of aggression was proposed by the Nobel Prize-winning animal researcher Konrad Lorenz (1966). According to Lorenz, both animals and human beings have evolved an instinct for aggression as a means of promoting their survival. But, because animals have evolved natural weapons such as fangs and claws that can kill, they have also evolved ritualistic behaviors to inhibit aggression and prevent unnecessary injuries and deaths. In contrast, because human beings have not evolved natural weapons that can kill, they have not evolved ritualistic behaviors to inhibit aggression against their own species. As a consequence, human beings are less inhibited in using artificial weapons such as guns, clubs, spears, and missiles against one another. Lorenz, too, believed that outbursts of aggression could be avoided only by providing for the periodic release of aggressive energy through means such as sports (Leakey & Lewin, 1977).

Catharsis   According to Freud, both the participants and the spectators at this wrestling match should show a decrease in their tendencies toward violence as the result of catharsis. But research has found that, on the contrary, watching or taking part in violence will increase one's tendency to engage in it.

Aggressive Rituals According to Konrad Lorenz, human beings lack the inborn ritualistic forms of aggression that generally prevent animals from trying to injure members of their own species.

One of the great weaknesses of instinct theories of aggression is that they provide circular explanations for it. If someone asked you, Why are people aggressive? you might reply by saying they have an instinct for aggression. But if the person then asked you, How do you know that people have an instinct for aggression? you might reply by saying it is because people act aggressively.

Though few psychologists today accept instinct theories of human aggression, many do believe that there is a hereditary basis for it. The relatively new field called **sociobiology** assumes there is a strong hereditary basis for aggression and other behaviors (Wilson, 1975). Studies of twins have provided evidence supporting this. Psychologists who study twins may compare the aggressiveness of identical twins reared together to the aggressiveness of fraternal twins reared together. These researchers assume that if heredity plays a role in aggression, identical twins (who are genetically identical) will be more similar in aggressiveness than will be fraternal twins (who are no more alike genetically than ordinary siblings). Twin studies have, indeed, found this, providing evidence supporting the hereditary basis of differences in aggressiveness (Rushton, Fulker, Neale, Nias, & Eysenck, 1986).

Another source of evidence for the hereditary basis of aggression is research showing that sex differences in aggression may be attributable to differences in levels of the male sex hormone testosterone. Males with abnormally low levels of testosterone are less aggressive than males with normal levels, and violent criminals have higher levels of testosterone than do nonviolent criminals (Rubin, Reinisch, & Haskett, 1981). The possible role of testosterone in accounting for sex differences in aggressiveness has been shown in studies finding that males and females whose mothers received a synthetic form of testosterone during pregnancy become more aggressive children than

Sociobiology The study of the hereditary basis of human and animal social behavior.

their same-sex siblings who had not been exposed to the hormone prenatally (Reinisch, 1981).

Aggression as the Product of Experience   While some researchers look to hereditary factors, most look to life experiences as the main determinants of aggression. In the late 1930s a team of behaviorists concluded that aggression is caused by frustration (Dollard, Doob, Miller, Mowrer, & Sears, 1939). As noted in chapter 16, we experience frustration when we are blocked from reaching a goal. As an example of how frustration might lead to aggression, suppose that a student has just found out that he failed a midterm exam and might fail the course. He might respond by angrily shoving students out of his way. According to the **frustration-aggression hypothesis,** aggression can best be prevented by avoiding frustrations. So, the student could avoid frustration by being better prepared for the exam.

The frustration-aggression hypothesis is an inadequate explanation of aggression, however, because experiences other than frustration can cause aggression and frustration does not always lead to aggression. The inadequacies of the frustration-aggression hypothesis led psychologist Leonard Berkowitz to develop what became known as the *revised frustration-aggression hypothesis.* According to Berkowitz (1974), frustration does not directly provoke aggression. Instead, it directly provokes anger. Anger, in turn, will provoke aggression when stimuli (such as guns) that have been associated with aggression are present.

Berkowitz demonstrated this in a study in which male college students gave electric shocks to other students to induce feelings of anger in the shock recipients. When students who had received shocks were given the opportunity to give shocks to those who had shocked them, they gave more shocks when an aggressive stimulus such as a revolver, rather than a neutral stimulus such as a badminton racket, was left on the table (Berkowitz & LePage, 1967). Though some studies have failed to support the revised frustration-aggression hypothesis (Buss, Booker, & Buss, 1972), most have found that anger in the presence of aggressive stimuli does tend to provoke aggression (Rule & Nesdale, 1976).

As described in chapter 6, much of our behavior is the product of social learning—learning by observing the behavior of others. Aggression is no exception to this. We may learn to be aggressive by observing people who act aggressively. In a classic experiment by Albert Bandura, children in nursery school who observed an adult punching an inflated "Bobo doll" were more likely to engage in similar aggression against the Bobo doll than were children who had not observed the aggressive model (figure 18.11) (Bandura, Ross, & Ross, 1963). The observational learning of aggression is promoted by observing models who are rewarded for aggression and is inhibited by observing models who are punished for aggression. Today social learning theory is probably the most widely studied and widely accepted theory of aggression.

Group Violence

In A.D. 59, opposing fans rioted at the Pompeii amphitheater during a gladiatorial contest, prompting the Roman Senate to ban such contests in Pompeii for ten years. The twentieth century has also seen its share of riots instigated by athletic events. Following the final game of the 1984 World Series, fans of the victorious Detroit Tigers threw rocks, burned cars, and fought with police. And in 1985 a riot at a soccer game in Brussels killed four hundred people (Bredemeier & Shields, 1985).

What causes normally peaceful people to engage in violence when they are in groups? Normally we are aware of our own thoughts, feelings, and per-

Frustration-Aggression Hypothesis The assumption that frustration causes aggression.

FIGURE 18.11
Observational Learning of Aggression
Bandura, Ross, and Ross (1963) found that
children exposed to an aggressive adult
model acted more aggressively themselves.

Group Violence As has too often
been the case, rival British and
Italian soccer fans rioted at a 1985
game in Brussels, leaving dozens
dead and hundreds injured.
Knowing the factors that promote
group violence may help us
prevent incidents like this in the
future.

ceptions and are concerned about being socially evaluated. But, when in
groups, we may become less aware of ourselves and less concerned about
being socially evaluated. In the 1950s, Leon Festinger called this process
deindividuation (Festinger, Pepitone, & Newcomb, 1952). As the result of
deindividuation, our behavior may no longer be governed by our social values.

Deindividuation The process by
which group members become
less aware of themselves as
individuals and less concerned
about being socially evaluated.

This may, in turn, lead to the loss of normal restraints against undesirable behavior, making us more likely to participate in group violence. Moreover, the
anonymity provided by group membership may make us less concerned with
the impression we make on other people, because we feel less accountable
for our own actions (Prentice-Dunn & Rogers, 1982).

Deindividuation is more likely when the group is large, when the group
members feel anonymous, and when the group members are emotionally
aroused. This means that large groups of people, wearing masks, uniforms, or
disguises and aroused by drugs, dancing, chanting, or oratory will be more
likely to engage in violence. These factors account for the use of hooded uniforms and frenzied meetings by members of the Ku Klux Klan.

Television and Aggression

As you might expect, social learning theory would predict that televised violence might promote real-life violence. An early study of the effects of televised violence presented excerpts of television programs (the violent show
"The Untouchables" or track and field events) to children between five and
nine years old. Children who viewed the aggressive scenes were more likely
to act aggressively toward another child and for a longer time (Liebert & Baron,
1972). In a more recent study, groups of second- and third-grade boys who
watched a violent television program were later more violent during a game
of floor hockey than were groups of boys who had watched a nonviolent television program (Josephson, 1987). Because the typical four-year-old child
watches four hours of television a day (Singer, 1983), findings such as these
have provoked concern.

Concern about the effects of televised violence on aggression is not new.
It has existed ever since television became a popular medium in the 1950s
(Carpenter, 1955). The first congressional report on the effects of television
was a 1954 report on its impact on juvenile delinquency. Since then, reports
on the social effects of television have appeared every few years. Major reports,
sponsored by the National Institute of Mental Health, on the social effects of
television appeared in 1972 and 1982. Both reports found that violence on

Television and Aggression
Researchers have yet to reach a
consensus on the effects of
televised violence on real-life
aggression.

television lead to aggressive behavior by children and adolescents and recommended a decrease in televised violence (Walsh, 1983). But critics of these reports claimed that the results of laboratory experiments on the effects of televised violence might not generalize to real life and that the results of field studies on the effects of televised violence failed to control all of the other variables that might encourage violence (Fisher, 1983).

Psychologists themselves have not reached a consensus on the effects of televised violence. One view is that the relationship between televised violence and real-life aggression is moderate in strength and bidirectional. This means that televised violence makes people more aggressive and that people who are aggressive choose to watch more televised violence (Friedrich-Cofer & Huston, 1986). This view is countered by evidence from field studies has shown only a weak relationship between televised violence and aggression (Freedman, 1986). Because of these contradictory findings, we still do not know the extent to which televised violence is responsible for real-life violence.

Some researchers, rather than just urging that violent television shows be curtailed, have sought to reduce the effects of violent television shows on the aggressiveness of children. In one study, first- and third-graders who tended to watch many hours of television shows depicting violence were randomly assigned to either an experimental group or a control group. The experimental group was taught that real people did not behave as aggressively as television characters, that special effects created the illusion that television characters are performing highly aggressive acts, and that most people use nonviolent methods of solving problems like those encountered by television characters. They were also taught that watching television violence was undesirable and it should not be imitated. Two years after the study began, children in the experimental group were rated as being less aggressive by their peers than were children in the control group, who had not been given the treatment, and expressed less favorable attitudes toward television violence (Huesmann, Eron, Klein, Brice, & Fisher, 1983).

THINKING ABOUT PSYCHOLOGY

Does Pornography Cause Sexual Aggression?

next pg.

One of the most distressing social statistics is that one American woman in ten is raped during her lifetime (Dowd, 1983). Women in colleges and universities are not immune to sexual aggression, including so-called date rape. A nationwide sample of 6,159 men and women enrolled in colleges or universities found that 27.5 percent of women reported being sexually assaulted and 7.7 percent of men reported committing or attempting rape (Koss, Gidycz, & Wisniewski, 1987). This high incidence of sexual aggression has prompted researchers to study the factors that might promote it. One of the most controversial and extensively studied of these factors is **pornography**, which is sexually explicit material intended to create sexual arousal.

Pornography Sexually explicit material intended to create sexual arousal.

Reports on Pornography and Aggression

The issue of pornography is not only a scientific issue but also a social, cultural, religious, and political one. In 1970, the President's Commission on Obscenity and Pornography concluded that men exposed to pornography are not more likely to commit sexual aggression. More recently, in ceremonies associated with the signing of the Child Protection Act of 1984, President Reagan announced his intention to sponsor a study of the effects of pornography. In 1985 he appointed an eleven-member commission headed by Attorney General Edwin Meese—the Attorney General's Commission on Pornography.

But even before submitting its findings, the commission was criticized for including few social scientists while including several individuals who had previously expressed their belief that there is a causal link between pornography and sexual aggression. Unlike the 1970 study, this one sponsored no research studies. Instead, it merely gathered and analyzed existing data. The commission's report was published in 1986 and concluded that exposure to either violent or nonviolent pornography may cause aggression against women. Two members of the commission, Ellen Levine, editor of *Woman's Day,* and Judith Becker, a Columbia University psychologist, wrote a dissenting opinion in which they claimed that the report incorrectly characterized the scientific evidence as supporting a *causal* link between pornography and sexual aggression (Wilcox, 1987). You will recall that it is important to distinguish between causation and correlation when interpreting research findings. For example, pornography may cause sexual aggression, men who commit aggression may be more likely to enjoy pornography, or some men may share personal characteristics that predispose them to enjoy pornography *and* commit sexual aggression.

The results of a 1986 conference sponsored by Surgeon General C. Everett Koop, the *Report of the Surgeon General's Workshop on Pornography and Public Health,* were published several months after the attorney general's report was published. Unlike Meese, Koop, also morally appalled by pornography—but committed to objective scientific discourse—relied on testimony from many of the most eminent researchers in the field. The workshop met with political opposition. While liberals attacked the workshop as a threat to civil liberties, conservatives attacked it as a threat to the nation's moral fiber.

Based on the data presented at the workshop Koop concluded that children and adolescents who participate in the production of pornography experience adverse, enduring effects, such as eventual involvement in child prostitution. He also concluded that rape portraying sexual aggression as pleasurable for the victim increases the acceptance of coercion in sexual relations, and, conceivably, *might* increase the the incidence of rape by promoting the view that women enjoy being forced to have sex. Koop's report, unlike Meese's, did not conclude that nonviolent pornography causes aggression against women (Koop, 1987).

Research on Pornography and Aggression

What kinds of research studies were Meeses's and Koop's reports based on? Consider an experiment in which male and female college students read erotic passages, either portraying consenting sex or the rape of a woman. The rape victim was portrayed as either being distressed or as enjoying herself and having an orgasm. The subjects reported that they were more sexually aroused by the portrayal of consenting sex than by the portrayal of rape. But, when the victim was portrayed as having an orgasm, the subjects reported that they were as sexually aroused as they were by the portrayal of consenting sex. Moreover, females were more aroused when the victim experienced orgasm and no pain.

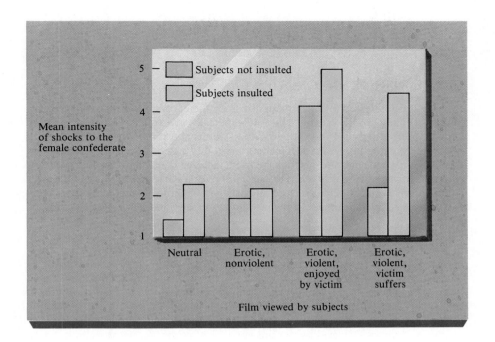

FIGURE 18.12
Pornography and Aggression
The results of the study by Donnerstein and Berkowitz (1981) showed that men who had been provoked and then watched an aggressive erotic film in which a woman acted as though she enjoyed being raped behaved the most aggressively.

In contrast, males were more aroused when the victim experienced orgasm and pain. These results indicate that portrayals of violent sexual attacks may condition people, especially males, to associate sex and aggression, with sexual pleasure reinforcing sexual attacks (Malamuth, Heim, & Feshbach, 1980).

Evidence for this effect has also come from other experiments. In one experiment, men watched one of four films: a talk show; a couple making love; a woman enjoying being raped by two men; and a woman suffering during a rape by two men. Half of the men in each group were also insulted and angered by a woman (who was the experimenter's confederate). The men were given the opportunity to retaliate against her by giving her electric shocks. The intensity of the shock was used as a measure of aggression.

The results showed that men who had seen the neutral or nonviolent erotic film displayed relatively little aggression (figure 18.12). Both angered and nonangered men who had seen the film of the rape in which the woman enjoyed it displayed higher levels of aggression. And, of the men who had seen the rape during which the woman suffered, those who had been angered behaved more aggressively than those who had not (Donnerstein & Berkowitz, 1981). These results may also hold outside of the laboratory, because men who are sexually aroused by portrayals of sexual aggression against women report that they are more likely to attack women (Malamuth, 1986).

Today, findings are more consistent with the conclusions of former Surgeon General Koop than those of former Attorney General Meese. There is little evidence that nonviolent pornography causes sexual aggression against women. There is somewhat stronger evidence that violent pornography may cause aggression against women. But this conclusion is based mainly on the results of laboratory experiments that have only considered short-term effects of violent pornography and that may not generalize outside of the laboratory. Of course, whether violent erotic movies, such as the "teenage slasher" movies of the past decade, cause aggression against women is a scientific question. Yet, whether such films are harmful in other ways is also a moral and social dilemma.

SUMMARY

RELATIONSHIPS IN GROUPS

Psychologists interested in social influence study the effects of social relationships on thinking, feeling, and behaving. They are especially interested in studying relationships in groups, including the importance of norms and roles, which are influenced by our reference groups. Decision making in groups may be affected by group polarization, the tendency for groups to make more extreme decisions than their members would make as individuals. Group decisions are also characterized by groupthink, in which group members place greater emphasis on unanimity than on critical thinking. Minorities can affect group decisions by being rational, confident, consistent, and patient.

Groups are run by leaders, individuals who exert more influence on the group than do any other group members. There is no set of personal characteristics that predisposes someone to become a leader. Leaders emerge whose characteristics meet the requirements of specific situations. One of the most influential explanations of leadership is Fred Fiedler's contingency theory of leadership, which distinguishes between task-oriented and relationship-oriented leaders.

Groups may affect performance through social facilitation, which is the improvement of performance caused by the presence of other people, and social inhibition, which is the impairment of performance caused by the presence of other people. Our performance may also be affected by social loafing, which is the tendency of individuals to exert less effort when performing in groups.

INTERPERSONAL INFLUENCE

Human relationships are characterized by conformity, compliance, and obedience. Conformity is behaving in accordance with group norms with little or no overt pressure to do so. Compliance is agreeing to a request that is backed by little or no threat of punishment. Two of the chief techniques for inducing compliance are the foot-in-the-door technique and the door-in-the-face technique. Obedience is following orders given by an authority.

ENVIRONMENTAL PSYCHOLOGY

Environmental psychology is the study of the interrelationship between the physical environment and human behavior and experience. One of the main topics of research in environmental psychology is proxemics, the study of the role of social space in interpersonal relationships. Personal space is the distance at which we prefer to carry out the everyday social relations that are neither formal nor intimate. Our social interactions take place in territories to which we feel attached to varying degrees. Environmental psychologists distinguish between social density, which is the number of persons in a given area, and crowding, which is an unpleasant state of arousal that is a subjective response to social density. Urban dwellers suffer adverse physical and psychological effects from chronic exposure to noise. Even temperature affects our behavior, with a general tendency for violence to increase as temperature increases.

PROSOCIAL BEHAVIOR

Prosocial behavior involves helping others in need. Altruism is helping others without the expectation of a reward in return. Some researchers have found that true altruism occurs only when prosocial behavior occurs out of empathy, rather than out of a desire to reduce one's own distress at the plight of another person. Other researchers have found, instead, that even prosocial behavior is never truly altruistic—it always depends on the desire to reduce our own distress. Psychologists who study prosocial behavior are especially concerned with bystander intervention, the act of helping someone who is in immediate need of help. Bystander intervention depends on noticing the victim, interpreting the situation as an emergency, taking personal responsibility, deciding on a course of action, and taking action to help.

AGGRESSION

Aggression is behavior aimed at causing harm to someone else. Some theories of aggression view it as inborn. Freud and Lorenz believed that aggression is instinctive, meaning that we have no choice but to engage in it periodically. Today, most researchers reject the instinct theory of aggression but still study genetic influences on it. Most researchers look to life experiences as the main determinants of aggression. Acccording to the frustration-aggression hypothesis, aggression becomes more likely after we have been blocked from reaching a goal. According to social learning theory, we may learn to be aggressive by observing people who act aggressively. Group violence is promoted by deindividuation, which is the loss of self-awareness and the feeling of anonymity that comes from being part of a group. The past two decades have seen yet-unresolved controversy about the effects of televised violence on real-life aggression.

THINKING ABOUT PSYCHOLOGY: DOES PORNOGRAPHY CAUSE SEXUAL AGGRESSION?

Pornography is sexually explicit material intended to create sexual arousal. Reports by the attorney general and the surgeon general published in 1986 disagree about the strength of the relationship between pornography and sexual aggression. Perhaps the only generally accepted finding is that violent pornography is more likely than nonviolent pornography to contribute to sexual aggression.

IMPORTANT CONCEPTS

IMPORTANT PEOPLE

RECOMMENDED READINGS

For More on Relationships in Groups:

Forsyth, D. (1983). *An introduction to group dynamics.* Monterey, CA: Brooks/Cole.
A textbook describing the principles guiding relationships in groups, including numerous practical examples.

Janis, I. L. (1982). *Groupthink: Psychological studies of policy decisions and fiascoes* (2nd ed.). Boston: Houghton Mifflin.
An intriguing discussion of groupthink, including several notorious real-life examples, such as the Watergate burglary and cover-up.

For More on Interpersonal Influence:

Cialdini, R. B. (1988). *Influence: Science and practice* (2nd ed.). Glenview, IL: Scott, Foresman.
An interesting account of different kinds of influence, with many examples from everyday life.

Milgram, S. (1974). *Obedience to authority: An experimental view.* New York: Harper & Row.
A description of Milgram's famous series of experiments on obedience.

For More on Environmental Psychology:

Fisher, J. D., Bell, P. A., & Baum, A. (1984). *Environmental psychology* (2nd ed.). New York: Holt, Rinehart, & Winston.
A comprehensive textbook covering all aspects of environmental psychology.

For More on Prosocial Behavior:

Latané, B., & Darley, J. M. (1970). *The unresponsive bystander: Why doesn't he help?* New York: Appleton-Century-Crofts.
A discussion of classic research studies on bystander intervention.

Piliavin, J. A., Dovidio, J. F., Gaertner, S. L., & Clark, R. D. (1981). *Emergency intervention.* New York: Academic Press.
A discussion of the factors that influence bystander intervention.

For More on Aggression:

Geen, R. G., & Donnerstein, E. I. (Eds.). (1983). *Aggression: Theoretical and empirical reviews.* New York: Academic Press.
A collection of scholarly papers on the nature of aggression.

Liebert, R. M., Sprafkin, J. N., & Davidson, E. S. (1982). *The early window: Effects of television on children and youth* (2nd ed.). New York: Pergamon.
A summary of the influence of television on the behavior of children and adolescents, including the effects of televised violence on aggression.

For More on the Effects of Pornography:

Donnerstein, E. I., Linz, D. G., & Penrod, S. D. (1987). *The question of pornography.* New York: Free Press.
A comprehensive survey of research on the relationship between pornography and sexual aggression.

APPENDIX

CAREERS IN PSYCHOLOGY

Now that you know what psychologists do and the fields in which they specialize, you may be interested in pursuing a career in psychology. Table A lists the divisions of the American Psychological Association, providing further evidence of the diversity of interests of psychologists. A career as a psychologist would permit you to combine teaching, research, and practice in any of a wide variety of fields.

A psychology major is particularly attractive because it is interesting, provides marketable skills, and prepares students for further education or for employment (Lunneborg, 1978). A psychology major is also attractive because it does more than provide training in a narrow discipline aimed primarily at getting a first job. It provides personal and practical skills that make students more adaptable to many career opportunities. A psychology major improves abilities in writing, speaking, and problem solving. Students who major in psychology learn to be open-minded skeptics capable of objectively evaluating claims made by scientists, advertisers, and people in everyday life. Most undergraduate psychology programs also provide experience in using statistics and computers. And, of course, no major enhances one's ability to understand human and animal behavior more than psychology.

If you decide to major in psychology as preparation for a career as a psychologist, you must first realize that the bachelor's degree is not sufficient preparation—you must pursue graduate studies. Though psychologists may have a bachelor's degree in a field other than psychology, they usually have a bachelor's degree (B.A. or B.S.) in psychology. You would need one to two years of study beyond the bachelor's level to earn a master's degree (M.A. or M.S.). A master's degree would usually require advanced courses in psychology related to a field of specialization and completion of a written thesis or original research study. The most popular fields of specialization for those with a master's degree are clinical psychology, counseling psychology, and school psychology.

You would need four to six more years of study beyond the bachelor's level to earn a doctoral degree (Ph.D., Psy.D., or Ed.D.). The Ph.D. requires advanced courses in research methods, statistics, and a particular field of study. It also requires completion of an ambitious original research study that is then described in a written doctoral dissertation. The Psy.D. requires advanced courses in a particular field of study, usually clinical or counseling psychology, and an internship in an applied setting. While the Ph.D. indicates expertise in conducting research, the Psy.D. indicates expertise in providing therapy. Many psychologists who practice clinical or counseling psychology have a Ph.D., which means that they, too, are experts in providing therapy and have served an internship in an applied setting. Almost all states require that a person

TABLE A   Divisions of the American Psychological Association

1. General psychology
2. Teaching of psychology
3. Experimental psychology
4. There is no division 4
5. Evaluation and measurement
6. Physiological and comparative psychology
7. Developmental psychology
8. Personality and social psychology
9. Society for the psychological study of social issues
10. Psychology and the arts
11. There is no division 11
12. Clinical psychology
13. Consulting psychology
14. Society for industrial and organizational psychology
15. Educational psychology
16. School psychology
17. Counseling psychology
18. Psychologists in public service
19. Military psychology
20. Adult development and aging
21. Applied experimental and engineering psychology
22. Rehabilitation psychology
23. Consumer psychology
24. Theoretical and philosophical psychology
25. Experimental analysis of behavior
26. History of psychology
27. Community psychology
28. Psychopharmacology
29. Psychotherapy
30. Psychological hypnosis
31. State psychological association affairs
32. Humanistic psychology
33. Mental retardation
34. Population and environmental psychology
35. Psychology of women
36. Psychologists interested in religious issues
37. Child, youth, and family services
38. Health psychology
39. Psychoanalysis
40. Neuropsychology
41. American psychology-law society
42. Psychologists in independent practice
43. Family psychology
44. Society for the psychological study of lesbian and gay issues
45. Society for the psychological study of ethnic minority issues
46. Media psychology
47. Exercise and sport psychology

earn a doctoral degree, serve an internship, and pass a licensing exam to be licensed as a psychologist. The Ed.D. is normally offered by an education department and usually signifies expertise in relating psychology to education or counseling.

As an undergraduate preparing for a career as a psychologist, you should be aware of ways to make yourself more attractive to prospective graduate programs:

1. You must earn high grades—at least a B average for desirable graduate programs and a B+ or A− average for the most competitive graduate programs.
2. You must perform well on the Graduate Record Examination (GRE), which is analogous to the SAT or ACT exams that you probably took for entrance into your undergraduate school. The GRE includes three subtests measuring verbal ability, mathematical ability, and reasoning ability and an advanced test of your knowledge of psychology.
3. You may also be required to take the Miller Analogies Test, which assesses your ability to do analogies.
4. You should perform research under faculty supervision and, preferably, present your findings at one of the many undergraduate psychology research conferences each spring. These conferences are announced in the *APA Monitor,* the *American Psychologist,* and the *Teaching of Psychology,* one or more of which should be available in your library or from your psychology faculty members.
5. You should serve an undergraduate internship in a setting geared to your career goal. You may even be able to serve a teaching internship or a peer counseling internship at your school.
6. Get to know several psychology faculty members so that they can guide you and, eventually, write letters of reference for you. It is impossible for professors to write sterling letters for students they hardly know.
7. Be active in your psychology club or Psi Chi (psychology honor society) chapter.
8. Do summer work or volunteer work related to your career goals.
9. Broaden yourself by taking courses in disciplines other than psychology. These might include courses in logic, writing, public speaking, and computer science.
10. Discuss your career goals and graduate programs of interest with your faculty advisor. If you intend to proceed immediately to graduate school, you should begin considering graduate schools no later than your junior year.

You can get information about psychology and graduate training from psychological associations. These include the American Psychological Association, regional associations, state associations, and local associations.

Individuals who major in psychology may also choose to pursue graduate study in disciplines other than psychology. Many psychology majors pursue graduate study in law, medicine, computer science, or business administration. Of course, to pursue any of these careers, you should take courses that will prepare you for graduate study in your discipline of interest. For example, psychology majors who plan to attend medical school must also take courses in biology, chemistry, physics, and mathematics.

Though a bachelor's degree in psychology can be the first step toward a career as a psychologist, it can also lead to an attractive career outside of psychology. For example, with proper course work and student teaching experience, you can become a high school teacher. The combination of a bachelor's degree in psychology, appropriate elective courses, and experience in a relevant setting can make a graduate attractive to prospective employers. If you major in psychology, it is advisable to minor in a discipline related to your career interests.

With a proper background, psychology majors can even compete with business majors. Business firms consider the following attributes for entry-level employees: first, technical skills such as accounting and interviewing skills; second, conceptual skills such as problem-solving ability and the ability to fit into the organization; third, social skills such as understanding human behavior; and fourth, communication skills such as writing, speaking, and listening (Carducci & Wheat, 1984). If you intend to enter the business world with a degree in psychology, you should consider taking courses in accounting, management, marketing, and other related areas. You might even serve as an undergraduate intern in a local business or industry and seek part-time and summer employment with a business or industry.

Psychology majors are especially attractive to employers of all kinds because the psychology curriculum enhances their social, communication, and problem-solving skills. For example, American Telephone and Telegraph (AT&T) has found that students with bachelor's degrees in liberal arts majors that provide a broad background, such as psychology, philosophy, history, and English, progress more rapidly in management than do business and engineering majors (Candland, 1982).

RECOMMENDED READINGS

For Information on Careers for Psychology Majors:

American Psychological Association. (1986). *Careers in psychology.* Washington, DC: American Psychological Association.
A booklet describing a variety of careers in psychology. You can obtain a free copy by writing to Order Department, American Psychological Association, P.O. Box 2710, Hyattsville, MD 20784.

Fretz, B. R., & Stang, D. J. (1980). *Not for seniors only!* Washington, DC: American Psychological Association.
Helpful hints on long-range preparation for graduate study in psychology.

Woods, P. (Ed.). (1986). *The psychology major.* Washington, DC: American Psychological Association.
A collection of articles on the undergraduate psychology curriculum, career preparation, and employment trends in psychology.

Woods, P. J., & Wilkinson, C. S. (Eds.). (1987). *Is psychology the major for you?* Washington, DC: American Psychological Association.
A book advising you on how to plan for your undergraduate years.

For Further Information About Any Aspect of Psychology, Write:

American Psychological Association
1200 17th Street, N.W.
Washington, DC 20036

GLOSSARY

Absolute Threshold The minimum amount of stimulation that an individual can detect through a given sense. (p. 98)

Accommodation 1. The process by which the thickness of the lens in the eye changes to focus images of objects located at different distances from the retina. (p. 103) 2. The cognitive process that revises existing schemas to incorporate new information. (p. 400)

Achievement Motive The desire for mastery, excellence, and accomplishment. (p. 344)

Achievement Test A test that measures knowledge of a particular subject. (p. 292)

Acronym A mnemonic device that involves forming a term from the first letters of a series of words that are to be recalled. (p. 241)

Action Potential A series of changes in the electrical charge across the axonal membrane that occurs after the axon has reached its firing threshold. (p. 62)

Activation-Synthesis Theory The theory that dreams are the by-products of the brain's attempt to make sense of the spontaneous changes in physiological activity generated by the pons during REM sleep. (p. 159)

Actor-Observer Bias The tendency of observers to make dispositional attributions for the behaviors of others but to make situational attributions for their own behaviors. (p. 593)

Acupuncture The technique that involves the insertion of fine needles into various sites on the body to provide pain relief, apparently by stimulating the release of endorphins. (p. 135)

Adaptation Level Theory The theory that happiness depends on comparing one's present circumstances with one's past circumstances. (p. 368)

Adolescence The transition period lasting from the onset of puberty to the beginning of adulthood. (p. 409)

Adulthood The period beginning when the individual assumes responsibility for his or her own life. (p. 416)

Afterimage A visual image that persists after the removal of a stimulus. (p. 109)

Age Regression A hypnotic state in which the individual apparently behaves as he or she did as a child. (p. 164)

Aggression Behavior that is intended to hurt someone either physically or psychologically. (p. 647)

Agoraphobia A phobia associated with fear of being in public, usually because the person fears the embarrassment of a panic attack. (p. 486)

Alcohol A depressant, ethyl alcohol, found in beverages and commonly used to reduce social inhibitions. (p. 166)

Algorithm A problem-solving rule or procedure that, when followed step by step, assures that a correct solution will be found. (p. 261)

All-or-None Law The principle that once a neuron reaches its firing threshold a neural impulse travels at full strength along the entire length of its axon. (p. 62)

Altruism The helping of others without the expectation of a reward. (p. 643)

Alzheimer's Disease A brain disorder characterized by anterograde amnesia and general mental deterioration. (p. 246)

Amphetamines Stimulants used to maintain alertness and wakefulness. (p. 170)

Amygdala A limbic system structure that evaluates information from the immediate environment, contributing to feelings of fear, anger, or relief. (p. 75)

Anal Stage In Freud's theory, the stage of personality development, between ages one and three, during which the child gains pleasure from defecation and faces a conflict over toilet training. (p. 442)

Analysis of Dreams In psychoanalysis, the process by which the therapist interprets the symbolic, manifest content of dreams to reveal their true, latent content to the client. (p. 520)

Analysis of Free Associations In psychoanalysis, the process by which the therapist interprets the underlying meaning of the client's uncensored reports of anything that comes to mind. (p. 519)

Analysis of Resistances In psychoanalysis, the process by which the therapist interprets client behaviors that interfere with therapeutic progress toward uncovering unconscious conflicts. (p. 520)

Analysis of Transference In psychoanalysis, the process by which the therapist interprets the feelings expressed by the client toward the therapist as being indicative of the feelings typically expressed by the client toward important people in his or her personal life. (p. 520)

Analysis of Variance An inferential statistical procedure used to determine whether two or more sets of scores are different from each other. (p. 47)

Analytic Introspection A research method in which highly trained subjects report the contents of their conscious mental experiences. (p. 7)

Anorexia Nervosa An eating disorder marked by self-starvation. (p. 333)

Anterograde Amnesia A memory disorder in which the individual is unable to form new long-term memories. (p. 244)

Antianxiety Drugs Psychoactive drugs, commonly known as minor tranquilizers, that are used to treat anxiety disorders. (p. 539)

Antidepressant Drugs Psychoactive drugs that are used to treat major depression. (p. 540)

Antipsychotic Drugs Psychoactive drugs, commonly known as major tranquilizers, that are used to treat schizophrenia. (p. 539)

Antisocial Personality Disorder A personality disorder marked by impulsive, manipulative, often criminal behavior, without any feelings of guilt in the perpetrator. (p. 502)

Anxiety Disorders Psychological disorders marked by persistent anxiety that disrupts everyday functioning. (p. 483)

Applied Research Research aimed at applying research findings to solve practical problems and to improve the quality of life. (p. 18)

Aptitude Test A test designed to predict a person's potential to benefit from instruction in a particular academic or vocational setting. (p. 292)

Archetypes In Jung's theory, inherited images that are passed down from our prehistoric ancestors and that reveal themselves as universal symbols in art, dreams, and religion. (p. 446)

Arousal Motive The motive to maintain an optimal level of physiological activation. (p. 341)

Artifical Intelligence (AI) A field that integrates computer science and cognitive psychology in studying information processing through the design of computer programs that appear to exhibit intelligence. (p. 269)

Assertiveness Training A form of social skills training that teaches clients to express their feelings directly, instead of passively or aggressively. (p. 534)

Assimilation The cognitive process that interprets new information in light of existing schemas. (p. 400)

Association Areas Areas of the cerebral cortex that integrate information from the primary cortical areas and other brain areas. (p. 77)

Atherosclerosis The narrowing of arteries caused by the accumulation of fatty deposits. (p. 562)

Attention The process by which the individual focuses awareness on certain contents of consciousness while ignoring others. (p. 147)

Attitude An evaluation, containing cognitive, emotional, and behavioral components, of an idea, event, object, or person. (p. 605)

Audition The sense of hearing. (p. 122)

Auditory Cortex The area of the temporal lobes that processes sounds. (pp. 78, 123)

Auditory Nerve The nerve that conducts impulses from the cochlea to the brain. (p. 123)

Authoritarian Personality A personality type marked by the tendency to obey superiors while dominating subordinates, to favor one's own group while being prejudiced against other groups, and to be unwilling to admit one's own faults while placing them on members of other groups. (p. 616)

Autism A condition, arising in infancy, in which the individual is motivated to avoid stimulation, including social interaction. (p. 343)

Automatic Processing Information processing that does not require conscious awareness and mental effort, and that does not interfere with the performance of other ongoing activities. (p. 177)

Autonomic Nervous System The division of the peripheral nervous system that controls automatic, involuntary physiological processes. (pp. 56, 360)

Availability Heuristic In decision making, the tendency to estimate the probability of an event by how easily relevant instances of it come to mind. (p. 268)

Aversion Therapy A form of behavior therapy that inhibits maladaptive behavior by pairing it with an unpleasant stimulus. (p. 523)

Avoidance Learning Learning to prevent the occurrence of an aversive stimulus by giving an appropriate response to a warning stimulus. (p. 200)

Axon The relatively long fiber of the neuron that conducts neural impulses. (p. 58)

Axonal Conduction The transmission of a neural impulse along the length of an axon. (p. 61)

Barbiturates Depressants used to induce sleep or anesthesia. (p. 168)

Basal Metabolic Rate The rate at which the body burns calories merely to keep itself alive. (p. 331)

Basic Research Research aimed at finding answers to psychological questions for their own sakes. (p. 18)

Basilar Membrane A membrane running the length of the cochlea that contains the auditory receptor (hair) cells. (p. 123)

Behavioral Contingencies Relationships between behaviors and their consequences, such as positive reinforcement, negative reinforcement, extinction, and punishment. (p. 193)

Behavioral Genetics The study of the relationship between heredity and behavior. (p. 435)

Behavioral Perspective The psychological viewpoint, descended from behaviorism, that emphasizes the importance of studying environmental influences on overt behavior, yet, in some cases, permits the study of mental processes. (p. 14)

Behaviorism The early school of psychology that rejected the study of mental processes in favor of the study of overt behavior. (p. 10)

Behavior Modification The application of the principles of operant conditioning to change maladaptive behaviors. (p. 523)

Behavior Therapy The therapeutic application of the principles of learning in order to change maladaptive behaviors. (p. 520)

Binocular Cues Depth perception cues that require input from the two eyes. (p. 114)

Biofeedback A form of operant conditioning that enables an individual either to learn to control a normally involuntary physiological process or to gain better control of a normally voluntary one when provided with visual or auditory feedback of the state of that process. (p. 209)

Bipolar Disorder A mood disorder marked by periods of mania alternating with longer periods of major depression. (p. 493)

Blind Spot The point, lacking any rods or cones, at which the optic nerve leaves the eye. (p. 106)

Blocking The process by which a neutral stimulus paired with a conditioned stimulus that already elicits a conditioned response fails to become a conditioned stimulus itself. (p. 206)

Brain The portion of the central nervous system located in the skull, and which plays important roles in sensation, movement, and information processing. (p. 56)

Brain Graft The transplantation of brain tissue or, in some cases, adrenal gland tissue into a brain to restore functions lost because of brain damage. (p. 84)

Brightness Constancy The perceptual process that makes an object maintain a particular level of brightness despite changes in the amount of light reflected from it. (p. 118)

Broca's Area The area of the frontal lobe responsible for the production of speech. (p. 81)

Bulimia Nervosa An eating disorder marked by binging and purging. (p. 334)

Burnout A state of cognitive, emotional, and physical exhaustion caused by exposure to chronic uncontrollable stressors. (p. 569)

Bystander Intervention The act of helping someone who is in immediate need of aid. (p. 644)

Caffeine A stimulant used to increase mental alertness. (p. 169)

Cannabis Sativa A hallucinogen derived from the hemp plant and ingested in the form of marijuana or hashish. (p. 172)

Cannon-Bard Theory The theory that an emotion is produced when an event or object is perceived by the thalamus, which conveys this information simultaneously to the cerebral cortex and the skeletal muscles and autonomic nervous system. (p. 374)

Case Study An in-depth study of an individual. (p. 35)

Catatonic Schizophrenia A type of schizophrenia marked by unusual motor behavior, such as bizarre actions, extreme agitation, or immobile stupor. (p. 499)

Catharsis In psychoanalysis, the release of repressed emotional energy as a consequence of insight into the unconscious causes of one's psychological problems. (p. 518)

Causation The demonstration of an effect of particular factors on other factors. (p. 35)

Central Nervous System The division of the nervous system consisting of the brain and the spinal cord. (p. 56)

Cerebellum A hindbrain structure that controls the timing of well-learned movements. (p. 72)

Cerebral Cortex The outer covering of the forebrain. (p. 76)

Cerebral Hemispheres The left and right halves of the cerebrum. (p. 77)

Cerebral Palsy A movement disorder caused by brain damage, which is often accompanied by mental retardation. (p. 304)

Chaining An operant conditioning procedure used to establish a desired sequence of behaviors by positively reinforcing each behavior in the sequence, beginning with the last behavior. (p. 196)

Childhood The period that extends from the end of infancy until the onset of puberty. (p. 396)

Circadian Rhythms Twenty-four-hour cycles of psychological and physiological changes, most notably the sleep-wake cycle. (p. 148)

Clairvoyance The ability to perceive objects or events without any sensory contact with them. (p. 138)

Classical Conditioning A form of learning in which a neutral stimulus comes to elicit a response after being associated with a stimulus that already elicits that response. (p. 186)

Clinical Psychology The field that applies psychological principles to the prevention, diagnosis, and treatment of psychological disorders. (p. 18)

Cocaine A stimulant used to induce mental alertness and euphoria. (p. 170)

Cochlea The spiral, fluid-filled structure of the inner ear that contains the receptor cells for hearing. (p. 123)

Cognitive Appraisal Theory The theory that one's emotion at a given time depends on one's interpretation of the situation one is in at that time. (p. 380)

Cognitive Behavior Modification A type of therapy, developed by Donald Meichenbaum, that promotes more positive thinking. (p. 528)

Cognitive Developmental Theory A theory of gender-role development that assumes the child must first understand the concept of gender before adopting behaviors that are gender related. (p. 408)

Cognitive Dissonance Theory Leon Festinger's theory that attitude change is motivated by the desire to relieve the unpleasant state of tension caused when one holds cognitions that are inconsistent with each other. (p. 612)

Cognitive Evaluation Theory The theory that a person's intrinsic motivation will increase when a reward is perceived as a source of information but will decrease when a reward is perceived as an attempt to exert control. (p. 349)

Cognitive Perspective The psychological viewpoint that favors the study of how the mind organizes perceptions, processes information, and interprets experiences. (p. 15)

Cognitive Therapy A type of therapy, developed by Aaron Beck, that aims at eliminating exaggerated negative beliefs. (p. 527)

Collective Unconscious In Jung's theory, the unconscious mind that is shared by all human beings and that contains archetypal images passed down from our prehistoric ancestors. (p. 446)

Color Blindness The inability to distinguish between certain colors, most often red and green. (p. 111)

Companionate Love Love characterized by feelings of affection and commitment to a relationship with another person. (p. 603)

Comparative Psychology The field that studies similarities and differences in the physiology, behaviors, and abilities of animals, including human beings. (p. 18)

Compliance Behaving in accordance with a direct request that is backed by little or no threat of punishment. (p. 634)

Computer-Assisted Instruction The use of computers to provide programmed instruction. (p. 204)

Concept A category of objects, events, qualities, or relations that share certain features. (p. 256)

Concrete Operational Stage The Piagetian stage, extending from age seven until age twelve, during which the child learns to reason logically about objects that are physically present. (p. 401)

Conditioned Response (CR) In classical conditioning, the learned response given to a particular "conditioned" stimulus. (p. 186)

Conditioned Stimulus (CS) In classical conditioning, a neutral stimulus that comes to elicit a particular "conditioned" response after being paired with a particular "unconditioned" stimulus that already elicits that response. (p. 186)

Conduction Deafness Hearing loss usually caused by deterioration of the ossicles of the middle ear. (p. 126)

Cones Receptor cells of the retina that play an important role in daylight vision and color vision. (p. 104)

Conflict The emotional state induced when one is torn between two or more potential courses of action. (p. 557)

Confluence Model The view that each child is born into an intellectual environment that is dependent on the intelligence levels of his or her parents and siblings, with the number of children and the interval between births affecting the intelligence of each successive child. (p. 317)

Conformity Behaving in accordance with group norms when there is little or no overt pressure to do so. (p. 632)

Conscious The level of consciousness that includes the mental experiences which we are aware of at a given moment. (pp. 173, 438)

Consciousness The awareness of one's own mental activity, including thoughts, feelings, and sensations. (p. 146)

Consensus The extent to which, in a given situation, other people perform the same behavior as the person being observed. (p. 591)

Conservation The realization that changing the appearance of something does not change its amount or number. (p. 402)

Consistency The extent to which a person behaves in the same way in a given situation on different occasions. (p. 590)

Constructive Recall The distortion of memories by adding, dropping, or changing details to fit a schema. (p. 232)

Construct Validity The extent to which a test measures the supposed concept, or construct, it presumably measures. (p. 300)

Content Validity The extent to which the items in a test are a representative sample of the knowledge or behavior that is being tested. (p. 300)

Context-Dependent Memory The tendency for recall to be best when the environmental context present during the encoding of a memory is also present during attempts at retrieving it. (p. 237)

Contingency Theory of Leadership The theory that the effectiveness of a leader is a function of the interaction between the style of leadership and the favorableness of the leadership situation. (p. 629)

Continuous Schedule of Reinforcement A schedule of reinforcement that provides reinforcement for each instance of a desired response. (p. 196)

Control 1. The ability to manipulate factors to bring about particular events. 2. The procedure by which experimenters keep extraneous variables from affecting dependent variables. (p. 40)

Control Group The subjects in an experiment who are not exposed to the experimental condition of interest. (p. 39)

Controlled Processing Information processing that involves conscious awareness and mental effort, and that interferes with the performance of other ongoing activities. (p. 177)

Conventional Level In Kohlberg's theory, the level of moral reasoning characterized by concern with upholding laws and values and by favoring obedience to authority. (p. 412)

Convergent Thinking The cognitive process that focuses on finding conventional solutions to problems. (p. 266)

Conversion Disorder A somatoform disorder in which the person exhibits motor or sensory loss or the alteration of a physiological function without any apparent physical cause. (p. 489)

Cornea The round, transparent area at the front of the sclera that allows light to enter the eye. (p. 102)

Corpus Callosum A thick bundle of axons that provides a means of communication between the cerebral hemispheres, which is severed in so-called split-brain surgery. (p. 89)

Correlation The degree of relationship among events, behaviors, or characteristics. (p. 33)

Correlational Research Research that studies the degree of relationship among events, behaviors, or characteristics. (p. 38)

Counseling Psychology The field that applies psychological principles to help individuals deal with personal problems, generally less severe ones than those seen by clinical psychologists. (p. 18)

Counterconditioning A behavior therapy technique that applies the principles of classical conditioning to replace undesirable responses to stimuli with desirable ones. (p. 521)

Creativity A form of problem solving that generates novel, useful solutions to problems. (p. 265)

Critical Period A period in childhood when experience with language produces optimal language acquisition. (p. 277)

Cross-Sectional Research Design A research design in which groups of subjects of different ages are compared at the same point in time. (pp. 299, 391)

Crowding An unpleasant state of arousal that is a subjective response to social density. (p. 639)

Crystallized Intelligence The form of intelligence that reflects knowledge acquired through schooling and in everyday life. (p. 310)

Cultural-Familial Retardation Mental retardation apparently caused by social or cultural deprivation. (p. 304)

Dark Adaptation The process by which the eyes become more sensitive to light when under low illumination. (p. 108)

Daydreaming A state of consciousness that involves shifting attention from external stimuli to self-generated thoughts and images. (p. 147)

Decay Theory The theory that forgetting occurs because memories naturally fade over time. (p. 233)

Decision Making A form of problem solving in which one tries to make the best choice from among alternative judgments or courses of actions. (p. 267)

Declarative Memory The part of long-term memory that contains memories of facts. (p. 227)

Deep Structure The underlying meaning of a statement. (p. 274)

Defense Mechanism In Freud's theory, a process that distorts reality to prevent the individual from being overwhelmed by anxiety. (p. 440)

Deindividuation The process by which group members become less aware of themselves as individuals and less concerned about being socially evaluated. (p. 651)

Deinstitutionalization The movement toward treating people with psychological disorders in community settings instead of in mental hospitals. (p. 541)

Dendrites The branchlike structures of the neuron that receive neural impulses. (p. 58)

Dependent Variable A variable showing the effect of the independent variable. (p. 40)

Depressants Psychoactive drugs that inhibit activity in the central nervous system. (p. 166)

Depth Perception The perception of the relative distance of objects. (p. 114)

Descriptive Research Research that involves the recording of behaviors that have been observed systematically. (p. 35)

Descriptive Statistics Statistics that summarize research data. (p. 44)

Developmental Psychology The field that studies physical, cognitive, and psychosocial changes across the life span. (pp. 18, 390)

Diathesis-Stress Viewpoint The assumption that psychological disorders are consequences of the interaction of a biological, inherited predisposition (diathesis) and exposure to stressful life experiences. (p. 479)

Difference Threshold The minimum amount of change in stimulation that can be detected. (p. 100)

Differential Psychology The field concerned with studying cognitive and behavioral variations among individuals. (p. 293)

Discrimination The treatment of a person differently, usually negatively, based on his or her group membership. (p. 614)

Discriminative Stimulus In operant conditioning, a stimulus that indicates the likelihood that a particular response will be reinforced. (p. 195)

Disorganized Schizophrenia A type of schizophrenia marked by severe personality deterioration and extremely bizarre behavior. (p. 498)

Disparagement Theory The theory that humor is amusing when it makes one feel superior to other people. (p. 369)

Displacement The characteristic of language marked by the ability to refer to objects and events that are not present. (p. 272)

Dissociation A state in which the mind is split into two or more independent streams of consciousness. (p. 163)

Dissociative Disorders Psychological disorders in which thoughts, feelings, and memories become separated from conscious awareness. (p. 490)

Distinctiveness The extent to which a person behaves in the same way across different situations. (p. 590)

Distributed Practice Spreading out the memorization of information or the learning of a motor skill over several sessions. (p. 240)

Divergent Thinking The cognitive process by which an individual freely considers a variety of potential solutions to artistic, scientific, or practical problems. (p. 266)

Door-in-the-Face Technique Increasing the likelihood that someone will comply with a request by first getting them to reject a larger request. (p. 634)

Double-Blind Technique A research technique in which neither the experimenter nor the subjects know which subjects have received an active treatment and which subjects have received a placebo treatment. (p. 363)

Down Syndrome A form of mental retardation associated with certain physical deformities, which is caused by an extra, third chromosome on the twenty-first pair. (p. 305)

Dream A storylike sequence of visual images, usually occurring during REM sleep. (p. 156)

Drive A state of psychological tension induced by a need. (p. 326)

Drive-Reduction Theory The theory that behavior is motivated by the need to reduce drives such as sex or hunger. (p. 326)

Echoic Memory Auditory sensory memory, which lasts up to about three or four seconds. (p. 220)

Educational Psychology The field that applies psychological principles to improving curriculums, teaching methods, and administrative procedures. (p. 19)

Ego In Freud's theory, the part of the personality that helps the individual adapt to external reality by making compromises between the id, the superego, and the environment. (p. 439)

Egocentrism The inability to perceive physical reality from the perspective of another person. (p. 401)

Elaborative Rehearsal Actively organizing new information to make it more meaningful, and integrating it with information already stored in long-term memory. (p. 226)

Electra Complex A term used by some psychoanalysts, but not by Freud, to refer to the Oedipus complex in females. (p. 442)

Electroconvulsive Therapy (ECT) A biomedical therapy in which brief electrical currents are used to induce brain seizures in victims of major depression. (p. 538)

Electroencephalograph (EEG) A device used to record patterns of electrical activity produced by neuronal activity in the brain. (p. 71)

Embryonic Stage The prenatal period that lasts from the end of the second week through the eighth week. (p. 393)

Emotion A motivated state marked by physiological arousal, expressive behavior, and mental experience. (p. 360)

Empathy The ability to experience the emotions that someone else feels. (p. 643)

Empiricism The philosophical position that true knowledge comes through the senses. (p. 5)

Encoding The placing of information into a form that can be stored in memory. (p. 219)

Encoding Specificity The principle that recall will be best when cues that were associated with the encoding of a memory are also present during attempts at retrieving it. (p. 236)

Encounter Group A derivative of humanistic therapy in which group members learn to be themselves by openly expressing their true feelings to one another. (p. 535)

Endocrine System Glands that secrete hormones into the bloodstream. (p. 67)

Endorphins Neurotransmitters that play a role in pleasure, pain relief, and other functions. (p. 66)

Engineering Psychology The field that applies psychological principles to the design of equipment and instruments. (p. 19)

Engram A memory trace in the brain. (p. 244)

Environmental Psychology The field that applies psychological principles to improve the physical environment, including the design of buildings and the reduction of noise. (pp. 19, 637)

Episodic Memory The part of declarative memory that contains memories of personal experiences tied to particular times and places. (p. 227)

Escape Learning Learning to perform a behavior that terminates an aversive stimulus, as in negative reinforcement. (p. 199)

Eugenics The practice of encouraging supposedly superior people to reproduce, while preventing supposedly inferior people from reproducing. (p. 313)

Expectancy In achievement situations, the perceived probability of success in a particular area. (p. 346)

Experimental Group The subjects in an experiment who are exposed to the experimental condition of interest. (p. 39)

Experimental Psychology The field primarily concerned with laboratory research on basic psychological processes, including perception, learning, memory, thinking, language, motivation, and emotion. (p. 18)

Experimental Research Research that manipulates one or more variables, while controlling others, to determine the effects on behavior, mental processes, or physiological activity. (p. 39)

Experimenter Bias The tendency of experimenters to let their expectancies alter the way they treat their subjects or record the behavior of their subjects. (p. 41)

Expert System A computer program that displays expertise in a specific domain of knowledge. (p. 270)

Extinction 1. In classical conditioning, the gradual disappearance of the conditioned response when the conditioned stimulus is repeatedly presented without being paired with the unconditioned stimulus. (p. 188) 2. In operant conditioning, the gradual disappearance of a response that is no longer followed by a reinforcer. (p. 200)

Extraneous Variable A variable that may affect the dependent variable against the wishes of the experimenter. (p. 40)

Extrasensory Perception (ESP) The ability to perceive events without the use of sensory receptors. (p. 137)

Extravert A person who is socially outgoing and prefers to pay attention to the external environment. (p. 448)

Extrinsic Motivation The desire to perform a behavior to obtain an external reward, such as praise, grades, or money. (p. 348)

Face Validity The extent to which a test appears, on superficial observation, to be valid. (p. 299)

Facial-Feedback Theory The theory that particular facial expressions induce particular emotional experiences. (p. 376)

Factor Analysis A statistical technique that determines the degree of correlation between performances on various tasks to determine the extent to which they reflect particular underlying characteristics, which are known as factors. (p. 308)

Family Therapy A form of group therapy that encourages the constructive expression of feelings and the establishment of rules that family members agree to follow. (p. 535)

Fear of Failure The motivation to avoid achievement situations that might bring failure. (p. 347)

Feature-Detector Theory The view that we construct our perceptions from neurons of the brain that are sensitive to specific features of stimuli. (p. 113)

Fetal Alcohol Syndrome A disorder, marked by physical defects and mental retardation, that may afflict the offspring of women who drink alcohol during pregnancy. (pp. 304, 395)

Fetal Stage The prenatal period that lasts from the end of the eighth week through birth. (p. 394)

Fight-or-Flight Response A state of physiological arousal that enables us to meet sudden threats by either confronting them or running away from them. (p. 360)

Figure-Ground Perception The distinguishing of an object (the figure) from its surroundings (the ground). (p. 112)

Fixation In Freud's theory, the failure to mature beyond a particular stage of psychosexual development. (p. 442)

Fixed-Interval Schedule of Reinforcement A partial schedule of reinforcement that provides reinforcement for the first desired response made after a set length of time. (p. 198)

Fixed-Ratio Schedule of Reinforcement A partial schedule of reinforcement that provides reinforcement after a set number of desired responses. (p. 197)

Fixed-Role Therapy A kind of therapy, derived from Kelly's personality theory, that encourages clients to adopt roles that promote new, more adaptive personal constructs. (p. 462)

Flashbulb Memory A vivid, long-lasting memory of a surprising, important, emotionally arousing event. (p. 218)

Fluid Intelligence The form of intelligence that reflects reasoning ability, memory capacity, and speed of information processing. (p. 310)

Foot-in-the-Door Technique Increasing the likelihood that someone will comply with a request by first getting them to comply with a smaller request. (p. 634)

Forensic Psychology The field that applies psychological principles to improve the legal system, including the work of police and juries. (p. 19)

Forgetting The failure to retrieve information from memory. (p. 219)

Forgetting Curve A graph showing that forgetting is initially rapid and then slows. (p. 233)

Formal Operational Stage The Piagetian stage, beginning at about age twelve, marked by the ability to use abstract reasoning and to solve problems by testing hypotheses. (p. 411)

Fovea A small area at the center of the retina that contains only cones and provides the most acute vision. (p. 104)

Framing Effect In decision making, biases introduced into the decision-making process by presenting an issue or situation in a certain manner. (p. 269)

Frequency Theory The theory of pitch perception assuming that the basilar membrane vibrates as a whole in direct proportion to the frequency of the sound waves striking the eardrum. (p. 125)

Frontal Lobe A lobe of the cerebral cortex responsible for motor control and higher mental processes. (p. 78)

Frustration The emotional state induced when one is blocked from reaching a goal. (p. 556)

Frustration-Aggression Hypothesis The assumption that frustration causes aggression. (p. 650)

Functional Fixedness The inability to realize that a problem can be solved by using a familiar object in an unusual way. (p. 263)

Functionalism The early school of psychology that studied how the conscious mind helps the individual adapt to the environment. (p. 7)

Garcia Effect A conditioned taste aversion produced by pairing a taste with gastrointestinal distress. (p. 191)

Gate-Control Theory The theory that pain impulses can be blocked by the closing of a neuronal gate in the spinal cord. (p. 133)

Gender Identity A person's self-perceived sex. (p. 339)

Gender Roles The behaviors that are considered to be appropriate for males or females in a given culture. (p. 407)

Gender Schema Theory A theory of gender role development that combines aspects of social learning theory and cognitive-developmental theory. (p. 409)

General Adaptation Syndrome As first identified by Hans Selye, the body's stress response, which includes the stages of alarm, resistance, and exhaustion. (p. 561)

Generalizability The extent to which the results of a research study hold true for other people or animals and in other settings. (p. 42)

Generalized Anxiety Disorder An anxiety disorder marked by a persistent state of anxiety that exists independently of any particular stressful situation. (p. 483)

Generativity The characteristic of language marked by the ability to combine words in novel, meaningful ways. (p. 271)

Genital Stage In Freud's theory, the last stage, associated with puberty, during which the individual develops erotic attachments to others. (p. 442)

Germinal Stage The prenatal period that lasts from conception through the second week. (p. 392)

Gestalt Psychology The early school of psychology that claimed that we perceive and think about wholes rather than simply combinations of separate elements. (p. 12)

Gestalt Therapy A type of humanistic therapy, developed by Fritz Perls, that encourages the client to become aware of his or her true feelings and to take responsibility for his or her own actions. (p. 530)

Goal Setting The establishment of a particular level of performance to achieve in the future. (p. 347)

Gonads The male and female sex glands, the testes and the ovaries. (p. 335)

Grammar The set of rules that governs the proper use and combination of language symbols. (p. 273)

Group A collection of two or more persons who have mutual influence on each other. (p. 624)

Group Polarization The tendency for groups to make more extreme decisions than their members would make as individuals. (p. 626)

Groupthink The tendency of small, cohesive groups to place unanimity ahead of critical thinking in making decisions. (p. 626)

Guilty Knowledge Test A method that assesses lying by measuring physiological arousal in response to words that are relevant to a transgression and physiological arousal in response to words that are irrelevant to that transgression. (p. 385)

Gustation The sense of taste, which detects molecules dissolved in the saliva. (p. 130)

Hallucinogens Psychoactive drugs that induce extreme alterations in consciousness, including visual hallucinations, a sense of timelessness, and feelings of depersonalization. (p. 171)

Hardiness A personality characteristic, marked by feelings of commitment, challenge, and control, that promotes resistance to stress. (p. 567)

Health Psychology The field that applies psychological principles to the prevention and treatment of physical illness. (pp. 19, 556)

Heritability The extent to which variability in a characteristic within a group can be attributed to heredity. (p. 314)

Heuristic A general principle, or "rule of thumb," that guides problem solving, though it does not guarantee a correct solution. (p. 261)

Hidden Observer Ernest Hilgard's term for the part of the hypnotized person's consciousness that is not under the control of the hypnotist. (p. 164)

Hierarchy of Needs Abraham Maslow's arrangement of needs in order of their motivational priority, ranging from physiological needs to the need for self-actualization. (p. 326)

Hippocampus A limbic system structure that contributes to the formation of memories. (p. 75)

Holophrastic Speech The use of single words to represent whole phrases or sentences. (p. 276)

Homeostasis A steady state of physiological equilibrium. (p. 326)

Homosexuality A consistent preference for sexual relations with members of one's own sex. (p. 339)

Hormones Chemicals, secreted by endocrine glands, that play a role in a variety of functions, including synaptic transmission. (p. 67)

Hospice Movement The movement to provide care for the terminally ill in settings that are as close to everyday life as possible, and that emphasizes the need to reduce pain and suffering. (p. 422)

Humanistic Perspective The psychological viewpoint that holds that the proper subject matter of psychology should be the individual's subjective experience of the world. (p. 15)

Hyperactivity A condition, arising in childhood, in which the individual is motivated to seek constant stimulation and has difficulty focusing his or her attention. (p. 343)

Hypermnesia The hypnotic enhancement of recall. (p. 162)

Hypnosis An induced state of consciousness in which one person responds to suggestions by another person for alterations in perception, thinking, and behavior. (p. 159)

Hypochondriasis A somatoform disorder in which the person interprets the slightest physical changes as evidence of a serious illness. (p. 488)

Hypothalamus A forebrain structure that helps to regulate aspects of motivation and emotion, including eating, drinking, sexual behavior, body temperature, and stress responses through its effects on the pituitary gland and the autonomic nervous system. (p. 74)

Hypothesis A testable prediction about the relationship between two or more variables, typically concerning the outcome of a research study. (p. 31)

Iconic Memory Visual sensory memory, which lasts up to about a second. (p. 220)

Id In Freud's theory, the part of the personality that contains inborn biological drives and that seeks immediate gratification. (p. 439)

Illusory Contours The perception of edges that do not actually exist, as though they were the outlines of real objects. (p. 114)

Impression Formation The process of making judgments about the personal characteristics of others. (p. 595)

Incentive An external stimulus that pulls an individual toward a goal. (p. 326)

Incentive Value In achievement situations, the perceived rewards that would accompany success in a particular area. (p. 346)

Incongruity Theory The theory that humor is amusing when it brings together incompatible ideas in a surprising outcome that violates one's expectations. (p. 370)

Independent Variable A variable manipulated by the experimenter to determine its effect on another, dependent, variable. (p. 40)

Industrial/Organizational Psychology The field that applies psychological principles to improve productivity in businesses, industries, and government agencies. (p. 19)

Infancy The period that extends from birth through two years of age. (p. 396)

Inferential Statistics Statistics used to determine whether the results of experiments are due to the effects of their independent variables. (p. 47)

Information-Processing Model The view that the processing of memories involves encoding, storage, and retrieval. (p. 219)

Inhalants Depressants that are inhaled to induce altered states of consciousness. (p. 168)

Insanity A legal term attesting that a person is not responsible for his or her own actions, including criminal behavior. (p. 505)

Insight An approach to problem solving that depends on mental manipulation of information rather than overt trial and error, and produces sudden solutions to problems. (p. 260)

Insomnia Chronic difficulty in either falling asleep or staying asleep. (p. 155)

Instinct A relatively complex, inherited behavior pattern characteristic of a species. (p. 324)

Instinctive Drift The reversion of animals to behaviors characteristic of their species even when being reinforced for performing other behaviors. (p. 204)

Instrumental Conditioning A form of learning in which a behavior becomes more or less probable, depending on its consequences. (p. 193)

Insulin A hormone secreted by the pancreas that helps blood sugar enter body cells. (p. 329)

Intelligence The global capacity to act purposefully, to think rationally, and to deal effectively with the environment. (p. 292)

Intelligence Quotient (IQ)
1. Originally, the ratio of mental age to chronological age; that is, MA/CA × 100. 2. Today, the score on an intelligence test, calculated by comparing a person's performance to norms for his or her age group. (p. 294)

Intelligence Test A test that assesses overall mental ability. (p. 292)

Interference Theory The theory that forgetting results from some memories interfering with the ability to remember other memories. (p. 234)

Interneuron A neuron that conveys messages between neurons in the brain or spinal cord. (p. 58)

Intrinsic Motivation The desire to perform a behavior for its own sake. (p. 348)

Introvert A person who is socially reserved and prefers to pay attention to his or her private mental experiences. (p. 448)

Iodopsin The photopigment that accounts for cone vision. (p. 107)

Iris The donut-shaped band of muscles behind the cornea that gives the eye its color and controls the size of the pupil. (p. 102)

James-Lange Theory The theory that specific patterns of physiological changes evoke specific emotional experiences. (p. 371)

Justification Theory The theory that an extrinsic reward will decrease intrinsic motivation when a person attributes his or her performance to that reward. (p. 348)

Just Noticeable Difference (jnd) Weber and Fechner's term for the difference threshold. (p. 100)

Kinesthetic Sense The sense that provides information about the position of the joints, the degree of tension in the muscles, and the movement of the arms and legs. (p. 135)

Korsakoff's Syndrome A brain disorder caused by alcoholism and marked by difficulty in forming new long-term memories. (p. 225)

Language A formal system of communication involving symbols—whether spoken, written, or gestured—and rules for combining them. (p. 271)

Latency Stage In Freud's theory, the stage, between age five and puberty, during which there is little psychosexual development. (p. 442)

Latent Content Sigmund Freud's term for the true, though disguised, meaning of a dream. (p. 158)

Latent Learning Learning that occurs without the reinforcement of overt behavior. (p. 207)

Law of Effect Edward Thorndike's principle that a behavior followed by a satisfying state of affairs is strengthened and a behavior followed by an annoying state of affairs is weakened. (p. 193)

Leader A group member who exerts more influence on the group than does any other member. (p. 628)

Learned Helplessness A feeling of futility caused by the belief that one has little or no control over events in one's life, which may make one stop trying and develop feelings of depression. (pp. 204, 569)

Learning A relatively permanent change in knowledge or behavior as a result of experience. (p. 184)

Lens The transparent structure behind the pupil that focuses light onto the retina. (p. 103)

Levels of Processing Theory The theory that the "depth" at which we process information determines how well it is encoded, stored, and retrieved. (p. 266)

Libido Freud's term for the sexual energy of the id. (p. 441)

Limbic System A group of forebrain structures that promote the survival of the individual and, as a result, the continuation of the species by its influence on emotion, motivation, and memory. (p. 75)

Linguistic Relativity Hypothesis The assumption that one's perception of the world is molded by one's language. (p. 279)

Link Method A mnemonic device that involves connecting images of items to be memorized in sequence to make them easier to recall. (p. 242)

Logical Concept A concept formed by identifying the specific features possessed by all of its members. (p. 257)

Longitudinal Research Design A research design in which the same group of subjects is tested or observed repeatedly over a period of time. (pp. 299, 391)

Long-Term Memory The stage of memory that can store a virtually unlimited amount of information relatively permanently. (p. 219)

Loudness Perception The subjective experience of the intensity of a sound, which corresponds most closely to the amplitude of the sound waves composing it. (p. 126)

LSD A hallucinogen derived from a fungus that grows on rye grain. (p. 171)

Maintenance Rehearsal Repeating information to oneself to keep it in short-term memory. (p. 226)

Major Depression A mood disorder marked by depression so intense and prolonged that the person may be completely unable to function in everyday life. (p. 492)

Mania A mood disorder marked by euphoria, hyperactivity, grandiose ideas, annoying talkativeness, unrealistic optimism, and inflated self-esteem. (p. 493)

Manifest Content Sigmund Freud's term for the verbally reported dream. (p. 158)

Massed Practice Cramming the memorization of information or the learning of a motor skill into one session. (p. 240)

Mean The arithmetic average of a set of scores. (p. 44)

Mean Length of Utterance (MLU) The average length of spoken statements, which is used as a measure of language development in children. (p. 276)

Measure of Central Tendency A statistic that represents the typical score in a set of scores. (p. 44)

Measure of Correlation A statistic that assesses the degree of association between two or more sets of scores. (p. 45).

Measure of Variability A statistic describing the degree of dispersion in a set of scores. (p. 45)

Median The middle score in a set of scores that have been ordered from lowest to highest. (p. 44)

Meditation A procedure that uses mental exercises to achieve a highly focused state of consciousness. (p. 165)

Medulla A hindbrain structure that regulates breathing, heart rate, blood pressure, and other life functions. (p. 72)

Memory The process by which information is stored in the brain and later retrieved. (p. 218)

Mental Giftedness Intellectual superiority marked by an IQ above 130 and exceptionally high scores on achievement tests in specific subjects, such as mathematics. (p. 306)

Mental Retardation Intellectual deficiency marked by an IQ below 70 and difficulties performing in everyday life. (p. 303)

Mental Set A tendency to use a particular problem-solving strategy that has succeeded in the past but that may interfere with solving a problem requiring a new strategy. (p. 262)

Mental Telepathy The ability to perceive the thoughts of others without any sensory contact with them. (p. 137)

Mere Exposure Effect The tendency to like stimuli, including people, more as we are exposed to them repeatedly. (p. 599)

Method of Loci A mnemonic device in which items to be recalled are associated with landmarks in a familiar place and then recalled during a mental walk from one landmark to another. (p. 241)

Method of Savings The assessment of memory by comparing the number of trials needed to memorize a given amount of information and the number of trials needed to memorize it again at a later time. (p. 233)

Mnemonic Device A technique for organizing information to be memorized to make it easier to remember. (p. 241)

Mode The score that occurs most frequently in a set of scores. (p. 44)

Monocular Cues Depth perception cues that require input from only one eye. (p. 115)

Mood Disorders Psychological disorders marked by prolonged periods of extreme depression or elation, often unrelated to the person's current situation. (p. 492)

Moon Illusion The misperception that the moon is larger when it is at the horizon than when it is overhead. (p. 118)

Moral Therapy An approach to therapy, developed by Phillippe Pinel, that provided mental patients with humane treatment. (p. 515)

Morpheme The smallest meaningful unit of language. (p. 274)

Motivation The psychological process that arouses, directs, and maintains behavior. (p. 324)

Motor Cortex The area of the frontal lobes that controls specific voluntary body movements. (p. 78)

Motor Neuron A neuron that sends messages from the central nervous system to glands, cardiac muscle, or skeletal muscles. (p. 58)

Multiple Personality A dissociative disorder in which the person has two or more distinct personalities that alternate with one another. (p. 491)

Myelin A fatty substance that forms a sheath around many axons. (p. 62)

Narcolepsy A condition in which an awake person suffers from repeated, sudden, and irresistible REM sleep attacks. (p. 156)

Natural Concept A concept, typically formed through everyday experience, whose members may not all possess a common set of features. (p. 258)

Naturalistic Observation The recording of the behavior of subjects in their natural environments, with little or no intervention by the researcher. (p. 36)

Near-Death Experiences The experiences reported by persons as they die or by persons who have apparently died and then been revived. (p. 422)

Need A motivated state caused by physiological deprivation, such as a lack of food or water. (p. 326)

Negative Correlation A relationship in which scores on one variable increase as scores on another decrease. (p. 38)

Negative Reinforcement In operant conditioning, an increase in the probability of a behavior that is followed by the removal of an aversive stimulus. (p. 199)

Neodissociation Theory The theory that hypnosis induces a dissociated state of consciousness. (p. 163)

Nerve A bundle of axons that conveys information to and from the central nervous system. (p. 56)

Nerve Deafness Hearing loss caused by damage to the hair cells of the basilar membrane or the axons of the auditory nerve. (p. 126)

Neuron A cell specialized for the transmission of information in the nervous system. (p. 56)

Neuroses A general category, no longer widely used, that comprises psychological disorders associated with maladaptive attempts to deal with anxiety but with relatively good contact with reality. (p. 480)

Neurotransmitters Chemicals secreted by neurons, which provide the means of synaptic transmission. (p. 64)

Nicotine A stimulant used to regulate physical and mental arousal. (p. 170)

Nightmare A frightening REM dream. (p. 157)

Night Terror A frightening NREM experience, common in childhood, in which the individual may suddenly sit up, let out a bloodcurdling scream, speak incoherently, and quickly fall back to sleep, yet usually fail to recall it on awakening. (p. 157)

Norm A rule of proper social behavior that guides group members. (p. 624)

Norms Scores based on the test performances of large numbers of subjects that are used as standards for assessing the performances of individual test takers. (p. 295)

NREM Sleep The stages of sleep not associated with rapid eye movements and marked by relatively little dreaming. (p. 151)

Obedience Behaving in accordance with orders given by an authority. (p. 635)

Obesity A body weight more than 20 percent above normal for one's height and build. (p. 331)

Object Permanence The realization that objects exist even when they are no longer visible. (p. 400)

Observational Learning Learning a behavior by observing the consequences that others receive for performing it. (p. 207)

Obsessive-Compulsive Disorder An anxiety disorder in which the person has recurrent, intrusive thoughts (obsessions) and recurrent urges to perform ritualistic actions (compulsions). (p. 487)

Occipital Lobe A lobe of the cerebral cortex responsible for processing vision. (p. 79)

Oedipus Complex In Freud's theory, a conflict, during the phallic stage, between the child's desire for the parent of the opposite sex and fear of punishment from the same-sex parent. (p. 442)

Olfaction The sense of smell, which detects molecules carried in the air. (p. 129)

Operant Conditioning B. F. Skinner's term for instrumental conditioning. (p. 193)

Operational Definition The definition of behaviors or qualities in terms of the procedures used to measure them. (p. 32)

Opiates Depressant drugs, derived from opium, used to relieve pain or to induce a euphoric state of consciousness. (p. 168)

Opponent-Process Theory of Emotion The theory that the brain counteracts a strong positive or negative emotion by evoking an opposite emotional response. (p. 375)

Opponent-Process Theory of Color Vision The theory that color vision depends on red-green, blue-yellow, and black-white opponent processes in the brain. (p. 109)

Optic Chiasm The point under the frontal lobes at which some axons from each of the optic nerves cross over to the opposite side of the brain. (p. 106)

Optic Nerve The nerve formed from the axons of ganglion cells that carries visual impulses from the retina to the brain. (p. 105)

Oral Stage In Freud's theory, the stage of personality development, between birth and age one, during which the infant gains pleasure from oral activities and faces a conflict over weaning. (p. 442)

Overextension The tendency to apply a word to more objects or actions than it actually represents. (p. 275)

Overlearning Studying material beyond the point of initial mastery. (p. 240)

Overregularization The application of a grammatical rule without making necessary exceptions to it. (p. 277)

Panic Disorder An anxiety disorder marked by sudden, unexpected attacks of overwhelming anxiety, often associated with the fear of dying or "losing one's mind." (p. 484)

Paradoxical Intention A therapy technique that requires clients to perform the very acts that would normally cause them emotional distress. (p. 526)

Parallel Processing The processing of different information simultaneously. (p. 270)

Paranoid Schizophrenia A type of schizophrenia marked by hallucinations, delusions, suspiciousness, and argumentativeness. (p. 499)

Paraphilia A way of obtaining sexual gratification that violates legal or cultural norms concerning proper sex objects and sexual practices. (p. 336)

Parapsychology The study of extrasensory perception, psychokinesis, and related phenomena. (p. 137)

Parasympathetic Nervous System The division of the autonomic nervous system that calms the body and serves maintenance functions. (pp. 56, 360)

Parietal Lobe A lobe of the cerebral cortex responsible for processing body sensations and perceiving spatial relations. (p. 78)

Partial Schedule of Reinforcement A schedule of reinforcement that reinforces some, but not all, instances of a desired response. (p. 197)

Participatory Modeling A form of social learning therapy in which the client learns to perform more adaptive behaviors by first observing the therapist model the desired behaviors. (p. 525)

Passionate Love Love characterized by intense emotional arousal and sexual feelings. (p. 603)

Pegword Method A mnemonic device that involves associating items to be recalled with objects that rhyme with the numbers 1, 2, 3, and so on, to make the items easier to recall. (p. 242)

Perception The process that organizes sensations into meaningful patterns. (p. 98)

Perception without Awareness The unconscious perception of stimuli that normally exceed the absolute threshold but fall outside our focus of attention. (p. 175)

Peripheral Nervous System The division of the nervous system composed of the nerves, which conveys sensory information to the central nervous system and motor commands from the central nervous system to the glands and muscles. (p. 56)

Personality An individual's unique, relatively consistent pattern of thoughts, feelings, and behaviors. (p. 432)

Personality Disorders Psychological disorders characterized by enduring, inflexible, maladaptive patterns of behavior. (p. 502)

Personality Psychology The field that focuses on factors accounting for the differences in behavior and enduring personal characteristics among individuals. (p. 18)

Personal Space The distance at which we prefer to carry out the everyday social relations that are neither formal nor intimate. (p. 638)

Personal Unconscious In Jung's theory, the individual's own unconscious mind, which contains repressed memories. (p. 446)

Person-Centered Therapy A type of humanistic therapy, developed by Carl Rogers, that helps clients find their own answers to their problems. (p. 529)

Persuasion The intentional attempt to influence the attitudes of other people. (p. 607)

Phallic Stage In Freud's theory, the stage of personality development, between ages three and five, during which the child gains pleasure from the genitals and must resolve the Oedipus complex. (p. 442)

Phase Advance Shortening the sleep-wake cycle, as occurs when traveling from west to east. (p. 149)

Phase Delay Lengthening the sleep-wake cycle, as occurs when traveling from east to west. (p. 149)

Phenylketonuria (PKU) A hereditary enzyme deficiency that, if left untreated in the infant, causes mental retardation. (p. 304)

Pheromones Odorous chemicals secreted by animals that affect the behavior of other animals. (p. 130)

Phi Phenomenon Apparent motion caused by the presentation of different stimuli in rapid succession. (p. 117)

Phobia An anxiety disorder marked by excessive or inappropriate fear. (p. 486)

Phoneme The smallest unit of sound in a language. (p. 273)

Phrenology A discredited technique for determining intellectual abilities and personality traits by examining the bumps and depressions of the skull. (p. 82)

Physiological Psychology The field that emphasizes the biological basis of overt behavior and mental processes. (p. 18)

Pineal Gland An endocrine gland that affects circadian rhythms through its secretion of the hormone melatonin. (p. 149)

Pitch Perception The subjective experience of the highness or lowness of a sound, which corresponds most closely to the frequency of the sound waves that compose it. (p. 125)

Pituitary Gland An endocrine gland that regulates many of the other endocrine glands by secreting hormones that affect those glands. (p. 67)

Placebo An inactive substance that may induce some of the effects of the drug for which it has been substituted. (p. 135)

Place Theory The theory of pitch perception assuming that hair cells at particular points on the basilar membrane are maximally responsive to sound waves of particular frequencies. (p. 125)

Plasticity The ability of intact brain areas to take over the functions of damaged ones. (p. 84)

Pleasure Principle The process by which the id seeks immediate gratification of its impulses. (p. 439)

Polygraph Test The "lie detector" test, which assesses lying by measuring changing patterns of physiological arousal in response to particular questions. (p. 383)

Pons A hindbrain structure that regulates the sleep-wake cycle. (p. 72)

Population A group of individuals who share certain characteristics. (p. 37)

Pornography Sexually explicit material intended to create sexual arousal. (p. 653)

Positive Correlation A relationship in which scores on two variables increase and decrease together. (p. 38)

Positive Reinforcement In operant conditioning, an increase in the probability of a behavior that is followed by a desirable stimulus. (p. 194)

Positron-Emission Tomography (PET Scan) A brain-scanning technique that produces color-coded pictures showing the relative activity of different brain areas. (p. 79)

Postconventional Level In Kohlberg's theory, the level of moral reasoning characterized by concern with obeying mutually agreed upon laws and by the need to uphold human dignity. (p. 412)

Posthypnotic Suggestions Suggestions directing subjects to carry out particular behaviors or to have particular experiences after leaving hypnosis. (p. 162)

Posttraumatic Stress Disorder A syndrome of physical and psychological symptoms that appears as a delayed response after exposure to an extremely emotionally distressing event. (p. 559)

Pragmatics The relationship between language and its social context. (p. 275)

Precognition The ability to perceive events in the future. (p. 138)

Preconscious The level of consciousness that contains feelings and memories which we are unaware of at the moment, but which we can become aware of at will. (pp. 173, 438)

Preconventional Level In Kohlberg's theory, the level of moral reasoning characterized by concern with the consequences that behavior has to oneself. (p. 412)

Predictive Validity The extent to which a test accurately predicts behavior it is supposed to predict. (p. 300)

Prejudice An attitude, usually negative, toward a person based on his or her membership in a particular group. (p. 614)

Preoperational Stage The Piagetian stage, extending from age two until age seven, during which the child's use of language becomes more sophisticated but the child has difficulty in the logical mental manipulation of information. (p. 400)

Preparedness The degree to which members of a species are innately prepared to learn particular behaviors. (p. 205)

Pressure The emotional state induced when one is confronted by personal responsibilities. (p. 556)

Primary Cortical Areas Areas of the cerebral cortex that serve motor or sensory functions. (p. 77)

Primary Reinforcer In operant conditioning, an unlearned reinforcer, which satisfies a biological need such as air, food, or water. (p. 195)

Proactive Interference The process by which old memories interfere with the ability to remember new memories. (p. 234)

Problem Solving The thought process by which an individual overcomes obstacles to reach a goal. (p. 259)

Procedural Memory The part of long-term memory that contains memories of how to perform particular actions or skills. (p. 227)

Program Evaluation The field that applies psychological principles in evaluating programs sponsored by health, social, educational, industrial, and governmental organizations. (p. 19)

Programmed Instruction A step-by-step approach, based on operant conditioning, in which the learner proceeds at his or her own pace through more and more difficult material and receives immediate knowledge of the results of each response. (p. 203)

Progressive Relaxation A procedure that involves the successive tensing and relaxing of each of the major muscle groups of the body. (p. 571)

Projective Test A Freudian personality test based on the assumption that individuals will project their unconscious feelings when responding to ambiguous stimuli. (p. 448)

Prosocial Behavior Behavior that helps others in need. (p. 643)

Prototype The best representative of a concept. (p. 258)

Proxemics The study of the role of social space in interpersonal relationships. (p. 638)

Psychiatry The field of medicine that diagnoses and treats psychological disorders by using medical or psychological forms of therapy. (p. 18)

Psychic Determinism The Freudian assumption that all behaviors are influenced by unconscious motives. (pp. 9, 439)

Psychoactive Drugs Chemicals that induce changes in mood, thinking, perception, and behavior by affecting neuronal activity in the brain. (p. 166)

Psychoanalysis 1. The early school of psychology that emphasized the importance of unconscious causes of behavior. (p. 9) 2. A type of psychotherapy, developed by Sigmund Freud, aimed at uncovering the unconscious causes of psychological disorders. (p. 519)

Psychoanalytic Perspective The psychological viewpoint, descended from psychoanalysis, that places less emphasis on biological motives and more emphasis on the importance of interpersonal relationships. (p. 14)

Psychobiological Perspective The psychological viewpoint that supports the study of the relationship between biological and psychological factors. (p. 16)

Psychobiology The field that studies the relationship between psychological and physiological processes. (p. 56)

Psychodrama A form of psychoanalytic group therapy, developed by Jacob Moreno, that aims at achieving insight and catharsis through acting out real-life situations. (p. 532)

Psychogenic Amnesia A dissociative disorder marked by the inability to recall personally significant memories. (p. 490)

Psychogenic Fugue A dissociative disorder marked by the memory loss characteristic of psychogenic amnesia, the loss of one's identity, and fleeing from one's home. (p. 490)

Psychokinesis (PK) The ability to control objects with the mind alone. (p. 138)

Psychology The science of behavior and mental processes. (p. 4)

Psychoneuroimmunology The interdisciplinary field that studies the relationship between psychological factors and physical illness. (p. 563)

Psychopathology The study of psychological disorders. (p. 474)

Psychophysics The study of the relationship between the physical characteristics of stimuli and the conscious psychological experiences they produce. (pp. 6, 98)

Psychoses A general category, no longer widely used, that comprises severe psychological disorders associated with thought disturbances, bizarre behavior, severe disruption of social relations, and relatively poor contact with reality. (p. 480)

Psychosurgery The treatment of psychological disorders by the destruction of specific areas of the brain. (p. 537)

Psychotherapy The treatment of psychological disorders through psychological, as opposed to biomedical, means, generally involving verbal interaction with a professional therapist. (p. 518)

Puberty The period of rapid physical change that occurs during adolescence, including the development of the ability to reproduce sexually. (p. 410)

Punishment In operant conditioning, the process by which an aversive stimulus decreases the probability of a response that precedes it. (p. 200)

Pupil The opening at the center of the iris that controls how much light will enter the eye. (p. 102)

Quasiexperimental Research The use of experimental research methods in situations in which the researcher may not be able to randomly assign subjects to the experimental and control conditions. (p. 40)

Random Assignment The assignment of subjects to experimental and control conditions so that each subject is as likely to be assigned to one condition as to another. (p. 41)

Random Sampling The selection of a sample from a population so that each member of the population has an equal chance of being included. (p. 38)

Range A statistic representing the difference between the highest and lowest scores in a set of scores. (p. 45)

Rational-Emotive Therapy (R-E-T) A type of cognitive therapy, developed by Albert Ellis, that treats psychological disorders by forcing the client to give up irrational ways of thinking. (p. 526)

Rationalism The philosophical position that true knowledge comes through correct reasoning. (p. 5)

Reality Principle The process by which the ego directs the individual to express sexual and aggressive impulses in socially acceptable ways. (p. 439)

Reciprocal Determinism Bandura's belief that personality traits, environmental factors, and overt behavior affect each other. (p. 458)

Reflex An automatic, involuntary motor response to sensory stimulation. (p. 58)

Relaxation Response A variation of transcendental meditation in which the individual may repeat a sound other than a mantra. (p. 165)

Release Theory The theory that humor is amusing when it raises one's level of anxiety and then suddenly lowers it. (p. 370)

Reliability The degree to which a test gives consistent results. (p. 298)

REM Sleep The stage of sleep associated with rapid eye movements, an active brain-wave pattern, and vivid dreams. (p. 151)

Replication The repetition of a research study, usually with some alterations in its subjects, methods, or setting, to determine whether the principles derived from earlier findings hold up under similar circumstances. (p. 43)

Representativeness Heuristic In decision making, the assumption that characteristics of a small sample are representative of its population. (p. 268)

Repression The process by which emotionally threatening experiences are banished from the conscious mind to the unconscious mind; a defense mechanism. (pp. 235, 438)

Resting Potential The electrical charge of a neuron when it is not firing a neural impulse. (p. 61)

Reticular Formation A diffuse network of neurons extending from the hindbrain through the midbrain and into the forebrain that helps maintain vigilance and an optimal level of brain arousal. (p. 73)

Retina The light-sensitive inner membrane of the eye that contains the receptor cells for vision. (p. 103)

Retrieval The recovering of information from memory. (p. 219)

Retroactive Interference The process by which new memories interfere with the ability to remember old memories. (p. 234)

Rhodopsin The photopigment that accounts for rod vision. (p. 107)

Rods Receptor cells of the retina that play an important role in night vision and peripheral vision. (p. 104)

Role A social position that is associated with norms that determine the proper behavior of individuals who hold that position. (p. 624)

Saccadic Movements Continuous small darting movements of the eyes that bring new portions of scenes into focus on the foveae. (p. 104)

Sample A group of subjects selected from a population. (p. 37)

Schema A mental model incorporating the characteristics of particular persons, objects, events, or situations. (p. 400)

Schema Theory The theory that long-term memories are stored as parts of schemas, which are cognitive structures that organize knowledge about events or objects. (p. 230)

Schizophrenia A class of psychological disorders characterized by grossly impaired social, emotional, cognitive, and perceptual functioning. (p. 496)

School Psychology The field that applies psychological principles to improving the academic performance and social behavior of students in elementary, junior high, and high schools. (p. 18)

Scientific Method A source of knowledge based on the assumption that knowledge comes from the objective, systematic observation and measurement of particular factors and the events they influence. (p. 30)

Sclera The tough, white outer membrane of the eye. (p. 102)

Secondary Reinforcer In operant conditioning, a neutral stimulus that becomes reinforcing after being associated with a primary reinforcer. (p. 195)

Self-Actualization In Maslow's theory, the individual's predisposition to try to reach his or her potentials. (p. 463)

Self-Disclosure The extent to which we reveal our private beliefs, feelings, and experiences to others. (p. 602)

Self-Efficacy In Bandura's theory, a person's belief that he or she can perform behaviors that are necessary to bring about a desired outcome. (p. 458)

Self-Fulfilling Prophecy The tendency for one person's expectations to influence another person to behave in accordance with those expectations. (p. 598)

Self-Perception Theory Daryl Bem's theory that when we are unsure of our attitudes we infer them from our own behavior. (p. 613)

Self-Serving Bias The tendency to make dispositional attributions for one's successes and situational attributions for one's failures. (p. 594)

Semanticity The characteristic of language marked by the use of symbols to convey thoughts in a meaningful way. (p. 271)

Semantic Memory The part of declarative memory that contains general information about the world. (p. 227)

Semantic Network Theory The theory that memories are stored as nodes interconnected by links representing their relationships. (p. 228)

Semantics The study of how language conveys meaning. (p. 274)

Semicircular Canals The curved vestibular organs of the inner ear that detect movements of the head in any direction. (p. 136)

Sensate Focusing A sex therapy technique that, at first, involves nongenital caressing and gradually progresses to sexual intercourse. (p. 339)

Sensation The process that detects stimuli from the body or surroundings. (p. 98)

Sensation Seeking The extent to which an individual seeks sensory stimulation. (p. 343)

Sensorimotor Stage The Piagetian stage, from birth through the second year, during which the infant learns to coordinate sensory experiences and motor behavior. (p. 400)

Sensory Adaptation The tendency of the sensory receptors to respond less and less to a constant stimulus. (p. 101)

Sensory Deprivation The prolonged withdrawal of normal levels of external stimulation. (p. 342)

Sensory Neuron A neuron that sends messages from sensory receptors toward the central nervous system. (p. 58)

Sensory Memory The stage of memory that briefly, for at most a few seconds, stores exact replicas of sensations. (p. 219)

Sensory Receptors Specialized cells that detect stimuli and convert their energy into neural impulses. (p. 98)

Sensory Transduction The process by which sensory receptors convert stimuli into neural impulses. (p. 98)

Serial-Position Effect The superiority of immediate recall for items at the beginning and end of a list. (p. 232)

Serial Processing The processing of information one step at a time. (p. 270)

Set Point A specific body weight that the brain tries to maintain through the regulation of diet, activity, and metabolism. (p. 330)

Sexual Dysfunction A chronic problem at one or more phases of the sexual response cycle. (p. 338)

Sexual Orientation One's sexual attraction toward members of either one's own sex or opposite sex. (p. 339)

Sexual Response Cycle During sexual activity, the phases of excitement, plateau, orgasm, and resolution. (p. 338)

Shape Constancy The perceptual process that makes an object appear to maintain its normal shape regardless of the angle from which it is viewed. (p. 118)

Shaping An operant conditioning procedure involving the positive reinforcement of successive approximations of an initially improbable behavior to eventually bring about that behavior. (p. 196)

Short-Term Memory The stage of memory that can store a few items of unrehearsed information for up to about twenty seconds. (p. 219)

Signal Detection Theory The theory holding that the detection of a stimulus depends on both the intensity of the stimulus and the physical and psychological state of the individual. (p. 100)

Simple Phobia A phobia of a specific object or situation. (p. 486)

Size Constancy The perceptual process that makes an object appear to remain the same size despite changes in the size of the image it casts on the retina. (p. 117)

Skinner Box An enclosure containing a bar or key that can be pressed to obtain food or water, which is used to study operant conditioning in rats, pigeons, or other small animals. (p. 193)

Skin Senses The senses of touch, temperature, and pain. (p. 132)

Sleep Apnea A condition in which a person awakens repeatedly in order to breathe. (p. 156)

Smooth Pursuit Movements Eye movements that track objects. (p. 104)

Social Attachment A strong, enduring emotional tie between an infant and a caregiver. (p. 402)

Social Attribution The cognitive process by which we infer the causes of both our own and other people's social behavior. (p. 590)

Social Comparison Theory The theory that happiness is the result of estimating that one's life circumstances are more favorable than those of others. (p. 368)

Social Density The number of persons in a given area. (p. 693)

Social Facilitation The improvement in a person's task performance when in the presence of other people. (p. 630)

Social Influence The effects of social relationships on thinking, feeling, and behaving. (p. 624)

Social Learning Theory A theory that assumes that people learn social behaviors mainly through observation and mental processing of information. (p. 208)

Social Loafing A decrease in the individual effort exerted by group members when working together on a task than when working independently. (p. 631)

Social Phobia A phobia of situations that involve public scrutiny. (p. 486)

Social Psychology The field that studies the effects that people have on one another's thoughts, feelings, and behaviors. (pp. 18, 590)

Social Schema A cognitive structure comprising the presumed characteristics of a role, event, person, or group. (p. 595)

Social Skills Training A form of behavioral group therapy that improves the client's social relationships by improving his or her interpersonal skills. (p. 534)

Sociobiology The study of the hereditary basis of human and animal social behavior. (pp. 325, 649)

Soma The part of the neuron that serves as its control center. (p. 58)

Somatic Nervous System The division of the peripheral nervous system that sends messages from the sensory organs to the central nervous system and messages from the central nervous system to the skeletal muscles. (p. 56)

Somatoform Disorders Psychological disorders characterized by physical symptoms in the absence of disease or injury. (p. 488)

Somatosensory Cortex The area of the parietal lobes that processes information from sensory receptors in the skin. (pp. 78, 132)

Somatotype A person's body type, whether an ectomorph (thin), a mesomorph (muscular), or an endomorph (fat). (p. 434)

Sound Localization The process by which the individual determines the location of a sound. (p. 128)

Spinal Cord The portion of the central nervous system located in the spine, which plays a role in body reflexes and in communicating information between the brain and the peripheral nervous system. (p. 56)

Split-Half Reliability Assessing a test's consistency by dividing it into two halves, usually with odd-numbered items in one half and even-numbered items in the other, and then correlating scores on the two halves. (p. 298)

Spontaneous Recovery 1. In classical conditioning, the reappearance after a period of time of a conditioned response that has been subjected to extinction. (p. 188) 2. In operant conditioning, the reappearance after a period of time of a behavior that has been subjected to extinction. (p. 200)

Spontaneous Remission The improvement of some victims of psychological disorders without their undergoing formal therapy. (p. 547)

Sport Psychology The field that applies psychological principles to help amateur and professional athletes improve their performance. (pp. 19, 350)

SQ3R Method A study technique that requires the student to survey, question, read, recite, and review course material. (p. 239)

Standard Deviation A statistic representing the degree of dispersion of a set of scores around their mean. (p. 45)

Standardization (1) A procedure assuring that a test is administered and scored in a consistent manner. (2) A procedure for establishing test norms by giving a test to large samples of people who are representative of those for whom the test is designed. (p. 295)

State-Dependent Memory The tendency for recall to be best when one's emotional or physiological state is the same during the recall of a memory as it was during the encoding of that memory. (p. 237)

Statistical Significance A low probability (usually less than 5 percent) that the results of a research study are due to chance factors. (p. 47)

Statistics Mathematical techniques used to summarize research data or to determine whether the data support the researcher's hypothesis. (p. 32)

Stereochemical Theory The theory of taste assuming that taste receptors in different areas of the tongue are maximally responsive to molecules of different shapes. (p. 132)

Stereotype A social schema that incorporates characteristics, both positive and negative, supposedly shared by almost all members of a group. (p. 615)

Stimulants Psychoactive drugs that increase central nervous system activity. (p. 169)

Stimulus Discrimination In classical conditioning, a conditioned response to the conditioned stimulus but not to stimuli similar to it. (p. 188)

Stimulus Generalization In classical conditioning, a conditioned response to stimuli similar to the conditioned stimulus. (p. 188)

Storage The retaining of information in memory. (p. 219)

Stress The body's physiological adjustment to physical and psychological demands. (p. 556)

Stressor A physical or psychological demand to which the body must adjust. (p. 556)

Structuralism The early school of psychology that sought to identify the components of the conscious mind. (p. 6)

Subject Bias The tendency of people who know they are subjects in a study to behave in a way other than they normally would. (p. 41)

Subliminal Perception The unconscious perception of stimuli that are too weak to exceed the absolute threshold for detection. (p. 174)

Substantia Nigra A midbrain structure that promotes smooth voluntary body movements. (p. 73)

Superego In Freud's theory, the part of the personality that acts as a moral guide telling us what we should and should not do. (p. 440)

Surface Structure The word arrangements used to express thoughts. (p. 274)

Survey A set of questions related to a particular topic of interest administered through an interview or questionnaire. (p. 37)

Sympathetic Nervous System The division of the autonomic nervous system that arouses the body to prepare it for action. (pp. 56, 360)

Synapse The junction between a neuron and another neuron, a gland, a muscle, or a sensory organ. (p. 63)

Synaptic Transmission The conveying of a neural impulse from one neuron to another. (p. 63)

Syntax The rules that govern the acceptable arrangement of words in phrases and sentences. (p. 274)

Systematic Desensitization A form of counterconditioning that trains the client to maintain a state of relaxation in the presence of anxiety-inducing stimuli. (p. 521)

Taste Buds Structures lining the grooves of the tongue that contain the taste receptor cells. (p. 131)

Tectum A midbrain structure that mediates reflexive responses to visual and auditory stimuli. (p. 73)

Telegraphic Speech Speech marked by reliance on nouns and verbs, while omitting other parts of speech, including articles and prepositions. (p. 276)

Temperament A person's characteristic emotional state, first apparent in early infancy and possibly inborn. (p. 433)

Temporal Lobe A lobe of the cerebral cortex responsible for processing hearing. (p. 78)

Test-Retest Reliability Assessing a test's consistency by giving it to a group of people on two occasions and then correlating scores on the first occasion with scores on the second. (p. 298)

Thalamus A forebrain structure that acts as a sensory relay station for taste, body, visual, and auditory sensations. (p. 75)

Theory An integrated set of statements that summarizes and explains research findings, and from which research hypotheses may be derived. (p. 33)

Theory of Multiple Intelligences Howard Gardner's theory of intelligence, which assumes that the brain has evolved separate systems for seven kinds of intelligence. (p. 311)

Thinking The mental manipulation of words and images, as in concept formation, problem solving, and decision making. (p. 256)

Timbre The subjective experience that identifies a particular sound and corresponds most closely to the mixture of sound waves composing it. (p. 126)

Tip-of-the-Tongue Phenomenon The inability to recall information that one knows has been stored in long-term memory. (p. 236)

Token Economy An operant conditioning procedure that uses tokens as positive reinforcers in programs designed to promote positive behaviors, with the tokens later used to purchase desired items or privileges. (pp. 203, 524)

Trait A relatively enduring, cross-situationally consistent personality characteristic that is inferred from a person's behavior. (p. 452)

Transactional Analysis (TA) A form of psychoanalytic group therapy, developed by Eric Berne, that helps clients change their immature or inappropriate ways of relating to other people. (p. 533)

Transcendental Meditation (TM) A form of meditation in which the individual relaxes and repeats a sound called a mantra for two 20-minute periods a day. (p. 165)

Transcutaneous Nerve Stimulation (TENS) The use of electrical stimulation of sites on the body to provide pain relief, apparently by stimulating the release of endorphins. (p. 135)

Transductive Reasoning The assumption that if two objects have a characteristic in common, then the objects are identical. (p. 401)

Transformational Grammar The rules by which languages generate surface structures from deep structures, and deep structures from surface structures. (p. 274)

Transitive Inferences The application of previously learned relationships to infer new relationships. (p. 402)

Transsexualism A condition in which a genetic male or female has the gender identity of the opposite sex. (p. 339)

Trephining An ancient technique that involved the use of sharp stones to chip holes in the skull, presumably to let out evil spirits that caused abnormal behavior. (p. 514)

Trial and Error An approach to problem solving in which the individual tries one possible solution after another until one works. (p. 260)

Triangular Theory of Love Robert Sternberg's theory that love comprises passion, intimacy, and decision/commitment. (p. 604)

Triarchic Theory of Intelligence Robert Sternberg's theory of intelligence, which assumes that there are three main kinds of intelligence: componential, experiential, and contextual. (p. 311)

Trichromatic Theory The theory that color vision depends on the relative degree of stimulation of red, green, and blue receptors. (p. 109)

t-test An inferential statistic used to determine whether two sets of scores are significantly different from each other. (p. 47)

Two-Factor Theory The theory that emotional experience is the outcome of physiological arousal and the attribution of a cause for that arousal. (p. 378)

Tympanic Membrane The eardrum; a membrane separating the outer and inner ears that vibrates in response to sound waves that strike it. (p. 123)

Type A Behavior A syndrome, marked by impatience, hostility, and extreme competitiveness, that has been associated with the development of coronary heart disease. (p. 582)

Unconditioned Response (UCR) In classical conditioning, an unlearned, automatic response to a particular "unconditioned" stimulus. (p. 186)

Unconditioned Stimulus (UCS) In classical conditioning, a stimulus that automatically elicits a particular "unconditioned" response. (p. 186)

Unconscious The level of consciousness that contains thoughts, feelings, and memories that influence us without our awareness and that we cannot become aware of at will. (pp. 173, 438)

Underextension The tendency to apply a word to fewer objects or actions than it actually represents. (p. 276)

Undifferentiated Schizophrenia A catchall category for cases that do not fall neatly into any single type of schizophrenia. (p. 499)

Validity The extent to which a test measures what it is supposed to measure. (p. 299)

Variable An event, behavior, condition, or characteristic that has two or more values. (p. 39)

Variable-Interval Schedule of Reinforcement A partial schedule of reinforcement that provides reinforcement for the first desired response made after varying, unpredictable lengths of time. (p. 199)

Variable-Ratio Schedule of Reinforcement A partial schedule of reinforcement that provides reinforcement after varying, unpredictable numbers of desired responses. (p. 198)

Vestibular Sense The sense that provides information about one's position in space and helps in the maintenance of balance. (p. 136)

Visible Spectrum The portion of the electromagnetic spectrum that we commonly call light. (p. 101)

Vision The sense that detects objects by the light reflected from them into the eyes. (p. 101)

Visual Cortex The area of the occipital lobes that processes visual input. (pp. 79, 106)

Visual Illusion A misperception of physical reality usually caused by the misapplication of visual cues. (p. 118)

Volley Theory The theory of pitch perception assuming that sound waves of particular frequencies induce auditory neurons to fire in volleys, with one volley following another. (p. 125)

Weber-Fechner Law The principle that the amount of change in stimulation needed to produce a just noticeable difference is a constant proportion of the original stimulus. (p. 100)

Wernicke's Area The area of the temporal lobe responsible for the comprehension of speech. (p. 81)

Yerkes-Dodson Law The principle that the relationship between arousal and performance is best represented by an inverted U-shaped curve. (p. 341)

REFERENCES

Aarons, L. (1976). Sleep-assisted instruction. *Psychological Bulletin, 83,* 1–40.

Abel, E. L. (1977). The relationship between cannabis and violence: A review. *Psychological Bulletin, 84,* 193–211.

Abelson, R. P. (1981). Psychological status of the script concept. *American Psychologist, 36,* 715–729.

Abernethy, E. M. (1940). The effect of changed environmental conditions upon the results of college examinations. *Journal of Psychology, 10,* 293–301.

Abramowitz, S. I. (1986). Psychosocial outcomes of sex reassignment surgery. *Journal of Consulting and Clinical Psychology, 54,* 183–189.

Abramson, L. Y., Seligman, M. E. P., & Teasdale, J. D. (1978). Learned helplessness in humans: Critique and reformulation. *Journal of Abnormal Psychology, 87,* 49–74.

Adams, P. R., & Adams, G. R. (1984). Mount Saint Helen's ashfall: Evidence for a disaster stress reaction. *American Psychologist, 39,* 252–260.

Adams, V. (1981, June). The sibling bond: A lifelong love/hate dialectic. *Psychology Today,* pp. 32–38, 40–41, 43–47.

Adelson, B. (1984). When novices surpass experts: The difficulty of a task may increase with expertise. *Journal of Experimental Psychology: Learning, Memory, and Cognition, 10,* 483–495.

Ader, R., & Cohen, N. (1982). Behaviorally conditioned immunosuppression and murine systemic lupus erythematosus. *Science, 215,* 1534–1536.

Adler, J., & Carey, J. (1980, February 25). The science of love. *Newsweek,* pp. 89–90.

Adler, T. (1989, November). Revision brings test "to the twenty-first century." *APA Monitor,* pp. 1, 6.

Adorno, T. W., Frenkel-Brunswik, E., Levinson, D. J., & Sanford, R. N. (1950). *The authoritarian personality.* New York: Harper & Row.

Agras, W. S., & McCann, U. (1987). The efficacy and role of antidepressants in the treatment of bulimia nervosa. *Annals of Behavioral Medicine, 9,* 18–22.

Aichner, H. C. (1956). Bravo, Dr. Brothers! *American Psychologist, 11,* 53.

Aiken, L. R. (1982). *Psychological testing and assessment.* Boston: Allyn & Bacon.

Ainsworth, M. D. S. (1979). Infant-mother attachment. *American Psychologist, 34,* 932–937.

Ajzen, I., Timko, C., & White, J. B. (1982). Self-monitoring and the attitude-behavior relation. *Journal of Personality and Social Psychology, 42,* 426–435.

Alexopoulos, G. S., Inturrisi, C. E., Lipman, R., Frances, R., Haycox, J., Dougherty, J. H., & Rossier, J. (1983). Plasma immunoreactive beta-endorphin levels in depression: Effect of electroconvulsive therapy. *Archives of General Psychiatry, 40,* 181–183.

Allen, M. G. (1976). Twin studies of affective illness. *Archives of General Psychiatry, 33,* 1476–1478.

Allison, P. D., & Furstenberg, F. F., Jr. (1989). How marital dissolution affects children: Variation by age and sex. *Developmental Psychology, 25,* 540–549.

Allport, F. H. (1920). The influence of the group upon association and thought. *Journal of Experimental Psychology, 3,* 159–182.

Allport, G. W. (1954). *The nature of prejudice.* Reading, MA: Addison-Wesley.

Allport, G. W. (1967). Autobiography. In E. G. Boring & G. Lindzey (Eds.), *A history of psychology in autobiography* (Vol. 5). New York: Appleton-Century-Crofts.

Allport, G. W., & Postman, L. J. (1947). *The psychology of rumor.* New York: Holt, Rinehart & Winston.

Amabile, T. M. (1985). Motivation and creativity effects of motivational orientation on creative writers. *Journal of Personality and Social Psychology, 48,* 393–399.

American Psychiatric Association. (1987). *Diagnostic and statistical manual of mental disorders* (3rd ed.—Revised). Washington, DC: American Psychological Association.

American Psychological Association. (1981). Ethical principles of psychologists. *American Psychologist, 36,* 633–638.

Amoore, J. E. (1963). Stereochemical theory of olfaction. *Nature, 198,* 271–277.

Anand, B. K., & Brobeck, J. R. (1951). Hypothalamic control of food intake in rats and cats. *Yale Journal of Biology and Medicine, 24,* 123–140.

Andersen, S. M., & Ross, L. (1984). Self-knowledge and social inference: I. The impact of cognitive/affective and behavioral data. *Journal of Personality and Social Psychology, 46,* 280–293.

Anderson, C. A. (1987). Temperature and aggression: Effects on quarterly, yearly, and city rates of violent and nonviolent crime. *Journal of Personality and Social Psychology, 52,* 1161–1173.

Anderson, C. A., & Anderson, D. C. (1984). Ambient temperature and violent crime: Tests of the linear and curvilinear hypotheses. *Journal of Personality and Social Psychology, 46,* 91–97.

Anderson, D. C., Crowell, C. R., Doman, M., & Howard, G. S. (1988). Performance posting, goal setting, and activity-contingent praise as applied to a university hockey team. *Journal of Applied Psychology, 73,* 87–95.

Anderson, J. R. (1983). Retrieval of information from long-term memory. *Science, 220,* 25–30.

Andreasen, N. C., Olsen, S. A., Dennert, J. W., & Smith, M. R. (1982). Ventricular enlargement in schizophrenia: Relationship to positive and negative symptoms. *American Journal of Psychiatry, 139,* 297–302.

Angus, R. G., Heslegrave, R. J., & Myles, W. S. (1985). Effects of prolonged sleep deprivation, with and without chronic physical exercise, on mood and performance. *Psychophysiology, 22,* 276–282.

Ape language. (1981). Comments. *Science, 211,* 86–88.

Appelbaum, P. S., & Gutheil, T. G. (1980). The Boston State Hospital case: "Involuntary mind control," the Constitution, and the "right to rot." *American Journal of Psychiatry, 137,* 720–723.

Arehart-Treichel, J. (1981). Beta-endorphins in the placenta. *Science News, 120,* 89.

Aronov, B. M. (1955). Aren't we forgetting something?: A note on psychology via TV. *American Psychologist, 10,* 88.

Aronson, E., & Bridgeman, D. (1979). Jigsaw groups and the desegregated classroom: In pursuit of common goals. *Personality and Social Psychology Bulletin, 5,* 438–446.

Arvidson, K., & Friberg, U. (1980). Human taste: Response and taste bud number in fungiform papillae. *Science, 209,* 807–808.

Asch, S. E. (1955, November). Opinions and social pressure. *Scientific American,* pp. 31–35.

Asendorpf, J. B. (1987). Videotape reconstruction of emotions and cognitions related to shyness. *Journal of Personality and Social Psychology, 53,* 542–549.

Aserinsky, E., & Kleitman, N. (1953). Regularly occurring periods of eye motility and concomitant phenomena during sleep. *Science, 118,* 273–274.

Aserinsky, E., Lynch, J. A., Mack, M. E., Tzankoff, S. P., & Hurn, E. (1985). Comparison of eye motion in wakefulness and REM sleep. *Psychophysiology, 22,* 1–10.

Atkinson, A. K., & Rickel, A. U. (1984). Postpartum depression in primiparous parents. *Journal of Abnormal Psychology, 93,* 115–119.

Atkinson, J., & Huston, T. L. (1984). Sex role orientation and division of labor early in marriage. *Journal of Personality and Social Psychology, 46,* 330–345.

Atkinson, J. W. (1981). Studying personality in the context of an advanced motivational psychology. *American Psychologist, 36,* 117–128.

Atkinson, J. W., & Litwin, G. H. (1960). Achievement motive and test anxiety concerned as motive to approach success and motive to avoid failure. *Journal of Abnormal and Social Psychology, 60,* 52–63.

Atkinson, R. C. (1975). Mnemotechnics in second-language learning. *American Psychologist, 30,* 821–828.

Attie, I., & Brooks-Gunn, J. (1989). Development of eating problems in adolescent girls: A longitudinal study. *Developmental Psychology, 25,* 70–79.

Ayllon, T., & Azrin, N. H. (1968). *The token economy: A motivational system for therapy and rehabilitation.* New York: Appleton-Century-Crofts.

Baddeley, A. D. (1982). Domains of recollection. *Psychological Review, 89,* 708–729.

Bahill, A. T., & LaRitz, T. (1984). Why can't batters keep their eyes on the ball? *American Scientist, 72,* 249–253.

Bahrick, H. P. (1984). Semantic memory content in permastore: Fifty years of memory for Spanish learned in school. *Journal of Experimental Psychology: General, 113,* 1–29.

Bahrick, H. P., Bahrick, P. O., & Wittlinger, R. P. (1975). Fifty years of memory for names and faces: A cross-sectional approach. *Journal of Experimental Psychology: General, 104,* 54–75.

Baillargeon, R. (1987). Object permanence in 3 1/2- and 4 1/2-month-old infants. *Developmental Psychology, 23,* 655–664.

Baird, J. C., & Wagner, M. (1982). The moon illusion: I. How high is the sky? *Journal of Experimental Psychology: General, 111,* 296–303.

Baker, G. H. B. (1987). Psychological factors and immunity. *Journal of Psychosomatic Research, 31,* 1–10.

Baker, T. B., & Tiffany, S. T. (1985). Morphine tolerance as habituation. *Psychological Review, 92,* 78–108.

Balanovski, E., & Taylor, J. G. (1978). Can electromagnetism account for extra sensory phenomena? *Nature, 276,* 64–67.

Baldwin, M. W. (1954). Subjective measurements in television. *American Psychologist, 9,* 231–234.

Bales, J. (1986, September). Pastoral counseling. *APA Monitor,* p. 16.

Bales, J. (1988, March). Court rules no duty to commit in N. C. *APA Monitor,* p. 20.

Bales, J. (1988, August). Pre-work polygraph ban signed by Reagan. *APA Monitor,* p. 5.

Baltes, P. B., & Schaie, K. W. (1976). On the plasticity of intelligence in adulthood and old age: Where Horn and Donaldson fail. *American Psychologist, 31,* 720–725.

Bandura, A. (1965). Influence of model's reinforcement contingencies on the acquisition of imitative responses. *Journal of Personality and Social Psychology, 1,* 589–595.

Bandura, A. (1977). *Social learning theory.* Englewood Cliffs, NJ: Prentice-Hall.

Bandura, A. (1982). The psychology of chance encounters and life paths. *American Psychologist, 37,* 747–755.

Bandura, A. (1986). *Social foundations of thought and action: A social-cognitive theory.* Englewood Cliffs, NJ: Prentice-Hall.

Bandura, A., Blanchard, E. B., & Ritter, B. (1969). The relative efficacy of desensitization and modeling approaches for inducing behavioral, affective, and attitudinal changes. *Journal of Personality and Social Psychology, 13,* 173–199.

Bandura, A., Reese, L., & Adams, N. E. (1982). Microanalysis of action and fear arousal as a function of differential levels of perceived self-efficacy. *Journal of Personality and Social Psychology, 43,* 5–21.

Bandura, A., Ross, D., & Ross, S. A. (1963). Imitation of film-mediated aggressive models. *Journal of Abnormal and Social Psychology, 66,* 3–11.

Bandura, A., & Schunk, D. H. (1981). Cultivating competence, self-efficacy, and intrinsic interest through proximal self-motivation. *Journal of Personality and Social Psychology, 41,* 586–598.

Bank, S. P., & Kahn, M. D. (1982). *The sibling bond.* New York: Basic Books.

Barchas, P. R., & Perlaki, K. M. (1986). Processing of preconsciously acquired information measured by hemispheric asymmetry and selection accuracy. *Behavioral Neuroscience, 100,* 343–349.

Bard, P. (1934). On emotional experience after decortication with some remarks on theoretical views. *Psychological Review, 41,* 309–329.

Baribeau-Braun, J., Picton, T. W., & Gosselin, J. Y. (1983). Schizophrenia: A neuro-psychological evaluation of abnormal information processing. *Science, 219,* 874–876.

Barnes, D. M. (1987). Hippocampus studied for learning mechanisms. *Science, 236,* 1628–1629.

Baron, R. (1983). "Sweet smell of success"? The impact of pleasant artificial scents on evaluations of job applicants. *Journal of Applied Psychology, 68,* 709–713.

Baron, R. A., & Ransberger, V. M. (1978). Ambient temperature and the occurrence of collective violence: The "long, hot, summer" revisited. *Journal of Personality and Social Psychology, 36,* 351–360.

Barr, B. P., & Benson, H. (1984). The relaxation response and cardiovascular disorders. *Behavioral Medicine Update, 6*(4), pp. 28–30.

Barron, F., & Harrington, D. M. (1981). Creativity, intelligence, and personality. *Annual Review of Psychology, 32,* 439–476.

Barsky, A. J., & Klerman, G. L. (1983). Overview: Hypochondriasis, bodily complaints, and somatic styles. *American Journal of Psychiatry, 140,* 273–283.

Bartlett, F. C. (1932). *Remembering: A study in experimental and social psychology.* Cambridge, England: Cambridge University Press.

Bartus, R. T., Dean, R. L., III, Beer, B., & Lippa, A. S. (1982). The cholinergic hypothesis of geriatric memory application. *Science, 217,* 408–409.

Bartusiak, M. (1980, November). Beeper man. *Discover,* p. 57.

Basadur, M., Graen, G. B., & Scandura, T. A. (1986). Training effects on attitudes toward divergent thinking among manufacturing engineers. *Journal of Applied Psychology, 71,* 612–617.

Baskett, L. M. (1984). Ordinal position differences in children's family interactions. *Developmental Psychology, 20,* 1026–1031.

Baskin, Y. (1983, August). Interview with Roger Sperry. *Omni,* pp. 68–73, 98–100.

Basmajian, J. V. (1963). Control and training of individual motor units. *Science, 141,* 440–441.

Bassuk, E. L. (1984, July). The homelessness problem. *Scientific American,* pp. 40–45.

Batson, C. D., Bolen, M. H., Cross, J. A., & Neuringer-Benefiel, H. E. (1986). Where is the altruism in the altruistic personality? *Journal of Personality and Social Psychology, 50,* 212–220.

Baucom, D. H., Besch, P. J., & Callahan, S. (1985). Relation between testosterone concentration, sex role identity, and personality among females. *Journal of Personality and Social Psychology, 48,* 1218–1226.

Baum, A., Aiello, J. R., & Calesnick, L. E. (1978). Crowding and personal control: Social density and the development of learned helplessness. *Journal of Personality and Social Psychology, 36,* 1000–1001.

Baum, A., & Davis, G. E. (1980). Reducing the stress of high-density living: An architectural intervention. *Journal of Personality and Social Psychology, 38,* 471–481.

Baumeister, R. F. (1982). A self-presentational view of social phenomena. *Psychological Bulletin, 91,* 3–26.

Baumeister, R. F. (1984). Choking under pressure: Self-consciousness, and paradoxical effects of incentives on skillful performance. *Journal of Personality and Social Psychology, 46,* 610–620.

Baumeister, R. F. (1988). Should we stop studying sex differences altogether? *American Psychologist, 43,* 1092–1095.

Baumeister, R. F., & Scher, S. J. (1988). Self-defeating behavior patterns among normal individuals: Review and analysis of common self-destructive tendencies. *Psychological Bulletin, 104,* 3–22.

Baumeister, R. F., & Steinhilber, A. (1984). Paradoxical effects of supportive audiences on performance under pressure: The home field disadvantage in sports championships. *Journal of Personality and Social Psychology, 47,* 85–93.

Baumrind, D. (1964). Some thoughts on ethics of research: After reading Milgram's "Behavioral Study of Obedience." *American Psychologist, 19,* 421–423.

Baumrind, D. (1983). Rejoinder to Lewis's reinterpretation of parental firm control effects: Are authoritative families really harmonious? *Psychological Bulletin, 94,* 132–142.

Baumrind, D. (1985). Research using intentional deception: Ethical issues revisited. *American Psychologist, 40,* 165–174.

Bayley, N. (1955). On the growth of intelligence. *American Psychologist, 10,* 805–818.

Bayton, J. A. (1975). Francis Sumner, Max Meenes, and the training of black psychologists. *American Psychologist, 30,* 185–186.

Beatty, W. W. (1984). Discriminating drunkenness: A replication. *Bulletin of the Psychonomic Society, 22,* 431–432.

Beck, A. T. (1967). *Depression: Clinical, experimental and theoretical aspects.* New York: Harper & Row.

Beck, A. T., Rush, A. J., Shaw, B. F., & Emery, G. (1979). *Cognitive therapy of depression.* New York: Guilford Press.

Beers, C. W. (1908/1970). *A mind that found itself.* New York: Doubleday.

Beiser, M., Shore, J. H., Peters, R., & Tatum, W. (1985). Does community care for the mentally ill make a difference? A tale of two cities. *American Journal of Psychiatry, 142,* 1047–1052.

Belisle, M., Roskies, E., & Levesque, J. M. (1987). Improving adherence to physical activity. *Health Psychology, 6,* 159–172.

Bell, A. P., Weinberg, M. S., & Hammersmith, S. J. (1981). *Sexual preference: Its development in men and women.* Bloomington: Indiana University Press.

Belmont, L., & Marolla, F. A. (1973). Birth order, family size, and intelligence. *Science, 182,* 1096–1101.

Bem, D. J. (1967). Self-perception: An alternative interpretation of cognitive dissonance phenomena. *Psychological Review, 74,* 183–200.

Bem, D. J., & Allen, A. (1974). On predicting some of the people some of the time: The search for cross-situational consistencies in behavior. *Psychological Review, 81,* 506–520.

Bem, S. L. (1981). Gender schema theory: A cognitive account of sex typing. *Psychological Review, 88,* 354–364.

Bemis, K. M. (1978). Current approaches to the etiology and treatment of anorexia nervosa. *Psychological Bulletin, 85,* 593–617.

Benbow, C. P., & Stanley, J. C. (1983). Sex differences in mathematical reasoning ability: More facts. *Science, 222,* 1029–1031.

Benjamin, L. T., Jr. (1986). Why don't they understand us?: A history of psychology's public image. *American Psychologist, 41,* 941–946.

Benjamin, L. T., Jr. (1988). A history of teaching machines. *American Psychologist, 43,* 703–712.

Bennett, W., & Gurin, J. (1982). *The dieter's dilemma.* New York: Basic Books.

Ben-Shakhar, G., Bar-Hillel, M., Bilu, Y., Ben-Abba, E., & Flug, A. (1986). Can graphology predict occupational success? Two empirical studies and some methodological ruminations. *Journal of Applied Psychology, 71,* 645–653.

Benson, H., & Friedman, R. (1985). A rebuttal to the conclusions of David S. Holme's article: "Meditation and somatic arousal reduction." *American Psychologist, 40,* 725–728.

Berg, J. H. (1984). Development of friendship between roommates. *Journal of Personality and Social Psychology, 46,* 346–356.

Berg, J. H., & McQuinn, R. D. (1986). Attraction and exchange in continuing and noncontinuing dating relationships. *Journal of Personality and Social Psychology, 50,* 942–952.

Bergin, A. E., & Lambert, E. (1978). The evaluation of therapeutic outcome. In S. L. Garfield & A. E. Bergin (Eds.), *Handbook of psychotherapy and behavior change* (pp. 139–189). New York: Wiley.

Berko, J. (1958). The child's learning of English morphology. *Word, 14,* 150–177.

Berkowitz, L. (1974). Some determinants of impulsive aggression. *Psychological Review, 81,* 165–176.

Berkowitz, L., & LePage, A. (1967). Weapons as aggression-eliciting stimuli. *Journal of Personality and Social Psychology, 7,* 202–207.

Berkowitz, M. W., Mueller, C. W., Schnell, S. V., & Padberg, U. (1986). Moral reasoning and judgments of aggression. *Journal of Personality and Social Psychology, 51,* 885–891.

Bernard, J. (1981). The good-provider role: Its rise and fall. *American Psychologist, 36,* 1–12.

Berndt, T. J., & Hoyle, S. G. (1985). Stability and change in childhood and adolescent friendships. *Developmental Psychology, 21,* 1007–1015.

Berne, E. (1964). *Games people play.* New York: Grove Press.

Bernstein, I. L. (1978). Learned taste aversions in children receiving chemotherapy. *Science, 200,* 1302–1303.

Bernstein, W. M., Stephan, W. G., & Davis, M. H. (1979). Explaining attributions for achievement: A path analytic approach. *Journal of Personality and Social Psychology, 37,* 1810–1821.

Berra, Y. (1984, May). Continuum. *Omni,* p. 38.

Berry, D. S., & McArthur, L. Z. (1985). Some components and consequences of a baby face. *Journal of Personality and Social Psychology, 48,* 312–323.

Berscheid, E., & Walster, E. (1974). A little bit about love. In T. L. Houston (Ed.), *Foundations of interpersonal attraction.* New York: Academic Press.

Bexton, W. H., Heron, W., & Scott, T. H. (1954). Effects of decreased variation in the sensory environment. *Canadian Journal of Psychology, 8,* 70–76.

Bjork, E. L., & Cummings, E. M. (1984). Infant search errors: Stage of concept development or stage of memory development. *Memory and Cognition, 12,* 1–19.

Blair, M. C., & Fretz, B. R. (1980). Interpersonal skills training for premedical students. *Journal of Counseling Psychology, 27,* 380–384.

Blakemore, C. (1977). *Mechanics of the mind.* New York: Cambridge University Press.

Blakemore, C., & Cooper, G. F. (1970). Development of the brain depends on the visual environment. *Nature, 228,* 477–478.

Blasi, A. (1980). Bridging moral cognition and moral action: A critical review of the literature. *Psychological Bulletin, 88,* 1–45.

Blechman, E. A., Tinsley, B., Carella, E. T., & McEnroe, M. J. (1985). Childhood competence and behavior problems. *Journal of Abnormal Psychology, 94,* 70–77.

Bohannon, J. N., III, & Stanowicz, L. (1988). The issue of negative evidence: Adult responses to children's language errors. *Developmental Psychology, 24,* 684–689.

Bolles, R. C. (1979). *Learning theory.* New York: Holt, Rinehart & Winston.

Bond, C. F., Jr., & Titus, L. J. (1983). Social facilitation: A meta-analysis of 241 studies. *Psychological Bulletin, 94,* 265–292.

Boneau, C. A. (1974). Paradigm regained?: Cognitive behaviorism revisited. *American Psychologist, 29,* 297–309.

Boring, E. G. (1957). *A history of experimental psychology.* New York: Appleton-Century-Crofts.

Bornstein, R. F., Leone, D. R., Galley, D. J. (1987). The generalizability of subliminal mere exposure effects: Influence of stimuli perceived without awareness on social behavior. *Journal of Personality and Social Psychology, 53,* 1070–1079.

Bouchard, T. J., Jr., & McGue, M. (1981). Familial studies of intelligence: A review. *Science, 212,* 1055–1059.

Bower, G. H. (1970). Analysis of a mnemonic device. *American Scientist, 58,* 496–510.

Bower, G. H. (1981). Mood and memory. *American Psychologist, 36,* 129–148.

Bower, G. H., & Clark, M. C. (1969). Narrative stories as mediators for serial learning. *Psychonomic Science, 14,* 181–182.

Bower, G. H., & Mayer, J. D. (1985). Failure to replicate mood-dependent retrieval. *Bulletin of the Psychonomic Society, 23,* 39–42.

Bowers, T. G., & Clum, G. A. (1988). Relative contribution of specific and nonspecific treatment effects: Meta-analysis of placebo-controlled behavior therapy research. *Psychological Bulletin, 103,* 315–323.

Boyd, J. (1986). Use of mental health services for the treatment of panic disorder. *American Journal of Psychiatry, 143,* 1569–1574.

Boynton, R. M. (1988). Color vision. *Annual Review of Psychology, 39,* 69–100.

Brackbill, Y., & Nichols, P. L. (1982). A test of the confluence model of intellectual development. *Developmental Psychology, 18,* 192–198.

Brantley, P. J., Dietz, L. S., McKnight, G. T., Jones, G. N., & Tulley, R. (1988). Convergence between the Daily Stress Inventory and endocrine measures of stress. *Journal of Consulting and Clinical Psychology, 56,* 549–551.

Brecher, E. M. (1972). *Licit and illicit drugs.* Boston: Little, Brown.

Breckler, S. J. (1984). Empirical validation of affect, behavior, and cognition as distinct components of attitude. *Journal of Personality and Social Psychology, 47*, 1191–1205.

Bredemeier, B. J., & Shields, D. L. (1985, October). Values and violence in sports today. *Psychology Today*, pp. 22–32.

Breland, K., & Breland, M. (1961). The misbehavior of organisms. *American Psychologist, 16*, 681–684.

Breslow, L. (1981). Reevaluation of the literature on the development of transitive inferences. *Psychological Bulletin, 89*, 325–351.

Brewer, M. B., & Kramer, R. M. (1985). The psychology of intergroup attitudes and behavior. *Annual Review of Psychology, 36*, 219–243.

Brewin, C. R. (1985). Depression and causal attributions: What is their relation? *Psychological Bulletin, 98*, 297–309.

Brickman, P., Coates, D., & Janoff-Bulman, R. (1978). Lottery winners and accident victims: Is happiness relative? *Journal of Personality and Social Psychology, 36*, 917–927.

Briggs, K. C., & Myers, I. B. (1943). *Myers-Briggs type indicator*. Palo Alto, CA: Consulting Psychologists Press.

Brigham, C. C. (1923). *A study of American intelligence*. Princeton, NJ: Princeton University Press.

Brigham, C. C. (1930). Intelligence tests of immigrant groups. *Psychological Review, 37*, 158–165.

Brigham, J. C., Maas, A., Snyder, L. D., & Spaulding, K. (1982). Accuracy of eyewitness identifications in a field setting. *Journal of Personality and Social Psychology, 42*, 673–681.

Broad, W. J. (1981). Sir Isaac Newton: Mad as a hatter. *Science, 213*, 1341–1344.

Brock, T. (1965). Communicator-recipient similarity and decision change. *Journal of Personality and Social Psychology, 1*, 650–654.

Bromberg, W. (1954). *Man above humanity: A history of psychotherapy*. Philadelphia: J. B. Lippincott.

Bronstein, P. (1984). Differences in mothers' and fathers' behaviors toward children: A cross-cultural comparison. *Developmental Psychology, 20*, 995–1003.

Brooks-Gunn, J., & Furstenberg, F. F., Jr. (1989). Adolescent sexual behavior. *American Psychologist, 44*, 249–257.

Brown, J. D., & Siegel, J. M. (1988). Exercise as a buffer of life stress: A prospective study of adolescent health. *Health Psychology, 7*, 341–353.

Brown, R. (1973). *A first language: The early stages*. Cambridge, MA: Harvard University Press.

Brown, R., & Kulik, J. (1977). Flashbulb memories. *Cognition, 5*, 73–99.

Brown, R., & McNeill, D. (1966). The "tip of the tongue" phenomenon. *Journal of Verbal Learning and Verbal Behavior, 5*, 325–337.

Brownell, K. D. (1982). Obesity: Understanding and treating a serious, prevalent and refractory disorder. *Journal of Consulting and Clinical Psychology, 50*, 820–840.

Bruner, J. S. (1956). Freud and the image of man. *American Psychologist, 11*, 463–466.

Bruning, N. S., & Frew, D. R. (1987). Effects of exercise, relaxation, and management skills training on physiological stress indicators: A field experiment. *Journal of Applied Psychology, 72*, 515–521.

Brustad, R. J. (1988). Affective outcomes in competitive youth sport: The influence of intrapersonal and socialization factors. *Journal of Sport and Exercise Psychology, 10*, 307–321.

Buchsbaum, M. S., & Haier, R. J. (1983). Psychopathology: Biological approaches. *Annual Review of Psychology, 34*, 401–430.

Buck, R. (1980). Nonverbal behavior and the theory of emotion: The facial feedback hypothesis. *Journal of Personality and Social Psychology, 38*, 811–824.

Buck, R. (1985). Prime theory: An integrated view of motivation and emotion. *Psychological Review, 92*, 389–413.

Buckley, K. W. (1982). The selling of a psychologist: John Broadus Watson and the application of behavioral techniques to advertising. *Journal of the History of the Behavioral Sciences, 18*, 207–221.

Buckley, W. F. (1982). The Hinckley mess. *National Review, 34*, 916–917.

Bullock, M. (1985). Animism in childhood thinking: A new look at an old question. *Developmental Psychology, 21*, 217–225.

Burnette, M. M., & Adams, H. E. (1987). Detection of noncontingent feedback in EMG biofeedback. *Biofeedback and Self-Regulation, 12*, 281–293.

Burton, D. (1988). Do anxious swimmers swim slower? Reexamining the elusive anxiety-performance relationship. *Journal of Sport and Exercise Psychology, 10*, 45–61.

Buss, A., Booker, A., & Buss, E. (1972). Firing a weapon and aggression. *Journal of Personality and Social Psychology, 22*, 296–302.

Buss, A. B. (1976). Galton and sex differences: An historical note. *Journal of the History of the Behavioral Sciences, 12*, 283–285.

Buss, D. M. (1984). Evolutionary biology and personality psychology. *American Psychologist, 39*, 1135–1147.

Buss, D. M. (1985). Human mate selection. *American Scientist, 73*, 47–51.

Buss, D. M. (1988). The evolution of human intrasexual competition. *Journal of Personality and Social Psychology, 54*, 616–628.

Buss, D. M., & Barnes, M. (1986). Preferences in human mate selection. *Journal of Personality and Social Psychology, 50*, 559–570.

Busse, T. V., & Mansfield, R. S. (1980). Theories of the creative process: A review and a perspective. *Journal of Creative Behavior, 14*, 91–103.

Bussey, K., & Bandura, A. (1984). Influence of gender constancy and social power on sex-linked modeling. *Journal of Personality and Social Psychology, 47*, 1292–1302.

Butterfield-Picard, H., & Magno, J. B. (1982). Hospice the adjective, not the noun: The future of a national priority. *American Psychologist, 37*, 1254–1259.

Byck, R. (Ed.). (1974). *Cocaine papers: Sigmund Freud*. New York: Stonehill.

Byrne, D., Clore, G. L., & Smeaton, G. (1986). The attraction hypothesis: Do similar attitudes affect anything? *Journal of Social Psychology, 51*, 1167–1170.

Byrne, D., Ervin, C. R., & Lamberth, J. (1970). Continuity between the experimental study of attraction and real-life computer dating. *Journal of Personality and Social Psychology, 16*, 157–165.

Byrne, D., & Kelley, K. C. (1981). *An introduction to personality*. Englewood Cliffs, NJ: Prentice-Hall.

Byrne, W., Bleier, R., & Houston, L. (1988). Variations in human corpus callosum do not predict gender: A study using magnetic resonance imaging. *Behavioral Neuroscience, 102*, 222–227.

Calantone, R. J., & Warshaw, P. R. (1985). Negating the effects of fear appraisals in election campaigns. *Journal of Applied Psychology, 70,* 627–633.

Calhoun, J. B. (1962, February). Population density and social pathology. *Scientific American,* pp. 139–148.

Calkins, M. (1893). Statistics of dreams. *American Journal of Psychology, 5,* 311–343.

Calkins, M. W. (1930). Mary Whiton Calkins. In C. Murchison (Ed.), *A history of psychology in autobiography* (Vol. 1, pp. 31–62). New York: Russell & Russell.

Camel, J. E., Withers, G. S., & Greenough, W. T. (1986). Persistence of visual cortex dendritic alterations induced by postweaning exposure to a "superenriched" environment in rats. *Behavioral Neuroscience, 100,* 810–813.

Campione, J. E., & Brown, A. L. (1979). Toward a theory of intelligence: Contributions from research with retarded children. *Intelligence, 2,* 279–304.

Candland, D. K. (1982). Selective pressure and the teaching of psychology: The fox and the hedgehog. *Teaching of Psychology, 9,* 20–23.

Cann, A., Sherman, S. J., & Elkes, R. (1975). Effects of initial request size and timing of a second request on compliance: The foot in the door and the door in the face. *Journal of Personality and Social Psychology, 32,* 774–782.

Cannon, D. S., & Baker, T. B. (1981). Emetic and electric shock alcohol aversion therapy: Assessment of conditioning. *Journal of Consulting and Clinical Psychology, 49,* 20–33.

Cannon, J. G., & Kluger, M. J. (1983). Endogenous pyrogen activity in human plasma after exercise. *Science, 220,* 617–619.

Cannon, W. B. (1927). The James-Lange theory of emotions: A critical examination and an alternative. *American Journal of Psychology, 39,* 106–124.

Cannon, W. B., & Washburn, A. L. (1912). An explanation of hunger. *American Journal of Physiology, 29,* 444–454.

Caplan, P. J., MacPherson, G. M., & Tobin, P. (1985). Do sex-related differences in spatial abilities exist?: A multilevel critique with new data. *American Psychologist, 40,* 786–799.

Carducci, B. J., & Wheat, J. E. (1984, September). Business: An open door for psych majors. *APA Monitor,* p. 20.

Carey, M. P., & Burish, T. G. (1987). Providing relaxation training to cancer chemotherapy patients: A comparison of three delivery techniques. *Journal of Consulting and Clinical Psychology, 55,* 732–737.

Carlson, E. T. (1981). The history of multiple personality in the United States: I. The beginnings. *American Journal of Psychiatry, 138,* 666–668.

Carmichael, L., Hogan, H. P., & Walter, A. (1932). An experimental study of the effect of language on the reproduction of visually perceived form. *Journal of Experimental Psychology, 15,* 73–86.

Carpenter, C. R. (1955). Psychological research using television. *American Psychologist, 10,* 606–610.

Carr, D. B., Bullen, B. A., Skrinar, G. S., Arnold, M. A., Rosenblatt, M., Beitins, I. Z., Martin, J. B., & McArthur, J. W. (1981). Physical conditioning facilitates the exercise-induced secretion of beta-endorphin and beta-lipotropin in women. *New England Journal of Medicine, 305,* 560–563.

Carskadon, M. A., & Dement, W. C. (1981). Cumulative effect of sleep deprivation on daytime sleepiness. *Psychophysiology, 18,* 107–113.

Carson, R. C., Butcher, J. N., & Coleman, J. C. (1988). *Abnormal psychology and modern life.* Glenview, IL: Scott, Foresman.

Cartwright, R. D. (1978). *A primer on sleep and dreaming.* Reading, MA: Addison-Wesley.

Carver, C. S., & Ganellen, R. J. (1983). Depression and components of self-punitiveness: High standards, self-criticism, and overgeneralization. *Journal of Abnormal Psychology, 92,* 330–337.

Castelnuovo-Tedesco, P., Weinberg, J., Buchanan, D. C., & Scott, H. W., Jr. (1982). Long-term outcome of a jejuno-ileal bypass surgery for super obesity: A psychiatric assessment. *American Journal of Psychiatry, 139,* 1248–1252.

Cattell, R. B. (1940). A culture free intelligence test I. *Journal of Educational Psychology, 31,* 161–179.

Cattell, R. B. (1949). *Sixteen personality factor questionnaire.* Champaign, IL: Institute for Personality and Ability Testing.

Ceci, S. J., & Liker, J. J. (1986). A day at the races: A study of IQ expertise, and cognitive complexity. *Journal of Experimental Psychology: General, 115,* 255–266.

Ceci, S. J., Ross, D. F., & Toglia, M. P. (1987). Suggestibility of children's memory: Psychological implications. *Journal of Experimental Psychology: General, 116,* 38–49.

Cerella, J. (1985). Information processing rates in the elderly. *Psychological Bulletin, 98,* 67–83.

Chaiken, S., & Baldwin, M. W. (1981). Affective-cognitive consistency and the effect of salient behavioral information on the self-perception of attitudes. *Journal of Personality and Social Psychology, 41,* 1–12.

Charness, N. (1981). Aging and skilled problem solving. *Journal of Experimental Psychology: General, 110,* 21–38.

Chase, M. H., & Morales, F. R. (1983). Subthreshold excitatory activity and motoneuron discharge during REM periods of active sleep. *Science, 221,* 1195–1198.

Chase, W. G., & Simon, H. A. (1973). Perception in chess. *Cognitive Psychology, 4,* 55–81.

Chassin, A., Presson, C. C., Sherman, S. J., Montello, D., & McGrew, J. (1986). Changes in peer and parent influence during adolescence: Longitudinal versus cross-sectional perspectives on smoking initiation. *Developmental Psychology, 22,* 327–334.

Chen, D. M., Collins, J. S., & Goldsmith, T. H. (1984). The ultraviolet receptor of bird retinas. *Science, 225,* 337–340.

Cherry, E. C. (1953). Some experiments on the recognition of speech with one and two ears. *Journal of the Acoustical Society of America, 25,* 975–979.

Chi, M. T. H., & Koeske, R. D. (1983). Network representation of a child's dinosaur knowledge. *Developmental Psychology, 19,* 29–39.

Child, I. L. (1985). Psychology and anomalous observations: The question of ESP in dreams. *American Psychologist, 40,* 1219–1230.

Chomsky, N. (1986). *Knowledge of language: Its nature, origin, and use.* New York: Praeger.

Chrisler, J. C. (1988). Conditioning the instructor's behavior: A class project in psychology of learning. *Teaching of Psychology, 15,* 135–137.

Christianson, S., & Nilsson, L. (1984). Functional amnesia as induced by a psychological trauma. *Memory and Cognition, 12,* 142–155.

Chwalisz, K., Diener, E., & Gallagher, D. (1988). Autonomic arousal feedback and emotional experience: Evidence from the spinal cord injured. *Journal of Personality and Social Psychology, 54,* 820–828.

Cialdini, R. B., Schaller, M., Houlihan, D., Arps, K., Fultz, J., & Beaman, A. L. (1987). Empathy-based helping: Is it selflessly motivated? *Journal of Personality and Social Psychology, 52,* 749–758.

Cialdini, R. B., Vincent, J. E., Lewis, S. J., Catalan, J., Wheeler, D., & Darley, B. L. (1975). Reciprocal concessions procedure for inducing compliance: The door-in-the-face technique. *Journal of Personality and Social Psychology, 31,* 206–215.

Clark, R. D., & Word, L. E. (1974). Where is the apathetic bystander?: Situational characteristics of the emergency. *Journal of Personality and Social Psychology, 29,* 279–287.

Clore, G. L., Bray, R. M., Itkin, S. M., & Murphy, P. (1978). Interracial attitudes and behavior at a summer camp. *Journal of Personality and Social Psychology, 36,* 107–116.

Cogan, D., & Cogan, R. (1984). Classical salivary conditioning: An easy demonstration. *Teaching of Psychology, 11,* 170–171.

Cohen, C. E. (1981). Person categories and social perception: Testing some boundaries of the processing effects of prior knowledge. *Journal of Personality and Social Psychology, 40,* 441–452.

Cohen, D. B. (1979). *Sleep and dreaming: Origins, nature and functions.* New York: Pergamon Press.

Cohen, N. J., & Squire, L. R. (1980). Preserved learning and retention of pattern-analyzing skill in amnesia: Dissociation of knowing how and knowing that. *Science, 210,* 207–210.

Cohen, S. (1981, October). Sound effects of behavior. *Psychology Today,* pp. 38–49.

Cohen, S., Evans, G. W., Krantz, D. S., Stokols, D., & Kelly, S. (1981). Aircraft noise and children: Longitudinal cross-sectional evidence on adaptation to noise and the effectiveness of noise abatement. *Journal of Personality and Social Psychology, 40,* 331–345.

Coke-Pepsi slugfest. (1976, July 26). *Time,* pp. 64–65.

Colegrove, F. W. (1899). Individual memories. *American Journal of Psychology, 10,* 228–255.

Collins, A. M., & Loftus, E. F. (1975). A spreading-activation theory of semantic processing. *Psychological Review, 82,* 407–428.

Colombo, J. (1982). The critical period concept: Research, methodology, and theoretical issues. *Psychological Bulletin, 91,* 260–275.

Comrey, A. L., Michael, W. B., & Fruchter, B. (1988). J. P. Guilford (1897–1987). *American Psychologist, 43,* 1086–1087.

Connelly, D. (1988). Increasing intensity of play of nonassertive athletes. *The Sport Psychologist, 2,* 255–265.

Conrad, R. (1962). An association between memory errors and errors due to acoustic masking of speech. *Nature, 193,* 1314–1315.

Constantinople, A. (1969). An Eriksonian measure of personality development in college students. *Developmental Psychology, 1,* 357–372.

Conway, M., & Ross, M. (1984). Getting what you want by revising what you had. *Journal of Personality and Social Psychology, 47,* 738–748.

Cook, S. W. (1985). Experimenting on social issues: The case of school desegregation. *American Psychologist, 40,* 452–460.

Coon, D. J. (1982). Eponymy, obscurity, Twitmyer, and Pavlov. *Journal of the History of the Behavioral Sciences, 18,* 255–262.

Cooney, J. L., & Zeichner, A. (1985). Selective attention to negative feedback in Type A and Type B individuals. *Journal of Abnormal Psychology, 94,* 110–112.

Cooper, J., & Croyle, R. T. (1984). Attitudes and attitude change. *Annual Review of Psychology, 35,* 395–426.

Cordes, C. (March, 1984). Researchers flunk Reagan on discipline theme. *APA Monitor,* pp. 12–13.

Corsini, R. J. (1984). *Current psychotherapies.* Itasca, IL: F. E. Peacock Publishers.

Costa, P. T., Jr., & McCrae, R. R. (1980). Influence of extraversion and neuroticism on subjective well-being: Happy and unhappy people. *Journal of Personality and Social Psychology, 38,* 668–678.

Cousins, N. (1979). *Anatomy of an illness as perceived by the patient.* New York: Norton.

Cousins, N. (1983). *The healing heart: Antidotes to panic and helplessness.* New York: Norton.

Cowan, N. (1984). On short and long auditory stories. *Psychological Bulletin, 96,* 341–370.

Cowen, E. L. (1982). Help is where you find it: Four informal helping groups. *American Psychologist, 37,* 385–395.

Coyle, J. T., Price, D. L., DeLong, M. R. (1983). Alzheimer's disease: A disorder of cortical cholinergic innervation. *Science, 219,* 1184–1190.

Craik, F. I. M., & Lockhart, R. S. (1972). Levels of processing: A framework for memory research. *Journal of Verbal Learning and Verbal Behavior, 11,* 671–684.

Craik, F. I. M., & Tulving, E. (1975). Depth of processing and the retention of words in episodic memory. *Journal of Experimental Psychology: General, 104,* 268–294.

Crandall, J. E. (1980). Adler's concept of social interest: Theory, measurement, and implications for adjustment. *Journal of Personality and Social Psychology, 39,* 481–495.

Critelli, J. W., & Neumann, K. F. (1984). The placebo: Conceptual analysis of a construct in transition. *American Psychologist, 39,* 32–39.

Croce, R. V. (1986). The effects of EMG biofeedback on strength acquisition. *Biofeedback and Self-Regulation, 11,* 299–310.

Crocker, J., Alloy, L. B., & Kayne, N. T. (1988). Attributional style, depression, and perceptions of consensus for events. *Journal of Personality and Social Psychology, 54,* 840–846.

Crook, T., & Eliot, J. (1980). Parental death during childhood and adult depression: A critical review of the literature. *Psychological Bulletin, 87,* 252–259.

Cunningham, S. (1983, March). Superior court retarts electroshock in Berkeley. *APA Monitor,* p. 17.

Cunningham, S. (1984, January). Bulimia's cycle shames patient, tests therapists. *APA Monitor,* pp. 16–17.

Cunningham, S. (1984, August). Chronic patients sue for community housing. *APA Monitor,* p. 21.

Cunningham, S. (1985, July). Chimps use sign language to talk to each other. *APA Monitor,* p. 11.

Curcio, C. A., Sloan, K. R., Jr., Packer, O., Hendrickson, A. E., & Kalina, R. E. (1987). Distribution of cones in human and monkey retina: Individual variability and radial asymmetry. *Science, 236,* 579–582.

Cusick, F. (1987, January 23). No one saw signs until it was over. *The Philadelphia Inquirer,* p. 1–A.

Cutting, J. E. (1987). Perception and information. *Annual Review of Psychology, 38,* 61–90.

Czeisler, C. A., Moore-Ede, M. C., & Coleman, R. M. (1982). Rotating shift work schedules that disrupt sleep are improved by applying circadian principles. *Science, 217,* 460–463.

Dabbs, J. M., Jr., & Leventhal, H. (1966). Effects of varying the recommendations in a fear-arousing communication. *Journal of Personality and Social Psychology, 4,* 525–531.

Dallenbach, K. M. (1927). The temperature spots and end organs. *American Journal of Psychology, 54,* 431–433.

Daniels, D. (1986). Differential experiences of siblings in the same family as predictors of adolescent sibling personality differences. *Journal of Personality and Social Psychology, 51,* 339–346.

Daniels, D., & Plomin, R. (1985). Origins of individual differences in infant shyness. *Developmental Psychology, 21,* 118–121.

Darian-Smith, I. (1982). Touch in primates. *Annual Review of Psychology, 33,* 155–194.

Darley, J. M., & Fazio, R. H. (1980). Expectancy confirmation processes arising in the social interaction sequence. *American Psychologist, 35,* 867–881.

Darley, J. M., & Latané, B. (1968). Bystander intervention in emergencies: Diffusion of responsibility. *Journal of Personality and Social Psychology, 8,* 377–383.

Darrach, B., & Norris, J. (1984, August). An American tragedy. *Life,* pp. 58–74.

Darwin, C. (1859/1959). *On the origin of species by means of natural selection.* Philadelphia: University of Pennsylvania Press.

Darwin, C. (1872/1965). *The expression of the emotions in man and animals.* Chicago: University of Chicago Press.

Darwin, C. (1877/1977). A biographical sketch of an infant. In P. H. Barrett (Ed.), *The collected papers of Charles Darwin* (pp. 191–200). Chicago: University of Chicago Press.

Davis, A., & Eels, K. (1953). *Davis-Eels games.* Yonkers, NY: World Book.

Davis, H., & Memmott, J. (1982). Counting behavior in animals: A critical evaluation. *Psychological Bulletin, 92,* 547–571.

Davis, H. P., & Squire, L. R. (1984). Protein synthesis and memory: A review. *Psychological Bulletin, 96,* 518–559.

Davis, J. O. (1988). Strategies for managing athlete's jet lag. *The Sport Psychologist, 2,* 154–160.

Davis, M. H., & Oathout, H. A. (1987). Maintenance of satisfaction in romantic relationships: Empathy and relational competence. *Journal of Personality and Social Psychology, 53,* 397–410.

Davis, P. J. (1987). Repression and the inaccessibility of affective memories. *Journal of Personality and Social Psychology, 53,* 585–593.

Davis, R. (1986). Knowledge-based systems. *Science, 231,* 957–963.

Davis, S. F., Thomas, R. L., & Weaver, M. S. (1982). Psychology's contemporary and all-time notables: Student, faculty, and chairperson viewpoints. *Bulletin of the Psychonomic Society, 20,* 3–6.

Deaux, K. (1985). Sex and gender. *Annual Review of Psychology, 36,* 49–81.

DeCharms, R., & Moeller, G. H. (1962). Values expressed in American children's readers: 1800–1950. *Journal of Abnormal and Social Psychology, 64,* 136–142.

Deci, E. L., Nezlek, J., & Sheinman, L. (1981). Characteristics of the rewarder and intrinsic motivation of the rewardee. *Journal of Personality and Social Psychology, 40,* 1–10.

DeLacoste-Utamsing, C., & Holloway, R. L. (1982). Sexual dimorphism in the human corpus callosum. *Science, 216,* 1431–1432.

Delmonte, M. M. (1984). Physiological responses during meditation and rest. *Biofeedback and Self-Regulation, 9,* 181–200.

DeLongis, A., Folkman, S., & Lazarus, R. S. (1988). The impact of daily stress on health and mood: Psychological and social resources as mediators. *Journal of Personality and Social Psychology, 54,* 486–495.

Dembroski, T. M., & Costa, P. T., Jr. (1988). Assessment of coronary-prone behavior: A current overview. *Annals of Behavioral Medicine, 10,* 60–63.

Dement, W. C. (1976). *Some must watch while some must sleep.* San Francisco: W. H. Freeman.

Dement, W. C., & Wolpert, E. (1958). The relation of eye movements, body motility, and external stimuli to dream content. *Journal of Experimental Psychology, 53,* 543–553.

Dempster, F. N. (1985). Proactive interference in sentence recall: Topic similarity effects and individual differences. *Memory and Cognition, 13,* 81–89.

Detera-Wadleigh, S. D., Berrettini, W. H., Goldin, L. R., Boorman, D., Anderson, S., & Gershon, E. S. (1987). Close linkage of c-Harvey-ras-I and the insulin gene to affective disorder is ruled out in three North American pedigrees. *Nature, 325,* 806–808.

Detjen, J. (1986, December 21). Scientists seek new uses for the "neglected sense." *The Philadelphia Inquirer,* pp. 1–B, 6–B.

DeValois, R. L., Abramov, I., & Jacobs, G. H. (1966). Analysis of response patterns of LGN cells. *Journal of the Optical Society of America, 56,* 966–977.

Devins, G. M., & Seland, T. P. (1987). Emotional impact of multiple sclerosis: Recent findings and suggestions for future research. *Psychological Bulletin, 101,* 363–375.

de Vries, B., & Walker, L. J. (1986). Moral reasoning and attitudes toward capital punishment. *Developmental Psychology, 22,* 509–513.

Diaconis, P. (1978). Statistical problems in ESP research. *Science, 201,* 131–136.

Dickey-Bryant, L., Lautenschlager, G. J., Mendoza, J. L., & Abrahams, N. (1986). Facial attractiveness and its relation to occupational success. *Journal of Applied Psychology, 71,* 16–19.

Dickson, D. (1984). Edinburgh sets up parapsychology chair. *Science, 223,* 1274.

Diener, E. (1984). Subjective well-being. *Psychological Bulletin, 95,* 542–575.

Diener, E., & Larsen, R. J. (1984). Temporal stability and cross-situational consistency of affective, behavioral, and cognitive responses. *Journal of Personality and Social Psychology, 47,* 871–883.

Diener, E., Larsen, R. J., Levine, S., & Emmons, R. A. (1985). Intensity and frequency: Dimensions underlying positive and negative affect. *Journal of Personality and Social Psychology, 48,* 1253–1265.

Digman, J. M., & Inouye, J. (1986). Further specification of the five robust factors of personality. *Journal of Personality and Social Psychology, 50,* 116–123.

Dishman, R. J., & Gettman, L. R. (1980). Psychobiologic influences on exercise adherence. *Journal of Sport Psychology, 2,* 295–310.

Doane, J. A., West, K. L., Goldstein, M. J., Rodnick, E. H., & Jones, J. E. (1981). Parental communication deviance and affective style: Predictors of subsequent schizophrenia spectrum disorders in vulnerable adolescents. *Archives of General Psychiatry, 38,* 679–685.

Dobelle, W. H., Madejovsky, M. G., Evans, J. R., Roberts, T. S., & Girvin, J. P. (1976). "Braille" reading by a blind volunteer by visual cortex stimulation. *Nature, 259,* 111–112.

Dolce, J. J., & Raczynski, J. M. (1985). Neuromuscular activity and electromyography in painful backs: Psychological and biomechanical models in assessment and treatment. *Psychological Bulletin, 97,* 502–520.

Dollard, J., Doob, I. W., Miller, N. E., Mowrer, O. H., & Sears, R. R. (1939). *Frustration and aggression.* New York: McGraw-Hill.

Donnerstein, E., & Berkowitz, L. (1981). Victim reactions in aggressive erotic films as a factor in violence against women. *Journal of Personality and Social Psychology, 41,* 710–724.

Dowd, M. (1983, September 5). Rape: The sexual weapon. *Time,* pp. 27–29.

Doyle, A. C. (1930). *The complete Sherlock Holmes.* Garden City, NY: Doubleday.

Doyle, J. (1989). *The male experience* (2nd ed.). Dubuque, IA: Wm. C. Brown.

Dudycha, G. J. (1936). An objective study of punctuality in relation to personality and achievement. *Archives of Psychology, 29,* 1–53.

Duke, M. P., & Nowicki, S., Jr. (1986). *Abnormal psychology: A new look.* New York: Holt, Rinehart & Winston.

Dutton, D. G., & Aron, A. P. (1974). Some evidence for heightened sexual attraction under conditions of high anxiety. *Journal of Personality and Social Psychology, 30,* 510–517.

Duyme, M. (1988). School success and social class: An adoption study. *Developmental Psychology, 24,* 203–209.

Dworkin, B. R., & Miller, N. E. (1986). Failure to replicate visceral learning in the acute curarized rat preparation. *Behavioral Neuroscience, 100,* 299–314.

Dwyer, T. (1986, June 15). How the will to win drove an athlete to the edge. *The Philadelphia Inquirer,* pp. 1–A, 8–A.

Eagly, A. H. (1984). Gender and social influence: A social psychological analysis. *American Psychologist, 38,* 971–981.

Eagly, A. H., & Steffen, V. J. (1986). Gender and aggressive behavior: A meta-analytic review of the social psychological literature. *Psychological Bulletin, 100,* 309–330.

Eagly, A. H., & Warren, R. (1976). Intelligence, comprehension, and opinion change. *Journal of Personality, 44,* 226–242.

Easterbrooks, M. A., & Goldberg, W. A. (1985). Effects of early maternal employment on toddlers, mothers, and fathers. *Developmental Psychology, 21,* 774–783.

Ebbeck, V., & Weiss, M. R. (1988). The arousal-performance relationship: Task characteristics and performance measures in track and field athletics. *The Sport Psychologist, 2,* 13–27.

Ebbinghaus, H. (1885/1913). *Memory: A contribution to experimental psychology.* New York: Columbia University Press.

Ecenbarger, W. (1987, June 4). The forgotten sense. *The Philadelphia Inquirer Magazine,* pp. 24–26, 34–35.

Eckenrode, J. (1984). Impact of chronic and acute stressors on daily reports of mood. *Journal of Personality and Social Psychology, 46,* 907–918.

Eckert, E. D., Bouchard, T. J., Bohlen, J., & Heston, L. L. (1986). Homosexuality in monozygotic twins reared apart. *British Journal of Psychiatry, 148,* 421–425.

Edelman, G. M. (1984, April). Cell-adhesion molecules: A molecular basis for animal form. *Scientific American,* pp. 118–129.

Egan, K. J., Carr, J. E., Hunt, D. D., & Adamson, R. (1988). Endogenous opiate system and systematic desensitization. *Journal of Consulting and Clinical Psychology, 56,* 287–291.

Egeland, J. A., Gerhard, D. S., Pauls, D. L., Sussex, J. N., Kidd, K. K., Allen, C. R., Hostetter, A. M., & Housman, D. E. (1987). Bipolar affective disorders linked to DNA markers on chromosome 11. *Nature, 325,* 783–787.

Ehara, T. H. (1980, December). On the electronic chess circuit. *Science 80,* pp. 78, 80.

Ehrlichman, H., & Halpern, J. N. (1988). Affect and memory: Effects of pleasant and unpleasant odors on retrieval of happy and unhappy memories. *Journal of Personality and Social Psychology, 55,* 769–779.

Eich, J. E. (1980). The cue-dependent nature of state-dependent retrieval. *Memory and Cognition, 8,* 157–173.

Eich, J. E., Weingartner, H., Stillman, R. C., & Gillin, J. C. (1975). State-dependent accessibility of retrieval cues in the retention of a categorized list. *Journal of Verbal Learning and Verbal Behavior, 14,* 408–417.

Eisdorfer, C. (1983). Conceptual models of aging: The challenge of a new frontier. *American Psychologist, 38,* 197–202.

Eisen, S. V. (1979). Actor-observer differences in information inference and casual attribution. *Journal of Personality and Social Psychology, 37,* 261–272.

Eisenberg, N., Cialdini, R. B., McCreath, H., & Shell, R. (1987). Consistency-based compliance: When and why do children become vulnerable? *Journal of Personality and Social Psychology, 52,* 1174–1181.

Eisenberg, N., & Lennon, R. (1983). Sex differences in empathy and related capacities. *Psychological Bulletin, 94,* 100–131.

Ekman, P., & Friesen, W. V. (1971). Constants across cultures in the face and emotion. *Journal of Personality and Social Psychology, 17,* 124–129.

Ekman, P., Friesen, W. V., O'Sullivan, M., Chan, A., Diacoyanni-Tarlatzis, I., Heider, K., Krause, R., LeCompte, W. A., Pitcairn, T., Ricci-Bitti, P. E., Scherer, K., Tomita, M., & Tzavaras, A. (1987). Universals and cultural differences in the judgments of facial expressions of emotion. *Journal of Personality and Social Psychology, 53,* 712–717.

Ekman, P., Levenson, R. W., & Friesen, W. V. (1983). Autonomic nervous system activity distinguishes among emotions. *Science, 221,* 1208–1210.

Elkin, R. A., & Leippe, M. R. (1986). Physiological arousal, dissonance, and attitude change: Evidence for a dissonance-arousal link and a "don't remind me" effect. *Journal of Personality and Social Psychology, 51,* 55–65.

Ellenberger, H. F. (1970). *The discovery of the unconscious: The history and evolution of dynamic psychiatry.* New York: Basic Books.

Ellis, A. (1962). *Reason and emotion in psychotherapy.* New York: Lyle Stuart.

Ellis, A. (1971). *Growth through reason.* Palo Alto, CA: Science and Behavior Books.

Ellis, L., & Ames, M. A. (1987). Neurohormonal functioning and sexual orientation: A theory of homosexuality-heterosexuality. *Psychological Bulletin, 101,* 233–258.

Elmore, R. T., Jr., Wildman, R. W., II, & Westefeld, J. S. (1980). The use of systematic desensitization in the treatment of blood phobia. *Journal of Behavior Therapy and Experimental Psychiatry, 11,* 277–279.

Emler, N., Renwick, S., & Malone, B. (1983). The relationship between moral reasoning and political orientation. *Journal of Personality and Social Psychology, 45,* 1073–1080.

Emmons, R. A. (1987). Narcissism: Theory and measurement. *Journal of Personality and Social Psychology, 52,* 11–17.

Epstein, R., Kirshnit, C. E., Lanza, R. P., & Rubin, L. C. (1984). "Insight" in the pigeon: Antecedents and determinants of an intelligent performance. *Nature, 308,* 61–62.

Epstein, S., & Feist, G. J. (1988). Relation between self- and other-acceptance and its moderation by identification. *Journal of Personality and Social Psychology, 54,* 309–315.

Epstein, S., & O'Brien, E. J. (1985). The person-situation debate in historical and current perspective. *Psychological Bulletin, 98,* 513–537.

Ericsson, K. A., Chase, W. G., & Faloon, S. (1980). Acquisition of a memory skill. *Science, 208,* 1181–1182.

Erikson, E. (1963). *Childhood and society.* New York: Norton.

Erikson, E. (1968). *Identity : Youth and crisis.* New York: Norton.

Eron, L. D. (1966). *The classification of behavior disorders.* Chicago: Aldine Publishing Co.

Etaugh, C. (1980). Effects of nonmaternal care on children: Research evidence and popular views. *American Psychologist, 35,* 309–319.

Everstine, L., Everstine, D. S., Heymann, G. M., True, R. H., Frey, D. H., Johnson, H. G., & Seiden, R. H. (1980). Privacy and confidentiality in psychotherapy. *American Psychologist, 35,* 828–840.

Eysenck, H. J. (1952). The effects of psychotherapy: An evaluation. *Journal of Consulting Psychology, 16,* 319–324.

Eysenck, H. J., & Eysenck, M. W. (1985). *Personality and individual differences.* New York: Plenum.

Eysenck, H. J., Wakefield, J. A., Jr., & Friedman, A. F. (1983). Diagnosis and clinical assessment: The DSM-III. *Annual Review of Psychology, 34,* 167–193.

Fagot, B. I., Leinbach, M. D., & Hagan, R. (1986). Gender labeling and the adoption of sex-typed behaviors. *Developmental Psychology, 22,* 440–443.

Falbo, T., & Polit, D. F. (1986). Quantitative review of the only-child literature: Research evidence and theory development. *Psychological Bulletin, 100,* 176–189.

Fallon, A. E., & Rozin, P. (1985). Sex differences in perceptions of desirable body shape. *Journal of Abnormal Psychology, 94,* 102–105.

Fancher, R. E. (1979). *Pioneers of psychology.* New York: Norton.

Fancher, R. E. (1984). Not Conley, but Burt and others: A reply. *Journal of the History of the Behavioral Sciences, 20,* 186.

Faraone, S. (1982). Psychiatry and political repression in the Soviet Union. *American Psychologist, 37,* 1105–1112.

Faraone, S. V., & Tsuang, M. T. (1985). Quantitative models of the genetic transmission of schizophrenia. *Psychological Bulletin, 98,* 41–46.

Farthing, G. W., Venturino, M., & Brown, S. W. (1984). Suggestion and distraction in the control of pain—test of two hypotheses. *Journal of Abnormal Psychology, 93,* 266–276.

Feder, H. H. (1984). Hormones and sexual behavior. *Annual Review of Psychology, 35,* 165–200.

Fehr, B., & Russell, J. A. (1984). Concept of emotion viewed from a prototypic perspective. *Journal of Experimental Psychology: General, 113,* 464–486.

Fellman, B. (1985, May). A clockwork gland. *Science 85,* pp. 76–81.

Festinger, L., & Carlsmith, J. M. (1959). Cognitive consequences of forced compliance. *Journal of Abnormal and Social Psychology, 58,* 203–210.

Festinger, L., & Maccoby, N. (1964). On resistance to persuasive communications. *Journal of Abnormal and Social Psychology, 68,* 359–366.

Festinger, L., Pepitone, A., & Newcomb, T. (1952). Some consequences of deindividuation in a group. *Journal of Abnormal and Social Psychology, 47,* 382–389.

Festinger, L., Riecken, H. W., & Schachter, S. (1956). *When prophecy fails.* New York: Harper & Row.

Festinger, L., Schachter, S., & Back, K. (1950). *Social pressures in informal groups: A study of a housing community.* Stanford, CA: Stanford University Press.

Fichten, C. (1984, May). Scientist denies astrology breakthrough: Or beware the press. *APA Monitor,* p. 5.

Fiedler, F. E. (1971). Validation and extension of the contingency model of leadership effectiveness: A review of empirical findings. *Psychological Bulletin, 76,* 128–148.

Field, T. M., Woodson, R., Greenberg, R., & Cohen, D. (1982). Discrimination and imitation of facial expressions by neonates. *Science, 218,* 179–181.

Filsinger, E. E., Braun, J. J., Monte, W. C., & Linder, D. E. (1984). Human (*Homo sapiens*) responses to the pig (*Sus scrofa*) sex pheromone 5 alpha-androst-16-en-3-one. *Journal of Comparative Psychology, 98,* 219–222.

Finkelstein, P., Wenegrat, B., & Yalom, I. (1982). Large group awareness training. *Annual Review of Psychology, 33,* 515–539.

Fisher, J. D., & Byrne, D. (1975). Too close for comfort: Sex differences in response to invasions of personal space. *Journal of Personality and Social Psychology, 32,* 15–21.

Fisher, K. (1983, February). TV violence. *APA Monitor,* pp. 7, 9.

Fisher, K. (1984, April). Strangler's mind becomes a trap for psychologists. *APA Monitor,* pp. 10–11, 13.

Fisher, K. (1985, November). Duty to warn: Where does it end? *APA Monitor*, pp. 24–25.

Fisher, K. (1986, March). Animal research: Few alternatives seen for behavioral studies. *APA Monitor*, pp. 16–17.

Fisher, S., & Fisher, R. L. (1981). *Pretend the world is funny and forever: A psychological analysis of comedians, clowns, and actors*. Hillsdale, NJ: Erlbaum.

Fisher, S., & Greenberg, R. P. (1985). *The scientific credibility of Freud's theories and therapy*. New York: Columbia University Press.

Fiske, D. W., Conley, J. J., & Goldberg, L. R. (1987). E. Lowell Kelly (1905–1986). *American Psychologist, 42,* 511–512.

Flavell, J. H., Shipstead, S. G., & Croft, K. (1980). What young children think you see when their eyes are closed. *Cognition, 8,* 369–387.

Flay, B. R. (1985). Psychosocial approaches to smoking prevention: A review of findings. *Health Psychology, 4,* 449–488.

Fleming, I., Baum, A., Davidson, L. M., Rectanus, E., & McArdle, S. (1987). Chronic stress as a factor in physiologic reactivity to challenge. *Health Psychology, 6,* 221–237.

Flynn, J. R. (1987). Massive IQ gains in 14 nations: What IQ tests really measure. *Psychological Bulletin, 101,* 171–191.

Foa, E. B., & Kozak, M. J. (1986). Emotional processing of fear: Exposure to corrective information. *Psychological Bulletin, 99,* 20–35.

Ford, M. R., & Lowery, C. R. (1986). Gender differences in moral reasoning: A comparison of the use of justice and care orientations. *Journal of Personality and Social Psychology, 50,* 777–783.

Foreyt, J. P. (1987). Issues in the assessment and treatment of obesity. *Journal of Consulting and Clinical Psychology, 55,* 677–684.

Fox, J. L. (1984). The brain's dynamic way of keeping in touch. *Science, 225,* 820–821.

Fox, L. H. (1981). Identification of the academically gifted. *American Psychologist, 36,* 1103–1111.

Fox, N. A., & Davidson, R. J. (1988). Patterns of brain electrical activity during facial signs of emotion in 10-month-old infants. *Developmental Psychology, 24,* 230–236.

Franzoi, S. L., Davis, M. H., Young, R. D. (1985). The effects of private self-consciousness and perspective talking in close relationships. *Journal of Personality and Social Psychology, 48,* 1584–1594.

Frayne, C. A., & Latham, G. P. (1987). Application of social learning theory to employee self-management of attendance. *Journal of Applied Psychology, 72,* 387–392.

Frazier, K. (1984). Gallup youth poll finds high belief in ESP, astrology. *The Skeptical Inquirer, 9,* 113–115.

Frederiksen, N. (1986). Toward a broader conception of human intelligence. *American Psychologist, 41,* 445–452.

Free, N. K., Green, B. L., Grace, M. C., Chernus, L. A., & Whitman, R. M. (1985). Empathy and outcome in brief focal dynamic therapy. *American Journal of Psychiatry, 142,* 917–921.

Freedman, J. L. (1986). Television violence and aggression: A rejoinder. *Psychological Bulletin, 100,* 372–378.

Freedman, J. L., & Fraser, S. C. (1966). Compliance without pressure. *Journal of Personality and Social Psychology, 4,* 195–202.

Freedman, M., & Oscar-Berman, M. (1986). Bilateral frontal lobe disease and selective delayed response deficits in humans. *Behavioral Neuroscience, 100,* 337–342.

Freud, S. (1900/1955). *The interpretation of dreams*. New York: Basic Books.

Freud, S. (1901/1965). *Psychopathology of everyday life*. New York: Norton.

Freud, S. (1905). *Jokes and their relationship to the unconscious*. London: Hogarth Press.

Freud, S. (1914/1957). On the history of the psychoanalytic movement. In J. Strachey (Ed.), *The standard edition of the complete psychological works of Sigmund Freud* (Vol. 14, pp. 7–66). London: Hogarth Press.

Freud, S. (1917/1963). Mourning and melancholia. In J. Strachey (Ed.), *The standard edition of the complete psychological works of Sigmund Freud* (Vol. 14, pp. 243–258). London: Hogarth Press.

Freud, S. (1920). *The psychopathology of everyday life*. New York: Mentor.

Frick, R. W. (1985). Communicating emotion: The role of prosodic features. *Psychological Bulletin, 97,* 412–429.

Fried, R. (1987). Relaxation with biofeedback-assisted guided imagery: The importance of breathing rate as an index of hypoarousal. *Biofeedback and Self-Control, 12,* 273–279.

Friedman, M., & Rosenman, R. H. (1974). *Type A behavior and your heart*. New York: Knopf.

Friedrich-Cofer, L., & Huston, A. C. (1986). Television violence and aggression: The debate continues. *Psychological Bulletin, 100,* 364–371.

Fromm, E. (1941). *Escape from freedom*. New York: Holt, Rinehart & Winston.

Fromm, E. (1956). *The art of loving*. New York: Harper & Row.

Furedy, J. J. (1987). Specific versus placebo effects in biofeedback training: A critical perspective. *Biofeedback and Self-Regulation, 12,* 169–184.

Galanter, E. (1962). *New directions in psychology*. New York: Holt, Rinehart & Winston.

Galef, B. G., Jr. (1980). Diving for food: Analysis of a possible case of social learning in wild rats (*Rattus norvegicus*). *Journal of Comparative and Physiological Psychology, 94,* 416–425.

Galef, B. G., Jr. (1986). Social identification of toxic diets by Norway rats (*Rattus norvegicus*). *Journal of Comparative Psychology, 100,* 331–334.

Gallup, G. G., Jr., & Suarez, S. D. (1985). Alternatives to the use of animals in psychological research. *American Psychologist, 40,* 1104–1111.

Galton, F. (1869). *Hereditary genius*. London: Macmillan.

Gangestad, S., & Snyder, M. (1985). "To carve nature at its joints": On the existence of discrete classes in personality. *Psychological Review, 92,* 317–349.

Gansberg, M. (1964, March 27). 37 who saw murder didn't call the police. *The New York Times*, pp. 1, 38.

Garcia, J. (1981). Tilting at the paper mills of academe. *American Psychologist, 36,* 149–158.

Garcia, J., & Koelling, R. A. (1966). The relation of cue to consequence in avoidance learning. *Psychonomic Science, 4,* 123–124.

Gardner, D. G. (1986). Activation theory and task design: An empirical test of several new predictions. *Journal of Applied Psychology, 71,* 411–418.

Gardner, H. (1983). *Frames of mind: The theory of multiple intelligences.* New York: Basic Books.

Gardner, R. A., & Gardner, B. T. (1969). Teaching sign language to a chimpanzee. *Science, 165,* 664–672.

Gardos, G., Cole, J. O., Salomon, M., & Schniebolk, S. (1987). Clinical forms of severe tardive dyskinesia. *American Journal of Psychiatry, 144,* 895–902.

Garfield, S. L. (1983). Effectiveness of psychotherapy: The perennial controversy. *Professional Psychology, 14,* 35–43.

Gathercole, S. E., & Conway, M. A. (1988). Exploring long-term modality effects: Vocalization leads to best retention. *Memory and Cognition, 16,* 110–119.

Gazzaniga, M. S. (1967, August). The split brain in man. *Scientific American,* pp. 24–29.

Gazzaniga, M. S. (1983). Right hemisphere language following brain bisection: A 20-year perspective. *American Psychologist, 38,* 525–537.

Geen, R. G. (1984). Preferred stimulation levels in introverts and extraverts: Effects on arousal and performance. *Journal of Personality and Social Psychology, 46,* 1303–1312.

Geen, R. G., Stonner, D., & Shope, G. L. (1975). The facilitation of aggression by aggression: Evidence against the catharsis hypothesis. *Journal of Personality and Social Psychology, 31,* 721–726.

Gelb, S. A. (1986). Henry H. Goddard and the immigrants, 1910–1917: The studies and their social context. *Journal of the History of the Behavioral Sciences, 22,* 324–332.

Geller, L. (1982, Spring). The failure of self-actualization theory: A critique of Carl Rogers and Abraham Maslow. *Journal of Humanistic Psychology, 22,* 56–73.

Geller, L. (1984, Spring). Another look at self-actualization. *Journal of Humanistic Psychology, 24,* 93–106.

Gendlin, E. T. (1988). Obituary: Carl Rogers (1902–1987). *American Psychologist, 43,* 127–128.

Gerrard, M. (1987). Sex, sex guilt, and contraceptive use revisited: The 1980s. *Journal of Personality and Social Psychology, 52,* 975–980.

Geschwind, N. (1979, September). Specializations of the human brain. *Scientific American,* pp. 180–199.

Gesten, E. L., & Jason, L. A. (1987). Social and community interventions. *Annual Review of Psychology, 38,* 427–460.

Gibbons, B. (1986). The intimate sense of smell. *National Geographic, 170,* 324–361.

Gibbs, J., Maddison, S. P., & Rolls, E. T. (1981). Satiety role of the small intestine examined in sham-feeding rhesus monkeys. *Journal of Comparative and Physiological Psychology, 95,* 1003–1015.

Gibbs, J. C., & Schnell, S. V. (1985). Moral development 'versus' socialization: A critique. *American Psychologist, 40,* 1071–1080.

Gibson, E. J. (1987). What does infant perception tell us about theories of perception. *Journal of Experimental Psychology, 13,* 515–523.

Gibson, E. J., & Walk, R. D. (1960, April). The visual cliff. *Scientific American,* pp. 67–71.

Gibson, J. J. (1968). What gives rise to the perception of motion? *Psychological Review, 75,* 335–346.

Gilbert, D. G., & Spielberger, C. D. (1987). Effects of smoking on heart rate, anxiety, and feelings of success during social interaction. *Journal of Behavioral Medicine, 10,* 629–638.

Gilbert, J. H. V. (1982). Babbling and the deaf child: A commentary on Lenneborg et al. (1964) and Lenneborg (1967). *Journal of Child Language, 9,* 511–515.

Giles, T. R. (1983). Probable superiority of behavioral interventions—I: Traditional comparative outcome. *Journal of Behavior Therapy and Experimental Psychiatry, 14,* 29–32.

Gillam, B. (1980, January). Geometrical illusions. *Scientific American,* pp. 102–111.

Gilligan, C. (1982). *In a different voice: Psychological theory and women's development.* Cambridge, MA: Harvard University Press.

Gilliland, K., & Andress, D. (1981). Ad lib caffeine consumption, symptoms of caffeinism, and academic performance. *American Journal of Psychiatry, 138,* 512–514.

Gilovich, T., Vallone, R., & Tversky, A. (1985). The hot hand in basketball: On misperception of random sequences. *Cognitive Psychology, 17,* 295–314.

Gist, R., & Stolz, S. B. (1982). Mental health promotion and the media: Community response to the Kansas City hotel disaster. *American Psychologist, 37,* 1136–1139.

Gladue, B. A., Green, R., & Hellman, R. E. (1984). Neuroendocrine response to estrogen and sexual orientation. *Science, 225,* 1496–1499.

Glaser, R., Rice, J., Speicher, C. E., Stout, J. C., & Kiecolt-Glaser, J. K. (1986). Stress depresses interferon production by leukocytes concomitant with a decrease in natural killer cell activity. *Behavioral Neuroscience, 100,* 675–678.

Glick, P., Zion, C., & Nelson, C. (1988). What mediates sex discrimination in hiring decisions? *Journal of Personality and Social Psychology, 55,* 178–186.

Gliedman, J. (1983, November). Interview with Noam Chomsky. *Omni,* pp. 112–118, 171–174.

Glucksberg, S., & Danks, J. H. (1968). Effects of discriminative labels and of nonsense labels upon availability of novel functions. *Journal of Verbal Learning and Verbal Behavior, 7,* 72–76.

Godden, D. R., & Baddeley, A. D. (1975). Context-dependent memory in two natural environments: On land and underwater. *British Journal of Psychology, 66,* 325–331.

"God's hand": Legless veteran crawls to save life of a baby. (1986, June 6). *The Philadelphia Inquirer,* pp. 1–A, 24–A.

Goebel, B. L., & Brown, D. R. (1981). Age differences in motivation related to Maslow's need hierarchy. *Developmental Psychology, 17,* 809–815.

Gold, M., & Yanof, D. S. (1985). Mothers, daughters, and girlfriends. *Journal of Personality and Social Psychology, 49,* 654–659.

Gold, M. S., Pottash, A. L. C., Sweeney, D. R., Martin, D. M., & Davies, R. K. (1980). Further evidence of hypothalamic-pituitary dysfunction in anorexia nervosa. *American Journal of Psychiatry, 137,* 101–102.

Goldberg, L., Elliot, D. L., Schutz, R. W., & Kloster, F. E. (1984). Changes in lipid and lipoprotein levels after weight training. *Journal of the American Medical Association, 252,* 504–506.

Goldberg, W., & Easterbrooks, M. A. (1984). Role of marital quality in toddler development. *Developmental Psychology, 20,* 504–514.

Goldin-Meadow, S., & Mylander, C. (1983). Gestural communication in deaf children: Noneffect of parental input on language development. *Science, 221,* 372–373.

Goldsmith, H. H., & Alansky, J. A. (1987). Maternal and infant temperamental predictors of attachment: A meta-analytic review. *Journal of Consulting and Clinical Psychology, 55,* 805–816.

Goldstein, A. (1980). Thrills in response to music and other stimuli. *Physiological Psychology, 8,* 126–129.

Goldstein, A. G., Chance, J. E., & Gilbert, B. (1984). Facial stereotypes of good guys and bad guys: A replication and extension. *Bulletin of the Psychonomic Society, 22,* 549–552.

Goleman, D. (1981, August). Deadlines for change: Therapy in the age of Reaganomics. *Psychology Today,* pp. 60–69.

Goleman, D. (1981, December). Will the next problem sign in please! *Psychology Today,* pp. 31, 33–34, 37, 39.

Gonzalez, E. R. (1980). Treating the brain by cingulotomy. *Journal of the American Medical Association, 244,* 2141–2143, 2146–2147.

Gonzalez, M. F., & Deutsch, J. A. (1981). Vagotomy abolishes cues of satiety produced by gastric distension. *Science, 212,* 1283–1284.

Goodall, J. (1986). *The chimpanzees of Gombe.* Cambridge, MA: Belknap Press/Harvard University Press.

Goodenough, F. L. (1932). Expression of the emotions in a blind-deaf child. *Journal of Abnormal and Social Psychology, 27,* 328–333.

Goodman, C. S., & Bastiani, M. J. (1984, December). How embryonic nerve cells recognize one another. *Scientific American,* pp. 58–66.

Goodwin, C. J. (1987). In Hall's shadow: Edmund Clark Sanford (1859–1924). *Journal of the History of the Behavioral Sciences, 23,* 153–168.

Gorman, J. (1985, February). My fair software. *Discover,* pp. 64–65.

Gosnell, B. A., & Hsiao, S. (1984). Effects of cholecystokinin on taste preference and sensitivity in rats. *Behavioral Neuroscience, 98,* 452–460.

Gotlib, I. H., & Robinson, L. A. (1982). Responses to depressed individuals: Discrepancies between self-report and observer-rated behavior. *Journal of Abnormal Psychology, 91,* 231–240.

Gottesman, I. L., & Shields, J. (1982). *Schizophrenia: The epigenetic puzzle.* Cambridge, MA: Cambridge University Press.

Gottman, J. M., & Katz, F. (1989). Effects of marital discord on young children's peer interactions and health. *Developmental Psychology, 25,* 373–381.

Gough, H. G., Fioravanti, M., & Lazzari, R. (1983). Some implications of self versus ideal-self congruence on the revised Adjective Check List. *Journal of Personality and Social Psychology, 44,* 1214–1220.

Gould, S. J. (1981). *The mismeasure of man.* New York: Norton.

Grady, K. E., Goodenow, C., & Psorkin, J. R. (1988). The effect of reward on compliance with breast self-examination. *Journal of Behavioral Medicine, 11,* 43–57.

Gray, P. H. (1980). Behaviorism: Some truths that need telling, some errors that need correcting. *Bulletin of the Psychonomic Society, 15,* 357–360.

Gray-Little, B., & Burks, N. (1983). Power and satisfaction in marriage: A review and critique. *Psychological Bulletin, 93,* 513–538.

Greenberg, L. S., & Dompierre, L. M. (1981). Specific effects of Gestalt two-chair dialogue on intrapsychic conflict in counseling. *Journal of Counseling Psychology, 28,* 288–294.

Greenblatt, D. J., Shader, R. I., & Abernathy, D. R. (1983). Drug therapy: Current status of benzodiazepines. *New England Journal of Medicine, 309,* 354–358.

Greene, E., Flynn, M. S., & Loftus, E. F. (1982). Inducing resistance to misleading information. *Journal of Verbal Learning and Verbal Behavior, 21,* 207–219.

Greene, R. L. (1986). Sources of recency effects in free recall. *Psychological Bulletin, 99,* 221–228.

Greene, R. L. (1987). Effects of maintenance rehearsal on human memory. *Psychological Bulletin, 102,* 403–413.

Greeno, J. G. (1980). Psychology of learning, 1960–1980. One participant's observations. *American Psychologist, 35,* 713–728.

Gregg, R. H. (1983). Biofeedback and biophysical monitoring during pregnancy and labor. In J. V. Basmajian (Ed.), *Biofeedback: Principles and practice for clinicians* (pp. 282–288). Baltimore: Williams & Wilkins.

Gregory, R. L. (1987). *The Oxford companion to the mind.* New York: Oxford University Press.

Guilford, J. P. (1950). Creativity. *American Psychologist, 5,* 444–454.

Guilford, J. P. (1959). Three faces of intellect. *American Psychologist, 14,* 469–479.

Guilford, J. P. (1980). Fluid and crystallized intelligences: Two fanciful concepts. *Psychological Bulletin, 88,* 406–412.

Guilford, J. P. (1984). Varieties of divergent production. *The Journal of Creative Behavior, 18,* 1–10.

Gulevich, G., Dement, W., & Johnson, L. (1966). Psychiatric and EEG observations on a case of prolonged (264 hours) wakefulness. *Archives of General Psychiatry, 15,* 29–35.

Gundersheim, J. (1982). A comparison of male and female athletes and nonathletes on measures of self-actualization. *Journal of Sport Behavior, 5,* 186–201.

Gustavson, C. R., Garcia, J., Hawkins, W. G., Rusiniak, K. W. (1974). Coyote predation control by aversive conditioning. *Science, 184,* 581–583.

Gutheil, T. G. (1985). *Rogers v. Commissioner.* Denouement of an important right-to-refuse case. *American Journal of Psychiatry, 142,* 213–216.

Haber, R. N. (1980). How we perceive depth from flat pictures. *American Scientist, 68,* 370–380.

Hackett, G. (1985). Role of mathematics self-efficacy in the choice of math-related majors of college women and men: A path analysis. *Journal of Counseling Psychology, 32,* 47–56.

Hahlweg, K., Goldstein, M. J., Nuechterlein, K. H., Doane, J. A., Miklowitz, D. J., & Snyder, K. S. (1989). Expressed emotion and patient-relative interaction in families of recent onset of schizophrenia. *Journal of Consulting Psychology, 57,* 11–18.

Hall, C. S. (1966). *The meaning of dreams.* New York: McGraw-Hill.

Hall, C. S. (1984). "A ubiquitous sex difference in dreams" revisited. *Journal of Personality and Social Psychology, 46,* 1109–1117.

Hall, E. T. (1959). *The silent language.* New York: Fawcet.

Hall, G. S. (1904). *Adolescence.* New York: Appleton.

Hall, H. K., & Byrne, A. T. J. (1988). Goal setting in sport: Clarifying recent anomalies. *Journal of Sport and Exercise Psychology, 10,* 184–198.

Hall, J. B. (1986). The cardiopulmonary failure of sleep-disordered breathing. *Journal of the American Medical Association, 255,* 930–933.

Halpern, L., Blake, R., & Hillerbrand, J. (1986). Psychoacoustics of a chilling sound. *Perception and Psychophysics, 39,* 77–80.

Hamburg, D. A. (1982). Health and behavior. *Science, 217,* 399.

Hamill, R., Decamp Wilson, T., & Nisbett, R. E. (1980). Insensitivity to sample bias: Generalizing from atypical cases. *Journal of Personality and Social Psychology, 39,* 578–589.

Hansen, C. H., & Hansen, R. D. (1988). Finding the face in the crowd: An anger superiority effect. *Journal of Personality and Social Psychology, 54,* 917–924.

Hardy, C. J., & Latané, B. (1988). Social loafing in cheerleaders: Effects of team membership and competition. *Journal of Sport and Exercise Psychology, 10,* 109–114.

Hare, R. D., McPherson, L. M., & Forth, A. E. (1988). Male psychopaths and their criminal careers. *Journal of Consulting and Clinical Psychology, 56,* 710–714.

Harlow, H. F., & Zimmerman, R. R. (1959). Affectional responses in the infant monkey. *Science, 130,* 421–432.

Harrell, L. E., Barlow, T. S., & Parsons, D. (1987). Cholinergic neurons, learning, and recovery of function. *Behavioral Neuroscience, 101,* 644–652.

Harrington, D. M., Block, J. H., & Block, J. (1987). Testing aspects of Carl Rogers' theory of creative environments: Child-rearing antecedents of creative potential in young adolescents. *Journal of Personality and Social Psychology, 52,* 851–856.

Harris, B. (1979). Whatever happened to Little Albert? *American Psychologist, 34,* 151–160.

Harris, D. B. (1955). Courses for credit. *American Psychologist, 10,* 593–597.

Harris, M. J., & Rosenthal, R. (1985). Mediation of interpersonal expectancy effects: 31 meta-analyses. *Psychological Bulletin, 97,* 363–386.

Harris, R. L., Ellicott, A. M., & Holmes, D. S. (1986). The timing of psychosocial transitions and changes in women's lives: An examination of women aged 45 to 60. *Journal of Personality and Social Psychology, 51,* 409–416.

Harrison, A. A. (1977). Let's make a deal: An analysis of revelations and stipulations in lonely hearts advertisements. *Journal of Personality and Social Psychology, 35,* 257–264.

Hart, J. D., & Cichanski, K. A. (1981). A comparison of frontal EMG biofeedback in the treatment of muscle-contraction headache. *Biofeedback and Self-Regulation, 6,* 63–74.

Hart, S. D., Knapp, P. R., & Hare, R. D. (1988). Performance of male psychopaths following conditional release from prison. *Journal of Consulting and Clinical Psychology, 56,* 227–232.

Hartley, D., Roback, H. B., & Abramowitz, S. I. (1976). Deterioration effects in encounter groups. *American Psychologist, 31,* 247–255.

Hartley, J., & Homa, D. (1981). Abstraction of stylistic concepts. *Journal of Experimental Psychology: Human Learning and Memory, 7,* 33–46.

Hartshorne, H., & May, M. A. (1928). *Studies in deceit.* New York: Macmillan.

Hartup, W. W. (1989). Social relationships and their developmental significance. *American Psychologist, 44,* 120–126.

Harvey, J. H., & Weary, G. (1984). Current issues in attribution theory and research. *Annual Review of Psychology, 35,* 427–457.

Hassett, J. (1978). *A primer of psychophysiology.* San Francisco: Freeman.

Hatfield, E. (1988). Passionate and companionate love. In R. J. Sternberg & M. L. Barnes (Eds.), *The psychology of love.* New Haven, CT: Yale University Press.

Hathaway, S. R., & McKinley, J. C. (1943). *Minnesota multiphasic personality inventory.* New York: The Psychological Corporation.

Hattie, J. A., Sharpley, C. F., & Rogers, H. J. (1984). Comparative effectiveness of professional and paraprofessional helpers. *Psychological Bulletin, 95,* 534–541.

Hawkes, N. (1979). Tracing Burt's descent to scientific fraud. *Science, 205,* 673–675.

Hayden, T., & Mischel, W. (1976). Maintaining trait consistency in the resolution of behavioral inconsistency: The wolf in sheep's clothing? *Journal of Personality, 44,* 109–132.

Hayes, C. (1951). *The ape in our house.* New York: Harper & Row.

Hayes, D. S., Chemelski, B. E., & Palmer, M. (1982). Nursery rhymes and prose passages: Preschoolers' liking and short-term retention of story events. *Developmental Psychology, 18,* 49–56.

Hayes, R. L., Pechura, C. M., Katayama, Y., Povlishuck, J. T., Giebel, M. L., & Becker, D. P. (1984). Activation of pontine cholinergic sites implicated in unconsciousness following cerebral concussions in the cat. *Science, 223,* 301–303.

Hayflick, L. (1980, January). The cell biology of human aging. *Scientific American,* pp. 58–65.

Haywood, H. C., Meyers, C. E., & Switzky, H. N. (1982). Mental retardation. *Annual Review of Psychology, 33,* 309–342.

Hazelrigg, M. D., Cooper, H. M., & Borduin, C. M. (1987). Evaluating the effectiveness of family therapies: An integrative review and analysis. *Psychological Bulletin, 101,* 428–442.

Hearnshaw, L. S. (1979). *Cyril Burt: Psychologist.* Ithaca: Cornell University Press.

Heath, R. G., Martens, S., Leach, B. E., Cohen, M., & Feigley, L. A. (1958). Behavioral changes in nonpsychotic volunteers following administration of taraxein, a substance obtained from serum of schizophrenic patients. *American Journal of Psychiatry, 11,* 917–920.

Hebb, D. O. (1955). Drives and the C.N.S. (conceptual nervous system). *Psychological Review, 62,* 243–254.

Hebb, D. O. (1958). The motivating effects of exteroceptive stimulation. *American Psychologist, 13,* 109–113.

Hechinger, N. (1981, March). Seeing without eyes. *Science 81,* pp. 38–43.

Hedges, L. V. (1987). How hard is hard science, how soft is soft science?: The empirical cumulativeness of research. *American Psychologist, 42,* 443–455.

Heffner, H. E. (1983). Hearing in large and small dogs: Absolute thresholds and size of the tympanic membrane. *Behavioral Neuroscience, 97,* 310–318.

Heider, E. R., & Olivier, D. C. (1972). The structure of the color space in naming and memory for two languages. *Cognitive Psychology, 3,* 337–354.

Heider, F. (1944). Social perception and phenomenal causality. *Psychological Review, 51,* 358–374.

Heilman, M. E., & Stopeck, M. H. (1985). Attractiveness and corporate success: Different causal attributions for males and females. *Journal of Applied Psychology, 70,* 379–388.

Heitzmann, C. A., & Kaplan, M. (1988). Assessment of methods for measuring social support. *Health Psychology, 7,* 75–109.

Helmreich, R. L., Spence, J. T., Beane, W. E., Lucker, G. W., & Matthews, K. A. (1980). Making it in academic psychology: Demographic and personality correlates of attainment. *Journal of Personality and Social Psychology, 39,* 896–908.

Hendrick, S., Hendrick, C., Slapion-Foote, M., & Foote, F. (1985). Gender differences in sexual attitudes. *Journal of Personality and Social Psychology, 48,* 1630–1642.

Henke, P. G. (1988). Electrophysiological activity in the central nucleus of the amygdala: Emotionality and stress ulcers in rats. *Behavioral Neuroscience, 102,* 77–83.

Henle, M. (1978). Gestalt psychology and gestalt therapy. *Journal of the History of the Behavioral Sciences, 14,* 23–32.

Henle, M. (1978). One man against the Nazis: Wolfgang Kohler. *American Psychologist, 33,* 939–944.

Herbert, W. (1983). MMPI: Redefining normality for modern times. *Science News, 134,* 228.

Herbert, W. (1983). Remembrance of things partly. *Science News, 124,* 378–381.

Herbert, W. (1983). Shrinking the insanity defense. *Science News, 123,* 68.

Hergenhahn, B. R. (1984). *An introduction to theories of personality.* Englewood Cliffs, NJ: Prentice-Hall.

Herman, C. P., Olmsted, M. P., & Polivy, J. (1983). Obesity, externality, and susceptibility to social influence: An integrated analysis. *Journal of Personality and Social Psychology, 45,* 926–934.

Herrnstein, R. J., Nickerson, R. S., de Sanchez, M., & Swets, J. A. (1986). Teaching thinking skills. *American Psychologist, 41,* 1279–1289.

Hersen, M., Kazdin, A. E., & Bellack, A. S. (Eds.). (1983). *The clinical psychology handbook.* New York: Pergamon Press.

Hertzog, C. (1989). Influences of cognitive slowing on age differences

Hertzog, C. (1989). Influences of cognitive slowing on age differences in intelligence. *Developmental Psychology, 25,* 636–651.

Hess, E. H. (1975, November). The role of pupil size in communication. *Scientific American,* pp. 110–112, 116–119.

Hesse, H. (1930/1968). *Narcissus and Goldmund.* New York: Farrar, Strauss, & Giroux.

Hetherington, A. W., & Ranson, S. W. (1942). The spontaneous activity and food intake of rats with hypothalamic lesions. *American Journal of Physiology, 136,* 609–617.

Hetherington, E. M. (1979). Divorce: A child's perspective. *American Psychologist, 34,* 851–858.

Higgins, E. T. (1987). Self-discrepancy: A theory relating self and affect. *Psychological Review, 94,* 319–340.

Hilgard, E. (1973). A neodissociation interpretation of pain reduction in hypnosis. *Psychological Review, 80,* 396–411.

Hilgard, E. (1978, January). Hypnosis and consciousness. *Human Nature,* pp. 42–49.

Hilgard, E. R. (1987). *Psychology in America: A historical survey.* San Diego: Harcourt Brace Jovanovich.

Hill, A. L. (1975). An investigation of calendar calculating by an idiot savant. *American Journal of Psychiatry, 132,* 557–562.

Hinckley, J. W. (1982, September 20). The insanity defense and me. *Newsweek,* p. 30.

Hines, M. (1982). Prenatal gonadal hormones and sex differences in human behavior. *Psychological Bulletin, 92,* 56–80.

Hjelle, L. A., & Ziegler, D. J. (1981). *Personality theories: Basic assumptions, research, and applications.* New York: McGraw-Hill.

Hobson, J. A. (1985, November/December). Can psychoanalysis be saved? *The Sciences,* pp. 52–58.

Hobson, J. A., & McCarley, R. W. (1977). The brain as a dream state generator: An activation-synthesis hypothesis of the dream process. *American Journal of Psychiatry, 134,* 1335–1348.

Hodgkin, A. L., & Huxley, A. F. (1952). A quantitative description of membrane current and its application to conduction within excitation in neurons. *Journal of Physiology, 117,* 500–544.

Hoelscher, T. J. (1987). Maintenance of relaxation-induced blood pressure reductions: The importance of continued relaxation practice. *Biofeedback and Self-Regulation, 12,* 3–12.

Hoff-Ginsberg, E. (1986). Function and structure in maternal speech: Their relation to the child's development of syntax. *Developmental Psychology, 22,* 155–163.

Hoffman, C., Lau, I., & Johnson, D. R. (1986). The linguistic relativity of person cognition: An English-Chinese comparison. *Journal of Personality and Social Psychology, 51,* 1097–1105.

Hoffman, L. W. (1989). Effects of maternal employment in the two-parent family. *American Psychologist, 44,* 283–292.

Holahan, C. J. (1986). Environmental psychology. *Annual Review of Psychology, 37,* 381–407.

Holden, C. (1980, November). Twins reunited: More than the faces are familiar. *Science 80,* pp. 55–59.

Holden, C. (1983). Insanity defense reexamined. *Science, 222,* 994–995.

Holden, C. (1985). A guarded endorsement for shock therapy. *Science, 228,* 1510–1511.

Holden, C. (1986). Depression research advances, treatment lags. *Science, 233,* 723–726.

Holden, C. (1986). Researchers grapple with problems of updating classic psychological test. *Science, 233,* 1249–1251.

Holden, C. (1987). Animal regulations: So far, so good. *Science, 238,* 880–882.

Holden, C. (1987). The genetics of personality. *Science, 237,* 598–601.

Holden, C. (1987). A top priority at NIMH. *Science, 235,* 431.

Hollender, M. H. (1983). The 51st landmark article. *Journal of the American Medical Association, 250,* 228–229.

Holmes, D. S. (1974). Investigations of repression: Differential recall of material experimentally or naturally associated with ego threat. *Psychology Bulletin, 81,* 632–653.

Holmes, D. S. (1984). Meditation and somatic arousal reduction: A review of the experimental evidence. *American Psychologist, 39,* 1–10.

Holmes, M. (1986, August 3). 20 years ago, the Texas tower massacre. *The Philadelphia Inquirer,* p. 3-E.

Holmes, T. H., & Rahe, R. H. (1967). The Social Readjustment Rating Scale. *Journal of Psychosomatic Research, 11,* 213–218.

Homa, D. (1983). An assessment of two extraordinary speed-readers. *Bulletin of the Psychonomic Society, 21,* 123–126.

Honchar, M. P., Olney, J. W., & Sherman, W. R. (1983). Systematic cholinergic agents induce seizures and brain damage in lithium-treated rats. *Science, 220,* 323–325.

Honts, C. R., Hodes, R. L., & Raskin, D. C. (1985). Effects of physical countermeasures on the physiological detection of deception. *Journal of Applied Psychology, 70,* 177–187.

Hood, R. W., Jr., & Morris, R. J. (1981). Sensory isolation and the differential elicitation of religious imagery in intrinsic and extrinsic persons. *Journal for the Scientific Study of Religion, 20,* 261–273.

Hoon, P. W., Bruce, K., & Kinchloe, B. (1982). Does the menstrual cycle play a role in sexual arousal? *Psychophysiology, 19,* 21–26.

Hoppe, R. B. (1988). In search of a phenomenon: Research in parapsychology [Review of *Foundations of parapsychology*]. *Contemporary Psychology, 33,* 129–130.

Hormuth, S. E. (1986). The sampling of experiences *in situ. Journal of Personality, 54,* 262–293.

Horn, J. C. (1988, December). Sporting life: The peak years. *Psychology Today,* pp. 62–63.

Horn, J. L., & Cattell, R. C. (1966). Refinement and test of the theory of fluid and crystallized general intelligences. *Journal of Educational Psychology, 57,* 253–270.

Horn, J. L., & Donaldson, G. (1976). On the myth of intellectual decline in adulthood. *American Psychologist, 31,* 701–719.

Horney, K. (1937). *The neurotic personality of our time.* New York: Norton.

Horton, D. L., & Mills, C. B. (1984). Human learning and memory. *Annual Review of Psychology, 35,* 361–394.

Hosch, H. M., & Cooper, D. S. (1982). Victimization as a determinant of eyewitness accuracy. *Journal of Applied Psychology, 67,* 649–652.

Hovland, C. I., Lumsdaine, A., & Sheffield, F. (1949). *Experiments on mass communication.* Princeton: Princeton University Press.

Howard, K. I., Kopta, S. M., Krausse, M. S., & Orlinsky, D. E. (1986). The dose-effect relationship in psychotherapy. *American Psychologist, 41,* 159–164.

Hubel, D. H., & Wiesel, T. N. (1979, September). Brain mechanisms of vision. *Scientific American,* pp. 130–144.

Hudspeth, A. J. (1983, January). The hair cells of the inner ear. *Scientific American,* pp. 54–64.

Huesmann, L. R., Eron, L. D., Klein, R., Brice, P., & Fischer, P. (1983). Mitigating the imitation of aggressive behaviors by changing children's attitudes about media violence. *Journal of Personality and Social Psychology, 44,* 899–910.

Hughes, J., Smith, T. W., Kosterlitz, H. W., Fothergill, L. A., Morgan, B. A., & Morris, H. R. (1975). Identification of two related pentapeptides from the brain with potent opiate agonistic activity. *Nature, 258,* 577–579.

Hull, C. L. (1943). *Principles of behavior.* New York: Appleton-Century-Crofts.

Hull, J. G., & Bond, C. F., Jr. (1986). Social and behavioral consequences of alcohol consumption and expectancy: A meta-analysis. *Psychological Bulletin, 99,* 347–360.

Humphreys, M. S., & Revelle, W. (1984). Personality, motivation, and performance: A theory of the relationship between individual differences and information processing. *Psychological Review, 91,* 153–184.

Hunt, J. M. (1979). Psychological development: Early experience. *Annual Review of Psychology, 30,* 103–143.

Huston, A. C., Watkins, B. A., & Kunkel, E. (1989). Public policy and children's television. *American Psychologist, 44,* 424–433.

Huston, T. L., & Levinger, G. (1978). Interpersonal attraction and relationships. *Annual Review of Psychology, 29,* 115–156.

Hutchins, C. M. (1981, October). The acoustics of violin plates. *Scientific American,* pp. 170–174, 177–180, 182–186.

Huxley, A. (1932). *Brave new world.* New York: Harper & Row.

Huyghe, P. (1982, July). Imaginary friends. *Omni,* pp. 22, 121.

Hyde, J. S. (1984). Children's understanding of sexist language. *Developmental Psychology, 20,* 697–706.

Hyde, J. S., & Linn, M. C. (1988). Gender differences in verbal ability: A meta-analysis. *Psychological Bulletin, 104,* 53–69.

Immergluck, L. (1964). Determinism-freedom in contemporary psychology: An ancient problem revisited. *American Psychologist, 19,* 270–281.

Ingelfinger, F. J. (1944). The late effects of total and subtotal gastrectomy. *New England Journal of Medicine, 231,* 321–327.

Insko, C. A. (1965). Verbal reinforcement of attitude. *Journal of Personality and Social Psychology, 2,* 621–623.

Isen, A. M., Daubman, K. A., & Nowicki, G. P. (1987). Positive affect facilitates creative problem solving. *Journal of Personality and Social Psychology, 52,* 1122–1131.

Isenberg, D. J. (1986). Group polarization: A critical review and meta-analysis. *Journal of Personality and Social Psychology, 50,* 1141–1151.

Isle, S. (1988, September 12). Color braves blue for second-class feeling. *The Sporting News,* p. 6.

Iyer, P. (1986, October). A mysterious sect gives its name to political murder. *Smithsonian,* pp. 145–162.

Izard, C. E., Huebner, R. R., Risser, D., McGinnes, G. C., & Dougherty, L. M. (1980). The young infant's ability to produce discrete emotion expressions. *Developmental Psychology, 16,* 132–140.

Jacklin, C. N. (1989). Female and male: Issues of gender. *American Psychologist, 44,* 127–133.

Jackson, J. M., & Harkins, S. G. (1985). Equity in effort: An explanation of the social loafing effect. *Journal of Personality and Social Psychology, 49,* 1199–1206.

Jacobs, B. L. (1987). How hallucinogenic drugs work. *American Scientist, 75,* 386–392.

Jacobson, E. (1979, September/October). I was there. *APA Monitor,* p. 13.

James, W. (1882). Subjective effects of nitrous oxide. *Mind, 7,* 186–208.

James, W. (1884). What is an emotion? *Mind, 9,* 188–205.

James, W. (1890/1950). *The principles of psychology.* New York: Dover.

James, W. (1902/1958). *The varieties of religious experience.* New York: Mentor.

James, W. (1904). Does consciousness exist? *Journal of Philosophy, Psychology, and Scientific Methods, 1,* 477–491.

Jamieson, D. G., & Morosan, D. E. (1986). Training non-native speech contrasts in adults: Acquisition of the English Ŏ-Ə contrast by Francophones. *Perception and Psychophysics, 40,* 205–215.

Janis, I. L. (1983). *Groupthink: Psychological studies of policy decisions and fiascoes.* Boston: Houghton Mifflin.

Janis, I. L., Kaye, D., & Kirschner, P. (1965). Facilitating effects of "eating-while-reading" on responsiveness to persuasive communications. *Journal of Personality and Social Psychology, 1,* 181–186.

Jankowicz, A. D. (1987). Whatever became of George Kelly. *American Psychologist, 42,* 481–487.

Jedlicka, D. (1980). A test of the psychoanalytic theory of mate selection. *Journal of Social Psychology, 112,* 295–299.

Jeffery, R. W. (1988). Dietary risk factors and their modification in cardiovascular disease. *Journal of Consulting and Clinical Psychology, 56,* 350–357.

Jemmott, J. B., & Locke, S. E. (1984). Psychosocial factors, immunologic mediation, and human susceptibility to infectious diseases: How much do we know? *Psychological Bulletin, 95,* 78–108.

Jemmott, J. B., & Magloire, K. (1988). Academic stress, social support, and secretory immunoglobulin A. *Journal of Personality and Social Psychology, 55,* 803–810.

Jenkins, J. G., & Dallenbach, K. M. (1924). Obliviscence during sleep and waking. *American Journal of Psychology, 35,* 605–612.

Jensen, A. J. (1969). How much can we boost IQ and scholastic achievement? *Harvard Educational Review, 39,* 1–123.

Jensen, A. R. (1980). *Bias in mental testing.* New York: The Free Press.

Johnson, C., & Flach, A. (1985). Family characteristics of 105 patients with bulimia. *American Journal of Psychiatry, 142,* 1321–1324.

Johnson, J. T., Cain, L. M., Falke, T. L., Hayman, J., & Perillo, E. (1985). The "Barnum effect" revisited: Cognitive and motivational factors in the acceptance of personality descriptions. *Journal of Personality and Social Psychology, 49,* 1378–1391.

Johnson, R. C., McClearn, G. E., Yuen, S., Nagoshi, C. T., Ahern, F. M., & Cole, R. E. (1985). Galton's data a century later. *American Psychologist, 40,* 875–892.

Jonah, B. A., & Grant, B. A. (1985). Long-term effectiveness of selective traffic enforcement programs for increasing seat belt use. *Journal of Applied Psychology, 70,* 257–263.

Jonas, G. (1972). *Visceral learning: Toward a science of self-control.* New York: Viking.

Jones, L. (1900). Education during sleep. *Suggestive Therapeutics, 8,* 283–285.

Jones, L. V. (1984). White-black achievement differences: The narrowing gap. *American Psychologist, 39,* 1207–1213.

Jones, M. C. (1924). The elimination of children's fears. *Journal of Experimental Psychology, 7,* 383–390.

Jones, M. M. (1980). Conversion disorder: Anachronism or evolutionary form? A review of the neurologic, behavioral, and psychoanalytic literature. *Psychological Bulletin, 87,* 427–441.

Jorgensen, R. S., Nash, J. K., Lasser, N. L., Hymowitz, N., & Langer, A. W. (1988). Heart rate acceleration and its relationship to total serum cholesterol, triglycerides, and blood pressure. *Psychophysiology, 25,* 39–44.

Josephson, W. L. (1987). Television violence and children's aggression: Testing the priming, social script, and disinhibition predictions. *Journal of Personality and Social Psychology, 53,* 882–890.

Julien, R. M. (1981). *A primer of drug action.* San Francisco: Freeman.

Jung, C. G. (1959/1969). *Flying saucers: A modern myth of things seen in the sky.* New York: Signet.

Jurkovic, G. J. (1980). The juvenile delinquent as a moral philosopher: A structural-developmental perspective. *Psychological Bulletin, 88,* 709–727.

Justice, A. (1985). Review of the effects of stress on cancer in laboratory animals: Importance of time of stress application and type of tumor. *Psychological Bulletin, 98,* 108–138.

Kahneman, D., & Tversky, A. (1973). On the psychology of prediction. *Psychological Review, 80,* 237–251.

Kahneman, D., & Tversky, A. (1982, January). The psychology of preferences. *Scientific American,* pp. 160–173.

Kalmun, A. J. (1982). Electric and magnetic field detection in elasmobranch fishes. *Science, 218,* 916–918.

Kamarck, T. W., & Lichtenstein, E. (1985). Current trends in clinic-based smoking control. *Annals of Behavioral Medicine, 7*(2), pp. 19–23.

Kamin, L. (1969). Predictability, surprise, attention, and conditioning. In B. Campbell & R. Church (Eds.), *Punishment and aversive behavior.* New York: Appleton-Century-Crofts.

Kamin, L. J. (1974). *The science and politics of IQ.* New York: Wiley.

Kamiya, J. (1969). Operant control of the EEG alpha rhythm and some of its reported effects on consciousness. In C. Tart (Ed.), *Altered states of consciousness* (pp. 489–501). New York: Wiley.

Kandel, E., Mednick, S. A., Kirkegaard-Sorensen, L., Hutchings, B., Knop, J., Rosenberg, R., & Schulsinger, R. (1988). IQ as a protective factor for subjects at high risk for antisocial behavior. *Journal of Consulting and Clinical Psychology, 56,* 224–226.

Kandel, E. R., & Schwartz, J. H. (1982). Molecular biology of learning: Modulation of transmitter release. *Science, 218,* 433–443.

Kanner, A. D., Coyne, J. C., Schaefer, C., & Lazarus, R. S. (1981). Comparisons of two modes of stress measurement: Daily hassles and uplifts versus major life events. *Journal of Behavioral Medicine, 4,* 1–39.

Kaplan, G. A., & Reynolds, P. (1988). Depression and cancer mortality and morbidity: Prospective evidence from the Alameda county study. *Journal of Behavioral Medicine, 11,* 1–13.

Kaplan, M. (1983). A woman's view of DSM-III. *American Psychologist, 38,* 786–792.

Kaplan, R. M., & Saccuzzo, D. P. (1982). *Psychological testing: Principles, applications, and issues.* Belmont, CA: Brooks/Cole.

Karen, G., & Wagenaar, W. A. (1985). On the psychology of playing blackjack: Normative and descriptive considerations with implications for decision theory. *Journal of Experimental Psychology: General, 114,* 133–158.

Kass, F., Spitzer, R. L., & Williams, J. B. W. (1983). An empirical study of the issue of sex bias in the diagnostic criteria of DSM-III axis II personality disorders. *American Psychologist, 38,* 799–801.

Kaufman, J., & Cicchetti, D. (1989). Effects of maltreatment on school-age children's socioemotional development: Assessments in a day-camp setting. *Developmental Psychology, 25,* 516–524.

Kaufman, L., & Rock, I. (1962, July). The moon illusion. *Scientific American,* pp. 120–130.

Kaylor, J. A., King, D. W., & King, L. A. (1987). Psychological effects of military service in Vietnam: A meta-analysis. *Psychological Bulletin, 102,* 257–271.

Kazdin, A. E. (1982). Symptom substitution, generalization, and response covariation: Implications for psychotherapy outcome. *Psychological Bulletin, 91,* 349–365.

Kazdin, A. E. (1982). The token economy: A decade later. *Journal of Applied Behavior Analysis, 15,* 431–445.

Keesey, R. E., & Powley, T. L. (1986). The regulation of body weight. *Annual Review of Psychology, 37,* 109–133.

Keith, J. R., & McVety, K. M. (1988). Latent place learning in a novel environment and the influences of prior training in rats. *Psychobiology, 16,* 146–151.

Kelley, H. H. (1950). The warm-cold variable in first impressions of personality. *Journal of Personality, 18,* 431–439.

Kelley, H. H. (1973). The processes of causal attributions. *American Psychologist, 28,* 107–128.

Kellogg, R. L. (1984). Conan Doyle and graphology. *Teaching of Psychology, 11,* 112–113.

Kellogg, W. N., & Kellogg, L. A. (1933). *The ape and the child.* New York: McGraw-Hill.

Kelly, G. A. (1963). *A theory of personality: The psychology of personal constructs.* New York: Norton.

Kendall, P. C., Williams, L., Pechacek, T. F., Graham, T. F., Shisslak, C., & Horzoff, N. (1979). Cognitive-behavioral and patient education interventions in cardiac catheterization procedures. *Journal of Consulting and Clinical Psychology, 47,* 49–58.

Kendrick, K. M., & Baldwin, B. A. (1987). Cells in temporal cortex of conscious sheep can respond preferentially to the sight of faces. *Science, 236,* 448–450.

Kendrick, M. J., Craig, K. D., Lawson, D. M., & Davidson, P. O. (1982). Cognitive behavioral therapy for musical performance anxiety. *Journal of Consulting and Clinical Psychology, 50,* 353–362.

Kenrick, D. T., & Dantchik, A. (1983). Interactionism, idiographics, and the social psychological invasion of personality. *Journal of Personality, 51,* 286–307.

Kenrick, D. T., & Funder, D. C. (1988). Profiting from controversy: Lessons from the person-situation debate. *American Psychologist, 43,* 23–34.

Kenrick, D. T., & Gutierres, S. E. (1980). Contrast effects and judgments of physical attractiveness: When beauty becomes a social problem. *Journal of Personality and Social Psychology, 38,* 131–140.

Kershner, J. R., & Ledger, G. (1985). Effect of sex, intelligence, and style of thinking on creativity: A comparison of gifted and average IQ children. *Journal of Personality and Social Psychology, 48,* 1033–1040.

Kessler, S. (1984). The myth of mythical disease [Review of *Schizophrenia: Medical diagnosis or moral verdict?*]. *Contemporary Psychology, 29,* 380–381.

Keys, A., Brozek, J., Henschel, A., Mickelson, O., & Taylor, H. L. (1950). *The biology of human starvation.* Minneapolis: University of Minnesota Press.

Kiecolt-Glaser, J. K., & Glaser, R. (1988). Psychological influences on immunity: Implications for AIDS. *American Psychologist, 43,* 892–898.

Kiecolt-Glaser, J. K., Glaser, R., Strain, E. C., Stout, J. C., Tarr, K. L., Holliday, J. E., & Speicher, C. E. (1986). Modulation of cellular immunity in medical students. *Journal of Behavioral Medicine, 9,* 5–21.

Kiesler, C. A. (1982). Mental hospitals and alternative care: Noninstitutionalization as potential public policy for mental patients. *American Psychologist, 37,* 349–360.

Kiesler, C. A., & Lowman, R. P. (1980). Hutchinson versus Proxmire. *American Psychologist, 35,* 689–690.

Kihlstrom, J. F. (1987). The cognitive unconscious. *Science, 237,* 1445–1452.

Killian, G. A., Holzman, P. S., Davis, J. M., & Gibbons, R. (1984). Effects of psychotropic medication on selected cognitive and perceptual measures. *Journal of Abnormal Psychology, 93,* 58–70.

Kilmann, P. R., & Sotile, W. M. (1976). The marathon encounter group: A review of the outcome literature. *Psychological Bulletin, 83,* 827–850.

Kimball, M. M. (1989). A new perspective on women's math achievement. *Psychological Bulletin, 105,* 198–214.

Kinsey, A. C., Pomeroy, W. D., & Martin, C. E. (1948). *Sexual behavior in the human male.* Philadelphia: Saunders.

Kinsey, A. C., Pomeroy, W. D., Martin, C. E., & Gebhard, T. H. (1953). *Sexual behavior in the human female.* Philadelphia: Saunders.

Kirmeyer, S. L., & Biggers, K. (1988). Environmental demand and demand engineering behavior: An observational analysis of the Type A patterns. *Journal of Personality and Social Psychology, 54,* 997–1005.

Klein, M., Coles, M. G. H., & Donchin, E. (1984). People with absolute pitch process tones without producing a P300. *Science, 223,* 1306–1309.

Klein, S. B. (1982). *Motivation: Biosocial approaches.* New York: McGraw-Hill.

Kleinmuntz, B., & Szucko, J. J. (1984a). A field study of the fallibility of polygraph lie detection. *Nature, 308,* 449–450.

Kleinmuntz, B., & Szucko, J. J. (1984b). Lie detection in ancient and modern times: A call for contemporary scientific study. *American Psychologist, 39,* 766–776.

Klepac, R. K. (1986). Fear and avoidance of dental treatment in adults. *Annals of Behavioral Medicine, 8,* 17–22.

Klonoff, E. A., Janata, J. W., & Kaufman, B. (1986). The use of systematic desensitization to overcome resistance to magnetic resonance imaging (MRI) scanning. *Journal of Behavior Therapy and Experimental Psychiatry, 17,* 189–192.

Klonoff, E. A., & Moore, D. J. (1986). "Conversion reactions" in adolescents: A biofeedback-based operant approach. *Journal of Behavior Therapy and Experimental Psychiatry, 17,* 179–184.

Kluger, M. A., Jamner, L. D., & Tursky, B. (1985). Comparison of the effectiveness of biofeedback and relaxation training on handwarming. *Psychophysiology, 22,* 162–166.

Knapp, T. J., & Shodahl, S. A. (1974). Ben Franklin as a behavior modifier: A note. *Behavior Therapy, 5,* 656–660.

Knight, I. F. (1984). Freud's "Project": A theory for studies on hysteria. *Journal of the History of the Behavioral Sciences, 20,* 340–358.

Knudsen, E. I. (1981, December). The hearing of the barn owl. *Scientific American,* pp. 112–113, 115–116, 118–125.

Kobasa, S. C., Maddi, S. R., & Kahn, S. (1982). Hardiness and health: A prospective study. *Journal of Personality and Social Psychology, 42,* 168–177.

Koenigsberg, H. W., & Hadley, R. (1986). Expressed emotion: From predictive index to clinical construct. *American Journal of Psychiatry, 143,* 1361–1373.

Kohlberg, L. (1966). A cognitive-developmental analysis of children's sex-role concepts and attitudes. In E. E. Maccoby (Ed.), *The development of sex differences.* Stanford, CA: Stanford University Press.

Kohlberg, L. (1981). *Essays on moral development.* New York: Harper & Row.

Kohlberg, L. (1981). *The philosophy of moral development: Essays on moral development* (Vol. I). New York: Harper & Row.

Kohlberg, L. (1984). *Essays on moral development: The psychology of moral development.* San Francisco: Harper & Row.

Kohler, W. (1925). *The mentality of apes.* New York: Harcourt Brace Jovanovich.

Kohler, W. (1959). Gestalt psychology today. *American Psychologist, 14,* 727–734.

Kohnken, G., & Maass, A. (1988). Eyewitness testimony: False alarms on biased instructions. *Journal of Applied Psychology, 73,* 363–370.

Kolata, G. (1984a). Puberty mystery solved. *Science, 223,* 272.

Kolata, G. (1984b). Studying learning in the womb. *Science, 225,* 302–303.

Kolata, G. (1985). Why do people get fat? *Science, 227,* 1327–1328.

Kolata, G. (1987). Associations or rules in learning language? *Science, 237,* 133–134.

Koop, C. E. (1987). Report of the Surgeon General's Workshop on Pornography and Public Health. *American Psychologist, 42,* 944–945.

Koss, M. P., Gidycz, C. A., & Wisniewski, N. (1987). The scope of rape: Incidence and prevalence of sexual aggression and victimization in a national sample of higher education students. *Journal of Consulting and Clinical Psychology, 55,* 162–170.

Krafka, C., & Penrod, S. (1985). Reinstatement of context in a field experiment on eyewitness identification. *Journal of Personality and Social Psychology, 49,* 58–69.

Kral, J. G., & Kissileff, H. R. (1987). Surgical approaches to the treatment of obesity. *Annals of Behavioral Medicine, 9* (1), pp. 15–19.

Kramer, D. E., & Bayern, C. D. (1984). The effects of behavioral strategies on creativity training. *Journal of Creative Behavior, 18,* 23–24.

Kramer, T. H., Buckhout, R., Eugenio, P., & Cohen, R. (1985). Presence of malice: Scientific evaluation of reader response to innuendo. *Bulletin of the Psychonomic Society, 23,* 61–63.

Krantz, D. S., Contrada, R. J., Hill, D. R., & Friedler, E. (1988). Environmental stress and biobehavioral antecedents of coronary heart disease. *Journal of Consulting and Clinical Psychology, 56,* 333–341.

Krantz, D. S., & Manuck, S. B. (1984). Acute psychophysiologic reactivity and risk of cardiovascular disease: A review and methodologic critique. *Psychological Bulletin, 96,* 435–464.

Kravitz, D. A., & Martin, B. (1986). Ringelmann rediscovered: The original article. *Journal of Personality and Social Psychology, 50,* 936–941.

Kretschmer, E. (1925). *Physique and character.* New York: Harcourt, Brace.

Kromer, L. F. (1987). Nerve growth factor treatment after brain injury prevents neuronal death. *Science, 235,* 214–216.

Kübler-Ross, E. (1969). *On death and dying.* New York: Macmillan.

Kübler-Ross, E. (1974). *Questions and answers on death and dying.* New York: Macmillan.

Kuhlman, T. L. (1985). A study of salience and motivational theories of humor. *Journal of Personality and Social Psychology, 49,* 281–286.

Kuhn, T. S. (1970). *The structure of scientific revolutions.* Chicago: University of Chicago Press.

Kulik, J. A. (1983). Confirmatory attribution and the perpetuation of social beliefs. *Journal of Personality and Social Psychology, 44,* 1171–1181.

Kulik, J. A., & Mahler, H. I. M. (1987). Effects of preoperative roommate assignment on preoperative anxiety and recovery from coronary-bypass surgery. *Health Psychology, 6,* 525–543.

Kurzweil, R. (1985). What is artificial intelligence anyway? *American Scientist, 73,* 258–264.

Ladouceur, R. (1983). Participant modeling with or without cognitive treatment for phobias. *Journal of Consulting and Clinical Psychology, 51,* 942–944.

Ladouceur, R., & Gros-Louis, Y. (1986). Paradoxical intention vs. stimulus control in the treatment of severe insomnia. *Journal of Behavior Therapy and Experimental Psychiatry, 17,* 267–269.

LaFreniere, P. J., & Sroufe, L. A. (1985). Profiles of peer competence in the preschool: Interrelations between measures, influence of social ecology, and relation to attachment history. *Developmental Psychology, 21,* 56–69.

Laing, R. D. (1967). *The politics of experience.* New York: Ballantine Books.

Lambert, N. M. (1981). Psychological evidence in Larry P. v. Wilson Riles. *American Psychologist, 36,* 937–952.

Landers, S. (1987, December). Aversive device sparks controversy. *APA Monitor,* p. 15.

Landesman, S., & Butterfield, E. C. (1987). Normalization and deinstitutionalization of mentally retarded individuals: Controversy and facts. *American Psychologist, 42,* 809–816.

Landesman, S., & Ramey, C. (1989). Developmental psychology and mental retardation: Integrating scientific principles with treatment practices. *American Psychologist, 44,* 409–415.

Langenbucher, J. W., & Nathan, P. E. (1983). Psychology, public policy, and the evidence for alcohol intoxication. *American Psychologist, 38,* 1070–1077.

Langlois, J. H., Roggman, L. A., Casey, R. J., Ritter, J. M., Rieser-Danner, L. A., & Jenkins, V. Y. (1987). Infant preferences for attractive faces: Rudiments of a stereotype? *Developmental Psychology, 23,* 363–369.

Langone, J. (1981, November). [Review of *The minds of Billy Milligan*]. *Discover*, pp. 293–294.

Langone, J. (1983, September). B. F. Skinner: Beyond reward and punishment. *Discover*, pp. 38–46.

La Piere, R. T. (1934). Attitudes versus action. *Social Forces, 13*, 230–237.

La Pointe, F. H. (1970). Origin and evolution of the term "psychology." *American Psychologist, 25*, 640–646.

Lashley, K. S. (1950). In search of the engram. In *Symposium of the Society for Experimental Biology* (Vol. 4, pp. 454–482). New York: Cambridge University Press.

Latané, B., & Darley, J. M. (1968). Group inhibition of bystander intervention in emergencies. *Journal of Personality and Social Psychology, 10*, 215–221.

Latham, G. P., & Saari, L. M. (1984). Do people do what they say? Further studies on the situational interview. *Journal of Applied Psychology, 69*, 569–573.

Lau, R. R., & Russell, D. (1980). Attributions in the sports pages. *Journal of Personality and Social Psychology, 39*, 29–38.

Lauer, C., Riemann, D., Lund, R., & Berger, M. (1987). Shortened REM latency: A consequence of psychological strain? *Psychophysiology, 24*, 263–271.

Laurence, J. R., & Perry, C. (1983). Hypnotically created memory among highly hypnotizable subjects. *Science, 222*, 523–524.

Laver, A. B. (1972). Precursors of psychology in ancient Egypt. *Journal of the History of the Behavioral Sciences, 8*, 181–195.

Lazarus, R. S. (1984). On the primacy of cognition. *American Psychologist, 39*, 124–129.

Lazarus, R. S., DeLongis, A., Folkman, S., & Gruen, R. (1985). Stress and adaptational outcomes: The problem of confounded measures. *American Psychologist, 40*, 770–779.

Leahey, T. H. (1981). The mistaken mirror: On Wundt's and Titchener's psychologies. *Journal of the History of the Behavioral Sciences, 17*, 273–282.

Leakey, R. E., & Lewin, R. (1977, November). Is it our culture, not our genes, that makes us killers? *Smithsonian*, pp. 56–64.

Lebow, J. (1982). Consumer satisfaction with mental health treatment. *Psychological Bulletin, 91*, 244–259.

Lee, M. K., Graham, S. N., & Gold, P. E. (1988). Memory enhancement with posttraining intraventricular glucose injections in rats. *Behavioral Neuroscience, 102*, 591–595.

Lee, V. E., Brooks-Gunn, J., & Schnur, E. (1988). Does Head Start work? A 1-year follow-up comparison of disadvantaged children attending Head Start, no preschool, and other preschool programs. *Developmental Psychology, 24*, 210–222.

Leibowitz, H. W., & Pick, H. A., Jr. (1972). Cross-cultural and educational aspects of the Ponzo perspective illusion. *Perception and Psychophysics, 12*, 430–432.

Leikin, L., Firestone, P., & McGrath, P. (1988). Physical symptom reporting in Type A and Type B children. *Journal of Consulting and Clinical Psychology, 56*, 721–726.

Leitenberg, H., Rosen, J. C., Gross, J., Nudelman, S., & Vara, L. S. (1988). Exposure plus response-prevention treatment of bulimia nervosa. *Journal of Consulting and Clinical Psychology, 56*, 535–541.

Lenneborg, E. H., Rebelsky, F. G., & Nichols, I. A. (1965). The vocalizations of infants born to deaf and hearing parents. *Human Development, 8*, 23–27.

Leonard, J. (1970, May 8). Ghetto for blue-eyes in the classroom. *Life*, p. 16.

Lepper, M. R., Greene, D., & Nisbett, R. E. (1973). Undermining children's intrinsic interest with extrinsic reward: A test of the "overjustification" hypothesis. *Journal of Personality and Social Psychology, 28*, 129–137.

Lettvin, J. Y., Maturana, H. R., McCulloch, W. S., & Pitts, W. H. (1959). What the frog's eye tells the frog brain. *Proceedings of the Institute of Radio Engineering, 47*, 1940–1951.

Levander, S., & Sachs, C. (1985). Vigilance performance and autonomic function in narcolepsy: Effects of central stimulants. *Psychophysiology, 22*, 24–31.

Leventhal, H., & Cleary, P. D. (1980). The smoking problem: A review of the research and theory in behavioral risk modification. *Psychological Bulletin, 88*, 370–405.

Leventhal, H., & Tomarken, A. J. (1986). Emotion: Today's problems. *Annual Review of Psychology, 37*, 565–610.

Levine, J. D., Clark, R., Devor, M., Helms, C., Moskowitz, M. A., & Basbaum, A. I. (1984). Interneuronal substance P contributes to the severity of experimental arthritis. *Science, 226*, 547–549.

Levine, J. S., & MacNichol, E. F., Jr. (1982, February). Color vision in fishes. *Scientific American*, pp. 140–149.

Levine, M. (1976). The academic achievement test: Its historical context and social functions. *American Psychologist, 31*, 228–238.

LeVine, W. R., & Irvine, J. J. (1984). In vivo EMG biofeedback in violin and viola pedagogy. *Biofeedback and Self-Regulation, 9*, 161–168.

Levinson, S. E., & Liberman, M. Y. (1981, April). Speech recognition by computer. *Scientific American*, pp. 64–76.

Levinthal, C. F. (1988). *Messengers of paradise*. New York: Anchor Press.

Levitt, M. J., Weber, R. A., & Clark, M. C. (1986). Social network relationships as sources of maternal support and well-being. *Developmental Psychology, 22*, 310–316.

Levitz-Jones, E. M., & Orlofsky, J. L. (1985). Separation-individuation and intimacy capacity in college women. *Journal of Personality and Social Psychology, 49*, 156–169.

Levy, J. (1983). Language, cognition, and the right hemisphere: A response to Gazzaniga. *American Psychologist, 38*, 538–541.

Levy, J. (1985, May). Right brain, left brain: Fact and fiction. *Psychology Today*, pp. 38–39.

Lewicki, P. (1985). Nonconscious biasing effects of single instances on subsequent judgments. *Journal of Personality and Social Psychology, 48*, 563–574.

Lewin, R. (1984). Trail of ironies to Parkinson's disease. *Science, 224*, 1083–1085.

Lewin, R. (1986). How unusual are unusual events? *Science, 233*, 1385.

Lewin, R. (1988). Cloud over Parkinson's therapy. *Science, 240*, 390–392.

Lewis, D. (1899/1983). The gynecologic consideration of the sexual act. *Journal of the American Medical Association, 250*, 222–227.

Libo, L. M., & Arnold, G. E. (1983). Relaxation practice after biofeedback therapy: A long-term follow-up study of utilization and effectiveness. *Biofeedback and Self-Regulation, 8*, 217–227.

Lieberman, D. A. (1979). Behaviorism and the mind: A (limited) call for a return to introspection. *American Psychologist, 34,* 319–333.

Liebert, R. M., & Baron, R. A. (1972). Some immediate effects of television violence on children's behavior. *Developmental Psychology, 6,* 469–475.

Liegois, M. J. (1899). The relation of hypnotism to crime. *Suggestive Therapeutics, 6,* 18–21.

Liem, R., & Rayman, P. (1982). Health and social costs of unemployment: Research and policy considerations. *American Psychologist, 37,* 1116–1123.

Linn, L., & Spitzer, R. L. (1982). DSM-III: Implications for liaison psychiatry and psychosomatic medicine. *Journal of the American Medical Association, 247,* 3207–3209.

Linn, R. L. (1982). Admissions testing on trial. *American Psychologist, 37,* 279–291.

Liuzzi, F. J., & Lasek, R. J. (1987). Astrocytes block axonal regeneration in mammals by activating the physiological stop pathway. *Science, 237,* 642–645.

Livingstone, M., & Hubel, D. (1988). Segregation of form, color, movement, and depth: Anatomy, physiology, and perception. *Science, 240,* 740–749.

Lloyd, J., & Barenblatt, L. (1984). Intrinsic intellectuality: Its relations to social class, intelligence, and achievement. *Journal of Personality and Social Psychology, 46,* 646–654.

Locke, E. A., & Latham, G. P. (1985). The application of goal setting to sports. *Journal of Sport Psychology, 7,* 205–222.

Locke, J. (1690/1956). *An essay concerning human understanding.* New York: Oxford University Press.

Loeb, G. E. (1985, February). The functional replacement of the ear. *Scientific American,* pp. 104–111.

Loeber, R., & Dishion, T. (1983). Early predictors of male delinquency: A review. *Psychological Bulletin, 94,* 68–99.

Loftus, E., & Hoffman, H. G. (1989). Misinformation and memory: The creation of new memories. *Journal of Experimental Psychology: General, 118,* 100–104.

Loftus, E. F., & Burns, T. E. (1982). Mental shock can produce retrograde amnesia. *Memory and Learning, 10,* 318–323.

Loftus, E. F., & Palmer, J. C. (1974). Reconstruction of automobile destruction: An example of the interaction between language and memory. *Journal of Verbal Learning and Verbal Behavior, 13,* 585–589.

Loomis, M., & Saltz, E. (1984). Cognitive styles as predictors of artistic styles. *Journal of Personality, 52,* 22–35.

LoPiccolo, J., & Stock, W. E. (1986). Treatment of sexual dysfunction. *Journal of Consulting and Clinical Psychology, 54,* 158–167.

Lord, C. G. (1982). Predicting behavioral consistency from an individual's perception of situational similarities. *Journal of Personality and Social Psychology, 42,* 1076–1088.

Lorenz, K. Z. (1966). *On aggression.* New York: Harcourt Brace Jovanovich.

Loring, D. W., & Sheer, D. E. (1984). Laterality of 40 Hz EEG and EMG during cognitive performance. *Psychophysiology, 21,* 34–38.

Lovass, O. I. (1987). Behavioral treatment and normal educational and intellectual functioning in young autistic children. *Journal of Consulting and Clinical Psychology, 55,* 3–9.

Lubin, B., Larsen, R. M., Matarazzo, J. D., & Seever, M. (1985). Psychological test usage patterns in five professional settings. *American Psychologist, 40,* 857–861.

Luborsky, L., Chandler, M., Auerbach, A. H., Cohen, J., & Bachrach, H. M. (1971). Factors influencing the outcome of psychotherapy: A review of quantitative research. *Psychological Bulletin, 75,* 145–185.

Luchins, A. (1946). Classroom experiments on mental sets. *American Journal of Psychology, 59,* 295–298.

Lunneborg, P. W. (1978). *Why study psychology?* Monterey, CA: Brooks/Cole.

Lykken, D. T. (1974). Psychology and the lie detector industry. *American Psychologist, 29,* 725–739.

Lykken, D. T. (1981). *A tremor in the blood: Uses and abuses of the lie detector.* New York: McGraw-Hill.

Lynn, R. (1982). IQ in Japan and the United States shows a growing disparity. *Nature, 297,* 222–223.

Lynn, S. J., & Rhue, J. W. (1988). Fantasy proneness: Hypnosis, developmental antecedents, and psychopathology. *American Psychologist, 43,* 35–44.

Maccoby, E. E., & Jacklin, C. N. (1974). *The psychology of sex differences.* Stanford, CA: Stanford University Press.

MacCracken, M. J., & Stadulis, R. E. (1985). Social facilitation of young children's dynamic balance performance. *Journal of Sport Psychology, 7,* 150–165.

Mack, A., Heuer, F., Villardi, K., & Chambers, D. (1985). The dissociation of position and extent in Müller-Lyer figures. *Perception and Psychophysics, 37,* 335–344.

Mack, S. (1981). Novel help for the handicapped. *Science, 212,* 26–27.

Mackenzie, B. (1984). Explaining race differences in IQ: The logic, the methodology, and the evidence. *American Psychologist, 39,* 1214–1233.

MacLeod, C. M. (1988). Forgotten but not gone: Savings for pictures and words in long-term memory. *Journal of Experimental Psychology: Learning, Memory, and Cognition, 14,* 195–212.

MacTurk, R. H., McCarthy, M. E., Vietze, P. M., & Yarrow, L. J. (1987). Sequential analysis of mastery behavior in 6- and 12-month-old infants. *Developmental Psychology, 23,* 199–203.

Madrazo, I., Drucker-Colin, R., Diaz, V., Martinez-Mata, J., Torres, C., & Becerril, J. J. (1987). Open microsurgical autograft of adrenal medulla to the right caudate nucleus in two patients with intractable Parkinson's disease. *New England Journal of Medicine, 316,* 831–834.

Maier, N. R. (1931). Reasoning in humans. *Journal of Comparative Psychology, 12,* 181–194.

Main, M., & George, C. (1985). Responses of abused and disadvantaged toddlers to distress in agemates: A study in the day care setting. *Developmental Psychology, 21,* 407–412.

Malamuth, N. M. (1986). Predictors of naturalistic sexual aggression. *Journal of Personality and Social Psychology, 50,* 953–962.

Malamuth, N. M., Heim, M., & Feshbach, S. (1980). Sexual responsiveness of college students to rape depictions: Inhibitory and disinhibitory effects. *Journal of Personality and Social Psychology, 38,* 399–408.

Malinowski, C. I., & Smith, C. P. (1985). Moral reasoning and moral conduct: An investigation prompted by Kohlberg's theory. *Journal of Personality and Social Psychology, 49,* 1016–1027.

Manicas, P. T., & Secord, P. F. (1983). Implications for psychology of the new philosophy of science. *American Psychologist, 38,* 399–413.

Maranto, G. (1984, December). Aging: Can we slow the inevitable? *Discover,* pp. 17–21.

Marquis, K. S., & Detweiler, R. A. (1985). Does adopted mean different? An attributional analysis. *Journal of Personality and Social Psychology, 48,* 1054–1066.

Marshall, G. D., & Zimbardo, P. G. (1979). Affective consequences of inadequately explained physiological arousal. *Journal of Personality and Social Psychology, 37,* 970–988.

Martin, J. E., & Dubbert, P. M. (1985). Exercise in hypertension. *Annals of Behavioral Medicine, 7* (1), pp. 13–18.

Martin, R. A., & Lefcourt, H. M. (1984). Situational Humor Response Questionnaire: Quantitative measure of sense of humor. *Journal of Personality and Social Psychology, 47,* 145–155.

Marx, J. L. (1980). Ape-language controversy flares up. *Science, 207,* 1330–1332.

Marx, M. H., & Hillix, W. A. (1979). *Systems and theories in psychology.* New York: McGraw-Hill.

Maslow, A. H. (1970). *Motivation and personality.* New York: Harper & Row.

Masserano, J. M., Takimoto, G. S., & Weiner, N. (1981). Electroconvulsive shock increases tyrosine hydroxylase activity via the brain and adrenal gland of the rat. *Science, 214,* 662–665.

Masters, W. H., & Johnson, V. E. (1966). *Human sexual response.* Boston: Little, Brown.

Masters, W. H., & Johnson, V. E. (1970). *Human sexual inadequacy.* Boston: Little, Brown.

Matheny, A. P., Jr., Riese, M. L., & Wilson, R. S. (1985). Rudiments of infant temperament: Newborn to 9 months. *Developmental Psychology, 21,* 486–494.

Matson, J. L., DiLorenzo, T. M., & Esveldt-Dawson, K. (1981). Independence training as a method of enhancing self-help skills acquisition of the mentally retarded. *Behaviour Research and Therapy, 19,* 399–405.

Matsumoto, D. (1987). The role of facial response in the experience of emotion: More methodological problems and a meta-analysis. *Journal of Personality and Social Psychology, 52,* 769–774.

Matthews, K. A., & Woodall, K. L. (1988). Childhood origins of overt Type A behaviors and cardiovascular reactivity to behavioral stressors. *Annals of Behavioral Medicine, 10,* 71–77.

Matthews, T., Harper, C. J., Fuller, T., Nater, T., & Lubenow, C. G. (1978, December 4). The cult of death. *Newsweek,* pp. 38–53.

Maugh, T. (1982). Sleep-promoting factor isolated. *Science, 216,* 1400.

Maugh, T. (1982). The scent makes sense. *Science, 215,* 1224.

Mauskopf, S., & McVaugh, M. (1981). Joseph Banks Rhine (1895–1980). *American Psychologist, 36,* 310–311.

May, R. (1982, Summer). The problem of evil: An open letter to Carl Rogers. *Journal of Humanistic Psychology,* pp. 10–21.

McAuley, E. (1985). Success and causality in sport: The influence of perception. *Journal of Sport Psychology, 7,* 13–22.

McCall, R. B. (1988). Science and the press: Like oil and water. *American Psychologist, 43,* 87–94.

McCann, B. S., & Matthews, K. A. (1988). Influences of potential for hostility, Type A behavior, and parental history of hypertension on adolescents' cardiovascular responses during stress. *Psychophysiology, 25,* 503–511.

McCanne, T. R., & Anderson, J. A. (1987). Emotional responding following experimental manipulation of facial electromyographic activity. *Journal of Personality and Social Psychology, 52,* 759–768.

McCarthy, T. (1981). Freud and the problem of sexuality. *Journal of the History of the Behavioral Sciences, 17,* 332–339.

McCaul, K. D., & Malott, J. M. (1984). Distraction and coping with pain. *Psychological Bulletin, 95,* 516–533.

McCauley, C., Woods, K., Coolidge, C., & Kulick, W. (1983). More aggressive cartoons are funnier. *Journal of Personality and Social Psychology, 44,* 817–823.

McClelland, D. C. (1978). Managing motivation to expand human freedom. *American Psychologist, 33,* 201–210.

McClelland, D. C. (1985). How motives, skills, and values determine what people do. *American Psychologist, 40,* 812–825.

McCloskey, M., & Egeth, H. E. (1983). Eyewitness identification: What can a psychologist tell a jury? *American Psychologist, 38,* 550–563.

McCloskey, M., Wible, C. G., & Cohen, N. J. (1988). Is there a special flashbulb-memory mechanism? *Journal of Experimental Psychology: General, 117,* 171–181.

McConnell, J. V., Cutter, R. L., & NcNeil, E. B. (1958). Subliminal stimulation: An overview. *American Psychologist, 13,* 229–242.

McConnell, J. V., Jacobson, A. L., & Kimble, D. P. (1959). The effects of regeneration upon retention of a conditioned response in the planarian. *Journal of Comparative and Physiological Psychology, 52,* 1–5.

McCormick, D. A., & Thompson, R. F. (1984). Cerebellum: Essential involvement in the classically conditioned eyelid response. *Science, 223,* 296–299.

McCoy, R. W. (1985). Phrenology and popular gullibility. *Skeptical Inquirer, 9,* 261–268.

McCurdy, H. E. (1981, April). Crowding and behavior in the White House. *Psychology Today,* pp. 21–25.

McDougall, W. (1908). *Social psychology.* New York: G. Putnam & Sons.

McFadden, D., & Wightman, F. L. (1983). Audition: Some relations between normal and pathological hearing. *Annual Review of Psychology, 34,* 94–128.

McGrady, A., Woerner, M., Bernal, G. A. A., & Higgins, J. T., Jr. (1987). Effect of biofeedback-assisted relaxation on blood pressure and cortisol levels in normotensives and hypertensives. *Journal of Behavioral Medicine, 10,* 301–310.

McGuigan, F. J. (1970). Covert oral behavior during the silent performance of language tasks. *Psychological Bulletin, 74,* 309–326.

McGuire, W. (Ed.). (1974). *The Freud/Jung letters.* Princeton, NJ: Princeton University Press.

McKeachie, W. J. (1952). Teaching psychology on television. *American Psychologist, 7,* 503–506.

McKinney, F., & Hillix, W. A. (1956). A personal adjustment television program. *American Psychologist, 11,* 672–676.

McMinn, M. R. (1984). Mechanisms of energy balance in obesity. *Behavioral Neuroscience, 98,* 375–393.

McNally, R. J. (1987). Preparedness and phobias: A review. *Psychological Bulletin, 101,* 283–303.

McNeal, E. T., & Cimbolic, P. (1986). Antidepressants and biochemical theories of depression. *Psychological Bulletin, 99,* 361–374.

McReynolds, P. (1989). Diagnosis and clinical assessment: Current status and major issues. *Annual Review of Psychology, 40,* 83–108.

Mednick, S. A. (1962). The associative basis of the creative process. *Psychological Review, 69,* 220–232.

Mednick, S. A., Gabrielli, W. F., & Hutchings, B. (1984). Genetic influences in criminal convictions: Evidence from an adoption cohort. *Science, 224,* 891–894.

Meehl, P. E. (1956). Wanted—A good cookbook. *American Psychologist, 11,* 263–272.

Meeker, W. B., & Barber, T. X. (1971). Toward an explanation of stage hypnosis. *Journal of Abnormal Psychology, 77,* 61–70.

Meichenbaum, D. (1985). *Stress-inoculation training.* New York: Pergamon Press.

Melanoma risk and socio-economic class. (1983). *Science News, 124,* 232.

Melzack, R., & Wall, P. D. (1965). Pain mechanisms: A new theory. *Science, 150,* 971–979.

Memory transfer. (1966). *Science, 153,* 658–659.

Meredith, M. A., & Stein, B. E. (1985). Descending efferents from the superior colliculus relay integrated multisensory information. *Science, 227,* 657–659.

Mervis, J. (1984, March). Council ends forums trial, opens way for new divisions. *APA Monitor,* pp. 10–11.

Mervis, J. (1986, July). NIMH data point way to effective treatment. *APA Monitor,* pp. 1, 13.

Metcalfe, J., & Wiebe, D. (1987). Intuition in insight and noninsight problem solving. *Memory and Cognition, 15,* 238–246.

Meyer, D. R., Gurklis, J. A., & Cloud, M. D. (1985). An equipotential function of the cerebral cortex. *Physiological Psychology, 13,* 48–50.

Michaels, R. R., Huber, M. J., & McCann, D. S. (1976). Evaluation of transcendental meditation as a method of reducing stress. *Science, 192,* 1242–1244.

Miczek, K. A., Thompson, M. L., & Shuster, L. (1982). Opioid-like analgesia in defeated mice. *Science, 215,* 1520–1523.

Milgram, S. (1963). Behavioral study of obedience. *Journal of Abnormal and Social Psychology, 67,* 371–378.

Milgram, S. (1964). Issues in the study of obedience: A reply to Baumrind. *American Psychologist, 19,* 848–852.

Milgram, S. (1970). The experience of living in cities. *Science, 167,* 1461–1468.

Milgram, S. (1974). *Obedience to authority.* New York: Harper & Row.

Miller, G. A. (1956). The magical number seven, plus or minus two: Some limits on our capacity for processing information. *Psychological Review, 63,* 81–97.

Miller, J. (1983). Three constructions of transference in Freud, 1895–1915. *Journal of the History of the Behavioral Sciences, 19,* 153–172.

Miller, J. A. (1984). Sexual ambiguity: Getting down to the gene. *Science News, 125,* 230.

Miller, L. L., & Branconnier, R. J. (1983). Cannabis: Effects on memory and the cholinergic limbic system. *Psychological Bulletin, 93,* 441–456.

Miller, M. G. (1984). Oral somatosensory factors in dietary self-selection in rats. *Behavioral Neuroscience, 98,* 416–423.

Miller, N. E. (1985). The value of behavioral research on animals. *American Psychologist, 40,* 423–440.

Miller, N. E., & Coile, D. C. (1984). How radical animal activists try to mislead humane people. *American Psychologist, 39,* 700–701.

Miller, P. C., Lefcourt, H. M., Holmes, J. G., Ware, E. E., & Saleh, W. E. (1986). Marital locus of control and marital problem solving. *Journal of Personality and Social Psychology, 51,* 161–169.

Miller, R. J., Pigion, R. G., & Martin, K. D. (1985). The effects of ingested alcohol on accommodation. *Perception and Psychophysics, 37,* 407–414.

Miller-Jones, D. (1989). Culture and testing. *American Psychologist, 44,* 360–366.

Minuchin, S. (1974). *Families and family therapy.* Cambridge, MA: Harvard University Press.

Mirsky, A. F., & Duncan, C. C. (1986). Etiology and expression of schizophrenia: Neurobiological and psychosocial factors. *Annual Review of Psychology, 37,* 291–319.

Mischel, W. (1968). *Personality and assessment.* New York: Wiley.

Mischel, W., & Peake, P. J. (1982). Beyond déjà vu in the search for cross-situational consistency. *Psychological Review, 89,* 730–755.

Mita, T. H., Dermer, M., & Knight, J. (1977). Reversed facial images and the mere-exposure hypothesis. *Journal of Personality and Social Psychology, 35,* 597–601.

Mitchell, J. E., & Eckert, E. D. (1987). Scope and significance of eating disorders. *Journal of Consulting and Clinical Psychology, 55,* 628–634.

Mollon, J. D. (1982). Color vision. *Annual Review of Psychology, 33,* 41–85.

Money, J. (1986). *Venuses penuses: Sexology, sexosophy, and exigency theory.* Buffalo, NY: Prometheus.

Money, J. (1987). Sin, sickness, or status? Homosexual gender identity and psychoneuroendocrinology. *American Psychologist, 42,* 384–399.

Monroe, S. M. (1982). Life events and disorder: Event-symptom associations and the course of disorder. *Journal of Abnormal Psychology, 91,* 14–24.

Monson, T. C., Hesley, J. W., & Chernick, L. (1982). Specifying when personality traits can and cannot predict behavior: An alternative to abandoning the attempt to predict single-act criteria. *Journal of Personality and Social Psychology, 43,* 385–399.

Montag, I., & Comrey, A. L. (1987). Internality and externality as correlates of involvement in fatal driving accidents. *Journal of Applied Psychology, 72,* 339–343.

Monte, C. F. (1980). *Beneath the mask: An introduction to theories of personality.* New York: Holt, Rinehart & Winston.

Monti, P. M., Curran, J. P., Corriveau, D. P., DeLancey, A. L., & Hagerman, S. M. (1980). Effects of social skills training groups and sensitivity training groups with psychiatric patients. *Journal of Consulting and Clinical Psychology, 48,* 241–248.

Montour, K. (1977). William James Sidis: The broken twig. *American Psychologist, 32,* 265–279.

Morawski, J. G. (1982). Assessing psychology's moral heritage through our neglected utopias. *American Psychologist, 37,* 1082–1095.

Moray, N. (1959). Attention in dichotic listening: Affective cues and the influence of instructions. *Quarterly Journal of Experimental Psychology, 11,* 56–60.

Moreland, R. L., & Zajonc, R. B. (1982). Exposure effects in person perception: Familiarity, similarity, and attraction. *Journal of Experimental Social Psychology, 18,* 395–415.

Morgan, C., & Murray, H. A. (1935). A method of investigating fantasies. *Archives of Neurology and Psychiatry, 4,* 310–329.

Morley, J. E., & Levine, A. S. (1980). Stress-induced eating is mediated through endogenous opiates. *Science, 209,* 1259–1261.

Morris, S. (1980, April). Interview: James Randi. *Omni,* pp. 76–78, 104, 106, 108.

Morris, W., & Morris, M. (1985). *Harper dictionary of contemporary usage.* New York: Harper & Row.

Morrison, A. R. (1983, April). A window on the sleeping brain. *Scientific American,* pp. 94–102.

Moruzzi, G., & Magoun, H. W. (1949). Brain stem reticular formation and activation of the EEG. *Electroencephalography and Clinical Neurophysiology, 1,* 455–473.

Moskowitz, D. S. (1982). Coherence and cross-situational generality in personality: A new analysis of old problems. *Journal of Personality and Social Psychology, 43,* 754–768.

Moskowitz, D. S., & Schwarz, J. C. (1982). Validity comparison of behavior counts and ratings by knowledgeable informants. *Journal of Personality and Social Psychology, 42,* 518–528.

Moss, G. R., & Rick, G. R. (1981). Application of a token economy for adolescents in a private psychiatric hospital. *Behavior Therapy, 12,* 585–590.

Mowrer, O. H. (1947). On the dual nature of learning—A reinterpretation of "conditioning" and "problem solving." *Harvard Educational Review, 17,* 102–148.

Mueller, C., & Rudolph, M. (1966). *Light and vision.* New York: Time.

Mueller, C. G. (1979). Some origins of psychology as a science. *Annual Review of Psychology, 30,* 9–29.

Mullen, B., Futrell, D., Stairs, D., Tice, D. M., Baumeister, R. F., Dawson, K. E., Radloff, C. E., Goethals, G. R., Kennedy, J. G., & Rosenfeld, P. (1986). Newscasters' facial expressions and voting behavior of viewers: Can a smile elect a president? *Journal of Personality and Social Psychology, 51,* 291–295.

Mumford, M. D., & Gustafson, S. B. (1988). Creativity syndrome: Integration, application, and innovation. *Psychological Bulletin, 103,* 27–43.

Munsterberg, H. (1908). *On the witness stand.* New York: Doubleday.

Murphy, G. L., & Medin, D. L. (1985). The role of theories in conceptual coherence. *Psychological Review, 92,* 289–316.

Murray, H. A. (1938). *Explorations in personality.* New York: Oxford University Press.

Murstein, B. (1972). Physical attractiveness and marital choice. *Journal of Personality and Social Psychology, 22,* 8–12.

Mustillo, P. (1985). Binocular mechanisms mediating crossed and uncrossed stereopsis. *Psychological Bulletin, 97,* 187–201.

Myers, D. G., & Bishop, G. D. (1970). Discussion effects on racial attitudes. *Science, 169,* 778–779.

Myerscough, R., & Taylor, S. (1985). The effects of marijuana on human physical aggression. *Journal of Personality and Social Psychology, 49,* 1541–1546.

Nahai, F., & Brown, D. M. (1983). Further applications of electromyographic muscle reeducation. In J. V. Basmajian (Ed.), *Biofeedback: Principles and practice for clinicians* (pp. 107–110). Baltimore: Williams & Wilkins.

NAS calls tests fair but limited. (1982, April). *APA Monitor,* p. 2.

Nash, M. (1987). What, if anything, is regressed about hypnotic age regression? A review of the empirical literature. *Psychological Bulletin, 102,* 42–52.

Navon, D. (1974). Forest before trees: The precedence of global features in visual perception. *Cognitive Psychology, 9,* 353–383.

Neisser, U. (1968, September). The processes of vision. *Scientific American,* pp. 204–214.

Neisser, U. (1981). John Dean's memory: A case study. *Cognition, 9,* 1–22.

Neisser, U. (1984). Interpreting Harry Bahrick's discovery: What confers immunity against forgetting? *Journal of Experimental Psychology: General, 113,* 32–35.

Neisser, U., & Becklen, R. (1975). Selective looking: Attending to visually specified events. *Cognitive Psychology, 7,* 480–494.

Nelson, K. E. (1977). Facilitating children's syntax acquisition. *Developmental Psychology, 13,* 101–107.

Nelson, T. O., Leonesio, R. J., Shimamura, A. P., Landwehr, R. F., & Narens, L. (1982). Overlearning and the feeling of knowing. *Journal of Experimental Psychology: Learning, Memory, and Cognition, 8,* 279–288.

Nemeth, C. J. (1986). Differential contributions of majority and minority influence. *Psychological Review, 93,* 23–32.

Nestoros, J. N. (1980). Ethanol specificity potentiates GABA-mediated neurotransmission in feline cerebral cortex. *Science, 209,* 708–710.

Nevo, O. (1985). Does one ever really laugh at one's own expense? *Journal of Personality and Social Psychology, 49,* 799–807.

Newcomb, M. D., & Bentler, P. M. (1989). Substance use and abuse among children and teenagers. *American Psychologist, 44,* 242–248.

Newcomb, M. D., & Harlow, L. L. (1986). Life events and substance use among adolescents: Mediating effects of perceived loss of control and meaningfulness in life. *Journal of Personality and Social Psychology, 51,* 564–577.

Newcomb, T. M. (1943). *Personality and social change.* New York: Dryden Press.

Newcomb, T. M., Koening, K., Flacks, R., & Warwick, D. (1967). *Persistence and change: Bennington College and its students after 25 years.* New York: Wiley.

Newell, A., & Simon, H. (1972). *Human problem solving.* Englewood Cliffs, NJ: Prentice-Hall.

Newman, E. A., & Hartline, P. H. (1982, March). The infrared "vision" of snakes. *Scientific American,* pp. 116–124, 127.

Nezu, A. M., Nezu, C. M., & Blissett, S. E. (1988). Sense of humor as a moderator of the relation between stressful events and psychological distress: A prospective analysis. *Journal of Personality and Social Psychology, 54,* 520–525.

Nicholls, J. G. (1972). Creativity in the person who will never produce anything original or useful: The concept of creativity as a normally distributed trait. *American Psychologist, 27,* 717–727.

Nicholls, J. G. (1984). Achievement motivation: Conceptions of ability, subjective experience, task choice, and performance. *Psychological Review, 91,* 328–346.

Nickerson, R. S., & Adams, M. J. (1979). Long-term memory for a common object. *Cognitive Psychology, 11,* 287–307.

Nicol, S. E., & Gottesman, I. I. (1983). Clues to the genetics and neurobiology of schizophrenia. *American Scientist, 71,* 398–404.

Nicoll, R. A., & Madison, D. V. (1982). General anesthetics hyperpolarize neurons in the vertebrate nervous system. *Science, 217,* 1055–1057.

Nisbett, R. E., Caputo, C. C., Legant, P., & Marecek, J. (1973). Behavior as seen by the actor and by the observer. *Journal of Personality and Social Psychology, 27,* 154–164.

Nolen-Hoeksema, S. (1987). Sex differences in unipolar depression: Evidence and theory. *Psychological Bulletin, 101,* 259–282.

Nonneman, A. J., & Corwin, J. V. (1981). Differential effects of prefrontal cortex ablation in neonatal, juvenile, and young adult rats. *Journal of Comparative and Physiological Psychology, 95,* 588–602.

Notz, W. W. (1975). Work motivation and the negative effects of extrinsic rewards: A review with implications for theory and practice. *American Psychologist, 30,* 884–891.

Nowack, K. M. (1986). Type A, hardiness, and psychological distress. *Journal of Behavioral Medicine, 9,* 537–548.

O'Connor, K. P. (1981). The intentional paradigm and cognitive psychophysiology. *Psychophysiology, 18,* 121–128.

Oden, G. C. (1984). Dependence, independence, and emergence of word features. *Journal of Experimental Psychology: Human Perception and Performance, 10,* 394–405.

Ogilvie, D. M. (1987). The undesired self: A neglected variable in personality research. *Journal of Personality and Social Psychology, 52,* 379–385.

Ogilvie, R. D., McDonagh, D. M., Stone, S. N., & Wilkinson, R. T. (1988). Eye movements and the detection of sleep onset. *Psychophysiology, 25,* 81–91.

Okwumabua, T. M. (1985). Psychological and physical contributions to marathon performance: An exploratory investigation. *Journal of Sport Behavior, 8,* 163–171.

Oldham, G. R. (1988). Effects of changes in workspace partitions and spatial density on employee reactions: A quasi-experiment. *Journal of Applied Psychology, 73,* 253–258.

Olds, J. (1956, October). Pleasure centers in the brain. *Scientific American,* pp. 105–116.

Olds, J., & Milner, P. (1954). Positive reinforcement produced by electrical stimulations of septal area and other regions of rat brain. *Journal of Comparative and Physiological Psychology, 47,* 419–427.

Olmo, R. J., & Stevens, G. L. (1984, August). Chess champs: Introverts at play. *Psychology Today,* pp. 72, 74.

Olson, J. M. (1988). Misattribution, preparatory information, and speech anxiety. *Journal of Personality and Social Psychology, 54,* 758–767.

Olson, R. P., Ganley, R., Devine, V. T., & Dorsey, G. C., Jr. (1981). Long-term effects of behavioral versus insight-oriented therapy with inpatient alcoholics. *Journal of Consulting and Clinical Psychology, 49,* 866–877.

Orne, M. T. (1951). The mechanisms of hypnotic age regression: An experimental study. *Journal of Abnormal and Social Psychology, 46,* 213–225.

Orne, M. T., & Evans, F. J. (1965). Social control in the psychological experiment: Antisocial behavior and hypnosis. *Journal of Personality and Social Psychology, 1,* 189–200.

Orwell, G. (1949). *1984.* New York: Harcourt Brace Jovanovich.

Overweight: It's a matter of culture. (1986, March 16). *The Philadelphia Inquirer,* p. 3-A.

Pacht, A. R. (1984). Reflections on perfection. *American Psychologist, 39,* 386–390.

Paivio, A., & te Linde, J. (1982). Imagery, memory, and the brain. *Canadian Journal of Psychology, 36,* 243–272.

Parker, D. E. (1980, November). The vestibular apparatus. *Scientific American,* pp. 118–121, 125–130, 132, 134–135.

Parker, J. G., & Asher, S. R. (1987). Peer relations and later personal adjustment. *Psychological Bulletin, 102,* 357–389.

Parker, K. C. H., Hanson, R. K., & Hunsley, J. (1988). MMPI, Rorschach, and WAIS: A meta-analytic comparison of reliability, stability, and validity. *Psychological Bulletin, 103,* 367–373.

Parker, R. C. T. (1987). Dreams in ancient Greece. In R. L. Gregory (Ed.), *The Oxford companion to the mind* (pp. 203–204). New York: Oxford University Press.

Patterson, D. (1987, August). The causes of Down syndrome. *Scientific American,* pp. 52–60.

Patton, J. E., Routh, D. K., & Stinard, T. A. (1986). Where do children study? Behavioral observations. *Bulletin of the Psychonomic Society, 24,* 439–440.

Paul, S. M., Hulihan-Giblin, B., & Skolnick, P. (1982). (+)-amphetamine binding to rat hypothalamus: Relation to anorexic potency of phenylethylamines. *Science, 218,* 487–490.

Pavlov, I. P. (1928). *Lectures on conditioned reflexes.* New York: Liveright.

Penfield, W. (1975). *The mystery of the mind.* Princeton, NJ: Princeton University Press.

Pennebaker, J. W., Kiecolt-Glaser, J. K., & Glaser, R. (1988). Disclosure of traumas and immune function: Health implications for psychotherapy. *Journal of Consulting and Clinical Psychology, 56,* 239–245.

Pennebaker, J. W., & Watson, D. (1988). Blood pressure estimation and beliefs among normotensives and hypertensives. *Health Psychology, 7,* 309–328.

Pepitone, A. (1981). Lessons from the history of social psychology. *American Psychologist, 36*, 972–985.

Perkins, K. A. (1985). The synergestic effect of smoking and serum cholesterol on coronary heart disease. *Health Psychology, 4*, 337–360.

Perlow, M. J., Freed, W. J., Hoffer, B. J., Seiger, A., Olson, L., & Wyatt, R. J. (1979). Brain grafts reduce motor abnormalities produced by destruction of nigrostriatal dopamine system. *Science, 204*, 643–647.

Perls, F. (1972). Interview with Frederick Perls. In A. Bry (Ed.), *Inside psychotherapy* (pp. 58–70). New York: Basic Books.

Perls, F. (1973). *The Gestalt approach and eyewitness to therapy.* Palo Alto, CA: Science and Behavior Books.

Perr, I. N. (1983). The insanity defense: A tale of two cities. *American Journal of Psychiatry, 140*, 873–874.

Perri, M. G., McAllister, D. A., Gange, J. J., Jordan, R. C., McAdoo, W. G., & Nezu, A. M. (1988). Effects of four maintenance programs on the long-term management of obesity. *Journal of Consulting and Clinical Psychology, 56*, 529–534.

Pervin, L. A. (1984). *Personality: Theory and research.* New York: Wiley.

Peters, L. H., Hartke, D. D., & Pohlmann, J. T. (1985). Fiedler's contingency theory of leadership: An application of the meta-analysis procedures of Schmidt and Hunter. *Psychological Bulletin, 97*, 274–285.

Petersik, J. T. (1989). The two-process distinction in apparent motion. *Psychological Bulletin, 106*, 107–127.

Petersen, A. C. (1988). Adolescent development. *Annual Review of Psychology, 39*, 583–607.

Peterson, C., & Barrett, L. C. (1987). Explanatory style and academic performance among university freshmen. *Journal of Personality and Social Psychology, 53*, 603–607.

Peterson, C., Seligman, M. E. P., & Vaillant, G. E. (1988). Pessimistic explanatory style is a risk factor for physical illness: A thirty-five-year longitudinal study. *Journal of Personality and Social Psychology, 55*, 23–27.

Peterson, I. (1983). Playing chess bit by bit. *Science News, 124*, 236–237.

Peterson, L. R., & Peterson, M. (1959). Short-term retention of individual verbal items. *Journal of Experimental Psychology, 58*, 193–198.

Pettigrew, T. F. (1959). Regional differences in anti-Negro prejudice. *Journal of Abnormal and Social Psychology, 59*, 28–36.

Petty, R. E., Cacioppo, J. T., & Goldman, R. (1981). Personal involvement as a determinant of argument-based persuasion. *Journal of Personality and Social Psychology, 41*, 847–855.

Phelps, M. E., & Mazziotta, J. C. (1985). Positron-emission tomography: Human brain function and biochemistry. *Science, 228*, 799–809.

Phillips, D. P., & Brugge, J. F. (1985). Progress in neurophysiology of sound localization. *Annual Review of Psychology, 36*, 245–274.

Piaget, J. (1932). *The moral judgment of the child.* New York: Harcourt, Brace & World.

Piaget, J. (1952). *The origins of intelligence in children.* New York: International Universities Press.

Piliavin, J. A., Callero, P. L., & Evans, E. E. (1982). Addiction to altruism: Opponent-process theory and habitual blood donation. *Journal of Personality and Social Psychology, 43*, 1200–1213.

Pincomb, G. A., Lovallo, W. R., Passey, R. B., Brackett, D. J., & Wilson, M. F. (1987). Caffeine enhances the physiological response to occupational stress in medical students. *Health Psychology, 6*, 101–112.

Pine, C. J. (1985). Anxiety and eating behavior in obese and nonobese American Indians and White Americans. *Journal of Personality and Social Psychology, 49*, 774–780.

Piner, K. E., & Kahle, L. R. (1984). Adapting to the stigmatizing label of mental illness: Foregone but not forgotten. *Journal of Personality and Social Psychology, 47*, 805–811.

Pines, M. (1981, September). The civilizing of Genie. *Psychology Today*, pp. 28–34.

Plass, J. A., & Hill, K. T. (1986). Children's achievement strategies and test performance: The role of time pressure, evaluation anxiety, and sex. *Developmental Psychology, 22*, 31–36.

Plomin, R., Loehlin, J. C., & Defries, J. C. (1985). Genetic and environmental components of "environmental" influences. *Developmental Psychology, 21*, 391–402.

Plotkin, W. B. (1979). The alpha experience revisited: Biofeedback in the transformation of psychological state. *Psychological Bulletin, 86*, 1132–1148.

Plutchik, R. (1980, February). A language for the emotions. *Psychology Today*, pp. 68–78.

Poincaré, H. (1948, August). Mathematical creation. *Scientific American*, pp. 14–17.

Pollak, S., & Gilligan, C. (1982). Images of violence in Thematic Apperception Test stories. *Journal of Personality and Social Psychology, 42*, 159–167.

Pomerleau, C. S., & Pomerleau, O. F. (1987). The effects of a psychological stressor on cigarette smoking and subsequent behavioral and physiological responses. *Psychophysiology, 24*, 278–285.

Port, R. L., Mikhail, A. A., Kline, M. A., & Patterson, M. M. (1985). Neural and endocrine effects on classical conditioning: A comparison of ACTH and hippocampectomy. *Physiological Psychology, 13*, 15–20.

Posner, M. I., Inhoff, A. W., Friedrich, F. J., & Cohen, A. (1987). Isolating attentional systems: A cognitive-anatomical analysis. *Psychobiology, 15*, 107–121.

Potter, M. C., Kroll, J. F., Yachzel, B., Carpenter, E., & Sherman, J. (1986). Pictures in sentences: Understanding without words. *Journal of Experimental Psychology: General, 115*, 281–294.

Prasinos, S., & Tittler, B. I. (1981). The family relationships of humor-oriented adolescents. *Journal of Personality, 47*, 295–305.

Pratt, K. J. (1962). Motivation and learning in medieval writings. *American Psychologist, 17*, 496–500.

Premack, D. (1971). Language in chimpanzee? *Science, 172*, 808–822.

Prentice-Dunn, S., & Rogers, R. W. (1982). Effects of public and private self-awareness on deindividuation and aggression. *Journal of Personality and Social Psychology, 3*, 503–513.

Pribram, K. H. (1985, September). "Holism" could close cognition era. *APA Monitor*, pp. 5–6.

Price-Williams, E., Gordon, W., & Ramirez, M. (1969). Skill and conservation: A study of pottery-making children. *Development Psychology, 1*, 769.

Prochaska, J. O. (1984). *Systems of psychotherapy: A transtheoretical approach.* Homewood, IL: Dorsey.

Program power. (1981, April). *Scientific American*, pp. 83–85.

Psychic abscam. (1983, March). *Discover,* pp. 10, 13.

A psychic Watergate. (1981, June). *Discover,* p. 8.

Rabun, M. (1978, April). Frightening sight greets Rangers in dressing room. *Altoona Mirror.*

Ragland, D. R., & Brand, R. J. (1988). Type A behavior and mortality from coronary heart disease. *New England Journal of Medicine, 318,* 65–69.

Raloff, J. (1982). Noise can be hazardous to your health. *Science News, 121,* 377–381.

Rambo, L. R. (1980). Ethics, evolution, and the psychology of William James. *Journal of the History of the Behavioral Sciences, 16,* 50–57.

Rapee, R., Mattick, R., & Murrell, E. (1986). Cognitive mediation in the affective compenent of spontaneous panic attacks. *Journal of Behavior Therapy and Experimental Psychiatry, 17,* 245–253.

Rapp, D. (1988). The reception of Freud by the British press: General interest and literary magazines, 1920–1925. *Journal of the History of the Behavioral Sciences, 24,* 191–201.

Raps, C. S., Peterson, C., Jonas, M., & Seligman, M. E. P. (1982). Patient behavior in hospitals: Helplessness, reactance, or both? *Journal of Personality and Social Psychology, 42,* 1036–1041.

Raskin, D. C., & Podlesny, J. A. (1979). Truth and deception: A reply to Lykken. *Psychological Bulletin, 86,* 54–59.

Raskin, V. (1985, October). Jokes. *Psychology Today,* pp. 34–39.

Ratner, H. H., Schell, D. A., Crimmins, A., Mittelman, D., & Baldinelli, L. (1987). Changes in adults' prose recall: Aging or cognitive demands? *Developmental Psychology, 23,* 521–525.

Ravelli, G. P., Stein, Z. A., & Susser, M. W. (1976). Obesity in young men after famine exposure in utero in early infancy. *New England Journal of Medicine, 295,* 349–353.

Ray, O. (1983). *Drugs, society, and human behavior.* St. Louis: Mosby.

Rayner, K., Slowiaczek, M. L., Clifton, C., Jr., & Bertera, J. H. (1983). Latency of sequential eye movements: Implications for reading. *Journal of Experimental Psychology: Human Perception and Performance, 9,* 912–922.

Read, P. P. (1974). *Alive: The story of the Andes survivors.* Philadelphia: Lippincott.

Redd, W. H., Jacobsen, P. B., Die-Trill, M., Dermatis, H., McEvoy, M., & Holland, J. C. (1987). Cognitive/attentional distraction in the control of conditioned nausea in pediatric cancer patients receiving chemotherapy. *Journal of Consulting and Clinical Psychology, 55,* 391–395.

Rees, L. (1983). The development of psychosomatic medicine during the past 25 years. *Journal of Psychosomatic Medicine, 27,* 157–164.

Reese, H. W., & Fremouw, W. J. (1984). Normal and normative ethics in behavioral sciences. *American Psychologist, 39,* 863–876.

Regan, D. (1982). Visual information channeling in normal and disordered vision. *Psychological Review, 89,* 407–444.

Reinisch, J. M. (1981). Prenatal exposure to synthetic progestins increases potential for aggression in humans. *Science, 211,* 1171–1173.

Reis, S. (1989). Reflections on policy affecting the education of gifted and talented students: Past and future perspectives. *American Psychologist, 44,* 399–408.

Reisenzein, R. (1983). The Schachter theory of emotion: Two decades later. *Psychological Bulletin, 94,* 239–264.

Reitman, J. S. (1974). Without surreptitious rehearsal, information in short-term memory decays. *Journal of Verbal Learning and Verbal Behavior, 13,* 365–377.

Relinger, H. (1984). Hypnotic hypermnesia: A critical review. *American Journal of Clinical Hypnosis, 26,* 212–225.

Rescorla, R. A. (1988). Pavlovian conditioning: It's not what you think it is. *American Psychologist, 43,* 151–160.

Resnick, S. M., Berenbaum, S. A., Gottesman, I. I., & Bouchard, T. J., Jr. (1986). Early hormonal influences on cognitive functioning in congenital adrenal hyperplasia. *Developmental Psychology, 22,* 191–198.

Restle, F. (1970). Moon illusion explained on the basis of relative size. *Science, 167,* 1092–1096.

Rheingold, H. L., & Adams, J. L. (1980). The significance of speech to newborns. *Developmental Psychology, 16,* 397–403.

Rice, M. L. (1989). Children's language acquisition. *American Psychologist, 44,* 149–156.

Rinn, W. E. (1984). The neuropsychology of facial expression: A review of the neurological and psychological mechanisms for producing facial expressions. *Psychological Bulletin, 95,* 52–77.

Riordan, C. A., & Tedeschi, J. T. (1983). Attraction in aversive environments: Some evidence for classical conditioning and negative reinforcement. *Journal of Personality and Social Psychology, 44,* 683–692.

Roberts, G. C., Kleiber, D. A., & Duda, J. L. (1981). An analysis of motivation in children's sport: The role of perceived competence in participation. *Journal of Sport Psychology, 3,* 206–216.

Roberts, M. C., & Fanurik, D. (1986). Rewarding elementary school children for their use of safety belts. *Health Psychology, 5,* 185–196.

Robins, L. N., Helzer, J. E., Weissman, M. M., Orvaschel, H., Gruenberg, E., Burke, J. D., Jr., & Regier, D. A. (1984). Lifetime prevalence of specific psychiatric disorders in three sites. *Archives of General Psychiatry, 41,* 949–958.

Robinson, D. (1982). Cerebral plurality and the unity of the self. *American Psychologist, 37,* 904–910.

Robinson, F. P. (1970). *Effective study.* New York: Harper & Row.

Robinson, P. (1981, March). Five models for dying. *Psychology Today,* pp. 85, 87, 90–91.

Rockwell, T. (1979). Pseudoscience or pseudocriticism? *Journal of Parapsychology, 43,* 221–231.

Rodgers, J. E. (1982, June). The malleable memory of eyewitnesses. *Science 82,* pp. 32–35.

Rodgers, J. L., & Rowe, D. C. (1988). Influence of siblings on adolescent sexual behavior. *Developmental Psychology, 24,* 722–728.

Rodin, J. (1981). Current status of the internal-external hypothesis for obesity: What went wrong? *American Psychologist, 36,* 361–372.

Rodin, J. (1985). Insulin levels, hunger, and food intake: An example of feedback loops in body weight regulation. *Health Psychology, 4,* 1–24.

Rodin, J. (1986). Aging and health: Effects of the sense of control. *Science, 233,* 1271–1276.

Rodman, H., Pratto, D. J., & Nelson, R. S. (1985). Child care arrangements and children's functioning: A comparison of self-care and adult-care children. *Developmental Psychology, 21,* 413–418.

Rogers, C. R. (1951). *Client-centered therapy.* Boston: Houghton Mifflin.

Rogers, C. R. (1961). *On becoming a person: A therapist's view of psychotherapy.* Boston: Houghton Mifflin.

Rogers, C. R. (1968). Interpersonal relationships. *Journal of Applied Behavioral Science, 4,* 1–12.

Rogers, C. R. (1980). *A way of being.* Boston: Houghton Mifflin.

Rogers, C. R. (1985). Toward a more human science of the person. *Journal of Humanistic Psychology, 25,* 7–24.

Rogers, R. C. (1985). The chemical senses. *Science, 229,* 374–375.

Rogers, R. W., & Mewborn, C. R. (1976). Fear appeals and attitude change: Effects of a threat's noxiousness, probability of occurrence, and the efficacy of coping responses. *Journal of Personality and Social Psychology, 34,* 54–61.

Rokeach, M. (1964). *The three Christs of Ypsilanti.* New York: Random House.

Rokeach, M., & Mezei, L. (1966). Race and shared belief as factors in social choice. *Science, 151,* 167–172.

Rollin, B. E. (1985). The moral status of research animals in psychology. *American Psychologist, 40,* 920–926.

Romani, G. L., Williamson, S. J., & Kaufman, L. (1982). Tonotopic organization of the human auditory cortex. *Science, 216,* 1339–1340.

Rorer, L. G., & Widiger, T. A. (1983). Personality structure and assessment. *Annual Review of Psychology, 34,* 431–463.

Rosch, E. (1975). Cognitive representations of semantic categories. *Journal of Experimental Psychology: General, 104,* 192–233.

Rose, J. E., & Fantino, E. (1978). Conditioned reinforcement and discrimination in second-order schedules. *Journal of Experimental Analysis of Behavior, 29,* 393–418.

Rosenbaum, M. E. (1986). The repulsion hypothesis: On the nondevelopment of relationships. *Journal of Personality and Social Psychology, 51,* 1156–1166.

Rosenhan, D. L. (1973). On being sane in insane places. *Science, 179,* 250–258.

Rosenman, R. H., Brand, R. J., Jenkins, D., Friedman, M., Straus, R., & Wurm, M. (1975). Coronary heart disease in the Western Collaborative Group Study: Final follow-up experience of 8 1/2 years. *Journal of the American Psychological Association, 233,* 872–877.

Rosenthal, R., & Fode, K. L. (1963). The effect of experimenter bias on the performance of the albino rat. *Behavioral Science, 8,* 183–189.

Rosenthal, R., & Jacobson, L. (1968). *Pygmalion in the classroom.* New York: Holt, Rinehart & Winston.

Rosenzweig, M. R. (1984). Experience, memory, and the brain. *American Psychologist, 39,* 365–376.

Ross, J. (1980). The use of former phobics in the treatment of phobias. *American Journal of Psychiatry, 137,* 715–717.

Rossi, F. (1988, November 8). Stress test. *The Philadelphia Inquirer,* pp. 1–E, 10–E.

Rotter, J. B. (1966). Generalized expectancies for internal versus external control of reinforcement. *Psychological Monographs, 80* (1, Whole No. 609).

Rotton, J., & Kelly, I. W. (1985). Much ado about the full moon: A meta-analysis of lunar-lunacy research. *Psychological Bulletin, 97,* 286–306.

Routh, D. K. (1969). Conditioning of vocal response differentiation in infants. *Developmental Psychology, 1,* 219–226.

Rowley, P. T. (1984). Genetic screening: Marvel or menace? *Science, 225,* 138–144.

Rozin, P., & Fallon, A. E. (1987). A perspective on disgust. *Psychological Review, 94,* 23–41.

Rubin, J. R., Provenzano, F. J., Luria, Z. (1974). The eye of the beholder: Parents' views on sex of newborns. *American Journal of Orthopsychiatry, 44,* 512–519.

Rubin, L. C., & Mills, M. J. (1983). Behavioral precipitants to civil commitment. *American Journal of Psychiatry, 140,* 603–606.

Rubin, R. T., Reinisch, J. M., & Haskett, R. F. (1981). Postnatal gonadal steroid effects on human behavior. *Science, 211,* 1318–1324.

Ruda, M. A. (1982). Opiates and pain pathways: Demonstration of enkephalin synapses on dorsal horn projection neurons. *Science, 215,* 1523–1525.

Rule, B. G., & Nesdale, A. R. (1976). Emotional arousal and aggressive behavior. *Psychological Bulletin, 83,* 851–863.

Rumbaugh, D. M., Gill, T. V., & von Glasersfeld, E. C. (1973). Reading and sentence completion by a chimpanzee (*Pan*). *Science, 182,* 731–733.

Rush, A. J., Beck, A. T., Kovacs, M., Weissenburger, M. A., & Hollon, S. D. (1982). Comparison of the effects of cognitive therapy and pharmacotherapy on hopelessness and self-concept. *American Journal of Psychiatry, 139,* 862–866.

Rushton, J. P., Fulker, D. W., Neale, M. C., Nias, D. K. B., & Eysenck, H. J. (1986). Altruism and aggression: The heritability of individual differences. *Journal of Personality and Social Psychology, 50,* 1192–1198.

Russell, D. W., Altmaier, E., & Van Velzen, D. (1987). Job-related stress, social support, and burnout among classroom teachers. *Journal of Applied Psychology, 72,* 269–274.

Russell, J. A., & Fehr, B. (1987). Relativity in the perception of emotion in facial expressions. *Journal of Experimental Psychology: General, 116,* 223–237.

Russell, M. J. (1976). Human olfactory communication. *Nature, 260,* 520–522.

Russo, N. F., & Denmark, F. L. (1987). Contributions of women to psychology. *Annual Review of Psychology, 38,* 279–298.

Ryan, E. D. (1980). Attribution, intrinsic motivation, and athletics: A replication and extension. In C. H. Nadeau, W. R. Halliwell, K. M. Newell, & G. C. Roberts (Eds.), *Psychology of motor behavior and sport—1979* (pp. 19–26). Champaign, IL: Human Kinetics Press.

Santee, J. L., Keister, M. F., & Kleinman, K. M. (1980). Incentives to enhance the effects of electromyographic feedback training in stroke patients. *Biofeedback and Self-Regulation, 5,* 51–56.

Sarason, S. (1984). If it can be studied or developed, should it be? *American Psychologist, 39,* 477–485.

Savage-Rumbaugh, E. S., Rumbaugh, D. M., Smith, S. T., & Lawson, J. (1980). Reference: The linguistic essential. *Science, 210,* 922–925.

Savage-Rumbaugh, S. (1987). Communication, symbolic communication, and language: Reply to Seidenberg and Petitto. *Journal of Experimental Psychology: General, 116,* 288–292.

Savage-Rumbaugh, S., McDonald, K., Sevcik, R. A., Hopkins, W. D., & Rupert, E. (1986). Spontaneous symbol acquisition and communicative use by pygmy chimpanzees (*Pan paniscus*). *Journal of Experimental Psychology: General, 115,* 211–235.

Savin-Williams, R. C., & Demo, D. H. (1984). Developmental change and stability in adolescent self-concept. *Developmental Psychology, 20,* 1100–1110.

Saxe, L., Dougherty, D., & Cross, T. (1985). The validity of polygraph testing: Scientific analysis and public controversy. *American Psychologist, 40,* 355–366.

Scarr, S. (1985). Constructing psychology: Making facts and fables for our times. *American Psychologist, 40,* 499–512.

Scarr, S. (1988). Race and gender as psychological variables: Social and ethical issues. *American Psychologist, 43,* 56–59.

Scarr, S., Webber, P. L., Weinberg, R. A., & Wittig, M. A. (1981). Personality resemblance among adolescents and their parents in biologically related and adoptive families. *Journal of Personality and Social Psychology, 40,* 885–898.

Scarr, S., & Weinberg, R. A. (1976). IQ test performance of black children adopted by white families. *American Psychologist, 31,* 726–739.

Scarr, S., & Weinberg, R. A. (1983). The Minnesota Adoption Studies: Genetic differences and malleability. *Child Development, 54,* 260–267.

Schachter, D. L. (1976). The hypnagogic state: A critical review of the literature. *Psychological Bulletin, 83,* 452–481.

Schachter, D. L. (1983). Amnesia observed: Remembering and forgetting in a natural environment. *Journal of Abnormal Psychology, 92,* 236–242.

Schachter, S. (1971). Some extraordinary facts about obese humans and rats. *American Psychologist, 26,* 129–144.

Schachter, S. (1982). Recidivism and self-cure of smoking and obesity. *American Psychologist, 37,* 436–444.

Schachter, S., & Singer, J. E. (1962). Cognitive, social and physiological determinants of emotional state. *Psychological Review, 69,* 379–399.

Schein, E. H. (1956). The Chinese indoctrination program for prisoners of war: A study of attempted "brainwashing." *Psychiatry: Journal for the Study of Interpersonal Processes, 19,* 149–172.

Schiff, M., Duyme, M., Dumaret, A., & Tomkiewicz, S. (1982). How much could we boost scholastic achievement and IQ scores? A direct answer from a French adoption study. *Cognition, 12,* 165–196.

Schiffman, S. S. (1974). Physicochemical correlates of olfactory quality. *Science, 185,* 112–117.

Schilling, R. F., & Weaver, G. E. (1983). Effects of extraneous verbal information on memory for telephone numbers. *Journal of Applied Psychology, 68,* 559–564.

Schleifer, S. J., Keller, S. E., Camerino, M., Thornton, J. C., & Stein, M. (1983). Suppression of lymphocytic stimulation following bereavement. *Journal of the American Medical Association, 250,* 374–377.

Schneider, B., Trehub, S. E., & Bull, D. (1980). High frequency hearing in infants. *Science, 207,* 1003–1004.

Schneider, W., & Shiffrin, R. M. (1977). Controlled and automatic human information processing: I. Detection, search, and attention. *Psychological Review, 84,* 1–66.

Schoeneman, T. J., & Rubanowitz, D. E. (1985). Attributions in the advice columns: Actors and observers, causes and reasons. *Personality and Social Psychology Bulletin, 11,* 315–325.

Schroeder, D. A., Dovidio, J. F., Sibicky, M. E., Matthews, L. L., & Allen, J. L. (1988). Empathic concern and helping behavior: Egoism or altruism? *Journal of Experimental Social Psychology, 24,* 333–353.

Schroeder, S. R., Schroeder, C. S., & Landesman, S. (1987). Psychological services in educational settings to persons with mental retardation. *American Psychologist, 42,* 805–808.

Schulman, S. (1986, February). Facing the invisible handicap. *Psychology Today,* pp. 58–64.

Schurr, K. T., Ruble, V. E., Nisbet, J., & Wallace, D. (1984). Myers-Briggs Type Inventory characteristics of more and less successful players on an American football team. *Journal of Sport Behavior, 7,* 47–57.

Schweizer, E., Winokur, A., & Rickels, K. (1986). Insulin-induced hypoglycemia and panic attacks. *American Journal of Psychiatry, 143,* 654–655.

Scott, K. G., & Carran, D. T. (1987). The epidemiology and prevention of mental retardation. *American Psychologist, 42,* 801–804.

Scovern, A. W., & Kilmann, P. R. (1980). Status of electroconvulsive therapy: Review of the outcome literature. *Psychological Bulletin, 87,* 260–303.

Scoville, W. B., & Milner, B. (1957). Loss of recent memory after bilateral hippocampal lesions. *Journal of Neurology, Neurosurgery, and Psychiatry, 20,* 11–21.

Sears, D. O. (1986). College sophomores in the laboratory: Influences of a narrow data base on social psychology's view of human nature. *Journal of Personality and Social Psychology, 51,* 515–530.

Sears, R. R. (1977). Source of life satisfaction of the Terman gifted men. *American Psychologist, 32,* 119–128.

Sechrest, L. (1984). [Review of *The development and application of social language theory: Selected papers*]. Journal of the History of the Behavioral Sciences, 20, 228–230.

Segal, J., & Luce, G. G. (1966). *Sleep.* New York: Arena Books.

Segal, M. W. (1974). Alphabet and attraction: An unobtrusive measure of the effect of propinquity in a field setting. *Journal of Personality and Social Psychology, 30,* 654–657.

Seidman, L. J. (1983). Schizophrenia and brain dysfunction: An integration of recent neurodiagnostic findings. *Psychological Bulletin, 94,* 195–238.

Seligman, M. E. P. (1970). On the generality of the laws of learning. *Psychological Review, 77,* 406–418.

Seligman, M. E. P. (1971). Phobias and preparedness. *Behavior Therapy, 2,* 307–320.

Selye, H. (1936). A syndrome produced by diverse nocuous agents. *Nature, 138,* 32.

Selye, H. (1980). The stress concept today. In I. L. Kutash, L. B. Schlesinger, & Associates (Eds.), *Handbook on stress and anxiety* (pp. 127–143). San Francisco: Jossey-Bass.

Seyfarth, R. M., Cheney, D. L., & Marler, P. (1980). Monkey responses to three different alarm calls: Evidence of predator classification and semantic communication. *Science, 210,* 801–803.

Shaffer, D. R., & Ogden, J. K. (1986). On sex differences in self-disclosure during the acquaintance process. *Journal of Personality and Social Psychology, 51,* 92–101.

Shaffer, J. W., Graves, P. L., Swank, R. T., & Pearson, T. A. (1987). Clustering of personality traits in youth and the subsequent development of cancer among physicians. *Journal of Behavioral Medicine, 10,* 441–447.

Shaffer, L. S. (1977). The Golden Fleece: Anti-intellectualism and social science. *American Psychologist, 32,* 814–823.

Shanab, M. E., & Yahya, K. A. (1970). A behavioral study of obedience in children. *Journal of Personality and Social Psychology, 35,* 530–536.

Shapiro, C. M., Bortz, R., Mitchell, D., Bartel, P., & Jooste, P. (1981). Slow-wave sleep: A recovery period after exercise. *Science, 214,* 1253–1254.

Shattuck, R. (1980). *The forbidden experiment: The story of the wild boy of Aveyron.* New York: Washington Square Press.

Shearn, D. W. (1962). Operant conditioning of heart rate. *Science, 137,* 530–531.

Sheehan, P. W., & Tilden, J. (1983). Effects of suggestibility and hypnosis on accurate and distorted retrieval from memory. *Journal of Experimental Psychology: Learning, Memory, and Cognition, 9,* 283–293.

Sheldon, W. H. (1942). *The varieties of temperament: A psychology of constitutional differences.* New York: Harper.

Shepard, R. N. (1984). Ecological constraints on internal representation: Resonant kinematics of perceiving, imagining, thinking, and dreaming. *Psychological Review, 91,* 417–447.

Sherry, D. F., & Schachter, D. L. (1987). The evolution of multiple memory systems. *Psychological Review, 94,* 439–454.

Shettleworth, S. J., & Juergensen, M. R. (1980). Reinforcement of the organization of behavior in golden hamsters: Brain stimulation reinforcement for seven action patterns. *Journal of Experimental Psychology: Animal Behavior Processes, 6,* 352–375.

Shevrin, H., & Dickman, S. (1980). The psychological unconscious: A necessary assumption for all psychological theory? *American Psychologist, 35,* 421–434.

Shields, S. A. (1975). Functionalism, Darwinism, and the psychology of women: A study in social myth. *American Psychologist, 30,* 739–754.

Shiffrin, R. M., & Atkinson, R. C. (1969). Storage and retrieval processes in long-term memory. *Psychological Review, 76,* 179–193.

Shneidman, E. (1987, March). At the point of no return. *Psychology Today,* pp. 54–58.

Shneidman, E. (1989). The Indian summer of life: A preliminary study of septuagenerarians. *American Psychologist, 44,* 684–694.

Shockley, W. (1972). Dysgenics, geneticity, raceology: A challenge to the intellectual responsibility of educators. *Phi Delta Kappan, 53,* 297–307.

Shohan-Salomon, V., & Rosenthal, R. (1987). Paradoxical interventions: A meta-analysis. *Journal of Consulting and Clinical Psychology, 55,* 22–28.

Shostrom, E. L. (1962). *Personal orientation inventory.* San Diego: EDITS.

Shotland, R. L., & Straw, M. J. (1976). Bystander response to an assault: When a man attacks a woman. *Journal of Personality and Social Psychology, 34,* 990–999.

Shulins, N. (1987, August 30). Hemispherectomy. *Allentown Morning Call,* p. E-3.

Shweder, R. A. (1982). Liberalism as destiny. *Contemporary Psychology, 27,* 421–424.

Siberstein, A. (1988). An Aristotlean resolution of the idographic versus nomothetic tension. *American Psychologist, 43,* 425–430.

Sibicky, M., & Dovidio, J. F. (1986). Stigma of psychological therapy: Stereotypes, interpersonal reactions, and the self-fulfilling prophecy. *Journal of Counseling Psychology, 33,* 148–154.

Siegal, J. M., & Brown, J. D. (1988). A prospective study of stressful circumstances, illness symptoms, and depressed mood among adolescents. *Developmental Psychology, 24,* 715–721.

Siegel, M. (1983). Crime and violence in America: The victims. *American Psychologist, 38,* 1267–1273.

Siegel, M., & Barclay, M. S. (1985). Children's evaluations of fathers' socialization behavior. *Developmental Psychology, 21,* 1090–1096.

Siegel, R. K. (1980). The psychology of life after death. *American Psychologist, 35,* 911–931.

Siegel, S., Hinson, R., Krank, M. D., & McCully, J. (1982). Heroin "overdose" death: Contribution of drug-associated environmental cues. *Science, 216,* 436–437.

Silva, J. M., III, & Weinberg, R. S. (1984). *Psychological foundations of sport.* Champaign, IL: Human Kinetics Publishers.

Simons, A. D., Garfield, S. L., & Murphy, G. E. (1984). The process of change in cognitive therapy and pharmacotherapy for depression. *Archives of General Psychiatry, 41,* 45–51.

Simonton, D. K. (1988). Age and outstanding achievement: What do we know after a century of research. *Psychological Bulletin, 104,* 251–267.

Sims, J. H., & Baumann, D. D. (1972). The tornado threat: Coping styles of the north and south. *Science, 176,* 1386–1392.

Singer, D. G. (1983). A time to reexamine the role of television in our lives. *American Psychologist, 38,* 815–816.

Singer, J. L. (1975). Navigating the stream of consciousness. *American Psychologist, 30,* 727–738.

Singer, J. L., & Kolligian, J., Jr. (1987). Personality: Developments in the study of private experience. *Annual Review of Psychology, 38,* 533–574.

Singer, J. L., & Singer, D. G. (1979, March). Come back, Mister Rogers, come back. *Psychology Today,* pp. 56, 59–60.

Singer, J. L., & Singer, D. G. (1983). Psychologists look at television: Cognitive, developmental, personality, and social policy implications. *American Psychologist, 38,* 826–834.

Skinner, B. F. (1938). *The behavior of organisms.* Englewood Cliffs, NJ: Prentice-Hall.

Skinner, B. F. (1945, October). Baby in a box. *Ladies' Home Journal,* pp. 30–31.

Skinner, B. F. (1948). *Walden two.* New York: Macmillan.

Skinner, B. F. (1953). *Science and human behavior.* New York: Macmillan.

Skinner, B. F. (1957). *Verbal behavior.* New York: Appleton-Century-Crofts.

Skinner, B. F. (1960). Pigeons in a pelican. *American Psychologist, 15,* 28–37.

Skinner, B. F. (1971). *Beyond freedom and dignity.* New York: Knopf.

Skinner, B. F. (1983). Intellectual self-management in old age. *American Psychologist, 38,* 239–244.

Skinner, B. F. (1984). The shame of American education. *American Psychologist, 39,* 947–954.

Skinner, B. F. (1986). What is wrong with daily life in the Western World? *American Psychologist, 41,* 568–574.

Skinner, N. F. (1983). Switching answers on multiple-choice questions: Shrewdness or shibboleth? *Teaching of Psychology, 10,* 220–222.

Slater, J., & Depue, R. A. (1981). The contribution of environmental events and social support to serious suicide attempts in primary depressive disorder. *Journal of Abnormal Psychology, 90,* 275–285.

Smeaton, G., Byrne, D., & Murnen, S. K. (1989). The repulsion hypothesis revisited: Similarity irrelevance or dissimilarity bias. *Journal of Personality and Social Psychology, 56,* 54–59.

Smith, B. M., Schumaker, J. B., Schaeffer, J., & Sherman, J. A. (1982). Increasing participation and improving the quality of discussion in seventh-grade social studies classes. *Journal of Applied Behavior Analysis, 15,* 97–110.

Smith, C. A., & Ellsworth, P. C. (1985). Patterns of cognitive appraisal in emotion. *Journal of Personality and Social Psychology, 48,* 813–838.

Smith, D. (1982). Trends in counseling and psychotherapy. *American Psychologist, 37,* 802–809.

Smith, D., & Kraft, W. A. (1983). DSM-III: Do psychologists really want an alternative? *American Psychologist, 38,* 777–785.

Smith, L. T. (1974). The interanimal transfer phenomenon: A review. *Psychological Bulletin, 81,* 1078–1095.

Smith, M. C. (1983). Hypnotic memory enhancement of witnesses: Does it work? *Psychological Bulletin, 94,* 387–407.

Smith, M. L., Glass, G. V., & Miller, T. I. (1980). *The benefits of psychotherapy.* Baltimore: Johns Hopkins University Press.

Smith, S. M. (1984). A comparison of two techniques for reducing context-dependent forgetting. *Memory and Cognition, 12,* 477–482.

Smith, S. M., Brown, H. O., Toman, J. E. P., & Goodman, L. S. (1947). The lack of cerebral effects of d-tubercurarine. *Anesthesiology, 8,* 1–14.

Smith, T. W. (1983). Change in irrational beliefs and the outcome of rational-emotive psychotherapy. *Journal of Consulting and Clinical Psychology, 51,* 156–157.

Snarey, J., Son, L., Kuehne, V. S., Hauser, S., & Vaillant, G. (1987). The role of parenting in men's psychosocial development: A longitudinal study of early adulthood infertility and midlife generativity. *Developmental Psychology, 23,* 593–603.

Snarey, J. R. (1985). Cross-cultural universality of social-moral development: A critical review of Kohlbergian research. *Psychological Bulletin, 97,* 202–232.

Snarey, J. R., Reimer, J., & Kohlberg, L. (1985). Development of social-moral reasoning among kibbutz adolescents: A longitudinal cross-cultural study. *Developmental Psychology, 21,* 3–17.

Snow, C. E. (1981). The uses of imitation. *Journal of Child Language, 8,* 205–212.

Snyder, C. R., & Higgins, R. L. (1988). Excuses: Their effective role in the negotiation of reality. *Psychological Bulletin, 104,* 23–35.

Snyder, M. (1983). The influence of individuals on situations: Implications for understanding the links between personality and social behavior. *Journal of Personality, 51,* 497–516.

Solomon, P. R., & Morse, D. L. (1981). Teaching the principles of operant conditioning through laboratory experience: The rat olympics. *Teaching of Psychology, 8,* 111–112.

Solomon, R. L. (1980). The opponent-process theory of acquired motivation: The costs of pleasure and the benefits of pain. *American Psychologist, 35,* 691–712.

Sommers, S. (1984). Reported emotions and conventions of emotionality among college students. *Journal of Personality and Social Psychology, 46,* 207–215.

Sonstroem, R. J., & Bernardo, P. (1982). Intraindividual pregame state anxiety and basketball performance: A re-examination of the inverted-U curve. *Journal of Sport Psychology, 4,* 235–245.

Sothmann, M. S., Horn, T. S., Hart, B. A., & Gustafson, A. B. (1987). Comparison of discrete cardiovascular fitness groups on plasma, catecholamine and selected behavioral responses to psychological stress. *Psychophysiology, 24,* 47–54.

Spanos, N. P. (1985). Witchcraft and social history: An essay review. *Journal of the History of the Behavioral Sciences, 24,* 60–67.

Spanos, N. P., & Hewitt, E. C. (1980). The hidden observer in hypnotic amnesia: Discovery or experimental creation? *Journal of Personality and Social Psychology, 39,* 1201–1214.

Spanos, N. P., McNeil, C., & Stam, H. J. (1982). Hypnotically "reliving" a prior burn: Effects on blister formation and localized skin temperature. *Journal of Abnormal Psychology, 91,* 303–305.

Spanos, N. P., Weekes, J. R., & Bertrand, L. D. (1985). Multiple personality: A social psychological perspective. *Journal of Abnormal Psychology, 94,* 362–376.

Spearman, C. (1927). *The abilities of man.* London: Macmillan.

Speisman, J. C., Lazurus, R. S., Mordkoff, A., & Davison, L. (1964). Experimental reduction of stress based on ego-defense theory. *Journal of Abnormal and Social Psychology, 68,* 367–380.

Sperling, G. (1960). The information available in brief visual presentations. *Psychological Monographs, 74* (11, Whole No. 498).

Sperry, R. (1982). Some effects of disconnecting the cerebral hemispheres. *Science, 217,* 1223–1226.

Sperry, R. W. (1988). Psychology's mentalist paradigm and the religion/science tension. *American Psychologist, 43,* 607–613.

Spetch, M. L., Wilkie, D. M., & Pinel, J. P. J. (1981). Backward conditioning: A reevaluation of the empirical evidence. *Psychological Bulletin, 89,* 163–175.

Spiegel, D., Cutcomb, S., Ren, C., & Pribram, K. (1985). Hypnotic hallucination alters evoked potentials. *Journal of Abnormal Psychology, 94,* 249–255.

Springer, S. P., & Deutsch, G. (1985). *Left brain, right brain.* San Francisco: Freeman.

Stafford-Clark, D. (1965). *What Freud really said.* New York: Schocken Books.

Staines, G. L., Pottick, K. J., & Fudge, D. A. (1986). Wives' employment and husbands' attitudes toward work and life. *Journal of Applied Psychology, 71,* 118–128.

Stake, J. E., & Pearlman, J. (1980). Assertiveness training as an intervention technique for low performance self-esteem women. *Journal of Counseling Psychology, 27,* 276–281.

Stapp, J., Tucker, A. M., & VandenBos, G. R. (1985). Census of psychological personnel: 1983. *American Psychologist, 40,* 1317–1351.

Stark, E. (1981, September). Pigeon patrol. *Science 81,* pp. 85–86.

Steele, C. M., Critchlow, B., & Liu, T. J. (1985). Alcohol and social behavior II: The helpful drunkard. *Journal of Personality and Social Psychology, 48,* 35–46.

Steiner, S. S., & Dince, W. M. (1981). Biofeedback efficacy studies: A critique of critiques. *Biofeedback and Self-Regulation, 6,* 275–288.

Sternberg, D. E., Van Kammen, D. P., Lerner, P., & Bunney, W. E. (1982). Schizophrenia: Dopamine beta-hydroxylase activity and treatment response. *Science, 216,* 1423–1425.

Sternberg, R. J. (1984). *Beyond IQ: A triarchic theory of intelligence.* New York: Cambridge University Press.

Sternberg, R. J. (1986). *Intelligence applied.* San Diego: Harcourt Brace Jovanovich.

Sternberg, R. J. (1986). A triangular theory of love. *Psychological Review, 93,* 119–135.

Sternberg, R. J., Conway, B. E., Ketron, J. L., & Bernstein, M. (1981). People's conceptions of intelligence. *Journal of Personality and Social Psychology, 41,* 37–55.

Sternberg, S. (1966). High-speed scanning in human memory. *Science, 153,* 652–654.

Stokols, D. (1972). On the distinction between density and crowding: Some implications for future research. *Psychological Review, 79,* 275–277.

Stone, A. A., Cox, D. S., Validmarsdottir, H., Jandorf, L., & Neale, J. M. (1987). Evidence that secretory IgA antibody is associated with daily mood. *Journal of Personality and Social Personality, 52,* 988–993.

Stone, A. A., Hedges, S. M., Neale, J. M., & Satin, M. S. (1985). Prospective and cross-sectional mood reports offer no evidence of a "blue Monday" phenomenon. *Journal of Personality and Social Psychology, 49,* 129–134.

Stoner, J. A. F. (1961). *A comparison of individual and group decisions involving risk.* Unpublished master's thesis, Massachusetts Institute of Technology.

Stoney, C. M., Davis, M. C., & Matthews, K. A. (1987). Sex differences in physiological responses to stress and in coronary heart disease: A causal link? *Psychophysiology, 24,* 127–131.

Storms, M. D. (1981). A theory of erotic orientation development. *Psychological Review, 88,* 340–353.

Strange, W., & Dittmann, S. (1984). Effects of discrimination training on the perception of r-l by Japanese adults learning English. *Perception and Psychophysics, 36,* 131–145.

Stratton, G. M. (1917). The mnemonic feat of the "Shass Pollak." *Psychological Review, 24,* 244–247.

Straub, W. F. (1982). Sensation seeking among high and low-risk male athletes. *Journal of Sport Psychology, 4,* 246–253.

Streissguth, A. P., Barr, H. M., Sampson, P. D., Darby, B. L., & Martin, D. C. (1989). IQ at age four in relation to maternal alcohol use and smoking during pregnancy. *Developmental Psychology, 25,* 3–11.

Stricker, E. M., & Verbalis, J. G. (1987). Biological bases of hunger and satiety. *Annals of Behavioral Medicine, 9,* 3–8.

Striegel-Moore, R. H., Silberstein, L. R., & Rodin, J. (1986). Toward an understandng of risk factors in bulimia. *American Psychologist, 41,* 246–263.

Strober, M., & Humphrey, L. L. (1987). Familial contributions to the etiology and course of anorexia nervosa and bulimia. *Journal of Consulting and Clinical Psychology, 55,* 654–659.

Stroebe, M. S., & Stroebe, W. (1983). Who suffers more? Sex differences in health risks of the widowed. *Psychological Bulletin, 93,* 279–301.

Strube, M. J. (1988). The decision to leave an abusive relationship: Empirical evidence and theoretical issues. *Psychological Bulletin, 104,* 236–250.

Strupp, H. H., & Hadley, S. W. (1979). Specific versus nonspecific factors in psychotherapy: A controlled study of outcome. *Archives of General Psychiatry, 36,* 1125–1136.

Stunkard, A. J., Sorensen, T., Hanis, C., Teasdale, T. W., Chakraborty, R., Schull, W. J., & Schulsinger, F. (1986). An adoption study of human obesity. *New England Journal of Medicine, 314,* 193–198.

Suler, J. R. (1980). Primary process thinking and creativity. *Psychological Bulletin, 88,* 144–165.

Sulin, R. A., & Dooling, D. J. (1974). Intrusion of a thematic idea in retention of prose. *Journal of Experimental Psychology, 103,* 255–262.

Sullivan, H. S. (1953). *An interpersonal theory of psychiatry.* New York: Norton.

Superkids?: A sperm bank for Nobelists. (1980, March 10). *Time,* p. 49.

Sussman, N. M., & Rosenfeld, H. M. (1982). Influence of culture, language, and sex on conversational distance. *Journal of Personality and Social Psychology, 42,* 66–74.

Swain, J. J., Allard, G. B., & Holborn, S. W. (1982). The good toothbrushing game: A school-based dental hygiene program for increasing the toothbrushing effectiveness of children. *Journal of Applied Behavior Analysis, 15,* 171–176.

Swain, R. B. (1984, August). Message from a heaving deck. *Discover,* pp. 60–62, 64.

Sweeney, P. D., Anderson, K., & Bailey, S. (1986). Attributional style in depression: A meta-analytic review. *Journal of Personality and Social Psychology, 50,* 974–991.

Sweeney, P. D., & Gruber, K. L. (1984). Selective exposure: Voter information preferences and the Watergate affair. *Journal of Personality and Social Psychology, 46,* 1208–1221.

Szasz, T. (1960). The myth of mental illness. *American Psychologist, 15,* 113–118.

Tarchanoff, J. R. (1885). Uber die willkurliche acceleration der herzschlage beim menschen (Voluntary acceleration of the heart beat in man). *Pflugers Archives, 35,* 109–135. Reprinted in D. Shapiro et al. (Eds.). (1973). *Biofeedback and Self-Control, 1972* (pp. 3–20). Chicago: Aldine-Atherton.

Task Force on the Use of Laboratory Tests in Psychiatry. (1985). Tricyclic antidepressants—Blood level measurements and clinical outcome: An APA task force report. *American Journal of Psychiatry, 142,* 155–162.

Taulbee, P. (1983). Solving the mystery of anxiety. *Science News, 124,* 45.

Taylor, S. E., & Brown, J. D. (1988). Illusion and well-being: A social psychological perspective on mental health. *Psychological Bulletin, 103,* 193–210.

Teaching a machine the shades of gray. (1981). *Science News, 119,* 38–39.

Teevan, R. C., & McGhee, P. E. (1972). Childhood development of fear of failure motivation. *Journal of Personality and Social Psychology, 21,* 345–348.

Tellegen, A., Lykken, D. T., Bouchard, T. J., Jr., Wilcox, K. J., Segal, N. L., & Rich, S. (1988). Personality similarity in twins reared apart and together. *Journal of Personality and Social Psychology, 54,* 1031–1039.

Terman, L. M. (1917). The intelligence quotient of Francis Galton in childhood. *American Journal of Psychology, 28,* 209–215.

Terrace, H. S. (1985). In the beginning was the "name." *American Psychologist, 40,* 1011–1028.

Terrace, H. S., Petitto, L. A., Sanders, R. J., & Bever, T. G. (1979). Can an ape create a sentence? *Science, 206,* 891–902.

Thase, M. E., Hersen, M., Bellack, A. S., Himmelhoch, J. M., Kornblith, S. J., & Greenwald, D. P. (1984). Social skills training and endogenous depression. *Journal of Behavior Therapy and Experimental Psychiatry, 15,* 101–108.

Thomas, J. R., & French, K. E. (1985). Gender differences across age in motor performance: A meta-analysis. *Psychological Bulletin, 98,* 260–282.

Thomas, L. (1981, December). On the need for asylums. *Discover,* pp. 68, 71.

Thompson, J. K., Jarvie, G. J., Lahey, B. B., & Cureton, K. J. (1982). Exercise and obesity: Etiology, physiology, and intervention. *Psychological Bulletin, 91,* 55–79.

Thorndike, E. L. (1898). Animal intelligence: An experimental study of the associative processes in animals. *Psychological Review Monograph Supplement, 2* (No. 8).

Thorndike, E. L. (1961). Edward Lee Thorndike. In C. Murchison (Ed.), *A history of psychology in autobiography* (Vol. 3, pp. 263–270). New York: Russell & Russell. .

Thurman, C. W. (1985). Effectiveness of cognitive-behavioral treatments in reducing Type A behavior among university faculty—one year later. *Journal of Counseling Psychology, 32,* 445–448.

Thurstone, L. L. (1938). *Primary mental abilities.* Chicago: University of Chicago Press.

Timberlake, W., & Melcer, T. (1988). Effects of poisoning on predatory and ingestive behavior toward artificial prey in rats (*Rattus norvegicus*). *Journal of Comparative Psychology, 102,* 182–187.

Titchener, E. B. (1910). *A textbook of psychology.* New York: Macmillan.

Tolman, E. C. (1932). *Purposive behavior in animals and man.* New York: Appleton-Century-Crofts.

Tolman, E. C., & Honzik, C. H. (1930). Introduction and removal of reward, and maze performance in rats. *University of California Publications in Psychology, 4,* 257–275.

Tomizuka, C., & Tobias, S. (1981). Mathematical ability: Is sex a factor? *Science, 212,* 114.

Tordoff, M. G., Novin, D., & Russek, M. (1982). Effects of hepatic denervation of the anorexic response to epinephrine, amphetamine, and lithium chloride: A behavioral identification of glucostatic afferents. *Journal of Comparative and Physiological Psychology, 96,* 361–375.

Torgersen, S. (1986). Genetics of somatoform disorders. *Archives of General Psychiatry, 43,* 502–505.

Torrey, E. F. (1981, November). The protection of Ezra Pound. *Psychology Today,* pp. 57–66.

Tosteson, D. C. (1981, April). Lithium and mania. *Scientific American,* pp. 164–174.

Tourney, G. (1965). Freud and the Greeks: A study of the influence of classical Greek mythology and philosophy upon the development of Freudian thought. *Journal of the History of the Behavioral Sciences, 1,* 67–87.

Tranel, D., & Damasio, A. R. (1985). Knowledge without awareness: An automatic index of facial recognition by prosopagnosics. *Science, 228,* 1453–1454.

Traskman, L., Asberg, M., Bertilsson, L., & Sjostrand, L. (1981). Monoamine metabolites in CSF and suicidal behavior. *Archives of General Psychiatry, 38,* 631–636.

Treisman, M. (1977). Motion sickness: An evolutionary hypothesis. *Science, 197,* 493–495.

Triplett, N. (1898). The dynamogenic factors in pacemaking and competition. *American Journal of Psychology, 9,* 507–533.

Trotter, R. J. (1981). Psychiatry for the 80's. *Science News, 119,* 348–349.

Trotter, R. J. (1986, August). Three heads are better than one. *Psychology Today,* pp. 56–62.

Truax, C. B. (1966). Reinforcement and nonreinforcement in Rogerian psychotherapy. *Journal of Abnormal Psychology, 71,* 1–9.

Trujillo, C. M. (1983). The effect of weight training and running exercise intervention programs on the self-esteem of college women. *International Journal of Sport Psychology, 14,* 162–173.

Tucker, L. A. (1982). Effect of a weight training program on the self-concept of college males. *Perceptual and Motor Skills, 54,* 1055–1061.

Tucker, L. A. (1983). Muscular strength: A predictor of personality in males. *Journal of Sports Medicine and Physical Fitness, 23,* 213–220.

Tulsky, F. N. (1986, March 28). $988,000 is awarded in suit over lost psychic power. *The Philadelphia Inquirer,* p. 1-A.

Tulving, E. (1985). How many memory systems are there? *American Psychologist, 40,* 385–398.

Tulving, E., & Thomson, D. M. (1973). Encoding specificity and retrieval processes in episodic memory. *Psychological Review, 80,* 352–373.

Turkington, C. (1984, January). Ideology affects approach taken to alleviate PMS. *APA Monitor,* pp. 28–29.

Turkington, C. (1984, August). Supportive homes few, barriers many. *APA Monitor,* pp. 20, 22.

Turkington, C. (1986, October). Neuron deaths balanced by growth of neurons. *APA Monitor,* p. 25.

Turnbull, C. M. (1961). Some observations regarding the experiences of the Bambuti pygmies. *American Journal of Psychology, 74,* 304–308.

Turner, S. M., Beidel, D. C., & Costello, A. (1987). Psychopathology in the offspring of anxiety disorder patients. *Journal of Consulting and Clinical Psychology, 55,* 229–235.

Turner, S. M., Beidel, D. C., & Nathan, R. S. (1985). Biological factors in obsessive-compulsive disorders. *Psychological Bulletin, 97*, 430–450.

Tversky, A., & Kahneman, D. (1973). Availability: A heuristic for judging frequency and probability. *Cognitive Psychology, 5*, 207–232.

Type A: A change of heart and mind. (1984). *Science News, 126*, 109.

Ullman, M., Krippner, S., & Vaughan, A. (1973). *Dream telepathy.* New York: Macmillan.

Ullmann, L. P., & Krasner, L. (1975). *Psychological approaches to abnormal behavior.* Englewood Cliffs, NJ: Prentice-Hall.

Ulrich, R. E., Stachnik, T. J., & Stainton, N. R. (1963). Student acceptance of generalized personality interpretations *Psychological Reports, 13*, 831–834.

Unger, G., Desiderio, D. M., & Parr, W. (1972). Isolation, identification and synthesis of a specific-behavior-inducing brain peptide. *Nature, 238*, 198–202.

Valenstein, E. S. (1980). *The psychosurgery debate.* San Francisco: Freeman.

Van Doornen, L. J. P., & van Blokland, R. (1987). Serum-cholesterol: Sex specific psychological correlates during rest and stress. *Journal of Psychosomatic Research, 31*, 239–249.

Van Dyke, C., & Byck, R. (1982, March). Cocaine. *Scientific American,* pp. 128–134, 139–141.

Van Hasselt, V. B., Griest, D. L., Kazdin, A. E., Esveldt-Dawson, K., & Unis, A. S. (1984). Poor peer interactions and social isolation: A case report of successful *in vivo* social skills training on a child psychiatric inpatient unit. *Journal of Behavior Therapy and Experimental Psychiatry, 15*, 271–276.

Vance, F. L. (1965). I was an imaginary playmate. *American Psychologist, 20*, 990.

Vanden Pol, R. A., Iwata, B. A., Ivancic, M. T., Page, T. J., Neef, N. A., & Whitley, F. P. (1981). Teaching the handicapped to eat in public places: Acquisition, generalization, and maintenance of restaurant skills. *Journal of Applied Behavior Analysis, 14*, 64–69.

Vander Plate, C., Aral, S. O., & Magder, L. (1988). The relationship among genital herpes simplex virus, stress, and social support. *Health Psychology, 7*, 159–168.

Vanherweghen, J. L., Linkowski, P., & Mendlewicz, J. (1983). Hemodialysis in schizophrenics: A double-blind study. *Archives of General Psychiatry, 40*, 211–214.

Veroff, J., Depner, C., Kulka, R., & Douvan, E. (1980). Comparison of American motives: 1957 versus 1976. *Journal of Personality and Social Psychology, 39*, 1249–1262.

Vetter, H. J. (1969). *Language behavior and psychopathology.* Chicago: Rand McNally.

Vidal, F., Buscaglia, M., & Voneche, J. J. (1983). Darwinism and developmental psychology. *Journal of the History of the Behavioral Sciences, 19*, 81–94.

Viney, W., Michaels, T., & Ganong, A. (1981). A note on the history of psychology in magazines. *Journal of the History of the Behavioral Sciences, 17*, 270–272.

Vogel, G. W. (1978). An alternative view of the neurobiology of dreaming. *American Journal of Psychiatry, 135*, 1531–1535.

Vokey, J. R., & Read, J. D. (1985). Subliminal messages: Between the devil and the media. *American Psychologist, 40*, 1231–1239.

von Békésy, G. (1957, August). The ear. *Scientific American,* pp. 66–78.

von der Heydt, R., Peterhans, E., & Baumgartner, G. (1984). Illusory contours and cortical neuron responses. *Science, 224*, 1260–1262.

von Frisch, K. (1974). Decoding the language of a bee. *Science, 185*, 663–668.

von Hofsten, C. (1983). Eye-hand coordination in the newborn. *Developmental Psychology, 18*, 450–461.

Vonnegut, M. (1974, April). Why I want to bite R. D. Laing. *Harper's Magazine,* pp. 90–92.

Vonnegut, M. (1975). *The Eden express.* New York: Bantam Books.

Wadden, T. A., & Anderton, C. H. (1982). The clinical use of hypnosis. *Psychological Bulletin, 91*, 215–243.

Waid, W. M., Wilson, S. K., & Orne, M. T. (1981). Cross-modal physiological effects of electrodermal ability in the detection of deception. *Journal of Personality and Social Psychology, 40*, 1118–1125.

Wald, G. (1964). The receptors of human color vision. *Science, 145*, 1007–1017.

Waldrop, M. M. (1984). Artificial intelligence in parallel. *Science, 225*, 608–610.

Waldrop, M. M. (1984, June). Astrology's off target. *Science 84,* pp. 80, 82.

Walgren, D. (1982). Problems of the behavioral and social sciences in national science foundation budget debates. *American Psychologist, 37*, 927–933.

Walk, R. D., & Homan, C. P. (1984). Emotion and dance in dynamic light displays. *Bulletin of the Psychonomic Society, 22*, 437–440.

Walker, E., Hoppes, E., Emory, E., Mednick, S., & Schulsinger, F. (1981). Environmental factors related to schizophrenia in psychophysiologically labile high-risk males. *Journal of Abnormal Psychology, 90*, 313–320.

Wallace, A. (1986). *The prodigy.* New York: Dutton.

Wallace, R. K., & Benson, H. (1972, February). The physiology of meditation. *Scientific American,* pp. 84–90.

Wallach, H., & Marshall, F. J. (1985). Shape constancy in pictorial representation. *Perception and Psychophysics, 39*, 233–235.

Wallach, M. A., Kogan, N., & Bem, D. J. (1962). Group influence on individual risk taking. *Journal of Abnormal and Social Psychology, 65*, 75–86.

Wallis, C. (1984, June 11). Unlocking pain's secrets. *Time,* pp. 58–66.

Walsh, J. (1981). A plenipotentiary for human intelligence. *Science, 214*, 640–641.

Walsh, J. (1983). Wide world of reports. *Science, 220*, 804–805.

Walster, E., Aronson, V., Abrahams, D., & Rottman, L. (1966). Importance of physical attractiveness in dating behavior. *Journal of Personality and Social Psychology, 4*, 508–516.

Walster, E., Walster, G. W., & Traupmann, J. (1978). Equity and premarital sex. *Journal of Personality and Social Psychology, 36*, 82–92.

Waltz, D. L. (1982, October). Artificial intelligence. *Scientific American,* pp. 118–133.

Watkins, C. E., Jr., Lopez, F. G., Campbell, V. L., & Himmell, C. D. (1986). Counseling psychology and clinical psychology: Some preliminary comparative data. *American Psychologist, 41*, 581–584.

Watkins, L. R., & Mayer, D. J. (1982). Organization of endogenous opiate and nonopiate pain control systems. *Science, 216,* 1185–1192.

Watson, D. (1982). The actor and the observer: How are their perceptions of causality divergent? *Psychological Bulletin, 92,* 682–700.

Watson, D., & Clark, L. A. (1984). Negative affectivity: The disposition to experience aversive emotional states. *Psychological Bulletin, 96,* 465–490.

Watson, J. B. (1913). Psychology as the behaviorist views it. *Psychological Review, 20,* 158–177.

Watson, J. B. (1930). *Behaviorism.* New York: Norton.

Watson, J. B. (1961). John Broadus Watson. In C. Murchison (Ed.), *A history of psychology in autobiography* (Vol. 3, pp. 271–281). New York: Russell & Russell.

Watson, J. B., & Rayner, R. (1920). Conditioned emotional reactions. *Journal of Experimental Psychology, 3,* 1–14.

Watts, B. L. (1982). Individual differences in circadian activity rhythms and their effects on roommate relationships. *Journal of Personality, 50,* 374–384.

Weaver, J. B., Masland, J. L., Kharazmi, S., & Zillman, D. (1985). Effect of alcoholic intoxication on the appreciation of different types of humor. *Journal of Personality and Social Psychology, 49,* 781–787.

Webb, C. (1977). The use of myoelectric facial feedback in teaching facial expression to the blind. *Biofeedback and Self-Regulation, 2,* 147–160.

Webb, E. J., Campbell, D. T., Schwartz, R. D., & Sechrest, L. (1966). *Unobtrusive measures: Nonreactive research in the social sciences.* Chicago: Rand McNally.

Webb, W. B. (1975). *Sleep: The gentle tyrant.* Englewood Cliffs, NJ: Prentice-Hall.

Webb, W. B. (1981). An essay on consciousness. *Teaching of Psychology, 8,* 15–19.

Webb, W. B. (1987). The proximal effects of two and four hour naps within extended performance without sleep. *Psychophysiology, 24,* 426–429.

Webb, W. B., & Agnew, H. W., Jr. (1975). Are we chronically sleep deprived? *Bulletin of the Psychonomic Society, 6,* 47–48.

Weber, J. M., Klesges, R. C., & Klesges, L. M. (1988). Dietary restraint and obesity: Their effects on dietary intake. *Journal of Behavioral Medicine, 11,* 185–199.

Weber, R., & Crocker, J. (1983). Cognitive processes in the revision of stereotype beliefs. *Journal of Personality and Social Psychology, 45,* 961–977.

Wechsler, D. (1958). *Measurement and appraisal of adult intelligence.* Baltimore: Williams & Wilkins.

Weigel, R. H., Vernon, D. T. A., & Tognacci, L. N. (1974). Specificity of the attitude as a determinant of attitude-behavior congruence. *Journal of Personality and Social Psychology, 30,* 724–728.

Weinberg, R. A. (1989). Intelligence and IQ: Landmark issues and great debates. *American Psychologist, 44,* 98–104.

Weinberger, M., Hiner, S. L., & Tierney, W. M. (1987). In support of hassles as a measure of stress in predicting health outcomes. *Journal of Behavioral Medicine, 10,* 19–31.

Weiner, B. (1980). A cognitive (attribution)-emotion-action model of motivated behavior: An analysis of judgments of help-giving. *Journal of Personality and Social Psychology, 39,* 186–200.

Weiner, B. (1985a). An attributional theory of achievement motivation and emotion. *Psychological Review, 92,* 548–573.

Weiner, B. (1985b). "Spontaneous" causal thinking. *Psychological Bulletin, 97,* 74–84.

Weiner, B., Amirkhan, J., Folkes, V. S., & Verette, J. A. (1987). An attributional analysis of excuse giving: Studies of a naive theory of emotion. *Journal of Personality and Social Psychology, 52,* 316–324.

Weinstein, L., & Almaguer, L. L. (1987). "I'm bored!" *Bulletin of the Psychonomic Society, 25,* 389–390.

Weinstein, N. D. (1984). Reducing unrealistic optimism about illness susceptibility. *Health Psychology, 3,* 431–457.

Weisburd, S. (1984). Whales and dolphins use magnetic "roads." *Science News, 126,* 391.

Weisman, J. (1988, November 19–25). Remembering JFK: Our first TV president. *TV Guide,* pp. 2–4, 6–8.

Weiss, J. M. (1972, June). Psychological factors in stress and disease. *Scientific American,* pp. 104–113.

Wells, G. L., & Lindsay, R. C. L. (1985). Methodological notes on the accuracy-confidence relation in eyewitness identification. *Journal of Applied Psychology, 70,* 413–419.

Wertheimer, M. (1912). Experimental studies of the perception of movement. *Zeitschrift fuer psychologie, 61,* 161–265.

Wertheimer, M. (1978). Humanistic psychology and the humane but tough-minded psychologist. *American Psychologist, 33,* 739–745.

Wever, E. G., & Bray, C. W. (1937). The perception of low tones and the resonance volley theory. *Journal of Psychology, 3,* 101–114.

White, G. L., Fishbein, S., & Rutstein, J. (1981). Passionate love and the misattribution of arousal. *Journal of Personality, 41,* 56–62.

Whitehurst, G. J., Falco, F. L., Lonigan, C. J., Fischel, J. E., DeBaryshe, B. D., Valdez-Menchaca, M. C., & Caulfield, M. (1988). Accelerating language development through picture book reading. *Developmental Psychology, 24,* 552–559.

Whitlock, F. A. (1987). Addiction. In R. L. Gregory (Ed.), *The Oxford companion to the mind* (pp. 3–5). New York: Oxford University Press.

Whorf, B. L. (1956). Science and linguistics. In J. B. Carroll (Ed.), *Language, thought, and reality: Selected writings of Benjamin Lee Whorf.* Cambridge, MA: MIT Press.

Whyte, W. H. (1956). *The organization man.* New York: Simon & Schuster.

Wickelgren, W. A. (1981). Human learning and memory. *Annual Review of Psychology, 32,* 21–52.

Wicker, F. W., Barron, W. L., III, & Willis, A. C. (1980). Disparagement humor: Dispositions and resolutions. *Journal of Personality and Social Psychology, 39,* 701–709.

Wideman, M. V., & Singer, J. E. (1984). The role of psychological mechanisms in preparation for childbirth. *American Psychologist, 39,* 1357–1371.

Wiebe, D. J., & McCallum, D. M. (1986). Health practices and hardiness as mediators in the stress-illness relationship. *Health Psychology, 5,* 425–438.

Wiens, A. N., & Menustik, C. E. (1983). Treatment outcome and patient characteristics in an aversion therapy program for alcoholism. *American Psychologist, 38,* 1089–1096.

Wilcox, B. L. (1987). Pornography, social science, and politics: When research and ideology collide. *American Psychologist, 42,* 941–943.

Williams, C. D. (1959). The elimination of tantrum behavior by extinction procedures. *Journal of Abnormal and Social Psychology, 59,* 269.

Williams, K., Harkins, S., & Latané, B. (1981). Identifiability as a determinant to social loafing: Two cheering experiments. *Journal of Personality and Social Psychology, 40,* 303–311.

Williams, R. B., Jr., Kuhn, C. M., Melosh, W., White, A. D., & Schonberg, S. M. (1982). Type A behavior and elevated physiological and neuroendocrine responses to cognitive tasks. *Science, 218,* 483–485.

Wills, T. A. (1981). Downward comparison principles in social psychology. *Psychological Bulletin, 90,* 245–271.

Wilson, E. O. (1975). *Sociobiology: The new synthesis.* Cambridge, MA: Harvard University Press.

Wilson, J. P., & Petruska, R. (1984). Motivation, model attributes, and prosocial behavior. *Journal of Personality and Social Psychology, 46,* 458–468.

Wilson, J. R. (1964). *The mind.* New York: Time.

Wilson, T. D., & Linville, P. W. (1982). Improving the academic performance of college freshmen: Attribution theory revisited. *Journal of Personality and Social Psychology, 42,* 367–376.

Wilson, V. E., & Bird, E. I. (1981). Effects of relaxation and/or biofeedback training upon hip flexion in gymnasts. *Biofeedback and Self-Regulation, 6,* 25–34.

Winter, L., & Uleman, J. S. (1984). When are social judgments made? Evidence for the spontaneousness of trait inferences. *Journal of Personality and Social Psychology, 47,* 237–252.

Wittig, M. A. (1985). Metatheoretical dilemmas in the psychology of gender. *American Psychologist, 40,* 400–411.

Wolf, T. H. (1961). An individual who made a difference. *American Psychologist, 16,* 245–248.

Wolfe, D. A. (1985). Child-abusive parents: An empirical review and analysis. *Psychological Bulletin, 97,* 462–482.

Wolfe, J. (1936). Effectiveness of token rewards for chimpanzees. *Comparative Psychological Monographs (12,* Whole No. 5).

Wolfe, T. (1979). *The right stuff.* New York: Bantam Books.

Wolfensberger, W. (1972). *Normalization.* Toronto: National Institute on Mental Retardation.

Wolff, J., & Desiderato, O. (1980). Transfer of assertion-training effects to roommates of program participants. *Journal of Counseling Psychology, 27,* 484–491.

Wollen, K. A., Weber, A., Lowry, D. H. (1972). Bizarreness versus interaction of mental images as determinants of learning. *Cognitive Psychology, 3,* 518–523.

Wolpe, J. (1958). *Psychotherapy by reciprocal inhibition.* Stanford, CA: Stanford University Press.

Wolpe, J. (1988). Obituary: Mary Cover Jones 1896–1987. *Journal of Behavior Therapy and Experimental Psychiatry, 19,* 3–4.

Wood, W., & Eagly, A. H. (1981). Stages in the analysis of persuasive messages: The role of causal attributions and message comprehension. *Journal of Experimental and Social Psychology, 40,* 246–259.

Wood, W., & Karten, S. J. (1986). Sex differences in interaction style as a product of perceived sex differences in competence. *Journal of Personality and Social Psychology, 50,* 341–347.

Worringham, C. J., & Messick, D. M. (1983). Social facilitation of running: An unobtrusive study. *Journal of Social Psychology, 121,* 23–29.

Wright, J. C., Huston, A. C., Ross, R. P., Calvert, S. L., Rolandelli, D., Weeks, L. A., Raeissi, P., & Potts, R. (1984). Pace and continuity of television programs: Effects on children's attention and comprehension. *Developmental Psychology, 20,* 653–666.

Wright, L. (1988). The Type A behavior pattern and coronary artery disease. *American Psychologist, 43,* 2–14.

Wurtman, R. J. (1985, January). Alzheimer's disease. *Scientific American,* pp. 62–66, 71–74.

Wyatt, J. W., Posey, A., Welker, W., & Seamonds, C. (1984). Natural levels of similarities between identical twins and between unrelated people. *The Skeptical Inquirer, 9,* 62–66.

Yates, J. (1985). The content of awareness is a model of the world. *Psychological Review, 92,* 249–284.

Yerkes, R. M. (1925). *Almost human.* New York: Century.

Yerkes, R. M., & Dodson, J. D. (1908). The relation of strength of stimulus to rapidity of habit-formation. *Journal of Comparative Neurology and Psychology, 18,* 459–482.

Young, L. D., Richter, J. E., Bradley, L. A., & Anderson, K. O. (1987). Disorders of the upper gastrointestinal system: An overview. *Annals of Behavioral Medicine, 9* (3), pp. 7–12.

Youngren, M. A., & Lewinsohn, P. M. (1980). The functional relation between depression and problematic interpersonal behavior. *Journal of Abnormal Psychology, 89,* 333–341.

Zajonc, R. B. (1965). Social facilitation. *Science, 149,* 269–274.

Zajonc, R. B. (1976). Family configuration and intelligence. *Science, 192,* 227–236.

Zajonc, R. B. (1983). Validating the confluence model. *Psychological Bulletin, 93,* 457–480.

Zajonc, R. B. (1984). On the primacy of affect. *American Psychologist, 39,* 117–123.

Zajonc, R. B. (1985). Emotion and facial efference: A theory revisited. *Science, 228,* 15–21.

Zajonc, R. B. (1986). The decline and rise of Scholastic Aptitude scores: A prediction derived from the confluence model. *American Psychologist, 41,* 862–867.

Zaldivar, R. A. (1986, June 10). Panel faults NASA on shuttle. *The Philadelphia Inquirer,* pp. 1–A, 12–A.

Zamble, E., Mitchell, J. B., & Findlay, H. (1986). Pavlovian conditioning of sexual arousal: Parametric and background manipulations. *Journal of Experimental Psychology: Animal Behavior Processes, 12,* 403–411.

Zander, A. (1979). The psychology of group processes. *Annual Review of Psychology, 30,* 417–451.

Zanna, M. P., Olson, J. M., & Fazio, R. H. (1980). Attitude-behavior consistency: An individual difference perspective. *Journal of Personality and Social Psychology, 38,* 432–440.

Zentall, S. S., & Zentall, T. R. (1983). Optimal stimulation: A model of disordered activity and performance in normal and deviant children. *Psychological Bulletin, 94,* 466–471.

Zigler, E., Abelson, W. D., Trickett, P. K., & Seitz, V. (1982). Is an intervention program necessary in order to improve economically disadvantaged children's IQ scores? *Child Development, 33,* 340–348.

Zimbardo, P. G., Haney, C., & Banks, W. C. (1973, April 8). A Pirandellian prison. *The New York Times Magazine,* pp. 38–60.

Ziporyn, T. (1982). Taste and smell: The neglected senses. *Journal of the American Medical Association, 247,* 277–285.

Zuckerman, M. (1979). *Sensation seeking: Beyond the optimal level of arousal.* Hillside, NJ: Erlbaum.

Zuckerman, M., Buchsbaum. M. S., & Murphy, D. L. (1980). Sensation seeking and its biological correlates. *Psychological Bulletin, 88,* 187–214.

Zuckerman, M., Koestner, R., DeBoy, T., Garcia, T., Maresca, B. C., & Sartoris, J. M. (1988). To predict some of the people some of the time: A reexamination of the moderator variable approach in personality theory. *Journal of Personality and Social Psychology, 54,* 1006–1019.

Zwislocki, J. J. (1981). Sound analysis in the ear: A history of discoveries. *American Scientist, 69,* 184–192.

CREDITS

Photographs

Photo Research by Toni Michaels

Chapter 1

Table of Contents and Opener: Mark Rothko *Vessels of Magic,* 1946, watercolor, 98.8 × 66″. The Brooklyn Museum, 47.106, Museum Collection Fund; **page 4:** © Wesley Bocxe/Photo Researchers; **page 5, 6:** National Library of Medicine; **page 7: (top)** Archives of the History of American Psychology, **(bottom)** Dover Publications, Inc.; **page 8: (top)** Dover Publications, Inc., **(bottom)** Archives of the History of American Psychology; **page 9:** Howard University/Photo: Scurlock Studios; **page 10:** Mary Evans Picture Library; **page 11:** Culver Pictures; **page 13:** Archives of the History of American Psychology; **page 14: (top)** The Bettmann Archive, **(bottom)** © Christopher S. Johnson/ Stock Boston; **page 15:** The Granger Collection; **page 16: (top)** Andrew Schwebel, **(bottom)** Courtesy Roger Sperry; **page 17:** © NIH/Science Source/ Photo Reseachers; **1.2: (left)** © Doug Lee/Tom Stack and Associates, **(right)** © Peter D'Angelo/Comstock, **(bottom)** © David H. Wells/The Image Works; **page 22:** © Shepard Sherbell/Picture Group.

Chapter 2

Table of Contents and Opener: Vasily Kandinsky *Compositon 8,* July 1923, oil on canvas, 55 1/8 × 79 1/8″. Solomon R. Guggenheim Museum, New York, Photo: David Heald; **page 28:** © Bob Daemmrich/The Image Works; **2.1:** © Annie Hunter; **page 32:** © Bob Daemmrich/The Image Works; **page 36:** © Photofest; **page 37:** Bettmann Newsphotos; **page 38: (top)** Bettmann Newsphotos, **(bottom)** © Lorraine Rorke/The Image Works; **page 50:** © Paul Conklin.

Chapter 3

Table of Contents and Opener: Joseph Stella *Brooklyn Bridge,* oil on canvas, 84 × 76″. Yale University Art Collection. (Gift of Collection Societe Anonyme); **3.3b:** © Dr. Christopher Frederickson; **page 63:** Historical Pictures Services;

page 66: © Jules Asher; **page 67:** © John Colette/The Picture Cube; **page 70:** © A. Glauberman/Photo Researchers, Inc.; **3.8:** © Betsy Cole/The Picture Cube; **page 74:** National Library of Medicine; **page 78:** Bettmann Newsphotos; **3.13:** Courtesy Dr. Michael Phelps; **3.17:** Wurtz, *Scientific American,* June, 1982; **3.18:** Courtesy Dr. Michael Phelps; **3.19b:** © Fred Hossler/Visuals Unlimited.

Chapter 4

Table of Contents and Opener: Carol Colburn *After the Rain,* acrylic on canvas, 54 × 60″. Gallery 3, Phoenix, Arizona; **page 98:** UPI/Bettmann Newsphotos; **page 100:** © David M. Grossman/Photo Researchers; **4.3: (left)** Courtesy of Munsell Color, Baltimore, MD; **page 108:** © Villafuerte/Texastock; **page 109:** © Roy/Photo Researchers; **4.10:** Fritz Goreau/LIFE Magazine © 1944 Time, Inc.; **page 111:** *Sunday Afternoon on the Island of La Grande Jatte,* 1984–86, by Georges Seurat. Oil on Canvas, 207.6 × 308cm. Helen Birch Bartlett Memorial Collection, Art Institute of Chicago; **4.13:** Kaiser Porcelain, Ltd.; **page 113:** © Ira Wyman/ Sygma; **4.18: (top)** © Thomas Kitchin/ Tom Stack and Associates, **(left)** © Spenser Grant/The Picture Cube **(middle right)** © Greg Vaughn/Tom Stack and Associates, **(bottom right)** © IPA/The Image Works; **4.20: (both)** © Mark Antman/The Image Works; **4.21:** © Arthur Sirdofsky; **4.23b:** © Van Bucher/Photo Researchers; **page 124, 125:** AP/Wide World; **page 129: (both)** © Louie Psihoyos/Contact Press Images; **4.30:** © Christopher Springmann; **page 137:** © Tom Stack/Tom Stack and Associates; **page 139:** © Ana Fineman/ Sygma.

Chapter 5

Table of Contents and Opener: Marc Chagall *I and the Village,* 1911, oil on canvas, 6′6 5/8″ × 59 5/8″. Collection, The Museum of Modern Art, New York. Mrs. Simon Guggenheim Fund; **page 146:** AP/Wide World Photos; **page 147:** © Richard Hutchings/Photo Researchers; **5.2a:** © Topham/The Image Works; **page 154:** Courtesy Wilse Webb; **page 155:** © Annie Hunter; **page 157:** The Bettmann Archive; **page 161: (top)**

National Library of Medicine, **(bottom)** © Bob Daemmrich/The Image Works; **page 163:** The Bettmann Archive; **page 164:** News and Publication Service, Stanford University; **page 165:** © Annie Hunter; **page 168: (left)** © Bob Daemmrich/The Image Works, **(right)** © Arthur Grace/Stock Boston; **page 169:** The Bettmann Archive; **page 170:** © Dion Ogust/The Image Works; **page 172: (all)** © Ronald K. Siegel; **5.10: (left)** © David Lissy/The Picture Cube, **(right)** © Annie Hunter.

Chapter 6

Table of Contents and Opener: Henry O. Tanner *The Banjo Lesson,* 1933, oil on canvas, 4′1/2″ × 3′11″. Hampton University Museum, Hampton, Virginia; **page 185:** The Bettmann Archive; **page 189:** © Bruce Lkiewe/The Picture Cube; **page 190:** Courtesy Dr. Ben Harris; **page 191: (top)** © Leonard Lee Rue III/ Animals, Animals, **(bottom)** Courtesy John Garcia; **page 192:** Courtesy Ilene Berstein; **page 193:** Archives of the History of American Psychology; **page 195:** © Richard Wood/The Picture Cube; **page 198: (all)** Robert W. Kelley/Life Magazine © 1952 Time Inc.; **page 199: (top)** © Suzanne Goldstein/Photo Researchers, **(bottom)** © Michael P. Gadomski/Photo Researchers; **page 201: (left)** © Elisabeth Weiland/Photo Researchers, **(top right)** © Eastcott/ Momatiuk/The Image Works, **(bottom right)** © Norman Prince; **page 203:** Courtesy B. F. Skinner; **page 207:** Archives of the History of American Psychology; **page 208: (both)** Courtesy Albert Bandura; **page 209:** © Russ Kinne/Comstock; **page 210:** Courtesy Neal Miller; **page 211:** © Kennedy/ Texastock.

Chapter 7

Table of Contents and Opener: Salvador Dali *The Persistence of Memory,* 1931, oil on canvas, 9 1/4 × 13″. Collection, The Museum of Modern Art, New York. Given anonymously; **page 218: (top)** The Bettmann Archive, **(bottom left)** © Carlin/The Picture Cube, **(bottom right)** © Sylvia Johnson/ Woodfin Camp and Associates; **page 221:** © Stuart Cohen/Comstock; **page 231:** © Steve Northup/Picture Group;

Dept.; **page 464:** Center for the Studies of the Person; **page 466:** © Howard Frank; **page 467:** Courtesy Walter Mischel.

Chapter 14

Table of Contents and Opener: Willem De Kooning, *Excavation,* 1950, oil on canvas, 203.2 × 254.3cm. Mr. and Mrs. Frank G. Logan Purchase Prize, Gift of Mr. and Mrs. Noah Goldowsky and Edgar Kaufmann Jr., 1952. The Art Institute of Chicago; **page 476:** AP/Wide World Photos; **page 477: (both)** The Bettmann Archive; **page 483:** UPI/Bettmann Newsphotos; **page 485:** Scala/Art Resource; **page 487:** AP/Wide World Photos; **page 490:** © Susan Greenwood/Gamma Liaison; **page 491a-c:** Museum of Modern Art Film Stills Archive, **(d)** AP/Wide World Photos; **page 494:** © Joe McDonald/Tom Stack and Associates; **14.3:** Courtesy Dr. Michael Phelps; **page 498: (all)** © Derek Bayes/Life Magazine; **page 499:** © Grunnitus/Monkmeyer Press; **14.5: (left)** © Alexander Tsiaras/Science Source/Photo Researchers, **(right)** Courtesy Dr. Daniel R. Weinberger; **page 501:** Courtesy Nancy Andreasen; **page 504:** © Grey Villet/Black Star; **page 505:** Wide World Photos.

Chapter 15

Table of Contents and Opener: Richard Diebenkorn, *Ocean Park No. 66,* 1973, oil on canvas, 93 × 81″. Albright-Knox Art Gallery, Buffalo, Gift of Seymour H. Knox; **page 514:** National Museum of Denmark; **page 515:** The Bettmann Archive; **15.1a-b:** The Bettmann Archive; **15.1c:** National Library of Medicine; **page 516:** Historical Pictures Service; **page 517: (bottom left)** The Granger Collection, **(bottom right)** Andrew Schwebel; **page 518:** Historical Pictures Service; **page 519:** © Ann Chwatsky/Phototake; **page 521: (top to bottom)** Courtesy Joseph Wolpe, Archives of the History of American Psychology; **page 523:** © Jacques M. Chenet/Woodfin Camp and Associates; **15.2:** John Hopkins University; **15.3a:** Courtesy Albert Bandura; **page 526:** Courtesy Albert Ellis; **page 527:** Courtesy Aaron Beck; **page 530:** Paul Herbert/Esalen Institute; **page 532:** © Bob Daemmrich/The Image Works; **page 535:** © Richard Hutchings/Photo Researchers; **page 536:** © Bob Daemmrich/The Image Works; **15.6:** © Will McIntyre/Photo Researchers; **page 542:** © Mark Antman/The Image Works; **page 543:** © Charles Steiner/Picture Group; **page 544:** © Jerruy Berndt.

Chapter 16

Table of Contents and Opener: Henri Matisse, *La Negresse.* National Gallery of Art, Washington; Ailsa Mellon Bruce Fund; **page 556:** © MacDonald/The Picture Cube; **page 557:** © Focus on Sports; **page 559:** © C. Simonpietri/

Sygma; **page 562:** AP/Wide World Photos; **16.2: (both)** © Custom Medical Stock; **page 565:** © John Griffin/The Image Works; **page 567:** Courtesy Suzanne Kobasa; **page 570: (top)** © Kindra Clineff/The Picture Cube, **(bottom)** © Photofest; **page 574:** © Steve Schapiro/Sygma; **16.10: (top left)** Scala/Art Resource, **(top right and bottom)** AP Wide World Photos; **page 578:** AP Wide World Photos; **page 580:** © John Griffin/The Image Works; **page 581:** UPI/Bettmann Newsphotos; **page 582, 583:** © Dion Ogust/The Image Works; **page 585:** Courtesy Karen Matthews.

Chapter 17

Table of Contents and Opener: Auguste Renoir, *Le Moulin de la Galette,* 1876, 5 1/4 × 69″. The Louvre, Paris; **page 594:** © Chet Seymour/The Picture Cube; **page 595:** © Focus on Sports; **page 598: (left)** © Hangarter/The Picture Cube, **(right)** © Alan Carey/The Image Works; **page 599:** © Bob Daemmrich/The Image Works; **page 600:** © B. Bartholomew/Black Star; **page 601: (left to right)** © Eastcott/Momatiuk/The Image Works, © Roger Sakolove/The Picture Cube, © Alan Carey/The Image Works; **page 603: (top)** Courtesy Ellen Bersceid, **(middle)** Courtesy Elaine Hatfield, **(bottom)** © Alan Carey/The Image Works; **17.3:** © Georg Gerster/Photo Researchers; **page 609:** © Philip Drell/Black Star; **page 610: (top)** © Bob Daemmrich/The Image Works, **(bottom)** © Miro Vintoniv/Stock Boston; **page 613:** © Karen Zebulon/New School for Social Research; **page 615: (left)** © Rick Friedman/The Picture Cube, **(right)** © Larry Kolvoord/The Image Works; **page 617:** © MacDonald/The Picture Cube; **page 618:** © Dan Burns/Monkmeyer Press.

Chapter 18

Table of Contents and Opener: Joan Miro, *The Birth of the World,* Monroig, 1925, oil on Canvas, 8′2 3/4″ × 6′6 3/4″ Collection, The Museum of Modern Art, New York. Acquired through an anonymous fund, the Mr. and Mrs. Joseph Slifka and Armand G. Erpf Funds, and by gift of the artist; **page 625: (both)** Courtesy Philip G. Zimbardo, Stanford University; **page 626:** © Billy Barnes/Stock Boston; **page 627:** © Arthur Rickerby/Time-Life; **page 629:** © Andy Hernandez/Picture Group; **page 631: (top)** © R. M. Collins III/The Image Works, **(bottom)** © Alan Carey/The Image Works; **page 632: (top)** © Bob Daemmrich/The Image Works, **(middle)** © Miro Vintoniv/The Picture Cube, **(bottom)** © Bob Daemmrich/The Image Works; **18.1a: (both)** © William Vandivert; **page 634:** © Alan Carey/The Image Works; **page 635:** © Frank Johnston/Woodfin Camp and Associates; **18.3a-b:** Courtesy Mrs. Alexandra Milgram; **page 638:** UPI/Bettmann Newsphotos; **page 639: (left)** © Lee

Balterman/The Picture Cube, **(right)** © John Griffin/The Image Works; **page 641:** © Mike J. Howell/The Picture Cube; **page 643:** © Rich Frishman/The Picture Cube; **18.8: (both)** AP/Wide World Photos; **page 647: (both)** UPI/Bettmann Newsphotos; **page 648:** © Bob Daemmrich/The Image Works; **page 649: (top)** © Mark Newman/Tom Stack and Associates, **(bottom)** © IPA/The Image Works; **8.11:** Courtesy Albert Bandura; **page 651:** Bettmann Newsphotos; **page 652:** © Mike Greenlar/The Image Works.

Illustrators

Keith Kasnot: Figures 3.1, 3.2, 3.3a, 3.6, 3.7, 3.9, 3.10, 3.11, 3.12, 3.14, 3.16, 3.19, 3.20, 4.5, 4.7, 4.26, 4.27, 4.28, 4.29, 4.32, 4.33, 10.3, 10.5, 11.1, 11.6, 11.8, 11.10, 11.11.
Chris Creek: Figures 12.1, 12.4.
Laurie O'Keefe: Figures 4.1, 4.6, 4.16, 4.22, 4.31, 5.5, 5.9, 6.2, 6.6, 7.13, 7.18, 8.6, 8.7, 8.8, 8.9, 13.2, 14.2, 15.5.
Benoit & Associates: Figures 1.1, 2.2, 2.3, 2.4, 2.5, 2.6, 4.8, 4.9, 4.17, 4.19, 5.1, 5.3, 5.4, 5.7, 5.8, 6.3, 6.4, 6.5, 6.7, 7.1, 7.2, 7.3, 7.4, 7.6, 7.7, 7.9, 7.10, 7.11, 7.12, 7.14, 7.15, 7.16, 8.5, 8.10, 9.5, 9.6, 9.7, 9.8, 10.1, 10.4, 10.7, 10.9, 10.11, 11.4, 11.7, 11.9, 11.13, 11.14, 11.15, 12.11, 13.7, 13.8, 13.9, 14.1, 14.4, 15.3, 15.4, 15.7, 15.8, 15.9, 16.3, 16.4, 16.5, 16.6, 16.7, 16.8, 16.9, 16.11, 17.1, 17.2, 17.4, 17.5, page 608, 17.16, 18.1b, 18.2, 18.4, 18.5, 18.6, 18.7, 18.9, 18.10, 18.12.

Line Art

Chapter 1

Figure 1.1: From Joy Stapp, et al., "Census of Psychological Personnel:1983" in *American Psychologist,* 40:1317–1351. Copyright 1985 by the American Psychological Association. Reprinted by permission.

Chapter 3

Figure 3.1: From Benjamin B. Lahey, *Psychology: An Introduction,* 3d ed. Copyright © 1989 Wm. C. Brown Publishers, Dubuque, Iowa. All Rights Reserved. Reprinted by permission.
Figure 3.4: From Kurt Schlesinger and Philip M. Groves, *Psychology: A Dynamic Science.* Copyright © 1976 Wm. C. Brown Publishers, Dubuque, Iowa. Reprinted by permission of the author.
Figure 3.5: From Leland G. Johnson, *Biology,* 2d ed. Copyright © 1987 Wm. C. Brown Publishers, Dubuque, Iowa. All Rights Reserved. Reprinted by permission.
Figure 3.10: Mitchell Beazley Publishers, London. Reprinted by permission.
Figure 3.15: From John W. Santrock, *Psychology,* 2d ed. Copyright © 1988 Wm. C. Brown Publishers, Dubuque, Iowa. All Rights Reserved. Reprinted by permission.

Figure 9.6: From J. L. Horn and G. Donaldson, "On the Myth of Intellectual Decline in Adulthood" in *American Psychologist,* 31:701–719. Copyright 1976 by the American Psychological Association. Reprinted by permission.
Figure 9.8: From R. B. Zajonc, "The Decline and Rise of Scholastic Aptitude Scores: A Prediction Derived from the Confluence Model" in *American Psychologist,* 41:862–867. Copyright by the American Psychological Association. Reprinted by permission.

Chapter 10

Figure 10.2: This diagram was taken from *Foundations of Experimental Psychology* (C. Murchison, ed.), 1929 and is reprinted by permission of Clark University Press.
Figure 10.4: Adapted from information appearing in *The New England Journal of Medicine,* 314:193–198, 1986. A. J. Stunkard, et al., "An Adoption Study of Human Obesity."
Figure 10.6: From *Human Sexuality* by William H. Masters, Virginia E. Johnson, and Robert C. Kolodny. Copyright © 1982 by William H. Masters, Virginia E. Johnson, and Robert C. Kolodny. Reprinted by permission of Scott, Foresman and Company.
Figure 10.9: From R. de Charms and G. H. Moeller, "Values Expressed in American Children's Readers: 1800–1950" in *Journal of Abnormal and Social Psychology,* 64:136–142. Copyright 1962 by the American Psychological Association. Reprinted by permission.
Figure 10.11: From D. C. Anderson, et al., "Performance Posting, Goal Setting, and Activity-Contingent Praise as Applied to a University Hockey Team" in *Journal of Applied Psychology,* 73:87–95. Copyright 1988 by the American Psychological Association. Reprinted by permission.

Chapter 11

Figure 11.9: From R. L. Solomon, "The Opponent-Process Theory of Acquired Motivation: The Costs of Pleasure and the Benefits of Pain" in *American Psychologist,* 35:691–712. Copyright 1980 by the American Psychological Association. Reprinted by permission.
Figure 11.13: From J. C. Speisman, et al., "Experimental Reduction of Stress Based on Ego-Defense Theory" in *Journal of Abnormal and Social Psychology,* 68:367–380. Copyright 1964 by the American Psychological Association. Reprinted by permission.
Figure 11.15: Reprinted by permission from *Nature,* 308:449–450. Copyright © 1984 Macmillan Magazines Ltd.

Chapter 12

Figure 12.9: From J. M. Tanner, et al., "Standards from Birth to Maturity for Height, Weight, Height Velocity, and Weight Velocity" in *Archives of Diseases in Childhood.* Copyright © 1966 British Medical Association, London, England.
Figure 12.10: Data from D. K. Simonton, "Age and Outstanding Achievement: What Do We Know after a Century of Research?" in *Psychological Bulletin,* 104:251–267. Copyright 1988 by the American Psychological Association. Reprinted by permission.

Chapter 13

Figure 13.6: Figure 22 from *Introduction to Personality,* Second Edition, by Walter Mischel and Harriet N. Michel, copyright © 1971 by Holt, Rinehart and Winston, Inc., reprinted by permission of the publisher.
Figure 13.8: Adapted from R. B. Cattell, "Personality Pinned Down" in *Psychology Today,* July 1973. Copyright © 1973 Institute for Personality and Ability Testing, Inc., Champaign, IL.

Chapter 14

Figure 14.1: Data adapted from L. N. Robins, et al., "Lifetime Prevalence of Specific Psychiatric Disorders in Three Sites" in *Archives of General Psychiatry,* 41:949–958. Copyright 1984, American Medical Association.
Figure 14.4: Data from I. I. Gottesman and J. Shields, *Schizophrenia: The Epigenetic Puzzle.* Copyright © 1982 Cambridge University Press, New York, NY. Reprinted with the permission of Cambridge University Press.

Chapter 15

Figure 15.3b: From A. Bandura, et al., "The Relative Efficacy of Desensitization and Modeling Approaches for Inducing Behavioral, Affective, and Attitudinal Changes" in *Journal of Personality and Social Psychology,* 13:173–199. Copyright 1969 by the American Psychological Association. Reprinted by permission.
Figure 15.8: Smith, Mary Lee, Gene V. Glass, Thomas I. Miller: *The Benefits of Psychotherapy.* The Johns Hopkins University Press, Baltimore/London, 1981, p. 89.
Figure 15.9: From K. I. Howard, et al., "The Dose-Effect Relationship in Psychotherapy" in *American Psychologist,* 1986. Copyright 1986 by the American Psychological Association. Reprinted by permission.

Chapter 16

Figure 16.1: From Benjamin B. Lahey, *Psychology,* 3d ed. Copyright © 1989 Wm. C. Brown Publishers, Dubuque, Iowa. All Rights Reserved. Reprinted by permission.

Figure 16.3: Data from Schleifer, et al., *Journal of the American Medical Association,* 250:375. Copyright 1983 American Medical Association.
Figure 16.7: From T. J. Hoelscher, "Maintenance of Relaxation-Induced Blood Pressure Reductions: The Importance of Continued Relaxation Practices" in *Biofeedback and Self-Regulation,* 12:3–12. Copyright © 1987 Plenum Publishing Corporation, New York, NY. Reprinted by permission.
Figure 16.8: From J. D. Brown and J. M. Siegel, "Exercise as a Buffer of Life Stress: A Prospective Study of Adolescent Health" in *Health Psychology,* 7:341–353. Copyright by the American Psychological Association. Reprinted by permission.
Figure 16.9: From J. W. Pennebaker, et al., "Disclosure of Traumas and Immune Function" in *Journal of Consulting and Clinical Psychology,* 56:239–245. Copyright 1988 by the American Psychological Association. Reprinted by permission.
Figure 16.11: From W. H. Redd, et al., "Cognitive/Attentional Distraction in the Control of Conditional Nausea in Pediatric Cancer Patients Receiving Chemotherapy" in *Journal of Consulting and Clinical Psychology,* 55:391–395. Copyright © 1987 by the American Psychological Association. Reprinted by permission.

Chapter 17

Figure 17.4: Data from Robert J. Sternberg, "A Triangular Theory of Love" in *Psychological Review,* 93:119–135, 1986. Copyright 1986 by the American Psychological Association. Reprinted by permission.

Chapter 18

Figure 18.3a: Figure 1 from *Obedience to Authority* by Stanley Milgram. Copyright © 1974 by Stanley Milgram. Reprinted by permission of Harper & Row, Publishers, Inc.
Figure 18.4: Data from S. Milgram, "Behavioral Study of Obedience" in *Journal of Abnormal and Social Psychology,* 67:371–378. Copyright 1963 by the American Psychological Association. Reprinted by permission. Graph from S. Milgram, *Obedience to Authority.* Copyright © 1974 Harper & Row, Publishers, Inc., New York, NY.
Figure 18.5: From A. Baum and G. E. Davis, "Reducing the Stress of High-Density Living: An Architectural Intervention" in *Journal of Personality and Social Psychology,* 38:471–481. Copyright 1980 by the American Psychological Association. Reprinted by permission.

NAME INDEX

SUBJECT INDEX